PRAYERS FOR WORSHIP

On entering a church

Lord, I love the habitation of Your house and the place where Your glory dwells. In the multitude of Your tender mercies prepare my heart that I may enter Your house to worship and confess Your holy name; through Jesus Christ, my God and Lord. Amen.

Before worship

O Lord, my creator, redeemer, and comforter, as I come to worship You in spirit and in truth, I humbly pray that You would open my heart to the preaching of Your Word so that I may repent of my sins, believe in Jesus Christ as my only Savior, and grow in grace and holiness. Hear me for the sake of His name. Amen.

After worship

Almighty and merciful God, I have again worshiped in Your presence and received both forgiveness for my many sins and the assurance of Your love in Jesus Christ. I thank You for this undeserved grace and ask You to keep me in faith until, with all Your saints, I inherit eternal salvation; through Jesus Christ, my Lord. Amen.

Before confession and absolution

Almighty, everlasting God, for my many sins I justly deserve eternal condemnation. In Your mercy You sent Your dear Son, my Lord Jesus Christ, who won for me forgiveness of sins and everlasting salvation. Grant me a true confession that, dead to sin, I may be raised up by Your life-giving absolution. Grant me Your Holy Spirit that I may be ever watchful and live a true and godly life in Your service; through Jesus Christ, my Lord. Amen.

Before communing

Dear Savior, at Your gracious invitation I come to Your table to eat and drink Your holy body and blood. Let me find favor in Your eyes to receive this holy Sacrament in faith for the salvation of my soul and to the glory of Your holy name; for You live and reign with the Father and the Holy Spirit, one God, now and forever. Amen.

Thanksgiving after receiving the Sacrament

Almighty and everlasting God, I thank and praise You for feeding me the life-giving body and blood of Your beloved Son, Jesus Christ. Send Your Holy Spirit that, having with my mouth received the holy Sacrament, I may by faith obtain and eternally enjoy Your divine grace, the forgiveness of sins, unity with Christ, and life eternal; through Jesus Christ, my Lord. Amen.

For blessing on the Word

Lord God, bless Your Word wherever it is proclaimed. Make it a word of power and peace to convert those not yet Your own and to confirm those who have come to saving faith. May Your Word pass from the ear to the heart, from the heart to the lip, and from the lip to the life that, as You have promised, Your Word may achieve the purpose for which You send it; through Jesus Christ, my Lord. Amen.

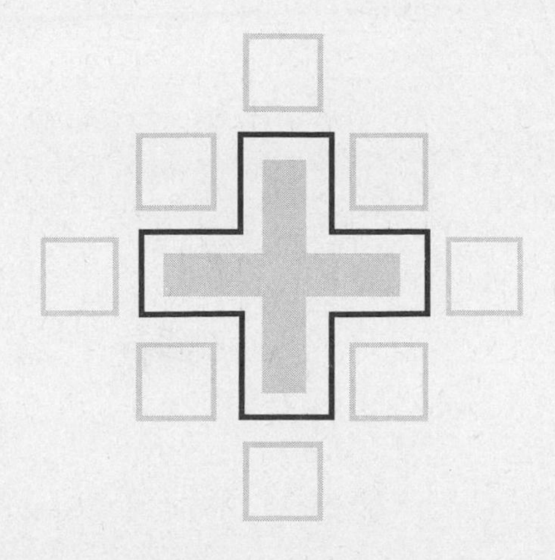

LUTHERAN SERVICE BOOK

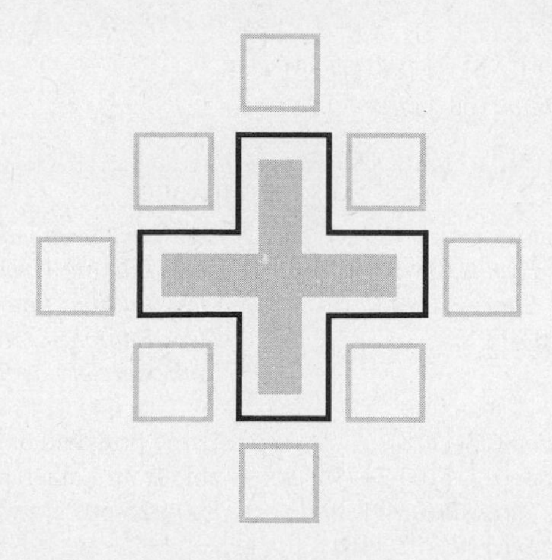

LUTHERAN SERVICE BOOK

Prepared by
The Commission on Worship
of
The Lutheran Church—Missouri Synod

CONCORDIA PUBLISHING HOUSE • SAINT LOUIS

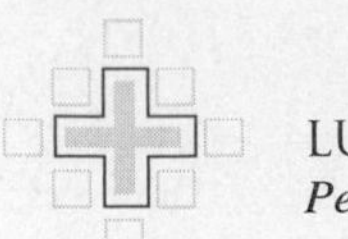

LUTHERAN SERVICE BOOK
Pew Edition (03-1170)

ALSO AVAILABLE:

Gift Edition (03-1171)
Accompaniment for the Hymns (03-1173)
Accompaniment for the Liturgy (03-1174)
Guitar Chord Edition (03-1175)
Altar Book (03-1176)
Agenda (03-1177)
Pastoral Care Companion (03-1178)
Three-Year Lectionary, Series A (03-1179)
Three-Year Lectionary, Series B (03-1180)
Three-Year Lectionary, Series C (03-1181)
One-Year Lectionary (03-1182)
Desk Edition: Hymns
Desk Edition: Liturgy
Desk Edition: Lectionary
Lutheran Service Builder—Electronic Edition

Large print and braille editions may be available from Lutheran Braille Workers. Phone 800-925-6092. www.lbwinc.org.

3558 S. Jefferson Ave., St. Louis, MO 63118-3968
1-800-325-3040 • www.cph.org

Manufactured in the United States of America

ISBN 0-7586-1217-6
ISBN 978-0-7586-1217-5

Cataloging-in-Publication Data can be found on page 1024.

12 13 14 15 16 17 18 19 18 17 16 15 14 13

CONTENTS

THE HYMNS

The Church Year

Person and Work of Christ

The Christian Church

The Christian Life

Terms and Abbreviations Used in Hymns

abbr.	abbreviated
abr.	abridged
adapt.	adapted/adapted by
admin.	administered by
alt.	altered
arr.	arranged
attr.	attributed to
b.	born
c.	*circa*, about
cent.	century
coll.	collected
composite	a combined translation from the works of various authors
d.	died
ed.	edited by/edition
harm.	harmonized by
para.	paraphrased by
ren.	renewed
rev.	revised
st.	stanza
sts.	stanzas
tr.	translated by/translation/ translator
vol.	volume

INTRODUCTION

Our Lord is the Lord who serves. Jesus Christ came into the flesh not to be served, but to serve and to give His life as a ransom for many. On the cross He offered Himself as a spotless sacrifice for the sin of the whole world. Through His perfect life and death, He accomplished forgiveness and salvation for all before the Father in heaven. By His empty tomb and ascension into heaven, He declared His victory over sin and death to all the world. Seated now at the Father's right hand, He graciously serves His Church with the gifts of salvation. On the Last Day, He will come again to gather His elect from every nation to celebrate the feast that will have no end.

Our Lord serves us today through His holy Word and Sacraments. Through these means, He comes among us to deliver His forgiveness and salvation, freeing us from our sins and strengthening us for service to one another and to the world. At Holy Baptism, He puts His name upon us, pours His Holy Spirit into our hearts, and rescues us from sin, death, and the devil. Through Holy Absolution, He pronounces His forgiveness again and again. With His holy Word, written in Scripture and preached into our ears, He daily proclaims His abiding love for us through all the joys and sorrows of life in this world. In His Holy Supper, He gives us His own body and blood to eat and drink as a priceless gift to nourish and strengthen us in both body and soul.

The Lord's service calls forth our service—in sacrifices of praise and thanksgiving to Him and in loving service to one another. Having been called, gathered, enlightened, and sanctified by the Holy Spirit, we receive His gifts with thankfulness and praise. With psalms, hymns, and spiritual songs, we joyfully confess all that God has done for us, declaring the praises of Him who called us out of darkness into His marvelous light. Our song joins with the song of every saint from every age, the new song of Christ's holy people, declaring: "Worthy is the Lamb who was slain, to receive power and wealth and wisdom and might and honor and glory and blessing!" (Rev. 5:12).

Within the Lutheran tradition, the wedding of the Word of God to melody was modeled by the reformer himself. Martin Luther had a high regard for music and urged the Church to use it wisely as a vehicle for proclaiming the Gospel. "Next to theology," he wrote, "I accord to music the highest place and the greatest honor." Retaining the best of pre-Reformation hymnody, as well as adding a great number of new hymns to the Church's song, Luther and succeeding generations of hymnwriters continue to inspire the faithful to lift their voices in praise and thanksgiving to the triune God.

This heritage of word and song has been highly valued throughout the history of The Lutheran Church—Missouri Synod. Even before the Synod's formation, a new, German-language hymnal was already in development, edited by the Synod's first president, C. F. W. Walther. With the transition to English came several books: *Evangelical Lutheran Hymn-Book* (1889, 1912), *The Lutheran Hymnal* (1941), and, most recently,

Lutheran Worship (1982). Each of these hymnals not only handed on the treasures of the past but also offered contemporary expressions of word and song in service to the Gospel.

Lutheran Service Book now continues the Church's song into the twenty-first century. Officially accepted at the Synod's 2004 Convention, *Lutheran Service Book* is a careful blending of the best of *The Lutheran Hymnal* and *Lutheran Worship*. It offers treasured melodies and texts that have nourished God's people for generations.

In every age God also blesses His people by raising up hymnwriters who have honed their craft to create rich and fresh expressions of praise. Produced during the most prolific period of English-language hymn writing in the history of Christendom, *Lutheran Service Book* delivers a rich feast of Gospel-centered hymns from every age and from many lands.

Lutheran Service Book is offered with the prayer that it may be used in all its fullness to give voice to the prayer, praise, and thanksgiving of God's holy people as they are graciously served by Him through Word and Sacrament.

ABOUT THE COVER

The most prominent feature of the cover design is the cross. The dark, innermost portion of the cross is a reminder of the darkness of Good Friday, when our Lord "humbled Himself by becoming obedient to the point of death, even death on a cross" (Phil. 2:8). The prominent, gold leaf cross is a reminder of the resurrection of our Lord. God raised Him "from the dead and gave Him glory, so that [our] faith and hope are in God" (1 Peter 1:21). The eight embossed squares surrounding the cross remind us of Christ's resurrection on Sunday, the eighth day, and the inauguration of a new creation through our Baptism into the death and resurrection of Christ (2 Cor. 5:17). Taken as a whole, the cross design gives the impression of ongoing expansion—even as the Gospel continues to be proclaimed until the end of time "in Jerusalem and in Judea and Samaria, and to the end of the earth" (Acts 1:8).

To the left of the cross are depicted the means of grace, through which the Gospel goes forth into our lives and to all the world. From top to bottom are an open Bible (Word of God), a shell with drops of water (Holy Baptism), and Communion vessels with grains of wheat and fruit of the vine (Lord's Supper). On the back cover, the Holy Trinity is pictured in the form of the hand of God (the Father), a cross (the Son), and a dove (the Holy Spirit).

THE CHURCH YEAR

SUNDAYS AND SEASONS

The Time of Christmas

Advent Season

First Sunday in Advent B/V
Second Sunday in Advent B/V
Third Sunday in Advent B/V
Fourth Sunday in Advent B/V

Christmas Season

THE NATIVITY OF OUR LORD W
Christmas Eve
Christmas Midnight
Christmas Dawn
Christmas Day
First Sunday after Christmas W
Second Sunday after Christmas W

Epiphany Season

The Epiphany of Our Lord W
First Sunday after the Epiphany W
The Baptism of Our Lord
Second Sunday after the Epiphany G
Third Sunday after the Epiphany G
Fourth Sunday after the Epiphany G
Fifth Sunday after the Epiphany G
Sixth Sunday after the Epiphany G
Seventh Sunday after the Epiphany G
Eighth Sunday after the Epiphany G
(Sixth through Eighth: *3-Year Lect.*)
Last Sunday after the Epiphany W
The Transfiguration of Our Lord

The Time of Easter

Pre-Lent Season

Septuagesima G
Sexagesima G
Quinquagesima G
(*1-Year Lect.*)

Lenten Season

Ash Wednesday BK/V
First Sunday in Lent V
Second Sunday in Lent V
Third Sunday in Lent V
Fourth Sunday in Lent V
Fifth Sunday in Lent V

Holy Week

Palm Sunday S/V
Sunday of the Passion
Monday in Holy Week S/V
Tuesday in Holy Week S/V
Wednesday in Holy Week S/V
Holy (Maundy) Thursday W/S/V
Good Friday BK
Holy Saturday BK

Easter Season

THE RESURRECTION OF OUR LORD W/GO
Vigil of Easter
Easter Sunrise
Easter Day
Easter Evening/Easter Monday
Easter Tuesday
Easter Wednesday
Second Sunday of Easter W
Third Sunday of Easter W
Fourth Sunday of Easter W
Fifth Sunday of Easter W
Sixth Sunday of Easter W
The Ascension of Our Lord W
Seventh Sunday of Easter W
PENTECOST R
Pentecost Eve
The Day of Pentecost
Pentecost Evening/Pentecost Monday
Pentecost Tuesday

The Time of the Church

The Season after Pentecost

The Holy Trinity W
Second through Twenty-seventh Sunday after Pentecost *(3-Year Lectionary)* G
First through Twenty-sixth Sunday after Trinity *(1-Year Lectionary)* G
Last Sunday of the Church Year G

FEASTS AND FESTIVALS

November
30 St. Andrew, Apostle R

December
21 St. Thomas, Apostle R
26 St. Stephen, Martyr R
27 St. John, Apostle and Evangelist W
28 The Holy Innocents, Martyrs R
31 **Eve of the Circumcision and Name of Jesus** W
New Year's Eve

January
1 **Circumcision and Name of Jesus** W
18 The Confession of St. Peter W
24 St. Timothy, Pastor and Confessor W
25 The Conversion of St. Paul W
26 St. Titus, Pastor and Confessor W

February
2 **The Purification of Mary and the Presentation of Our Lord** W
24 St. Matthias, Apostle R

March
19 St. Joseph, Guardian of Jesus W
25 **The Annunciation of Our Lord** W

April
25 St. Mark, Evangelist R

May
1 St. Philip and St. James, Apostles R
31 **The Visitation** *(3-Year Lectionary)* W

June
11 St. Barnabas, Apostle R
24 **The Nativity of St. John the Baptist** W
29 St. Peter and St. Paul, Apostles R

July
2 **The Visitation** *(1-Year Lectionary)* W
22 St. Mary Magdalene W
25 St. James the Elder, Apostle R

August
15 St. Mary, Mother of Our Lord W
24 St. Bartholomew, Apostle R
29 The Martyrdom of St. John the Baptist R

September
14 Holy Cross Day R
21 St. Matthew, Apostle and Evangelist R
29 **St. Michael and All Angels** W

October
18 St. Luke, Evangelist R
23 St. James of Jerusalem, Brother of Jesus and Martyr R
28 St. Simon and St. Jude, Apostles R
31 Reformation Day R

November
1 **All Saints' Day** W

OCCASIONS

Anniversary of a Congregation R
Mission Observance W
Christian Education Color of Season
Harvest Observance Color of Season
Day of Thanksgiving W
Day of Supplication and Prayer V
Day of National or Local Tragedy V

The observances listed in **boldface** *are principal feasts of Christ and are normally observed when they occur on a Sunday. The other festivals may be observed according to local custom and preference.*

The letters indicate the suggested colors: B = *blue,* BK = *black,* G = *green,* GO = *gold,* R = *red,* S = *scarlet,* V = *violet,* W = *white.*

COMMEMORATIONS

Our churches teach that the remembrance of the saints is to be commended in order that we may imitate their faith and good works according to our calling.

Augsburg Confession 21

The Lutheran reformers understood that there was great benefit in remembering the saints whom God has given to His Church. The Apology of the Augsburg Confession (Article 21) gives three reasons for such honor. First, we thank God for giving faithful servants to His Church. Second, through such remembrance our faith is strengthened as we see the mercy that God extended to His saints of old. Third, these saints are examples by which we may imitate both their faith and their holy living according to our calling in life.

The calendar of commemorations given below lists a number of men and women from both the Old and New Testaments and from the first 19 centuries of the Church's life. (Other New Testament persons and events are given with the Feasts and Festivals calendar on page xi.) Their defense of the fundamental beliefs of the Christian faith and/or their virtuous living have caused these individuals to stand out over time as persons worthy of recognition. In every case, the purpose of our remembrance is not that we honor these saints for their own sake, but as examples of those in whom the saving work of Jesus Christ has been made manifest to the glory of His holy name and to the praise of His grace and mercy.

Therefore, since we are surrounded by so great a cloud of witnesses, let us also lay aside every weight, and sin which clings so closely, and let us run with endurance the race that is set before us.

Hebrews 12:1

January

2 J. K. Wilhelm Loehe, *Pastor*
10 Basil the Great of Caesarea, Gregory of Nazianzus, and Gregory of Nyssa, *Pastors and Confessors*
20 Sarah
27 John Chrysostom, *Preacher*

February

5 Jacob (Israel), *Patriarch*
10 Silas, *Fellow Worker of St. Peter and St. Paul*
13 Aquila, Priscilla, Apollos
14 Valentine, *Martyr*
15 Philemon and Onesimus
16 Philipp Melanchthon (birth), *Confessor*
18 Martin Luther, *Doctor and Confessor*
23 Polycarp of Smyrna, *Pastor and Martyr*

March

7 Perpetua and Felicitas, *Martyrs*
17 Patrick, *Missionary to Ireland*
31 Joseph, *Patriarch*

April

6 Lucas Cranach and Albrecht Dürer, *Artists*
20 Johannes Bugenhagen, *Pastor*
21 Anselm of Canterbury, *Theologian*
24 Johann Walter, *Kantor*

May

2 Athanasius of Alexandria, *Pastor and Confessor*
4 Friedrich Wyneken, *Pastor and Missionary*
5 Frederick the Wise, *Christian Ruler*
7 C. F. W. Walther, *Theologian*
9 Job
11 Cyril and Methodius, *Missionaries to the Slavs*
21 Emperor Constantine, *Christian Ruler,* and Helena, *Mother of Constantine*
24 Esther
25 Bede the Venerable, *Theologian*

June

1 Justin, *Martyr*
5 Boniface of Mainz, *Missionary to the Germans*
12 The Ecumenical Council of Nicaea, AD 325
14 Elisha
25 Presentation of the Augsburg Confession
26 Jeremiah
27 Cyril of Alexandria, *Pastor and Confessor*
28 Irenaeus of Lyons, *Pastor*

July

6 Isaiah
16 Ruth
20 Elijah
21 Ezekiel
28 Johann Sebastian Bach, *Kantor*
29 Mary, Martha, and Lazarus of Bethany
30 Robert Barnes, *Confessor and Martyr*
31 Joseph of Arimathea

August

3 Joanna, Mary, and Salome, *Myrrhbearers*
10 Lawrence, *Deacon and Martyr*
16 Isaac
17 Johann Gerhard, *Theologian*
19 Bernard of Clairvaux, *Hymnwriter and Theologian*
20 Samuel
27 Monica, *Mother of Augustine*
28 Augustine of Hippo, *Pastor and Theologian*

September

1 Joshua
2 Hannah
3 Gregory the Great, *Pastor*
4 Moses
5 Zacharias and Elizabeth
16 Cyprian of Carthage, *Pastor and Martyr*
22 Jonah
30 Jerome, *Translator of Holy Scripture*

October

7 Henry Melchior Muhlenberg, *Pastor*
9 Abraham
11 Philip the Deacon
17 Ignatius of Antioch, *Pastor and Martyr*
25 Dorcas (Tabitha), Lydia, and Phoebe, *Faithful Women*
26 Philipp Nicolai, Johann Heermann, and Paul Gerhardt, *Hymnwriters*

November

8 Johannes von Staupitz, *Luther's Father Confessor*
9 Martin Chemnitz (birth), *Pastor and Confessor*
11 Martin of Tours, *Pastor*
14 Emperor Justinian, *Christian Ruler and Confessor of Christ*
19 Elizabeth of Hungary
23 Clement of Rome, *Pastor*
29 Noah

December

4 John of Damascus, *Theologian and Hymnwriter*
6 Nicholas of Myra, *Pastor*
7 Ambrose of Milan, *Pastor and Hymnwriter*
13 Lucia, *Martyr*
17 Daniel the Prophet and the Three Young Men
19 Adam and Eve
20 Katharina von Bora Luther
29 David

LECTIONARIES

SUNDAYS AND SEASONS

Three-Year Lectionary: Series A

Sunday/Festival	Old Testament/ First Reading	Epistle/ Second Reading	Holy Gospel
Advent 1	Is. 2:1–5	Rom. 13:(8–10) 11–14	Matt. 21:1–11 *or* Matt. 24:36–44
Advent 2	Is. 11:1–10	Rom. 15:4–13	Matt. 3:1–12
Advent 3	Is. 35:1–10	James 5:7–11	Matt. 11:2–15
Advent 4	Is. 7:10–17	Rom. 1:1–7	Matt. 1:18–25
Christmas Eve	Is. 7:10–14	1 John 4:7–16	Matt. 1:18–25
Christmas Midnight	Is. 9:2–7	Titus 2:11–14	Luke 2:1–14 (15–20)
Christmas Dawn	Is. 62:10–12	Titus 3:4–7	Luke 2:(1–14) 15–20
Christmas Day	Is. 52:7–10	Heb. 1:1–6 (7–12)	John 1:1–14 (15–18)
Christmas 1	Is. 63:7–14	Gal. 4:4–7	Matt. 2:13–23
Christmas 2	1 Kings 3:4–15	Eph. 1:3–14	Luke 2:40–52
Epiphany	Is. 60:1–6	Eph. 3:1–12	Matt. 2:1–12
Baptism of Our Lord	Is. 42:1–9	Rom. 6:1–11	Matt. 3:13–17
Epiphany 2	Is. 49:1–7	1 Cor. 1:1–9	John 1:29–42a
Epiphany 3	Is. 9:1–4	1 Cor. 1:10–18	Matt. 4:12–25
Epiphany 4	Micah 6:1–8	1 Cor. 1:18–31	Matt. 5:1–12
Epiphany 5	Is. 58:3–9a	1 Cor. 2:1–12 (13–16)	Matt. 5:13–20
Epiphany 6	Deut. 30:15–20	1 Cor. 3:1–9	Matt. 5:21–37
Epiphany 7	Lev. 19:1–2, 9–18	1 Cor. 3:10–23	Matt. 5:38–48
Epiphany 8	Is. 49:8–16a	1 Cor. 4:1–13	Matt. 6:24–34
Transfiguration	Ex. 24:8–18	2 Peter 1:16–21	Matt. 17:1–9
Ash Wednesday	Joel 2:12–19	2 Cor. 5:20b—6:10	Matt. 6:1–6, 16–21
Lent 1	Gen. 3:1–21	Rom. 5:12–19	Matt. 4:1–11
Lent 2	Gen. 12:1–9	Rom. 4:1–8, 13–17	John 3:1–17
Lent 3	Ex. 17:1–7	Rom. 5:1–8	John 4:5–26 (27–30, 39–42)
Lent 4	Is. 42:14–21	Eph. 5:8–14	John 9:1–41 *or* John 9:1–7, 13–17, 34–39
Lent 5	Ezek. 37:1–14	Rom. 8:1–11	John 11:1–45 (46–53) *or* John 11:17–27, 38–53
Palm Sunday Procession			John 12:12–19
Sunday of the Passion	Is. 50:4–9a	Phil. 2:5–11	Matt. 26:1—27:66 *or* Matt. 27:11–66 *or* John 12:20–43
Monday in Holy Week	Is. 50:5–10	Heb. 9:11–15	Matt. 26:1—27:66 *or* John 12:1–23
Tuesday in Holy Week	Is. 49:1–7	1 Cor. 1:18–25 (26–31)	Mark 14:1—15:47 *or* John 12:23–50
Wednesday in Holy Week	Is. 62:11—63:7	Rom. 5:6–11	Luke 22:1—23:56 *or* John 13:16–38
Holy Thursday	Ex. 24:3–11	Heb. 9:11–22	Matt. 26:17–30
Holy Thursday (alt)	Ex. 12:1–14	1 Cor. 11:23–32	John 13:1–17, 31b–35
Good Friday	Is. 52:13—53:12	Heb. 4:14–16; 5:7–9	John 18:1—19:42 *or* John 19:17–30
Holy Saturday	Dan. 6:1–24	1 Peter 4:1–8	Matt. 27:57–66

Sunday/Festival	Old Testament/ First Reading	Epistle/ Second Reading	Holy Gospel
Vigil of Easter	Selected Readings		
Easter Sunrise	Ex. 14:10—15:1	1 Cor. 15:1–11	John 20:1–18
Easter Day	Acts 10:34–43 *or* Jer. 31:1–6	Col. 3:1–4	Matt. 28:1–10
Easter Evening/Monday	Ex. 15:1–18 *or* Dan. 12:1c–3	Acts 10:34–43 *or* 1 Cor. 5:6b–8	Luke 24:13–35 (36–49)
Easter Tuesday	Dan. 3:8–28	Acts 13:26–33	Luke 24:36–49
Easter Wednesday	Acts 3:13–15, 17–19	Col. 3:1–7 *or* 1 Cor. 11:23–26	John 21:1–14
Easter 2	Acts 5:29–42	1 Peter 1:3–9	John 20:19–31
Easter 3	Acts 2:14a, 36–41	1 Peter 1:17–25	Luke 24:13–35
Easter 4	Acts 2:42–47	1 Peter 2:19–25	John 10:1–10
Easter 5	Acts 6:1–9; 7:2a, 51–60	1 Peter 2:2–10	John 14:1–14
Easter 6	Acts 17:16–31	1 Peter 3:13–22	John 14:15–21
Ascension	Acts 1:1–11	Eph. 1:15–23	Luke 24:44–53
Easter 7	Acts 1:12–26	1 Peter 4:12–19; 5:6–11	John 17:1–11
Pentecost Eve	Ex. 19:1–9	Rom. 8:12–17 (22–27)	John 14:8–21
Day of Pentecost	Num. 11:24–30	Acts 2:1–21	John 7:37–39
Pentecost Evening/Monday	Is. 57:15–21	Acts 10:34a, 42–48	John 3:16–21
Pentecost Tuesday	Is. 32:14–20	Acts 8:14–17	John 10:1–10
Holy Trinity	Gen. 1:1—2:4a	Acts 2:14a, 22–36	Matt. 28:16–20
Proper 3 (May 24–28)	Is. 49:8–16a	Rom. 1:8–17	Matt. 6:24–34
Proper 4 (May 29—June 4)	Deut. 11:18–21, 26–28	Rom. 3:21–28	Matt. 7:15–29
Proper 5 (June 5–11)	Hos. 5:15—6:6	Rom. 4:13–25	Matt. 9:9–13
Proper 6 (June 12–18)	Ex. 19:2–8	Rom. 5:6–15	Matt. 9:35—10:8 (9–20)
Proper 7 (June 19–25)	Jer. 20:7–13	Rom. 6:12–23	Matt. 10:5a, 21–33
Proper 8 (June 26—July 2)	Jer. 28:5–9	Rom. 7:1–13	Matt. 10:34–42
Proper 9 (July 3–9)	Zech. 9:9–12	Rom. 7:14–25a	Matt. 11:25–30
Proper 10 (July 10–16)	Is. 55:10–13	Rom. 8:12–17	Matt. 13:1–9, 18–23
Proper 11 (July 17–23)	Is. 44:6–8	Rom. 8:18–27	Matt. 13:24–30, 36–43
Proper 12 (July 24–30)	Deut. 7:6–9	Rom. 8:28–39	Matt. 13:44–52
Proper 13 (July 31—Aug. 6)	Is. 55:1–5	Rom. 9:1–5 (6–13)	Matt. 14:13–21
Proper 14 (Aug. 7–13)	Job 38:4–18	Rom. 10:5–17	Matt. 14:22–33
Proper 15 (Aug. 14–20)	Is. 56:1, 6–8	Rom. 11:1–2a, 13–15, 28–32	Matt. 15:21–28
Proper 16 (Aug. 21–27)	Is. 51:1–6	Rom. 11:33—12:8	Matt. 16:13–20
Proper 17 (Aug. 28—Sept. 3)	Jer. 15:15–21	Rom. 12:9–21	Matt. 16:21–28
Proper 18 (Sept. 4–10)	Ezek. 33:7–9	Rom. 13:1–10	Matt. 18:1–20
Proper 19 (Sept. 11–17)	Gen. 50:15–21	Rom. 14:1–12	Matt. 18:21–35
Proper 20 (Sept. 18–24)	Is. 55:6–9	Phil. 1:12–14, 19–30	Matt. 20:1–16
Proper 21 (Sept. 25—Oct. 1)	Ezek. 18:1–4, 25–32	Phil. 2:1–4 (5–13) 14–18	Matt. 21:23–27 (28–32)
Proper 22 (Oct. 2–8)	Is. 5:1–7	Phil. 3:4b–14	Matt. 21:33–46
Proper 23 (Oct. 9–15)	Is. 25:6–9	Phil. 4:4–13	Matt. 22:1–14
Proper 24 (Oct. 16–22)	Is. 45:1–7	1 Thess. 1:1–10	Matt. 22:15–22
Proper 25 (Oct. 23–29)	Lev. 19:1–2, 15–18	1 Thess. 2:1–13	Matt. 22:34–46
Proper 26 (Oct. 30—Nov. 5)	Micah 3:5–12	1 Thess. 4:1–12	Matt. 23:1–12
Proper 27 (Nov. 6–12)	Amos 5:18–24	1 Thess. 4:13–18	Matt. 25:1–13
Proper 28 (Nov. 13–19)	Zeph. 1:7–16	1 Thess. 5:1–11	Matt. 25:14–30
Proper 29 (Nov. 20–26)	Ezek. 34:11–16, 20–24	1 Cor. 15:20–28	Matt. 25:31–46

Because the date of Easter changes from year to year, its place on the calendar during a particular year determines whether there will be a greater or lesser number of Sundays during the season after Pentecost.

For the Three-Year Lectionary, each set of appointed readings is assigned to a specific seven-day period during the season after Pentecost and given a "proper" number. When Easter falls late, the proper numbers immediately following Trinity Sunday are skipped, and the readings resume with the proper number appropriate to the seven-day period. For the One-Year Lectionary, the propers appointed for the Trinity Season follow immediately after Trinity Sunday, and the Sundays immediately prior to the Last Sunday of the Church Year are skipped.

Three-Year Lectionary: Series B

Sunday/Festival	Old Testament/ First Reading	Epistle/ Second Reading	Holy Gospel
Advent 1	Is. 64:1–9	1 Cor. 1:3–9	Mark 11:1–10 *or* Mark 13:24–37
Advent 2	Is. 40:1–11	2 Peter 3:8–14	Mark 1:1–8
Advent 3	Is. 61:1–4, 8–11	1 Thess. 5:16–24	John 1:6–8, 19–28
Advent 4	2 Sam. 7:1–11, 16	Rom. 16:25–27	Luke 1:26–38
Christmas Eve	Is. 7:10–14	1 John 4:7–16	Matt. 1:18–25
Christmas Midnight	Is. 9:2–7	Titus 2:11–14	Luke 2:1–14 (15–20)
Christmas Dawn	Is. 62:10–12	Titus 3:4–7	Luke 2:(1–14) 15–20
Christmas Day	Is. 52:7–10	Heb. 1:1–6 (7–12)	John 1:1–14 (15–18)
Christmas 1	Is. 61:10—62:3	Gal. 4:4–7	Luke 2:22–40
Christmas 2	1 Kings 3:4–15	Eph. 1:3–14	Luke 2:40–52
Epiphany	Is. 60:1–6	Eph. 3:1–12	Matt. 2:1–12
Baptism of Our Lord	Gen. 1:1–5	Rom. 6:1–11	Mark 1:4–11
Epiphany 2	1 Sam. 3:1–10 (11–20)	1 Cor. 6:12–20	John 1:43–51
Epiphany 3	Jonah 3:1–5, 10	1 Cor. 7:29–31 (32–35)	Mark 1:14–20
Epiphany 4	Deut. 18:15–20	1 Cor. 8:1–13	Mark 1:21–28
Epiphany 5	Is. 40:21–31	1 Cor. 9:16–27	Mark 1:29–39
Epiphany 6	2 Kings 5:1–14	1 Cor. 10:(19–30) 10:31—11:1	Mark 1:40–45
Epiphany 7	Is. 43:18–25	2 Cor. 1:18–22	Mark 2:1–12
Epiphany 8	Hos. 2:14–20	2 Cor. 2:12—3:6	Mark 2:(13–17) 18–22
Transfiguration	2 Kings 2:1–12 *or* Ex. 34:29–35	2 Cor. 3:12–13 (14–18); 4:1–6	Mark 9:2–9
Ash Wednesday	Joel 2:12–19	2 Cor. 5:20b—6:10	Matt. 6:1–6, 16–21
Lent 1	Gen. 22:1–18	James 1:12–18	Mark 1:9–15
Lent 2	Gen. 17:1–7, 15–16	Rom. 5:1–11	Mark 8:27–38
Lent 3	Ex. 20:1–17	1 Cor. 1:18–31	John 2:13–22 (23–25)
Lent 4	Num. 21:4–9	Eph. 2:1–10	John 3:14–21
Lent 5	Jer. 31:31–34	Heb. 5:1–10	Mark 10:(32–34) 35–45
Palm Sunday Procession			John 12:12–19
Sunday of the Passion	Zech. 9:9–12	Phil. 2:5–11	Mark 14:1—15:47 *or* Mark 15:1–47 *or* John 12:20–43
Monday in Holy Week	Is. 50:5–10	Heb. 9:11–15	Matt. 26:1—27:66 *or* John 12:1–23
Tuesday in Holy Week	Is. 49:1–7	1 Cor. 1:18–25 (26–31)	Mark 14:1—15:47 *or* John 12:23–50
Wednesday in Holy Week	Is. 62:11—63:7	Rom. 5:6–11	Luke 22:1—23:56 *or* John 13:16–38
Holy Thursday	Ex. 24:3–11	1 Cor. 10:16–17	Mark 14:12–26
Holy Thursday (alt)	Ex. 12:1–14	1 Cor. 11:23–32	John 13:1–17, 31b–35
Good Friday	Is. 52:13—53:12	Heb. 4:14–16; 5:7–9	John 18:1—19:42 *or* John 19:17–30
Holy Saturday	Dan. 6:1–24	1 Peter 4:1–8	Matt. 27:57–66
Vigil of Easter	Selected Readings		
Easter Sunrise	Ex. 15:1–11	1 Cor. 5:6b–8	John 20:1–18
Easter Day	Is. 25:6–9	1 Cor. 15:1–11	Mark 16:1–8
Easter Evening/Monday	Ex. 15:1–18 *or* Dan. 12:1c–3	Acts 10:34–43 *or* 1 Cor. 5:6b–8	Luke 24:13–35 (36–49)
Easter Tuesday	Dan. 3:8–28	Acts 13:26–33	Luke 24:36–49
Easter Wednesday	Acts 3:13–15, 17–19	Col. 3:1–7 *or* 1 Cor. 11:23–26	John 21:1–14
Easter 2	Acts 4:32–35	1 John 1:1—2:2	John 20:19–31
Easter 3	Acts 3:11–21	1 John 3:1–7	Luke 24:36–49

Sunday/Festival	Old Testament/ First Reading	Epistle/ Second Reading	Holy Gospel
Easter 4	Acts 4:1–12	1 John 3:16–24	John 10:11–18
Easter 5	Acts 8:26–40	1 John 4:1–11 (12–21)	John 15:1–8
Easter 6	Acts 10:34–48	1 John 5:1–8	John 15:9–17
Ascension	Acts 1:1–11	Eph. 1:15–23	Luke 24:44–53
Easter 7	Acts 1:12–26	1 John 5:9–15	John 17:11b–19
Pentecost Eve	Ex. 19:1–9	Rom. 8:12–17 (22–27)	John 14:8–21
Day of Pentecost	Ezek. 37:1–14	Acts 2:1–21	John 15:26–27; 16:4b–15
Pentecost Evening/Monday	Is. 57:15–21	Acts 10:34a, 42–48	John 3:16–21
Pentecost Tuesday	Is. 32:14–20	Acts 8:14–17	John 10:1–10
Holy Trinity	Is. 6:1–8	Acts 2:14a, 22–36	John 3:1–17
Proper 3 (May 24–28)	Hos. 2:14–20	Acts 2:14a, 36–47	Mark 2:(13–17) 18–22
Proper 4 (May 29—June 4)	Deut. 5:12–15	2 Cor. 4:5–12	Mark 2:23–28 (3:1–6)
Proper 5 (June 5–11)	Gen. 3:8–15	2 Cor. 4:13—5:1	Mark 3:20–35
Proper 6 (June 12–18)	Ezek. 17:22–24	2 Cor. 5:1–10 (11–17)	Mark 4:26–34
Proper 7 (June 19–25)	Job 38:1–11	2 Cor. 6:1–13	Mark 4:35–41
Proper 8 (June 26—July 2)	Lam. 3:22–33	2 Cor. 8:1–9, 13–15	Mark 5:21–43
Proper 9 (July 3–9)	Ezek. 2:1–5	2 Cor. 12:1–10	Mark 6:1–13
Proper 10 (July 10–16)	Amos 7:7–15	Eph. 1:3–14	Mark 6:14–29
Proper 11 (July 17–23)	Jer. 23:1–6	Eph. 2:11–22	Mark 6:30–44
Proper 12 (July 24–30)	Gen. 9:8–17	Eph. 3:14–21	Mark 6:45–56
Proper 13 (July 31—Aug. 6)	Ex. 16:2–15	Eph. 4:1–16	John 6:22–35
Proper 14 (Aug. 7–13)	1 Kings 19:1–8	Eph. 4:17—5:2	John 6:35–51
Proper 15 (Aug. 14–20)	Prov. 9:1–10 *or* Josh. 24:1–2a, 14–18	Eph. 5:6–21	John 6:51–69
Proper 16 (Aug. 21–27)	Is. 29:11–19	Eph. 5:22–33	Mark 7:1–13
Proper 17 (Aug. 28—Sept. 3)	Deut. 4:1–2, 6–9	Eph. 6:10–20	Mark 7:14–23
Proper 18 (Sept. 4–10)	Is. 35:4–7a	James 2:1–10, 14–18	Mark 7:(24–30) 31–37
Proper 19 (Sept. 11–17)	Is. 50:4–10	James 3:1–12	Mark 9:14–29
Proper 20 (Sept. 18–24)	Jer. 11:18–20	James 3:13—4:10	Mark 9:30–37
Proper 21 (Sept. 25—Oct. 1)	Num. 11:4–6, 10–16, 24–29	James 5:(1–12) 13–20	Mark 9:38–50
Proper 22 (Oct. 2–8)	Gen. 2:18–25	Heb. 2:1–13 (14–18)	Mark 10:2–16
Proper 23 (Oct. 9–15)	Amos 5:6–7, 10–15	Heb. 3:12–19	Mark 10:17–22
Proper 24 (Oct. 16–22)	Eccl. 5:10–20	Heb. 4:1–13 (14–16)	Mark 10:23–31
Proper 25 (Oct. 23–29)	Jer. 31:7–9	Heb. 7:23–28	Mark 10:46–52
Proper 26 (Oct. 30—Nov. 5)	Deut. 6:1–9	Heb. 9:11–14 (15–22)	Mark 12:28–37
Proper 27 (Nov. 6–12)	1 Kings 17:8–16	Heb. 9:24–28	Mark 12:38–44
Proper 28 (Nov. 13–19)	Dan. 12:1–3	Heb. 10:11–25	Mark 13:1–13
Proper 29 (Nov. 20–26)	Is. 51:4–6 *or* Dan. 7:9–10, 13–14	Jude 20–25 *or* Rev. 1:4b–8	Mark 13:24–37 *or* John 18:33–37

Three-Year Lectionary: Series C

Sunday/Festival	Old Testament/ First Reading	Epistle/ Second Reading	Holy Gospel
Advent 1	Jer. 33:14–16	1 Thess. 3:9–13	Luke 19:28–40 *or* Luke 21:25–36
Advent 2	Mal. 3:1–7b	Phil. 1:2–11	Luke 3:1–14 (15–20)
Advent 3	Zeph. 3:14–20	Phil. 4:4–7	Luke 7:18–28 (29–35)
Advent 4	Micah 5:2–5a	Heb. 10:5–10	Luke 1:39–45 (46–56)
Christmas Eve	Is. 7:10–14	1 John 4:7–16	Matt. 1:18–25
Christmas Midnight	Is. 9:2–7	Titus 2:11–14	Luke 2:1–14 (15–20)
Christmas Dawn	Is. 62:10–12	Titus 3:4–7	Luke 2:(1–14) 15–20
Christmas Day	Is. 52:7–10	Heb. 1:1–6 (7–12)	John 1:1–14 (15–18)
Christmas 1	Ex. 13:1–3a, 11–15	Col. 3:12–17	Luke 2:22–40
Christmas 2	1 Kings 3:4–15	Eph. 1:3–14	Luke 2:40–52
Epiphany	Is. 60:1–6	Eph. 3:1–12	Matt. 2:1–12
Baptism of Our Lord	Is. 43:1–7	Rom. 6:1–11	Luke 3:15–22
Epiphany 2	Is. 62:1–5	1 Cor. 12:1–11	John 2:1–11
Epiphany 3	Neh. 8:1–3, 5–6, 8–10	1 Cor. 12:12–31a	Luke 4:16–30
Epiphany 4	Jer. 1:4–10 (17–19)	1 Cor. 12:31b—13:13	Luke 4:31–44
Epiphany 5	Is. 6:1–8 (9–13)	1 Cor. 14:12b–20	Luke 5:1–11
Epiphany 6	Jer. 17:5–8	1 Cor. 15:(1–11) 12–20	Luke 6:17–26
Epiphany 7	Gen. 45:3–15	1 Cor. 15:21–26, 30–42	Luke 6:27–38
Epiphany 8	Jer. 7:1–7 (8–15)	1 Cor. 15:42–52 (53–58)	Luke 6:39–49
Transfiguration	Deut. 34:1–12	Heb. 3:1–6	Luke 9:28–36
Ash Wednesday	Joel 2:12–19	2 Cor. 5:20b—6:10	Matt. 6:1–6, 16–21
Lent 1	Deut. 26:1–11	Rom. 10:8b–13	Luke 4:1–13
Lent 2	Jer. 26:8–15	Phil. 3:17—4:1	Luke 13:31–35
Lent 3	Ezek. 33:7–20	1 Cor. 10:1–13	Luke 13:1–9
Lent 4	Is. 12:1–6	2 Cor. 5:16–21	Luke 15:1–3, 11–32
Lent 5	Is. 43:16–21	Phil. 3:(4b–7) 8–14	Luke 20:9–20
Palm Sunday Procession			John 12:12–19
Sunday of the Passion	Deut. 32:36–39	Phil. 2:5–11	Luke 22:1—23:56 *or* Luke 23:1–56 *or* John 12:20–43
Monday in Holy Week	Is. 50:5–10	Heb. 9:11–15	Matt. 26:1—27:66 *or* John 12:1–23
Tuesday in Holy Week	Is. 49:1–7	1 Cor. 1:18–25 (26–31)	Mark 14:1—15:47 *or* John 12:23–50
Wednesday in Holy Week	Is. 62:11—63:7	Rom. 5:6–11	Luke 22:1—23:56 *or* John 13:16–38
Holy Thursday	Jer. 31:31–34	Heb. 10:15–25	Luke 22:7–20
Holy Thursday (alt)	Ex. 12:1–14	1 Cor. 11:23–32	John 13:1–17, 31b–35
Good Friday	Is. 52:13—53:12	Heb. 4:14–16; 5:7–9	John 18:1—19:42 *or* John 19:17–30
Holy Saturday	Dan. 6:1–24	1 Peter 4:1–8	Matt. 27:57–66
Vigil of Easter	Selected Readings		
Easter Sunrise	Job 19:23–27	1 Cor. 15:51–57	John 20:1–18
Easter Day	Is. 65:17–25	1 Cor. 15:19–26	Luke 24:1–12
Easter Evening/Monday	Ex. 15:1–18 *or* Dan. 12:1c–3	Acts 10:34–43 *or* 1 Cor. 5:6b–8	Luke 24:13–35 (36–49)
Easter Tuesday	Dan. 3:8–28	Acts 13:26–33	Luke 24:36–49
Easter Wednesday	Acts 3:13–15, 17–19	Col. 3:1–7 *or* 1 Cor. 11:23–26	John 21:1–14
Easter 2	Acts 5:12–20 (21–32)	Rev. 1:4–18	John 20:19–31
Easter 3	Acts 9:1–22	Rev. 5:(1–7) 8–14	John 21:1–14 (15–19)
Easter 4	Acts 20:17–35	Rev. 7:9–17	John 10:22–30

Sunday/Festival	Old Testament/ First Reading	Epistle/ Second Reading	Holy Gospel
Easter 5	Acts 11:1–18	Rev. 21:1–7	John 16:12–22 *or* John 13:31–35
Easter 6	Acts 16:9–15	Rev. 21:9–14, 21–27	John 16:23–33 *or* John 5:1–9
Ascension	Acts 1:1–11	Eph. 1:15–23	Luke 24:44–53
Easter 7	Acts 1:12–26	Rev. 22:1–6 (7–11) 12–20	John 17:20–26
Pentecost Eve	Ex. 19:1–9	Rom. 8:12–17 (22–27)	John 14:8–21
Day of Pentecost	Gen. 11:1–9	Acts 2:1–21	John 14:23–31
Pentecost Evening/Monday	Is. 57:15–21	Acts 10:34a, 42–48	John 3:16–21
Pentecost Tuesday	Is. 32:14–20	Acts 8:14–17	John 10:1–10
Holy Trinity	Prov. 8:1–4, 22–31	Acts 2:14a, 22–36	John 8:48–59
Proper 3 (May 24–28)	Gen. 50:15–21	Acts 2:14a, 36–47	Luke 6:(20–26) 27–42
Proper 4 (May 29—June 4)	1 Kings 8:22–24, 27–29, 41–43	Gal. 1:1–12	Luke 7:1–10
Proper 5 (June 5–11)	1 Kings 17:17–24	Gal. 1:11–24	Luke 7:11–17
Proper 6 (June 12–18)	2 Sam. 11:26—12:10, 13–14	Gal. 2:15–21; 3:10–14	Luke 7:36—8:3
Proper 7 (June 19–25)	Is. 65:1–9	Gal. 3:23—4:7	Luke 8:26–39
Proper 8 (June 26—July 2)	1 Kings 19:9b–21	Gal. 5:1, 13–25	Luke 9:51–62
Proper 9 (July 3–9)	Is. 66:10–14	Gal. 6:1–10, 14–18	Luke 10:1–20
Proper 10 (July 10–16)	Lev. (18:1–5) 19:9–18	Col. 1:1–14	Luke 10:25–37
Proper 11 (July 17–23)	Gen. 18:1–10a (10b–14)	Col. 1:21–29	Luke 10:38–42
Proper 12 (July 24–30)	Gen. 18:(17–19) 20–33	Col. 2:6–15 (16–19)	Luke 11:1–13
Proper 13 (July 31—Aug. 6)	Eccl. 1:2, 12–14; 2:18–26	Col. 3:1–11	Luke 12:13–21
Proper 14 (Aug. 7–13)	Gen. 15:1–6	Heb. 11:1–16	Luke 12:22–34 (35–40)
Proper 15 (Aug. 14–20)	Jer. 23:16–29	Heb. 11:17–31 (32–40); 12:1–3	Luke 12:49–53 (54–56)
Proper 16 (Aug. 21–27)	Is. 66:18–23	Heb. 12:4–24 (25–29)	Luke 13:22–30
Proper 17 (Aug. 28—Sept. 3)	Prov. 25:2–10	Heb. 13:1–17	Luke 14:1–14
Proper 18 (Sept. 4–10)	Deut. 30:15–20	Philemon 1–21	Luke 14:25–35
Proper 19 (Sept. 11–17)	Ezek. 34:11–24	1 Tim. 1:(5–11) 12–17	Luke 15:1–10
Proper 20 (Sept. 18–24)	Amos 8:4–7	1 Tim. 2:1–15	Luke 16:1–15
Proper 21 (Sept. 25—Oct. 1)	Amos 6:1–7	1 Tim. 3:1–13 *or* 1 Tim. 6:6–19	Luke 16:19–31
Proper 22 (Oct. 2–8)	Hab. 1:1–4; 2:1–4	2 Tim. 1:1–14	Luke 17:1–10
Proper 23 (Oct. 9–15)	Ruth 1:1–19a	2 Tim. 2:1–13	Luke 17:11–19
Proper 24 (Oct. 16–22)	Gen. 32:22–30	2 Tim. 3:14—4:5	Luke 18:1–8
Proper 25 (Oct. 23–29)	Gen. 4:1–15	2 Tim. 4:6–8, 16–18	Luke 18:9–17
Proper 26 (Oct. 30—Nov. 5)	Is. 1:10–18	2 Thess. 1:1–5 (6–10) 11–12	Luke 19:1–10
Proper 27 (Nov. 6–12)	Ex. 3:1–15	2 Thess. 2:1–8, 13–17	Luke 20:27–40
Proper 28 (Nov. 13–19)	Mal. 4:1–6	2 Thess. 3:(1–5) 6–13	Luke 21:5–28 (29–36)
Proper 29 (Nov. 20–26)	Mal. 3:13–18	Col. 1:13–20	Luke 23:27–43

One-Year Lectionary

Sunday/Festival	Old Testament	Epistle	Holy Gospel
Advent 1	Jer. 23:5–8	Rom. 13:(8–10) 11–14	Matt. 21:1–9
Advent 2	Mal. 4:1–6	Rom. 15:4–13	Luke 21:25–36
Advent 3	Is. 40:1–8 (9–11)	1 Cor. 4:1–5	Matt. 11:2–10 (11)
Advent 4	Deut. 18:15–19	Phil. 4:4–7	John 1:19–28 *or* Luke 1:39–56
Christmas Eve	Is. 7:10–14	1 John 4:7–16	Matt. 1:18–25
Christmas Midnight	Is. 9:2–7	Titus 2:11–14	Luke 2:1–14 (15–20)
Christmas Dawn	Micah 5:2–5a	Titus 3:4–7	Luke 2:(1–14) 15–20
Christmas Day	Ex. 40:17–21, 34–38	Titus 3:4–7	John 1:1–14 (15–18)
Christmas 1	Is. 11:1–5 *or* 2 Sam. 7:1–16	Gal. 4:1–7	Luke 2:(22–32) 33–40
Christmas 2	Gen. 46:1–7	1 Peter 4:12–19	Matt. 2:13–23
Epiphany	Is. 60:1–6	Eph. 3:1–12	Matt. 2:1–12
Epiphany 1	1 Kings 8:6–13	Rom. 12:1–5	Luke 2:41–52
or Baptism of Our Lord	Joshua 3:1–3, 7–8, 13–17 *or* Is. 42:1–7	1 Cor. 1:26–31	Matt. 3:13–17
Epiphany 2	Ex. 33:12–23 *or* Amos 9:11–15	Eph. 5:22–33 *or* Rom. 12:6–16	John 2:1–11
Epiphany 3	2 Kings 5:1–15a	Rom. 1:8–17 *or* Rom. 12:16–21	Matt. 8:1–13
Epiphany 4	Jonah 1:1–17	Rom. 8:18–23 *or* Rom. 13:8–10	Matt. 8:23–27
Epiphany 5	Gen. 18:20–33	Col. 3:12–17	Matt. 13:24–30 (36–43)
Transfiguration	Ex. 34:29–35 *or* Ex. 3:1–14	2 Peter 1:16–21	Matt. 17:1–9
Septuagesima	Ex. 17:1–7	1 Cor. 9:24—10:5	Matt. 20:1–16
Sexagesima	Is. 55:10–13	2 Cor. 11:19—12:9 *or* Heb. 4:9–13	Luke 8:4–15
Quinquagesima	1 Sam. 16:1–13 *or* Is. 35:3–7	1 Cor. 13:1–13	Luke 18:31–43
Ash Wednesday	Joel 2:12–19 *or* Jonah 3:1–10	2 Peter 1:2–11	Matt. 6:(1–6) 16–21
Lent 1	Gen. 3:1–21 *or* 1 Sam. 17:40–51	2 Cor. 6:1–10 *or* Heb. 4:14–16	Matt. 4:1–11
Lent 2	Gen. 32:22–32	1 Thess. 4:1–7 *or* Rom. 5:1–5	Matt. 15:21–28
Lent 3	Ex. 8:16–24 *or* Jer. 26:1–15	Eph. 5:1–9	Luke 11:14–28
Lent 4	Ex. 16:2–21 *or* Is. 49:8–13	Gal. 4:21–31 *or* Acts 2:41–47	John 6:1–15
Lent 5	Gen. 22:1–14	Heb. 9:11–15	John 8:(42–45) 46–59
Palm Sunday Procession			Matt. 21:1–9 *or* John 12:12–19
Sunday of the Passion	Zech. 9:9–12	Phil. 2:5–11	Matt. 26:1—27:66 *or* Matt. 27:11–54
Monday in Holy Week	Is. 50:5–10	1 Peter 2:21–24	John 12:1–36 (37–43)
Tuesday in Holy Week	Jer. 11:18–20	1 Tim. 6:12–14	Mark 14:1—15:47
Wednesday in Holy Week	Is. 62:11—63:7	Rev. 1:5b–7	Luke 22:1—23:56
Holy Thursday	Ex. 12:1–14 *or* Ex. 24:3–11	1 Cor. 11:23–32	John 13:1–15 (34–35)
Good Friday	Is. 52:13—53:12	2 Cor. 5:14–21	John 18:1—19:42
Holy Saturday	Dan. 6:1–24	1 Peter 3:17–22	Matt. 27:57–66
Vigil of Easter	Selected Readings		
Easter Sunrise	Is. 25:6–9 *or* Ex. 14:10—15:1	1 Cor. 15:1–11 *or* 1 Cor. 15:12–25	John 20:1–18

Sunday/Festival	Old Testament	Epistle	Holy Gospel
Easter Day	Job 19:23–27	1 Cor. 5:6–8 *or* 1 Cor. 15:51–57	Mark 16:1–8
Easter Evening/Monday	Ex. 15:1–18	Acts 10:34–43	Luke 24:13–35
Easter Tuesday	Dan. 3:8–28	Acts 13:26–33	Luke 24:36–48 (49)
Easter Wednesday	Acts 3:13–15, 17–19	Col. 3:1–7 *or* 1 Cor. 11:23–26	John 21:1–14
Easter 2	Ezek. 37:1–14	1 John 5:4–10	John 20:19–31
Easter 3	Ezek. 34:11–16	1 Peter 2:21–25	John 10:11–16
Easter 4	Is. 40:25–31 *or* Lam. 3:22–33	1 Peter 2:11–20 *or* 1 John 3:1–3	John 16:16–22
Easter 5	Is. 12:1–6	James 1:16–21	John 16:5–15
Easter 6	Num. 21:4–9	1 Tim. 2:1–6 *or* James 1:22–27	John 16:23–30 (31–33)
Ascension	2 Kings 2:5–15	Acts 1:1–11	Mark 16:14–20 *or* Luke 24:44–53
Easter 7	Ezek. 36:22–28	1 Peter 4:7–11 (12–14)	John 15:26—16:4
Pentecost Eve	Joel 3:1–5	Rom. 8:12–17	John 14:15–21
Day of Pentecost	Gen. 11:1–9	Acts 2:1–21	John 14:23–31
Pentecost Evening/Monday	Is. 57:15–21	Acts 10:34a, 42–48	John 3:16–21
Pentecost Tuesday	Is. 32:14–20	Acts 8:14–17	John 10:1–10
Holy Trinity	Is. 6:1–7	Rom. 11:33–36	John 3:1–15 (16–17)
Trinity 1	Gen. 15:1–6	1 John 4:16–21	Luke 16:19–31
Trinity 2	Prov. 9:1–10	Eph. 2:13–22 *or* 1 John 3:13–18	Luke 14:15–24
Trinity 3	Micah 7:18–20	1 Tim. 1:12–17 *or* 1 Peter 5:6–11	Luke 15:1–10 *or* Luke 15:11–32
Trinity 4	Gen. 50:15–21	Rom. 12:14–21 *or* Rom. 8:18–23	Luke 6:36–42
Trinity 5	1 Kings 19:11–21	1 Cor. 1:18–25 *or* 1 Peter 3:8–15	Luke 5:1–11
Trinity 6	Ex. 20:1–17	Rom. 6:(1–2) 3–11	Matt. 5:(17–19) 20–26
Trinity 7	Gen. 2:7–17	Rom. 6:19–23	Mark 8:1–9
Trinity 8	Jer. 23:16–29	Acts 20:27–38 *or* Rom. 8:12–17	Matt. 7:15–23
Trinity 9	2 Sam. 22:26–34	1 Cor. 10:6–13	Luke 16:1–9 (10–13)
Trinity 10	Jer. 8:4–12 *or* Jer. 7:1–11	Rom. 9:30—10:4 *or* 1 Cor. 12:1–11	Luke 19:41–48
Trinity 11	Gen. 4:1–15	Eph. 2:1–10 *or* 1 Cor. 15:1–10	Luke 18:9–14
Trinity 12	Is. 29:17–24	2 Cor. 3:4–11 *or* Rom. 10:9–17	Mark 7:31–37
Trinity 13	2 Chron. 28:8–15	Gal. 3:15–22	Luke 10:23–37
Trinity 14	Prov. 4:10–23	Gal. 5:16–24	Luke 17:11–19
Trinity 15	1 Kings 17:8–16	Gal. 5:25—6:10	Matt. 6:24–34
Trinity 16	1 Kings 17:17–24	Eph. 3:13–21	Luke 7:11–17
Trinity 17	Prov. 25:6–14	Eph. 4:1–6	Luke 14:1–11
Trinity 18	Deut. 10:12–21	1 Cor. 1:(1–3) 4–9	Matt. 22:34–46
Trinity 19	Gen. 28:10–17	Eph. 4:22–28	Matt. 9:1–8
Trinity 20	Is. 55:1–9	Eph. 5:15–21	Matt. 22:1–14 *or* Matt. 21:33–44
Trinity 21	Gen. 1:1—2:3	Eph. 6:10–17	John 4:46–54
Trinity 22	Micah 6:6–8	Phil. 1:3–11	Matt. 18:21–35
Trinity 23	Prov. 8:11–22	Phil. 3:17–21	Matt. 22:15–22
Trinity 24	Is. 51:9–16	Col. 1:9–14	Matt. 9:18–26
Trinity 25	Ex. 32:1–20 *or* Job 14:1–6	1 Thess. 4:13–18	Matt. 24:15–28 *or* Luke 17:20–30
Trinity 26	Dan. 7:9–14	2 Peter 3:3–14	Matt. 25:31–46
Last Sunday	Is. 65:17–25	1 Thess. 5:1–11	Matt. 25:1–13

FEASTS AND FESTIVALS

Feast/Festival	Old Testament/ First Reading	Epistle/ Second Reading	Holy Gospel
St. Andrew November 30	Ezek. 3:16–21	Rom. 10:8b–18	John 1:35–42a
St. Thomas December 21	Judg. 6:36–40	Eph. 4:7, 11–16	John 20:24–29
St. Stephen December 26	2 Chron. 24:17–22	Acts 6:8—7:2a, 51–60	Matt. 23:34–39
St. John December 27	Rev. 1:1–6	1 John 1:1—2:2	John 21:20–25
Holy Innocents December 28	Jer. 31:15–17	Rev. 14:1–5	Matt. 2:13–18
New Year's Eve December 31	Is. 30:(8–14) 15–17	Rom. 8:31b–39	Luke 12:35–40
Circumcision and Name of Jesus January 1	Num. 6:22–27	Gal. 3:23–29	Luke 2:21
Confession of St. Peter January 18	Acts 4:8–13	2 Peter 1:1–15	Mark 8:27–35 (36—9:1)
St. Timothy January 24	Acts 16:1–5	1 Tim. 6:11–16	Matt. 24:42–47
Conversion of St. Paul January 25	Acts 9:1–22	Gal. 1:11–24	Matt. 19:27–30
St. Titus January 26	Acts 20:28–35	Titus 1:1–9	Luke 10:1–9
Purification of Mary and Presentation of Our Lord February 2	1 Sam. 1:21–28	Heb. 2:14–18	Luke 2:22–32 (33–40)
St. Matthias February 24	Is. 66:1–2	Acts 1:15–26	Matt. 11:25–30
St. Joseph March 19	2 Sam. 7:4–16	Rom. 4:13–18	Matt. 2:13–15, 19–23
Annunciation of Our Lord March 25	Is. 7:10–14	Heb. 10:4–10	Luke 1:26–38
St. Mark April 25	Is. 52:7–10	2 Tim. 4:5–18	Mark 16:14–20
St. Philip and St. James May 1	Is. 30:18–21	Eph. 2:19–22	John 14:1–14
The Visitation May 31 *(3-Yr. Lect.)*	Is. 11:1–5	Rom. 12:9–16	Luke 1:39–45 (46–56)
St. Barnabas June 11	Is. 42:5–12	Acts 11:19–30; 13:1–3	Mark 6:7–13
Nativity of St. John the Baptist June 24	Is. 40:1–5	Acts 13:13–26	Luke 1:57–80
St. Peter and St. Paul June 29	Acts 15:1–12 (13–21)	Gal. 2:1–10	Matt. 16:13–19
The Visitation July 2 *(1-Yr. Lect.)*	Is. 11:1–5	Rom. 12:9–16	Luke 1:39–45 (46–56)
St. Mary Magdalene July 22	Prov. 31:10–31	Acts 13:26–31	John 20:1–2, 10–18
St. James the Elder July 25	Acts 11:27—12:5	Rom. 8:28–39	Mark 10:35–45
St. Mary, Mother of Our Lord August 15	Is. 61:7–11	Gal. 4:4–7	Luke 1:(39–45) 46–55
St. Bartholomew August 24	Prov. 3:1–8	2 Cor. 4:7–10	Luke 22:24–30 *or* John 1:43–51

Feast/Festival	Old Testament/ First Reading	Epistle/ Second Reading	Holy Gospel
Martyrdom of St. John the Baptist August 29	Rev. 6:9–11	Rom. 6:1–5	Mark 6:14–29
Holy Cross Day September 14	Num. 21:4–9	1 Cor. 1:18–25	John 12:20–33
St. Matthew September 21	Ezek. 2:8—3:11	Eph. 4:7–16	Matt. 9:9–13
St. Michael and All Angels September 29	Dan. 10:10–14; 12:1–3	Rev. 12:7–12	Matt. 18:1–11 *or* Luke 10:17–20
St. Luke October 18	Is. 35:5–8	2 Tim. 4:5–18	Luke 10:1–9
St. James of Jerusalem October 23	Acts 15:12–22a	James 1:1–12	Matt. 13:54–58
St. Simon and St. Jude October 28	Jer. 26:1–16	1 Peter 1:3–9	John 15:(12–16) 17–21
Reformation Day October 31	Rev. 14:6–7	Rom. 3:19–28	John 8:31–36 *or* Matt. 11:12–19
All Saints' Day November 1	Rev. 7:(2–8) 9–17	1 John 3:1–3	Matt. 5:1–12

OCCASIONS

Occasion	Old Testament/ First Reading	Epistle/ Second Reading	Holy Gospel
Anniversary of a Congregation	1 Kings 8:22–30	Rev. 21:1–5	Luke 19:1–10
Mission Observance	Is. 62:1–7	Rom. 10:11–17	Luke 24:44–53
Christian Education	Deut. 6:4–15	Acts 2:37–41	Luke 18:15–17
Harvest Observance	Deut. 26:1–11	2 Cor. 9:6–15	Luke 12:13–21
Day of Thanksgiving	Deut. 8:1–10	Phil. 4:6–20 *or* 1 Tim. 2:1–4	Luke 17:11–19
Day of Supplication and Prayer	Joel 2:12–19	1 John 1:5—2:2	Matt. 6:16–21
Day of National or Local Tragedy	Job 30:16–24 *or* Rev. 7:13–17	Rom. 8:31–39 *or* Heb. 12:4–13	Luke 13:1–9 *or* Matt. 24:32–35

DATES OF EASTER

Easter Day is always the Sunday after the full moon that occurs on or after the spring equinox on March 21. This full moon may happen on any date between March 21 and April 18 inclusive. If the full moon falls on a Sunday, Easter Day is the Sunday following. Easter Day cannot be earlier than March 22 or later than April 25.

Ash Wednesday, the first day of Lent, falls in the seventh week before Easter. The Ascension of Our Lord occurs on a Thursday, forty days after Easter Day. The Day of Pentecost is seven weeks, or the fiftieth day, after Easter Day.

2007—April 8
2008—March 23
2009—April 12
2010—April 4
2011—April 24
2012—April 8
2013—March 31
2014—April 20
2015—April 5
2016—March 27
2017—April 16

2018—April 1
2019—April 21
2020—April 12
2021—April 4
2022—April 17
2023—April 9
2024—March 31
2025—April 20
2026—April 5
2027—March 28
2028—April 16

2029—April 1
2030—April 21
2031—April 13
2032—March 28
2033—April 17
2034—April 9
2035—March 25
2036—April 13
2037—April 5
2038—April 25
2039—April 10

2040—April 1
2041—April 21
2042—April 6
2043—March 29
2044—April 17
2045—April 9
2046—March 25
2047—April 14
2048—April 5
2049—April 18
2050—April 10

GLOSSARY

Absolution. Announcement of forgiveness following the confession of sins. See page 151, left-hand column, and pages 291 and 293.

Agnus Dei (AHG-noose DAY-ee). Latin for "Lamb of God" (John 1:29). See page 163.

Alleluia. Hebrew word meaning "praise the LORD." Also spelled "Hallelujah."

Amen. Hebrew word meaning "it is true, reliable." Spoken as the congregation's affirmation of a prayer or blessing.

Antiphon. A verse of Scripture repeated at the beginning and end of a psalm or Introit.

Benedicamus (beh-neh-dih-KAH-moose). Latin for "bless we [the Lord]." See page 202.

Benediction. A blessing from the Lord, spoken by the pastor at the conclusion of the service. The Aaronic Benediction is from Numbers 6:24–26 (page 166). The Apostolic Benediction is from 2 Corinthians 13:14 (page 228).

Benedictus (beh-neh-DIK-toose). Latin for "blessed." Song of Zechariah (Luke 1:68–79), one of the canticles in Matins. See page 226.

Canticle. Sung liturgical text, usually drawn from the Bible (for example, the Magnificat and Benedictus).

Collect (KAH-lekt). A brief, structured prayer, usually consisting of five parts: address to God, basis for the prayer, petition, desired benefit or result, and trinitarian conclusion.

Compline (KOM-plin). Service of prayer at the close of the day. See pages 253–59.

Creed. From the Latin for "I believe." Words of faith confessing the teachings of Holy Scripture. The three Ecumenical Creeds are the Apostles' Creed (page 159), the Nicene Creed (page 158), and the Athanasian Creed (pages 319–20).

Divine Service. The name for the regular, weekly service that includes the celebration of the Lord's Supper.

Doxology. Words of praise addressed to the triune God. Hymns that conclude with a doxological stanza are so indicated with a △.

Epistle. From the Greek word for "letter." In the Divine Service, the Epistle is the second reading, usually drawn from a letter in the New Testament.

Funeral Pall. Large, white cloth that covers the casket, reminding us that we are clothed in Christ's righteousness through Baptism (Gal. 3:27).

Gloria in Excelsis (GLOW-ree-uh in ek-SHELL-sis). Latin meaning "glory in the highest" (Luke 2:14). The traditional Hymn of Praise in the Divine Service. See page 154.

Gloria Patri (GLOW-ree-uh PAH-tree). Latin for "glory to the Father." A trinitarian doxology used to conclude a psalm or Introit.

Gradual. A liturgical response, drawn from the Bible, that follows the Old Testament Reading.

Hosanna. Hebrew word of praise meaning "save us now" (Matt. 21:9). Included in the Sanctus.

Introit (inn-TRO-it). From the Latin for "enter." Psalm verses sung or spoken at the beginning of the Divine Service.

Many of these entries occur more than once in Lutheran Service Book. *Page references are generally given for only the first occurrence. Pronunciation of some words may vary.*

Invocation. From the Latin "to call upon." The words "In the name of the Father and of the ☩ Son and of the Holy Spirit" (Matt. 28:19b) are spoken at the beginning of the service and remind us of our Baptism. See page 151.

Kyrie (KIH-ree-ay). From the Greek "Kyrie eleison," which means "Lord, have mercy" (Mark 10:47). See page 152.

Lectionary. A list of appointed Scripture readings for the Sundays, festivals, and occasions of the Church Year.

Litany. A structured form of prayer for all conditions of humanity, consisting of a series of petitions and responses. See pages 288–89.

Liturgy. From a Greek word meaning "public service." See also Divine Service.

Magnificat (mag-NIH-fih-kaht). Latin for "magnify, praise" from the Song of Mary (Luke 1:46–55). A canticle sung in Vespers and Evening Prayer. See pages 248–49.

Matins. Morning service of psalms, readings, and prayers. See pages 219–28.

Nunc Dimittis (NUNK dih-MIH-tuss). Latin for "now [let your servant] depart," from the Song of Simeon (Luke 2:29–32). See page 165.

Ordinary. The parts of the service that remain the same from week to week, such as the Kyrie and Sanctus.

Paschal Candle. A large candle used during Eastertide and at baptisms and funerals to signify the presence of the risen Christ among His people.

Pax Domini (PAHKS DOH-mee-nee). Latin for "peace of the Lord" (John 20:19). See page 163.

Phos Hilaron (FOHS HILL-uh-rahn). Greek for "joyous light." See page 244.

Preface. The versicles and responses at the beginning of the Service of the Sacrament, followed by the Proper Preface, which changes from season to season. See pages 160–61.

Propers. The parts of the service, such as the Scripture readings, Introit, and hymns, that change according to the Sunday or festival of the Church Year.

Responsory. Scripture verses sung or spoken after the reading of Scripture in Matins, Vespers, and Compline. See pages 221–22.

Rubrics. From the Latin for "red." Instructions, which are often printed in red, for the minister(s) and congregation concerning how to conduct a service.

Sabaoth (SAH-bay-oath). Hebrew for "heavenly hosts," including "angels, archangels, and all the company of heaven." See page 195.

Salutation. "The Lord be with you" (2 Tim. 4:22), followed by the response "And also with you," or "And with your Spirit." See page 172.

Sanctus (SAHNK-toose). Latin for "holy." The Sanctus follows the Preface in the Service of the Sacrament. From Isaiah 6:3 and Matthew 21:9. See page 161.

Suffrages (SUFF-ruh-jez). "Petitions" of prayer to God. See page 282.

Te Deum (tay DAY-oom). Latin for "[we praise] You, O God." Ancient canticle of praise sung in Matins. See pages 223–25.

Venite (veh-NEE-tay). Latin for "O come." Initial words of Psalm 95, sung as the first psalm in Matins. See pages 220–21.

Verse. Portions of Scripture sung or spoken immediately before the Holy Gospel in the Divine Service, usually with Alleluias before and after.

Vespers. Evening service of psalms, readings, and prayers. See pages 229–34.

Words of Our Lord. The words of Jesus, spoken by the pastor over the bread and wine in the Service of the Sacrament, by which the body and blood of Christ are truly present, distributed, and received. Also known as the Words of Institution. See page 162.

SINGING THE PSALMS

The psalms are pointed for singing. Each psalm verse is divided into two parts, with an asterisk (*) indicating the point of division. Most of the text of each half verse is sung to a reciting tone (𝅜). At the point of the vertical line (|) the final two or three syllables are sung to the notes provided. Ordinarily there is one syllable of text for each note. When there are only two syllables, the first syllable is sung to two notes.

In addition to a number of single tones, three double tones are also provided. Two verses of text are sung to these tones. Double tones are especially appropriate for longer psalms and work best when sung to a psalm with an even number of verses.

Any psalm can be sung to any tone. It is best, however, that the tone, which can range from cheerful and bright to somber and austere, be appropriate to the text.

A
E
B
F
C
G
D
H
I
J
K

THE PSALMS

1

[1] Blessèd is the man who walks not in the counsel of the | wicked,*
nor stands in the way of sinners, nor sits in the seat of | scoffers;

[2] but his delight is in the law | of the LORD,*
and on his law he meditates | day and night.

[3] He is like a tree planted by streams of water that yields its fruit in its season, and its leaf does not | wither.*
In all that he does, he | prospers.

[4] The wicked | are not so,*
but are like chaff that the wind | drives away.

[5] Therefore the wicked will not stand in the | judgment,*
nor sinners in the congregation of the | righteous;

[6] for the LORD knows the way of the | righteous,*
but the way of the wicked will | perish.

Glory be to the Father and | to the Son*
and to the Holy | Spirit;
as it was in the be- | ginning,*
is now, and will be forever. | Amen.

2

[1] Why do the | nations rage*
and the peoples | plot in vain?

[2] The kings of the earth set themselves, and the rulers take counsel to- | gether,*
against the LORD and against his anointed, | saying,

[3] "Let us burst their | bonds apart*
and cast away their | cords from us."

[4] He who sits in the | heavens laughs;*
the Lord holds them in de- | rision.

[5] Then he will speak to them | in his wrath,*
and terrify them in his fury, | saying,

[6] "As for me, I have | set my King*
on Zion, my | holy hill."

[7] I will tell of | the decree:*
The LORD said to me, "You are my Son; today I have be- | gotten you.

[8] Ask of me, and I will make the nations your | heritage,*
and the ends of the earth your pos- | session.

[9] You shall break them with a | rod of iron*
and dash them in pieces like a potter's | vessel."

[10] Now therefore, O | kings, be wise;*
be warned, O rulers | of the earth.

[11] Serve the | LORD with fear,*
and rejoice with | trembling.

[12] Kiss the Son, lest he be angry, and you perish in the way, for his wrath is quickly | kindled.*
Blessèd are all who take ref- | uge in him.

Glory be to the Father and | to the Son*
and to the Holy | Spirit;
as it was in the be- | ginning,*
is now, and will be forever. | Amen.

3

[1] O LORD, how many | are my foes!*
Many are rising a- | gainst me;

[2] many are saying | of my soul,*
there is no salvation for | him in God.

[3] But you, O LORD, are a shield a- | bout me,*
my glory, and the lifter | of my head.

[4] I cried aloud | to the LORD,*
and he answered me from his | holy hill.

[5] I lay | down and slept;*
I woke again, for the LORD sus- | tained me.

[6] I will not be afraid of many thousands of | people*
who have set themselves against me | all around.

[7] Arise, O LORD! Save me, O my God! For you strike all my enemies | on the cheek;*
you break the teeth of the | wicked.

[8] Salvation belongs | to the LORD;*
your blessing be on your | people!

Glory be to the Father and | to the Son*
and to the Holy | Spirit;
as it was in the be- | ginning,*
is now, and will be forever. | Amen.

4

[1] Answer me when I call, O God of my righteousness! You have given me relief when I was | in distress.*
Be gracious to me and | hear my prayer!

[2] O men, how long shall my honor be turned | into shame?*
How long will you love vain words and seek | after lies?

[3] But know that the LORD has set apart the godly | for himself;*
the LORD hears when I | call to him.

[4] Be angry, and | do not sin;*
ponder in your own hearts on your beds, and be | silent.

[5] Offer right sacri- | fices,*
and put your trust | in the LORD.

[6] There are many who say, "Who will show | us some good?*
Lift up the light of your face upon us, | O LORD!"

[7] You have put more joy | in my heart*
than they have when their grain and | wine abound.

[8] In peace I will both lie | down and sleep;*
for you alone, O LORD, make me dwell in | safety.

Glory be to the Father and | to the Son*
and to the Holy | Spirit;
as it was in the be- | ginning,*
is now, and will be forever. | Amen.

5

[1] Give ear to my words, | O LORD;*
consider my | groaning.

[2] Give attention to the sound of my cry, my King | and my God,*
for to you | do I pray.

[3] O LORD, in the morning you | hear my voice;*
in the morning I prepare a sacrifice for | you and watch.

[4] For you are not a God who delights in | wickedness;*
evil may not | dwell with you.

[5] The boastful shall not stand be- | fore your eyes;*
you hate all evil- | doers.

[6] You destroy those | who speak lies;*
the LORD abhors the bloodthirsty and de- | ceitful man.

[7] But I, through the abundance of your steadfast love, will en- | ter your house.*

I will bow down toward your holy temple in the | fear of you.

[8] Lead me, O LORD, in your righteousness because of my | enemies;*
make your way straight be- | fore me.

[9] For there is no truth in their mouth; their inmost self is de- | struction;*
their throat is an open grave; they flatter | with their tongue.

[10] Make them bear their guilt, O God; let them fall by their own | counsels;*
because of the abundance of their transgressions cast them out, for they have rebelled a- | gainst you.

[11] But let all who take refuge in you rejoice; let them ever | sing for joy,*
and spread your protection over them, that those who love your name may ex- | ult in you.

[12] For you bless the righteous, | O LORD;*
you cover him with favor as | with a shield.

Glory be to the Father and | to the Son*
and to the Holy | Spirit;
as it was in the be- | ginning,*
is now, and will be forever. | Amen.

6

[1] O LORD, rebuke me not in your | anger,*
nor discipline me | in your wrath.

[2] Be gracious to me, O LORD, for I am | languishing;*
heal me, O LORD, for my bones are | troubled.

[3] My soul also is greatly | troubled.*
But you, O LORD— | how long?

[4] Turn, O LORD, deliv- | er my life;*
save me for the sake of your | steadfast love.

[5] For in death there is no remem- | brance of you;*
in Sheol who will | give you praise?

[6] I am weary with my moaning; every night I flood my | bed with tears;*
I drench my couch with my | weeping.

[7] My eye wastes away be- | cause of grief;*
it grows weak because of | all my foes.

[8] Depart from me, all you workers of | evil,*
for the LORD has heard the sound of my | weeping.

[9] The LORD has | heard my plea;*
the LORD ac- | cepts my prayer.

[10] All my enemies shall be ashamed and greatly | troubled;*
they shall turn back and be put to shame in a | moment.

Glory be to the Father and | to the Son*
and to the Holy | Spirit;
as it was in the be- | ginning,*
is now, and will be forever. | Amen.

8

[1] O LORD, our Lord, how majestic is your name in | all the earth!*
You have set your glory above the | heavens.

[2] Out of the mouth of babes and infants, you have established strength because | of your foes,*
to still the enemy and the a- | venger.

[3] When I look at your heavens, the work of your | fingers,*
the moon and the stars, which you have | set in place,

[4] what is man that you are mind- | ful of him,*
and the son of man that you | care for him?

[5] Yet you have made him a little lower than the heavenly | beings*
and crowned him with glory and | honor.

[6] You have given him dominion over the works | of your hands;*
you have put all things under | his feet,

[7] all sheep and | oxen,*
and also the beasts | of the field,

[8] the birds of the heavens, and the fish | of the sea,*
whatever passes along the paths | of the seas.

[9] O | LORD, our Lord,*
how majestic is your name in | all the earth!

Glory be to the Father and | to the Son*
and to the Holy | Spirit;
as it was in the be- | ginning,*
is now, and will be forever. | Amen.

11

[1] In the LORD I take refuge; how can you say | to my soul,*
"Flee like a bird to your | mountain,

[2] for behold, the wicked | bend the bow;*
they have fitted their arrow to the string to shoot in the dark at the up- | right in heart;

[3] if the foundations | are destroyed,*
what can the | righteous do?"

[4] The LORD is in his holy temple; the LORD's throne is in | heaven;*
his eyes see, his eyelids test, the chil- | dren of man.

[5] The LORD tests the | righteous,*
but his soul hates the wicked and the one who loves | violence.

[6] Let him rain coals on the | wicked;*
fire and sulfur and a scorching wind shall be the portion | of their cup.

[7] For the LORD is righteous; he loves | righteous deeds;*
the upright shall be- | hold his face.

Glory be to the Father and | to the Son*
and to the Holy | Spirit;
as it was in the be- | ginning,*
is now, and will be forever. | Amen.

13

[1] How long, O LORD? Will you forget me for- | ever?*
How long will you hide your | face from me?

[2] How long must I take counsel in my soul and have sorrow in my heart | all the day?*
How long shall my enemy be exalted | over me?

[3] Consider and answer me, O | LORD my God;*
light up my eyes, lest I sleep the | sleep of death,

[4] lest my enemy say, "I have prevailed | over him,"*
lest my foes rejoice because I am | shaken.

[5] But I have trusted in your | steadfast love;*
my heart shall rejoice in your sal- | vation.

[6] I will sing | to the LORD,*
because he has dealt bountifully | with me.

Glory be to the Father and | to the Son*
and to the Holy | Spirit;
as it was in the be- | ginning,*
is now, and will be forever. | Amen.

14

[1] The fool says in his heart, "There | is no God."*
They are corrupt, they do abominable deeds, there is none | who does good.

[2] The LORD looks down from heaven on the chil- | dren of man,*

to see if there are any who understand, who seek | after God.

[3] They have all turned aside; together they have be- | come corrupt;*
there is none who does good, not | even one.

[4] Have they no knowledge, all the evil- | doers*
who eat up my people as they eat bread and do not call up- | on the LORD?

[5] There they are in great | terror,*
for God is with the generation of the | righteous.

[6] You would shame the plans | of the poor,*
but the LORD is his | refuge.

[7] Oh, that salvation for Israel would come out of | Zion!*
When the LORD restores the fortunes of his people, let Jacob rejoice, let Israel | be glad.

Glory be to the Father and | to the Son*
and to the Holy | Spirit;
as it was in the be- | ginning,*
is now, and will be forever. | Amen.

15

[1] O LORD, who shall sojourn | in your tent?*
Who shall dwell on your | holy hill?

[2] He who walks blamelessly and does | what is right*
and speaks truth | in his heart;

[3] who does not slander with his tongue and does no evil to his | neighbor,*
nor takes up a reproach a- | gainst his friend;

[4] in whose eyes a vile person is despised, but who honors those who | fear the LORD;*
who swears to his own hurt and | does not change;

[5] who does not put out his money at interest and does not take a bribe against the | innocent.*
He who does these things shall nev- | er be moved.

Glory be to the Father and | to the Son*
and to the Holy | Spirit;
as it was in the be- | ginning,*
is now, and will be forever. | Amen.

16

[1] Preserve me, | O God,*
for in you I take | refuge.

[2] I say to the LORD, "You | are my Lord;*
I have no good a- | part from you."

[3] As for the saints | in the land,*
they are the excellent ones, in whom is all | my delight.

[4] The sorrows of those who run after another god shall | multiply;*
their drink offerings of blood I will not pour out or take their names | on my lips.

[5] The LORD is my chosen portion | and my cup;*
you | hold my lot.

[6] The lines have fallen for me in pleasant | places;*
indeed, I have a beautiful in- | heritance.

[7] I bless the LORD who gives me | counsel;*
in the night also my heart in- | structs me.

[8] I have set the LORD always be- | fore me;*
because he is at my right hand, I shall not be | shaken.

[9] Therefore my heart is glad, and my whole being re- | joices;*
my flesh also | dwells secure.

[10] For you will not abandon my soul | to Sheol,*
or let your holy one see cor- | ruption.

[11] You make known to me the | path of life;*
in your presence there is fullness of joy; at your right hand are pleasures for- | evermore.

Glory be to the Father and | to the Son*
and to the Holy | Spirit;
as it was in the be- | ginning,*
is now, and will be forever. | Amen.

18

[1] I | love you,*
O | LORD, my strength.

[2] The LORD is my rock and my fortress and my de- | liverer,*
my God, my rock, in whom I take refuge, my shield, and the horn of my salvation, my | stronghold.

[3] I call upon the LORD, who is worthy | to be praised,*
and I am saved from my | enemies.

[4] The cords of death en- | compassed me;*
the torrents of destruction as- | sailed me;

[5] the cords of Sheol en- | tangled me;*
the snares of death con- | fronted me.

[6] In my distress I called upon the LORD; to my God I | cried for help.*
From his temple he heard my voice, and my cry to him | reached his ears.

[7] Then the earth | reeled and rocked;*
the foundations also of the mountains trembled and quaked, because he was | angry.

[8] Smoke went up from his nostrils, and devouring fire | from his mouth;*
glowing coals flamed | forth from him.

[9] He bowed the heavens and | came down;*
thick darkness was un- | der his feet.

[10] He rode on a cher- | ub and flew;*
he came swiftly on the wings | of the wind.

[11] He made darkness his covering, his canopy a- | round him,*
thick clouds dark with | water.

[12] Out of the brightness be- | fore him*
hailstones and coals of fire broke | through his clouds.

[13] The LORD also thundered in the | heavens,*
and the Most High uttered his voice, hailstones and | coals of fire.

[14] And he sent out his arrows and | scattered them;*
he flashed forth lightnings and | routed them.

[15] Then the channels of the sea were seen, and the foundations of the world were | laid bare*
at your rebuke, O LORD, at the blast of the breath of your | nostrils.

[16] He sent from on high, he | took me;*
he drew me out of many | waters.

[17] He rescued me from my strong | enemy*
and from those who hated me, for they were too might- | y for me.

[18] They confronted me in the day of my ca- | lamity,*
but the LORD was | my support.

[19] He brought me out into a | broad place;*
he rescued me, because he delight- | ed in me.

[20] The LORD dealt with me according to my | righteousness;*
according to the cleanness of my hands he re- | warded me.

[21] For I have kept the ways | of the LORD,*
and have not wickedly departed | from my God.

[22] For all his just decrees were be- | fore me,*
and his statutes I did not put a- | way from me.

[23] I was blameless be- | fore him,*
and I kept myself | from my guilt.

[24] So the LORD has rewarded me according to my | righteousness,*
according to the cleanness of my hands | in his sight.

[25] With the merciful you show yourself | merciful;*
with the blameless man you show yourself | blameless;

[26] with the purified you show your- | self pure;*
and with the crooked you make yourself seem | tortuous.

[27] For you save a humble | people,*
but the haughty eyes | you bring down.

[28] For it is you who | light my lamp;*
the LORD my God lightens my | darkness.

[29] For by you I can run a- | gainst a troop,*
and by my God I can leap o- | ver a wall.

[30] This God—his way is | perfect;*
the word of the LORD proves true;
he is a shield for all those who take ref- | uge in him.

[31] For who is God, | but the LORD?*
And who is a rock, ex- | cept our God?—

[32] the God who equipped | me with strength*
and made my way | blameless.

[33] He made my feet like the feet | of a deer*
and set me secure | on the heights.

[34] He trains my | hands for war,*
so that my arms can bend a | bow of bronze.

[35] You have given me the shield of your sal- | vation,*
and your right hand supported me,
and your gentleness | made me great.

[36] You gave a wide place for my steps | under me,*
and my feet | did not slip.

[37] I pursued my enemies and over- | took them,*
and did not turn back till they | were consumed.

[38] I thrust them through, so that they were not a- | ble to rise;*
they fell un- | der my feet.

[39] For you equipped me with strength for the | battle;*
you made those who rise against me sink | under me.

[40] You made my enemies turn their | backs to me,*
and those who hated me | I destroyed.

[41] They cried for help, but there was | none to save;*
they cried to the LORD, but he did not | answer them.

[42] I beat them fine as dust be- | fore the wind;*
I cast them out like the mire | of the streets.

[43] You delivered me from strife with the | people;*
you made me the head of the nations;
people whom I had not known | served me.

[44] As soon as they heard of me they o- | beyed me;*
foreigners came cring- | ing to me.

[45] Foreigners | lost heart*
and came trembling out of their | fortresses.

[46] The LORD lives, and blessèd | be my rock,*
and exalted be the God of my sal- | vation—

[47] the God who gave me | vengeance*
and subdued peoples | under me,

[48] who delivered me from my enemies;
yes, you exalted me above those who rose a- | gainst me;*
you rescued me from the man of | violence.

[49] For this I will praise you, O LORD, among the | nations,*
and sing | to your name.

[50] Great salvation he brings | to his king,*
and shows steadfast love to his anointed, to David and his offspring for- | ever.

Glory be to the Father and | to the Son*
and to the Holy | Spirit;
as it was in the be- | ginning,*
is now, and will be forever. | Amen.

19

[1] The heavens declare the glo- | ry of God,*
and the sky above proclaims his | handiwork.

[2] Day to day | pours out speech,*
and night to night reveals | knowledge.

[3] There is no speech, nor | are there words,*
whose voice | is not heard.

[4] Their measuring line goes out through all the earth, and their words to the end | of the world.*
In them he has set a tent | for the sun,

[5] which comes out like a bridegroom leaving his | chamber,*
and, like a strong man, runs its | course with joy.

[6] Its rising is from the end of the heavens, and its circuit to the | end of them,*
and there is nothing hidden | from its heat.

[7] The law of the LORD is perfect, reviv- | ing the soul;*
the testimony of the LORD is sure, making wise the | simple;

[8] the precepts of the LORD are right, rejoicing | the heart;*
the commandment of the LORD is pure, enlightening | the eyes;

[9] the fear of the LORD is clean, enduring for- | ever;*
the just decrees of the LORD are true, and righteous alto- | gether.

[10] More to be desired are they than gold, even | much fine gold;*
sweeter also than honey and drippings of the | honeycomb.

[11] Moreover, by them is your | servant warned;*
in keeping them there is | great reward.

[12] Who can dis- | cern his errors?*
Declare me innocent from | hidden faults.

[13] Keep back your servant also from presumptuous sins; let them not have dominion | over me!*
Then I shall be blameless, and innocent of great trans- | gression.

[14] Let the words of my mouth and the meditation of my heart be acceptable | in your sight,*
O LORD, my rock and my re- | deemer.

Glory be to the Father and | to the Son*
and to the Holy | Spirit;
as it was in the be- | ginning,*
is now, and will be forever. | Amen.

22

[1] My God, my God, why have you for- | saken me?*
Why are you so far from saving me, from the words of my | groaning?

[2] O my God, I cry by day, but you do not | answer,*
and by night, but I | find no rest.

[3] Yet you are | holy,*
enthroned on the praises of | Israel.

[4] In you our fathers | trusted;*
they trusted, and you de- | livered them.

[5] To you they cried and were | rescued;*
in you they trusted and were not | put to shame.

[6] But I am a worm and | not a man,*
scorned by mankind and despised by the | people.

[7] All who see me | mock me;*
they make mouths at me; they | wag their heads;

[8] "He trusts in the LORD; let him de- | liver him;*
let him rescue him, for he de- | lights in him!"

[9] Yet you are he who took me | from the womb;*
you made me trust you at my | mother's breasts.

[10] On you was I cast | from my birth,*
and from my mother's womb you have | been my God.

[11] Be not far from me, for trouble | is near,*
and there is | none to help.

[12] Many bulls en- | compass me;*
strong bulls of Bashan sur- | round me;

[13] they open wide their | mouths at me,*
like a ravening and roaring | lion.

[14] I am poured out like water, and all my bones are | out of joint;*
my heart is like wax; it is melted with- | in my breast;

[15] my strength is dried up like a potsherd, and my tongue sticks | to my jaws;*
you lay me in the | dust of death.

[16] For dogs en- | compass me;*
a company of evildoers encircles me; they have pierced my | hands and feet—

[17] I can count | all my bones—*
they stare and gloat | over me;

[18] they divide my garments a- | mong them,*
and for my clothing they | cast lots.

[19] But you, O LORD, do not be | far off!*
O you my help, come quickly | to my aid!

[20] Deliver my soul | from the sword,*
my precious life from the power | of the dog!

[21] Save me from the mouth of the | lion!*
You have rescued me from the horns of the wild | oxen!

[22] I will tell of your name to my | brothers;*
in the midst of the congregation I will | praise you:

[23] You who fear the LORD, praise him! All you offspring of Jacob, glo- | rify him,*
and stand in awe of him, all you offspring of | Israel!

[24] For he has not despised or abhorred the affliction of the afflicted, and he has not hidden his | face from him,*
but has heard, when he | cried to him.

[25] From you comes my praise in the great congre- | gation;*
my vows I will perform before those who | fear him.

[26] The afflicted shall eat and be satisfied; those who seek him shall | praise the LORD!*
May your hearts live for- | ever!

[27] All the ends of the earth shall remember and turn | to the LORD,*
and all the families of the nations shall worship be- | fore you.

[28] For kingship belongs | to the LORD,*
and he rules over the | nations.

[29] All the prosperous of the earth eat and | worship;*
before him shall bow all who go down to the dust, even the one who could not keep him- | self alive.

[30] Posterity shall | serve him;*
it shall be told of the Lord to the coming gener- | ation;

[31] they shall come and proclaim his righteousness to a people | yet unborn,*
that he has | done it.

Glory be to the Father and | to the Son*
and to the Holy | Spirit;
as it was in the be- | ginning,*
is now, and will be forever. | Amen.

23

[1] The LORD is my | shepherd;*
I | shall not want.

[2] He makes me lie down in green | pastures.*
He leads me beside still | waters.

[3] He re- | stores my soul.*
He leads me in paths of righteousness for his | name's sake.

[4] Even though I walk through the valley of the shadow of death, I will fear no evil, for you are | with me;*
your rod and your staff, they | comfort me.

[5] You prepare a table before me in the presence of my | enemies;*
you anoint my head with oil; my cup | overflows.

[6] Surely goodness and mercy shall follow me all the days | of my life,*
and I shall dwell in the house of the LORD for- | ever.

Glory be to the Father and | to the Son*
and to the Holy | Spirit;
as it was in the be- | ginning,*
is now, and will be forever. | Amen.

24

[1] The earth is the LORD'S and the full- | ness thereof,*
the world and those who | dwell therein,

[2] for he has founded it up- | on the seas*
and established it upon the | rivers.

[3] Who shall ascend the hill | of the LORD?*
And who shall stand in his | holy place?

[4] He who has clean hands and a | pure heart,*
who does not lift up his soul to what is false and does not swear de- | ceitfully.

[5] He will receive blessing | from the LORD*
and righteousness from the God of his sal- | vation.

[6] Such is the generation of those who | seek him,*
who seek the face of the God of | Jacob.

[7] Lift up your heads, O gates! And be lifted up, O | ancient doors,*
that the King of glory | may come in.

[8] Who is this King of | glory?*
The LORD, strong and mighty,
the LORD, mighty in | battle!

[9] Lift up your heads, O gates! And lift them up, O | ancient doors,*
that the King of glory | may come in.

[10] Who is this King of | glory?*
The LORD of hosts, he is the King of | glory!

Glory be to the Father and | to the Son*
and to the Holy | Spirit;
as it was in the be- | ginning,*
is now, and will be forever. | Amen.

25

[1] To you, | O LORD,*
I lift | up my soul.

[2] O my God, in you I trust; let me not be | put to shame;*
let not my enemies exult | over me.

[3] Indeed, none who wait for you shall be | put to shame;*
they shall be ashamed who are wantonly | treacherous.

[4] Make me to know your ways, | O LORD;*
teach me | your paths.

[5] Lead me in your truth and teach me, for you are the God of my sal- | vation; *
for you I wait all the | day long.

[6] Remember your mercy, O LORD, and your | steadfast love, *
for they have been | from of old.

[7] Remember not the sins of my youth or my trans- | gressions; *
according to your steadfast love remember me, for the sake of your goodness, | O LORD!

[8] Good and upright | is the LORD; *
therefore he instructs sinners | in the way.

[9] He leads the humble in | what is right, *
and teaches the humble | his way.

[10] All the paths of the LORD are steadfast love and | faithfulness, *
for those who keep his covenant and his testi- | monies.

[11] For your name's sake, | O LORD, *
pardon my guilt, for | it is great.

[12] Who is the man who | fears the LORD? *
Him will he instruct in the way that | he should choose.

[13] His soul shall abide in well- | being, *
and his offspring shall inher- | it the land.

[14] The friendship of the LORD is for those who | fear him, *
and he makes known to them his | covenant.

[15] My eyes are ever | toward the LORD, *
for he will pluck my feet out | of the net.

[16] Turn to me and be gra- | cious to me, *
for I am lonely and af- | flicted.

[17] The troubles of my heart | are enlarged; *
bring me out of my dis- | tresses.

[18] Consider my affliction and my | trouble, *
and forgive | all my sins.

[19] Consider how many | are my foes, *
and with what violent hatred they | hate me.

[20] Oh, guard my soul, and de- | liver me! *
Let me not be put to shame, for I take ref- | uge in you.

[21] May integrity and uprightness pre- | serve me, *
for I | wait for you.

[22] Redeem Israel, | O God, *
out of all his | troubles.

**Glory be to the Father and | to the Son *
and to the Holy | Spirit;
as it was in the be- | ginning, *
is now, and will be forever. | Amen.**

26

[1] Vindicate me, O LORD, for I have walked in my in- | tegrity, *
and I have trusted in the LORD without | wavering.

[2] Prove me, O LORD, and | try me; *
test my heart | and my mind.

[3] For your steadfast love is be- | fore my eyes, *
and I walk in your | faithfulness.

[4] I do not sit with men of | falsehood, *
nor do I consort with | hypocrites.

[5] I hate the assembly of evil- | doers, *
and I will not sit with the | wicked.

[6] I wash my hands in | innocence *
and go around your altar, | O LORD,

[7] proclaiming thanksgiving | aloud, *
and telling all your | wondrous deeds.

[8] O LORD, I love the habitation | of your house *
and the place where your | glory dwells.

[9] Do not sweep my soul away with | sinners, *
nor my life with blood- | thirsty men,

[10] in whose hands are evil de- | vices,*
and whose right hands are | full of bribes.

[11] But as for me, I shall walk in my in- | tegrity;*
redeem me, and be gra- | cious to me.

[12] My foot stands on | level ground;*
in the great assembly I will | bless the LORD.

**Glory be to the Father and | to the Son*
and to the Holy | Spirit;
as it was in the be- | ginning,*
is now, and will be forever. | Amen.**

27

[1] The LORD is my light and my salvation; whom | shall I fear?*
The LORD is the stronghold of my life; of whom shall I | be afraid?

[2] When evildoers assail me to eat | up my flesh,*
my adversaries and foes, it is they who stum- | ble and fall.

[3] Though an army encamp against me, my heart | shall not fear;*
though war arise against me, yet I will be | confident.

[4] One thing have I asked of the LORD, that will I seek | after:*
that I may dwell in the house of the LORD all the days of my life, to gaze upon the beauty of the LORD and to inquire in his | temple.

[5] For he will hide me in his shelter in the day of | trouble;*
he will conceal me under the cover of his tent; he will lift me high up- | on a rock.

[6] And now my head shall be lifted up above my enemies all around me, and I will offer in his tent sacrifices with | shouts of joy;*
I will sing and make melody | to the LORD.

[7] Hear, O LORD, when I | cry aloud;*
be gracious to me and | answer me!

[8] You have said, | "Seek my face."*
My heart says to you, "Your face, LORD, | do I seek."

[9] Hide not your face from me. Turn not your servant away in | anger,*
O you who have been my help. Cast me not off; forsake me not, O God of my sal- | vation!

[10] For my father and my mother have for- | saken me,*
but the LORD will | take me in.

[11] Teach me your way, | O LORD,*
and lead me on a level path because of my | enemies.

[12] Give me not up to the will of my adver- | saries;*
for false witnesses have risen against me, and they breathe out | violence.

[13] I believe that I shall look upon the goodness | of the LORD*
in the land of the | living!

[14] Wait | for the LORD;*
be strong, and let your heart take courage; wait | for the LORD!

**Glory be to the Father and | to the Son*
and to the Holy | Spirit;
as it was in the be- | ginning,*
is now, and will be forever. | Amen.**

28

[1] To you, O LORD, I call; my rock, be not | deaf to me,*
lest, if you be silent to me, I become like those who go down | to the pit.

[2] Hear the voice of my pleas for mercy, when I cry to | you for help,*
when I lift up my hands toward your most holy sanctu- | ary.

[3] Do not drag me off with the wicked,
with the workers of | evil,*
who speak peace with their neighbors
while evil is | in their hearts.

[4] Give to them according to their work
and according to the evil | of their deeds;*
give to them according to the work of
their hands; render them their | due
reward.

[5] Because they do not regard the works
of the LORD or the work | of his hands,*
he will tear them down and build
them | up no more.

[6] Blessèd | be the LORD!*
For he has heard the voice of my pleas
for | mercy.

[7] The LORD is my strength and my
shield; in him my heart trusts,
and | I am helped;*
my heart exults, and with my song I
give | thanks to him.

[8] The LORD is the strength of his | people;*
he is the saving refuge of his
a- | nointed.

[9] Oh, save your people and bless
your | heritage!*
Be their shepherd and carry them
for- | ever.

Glory be to the Father and | to the Son*
and to the Holy | Spirit;
as it was in the be- | ginning,*
is now, and will be forever. | Amen.

29

[1] Ascribe to the LORD, O heavenly | beings,*
ascribe to the LORD glo- | ry and
strength.

[2] Ascribe to the LORD the glory | due his
name;*
worship the LORD in the splendor
of | holiness.

[3] The voice of the LORD is over
the | waters;*
the God of glory thunders, the LORD,
over many | waters.

[4] The voice of the LORD is | powerful;*
the voice of the LORD is full
of | majesty.

[5] The voice of the LORD breaks
the | cedars;*
the LORD breaks the cedars
of | Lebanon.

[6] He makes Lebanon to skip | like a
calf,*
and Sirion like a young | wild ox.

[7] The voice | of the LORD*
flashes forth | flames of fire.

[8] The voice of the LORD shakes
the | wilderness;*
the LORD shakes the wilderness | of
Kadesh.

[9] The voice of the LORD makes the deer
give birth and strips the | forests bare,*
and in his temple all cry, | "Glory!"

[10] The LORD sits enthroned o- | ver the
flood;*
the LORD sits enthroned as king
for- | ever.

[11] May the LORD give strength to
his | people!*
May the LORD bless his people | with
peace!

Glory be to the Father and | to the Son*
and to the Holy | Spirit;
as it was in the be- | ginning,*
is now, and will be forever. | Amen.

30

[1] I will extol you, O LORD, for you
have | drawn me up*
and have not let my foes rejoice | over
me.

[2] O LORD my God, I cried to | you for
help,*
and you have | healed me.

[3] O LORD, you have brought up my soul | from Sheol;*
you restored me to life from among those who go down | to the pit.

[4] Sing praises to the LORD, O | you his saints,*
and give thanks to his | holy name.

[5] For his anger is but for a moment, and his favor is for a | lifetime.*
Weeping may tarry for the night, but joy comes with the | morning.

[6] As for me, I said in my pros- | perity,*
"I shall nev- | er be moved."

[7] By your favor, O LORD, you made my mountain | stand strong;*
you hid your face; I | was dismayed.

[8] To you, O | LORD, I cry,*
and to the Lord I plead for | mercy:

[9] "What profit is there in my death, if I go down | to the pit?*
Will the dust praise you? Will it tell of your | faithfulness?

[10] Hear, O LORD, and be merci- | ful to me!*
O LORD, be my | helper!"

[11] You have turned for me my mourning into | dancing;*
you have loosed my sackcloth and clothed me with | gladness,

[12] that my glory may sing your praise and not be | silent.*
O LORD my God, I will give thanks to you for- | ever!

Glory be to the Father and | to the Son*
and to the Holy | Spirit;
as it was in the be- | ginning,*
is now, and will be forever. | Amen.

31

[1] In you, O LORD, do I take refuge;
let me never be | put to shame;*
in your righteousness de- | liver me!

[2] Incline your ear to me; rescue me | speedily!*
Be a rock of refuge for me, a strong fortress to | save me!

[3] For you are my rock and my | fortress;*
and for your name's sake you lead me and | guide me;

[4] you take me out of the net they have hidden | for me,*
for you are my | refuge.

[5] Into your hand I commit my | spirit;*
you have redeemed me,
O LORD, | faithful God.

[6] I hate those who pay regard to worthless | idols,*
but I trust | in the LORD.

[7] I will rejoice and be glad in your | steadfast love,*
because you have seen my affliction;
you have known the distress | of my soul,

[8] and you have not delivered me into the hand of the | enemy;*
you have set my feet in a | broad place.

[9] Be gracious to me, O LORD,
for I am | in distress;*
my eye is wasted from grief; my soul and my body | also.

[10] For my life is spent with sorrow, and my years with | sighing;*
my strength fails because of my iniquity, and my bones | waste away.

[11] Because of all my adversaries I have become a reproach, especially to my neighbors, and an object of dread to my ac- | quaintances;*
those who see me in the street | flee from me.

[12] I have been forgotten like one | who is dead;*
I have become like a broken | vessel.

[13] For I hear the whispering of many—
terror on | every side!—*

as they scheme together against me,
as they plot to | take my life.

[14] But I trust in you, | O LORD;*
I say, "You | are my God."

[15] My times are | in your hand;*
rescue me from the hand of my enemies and from my perse- | cutors!

[16] Make your face shine on your | servant;*
save me in your | steadfast love!

[17] O LORD, let me not be put to shame, for I call up- | on you;*
let the wicked be put to shame;
let them go silently | to Sheol.

[18] Let the lying | lips be mute,*
which speak insolently against the righteous in pride | and contempt.

[19] Oh, how abundant is your goodness, which you have stored up for those who | fear you*
and worked for those who take refuge in you, in the sight of the children of | mankind!

[20] In the cover of your presence you hide them from the | plots of men;*
you store them in your shelter from the | strife of tongues.

[21] Blessèd | be the LORD,*
for he has wondrously shown his steadfast love to me when I was in a besieged | city.

[22] I had said in my alarm, "I am cut off | from your sight."*
But you heard the voice of my pleas for mercy when I cried to | you for help.

[23] Love the LORD, all | you his saints!*
The LORD preserves the faithful but abundantly repays the one who | acts in pride.

[24] Be strong, and let your heart take | courage,*
all you who wait | for the LORD!

Glory be to the Father and | to the Son*
and to the Holy | Spirit;
as it was in the be- | ginning,*
is now, and will be forever. | Amen.

32

[1] Blessèd is the one whose transgression is for- | given,*
whose sin is | covered.

[2] Blessèd is the man against whom the LORD counts no in- | iquity,*
and in whose spirit there is | no deceit.

[3] For when I kept silent, my bones wast- | ed away*
through my groaning | all day long.

[4] For day and night your hand was heavy up- | on me;*
my strength was dried up as by the heat of | summer.

[5] I acknowledged my sin to you, and I did not cover my in- | iquity;*
I said, "I will confess my transgressions to the LORD," and you forgave the iniquity | of my sin.

[6] Therefore let everyone who is godly offer prayer to you at a time when you | may be found;*
surely in the rush of great waters, they shall not | reach him.

[7] You are a hiding place for me; you preserve me from | trouble;*
you surround me with shouts of de- | liverance.

[8] I will instruct you and teach you in the way | you should go;*
I will counsel you with my eye up- | on you.

[9] Be not like a horse or a mule, without under- | standing,*
which must be curbed with bit and bridle, or it will not stay | near you.

[10] Many are the sorrows of the | wicked,*
but steadfast love surrounds the one who trusts | in the LORD.

[11] Be glad in the LORD, and rejoice, O | righteous,*
and shout for joy, all you up- | right in heart!

Glory be to the Father and | to the Son*
and to the Holy | Spirit;
as it was in the be- | ginning,*
is now, and will be forever. | Amen.

33

[1] Shout for joy in the LORD, O you | righteous!*
Praise befits the | upright.

[2] Give thanks to the LORD | with the lyre;*
make melody to him with the harp of | ten strings!

[3] Sing to him a | new song;*
play skillfully on the strings, with | loud shouts.

[4] For the word of the LORD is | upright,*
and all his work is done in | faithfulness.

[5] He loves righteousness and | justice;*
the earth is full of the steadfast love | of the LORD.

[6] By the word of the LORD the heav- | ens were made,*
and by the breath of his mouth | all their host.

[7] He gathers the waters of the sea | as a heap;*
he puts the deeps in | storehouses.

[8] Let all the earth | fear the LORD;*
let all the inhabitants of the world stand in | awe of him!

[9] For he spoke, and it | came to be;*
he commanded, and it | stood firm.

[10] The LORD brings the counsel of the nations to | nothing;*
he frustrates the plans of the | peoples.

[11] The counsel of the LORD stands for- | ever,*
the plans of his heart to all gener- | ations.

[12] Blessèd is the nation whose God | is the LORD,*
the people whom he has chosen as his | heritage!

[13] The LORD looks down from | heaven;*
he sees all the chil- | dren of man;

[14] from where he sits enthroned he | looks out*
on all the inhabitants | of the earth,

[15] he who fashions the hearts | of them all*
and observes | all their deeds.

[16] The king is not saved by his great | army;*
a warrior is not delivered by his | great strength.

[17] The war horse is a false hope for sal- | vation,*
and by its great might it cannot | rescue.

[18] Behold, the eye of the LORD is on those who | fear him,*
on those who hope in his | steadfast love,

[19] that he may deliver their | soul from death*
and keep them alive in | famine.

[20] Our soul waits | for the LORD;*
he is our help | and our shield.

[21] For our heart is | glad in him,*
because we trust in his | holy name.

[22] Let your steadfast love, O LORD, be up- | on us,*
even as we | hope in you.

Glory be to the Father and | to the Son*
and to the Holy | Spirit;
as it was in the be- | ginning,*
is now, and will be forever. | Amen.

34

[1] I will bless the LORD at |all times; *
his praise shall continually be |in my mouth.

[2] My soul makes its boast |in the LORD; *
let the humble hear |and be glad.

[3] Oh, magnify the |LORD with me, *
and let us exalt his name to- |gether!

[4] I sought the LORD, and he |answered me *
and delivered me from |all my fears.

[5] Those who look to him are |radiant, *
and their faces shall never |be ashamed.

[6] This poor man cried, and the LORD |heard him *
and saved him out of all his |troubles.

[7] The angel of the LORD encamps around those who |fear him, *
and de- |livers them.

[8] Oh, taste and see that the |LORD is good! *
Blessèd is the man who takes ref- |uge in him!

[9] Oh, fear the LORD, |you his saints, *
for those who fear him |have no lack!

[10] The young lions suffer want and |hunger; *
but those who seek the LORD lack |no good thing.

[11] Come, O children, lis- |ten to me; *
I will teach you the fear |of the LORD.

[12] What man is there who de- |sires life *
and loves many days, that he may |see good?

[13] Keep your tongue from |evil *
and your lips from speak- |ing deceit.

[14] Turn away from evil |and do good; *
seek peace and pur- |sue it.

[15] The eyes of the LORD are toward the |righteous *
and his ears |toward their cry.

[16] The face of the LORD is against those who do |evil, *
to cut off the memory of them |from the earth.

[17] When the righteous cry for help, the |LORD hears *
and delivers them out of all their |troubles.

[18] The LORD is near to the broken- |hearted *
and saves the crushed in |spirit.

[19] Many are the afflictions of the |righteous, *
but the LORD delivers him out |of them all.

[20] He keeps |all his bones; *
not one of them is |broken.

[21] Affliction will slay the |wicked, *
and those who hate the righteous will |be condemned.

[22] The LORD redeems the life of his |servants; *
none of those who take refuge in him will |be condemned.

Glory be to the Father and |to the Son *
and to the Holy |Spirit;
as it was in the be- |ginning, *
is now, and will be forever. |Amen.

36

[1] Transgression speaks to the wicked deep |in his heart; *
there is no fear of God be- |fore his eyes.

[2] For he flatters himself in |his own eyes *
that his iniquity cannot be found out and |hated.

[3] The words of his mouth are trouble |and deceit; *
he has ceased to act wisely |and do good.

[4] He plots trouble while | on his bed;*
he sets himself in a way that is not good; he does not reject | evil.

[5] Your steadfast love, O LORD, extends to the | heavens,*
your faithfulness | to the clouds.

[6] Your righteousness is like the moun- | tains of God;*
your judgments are like the great deep; man and beast you save, | O LORD.

[7] How precious is your steadfast love, | O God!*
The children of mankind take refuge in the shadow | of your wings.

[8] They feast on the abundance | of your house,*
and you give them drink from the river of | your delights.

[9] For with you is the foun- | tain of life;*
in your light do | we see light.

[10] Oh, continue your steadfast love to those who | know you,*
and your righteousness to the up- | right of heart!

[11] Let not the foot of arrogance come up- | on me,*
nor the hand of the wicked drive | me away.

[12] There the evildoers lie | fallen;*
they are thrust down, unable | to rise.

Glory be to the Father and | to the Son*
and to the Holy | Spirit;
as it was in the be- | ginning,*
is now, and will be forever. | Amen.

38

[1] O LORD, rebuke me not in your | anger,*
nor discipline me | in your wrath!

[2] For your arrows have sunk | into me,*
and your hand has come | down on me.

[3] There is no soundness in my flesh because of your indig- | nation;*
there is no health in my bones because | of my sin.

[4] For my iniquities have gone o- | ver my head;*
like a heavy burden, they are too heav- | y for me.

[5] My wounds stink and | fester*
because of my | foolishness,

[6] I am utterly bowed down and | prostrate;*
all the day I go about | mourning.

[7] For my sides are filled with | burning,*
and there is no soundness | in my flesh.

[8] I am feeble | and crushed;*
I groan because of the tumult | of my heart.

[9] O Lord, all my longing is be- | fore you;*
my sighing is not hid- | den from you.

[10] My heart throbs; my strength | fails me,*
and the light of my eyes—it also has | gone from me.

[11] My friends and companions stand aloof | from my plague,*
and my nearest kin stand | far off.

[12] Those who seek my life lay their snares; those who seek my hurt speak of | ruin*
and meditate treachery | all day long.

[13] But I am like a deaf man; I | do not hear,*
like a mute man who does not o- | pen his mouth.

[14] I have become like a man who | does not hear,*
and in whose mouth are | no rebukes.

[15] But for you, O LORD, | do I wait;*
it is you, O Lord my God, who will | answer.

[16] For I said, "Only let them not rejoice | over me,*

who boast against me when my | foot slips!"

[17] For I am read- | y to fall,*
and my pain is ever be- | fore me.

[18] I confess my in- | iquity;*
I am sorry | for my sin.

[19] But my foes are vigorous, they are | mighty,*
and many are those who hate me | wrongfully.

[20] Those who render me e- | vil for good*
accuse me because I follow | after good.

[21] Do not forsake me, | O LORD!*
O my God, be not | far from me!

[22] Make haste to | help me,*
O Lord, my sal- | vation!

Glory be to the Father and | to the Son*
and to the Holy | Spirit;
as it was in the be- | ginning,*
is now, and will be forever. | Amen.

40

[1] I waited patiently | for the LORD;*
he inclined to me and | heard my cry.

[2] He drew me up from the pit of destruction, out of the | miry bog,*
and set my feet upon a rock, making my | steps secure.

[3] He put a new song in my mouth, a song of praise | to our God.*
Many will see and fear, and put their trust | in the LORD.

[4] Blessèd is the man who makes the | LORD his trust,*
who does not turn to the proud, to those who go astray af- | ter a lie!

[5] You have multiplied, O LORD my God, your wondrous deeds and your thoughts toward us; none can com- | pare with you!*
I will proclaim and tell of them, yet they are more than | can be told.

[6] Sacrifice and offering you have not desired, but you have given me an | open ear.*
Burnt offering and sin offering you have | not required.

[7] Then I said, "Behold, | I have come;*
in the scroll of the book it is writ- | ten of me:

[8] I desire to do your will, | O my God;*
your law is with- | in my heart."

[9] I have told the glad news of deliverance in the great congre- | gation;*
behold, I have not restrained my lips, as you know, | O LORD.

[10] I have not hidden your deliverance within my heart; I have spoken of your faithfulness and your sal- | vation;*
I have not concealed your steadfast love and your faithfulness from the great congre- | gation.

[11] As for you, O LORD, you will not restrain your mer- | cy from me;*
your steadfast love and your faithfulness will ever pre- | serve me!

[12] For evils have encompassed me beyond number; my iniquities have overtaken me, and I | cannot see;*
they are more than the hairs of my head; my heart | fails me.

[13] Be pleased, O LORD, to de- | liver me!*
O LORD, make haste to | help me!

[14] Let those be put to shame and disappointed altogether who seek to snatch a- | way my life;*
let those be turned back and brought to dishonor who de- | sire my hurt!

[15] Let those be appalled because | of their shame*
who say to me, "A- | ha, Aha!"

[16] But may all who seek you rejoice and be | glad in you;*
may those who love your salvation say continually, "Great | is the LORD!"

[17] As for me, I am poor and needy, but the Lord takes | thought for me.*
You are my help and my deliverer; do not delay, | O my God!

Glory be to the Father and | to the Son*
and to the Holy | Spirit;
as it was in the be- | ginning,*
is now, and will be forever. | Amen.

41

[1] Blessèd is the one who consid- | ers the poor!*
In the day of trouble the LORD de- | livers him;

[2] the LORD protects him and keeps him alive; he is called blessèd | in the land;*
you do not give him up to the will of his | enemies.

[3] The LORD sustains him on his | sickbed;*
in his illness you restore him to | full health.

[4] As for me, I said, "O LORD, be gra- | cious to me;*
heal me, for I have sinned a- | gainst you!"

[5] My enemies say of me in | malice,*
"When will he die and his name | perish?"

[6] And when one comes to see me, he utters empty words, while his heart gathers in- | iquity;*
when he goes out, he tells | it abroad.

[7] All who hate me whisper together a- | bout me;*
they imagine the | worst for me.

[8] They say, "A deadly thing is poured | out on him;*
he will not rise again from | where he lies."

[9] Even my close friend in whom I | trusted,*
who ate my bread, has lifted his heel a- | gainst me.

[10] But you, O LORD, be gra- | cious to me,*
and raise me up, that I may re- | pay them!

[11] By this I know that you de- | light in me:*
my enemy will not shout in triumph | over me.

[12] But you have upheld me because of my in- | tegrity,*
and set me in your presence for- | ever.

[13] Blessèd be the LORD, the God of | Israel,*
from everlasting to everlasting! Amen and | Amen.

Glory be to the Father and | to the Son*
and to the Holy | Spirit;
as it was in the be- | ginning,*
is now, and will be forever. | Amen.

42

[1] As a deer pants for | flowing streams,*
so pants my soul for you, | O God.

[2] My soul thirsts for God, for the | living God.*
When shall I come and appear be- | fore God?

[3] My tears have been my food | day and night,*
while they say to me continually, "Where | is your God?"

[4] These things I remember, as I pour | out my soul:*
how I would go with the throng and lead them in procession to the | house of God

with glad shouts and | songs of praise,*
a multitude keeping | festival.

[5] Why are you cast down, O my soul, and why are you in turmoil with- | in me?*
Hope in God; for I shall again praise him, my salvation | [6] and my God.

My soul is cast down with- | in me;*
therefore I remember you from the land of Jordan and of Hermon, from Mount | Mizar.

[7] Deep calls to deep at the roar of your | waterfalls;*
all your breakers and your waves have gone | over me.

[8] By day the LORD commands his steadfast love, and at night his song is | with me,*
a prayer to the God | of my life.

[9] I say to God, my rock: "Why have you for- | gotten me?*
Why do I go mourning because of the oppression of the | enemy?"

[10] As with a deadly wound in my bones, my adversaries | taunt me,*
while they say to me continually, "Where | is your God?"

[11] Why are you cast down, O my soul, and why are you in turmoil with- | in me?*
Hope in God; for I shall again praise him, my salvation | and my God.

Glory be to the Father and | to the Son*
and to the Holy | Spirit;
as it was in the be- | ginning,*
is now, and will be forever. | Amen.

43

[1] Vindicate me, O God, and defend my cause against an ungodly | people,*
from the deceitful and unjust man de- | liver me!

[2] For you are the God in whom I take refuge; why have you re- | jected me?*
Why do I go about mourning because of the oppression of the | enemy?

[3] Send out your light and your truth; let them | lead me;*
let them bring me to your holy hill and to your | dwelling!

[4] Then I will go to the altar of God, to God my ex- | ceeding joy,*
and I will praise you with the lyre, O | God, my God.

[5] Why are you cast down, O my soul, and why are you in turmoil with- | in me?*
Hope in God; for I shall again praise him, my salvation | and my God.

Glory be to the Father and | to the Son*
and to the Holy | Spirit;
as it was in the be- | ginning,*
is now, and will be forever. | Amen.

45

[1] My heart overflows with a pleasing theme; I address my verses | to the king;*
my tongue is like the pen of a | ready scribe.

[2] You are the most handsome of the sons of men; grace is poured up- | on your lips;*
therefore God has blessed you for- | ever.

[3] Gird your sword on your thigh, O | mighty one,*
in your splendor and | majesty!

[4] In your majesty ride out victoriously for the cause of truth and meekness and | righteousness;*
let your right hand teach you | awesome deeds!

[5] Your arrows are sharp in the heart of the king's | enemies;*
the peoples fall | under you.

[6] Your throne, O God, is forever and ever. The scepter of your kingdom is a scepter of up- | rightness;*
[7] you have loved righteousness and hated | wickedness.

Therefore God, your God, has anointed you with the oil of gladness beyond your com- | panions;*
[8] your robes are all fragrant with myrrh and aloes and | cassia.

From ivory palaces stringed instruments | make you glad;*
[9] daughters of kings are among your ladies of honor; at your right hand stands the queen in gold of | Ophir.

[10] Hear, O daughter, and consider, and in- | cline your ear:*
forget your people and your | father's house,

[11] and the king will desire your | beauty.*
Since he is your lord, | bow to him.

[12] The people of Tyre will seek your fa- | vor with gifts,*
the richest of the | people.

[13] All glorious is the princess in her chamber, with robes interwoven | with gold.*
[14] In many-colored robes she is led to the king, with her virgin companions following be- | hind her.

[15] With joy and gladness they are | led along*
as they enter the palace | of the king.

[16] In place of your fathers shall | be your sons;*
you will make them princes in | all the earth.

[17] I will cause your name to be remembered in all gener- | ations;*
therefore nations will praise you forever and | ever.

Glory be to the Father and | to the Son*
and to the Holy | Spirit;
as it was in the be- | ginning,*
is now, and will be forever. | Amen.

46

[1] God is our ref- | uge and strength,*
a very present help in | trouble.

[2] Therefore we will not fear though the | earth gives way,*
though the mountains be moved into the heart | of the sea,

[3] though its waters | roar and foam,*
though the mountains tremble at its | swelling.

[4] There is a river whose streams make glad the cit- | y of God,*
the holy habitation of the | Most High.

[5] God is in the midst of her; she shall | not be moved;*
God will help her when | morning dawns.

[6] The nations rage, the kingdoms | totter;*
he utters his voice, the | earth melts.

[7] The LORD of hosts is | with us;*
the God of Jacob is our | fortress.

[8] Come, behold the works | of the LORD,*
how he has brought desolations | on the earth.

[9] He makes wars cease to the end | of the earth;*
he breaks the bow and shatters the spear; he burns the chariots | with fire.

[10] "Be still, and know that | I am God.*
I will be exalted among the nations, I will be exalted | in the earth!"

[11] The LORD of hosts is | with us;*
the God of Jacob is our | fortress.

Glory be to the Father and | to the Son*
and to the Holy | Spirit;
as it was in the be- | ginning,*
is now, and will be forever. | Amen.

47

[1] Clap your hands, all | peoples!*
Shout to God with loud | songs of joy!

[2] For the LORD, the Most High, is | to be feared,*
a great king over | all the earth.

[3] He subdued peoples | under us,*
and nations un- | der our feet.

[4] He chose our heritage | for us,*
the pride of Jacob | whom he loves.

[5] God has gone up | with a shout,*
the LORD with the sound of a | trumpet.

[6] Sing praises to God, sing | praises!*
Sing praises to our King, sing | praises!

[7] For God is the King of | all the earth;*
sing praises | with a psalm!

[8] God reigns over the | nations;*
God sits on his | holy throne.

[9] The princes of the peoples gather as the people of the God of | Abraham.*
For the shields of the earth belong to God; he is highly ex- | alted!

Glory be to the Father and | to the Son*
and to the Holy | Spirit;
as it was in the be- | ginning,*
is now, and will be forever. | Amen.

48

[1] Great is the LORD and greatly | to be praised*
in the city | of our God!

His holy mountain, [2] beautiful in elevation, is the joy of | all the earth,*
Mount Zion, in the far north, the city of the | great King.

[3] Within her | citadels*
God has made himself known as a | fortress.

[4] For behold, the kings as- | sembled;*
they came on to- | gether.

[5] As soon as they saw it, they were as- | tounded;*
they were in panic; they | took to flight.

[6] Trembling took hold | of them there,*
anguish as of a woman in | labor.

[7] By the | east wind*
you shattered the ships of | Tarshish.

[8] As we have heard, so have we seen in the city of the LORD of hosts, in the city | of our God,*
which God will establish for- | ever.

[9] We have thought on your steadfast love, | O God,*
in the midst of your | temple.

[10] As your name, O God, so your praise reaches to the ends | of the earth.*
Your right hand is filled with | righteousness.

[11] Let Mount Zion | be glad!*
Let the daughters of Judah rejoice because of your | judgments!

[12] Walk about Zion, go around her, number her | towers,*
[13] consider well her ramparts, go through her | citadels,

that you may tell the next generation
[14] that this is God, our God forever and | ever.*
He will guide us for- | ever.

Glory be to the Father and | to the Son*
and to the Holy | Spirit;
as it was in the be- | ginning,*
is now, and will be forever. | Amen.

50

[1] The Mighty One, God the LORD, speaks and sum- | mons the earth*
from the rising of the sun to its | setting.

[2] Out of Zion, the perfection of | beauty,*
God | shines forth.

[3] Our God comes; he does not keep | silence;*
before him is a devouring fire, around him a mighty | tempest.

[4] He calls to the heav- | ens above*
and to the earth, that he may judge his | people:

[5] "Gather to me my | faithful ones,*
who made a covenant with me by | sacrifice!"

[6] The heavens declare his | righteousness,*
for God him- | self is judge!

[7] "Hear, O my people, and I will speak;
O Israel, I will testify a- | gainst you.*
I am | God, your God.

[8] Not for your sacrifices do I re- | buke you;*
your burnt offerings are continually be- | fore me.

[9] I will not accept a bull | from your house*
or goats | from your folds.

[10] For every beast of the for- | est is mine,*
the cattle on a | thousand hills.

[11] I know all the birds | of the hills,*
and all that moves in the | field is mine.

[12] "If I were hungry, I would not | tell you,*
for the world and its full- | ness are mine.

[13] Do I eat the | flesh of bulls*
or drink the | blood of goats?

[14] Offer to God a sacrifice of thanks- | giving,*
and perform your vows to the | Most High,

[15] and call upon me in the day of | trouble;*
I will deliver you, and you shall glo- | rify me."

[16] But to the wicked | God says:*
"What right have you to recite my statutes or take my covenant | on your lips?

[17] For you hate | discipline,*
and you cast my words be- | hind you.

[18] If you see a thief, you are | pleased with him,*
and you keep company with a- | dulterers.

[19] "You give your mouth free rein for | evil,*
and your tongue | frames deceit.

[20] You sit and speak against your | brother;*
you slander your own | mother's son.

[21] These things you have done, and I have been silent; you thought that I was one | like yourself.*
But now I rebuke you and lay the charge be- | fore you.

[22] "Mark this, then, you who for- | get God,*
lest I tear you apart, and there be none to de- | liver!

[23] The one who offers thanksgiving as his sacrifice glo- | rifies me;*
to one who orders his way rightly I will show the salva- | tion of God!"

Glory be to the Father and | to the Son*
and to the Holy | Spirit;
as it was in the be- | ginning,*
is now, and will be forever. | Amen.

51

[1] Have mercy on me, O God, according to your | steadfast love;*
according to your abundant mercy blot out my trans- | gressions.

[2] Wash me thoroughly from my in- | iquity,*
and cleanse me | from my sin!

[3] For I know my trans- | gressions,*
and my sin is ever be- | fore me.

[4] Against you, you only, have I sinned and done what is evil | in your sight,*
so that you may be justified in your words and blameless in your | judgment.

[5] Behold, I was brought forth in in- | iquity,*
and in sin did my mother con- | ceive me.

[6] Behold, you delight in truth in the inward | being,*
and you teach me wisdom in the | secret heart.

[7] Purge me with hyssop, and I | shall be clean;*

wash me, and I shall be whit- | er than snow.

[8] Let me hear joy and | gladness; *
let the bones that you have bro- | ken rejoice.

[9] Hide your face | from my sins, *
and blot out all my in- | iquities.

[10] Create in me a clean heart, | O God, *
and renew a right spirit with- | in me.

[11] Cast me not away from your | presence, *
and take not your Holy Spirit | from me.

[12] Restore to me the joy of your sal- | vation, *
and uphold me with a willing | spirit.

[13] Then I will teach transgressors | your ways, *
and sinners will re- | turn to you.

[14] Deliver me from bloodguiltiness, O God, O God of my sal- | vation, *
and my tongue will sing aloud of your | righteousness.

[15] O Lord, open | my lips, *
and my mouth will de- | clare your praise.

[16] For you will not delight in sacrifice, or I would | give it; *
you will not be pleased with a burnt | offering.

[17] The sacrifices of God are a broken | spirit; *
a broken and contrite heart, O God, you will | not despise.

[18] Do good to Zion in your good | pleasure; *
build up the walls of Je- | rusalem;

[19] then will you delight in right sacrifices, in burnt offerings and whole burnt | offerings; *
then bulls will be offered on your | altar.

**Glory be to the Father and | to the Son *
and to the Holy | Spirit;
as it was in the be- | ginning, *
is now, and will be forever. | Amen.**

54

[1] O God, save me, | by your name, *
and vindicate me | by your might.

[2] O God, | hear my prayer; *
give ear to the words | of my mouth.

[3] For strangers have risen against me; ruthless men | seek my life; *
they do not set God be- | fore themselves.

[4] Behold, God is my | helper; *
the Lord is the upholder | of my life.

[5] He will return the evil to my | enemies; *
in your faithfulness put an | end to them.

[6] With a freewill offering I will sacri- | fice to you; *
I will give thanks to your name, O LORD, for | it is good.

[7] For he has delivered me from every | trouble, *
and my eye has looked in triumph on my | enemies.

**Glory be to the Father and | to the Son *
and to the Holy | Spirit;
as it was in the be- | ginning, *
is now, and will be forever. | Amen.**

56

[1] Be gracious to me, O God, for man tramples | on me; *
all day long an attacker op- | presses me;

[2] my enemies trample on me | all day long, *
for many attack me | proudly.

[3] When I | am afraid,*
I put my | trust in you.

[4] In God, whose word I praise, in God I trust; I shall not | be afraid.*
What can flesh | do to me?

[5] All day long they in- | jure my cause;*
all their thoughts are against me for | evil.

[6] They stir up strife, they lurk; they | watch my steps,*
as they have waited | for my life.

[7] For their crime will | they escape?*
In wrath cast down the peoples, | O God!

[8] You have kept count of my tossings; put my tears in your | bottle.*
Are they not | in your book?

[9] Then my enemies will turn back in the day | when I call.*
This I know, that God is | for me.

[10] In God, whose | word I praise,*
in the LORD, whose | word I praise,

[11] in God I trust; I shall not | be afraid.*
What can man | do to me?

[12] I must perform my vows to you, | O God;*
I will render thank offerings | to you.

[13] For you have delivered my soul from death, yes, my feet from | falling,*
that I may walk before God in the | light of life.

Glory be to the Father and | to the Son*
and to the Holy | Spirit;
as it was in the be- | ginning,*
is now, and will be forever. | Amen.

61

[1] Hear my cry, | O God,*
listen | to my prayer;

[2] from the end of the earth I call to you when my | heart is faint.*
Lead me to the rock that is high- | er than I,

[3] for you have been my | refuge,*
a strong tower against the | enemy.

[4] Let me dwell in your tent for- | ever!*
Let me take refuge under the shelter | of your wings!

[5] For you, O God, have | heard my vows;*
you have given me the heritage of those who | fear your name.

[6] Prolong the life | of the king;*
may his years endure to all gener- | ations!

[7] May he be enthroned forever be- | fore God;*
appoint steadfast love and faithfulness to watch | over him!

[8] So will I ever sing praises | to your name,*
as I perform my vows day | after day.

Glory be to the Father and | to the Son*
and to the Holy | Spirit;
as it was in the be- | ginning,*
is now, and will be forever. | Amen.

62

[1] For God alone my soul waits in | silence;*
from him comes my sal- | vation.

[2] He only is my rock and my salvation, my | fortress;*
I shall not be greatly | shaken.

[3] How long will all of you attack a man to | batter him,*
like a leaning wall, a | tottering fence?

[4] They only plan to thrust him down from his high position. They take pleasure in | falsehood.*
They bless with their mouths, but inwardly | they curse.

[5] For God alone, O my soul, wait in | silence,*
for my hope is | from him.

[6] He only is my rock and my salvation, my | fortress;*
I shall not be | shaken.

[7] On God rests my salvation and my | glory;*
my mighty rock, my refuge | is God.

[8] Trust in him at all times, O people; pour out your heart be- | fore him;*
God is a refuge | for us.

[9] Those of low estate are but a breath; those of high estate are a de- | lusion;*
in the balances they go up; they are together lighter | than a breath.

[10] Put no trust in extortion; set no vain hopes on | robbery;*
if riches increase, set not your | heart on them.

[11] Once God has spoken; twice have I | heard this:*
that power belongs to God, [12] and that to you, O Lord, belongs | steadfast love.

For you will render | to a man*
according | to his work.

Glory be to the Father and | to the Son*
and to the Holy | Spirit;
as it was in the be- | ginning,*
is now, and will be forever. | Amen.

65

[1] Praise is due to you, O God, in | Zion,*
and to you shall vows | be performed.

[2] O you who | hears prayer,*
to you shall | all flesh come.

[3] When iniquities prevail a- | gainst me,*
you atone for our trans- | gressions.

[4] Blessèd is the one you choose and bring near, to dwell | in your courts!*
We shall be satisfied with the goodness of your house, the holiness of your | temple!

[5] By awesome deeds you answer us with righteousness, O God of our sal- | vation,*
the hope of all the ends of the earth and of the | farthest seas;

[6] the one who by his strength established the | mountains,*
being girded | with might;

[7] who stills the roaring of the seas, the roaring | of their waves,*
the tumult of the | peoples,

[8] so that those who dwell at the ends of the earth are in awe | at your signs.*
You make the going out of the morning and the evening to | shout for joy.

[9] You visit the earth and water it; you greatly enrich it; the river of God is full of | water;*
you provide their grain, for so you have pre- | pared it.

[10] You water its furrows abundantly, settling its | ridges,*
softening it with showers, and bless- | ing its growth.

[11] You crown the year with your | bounty;*
your wagon tracks overflow with a- | bundance.

[12] The pastures of the wilderness | overflow,*
the hills gird them- | selves with joy,

[13] the meadows clothe themselves with flocks, the valleys deck them- | selves with grain,*
they shout and sing together | for joy.

Glory be to the Father and | to the Son*
and to the Holy | Spirit;
as it was in the be- | ginning,*
is now, and will be forever. | Amen.

66

[1] Shout for joy to God, | all the earth; *
[2] sing the glory of his name; give to him | glorious praise!

[3] Say to God, "How awesome | are your deeds! *
So great is your power that your enemies come cringing | to you.

[4] All the earth worships you and sings prais- | es to you; *
they sing praises | to your name."

[5] Come and see what | God has done: *
he is awesome in his deeds toward the chil- | dren of man.

[6] He turned the sea into | dry land; *
they passed through the riv- | er on foot.

There did we rejoice in him, [7] who rules by his might forever, whose eyes keep watch on the | nations— *
let not the rebellious ex- | alt themselves.

[8] Bless our God, O | peoples; *
let the sound of his | praise be heard,

[9] who has kept our soul among the | living *
and has not let our | feet slip.

[10] For you, O God, have | tested us; *
you have tried us as sil- | ver is tried.

[11] You brought us in- | to the net; *
you laid a crushing burden | on our backs;

[12] you let men ride o- | ver our heads; *
we went through fire and through water; yet you have brought us out to a place of a- | bundance.

[13] I will come into your house with burnt | offerings; *
I will perform my | vows to you,

[14] that which my lips | uttered *
and my mouth promised when I was in | trouble.

[15] I will offer to you burnt offerings of fattened animals, with the smoke of the sacri- | fice of rams; *
I will make an offering of | bulls and goats.

[16] Come and hear, all you who | fear God, *
and I will tell what he has done | for my soul.

[17] I cried to him | with my mouth, *
and high praise was | on my tongue.

[18] If I had cherished iniquity | in my heart, *
the Lord would not have | listened.

[19] But truly God has | listened; *
he has attended to the voice | of my prayer.

[20] Blessèd | be God, *
because he has not rejected my prayer or removed his steadfast | love from me!

**Glory be to the Father and | to the Son *
and to the Holy | Spirit;
as it was in the be- | ginning, *
is now, and will be forever. | Amen.**

67

[1] May God be gracious to us and | bless us *
and make his face to shine up- | on us,

[2] that your way may be | known on earth, *
your saving power among all | nations.

[3] Let the peoples praise you, | O God; *
let all the peoples | praise you!

[4] Let the nations be glad and | sing for joy, *
for you judge the peoples with equity and guide the nations up- | on earth.

[5] Let the peoples praise you, | O God; *
let all the peoples | praise you!

[6] The earth has yielded its | increase; *
God, our God, shall | bless us.

[7] God shall | bless us; *
let all the ends of the earth | fear him!

Glory be to the Father and | to the Son*
and to the Holy | Spirit;
as it was in the be- | ginning,*
is now, and will be forever. | Amen.

68

[1] God shall arise, his enemies shall be | scattered;*
and those who hate him shall flee be- | fore him!

[2] As smoke is driven away, so you shall drive | them away;*
as wax melts before fire, so the wicked shall perish be- | fore God!

[3] But the righteous shall be glad; they shall exult be- | fore God;*
they shall be jubilant | with joy!

[4] Sing to God, sing praises | to his name;*
lift up a song to him who rides through the deserts; his name is the LORD; exult be- | fore him!

[5] Father of the fatherless and protector of | widows*
is God in his holy habi- | tation.

[6] God settles the solitary in a home; he leads out the prisoners to pros- | perity,*
but the rebellious dwell in a | parched land.

[7] O God, when you went out before your | people,*
when you marched through the | wilderness,

[8] the earth quaked, the heavens poured down rain, before God, the One of | Sinai,*
before God, the God of | Israel.

[9] Rain in abundance, O God, you | shed abroad;*
you restored your inheritance as it | languished;

[10] your flock found a dwell- | ing in it;*
in your goodness, O God, you provided for the | needy.

[11] The Lord | gives the word;*
the women who announce the news are a | great host:

[12] "The kings of the armies—they | flee, they flee!"*
The women at home divide the | spoil—

[13] though you men lie among the | sheepfolds—*
the wings of a dove covered with silver, its pinions with | shimmering gold.

[14] When the Almighty scatters | kings there,*
let snow fall on | Zalmon.

[15] O mountain of God, mountain of | Bashan;*
O many-peaked mountain, mountain of | Bashan!

[16] Why do you look with hatred, O many-peaked | mountain,*
at the mount that God desired for his abode, yes, where the LORD will dwell for- | ever?

[17] The chariots of God are twice ten thousand, thousands upon | thousands;*
the Lord is among them; Sinai is now in the sanctu- | ary.

[18] You ascended on high, leading a host of captives in your train and receiving gifts a- | mong men,*
even among the rebellious, that the LORD God may | dwell there.

[19] Blessèd be the Lord, who daily | bears us up;*
God is our sal- | vation.

[20] Our God is a God of sal- | vation,*
and to GOD, the Lord, belong deliverances | from death.

[21] But God will strike the heads of his | enemies,*
the hairy crown of him who walks in his | guilty ways.

[22] The Lord said, "I will bring them back from | Bashan,*
I will bring them back from the depths | of the sea,

[23] that you may strike your feet | in their blood,*
that the tongues of your dogs may have their portion | from the foe."

[24] Your procession is seen, | O God,*
the procession of my God, my King, into the sanctu- | ary—

[25] the singers in front, the mu- | sicians last,*
between them virgins playing | tambourines:

[26] "Bless God in the great congre- | gation,*
the LORD, O you who are of Israel's | fountain!"

[27] There is Benjamin, the least of them, in the lead, the princes of Judah | in their throng,*
the princes of Zebulun, the princes of | Naphtali.

[28] Summon your power, | O God,*
the power, O God, by which you have | worked for us.

[29] Because of your temple at Je- | rusalem*
kings shall bear | gifts to you.

[30] Rebuke the beasts that dwell among the reeds, the herd of bulls with the calves of the | peoples.*
Trample underfoot those who lust after tribute; scatter the peoples who de- | light in war.

[31] Nobles shall come from | Egypt;*
Cush shall hasten to stretch out her | hands to God.

[32] O kingdoms of the earth, | sing to God;*
sing praises | to the Lord,

[33] to him who rides in the heavens, the ancient | heavens;*
behold, he sends out his voice, his | mighty voice.

[34] Ascribe | power to God,*
whose majesty is over Israel, and whose power is | in the skies.

[35] Awesome is God from his sanctu- | ary;*
the God of Israel—he is the one who gives power and strength to his people. Blessèd | be God!

Glory be to the Father and | to the Son*
and to the Holy | Spirit;
as it was in the be- | ginning,*
is now, and will be forever. | Amen.

70

[1] Make haste, O God, to de- | liver me!*
O LORD, make haste to | help me!

[2] Let them be put to shame and confusion who | seek my life!*
Let them be turned back and brought to dishonor who de- | sire my hurt!

[3] Let them turn back because | of their shame*
who say, "A- | ha, Aha!"

[4] May all who seek you rejoice and be | glad in you!*
May those who love your salvation say evermore, | "God is great!"

[5] But I am poor and needy; hasten to me, | O God!*
You are my help and my deliverer; O LORD, do | not delay!

Glory be to the Father and | to the Son*
and to the Holy | Spirit;
as it was in the be- | ginning,*
is now, and will be forever. | Amen.

71

[1] In you, O LORD, do I take | refuge;*
let me never be | put to shame!

[2] In your righteousness deliver me and | rescue me;*
incline your ear to me, and | save me!

[3] Be to me a rock of refuge, to which I may contin- | ually come;*
you have given the command to save me, for you are my rock and my | fortress.

[4] Rescue me, O my God, from the hand of the | wicked,*
from the grasp of the unjust and | cruel man.

[5] For you, O Lord, | are my hope,*
my trust, O LORD, | from my youth.

[6] Upon you I have leaned from before my birth; you are he who took me from my | mother's womb.*
My praise is continually | of you.

[7] I have been as a portent to | many,*
but you are my strong | refuge.

[8] My mouth is filled | with your praise,*
and with your glory | all the day.

[9] Do not cast me off in the time of | old age;*
forsake me not when my | strength is spent.

[10] For my enemies speak con- | cerning me;*
those who watch for my life consult together [11] and say,
"God has for- | saken him;

pursue and | seize him,*
for there is none to de- | liver him."

[12] O God, be not | far from me;*
O my God, make haste to | help me!

[13] May my accusers be put to shame | and consumed;*
with scorn and disgrace may they be covered who | seek my hurt.

[14] But I will hope con- | tinually*
and will praise you yet | more and more.

[15] My mouth will tell of your righteous acts, of your deeds of salvation | all the day,*
for their number is past my | knowledge.

[16] With the mighty deeds of the Lord GOD | I will come;*
I will remind them of your righteousness, | yours alone.

[17] O God, from my youth you have | taught me,*
and I still proclaim your | wondrous deeds.

[18] So even to old age and gray hairs, O God, do not for- | sake me,*
until I proclaim your might to another generation, your power to all | those to come.

[19] Your righteousness, O God, reaches the high | heavens.*
You who have done great things, O God, who is | like you?

[20] You who have made me see many troubles and calamities will revive | me again;*
from the depths of the earth you will bring me | up again.

[21] You will increase my | greatness*
and comfort | me again.

[22] I will also praise you with the harp for your faithfulness, | O my God;*
I will sing praises to you with the lyre, O Holy One of | Israel.

[23] My lips will shout for joy, when I sing prais- | es to you;*
my soul also, which you | have redeemed.

[24] And my tongue will talk of your righteous help all | the day long,*
for they have been put to shame and disappointed who sought to | do me hurt.

Glory be to the Father and | to the Son*
and to the Holy | Spirit;
as it was in the be- | ginning,*
is now, and will be forever. | Amen.

72

[1] Give the king your justice, | O God,*
and your righteousness to the | royal son!

[2] May he judge your people with | righteousness,*
and your poor with | justice!

[3] Let the mountains bear prosperity for the | people,*
and the hills, in | righteousness!

[4] May he defend the cause of the poor of the people, give deliverance to the children of the | needy,*
and crush the op- | pressor!

[5] May they fear you while the | sun endures,*
and as long as the moon, throughout all gener- | ations!

[6] May he be like rain that falls on the | mown grass,*
like showers that wa- | ter the earth!

[7] In his days may the righteous | flourish,*
and peace abound, till the moon | be no more!

[8] May he have dominion from | sea to sea,*
and from the River to the ends | of the earth!

[9] May desert tribes bow down be- | fore him*
and his enemies | lick the dust!

[10] May the kings of Tarshish and of the coastlands render him | tribute;*
may the kings of Sheba and Seba | bring gifts!

[11] May all kings fall down be- | fore him,*
all nations | serve him!

[12] For he delivers the needy | when he calls,*
the poor and him who has no | helper.

[13] He has pity on the weak and the | needy,*
and saves the lives of the | needy.

[14] From oppression and violence he re- | deems their life,*
and precious is their blood | in his sight.

[15] Long may he live; may gold of Sheba be giv- | en to him!*
May prayer be made for him continually, and blessings invoked for him | all the day!

[16] May there be abundance of grain in the land; on the tops of the mountains may it wave; may its fruit be like | Lebanon;*
and may people blossom in the cities like the grass | of the field!

[17] May his name endure forever, his fame continue as long | as the sun!*
May people be blessed in him, all nations call him | blessèd!

[18] Blessèd be the LORD, the God of | Israel,*
who alone does | wondrous things.

[19] Blessèd be his glorious name for- | ever;*
may the whole earth be filled with his glory! Amen and | Amen!

Glory be to the Father and | to the Son*
and to the Holy | Spirit;
as it was in the be- | ginning,*
is now, and will be forever. | Amen.

73

[1] Truly God is good to | Israel,*
to those who are | pure in heart.

[2] But as for me, my feet had almost | stumbled,*
my steps had | nearly slipped.

[3] For I was envious of the | arrogant*
when I saw the prosperity of the | wicked.

[4] For they have no pangs | until death;*
their bodies are | fat and sleek.

[5] They are not in trouble as | others are;*
they are not stricken like the rest of | mankind.

[6] Therefore pride is their | necklace;*
violence covers them as a | garment.

[7] Their eyes swell out through | fatness;*
their hearts overflow with | follies.

[8] They scoff and speak with | malice;*
loftily they threaten op- | pression.

[9] They set their mouths against the | heavens,*
and their tongue struts | through the earth.

[10] Therefore his people turn | back to them,*
and find no | fault in them.

[11] And they say, "How can | God know?*
Is there knowledge in the | Most High?"

[12] Behold, these are the | wicked;*
always at ease, they increase in | riches.

[13] All in vain have I kept my | heart clean*
and washed my hands in | innocence.

[14] For all the day long I have been | stricken*
and rebuked every | morning.

[15] If I had said, "I will | speak thus,"*
I would have betrayed the generation of your | children.

[16] But when I thought how to under- | stand this,*
it seemed to me a | wearisome task,

[17] until I went into the sanctuary | of God;*
then I dis- | cerned their end.

[18] Truly you set them in slippery | places;*
you make them fall to | ruin.

[19] How they are destroyed in a | moment,*
swept away utterly by | terrors!

[20] Like a dream when | one awakes,*
O Lord, when you rouse yourself,
you despise them as | phantoms.

[21] When my soul was em- | bittered,*
when I was | pricked in heart,

[22] I was brutish and | ignorant;*
I was like a | beast toward you.

[23] Nevertheless, I am continually | with you;*
you hold my | right hand.

[24] You guide me with your | counsel,*
and afterward you will receive me to | glory.

[25] Whom have I in | heaven but you?*
And there is nothing on earth that I desire be- | sides you.

[26] My flesh and my | heart may fail,*
but God is the strength of my heart and my portion for- | ever.

[27] For behold, those who are far from you shall | perish;*
you put an end to everyone who is unfaithful | to you.

[28] But for me it is good to be | near God;*
I have made the Lord GOD my refuge,
that I may tell of | all your works.

Glory be to the Father and | to the Son*
and to the Holy | Spirit;
as it was in the be- | ginning,*
is now, and will be forever. | Amen.

77

[1] I cry a- | loud to God,*
aloud to God, and he will | hear me.

[2] In the day of my trouble I | seek the Lord;*
in the night my hand is stretched out without wearying; my soul refuses to be | comforted.

[3] When I remember | God, I moan;*
when I meditate, my | spirit faints.

[4] You hold my eyelids | open;*
I am so troubled that I | cannot speak.

[5] I consider the | days of old,*
the years | long ago.

[6] I said, "Let me remember my song in the night; let me meditate | in my heart."*
Then my spirit made a dil- | igent search:

[7] "Will the Lord spurn for- | ever,*
and never again be | favorable?

[8] Has his steadfast love for- | ever ceased?*
Are his promises at an end | for all time?

[9] Has God forgotten to be | gracious?*
Has he in anger shut up his com- | passion?"

[10] Then I said, "I will ap- | peal to this,*
to the years of the right hand of the | Most High."

[11] I will remember the deeds | of the LORD;*
yes, I will remember your won- | ders of old.

[12] I will ponder | all your work,*
and meditate on your | mighty deeds.

[13] Your way, O God, is | holy.*
What god is great | like our God?

[14] You are the God who works | wonders;*
you have made known your might among the | peoples.

[15] You with your arm redeemed your | people,*
the children of Jacob and | Joseph.

[16] When the waters saw you, O God, when the waters saw you, they | were afraid;*
indeed, the deep | trembled.

[17] The clouds poured out water; the skies gave forth | thunder;*
your arrows flashed on | every side.

[18] The crash of your thunder was in the whirlwind; your lightnings lighted | up the world;*
the earth trem- | bled and shook.

[19] Your way was through the sea, your path through the great | waters;*
yet your footprints | were unseen.

[20] You led your people | like a flock*
by the hand of Moses and | Aaron.

Glory be to the Father and | to the Son*
and to the Holy | Spirit;
as it was in the be- | ginning,*
is now, and will be forever. | Amen.

80

[1] Give ear, O Shepherd of Israel, you who lead Joseph | like a flock!*
You who are enthroned upon the cherubim, | shine forth.

[2] Before Ephraim and Benjamin and Ma- | nasseh,*
stir up your might and come to | save us!

[3] Restore us, | O God;*
let your face shine, that we | may be saved!

[4] O LORD | God of hosts,*
how long will you be angry with your | people's prayers?

[5] You have fed them with the | bread of tears*
and given them tears to drink in full | measure.

[6] You make us an object of contention for our | neighbors,*
and our enemies laugh a- | mong themselves.

[7] Restore us, O | God of hosts;*
let your face shine, that we | may be saved!

[8] You brought a vine out of | Egypt;*
you drove out the nations and | planted it.

[9] You cleared the | ground for it;*
it took deep root and | filled the land.

[10] The mountains were covered | with its shade,*
the mighty cedars with its | branches.

[11] It sent out its branches | to the sea*
and its shoots to the | River.

[12] Why then have you broken | down its walls,*
so that all who pass along the way | pluck its fruit?

[13] The boar from the forest rav- | ages it,*
and all that move in the field | feed on it.

[14] Turn again, O | God of hosts!*
Look down from | heaven, and see;

have regard for this vine, [15] the stock that your right hand | planted,*
and for the son whom you made strong | for yourself.

[16] They have burned it with fire; they have | cut it down;*
may they perish at the rebuke | of your face!

[17] But let your hand be on the man of your | right hand,*
the son of man whom you have made strong | for yourself!

[18] Then we shall not turn | back from you;*
give us life, and we will call up- | on your name!

[19] Restore us, O LORD | God of hosts!*
Let your face shine, that we | may be saved!

Glory be to the Father and | to the Son*
and to the Holy | Spirit;
as it was in the be- | ginning,*
is now, and will be forever. | Amen.

81

[1] Sing aloud to | God our strength;*
shout for joy to the God of | Jacob!

[2] Raise a song; sound the | tambourine,*
the sweet lyre | with the harp.

[3] Blow the trumpet at the | new moon,*
at the full moon, on our | feast day.

[4] For it is a statute for | Israel,*
a just decree of the God of | Jacob.

[5] He made it a decree in Joseph when he went out over the land of | Egypt.*
I hear a language I | had not known:

[6] "I relieved your shoulder of the | burden;*
your hands were freed from the | basket.

[7] In distress you called, and I de- | livered you;*
I answered you in the secret place of thunder; I tested you at the waters of | Meribah.

[8] Hear, O my people, while I ad- | monish you!*
O Israel, if you would but lis- | ten to me!

[9] There shall be no strange god a- | mong you;*
you shall not bow down to a | foreign god.

[10] I am the LORD your God, who brought you up out of the land of | Egypt.*
Open your mouth wide, and I will | fill it.

[11] "But my people did not listen | to my voice;*
Israel would not sub- | mit to me.

[12] So I gave them over to their | stubborn hearts,*
to follow their own | counsels.

[13] Oh, that my people would lis- | ten to me,*
that Israel would walk | in my ways!

[14] I would soon subdue their | enemies*
and turn my hand a- | gainst their foes.

[15] Those who hate the LORD would | cringe toward him,*
and their fate would last for- | ever.

[16] But he would feed you with the finest | of the wheat,*
and with honey from the rock I would sat- | isfy you."

Glory be to the Father and | to the Son*
and to the Holy | Spirit;
as it was in the be- | ginning,*
is now, and will be forever. | Amen.

84

[1] How lovely is your | dwelling place,*
O | LORD of hosts!

[2] My soul longs, yes, faints for the courts | of the LORD;*
my heart and flesh sing for joy to the | living God.

[3] Even the sparrow finds a home, and the swallow a nest for herself, where she may | lay her young,*
at your altars, O LORD of hosts, my King | and my God.

[4] Blessèd are those who dwell | in your house,*
ever sing- | ing your praise!

[5] Blessèd are those whose strength is | in you,*
in whose heart are the highways to | Zion.

[6] As they go through the Valley of Baca they make it a | place of springs;*
the early rain also covers | it with pools.

[7] They go from | strength to strength;*
each one appears before God in | Zion.

[8] O LORD God of hosts, | hear my prayer;*
give ear, O God of | Jacob!

[9] Behold our shield, | O God;*
look on the face of your a- | nointed!

[10] For a day in your courts is better than a thousand | elsewhere.*
I would rather be a doorkeeper in the house of my God than dwell in the tents of | wickedness.

[11] For the LORD God is a sun and shield; the LORD bestows favor and | honor.*
No good thing does he withhold from those who walk up- | rightly.

[12] O | LORD of hosts,*
blessèd is the one who | trusts in you!

Glory be to the Father and | to the Son*
and to the Holy | Spirit;
as it was in the be- | ginning,*
is now, and will be forever. | Amen.

85

[1] LORD, you were favorable | to your land;*
you restored the fortunes of | Jacob.

[2] You forgave the iniquity of your | people;*
you covered | all their sin.

[3] You withdrew | all your wrath;*
you turned from your hot | anger.

[4] Restore us again, O God of our sal- | vation,*
and put away your indignation | toward us!

[5] Will you be angry with us for- | ever?*
Will you prolong your anger to all gener- | ations?

[6] Will you not revive | us again,*
that your people may re- | joice in you?

[7] Show us your steadfast love, | O LORD,*
and grant us your sal- | vation.

[8] Let me hear what God the | LORD will speak,*
for he will speak peace to his people, to his saints; but let them not turn back to | folly.

[9] Surely his salvation is near to those who | fear him,*
that glory may dwell | in our land.

[10] Steadfast love and faith- | fulness meet;*
righteousness and peace kiss each | other.

[11] Faithfulness springs up | from the ground,*
and righteousness looks down | from the sky.

[12] Yes, the LORD will give | what is good,*
and our land will yield its | increase.

[13] Righteousness will go be- | fore him*
and make his foot- | steps a way.

Glory be to the Father and | to the Son*
and to the Holy | Spirit;
as it was in the be- | ginning,*
is now, and will be forever. | Amen.

86

[1] Incline your ear, O LORD, and | answer me,*
for I am poor and | needy.

[2] Preserve my life, for I am | godly;*
save your servant, who trusts in you—you | are my God.

[3] Be gracious to me, | O Lord,*
for to you do I cry | all the day.

[4] Gladden the soul of your | servant,*
for to you, O Lord, do I lift | up my soul.

[5] For you, O Lord, are good and for- | giving,*
abounding in steadfast love to all who call up- | on you.

[6] Give ear, O LORD, | to my prayer;*
listen to my | plea for grace.

[7] In the day of my trouble I call up- | on you,*
for you | answer me.

[8] There is none like you among the gods, | O Lord,*
nor are there any | works like yours.

[9] All the nations you have made shall come and worship before you, | O Lord,*
and shall glori- | fy your name.

[10] For you are great and do | wondrous things;*
you a- | lone are God.

[11] Teach me your way, O LORD, that I may walk | in your truth;*
unite my heart to | fear your name.

[12] I give thanks to you, O Lord my God, with | my whole heart,*
and I will glorify your name for- | ever.

[13] For great is your steadfast | love toward me;*
you have delivered my soul from the depths | of Sheol.

[14] O God, insolent men have risen up against me; a band of ruthless men | seek my life,*
and they do not set you be- | fore them.

[15] But you, O Lord, are a God merciful and | gracious,*
slow to anger and abounding in steadfast love and | faithfulness.

[16] Turn to me and be gra- | cious to me;*
give your strength to your servant, and save the son of your maid- | servant.

[17] Show me a sign of your | favor,*
that those who hate me may see and be put to shame because you, LORD, have helped me and com- | forted me.

Glory be to the Father and | to the Son*
and to the Holy | Spirit;
as it was in the be- | ginning,*
is now, and will be forever. | Amen.

89

[1] I will sing of the steadfast love of the LORD, for- | ever;*
with my mouth I will make known your faithfulness to all gener- | ations.

[2] For I said, "Steadfast love will be built up for- | ever;*
in the heavens you will establish your | faithfulness."

[3] You have said, "I have made a covenant with my | chosen one;*
I have sworn to David my | servant:

[4] 'I will establish your offspring for- | ever,*
and build your throne for all gener- | ations.' "

[5] Let the heavens praise your wonders, | O LORD,*
your faithfulness in the assembly of the | holy ones!

[6] For who in the skies can be compared | to the LORD?*
Who among the heavenly beings is | like the LORD,

[7] a God greatly to be feared in the council of the | holy ones,*
and awesome above all who are a- | round him?

[8] O LORD God of hosts, who is mighty as you are, | O LORD,*
with your faithfulness all a- | round you?

[9] You rule the raging | of the sea;*
when its waves rise, you | still them.

[10] You crushed Rahab like a | carcass;*
you scattered your enemies with your | mighty arm.

[11] The heavens are yours; the earth al- | so is yours;*
the world and all that is in it, you have | founded them.

[12] The north and the south, you have cre- | ated them;*
Tabor and Hermon joyously | praise your name.

[13] You have a | mighty arm;*
strong is your hand, high your | right hand.

[14] Righteousness and justice are the foundation | of your throne;*
steadfast love and faithfulness go be- | fore you.

[15] Blessèd are the people who know the | festal shout,*
who walk, O LORD, in the light | of your face,

[16] who exult in your name | all the day*
and in your righteousness are ex- | alted.

[17] For you are the glory | of their strength;*
by your favor our horn is ex- | alted.

[18] For our shield belongs | to the LORD,*
our king to the Holy One of | Israel.

[19] Of old you spoke in a vision to your godly one, and said: "I have granted help to one who is | mighty;*
I have exalted one chosen from the | people.

[20] I have found David, my | servant;*
with my holy oil I have a- | nointed him,

[21] so that my hand shall be estab- | lished with him;*
my arm also shall | strengthen him.

[22] The enemy shall not out- | wit him;*
the wicked shall not | humble him.

[23] I will crush his foes be- | fore him*
and strike down those who | hate him.

[24] My faithfulness and my steadfast love shall | be with him,*
and in my name shall his horn be ex- | alted.

[25] I will set his hand | on the sea*
and his right hand on the | rivers.

[26] He shall cry to me, 'You are my | Father,*
my God, and the Rock of my sal- | vation.'

[27] And I will make him the | firstborn,*
the highest of the kings | of the earth.

[28] My steadfast love I will keep for him for- | ever,*
and my covenant will stand | firm for him.

[29] I will establish his offspring for- | ever*
and his throne as the days of the | heavens.

[30] If his children for- | sake my law*
and do not walk according to my | just decrees,

[31] if they violate my | statutes*
and do not keep my com- | mandments,

[32] then I will punish their transgression | with the rod*
and their iniqui- | ty with stripes,

[33] but I will not remove from him my | steadfast love*
or be false to my | faithfulness.

[34] I will not violate my | covenant*
or alter the word that went forth | from my lips.

[35] Once for all I have sworn by my | holiness;*
I will not lie to | David.

[36] His offspring shall endure for- | ever,*
his throne as long as the sun be- | fore me.

[37] Like the moon it shall be established for- | ever,*
a faithful witness | in the skies."

[38] But now you have cast off and re- | jected;*
you are full of wrath against your a- | nointed.

[39] You have renounced the covenant with your | servant;*
you have defiled his crown | in the dust.

[40] You have breached | all his walls;*
you have laid his strongholds in | ruins.

[41] All who pass by | plunder him;*
he has become the scorn of his | neighbors.

[42] You have exalted the right hand | of his foes;*
you have made all his ene- | mies rejoice.

[43] You have also turned back the edge | of his sword,*
and you have not made him stand in | battle.

[44] You have made his splen- | dor to cease*
and cast his throne | to the ground.

[45] You have cut short the days | of his youth;*
you have covered | him with shame.

[46] How long, O LORD? Will you hide yourself for- | ever?*
How long will your wrath | burn like fire?

[47] Remember how short my | time is!*
For what vanity you have created all the chil- | dren of man!

[48] What man can live and never | see death?*
Who can deliver his soul from the power | of Sheol?

[49] Lord, where is your steadfast | love of old,*
which by your faithfulness you swore to | David?

[50] Remember, O Lord, how your ser- | vants are mocked,*
and how I bear in my heart the insults of all the many | nations,

[51] with which your enemies mock, | O LORD,*
with which they mock the footsteps of your a- | nointed.

[52] Blessèd be the LORD for- | ever!*
Amen and | Amen.

Glory be to the Father and | to the Son*
and to the Holy | Spirit;
as it was in the be- | ginning,*
is now, and will be forever. | Amen.

90

[1] Lord, you have been our | dwelling place*
in all gener- | ations.

[2] Before the mountains were brought forth, or ever you had formed the earth | and the world,*
from everlasting to everlasting | you are God.

[3] You return | man to dust*
and say, "Return, O chil- | dren of man!"

[4] For a thousand years in your sight are but as yesterday when | it is past,*
or as a watch | in the night.

[5] You sweep them away as | with a flood;*
they are like a dream, like grass that is renewed in the | morning:

[6] in the morning it flourishes and | is renewed;*
in the evening it fades and | withers.

[7] For we are brought to an end by your | anger;*
by your wrath we | are dismayed.

[8] You have set our iniquities be- | fore you,*
our secret sins in the light of your | presence.

[9] For all our days pass away un- | der your wrath;*
we bring our years to an end | like a sigh.

[10] The years of our life are seventy, or even by reason of strength | eighty;*
yet their span is but toil and trouble; they are soon gone, and we | fly away.

[11] Who considers the power of your | anger,*
and your wrath according to the | fear of you?

[12] So teach us to number | our days*
that we may get a heart of | wisdom.

[13] Return, O LORD! | How long?*
Have pity on your | servants!

[14] Satisfy us in the morning with your | steadfast love,*
that we may rejoice and be glad | all our days.

[15] Make us glad for as many days as you have af- | flicted us,*
and for as many years as we have seen | evil.

[16] Let your work be shown to your | servants,*
and your glorious power to their | children.

[17] Let the favor of the Lord our God be upon us, and establish the work of our hands up- | on us;*
yes, establish the work | of our hands!

Glory be to the Father and | to the Son*
and to the Holy | Spirit;
as it was in the be- | ginning,*
is now, and will be forever. | Amen.

91

[1] He who dwells in the shelter of the | Most High*
will abide in the shadow of the Al- | mighty.

[2] I will say to the LORD, "My refuge and my | fortress,*
my God, in | whom I trust."

[3] For he will deliver you from the snare of the | fowler*
and from the deadly | pestilence.

[4] He will cover you with his pinions, and under his wings you will find | refuge;*
his faithfulness is a shield and | buckler.

[5] You will not fear the terror | of the night,*
nor the arrow that | flies by day,

[6] nor the pestilence that stalks in | darkness,*

nor the destruction that wastes at | noonday.

[7] A thousand may fall at your side, ten thousand at your | right hand,*
but it will not come | near you.

[8] You will only look | with your eyes*
and see the recompense of the | wicked.

[9] Because you have made the LORD your | dwelling place—*
the Most High, who is my | refuge—

[10] no evil shall be allowed to be- | fall you,*
no plague come | near your tent.

[11] For he will command his angels con- | cerning you*
to guard you in | all your ways.

[12] On their hands they will | bear you up,*
lest you strike your foot a- | gainst a stone.

[13] You will tread on the lion and the | adder;*
the young lion and the serpent you will trample | underfoot.

[14] "Because he holds fast to me in love, I will de- | liver him;*
I will protect him, because he | knows my name.

[15] When he calls to me, I will answer him; I will be with him in | trouble;*
I will rescue him and | honor him.

[16] With long life I will sat- | isfy him*
and show him my sal- | vation."

Glory be to the Father and | to the Son*
and to the Holy | Spirit;
as it was in the be- | ginning,*
is now, and will be forever. | Amen.

92

[1] It is good to give thanks | to the LORD,*
to sing praises to your name, | O Most High;

[2] to declare your steadfast love in the | morning,*
and your faithful- | ness by night,

[3] to the music of the lute | and the harp,*
to the melody | of the lyre.

[4] For you, O LORD, have made me glad | by your work;*
at the works of your hands I | sing for joy.

[5] How great are your works, | O LORD!*
Your thoughts are | very deep!

[6] The stupid man cannot know; the fool cannot under- | stand this:*
[7] that though the wicked sprout like grass and all evildoers flourish, they are doomed to destruction for- | ever;

[8] but you, | O LORD,*
are on high for- | ever.

[9] For behold, your enemies, O LORD, for behold, your enemies shall | perish;*
all evildoers shall be | scattered.

[10] But you have exalted my horn like that of the | wild ox;*
you have poured over me | fresh oil.

[11] My eyes have seen the downfall of my | enemies;*
my ears have heard the doom of my evil as- | sailants.

[12] The righteous flourish like the | palm tree*
and grow like a cedar in | Lebanon.

[13] They are planted in the house | of the LORD;*
they flourish in the courts | of our God.

[14] They still bear fruit in | old age;*
they are ever full of | sap and green,

[15] to declare that the LORD is | upright;*
he is my rock, and there is no unrighteousness | in him.

Glory be to the Father and | to the Son*
and to the Holy | Spirit;
as it was in the be- | ginning,*
is now, and will be forever. | Amen.

93

[1] The LORD reigns; he is robed in | majesty;*
the LORD is robed; he has put on strength | as his belt.

Yes, the world is es- | tablished;*
it shall nev- | er be moved.

[2] Your throne is established | from of old;*
you are from ever- | lasting.

[3] The floods have lifted up, O LORD, the floods have lifted | up their voice;*
the floods lift up their | roaring.

[4] Mightier than the thunders of many waters, mightier than the waves | of the sea,*
the LORD on high is | mighty!

[5] Your decrees are very | trustworthy;*
holiness befits your house, O LORD, for- | evermore.

Glory be to the Father and | to the Son*
and to the Holy | Spirit;
as it was in the be- | ginning,*
is now, and will be forever. | Amen.

95

[1] Oh come, let us sing | to the LORD;*
let us make a joyful noise to the rock of our sal- | vation!

[2] Let us come into his presence with thanks- | giving;*
let us make a joyful noise to him with | songs of praise!

[3] For the LORD is a | great God,*
and a great King a- | bove all gods.

[4] In his hand are the depths | of the earth;*
the heights of the mountains are his | also.

[5] The sea is his, for he | made it,*
and his hands formed the | dry land.

[6] Oh come, let us worship and | bow down;*
let us kneel before the LORD, our | Maker!

[7] For he | is our God,*
and we are the people of his pasture, and the sheep | of his hand.

Today, if you | hear his voice,*
[8] do not harden your hearts, as at Meribah, as on the day at Massah in the | wilderness,

[9] when your fathers put me | to the test*
and put me to the proof, though they had | seen my work.

[10] For forty years I loathed that generation and said, "They are a people who go astray | in their heart,*
and they have not | known my ways."

[11] Therefore I swore | in my wrath,*
"They shall not enter | my rest."

Glory be to the Father and | to the Son*
and to the Holy | Spirit;
as it was in the be- | ginning,*
is now, and will be forever. | Amen.

96

[1] Oh sing to the LORD a | new song;*
sing to the LORD, | all the earth!

[2] Sing to the LORD, | bless his name;*
tell of his salvation from | day to day.

[3] Declare his glory among the | nations,*
his marvelous works among all the | peoples!

[4] For great is the LORD, and greatly | to be praised;*
he is to be feared a- | bove all gods.

[5] For all the gods of the peoples are worthless | idols,*
but the LORD made the | heavens.

[6] Splendor and majesty are be- | fore him;*
strength and beauty are in his sanctu- | ary.

[7] Ascribe to the LORD, O families of the | peoples,*
ascribe to the LORD glo- | ry and strength!

[8] Ascribe to the LORD the glory | due his name;*
bring an offering, and come in- | to his courts!

[9] Worship the LORD in the splendor of | holiness;*
tremble before him, | all the earth!

[10] Say among the nations, "The LORD reigns! Yes, the world is established; it shall nev- | er be moved;*
he will judge the peoples with | equity."

[11] Let the heavens be glad, and let the | earth rejoice;*
let the sea roar, and all that fills it;
[12] let the field exult, and every- | thing in it!

Then shall all the trees of the forest sing for joy [13] before the LORD, | for he comes,*
for he comes to | judge the earth.

He will judge the world in | righteousness,*
and the peoples in his | faithfulness.

Glory be to the Father and | to the Son*
and to the Holy | Spirit;
as it was in the be- | ginning,*
is now, and will be forever. | Amen.

97

[1] The LORD reigns, let the | earth rejoice;*
let the many coast- | lands be glad!

[2] Clouds and thick darkness are all a- | round him;*
righteousness and justice are the foundation | of his throne.

[3] Fire goes be- | fore him*
and burns up his adversaries | all around.

[4] His lightnings light | up the world;*
the earth sees and | trembles.

[5] The mountains melt like wax be- | fore the LORD,*
before the Lord of | all the earth.

[6] The heavens proclaim his | righteousness,*
and all the peoples see his | glory.

[7] All worshipers of images are put to shame, who make their boast in worthless | idols;*
worship him, | all you gods!

[8] Zion hears and is glad, and the daughters of Ju- | dah rejoice,*
because of your judgments, | O LORD.

[9] For you, O LORD, are most high over | all the earth;*
you are exalted far a- | bove all gods.

[10] O you who love the LORD, hate | evil!*
He preserves the lives of his saints;
he delivers them from the hand of the | wicked.

[11] Light is sown for the | righteous,*
and joy for the up- | right in heart.

[12] Rejoice in the LORD, O you | righteous,*
and give thanks to his | holy name!

Glory be to the Father and | to the Son*
and to the Holy | Spirit;
as it was in the be- | ginning,*
is now, and will be forever. | Amen.

98

[1] Oh sing to the LORD a new song, for he has done | marvelous things!*
His right hand and his holy arm have worked salva- | tion for him.

[2] The LORD has made known his sal- | vation;*
he has revealed his righteousness in the sight of the | nations.

[3] He has remembered his steadfast love and faithfulness to the house of | Israel.*
All the ends of the earth have seen the salvation | of our God.

[4] Make a joyful noise to the LORD, | all the earth;*
break forth into joyous song and sing | praises!

[5] Sing praises to the LORD | with the lyre,*
with the lyre and the sound of | melody!

[6] With trumpets and the sound | of the horn*
make a joyful noise before the | King, the LORD!

[7] Let the sea roar, and all that | fills it;*
the world and those who | dwell in it!

[8] Let the rivers clap their hands; let the hills sing for joy together [9] be- | fore the LORD,*
for he comes to | judge the earth.

He will judge the world with | righteousness,*
and the peoples with | equity.

Glory be to the Father and | to the Son*
and to the Holy | Spirit;
as it was in the be- | ginning,*
is now, and will be forever. | Amen.

99

[1] The LORD reigns;
let the peoples | tremble!*
He sits enthroned upon the cherubim;
let the | earth quake!

[2] The LORD is great in | Zion;*
he is exalted over all the | peoples.

[3] Let them praise your great and | awesome name!*
Ho- | ly is he!

[4] The King in his might loves | justice.*
You have established equity;
you have executed justice and righteousness in | Jacob.

[5] Exalt the LORD our God; worship at his | footstool!*
Ho- | ly is he!

[6] Moses and Aaron were among his priests, Samuel also was among those who called up- | on his name.*
They called to the LORD, and he | answered them.

[7] In the pillar of the cloud he | spoke to them;*
they kept his testimonies and the statute that he | gave them.

[8] O LORD our God, you | answered them;*
you were a forgiving God to them,
but an avenger of their wrong- | doings.

[9] Exalt the LORD our God, and worship at his holy | mountain;*
for the LORD our God is | holy!

Glory be to the Father and | to the Son*
and to the Holy | Spirit;
as it was in the be- | ginning,*
is now, and will be forever. | Amen.

100

[1] Make a joyful noise to the LORD, | all the earth!*
[2] Serve the LORD with gladness! Come into his presence with | singing!

[3] Know that the LORD, | he is God!*
It is he who made us, and we are his;
we are his people, and the sheep of his | pasture.

[4] Enter his gates with thanksgiving, and his | courts with praise!*
Give thanks to him; | bless his name!

[5] For the LORD is good; his steadfast love endures for- | ever,*
and his faithfulness to all gener- | ations.

Glory be to the Father and | to the Son*
and to the Holy | Spirit;
as it was in the be- | ginning,*
is now, and will be forever. | Amen.

102

[1] Hear my prayer, | O LORD;*
let my cry | come to you!

[2] Do not hide your face from me in the day of | my distress!*
Incline your ear to me; answer me speedily in the day | when I call!

[3] For my days pass a- | way like smoke,*
and my bones burn like a | furnace.

[4] My heart is struck down like grass and has | withered;*
I forget to | eat my bread.

[5] Because of my loud | groaning*
my bones cling | to my flesh.

[6] I am like a desert owl of the | wilderness,*
like an owl of the waste | places;

[7] I | lie awake;*
I am like a lonely sparrow on the | housetop.

[8] All the day my enemies | taunt me;*
those who deride me use my name | for a curse.

[9] For I eat ashes | like bread*
and mingle tears | with my drink,

[10] because of your indignation and | anger;*
for you have taken me up and | thrown me down.

[11] My days are like an evening | shadow;*
I wither a- | way like grass.

[12] But you, O LORD, are enthroned for- | ever;*
you are remembered throughout all gener- | ations.

[13] You will arise and have pity on | Zion;*
it is the time to favor her; the appointed | time has come.

[14] For your servants hold her | stones dear*
and have pity | on her dust.

[15] Nations will fear the name | of the LORD,*
and all the kings of the earth will fear your | glory.

[16] For the LORD builds up | Zion;*
he appears in his | glory;

[17] he regards the prayer of the | destitute*
and does not de- | spise their prayer.

[18] Let this be recorded for a genera- | tion to come,*
so that a people yet to be created may | praise the LORD:

[19] that he looked down from his | holy height;*
from heaven the LORD looked | at the earth,

[20] to hear the groans of the | prisoners,*
to set free those who were | doomed to die,

[21] that they may declare in Zion the name | of the LORD,*
and in Jerusa- | lem his praise,

[22] when peoples gather to- | gether,*
and kingdoms, to wor- | ship the LORD.

[23] He has broken my strength in | midcourse;*
he has shortened | my days.

[24] "O my God," I say, "take me not away in the midst | of my days—*
you whose years endure throughout all gener- | ations!"

[25] Of old you laid the foundation | of the earth,*
and the heavens are the work | of your hands.

[26] They will perish, but you | will remain;*
they will all wear out like a | garment.

You will change them like a robe, and they will | pass away,*
[27] but you are the same, and your years | have no end.

[28] The children of your servants shall | dwell secure;*
their offspring shall be established be- | fore you.

Glory be to the Father and | to the Son*
and to the Holy | Spirit;
as it was in the be- | ginning,*
is now, and will be forever. | Amen.

103

[1] Bless the LORD, | O my soul,*
and all that is within me, bless his | holy name!

[2] Bless the LORD, | O my soul,*
and forget not all his | benefits,

[3] who forgives all your in- | iquity,*
who heals all your dis- | eases,

[4] who redeems your life | from the pit,*
who crowns you with steadfast love and | mercy,

[5] who satisfies | you with good*
so that your youth is renewed like the | eagle's.

[6] The LORD works | righteousness*
and justice for all who | are oppressed.

[7] He made known his ways to | Moses,*
his acts to the people of | Israel.

[8] The LORD is merciful and | gracious,*
slow to anger and abounding in | steadfast love.

[9] He will not | always chide,*
nor will he keep his anger for- | ever.

[10] He does not deal with us according | to our sins,*
nor repay us according to our in- | iquities.

[11] For as high as the heavens are a- | bove the earth,*
so great is his steadfast love toward those who | fear him;

[12] as far as the east is | from the west,*
so far does he remove our transgres- | sions from us.

[13] As a father shows compassion to his | children,*
so the LORD shows compassion to those who | fear him.

[14] For he | knows our frame;*
he remembers that | we are dust.

[15] As for man, his days | are like grass;*
he flourishes like a flower | of the field;

[16] for the wind passes over it, and | it is gone,*
and its place knows | it no more.

[17] But the steadfast love of the LORD is from everlasting to everlasting on those who | fear him,*
and his righteousness to children's | children,

[18] to those who keep his | covenant*
and remember to do his com- | mandments.

[19] The LORD has established his throne in the | heavens,*
and his kingdom rules | over all.

[20] Bless the LORD, O you his | angels,*
you mighty ones who do his word, obeying the voice | of his word!

[21] Bless the LORD, | all his hosts,*
his ministers, who | do his will!

[22] Bless the LORD, all his works, in all places of his do- | minion.*
Bless the LORD, | O my soul!

Glory be to the Father and | to the Son*
and to the Holy | Spirit;
as it was in the be- | ginning,*
is now, and will be forever. | Amen.

104

[1] Bless the LORD, | O my soul!*
O LORD my God, you are | very great!

You are clothed with splendor and | majesty,*
[2] covering yourself with light as with a garment, stretching out the heavens | like a tent.

[3] He lays the beams of his chambers on the | waters;*
he makes the clouds his chariot; he rides on the wings | of the wind;

[4] he makes his mes- | sengers winds,*
his ministers a | flaming fire.

[5] He set the earth on its foun- | dations,*
so that it should nev- | er be moved.

[6] You covered it with the deep as with a | garment;*
the waters stood above the | mountains.

[7] At your re- | buke they fled;*
at the sound of your thunder they | took to flight.

[8] The mountains rose, the valleys | sank down*
to the place that you appoint- | ed for them.

[9] You set a boundary that they | may not pass,*
so that they might not again cov- | er the earth.

[10] You make springs gush forth in the | valleys;*
they flow be- | tween the hills;

[11] they give drink to every beast | of the field;*
the wild donkeys | quench their thirst.

[12] Beside them the birds of the | heavens dwell;*
they sing among the | branches.

[13] From your lofty abode you water the | mountains;*
the earth is satisfied with the fruit | of your work.

[14] You cause the grass to grow for the livestock and plants for man to | cultivate,*
that he may bring forth food from the earth [15] and wine to gladden the | heart of man,

oil to make his | face shine*
and bread to strengthen | man's heart.

[16] The trees of the LORD are watered a- | bundantly,*
the cedars of Lebanon that he | planted.

[17] In them the birds | build their nests;*
the stork has her home in the | fir trees.

[18] The high mountains are for the | wild goats;*
the rocks are a refuge for the rock | badgers.

[19] He made the moon to mark the | seasons;*
the sun knows its time for | setting.

[20] You make darkness, and | it is night,*
when all the beasts of the forest | creep about.

[21] The young lions roar | for their prey,*
seeking their | food from God.

[22] When the sun rises, they | steal away*
and lie down | in their dens.

[23] Man goes out | to his work*
and to his labor until the | evening.

[24] O LORD, how manifold are your works!
In wisdom have you | made them all;*
the earth is full of your | creatures.

[25] Here is the sea, | great and wide,*
which teems with creatures innumerable, living things both | small and great.

[26] There | go the ships,*
and Leviathan, which you formed to | play in it.

[27] These all | look to you,*
to give them their food in due | season.

[28] When you give it to them, they gath- | er it up;*
when you open your hand, they are filled with | good things.

[29] When you hide your face, they | are dismayed;*
when you take away their breath, they die and return | to their dust.

[30] When you send forth your Spirit, they are cre- | ated,*
and you renew the face | of the ground.

[31] May the glory of the LORD endure for- | ever;*
may the LORD rejoice | in his works,

[32] who looks on the earth and it | trembles,*
who touches the mountains | and they smoke!

[33] I will sing to the LORD as long | as I live;*
I will sing praise to my God while I have | being.

[34] May my meditation be pleas- | ing to him,*
for I rejoice | in the LORD.

[35] Let sinners be consumed from the earth, and let the wicked | be no more!*
Bless the LORD, O my soul! | Praise the LORD!

Glory be to the Father and | to the Son*
and to the Holy | Spirit;
as it was in the be- | ginning,*
is now, and will be forever. | Amen.

107

[1] Oh give thanks to the Lord, for | he is good,*
for his steadfast love endures for- | ever!

[2] Let the redeemed of the LORD | say so,*
whom he has redeemed from | trouble

[3] and gathered in | from the lands,*
from the east and from the west,
from the north and | from the south.

[4] Some wandered in | desert wastes,*
finding no way to a city to | dwell in;

[5] hungry and | thirsty,*
their soul fainted with- | in them.

[6] Then they cried to the LORD in their | trouble,*
and he delivered them from | their distress.

[7] He led them by a | straight way*
till they reached a city to | dwell in.

[8] Let them thank the LORD for his | steadfast love,*
for his wondrous works to the chil- | dren of men!

[9] For he satisfies the | longing soul,*
and the hungry soul he fills | with good things.

[10] Some sat in darkness and in the shad- | ow of death,*
prisoners in affliction | and in irons,

[11] for they had rebelled against the | words of God,*
and spurned the counsel of the | Most High.

[12] So he bowed their hearts down with hard | labor;*
they fell down, with | none to help.

[13] Then they cried to the LORD in their | trouble,*
and he delivered them from | their distress.

[14] He brought them out of darkness and the shad- | ow of death,*
and burst their | bonds apart.

[15] Let them thank the LORD for his | steadfast love,*
for his wondrous works to the chil- | dren of men!

[16] For he shatters the | doors of bronze*
and cuts in two the | bars of iron.

[17] Some were fools through their | sinful ways,*
and because of their iniquities suffered af- | fliction;

[18] they loathed any | kind of food,*
and they drew near to the | gates of death.

[19] Then they cried to the LORD in their | trouble,*
and he delivered them from | their distress.

[20] He sent out his word and | healed them,*
and delivered them from their de- | struction.

[21] Let them thank the LORD for his | steadfast love,*
for his wondrous works to the chil- | dren of men!

[22] And let them offer sacrifices of thanks- | giving,*
and tell of his deeds in | songs of joy!

[23] Some went down to the | sea in ships,*
doing business on the great | waters;

[24] they saw the deeds | of the LORD,*
his wondrous works | in the deep.

[25] For he commanded and raised the | stormy wind,*
which lifted up the waves | of the sea.

[26] They mounted up to heaven; they went down | to the depths;*
their courage melted away in their | evil plight;

[27] they reeled and staggered like | drunken men*
and were at their | wits' end.

[28] Then they cried to the LORD in their | trouble,*
and he delivered them from | their distress.

[29] He made the | storm be still,*
and the waves of the | sea were hushed.

[30] Then they were glad that the waters were | quiet,*
and he brought them to their desired | haven.

[31] Let them thank the LORD for his | steadfast love,*
for his wondrous works to the chil- | dren of men!

[32] Let them extol him in the congregation of the | people,*
and praise him in the assembly of the | elders.

[33] He turns rivers into a | desert,*
springs of water into | thirsty ground,

[34] a fruitful land into a | salty waste,*
because of the evil of its in- | habitants.

[35] He turns a desert into pools of | water,*
a parched land into springs of | water.

[36] And there he lets the | hungry dwell,*
and they establish a city to | live in;

[37] they sow fields and plant | vineyards*
and get a | fruitful yield.

[38] By his blessing they multiply | greatly,*
and he does not let their livestock di- | minish.

[39] When they are diminished and | brought low*
through oppression, evil, and | sorrow,

[40] he pours contempt on | princes*
and makes them wander in | trackless wastes;

[41] but he raises up the needy out of af- | fliction*
and makes their families | like flocks.

[42] The upright see it | and are glad,*
and all wickedness | shuts its mouth.

[43] Whoever is wise, let him attend | to these things;*
let them consider the steadfast love | of the LORD.

Glory be to the Father and | to the Son*
and to the Holy | Spirit;
as it was in the be- | ginning,*
is now, and will be forever. | Amen.

110

[1] The LORD says to my Lord: "Sit at my | right hand,*
until I make your enemies your | footstool."

[2] The LORD sends forth from Zion your mighty | scepter.*
Rule in the midst of your | enemies!

[3] Your people will offer themselves freely on the day of your power, in holy | garments;*
from the womb of the morning, the dew of your youth | will be yours.

[4] The LORD has sworn and will not | change his mind,*
"You are a priest forever after the order of Mel- | chizedek."

[5] The Lord is at your | right hand;*
he will shatter kings on the day | of his wrath.

[6] He will execute judgment among the nations, filling them with | corpses;*
he will shatter chiefs over the | wide earth.

[7] He will drink from the brook | by the way;*
therefore he will lift | up his head.

Glory be to the Father and | to the Son*
and to the Holy | Spirit;
as it was in the be- | ginning,*
is now, and will be forever. | Amen.

111

[1] Praise the LORD! I will give thanks to the LORD with my | whole heart,*
in the company of the upright, in the congre- | gation.

[2] Great are the works | of the LORD,*
studied by all who de- | light in them.

[3] Full of splendor and majesty | is his work,*
and his righteousness endures for- | ever.

[4] He has caused his wondrous works to be re- | membered;*
the LORD is gracious and | merciful.

[5] He provides food for those who | fear him;*
he remembers his covenant for- | ever.

[6] He has shown his people the power | of his works,*
in giving them the inheritance of the | nations.

[7] The works of his hands are faith- | ful and just;*
all his precepts are | trustworthy;

[8] they are established forever and | ever,*
to be performed with faithfulness and up- | rightness.

[9] He sent redemption to his people; he has commanded his covenant for- | ever.*
Holy and awesome | is his name!

[10] The fear of the LORD is the beginning of wisdom; all those who practice it have a good under- | standing.*
His praise endures for- | ever!

Glory be to the Father and | to the Son*
and to the Holy | Spirit;
as it was in the be- | ginning,*
is now, and will be forever. | Amen.

112

[1] Praise the LORD! Blessèd is the man who | fears the LORD,*
who greatly delights in his com- | mandments!

[2] His offspring will be mighty | in the land;*
the generation of the upright | will be blessed.

[3] Wealth and riches are | in his house,*
and his righteousness endures for- | ever.

[4] Light dawns in the darkness for the | upright;*

he is gracious, merciful, and | righteous.

[5] It is well with the man who deals generous- | ly and lends;*
who conducts his affairs with | justice.

[6] For the righteous will nev- | er be moved;*
he will be remembered for- | ever.

[7] He is not afraid of | bad news;*
his heart is firm, trusting | in the LORD.

[8] His heart is steady; he will not | be afraid,*
until he looks in triumph on his adver- | saries.

[9] He has distributed freely; he has given to the poor; his righteousness endures for- | ever;*
his horn is exalted in | honor.

[10] The wicked man sees it and is angry; he gnashes his teeth and | melts away;*
the desire of the wicked will | perish!

Glory be to the Father and | to the Son*
and to the Holy | Spirit;
as it was in the be- | ginning,*
is now, and will be forever. | Amen.

113

[1] Praise the LORD! Praise, O servants | of the LORD,*
praise the name | of the LORD!

[2] Blessèd be the name | of the LORD*
from this time forth and for- | evermore!

[3] From the rising of the sun to its | setting,*
the name of the LORD is | to be praised!

[4] The LORD is high above all | nations,*
and his glory above the | heavens!

[5] Who is like the | LORD our God,*
who is seated | on high,

[6] who looks | far down*
on the heavens | and the earth?

[7] He raises the poor | from the dust*
and lifts the needy from the | ash heap,

[8] to make them sit with | princes,*
with the princes of his | people.

[9] He gives the barren wom- | an a home,*
making her the joyous mother of children. | Praise the LORD!

Glory be to the Father and | to the Son*
and to the Holy | Spirit;
as it was in the be- | ginning,*
is now, and will be forever. | Amen.

114

[1] When Israel went out from | Egypt,*
the house of Jacob from a people of strange | language,

[2] Judah became his sanctu- | ary,*
Israel his do- | minion.

[3] The sea | looked and fled;*
Jordan | turned back.

[4] The mountains | skipped like rams,*
the | hills like lambs.

[5] What ails you, O sea, | that you flee?*
O Jordan, that you | turn back?

[6] O mountains, that you | skip like rams?*
O | hills, like lambs?

[7] Tremble, O earth, at the presence | of the Lord,*
at the presence of the God of | Jacob,

[8] who turns the rock into a pool of | water,*
the flint into a spring of | water.

Glory be to the Father and | to the Son*
and to the Holy | Spirit;
as it was in the be- | ginning,*
is now, and will be forever. | Amen.

115

[1] Not to us, O LORD, not to us, but to your name give | glory,*
for the sake of your steadfast love and your | faithfulness!

[2] Why should the | nations say,*
"Where | is their God?"

[3] Our God is in the | heavens;*
he does all that he | pleases.

[4] Their idols are sil- | ver and gold,*
the work of | human hands.

[5] They have mouths, but | do not speak;*
eyes, but | do not see.

[6] They have ears, but | do not hear;*
noses, but | do not smell.

[7] They have hands, but do not feel; feet, but | do not walk;*
and they do not make a sound | in their throat.

[8] Those who make them be- | come like them;*
so do all who | trust in them.

[9] O Israel, trust | in the LORD!*
He is their help | and their shield.

[10] O house of Aaron, trust | in the LORD!*
He is their help | and their shield.

[11] You who fear the LORD, trust | in the LORD!*
He is their help | and their shield.

[12] The LORD has remembered us;
he will | bless us;*
he will bless the house of Israel; he will bless the house of | Aaron;

[13] he will bless those who | fear the LORD,*
both the small | and the great.

[14] May the LORD give you | increase,*
you and your | children!

[15] May you be blessed | by the LORD,*
who made | heaven and earth!

[16] The heavens are the LORD's | heavens,*
but the earth he has given to the chil- | dren of man.

[17] The dead do not | praise the LORD,*
nor do any who go down into | silence.

[18] But we will | bless the LORD*
from this time forth and forevermore. | Praise the LORD!

Glory be to the Father and | to the Son*
and to the Holy | Spirit;
as it was in the be- | ginning,*
is now, and will be forever. | Amen.

116

[1] I love the LORD, because | he has heard*
my voice and my pleas for | mercy.

[2] Because he inclined his | ear to me,*
therefore I will call on him as long | as I live.

[3] The snares of death encompassed me;
the pangs of Sheol laid | hold on me;*
I suffered distress and | anguish.

[4] Then I called on the name | of the LORD:*
"O LORD, I pray, deliv- | er my soul!"

[5] Gracious is the LORD, and | righteous;*
our God is | merciful.

[6] The LORD preserves the | simple;*
when I was brought low, he | saved me.

[7] Return, O my soul, | to your rest;*
for the LORD has dealt bountifully | with you.

[8] For you have delivered my | soul from death,*
my eyes from tears, my feet from | stumbling;

[9] I will walk be- | fore the LORD*
in the land of the | living.

[10] I believed, even | when I spoke,*
"I am greatly af- | flicted";

[11] I said in | my alarm,*
"All mankind are | liars."

[12] What shall I render | to the LORD*
for all his bene- | fits to me?

[13] I will lift up the cup of sal- | vation*
and call on the name | of the LORD,

[14] I will pay my vows | to the LORD*
in the presence of all his | people.

[15] Precious in the sight | of the LORD*
is the death | of his saints.

[16] O LORD, I am your | servant;*
I am your servant, the son of your maidservant. You have | loosed my bonds.

[17] I will offer to you the sacrifice of thanks- | giving*
and call on the name | of the LORD.

[18] I will pay my vows | to the LORD*
in the presence of all his | people,

[19] in the courts of the house | of the LORD,*
in your midst, O Jerusalem. | Praise the LORD!

Glory be to the Father and | to the Son*
and to the Holy | Spirit;
as it was in the be- | ginning,*
is now, and will be forever. | Amen.

117

[1] Praise the LORD, all | nations!*
Extol him, all | peoples!

[2] For great is his steadfast | love toward us,*
and the faithfulness of the LORD endures forever. | Praise the LORD!

Glory be to the Father and | to the Son*
and to the Holy | Spirit;
as it was in the be- | ginning,*
is now, and will be forever. | Amen.

118

[1] Oh give thanks to the LORD, for | he is good;*
for his steadfast love endures for- | ever!

[2] Let | Israel say,*
"His steadfast love endures for- | ever."

[3] Let the house of | Aaron say,*
"His steadfast love endures for- | ever."

[4] Let those who fear the | LORD say,*
"His steadfast love endures for- | ever."

[5] Out of my distress I called | on the LORD;*
the LORD answered me and | set me free.

[6] The LORD is on my side; I | will not fear.*
What can man | do to me?

[7] The LORD is on my side as my | helper;*
I shall look in triumph on those who | hate me.

[8] It is better to take refuge | in the LORD*
than to | trust in man.

[9] It is better to take refuge | in the LORD*
than to trust in | princes.

[10] All nations sur- | rounded me;*
in the name of the LORD I | cut them off!

[11] They surrounded me, surrounded me on | every side;*
in the name of the LORD I | cut them off!

[12] They surrounded me like bees; they went out like a fire a- | mong thorns;*
in the name of the LORD I | cut them off!

[13] I was pushed hard, so that I was | falling,*
but the LORD | helped me.

[14] The LORD is my strength | and my song;*
he has become my sal- | vation.

[15] Glad songs of salvation are in the tents of the | righteous:*
"The right hand of the LORD does | valiantly,

[16] the right hand of the | LORD exalts,*
the right hand of the LORD
does | valiantly!"

[17] I shall not die, but | I shall live,*
and recount the deeds | of the LORD.

[18] The LORD has disciplined me se- | verely,*
but he has not given me o- | ver to
death.

[19] Open to me the gates of | righteousness,*
that I may enter through them and
give thanks | to the LORD.

[20] This is the gate | of the LORD;*
the righteous shall enter | through it.

[21] I thank you that you have | answered me*
and have become my sal- | vation.

[22] The stone that the builders re- | jected*
has become the | cornerstone.

[23] This is the LORD's | doing;*
it is marvelous | in our eyes.

[24] This is the day that the | LORD has made;*
let us rejoice and be | glad in it.

[25] Save us, we pray, | O LORD!*
O LORD, we pray, give | us success!

[26] Blessèd is he who comes in the name | of
the LORD!*
We bless you from the house | of the
LORD.

[27] The LORD is God, and he has made his
light to shine up- | on us.*
Bind the festal sacrifice with cords,
up to the horns of the | altar!

[28] You are my God, and I will give | thanks
to you;*
you are my God; I will ex- | tol you.

[29] Oh give thanks to the LORD, for | he is
good;*
for his steadfast love endures for- | ever!

Glory be to the Father and | to the Son*
and to the Holy | Spirit;
as it was in the be- | ginning,*
is now, and will be forever. | Amen.

119

ALEPH

[1] Blessèd are those whose way
is | blameless,*
who walk in the law | of the LORD!

[2] Blessèd are those who keep his
testi- | monies,*
who seek him with their | whole
heart,

[3] who also | do no wrong,*
but walk | in his ways!

[4] You have commanded your | precepts*
to be kept dil- | igently.

[5] Oh that my ways may be | steadfast*
in keeping your | statutes!

[6] Then I shall not be | put to shame,*
having my eyes fixed on all your
com- | mandments.

[7] I will praise you with an | upright
heart,*
when I learn your just and righ- | teous
decrees.

[8] I will keep your | statutes;*
do not utterly for- | sake me!

Glory be to the Father and | to the Son*
and to the Holy | Spirit;
as it was in the be- | ginning,*
is now, and will be forever. | Amen.

BETH

[9] How can a young man keep his | way
pure?*
By guarding it according | to your word.

[10] With my whole heart I | seek you;*
let me not wander from your
com- | mandments!

[11] I have stored up your word | in my
heart,*
that I might not sin a- | gainst you.

[12] Blessèd are you, | O LORD;*
teach me your | statutes!

[13] With my lips | I declare*
all the just decrees | of your mouth.

[14] In the way of your testimonies | I delight*
as much as in all | riches.

[15] I will meditate on your | precepts*
and fix my eyes | on your ways.

[16] I will delight in your | statutes;*
I will not for- | get your word.

Glory be to the Father and | to the Son*
and to the Holy | Spirit;
as it was in the be- | ginning,*
is now, and will be forever. | Amen.

GIMEL

[17] Deal bountifully with your | servant,*
that I may live and | keep your word.

[18] Open my eyes, that I | may behold*
wondrous things out | of your law.

[19] I am a sojourner | on the earth;*
hide not your command- | ments from me!

[20] My soul is consumed with | longing*
for your just decrees at | all times.

[21] You rebuke the insolent, ac- | cursèd ones,*
who wander from your com- | mandments.

[22] Take away from me scorn | and contempt,*
for I have kept your testi- | monies.

[23] Even though princes sit plotting a- | gainst me,*
your servant will meditate on your | statutes.

[24] Your testimonies are | my delight;*
they are my | counselors.

Glory be to the Father and | to the Son*
and to the Holy | Spirit;
as it was in the be- | ginning,*
is now, and will be forever. | Amen.

DALETH

[25] My soul clings | to the dust;*
give me life according | to your word!

[26] When I told of my ways, you | answered me;*
teach me your | statutes!

[27] Make me understand the way of your | precepts,*
and I will meditate on your | wondrous works.

[28] My soul melts away for | sorrow;*
strengthen me according | to your word!

[29] Put false ways | far from me*
and graciously teach | me your law!

[30] I have chosen the way of | faithfulness;*
I set your just decrees be- | fore me.

[31] I cling to your testimonies, | O Lord;*
let me not be | put to shame!

[32] I will run in the way of your com- | mandments*
when you en- | large my heart!

Glory be to the Father and | to the Son*
and to the Holy | Spirit;
as it was in the be- | ginning,*
is now, and will be forever. | Amen.

HE

[33] Teach me, O Lord, the way of your | statutes;*
and I will keep it | to the end.

[34] Give me understanding, that I may | keep your law*
and observe it with my | whole heart.

[35] Lead me in the path of your com- | mandments,*
for I de- | light in it.

[36] Incline my heart to your testi- | monies,*
and not to | selfish gain!

[37] Turn my eyes from looking at | worthless things;*
and give me life | in your ways.

[38] Confirm to your servant
your | promise,*
that you | may be feared.

[39] Turn away the reproach | that I dread,*
for your just de- | crees are good.

[40] Behold, I long for your | precepts;*
in your righteousness | give me life!

Glory be to the Father and | to the Son*
and to the Holy | Spirit;
as it was in the be- | ginning,*
is now, and will be forever. | Amen.

WAW

[41] Let your steadfast love come to
me, | O LORD,*
your salvation according to
your | promise;

[42] then shall I have an answer for him
who | taunts me,*
for I trust | in your word.

[43] And take not the word of truth utterly
out | of my mouth,*
for my hope is in your | just decrees.

[44] I will keep your law con- | tinually,*
forever and | ever,

[45] and I shall walk in a | wide place,*
for I have sought your | precepts.

[46] I will also speak of your testimonies
be- | fore kings*
and shall not be | put to shame,

[47] for I find my delight in your
com- | mandments,*
which | I love.

[48] I will lift up my hands toward your
commandments, | which I love,*
and I will meditate on your | statutes.

Glory be to the Father and | to the Son*
and to the Holy | Spirit;
as it was in the be- | ginning,*
is now, and will be forever. | Amen.

ZAYIN

[49] Remember your word to your | servant,*
in which you have | made me hope.

[50] This is my comfort in my
af- | fliction,*
that your promise | gives me life.

[51] The insolent utterly de- | ride me,*
but I do not turn away | from your law.

[52] When I think of your just
decrees | from of old,*
I take comfort, | O LORD.

[53] Hot indignation seizes me because of
the | wicked,*
who for- | sake your law.

[54] Your statutes have | been my songs*
in the house of my | sojourning.

[55] I remember your name in the
night, | O LORD,*
and | keep your law.

[56] This blessing has fal- | len to me,*
that I have kept your | precepts.

Glory be to the Father and | to the Son*
and to the Holy | Spirit;
as it was in the be- | ginning,*
is now, and will be forever. | Amen.

HETH

[57] The LORD is my | portion;*
I promise to | keep your words.

[58] I entreat your favor with | all my heart;*
be gracious to me according to
your | promise.

[59] When I think | on my ways,*
I turn my feet to your testi- | monies;

[60] I hasten and do | not delay*
to keep your com- | mandments.

[61] Though the cords of the wicked
en- | snare me,*
I do not for- | get your law.

[62] At midnight I rise to | praise you,*
because of your just and righ- | teous
decrees.

[63] I am a companion of all who | fear you,*
of those who keep your | precepts.

[64] The earth, O LORD, is full of your | steadfast love;*
teach me your | statutes!

Glory be to the Father and | to the Son*
and to the Holy | Spirit;
as it was in the be- | ginning,*
is now, and will be forever. | Amen.

TETH

[65] You have dealt well with your | servant,*
O LORD, according | to your word.

[66] Teach me good judgment and | knowledge,*
for I believe in your com- | mandments.

[67] Before I was afflicted I | went astray,*
but now I | keep your word.

[68] You are good and | do good;*
teach me your | statutes.

[69] The insolent smear | me with lies,*
but with my whole heart I keep your | precepts;

[70] their heart is unfeeling | like fat,*
but I delight | in your law.

[71] It is good for me that I was af- | flicted,*
that I might learn your | statutes.

[72] The law of your mouth is bet- | ter to me*
than thousands of gold and silver | pieces.

Glory be to the Father and | to the Son*
and to the Holy | Spirit;
as it was in the be- | ginning,*
is now, and will be forever. | Amen.

YODH

[73] Your hands have made and | fashioned me;*
give me understanding that I may learn your com- | mandments.

[74] Those who fear you shall see me | and rejoice,*
because I have hoped | in your word.

[75] I know, O LORD, that your just decrees are | righteous,*
and that in faithfulness you have af- | flicted me.

[76] Let your steadfast love | comfort me*
according to your promise to your | servant.

[77] Let your mercy come to me, that | I may live;*
for your law is | my delight.

[78] Let the insolent be put to shame, because they have wronged me with | falsehood;*
as for me, I will meditate on your | precepts.

[79] Let those who fear you | turn to me,*
that they may know your testi- | monies.

[80] May my heart be blameless in your | statutes,*
that I may not be | put to shame!

Glory be to the Father and | to the Son*
and to the Holy | Spirit;
as it was in the be- | ginning,*
is now, and will be forever. | Amen.

KAPH

[81] My soul longs for your sal- | vation;*
I hope | in your word.

[82] My eyes long for your | promise;*
I ask, "When will you | comfort me?"

[83] For I have become like a wineskin | in the smoke,*
yet I have not forgotten your | statutes.

[84] How long must your ser- | vant endure?*
When will you judge those who perse- | cute me?

[85] The insolent have dug pit- | falls for me;*
they do not live according | to your law.

[86] All your command- | ments are sure;*
they persecute me with
falsehood; | help me!

[87] They have almost made an end of me | on earth,*
but I have not forsaken your | precepts.

[88] In your steadfast love | give me life,*
that I may keep the testimonies | of
your mouth.

Glory be to the Father and | to the Son*
and to the Holy | Spirit;
as it was in the be- | ginning,*
is now, and will be forever. | Amen.

LAMEDH

[89] Forever, | O LORD,*
your word is firmly fixed in the | heavens.

[90] Your faithfulness endures to all
gener- | ations;*
you have established the earth,
and it | stands fast.

[91] By your appointment they | stand this day,*
for all things are your | servants.

[92] If your law had not been | my delight,*
I would have perished in my
af- | fliction.

[93] I will never forget your | precepts,*
for by them you have giv- | en me life.

[94] I am yours; | save me,*
for I have sought your | precepts.

[95] The wicked lie in wait to de- | stroy me,*
but I consider your testi- | monies.

[96] I have seen a limit to all per- | fection,*
but your commandment is
exceed- | ingly broad.

Glory be to the Father and | to the Son*
and to the Holy | Spirit;
as it was in the be- | ginning,*
is now, and will be forever. | Amen.

MEM

[97] Oh how I | love your law!*
It is my meditation | all the day.

[98] Your commandment makes me wiser
than my | enemies,*
for it is ever | with me.

[99] I have more understanding than all
my | teachers,*
for your testimonies are my
medi- | tation.

[100] I understand more than the | agèd,*
for I keep your | precepts.

[101] I hold back my feet from every | evil way,*
in order to | keep your word.

[102] I do not turn aside from your | just decrees,*
for you have | taught me.

[103] How sweet are your words | to my taste,*
sweeter than honey | to my mouth!

[104] Through your precepts I get
under- | standing;*
therefore I hate every | false way.

Glory be to the Father and | to the Son*
and to the Holy | Spirit;
as it was in the be- | ginning,*
is now, and will be forever. | Amen.

NUN

[105] Your word is a lamp | to my feet*
and a light | to my path.

[106] I have sworn an oath and con- | firmed it,*
to keep your just and righ- | teous
decrees.

[107] I am severely af- | flicted;*
give me life, O LORD, according | to
your word!

[108] Accept my freewill offerings of
praise, | O LORD,*
and teach me your | just decrees.

[109] I hold my life in my hand con- | tinually,*
but I do not for- | get your law.

[110] The wicked have laid a | snare for me,*
but I do not stray from your | precepts.

[111] Your testimonies are my heritage for- | ever,*
for they are the joy | of my heart.

[112] I incline my heart to perform your | statutes*
forever, | to the end.

Glory be to the Father and | to the Son*
and to the Holy | Spirit;
as it was in the be- | ginning,*
is now, and will be forever. | Amen.

SAMEKH

[113] I hate the double- | minded,*
but I | love your law.

[114] You are my hiding place | and my shield;*
I hope | in your word.

[115] Depart from me, you evil- | doers,*
that I may keep the commandments | of my God.

[116] Uphold me according to your promise, that | I may live,*
and let me not be put to shame | in my hope!

[117] Hold me up, that I | may be safe*
and have regard for your statutes con- | tinually!

[118] You spurn all who go astray from your | statutes,*
for their cunning | is in vain.

[119] All the wicked of the earth you dis- | card like dross,*
therefore I love your testi- | monies.

[120] My flesh trembles for | fear of you,*
and I am afraid of your | judgments.

Glory be to the Father and | to the Son*
and to the Holy | Spirit;
as it was in the be- | ginning,*
is now, and will be forever. | Amen.

AYIN

[121] I have done what is | just and right;*
do not leave me to my op- | pressors.

[122] Give your servant a | pledge of good;*
let not the insolent op- | press me.

[123] My eyes long for your sal- | vation*
and for the fulfillment of your righteous | promise.

[124] Deal with your servant according to your | steadfast love,*
and teach me your | statutes.

[125] I am your servant; give me under- | standing,*
that I may know your testi- | monies!

[126] It is time for the | LORD to act,*
for your law has been | broken.

[127] Therefore I love your com- | mandments*
above gold, above | fine gold.

[128] Therefore I consider all your precepts | to be right;*
I hate every | false way.

Glory be to the Father and | to the Son*
and to the Holy | Spirit;
as it was in the be- | ginning,*
is now, and will be forever. | Amen.

PE

[129] Your testimonies are | wonderful;*
therefore my soul | keeps them.

[130] The unfolding of your | words gives light;*
it imparts understanding to the | simple.

[131] I open my | mouth and pant,*
because I long for your com- | mandments.

[132] Turn to me and be gra- | cious to me,*
as is your way with those who | love your name.

[133] Keep steady my steps according to your | promise,*
and let no iniquity get dominion | over me.

[134] Redeem me from man's op- | pression,*
that I may keep your | precepts.

[135] Make your face shine upon your | servant,*
and teach me your | statutes.

[136] My eyes shed | streams of tears,*
because people do not | keep your law.

Glory be to the Father and | to the Son*
and to the Holy | Spirit;
as it was in the be- | ginning,*
is now, and will be forever. | Amen.

TSADHE

[137] Righteous are you, | O LORD,*
and right are your | just decrees.

[138] You have appointed your testimonies in | righteousness*
and in all | faithfulness.

[139] My zeal con- | sumes me,*
because my foes for- | get your words.

[140] Your promise is | well tried,*
and your servant | loves it.

[141] I am small | and despised,*
yet I do not forget your | precepts.

[142] Your righteousness is righteous for- | ever,*
and your | law is true.

[143] Trouble and anguish have | found me out,*
but your commandments are | my delight.

[144] Your testimonies are righteous for- | ever;*
give me understanding that | I may live.

Glory be to the Father and | to the Son*
and to the Holy | Spirit;
as it was in the be- | ginning,*
is now, and will be forever. | Amen.

QOPH

[145] With my whole heart I cry; answer me, | O LORD!*
I will keep your | statutes.

[146] I call to you; | save me,*
that I may observe your testi- | monies.

[147] I rise before dawn and | cry for help;*
I hope | in your words.

[148] My eyes are awake before the watches | of the night,*
that I may meditate on your | promise.

[149] Hear my voice according to your | steadfast love;*
O LORD, according to your justice | give me life.

[150] They draw near who persecute me with evil | purpose;*
they are far | from your law.

[151] But you are near, | O LORD,*
and all your command- | ments are true.

[152] Long have I known from your testi- | monies*
that you have founded them for- | ever.

Glory be to the Father and | to the Son*
and to the Holy | Spirit;
as it was in the be- | ginning,*
is now, and will be forever. | Amen.

RESH

[153] Look on my affliction and de- | liver me,*
for I do not for- | get your law.

[154] Plead my cause and re- | deem me;*
give me life according to your | promise!

[155] Salvation is far from the | wicked,*
for they do not seek your | statutes.

[156] Great is your mercy, | O LORD;*
give me life according to your | just decrees.

[157] Many are my persecutors and my adver- | saries,*

but I do not swerve from your testi- | monies.

[158] I look at the faithless | with disgust,*
because they do not keep | your commands.

[159] Consider how I love your | precepts!*
Give me life according to your | steadfast love.

[160] The sum of your | word is truth,*
and every one of your just and righteous decrees endures for- | ever.

Glory be to the Father and | to the Son*
and to the Holy | Spirit;
as it was in the be- | ginning,*
is now, and will be forever. | Amen.

SIN AND SHIN

[161] Princes persecute me with- | out cause,*
but my heart stands in awe | of your words.

[162] I rejoice | at your word*
like one who | finds great spoil.

[163] I hate and abhor | falsehood,*
but I | love your law.

[164] Seven times a day I | praise you*
for your just and righ- | teous decrees.

[165] Great peace have those who | love your law;*
nothing can make them | stumble.

[166] I hope for your salvation, | O LORD,*
and I do your com- | mandments.

[167] My soul keeps your testi- | monies;*
I love them ex- | ceedingly.

[168] I keep your precepts and testi- | monies,*
for all my ways are be- | fore you.

Glory be to the Father and | to the Son*
and to the Holy | Spirit;
as it was in the be- | ginning,*
is now, and will be forever. | Amen.

TAW

[169] Let my cry come before you, | O LORD;*
give me understanding according | to your word!

[170] Let my plea come be- | fore you;*
deliver me according | to your word.

[171] My lips will | pour forth praise,*
for you teach me your | statutes.

[172] My tongue will sing | of your word,*
for all your command- | ments are right.

[173] Let your hand be ready to | help me,*
for I have chosen your | precepts.

[174] I long for your salvation, | O LORD,*
and your law is | my delight.

[175] Let my soul live and | praise you,*
and let your just decrees | help me.

[176] I have gone astray like a lost sheep; seek your | servant,*
for I do not forget your com- | mandments.

Glory be to the Father and | to the Son*
and to the Holy | Spirit;
as it was in the be- | ginning,*
is now, and will be forever. | Amen.

121

[1] I lift up my eyes | to the hills.*
From where does my | help come?

[2] My help comes | from the LORD,*
who made | heaven and earth.

[3] He will not let your | foot be moved;*
he who keeps you will not | slumber.

[4] Behold, he who keeps | Israel*
will neither slum- | ber nor sleep.

[5] The LORD is your | keeper;*
the LORD is your shade on your | right hand.

[6] The sun shall not strike | you by day,*
nor the | moon by night.

[7] The LORD will keep you from all | evil;*
he will | keep your life.

[8] The LORD will keep your going out and your | coming in*
from this time forth and for- | evermore.

Glory be to the Father and | to the Son*
and to the Holy | Spirit;
as it was in the be- | ginning,*
is now, and will be forever. | Amen.

122

[1] I was glad when they | said to me,*
"Let us go to the house | of the LORD!"

[2] Our feet have been | standing*
within your gates, O Je- | rusalem!

[3] Jerusalem—built as a | city*
that is bound firmly to- | gether,

[4] to which the tribes go up, the tribes of the LORD, as was decreed for | Israel,*
to give thanks to the name | of the LORD.

[5] There thrones for judg- | ment were set,*
the thrones of the house of | David.

[6] Pray for the peace of Je- | rusalem!*
"May they be secure who | love you!

[7] Peace be with- | in your walls*
and security within your | towers!"

[8] For my brothers and com- | panions' sake*
I will say, "Peace be with- | in you!"

[9] For the sake of the house of the | LORD our God,*
I will | seek your good.

Glory be to the Father and | to the Son*
and to the Holy | Spirit;
as it was in the be- | ginning,*
is now, and will be forever. | Amen.

123

[1] To you I lift | up my eyes,*
O you who are enthroned in the | heavens!

[2] Behold, as the eyes of servants look to the hand of their master, as the eyes of a maidservant to the hand of her | mistress,*
so our eyes look to the LORD our God, till he has mercy up- | on us.

[3] Have mercy upon us, O LORD, have mercy up- | on us,*
for we have had more than enough | of contempt.

[4] Our soul has had more than enough of the scorn of those who | are at ease,*
of the contempt | of the proud.

Glory be to the Father and | to the Son*
and to the Holy | Spirit;
as it was in the be- | ginning,*
is now, and will be forever. | Amen.

124

[1] If it had not been the LORD who was | on our side—*
let Israel | now say—

[2] if it had not been the LORD who was | on our side*
when people rose up a- | gainst us,

[3] then they would have swallowed us | up alive,*
when their anger was kindled a- | gainst us;

[4] then the flood would have swept | us away,*
the torrent would have gone | over us;

[5] then over us | would have gone*
the raging | waters.

[6] Blessèd | be the LORD,*
who has not given us as prey | to their teeth!

[7] We have escaped like a bird from the snare of the | fowlers;*

the snare is broken, and we | have escaped!

[8] Our help is in the name | of the LORD,*
who made | heaven and earth.

Glory be to the Father and | to the Son*
and to the Holy | Spirit;
as it was in the be- | ginning,*
is now, and will be forever. | Amen.

125

[1] Those who trust in the LORD are like Mount | Zion,*
which cannot be moved, but abides for- | ever.

[2] As the mountains surround Jerusalem, so the LORD surrounds his | people,*
from this time forth and for- | evermore.

[3] For the scepter of wickedness shall not rest on the land allotted to the | righteous,*
lest the righteous stretch out their hands to | do wrong.

[4] Do good, O LORD, to those | who are good,*
and to those who are upright | in their hearts!

[5] But those who turn aside to their crooked ways the LORD will lead away with evil- | doers!*
Peace be upon | Israel!

Glory be to the Father and | to the Son*
and to the Holy | Spirit;
as it was in the be- | ginning,*
is now, and will be forever. | Amen.

126

[1] When the LORD restored the fortunes of | Zion,*
we were like | those who dream.

[2] Then our mouth was filled with | laughter,*
and our tongue with | shouts of joy;
then they said among the nations, "The LORD has done great | things for them."*
[3] The LORD has done great things for us; | we are glad.

[4] Restore our fortunes, | O LORD,*
like streams in the | Negeb!

[5] Those who | sow in tears*
shall reap with | shouts of joy!

[6] He who goes out weeping, bearing the seed for | sowing,*
shall come home with shouts of joy, bringing his | sheaves with him.

Glory be to the Father and | to the Son*
and to the Holy | Spirit;
as it was in the be- | ginning,*
is now, and will be forever. | Amen.

127

[1] Unless the LORD builds the house, those who build it la- | bor in vain.*
Unless the LORD watches over the city, the watchman stays a- | wake in vain.

[2] It is in vain that you rise up early and go late to rest, eating the bread of | anxious toil;*
for he gives to his be- | lovèd sleep.

[3] Behold, children are a heritage | from the LORD,*
the fruit of the womb | a reward.

[4] Like arrows in the hand of a | warrior*
are the children | of one's youth.

[5] Blessèd is the man who fills his quiver | with them!*
He shall not be put to shame when he speaks with his enemies | in the gate.

Glory be to the Father and | to the Son*
and to the Holy | Spirit;
as it was in the be- | ginning,*
is now, and will be forever. | Amen.

128

[1] Blessèd is everyone who | fears the LORD,*
who walks | in his ways!

[2] You shall eat the fruit of the labor | of your hands;*
you shall be blessed, and it shall be | well with you.

[3] Your wife will be like a fruitful vine with- | in your house;*
your children will be like olive shoots around your | table.

[4] Behold, thus shall the | man be blessed*
who | fears the LORD.

[5] The LORD bless you from | Zion!*
May you see the prosperity of Jerusalem all the days | of your life!

[6] May you see your children's | children!*
Peace be upon | Israel!

Glory be to the Father and | to the Son*
and to the Holy | Spirit;
as it was in the be- | ginning,*
is now, and will be forever. | Amen.

130

[1] Out | of the depths*
I cry to you, | O LORD!

[2] O Lord, | hear my voice!*
Let your ears be attentive to the voice of my pleas for | mercy!

[3] If you, O LORD, should mark in- | iquities,*
O Lord, | who could stand?

[4] But with you there is for- | giveness,*
that you | may be feared.

[5] I wait for the LORD, my | soul waits,*
and in his | word I hope;

[6] my soul waits for the Lord more than watchmen for the | morning,*
more than watchmen for the | morning.

[7] O Israel, hope in the LORD! For with the LORD there is | steadfast love,*
and with him is plentiful re- | demption.

[8] And he will redeem | Israel*
from all his in- | iquities.

Glory be to the Father and | to the Son*
and to the Holy | Spirit;
as it was in the be- | ginning,*
is now, and will be forever. | Amen.

131

[1] O LORD, my heart is not lifted up; my eyes are not | raised too high;*
I do not occupy myself with things too great and too marvel- | ous for me.

[2] But I have calmed and quieted my soul, like a weaned child with its | mother;*
like a weaned child is my soul with- | in me.

[3] O Israel, hope | in the LORD*
from this time forth and for- | evermore.

Glory be to the Father and | to the Son*
and to the Holy | Spirit;
as it was in the be- | ginning,*
is now, and will be forever. | Amen.

132

[1] Remember, O LORD, in David's | favor,*
all the hardships | he endured,

[2] how he swore | to the LORD*
and vowed to the Mighty One of | Jacob,

[3] "I will not en- | ter my house*
or get in- | to my bed,

[4] I will not give sleep | to my eyes*
or slumber to my | eyelids,

[5] until I find a place | for the LORD,*
a dwelling place for the Mighty One of | Jacob."

[6] Behold, we heard of it in | Ephrathah;*
we found it in the | fields of Jaar.

[7] "Let us go to his |dwelling place; *
let us worship at his |footstool!"

[8] Arise, O LORD, and go to your |resting place, *
you and the ark |of your might.

[9] Let your priests be clothed with |righteousness, *
and let your saints |shout for joy.

[10] For the sake of your servant |David, *
do not turn away the face of your a- |nointed one.

[11] The LORD swore to David a sure oath from which he will |not turn back: *
"One of the sons of your body I will set |on your throne.

[12] If your sons keep my covenant and my testimonies that I shall |teach them, *
their sons also forever shall sit |on your throne."

[13] For the LORD has chosen |Zion; *
he has desired it for his |dwelling place:

[14] "This is my resting place for- |ever; *
here I will dwell, for I have de- |sired it.

[15] I will abundantly bless her pro- |visions; *
I will satisfy her |poor with bread.

[16] Her priests I will clothe with sal- |vation, *
and her saints will |shout for joy.

[17] There I will make a horn to sprout for |David; *
I have prepared a lamp for my a- |nointed.

[18] His enemies I will |clothe with shame, *
but on him his |crown will shine."

**Glory be to the Father and |to the Son *
and to the Holy |Spirit;
as it was in the be- |ginning, *
is now, and will be forever. |Amen.**

133

[1] Behold, how good and pleas- |ant it is *
when brothers dwell in |unity!

[2] It is like the precious oil on the head, running down on the beard, on the beard of |Aaron, *
running down on the collar |of his robes!

[3] It is like the dew of Hermon, which falls on the mountains of |Zion! *
For there the LORD has commanded the blessing, life for- |evermore.

**Glory be to the Father and |to the Son *
and to the Holy |Spirit;
as it was in the be- |ginning, *
is now, and will be forever. |Amen.**

134

[1] Come, bless the LORD, all you servants |of the LORD, *
who stand by night in the house |of the LORD!

[2] Lift up your hands to the |holy place *
and |bless the LORD!

[3] May the LORD bless you from |Zion, *
he who made |heaven and earth!

**Glory be to the Father and |to the Son *
and to the Holy |Spirit;
as it was in the be- |ginning, *
is now, and will be forever. |Amen.**

136

[1] Give thanks to the LORD, for |he is good, *
for his steadfast love endures for- |ever.

[2] Give thanks to the |God of gods, *
for his steadfast love endures for- |ever.

[3] Give thanks to the |Lord of lords, *
for his steadfast love endures for- |ever;

[4] to him who alone does great |wonders, *
for his steadfast love endures for- |ever;

[5] to him who by understanding made the | heavens,*
for his steadfast love endures for- | ever;

[6] to him who spread out the earth above the | waters,*
for his steadfast love endures for- | ever;

[7] to him who made the | great lights,*
for his steadfast love endures for- | ever;

[8] the sun to rule o- | ver the day,*
for his steadfast love endures for- | ever;

[9] the moon and stars to rule o- | ver the night,*
for his steadfast love endures for- | ever;

[10] to him who struck down the firstborn of | Egypt,*
for his steadfast love endures for- | ever;

[11] and brought Israel out from a- | mong them,*
for his steadfast love endures for- | ever;

[12] with a strong hand and an | outstretched arm,*
for his steadfast love endures for- | ever;

[13] to him who divided the Red | Sea in two,*
for his steadfast love endures for- | ever;

[14] and made Israel pass through the | midst of it,*
for his steadfast love endures for- | ever;

[15] but overthrew Pharaoh and his host in the | Red Sea,*
for his steadfast love endures for- | ever;

[16] to him who led his people through the | wilderness,*
for his steadfast love endures for- | ever;

[17] to him who struck down | great kings,*
for his steadfast love endures for- | ever;

[18] and killed | mighty kings,*
for his steadfast love endures for- | ever;

[19] Sihon, king of the | Amorites,*
for his steadfast love endures for- | ever;

[20] and Og, king of | Bashan,*
for his steadfast love endures for- | ever;

[21] and gave their land as a | heritage,*
for his steadfast love endures for- | ever;

[22] a heritage to Israel his | servant,*
for his steadfast love endures for- | ever.

[23] It is he who remembered us in our | low estate,*
for his steadfast love endures for- | ever;

[24] and rescued us | from our foes,*
for his steadfast love endures for- | ever;

[25] he who gives food | to all flesh,*
for his steadfast love endures for- | ever.

[26] Give thanks to the God of | heaven,*
for his steadfast love endures for- | ever.

Glory be to the Father and | to the Son*
and to the Holy | Spirit;
as it was in the be- | ginning,*
is now, and will be forever. | Amen.

138

[1] I give you thanks, O LORD, with | my whole heart;*
before the gods I | sing your praise;

[2] I bow down toward your holy temple and give thanks to your name for your steadfast love and your | faithfulness,*
for you have exalted above all things your name | and your word.

[3] On the day I called, you | answered me;*
my strength of soul | you increased.

[4] All the kings of the earth shall give you thanks, | O LORD,*
for they have heard the words | of your mouth,

[5] and they shall sing of the ways | of the LORD,*
for great is the glory | of the LORD.

[6] For though the LORD is high, he regards the | lowly,*
but the haughty he knows | from afar.

[7] Though I walk in the midst of trouble, you pre- | serve my life;*

you stretch out your hand against the wrath of my enemies, and your right hand de- | livers me.

[8] The LORD will fulfill his pur- | pose for me;*
your steadfast love, O LORD, endures forever. Do not forsake the work | of your hands.

Glory be to the Father and | to the Son*
and to the Holy | Spirit;
as it was in the be- | ginning,*
is now, and will be forever. | Amen.

139

[1] O LORD, you have searched me and | known me!*
[2] You know when I sit down and when I rise up; you discern my thoughts | from afar.

[3] You search out my path and my | lying down*
and are acquainted with | all my ways.

[4] Even before a word is | on my tongue,*
behold, O LORD, you know it alto- | gether.

[5] You hem me in, behind | and before,*
and lay your hand up- | on me.

[6] Such knowledge is too wonder- | ful for me;*
it is high; I cannot | attain it.

[7] Where shall I go from your | Spirit?*
Or where shall I flee from your | presence?

[8] If I ascend to heaven, | you are there!*
If I make my bed in Sheol, | you are there!

[9] If I take the wings of the | morning*
and dwell in the uttermost parts | of the sea,

[10] even there your hand shall | lead me,*
and your right hand shall | hold me.

[11] If I say, "Surely the darkness shall | cover me,*
and the light about me | be night,"

[12] even the darkness is not | dark to you;*
the night is bright as the day, for darkness is as | light with you.

[13] For you formed my | inward parts;*
you knitted me together in my | mother's womb.

[14] I praise you, for I am fearfully and wonder- | fully made.*
Wonderful are your works; my soul knows it | very well.

[15] My frame was not hid- | den from you,*
when I was being made in secret, intricately woven in the depths | of the earth.

[16] Your eyes saw my unformed substance; in your book were written, every | one of them,*
the days that were formed for me, when as yet there were | none of them.

[17] How precious to me are your thoughts, | O God!*
How vast is the | sum of them!

[18] If I would count them, they are more | than the sand.*
I awake, and I am still | with you.

[19] Oh that you would slay the wicked, | O God!*
O men of blood, de- | part from me!

[20] They speak against you with mali- | cious intent;*
your enemies take your | name in vain!

[21] Do I not hate those who hate you, | O LORD?*
And do I not loathe those who rise up a- | gainst you?

[22] I hate them with complete | hatred;*
I count them my | enemies.

[23] Search me, O God, and | know my heart!*
Try me and | know my thoughts!

[24] And see if there be any grievous | way in me,*
and lead me in the way ever- | lasting!

Glory be to the Father and | to the Son*
and to the Holy | Spirit;
as it was in the be- | ginning,*
is now, and will be forever. | Amen.

141

[1] O LORD, I call upon you; hasten | to me!*
Give ear to my voice when I | call to you!

[2] Let my prayer be counted as incense be- | fore you,*
and the lifting up of my hands as the evening | sacrifice!

[3] Set a guard, O LORD, over | my mouth;*
keep watch over the door | of my lips!

[4] Do not let my heart incline to any evil, to busy myself with wicked deeds in company with men who work in- | iquity,*
and let me not eat of their del- | icacies!

[5] Let a righteous man strike me—it is a kindness; let him rebuke me—it is oil for my head; let my head not re- | fuse it.*
Yet my prayer is continually against their | evil deeds.

[6] When their judges are thrown o- | ver the cliff,*
then they shall hear my words, for they are | pleasant.

[7] As when one plows and breaks | up the earth,*
so shall our bones be scattered at the mouth | of Sheol.

[8] But my eyes are toward you, O | GOD, my Lord;*
in you I seek refuge; leave me not de- | fenseless!

[9] Keep me from the trap that they have | laid for me*
and from the snares of evil- | doers!

[10] Let the wicked fall into their | own nets,*
while I pass by | safely.

Glory be to the Father and | to the Son*
and to the Holy | Spirit;
as it was in the be- | ginning,*
is now, and will be forever. | Amen.

142

[1] With my voice I cry out | to the LORD;*
with my voice I plead for mercy | to the LORD.

[2] I pour out my complaint be- | fore him;*
I tell my trouble be- | fore him.

[3] When my spirit faints within me, you | know my way!*
In the path where I walk they have hidden a | trap for me.

[4] Look to the right and see: there is none who takes notice | of me;*
no refuge remains to me; no one cares | for my soul.

[5] I cry to you, | O LORD;*
I say, "You are my refuge, my portion in the land of the | living."

[6] Attend to my cry, for I am brought | very low!*
Deliver me from my persecutors, for they are too | strong for me!

[7] Bring me out of prison, that I may give thanks | to your name!*
The righteous will surround me, for you will deal bountifully | with me.

Glory be to the Father and | to the Son*
and to the Holy | Spirit;
as it was in the be- | ginning,*
is now, and will be forever. | Amen.

143

[1] Hear my prayer, O LORD; give ear to my pleas for | mercy!*
In your faithfulness answer me, in your | righteousness!

[2] Enter not into judgment with your | servant,*
for no one living is righteous be- | fore you.

[3] For the enemy has pursued my soul; he has crushed my life | to the ground;*
he has made me sit in darkness like | those long dead.

[4] Therefore my spirit faints with- | in me;*
my heart within me | is appalled.

[5] I remember the days of old; I meditate on all that | you have done;*
I ponder the work | of your hands.

[6] I stretch out my | hands to you;*
my soul thirsts for you like a | parched land.

[7] Answer me quickly, O LORD! My | spirit fails!*
Hide not your face from me, lest I be like those who go down | to the pit.

[8] Let me hear in the morning of your steadfast love, for in | you I trust.*
Make me know the way I should go, for to you I lift | up my soul.

[9] Deliver me from my enemies, | O LORD!*
I have fled to you for | refuge!

[10] Teach me to do your will, for you | are my God!*
Let your good Spirit lead me on | level ground!

[11] For your name's sake, O LORD, pre- | serve my life!*
In your righteousness bring my soul out of | trouble!

[12] And in your steadfast love you will cut off my | enemies,*
and you will destroy all the adversaries of my soul, for I am your | servant.

Glory be to the Father and | to the Son*
and to the Holy | Spirit;
as it was in the be- | ginning,*
is now, and will be forever. | Amen.

145

[1] I will extol you, my | God and King,*
and bless your name forever and | ever.

[2] Every day I will | bless you*
and praise your name forever and | ever.

[3] Great is the LORD, and greatly | to be praised,*
and his greatness is un- | searchable.

[4] One generation shall commend your works to an- | other,*
and shall declare your | mighty acts.

[5] On the glorious splendor of your | majesty,*
and on your wondrous works, I will | meditate.

[6] They shall speak of the might of your | awesome deeds,*
and I will declare your | greatness.

[7] They shall pour forth the fame of your abundant | goodness*
and shall sing aloud of your | righteousness.

[8] The LORD is gracious and | merciful,*
slow to anger and abounding in | steadfast love.

[9] The LORD is | good to all,*
and his mercy is over all that | he has made.

[10] All your works shall give thanks to you, | O LORD,*
and all your saints shall | bless you!

[11] They shall speak of the glory of your | kingdom*
and tell | of your power,

[12] to make known to the children of man your | mighty deeds,*
and the glorious splendor of your | kingdom.

[13] Your kingdom is an everlasting | kingdom,*
and your dominion endures throughout all gener- | ations.

The LORD is faithful in | all his words*
and kind in | all his works.

[14] The LORD upholds all who are | falling*
and raises up all who are | bowed down.

[15] The eyes of all | look to you,*
and you give them their food in due | season.

[16] You open | your hand;*
you satisfy the desire of every | living thing.

[17] The LORD is righteous in | all his ways*
and kind in | all his works.

[18] The LORD is near to all who | call on him,*
to all who call on | him in truth.

[19] He fulfills the desire of those who | fear him;*
he also hears their cry and | saves them.

[20] The LORD preserves all who | love him,*
but all the wicked he | will destroy.

[21] My mouth will speak the praise | of the LORD,*
and let all flesh bless his holy name forever and | ever.

Glory be to the Father and | to the Son*
and to the Holy | Spirit;
as it was in the be- | ginning,*
is now, and will be forever. | Amen.

146

[1] Praise | the LORD!*
Praise the LORD, | O my soul!

[2] I will praise the LORD as long | as I live;*
I will sing praises to my God while I have my | being.

[3] Put not your trust in | princes,*
in a son of man, in whom there is no sal- | vation.

[4] When his breath departs he returns | to the earth;*
on that very day his plans | perish.

[5] Blessèd is he whose help is the God of | Jacob,*
whose hope is in the | LORD his God,

[6] who made heaven and earth, the sea, and all that is | in them,*
who keeps faith for- | ever;

[7] who executes justice for | the oppressed,*
who gives food to the | hungry.

The LORD sets the prisoners free; [8] the LORD opens the eyes | of the blind.*
The LORD lifts up those who are bowed down; the LORD loves the | righteous.

[9] The LORD watches over the sojourners; he upholds the widow and the | fatherless,*
but the way of the wicked he brings to | ruin.

[10] The LORD will reign for- | ever,*
your God, O Zion, to all generations. | Praise the LORD!

Glory be to the Father and | to the Son*
and to the Holy | Spirit;
as it was in the be- | ginning,*
is now, and will be forever. | Amen.

147

[1] Praise the LORD! For it is good to sing praises | to our God;*
for it is pleasant, and a song of praise is | fitting.

[2] The LORD builds up Je- | rusalem;*
he gathers the outcasts of | Israel.

[3] He heals the broken- | hearted*
and binds | up their wounds.

[4] He determines the number | of the stars;*
he gives to all of | them their names.

[5] Great is our Lord, and abun- | dant in power;*
his understanding is beyond | measure.

[6] The LORD lifts up the | humble;*
he casts the wicked | to the ground.

[7] Sing to the LORD with thanks- | giving;*
make melody to our God | on the lyre!

[8] He covers the heavens with clouds; he prepares rain | for the earth;*
he makes grass grow | on the hills.

[9] He gives to the | beasts their food,*
and to the young ravens | that cry.

[10] His delight is not in the strength | of the horse,*
nor his pleasure in the legs | of a man,

[11] but the LORD takes pleasure in those who | fear him,*
in those who hope in his | steadfast love.

[12] Praise the LORD, O Je- | rusalem!*
Praise your God, O | Zion!

[13] For he strengthens the bars | of your gates;*
he blesses your children with- | in you.

[14] He makes peace in your | borders;*
he fills you with the finest | of the wheat.

[15] He sends out his command | to the earth;*
his word runs | swiftly.

[16] He gives | snow like wool;*
he scatters hoarfrost like | ashes.

[17] He hurls down his crystals of | ice like crumbs;*
who can stand be- | fore his cold?

[18] He sends out his word, and | melts them;*
he makes his wind blow and the | waters flow.

[19] He declares his word to | Jacob,*
his statutes and just decrees to | Israel.

[20] He has not dealt thus with any other | nation;*
they do not know his just decrees. | Praise the LORD!

Glory be to the Father and | to the Son*
and to the Holy | Spirit;
as it was in the be- | ginning,*
is now, and will be forever. | Amen.

148

[1] Praise the LORD! Praise the LORD from the | heavens;*
praise him | in the heights!

[2] Praise him, all his | angels;*
praise him, | all his hosts!

[3] Praise him, | sun and moon,*
praise him, all you | shining stars!

[4] Praise him, you highest | heavens,*
and you waters above the | heavens!

[5] Let them praise the name | of the LORD!*
For he commanded and they were cre- | ated.

[6] And he established them forever and | ever;*
he gave a decree, and it shall not | pass away.

[7] Praise the LORD | from the earth,*
you great sea creatures and | all deeps,

[8] fire and hail, | snow and mist,*
stormy wind fulfill- | ing his word!

[9] Mountains and | all hills,*
fruit trees and all | cedars!

[10] Beasts and all | livestock,*
creeping things and | flying birds!

[11] Kings of the earth and all | peoples,*
princes and all rulers | of the earth!

[12] Young men and maidens to- | gether,*
old men and | children!

[13] Let them praise the name of the LORD,
for his name alone is ex- | alted;*
his majesty is above earth and | heaven.

[14] He has raised up a horn for his people,
praise for | all his saints,*
for the people of Israel who are near
to him. | Praise the LORD!

Glory be to the Father and | to the Son*
and to the Holy | Spirit;
as it was in the be- | ginning,*
is now, and will be forever. | Amen.

149

[1] Praise the LORD! Sing to the LORD a | new
song,*
his praise in the assembly of the | godly!

[2] Let Israel be glad in his | Maker;*
let the children of Zion rejoice | in
their King!

[3] Let them praise his name with | dancing,*
making melody to him with
tambou- | rine and lyre!

[4] For the LORD takes pleasure in
his | people;*
he adorns the humble with sal- | vation.

[5] Let the godly exult in | glory;*
let them sing for joy | on their beds.

[6] Let the high praises of God be | in their
throats*
and two-edged swords | in their hands,

[7] to execute vengeance on the | nations*
and punishments on the | peoples,

[8] to bind their | kings with chains*
and their nobles with fet- | ters of iron,

[9] to execute on them the
judgment | written!*
This is honor for all his godly
ones. | Praise the LORD!

Glory be to the Father and | to the Son*
and to the Holy | Spirit;
as it was in the be- | ginning,*
is now, and will be forever. | Amen.

150

[1] Praise the LORD! Praise God in his
sanctu- | ary;*
praise him in his mighty | heavens!

[2] Praise him for his | mighty deeds;*
praise him according to his
excellent | greatness!

[3] Praise him with | trumpet sound;*
praise him with | lute and harp!

[4] Praise him with tambou- | rine and
dance;*
praise him with | strings and pipe!

[5] Praise him with sounding | cymbals;*
praise him with loud clashing | cymbals!

[6] Let everything that has breath | praise
the LORD!*
Praise | the LORD!

Glory be to the Father and | to the Son*
and to the Holy | Spirit;
as it was in the be- | ginning,*
is now, and will be forever. | Amen.

DIVINE SERVICE
Setting One

CONFESSION AND ABSOLUTION

A Hymn of Invocation may be sung.

Stand

The sign of the cross ☩ may be made by all in remembrance of their Baptism.

P In the name of the Father and of the ☩ Son and of the Holy Spirit.
C **Amen.** *Matthew 28:19b; [18:20]*

P If we say we have no sin, we deceive ourselves, and the truth is not in us.
C **But if we confess our sins, God, who is faithful and just, will forgive our sins and cleanse us from all unrighteousness.** *1 John 1:8–9*

Kneel/Stand

Silence for reflection on God's Word and for self-examination.

P Let us then confess our sins to God our Father.
C **Most merciful God, we confess that we are by nature sinful and unclean. We have sinned against You in thought, word, and deed, by what we have done and by what we have left undone. We have not loved You with our whole heart; we have not loved our neighbors as ourselves. We justly deserve Your present and eternal punishment. For the sake of Your Son, Jesus Christ, have mercy on us. Forgive us, renew us, and lead us, so that we may delight in Your will and walk in Your ways to the glory of Your holy name. Amen.**

P Almighty God in His mercy has given His Son to die for you and for His sake forgives you all your sins. As a called and ordained servant of Christ, and by His authority, I therefore forgive you all your sins in the name of the Father and of the ☩ Son and of the Holy Spirit. *[John 20:19–23]*
C **Amen.**

P In the mercy of almighty God, Jesus Christ was given to die for us, and for His sake God forgives us all our sins. To those who believe in Jesus Christ He gives the power to become the children of God and bestows on them the Holy Spirit. May the Lord, who has begun this good work in us, bring it to completion in the day of our Lord Jesus Christ.

John 1:12; Philippians 1:6

C **Amen.**

Stand

SERVICE OF THE WORD

INTROIT, PSALM, or ENTRANCE HYMN

KYRIE ~ *Lord, Have Mercy*

Mark 10:47

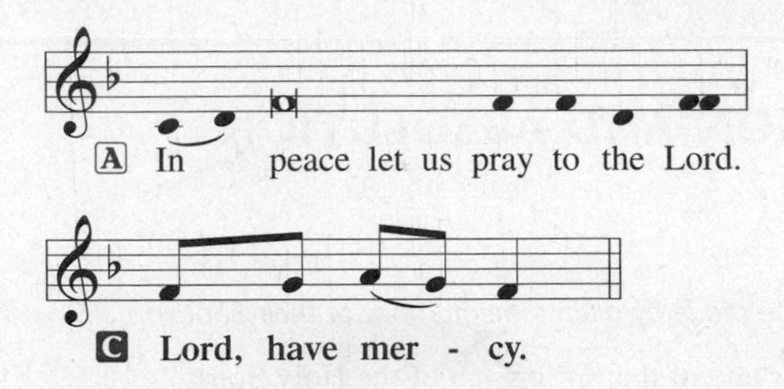
A In peace let us pray to the Lord.
C Lord, have mer - cy.

A For the peace from above and for our salvation let us pray to the Lord.
C Lord, have mer - cy.

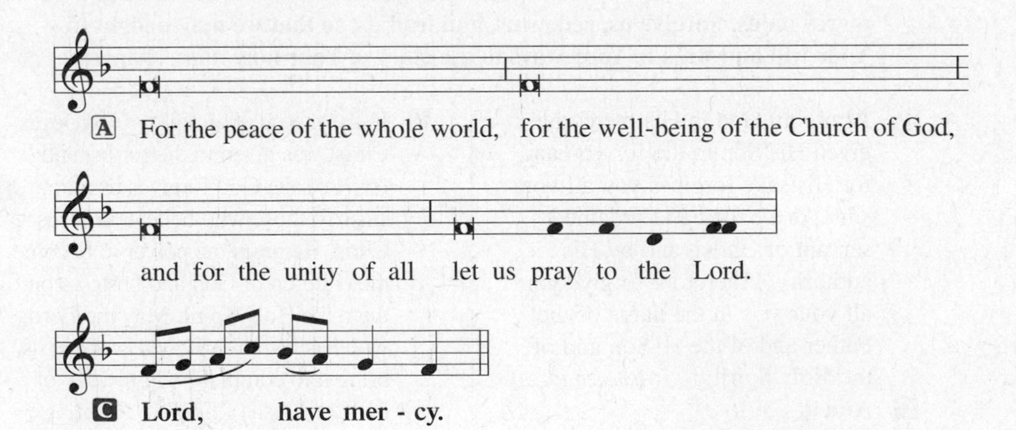
A For the peace of the whole world, for the well-being of the Church of God,
and for the unity of all let us pray to the Lord.
C Lord, have mer - cy.

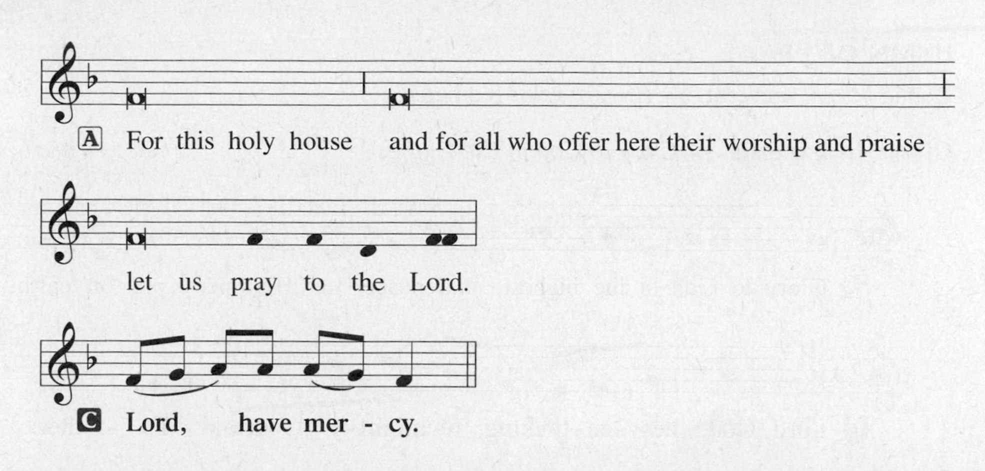
A For this holy house and for all who offer here their worship and praise
let us pray to the Lord.
C Lord, have mer - cy.

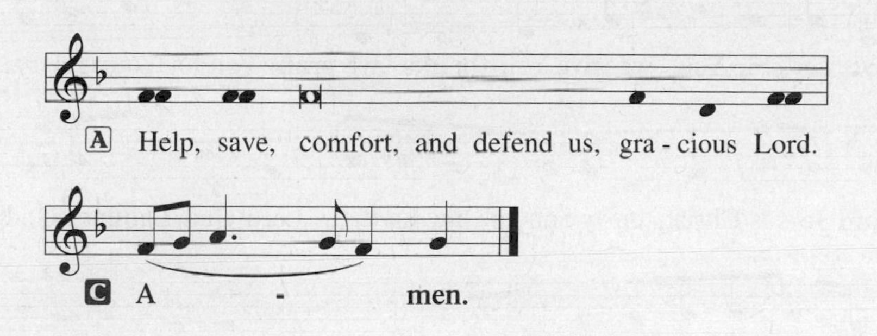
A Help, save, comfort, and defend us, gra - cious Lord.
C A - men.

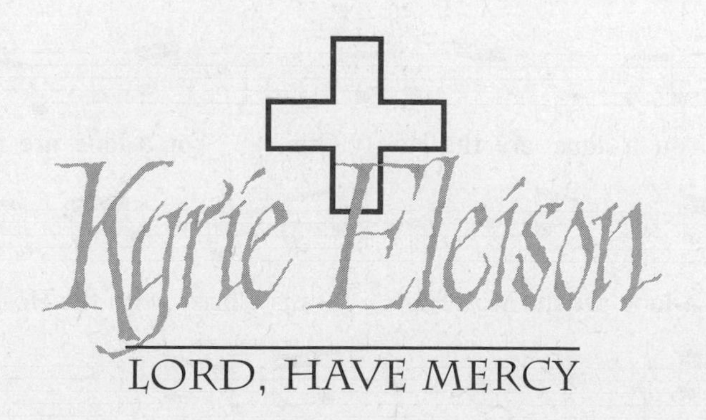
Kyrie Eleison
LORD, HAVE MERCY

HYMN OF PRAISE

During Advent and Lent, the HYMN OF PRAISE is omitted.

Gloria in Excelsis ~ *Glory to God in the Highest* *Luke 2:14; John 1:29*

A Glory to God in the highest, and peace to His peo - ple on earth.
C Lord God, heav-en-ly king, al-might-y God and Fa - ther:
We wor-ship You, we give You thanks, we praise You for Your glo-ry.
Lord Je-sus Christ, on-ly Son of the Fa-ther, Lord God, Lamb of God:
You take a-way the sin of the world; have mer-cy on us.
You are seat-ed at the right hand of the Fa-ther; re-ceive our prayer.
For You a-lone are the Ho-ly One, You a-lone are the Lord,
You a-lone are the Most High, Je-sus Christ, with the Ho-ly Spir-it,
in the glo-ry of God the Fa-ther. A - men.

The service continues with the SALUTATION on page 156.

OR

This Is the Feast

Revelation 5:12–13; 19:5–9

Refrain
C This is the feast of vic-to-ry for our God.
Al-le-lu-ia, al-le-lu-ia, al-le-lu-ia.
1 — Wor-thy is Christ, the Lamb who was slain, whose
2 Pow-er, rich-es, wis-dom, and strength, and
3 Sing with all the peo-ple of God, and
4 Bless-ing, hon-or, glo-ry, and might be to
5 For the Lamb who was slain has be-
blood set us free to be peo-ple of God. Refrain
hon-or, bless-ing, and glo-ry are His. Refrain
join in the hymn of all cre-a-tion: Stanza 4
God and the Lamb for-ev-er. A-men. Refrain
gun His reign. Al-le-lu-ia. Final Refrain
Final Refrain
This is the feast of vic-to-ry for our God.
Al-le-lu-ia, al-le-lu-ia, al-le-lu-ia.

SALUTATION and COLLECT OF THE DAY

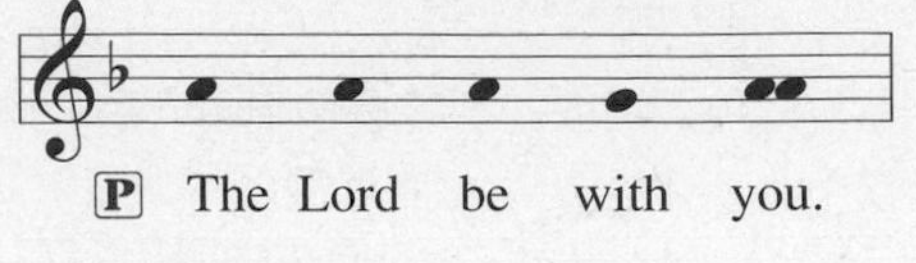

P The Lord be with you. *2 Timothy 4:22*

C **And al - so with you.**

P Let us pray.

The Collect of the Day is spoken or chanted.

C **Amen.** *OR*

C A - men.

Sit

OLD TESTAMENT or FIRST READING

After the reading:

A This is the Word of the Lord.

C **Thanks be to God.**

PSALM or GRADUAL

EPISTLE or SECOND READING

After the reading:

A This is the Word of the Lord.

C **Thanks be to God.**

Stand

ALLELUIA and VERSE

The congregation sings one of the following, or the choir may sing the appointed Verse.

Common

John 6:68

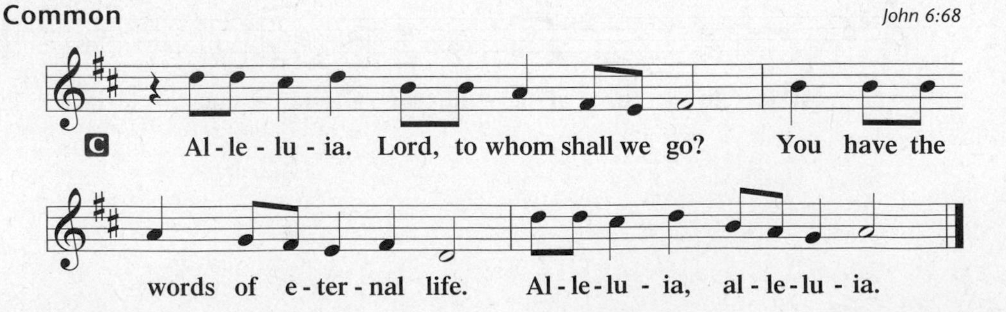

C **Al - le - lu - ia. Lord, to whom shall we go? You have the words of e - ter - nal life. Al - le - lu - ia, al - le - lu - ia.**

OR

Lent *Joel 2:13*

C Re - turn to the Lord, your God, for He is gra - cious and
mer - ci - ful, slow to an - ger, and a - bound - ing in
stead - fast love, and a - bound - ing in stead - fast love.

HOLY GOSPEL

P The Holy Gospel according to St. ________, the ________ chapter.

C Glo - ry to You, O Lord.

After the reading:

P This is the Gospel of the Lord.

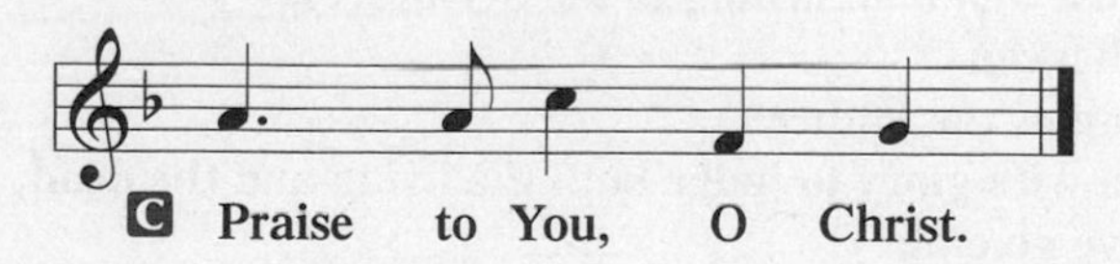
C Praise to You, O Christ.

Sola Scriptura
SCRIPTURE ALONE

The Creed *may be confessed here or after the* Sermon.

Sit

HYMN OF THE DAY

SERMON

Stand

CREED

Nicene Creed

C **I believe in one God,**
the Father Almighty,
maker of heaven and earth
and of all things visible and invisible.

And in one Lord Jesus Christ,
the only-begotten Son of God,
begotten of His Father before all worlds,
God of God, Light of Light,
very God of very God,
begotten, not made,
being of one substance with the Father,
by whom all things were made;
who for us men and for our salvation came down from heaven
and was incarnate by the Holy Spirit of the virgin Mary
and was made man;
and was crucified also for us under Pontius Pilate.
He suffered and was buried.
And the third day He rose again according to the Scriptures
and ascended into heaven
and sits at the right hand of the Father.
And He will come again with glory to judge both the living and the dead,
whose kingdom will have no end.

And I believe in the Holy Spirit,
the Lord and giver of life,
who proceeds from the Father and the Son,
who with the Father and the Son together is worshiped and glorified,
who spoke by the prophets.
And I believe in one holy Christian and apostolic Church,
I acknowledge one Baptism for the remission of sins,
and I look for the resurrection of the dead
and the life ☩ of the world to come. Amen.

Us men means all people.
Christian: the ancient text reads "catholic," meaning the whole Church as it confesses the wholeness of Christian doctrine.

OR

Apostles' Creed

C I believe in God, the Father Almighty,
maker of heaven and earth.

And in Jesus Christ, His only Son, our Lord,
who was conceived by the Holy Spirit,
born of the virgin Mary,
suffered under Pontius Pilate,
was crucified, died and was buried.
He descended into hell.
The third day He rose again from the dead.
He ascended into heaven
and sits at the right hand of God the Father Almighty.
From thence He will come to judge the living and the dead.

I believe in the Holy Spirit,
the holy Christian Church,
the communion of saints,
the forgiveness of sins,
the resurrection of the body,
and the life ☩ everlasting. Amen.

Christian: the ancient text reads "catholic," meaning the whole Church as it confesses the wholeness of Christian doctrine.

PRAYER OF THE CHURCH

[1 Timothy 2:1–4]

Following the prayers, the people may greet one another in the name of the Lord, saying, "Peace be with you," as a sign of reconciliation and of the unity of the Spirit in the bond of peace (Matt. 5:22–24; Eph. 4:1–3).

Sit

OFFERING

Stand

OFFERTORY

Psalm 116:12–13, 17–19

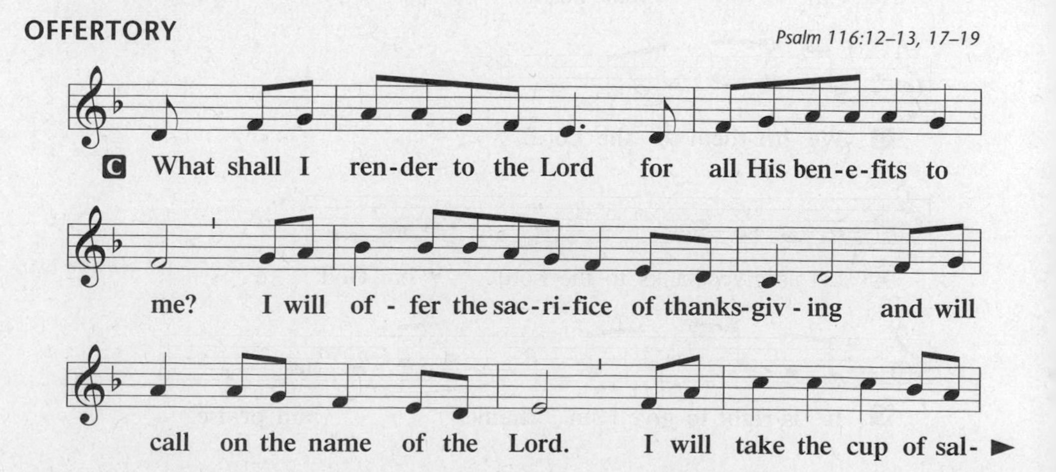
C What shall I ren-der to the Lord for all His ben-e-fits to
me? I will of - fer the sac-ri-fice of thanks-giv - ing and will
call on the name of the Lord. I will take the cup of sal- ►

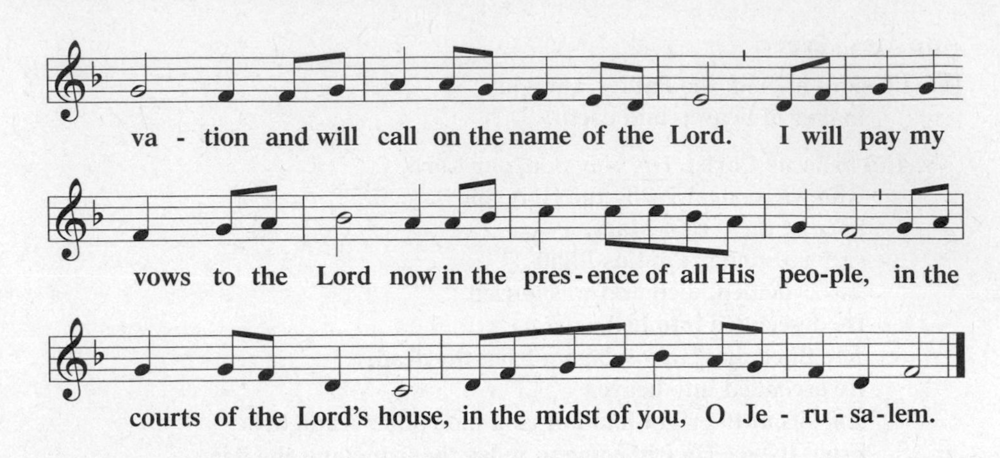
va - tion and will call on the name of the Lord. I will pay my
vows to the Lord now in the pres-ence of all His peo-ple, in the
courts of the Lord's house, in the midst of you, O Je - ru - sa-lem.

If there is no Communion, the service concludes with the LORD'S PRAYER (page 162), a concluding collect, and the BENEDICTION.

SERVICE OF THE SACRAMENT

PREFACE

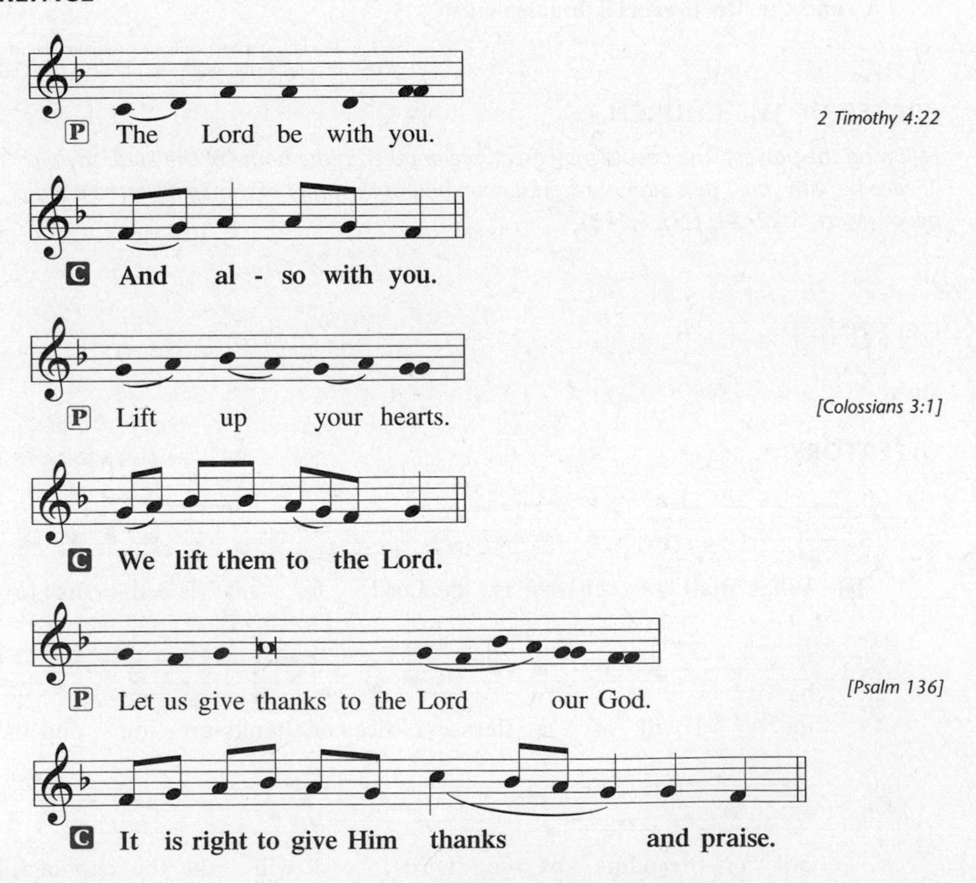
P The Lord be with you.
2 Timothy 4:22
C And al - so with you.
P Lift up your hearts.
[Colossians 3:1]
C We lift them to the Lord.
P Let us give thanks to the Lord our God.
[Psalm 136]
C It is right to give Him thanks and praise.

The Proper Preface *appropriate to the day or season is spoken or chanted:*

P It is truly good, right, and salutary . . . evermore praising You and saying:

SANCTUS ~ *Holy, Holy, Holy*

Isaiah 6:3; Matthew 21:9

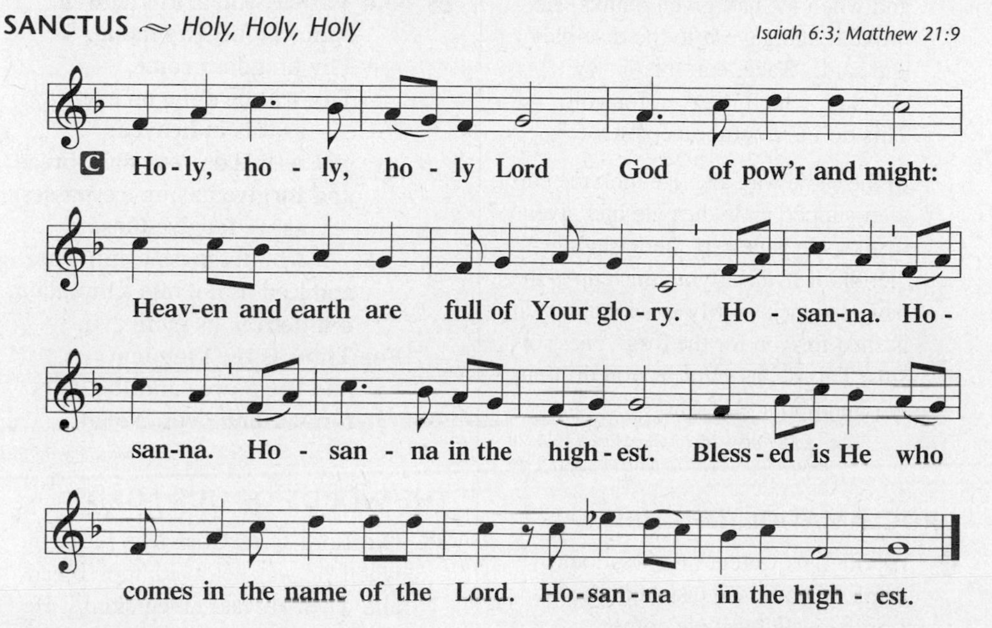
C Ho-ly, ho - ly, ho - ly Lord God of pow'r and might:
Heav-en and earth are full of Your glo-ry. Ho - san-na. Ho -
san-na. Ho - san - na in the high-est. Bless-ed is He who
comes in the name of the Lord. Ho-san-na in the high - est.

Hosanna is a Hebrew word of praise meaning "save us now."

PRAYER OF THANKSGIVING

P Blessed are You, Lord of heaven and earth, for You have had mercy on those whom You created and sent Your only-begotten Son into our flesh to bear our sin and be our Savior. With repentant joy we receive the salvation accomplished for us by the all-availing sacrifice of His body and His blood on the cross.

Gathered in the name and the remembrance of Jesus, we beg You, O Lord, to forgive, renew, and strengthen us with Your Word and Spirit. Grant us faithfully to eat His body and drink His blood as He bids us do in His own testament. Gather us together, we pray, from the ends of the earth to celebrate with all the faithful the marriage feast of the Lamb in His kingdom, which has no end. Graciously receive our prayers; deliver and preserve us. To You alone, O Father, be all glory, honor, and worship, with the Son and the Holy Spirit, one God, now and forever. (401)

C **Amen.**

THE WORDS OF OUR LORD

P Our Lord Jesus Christ, on the night when He was betrayed, took bread, and when He had given thanks, He broke it and gave it to the disciples and said: "Take, eat; this is My ☩ body, which is given for you. This do in remembrance of Me."

In the same way also He took the cup after supper, and when He had given thanks, He gave it to them, saying: "Drink of it, all of you; this cup is the new testament in My ☩ blood, which is shed for you for the forgiveness of sins. This do, as often as you drink it, in remembrance of Me."

Matthew 26:26–28; Mark 14:22–24
Luke 22:19–20; 1 Corinthians 11:23–25

PROCLAMATION OF CHRIST

P As often as we eat this bread and drink this cup, we proclaim the Lord's death until He comes.

1 Corinthians 11:26

C **Amen. Come, Lord Jesus.**

Revelation 22:20

P O Lord Jesus Christ, only Son of the Father, in giving us Your body and blood to eat and to drink, You lead us to remember and confess Your holy cross and passion, Your blessed death, Your rest in the tomb, Your resurrection from the dead, Your ascension into heaven, and Your coming for the final judgment. So remember us in Your kingdom and teach us to pray:

LORD'S PRAYER

C **Our Father who art in heaven,**
hallowed be Thy name,
Thy kingdom come,
Thy will be done on earth
as it is in heaven;
give us this day our daily bread;
and forgive us our trespasses

LORD'S PRAYER

P Lord, remember us in Your kingdom and teach us to pray:

C **Our Father who art in heaven,**
hallowed be Thy name,
Thy kingdom come,
Thy will be done on earth
as it is in heaven;
give us this day our daily bread;
and forgive us our trespasses
as we forgive those
who trespass against us;
and lead us not into temptation,
but deliver us from evil.
For Thine is the kingdom
and the power and the glory
forever and ever. Amen.

Matthew 6:9–13

THE WORDS OF OUR LORD

P Our Lord Jesus Christ, on the night when He was betrayed, took bread, and when He had given thanks, He broke it and gave it to the disciples and said: "Take, eat; this is My ☩ body, which is given for you. This do in remembrance of Me."

In the same way also He took the cup after supper, and when He had given thanks, He gave it to them, saying: "Drink of it, all of you; this cup is the new testament in My ☩ blood, which is shed for you for the forgiveness of sins. This do, as often as you drink it, in remembrance of Me."

Matthew 26:26–28; Mark 14:22–24
Luke 22:19–20; 1 Corinthians 11:23–25

The service continues with the PAX DOMINI on the following page.

as we forgive those
who trespass against us;
and lead us not into temptation,
but deliver us from evil.
For Thine is the kingdom
and the power and the glory
forever and ever. Amen.

Matthew 6:9–13

PAX DOMINI ~ *The Peace of the Lord*

John 20:19

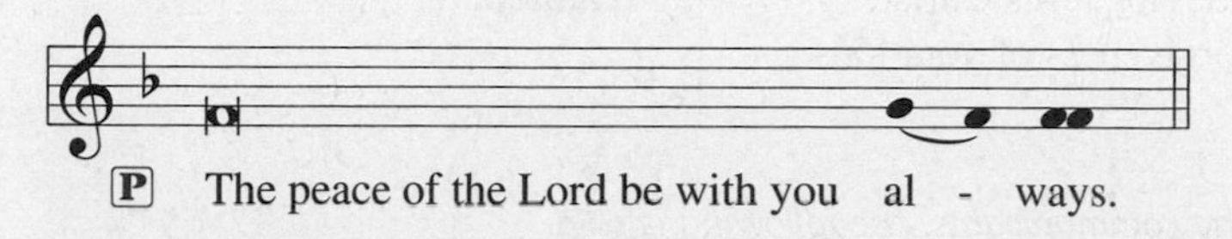
P The peace of the Lord be with you al - ways.

C A - men.

AGNUS DEI ~ *Lamb of God*

John 1:29

C Lamb of God, You take a - way the sin of the world; have
mer-cy on us. Lamb of God, You take a - way the sin of the
world; have mer-cy on us. Lamb of God, You take a - way the
sin of the world; grant us peace.

Sit

DISTRIBUTION

The pastor and those who assist him receive the body and blood of Christ first and then distribute them to those who come to receive, saying:

Take, eat; this is the true body of our Lord and Savior Jesus Christ, given into death for your sins.
Amen.

Take, drink; this is the true blood of our Lord and Savior Jesus Christ, shed for the forgiveness of your sins.
Amen.

The true body of Christ, given for you.
Amen.

The true blood of Christ, shed for you.
Amen.

In dismissing the communicants, the following is said:

P The body and blood of our Lord Jesus Christ strengthen and preserve you in body and soul to life everlasting. Depart ☩ in peace.

C **Amen.**

Stand

POST-COMMUNION CANTICLE

One of the following canticles or an appropriate hymn is sung. During Lent, "Thank the Lord" is not sung.

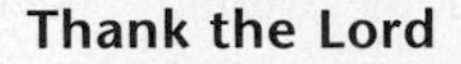

Thank the Lord

[Psalm 105:1–3, 42–43; 1 Chronicles 16:8–10]

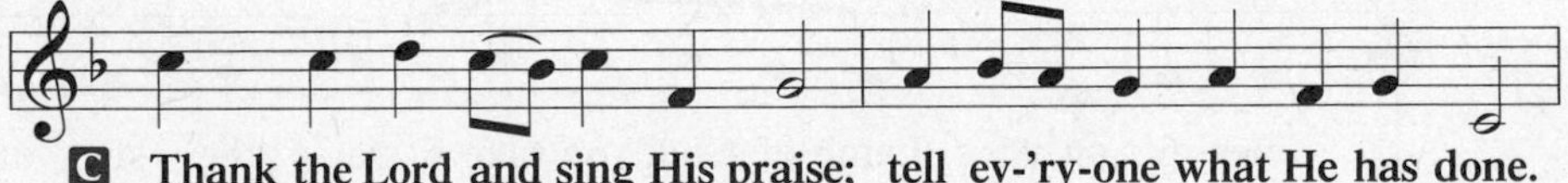
C Thank the Lord and sing His praise; tell ev-'ry-one what He has done.

Let all who seek the Lord re - joice and proud-ly bear His name.

He re-calls His prom-is - es and leads His peo-ple forth in joy

with shouts of thanks-giv-ing. Al-le-lu - ia, al-le-lu - ia.

OR

Nunc Dimittis ~ *Song of Simeon* *Luke 2:29–32*

C Lord, now You let Your ser-vant go in peace; Your word has been ful-
filled. My own eyes have seen the sal - va-tion which You have pre -
pared in the sight of ev - 'ry peo - ple: A light to re -
veal You to the na-tions and the glo-ry of Your peo-ple Is - ra - el.
Glo-ry be to the Fa-ther and to the Son and to the Ho-ly Spir-it;
as it was in the be-gin-ning, is now, and will be for-ev-er. A - men.

Nunc Dimittis
SONG OF SIMEON

POST-COMMUNION COLLECT

A Let us pray.

A We give thanks to You, almighty God, that You have refreshed us through this salutary gift, and we implore You that of Your mercy You would strengthen us through the same in faith toward You and in fervent love toward one another; through Jesus Christ, Your Son, our Lord, who lives and reigns with You and the Holy Spirit, one God, now and forever. (402)

O God the Father, the fountain and source of all goodness, who in loving-kindness sent Your only-begotten Son into the flesh, we thank You that for His sake You have given us pardon and peace in this Sacrament, and we ask You not to forsake Your children but always to rule our hearts and minds by Your Holy Spirit that we may be enabled constantly to serve You; through Jesus Christ, Your Son, our Lord, who lives and reigns with You and the Holy Spirit, one God, now and forever. (403)

Gracious God, our heavenly Father, You have given us a foretaste of the feast to come in the Holy Supper of Your Son's body and blood. Keep us firm in the true faith throughout our days of pilgrimage that, on the day of His coming, we may, together with all Your saints, celebrate the marriage feast of the Lamb in His kingdom which has no end; through Jesus Christ, Your Son, our Lord, who lives and reigns with You and the Holy Spirit, one God, now and forever. (404)

C **Amen.** *OR*

C A - men.

BENEDICTION

Numbers 6:24–26

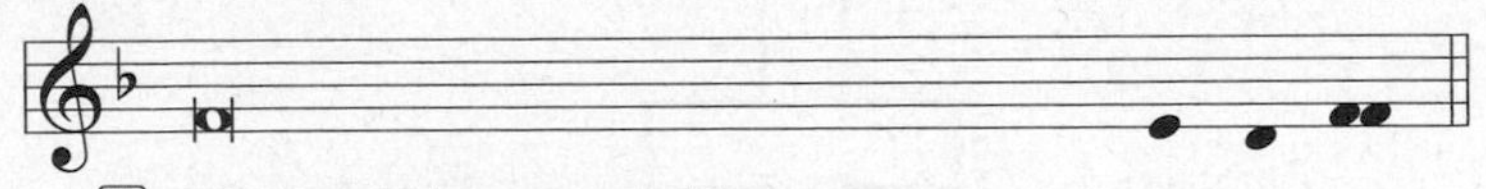

P The Lord bless you and keep you.
The Lord make His face shine on you
and be gracious to you.
The Lord look upon you with favor and ✝ give you peace.

C A - men.

DIVINE SERVICE
Setting Two

CONFESSION AND ABSOLUTION

A Hymn of Invocation may be sung.

Stand

The sign of the cross ☩ may be made by all in remembrance of their Baptism.

P In the name of the Father and of the ☩ Son and of the Holy Spirit.
C **Amen.** *Matthew 28:19b; [18:20]*

P If we say we have no sin, we deceive ourselves, and the truth is not in us.
C **But if we confess our sins, God, who is faithful and just, will forgive our sins and cleanse us from all unrighteousness.** *1 John 1:8–9*

Kneel/Stand

Silence for reflection on God's Word and for self-examination.

P Let us then confess our sins to God our Father.
C **Most merciful God, we confess that we are by nature sinful and unclean. We have sinned against You in thought, word, and deed, by what we have done and by what we have left undone. We have not loved You with our whole heart; we have not loved our neighbors as ourselves. We justly deserve Your present and eternal punishment. For the sake of Your Son, Jesus Christ, have mercy on us. Forgive us, renew us, and lead us, so that we may delight in Your will and walk in Your ways to the glory of Your holy name. Amen.**

P Almighty God in His mercy has given His Son to die for you and for His sake forgives you all your sins. As a called and ordained servant of Christ, and by His authority, I therefore forgive you all your sins in the name of the Father and of the ☩ Son and of the Holy Spirit. *[John 20:19–23]*
C **Amen.**

P In the mercy of almighty God, Jesus Christ was given to die for us, and for His sake God forgives us all our sins. To those who believe in Jesus Christ He gives the power to become the children of God and bestows on them the Holy Spirit. May the Lord, who has begun this good work in us, bring it to completion in the day of our Lord Jesus Christ.
John 1:12; Philippians 1:6
C **Amen.**

Stand

SERVICE OF THE WORD

INTROIT, PSALM, or ENTRANCE HYMN

KYRIE ~ *Lord, Have Mercy*

Mark 10:47

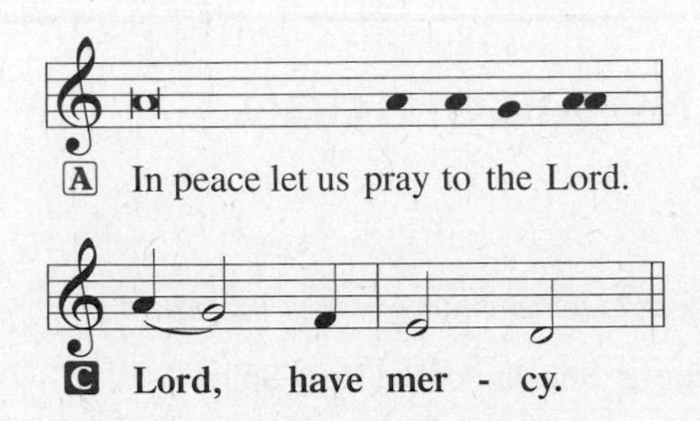
A In peace let us pray to the Lord.
C Lord, have mer - cy.

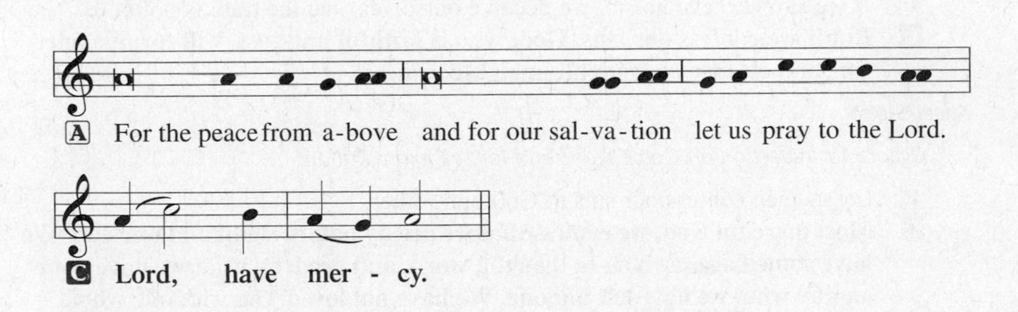
A For the peace from a-bove and for our sal-va-tion let us pray to the Lord.
C Lord, have mer - cy.

A For the peace of the whole world, for the well-being of the Church of God,
and for the uni-ty of all let us pray to the Lord.
C Lord, have mer - cy.

A For this holy house and for all who offer here their wor - ship and praise
let us pray to the Lord.
C Lord, have mer - cy.

A Help, save, comfort, and de - fend us, gra - cious Lord.
C A - men.

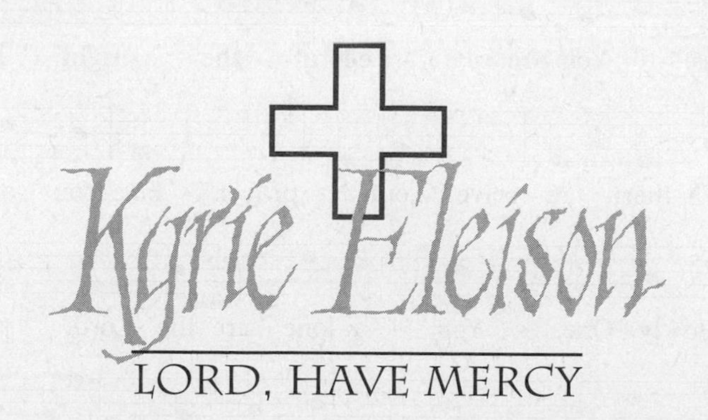
Kyrie Eleison
LORD, HAVE MERCY

HYMN OF PRAISE

During Advent and Lent, the Hymn of Praise is omitted.

Gloria in Excelsis ~ *Glory to God in the Highest* — *Luke 2:14; John 1:29*

A
Glo-ry to God in the high-est, and peace to His peo-ple on earth.
C
Lord God, heav-en-ly king, al-might-y God and
Fa-ther: We wor-ship You, we give You thanks, we
praise You for Your glo-ry. Lord Je-sus Christ, on-ly
Son of the Fa-ther, Lord God, Lamb of God: You
take a-way the sin of the world; have mer-cy on
us. You are seat-ed at the right hand of the
Fa-ther; re-ceive our prayer. For You a-lone are the
Ho-ly One, You a-lone are the Lord, You a-
lone are the Most High, Je-sus Christ, with the Ho-ly Spir-it,
in the glo-ry of God the Fa-ther. A-men.

The service continues with the Salutation on page 172.

OR

This Is the Feast

Revelation 5:12–13; 19:5–9

A This is the feast of vic-to-ry for our God. Al-le-lu-ia.
C Wor-thy is Christ, the Lamb who was slain,
whose blood set us free to be peo-ple of God.
Pow-er and rich-es and wis-dom and strength and
hon-or and bless-ing and glo-ry are His.
This is the feast of vic-to-ry for our God. Al-le-
lu-ia. Sing with all the peo-ple of
God, and join in the hymn of all cre-a-tion:
Bless-ing and hon-or and glo-ry and might be to
God and the Lamb for-ev-er. A-men.

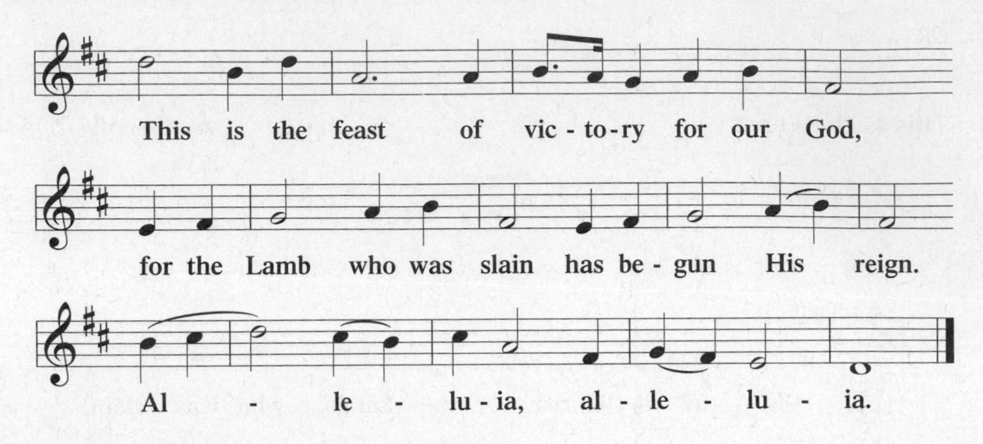
This is the feast of vic - to - ry for our God,
for the Lamb who was slain has be - gun His reign.
Al - le - lu - ia, al - le - lu - ia.

SALUTATION and COLLECT OF THE DAY

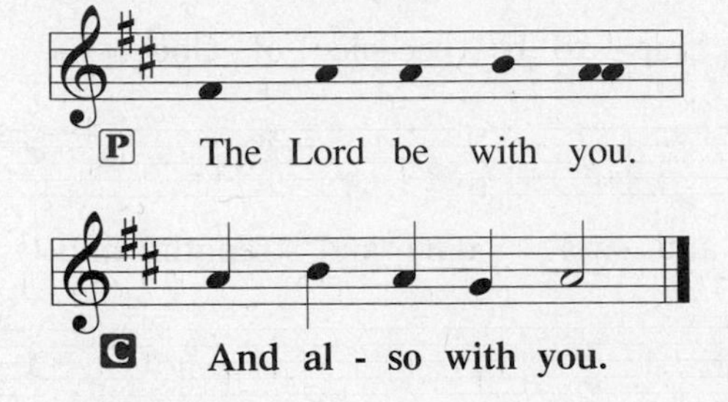
P The Lord be with you.
C And al - so with you.

2 Timothy 4:22

P Let us pray.

The Collect of the Day is spoken or chanted.

C **Amen.** *OR*

C A - men.

Sit

OLD TESTAMENT or FIRST READING

After the reading:

A This is the Word of the Lord.

C **Thanks be to God.**

PSALM or GRADUAL

EPISTLE or SECOND READING

After the reading:

A This is the Word of the Lord.

C **Thanks be to God.**

Stand

ALLELUIA and VERSE

The congregation sings one of the following, or the choir may sing the appointed Verse.

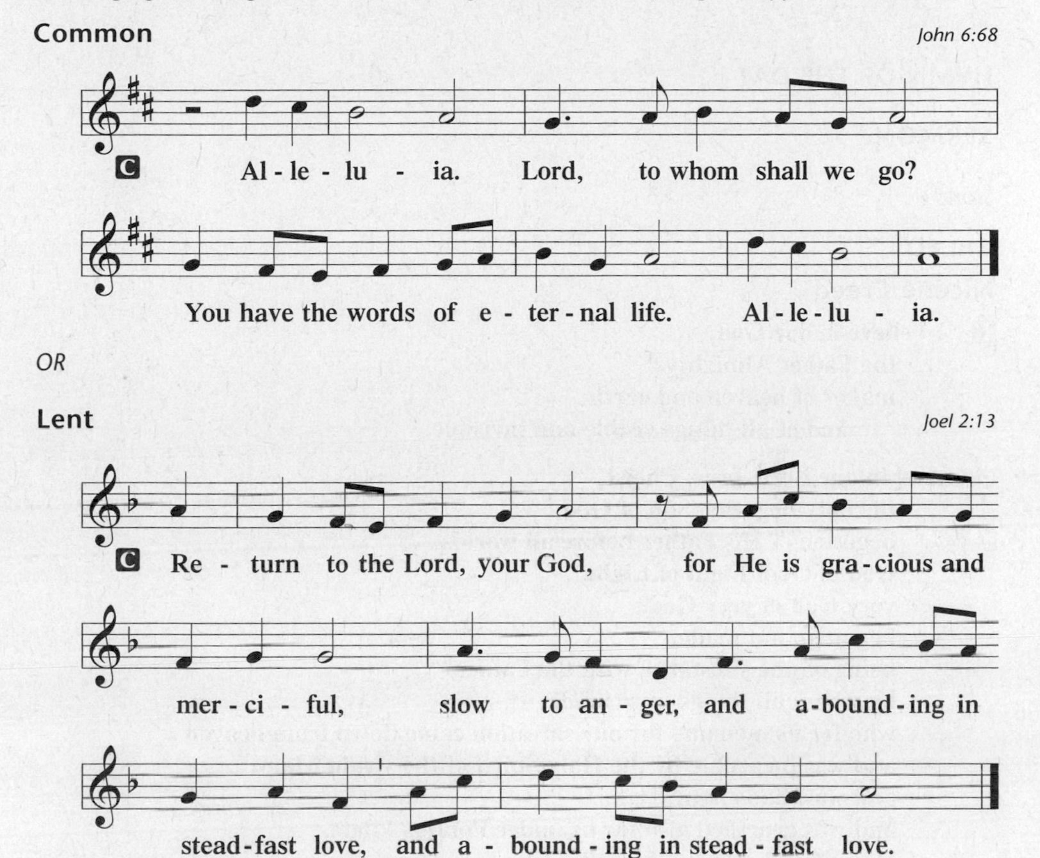
Common
John 6:68
C Al - le - lu - ia. Lord, to whom shall we go?
You have the words of e - ter - nal life. Al - le - lu - ia.
OR
Lent
Joel 2:13
C Re - turn to the Lord, your God, for He is gra - cious and
mer - ci - ful, slow to an - ger, and a - bound - ing in
stead - fast love, and a - bound - ing in stead - fast love.

HOLY GOSPEL

P The Holy Gospel according to St. _______, the _______ chapter.

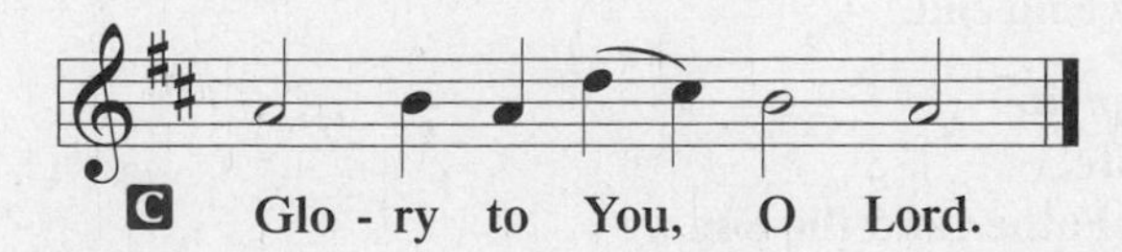
C Glo - ry to You, O Lord.

After the reading:

P This is the Gospel of the Lord.

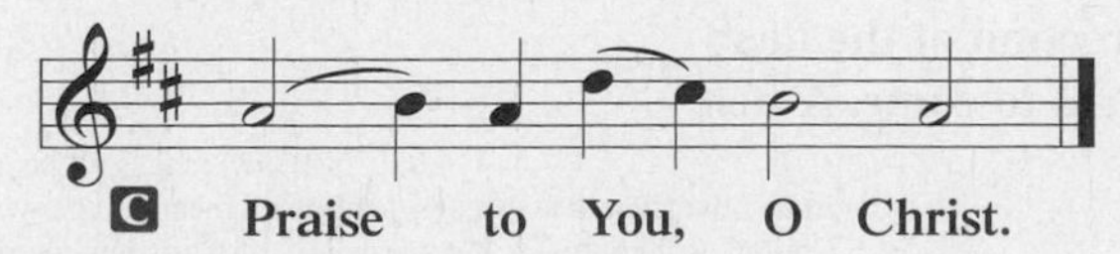
C Praise to You, O Christ.

The Creed may be confessed here or after the Sermon.

Sit

HYMN OF THE DAY

SERMON

Stand

CREED

Nicene Creed

C **I believe in one God,**
the Father Almighty,
maker of heaven and earth
and of all things visible and invisible.

And in one Lord Jesus Christ,
the only-begotten Son of God,
begotten of His Father before all worlds,
God of God, Light of Light,
very God of very God,
begotten, not made,
being of one substance with the Father,
by whom all things were made;
who for us men and for our salvation came down from heaven
and was incarnate by the Holy Spirit of the virgin Mary
and was made man;
and was crucified also for us under Pontius Pilate.
He suffered and was buried.
And the third day He rose again according to the Scriptures
and ascended into heaven
and sits at the right hand of the Father.
And He will come again with glory to judge both the living and the dead,
whose kingdom will have no end.

And I believe in the Holy Spirit,
the Lord and giver of life,
who proceeds from the Father and the Son,
who with the Father and the Son together is worshiped and glorified,
who spoke by the prophets.
And I believe in one holy Christian and apostolic Church,
I acknowledge one Baptism for the remission of sins,
and I look for the resurrection of the dead
and the life ☩ of the world to come. Amen.

Us men means all people.
Christian: the ancient text reads "catholic," meaning the whole Church as it confesses the wholeness of Christian doctrine.

OR

Apostles' Creed

C **I believe in God, the Father Almighty,**
maker of heaven and earth.

And in Jesus Christ, His only Son, our Lord,
who was conceived by the Holy Spirit,
born of the virgin Mary,
suffered under Pontius Pilate,
was crucified, died and was buried.
He descended into hell.
The third day He rose again from the dead.
He ascended into heaven
and sits at the right hand of God the Father Almighty.
From thence He will come to judge the living and the dead.

I believe in the Holy Spirit,
the holy Christian Church,
the communion of saints,
the forgiveness of sins,
the resurrection of the body,
and the life ☩ everlasting. Amen.

Christian: the ancient text reads "catholic," meaning the whole Church as it confesses the wholeness of Christian doctrine.

PRAYER OF THE CHURCH

[1 Timothy 2:1–4]

Following the prayers, the people may greet one another in the name of the Lord, saying, "Peace be with you," as a sign of reconciliation and of the unity of the Spirit in the bond of peace (Matt. 5:22–24; Eph. 4:1–3).

Sit

OFFERING

Deo Gratias
THANKS BE TO GOD

Stand

OFFERTORY

Psalm 116:12–13, 17–19

C
What shall I ren - der to the Lord for all His ben - e-fits to
me? I will of - fer the sac - ri - fice of thanks - giv - ing and will
call on the name of the Lord. I will take the cup of sal-
va - tion and will call on the name of the Lord. I will pay my
vows to the Lord now in the pres - ence of all His peo - ple, in the
courts of the Lord's house, in the midst of you, O Je - ru - sa - lem.

If there is no Communion, the service concludes with the Lord's Prayer *(page 179), a concluding collect, and the* Benediction.

SERVICE OF THE SACRAMENT

PREFACE

P The Lord be with you.
C And al-so with you.

2 Timothy 4:22

P Lift up your hearts.
C We lift them to the Lord.

[Colossians 3:1]

P Let us give thanks to the Lord our God.
C It is right to give Him thanks and praise.

[Psalm 136]

The Proper Preface *appropriate to the day or season is spoken or chanted:*

P It is truly good, right, and salutary . . . evermore praising You and saying:

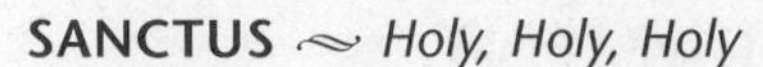

SANCTUS ~ *Holy, Holy, Holy*

Isaiah 6:3; Matthew 21:9

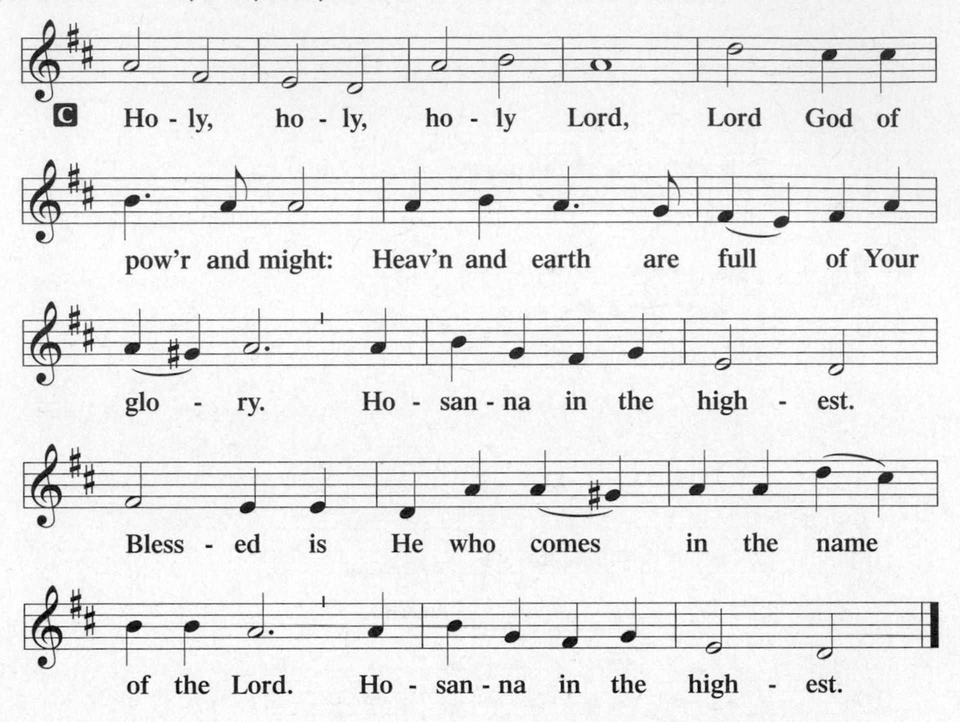

C Ho - ly, ho - ly, ho - ly Lord, Lord God of
pow'r and might: Heav'n and earth are full of Your
glo - ry. Ho - san - na in the high - est.
Bless - ed is He who comes in the name
of the Lord. Ho - san - na in the high - est.

Hosanna is a Hebrew word of praise meaning "save us now."

PRAYER OF THANKSGIVING

P Blessed are You, Lord of heaven and earth, for You have had mercy on those whom You created and sent Your only-begotten Son into our flesh to bear our sin and be our Savior. With repentant joy we receive the salvation accomplished for us by the all-availing sacrifice of His body and His blood on the cross.

Gathered in the name and the remembrance of Jesus, we beg You, O Lord, to forgive, renew, and strengthen us with Your Word and Spirit. Grant us faithfully to eat His body and drink His blood as He bids us do in His own testament. Gather us together, we pray, from the ends of the earth to celebrate with all the faithful the marriage feast of the Lamb in His kingdom, which has no end. Graciously receive our prayers; deliver and preserve us. To You alone, O Father, be all glory, honor, and worship, with the Son and the Holy Spirit, one God, now and forever. (401)

C **Amen.**

THE WORDS OF OUR LORD

P Our Lord Jesus Christ, on the night when He was betrayed, took bread, and when He had given thanks, He broke it and gave it to the disciples and said: "Take, eat; this is My ☩ body, which is given for you. This do in remembrance of Me."

In the same way also He took the cup after supper, and when He had given thanks, He gave it to them, saying: "Drink of it, all of you; this cup is the new testament in My ☩ blood, which is shed for you for the forgiveness of sins. This do, as often as you drink it, in remembrance of Me."

Matthew 26:26–28; Mark 14:22–24
Luke 22:19–20; 1 Corinthians 11:23–25

PROCLAMATION OF CHRIST

P As often as we eat this bread and drink this cup, we proclaim the Lord's death until He comes.

1 Corinthians 11:26

C **Amen. Come, Lord Jesus.**

Revelation 22:20

P O Lord Jesus Christ, only Son of the Father, in giving us Your body and blood to eat and to drink, You lead us to remember and confess Your holy cross and passion, Your blessed death, Your rest in the tomb, Your resurrection from the dead, Your ascension into heaven, and Your coming for the final judgment. So remember us in Your kingdom and teach us to pray:

LORD'S PRAYER

C **Our Father who art in heaven,**
hallowed be Thy name,
Thy kingdom come,
Thy will be done on earth
as it is in heaven;
give us this day our daily bread;
and forgive us our trespasses

LORD'S PRAYER

P Lord, remember us in Your kingdom and teach us to pray:

C **Our Father who art in heaven,**
hallowed be Thy name,
Thy kingdom come,
Thy will be done on earth
as it is in heaven;
give us this day our daily bread;
and forgive us our trespasses
as we forgive those
who trespass against us;
and lead us not into temptation,
but deliver us from evil.
For Thine is the kingdom
and the power and the glory
forever and ever. Amen.

Matthew 6:9–13

THE WORDS OF OUR LORD

P Our Lord Jesus Christ, on the night when He was betrayed, took bread, and when He had given thanks, He broke it and gave it to the disciples and said: "Take, eat; this is My ☩ body, which is given for you. This do in remembrance of Me."

In the same way also He took the cup after supper, and when He had given thanks, He gave it to them, saying: "Drink of it, all of you; this cup is the new testament in My ☩ blood, which is shed for you for the forgiveness of sins. This do, as often as you drink it, in remembrance of Me."

Matthew 26:26–28; Mark 14:22–24
Luke 22:19–20; 1 Corinthians 11:23–25

The service continues with the PAX DOMINI on the following page.

as we forgive those
who trespass against us;
and lead us not into temptation,
but deliver us from evil.
For Thine is the kingdom
and the power and the glory
forever and ever. Amen.

Matthew 6:9–13

PAX DOMINI ~ *The Peace of the Lord*

John 20:19

P The peace of the Lord be with you al - ways.
C A - men.

AGNUS DEI ~ *Lamb of God*

John 1:29

C Lamb of God, You take a-way the sin of the world;
have mer-cy on us. Lamb of God, You take a-way the
sin of the world; have mer-cy on us. Lamb of
God, You take a-way the sin of the world;
grant us peace, grant us peace.

Sit

DISTRIBUTION

The pastor and those who assist him receive the body and blood of Christ first and then distribute them to those who come to receive, saying:

Take, eat; this is the true body of our Lord and Savior Jesus Christ, given into death for your sins.
Amen.

Take, drink; this is the true blood of our Lord and Savior Jesus Christ, shed for the forgiveness of your sins.
Amen.

The true body of Christ, given for you.
Amen.

The true blood of Christ, shed for you.
Amen.

In dismissing the communicants, the following is said:

P The body and blood of our Lord Jesus Christ strengthen and preserve you in body and soul to life everlasting. Depart ☩ in peace.

C **Amen.**

Stand

POST-COMMUNION CANTICLE

One of the following canticles or an appropriate hymn is sung. During Lent, "Thank the Lord" is not sung.

Thank the Lord

[Psalm 105:1–3, 42–43; 1 Chronicles 16:8–10]

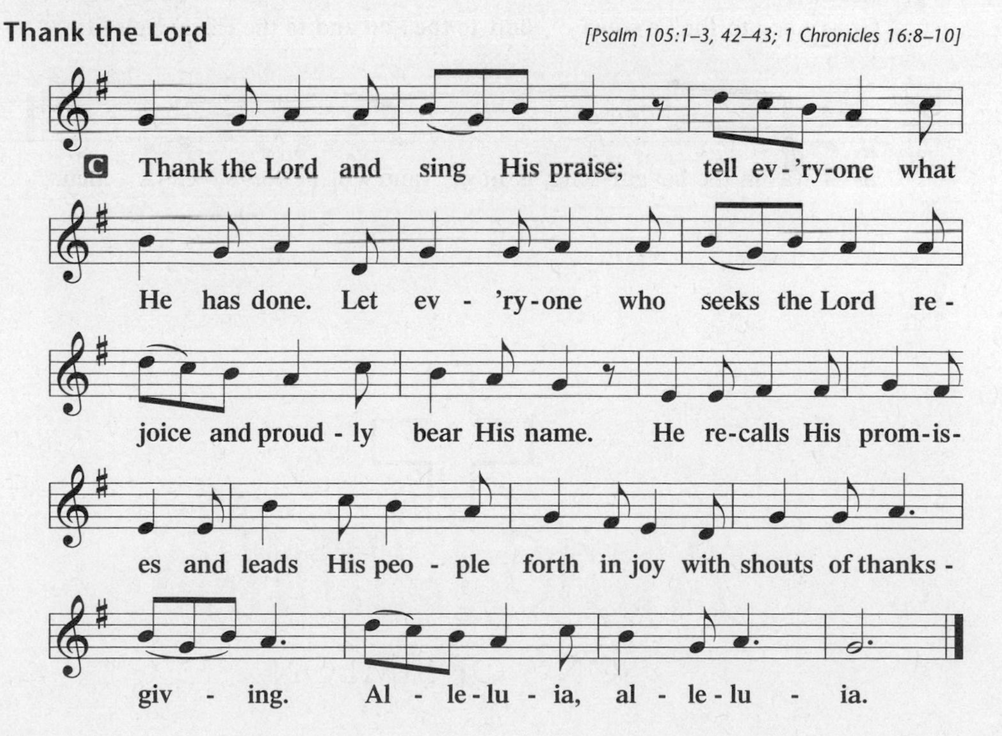
C Thank the Lord and sing His praise; tell ev - 'ry-one what
He has done. Let ev - 'ry-one who seeks the Lord re -
joice and proud - ly bear His name. He re-calls His prom-is-
es and leads His peo - ple forth in joy with shouts of thanks -
giv - ing. Al - le-lu - ia, al - le-lu - ia.

OR

Nunc Dimittis ~ *Song of Simeon* *Luke 2:29–32*

C Lord, now You let Your ser-vant go in peace; Your word has been ful -
filled. My own eyes have seen the sal - va-tion which You have pre -
pared in the sight of ev - 'ry peo - ple: A light to re -
veal You to the na-tions and the glo-ry of Your peo-ple Is - ra - el.
Glo-ry be to the Fa - ther and to the Son and to the Ho-ly Spir - it;
as it was in the be - gin - ning, is now, and will be for - ev - er. A - men.

Nunc Dimittis
SONG OF SIMEON

POST-COMMUNION COLLECT

A Let us pray.

A We give thanks to You, almighty God, that You have refreshed us through this salutary gift, and we implore You that of Your mercy You would strengthen us through the same in faith toward You and in fervent love toward one another; through Jesus Christ, Your Son, our Lord, who lives and reigns with You and the Holy Spirit, one God, now and forever. (402)

O God the Father, the fountain and source of all goodness, who in loving-kindness sent Your only-begotten Son into the flesh, we thank You that for His sake You have given us pardon and peace in this Sacrament, and we ask You not to forsake Your children but always to rule our hearts and minds by Your Holy Spirit that we may be enabled constantly to serve You; through Jesus Christ, Your Son, our Lord, who lives and reigns with You and the Holy Spirit, one God, now and forever. (403)

Gracious God, our heavenly Father, You have given us a foretaste of the feast to come in the Holy Supper of Your Son's body and blood. Keep us firm in the true faith throughout our days of pilgrimage that, on the day of His coming, we may, together with all Your saints, celebrate the marriage feast of the Lamb in His kingdom which has no end; through Jesus Christ, Your Son, our Lord, who lives and reigns with You and the Holy Spirit, one God, now and forever. (404)

C **Amen.** *OR*

C A - men.

BENEDICTION

Numbers 6:24–26

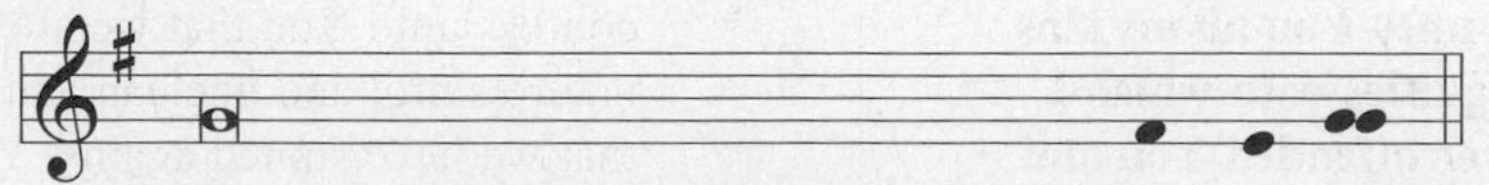

P The Lord bless you and keep you.
The Lord make His face shine on you
and be gracious to you.
The Lord look upon you with favor and ☩ give you peace.

C A - men.

DIVINE SERVICE

Setting Three

CONFESSION AND ABSOLUTION

A Hymn of Invocation may be sung.

Stand

The sign of the cross ☩ may be made by all in remembrance of their Baptism.

P In the name of the Father and of the ☩ Son and of the Holy Spirit.
C **Amen.** *Matthew 28:19b; [18:20]*

P Beloved in the Lord! Let us draw near with a true heart and confess our sins unto God our Father, beseeching Him in the name of our Lord Jesus Christ to grant us forgiveness. *[Hebrews 10:22]*

P Our help is in the name of the Lord,
C **who made heaven and earth.** *Psalm 124:8*
P I said, I will confess my transgressions unto the Lord,
C **and You forgave the iniquity of my sin.** *Psalm 32:5*

Kneel/Stand

Silence for reflection on God's Word and for self-examination.

P O almighty God, merciful Father,
C **I, a poor, miserable sinner, confess unto You all my sins and iniquities with which I have ever offended You and justly deserved Your temporal and eternal punishment. But I am heartily sorry for them and sincerely repent of them, and I pray You of Your boundless mercy and for the sake of the holy, innocent, bitter sufferings and death of Your beloved Son, Jesus Christ, to be gracious and merciful to me, a poor, sinful being.**

P Almighty God, our maker and redeemer, we poor sinners confess unto You that we are by nature sinful and unclean and that we have sinned against You by thought, word, and deed. Wherefore we flee for refuge to Your infinite mercy, seeking and imploring Your grace for the sake of our Lord Jesus Christ.

C **O most merciful God, who has given Your only-begotten Son to die for us, have mercy upon us and for His sake grant us remission of all our sins; and by Your Holy**

P Upon this your confession, I, by virtue of my office, as a called and ordained servant of the Word, announce the grace of God unto all of you, and in the stead and by the command of my Lord Jesus Christ I forgive you all your sins in the name of the Father and of the ☩ Son and of the Holy Spirit. *[John 20:19–23]*

C **Amen.**

Spirit increase in us true knowledge of You and of Your will and true obedience to Your Word, to the end that by Your grace we may come to everlasting life; through Jesus Christ, our Lord. Amen.

P Almighty God, our heavenly Father, has had mercy upon us and has given His only Son to die for us and for His sake forgives us all our sins. To those who believe on His name He gives power to become the children of God and has promised them His Holy Spirit. He that believes and is baptized shall be saved. Grant this, Lord, unto us all.

Mark 16:16; John 1:12

C **Amen.**

Stand

Sola Gratia
GRACE ALONE

SERVICE OF THE WORD

INTROIT, PSALM, or ENTRANCE HYMN

When the INTROIT is used, the following Gloria Patri may be sung.

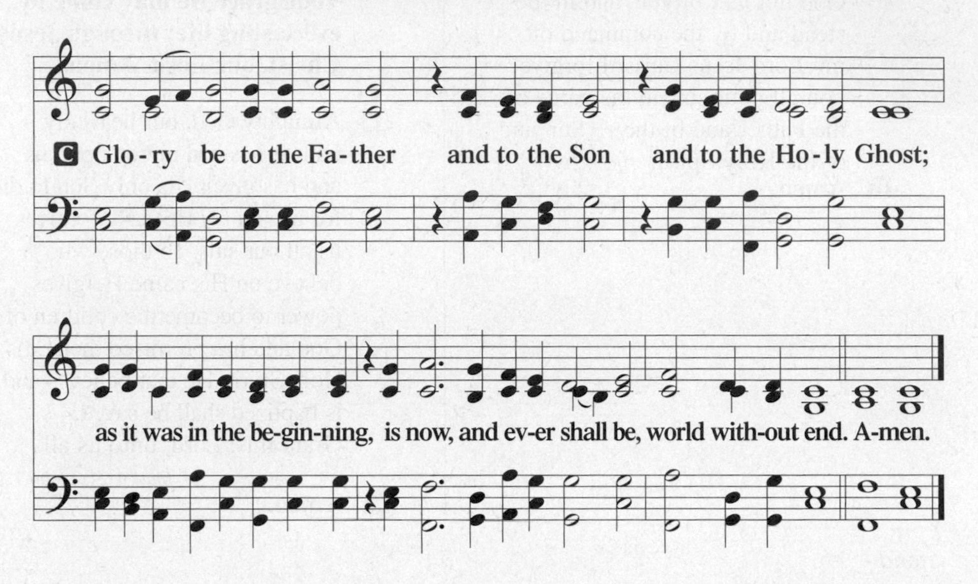

C Glo-ry be to the Fa-ther and to the Son and to the Ho-ly Ghost;
as it was in the be-gin-ning, is now, and ev-er shall be, world with-out end. A-men.

KYRIE ~ *Lord, Have Mercy*

Mark 10:47

C Lord, have mer-cy up-on us. Christ, have mer-cy upon us. Lord, have mer-cy up-on us.

GLORIA IN EXCELSIS ~ *Glory to God in the Highest*

Luke 2:14; John 1:29

During Advent and Lent, the Gloria in Excelsis *is omitted.*

P Glory be to God on high: C and on earth peace, good - will toward
men. We praise Thee, we bless Thee, we wor - ship Thee,
we glorify Thee, we give thanks to Thee, for Thy great glory.
O Lord God, heav'n - ly King, God the Fa - ther Al - mighty.
O Lord, the only - begotten Son, Je - sus Christ;

O Lord God, Lamb of God, Son of the Father,
that takest away the sin of the world, have mercy up-on us.
Thou that takest away the sin of the world, re-ceive our prayer.
Thou that sittest at the right hand of God the Father, have mercy up-
on us. For Thou only art holy; Thou on-ly art the Lord.

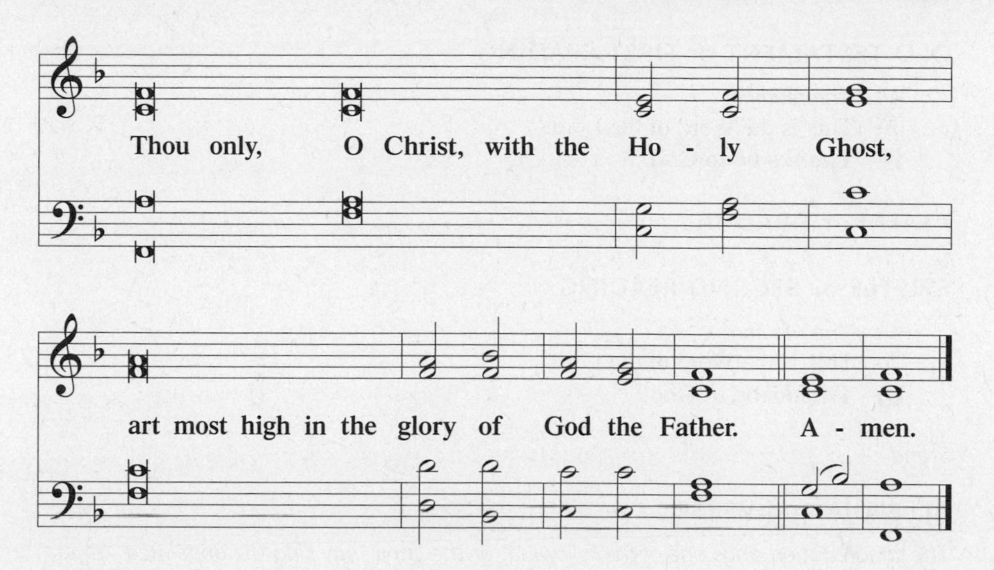
Thou only, O Christ, with the Ho - ly Ghost,
art most high in the glory of God the Father. A - men.

SALUTATION and COLLECT OF THE DAY

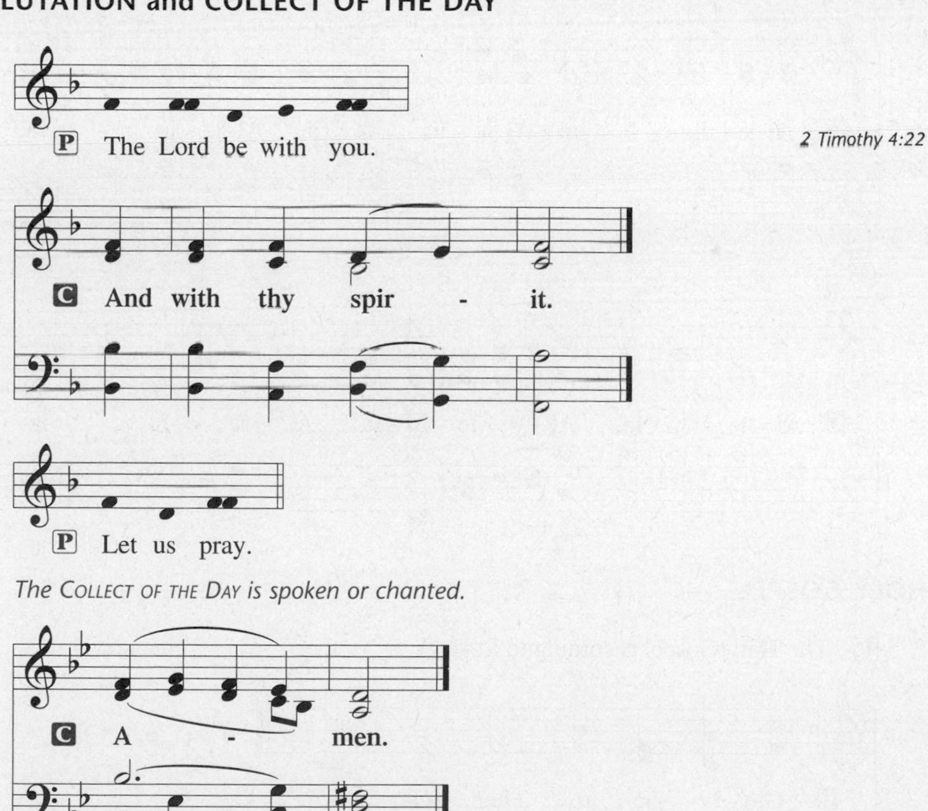
P The Lord be with you.
2 Timothy 4:22
C And with thy spir - it.
P Let us pray.
C A - men.

The COLLECT OF THE DAY *is spoken or chanted.*

Sit

OLD TESTAMENT or FIRST READING

After the reading:

A This is the Word of the Lord.

C **Thanks be to God.**

PSALM or GRADUAL

EPISTLE or SECOND READING

After the reading:

A This is the Word of the Lord.

C **Thanks be to God.**

Stand

ALLELUIA and VERSE

The congregation sings one of the following, or the choir may sing the appointed VERSE. During Lent, the ALLELUIA is omitted.

C Al-le - lu - ia. Al-le - lu - ia. Al-le - lu - ia.
OR
C Al - le - lu - ia. Al - le - lu - ia. Al - le - lu - ia.

HOLY GOSPEL

P The Holy Gospel according to St. ________, the ________ chapter.

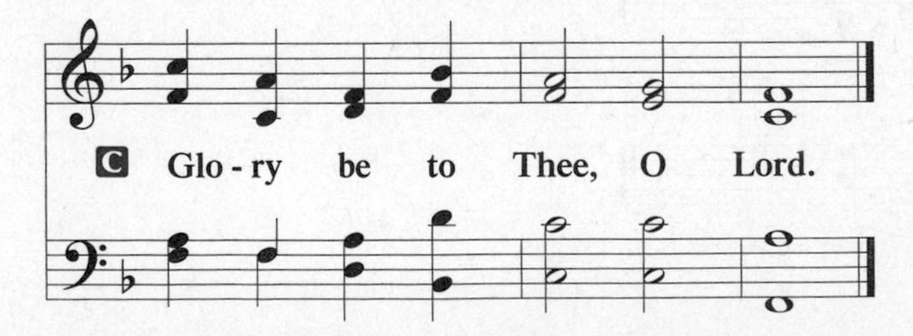
C Glo - ry be to Thee, O Lord.

After the reading:

P This is the Gospel of the Lord.

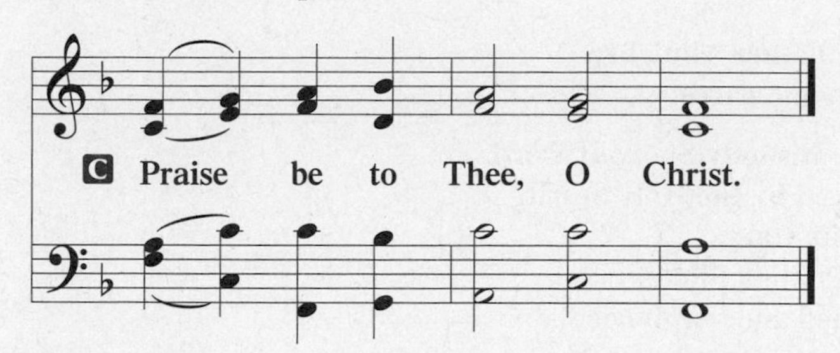
C Praise be to Thee, O Christ.

CREED

Nicene Creed

C **I believe in one God,**
the Father Almighty,
maker of heaven and earth
and of all things visible and invisible.

And in one Lord Jesus Christ,
the only-begotten Son of God,
begotten of His Father before all worlds,
God of God, Light of Light,
very God of very God,
begotten, not made,
being of one substance with the Father,
by whom all things were made;
who for us men and for our salvation came down from heaven
and was incarnate by the Holy Spirit of the virgin Mary
and was made man;
and was crucified also for us under Pontius Pilate.
He suffered and was buried.
And the third day He rose again according to the Scriptures
and ascended into heaven
and sits at the right hand of the Father.
And He will come again with glory to judge both the living and the dead,
whose kingdom will have no end.

And I believe in the Holy Spirit,
the Lord and giver of life,
who proceeds from the Father and the Son,
who with the Father and the Son together is worshiped and glorified,
who spoke by the prophets.
And I believe in one holy Christian and apostolic Church,
I acknowledge one Baptism for the remission of sins,
and I look for the resurrection of the dead
and the life ☩ of the world to come. Amen.

Us men means all people.
Christian: the ancient text reads "catholic," meaning the whole Church as it confesses the wholeness of Christian doctrine.

OR

Apostles' Creed

C **I believe in God, the Father Almighty,**
maker of heaven and earth.

And in Jesus Christ, His only Son, our Lord,
who was conceived by the Holy Spirit,
born of the virgin Mary,
suffered under Pontius Pilate,
was crucified, died and was buried.
He descended into hell.
The third day He rose again from the dead.
He ascended into heaven
and sits at the right hand of God the Father Almighty.
From thence He will come to judge the living and the dead.

I believe in the Holy Spirit,
the holy Christian Church,
the communion of saints,
the forgiveness of sins,
the resurrection of the body,
and the life ☩ everlasting. Amen.

Christian: the ancient text reads "catholic," meaning the whole Church as it confesses the wholeness of Christian doctrine.

Sit

HYMN OF THE DAY

SERMON

After the Sermon *the pastor may say:*

P The peace of God, which passes all understanding, keep your hearts and minds in Christ Jesus. *Philippians 4:7*

C **Amen.**

Stand

OFFERTORY

Psalm 51:10–12

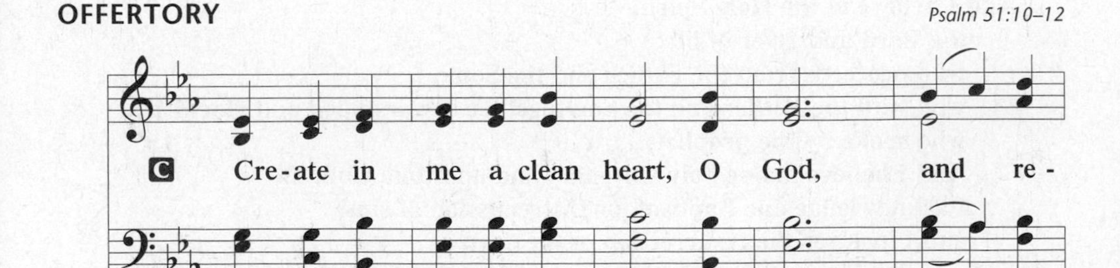
C
Cre - ate in me a clean heart, O God, and re -

new a right spir - it with - in me. Cast me not a -
way from Thy pres - ence, and take not Thy Ho - ly Spir - it
from me. Re - store un - to me the joy of Thy sal - va -
tion, and up - hold me with Thy free spir - it. A - men.

Sit

OFFERING

Stand

PRAYER OF THE CHURCH

[1 Timothy 2:1–4]

If there is no Communion, the service concludes with the LORD'S PRAYER *(page 196), a concluding collect, and the* BENEDICTION.

SERVICE OF THE SACRAMENT

PREFACE

P The Lord be with you.
2 Timothy 4:22
C And with thy spir - it.
P Lift up your hearts.
[Colossians 3:1]
C We lift them up un - to the Lord.
P Let us give thanks un - to the Lord, our God.
[Psalm 136]
C It is meet and right so to do.
Meet means fitting, proper.

The Proper Preface *appropriate to the day or season is spoken or chanted:*

P It is truly meet, right, and salutary . . . evermore praising You and saying:

SANCTUS ~ *Holy, Holy, Holy* *Isaiah 6:3; Matthew 21:9*

C Ho - ly, ho - ly, ho - ly Lord God of Sab - a - oth;
heav'n and earth are full of Thy glo - ry. Ho - san - na,
ho - san - na, ho - san - na in the high - est. Bless-ed is He,
bless-ed is He, bless-ed is He that com-eth in the name of the Lord.
Ho-san - na, ho - san - na, ho - san-na in the high - est.

Sabaoth (SAH-bay-oath) is Hebrew for "heavenly hosts."
Hosanna is a Hebrew word of praise meaning "save us now."

LORD'S PRAYER

Matthew 6:9–13

The LORD'S PRAYER may be spoken by all or sung as follows:

P Our Father who art in heav - en, hal - low - ed be Thy name,
Thy king - dom come, Thy will be done on earth as it
is in heav - en; give us this day our dai - ly bread;
and forgive us our tres - pass - es as we forgive those who
tres - pass a - gainst us; and lead us not in - to
temp - ta - tion, but deliver us from e - vil.
C For Thine is the kingdom and the power and the
glo - ry for - ev - er and ev - er. A - men.

THE WORDS OF OUR LORD

Matthew 26:26–28; Mark 14:22–24
Luke 22:19–20; 1 Corinthians 11:23–25

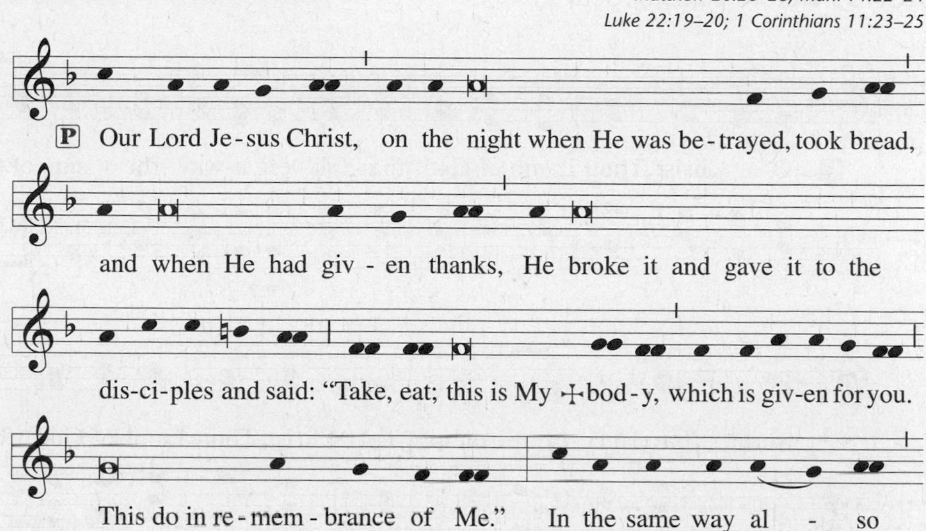
P Our Lord Je-sus Christ, on the night when He was be-trayed, took bread,
and when He had giv - en thanks, He broke it and gave it to the
dis-ci-ples and said: "Take, eat; this is My ☩ bod-y, which is giv-en for you.
This do in re-mem-brance of Me." In the same way al - so

He took the cup after sup-per, and when He had giv-en thanks, He gave it

to them, say-ing: "Drink of it, all of you; this cup is the new testament in

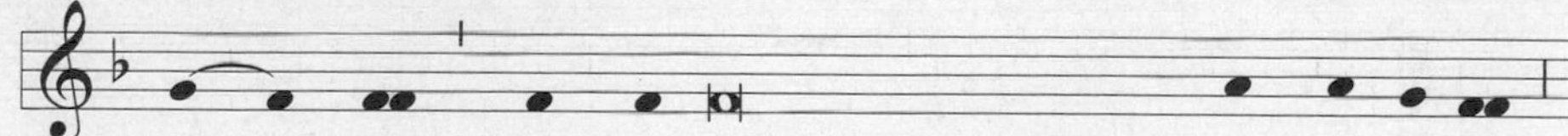
My ☩ blood, which is shed for you for the for-give-ness of sins.

This do, as often as you drink it, in re-mem-brance of Me."

PAX DOMINI ~ *The Peace of the Lord*

John 20:19

P The peace of the Lord be with you al - ways.

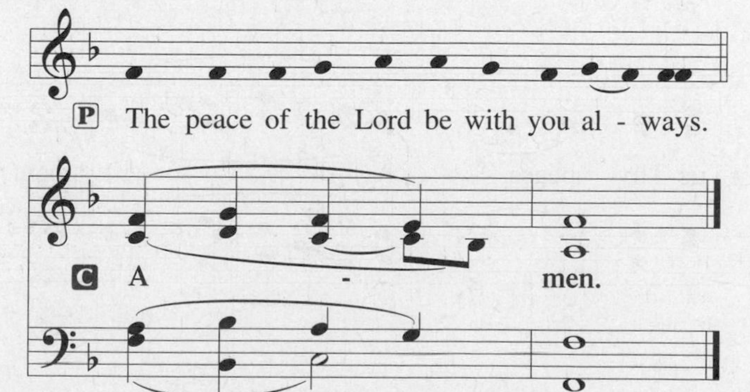
C A - men.

AGNUS DEI ~ *Lamb of God*

John 1:29

C O Christ, Thou Lamb of God, that tak - est a-way the sin of the
world, have mer - cy up - on us. O Christ, Thou Lamb of God, that
tak - est a-way the sin of the world, have mer - cy up - on us.
O Christ, Thou Lamb of God, that tak - est a-way the sin of the
world, grant us Thy peace. A - men.

Sit

DISTRIBUTION

The pastor and those who assist him receive the body and blood of Christ first and then distribute them to those who come to receive, saying:

Take, eat; this is the true body of our Lord and Savior Jesus Christ, given into death for your sins.
Amen.

Take, drink; this is the true blood of our Lord and Savior Jesus Christ, shed for the forgiveness of your sins.
Amen.

The true body of Christ, given for you.
Amen.

The true blood of Christ, shed for you.
Amen.

In dismissing the communicants, the following is said:

[P] The body and blood of our Lord Jesus Christ strengthen and preserve you in body and soul to life everlasting. Depart ☩ in peace.

[C] **Amen.**

Stand

NUNC DIMITTIS ~ *Song of Simeon*

Luke 2:29–32

C Lord, now lettest Thou Thy servant de - part in peace ac -
cord-ing to Thy word, for mine eyes have seen Thy salvation,
which Thou hast pre - pared be - fore the face of all people,

a light to light-en the Gen-tiles and the glo-ry of Thy
peo-ple Is-ra-el. Glo-ry be to the Father and
to the Son and to the Ho-ly Ghost; as it was in the beginning,
is now, and ev-er shall be, world with-out end. A-men.

THANKSGIVING

Psalm 107:1

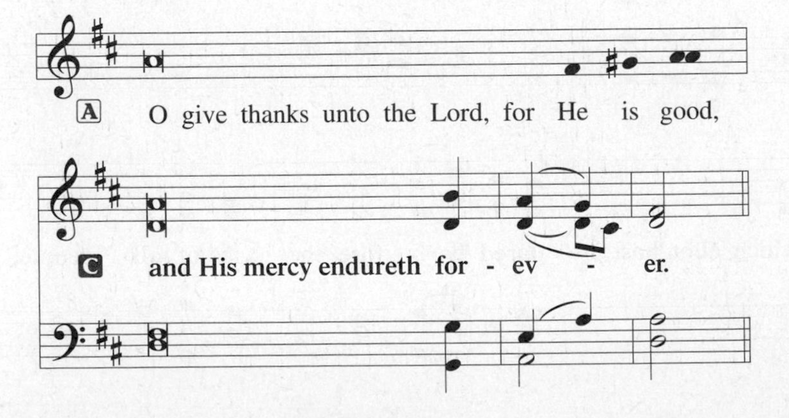
A O give thanks unto the Lord, for He is good,
C and His mercy endureth for-ev-er.

One of the following collects is spoken or chanted:

A Let us pray.

A We give thanks to You, almighty God, that You have refreshed us through this salutary gift, and we implore You that of Your mercy You would strengthen us through the same in faith toward You and in fervent love toward one another; through Jesus Christ, Your Son, our Lord, who lives and reigns with You and the Holy Spirit, one God, now and forever. (402)

O God the Father, the fountain and source of all goodness, who in loving-kindness sent Your only-begotten Son into the flesh, we thank You that for His sake You have given us pardon and peace in this Sacrament, and we ask You not to forsake Your children but always to rule our hearts and minds by Your Holy Spirit that we may be enabled constantly to serve You; through Jesus Christ, Your Son, our Lord, who lives and reigns with You and the Holy Spirit, one God, now and forever. (403)

C A - men.

SALUTATION and BENEDICAMUS

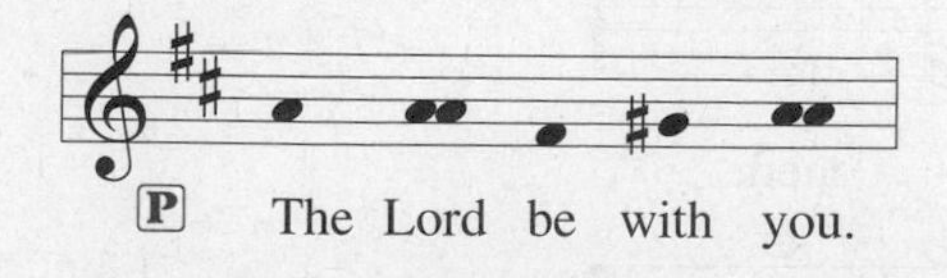
P The Lord be with you.

2 Timothy 4:22

C And with thy spir - it.

A Bless we the Lord.
[Psalm 103:1]
C Thanks be to God.

BENEDICTION

Numbers 6:24–26

P The Lord bless you and keep you. The Lord make
His face shine upon you and be gra - cious un - to you.
The Lord lift up His countenance upon you and ☩ give you peace.

C A - men, a - men, a - men.

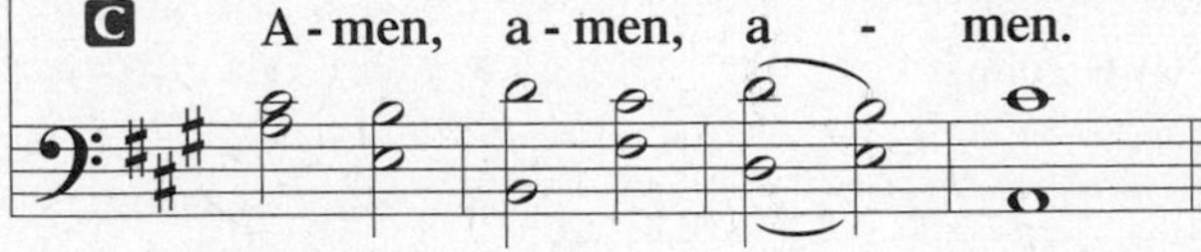

DIVINE SERVICE
Setting Four

CONFESSION AND ABSOLUTION

A Hymn of Invocation may be sung.

Stand

The sign of the cross ☩ may be made by all in remembrance of their Baptism.

P In the name of the Father and of the ☩ Son and of the Holy Spirit.
C **Amen.** *Matthew 28:19b; [18:20]*

P Our help is in the name of the Lord,
C **who made heaven and earth.** *Psalm 124:8*

P If You, O Lord, kept a record of sins, O Lord, who could stand?
C **But with You there is forgiveness; therefore You are feared.** *Psalm 130:3–4*

P Since we are gathered to hear God's Word, call upon Him in prayer and praise, and receive the body and blood of our Lord Jesus Christ in the fellowship of this altar, let us first consider our unworthiness and confess before God and one another that we have sinned in thought, word, and deed, and that we cannot free ourselves from our sinful condition. Together as His people let us take refuge in the infinite mercy of God, our heavenly Father, seeking His grace for the sake of Christ, and saying: God, be merciful to me, a sinner. *[Luke 18:13]*

Kneel/Stand

C **Almighty God, have mercy upon us, forgive us our sins, and lead us to everlasting life. Amen.**

P Almighty God, merciful Father, in Holy Baptism You declared us to be Your children and gathered us into Your one, holy Church, in which You daily and richly forgive us our sins and grant us new life through Your Spirit. Be in our midst, enliven our faith, and graciously receive our prayer and praise; through Your Son, Jesus Christ, our Lord. (407)
C **Amen.**

The pastor faces the congregation:
P Almighty God in His mercy has given His Son to die for you and for His sake forgives you all your sins. As a called and ordained servant of Christ, and by His authority, I therefore forgive you all your sins in the name of the Father and of the ☩ Son and of the Holy Spirit.
C **Amen.** *[John 20:19–23]*

Stand

SERVICE OF THE WORD

INTROIT, PSALM, or ENTRANCE HYMN

KYRIE ~ *Lord, Have Mercy*

Mark 10:47

The Kyrie may be sung once or several times in response to various petitions.

C Lord, have mer - cy; Christ, have mer - cy; Lord, have mer - cy.

GLORIA IN EXCELSIS ~ *Glory to God in the Highest*

Luke 2:14; John 1:29

During Advent and Lent, the Gloria in Excelsis is omitted.

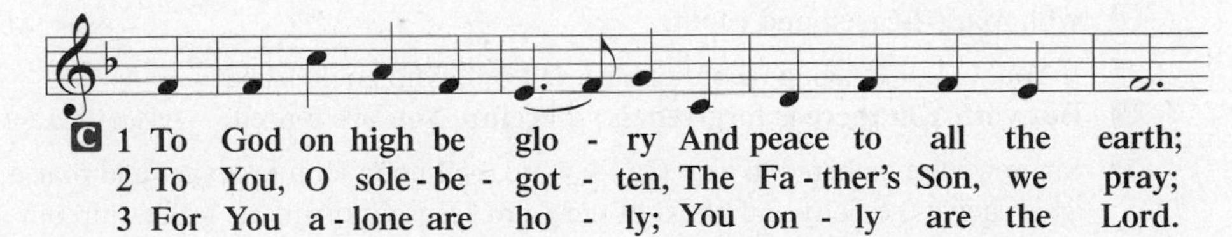

C 1 To God on high be glo - ry And peace to all the earth;
2 To You, O sole - be - got - ten, The Fa - ther's Son, we pray;
3 For You a - lone are ho - ly; You on - ly are the Lord.

Good - will from God in heav - en Pro - claimed at Je - sus' birth!
O Lamb of God, our Sav - ior, You take our sins a - way.
For - ev - er and for - ev - er, Be wor - shiped and a - dored;

We praise and bless You, Fa - ther; Your ho - ly name, we sing—
Have mer - cy on us, Je - sus; Re - ceive our heart - felt cry,
You with the Ho - ly Spir - it A - lone are Lord Most High,

Our thanks for Your great glo - ry, Lord God, our heav'n - ly King.
Where You in pow'r are seat - ed At God's right hand on high—
In God the Fa - ther's glo - ry. "A - men!" our glad re - ply.

SALUTATION and COLLECT OF THE DAY

P The Lord be with you. *2 Timothy 4:22*

C **And also with you.**

P Let us pray.

The COLLECT OF THE DAY is spoken.

C **Amen.**

Sit

OLD TESTAMENT or FIRST READING

After the reading:

A This is the Word of the Lord.

C **Thanks be to God.**

PSALM or GRADUAL

EPISTLE or SECOND READING

After the reading:

A This is the Word of the Lord.

C **Thanks be to God.**

Stand

ALLELUIA and VERSE

During Lent, the ALLELUIA is omitted.

C Al - le - lu - ia, al - le - lu - ia, al - le - lu - ia.

The congregation sings the following, or the choir may sing the appointed VERSE:

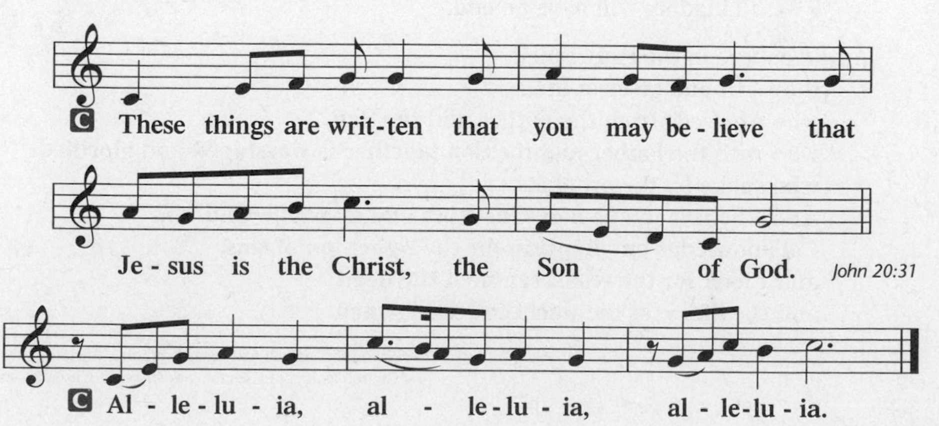
C These things are writ - ten that you may be - lieve that
Je - sus is the Christ, the Son of God.
John 20:31
C Al - le - lu - ia, al - le - lu - ia, al - le - lu - ia.

HOLY GOSPEL

P The Holy Gospel according to St. ________, the ________ chapter.

C Glory to You, O Lord.

After the reading:

P This is the Gospel of the Lord.

C Praise to You, O Christ.

CREED

Nicene Creed

C I believe in one God,
the Father Almighty,
maker of heaven and earth
and of all things visible and invisible.

And in one Lord Jesus Christ,
the only-begotten Son of God,
begotten of His Father before all worlds,
God of God, Light of Light,
very God of very God,
begotten, not made,
being of one substance with the Father,
by whom all things were made;
who for us men and for our salvation came down from heaven
and was incarnate by the Holy Spirit of the virgin Mary
and was made man;
and was crucified also for us under Pontius Pilate.
He suffered and was buried.
And the third day He rose again according to the Scriptures
and ascended into heaven
and sits at the right hand of the Father.
And He will come again with glory to judge both the living and the dead,
whose kingdom will have no end.

And I believe in the Holy Spirit,
the Lord and giver of life,
who proceeds from the Father and the Son,
who with the Father and the Son together is worshiped and glorified,
who spoke by the prophets.
And I believe in one holy Christian and apostolic Church,
I acknowledge one Baptism for the remission of sins,
and I look for the resurrection of the dead
and the life ☩ of the world to come. Amen.

Us men means all people.
Christian: the ancient text reads "catholic," meaning the whole Church as it confesses the wholeness of Christian doctrine.

OR

Apostles' Creed

C **I believe in God, the Father Almighty,**
maker of heaven and earth.

And in Jesus Christ, His only Son, our Lord,
who was conceived by the Holy Spirit,
born of the virgin Mary,
suffered under Pontius Pilate,
was crucified, died and was buried.
He descended into hell.
The third day He rose again from the dead.
He ascended into heaven
and sits at the right hand of God the Father Almighty.
From thence He will come to judge the living and the dead.

I believe in the Holy Spirit,
the holy Christian Church,
the communion of saints,
the forgiveness of sins,
the resurrection of the body,
and the life ☩ everlasting. Amen.

Christian: the ancient text reads "catholic," meaning the whole Church as it confesses the wholeness of Christian doctrine.

Sit

HYMN OF THE DAY

SERMON

Stand

The Creed may be confessed here.

PRAYER OF THE CHURCH

[1 Timothy 2:1–4]

Following the prayers, the people may greet one another in the name of the Lord, saying, "Peace be with you," as a sign of reconciliation and of the unity of the Spirit in the bond of peace (Matt. 5:22–24; Eph. 4:1–3).

Sit

OFFERING

SERVICE OF THE SACRAMENT

Stand

PREFACE

P The Lord be with you. *2 Timothy 4:22*
C And also with you.

P Lift up your hearts.
C We lift them to the Lord. *[Colossians 3:1]*

P Let us give thanks to the Lord our God.
C It is right to give Him thanks and praise. *[Psalm 136]*

P It is truly good, right, and salutary that we should at all times and in all places give thanks to You, O Lord, holy Father, almighty and everlasting God, for the countless blessings You so freely bestow on us and all creation. Above all, we give thanks for Your boundless love shown to us when You sent Your only-begotten Son, Jesus Christ, into our flesh and laid on Him our sin, giving Him into death that we might not die eternally. Because He is now risen from the dead and lives and reigns to all eternity, all who believe in Him will overcome sin and death and will rise again to new life. Therefore with angels and archangels and with all the company of heaven we laud and magnify Your glorious name, evermore praising You and saying:

SANCTUS ~ *Holy, Holy, Holy*

Isaiah 6:3; Matthew 21:9

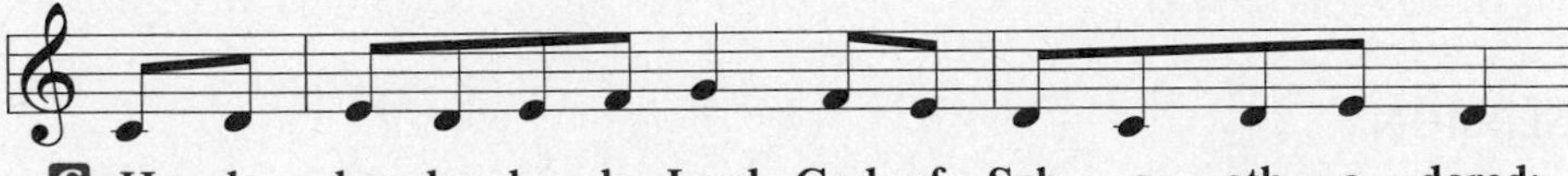

C Ho - ly, ho - ly, ho - ly Lord God of Sab - a - oth a - dored;

Heav'n and earth with full ac-claim shout the glo-ry of Your name.

Sing ho - san-na in the high-est, sing ho-san - na to the Lord;

Tru - ly blest is He who comes in the name of the Lord!

Sabaoth (SAH-bay-oath) is Hebrew for "heavenly hosts."
Hosanna is a Hebrew word of praise meaning "save us now."

PRAYER OF THANKSGIVING

P Blessed are You, O Lord our God, king of all creation, for You have had mercy on us and given Your only-begotten Son that whoever believes in Him should not perish but have eternal life.

The prayer continues with the following, or a prayer appropriate to the season is said:

In Your righteous judgment You condemned the sin of Adam and Eve, who ate the forbidden fruit, and You justly barred them and all their children from the tree of life. Yet, in Your great mercy, You promised salvation by a second Adam, Your Son, Jesus Christ, our Lord, and made His cross a life-giving tree for all who trust in Him.

We give You thanks for the redemption You have prepared for us through Jesus Christ. Grant us Your Holy Spirit that we may faithfully eat and drink of the fruits of His cross and receive the blessings of forgiveness, life, and salvation that come to us in His body and blood.

The prayer concludes:

Hear us as we pray in His name and as He has taught us:

LORD'S PRAYER

Matthew 6:9–13

C **Our Father who art in heaven,**
hallowed be Thy name,
Thy kingdom come,
Thy will be done on earth as it is in heaven;
give us this day our daily bread;
and forgive us our trespasses as we forgive those who trespass against us;
and lead us not into temptation,
but deliver us from evil.
For Thine is the kingdom and the power and the glory forever and ever. Amen.

THE WORDS OF OUR LORD

Matthew 26:26–28; Mark 14:22–24
Luke 22:19–20; 1 Corinthians 11:23–25

P Our Lord Jesus Christ, on the night when He was betrayed, took bread, and when He had given thanks, He broke it and gave it to the disciples and said: "Take, eat; this is My ☩ body, which is given for you. This do in remembrance of Me."

In the same way also He took the cup after supper, and when He had given thanks, He gave it to them, saying: "Drink of it, all of you; this cup is the new testament in My ☩ blood, which is shed for you for the forgiveness of sins. This do, as often as you drink it, in remembrance of Me."

PAX DOMINI ~ *The Peace of the Lord*

John 20:19

P The peace of the Lord be with you always.
C **Amen.**

AGNUS DEI ~ *Lamb of God*

John 1:29

C 1 O Je - sus Christ, true Lamb of God,
2 O Je - sus Christ, true Lamb of God,
You take the sin of the world a - way;
You take the sin of the world a - way;
O Je - sus Christ, true Lamb of God,
Have mer - cy on us, Je - sus Christ,
Have mer - cy on us, Lord, we pray.
And grant us peace, O Lord, we pray.

Sit

DISTRIBUTION

The pastor and those who assist him receive the body and blood of Christ first and then distribute them to those who come to receive, saying:

Take, eat; this is the true body of our Lord and Savior Jesus Christ, given into death for your sins.
Amen.

Take, drink; this is the true blood of our Lord and Savior Jesus Christ, shed for the forgiveness of your sins.
Amen.

The true body of Christ, given for you.
Amen.

The true blood of Christ, shed for you.
Amen.

In dismissing the communicants, the following is said:

P The body and blood of our Lord Jesus Christ strengthen and preserve you in body and soul to life everlasting. Depart ☩ in peace.

C **Amen.**

Stand

NUNC DIMITTIS ~ *Song of Simeon* *Luke 2:29–32*

The following canticle or an appropriate hymn is sung.

C 1 O Lord, now let Your ser - vant De - part in heav'n - ly peace, For I have seen the glo - ry Of Your re - deem - ing grace: A light to lead the Gen - tiles Un - to Your ho - ly hill, The glo - ry of Your peo - ple, Your cho - sen Is - ra - el.
2 All glo - ry to the Fa - ther, All glo - ry to the Son, All glo - ry to the Spir - it, For - ev - er Three in One; For as in the be - gin - ning, Is now, shall ev - er be, God's tri - une name re - sound - ing Through all e - ter - ni - ty.

Nunc Dimittis
SONG OF SIMEON

POST-COMMUNION COLLECT

[A] Let us pray.

[A] We give thanks to You, almighty God, that You have refreshed us through this salutary gift, and we implore You that of Your mercy You would strengthen us through the same in faith toward You and in fervent love toward one another; through Jesus Christ, Your Son, our Lord, who lives and reigns with You and the Holy Spirit, one God, now and forever. (402)

O God the Father, the fountain and source of all goodness, who in loving-kindness sent Your only-begotten Son into the flesh, we thank You that for His sake You have given us pardon and peace in this Sacrament, and we ask You not to forsake Your children but always to rule our hearts and minds by Your Holy Spirit that we may be enabled constantly to serve You; through Jesus Christ, Your Son, our Lord, who lives and reigns with You and the Holy Spirit, one God, now and forever. (403)

Gracious God, our heavenly Father, You have given us a foretaste of the feast to come in the Holy Supper of Your Son's body and blood. Keep us firm in the true faith throughout our days of pilgrimage that, on the day of His coming, we may, together with all Your saints, celebrate the marriage feast of the Lamb in His kingdom which has no end; through Jesus Christ, Your Son, our Lord, who lives and reigns with You and the Holy Spirit, one God, now and forever. (404)

[C] **Amen.**

BENEDICAMUS and BENEDICTION

[A] Let us bless the Lord. *[Psalm 103:1]*
[C] **Thanks be to God.**

[P] The Lord bless you and keep you.
The Lord make His face shine on you and be gracious to you.
The Lord look upon you with favor and ✠ give you peace. *Numbers 6:24–26*
[C] **Amen.**

DIVINE SERVICE
Setting Five

CONFESSION AND ABSOLUTION

A Hymn of Invocation may be sung.

Stand

The sign of the cross ☩ may be made by all in remembrance of their Baptism.

P In the name of the Father and of the ☩ Son and of the Holy Spirit.
C **Amen.** *Matthew 28:19b; [18:20]*

P Beloved in the Lord! Let us draw near with a true heart and confess our sins unto God our Father, beseeching Him in the name of our Lord Jesus Christ to grant us forgiveness. *[Hebrews 10:22]*

P Our help is in the name of the Lord,
C **who made heaven and earth.** *Psalm 124:8*
P I said, I will confess my transgressions unto the Lord,
C **and You forgave the iniquity of my sin.** *Psalm 32:5*

Kneel/Stand

Silence for reflection on God's Word and for self-examination.

P O almighty God, merciful Father,
C **I, a poor, miserable sinner, confess unto You all my sins and iniquities with which I have ever offended You and justly deserved Your temporal and eternal punishment. But I am heartily sorry for them and sincerely repent of them, and I pray You of Your boundless mercy and for the sake of the holy, innocent, bitter sufferings and death of Your beloved Son, Jesus Christ, to be gracious and merciful to me, a poor, sinful being.**

P Let us then confess our sins to God our Father.
C **Most merciful God, we confess that we are by nature sinful and unclean. We have sinned against You in thought, word, and deed, by what we have done and by what we have left undone. We have not loved You with our whole heart; we have not loved our neighbors as ourselves. We justly deserve Your present and eternal punishment. For the sake of Your Son, Jesus Christ, have mercy on us. Forgive us,**

P Upon this your confession, I, by virtue of my office, as a called and ordained servant of the Word, announce the grace of God unto all of you, and in the stead and by the command of my Lord Jesus Christ I forgive you all your sins in the name of the Father and of the ☩ Son and of the Holy Spirit. *[John 20:19–23]*

C **Amen.**

renew us, and lead us, so that we may delight in Your will and walk in Your ways to the glory of Your holy name. Amen.

P In the mercy of almighty God, Jesus Christ was given to die for us, and for His sake God forgives us all our sins. To those who believe in Jesus Christ He gives the power to become the children of God and bestows on them the Holy Spirit. May the Lord, who has begun this good work in us, bring it to completion in the day of our Lord Jesus Christ. *John 1:12; Philippians 1:6*

C **Amen.**

Stand

SERVICE OF THE WORD

INTROIT, PSALM, or ENTRANCE HYMN

KYRIE ~ *Lord, Have Mercy*

Mark 10:47

"Kyrie! God, Father" (Hymn 942)

GLORIA IN EXCELSIS ~ *Glory to God in the Highest*

Luke 2:14; John 1:29

During Advent and Lent, the GLORIA IN EXCELSIS is omitted.

"All Glory Be to God Alone" (Hymn 948)

OR "All Glory Be to God on High" (Hymn 947)

SALUTATION and COLLECT OF THE DAY

P The Lord be with you. *2 Timothy 4:22*

C **And also with you.**

P Let us pray.

The COLLECT OF THE DAY is spoken.

C **Amen.**

Sit

OLD TESTAMENT or FIRST READING

After the reading:

A This is the Word of the Lord.

C **Thanks be to God.**

PSALM or GRADUAL

EPISTLE or SECOND READING

After the reading:

A This is the Word of the Lord.

C **Thanks be to God.**

HYMN OF THE DAY

Stand

HOLY GOSPEL

P The Holy Gospel according to St. ________, the ________ chapter.

C **Glory to You, O Lord.**

After the reading:

P This is the Gospel of the Lord.

C **Praise to You, O Christ.**

CREED

"We All Believe in One True God" (Hymn 954)
OR "We All Believe in One True God" (Hymn 953)

Sit

SERMON

Stand

PRAYER OF THE CHURCH

[1 Timothy 2:1–4]

The following form may be used, or another form may be used according to local custom.

P Friends in Christ, I urge you all to lift up your hearts to God and pray with me as Christ our Lord has taught us and freely promised to hear us.

God, our Father in heaven, look with mercy on us, Your needy children on earth, and grant us grace that Your holy name be hallowed by us and all the world through the pure and true teaching of Your Word and the fervent love shown forth in our lives. Graciously turn from us all false doctrine and evil living whereby Your precious name is blasphemed and profaned. Lord, in Your mercy,

C **hear our prayer.**

P May Your kingdom come to us and expand. Bring all transgressors and those who are blinded and bound in the devil's kingdom to know Jesus Christ, Your Son, by faith that the number of Christians may be increased. Lord, in Your mercy,

C **hear our prayer.**

P Strengthen us by Your Spirit according to Your will, both in life and in death, in the midst of both good and evil things, that our own wills may be crucified daily and sacrificed to Your good and gracious will. Into Your merciful hands we commend _name(s)_ and all who are in need, praying for them at all times: Thy will be done. Lord, in Your mercy,

C **hear our prayer.**

P Grant us our daily bread, preserve us from greed and selfish cares, and help us trust in You to provide for all our needs. Lord, in Your mercy,

C **hear our prayer.**

P Forgive us our sins as we also forgive those who sin against us so that our hearts may be at peace and may rejoice in a good conscience before You, and that no sin may ever frighten or alarm us. Lord, in Your mercy,

C **hear our prayer.**

P Lead us not into temptation, O Lord, but help us by Your Spirit to subdue our flesh, to turn from the world and its ways, and to overcome the devil with all his wiles. Lord, in Your mercy,

C **hear our prayer.**

P And lastly, O heavenly Father, deliver us from all evil of both body and soul, now and forever. Lord, in Your mercy,

C **hear our prayer.**

P We trust, O Lord, in Your great mercy to hear and answer us; through Jesus Christ, our Lord.

C **Amen.** (408)

Sit

OFFERING

SERVICE OF THE SACRAMENT

Stand

PREFACE

P The Lord be with you. *2 Timothy 4:22*

C **And also with you.**

P Lift up your hearts.

C **We lift them to the Lord.** *[Colossians 3:1]*

P Let us give thanks to the Lord our God.

C **It is right to give Him thanks and praise.** *[Psalm 136]*

P It is truly good, right, and salutary that we should at all times and in all places give thanks to You, O Lord our God, king of all creation, for You have had mercy on us and given Your only-begotten Son that whoever believes in Him should not perish but have eternal life. Grant us Your Spirit, gracious Father, that we may give heed to the testament of Your Son in true faith and, above all, firmly take to heart the words with which Christ gives to us His body and blood for our forgiveness. By Your grace, lead us to remember and give thanks for the boundless love which He manifested to us when, by pouring out His precious blood, He saved us from Your righteous wrath and from sin, death, and hell. Grant that we may receive the bread and wine, that is, His body and blood, as a gift, guarantee, and pledge of His salvation. Graciously receive our prayers; deliver and preserve us. To You alone, O Father, be all glory, honor, and worship, with the Son and the Holy Spirit, one God, now and forever.

C **Amen.**

LORD'S PRAYER

Matthew 6:9–13

C **Our Father who art in heaven,**
hallowed be Thy name,
Thy kingdom come,
Thy will be done on earth as it is in heaven;
give us this day our daily bread;
and forgive us our trespasses as we forgive those who trespass against us;
and lead us not into temptation,
but deliver us from evil.
For Thine is the kingdom and the power and the glory forever and ever. Amen.

P In the name of our Lord and Savior Jesus Christ, at His command, and with His own words, we receive His testament:

THE WORDS OF OUR LORD

Matthew 26:26–28; Mark 14:22–24
Luke 22:19–20; 1 Corinthians 11:23–25

P Our Lord Jesus Christ, on the night when He was betrayed, took bread, and when He had given thanks, He broke it and gave it to the disciples and said: "Take, eat; this is My ☩ body, which is given for you. This do in remembrance of Me."

In the same way also He took the cup after supper, and when He had given thanks, He gave it to them, saying: "Drink of it, all of you; this cup is the new testament in My ☩ blood, which is shed for you for the forgiveness of sins. This do, as often as you drink it, in remembrance of Me."

SANCTUS ~ *Holy, Holy, Holy*

Isaiah 6:3; Matthew 21:9

"Isaiah, Mighty Seer in Days of Old" (Hymn 960)

PAX DOMINI ~ *The Peace of the Lord*

John 20:19

P The peace of the Lord be with you always.
C **Amen.**

AGNUS DEI ~ *Lamb of God*

John 1:29

"O Christ, Thou Lamb of God" (from Divine Service, Setting Three, page 198)
OR "Lamb of God, Pure and Holy" (Hymn 434)

Sit

DISTRIBUTION

The pastor and those who assist him receive the body and blood of Christ first and then distribute them to those who come to receive, saying:

Take, eat; this is the true body of our Lord and Savior Jesus Christ, given into death for your sins.
Amen.

Take, drink; this is the true blood of our Lord and Savior Jesus Christ, shed for the forgiveness of your sins.
Amen.

The true body of Christ, given for you.
Amen.

The true blood of Christ, shed for you.
Amen.

In dismissing the communicants, the following is said:

[P] The body and blood of our Lord Jesus Christ strengthen and preserve you in body and soul to life everlasting. Depart ☩ in peace.

[C] **Amen.**

Stand

POST-COMMUNION HYMN

"O Lord, We Praise Thee" (Hymn 617)
OR "May God Bestow on Us His Grace" (Hymn 823 or 824)
OR "In Peace and Joy I Now Depart" (Hymn 938)

POST-COMMUNION COLLECT

[A] Let us pray.

[A] We give thanks to You, almighty God, that You have refreshed us through this salutary gift, and we implore You that of Your mercy You would strengthen us through the same in faith toward You and in fervent love toward one another; through Jesus Christ, Your Son, our Lord, who lives and reigns with You and the Holy Spirit, one God, now and forever. (402)

O God the Father, the fountain and source of all goodness, who in loving-kindness sent Your only-begotten Son into the flesh, we thank You that for His sake You have given us pardon and peace in this Sacrament, and we ask You not to forsake Your children but always to rule our hearts and minds by Your Holy Spirit that we may be enabled constantly to serve You; through Jesus Christ, Your Son, our Lord, who lives and reigns with You and the Holy Spirit, one God, now and forever. (403)

[C] **Amen.**

BENEDICAMUS and BENEDICTION

[A] Let us bless the Lord. *[Psalm 103:1]*

[C] **Thanks be to God.**

[P] The Lord bless you and keep you.
The Lord make His face shine on you and be gracious to you.
The Lord look upon you with favor and ☩ give you peace. *Numbers 6:24–26*

[C] **Amen.**

MATINS

Stand

L O Lord, o - pen my lips,
C and my mouth will de - clare Your praise.
Psalm 51:15
L Make haste, O God, to de - liv - er me;
C make haste to help me, O Lord.
Psalm 70:1
C Glo-ry be to the Father and to the Son and to the Holy Spir - it;
as it was in the be - gin - ning, is now, and will be for-ev-er. A - men.
Common: Praise to You, O Christ. Al - le - lu - ia.
Advent: Praise to You, O Christ, King who comes to save us.
Lent: Praise to You, O Christ, Lamb of our sal - va - tion.

PSALMODY

Common (or Seasonal) Antiphon

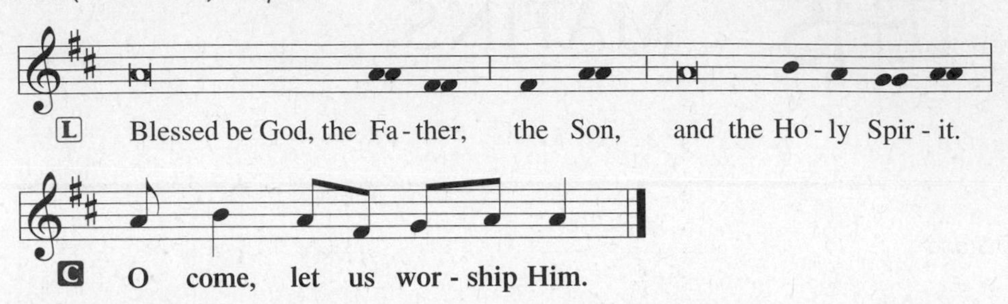
L Blessed be God, the Fa - ther, the Son, and the Ho - ly Spir - it.
C O come, let us wor - ship Him.

VENITE ~ *O Come, Let Us Sing*

Psalm 95:1–7

C 1 O come, let us sing . . . to the Lord,
2 For the Lord is a . . . great God
3 The sea is His, for He . . . made it,
5 Glory be to the Father and . . . to the Son
1 let us make a joyful noise to the rock of our sal - va - tion.
2 and a great . . . king a - bove all gods.
3 and His hand . . . formed the dry land.
5 and to the . . . Ho - ly Spir - it;
1 Let us come into His presence with thanks - giv - ing,
2 The deep places of the earth are . . . in His hand;
3 O come, let us worship and . . . bow down,
4 For He . . . is our God,
5 as it was in the be - - gin - ning,

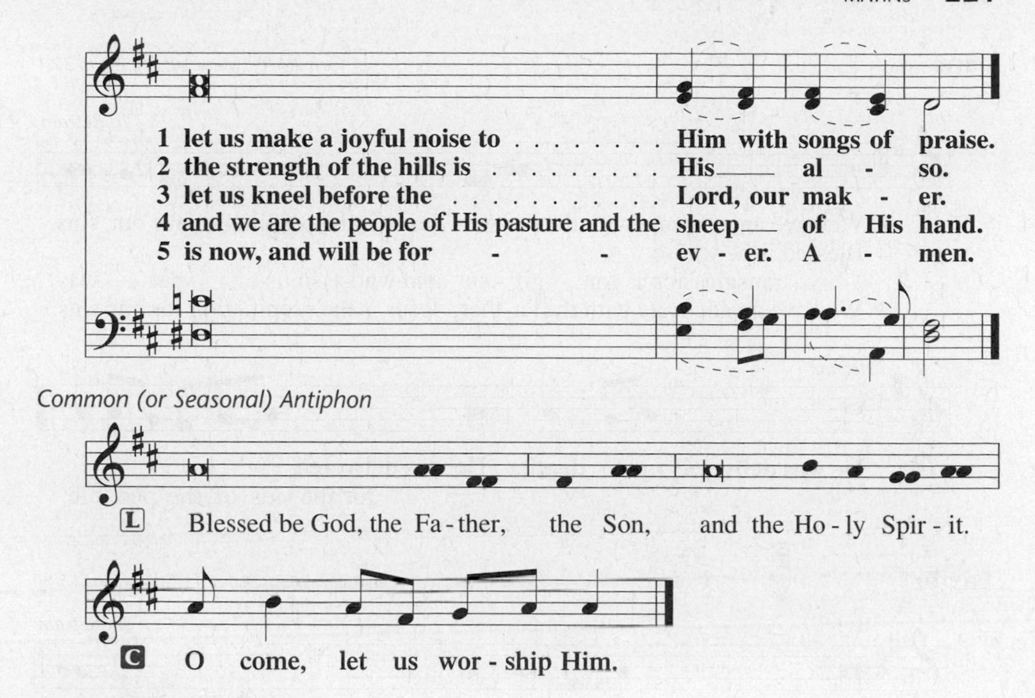
1 let us make a joyful noise to . . . . Him with songs of praise.
2 the strength of the hills is . . . . His___ al - so.
3 let us kneel before the . . . . Lord, our mak - er.
4 and we are the people of His pasture and the sheep___ of His hand.
5 is now, and will be for - - ev - er. A - men.
Common (or Seasonal) Antiphon
L Blessed be God, the Fa - ther, the Son, and the Ho - ly Spir - it.
C O come, let us wor - ship Him.

ADDITIONAL PSALMS

Sit

OFFICE HYMN

READINGS

READINGS FROM HOLY SCRIPTURE

After each reading:

L O Lord, have mercy on us.

C **Thanks be to God.**

RESPONSORY

Common

Psalm 119:89; 26:8; Luke 11:28

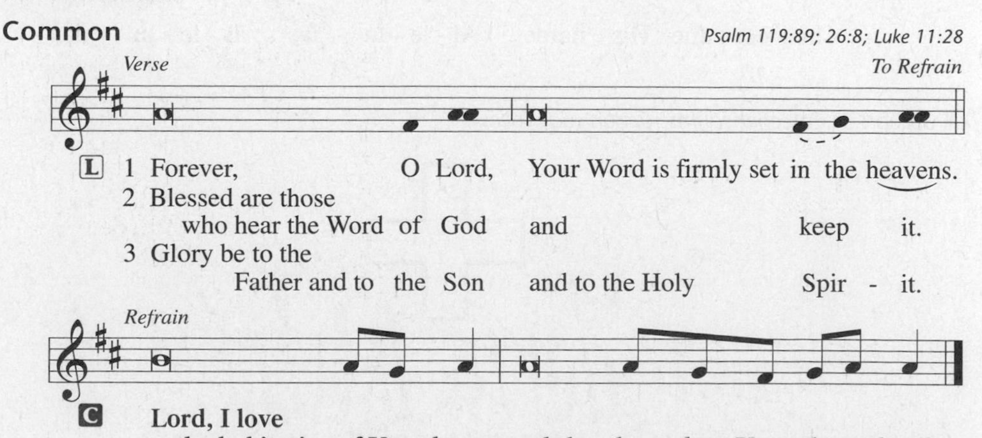
Verse
To Refrain
L 1 Forever, O Lord, Your Word is firmly set in the heavens.
2 Blessed are those who hear the Word of God and keep it.
3 Glory be to the Father and to the Son and to the Holy Spir - it.
Refrain
C Lord, I love the habitation of Your house and the place where Your glo-ry dwells.

Responsories for Lent and Easter are found on the following page.

Lent

1 John 2:1–2; [Mark 10:33]; Psalm 32:1

Verse *To Refrain*

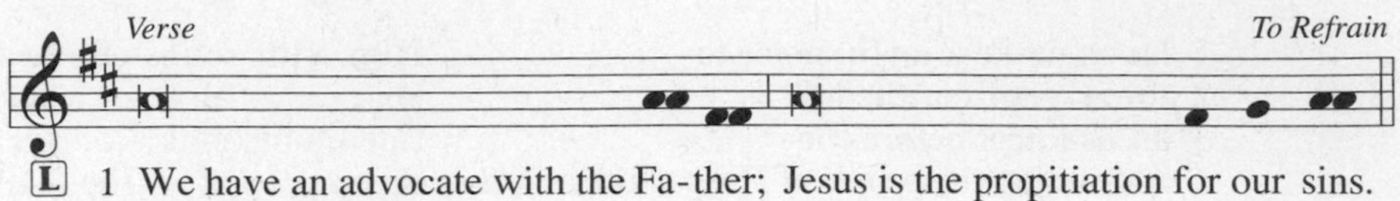

L 1 We have an advocate with the Fa-ther; Jesus is the propitiation for our sins.
2 Blessed is he whose transgression is for - giv - en and whose sin is put a - way.
3 We have an advocate with the Fa-ther; Jesus is the propitiation for our sins.

Refrain

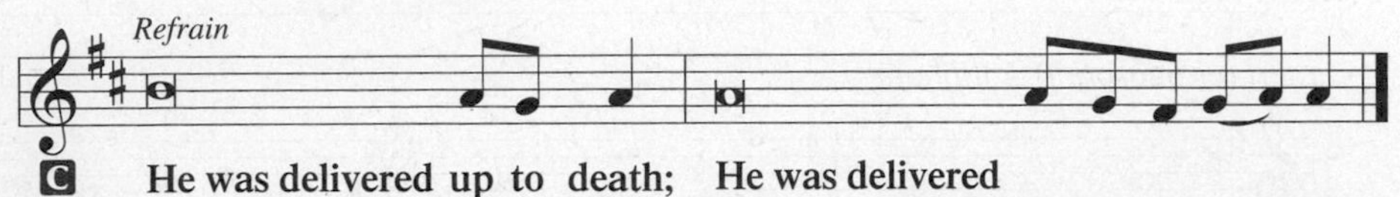

C He was delivered up to death; He was delivered for the sins of the peo-ple.

Easter

Psalm 96:2; 29:1–2; 1 Corinthians 15:20

Verse *To Refrain*

L 1 Sing to the Lord and bless His name, proclaim His salvation from day to day.
2 Now is Christ risen from the dead and become the firstfruits of them that sleep.
3 Glory be to the Father and to the Son and to the Holy Spir - it.

Refrain

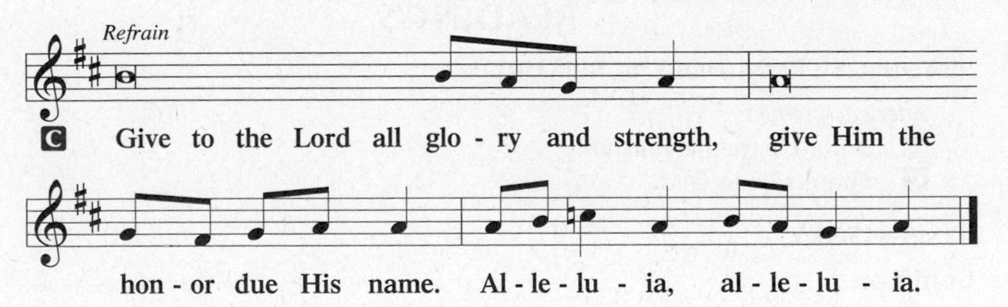

C Give to the Lord all glo - ry and strength, give Him the hon - or due His name. Al - le - lu - ia, al - le - lu - ia.

A Sermon or Catechetical Instruction may follow.

Gloria Patri

GLORY BE TO THE FATHER

CANTICLE

Stand

The Te Deum, Benedictus *(page 226), or another canticle (936, 939–941) is sung.*

TE DEUM ~ *We Praise You, O God*

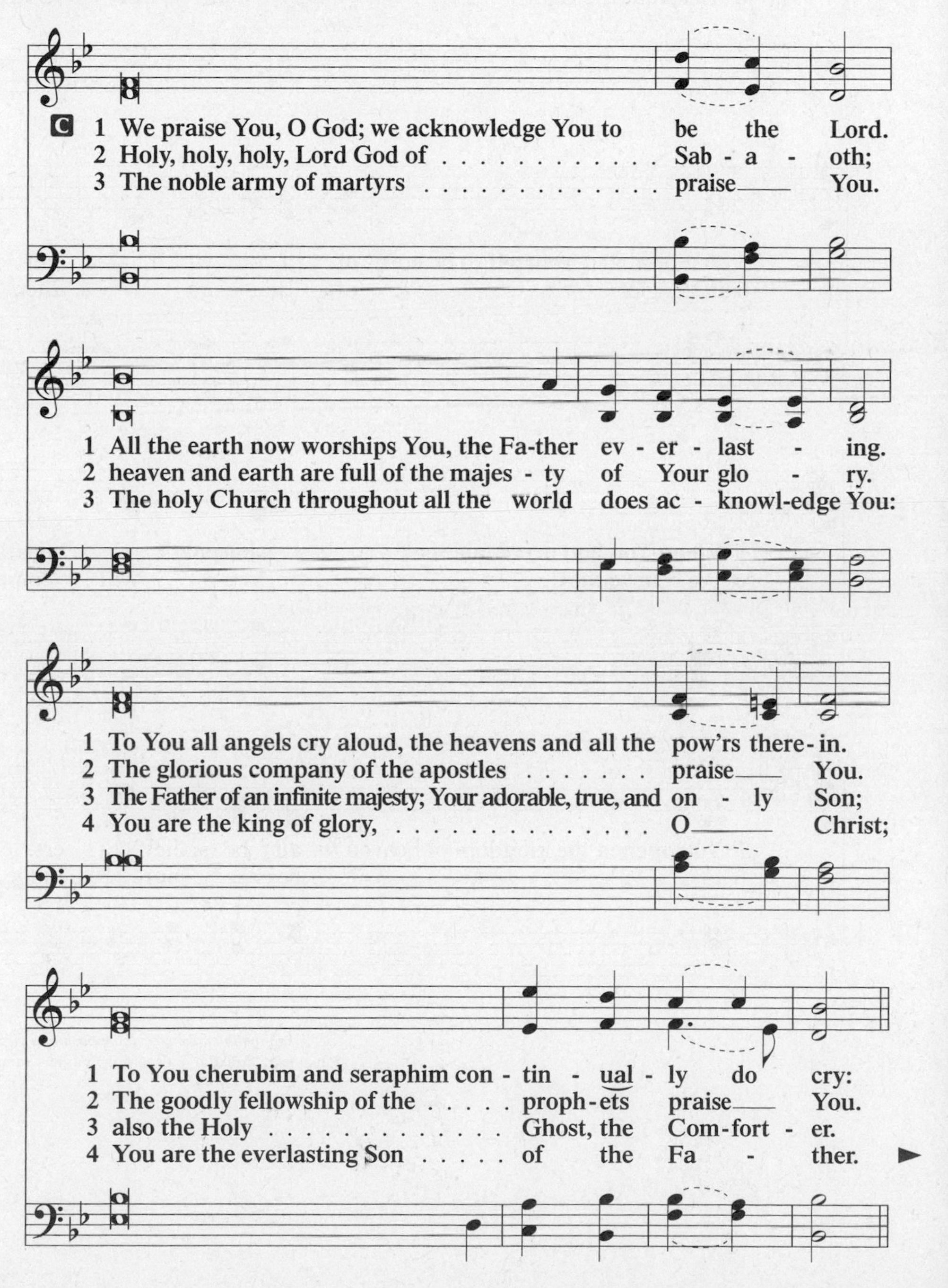
C
1 We praise You, O God; we acknowledge You to be the Lord.
2 Holy, holy, holy, Lord God of . . . . Sab - a - oth;
3 The noble army of martyrs . . . . praise You.
1 All the earth now worships You, the Fa-ther ev - er - last - ing.
2 heaven and earth are full of the majes - ty of Your glo - ry.
3 The holy Church throughout all the world does ac - knowl-edge You:
1 To You all angels cry aloud, the heavens and all the pow'rs there-in.
2 The glorious company of the apostles . . . . praise You.
3 The Father of an infinite majesty; Your adorable, true, and on - ly Son;
4 You are the king of glory, ... O Christ;
1 To You cherubim and seraphim con - tin - ual - ly do cry:
2 The goodly fellowship of the . . . . . proph-ets praise You.
3 also the Holy . . . . Ghost, the Com-fort - er.
4 You are the everlasting Son . . . . . of the Fa - ther.

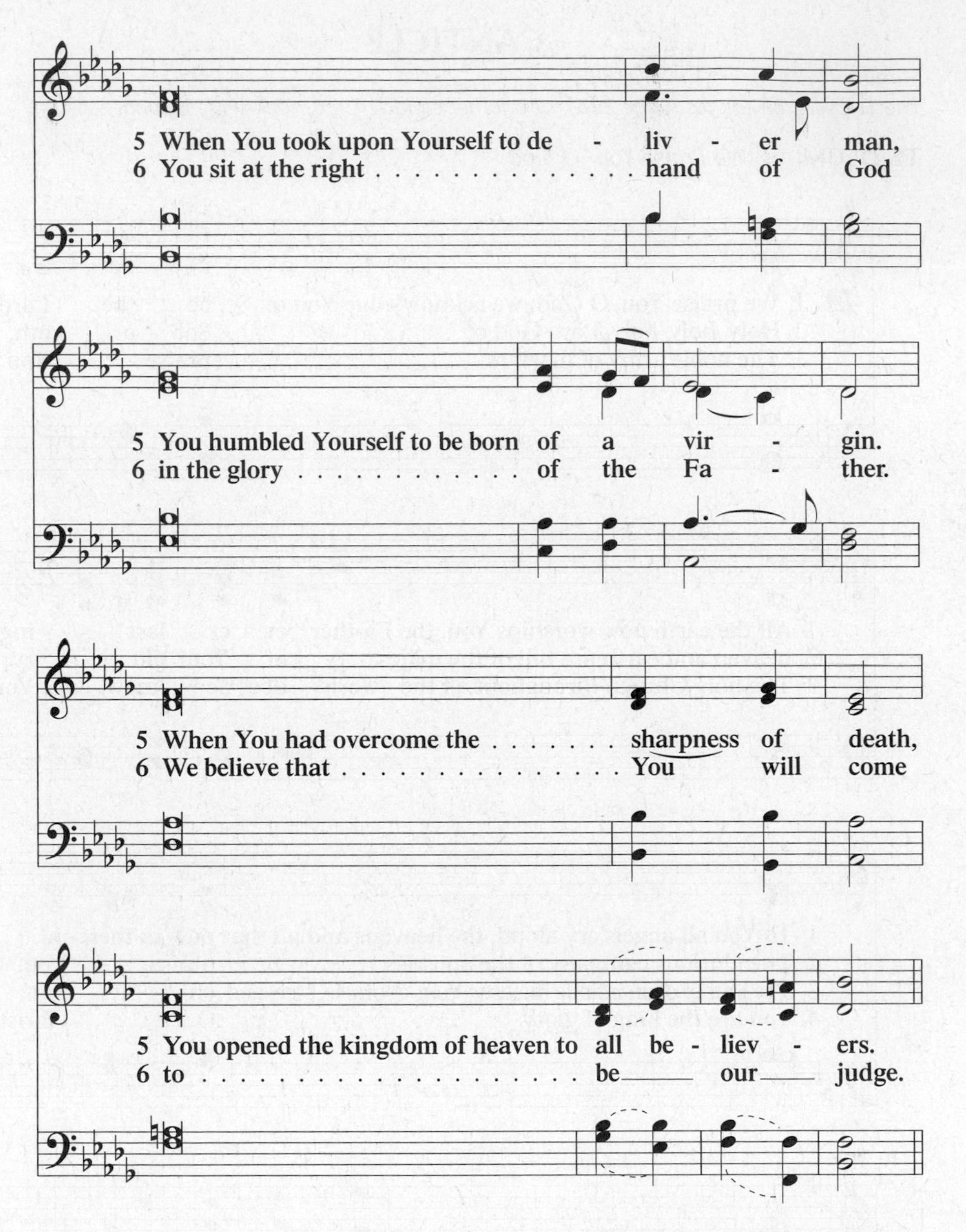
5 When You took upon Yourself to de - liv - er man,
6 You sit at the right . . . . hand of God
5 You humbled Yourself to be born of a vir - gin.
6 in the glory . . . . of the Fa - ther.
5 When You had overcome the . . . . sharpness of death,
6 We believe that . . . . You will come
5 You opened the kingdom of heaven to all be - liev - ers.
6 to . . . . be our judge.

You humbled Yourself to be born of a virgin:
original text, "You did not spurn the virgin's womb."

7 We therefore pray You to help Your . . . . . . ser - vants,
8 O Lord, save Your people and bless Your . . . . her - i - tage.
9 Grant, O Lord, to keep us this day with - out sin.
7 whom You have redeem - ed with Your pre - cious blood.
8 Govern them and lift . . . . . them up for - ev - er.
9 O Lord, have mercy upon us, have mercy up - on us.
7 Make them to be numbered . . . . with Your saints
8 Day by day we . . . . magni - fy You.
9 O Lord, let Your mercy be upon us, as our trust is in You.
7 in glory . . . . ev - er - last - ing.
8 And we worship Your name for - ever and ev - er.
9 O Lord, in You have I trusted; let me never be con - found - ed.

The earliest versions of the Te Deum omit verses 8–9.

OR

BENEDICTUS ~ *Song of Zechariah*

Luke 1:68–79

C
1 Blessed be the Lord God of . . . . Is - ra - el;
2 as He spoke by the mouth of His holy . . . . proph - ets,
3 to perform the mercy promised to our . . . . fa - thers
4 being delivered from the hand of our . . . . en - e - mies,
5 And you, child, will be called the prophet of the Most High;
6 through the tender mercy . . . . of our God;
7 Glory be to the Father and . . . . to the Son
1 for He has visited and re - deemed His peo - ple
2 who have . . . . been since the world be - gan:
3 and to remember . . . . . His ho - ly cov - e - nant,
4 might . . . . serve Him with - out fear,
5 for you will go before the Lord to pre - pare His ways;
6 when the day shall dawn up - on us from on high
7 and to . . . . the Ho - ly Spir - it;
1 and has raised up a horn of salvation . . . . for us
2 that we should be saved from our . . . . en - e - mies
3 the oath that He swore to our father . . . . A - bra - ham,
4 in holiness and righteousness be - fore Him
5 to give knowledge of salvation to His . . . . peo - ple
6 to give light to those who sit in darkness and in the shadow of death,
7 as it was in the be - - gin - ning,

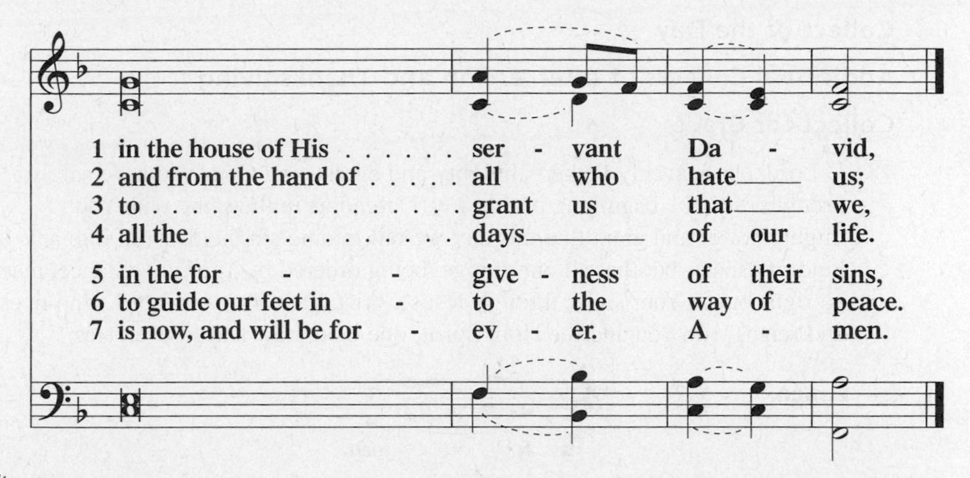
1 in the house of His . . . . . . ser - vant Da - vid,
2 and from the hand of . . . . . all who hate us;
3 to . . . . grant us that we,
4 all the . . . . days of our life.
5 in the for - - give - ness of their sins,
6 to guide our feet in - to the way of peace.
7 is now, and will be for - ev - er. A - men.

Sit

The Offering *may follow.*

PRAYER

Kneel/Stand

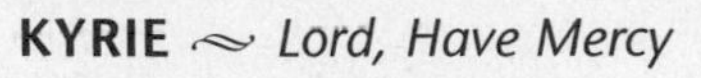

KYRIE ~ *Lord, Have Mercy* *Mark 10:47*

C Lord, have mer-cy; Christ, have mer-cy; Lord, have mer-cy.

LORD'S PRAYER *Matthew 6:9–13*

C **Our Father who art in heaven,**
hallowed be Thy name,
Thy kingdom come,
Thy will be done on earth as it is in heaven;
give us this day our daily bread;
and forgive us our trespasses as we forgive those who trespass against us;
and lead us not into temptation,
but deliver us from evil.
For Thine is the kingdom and the power and the glory forever and ever. Amen.

COLLECTS

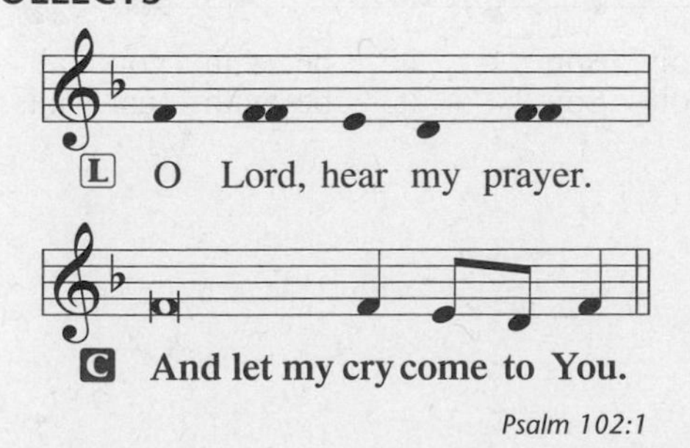
L O Lord, hear my prayer.
C And let my cry come to You.
Psalm 102:1

P The Lord be with you.
C And with your spir - it.
2 Timothy 4:22

Collect of the Day

Additional Collects of Intercession and Thanksgiving

Collect for Grace

L O Lord, our heavenly Father, almighty and everlasting God, You have safely brought us to the beginning of this day. Defend us in the same with Your mighty power and grant that this day we fall into no sin, neither run into any kind of danger, but that all our doings, being ordered by Your governance, may be righteous in Your sight; through Jesus Christ, Your Son, our Lord, who lives and reigns with You and the Holy Spirit, one God, now and forever. (409)

C **Amen.** *OR*

C A - men.

Stand

BENEDICAMUS

L Let us bless the Lord.
C Thanks be to God.

[Psalm 103:1]

BENEDICTION

2 Corinthians 13:14

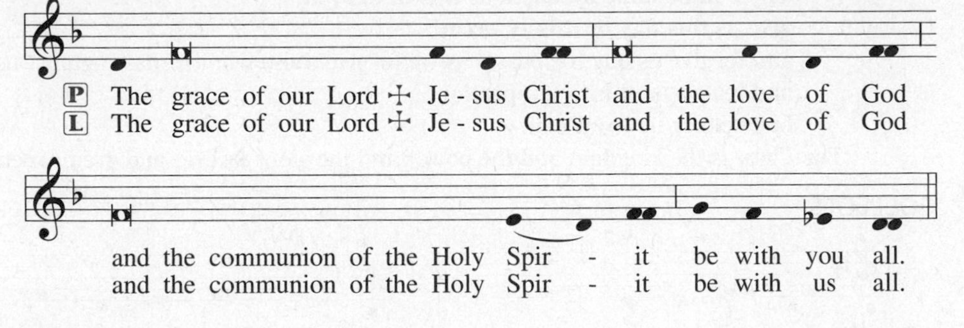
P The grace of our Lord ☩ Je - sus Christ and the love of God
L The grace of our Lord ☩ Je - sus Christ and the love of God
and the communion of the Holy Spir - it be with you all.
and the communion of the Holy Spir - it be with us all.

C A - men.

VESPERS

Stand

L O Lord, o - pen my lips,
C and my mouth will de - clare Your praise.
Psalm 51:15
L Make haste, O God, to de - liv - er me;
C make haste to help me, O Lord.
Psalm 70:1
C Glo-ry be to the Father and to the Son and to the Holy Spir - it;
as it was in the be - gin - ning, is now, and will be for-ev-er. A - men.
Common: Praise to You, O Christ. Al - le - lu - ia.
Advent: Praise to You, O Christ, King who comes to save us.
Lent: Praise to You, O Christ, Lamb of our sal - va - tion.

PSALMODY

PSALMS

One or more psalms are sung or spoken.

Sit

OFFICE HYMN

READINGS

READINGS FROM HOLY SCRIPTURE

After each reading:

L O Lord, have mercy on us.

C **Thanks be to God.**

RESPONSORY

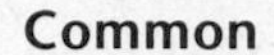

Common

Psalm 86:11; 119:105

Verse
To Refrain
L 1 Teach me Your way, O Lord, that I may walk in Your truth.
2 Unite my heart to fear Your name that I may walk in Your truth.
3 Glory be to the Father and to the Son and to the Holy Spir - it.
Refrain
C Your Word is a lamp to my feet and a light to my path.

Advent

Jeremiah 23:5a, 6

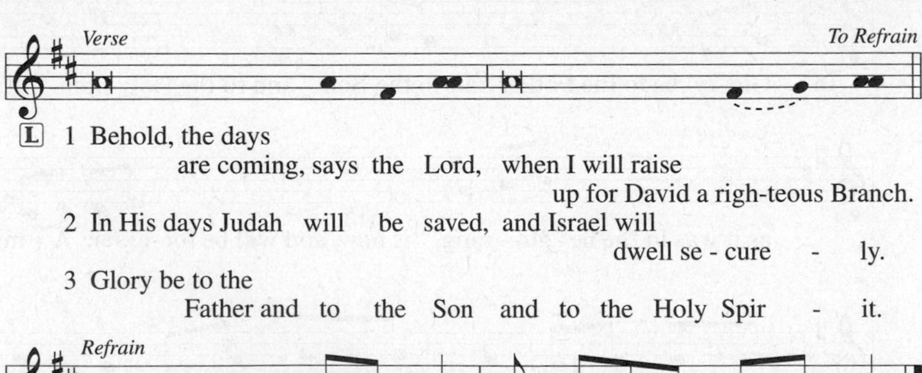
Verse
To Refrain
L 1 Behold, the days are coming, says the Lord, when I will raise up for David a righ-teous Branch.
2 In His days Judah will be saved, and Israel will dwell se - cure - ly.
3 Glory be to the Father and to the Son and to the Holy Spir - it.
Refrain

C **This is the name by which He will be called: The Lord Is Our Righ-teous-ness.**

Lent

Psalm 51:14; 59:1; 141:8

Verse
To Refrain
L 1 Deliver me, O Lord, my God, for You are the God of my sal - va - tion.
2 In You, O Lord, do I put my trust, leave me not, O Lord, my God.
3 Deliver me, O Lord, my God, for You are the God of my sal - va - tion.
Refrain
C Rescue me from my en - e - mies, protect me from those who rise a - gainst me.

A Sermon or Catechetical Instruction may follow.

CANTICLE

Stand

L Let my prayer rise before You as in - cense,
C and the lifting up of my hands as the eve - ning sac - ri - fice.
Psalm 141:2
MAGNIFICAT ~ Song of Mary
Luke 1:46–55
C My soul mag-ni-fies the Lord, and my spirit rejoices in God, my Sav-ior;
I for He has re-gard - ed the lowliness of His hand-maid - en.
II For be - hold, from this day all generations will call me bless - ed.
I For the Mighty One has done great things to me, and holy is His name;

►

II and His mercy is on those who fear Him from generation to gen - er - a - tion.
I He has shown strength with His arm; He has scattered the proud in the
imagination of their hearts. II He has cast down the
might-y from their thrones and has ex - alt - ed the low - ly.
I He has filled the hun - gry with good things,
and the rich He has sent emp - ty a - way.
II He has helped His servant Israel in remembrance of His mer - cy
as He spoke to our fathers, to Abraham and to his seed for-ev-er.
C Glo-ry be to the Fa-ther and to the Son and to the Ho - ly Spir-it;
as it was in the be-gin-ning, is now, and will be for-ev - er. A-men.

Sit

The Offering may follow.

PRAYER

Kneel/Stand

KYRIE ~ *Lord, Have Mercy* *Mark 10:47*

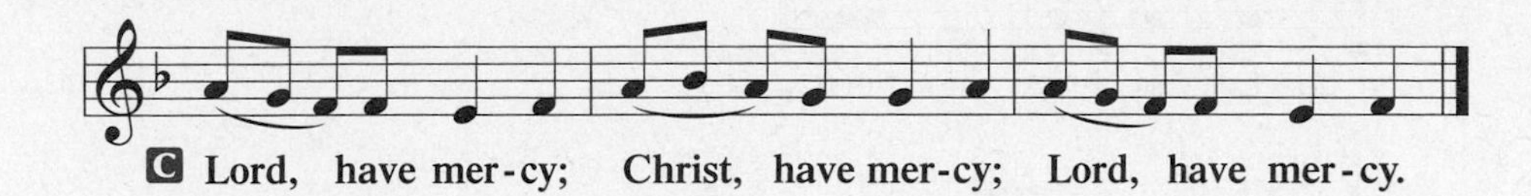
C Lord, have mer-cy; Christ, have mer-cy; Lord, have mer-cy.

LORD'S PRAYER *Matthew 6:9–13*

C **Our Father who art in heaven,**
hallowed be Thy name,
Thy kingdom come,
Thy will be done on earth as it is in heaven;
give us this day our daily bread;
and forgive us our trespasses as we forgive those who trespass against us;
and lead us not into temptation,
but deliver us from evil.
For Thine is the kingdom and the power and the glory forever and ever. Amen.

COLLECTS

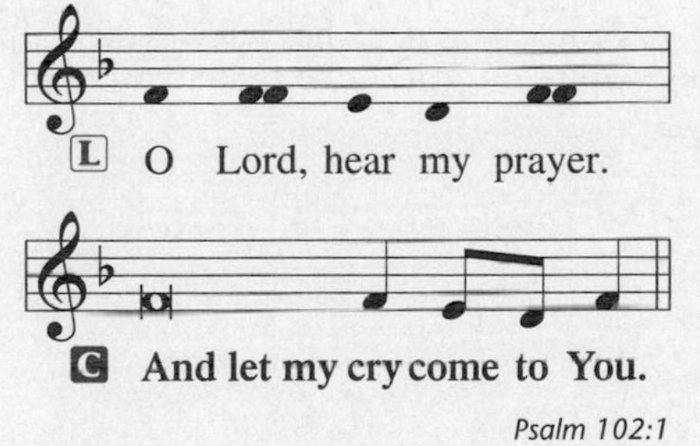
L O Lord, hear my prayer.
C And let my cry come to You.

Psalm 102:1

P The Lord be with you.
C And with your spir - it.

2 Timothy 4:22

Collect of the Day

Additional Collects of Intercession and Thanksgiving

Collect for Peace

L O God, from whom come all holy desires, all good counsels, and all just works, give to us, Your servants, that peace which the world cannot give, that our hearts may be set to obey Your commandments and also that we, being defended from the fear of our enemies, may live in peace and quietness; through Jesus Christ, Your Son, our Lord, who lives and reigns with You and the Holy Spirit, one God, now and forever. (410)

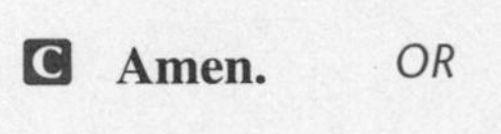
C Amen.

OR

C A - men.

Stand

BENEDICAMUS

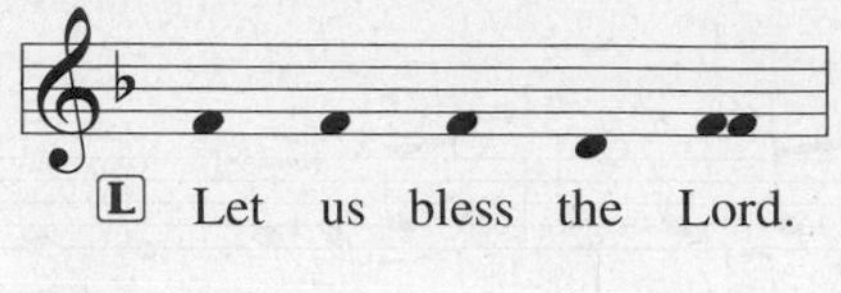
L Let us bless the Lord.

[Psalm 103:1]

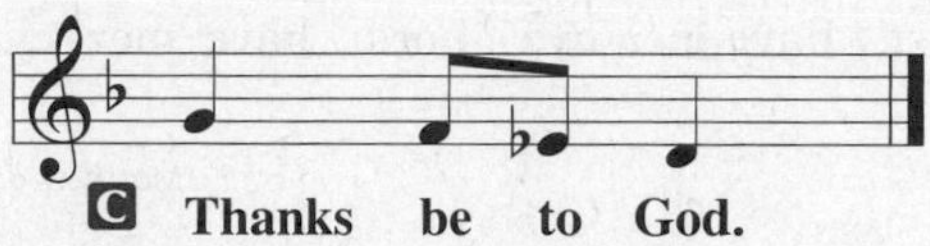
C Thanks be to God.

BENEDICTION

2 Corinthians 13:14

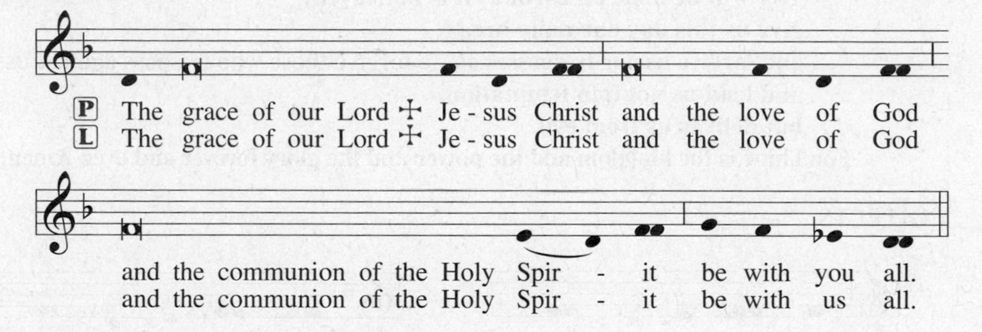
P The grace of our Lord ☩ Je - sus Christ and the love of God
L The grace of our Lord ☩ Je - sus Christ and the love of God
and the communion of the Holy Spir - it be with you all.
and the communion of the Holy Spir - it be with us all.

C A - men.

MORNING PRAYER

Stand

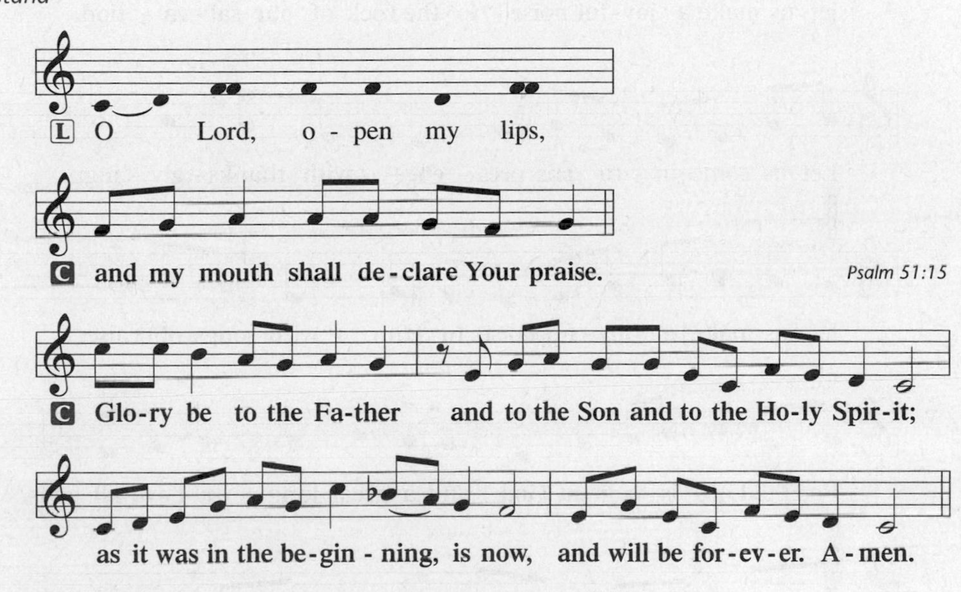
L O Lord, o - pen my lips,
C and my mouth shall de - clare Your praise.
Psalm 51:15
C Glo-ry be to the Fa-ther and to the Son and to the Ho-ly Spir-it;
as it was in the be-gin - ning, is now, and will be for-ev-er. A-men.

During Lent, the alleluia is omitted.

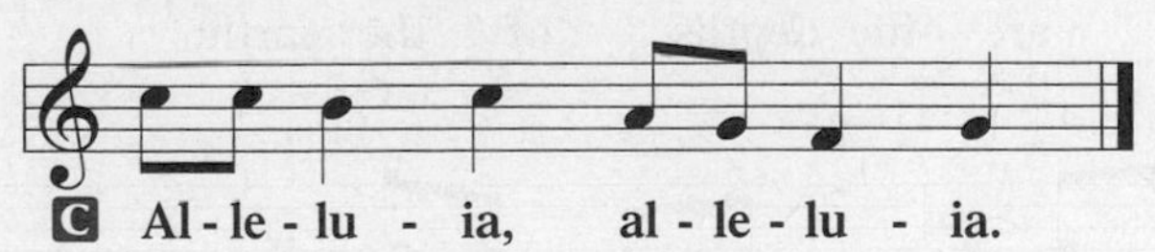
C Al - le - lu - ia, al - le - lu - ia.

PSALMODY

Common (or Seasonal) Antiphon

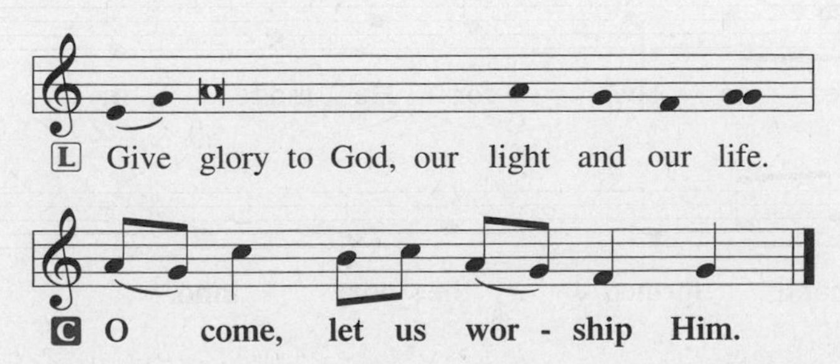
L Give glory to God, our light and our life.
C O come, let us wor - ship Him.

VENITE ⁓ *O Come, Let Us Sing* *Psalm 95:1–7*

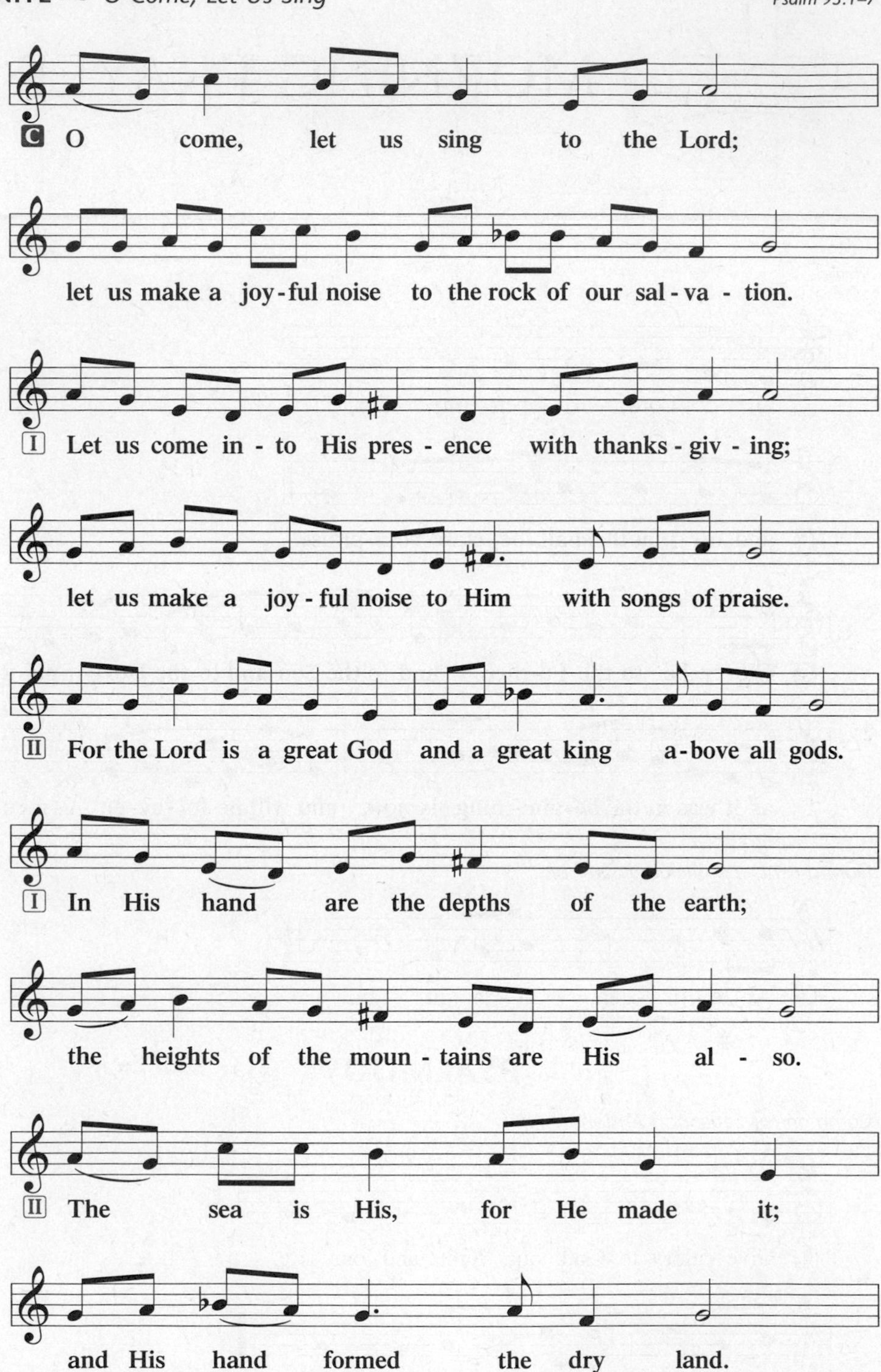
C O come, let us sing to the Lord;
let us make a joy-ful noise to the rock of our sal-va-tion.
I Let us come in-to His pres-ence with thanks-giv-ing;
let us make a joy-ful noise to Him with songs of praise.
II For the Lord is a great God and a great king a-bove all gods.
I In His hand are the depths of the earth;
the heights of the moun-tains are His al-so.
II The sea is His, for He made it;
and His hand formed the dry land.

I O come, let us wor - ship and bow down;
let us kneel be - fore the Lord, our mak - er.
II For He is our God, and we are the peo - ple
of His pas - ture and the sheep of His hand.
C Glo-ry be to the Fa - ther and to the Son and to the Ho-ly Spir-it;
as it was in the be-gin - ning, is now, and will be for-ev-er. A-men.

Common (or Seasonal) Antiphon

L Give glory to God, our light and our life.
C O come, let us wor - ship Him.

ADDITIONAL PSALMS

Sit

OFFICE HYMN

READINGS

READINGS FROM HOLY SCRIPTURE

After each reading:

L O Lord, have mercy on us.

C **Thanks be to God.**

Silence for reflection on God's Word may follow each reading. After the final reading:

L In many and various ways, God spoke to His people of old by the prophets.

C **But now in these last days, He has spoken to us by His Son.** *Hebrews 1:1–2a*

A SERMON or Catechetical Instruction may follow.

CANTICLE

Stand

BENEDICTUS ~ *Song of Zechariah*
Luke 1:68–79

C Bless - ed be the Lord, the God of Is - ra - el;
He has come to His peo - ple and re - deemed them.
He has raised up for us a might - y Sav - ior,
born of the house of His ser - vant Da - vid.
Through His ho - ly proph - ets He prom - ised of old
that He would save us from our en - e - mies, from the hands of all who

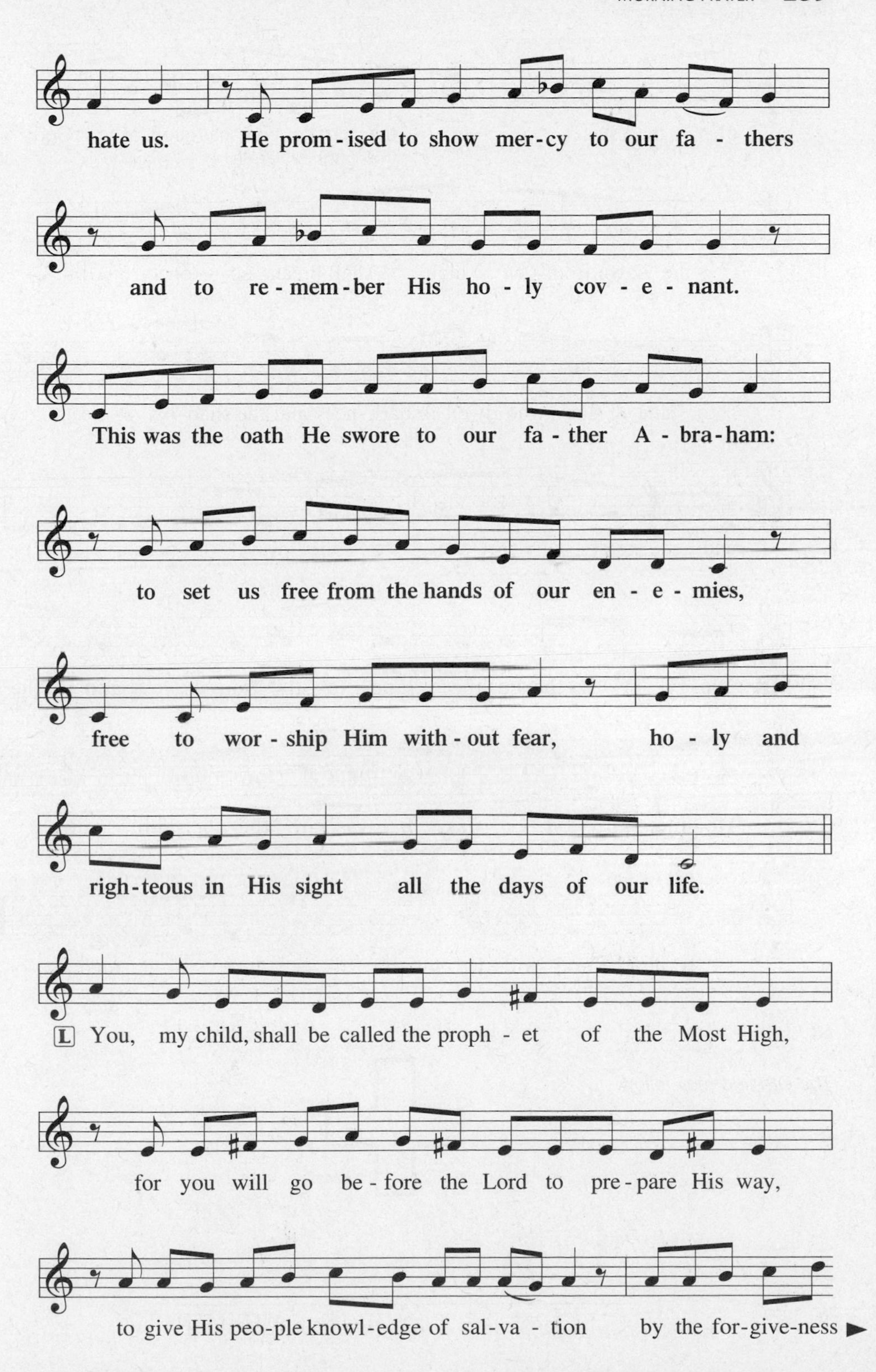
hate us. He prom - ised to show mer-cy to our fa - thers
and to re - mem - ber His ho - ly cov - e - nant.
This was the oath He swore to our fa - ther A - bra - ham:
to set us free from the hands of our en - e - mies,
free to wor - ship Him with - out fear, ho - ly and
righ - teous in His sight all the days of our life.
L You, my child, shall be called the proph - et of the Most High,
for you will go be - fore the Lord to pre - pare His way,
to give His peo - ple knowl - edge of sal - va - tion by the for - give - ness ►

of their sins. In the ten-der com-pas-sion of our God,
the dawn from on high shall break up - on us
to shine on those who dwell in dark-ness and the shad-ow of death
and to guide our feet in - to the way of peace.
C Glo-ry be to the Fa-ther and to the Son and to the
Ho-ly Spir - it; as it was in the be-gin - ning,
is now, and will be for - ev - er. A - men.

Sit

The Offering *may follow.*

Gloria Patri

GLORY BE TO THE FATHER

PRAYER

Kneel/Stand

COLLECTS

Collect of the Day

Additional Collects of Intercession and Thanksgiving

Collect for Grace

L O Lord, our heavenly Father, almighty and everlasting God, You have safely brought us to the beginning of this day. Defend us in the same with Your mighty power and grant that this day we fall into no sin, neither run into any kind of danger, but that all our doings, being ordered by Your governance, may be righteous in Your sight; through Jesus Christ, Your Son, our Lord, who lives and reigns with You and the Holy Spirit, one God, now and forever. (409)

C **Amen.** *OR*

C A - men.

LORD'S PRAYER

Matthew 6:9–13

L Taught by our Lord and trusting His promises, we are bold to pray:

C **Our Father who art in heaven,**
hallowed be Thy name,
Thy kingdom come,
Thy will be done on earth as it is in heaven;
give us this day our daily bread;
and forgive us our trespasses as we forgive those who trespass against us;
and lead us not into temptation,
but deliver us from evil.
For Thine is the kingdom and the power and the glory forever and ever. Amen.

Stand

BENEDICAMUS

L Let us bless the Lord.
[Psalm 103:1]
C Thanks be to God.

The service concludes with the following BENEDICTION. On Sundays, the TE DEUM WITH PASCHAL BLESSING (Hymn 939) may conclude the service.

BENEDICTION

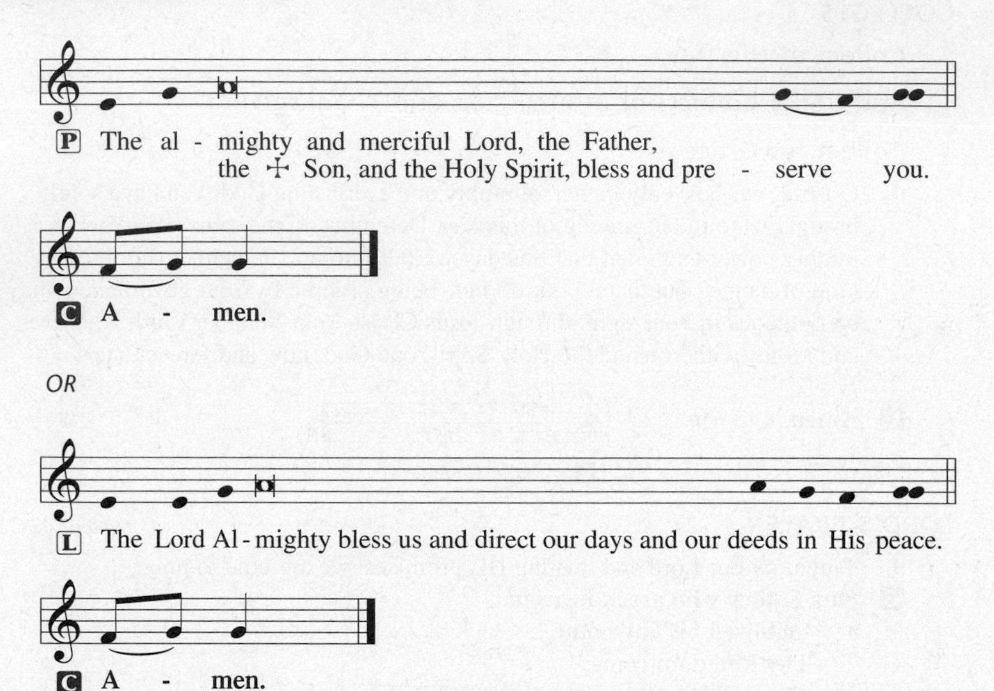
P The al - mighty and merciful Lord, the Father,
the ☩ Son, and the Holy Spirit, bless and pre - serve you.
C A - men.
OR
L The Lord Al - mighty bless us and direct our days and our deeds in His peace.
C A - men.

EVENING PRAYER

SERVICE OF LIGHT

Stand

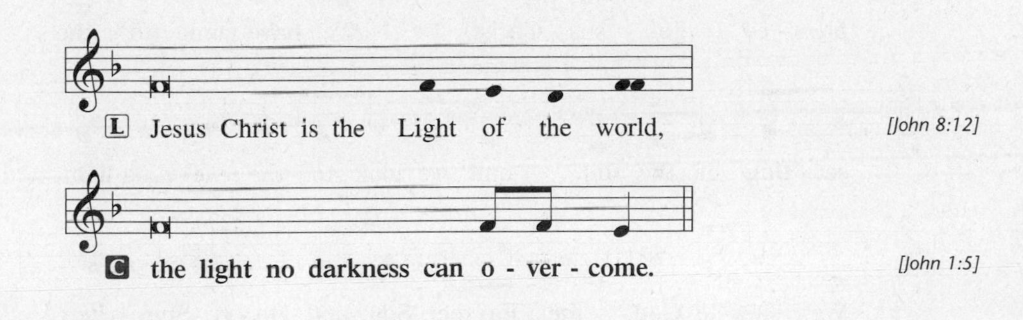
L Jesus Christ is the Light of the world,
[John 8:12]
C the light no darkness can o - ver - come.
[John 1:5]

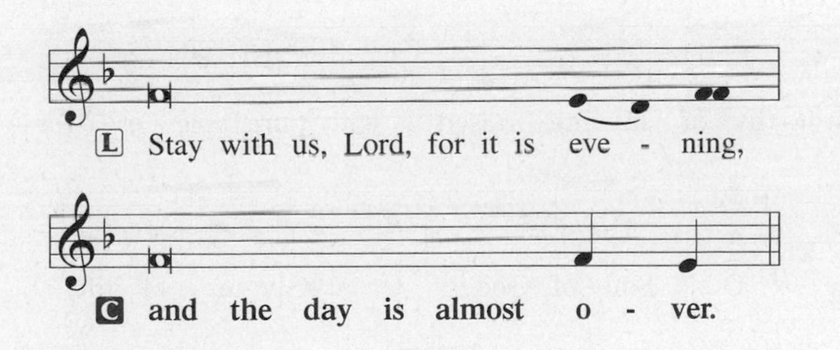
L Stay with us, Lord, for it is eve - ning,
C and the day is almost o - ver.

Luke 24:29

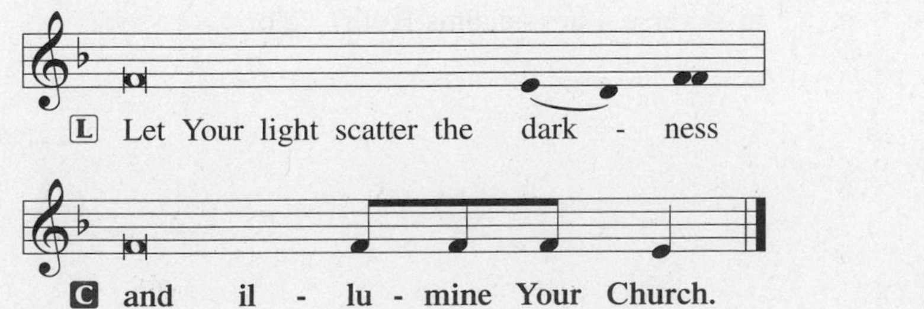
L Let Your light scatter the dark - ness
C and il - lu - mine Your Church.

1 Corinthians 4:5

[2 Corinthians 4:6]

PHOS HILARON ~ *Hymn of Light*

L Joy - ous light of glo - ry:
C of the im - mor - tal Fa - ther; heav - en - ly, ho - ly,
bless - ed Je - sus Christ. We have come to the
set - ting of the sun, and we look to the eve - ning light.
We sing to God, the Fa - ther, Son, and Ho - ly Spir - it:
You are wor - thy of be - ing praised with pure voic - es for -
ev - er. O Son of God, O Giv - er of life:
the u - ni - verse pro - claims Your glo - ry.

THANKSGIVING FOR LIGHT

L Blessèd are You, O Lord our God, king of the u - ni - verse,
who led Your people Israel by a pillar of cloud by day and a pillar of
fire by night. Enlighten our darkness by the light of Your Christ;
may His Word be a lamp to our feet and a light to our path;
for You are mer - ci - ful, and You love Your whole cre - a - tion
and we, Your creatures, glo - ri - fy You, Father, Son, and Ho - ly Spir - it.
(411)
C A - men.

Sit

PSALMODY

PSALM 141

Psalm 141:1–4, 8

C Let my prayer rise be - fore You as in - cense,
the lift - ing up of my hands as the eve - ning sac - ri - fice.

►

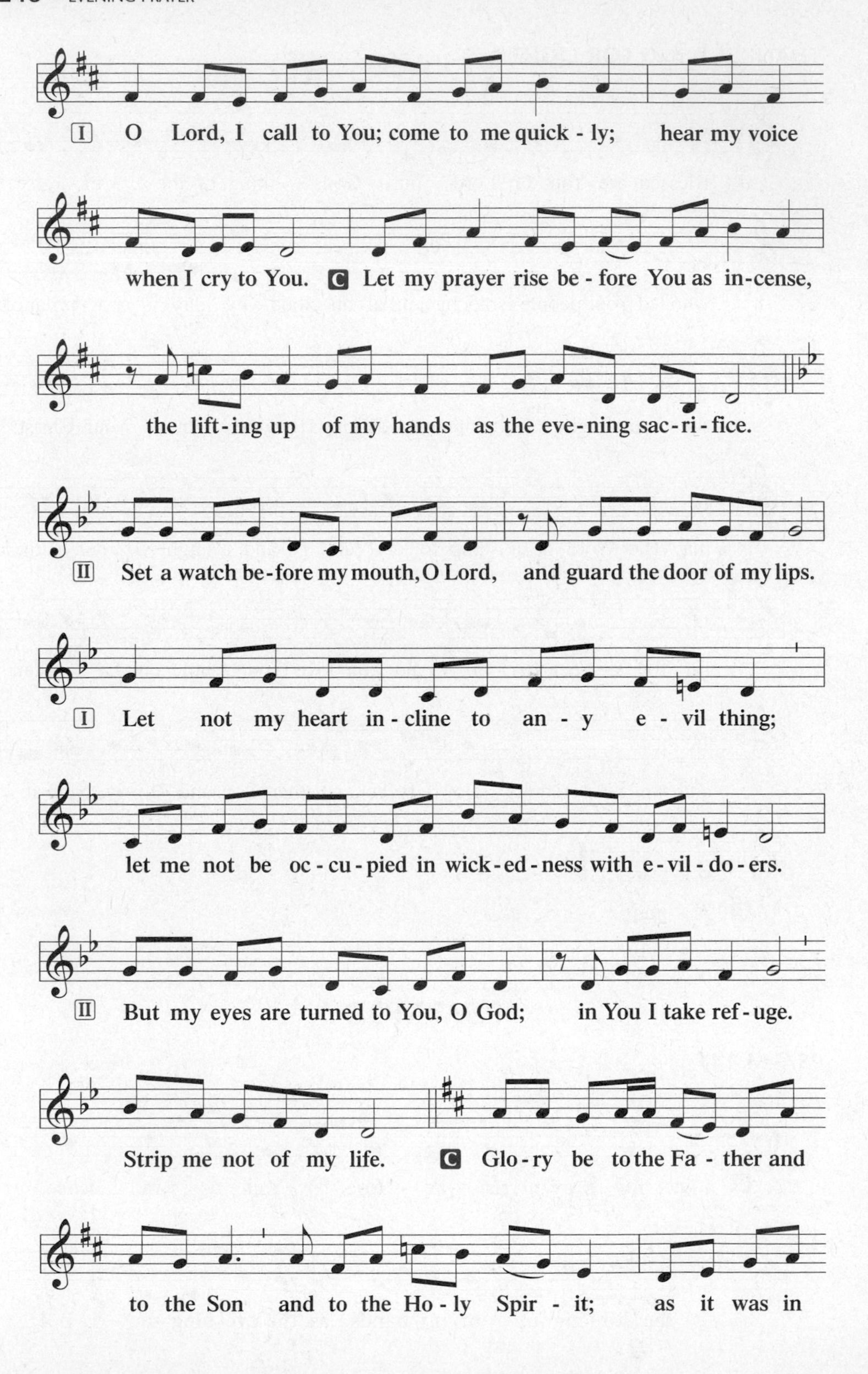
I O Lord, I call to You; come to me quick - ly; hear my voice
when I cry to You. C Let my prayer rise be - fore You as in-cense,
the lift-ing up of my hands as the eve-ning sac-ri-fice.
II Set a watch be-fore my mouth, O Lord, and guard the door of my lips.
I Let not my heart in-cline to an - y e - vil thing;
let me not be oc-cu-pied in wick-ed-ness with e-vil-do-ers.
II But my eyes are turned to You, O God; in You I take ref-uge.
Strip me not of my life. C Glo-ry be to the Fa - ther and
to the Son and to the Ho - ly Spir - it; as it was in

the be - gin - ning, is now, and will be for-ev-er. A - men.
Let my prayer rise be - fore You as in - cense,

the lift-ing up of my hands as the eve-ning sac-ri-fice.

L Let us pray.

Silence for individual prayer may follow.

L Let the incense of our repentant prayer ascend before You, O Lord, and let Your loving-kindness descend on us that, with purified minds, we may sing Your praises with the Church on earth and the whole heavenly host and may glorify You forever. (414)

C **Amen.**

ADDITIONAL PSALMS

OFFICE HYMN

READINGS

READINGS FROM HOLY SCRIPTURE

After each reading:

L O Lord, have mercy on us.

C **Thanks be to God.**

Silence for reflection on God's Word may follow each reading. After the final reading:

L In many and various ways, God spoke to His people of old by the prophets.

C **But now in these last days, He has spoken to us by His Son.** *Hebrews 1:1–2a*

A SERMON *or Catechetical Instruction may follow.*

CANTICLE

Stand

MAGNIFICAT ~ *Song of Mary*

Luke 1:46–55

Refrain

C My soul mag - ni - fies the Lord, and my spir - it re - joic - es in God, my Sav - ior. My soul mag - ni - fies the Lord, and my spir - it re - joic - es in God, my Sav - ior.

1 For He has re - - garded the lowliness of . . . . His hand - maiden.
2 For the Mighty One has done great things to . . . . . . me, and holy . . . . is His name;
3 He has shown strength with His . . . . arm; He has scattered the proud in the imagination of their hearts.
4 He has filled the hungry with good . . . . things, and the rich He has sent emp - - ty a - way.
5 Glo - ry be to the Father and to the . . . . Son and to the . . . . Ho - ly Spirit;

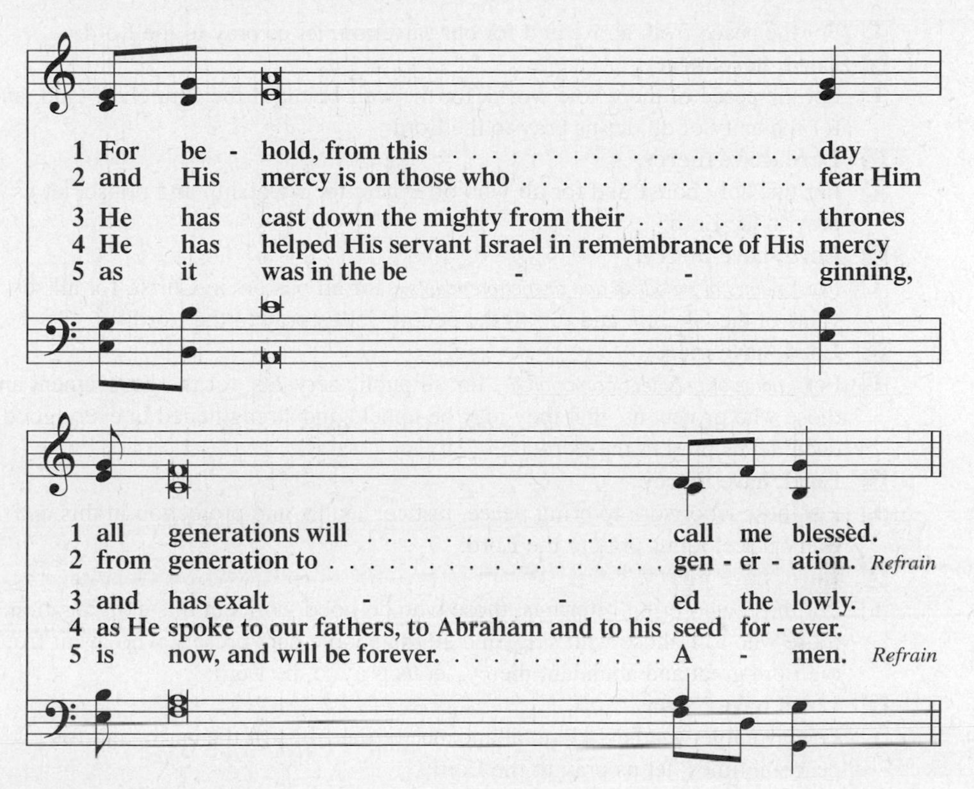
1 For be - hold, from this . . . . day
2 and His mercy is on those who . . . . fear Him
3 He has cast down the mighty from their . . . . thrones
4 He has helped His servant Israel in remembrance of His mercy
5 as it was in the be - - ginning,
1 all generations will . . . . call me blessèd.
2 from generation to . . . . gen - er - ation. Refrain
3 and has exalt - - ed the lowly.
4 as He spoke to our fathers, to Abraham and to his seed for - ever.
5 is now, and will be forever. . . . . A - men. Refrain

Sit

The Offering *may follow.*

PRAYER

Kneel/Stand

LITANY

The Litany *may be spoken, or it may be sung according to the following musical form. When sung, the congregation's response may begin just as the leader's petition ends so that the word "Lord" is sung simultaneously by both leader and congregation.*

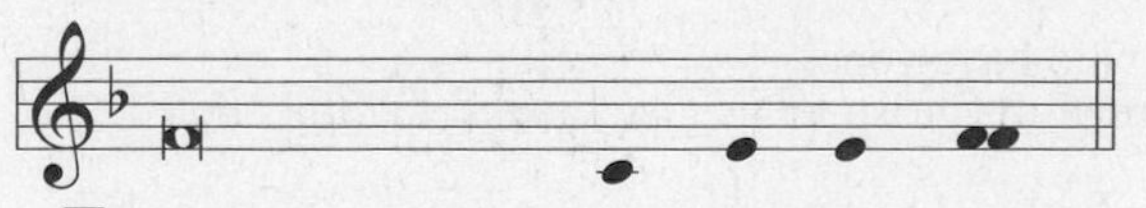
L In peace let us pray to the Lord:

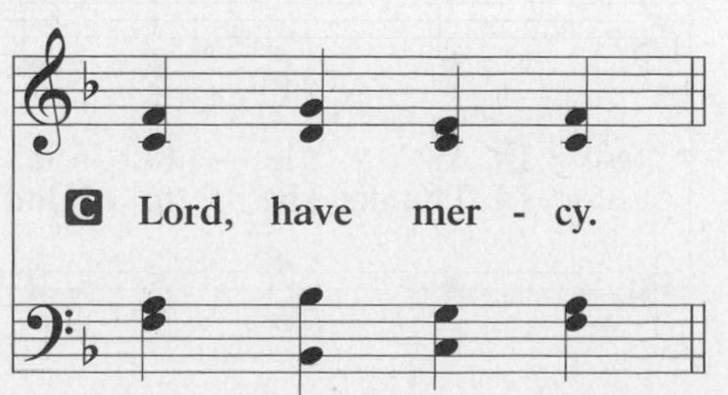
C Lord, have mer - cy.

L For the peace from above and for our salvation, let us pray to the Lord:
C **Lord, have mercy.**
L For the peace of the whole world, for the well-being of the Church of God, and for the unity of all, let us pray to the Lord:
C **Lord, have mercy.**
L For this holy house and for all who offer here their worship and praise, let us pray to the Lord:
C **Lord, have mercy.**
L For *names of synodical and district presidents*, for all pastors in Christ, for all servants of the Church, and for all the people, let us pray to the Lord:
C **Lord, have mercy.**
L For *name of president or monarch*, for all public servants, for the government and those who protect us, that they may be upheld and strengthened in every good deed, let us pray to the Lord:
C **Lord, have mercy.**
L For those who work to bring peace, justice, health, and protection in this and every place, let us pray to the Lord:
C **Lord, have mercy.**
L For those who bring offerings, those who do good works in this congregation, those who toil, those who sing, and all the people here present who await from the Lord great and abundant mercy, let us pray to the Lord:
C **Lord, have mercy.**
L For favorable weather, for an abundance of the fruits of the earth, and for peaceful times, let us pray to the Lord:
C **Lord, have mercy.**
L For our deliverance from all affliction, wrath, danger, and need, let us pray to the Lord:
C **Lord, have mercy.**
L For . . . *[additional bids for prayer may be inserted here]* . . . let us pray to the Lord:
C **Lord, have mercy.**

The prayers then continue:

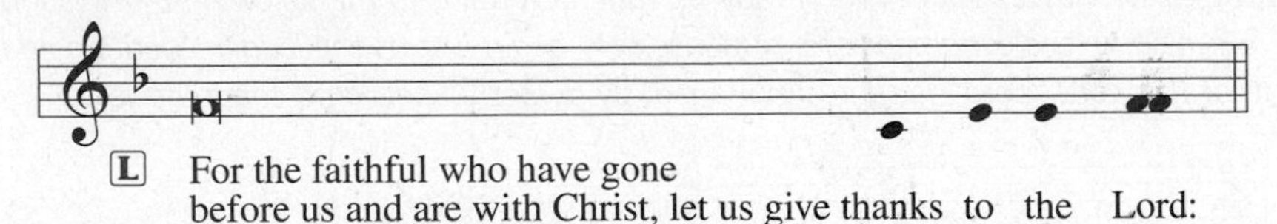
L For the faithful who have gone
before us and are with Christ, let us give thanks to the Lord:

Common: C **Al - le - lu - ia.**
Lent: C **Thanks be to God.**

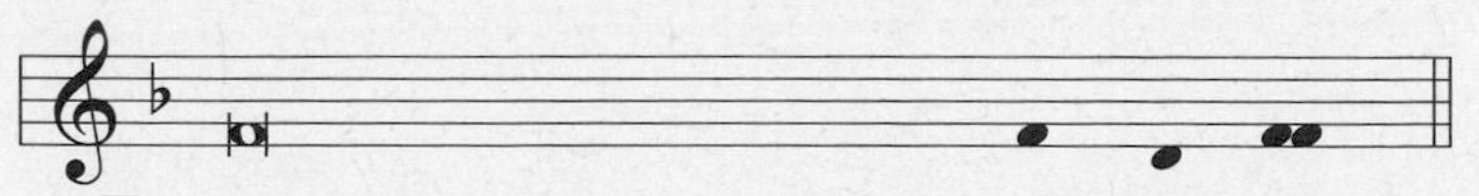

L Help, save, comfort, and defend us, gra - cious Lord. (415)

Silence for individual prayer may follow.

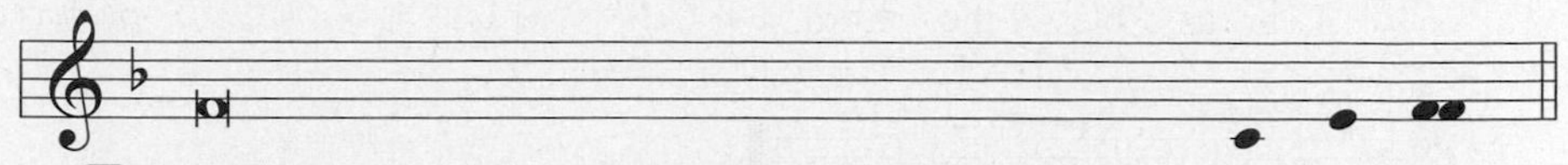

L Rejoicing in the fellowship of all the saints, let us
commend ourselves, one another, and our whole life to Christ, our Lord:

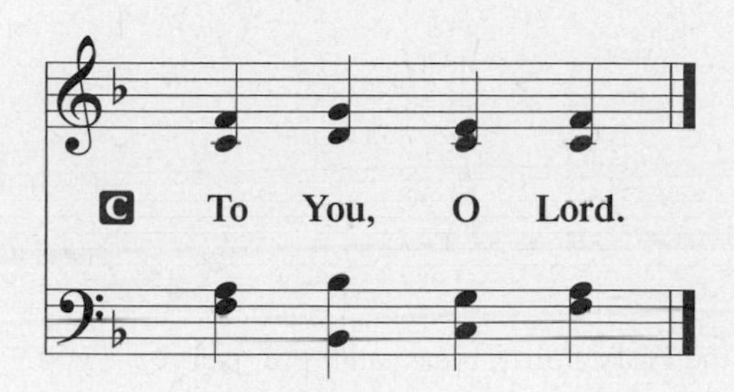
C To You, O Lord.

COLLECT FOR PEACE

L O God, from whom come all holy desires, all good counsels, and all just works, give to us, Your servants, that peace which the world cannot give, that our hearts may be set to obey Your commandments and also that we, being defended from the fear of our enemies, may live in peace and quietness; through Jesus Christ, Your Son, our Lord, who lives and reigns with You and the Holy Spirit, one God, now and forever. (410)

C **Amen.** *OR*

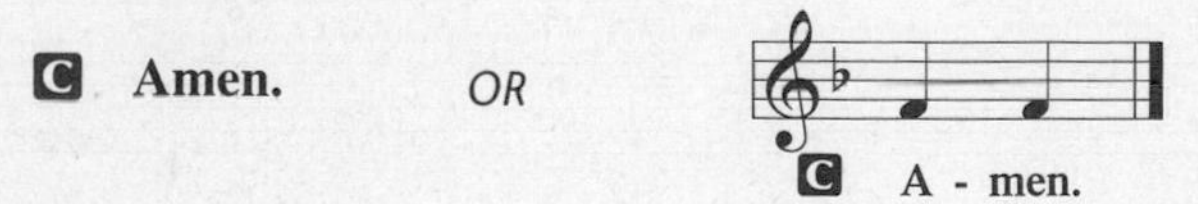
C A - men.

LORD'S PRAYER

Matthew 6:9–13

L Taught by our Lord and trusting His promises, we are bold to pray:

C **Our Father who art in heaven,**
hallowed be Thy name,
Thy kingdom come,
Thy will be done on earth as it is in heaven;
give us this day our daily bread;
and forgive us our trespasses as we forgive those who trespass against us;
and lead us not into temptation,
but deliver us from evil.
For Thine is the kingdom and the power and the glory forever and ever. Amen.

Stand

BENEDICAMUS

L Let us bless the Lord.
C Thanks be to God.

[Psalm 103:1]

BENEDICTION

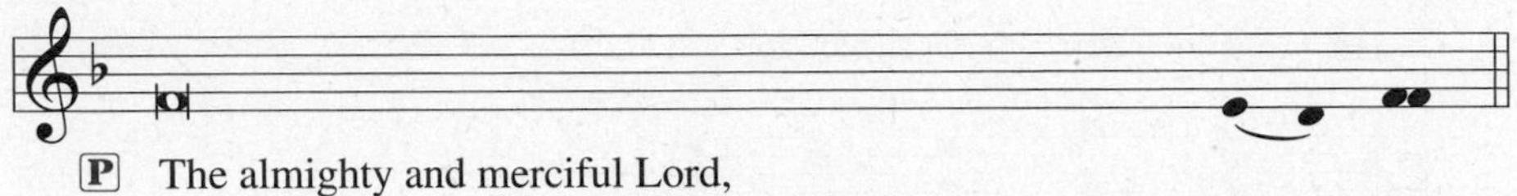

P The almighty and merciful Lord,
the Father, the ☩ Son, and the Holy Spirit, bless and pre - serve you.

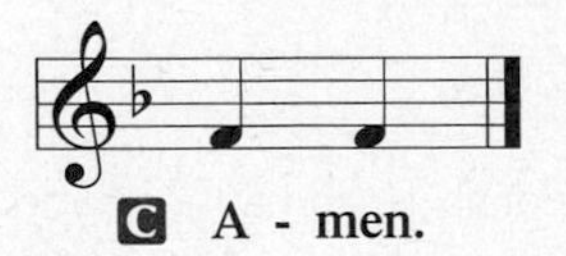
C A - men.

OR

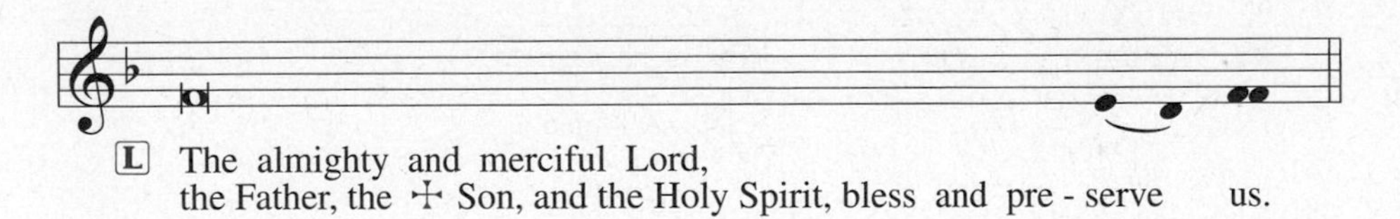
L The almighty and merciful Lord,
the Father, the ☩ Son, and the Holy Spirit, bless and pre - serve us.

C A - men.

COMPLINE

Prayer at the Close of the Day

The congregation assembles in silence.

Kneel/Stand

L The Lord Almighty grant us a qui - et night and peace at the last.

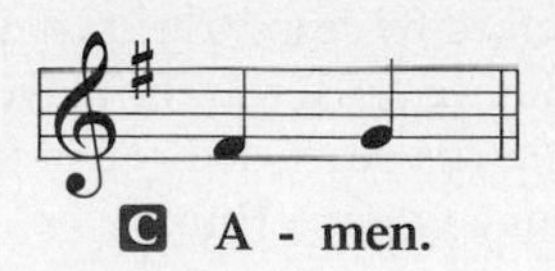

C A - men.

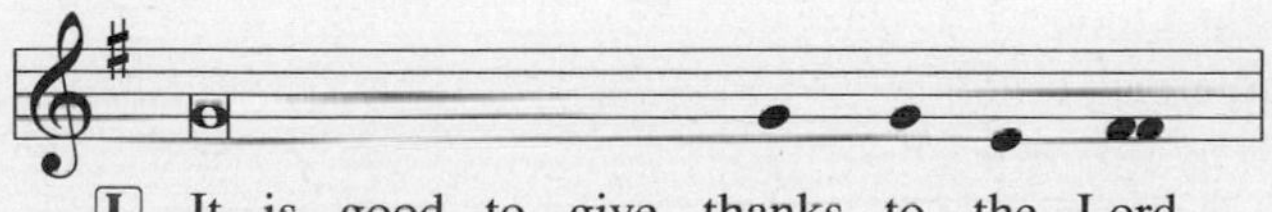

L It is good to give thanks to the Lord,

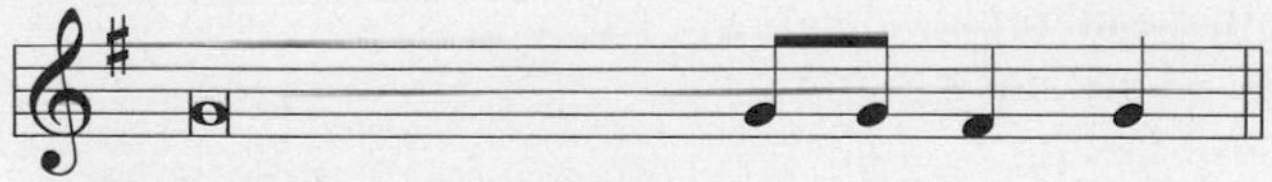

C to sing praise to Your name, O Most High;

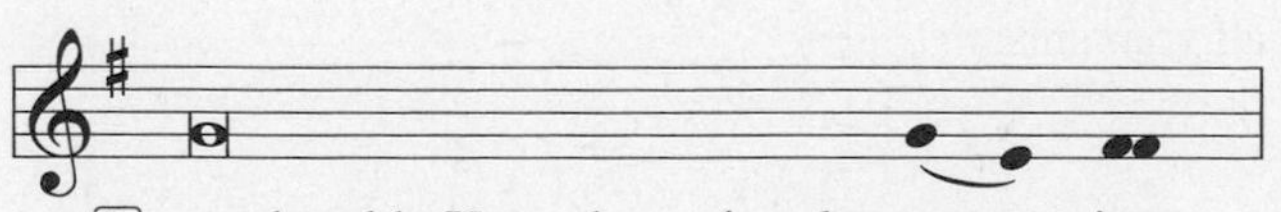

L to herald Your love in the morn - ing,

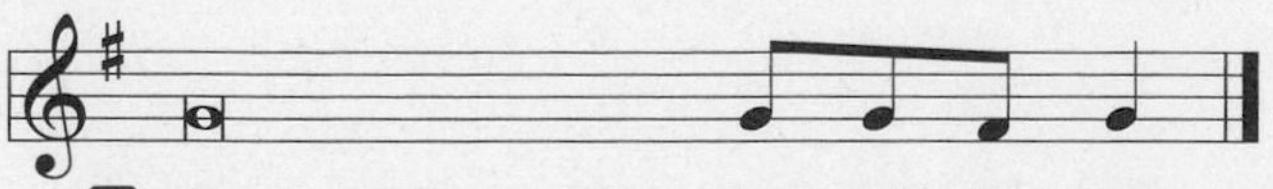

C Your truth at the close of the day.

Psalm 92:1

CONFESSION

L Let us confess our sin in the presence of God and of one another.

Silence for self-examination.

L I confess to God Almighty, before the whole company of heaven and to you, my brothers and sisters, that I have sinned in thought, word, and deed by my fault, by my own fault, by my own most grievous fault; wherefore I pray God Almighty to have mercy on me, forgive me all my sins, and bring me to everlasting life. Amen.

C **The almighty and merciful Lord grant you pardon, forgiveness, and remission of all your sins. Amen.**

C **I confess to God Almighty, before the whole company of heaven and to you, my brothers and sisters, that I have sinned in thought, word, and deed by my fault, by my own fault, by my own most grievous fault; wherefore I pray God Almighty to have mercy on me, forgive me all my sins, and bring me to everlasting life. Amen.**

L The almighty and merciful Lord grant you pardon, forgiveness, and remission of all your sins.

C **Amen.**

L Holy and gracious God,

C **I confess that I have sinned against You this day. Some of my sin I know—the thoughts and words and deeds of which I am ashamed—but some is known only to You. In the name of Jesus Christ I ask forgiveness. Deliver and restore me that I may rest in peace.**

L By the mercy of God we are redeemed by Jesus Christ, and in Him we are forgiven. We rest now in His peace and rise in the morning to serve Him.

C **Amen.**

Stand

PSALMODY

Sit

OFFICE HYMN

READINGS FROM HOLY SCRIPTURE

One or more of the following are read.

You, O Lord, are in the midst of us, and we are called by Your name; do not leave us. *(Jer. 14:9)*

Who is a God like You, pardoning iniquity and passing over transgression for the remnant of His inheritance? He does not retain His anger forever, because He delights in steadfast love. He will again have compassion on us; He will tread our iniquities under foot. You will cast all our sins into the depths of the sea. *(Micah 7:18–19)*

Come to Me, all who labor and are heavy laden, and I will give you rest. Take My yoke upon you, and learn from Me, for I am gentle and lowly in heart, and you will find rest for your souls. For My yoke is easy, and My burden is light. *(Matt. 11:28–30)*

Peace I leave with you; My peace I give to you. Not as the world gives do I give to you. Let not your hearts be troubled, neither let them be afraid. *(John 14:27)*

For I am sure that neither death nor life, nor angels nor rulers, nor things present nor things to come, nor powers, nor height nor depth, nor anything else in all creation, will be able to separate us from the love of God in Christ Jesus our Lord. *(Rom. 8:38–39)*

Humble yourselves, therefore, under the mighty hand of God so that at the proper time He may exalt you, casting all your anxieties on Him, because He cares for you. Be sober-minded; be watchful. Your adversary the devil prowls around like a roaring lion, seeking someone to devour. Resist him, firm in your faith. *(1 Peter 5:6–9a)*

RESPONSORY

Psalm 31:5

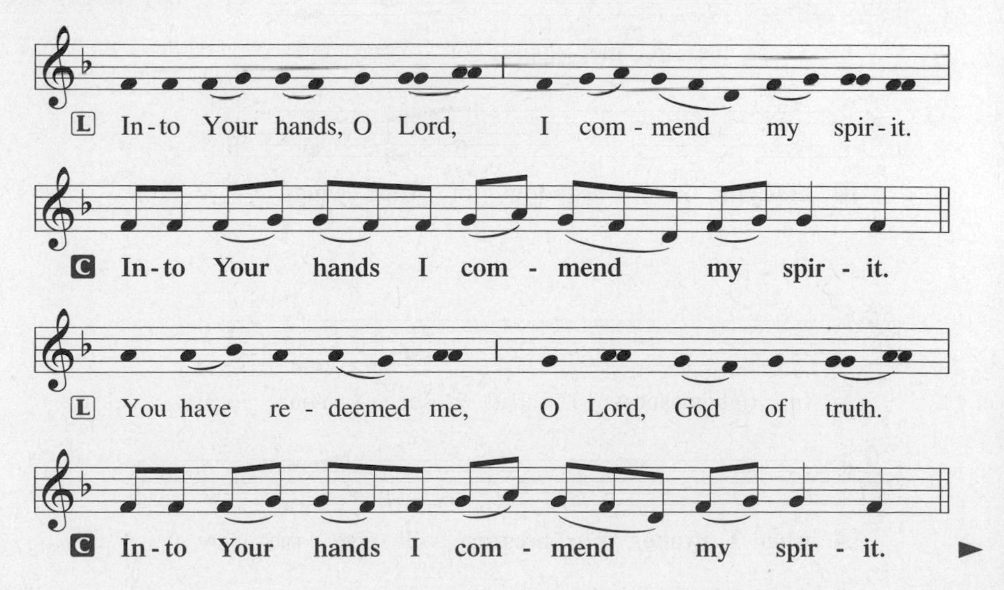
L In-to Your hands, O Lord, I com-mend my spir-it.
C In-to Your hands I com - mend my spir - it.
L You have re - deemed me, O Lord, God of truth.
C In-to Your hands I com - mend my spir - it.

►

L Glory be to the Fa - ther and to the Son and to the Ho-ly Spir-it.
C In-to Your hands I com - mend my spir - it.

A hymn may be sung.

Kneel/Stand

PRAYER

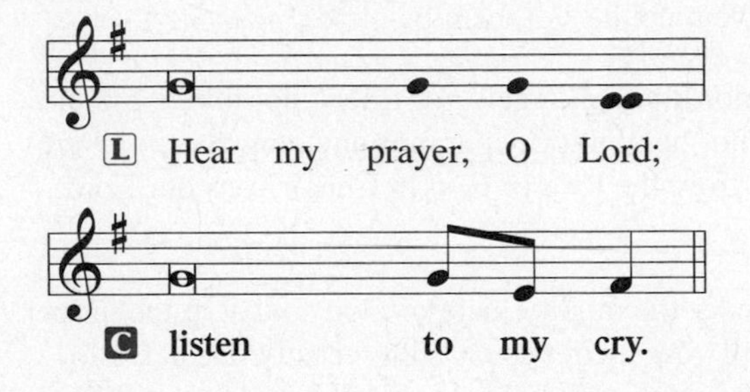
L Hear my prayer, O Lord;
C listen to my cry.

Psalm 102:1

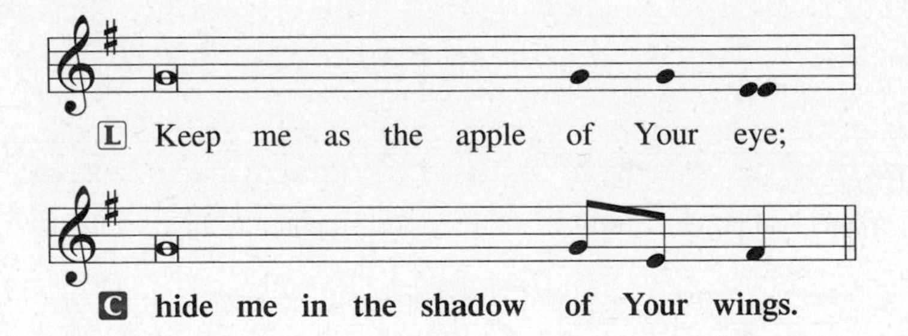
L Keep me as the apple of Your eye;
C hide me in the shadow of Your wings.

Psalm 17:8

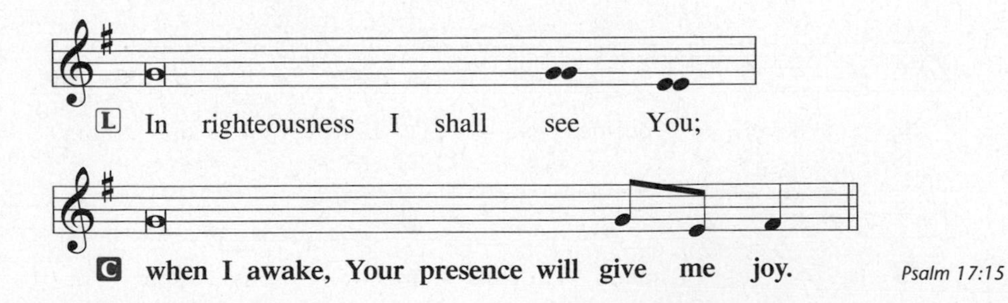
L In righteousness I shall see You;
C when I awake, Your presence will give me joy.

Psalm 17:15

One or more of the following are prayed.

L Be present, merciful God, and protect us through the hours of this night, so that we who are wearied by the changes and chances of life may find our rest in You; through Jesus Christ, our Lord. (416)

L O Lord, support us all the day long of this troubled life, until the shadows lengthen and the evening comes and the busy world is hushed, the fever of life is over, and our work is done. Then, Lord, in Your mercy grant us a safe lodging and a holy rest and peace at the last; through Jesus Christ, our Lord. (417)

L Be our light in the darkness, O Lord, and in Your great mercy defend us from all perils and dangers of this night; for the love of Your only Son, Jesus Christ, our Lord. (418)

L Visit our dwellings, O Lord, and drive from them all the snares of the enemy; let Your holy angels dwell with us to preserve us in peace; and let Your blessing be on us always; through Jesus Christ, our Lord. (419)

L Eternal God, the hours both of day and night are Yours, and to You the darkness is no threat. Be present, we pray, with those who labor in these hours of night, especially those who watch and work on behalf of others. Grant them diligence in their watching, faithfulness in their service, courage in danger, and competence in emergencies. Help them to meet the needs of others with confidence and compassion; through Jesus Christ, our Lord. (420)

L Abide with us, Lord, for it is toward evening, and the day is far spent. Abide with us and with Your whole Church. Abide with us at the end of the day, at the end of our life, at the end of the world. Abide with us with Your grace and goodness, with Your holy Word and Sacrament, with Your strength and blessing. Abide with us when the night of affliction and temptation comes upon us, the night of fear and despair, the night when death draws near. Abide with us and with all the faithful, now and forever. (421)

C **Amen.** *OR*

C **A - men.**

LORD'S PRAYER

Matthew 6:9–13

L Taught by our Lord and trusting His promises, we are bold to pray:

C **Our Father who art in heaven,**
hallowed be Thy name,
Thy kingdom come,
Thy will be done on earth as it is in heaven;
give us this day our daily bread;
and forgive us our trespasses as we forgive those who trespass against us;
and lead us not into temptation,
but deliver us from evil.
For Thine is the kingdom and the power and the glory forever and ever. Amen.

Stand

NUNC DIMITTIS ~ *Song of Simeon*

Luke 2:29–32

Antiphon
L Guide us wak - ing, O Lord, and guard us sleep - ing
that a - wake we may watch with Christ and asleep we may rest in peace.
C Lord, now You let Your ser - vant go in peace; Your word has been ful - filled.
My own eyes have seen the sal - va - tion which You have prepared
in the sight of ev'ry peo - ple: a light to reveal You to the na - tions
and the glory of Your peo - ple Is - ra - el. Glo - ry be to the
Fa - ther and to the Son and to the Ho - ly Spir - it;
as it was in the be - gin - ning, is now, and will be for -

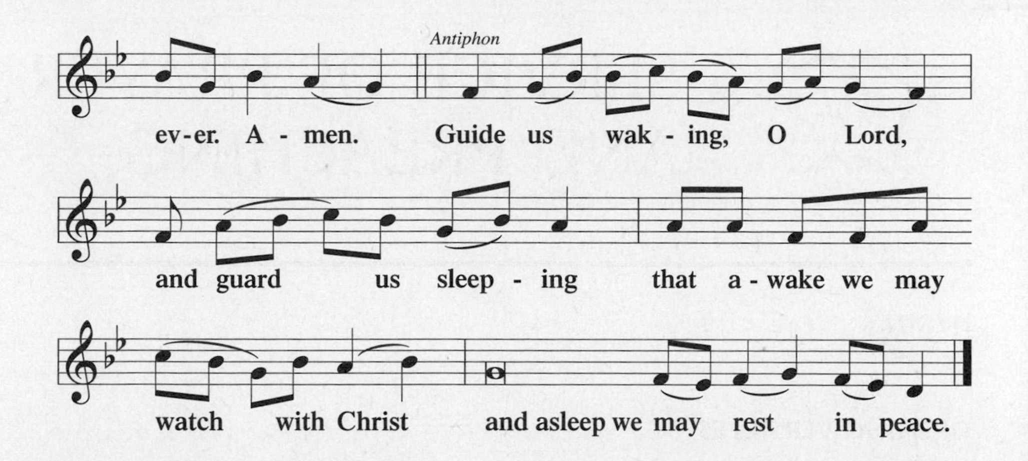
Antiphon
ev-er. A - men. Guide us wak - ing, O Lord,
and guard us sleep - ing that a - wake we may
watch with Christ and asleep we may rest in peace.

BENEDICTION

P The almighty and merciful Lord, the Fa - ther, the ☩ Son,
L The almighty and merciful Lord, the Fa - ther, the ☩ Son,
and the Holy Spir - it, bless you and keep you.
and the Holy Spir - it, bless us and keep us.

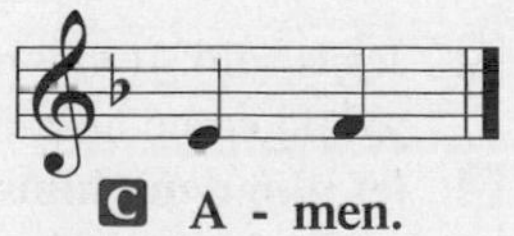
C A - men.

SERVICE OF PRAYER AND PREACHING

HYMN

Stand

OPENING VERSICLES

L This is the day which the Lord has made;
C **let us rejoice and be glad in it.** *Psalm 118:24*

L From the rising of the sun to its setting,
C **the name of the Lord is to be praised.** *Psalm 113:3*

Common

L Better is one day in Your courts than a thousand elsewhere;
C **I would rather be a doorkeeper in the house of my God than dwell in the tents of the wicked.**

L Make me to know Your ways, O Lord.
C **Teach me Your paths.**

L Sanctify us in Your truth.
C **Your Word is truth.**

Psalm 84:10; 25:4; John 17:17

Advent

L Out of Zion, the perfection of beauty, God shines forth.
C **Our God shall come; He does not keep silence.**

L Prepare the way of the Lord.
C **Make His paths straight.**

L Shower, O heavens, from above, and let the skies rain down righteousness.
C **Let the earth open, that salvation may sprout forth.**

Psalm 50:2–3a; Isaiah 40:3; 45:8

Lent

L Return to the Lord, your God, for He is gracious and merciful,
C **slow to anger, and abounding in steadfast love, and repents of evil.**

L Jesus said: If any man would come after Me,
C **let him deny himself and take up his cross and follow Me.**

L Christ was wounded for our transgressions.
C **He was bruised for our iniquities.**

Joel 2:13; Matthew 16:24; Isaiah 53:5

L From the rising of the sun to its setting,
C **the name of the Lord is to be praised.** *Psalm 113:3*

C **Glory be to the Father and to the Son and to the Holy Spirit; as it was in the beginning, is now, and will be forever. Amen.**

OLD TESTAMENT CANTICLE

Isaiah 12:2b–6

Refrain
C
The Lord God is my strength and my song, and
He has be - come my sal - va - tion.
Verse
With joy will you draw wa - ter from the
wells of sal - va - tion. And you will say in that
day: "Give thanks to the Lord, call up - on His name,
make known His deeds a - mong the peo - ples, pro -
claim that His name is ex - alt - ed."
Refrain
The Lord God is my strength and my song, and
He has be - come my sal - va - tion.
Verse
Sing prais - es to the Lord, for He has done
glo - rious - ly; let this be made known in all the

earth. Shout, and sing for joy, O in-
hab-i-tants of Zi-on, for great in your midst is the
Ho-ly One of Is-ra-el.
Refrain
The Lord God is my strength and my song, and
He has be-come my sal-va-tion.
Verse
Glo-ry be to the Fa-ther and to the Son
and to the Ho-ly Spir-it;
as it was in the be-gin-ning, is now, and will
be for-ev-er. A-men.
Refrain
The Lord God is my strength and my song, and
He has be-come my sal-va-tion.

Sit

READINGS FROM HOLY SCRIPTURE

After each reading:

L This is the Word of the Lord.

C **Thanks be to God.**

Psalms, hymns, or choral music may be sung between the readings.

RESPONSORY

Common

L Forever, O Lord, Your Word is firmly set in the heavens.

C **Lord, I love the habitation of Your house and the place where Your glory dwells.**

L Blessed are those who hear the Word of God and keep it.

C **Lord, I love the habitation of Your house and the place where Your glory dwells.**

L Glory be to the Father and to the Son and to the Holy Spirit.

C **Lord, I love the habitation of Your house and the place where Your glory dwells.**

Psalm 119:89; 26:8; Luke 11:28

Advent

L Behold, the days are coming, says the Lord, when I will raise up for David a righteous Branch.

C **This is the name by which He will be called: The Lord Is Our Righteousness.**

L He shall reign as king and deal wisely, and shall execute justice and righteousness in the land.

C **This is the name by which He will be called: The Lord Is Our Righteousness.**

L Glory be to the Father and to the Son and to the Holy Spirit.

C **This is the name by which He will be called: The Lord Is Our Righteousness.**

Jeremiah 23:5, 6b

Lent

L We have an advocate with the Father; Jesus Christ, the Righteous One.

C **He was delivered up to death; He was delivered for the sins of the people.**

L Blessed is the one whose transgression is forgiven, whose sin is covered.

C **He was delivered up to death; He was delivered for the sins of the people.**

L We have an advocate with the Father; Jesus Christ, the Righteous One.

C **He was delivered up to death; He was delivered for the sins of the people.**

1 John 2:1; [Mark 10:33]; Psalm 32:1

Stand

CATECHISM

One or more of the following parts of the Small Catechism may be spoken.

Ten Commandments

Exodus 20:2–17

C **You shall have no other gods.**
You shall not misuse the name of the Lord your God.
Remember the Sabbath day by keeping it holy.
Honor your father and your mother.
You shall not murder.
You shall not commit adultery.
You shall not steal.
You shall not give false testimony against your neighbor.
You shall not covet your neighbor's house.
You shall not covet your neighbor's wife, or his manservant or maidservant, his ox or donkey, or anything that belongs to your neighbor.

Apostles' Creed

C **I believe in God, the Father Almighty,**
maker of heaven and earth.

And in Jesus Christ, His only Son, our Lord,
who was conceived by the Holy Spirit,
born of the virgin Mary,
suffered under Pontius Pilate,
was crucified, died and was buried.
He descended into hell.
The third day He rose again from the dead.
He ascended into heaven
and sits at the right hand of God the Father Almighty.
From thence He will come to judge the living and the dead.

I believe in the Holy Spirit,
the holy Christian Church,
the communion of saints,
the forgiveness of sins,
the resurrection of the body,
and the life ☩ everlasting. Amen.

Christian: the ancient text reads "catholic," meaning the whole Church as it confesses the wholeness of Christian doctrine.

Lord's Prayer

Matthew 6:9–13

C **Our Father who art in heaven,**
hallowed be Thy name,
Thy kingdom come,
Thy will be done on earth as it is in heaven;
give us this day our daily bread;
and forgive us our trespasses as we forgive those who trespass against us;
and lead us not into temptation,
but deliver us from evil.
For Thine is the kingdom and the power and the glory forever and ever. Amen.

A responsive reading from the Small Catechism (pages 321–330) may follow.

Sit

SERMON or CATECHETICAL INSTRUCTION

HYMN

The Offering *may follow.*

Stand

PRAYER

L In peace let us pray to the Lord:
C Lord, have mercy.
L For the gift of divine peace and of pardon, with all our heart and with all our mind, let us pray to the Lord:
C Lord, have mercy.
L For the holy Christian Church, here and scattered throughout the world, and for the proclamation of the Gospel and the calling of all to faith, let us pray to the Lord:
C Lord, have mercy.
L For this nation, for our cities and communities, and for the common welfare of us all, let us pray to the Lord:
C Lord, have mercy.
L For seasonable weather and for the fruitfulness of the earth, let us pray to the Lord:
C Lord, have mercy.
L For those who labor, for those whose work is difficult or dangerous, and for all who travel, let us pray to the Lord:
C Lord, have mercy.
L For all those in need, for the hungry and homeless, for the widowed and orphaned, and for all those in prison, let us pray to the Lord:
C Lord, have mercy.
L For the sick and dying and for all those who care for them, let us pray to the Lord:
C Lord, have mercy.
L For . . . *[additional bids for prayer may be inserted here]* . . . let us pray to the Lord:
C Lord, have mercy.
L Finally, for these and for all our needs of body and soul, let us pray to the Lord:
C Lord, have mercy. Christ, have mercy. Lord, have mercy. (422)

Collect of the Day

L . . . one God, now and forever.
C Amen.

Collect for the Word

L Blessed Lord, You have caused all Holy Scriptures to be written for our learning. Grant that we may so hear them, read, mark, learn, and take them to heart that, by the patience and comfort of Your holy Word, we may embrace and ever hold fast the blessed hope of everlasting life; through Jesus Christ, Your Son, our Lord, who lives and reigns with You and the Holy Spirit, one God, now and forever. (405)
C Amen.

The prayers may conclude with one of the following:

Morning Prayer

C **I thank You, my heavenly Father, through Jesus Christ, Your dear Son, that You have kept me this night from all harm and danger; and I pray that You would keep me this day also from sin and every evil, that all my doings and life may please You. For into Your hands I commend myself, my body and soul, and all things. Let Your holy angel be with me, that the evil foe may have no power over me. Amen.** (423)

Small Catechism

Evening Prayer

C **I thank You, my heavenly Father, through Jesus Christ, Your dear Son, that You have graciously kept me this day; and I pray that You would forgive me all my sins where I have done wrong, and graciously keep me this night. For into Your hands I commend myself, my body and soul, and all things. Let Your holy angel be with me, that the evil foe may have no power over me. Amen.** (424)

Small Catechism

NEW TESTAMENT CANTICLE

1 Corinthians 15:20a; 5:7b; Romans 6:9–11

During Lent, another canticle is sung.

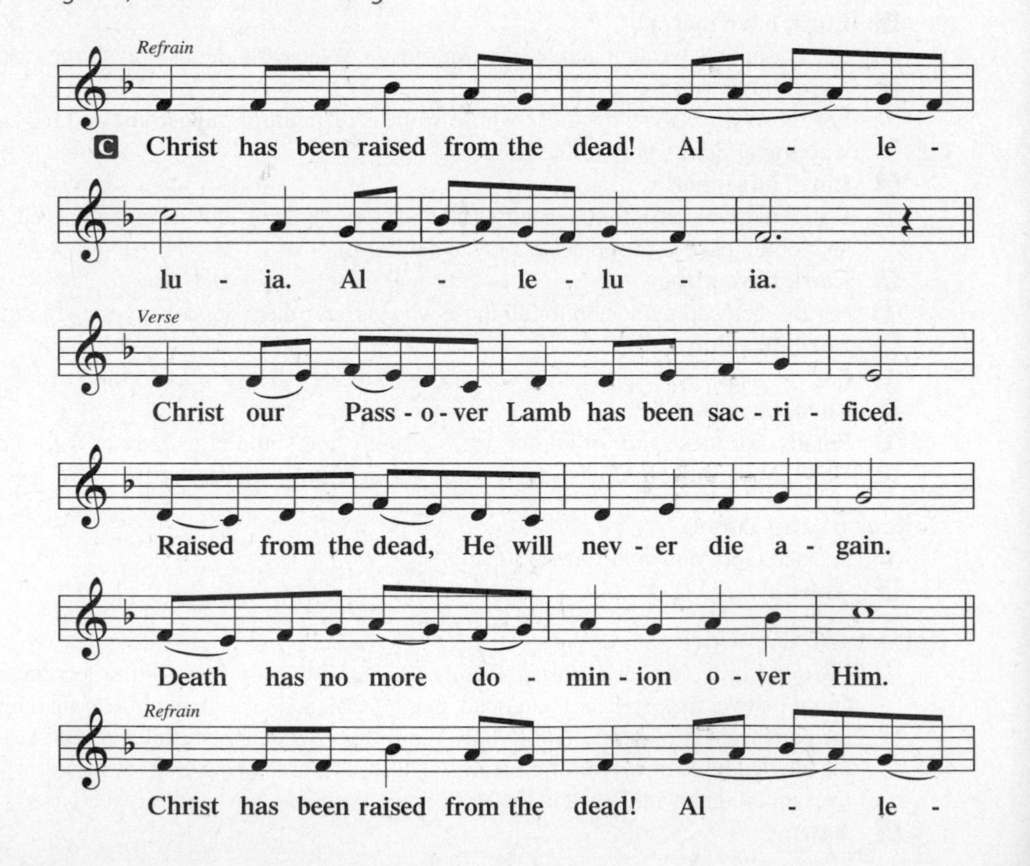
Refrain
C Christ has been raised from the dead! Al - le -
lu - ia. Al - le - lu - ia.
Verse
Christ our Pass - o - ver Lamb has been sac - ri - ficed.
Raised from the dead, He will nev - er die a - gain.
Death has no more do - min - ion o - ver Him.
Refrain
Christ has been raised from the dead! Al - le -

lu - ia. Al - le - lu - ia.
Verse
Dy-ing, Christ dies to sin, once for all. Liv-ing, He
lives to God. Count your-selves as dead to
sin and a-live to God in Christ Je - sus, our Lord.
Refrain
Christ has been raised from the dead! Al - le -
lu - ia. Al - le - lu - ia.

BLESSING

L Let us bless the Lord. [Psalm 103:1]

C **Thanks be to God.**

P The almighty and merciful Lord, the Father, the ☩ Son, and the Holy Spirit, bless and preserve you.

C **Amen.**

L The almighty and merciful Lord, the Father, the ☩ Son, and the Holy Spirit, bless and preserve us.

C **Amen.**

HOLY BAPTISM

An appropriate baptismal hymn may be sung. The candidate(s), sponsors, and family gather with the pastor at the entrance of the nave or at the font.

When candidates are unable to speak for themselves, the sponsors answer the questions on their behalf.

Stand

P In the name of the Father and of the ☩ Son and of the Holy Spirit. *Matthew 28:19b*

C **Amen.**

P Dearly beloved, Christ our Lord says in the last chapter of Matthew, "All authority in heaven and on earth has been given to Me. Therefore go and make disciples of all nations, baptizing them in the name of the Father and of the Son and of the Holy Spirit." In the last chapter of Mark our Lord promises, "Whoever believes and is baptized will be saved." And the apostle Peter has written, "Baptism now saves you."

Matthew 28:18b–19; Mark 16:16a; 1 Peter 3:21

The Word of God also teaches that we are all conceived and born sinful and are under the power of the devil until Christ claims us as His own. We would be lost forever unless delivered from sin, death, and everlasting condemnation. But the Father of all mercy and grace has sent His Son Jesus Christ, who atoned for the sin of the whole world, that whoever believes in Him should not perish but have eternal life.

The pastor addresses each candidate:

P How are you named?

R *Name*

The pastor makes the sign of the holy cross upon the forehead and heart of each candidate while saying:

P *Name*, receive the sign of the holy cross both upon your ☩ forehead and upon your ☩ heart to mark you as one redeemed by Christ the crucified.

P Let us pray.
Almighty and eternal God,
according to Your strict judgment You condemned the unbelieving world through
the flood,
yet according to Your great mercy You preserved believing Noah and his family,
eight souls in all.
You drowned hard-hearted Pharaoh and all his host in the Red Sea,
yet led Your people Israel through the water on dry ground,
foreshadowing this washing of Your Holy Baptism.

Through the Baptism in the Jordan of Your beloved Son, our Lord Jesus Christ,
You sanctified and instituted all waters to be a blessed flood
and a lavish washing away of sin.

We pray that You would behold _name(s)_ according to Your boundless mercy
and bless _him/her/them_ with true faith by the Holy Spirit,
that through this saving flood all sin in _him/her/them_,
which has been inherited from Adam
and which _he himself / she herself / they themselves_ _has/have_ committed since,
would be drowned and die.
Grant that _he/she/they_ be kept safe and secure in the holy ark of the
Christian Church,
being separated from the multitude of unbelievers
and serving Your name at all times with a fervent spirit and a joyful hope,
so that, with all believers in Your promise,
he/she/they would be declared worthy of eternal life;
through Jesus Christ, our Lord. (501)

C **Amen.**

If the sponsors were previously enrolled, the service continues below with the Holy Gospel.

P From ancient times the Church has observed the custom of appointing sponsors for baptismal candidates and catechumens. In the Evangelical Lutheran Church sponsors are to confess the faith expressed in the Apostles' Creed and taught in the Small Catechism. They are, whenever possible, to witness the Baptism of those they sponsor. They are to pray for them, support them in their ongoing instruction and nurture in the Christian faith, and encourage them toward the faithful reception of the Lord's Supper. They are at all times to be examples to them of the holy life of faith in Christ and love for the neighbor.

The pastor addresses the sponsors.

P Is it your intention to serve _name of candidate(s)_ as sponsors in the Christian faith?

R *Yes, with the help of God.*

P God enable you both to will and to do this faithful and loving work and with His grace fulfill what we are unable to do.

C **Amen.**

P Hear the Holy Gospel according to St. Mark.

They brought young children to [Jesus] that He might touch them; but the disciples rebuked those who brought them. But when Jesus saw it, He was greatly displeased and said to them, "Let the little children come to Me, and do not forbid them; for of such is the kingdom of God. Assuredly, I say to you, whoever does not receive the kingdom of God as a little child will by no means enter it." And He took them up in His arms, put His hands on them, and blessed them. *Mark 10:13–16 NKJV*

P This is the Word of the Lord.

C **Thanks be to God.**

The pastor places his hands on the head(s) of the candidate(s), and the congregation joins in praying:

C **Our Father who art in heaven,**
hallowed be Thy name,
Thy kingdom come,
Thy will be done on earth as it is in heaven;
give us this day our daily bread;
and forgive us our trespasses as we forgive those who trespass against us;
and lead us not into temptation,
but deliver us from evil. *Matthew 6:9–13*
For Thine is the kingdom and the power and the glory forever and ever. Amen.

If the baptismal party has stood at the entrance of the nave to this point, they now move to the font. A hymn may be sung during the procession. Then the pastor says:

P The Lord preserve your coming in and your going out from this time forth and even ☩ forevermore.

C **Amen.**

Sit

The pastor addresses the candidate(s) and asks the following questions:

P *Name(s)*, do you renounce the devil?

R *Yes, I renounce him.*

P Do you renounce all his works?

R *Yes, I renounce them.*

P Do you renounce all his ways?

R *Yes, I renounce them.*

P Do you believe in God, the Father Almighty, maker of heaven and earth?

R *Yes, I believe.*

P Do you believe in Jesus Christ, His only Son, our Lord, who was conceived by the Holy Spirit, born of the virgin Mary, suffered under Pontius Pilate, was crucified, died and was buried; He descended into hell; the third day He rose again from the dead; He ascended into heaven and sits at the right hand of God the Father Almighty; from thence He will come to judge the living and the dead?

R *Yes, I believe.*

P Do you believe in the Holy Spirit, the holy Christian Church, the communion of saints, the forgiveness of sins, the resurrection of the body, and the life everlasting?

R *Yes, I believe.*

P *Name*, do you desire to be baptized?

R *Yes, I do.*

The pastor pours water three times on the head of each candidate while saying:

P *Name*, I baptize you in the name of the Father and of the Son and of the Holy Spirit.

C **Amen.**

The pastor places his hands on the head of the newly baptized while saying:

P The almighty God and Father of our Lord Jesus Christ, who has given you the new birth of water and of the Spirit and has forgiven you all your sins, strengthen you with His grace to life ☩ everlasting.

C **Amen.**

The pastor may place a white garment on the newly baptized while saying:

P Receive this white garment to show that you have been clothed with the robe of Christ's righteousness that covers all your sin. So shall you stand without fear before the judgment seat of Christ to receive the inheritance prepared for you from the foundation of the world.

The pastor may light a baptismal candle from the paschal candle and give it to the newly baptized while saying:

P Receive this burning light to show that you have received Christ who is the Light of the world. Live always in the light of Christ, and be ever watchful for His coming, that you may meet Him with joy and enter with Him into the marriage feast of the Lamb in His kingdom, which shall have no end.

The newly baptized may be welcomed with the following:

A In Holy Baptism God the Father has made you *a member / members* of His Son, our Lord Jesus Christ, and *an heir / heirs* with us of all the treasures of heaven in the one holy Christian and apostolic Church. We receive you in Jesus' name as our *brother(s)/sister(s)* in Christ, that together we might hear His Word, receive His gifts, and proclaim the praises of Him who called us out of darkness into His marvelous light.

C **Amen. We welcome you in the name of the Lord.**

Stand

P Let us pray.
Almighty and most merciful God and Father, we thank and praise You that You graciously preserve and enlarge Your family and have granted *name(s)* the new birth in Holy Baptism and made *him/her/them* *a member / members* of Your Son, our Lord Jesus Christ, and *an heir / heirs* of Your heavenly kingdom. We humbly implore You that, as *he/she/they* *has/have* now become Your *child/children*, You would keep *him/her/them* in *his/her/their* baptismal grace, that according to Your good pleasure *he/she/they* may faithfully grow to lead a godly life to the praise and honor of Your holy name and finally, with all Your saints, obtain the promised inheritance in heaven; through Jesus Christ, our Lord. (503)

C **Amen.**

P Peace ☩ be with you.

C **Amen.**

All return to their places.

CONFIRMATION

The pastor addresses the catechumens.

P Beloved in the Lord, our Lord Jesus Christ said to His apostles: "All authority has been given to Me in heaven and on earth. Therefore go and make disciples of all nations, baptizing them in the name of the Father and of the Son and of the Holy Spirit, teaching them to observe all things that I have commanded you; and lo, I am with you always, even to the end of the age." You have been baptized and catechized in the Christian faith according to our Lord's bidding. Jesus said, "Whoever confesses Me before men, I will also confess before My Father who is in heaven. But whoever denies Me before men, I will also deny before My Father who is in heaven." Lift up your hearts, therefore, to the God of all grace and joyfully give answer to what I now ask you in the name of the Lord.

Matthew 28:18b–20 NKJV; Matthew 10:32–33 NKJV alt.

P Do you this day in the presence of God and of this congregation acknowledge the gifts that God gave you in your Baptism?

R *Yes, I do.*

P Do you renounce the devil?

R *Yes, I renounce him.*

P Do you renounce all his works?

R *Yes, I renounce them.*

P Do you renounce all his ways?

R *Yes, I renounce them.*

P Do you believe in God, the Father Almighty?

R *Yes, I believe in God, the Father Almighty, maker of heaven and earth.*

P Do you believe in Jesus Christ, His only Son, our Lord?

R *Yes, I believe in Jesus Christ, His only Son, our Lord, who was conceived by the Holy Spirit, born of the virgin Mary, suffered under Pontius Pilate, was crucified, died and was buried. He descended into hell. The third day He rose again from the dead. He ascended into heaven and sits at the right hand of God the Father Almighty. From thence He will come to judge the living and the dead.*

P Do you believe in the Holy Spirit?
R *Yes, I believe in the Holy Spirit, the holy Christian Church, the communion of saints, the forgiveness of sins, the resurrection of the body, and the life everlasting.*

P Do you hold all the prophetic and apostolic Scriptures to be the inspired Word of God?
R *I do.*

P Do you confess the doctrine of the Evangelical Lutheran Church, drawn from the Scriptures, as you have learned to know it from the Small Catechism, to be faithful and true?
R *I do.*

P Do you intend to hear the Word of God and receive the Lord's Supper faithfully?
R *I do, by the grace of God.*

P Do you intend to live according to the Word of God, and in faith, word, and deed to remain true to God, Father, Son, and Holy Spirit, even to death?
R *I do, by the grace of God.*

P Do you intend to continue steadfast in this confession and Church and to suffer all, even death, rather than fall away from it?
R *I do, by the grace of God.*

P We rejoice with thankful hearts that you have been baptized and have received the teaching of the Lord. You have confessed the faith and been absolved of your sins. As you continue to hear the Lord's Word and receive His blessed Sacrament, He who has begun a good work in you will bring it to completion at the day of Jesus Christ.
C **Amen.**

The catechumens kneel to receive the confirmation blessing. The pastor places his hands on the head of each catechumen and makes the sign of the cross on the forehead while saying:
P *Name*, the almighty God and Father of our Lord Jesus Christ, who has given you the new birth of water and of the Spirit and has forgiven you all your sins, strengthen you with His grace to life ☩ everlasting.
R *Amen.*

The pastor may read a text of Holy Scripture as a remembrance of confirmation. After all the catechumens have received the blessing, one or both of the following collects are prayed.

Stand

P Let us pray.
Lord God, heavenly Father, we thank and praise You for Your great goodness in bringing these Your sons and daughters to the knowledge of Your Son, our Savior, Jesus Christ, and enabling them both with the heart to believe and with the mouth to confess His saving name. Grant that, bringing forth the fruits of faith, they may continue steadfast and victorious to the day when all who have fought the good fight of faith shall

receive the crown of righteousness; through Jesus Christ, Your Son, our Lord, who lives and reigns with You and the Holy Spirit, one God, now and forever. (513)

C **Amen.**

P Almighty and most merciful Father, in the waters of Holy Baptism You have united Your children in the suffering and death of Your Son Jesus Christ, cleansing them by His blood. Renew in them the gift of Your Holy Spirit, that they may live in daily contrition and repentance with a faith that ever clings to their Savior. Deliver them from the power of Satan and preserve them from false and dangerous doctrines, that they may remain faithful in hearing Christ's Word and receiving His body and blood. By the Lord's Supper strengthen them to believe that no one can make satisfaction for sin but Christ alone. Enable them to find joy and comfort only in Him, learning from this Sacrament to love You and their neighbor and to bear their cross with patience and joy until the day of the resurrection of their bodies to life immortal; through Jesus Christ, Your Son, our Lord, who lives and reigns with You and the Holy Spirit, one God, now and forever. (514)

C **Amen.**

P Peace ☩ be with you.

C **Amen.**

The service continues with the Prayer of the Church.

HOLY MATRIMONY

This rite is designed for use at the beginning of the Divine Service or Daily Office. It may also stand by itself as an independent order of service.

Stand

P In the name of the Father and of the ☩ Son and of the Holy Spirit. *Matthew 28:19b*
C **Amen.**

P Dearly beloved, we are gathered here in the sight of God and before His Church to witness the union of this man and this woman in holy matrimony. This is an honorable estate instituted and blessed by God in Paradise, before humanity's fall into sin.

In marriage we see a picture of the communion between Christ and His bride, the Church. Our Lord blessed and honored marriage with His presence and first miracle at Cana in Galilee. This estate is also commended to us by the apostle Paul as good and honorable. Therefore, marriage is not to be entered into inadvisedly or lightly, but reverently, deliberately, and in accordance with the purposes for which it was instituted by God.

The union of husband and wife in heart, body, and mind is intended by God for the mutual companionship, help, and support that each person ought to receive from the other, both in prosperity and adversity. Marriage was also ordained so that man and woman may find delight in one another. Therefore, all persons who marry shall take a spouse in holiness and honor, not in the passion of lust, for God has not called us to impurity but in holiness. God also established marriage for the procreation of children who are to be brought up in the fear and instruction of the Lord so that they may offer Him their praise.

For these reasons God has established the holy estate that *name* and *name* wish to enter. They desire our prayers as they begin their marriage in the Lord's name and with His blessing.

If this wedding rite is being used as an independent service, the following or other appropriate passages from Holy Scripture are now read: Genesis 2:7, 18–24 or 1:26–28; Ephesians 5:1–2, 22–33; and Matthew 19:4–6 or Mark 10:1–9. A sermon is also preached. A hymn may precede or follow. The wedding party may be seated throughout.

If the wedding party has been seated, they now stand and take their places before the chancel steps.

The pastor asks the bridegroom and bride in turn:

P ___*Name of bridegroom*___, will you have this woman to be your wedded wife, to live together in the holy estate of matrimony as God ordained it? Will you nourish and cherish her as Christ loved His body, the Church, giving Himself up for her? Will you love, honor, and keep her in sickness and in health and, forsaking all others, remain united to her alone, so long as you both shall live? Then say: I will.

[Ephesians 5:29]

R *I will.*

P ___*Name of bride*___, will you have this man to be your wedded husband, to live together in the holy estate of matrimony as God ordained it? Will you submit to him as the Church submits to Christ? Will you love, honor, and keep him in sickness and in health and, forsaking all others, remain united to him alone, so long as you both shall live? Then say: I will. *[Ephesians 5:24]*

R *I will.*

The pastor may ask for the bride to be given in marriage or for the parents of the couple to give their consent and blessing.

The pastor leads the couple to the altar for them to speak their vows. The bridegroom says:

I, ___*name*___, take you, ___*name*___, to be my wedded wife, to have and to hold from this day forward, for better, for worse, for richer, for poorer, in sickness and in health, to love and to cherish, till death us do part, according to God's holy will; and I pledge to you my faithfulness.

The bride says:

I, ___*name*___, take you, ___*name*___, to be my wedded husband, to have and to hold from this day forward, for better, for worse, for richer, for poorer, in sickness and in health, to love and to cherish, till death us do part, according to God's holy will; and I pledge to you my faithfulness.

The rings are presented to the pastor.

P Almighty Father, You have generously created all things to serve us for our good. Send Your blessing upon this couple who shall wear these ☩ rings as a constant reminder of their marital fidelity. Grant that by Your mercy they may live gladly and faithfully in this holy estate; through Jesus Christ, Your Son, our Lord, who lives and reigns with You and the Holy Spirit, one God, now and forever. (525)

C **Amen.**

The bridegroom and bride exchange rings.

The couple kneels. The pastor continues:

P Now that ___*name*___ and ___*name*___ have committed themselves to each other in holy matrimony, have given themselves to each other by their solemn pledges, and have declared the same before God and these witnesses, I pronounce them to be husband and wife, in the name of the Father and of the ☩ Son and of the Holy Spirit.

C **Amen.**

P What God has joined together, let no one put asunder. *Matthew 19:6*

C **Amen.**

The pastor blesses the couple.

P The almighty and gracious God abundantly grant you His favor and sanctify and bless you with the blessing given to Adam and Eve in Paradise, that you may please Him in both body and soul and live together in holy love until your life's end.

C **Amen.**

If the wedding rite has not taken place within another order of service, it concludes with prayer, the Lord's Prayer, and the following blessing:

P The Lord bless you and keep you.
The Lord make His face shine upon you and be gracious unto you.
The Lord lift up His countenance upon you and ☩ give you peace. *Numbers 6:24–26*

C **Amen.**

FUNERAL SERVICE

A hymn or psalm may be sung or spoken.

Stand

INVOCATION

The sign of the cross ☩ may be made by all in remembrance of their Baptism.

P In the name of the Father and of the ☩ Son and of the Holy Spirit.

C **Amen.** *Matthew 28:19b*

REMEMBRANCE OF BAPTISM

The casket may be covered with a funeral pall.

P In Holy Baptism ___*name*___ was clothed with the robe of Christ's righteousness that covered all ___*his/her*___ sin. St. Paul says: "Do you not know that all of us who have been baptized into Christ Jesus were baptized into His death?"

C **We were buried therefore with Him by baptism into death, in order that, just as Christ was raised from the dead by the glory of the Father, we too might walk in newness of life. For if we have been united with Him in a death like His, we shall certainly be united with Him in a resurrection like His.**

Romans 6:3–5

INTROIT, PSALM, or ENTRANCE HYMN

KYRIE ~ *Lord, Have Mercy*

Mark 10:47

P Lord, have mercy upon us.

C **Christ, have mercy upon us.**
Lord, have mercy upon us.

SALUTATION and COLLECT OF THE DAY

P The Lord be with you. *2 Timothy 4:22*

C **And also with you.**

P Let us pray.
O God of grace and mercy, we give thanks for Your loving-kindness shown to ___*name*___ and to all Your servants who, having finished their course in faith, now rest from their labors. Grant that we also may be faithful unto death and receive the crown of eternal life; through Jesus Christ, Your Son, our Lord, who lives and reigns with You and the Holy Spirit, one God, now and forever. (546)

C **Amen.**

Sit

OLD TESTAMENT or FIRST READING

After the reading:

[A] This is the Word of the Lord.

[C] **Thanks be to God.**

PSALM or GRADUAL

EPISTLE or SECOND READING

After the reading:

[A] This is the Word of the Lord.

[C] **Thanks be to God.**

Stand

VERSE

General

[A] Alleluia, alle- | luia.*
Jesus Christ is the firstborn | of the dead;

[C] **to Him be glory and power for- | ever.***
Alle- | luia. *[Revelation 1:5–6]*

Lent

[A] If we have | died with Christ,*
we shall also | live with Him;

[C] **if we are faithful | to the end,***
we shall | reign with Him.

2 Timothy 2:11b–12a

HOLY GOSPEL

[P] The Holy Gospel according to St. ________, the ________ chapter.

[C] **Glory to You, O Lord.**

After the reading:

[P] This is the Gospel of the Lord.

[C] **Praise to You, O Christ.**

APOSTLES' CREED

[P] God has made us His people through our Baptism into Christ. Living together in trust and hope, we confess our faith.

[C] **I believe in God, the Father Almighty,**
maker of heaven and earth.

And in Jesus Christ, His only Son, our Lord,
who was conceived by the Holy Spirit,
born of the virgin Mary,
suffered under Pontius Pilate,
was crucified, died and was buried.
He descended into hell.
The third day He rose again from the dead.
He ascended into heaven
and sits at the right hand of God the Father Almighty.
From thence He will come to judge the living and the dead.

I believe in the Holy Spirit,
the holy Christian Church,
the communion of saints,
the forgiveness of sins,
the resurrection of the body,
and the life ☩ everlasting. Amen.

Christian: the ancient text reads "catholic," meaning the whole Church as it confesses the wholeness of Christian doctrine.

Sit

HYMN OF THE DAY

SERMON

Kneel/Stand

PRAYER OF THE CHURCH

[1 Timothy 2:1–4]

P Let us pray to the Lord, our God and Father, who raised Jesus from the dead.

After each portion of the prayers:

P Lord, in Your mercy,
C **hear our prayer.**

The prayers conclude:

C **Amen.**

When there is Holy Communion, the service continues with the Offertory in the Divine Service; otherwise, the service continues with the Lord's Prayer.

LORD'S PRAYER

Matthew 6:9–13

P Taught by our Lord and trusting His promises, we are bold to pray:
C **Our Father who art in heaven,**
hallowed be Thy name,
Thy kingdom come,
Thy will be done on earth as it is in heaven;
give us this day our daily bread;
and forgive us our trespasses as we forgive those who trespass against us;
and lead us not into temptation,
but deliver us from evil.
For Thine is the kingdom and the power and the glory forever and ever. Amen.

Following the Lord's Prayer (or the Distribution when there is Holy Communion), the pastor takes his place at the casket.

NUNC DIMITTIS ~ *Song of Simeon*

A "I am the resurrection and the life," says the Lord. "He who believes in Me will live, even though he dies; and whoever lives and believes in Me will never die."

John 11:25–26 NIV

C **Lord, now You let Your servant go in peace;**
Your word has been fulfilled.
My own eyes have seen the salvation
which You have prepared in the sight of every people:
a light to reveal You to the nations
and the glory of Your people Israel. *Luke 2:29–32*
Glory be to the Father and to the Son and to the Holy Spirit;
as it was in the beginning, is now, and will be forever. Amen.

A "I am the resurrection and the life," says the Lord. "He who believes in Me will live, even though he dies; and whoever lives and believes in Me will never die."

CONCLUDING COLLECT

P The Lord be with you. *2 Timothy 4:22*
C **And also with you.**

P Let us pray.
Lord God, our shepherd, You gather the lambs of Your flock into the arms of Your mercy and bring them home. Comfort us with the certain hope of the resurrection to everlasting life and a joyful reunion with those we love who have died in the faith; through Jesus Christ, Your Son, our Lord, who lives and reigns with You and the Holy Spirit, one God, now and forever. (549)
C **Amen.**

BENEDICAMUS and BENEDICTION

A Let us bless the Lord. *[Psalm 103:1]*
C **Thanks be to God.**

P The Lord bless you and keep you.
The Lord make His face shine upon you and be gracious unto you.
The Lord lift up His countenance upon you and ☩ give you peace.
C **Amen.** *Numbers 6:24–26*

P Let us go forth in peace,
C **in the name of the Lord. Amen.**

A hymn may be sung as the casket is led in procession out of the church.

RESPONSIVE PRAYER 1

Suffrages

L Holy God, holy and most gracious Father,
C **have mercy and hear us.**

C **Our Father who art in heaven,**
hallowed be Thy name,
Thy kingdom come,
Thy will be done on earth as it is in heaven;
give us this day our daily bread;
and forgive us our trespasses as we forgive those who trespass against us;
and lead us not into temptation,
but deliver us from evil. *Matthew 6:9–13*
For Thine is the kingdom and the power and the glory forever and ever. Amen.

C **I believe in God, the Father Almighty,**
maker of heaven and earth.

And in Jesus Christ, His only Son, our Lord,
who was conceived by the Holy Spirit,
born of the virgin Mary,
suffered under Pontius Pilate,
was crucified, died and was buried.
He descended into hell.
The third day He rose again from the dead.
He ascended into heaven
and sits at the right hand of God the Father Almighty.
From thence He will come to judge the living and the dead.

I believe in the Holy Spirit,
the holy Christian Church,
the communion of saints,
the forgiveness of sins,
the resurrection of the body,
and the life ✝ everlasting. Amen.

Christian: the ancient text reads "catholic," meaning the whole Church as it confesses the wholeness of Christian doctrine.

Morning

L I cry to You, O Lord;
C **in the morning my prayer comes before You.** *Psalm 88:13*

L Restore to me the joy of Your salvation,
C **and uphold me with a willing spirit.** *Psalm 51:12*

L My mouth is filled with Your praise,
C **and with Your glory all the day.** *Psalm 71:8*

L Every day I will bless You
C **and praise Your name forever and ever.** *Psalm 145:2*

L By awesome deeds You answer us with righteousness,
C **O God of our salvation, the hope of all the ends of the earth and of the farthest seas.** *Psalm 65:5*

L Bless the Lord, O my soul;
C **and all that is within me, bless His holy name!** *Psalm 103:1*

L He redeems your life from the pit
C **and crowns you with steadfast love and mercy.** *Psalm 103:4*

L Hear my prayer, O Lord;
C **let my cry come to You.** *Psalm 102:1*

Afternoon/Evening

L Show us Your steadfast love, O Lord,
C **and grant us Your salvation.** *Psalm 85:7*

L Let Your priests be clothed with righteousness;
C **and let Your saints shout for joy.** *Psalm 132:9*

L Lord, keep this nation under Your care,
C **and guide us in the way of justice and truth.** *Liturgical Text*

L Let the nations be glad and sing for joy,
C **for You judge the peoples with equity and guide the nations upon the earth.**

L Let the peoples praise You, O God;
C **let all the peoples praise You!** *Psalm 67:4–5*

L For the needy shall not always be forgotten,
C **and the hope of the poor shall not perish forever.** *Psalm 9:18*

L Create in me a clean heart, O God,
C **and renew a right spirit within me.** *Psalm 51:10*

L Hear my prayer, O Lord;
C **let my cry come to You.** *Psalm 102:1*

L Let us pray.

The COLLECT OF THE DAY *and other suitable collects may be prayed. The prayers conclude with one of the following:*

Morning

C **I thank You, my heavenly Father, through Jesus Christ, Your dear Son, that You have kept me this night from all harm and danger; and I pray that You would keep me this day also from sin and every evil, that all my doings and life may please You. For into Your hands I commend myself, my body and soul, and all things. Let Your holy angel be with me, that the evil foe may have no power over me. Amen.** (423) *Small Catechism*

OR

Noon

L Gracious Jesus, our Lord and our God, at this hour You bore our sins in Your own body on the tree so that we, being dead to sin, might live unto righteousness. Have mercy upon us now and at the hour of our death, and grant to us, Your servants, with all others who devoutly remember Your blessed passion, a holy and peaceful life in this world and through Your grace eternal glory in the life to come, where, with the Father and the Holy Spirit, You live and reign, one God, now and forever. (425)

C **Amen.**

OR

Afternoon

L Heavenly Father, in whom we live and move and have our being, we humbly pray You so to guide and govern us by Your Word and Spirit, that in all the cares and occupations of our life we may not forget You but remember that we are ever walking in Your sight; through Jesus Christ, our Lord. (426)

C **Amen.**

OR

Evening

C **I thank You, my heavenly Father, through Jesus Christ, Your dear Son, that You have graciously kept me this day; and I pray that You would forgive me all my sins where I have done wrong, and graciously keep me this night. For into Your hands I commend myself, my body and soul, and all things. Let Your holy angel be with me, that the evil foe may have no power over me. Amen.** (424)

Small Catechism

L Let us bless the Lord. *[Psalm 103:1]*

C **Thanks be to God.**

L The Lord bless us, defend us from all evil, and bring us to everlasting life.

C **Amen.**

RESPONSIVE PRAYER 2

OPENING VERSICLES

L O Lord, open my lips,
C **and my mouth will declare Your praise.** *Psalm 51:15*
L Make haste, O God, to deliver me;
C **make haste to help me, O Lord.** *Psalm 70:1*
Glory be to the Father and to the Son and to the Holy Spirit;
as it was in the beginning, is now, and will be forever. Amen.

A psalm may be sung or spoken.

READINGS

After each reading:
L This is the Word of the Lord.
C **Thanks be to God.**

A hymn or canticle may be sung.

KYRIE

Mark 10:47

L O Lord, C **have mercy.**
L O Christ, C **have mercy.**
L O Lord, C **have mercy.**

LORD'S PRAYER

Matthew 6:9–13

C **Our Father who art in heaven,**
hallowed be Thy name,
Thy kingdom come,
Thy will be done on earth as it is in heaven;
give us this day our daily bread;
and forgive us our trespasses as we forgive those who trespass against us;
and lead us not into temptation,
but deliver us from evil.
For Thine is the kingdom and the power and the glory forever and ever. Amen.

APOSTLES' CREED

C **I believe in God, the Father Almighty,
maker of heaven and earth.**

**And in Jesus Christ, His only Son, our Lord,
who was conceived by the Holy Spirit,
born of the virgin Mary,
suffered under Pontius Pilate,
was crucified, died and was buried.
He descended into hell.
The third day He rose again from the dead.
He ascended into heaven
and sits at the right hand of God the Father Almighty.
From thence He will come to judge the living and the dead.**

**I believe in the Holy Spirit,
the holy Christian Church,
the communion of saints,
the forgiveness of sins,
the resurrection of the body,
and the life ☩ everlasting. Amen.**

Christian: the ancient text reads "catholic," meaning the whole Church as it confesses the wholeness of Christian doctrine.

VERSICLES

L Hear my prayer, O Lord;
C **let my cry come to You.** *Psalm 102:1*

L In the day of my trouble I call upon You,
C **for You answer me.** *Psalm 86:7*

L Hide Your face from my sins,
C **and blot out all my iniquities.**

L Create in me a clean heart, O God,
C **and renew a right spirit within me.**

L Cast me not away from Your presence,
C **and take not Your Holy Spirit from me.**

L Restore to me the joy of Your salvation,
C **and uphold me with a willing spirit.** *Psalm 51:9–12*

L Because Your steadfast love is better than life,
C **my lips will praise You.**

L For You have been my help,
C **and in the shadow of Your wings I will sing for joy.** *Psalm 63:3, 7*

L Teach me Your way, O Lord, that I may walk in Your truth;
C **unite my heart to fear Your name.**

L I give thanks to You, O Lord my God, with my whole heart,
C **and I will glorify Your name forever.** *Psalm 86:11–12*

L May all who seek You rejoice and be glad in You.
C **May those who love Your salvation say evermore, "God is great!"** *Psalm 70:4*

L Save Your people and bless Your heritage!
C **Be their shepherd and carry them forever.** *Psalm 28:9*

L Give ear, O Lord, to my prayer;
C **listen to my plea for grace.** *Psalm 86:6*

COLLECTS

L Let us pray.

The COLLECT OF THE DAY *and other suitable collects may be prayed. The prayers may conclude with one of the following:*

Morning

C **I thank You, my heavenly Father, through Jesus Christ, Your dear Son, that You have kept me this night from all harm and danger; and I pray that You would keep me this day also from sin and every evil, that all my doings and life may please You. For into Your hands I commend myself, my body and soul, and all things. Let Your holy angel be with me, that the evil foe may have no power over me. Amen.** (423) *Small Catechism*

OR

Evening

C **I thank You, my heavenly Father, through Jesus Christ, Your dear Son, that You have graciously kept me this day; and I pray that You would forgive me all my sins where I have done wrong, and graciously keep me this night. For into Your hands I commend myself, my body and soul, and all things. Let Your holy angel be with me, that the evil foe may have no power over me. Amen.** (424) *Small Catechism*

OR

Before Travel

L Lord God our Father, You kept Abraham and Sarah in safety throughout the days of their pilgrimage, You led the children of Israel through the midst of the sea, and by a star You led the Wise Men to the infant Jesus. Protect and guide us now in this time as we set out to travel. Make our ways safe and our homecomings joyful, and bring us at last to our heavenly home, where You dwell in glory with Your Son and the Holy Spirit, one God, now and forever. (427)
C **Amen.**

BENEDICAMUS and BLESSING

L Let us bless the Lord. *[Psalm 103:1]*
C **Thanks be to God.**

L The Lord bless us, defend us from all evil, and bring us to everlasting life.
C **Amen.**

THE LITANY

A musical setting of the Litany is available in the Altar Book.

Kneel/Stand

L O Lord, C **have mercy.**

L O Christ, C **have mercy.**

L O Lord, C **have mercy.**

L O Christ, C **hear us.**

L God the Father in heaven, C **have mercy.**

L God the Son, Redeemer of the world, C **have mercy.**

L God the Holy Spirit, C **have mercy.**

L Be gracious to us. C **Spare us, good Lord.**

L Be gracious to us. C **Help us, good Lord.**

L From all sin, from all error, from all evil;
From the crafts and assaults of the devil; from sudden and evil death;
From pestilence and famine; from war and bloodshed; from sedition and from rebellion;
From lightning and tempest; from all calamity by fire and water; and from everlasting death:

C **Good Lord, deliver us.**

L By the mystery of Your holy incarnation; by Your holy nativity;
By Your baptism, fasting, and temptation; by Your agony and bloody sweat; by Your cross and passion; by Your precious death and burial;
By Your glorious resurrection and ascension; and by the coming of the Holy Spirit, the Comforter:

C **Help us, good Lord.**

L In all time of our tribulation; in all time of our prosperity; in the hour of death; and in the day of judgment:

C **Help us, good Lord.**

L We poor sinners implore You
C **to hear us, O Lord.**

L To rule and govern Your holy Christian Church; to preserve all pastors and ministers of Your Church in the true knowledge and understanding of Your wholesome Word and to sustain them in holy living;

To put an end to all schisms and causes of offense; to bring into the way of truth all who have erred and are deceived;

To beat down Satan under our feet; to send faithful laborers into Your harvest; and to accompany Your Word with Your grace and Spirit:

C **We implore You to hear us, good Lord.**

L To raise those who fall and to strengthen those who stand; and to comfort and help the weakhearted and the distressed:

C **We implore You to hear us, good Lord.**

L To give to all peoples concord and peace; to preserve our land from discord and strife; to give our country Your protection in every time of need;

To direct and defend our *president/queen/king* and all in authority; to bless and protect our magistrates and all our people;

To watch over and help all who are in danger, necessity, and tribulation; to protect and guide all who travel;

To grant all women with child, and all mothers with infant children, increasing happiness in their blessings; to defend all orphans and widows and provide for them;

To strengthen and keep all sick persons and young children; to free those in bondage; and to have mercy on us all:

C **We implore You to hear us, good Lord.**

L To forgive our enemies, persecutors, and slanderers and to turn their hearts; to give and preserve for our use the kindly fruits of the earth; and graciously to hear our prayers:

C **We implore You to hear us, good Lord.**

L Lord Jesus Christ, Son of God,
C **we implore You to hear us.**

L Christ, the Lamb of God, who takes away the sin of the world,
C **have mercy.**

L Christ, the Lamb of God, who takes away the sin of the world,
C **have mercy.**

L Christ, the Lamb of God, who takes away the sin of the world,
C **grant us Your peace.**

L O Christ, C **hear us.**
L O Lord, C **have mercy.**
L O Christ, C **have mercy.**
L O Lord, C **have mercy. Amen.**

The Litany may conclude with the LORD'S PRAYER *and a collect.*

CORPORATE CONFESSION AND ABSOLUTION

Stand

A hymn of confession or repentance may be sung.

The sign of the cross ☩ may be made by all in remembrance of their Baptism.

P In the name of the Father and of the ☩ Son and of the Holy Spirit.

C **Amen.**

P I will go to the altar of God,

C **to God my exceeding joy.** *Psalm 43:4*

P Our help is in the name of the Lord,

C **who made heaven and earth.** *Psalm 124:8*

Sit

The following Confessional Address is read.

P Beloved in the Lord, it is our intention to receive the Holy Supper of our Lord Jesus Christ, in which He strengthens our faith by giving us His body to eat and His blood to drink. Therefore, it is proper that we diligently examine ourselves, as St. Paul urges us to do, for this holy Sacrament has been instituted for the special comfort of those who are troubled because of their sin and who humbly confess their sins, fear God's wrath, and hunger and thirst for righteousness.

But when we examine our hearts and consciences, we find nothing in us but sin and death, from which we are incapable of delivering ourselves. Therefore, our Lord Jesus Christ has had mercy on us. For our benefit He became man so that He might fulfill for us the whole will and law of God and, to deliver us, took upon Himself our sin and the punishment we deserve.

So that we may more confidently believe this and be strengthened in the faith and in holy living, our Lord Jesus Christ took bread, broke it, and gave it to His disciples and said: "Take, eat; this is My body, which is given for you." It is as if He said, "I became man, and all that I do and suffer is for your good. As a pledge of this, I give you My body to eat."

In the same way also He took the cup, gave thanks, and gave it to them, saying: "Drink of it, all of you; this cup is the new testament in My blood, which is shed for you for the forgiveness of sins." Again, it is as if He said, "I have had mercy on you by taking into Myself all your iniquities. I give Myself into death, shedding My blood to obtain grace and forgiveness of sins, and to comfort and establish the new testament, which gives forgiveness and everlasting salvation. As a pledge of this, I give you My blood to drink."

Therefore, whoever eats this bread and drinks this cup, confidently believing this Word and promise of Christ, dwells in Christ and Christ in him and has eternal life.

We should also do this in remembrance of Him, showing His death—that He was delivered for our offenses and raised for our justification. Giving Him our most heartfelt thanks, we take up our cross and follow Him and, according to His commandment, love one another as He has loved us. For we are all one bread and one body, even as we are all partakers of this one bread and drink from the one cup. For just as the one cup is filled with wine of many grapes and one bread made from countless grains, so also we, being many, are one body in Christ. Because of Him, we love one another, not only in word, but in deed and in truth.

May the almighty and merciful God and Father of our Lord Jesus Christ, by His Holy Spirit, accomplish this in us.

C **Amen.**

P Having heard the Word of God, let us confess our sins to Him, imploring Him for the sake of His Son Jesus Christ to grant us forgiveness.

Kneel/Stand

C **O almighty God, merciful Father, I, a poor, miserable sinner, confess unto You all my sins and iniquities with which I have ever offended You and justly deserved Your temporal and eternal punishment. But I am heartily sorry for them and sincerely repent of them, and I pray You of Your boundless mercy and for the sake of the holy, innocent, bitter sufferings and death of Your beloved Son, Jesus Christ, to be gracious and merciful to me, a poor, sinful being.**

P God be merciful to you and strengthen your faith.

C **Amen.**

P Do you believe that the forgiveness I speak is not my forgiveness but God's?

C **Yes.**

P Let it be done for you as you believe.

The pastor absolves the penitents individually at the altar, laying his hands on the head of each and pronouncing the following absolution, or he may absolve all the penitents corporately from the altar.

P In the stead and by the command of my Lord Jesus Christ I forgive you all your sins in the name of the Father and of the ☩ Son and of the Holy Spirit.

C **Amen.**

After all have returned to their seats, the pastor speaks this blessing.

P Now may the God of peace Himself sanctify you completely, and may your whole spirit, soul, and body be kept blameless at the coming of our Lord Jesus Christ. He who calls you is faithful; He will surely do it. Go in ☩ peace.

C **Amen.**

1 Thessalonians 5:23–24

INDIVIDUAL CONFESSION AND ABSOLUTION

Based on the Rite in Luther's Small Catechism

You may prepare yourself by meditating on the Ten Commandments (pages 321–322). You may also pray the penitential psalms (6, 32, 38, 51, 102, 130, or 143).

If you are not burdened with particular sins, do not trouble yourself or search for or invent other sins, thereby turning confession into a torture. Instead, mention one or two sins that you know and let that be enough.

When you are ready, kneel and say:

Pastor, please hear my confession and pronounce forgiveness in order to fulfill God's will.

Proceed.

I, a poor sinner, plead guilty before God of all sins.
I have lived as if God did not matter and as if I mattered most.
My Lord's name I have not honored as I should;
my worship and prayers have faltered.
I have not let His love have its way with me,
and so my love for others has failed.
There are those whom I have hurt, and those whom I have failed to help.
My thoughts and desires have been soiled with sin.

> *If you wish to confess specific sins that trouble you, continue as follows:*
>
> **What troubles me particularly is that . . .**
>
> *Confess whatever you have done against the commandments of God, according to your own place in life.*
>
> *The pastor may gently question or instruct you—not to pry or judge—but to assist in self-examination.*

Then conclude by saying:

I am sorry for all of this and ask for grace. I want to do better.

God be merciful to you and strengthen your faith.
Amen.

Do you believe that my forgiveness is God's forgiveness?
Yes.

Let it be done for you as you believe.

The pastor places his hands on the head of the penitent and says:

In the stead and by the command of my Lord Jesus Christ I forgive you all your sins in the name of the Father and of the ☩ Son and of the Holy Spirit.
Amen.

The pastor may speak additional Scripture passages to comfort and strengthen the faith of those who have great burdens of conscience or are sorrowful and distressed.

The pastor concludes:
Go in peace.
Amen.

You may remain to say a prayer of thanksgiving. Psalms 30, 31, 32, 34, 103, or 118 are also appropriate.

DAILY PRAYER

For Individuals and Families

These brief services are intended as a simple form of daily prayer for individuals and families, and in other settings.

When more than one person is present, the versicles and responses may be spoken responsively, with one person reading the words in regular type and the others responding with the words in bold type. Prayers that are in bold type are to be prayed by all.

For the readings, several verses have been recommended for each particular time of day. These may be used on a rotating basis. The value in using these few texts lies in the opportunity to learn them well. For those desiring a more complete selection of readings, daily lectionaries, such as the one found on pages 299–304, may be followed. Readings from the Small Catechism (pages 321–330) may also be incorporated into the services.

In the prayers "for others and ourselves," the following suggestions may be used to establish a pattern of daily and weekly prayer.

Sunday: For the joy of the resurrection among us; for the fruit of faith nourished by the Word and the Sacraments.

Monday: For faith to live in the promises of Holy Baptism; for one's calling and daily work; for the unemployed; for the salvation and well-being of our neighbors; for schools, colleges, and seminaries; for good government and for peace.

Tuesday: For deliverance against temptation and evil; for the addicted and despairing, the tortured and oppressed; for those struggling with sin.

Wednesday: For marriage and family, that husbands and wives, parents and children live in ordered harmony according to the Word of God; for parents who must raise children alone; for our communities and neighborhoods.

Thursday: For the Church and her pastors; for teachers, deaconesses, and other church workers; for missionaries and for all who serve the Church; for fruitful and salutary use of the blessed Sacrament of Christ's body and blood.

Friday: For the preaching of the holy cross of our Lord Jesus Christ and for the spread of His knowledge throughout the whole world; for the persecuted and oppressed; for the sick and dying.

Saturday: For faithfulness to the end; for the renewal of those who are withering in the faith or have fallen away; for receptive hearts and minds to God's Word on the Lord's Day; for pastors and people as they prepare to administer and receive Christ's holy gifts.

MORNING

The sign of the cross ☩ may be made by all in remembrance of their Baptism.

In the name of the Father and of the ☩ Son and of the Holy Spirit.
Amen.

In the morning, O Lord, You hear my voice;
in the morning I prepare a sacrifice for You and watch. *Psalm 5:3*

My mouth is filled with Your praise,
and with Your glory all the day. *Psalm 71:8*

O Lord, open my lips,
and my mouth will declare Your praise. *Psalm 51:15*

Glory be to the Father and to the Son and to the Holy Spirit;
as it was in the beginning, is now, and will be forever. Amen.

A hymn, canticle, or psalm may be sung or spoken.

An appointed reading or one of the following is read: Colossians 3:1–4; Exodus 15:1–11; Isaiah 12:1–6; Matthew 20:1–16; Mark 13:32–36; Luke 24:1–9; John 21:4–14; Ephesians 4:17–24; Romans 6:1–4.

A portion of the Small or Large Catechism may be read.

The Apostles' Creed is confessed.

Lord's Prayer

Prayers for others and ourselves

Concluding prayers:
Almighty God, merciful Father, who created and completed all things, on this day when the work of our calling begins anew, we implore You to create its beginning, direct its continuance, and bless its end, that our doings may be preserved from sin, our life sanctified, and our work this day be well pleasing to You; through Jesus Christ, our Lord. (441)
Amen.

I thank You, my heavenly Father, through Jesus Christ, Your dear Son, that You have kept me this night from all harm and danger; and I pray that You would keep me this day also from sin and every evil, that all my doings and life may please You. For into Your hands I commend myself, my body and soul, and all things. Let Your holy angel be with me, that the evil foe may have no power over me. Amen. (423)
Small Catechism

Let us bless the Lord. *[Psalm 103:1]*
Thanks be to God.

Then go joyfully to your work.

NOON

The sign of the cross ☩ may be made by all in remembrance of their Baptism.

In the name of the Father and of the ☩ Son and of the Holy Spirit.
Amen.

Listen to my prayer, O God, do not ignore my plea;
hear me and answer me.

Evening, morning, and noon
I cry out in distress, and He hears my voice.

Cast your cares on the Lord and He will sustain you;
He will never let the righteous fall. *Psalm 55:1–2a, 17, 22 NIV*

Glory be to the Father and to the Son and to the Holy Spirit;
as it was in the beginning, is now, and will be forever. Amen.

A hymn, canticle, or psalm may be sung or spoken.

An appointed reading or one of the following is read: 1 Corinthians 7:17a, 23–24; Luke 23:44–46; Matthew 5:13–16; Matthew 13:1–9, 18–23; Mark 13:24–27; John 15:1–9; Romans 7:18–25; Romans 12:1–2; 1 Peter 1:3–9; Revelation 7:13–17.

O Lord,
have mercy upon us.
O Christ,
have mercy upon us.
O Lord,
have mercy upon us. *Mark 10:47*

Lord's Prayer

Prayers for others and ourselves

Concluding prayer:

Blessed Lord Jesus Christ, at this hour You hung upon the cross, stretching out Your loving arms to embrace the world in Your death. Grant that all people of the earth may look to You and see their salvation; for Your mercy's sake we pray. (442)
Amen.

Heavenly Father, send Your Holy Spirit into our hearts to direct and rule us according to Your will, to comfort us in all our afflictions, to defend us from all error, and to lead us into all truth; through Jesus Christ, our Lord. (443)
Amen.

Let us bless the Lord. *[Psalm 103:1]*
Thanks be to God.

EARLY EVENING

The sign of the cross ☩ may be made by all in remembrance of their Baptism.

In the name of the Father and of the ☩ Son and of the Holy Spirit.
Amen.

A candle may be lighted.

Let my prayer rise before You as incense,
the lifting up of my hands as the evening sacrifice. *Psalm 141:2*

Joyous light of glory:
of the immortal Father;
heavenly, holy, blessed Jesus Christ.
We have come to the setting of the sun,
and we look to the evening light.
We sing to God, the Father, Son, and Holy Spirit:
You are worthy of being praised with pure voices forever.
O Son of God, O Giver of life: the universe proclaims Your glory.

A hymn, canticle, or psalm may be sung or spoken.

An appointed reading or one of the following is read: Luke 24:28–31; Exodus 16:11–21, 31; Isaiah 25:6–9; Matthew 14:15–21; Matthew 27:57–60; Luke 14:15–24; John 6:25–35; John 10:7–18; Ephesians 6:10–18a.

A portion of the Small or Large Catechism may be read.

Lord's Prayer

Prayers for others and ourselves

Concluding prayer:
Lord Jesus, stay with us, for the evening is at hand and the day is past. Be our constant companion on the way, kindle our hearts, and awaken hope among us, that we may recognize You as You are revealed in the Scriptures and in the breaking of the bread. Grant this for Your name's sake. (444)
Amen.

Let us bless the Lord. *[Psalm 103:1]*
Thanks be to God.

Mealtime Prayers

Asking a blessing before the meal
Lord God, heavenly Father, bless us and these Your gifts which we receive from Your bountiful goodness, through Jesus Christ, our Lord. Amen. (445) *Small Catechism*

Returning thanks after the meal
We thank You, Lord God, heavenly Father, for all Your benefits, through Jesus Christ, our Lord, who lives and reigns with You and the Holy Spirit forever and ever. Amen. (446) *Small Catechism*

CLOSE OF THE DAY

The sign of the cross ☩ may be made by all in remembrance of their Baptism.

In the name of the Father and of the ☩ Son and of the Holy Spirit.
Amen.

The Lord Almighty grant us a quiet night and peace at the last.
Amen.

It is good to give thanks to the Lord,
to sing praise to Your name, O Most High;

To herald Your love in the morning,
Your truth at the close of the day. *Psalm 92:1–2*

An appointed reading or one of the following is read: Matthew 11:28–30; Micah 7:18–20; Matthew 18:15–35; Matthew 25:1–13; Luke 11:1–13; Luke 12:13–34; Romans 8:31–39; 2 Corinthians 4:16–18; Revelation 21:22—22:5.

The Apostles' Creed is confessed.

Lord, now You let Your servant go in peace;
Your word has been fulfilled.
My own eyes have seen the salvation
which You have prepared in the sight of every people:
a light to reveal You to the nations
and the glory of Your people Israel. *Luke 2:29–32*
Glory be to the Father and to the Son and to the Holy Spirit;
as it was in the beginning, is now, and will be forever. Amen.

Lord's Prayer

Prayers for others and ourselves

Concluding prayers:
Visit our dwellings, O Lord, and in Your great mercy defend us from all perils and dangers of this night; for the love of Your only Son, our Savior Jesus Christ. (447)
Amen.

I thank You, my heavenly Father, through Jesus Christ, Your dear Son, that You have graciously kept me this day; and I pray that You would forgive me all my sins where I have done wrong, and graciously keep me this night. For into Your hands I commend myself, my body and soul, and all things. Let Your holy angel be with me, that the evil foe may have no power over me. Amen. (424) *Small Catechism*

Let us bless the Lord. *[Psalm 103:1]*
Thanks be to God.

Then go to sleep at once and in good cheer.

DAILY LECTIONARY

Following historic practice, this lectionary presents a continuous reading through the books of the Bible, often associating certain books with particular seasons of the Church Year. The goal is not to read through the entire Bible each year. Rather, two readings of 15–25 verses each are provided for each day—one from the Old Testament, the other from the New Testament. Under this plan, nearly all of the New Testament and approximately one-third of the Old Testament are read each year. Please note the following:

- *The lectionary begins with Ash Wednesday. During the seasons of Lent and Easter—the movable seasons in the Church Year—the Church Year calendar is followed.*
- *Following Holy Trinity Sunday, the calendar year is followed. The calendar readings are continued until the beginning of Lent in the following year.*
- *Occasionally a third, optional reading is listed in italic type. This reading covers materials that would otherwise be omitted from the daily readings. Sometimes it provides parallel readings, for example, from the minor prophets.*
- *A chart for daily psalm readings has been provided on page 304.*

The Time of Easter

Lenten Season

Ash Wed.	Gen. 1:1–19 Mark 1:1–13
Th	Gen. 1:20—2:3 Mark 1:14–28
F	Gen. 2:4–25 Mark 1:29–45
S	Gen. 3:1–24 Mark 2:1–17
Lent 1	Gen. 4:1–26 Mark 2:18–28
M	Gen. 6:1—7:5 Mark 3:1–19
T	Gen. 7:11—8:12 Mark 3:20–35
W	Gen. 8:13—9:17 *Gen. 9:18—11:26* Mark 4:1–20
Th	Gen. 11:27—12:20 Mark 4:21–41
F	Gen. 13:1–18 *Gen. 14:1–24* Mark 5:1–20
S	Gen. 15:1–21 Mark 5:21–43
Lent 2	Gen. 16:1-9, 15—17:22 Mark 6:1–13
M	Gen. 18:1–15 *Gen. 18:16—20:18* Mark 6:14–34
T	Gen. 21:1–21 Mark 6:35–56
W	Gen. 22:1–19 Mark 7:1–23
Th	Gen. 24:1–31 Mark 7:24–37
F	Gen. 24:32–52, 61–67 *Gen. 25:1—26:35* Mark 8:1–21
S	Gen. 27:1–29 Mark 8:22–38
Lent 3	Gen. 27:30–45; 28:10–22 Mark 9:1–13
M	Gen. 29:1–30 *Gen. 29:31—34:31* Mark 9:14–32
T	Gen. 35:1–29 Mark 9:33–50
W	Gen. 37:1–36 Mark 10:1–12
Th	Gen. 39:1–23 Mark 10:13–31
F	Gen. 40:1–23 Mark 10:32–52
S	Gen. 41:1–27 Mark 11:1–19
Lent 4	Gen. 41:28–57 Mark 11:20–33
M	Gen. 42:1–34, 38 Mark 12:1–12
T	Gen. 43:1–28 Mark 12:13–27
W	Gen. 44:1–18, 32–34 Mark 12:28–44
Th	Gen. 45:1–20, 24–28 Mark 13:1–23
F	Gen. 47:1–31 *Gen. 48:1—49:28* Mark 13:24–37
S	Gen. 49:29—50:7, 14–26 Mark 14:1–11
Lent 5	Ex. 1:1–22 Mark 14:12–31
M	Ex. 2:1–22 Mark 14:32–52
T	Ex. 2:23—3:22 Mark 14:53–72
W	Ex. 4:1–18 Mark 15:1–15
Th	Ex. 4:19–31 Mark 15:16–32
F	Ex. 5:1—6:1 Mark 15:33–47
S	Ex. 7:1–25 Mark 16:1–20

Holy Week

Palm Sun. Ex. 8:1–32
Psalm 118
Heb. 1:1–14

M Ex. 9:1–28
Lam. 1:1–22
Heb. 2:1–18

T Ex. 9:29—10:20
Lam. 2:1–22
Heb. 3:1–19

W Ex. 10:21—11:10
Lam. 3:1–66
Heb. 4:1–16

Holy Thurs. Ex. 12:1–28
Lam. 4:1–22
Heb. 5:1–14
Psalm 31

Good Fri. Ex. 12:29–32; 13:1–16
Lam. 5:1–22
Heb. 6:1–20
Psalm 22

Holy Sat. Ex. 13:17—14:9
Heb. 7:1–22

Easter Season

Easter Sun. Ex. 14:10–31
Heb. 7:23—8:13

M Ex. 15:1–18
Heb. 9:1–28

T Ex. 15:19—16:12
Heb. 10:1–18

W Ex. 16:13–35
Heb. 10:19–39

Th Ex. 17:1–16
Heb. 11:1–29

F Ex. 18:5–27
Heb. 12:1–24

S Ex. 19:1–25
Heb. 13:1–21

Easter 2 Ex. 20:1–24
Luke 4:1–15

M Ex. 22:20—23:13
Luke 4:16–30

T Ex. 23:14–33
Luke 4:31–44

W Ex. 24:1–18
Luke 5:1–16

Th Ex. 25:1–22
Ex. 25:23—30:38
Luke 5:17–39

F Ex. 31:1–18
Luke 6:1–19

S Ex. 32:1–14
Luke 6:20–38

Easter 3 Ex. 32:15–35
Luke 6:39–49

M Ex. 33:1–23
Luke 7:1–17

T Ex. 34:1–28
Luke 7:18–35

W Ex. 34:29—35:21
Ex. 35:22—38:20
Luke 7:36–50

Th Ex. 38:21—39:8, 22–23, 27–31
Luke 8:1–21

F Ex. 39:32—40:16
Luke 8:22–39

S Ex. 40:17–38
Lev. 1:1—7:38
Luke 8:40–56

Easter 4 Lev. 8:1–13, 30–36
Luke 9:1–17

M Lev. 9:1–24
Luke 9:18–36

T Lev. 10:1–20
Lev. 11:1—15:33
Luke 9:37–62

W Lev. 16:1–24
Luke 10:1–22

Th Lev. 17:1–16
Luke 10:23–42

F Lev. 18:1–7, 20—19:8
Luke 11:1–13

S Lev. 19:9–18, 26–37
Luke 11:14–36

Easter 5 Lev. 20:1–16, 22–27
Luke 11:37–54

M Lev. 21:1–24
Luke 12:1–12

T Lev. 23:1–22
Luke 12:13–34

W Lev. 23:23–44
Luke 12:35–53

Th Lev. 24:1–23
Lev. 25:1–55
Luke 12:54—13:17

F Lev. 26:1–20
Luke 13:18–35

S Lev. 26:21–33, 39–44
Num. 1:1—2:34
Luke 14:1–24

Easter 6 Num. 3:1–16, 39–48
Num. 4:1—8:4
Luke 14:25—15:10

M Num. 8:5–26
Luke 15:11–32

T Num. 9:1–23
Luke 16:1–18

W Num. 10:11–36
Luke 16:19–31

Ascension Num. 11:1–23, 31–35
Luke 17:1–19

F Num. 11:24–29; 12:1–16
Luke 17:20–37

S Num. 13:1–3, 17–33
Luke 18:1–17

Easter 7 Num. 14:1–25
Luke 18:18–34

M Num. 14:26–45
Num. 15:1–41
Luke 18:35—19:10

T Num. 16:1–22
Luke 19:11–28

W Num. 16:23–40
Luke 19:29–48

Th Num. 16:41—17:13
Num. 18:1—19:22
Luke 20:1–18

F Num. 20:1–21
Luke 20:19–44

S Num. 20:22—21:9
Luke 20:45—21:19

Pentecost Day Num. 21:10–35
Luke 21:20–38

M Num. 22:1–20
Luke 22:1–23

T Num. 22:21—23:3
Luke 22:24–46

W Num. 23:4–28
Luke 22:47–71

Th Num. 24:1–25
Luke 23:1–25

F Num. 27:12–23
Luke 23:26–56

S Num. 32:1–6, 16–27
Luke 24:1–27

The Time of the Church

Holy Trinity Num. 35:9–30
Acts 1:1—7:60
Luke 24:28–53

18 May Song 1:1—2:7
John 5:1–18

19 May Song 2:8—3:11
John 5:19–29

20 May Song 4:1—5:1
John 5:30–47

21 May Song 5:2—6:3
John 6:1–21

22 May Song 6:4—7:5
John 6:22–40

23 May Song 7:6—8:14
John 6:41–59

24 May Eccl. 1:1–18
Esther 1:1—10:3
John 6:60–71

25 May Eccl. 2:1–26
John 7:1–13

26 May Eccl. 3:1–22
John 7:14–31

27 May Eccl. 4:1–16
John 7:32–53

28 May Eccl. 5:1–20
John 8:1–20

29 May Eccl. 6:1—7:10
John 8:21–38

30 May Eccl. 7:11–29
John 8:39–59

31 May Eccl. 8:1–17
John 9:1–23

1 June Eccl. 9:1–17
John 9:24–41

2 June Eccl. 10:1–20
John 10:1–21

3 June Eccl. 11:1–10
John 10:22–42

4 June Eccl. 12:1–14
John 11:1–16

5 June Prov. 1:8–33
John 11:17–37

6 June Prov. 3:5–24
John 11:38–57

7 June	Prov. 4:1–27
	John 12:1–19
8 June	Prov. 5:1–23
	Prov. 6:1—7:27
	John 12:20–36a
9 June	Prov. 8:1–21
	John 12:36b–50
10 June	Prov. 8:22–36
	John 13:1–20
11 June	Prov. 9:1–18
	John 13:21–38
12 June	Prov. 10:1–23
	Prov. 11:1—12:28
	John 14:1–17
13 June	Prov. 13:1–25
	John 14:18–31
14 June	Prov. 14:1–27
	John 15:1–11
15 June	Prov. 15:1–29
	John 15:12–27
16 June	Prov. 16:1–24
	John 16:1–16
17 June	Prov. 17:1–28
	Prov. 18:1—20:4
	John 16:17–33
18 June	Prov. 20:5–25
	Prov. 21:1–31
	John 17:1–26
19 June	Prov. 22:1–21
	John 18:1–14
20 June	Prov. 22:22—23:12
	John 18:15–40
21 June	Prov. 24:1–22
	John 19:1–22
22 June	Prov. 25:1–22
	Prov. 26:1–28
	John 19:23–42
23 June	Prov. 27:1–24
	Prov. 28:1—29:27
	John 20:1–18
24 June	Prov. 30:1–9, 18–33
	John 20:19–31
25 June	Prov. 31:10–31
	John 21:1–25
26 June	Joshua 1:1–18
	Acts 8:1–25
27 June	Joshua 2:1–24
	Acts 8:26–40
28 June	Joshua 3:1–17
	Acts 9:1–22
29 June	Joshua 4:1–24
	Acts 9:23–43
30 June	Joshua 5:1—6:5
	Acts 10:1–17
1 July	Joshua 6:6–27
	Acts 10:18–33
2 July	Joshua 7:1–26
	Acts 10:34–48
3 July	Joshua 8:1–28
	Acts 11:1–18
4 July	Joshua 10:1–25
	Joshua 10:28—22:34
	Acts 11:19–30
5 July	Joshua 23:1–16
	Acts 12:1–25
6 July	Joshua 24:1–31
	Judg. 1:1–36
	Acts 13:1–12
7 July	Judg. 2:6–23
	Acts 13:13–41
8 July	Judg. 3:7–31
	Acts 13:42–52
9 July	Judg. 4:1–24
	Judg. 5:1–31
	Acts 14:1–18
10 July	Judg. 6:1–24
	Acts 14:19—15:5
11 July	Judg. 6:25–40
	Acts 15:6–21
12 July	Judg. 7:1–23
	Judg. 7:24—12:15
	Gal. 1:1–24
13 July	Judg. 13:1–25
	Ruth 1:1—4:22
	Gal. 2:1–21
14 July	Judg. 14:1–20
	Gal. 3:1–22
15 July	Judg. 15:1—16:3
	Gal. 3:23—4:11
16 July	Judg. 16:4–30
	Judg. 17:1—21:25
	Gal. 4:12–31
17 July	1 Sam. 1:1–20
	Gal. 5:1–26
18 July	1 Sam. 1:21—2:17
	Gal. 6:1–18
19 July	1 Sam. 2:18–36
	Acts 15:22–41
20 July	1 Sam. 3:1–21
	Acts 16:1–22
21 July	1 Sam. 4:1–22
	Acts 17:1–34
	Acts 16:23–40
22 July	1 Sam. 5:1—6:3, 10–16
	Acts 18:1–11, 23–28
23 July	1 Sam. 6:19—7:17
	Acts 19:23—21:14
	Acts 19:1–22
24 July	1 Sam. 8:1–22
	Acts 21:15–36
25 July	1 Sam. 9:1–27
	Acts 21:37—22:16
26 July	1 Sam. 10:1–27
	Acts 22:17–29
27 July	1 Sam. 12:1–25
	Acts 22:30—23:11
28 July	1 Sam. 13:1–18
	Acts 23:12–35
29 July	1 Sam. 14:47—15:9
	Acts 24:1–23
30 July	1 Sam. 15:10–35
	Acts 24:24—25:12
31 July	1 Sam. 16:1–23
	Acts 25:13–27
1 Aug.	1 Sam. 17:1–19
	Acts 26:1–23
2 Aug.	1 Sam. 17:20–47
	Acts 26:24—27:8
3 Aug.	1 Sam. 17:48—18:9
	Acts 27:9–26
4 Aug.	1 Sam. 18:10–30
	Acts 27:27–44
5 Aug.	1 Sam. 19:1–24
	Acts 28:1–15
6 Aug.	1 Sam. 20:1–23
	Acts 28:16–31
7 Aug.	1 Sam. 20:24–42
	1 Sam. 21:1—23:29
	1 Cor. 1:1–25
8 Aug.	1 Sam. 24:1–22
	1 Cor. 1:26—2:16
9 Aug.	1 Sam. 25:1–22
	1 Cor. 3:1–23
10 Aug.	1 Sam. 25:23–44
	1 Cor. 4:1–21
11 Aug.	1 Sam. 26:1–25
	1 Sam. 27:1—28:2
	1 Cor. 5:1–13
12 Aug.	1 Sam. 28:3–25
	1 Sam. 29:1—30:31
	1 Cor. 6:1–20
13 Aug.	1 Sam. 31:1–13
	1 Cor. 7:1–24
14 Aug.	2 Sam. 1:1–27
	1 Cor. 7:25–40
15 Aug.	2 Sam. 5:1–25
	1 Cor. 8:1–13
16 Aug.	2 Sam. 6:1–19
	1 Cor. 9:1–23
17 Aug.	2 Sam. 7:1–17
	1 Cor. 9:24—10:22
18 Aug.	2 Sam. 7:18–29
	1 Cor. 10:23—11:16
19 Aug.	2 Sam. 11:1–27
	1 Cor. 11:17–34
20 Aug.	2 Sam. 12:1–25
	2 Sam. 13:1—19:43
	1 Cor. 12:1–13
21 Aug.	1 Kings 1:1–4, 15–35
	1 Cor. 12:14–31
22 Aug.	1 Kings 2:1–27
	1 Cor. 14:1—16:24
	1 Cor. 13:1–13
23 Aug.	1 Kings 3:1–15
	1 Kings 3:16—4:34
	2 Cor. 1:1–22
24 Aug.	1 Kings 5:1–18
	1 Kings 6:1—7:50
	2 Cor. 1:23—2:17
25 Aug.	1 Kings 7:51—8:21
	2 Cor. 3:1–18
26 Aug.	1 Kings 8:22–30, 46–63
	2 Cor. 4:1–18
27 Aug.	1 Kings 9:1–9; 10:1–13
	2 Cor. 5:1–21
28 Aug.	1 Kings 11:1–26
	2 Cor. 6:1–18
29 Aug.	1 Kings 11:42—12:19
	2 Cor. 7:1–16
30 Aug.	1 Kings 12:20—13:5, 33–34
	1 Kings 14:1—16:28
	2 Cor. 8:1–24
31 Aug.	1 Kings 16:29—17:24
	2 Cor. 10:1—13:14
	2 Cor. 9:1–15

1 Sept.	1 Kings 18:1–19 Eph. 1:1–23
2 Sept.	1 Kings 18:20–40 Eph. 2:1–22
3 Sept.	1 Kings 19:1–21 *1 Kings 20:1—22:53* Eph. 3:1–21
4 Sept.	2 Kings 2:1–18 Eph. 4:1–24
5 Sept.	2 Kings 2:19–25; 4:1–7 Eph. 4:25—5:14
6 Sept.	2 Kings 4:8–22, 32–37 Eph. 5:15–33
7 Sept.	2 Kings 4:38—5:8 Eph. 6:1–24
8 Sept.	2 Kings 5:9–27 Phil. 1:1–20
9 Sept.	2 Kings 6:1–23 *2 Kings 6:24—8:29* Phil. 1:21—2:11
10 Sept.	2 Kings 9:1–13; 10:18–29 *2 Kings 13:1—18:8* Phil. 2:12–30
11 Sept.	2 Chron. 29:1–24 Phil. 3:1–21
12 Sept.	2 Chron. 31:1–21 Phil. 4:1–23
13 Sept.	2 Chron. 32:1–22 *Hos. 1:1—14:9* Col. 1:1–23
14 Sept.	2 Chron. 33:1–25 *Jonah 1:1—4:11* Col. 1:24—2:7
15 Sept.	2 Chron. 34:1–4, 8–11, 14–33 *Nah. 1:1—3:19* Col. 2:8–23
16 Sept.	2 Chron. 35:1–7, 16–25 *Zeph. 1:1—3:20* Col. 3:1–25
17 Sept.	2 Chron. 36:1–23 *Philemon 1–25* Col. 4:1–18
18 Sept.	Neh. 1:1—2:10 *Hag. 1:1—2:23* 1 Tim. 1:1–20
19 Sept.	Neh. 2:11–20; 4:1–6 1 Tim. 2:1–15
20 Sept.	Neh. 4:7–23 1 Tim. 3:1–16
21 Sept.	Neh. 5:1–16; 6:1–9, 15–16 1 Tim. 4:1–16
22 Sept.	Neh. 7:1–4; 8:1–18 *Ezra 1:1—10:19* 1 Tim. 5:1–16
23 Sept.	Neh. 9:1–21 1 Tim. 5:17—6:2
24 Sept.	Neh. 9:22–38 *Neh. 10:1—13:31* 1 Tim. 6:3–21
25 Sept.	Mal. 1:1–14 Matt. 3:1–17
26 Sept.	Mal. 2:1—3:5 Matt. 4:1–11
27 Sept.	Mal. 3:6—4:6 Matt. 4:12–25
28 Sept.	Deut. 1:1–18 Matt. 5:1–20
29 Sept.	Deut. 1:19–36 Matt. 5:21–48
30 Sept.	Deut. 1:37—2:15 Matt. 6:1–15
1 Oct.	Deut. 2:16–37 Matt. 6:16–34
2 Oct.	Deut. 3:1–29 Matt. 7:1–12
3 Oct.	Deut. 4:1–20 Matt. 7:13–29
4 Oct.	Deut. 4:21–40 Matt. 8:1–17
5 Oct.	Deut. 5:1–21 Matt. 8:18–34
6 Oct.	Deut. 5:22—6:9 Matt. 9:1–17
7 Oct.	Deut. 6:10–25 Matt. 9:18–38
8 Oct.	Deut. 7:1–19 Matt. 10:1–23
9 Oct.	Deut. 8:1–20 Matt. 10:24–42
10 Oct.	Deut. 9:1–22 Matt. 11:1–19
11 Oct.	Deut. 9:23—10:22 Matt. 11:20–30
12 Oct.	Deut. 11:1–25 Matt. 12:1–21
13 Oct.	Deut. 11:26—12:12 Matt. 12:22–37
14 Oct.	Deut. 12:13–32 Matt. 12:38–50
15 Oct.	Deut. 13:1–18 Matt. 13:1–23
16 Oct.	Deut. 14:1–2, 22–23, 14:28—15:15 Matt. 13:24–43
17 Oct.	Deut. 15:19—16:22 Matt. 13:44–58
18 Oct.	Deut. 17:1–20 Matt. 14:1–21
19 Oct.	Deut. 18:1–22 Matt. 14:22–36
20 Oct.	Deut. 19:1–20 Matt. 15:1–20
21 Oct.	Deut. 20:1–20 Matt. 15:21–39
22 Oct.	Deut. 21:1–23 *Deut. 22:1—24:9* Matt. 16:1–12
23 Oct.	Deut. 24:10—25:10 Matt. 16:13–28
24 Oct.	Deut. 25:17—26:19 Matt. 17:1–13
25 Oct.	Deut. 27:1–26 Matt. 17:14–27
26 Oct.	Deut. 28:1–22 Matt. 18:1–20
27 Oct.	Deut. 29:1–29 Matt. 18:21–35
28 Oct.	Deut. 30:1–20 Matt. 19:1–15
29 Oct.	Deut. 31:1–29 Matt. 19:16–30
30 Oct.	Deut. 31:30—32:27 Matt. 20:1–16
31 Oct.	Deut. 32:28–52 *Deut. 33:1–29* Matt. 20:17–34
1 Nov.	Deut. 34:1–12 Matt. 21:1–22
2 Nov.	Jer. 1:1–19 Matt. 21:23–46
3 Nov.	Jer. 3:6—4:2 Matt. 22:1–22
4 Nov.	Jer. 5:1–19 Matt. 22:23–46
5 Nov.	Jer. 7:1–29 Matt. 23:1–12
6 Nov.	Jer. 8:18—9:12 Matt. 23:13–39
7 Nov.	Jer. 11:1–23 *Jer. 12:1—19:15* Matt. 24:1–28
8 Nov.	Jer. 20:1–18 Matt. 24:29–51
9 Nov.	Jer. 22:1–23 Matt. 25:1–13
10 Nov.	Jer. 23:1–20 Matt. 25:14–30
11 Nov.	Jer. 23:21–40 Matt. 25:31–46
12 Nov.	Jer. 25:1–18 Matt. 26:1–19
13 Nov.	Jer. 26:1–19 *Rev. 13:1–18* Matt. 26:20–35
14 Nov.	Jer. 29:1–19 *Rev. 14:1–20* Matt. 26:36–56
15 Nov.	Jer. 30:1–24 *Rev. 15:1–8* Matt. 26:57–75
16 Nov.	Jer. 31:1–17, 23–34 *Rev. 16:1–21* Matt. 27:1–10
17 Nov.	Jer. 33:1–22 *Jer. 34:1—36:32; 45:1—51:64* Matt. 27:11–32
18 Nov.	Jer. 37:1–21 *Rev. 17:1–18* Matt. 27:33–56
19 Nov.	Jer. 38:1–28 *Jer. 39:1—44:30* Matt. 27:57–66
20 Nov.	Dan. 1:1–21 Matt. 28:1–20
21 Nov.	Dan. 2:1–23 Rev. 18:1–24
22 Nov.	Dan. 2:24–49 Rev. 19:1–21
23 Nov.	Dan. 3:1–30 Rev. 20:1–15
24 Nov.	Dan. 4:1–37 Rev. 21:1–8
25 Nov.	Dan. 5:1–30 *Dan. 7:1—8:27* Rev. 21:9–27
26 Nov.	Dan. 6:1–28 *Dan. 9:1–27* Rev. 22:1–21

The Time of Christmas

Advent Season

27 Nov.	Is. 1:1–28
	1 Peter 1:1–12
28 Nov.	Is. 2:1–22
	Is. 3:1—4:6
	1 Peter 1:13–25
29 Nov.	Is. 5:1–25
	Amos 1:1—9:15
	1 Peter 2:1–12
30 Nov.	Is. 6:1—7:9
	1 Peter 2:13–25
1 Dec.	Is. 7:10—8:8
	1 Peter 3:1–22
2 Dec.	Is. 8:9—9:7
	1 Peter 4:1–19
3 Dec.	Is. 9:8—10:11
	1 Peter 5:1–14
4 Dec.	Is. 10:12–27a, 33–34
	2 Peter 1:1–21
5 Dec.	Is. 11:1—12:6
	2 Peter 2:1–22
6 Dec.	Is. 14:1–23
	2 Peter 3:1–18
7 Dec.	Is. 24:1–13
	1 John 1:1—2:14
8 Dec.	Is. 24:14—25:12
	Obad. 1–21
	1 John 2:15–29
9 Dec.	Is. 26:1–19
	1 John 3:1–24
10 Dec.	Is. 26:20—27:13
	1 John 4:1–21
11 Dec.	Is. 28:14–29
	1 John 5:1–21
	2 John 1–13
	3 John 1–15
12 Dec.	Is. 29:1–14
	Jude 1–25
13 Dec.	Is. 29:15—30:14
	Rev. 1:1–20
14 Dec.	Is. 30:15–26
	Rev. 2:1–29
15 Dec.	Is. 30:27—31:9
	Rev. 3:1–22
16 Dec.	Is. 32:1–20
	Rev. 4:1–11
17 Dec.	Is. 33:1–24
	Rev. 5:1–14
18 Dec.	Is. 34:1–2, 8—35:10
	Micah 1:1—7:20
	Rev. 6:1–17
19 Dec.	Is. 40:1–17
	Rev. 7:1–17
20 Dec.	Is. 40:18—41:10
	Rev. 8:1–13
21 Dec.	Is. 42:1–25
	Rev. 9:1–12
22 Dec.	Is. 43:1–24
	Rev. 9:13—10:11
23 Dec.	Is. 43:25—44:20
	Rev. 11:1–19

Christmas Season

24 Dec.	Is. 44:21—45:13, 20–25
	Dan. 10:1—12:13
	Is. 48:1–22
	Rev. 12:1–17
25 Dec.	Is. 49:1–18
	Matt. 1:1–17
26 Dec.	Is. 49:22–26; 50:4—51:8, 12–16
	Matt. 1:18–25
27 Dec.	Is. 51:17—52:12
	Matt. 2:1–12
28 Dec.	Is. 52:13—54:10
	Matt. 2:13–23
29 Dec.	Is. 55:1–13
	Luke 1:1–25
30 Dec.	Is. 58:1—59:3, 14–21
	Luke 1:26–38
31 Dec.	Is. 60:1–22
	Luke 1:39–56
1 Jan.	Is. 61:1–11
	Luke 1:57–80
2 Jan.	Is. 62:1–12
	Luke 2:1–20
3 Jan.	Is. 63:1–14
	Luke 2:21–40
4 Jan.	Is. 63:15—65:7
	Luke 2:41–52
5 Jan.	Is. 65:8–25
	Luke 3:1–20

Epiphany Season

6 Jan.	Is. 66:1–20
	Luke 3:21–38
7 Jan.	Ezek. 1:1–14, 22–28
	Hab. 1:1—3:19
	Rom. 1:1–17
8 Jan.	Ezek. 2:1—3:11
	Rom. 1:18–32
9 Jan.	Ezek. 3:12–27
	Ezek. 4:1—11:25
	Rom. 2:1–16
10 Jan.	Ezek. 18:1–4, 19–32
	Ezek. 19:1—24:27
	Rom. 2:17–29
11 Jan.	Ezek. 33:1–20
	Rom. 3:1–18
12 Jan.	Ezek. 34:1–24
	Rom. 3:19–31
13 Jan.	Ezek. 36:13–28
	Rom. 4:1–25
14 Jan.	Ezek. 36:33—37:14
	Rom. 5:1–21
15 Jan.	Ezek. 37:15–28
	Rom. 6:1–23
16 Jan.	Ezek. 38:1–23
	Rom. 7:1–20
17 Jan.	Ezek. 39:1–10, 17–29
	Rom. 7:21—8:17
18 Jan.	Ezek. 40:1–4; 43:1–12
	Ezek. 40:5—42:20; 43:13–27
	Rom. 8:18–39
19 Jan.	Ezek. 44:1–16, 23–29
	Rom. 9:1–18
20 Jan.	Ezek. 47:1–14, 21–23
	Rom. 9:19–33
21 Jan.	Joel 1:1–20
	Rom. 10:1–21
22 Jan.	Joel 2:1–17
	Rom. 11:1–24
23 Jan.	Joel 2:18–32
	Rom. 11:25—12:13
24 Jan.	Joel 3:1–21
	Rom. 12:14—13:14
25 Jan.	Zech. 1:1–21
	Rom. 14:1–23
26 Jan.	Zech. 2:1—3:10
	Rom. 15:1–13
27 Jan.	Zech. 4:1—5:11
	Rom. 15:14–33
28 Jan.	Zech. 6:1—7:14
	Rom. 16:17–27
29 Jan.	Zech. 8:1–23
	2 Tim. 1:1–18
30 Jan.	Zech. 9:1–17
	2 Tim. 2:1–26
31 Jan.	Zech. 10:1—11:3
	2 Tim. 3:1–17
1 Feb.	Zech. 11:4–17
	2 Tim. 4:1–18
2 Feb.	Zech. 12:1—13:9
	Titus 1:1—2:6
3 Feb.	Zech. 14:1–21
	Titus 2:7—3:15
4 Feb.	Job 1:1–22
	John 1:1–18
5 Feb.	Job 2:1—3:10
	John 1:19–34
6 Feb.	Job 3:11–26
	John 1:35–51
7 Feb.	Job 4:1–21
	John 2:1–12
8 Feb.	Job 5:1–27
	John 2:13–25
9 Feb.	Job 6:1–13
	John 3:1–21
10 Feb.	Job 6:14–30
	John 3:22—4:6
11 Feb.	Job 7:1–21
	John 4:7–26
12 Feb.	Job 8:1–22
	John 4:27–45
13 Feb.	Job 9:1–35
	John 4:46–54
14 Feb.	Job 10:1–22
	John 5:1–18
15 Feb.	Job 11:1–20
	John 5:19–29
16 Feb.	Job 12:1–6, 12–25
	John 5:30–47
17 Feb.	Job 13:1–12
	John 6:1–21
18 Feb.	Job 13:13–28
	John 6:22–40
19 Feb.	Job 14:1–22
	John 6:41–59
20 Feb.	Job 15:1–23, 30–35
	John 6:60–71
21 Feb.	Job 16:1–22
	John 7:1–13
22 Feb.	Job 17:1–16
	John 7:14–31

23 Feb. Job 18:1–21
John 7:32–53

24 Feb. Job 19:1–12, 21–27
John 8:1–20

25 Feb. Job 20:1–23, 29
John 8:21–38

26 Feb. Job 21:1–21
Job 21:22—30:15
John 8:39–59

27 Feb. Job 30:16–31
John 9:1–23

28 Feb. Job 31:1–12, 33–40
John 9:24–41

29 Feb. Job 32:1–22
John 10:1–21

1 Mar. Job 33:1–18
John 10:22–42

2 Mar. Job 33:19—34:9
John 11:1–16

3 Mar. Job 34:10–33
John 11:17–37

4 Mar. Job 36:1–21
John 11:38–57

5 Mar. Job 37:1–24
John 12:1–19

6 Mar. Job 38:1–18
Job 38:19—39:30
John 12:20–36a

7 Mar. Job 40:1–24
John 12:36b–50

8 Mar. Job 41:1–20, 31–34
John 13:1–20

9 Mar. Job 42:1–17
John 13:21–38

TABLE OF PSALMS FOR DAILY PRAYER

The following seasonal psalm cycle may be used with the assigned readings in the Daily Lectionary. In addition to the psalms appointed for each morning according to season, Psalms 145–150 may also be prayed in the morning throughout the year according to the following weekly schedule: Sunday—Psalm 150; Monday—Psalm 145; Tuesday—Psalm 146; Wednesday—Psalm 147:1–11; Thursday—Psalm 147:12–20; Friday—Psalm 148; Saturday—Psalm 149. The four weeks under "General" are used during The Time of the Church and the season of Epiphany and may be repeated as often as necessary.

	Sunday	Monday	Tuesday	Wednesday	Thursday	Friday	Saturday
LENT							
Morning	84	119:73–80	34	5	38	22	43
Evening	42; 32	121; 6	25; 91	27; 51	126; 102	107; 130	31; 143
EASTER							
Morning	93	97	98	99	47	96	92
Evening	136; 117	124; 115	66; 116	8; 118	68; 113	50; 138	23; 114
GENERAL							
Week 1							
Morning	103	5	42	89:1–18	97	51	104
Evening	117; 139	84; 29	102; 133	1; 33	16; 62	142; 65	118; 111
Week 2							
Morning	19	136	123	15	36	130	56
Evening	81; 113	97; 112	30; 86	48; 4	80; 27	32; 139	100; 62
Week 3							
Morning	67	51	54	65	143	86	122
Evening	46; 93	85; 47	28; 99	125; 91	81; 116	6; 19	141; 90
Week 4							
Morning	110	62	13	96	116	85	61
Evening	66; 23	73; 8	36; 5	132; 134	26; 130	25; 40	138; 98
ADVENT							
Morning	24	122	33	50	18:1–20	102	90
Evening	25; 110	40; 67	85; 91	14; 16	126; 62	130; 16	80; 72

CHRISTMAS

December 24	December 28	January 1	January 5
Morning: 19 Evening: 132; 114	Morning: 2 Evening: 110; 111	Morning: 97 Evening: 99; 8	Morning: 99 Evening: 96; 110
December 25 Morning: 2 Evening: 98; 96	*December 29* Morning: 96 Evening: 132; 97	*January 2* Morning: 48 Evening: 45; 29	*January 6* Morning: 72 Evening: 100; 67
December 26 Morning: 116 Evening: 119:1–24; 27	*December 30* Morning: 93 Evening: 89:1–18, 19–52	*January 3* Morning: 111 Evening: 107; 15	
December 27 Morning: 34 Evening: 19; 121	*December 31* Morning: 98 Evening: 45; 96	*January 4* Morning: 103 Evening: 93; 97	

EPIPHANY See GENERAL above.

PRAYERS, INTERCESSIONS, AND THANKSGIVINGS

THE CHURCH AND HER MISSION

For the Church

Merciful God, we humbly implore You to cast the bright beams of Your light upon Your Church that we, being instructed by the doctrine of the blessed apostles, may walk in the light of Your truth and finally attain to the light of everlasting life; through Jesus Christ, our Lord. (101)

Almighty God, grant to Your Church Your Holy Spirit and the wisdom that comes down from above, that Your Word may not be bound but have free course and be preached to the joy and edifying of Christ's holy people, that in steadfast faith we may serve You and, in the confession of Your name, abide unto the end; through Jesus Christ, our Lord. (102)

For the mission of the Church

Almighty God, You have called Your Church to witness that in Christ You have reconciled us to Yourself. Grant that by Your Holy Spirit we may proclaim the good news of Your salvation so that all who hear it may receive the gift of salvation; through Jesus Christ, our Lord. (104)

For those outside the Church

Almighty and everlasting God, You desire not the death of a sinner but that all would repent and live. Hear our prayers for those outside the Church. Take away their iniquity, and turn them from their false gods to You, the living and true God. Gather them into Your holy Church to the glory of Your name; through Jesus Christ, our Lord. (106)

Defending the Church from error

Almighty and everlasting God, You would have all to be saved and to come to the knowledge of the truth. By Your almighty power and unsearchable wisdom break and hinder all the counsels of those who hate Your Word and who, by corrupt teaching, would destroy it. Enlighten them with the knowledge of Your glory that they may know the riches of Your heavenly grace and, in peace and righteousness, serve You, the only true God; through Jesus Christ, our Lord. (109)

For our enemies

Almighty, everlasting God, through Your only Son, our blessed Lord, You commanded us to love our enemies, to do good to those who hate us, and to pray for those who persecute us. Therefore, we earnestly implore You that by Your gracious working our enemies may be led to true repentance, may have the same love toward us as we have toward them, and may be of one accord and of one mind and heart with us and with Your whole Church; through Jesus Christ, our Lord. (110)

For persecuted Christians

Lord Jesus Christ, before whom all in heaven and earth shall bow, grant courage that Your children may confess Your saving name in the face of any opposition from a world hostile to the Gospel. Help them to remember Your faithful people who sacrificed much and even faced death rather than dishonor You when called upon to deny the faith. By Your Spirit, strengthen them to be faithful and to confess You boldly, knowing that You will confess Your own before the Father in heaven, with whom You and the Holy Spirit live and reign, one God, now and forever. (111)

Return of the wayward and erring

Almighty and most gracious God and Father, we implore You to turn the hearts of all who have forsaken the faith once delivered to Your Church, especially those who have wandered from it or are in doubt through the corruption of Your truth. Mercifully visit and restore them that in gladness of heart they may take pleasure in Your Word and be made wise to salvation through faith in Your Son, Jesus Christ, our Lord. (112)

Seminaries and colleges

O God, source of all abiding knowledge, through Word and Spirit You both enlighten the minds and sanctify the lives of those whom You draw to Your service. Look with favor on the seminaries and colleges of the Church, blessing those who teach and those who learn, that all the baptized may apply themselves with ready diligence to their tasks and faithfully fulfill their service according to Your will; through Jesus Christ, our Lord. (116)

Increase of the holy ministry

Almighty and gracious God, the Father of our Lord Jesus Christ, You have commanded us to pray that You would send forth laborers into Your harvest. Of Your infinite mercy give us true teachers and ministers of Your Word who truly fulfill Your command and preach nothing contrary to Your holy Word. Grant that we, being warned, instructed, nurtured, comforted, and strengthened by Your holy Word, may do those things which are well pleasing to You and profitable for our salvation; through Jesus Christ, our Lord. (119)

For those who minister to the armed forces

O Lord, almighty God, as You have always granted special gifts of the Holy Spirit to Your Church on earth, grant Your continual blessing to all who minister in Your name in the armed forces, that by Your gracious working they may honor Christ and advance the good of those committed to their care; through Jesus Christ, our Lord. (126)

Calling a faithful pastor

O Gracious Father, You led Your holy apostles to ordain ministers for the proclamation of Your Word and the faithful administration of the Sacraments of Christ. Grant to this congregation the guidance of the Holy Spirit to choose a suitable pastor according to Your will for the blessing of Your Church in this place; through Jesus Christ, our Lord. (127)

Calling faithful church workers

Merciful Lord, for the benefit of Your people You call faithful men and women to serve in a variety of offices in Your Church. Grant that Your Holy Spirit may lead and guide us in calling a _teacher / musician / deaconess / other_ to serve among us according to Your gracious will; through Jesus Christ, our Lord. (130)

For church musicians and artists

God of majesty, whom saints and angels delight to worship in heaven, be with Your servants who make art and music for Your people that with joy we on earth may glimpse Your beauty. Bring us to the fulfillment of that hope of perfection that will be ours as we stand before Your unveiled glory; through Jesus Christ, our Lord. (136)

For women's organizations

Lord Jesus, in Your earthly ministry You were loved and served by devoted women, including Mary and Martha in whose home You enjoyed rest and refreshment. Give us grace to recognize and affirm the varied and singular gifts You bestow on women (and especially upon _name of women's organization_) that Your kingdom may be extended, Your Church enriched, and Your people lovingly served to the glory of Your holy name; for You live and reign with the Father and the Holy Spirit, one God, now and forever. (137)

For men's organizations

Almighty and gracious God, in every age You have inspired men to labor, with hearts united, in Your kingdom. Continue to grant to the men of this congregation (and especially _name of men's organization_) faithfulness in serving You and upholding the truth of Your Word that they, together with us all, may respond to Your redeeming love in Christ Jesus by devoting themselves to seeking and doing Your holy will and following in the footsteps of our Lord Jesus Christ, who lives and reigns with You and the Holy Spirit, one God, now and forever. (138)

To open a congregational meeting

Almighty God and Lord, as You have called us to labor in Your vineyard, so grant us now Your presence. Enlighten and guide us by Your Word that in all matters of deliberation we may always consider the best interests of Your Church and this congregation. Let Your Holy Spirit rule and direct our hearts that, in the spirit of Christian love, we may present and discuss matters and be kindly disposed toward one another, to the end that all we say and do may please You; through Jesus Christ, our Lord. (139)

To open a church council meeting

Almighty God, direct and guide us by Your Holy Spirit both to plan and to accomplish those things that will benefit Your Church and glorify Your name; through Jesus Christ, our Lord. (140)

To open a committee meeting

Almighty God, we give thanks that through the varied gifts of the members of this _committee / task force / group_ You provide for the ongoing care of this congregation. Cause us to recognize and to act on every opportunity for fruitful service. Send Your Holy Spirit that everything we think, say, and do may be for the common good of the Church and the glory of Your name; through Jesus Christ, our Lord. (141)

At a retreat

Lord Jesus Christ, You withdrew Yourself for times of prayer and brought Your disciples with You that they might also rest with You. Be present with us during this time of retreat that, gathered together in Your name, we may profitably meditate on Your Word and be strengthened with a good will to serve You and Your people; for You live and reign with the Father and the Holy Spirit, one God, now and forever. (142)

AT WORSHIP

Grace to receive the Word

Blessed Lord, You have caused all Holy Scriptures to be written for our learning. Grant that we may so hear them, read, mark, learn, and inwardly digest them that, by patience and comfort of Your holy Word, we may embrace and ever hold fast the blessed hope of everlasting life; through Jesus Christ, our Lord. (148)

For blessing on the Word

Lord Jesus Christ, giver and perfecter of our faith, we thank and praise You for continuing among us the preaching of Your Gospel for our instruction and edification. Send Your blessing upon the Word, which has been spoken to us, and by Your Holy Spirit increase our saving knowledge of You, that day by day we may be strengthened in the divine truth and remain steadfast in Your grace. Give us strength to fight the good fight and by faith to overcome all the temptations of Satan, the flesh, and the world so that we may finally receive the salvation of our souls; for You live and reign with the Father and the Holy Spirit, one God, now and forever. (149)

For obedience to the Word

O holy and most merciful God, You have taught us the way of Your commandments. We implore You to pour out Your grace into our hearts. Cause it to bear fruit in us that, being ever mindful of Your mercies and Your laws, we may always be directed to Your will and daily increase in love toward You and one another. Enable us to resist all evil and to live a godly life. Help us to follow the example of our Lord and Savior, Jesus Christ, and to walk in His steps until we shall possess the kingdom that has been prepared for us in heaven; through Jesus Christ, our Lord. (152)

For right reception of the Lord's Supper

O Lord, our God, in Holy Baptism You have called us to be Christians and granted us the remission of sins. Make us ready to receive the most holy body and blood of Christ for the forgiveness of all our sins, and grant us grateful hearts that we may give thanks to You, O Father, to Your Son, and to the Holy Spirit, one God, now and forever. (154)

Thanksgiving after receiving the Sacrament

Blessed Savior, Jesus Christ, You have given Yourself to us in this holy Sacrament. Keep us in Your faith and favor that we may live in You even as You live in us. May Your body and blood preserve us in the true faith to life everlasting. Hear us for the sake of Your name. (157)

General intercession

Lord God, heavenly Father, we offer before You our common supplications for the well-being of Your Church throughout the world. So guide and govern it by Your Holy Spirit that all who profess themselves Christians may be led into the way of truth and hold the faith in unity of spirit, in the bond of peace, and in righteousness of life. Send down upon all ministers of the Gospel and upon the congregations committed to their care the healthful spirit of Your grace that they may please You in all things.

Behold in mercy all who are in authority over us. Supply them with Your blessing that they may be inclined to Your will and walk according to Your commandments. We humbly ask Your abiding presence in every situation that You would make known Your ways among us. Preserve those who travel, satisfy the wants of Your creatures, and help those who call upon You in any need that they may have patience in the midst of suffering and, according to Your will, be released from their afflictions; through Christ Jesus, Your Son, our Lord, who lives and reigns with You and the Holy Spirit, one God, now and forever. (161)

For pardon, growth in grace, and divine protection

O Lord, our God, we acknowledge Your great goodness toward us and praise You for the mercy and grace that our eyes have seen, our ears have heard, and our hearts have known. We sincerely repent of the sins of this day and those in the past. Pardon our offenses, correct and reform what is lacking in us, and help us to grow in grace and in the knowledge of our Lord and Savior, Jesus Christ. Inscribe Your law upon our hearts, and equip us to serve You with holy and blameless lives. May each day remind us of the coming of the night when no one can work. In the emptiness of this present age keep us united by a living faith through the power of Your Holy Spirit with Him who is the resurrection and the life, that we may escape the eternal bitter pains of condemnation.

By Your Holy Spirit bless the preaching of Your Word and the administration of Your Sacraments. Preserve these gifts to us and to all Christians. Guard and protect us from all dangers to body and soul. Grant that we may with faithful perseverance receive from You our sorrows as well as our joys, knowing that health and sickness, riches and poverty, and all things come by permission of Your fatherly hand. Keep us this day under Your protective care and preserve us, securely trusting in Your everlasting goodness and love, for the sake of Your Son, Jesus Christ, our Lord, who lives and reigns with You and the Holy Spirit, one God, now and forever. (159)

BAPTISMAL LIFE

Morning

Faithful God, whose mercies are new to us every morning, we humbly pray that You would look upon us in mercy and renew us by Your Holy Spirit. Keep safe our going out and our coming in, and let Your blessing remain with us throughout this day. Preserve us in Your righteousness, and grant us a portion in that eternal life which is in Christ Jesus, our Lord. (168)

Thanksgiving at end of day

Gracious Lord, we give You thanks for the day, especially for the good we were permitted to give and to receive. The day is now past, and we commit it to You. We entrust to You the night and rest in Your peace, for You are our help, and You neither slumber nor sleep. Hear us for the sake of Your name. (172)

Protection during the night

Lighten our darkness, O Lord, and by Your great mercy defend us from all perils and dangers of this night; for the love of Your only Son, our Savior, Jesus Christ. (173)

Life as a baptized child of God

Merciful Father, through Holy Baptism You called us to be Your own possession. Grant that our lives may evidence the working of Your Holy Spirit in love, joy, peace, patience, kindness, goodness, faithfulness, gentleness, and self-control, according to the image of Your only-begotten Son, Jesus Christ, our Savior. (175)

Anniversary of a Baptism

Gracious Lord, we give thanks that in Holy Baptism we receive forgiveness of sins, deliverance from death and the devil, and eternal salvation. On this baptismal anniversary, bless _name_ continually by Your Word and Spirit that _he/she_ may faithfully keep the covenant into which _he/she_ has been called, boldly confess _his/her_ Savior, and finally share with all Your saints the joys of eternal life; through Jesus Christ, our Lord. (176)

For catechumens

Lord God, heavenly Father, in Holy Baptism You began Your good work in our catechumens, and You have blessed their instruction and training in Your Word. We implore You to pour out Your Holy Spirit on their hearts and minds so that they will truly love and revere You, confess the faith with joy and boldness, endeavor to live according to Your commandments, and praise and glorify You as their faithful God and Lord, for the sake of Your Son, Jesus Christ, our Lord. (178)

For the Holy Spirit

Almighty God, send Your Holy Spirit into our hearts that He may rule and direct us according to Your will, comfort us in all our temptations and afflictions, defend us from all error, and lead us into all truth that we, being steadfast in faith, may increase in all good works and in the end obtain everlasting life; through Jesus Christ, our Lord. (183)

For divine guidance

Almighty and ever-living God, You make us both to will and to do those things that are good and acceptable in Your sight. Let Your fatherly hand ever guide us and Your Holy Spirit ever be with us to direct us in the knowledge and obedience of Your Word that we may obtain everlasting life; through Jesus Christ, our Lord. (187)

Direct us, O Lord, in all our doings with Your most gracious favor, and further us with Your continual help, that in all our works begun, continued, and ended in You we may glorify Your holy name and finally, by Your mercy, obtain eternal salvation; through Jesus Christ, our Lord. (188)

Faith, hope, and love

Almighty God, grant us a steadfast faith in Jesus Christ, a cheerful hope in Your mercy, and a sincere love for You and one another; through Jesus Christ, our Lord. (190)

Thanksgiving to God

Heavenly Father, God of all grace, govern our hearts that we may never forget Your blessings but steadfastly thank and praise You for all Your goodness in this life until, with all Your saints, we praise You eternally in Your heavenly kingdom; through Jesus Christ, our Lord. (191)

Grace to use our gifts

Lord God Almighty, even as You bless Your servants with various and unique gifts of the Holy Spirit, continue to grant us the grace to use them always to Your honor and glory; through Jesus Christ, our Lord. (192)

For guidance in our calling

Lord God, You have called Your servants to ventures of which we cannot see the ending, by paths as yet untrodden, through perils unknown. Give us faith to go out with good courage, not knowing where we go but only that Your hand is leading us and Your love supporting us; through Jesus Christ, our Lord. (193)

Christian vocation

Heavenly Father, grant Your mercy and grace to Your people in their many and various callings. Give them patience, and strengthen them in their Christian vocation of witness to the world and of service to their neighbor in Christ's name; through Jesus Christ, our Lord. (194)

Against the love of money

Almighty God, heavenly Father, You have called us to be Your children and heirs of Your gracious promises in Christ Jesus. Grant us Your Holy Spirit that we may forsake all covetous desires and the inordinate love of riches. Deliver us from the pursuit of passing things that we may seek the kingdom of Your Son and trust in His righteousness and so find blessedness and peace; through Jesus Christ, our Lord. (195)

Proper use of wealth

Almighty God, all that we possess is from Your loving hand. Give us grace that we may honor You with all we own, always remembering the account we must one day give to Jesus Christ, our Lord. (196)

Proper use of leisure

O God, give us times of refreshment and peace in the course of this busy life. Grant that we may so use our leisure to rebuild our bodies and renew our minds that we may be opened to the goodness of Your creation; through Jesus Christ, our Lord. (197)

Newness of life in Christ

Almighty God, give us grace that we may cast away the works of darkness and put upon ourselves the armor of light now in the time of this mortal life in which Your Son, Jesus Christ, came to visit us in great humility, that in the Last Day, when He shall come again in glorious majesty to judge both the living and the dead, we may rise to life immortal; through Jesus Christ, our Lord. (198)

For steadfast faith

Almighty God, our heavenly Father, because of Your tender love toward us sinners You have given us Your Son that, believing in Him, we might have everlasting life. Continue to grant us Your Holy Spirit that we may remain steadfast in this faith to the end and finally come to life everlasting; through Jesus Christ, our Lord. (200)

For a right knowledge of Christ

Almighty God, whom to know is everlasting life, grant us perfectly to know Your Son, Jesus Christ, to be the way, the truth, and the life, that following His steps we may steadfastly walk in the way that leads to eternal life; through the same Jesus Christ, our Lord. (202)

Before the study of God's Word

Almighty God, our heavenly Father, without Your help our labor is useless, and without Your light our search is in vain. Invigorate our study of Your holy Word that, by due diligence and right discernment, we may establish ourselves and others in Your holy faith; through Jesus Christ, our Lord. (203)

For spiritual renewal

Almighty God, You gave Your only-begotten Son to take our nature upon Himself. Grant that we, Your adopted children by grace, may daily be renewed by Your Holy Spirit; through Jesus Christ, our Lord. (204)

For reconciliation

God of love, through Your Son You have commanded us to love one another. By the guidance of Your Word and Spirit, deliver us from impenitence and teach us the truth that we might confess our sins, receive Your forgiveness, and be reconciled to one another; through Jesus Christ, our Lord. (206)

For aid against temptation

O God, You justify the ungodly and desire not the death of the sinner. Graciously assist us by Your heavenly aid and evermore shield us with Your protection, that no temptation may separate us from Your love in Christ Jesus, our Lord. (208)

In times of temptation

Almighty and everlasting God, through Your Son You have promised us forgiveness of sins and everlasting life. Govern our hearts by Your Holy Spirit that in our daily need, and especially in all time of temptation, we may seek Your help and, by a true and lively faith in Your Word, obtain all that You have promised; through the same Jesus Christ, our Lord. (209)

For control of the tongue

We pray You, O Lord, to keep our tongues from evil and our lips from speaking deceit, that as Your holy angels continuously sing praises to You in heaven, so may we at all times glorify You on earth; through Jesus Christ, our Lord. (210)

For purity

Almighty God, unto whom all hearts are open, all desires known, and from whom no secrets are hidden, cleanse the thoughts of our hearts by the inspiration of Your Holy Spirit that we may perfectly love You and worthily magnify Your holy name; through Jesus Christ, our Lord. (211)

For humility

O God, You resist the proud and give grace to the humble. Grant us true humility after the likeness of Your only Son that we may never be arrogant and prideful and thus provoke Your wrath but in all lowliness be made partakers of the gifts of Your grace; through Jesus Christ, our Lord. (216)

For patience

O God, by the patient endurance of Your only-begotten Son You beat down the pride of the old enemy. Help us to treasure rightly in our hearts what our Lord has borne for our sakes that, after His example, we may bear with patience those things that are adverse to us; through Jesus Christ, our Lord. (217)

Answer to prayer

Almighty God, You have promised to hear the petitions of those who ask in Your Son's name. Mercifully incline Your ears to us who have now made our prayers and supplications to You, and grant that those things that we have faithfully asked according to Your will we may receive to meet our need and bring glory to You; through Jesus Christ, our Lord. (219)

For a blessed death

Almighty God, grant Your unworthy servants Your grace, that in the hour of our death the adversary may not prevail against us but that we may be found worthy of everlasting life; through Jesus Christ, our Lord. (220)

Hope of eternal life in Christ

Almighty, everlasting God, Your Son has assured forgiveness of sins and deliverance from eternal death. Strengthen us by Your Holy Spirit that our faith in Christ may increase daily and that we may hold fast to the hope that on the Last Day we shall be raised in glory to eternal life; through Jesus Christ, our Lord. (222)

CIVIL REALM

For the nation

Almighty God, You have given us this good land as our heritage. Grant that we remember Your generosity and constantly do Your will. Bless our land with honest industry, truthful education, and an honorable way of life. Save us from violence, discord, and confusion, from pride and arrogance, and from every evil course of action. Grant that we, who came from many nations with many different languages, may become a united people. Support us in defending our liberties, and give those to whom we have entrusted the authority of government the spirit of wisdom, that there may be justice and peace in our land. When times are prosperous, may our hearts be thankful, and in troubled times do not let our trust in You fail; through Jesus Christ, our Lord. (224)

Responsible citizenship

Lord, keep this nation under Your care. Bless the leaders of our land that we may be a people at peace among ourselves and a blessing to the other nations of the earth. Grant that we may choose trustworthy leaders, contribute to wise decisions for the general welfare, and serve You faithfully in our generation; through Jesus Christ, our Lord. (225)

Collect for peace

O God, from whom come all holy desires, all good counsels, and all just works, give to us, Your servants, that peace which the world cannot give, that our hearts may be set to obey Your commandments and also that we, being defended from the fear of our enemies, may live in peace and quietness; through Jesus Christ, Your Son, our Lord, who lives and reigns with You and the Holy Spirit, one God, now and forever. (410)

In times of war

Almighty God, You alone can establish lasting peace. Forgive our sins, we implore You, and deliver us from the hands of our enemies that we, being strengthened by Your defense, may be preserved from all danger and glorify You for the restoration of tranquility in our land; through the merits of Your Son, Jesus Christ, our Savior. (228)

For peace in the world

Heavenly Father, God of all concord, it is Your gracious will that Your children on earth live together in harmony and peace. Defeat the plans of all those who would stir up violence and strife, destroy the weapons of those who delight in war and bloodshed, and, according to Your will, end all conflicts in the world. Teach us to examine our hearts that we may recognize our own inclination toward envy, malice, hatred, and enmity. Help us, by Your Word and Spirit, to search our hearts and to root out the evil that would lead to strife and discord, so that in our lives we may be at peace with all people. Fill us with zeal for the work of Your Church and the proclamation of the Gospel of Jesus Christ, which alone can bring that peace which is beyond all understanding; through Jesus Christ, our Lord. (229)

Armed forces of our nation

Lord God of hosts, stretch forth Your almighty arm to strengthen and protect those who serve in the armed forces of our country. Support them in times of war, and in times of peace keep them from all evil, giving them courage and loyalty. Grant that in all things they may serve with integrity and with honor; through Jesus Christ, our Lord. (233)

Industry and commerce

Lord Jesus Christ, as once You shared in our human toil and thus hallowed the work of our hands, bless and prosper those who maintain the industries and service sectors of this land. Give them a right regard for their labors, and grant them the just reward for their work that they may find joy in serving You and in supplying our needs; for You live and reign with the Father and the Holy Spirit, one God, now and forever. (234)

Agriculture

Almighty God, You bless the earth to make it fruitful, bringing forth in abundance whatever is needed for the support of our lives. Prosper the work of farmers and all those who labor to bring food to our table. Grant them seasonable weather that they may gather in the fruits of the earth in abundance and proclaim Your goodness with thanksgiving; through Jesus Christ, our Lord. (235)

Time of drought

O God, most merciful Father, without Your care and preservation all things wither and die. Open the windows of heaven and send bountiful rain on us to revive and renew the land. Graciously hear our prayer that we may praise and glorify Your name forever and ever; through Jesus Christ, our Lord. (236)

Times of unseasonable weather

Lord God, gracious and merciful Father, because You have promised that You will hear us when we bring You our cares, we implore You not to deal with us according to our sins but according to Your mercy. Send seasonable weather so that in due time the earth may yield her increase. Remind us ever to receive with thanks our daily bread, trusting You as our gracious God; through Jesus Christ, our Lord. (237)

Thanksgiving for rain

Most gracious God and Father, we thank and praise You for sending rain to water the earth, causing it to be fruitful and to bring forth food in plenteous supply. Teach us ever to remember that we do not live on bread alone in order that we may receive Your blessings with thanksgiving and Your Word with grateful hearts; through Jesus Christ, our Lord. (238)

HOME AND FAMILY

For home and family

Visit, O Lord, the homes in which Your people dwell, and keep all harm and danger far from them. Grant that we may dwell together in peace under the protection of Your holy angels, sharing eternally in Your blessings; through Jesus Christ, our Lord. (239)

For those who are married

Most gracious God, we give thanks for the joy and blessings that You grant to husbands and wives. Assist them always by Your grace that with true fidelity and steadfast love they may honor and keep their marriage vows, grow in love toward You and for each other, and come at last to the eternal joys that You have promised; through Jesus Christ, our Lord. (243)

Care of children

Almighty God, heavenly Father, You have blessed us with the joy and care of children. Give us calm strength and patient wisdom that, as they grow in years, we may teach them to love whatever is just and true and good, following the example of our Savior, Jesus Christ, our Lord. (246)

For young persons

Gracious Father, Your Son grew in wisdom and stature and in favor with God and all people. Bless, guide, and govern the children and young people of Your Church by Your Holy Spirit, that they may grow in grace and in the knowledge of Your Word. Grant that they may serve You well and usefully, developing their talents not for their own sakes but to Your glory and for the welfare of their neighbor. Protect and defend them from all danger and harm, giving Your holy angels charge over them; through Jesus Christ, our Lord. (247)

For children in crisis

Almighty God, our heavenly Father, be a source of strength and hope for the children in our families. When they stray, protect them from all danger and grant Your abiding presence. Guide them by Your Word into paths of wisdom and righteousness, and send Your holy angels to watch over them, that the evil one may have no power over them; through Jesus Christ, our Lord. (250)

For the aged

Almighty God and gracious Father, in Your mercy look on those whose increasing years bring them weakness, anxiety, distress, or loneliness. Grant that they may always know care and respect, concern and understanding. Grant them willing hearts to accept help and, as their strength wanes, increase their faith with the constant assurance of Your love through Jesus Christ, their Savior. (251)

Asking a blessing at mealtime

Heavenly Father, we thank You for the gift of food You have provided and for all those whose labor brings Your blessings to our table. We pray that at this meal we may be strengthened for Your service and together may await with joy the feast You have prepared for all the faithful in Your eternal kingdom; through Jesus Christ, our Lord. (252)

For those who are moving

Lord God, Your gracious presence attends Your people wherever they go. Be with those whose lives are in transition as they move from a familiar home to a new community. Support them in times of challenge or loneliness, and surround them with caring Christian people so that they may find welcome and peace in their new location and joy in Your ongoing kindness and love; through Jesus Christ, our Lord. (253)

IN TIMES OF NEED

For the sick

O Father of mercies and God of all comfort, our only help in time of need, look with favor upon Your servant _name_. Assure _him/her_ of Your mercy, deliver _him/her_ from the temptations of the evil one, and give _him/her_ patience and comfort in _his/her_ illness. If it please You, restore _him/her_ to health, or give _him/her_ grace to accept this tribulation with courage and hope; through Jesus Christ, our Lord. (254)

For a sick child

Almighty God, Father in heaven, watch over Your child _name_ now afflicted with sickness. Mercifully spare the life You have given. Relieve _his/her_ pain, guard _him/her_ from all danger, and restore _his/her_ health according to Your gracious will, that _he/she_ may be raised to a life of faithful service to You; through Jesus Christ, our Lord. (258)

For those undergoing surgery

Lord Jesus Christ, hear our prayers on behalf of Your servant _name_ as _he/she_ undergoes surgery. Bless _him/her_ with faith in Your loving-kindness and protection. Endow the surgeon and the medical team with ability and skill so that, according to Your will, this surgery may bring Your servant to a full restoration of health and strength; for You live and reign with the Father and the Holy Spirit, one God, forever and ever. (259)

For one near death

Eternal Father, You alone make the decisions concerning life and death. We ask You to show mercy to Your servant _name_, whose death seems imminent. If it be Your gracious will, restore _him/her_ and lengthen _his/her_ earthly life; but if not, keep _him/her_ in _his/her_ baptismal grace and in Your abiding care. Give _him/her_ a repentant heart, firm faith, and a lively hope. Let not the fear of death cause _him/her_ to waver in confidence and trust. At Your chosen time, grant _him/her_ a peaceful departure and a joyous entrance into everlasting life with the glorious company of all Your saints; through Jesus Christ, our Savior. (262)

Time of bereavement

Heavenly Father, into whose keeping we entrust our loved ones, help us to look to You in our time of sorrow, remembering the cloud of faithful witnesses with which we are surrounded. Grant that we may one day share in the joys of those who now rest in Your presence; through Jesus Christ, our Lord. (265)

At a suicide

Merciful Father, how mysterious are Your judgments and Your will beyond understanding. We are troubled, but not crushed; sometimes in doubt, but never in despair; dejected, but not destroyed. Your grace in Christ is all we need, for Your power is greatest when we are weak. In these dark hours strengthen us by Your Word and Sacrament, and grant us Your abiding presence in the midst of what we cannot understand. Take into Your care those whose hearts are heavy with sorrow and grief, and lead them to look to You for confidence and strength as they face the future. Sustain them with Your comforting love, and finally receive them and us into glory; through Jesus Christ, our Lord. (277)

In times of affliction and distress

Almighty and most merciful God, in this earthly life we endure sufferings and death before we enter into eternal glory. Grant us grace at all times to subject ourselves to Your holy will and to continue steadfast in the true faith to the end of our lives that we may know the peace and joy of the blessed hope of the resurrection of the dead and of the glory of the world to come; through Jesus Christ, our Lord. (279)

For those who are lonely

Ever-present Lord, You have promised never to leave us nor forsake us but to abide with us to the end of time. Grant that those who live alone may not be lonely but find both comfort from Your promises and fulfillment in loving You and their neighbors all their days; through Jesus Christ, our Lord. (281)

For the mentally ill

O Lord, merciful Father, sustain and comfort Your servants who are mentally ill. Do not allow the evil one to trouble them, but provide them with people who, in wisdom and sympathy, will minister to them in their need. Strengthen them and their families in the knowledge of Your redeeming love so that they may evermore look to You for rescue and help; through Jesus Christ, our Lord. (283)

For the disabled

Lord God, heavenly Father, we thank You for the gift of life and everything in Your creation that enriches our physical lives. By Your merciful guidance, aid and strengthen those with physical disabilities, and enable them to find fulfillment in their lives and encouragement and support for all their endeavors; through Jesus Christ, our Lord. (285)

The unemployed

Heavenly Father, we commend to Your care those who suffer want and anxiety from lack of work. Grant that the wealth and resources of this rich land be profitably used so that all persons may find suitable and fulfilling employment and receive just payment for their labor; through Jesus Christ, our Lord. (289)

Time of disaster

Almighty God, merciful Father, Your thoughts are not our thoughts, Your ways are not our ways. In Your wisdom You have permitted this disastrous _fire / flood / earthquake / plane crash / terrorist attack / other_ to befall us. We implore You, let not the hearts of Your people despair nor our faith fail us, but sustain and comfort us. Direct all efforts to attend the injured, console the bereaved, and protect the helpless. Bring hope and healing that we may find relief and restoration; through Jesus Christ, our Lord. (292)

IN TIMES OF JOY

Restoration of health

Almighty and gracious God, we give thanks that You have restored the health of Your servant _name_, and for this blessing we praise Your name. Grant that _he/she_ may continue joyfully through the days You have given _him/her_ in this world and also share in eternal glory at the appearing of Your Son, Jesus Christ, our Lord. (297)

At the birth of a child

Almighty God, creator of all that exists, we thank You this day for the birth of _name_. As You have added _him/her_ to the human family, so also unite _him/her_ to Your holy Church through the waters of Holy Baptism. By the gracious working of Your Holy Spirit, help _him/her_ to grow in Your nurture and admonition that _he/she_ may bring glory to You and serve others in Your name; through Jesus Christ, our Lord. (301)

Anniversary of a marriage

O Lord Jesus, Your mercies are new every morning. We thank You for another year of married life together for _name_ and _name_. Open their hearts always to receive more of Your love that their love for each other may never grow weary but deepen and grow through every joy and sorrow shared; for You live and reign with the Father and the Holy Spirit, one God, now and forever. (304)

At a birthday

Heavenly Father, our times are in Your hands. Look with favor on _name_ as _he/she_ celebrates _his/her_ birthday. Grant that _he/she_ may continue to grow in wisdom and grace. Strengthen _his/her_ trust in Your goodness and bless _him/her_ with Your abiding love all the days of _his/her_ life; through Jesus Christ, our Lord. (306)

ATHANASIAN CREED

Early in the fourth century, a north African pastor named Arius began teaching that Jesus Christ was not truly God. The Church responded decisively in AD 325 with a statement of faith (The Nicene Creed), which confessed that Jesus is, in fact, true God. Toward the end of the fifth century, another creed was written that delved further into the mystery of the Trinity. Though attributed to Athanasius, a fourth-century opponent of Arius, this anonymous creed clearly came at a later stage in the debate.

The Athanasian Creed declares that its teachings concerning the Holy Trinity and our Lord's incarnation are "the catholic faith." In other words, this is what the true Church of all times and all places has confessed. More than fifteen centuries later, the Church continues to confess this truth, confident that the triune God, Father, Son, and Holy Spirit, has given Himself for our salvation.

The following translation may be spoken responsively by whole verse.

[1] Whoever desires to be saved must, above all, hold the catholic faith.

[2] Whoever does not keep it whole and undefiled will without doubt perish eternally.

[3] And the catholic faith is this,

[4] that we worship one God in Trinity and Trinity in Unity, neither confusing the persons nor dividing the substance.

[5] For the Father is one person, the Son is another, and the Holy Spirit is another.

[6] But the Godhead of the Father and of the Son and of the Holy Spirit is one: the glory equal, the majesty coeternal.

[7] Such as the Father is, such is the Son, and such is the Holy Spirit:

[8] the Father uncreated, the Son uncreated, the Holy Spirit uncreated;

[9] the Father infinite, the Son infinite, the Holy Spirit infinite;

[10] the Father eternal, the Son eternal, the Holy Spirit eternal.

[11] And yet there are not three Eternals, but one Eternal,

[12] just as there are not three Uncreated or three Infinites, but one Uncreated and one Infinite.

[13] In the same way, the Father is almighty, the Son almighty, the Holy Spirit almighty;

[14] and yet there are not three Almighties, but one Almighty.

[15] So the Father is God, the Son is God, the Holy Spirit is God;

[16] and yet there are not three Gods, but one God.

[17] So the Father is Lord, the Son is Lord, the Holy Spirit is Lord;

[18] and yet there are not three Lords, but one Lord.

[19] Just as we are compelled by the Christian truth to acknowledge each distinct person as God and Lord, so also are we prohibited by the catholic religion to say that there are three Gods or Lords.

[20] The Father is not made nor created nor begotten by anyone.

[21] The Son is neither made nor created, but begotten of the Father alone.

[22] The Holy Spirit is of the Father and of the Son, neither made nor created nor begotten, but proceeding.

[23] Thus, there is one Father, not three Fathers; one Son, not three Sons; one Holy Spirit, not three Holy Spirits.

[24] And in this Trinity none is before or after another; none is greater or less than another;

[25] but the whole three persons are coeternal with each other and coequal, so that in all things, as has been stated above, the Trinity in Unity and Unity in Trinity is to be worshiped.

[26] Therefore, whoever desires to be saved must think thus about the Trinity.

[27] But it is also necessary for everlasting salvation that one faithfully believe the incarnation of our Lord Jesus Christ.

[28] Therefore, it is the right faith that we believe and confess that our Lord Jesus Christ, the Son of God, is at the same time both God and man.

[29] He is God, begotten from the substance of the Father before all ages; and He is man, born from the substance of His mother in this age:

[30] perfect God and perfect man, composed of a rational soul and human flesh;

[31] equal to the Father with respect to His divinity, less than the Father with respect to His humanity.

[32] Although He is God and man, He is not two, but one Christ:

[33] one, however, not by the conversion of the divinity into flesh, but by the assumption of the humanity into God;

[34] one altogether, not by confusion of substance, but by unity of person.

[35] For as the rational soul and flesh is one man, so God and man is one Christ,

[36] who suffered for our salvation, descended into hell, rose again the third day from the dead,

[37] ascended into heaven, and is seated at the right hand of the Father, God Almighty, from whence He will come to judge the living and the dead.

[38] At His coming all people will rise again with their bodies and give an account concerning their own deeds.

[39] And those who have done good will enter into eternal life, and those who have done evil into eternal fire.

[40] This is the catholic faith; whoever does not believe it faithfully and firmly cannot be saved.

THE SMALL CATECHISM

Though not printed here, the official text of Luther's Small Catechism also includes the Preface.

SECTION 1

The Ten Commandments

AS THE HEAD OF THE FAMILY SHOULD TEACH THEM IN A SIMPLE WAY TO HIS HOUSEHOLD

The First Commandment

You shall have no other gods.

What does this mean?
We should fear, love, and trust in God above all things.

The Second Commandment

You shall not misuse the name of the Lord your God.

What does this mean?
We should fear and love God so that we do not curse, swear, use satanic arts, lie, or deceive by His name, but call upon it in every trouble, pray, praise, and give thanks.

The Third Commandment

Remember the Sabbath day by keeping it holy.

What does this mean?
We should fear and love God so that we do not despise preaching and His Word, but hold it sacred and gladly hear and learn it.

The Fourth Commandment

Honor your father and your mother.

What does this mean?
We should fear and love God so that we do not despise or anger our parents and other authorities, but honor them, serve and obey them, love and cherish them.

The Fifth Commandment

You shall not murder.

What does this mean?
We should fear and love God so that we do not hurt or harm our neighbor in his body, but help and support him in every physical need.

The Sixth Commandment

You shall not commit adultery.

What does this mean?
We should fear and love God so that we lead a sexually pure and decent life in what we say and do, and husband and wife love and honor each other.

The Seventh Commandment

You shall not steal.

What does this mean?
We should fear and love God so that we do not take our neighbor's money or possessions, or get them in any dishonest way, but help him to improve and protect his possessions and income.

The Eighth Commandment

You shall not give false testimony against your neighbor.

What does this mean?
We should fear and love God so that we do not tell lies about our neighbor, betray him, slander him, or hurt his reputation, but defend him, speak well of him, and explain everything in the kindest way.

The Ninth Commandment

You shall not covet your neighbor's house.

What does this mean?
We should fear and love God so that we do not scheme to get our neighbor's inheritance or house, or get it in a way which only appears right, but help and be of service to him in keeping it.

The Tenth Commandment

You shall not covet your neighbor's wife, or his manservant or maidservant, his ox or donkey, or anything that belongs to your neighbor.

What does this mean?
We should fear and love God so that we do not entice or force away our neighbor's wife, workers, or animals, or turn them against him, but urge them to stay and do their duty.

[The text of the Ten Commandments is from Exodus 20:3, 7, 8, 12–17.]

The Close of the Commandments

What does God say about all these commandments?
He says: "I, the Lord your God, am a jealous God, punishing the children for the sin of the fathers to the third and fourth generation of those who hate Me, but showing love to a thousand generations of those who love Me and keep My commandments." *Exodus 20:5–6*

What does this mean?
God threatens to punish all who break these commandments. Therefore, we should fear His wrath and not do anything against them. But He promises grace and every blessing to all who keep these commandments. Therefore, we should also love and trust in Him and gladly do what He commands.

The Creed

AS THE HEAD OF THE FAMILY SHOULD TEACH IT IN A SIMPLE WAY TO HIS HOUSEHOLD

The First Article

Creation

I believe in God, the Father Almighty, maker of heaven and earth.

What does this mean?
I believe that God has made me and all creatures; that He has given me my body and soul, eyes, ears, and all my members, my reason and all my senses, and still takes care of them.

He also gives me clothing and shoes, food and drink, house and home, wife and children, land, animals, and all I have. He richly and daily provides me with all that I need to support this body and life.

He defends me against all danger and guards and protects me from all evil. All this He does only out of fatherly, divine goodness and mercy, without any merit or worthiness in me. For all this it is my duty to thank and praise, serve and obey Him.

This is most certainly true.

The Second Article

Redemption

And in Jesus Christ, His only Son, our Lord, who was conceived by the Holy Spirit, born of the virgin Mary, suffered under Pontius Pilate, was crucified, died and was buried. He descended into hell. The third day He rose again from the dead. He ascended into heaven and sits at the right hand of God the Father Almighty. From thence He will come to judge the living and the dead.

What does this mean?
I believe that Jesus Christ, true God, begotten of the Father from eternity, and also true man, born of the virgin Mary, is my Lord,

who has redeemed me, a lost and condemned person, purchased and won me from all sins, from death, and from the power of the devil; not with gold or silver, but with His holy, precious blood and with His innocent suffering and death,

that I may be His own and live under Him in His kingdom and serve Him in everlasting righteousness, innocence, and blessedness,

just as He is risen from the dead, lives and reigns to all eternity.

This is most certainly true.

The Third Article
Sanctification

I believe in the Holy Spirit, the holy Christian Church, the communion of saints, the forgiveness of sins, the resurrection of the body, and the life everlasting. Amen.

What does this mean?
I believe that I cannot by my own reason or strength believe in Jesus Christ, my Lord, or come to Him; but the Holy Spirit has called me by the Gospel, enlightened me with His gifts, sanctified and kept me in the true faith.

In the same way He calls, gathers, enlightens, and sanctifies the whole Christian Church on earth, and keeps it with Jesus Christ in the one true faith.

In this Christian Church He daily and richly forgives all my sins and the sins of all believers.

On the Last Day He will raise me and all the dead, and give eternal life to me and all believers in Christ.

This is most certainly true.

The Lord's Prayer

AS THE HEAD OF THE FAMILY SHOULD TEACH IT IN A SIMPLE WAY TO HIS HOUSEHOLD

Our Father who art in heaven, hallowed be Thy name, Thy kingdom come, Thy will be done on earth as it is in heaven. Give us this day our daily bread; and forgive us our trespasses as we forgive those who trespass against us; and lead us not into temptation, but deliver us from evil. For Thine is the kingdom and the power and the glory forever and ever. Amen.

Our Father in heaven, hallowed be Your name, Your kingdom come, Your will be done on earth as in heaven. Give us today our daily bread. Forgive us our sins as we forgive those who sin against us. Lead us not into temptation, but deliver us from evil. For the kingdom, the power, and the glory are Yours now and forever. Amen.

The Introduction

Our Father who art in heaven.
Our Father in heaven.

What does this mean?
With these words God tenderly invites us to believe that He is our true Father and that we are His true children, so that with all boldness and confidence we may ask Him as dear children ask their dear father.

The First Petition

Hallowed be Thy name.
Hallowed be Your name.

What does this mean?
God's name is certainly holy in itself, but we pray in this petition that it may be kept holy among us also.

How is God's name kept holy?
God's name is kept holy when the Word of God is taught in its truth and purity, and we, as the children of God, also lead holy lives according to it. Help us to do this, dear Father in heaven! But anyone

who teaches or lives contrary to God's Word profanes the name of God among us. Protect us from this, heavenly Father!

The Second Petition

Thy kingdom come.
Your kingdom come.

What does this mean?
The kingdom of God certainly comes by itself without our prayer, but we pray in this petition that it may come to us also.

How does God's kingdom come?
God's kingdom comes when our heavenly Father gives us His Holy Spirit, so that by His grace we believe His holy Word and lead godly lives here in time and there in eternity.

The Third Petition

Thy will be done on earth as it is in heaven.
Your will be done on earth as in heaven.

What does this mean?
The good and gracious will of God is done even without our prayer, but we pray in this petition that it may be done among us also.

How is God's will done?
God's will is done when He breaks and hinders every evil plan and purpose of the devil, the world, and our sinful nature, which do not want us to hallow God's name or let His kingdom come; and when He strengthens and keeps us firm in His Word and faith until we die. This is His good and gracious will.

The Fourth Petition

Give us this day our daily bread.
Give us today our daily bread.

What does this mean?
God certainly gives daily bread to everyone without our prayers, even to all evil people, but we pray in this petition that God would lead us to realize this and to receive our daily bread with thanksgiving.

What is meant by daily bread?
Daily bread includes everything that has to do with the support and needs of the body, such as food, drink, clothing, shoes, house, home, land, animals, money, goods, a devout husband or wife, devout children, devout workers, devout and faithful rulers, good government, good weather, peace, health, self-control, good reputation, good friends, faithful neighbors, and the like.

The Fifth Petition

And forgive us our trespasses as we forgive those who trespass against us.
Forgive us our sins as we forgive those who sin against us.

What does this mean?
We pray in this petition that our Father in heaven would not look at our sins, or deny our prayer because of them. We are neither worthy of the things for which we pray, nor have we deserved them, but we ask that He would give them all to us by grace, for we daily sin much and surely deserve nothing but punishment. So we too will sincerely forgive and gladly do good to those who sin against us.

The Sixth Petition

And lead us not into temptation.
Lead us not into temptation.

What does this mean?
God tempts no one. We pray in this petition that God would guard and keep us so that the devil, the world, and our sinful nature may not deceive us or mislead us into false belief, despair, and other great shame and vice. Although we are attacked by these things, we pray that we may finally overcome them and win the victory.

The Seventh Petition

But deliver us from evil.
But deliver us from evil.

What does this mean?
We pray in this petition, in summary, that our Father in heaven would rescue us

from every evil of body and soul, possessions and reputation, and finally, when our last hour comes, give us a blessed end, and graciously take us from this valley of sorrow to Himself in heaven.

The Conclusion

For Thine is the kingdom and the power and the glory forever and ever.* Amen. *For the kingdom, the power, and the glory are Yours now and forever.* Amen.*

What does this mean?
This means that I should be certain that these petitions are pleasing to our Father in heaven, and are heard by Him; for He Himself has commanded us to pray in this way and has promised to hear us. Amen, amen means "yes, yes, it shall be so."

** These words were not originally in Luther's Small Catechism.*

The Sacrament of Holy Baptism

AS THE HEAD OF THE FAMILY SHOULD TEACH IT IN A SIMPLE WAY TO HIS HOUSEHOLD

FIRST

What is Baptism?
Baptism is not just plain water, but it is the water included in God's command and combined with God's word.

Which is that word of God?
Christ our Lord says in the last chapter of Matthew: "Therefore go and make disciples of all nations, baptizing them in the name of the Father and of the Son and of the Holy Spirit." *Matthew 28:19*

SECOND

What benefits does Baptism give?
It works forgiveness of sins, rescues from death and the devil, and gives eternal salvation to all who believe this, as the words and promises of God declare.

Which are these words and promises of God?
Christ our Lord says in the last chapter of Mark: "Whoever believes and is baptized will be saved, but whoever does not believe will be condemned." *Mark 16:16*

THIRD

How can water do such great things?
Certainly not just water, but the word of God in and with the water does these things, along with the faith which trusts this word of God in the water. For without God's word the water is plain water and no Baptism. But with the word of God it is a Baptism, that is, a life-giving water, rich in grace, and a washing of the new birth in the Holy Spirit, as St. Paul says in Titus, chapter three: "He saved us through the washing of rebirth and renewal by the Holy Spirit, whom He poured out on us generously through Jesus Christ our Savior, so that, having been justified by His grace, we might become heirs having the hope of eternal life. This is a trustworthy saying." *Titus 3:5–8*

FOURTH

What does such baptizing with water indicate?
It indicates that the Old Adam in us should by daily contrition and repentance be drowned and die with all sins and evil desires, and that a new man should daily emerge and arise to live before God in righteousness and purity forever.

Where is this written?
St. Paul writes in Romans, chapter six: "We were therefore buried with Him through baptism into death in order that, just as Christ was raised from the dead through the glory of the Father, we too may live a new life." *Romans 6:4*

Confession

HOW CHRISTIANS SHOULD BE TAUGHT TO CONFESS

What is Confession?
Confession has two parts. First, that we confess our sins, and second, that we receive absolution, that is, forgiveness, from the pastor as from God Himself, not doubting, but firmly believing that by it our sins are forgiven before God in heaven.

What sins should we confess?
Before God we should plead guilty of all sins, even those we are not aware of, as we do in the Lord's Prayer; but before the pastor we should confess only those sins which we know and feel in our hearts.

Which are these?
Consider your place in life according to the Ten Commandments: Are you a father, mother, son, daughter, husband, wife, or worker? Have you been disobedient, unfaithful, or lazy? Have you been hot-tempered, rude, or quarrelsome? Have you hurt someone by your words or deeds? Have you stolen, been negligent, wasted anything, or done any harm?

*What is the Office of the Keys?**
The Office of the Keys is that special authority which Christ has given to His Church on earth to forgive the sins of repentant sinners, but to withhold forgiveness from the unrepentant as long as they do not repent.

*Where is this written?**
This is what St. John the Evangelist writes in chapter twenty: The Lord Jesus breathed on His disciples and said, "Receive the Holy Spirit. If you forgive anyone his sins, they are forgiven; if you do not forgive them, they are not forgiven." *John 20:22–23*

*What do you believe according to these words?**
I believe that when the called ministers of Christ deal with us by His divine command, in particular when they exclude openly unrepentant sinners from the Christian congregation and absolve those who repent of their sins and want to do better, this is just as valid and certain, even in heaven, as if Christ our dear Lord dealt with us Himself.

** These questions may not have been composed by Luther himself but reflect his teachings and were included in editions of the Small Catechism during his lifetime.*

For an order of service based on "A Short Form of Confession" included in the Small Catechism, see pages 292–293.

The Sacrament of the Altar

AS THE HEAD OF THE FAMILY SHOULD TEACH IT IN A SIMPLE WAY TO HIS HOUSEHOLD

What is the Sacrament of the Altar?
It is the true body and blood of our Lord Jesus Christ under the bread and wine, instituted by Christ Himself for us Christians to eat and to drink.

Where is this written?
The holy Evangelists Matthew, Mark, Luke, and St. Paul write: Our Lord Jesus Christ, on the night when He was betrayed, took bread, and when He had given thanks, He broke it and gave it to the disciples and said: "Take, eat; this is My body, which is given for you. This do in remembrance of Me." In the same way also He took the cup after supper, and when He had given thanks, He gave it to them, saying: "Drink of it, all of you; this cup is the new testament in My blood, which is shed for you for the forgiveness of sins. This do, as often as you drink it, in remembrance of Me."

What is the benefit of this eating and drinking?
These words, "Given and shed for you for the forgiveness of sins," show us that in the Sacrament forgiveness of sins, life, and salvation are given us through these words. For where there is forgiveness of sins, there is also life and salvation.

How can bodily eating and drinking do such great things?
Certainly not just eating and drinking do these things, but the words written here: "Given and shed for you for the forgiveness of sins." These words, along with the bodily eating and drinking, are the main thing in the Sacrament. Whoever believes these words has exactly what they say: "forgiveness of sins."

Who receives this Sacrament worthily?
Fasting and bodily preparation are certainly fine outward training. But that person is truly worthy and well prepared who has faith in these words: "Given and shed for you for the forgiveness of sins." But anyone who does not believe these words or doubts them is unworthy and unprepared, for the words "for you" require all hearts to believe.

SECTION 2

Daily Prayers

HOW THE HEAD OF THE FAMILY SHOULD TEACH HIS HOUSEHOLD TO PRAY MORNING AND EVENING

Morning Prayer

In the morning when you get up, make the sign of the holy cross and say:
In the name of the Father and of the ☩ Son and of the Holy Spirit. Amen.

Then, kneeling or standing, repeat the Creed and the Lord's Prayer. If you choose, you may also say this little prayer:

I thank You, my heavenly Father, through Jesus Christ, Your dear Son, that You have kept me this night from all harm and danger; and I pray that You would keep me this day also from sin and every evil, that all my doings and life may please You. For into Your hands I commend myself, my body and soul, and all things. Let Your holy angel be with me, that the evil foe may have no power over me. Amen. (423)

Then go joyfully to your work, singing a hymn, like that of the Ten Commandments, or whatever your devotion may suggest.

Evening Prayer

In the evening when you go to bed, make the sign of the holy cross and say:
In the name of the Father and of the ☩ Son and of the Holy Spirit. Amen.

Then, kneeling or standing, repeat the Creed and the Lord's Prayer. If you choose, you may also say this little prayer:
I thank You, my heavenly Father, through Jesus Christ, Your dear Son, that You have graciously kept me this day; and I pray that You would forgive me all my sins where I have done wrong, and graciously keep me this night. For into Your hands I commend myself, my body and soul, and all things. Let Your holy angel be with me, that the evil foe may have no power over me. Amen. (424)

Then go to sleep at once and in good cheer.

HOW THE HEAD OF THE FAMILY SHOULD TEACH HIS HOUSEHOLD TO ASK A BLESSING AND RETURN THANKS

Asking a Blessing

The children and members of the household shall go to the table reverently, fold their hands, and say:
The eyes of all look to You, [O Lord,] and You give them their food at the proper time. You open Your hand and satisfy the desires of every living thing. *Psalm 145:15–16*

Then shall be said the Lord's Prayer and the following:
Lord God, heavenly Father, bless us and these Your gifts which we receive from Your bountiful goodness, through Jesus Christ, our Lord. Amen. (445)

Returning Thanks
Also, after eating, they shall, in like manner, reverently and with folded hands say:
Give thanks to the Lord, for He is good. His love endures forever. [He] gives food to every creature. He provides food for the cattle and for the young ravens when they call. His pleasure is not in the strength of the horse, nor His delight in the legs of a man; the Lord delights in those who fear Him, who put their hope in His unfailing love. *Psalm 136:1, 25; 147:9–11*

Then shall be said the Lord's Prayer and the following:
We thank You, Lord God, heavenly Father, for all Your benefits, through Jesus Christ, our Lord, who lives and reigns with You and the Holy Spirit forever and ever. Amen. (446)

SECTION 3

Table of Duties

CERTAIN PASSAGES OF SCRIPTURE FOR VARIOUS HOLY ORDERS AND POSITIONS, ADMONISHING THEM ABOUT THEIR DUTIES AND RESPONSIBILITIES

To Bishops, Pastors, and Preachers
1 Timothy 3:2–4
1 Timothy 3:6
Titus 1:9

What the Hearers Owe Their Pastors
1 Corinthians 9:14
Galatians 6:6–7
1 Timothy 5:17–18
1 Thessalonians 5:12–13
Hebrews 13:17

Of Civil Government
Romans 13:1–4

Of Citizens
Matthew 22:21
Romans 13:5–7
1 Timothy 2:1–3
Titus 3:1
1 Peter 2:13–14

To Husbands
1 Peter 3:7
Colossians 3:19

To Wives
Ephesians 5:22
1 Peter 3:5–6

To Parents
Ephesians 6:4

To Children
Ephesians 6:1–3

To Workers of All Kinds
Ephesians 6:5–8

To Employers and Supervisors
Ephesians 6:9

To Youth
1 Peter 5:5–6

To Widows
1 Timothy 5:5–6

To Everyone
Romans 13:9
1 Timothy 2:1

Let each his lesson learn with care,
And all the household well shall fare.

SECTION 4

Christian Questions with Their Answers

Prepared by Dr. Martin Luther for those who intend to go to the Sacrament

[The "Christian Questions with Their Answers," designating Luther as the author, first appeared in an edition of the Small Catechism in 1551, five years after Luther's death.]

After confession and instruction in the Ten Commandments, the Creed, the Lord's Prayer, and the Sacraments of Baptism and the Lord's Supper, the pastor may ask, or Christians may ask themselves these questions:

1. Do you believe that you are a sinner?
Yes, I believe it. I am a sinner.

2. How do you know this?
From the Ten Commandments, which I have not kept.

3. Are you sorry for your sins?
Yes, I am sorry that I have sinned against God.

4. What have you deserved from God because of your sins?
His wrath and displeasure, temporal death, and eternal damnation. See Romans 6:21, 23.

5. Do you hope to be saved?
Yes, that is my hope.

6. In whom then do you trust?
In my dear Lord Jesus Christ.

7. Who is Christ?
The Son of God, true God and man.

8. How many Gods are there?
Only one, but there are three persons: Father, Son, and Holy Spirit.

9. What has Christ done for you that you trust in Him?
He died for me and shed His blood for me on the cross for the forgiveness of sins.

10. Did the Father also die for you?
He did not. The Father is God only, as is the Holy Spirit; but the Son is both true God and true man. He died for me and shed His blood for me.

11. How do you know this?
From the Holy Gospel, from the words instituting the Sacrament, and by His body and blood given me as a pledge in the Sacrament.

12. What are the Words of Institution?
Our Lord Jesus Christ, on the night when He was betrayed, took bread, and when He had given thanks, He broke it and gave it to the disciples and said: "Take, eat; this is My body, which is given for you. This do in remembrance of Me." In the same way also He took the cup after supper, and when He had given thanks, He gave it to them, saying: "Drink of it, all of you; this cup is the new testament in My blood, which is shed for you for the forgiveness of sins. This do, as often as you drink it, in remembrance of Me."

13. Do you believe, then, that the true body and blood of Christ are in the Sacrament?
Yes, I believe it.

14. What convinces you to believe this?
The word of Christ: Take, eat, this is My body; drink of it, all of you, this is My blood.

15. What should we do when we eat His body and drink His blood, and in this way receive His pledge?
We should remember and proclaim His death and the shedding of His blood, as He taught us: This do, as often as you drink it, in remembrance of Me.

16. Why should we remember and proclaim His death?
First, so we may learn to believe that no creature could make satisfaction for our

sins. Only Christ, true God and man, could do that. Second, so we may learn to be horrified by our sins, and to regard them as very serious. Third, so we may find joy and comfort in Christ alone, and through faith in Him be saved.

17. What motivated Christ to die and make full payment for your sins?
His great love for His Father and for me and other sinners, as it is written in John 14; Romans 5; Galatians 2; and Ephesians 5.

18. Finally, why do you wish to go to the Sacrament?
That I may learn to believe that Christ, out of great love, died for my sin, and also learn from Him to love God and my neighbor.

19. What should admonish and encourage a Christian to receive the Sacrament frequently?
First, both the command and the promise of Christ the Lord. Second, his own pressing need, because of which the command, encouragement, and promise are given.

20. But what should you do if you are not aware of this need and have no hunger and thirst for the Sacrament?
To such a person no better advice can be given than this: first, he should touch his body to see if he still has flesh and blood. Then he should believe what the Scriptures say of it in Galatians 5 and Romans 7. Second, he should look around to see whether he is still in the world, and remember that there will be no lack of sin and trouble, as the Scriptures say in John 15–16 and in 1 John 2 and 5. Third, he will certainly have the devil also around him, who with his lying and murdering day and night will let him have no peace, within or without, as the Scriptures picture him in John 8 and 16; 1 Peter 5; Ephesians 6; and 2 Timothy 2.

NOTE

These questions and answers are no child's play, but are drawn up with great earnestness of purpose by the venerable and devout Dr. Luther for both young and old. Let each one pay attention and consider it a serious matter; for St. Paul writes to the Galatians in chapter six: "Do not be deceived: God cannot be mocked."

THE HYMNS

The Advent of Our King 331

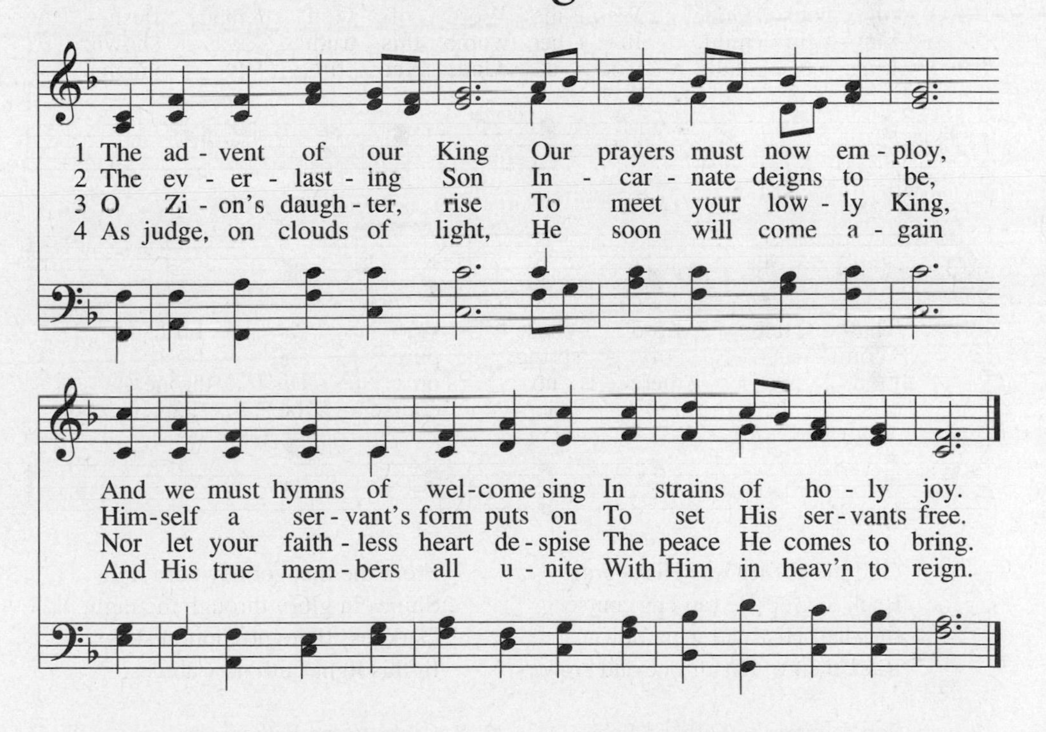
1 The ad - vent of our King Our prayers must now em - ploy,
2 The ev - er - last - ing Son In - car - nate deigns to be,
3 O Zi - on's daugh - ter, rise To meet your low - ly King,
4 As judge, on clouds of light, He soon will come a - gain
And we must hymns of wel - come sing In strains of ho - ly joy.
Him - self a ser - vant's form puts on To set His ser - vants free.
Nor let your faith - less heart de - spise The peace He comes to bring.
And His true mem - bers all u - nite With Him in heav'n to reign.

5 Before the dawning day
Let sin's dark deeds be gone,
The sinful self be put away,
The new self now put on.

△ 6 All glory to the Son,
Who comes to set us free,
With Father, Spirit, ever one
Through all eternity.

Text: Charles Coffin, 1676–1749; tr. John Chandler, 1806–76, alt.
Tune: Aaron Williams, 1731–76; setting: *The Lutheran Hymnal*, 1941

ST. THOMAS
S M

Luke 19:28–40; Phil. 2:5–11; Eph. 4:22–24; Dan. 7:13–14

332 Savior of the Nations, Come

1 Sav - ior of the na - tions, come, Vir - gin's Son, make here Your home! Mar - vel now, O heav'n and earth, That the Lord chose such a birth.
2 Not by hu - man flesh and blood, By the Spir - it of our God, Was the Word of God made flesh— Wom - an's off - spring, pure and fresh.
3 Here a maid was found with child, Yet re - mained a vir - gin mild. In her womb this truth was shown: God was there up - on His throne.
4 Then stepped forth the Lord of all From His pure and king - ly hall; God of God, yet ful - ly man, His he - ro - ic course be - gan.

5 God the Father was His source,
Back to God He ran His course.
Into hell His road went down,
Back then to His throne and crown.

6 For You are the Father's Son
Who in flesh the vict'ry won.
By Your mighty pow'r make whole
All our ills of flesh and soul.

7 From the manger newborn light
Shines in glory through the night.
Darkness there no more resides;
In this light faith now abides.

△ 8 Glory to the Father sing,
Glory to the Son, our king,
Glory to the Spirit be
Now and through eternity.

Text: attr. Ambrose of Milan, 340–397; German version, Martin Luther, 1483–1546; tr. William M. Reynolds, 1812–76, sts. 1–2; tr. *Lutheran Service Book*, 2006, sts. 3, 6; tr. F. Samuel Janzow, 1913–2001, sts. 4–5, 8; tr. Gifford A. Grobien, b. 1973, st. 7
Tune: *Geystliche gesangk Buchleyn*, Wittenberg, 1524, ed. Johann Walter; setting: *Lutheran Service Book*, 2006

NUN KOMM, DER HEIDEN HEILAND
77 77

John 1:1, 14; Luke 2:30–32

Once He Came in Blessing 333

1 Once He came in bless - ing, All our sins re -
2 Now He gent - ly leads us; With Him - self He
3 Soon will come that hour When with might - y
4 Come, then, O Lord Je - sus, From our sins re -
dress - ing; Came in like - ness low - ly,
feeds us Pre - cious food from heav - en,
pow - er Christ will come in splen - dor
lease us. Keep our hearts be - liev - ing,
Son of God most ho - ly; Bore the cross to
Pledge of peace here giv - en, Man - na that will
And will judg - ment ren - der, With the faith - ful
That we, grace re - ceiv - ing, Ev - er may con -
save us; Hope and free - dom gave us.
nour - ish Souls that they may flour - ish.
shar - ing Joy be - yond com - par - ing.
fess You Till in heav'n we bless You.

Text: Johann Horn, c. 1490–1547; tr. Catherine Winkworth, 1827–78, sts. 1, 4, alt.;
tr. *Lutheran Service Book*, 2006, sts. 2–3
Tune: Michael Weisse, c. 1480–1534; setting: Henry V. Gerike, b. 1948

GOTTES SOHN IST KOMMEN
66 66 66

Luke 4:17–19; Gal. 4:4; Rev. 22:20

334 O Lord, How Shall I Meet You

1 O Lord, how shall I meet You, How wel - come You a - right?
2 Your Zi - on strews be - fore You Green boughs and fair - est palms;
3 I lay in fet - ters, groan - ing; You came to set me free.
4 Love caused Your in - car - na - tion; Love brought You down to me.
Your peo - ple long to greet You, My hope, my heart's de - light!
And I too will a - dore You With joy - ous songs and psalms.
I stood, my shame be - moan - ing; You came to hon - or me.
Your thirst for my sal - va - tion Pro - cured my lib - er - ty.
O kin - dle, Lord most ho - ly, Your lamp with - in my breast
My heart shall bloom for - ev - er For You with prais - es new
A glo - rious crown You give me, A trea - sure safe on high
Oh, love be - yond all tell - ing, That led You to em - brace
To do in spir - it low - ly All that may please You best.
And from Your name shall nev - er With - hold the hon - or due.
That will not fail or leave me As earth - ly rich - es fly.
In love, all love ex - cel - ling, Our lost and fall - en race.

Alternate tune: VALET WILL ICH DIR GEBEN (442)

Text: Paul Gerhardt, 1607–76; tr. *The Lutheran Hymnal*, 1941, alt.
Tune: Johann Crüger, 1598–1662; setting: Richard J. Heschke, b. 1939

WIE SOLL ICH DICH EMPFANGEN
76 76 D

Matt. 21:1–9

5 Sin's debt, that fearful burden,
Cannot His love erase;
Your guilt the Lord will pardon
And cover by His grace.
He comes, for you procuring
The peace of sin forgiv'n,
His children thus securing
Eternal life in heav'n.

6 He comes to judge the nations,
A terror to His foes,
A light of consolations
And blessèd hope to those
Who love the Lord's appearing.
O glorious Sun, now come,
Send forth Your beams so cheering,
And guide us safely home.

O Bride of Christ, Rejoice 335

1 O bride of Christ, re - joice; Ex - ul - tant raise thy voice
2 Let shouts of glad-ness rise Tri - um - phant to the skies.
3 A hum - ble beast He rides, Yet as a King pre - sides;
4 The weak and tim - id find How meek He is and kind;
5 Then go thy Lord to meet; Strew palm leaves at His feet;
To hail the day of glo - ry Fore-told in sa - cred sto - ry.
Now comes the King most glo - rious To reign o'er all vic - to - rious.
Though not ar - rayed in splen-dor, He makes the grave sur - ren - der.
To them He gives a trea - sure Of bliss be - yond all mea - sure.
Thy gar-ments spread be - fore Him And hon - or and a - dore Him.
Refrain
Ho - san - na, praise, and glo - ry! Our King, we bow be - fore Thee.

Text: Danish, c. 1600; tr. Victor O. Petersen, 1864–1929, alt.
Tune: *Der Bussfertige Sünder*, Nürnberg, 1679; setting: *The Lutheran Hymnal*, 1941

WO SOLL ICH FLIEHEN HIN
66 77 77

Matt. 21:1–16; Zech. 9:9

336 Lo! He Comes with Clouds Descending

1 Lo! He comes with clouds de - scend - ing,
2 Ev - 'ry eye shall now be - hold Him
3 Those dear to - kens of His pas - sion
4 Yea, a - men, let all a - dore Thee,
Once for ev - 'ry sin - ner slain;
Robed in glo - rious maj - es - ty;
Still His daz - zling bod - y bears,
High on Thine e - ter - nal throne;
Thou - sand thou - sand saints at - tend - ing
Those who set at naught and sold Him,
Cause of end - less ex - ul - ta - tion
Sav - ior, take the pow'r and glo - ry,
Swell the tri - umph of His train:
Pierced and nailed Him to the tree,
To His ran - somed wor - ship - ers.
Claim the king - dom as Thine own.

Text: Charles Wesley, 1707–88, alt.
Tune: Thomas Olivers, 1725–99; setting: Ralph Vaughan Williams, 1872–1958, alt.

HELMSLEY
87 87 12 7

Rev. 1:7; John 20:24–31; Rev. 7:9–12

Al - le - lu - ia, al - le - lu - ia, al - le -
Deep - ly wail - ing, deep - ly wail - ing, deep - ly
With what rap - ture, with what rap - ture, with what
Al - le - lu - ia, al - le - lu - ia, al - le -
lu - ia! Christ the Lord re - turns to reign.
wail - ing, Shall their true Mes - si - ah see.
rap - ture Gaze we on those glo - rious scars!
lu - ia! Thou shalt reign, and Thou a - lone!

Stir up Your power, O Lord, and come, that by Your protection we may be rescued from the threatening perils of our sins and saved by Your mighty deliverance; for You live and reign with the Father and the Holy Spirit, one God, now and forever.

Collect for the First Sunday in Advent

337 The Night Will Soon Be Ending

1 The night will soon be end - ing; The dawn can - not be far. Let songs of praise as - cend - ing Now greet the Morn - ing Star! All you whom dark - ness fright - ens With guilt or grief or pain, God's ra - diant
2 The One whom an - gels tend - ed Comes near, a child, to serve; Thus God, the judge of - fend - ed, Bears all our sins de - serve. The guilt - y need not cow - er, For God has rec - on - ciled Through His re -
3 The earth in sure ro - ta - tion Will soon bring morn - ing bright, So run where God's sal - va - tion Glows in a sta - ble's light. As old as sin's per - ver - sion Is mer - cy's vast de - sign: God brings a
4 Yet nights will bring their sad - ness And rob our hearts of peace, And sin in all its mad - ness A - round us may in - crease. But now one Star is beam - ing Whose rays have pierced the night: God comes for

Text: Jochen Klepper, 1903–42; tr. Herman G. Stuempfle, Jr., 1923–2007
Tune: Welsh; setting: Ralph Vaughan Williams, 1872–1958, alt.

LLANGLOFFAN
76 76 D

Rom. 13:12a; Rev. 22:16–17; 1 Cor. 2:7; John 1:4–5; 3:19–21

Star now bright - ens And bids you sing a - gain.
demp - tive pow - er All those who trust this child.
new cre - a - tion— This child its seal and sign.
our re - deem - ing From sin's op - pres - sive might.

5 God dwells with us in darkness
 And makes the night as day;
Yet we resist the brightness
 And turn from God away.

But grace does not forsake us,
 However far we run.
God claims us still as children
 Through Mary's infant Son.

Come, Thou Long-Expected Jesus 338

1 Come, Thou long - ex - pect-ed Je-sus, Born to set Thy peo-ple free;
2 Born Thy peo - ple to de - liv - er; Born a child and yet a king!

From our fears and sins re-lease us; Let us find our rest in Thee.
Born to reign in us for-ev - er, Now Thy gra - cious king-dom bring.

Is - rael's strength and con-so - la-tion, Hope of all the earth Thou art,
By Thine own e - ter - nal Spir - it Rule in all our hearts a - lone;

Dear de - sire of ev - 'ry na-tion, Joy of ev - 'ry long-ing heart.
By Thine all - suf - fi - cient mer - it Raise us to Thy glo-rious throne.

Setting available in hymn accompaniment edition.

Text: Charles Wesley, 1707–88, alt.
Tune: *Southern Harmony*, New Haven, 1835

JEFFERSON
87 87 D

Is. 9:6; Luke 1:67–75; Is. 61:1–2; 2 Peter 1:3–4

339 Lift Up Your Heads, You Everlasting Doors

1 Lift up your heads, you ev - er - last - ing doors,
2 Who is this King of great and glo - rious fame?
3 Who may as - cend Mount Zi - on's ho - ly hill
4 "Wor - thy is Christ!" The Lamb who once was slain
And weep no more! O Zi - on's daugh - ter, sing,
What is His name? Lord God of Sab - a - oth,
To do God's will? The One whose un - stained hands
Now lives to reign. He rules our earth - ly ways
To greet your com - ing King; Now wave the vic - tor's
Of whom the proph - ets wrote, Whose cho - sen, hum - ble
Can meet the Law's de - mands, Whose pu - ri - ty with -
As Lord of An - cient Days— O join the end - less
palm And sing the an - cient psalm: "Lift up your
steed De - clares Him king in - deed! Ho - san - na,
in Re - veals One free from sin. Come, praise this
song Sung by the ran - somed throng: "Wor - thy is
heads, you ev - er - last - ing gates!" Your King a - waits!
Lord! Mes - si - ah, come and save From sin and grave.
King who claims the cross as throne— Praise Him a - lone!
Christ!" The Lamb be praised a - gain! A - men! A - men!

Setting available in hymn accompaniment edition.

Text: Stephen P. Starke, b. 1955
Tune: Paul Liljestrand, 1931–2011

CONRAD
14 12 12 14

Ps. 24:3–10; Rev. 5:6–14

Lift Up Your Heads, Ye Mighty Gates

1 Lift up your heads, ye might - y gates! Be - hold, the King of
2 A righ - teous Help - er comes to thee; His char - iot is hu -
3 How blest the land, the cit - y blest, Where Christ the rul - er
4 Fling wide the por - tals of your heart; Make it a tem - ple
5 Re - deem - er, come and o - pen wide My heart to Thee; here,
glo - ry waits. The King of kings is draw - ing near; The
mil - i - ty, His king - ly crown is ho - li - ness, His
is con-fessed! O peace - ful hearts and hap - py homes To
set a - part From earth - ly use for heav'n's em - ploy, A -
Lord, a - bide! O en - ter with Thy grace di - vine; Thy
Sav - ior of the world is here. Life and sal - va - tion
scep - ter, pit - y in dis - tress. The end of all our
whom this King in tri - umph comes! The cloud - less sun of
dorned with prayer and love and joy. So shall your Sov - 'reign
face of mer - cy on me shine. Thy Ho - ly Spir - it
He doth bring; There - fore re - joice and glad - ly sing. To
woe He brings; There - fore the earth is glad and sings. To
joy is He Who comes to set His peo - ple free. To
en - ter in And new and no - bler life be - gin. To
guide us on Un - til our glo - rious goal is won. E -
God the Fa - ther raise Your joy - ful songs of praise.
Christ the Sav - ior raise Your grate - ful hymns of praise.
God the Spir - it raise Your hap - py shouts of praise.
God a - lone be praise For word and deed and grace!
ter - nal praise and fame We of - fer to Thy name.

Setting available in hymn accompaniment edition.

Text: Georg Weissel, 1590–1635; tr. Catherine Winkworth, 1827–78, alt.
Tune: *Geist-reiches Gesang-Buch*, Halle, 1704, ed. Johann A. Freylinghausen, alt.

MACHT HOCH DIE TÜR
88 88 88 66

Ps. 24:7–10; Is. 60:4–5

341 Lift Up Your Heads, Ye Mighty Gates

1 Lift up your heads, ye might - y gates! Be - hold, the
2 A righ - teous Help - er comes to thee; His char - iot
3 How blest the land, the cit - y blest, Where Christ the
4 Fling wide the por - tals of your heart; Make it a
King of glo - ry waits. The King of kings is draw - ing
is hu - mil - i - ty, His king - ly crown is ho - li -
rul - er is con-fessed! O peace - ful hearts and hap - py
tem - ple set a - part From earth - ly use for heav'n's em -
near; The Sav - ior of the world is here. Life and sal -
ness, His scep - ter, pit - y in dis - tress. The end of
homes To whom this King in tri - umph comes! The cloud - less
ploy, A - dorned with prayer and love and joy. So shall your
va - tion He doth bring; There-fore re - joice and glad - ly sing.
all our woe He brings; There-fore the earth is glad and sings.
sun of joy is He Who comes to set His peo - ple free.
Sov - 'reign en - ter in And new and no - bler life be - gin.

Text: Georg Weissel, 1590–1635; tr. Catherine Winkworth, 1827–78, alt.
Tune: August Lemke, 1820–1913; setting: *The Lutheran Hymnal*, 1941

MILWAUKEE
88 88 88 66

Ps. 24:7–10; Is. 60:4–5

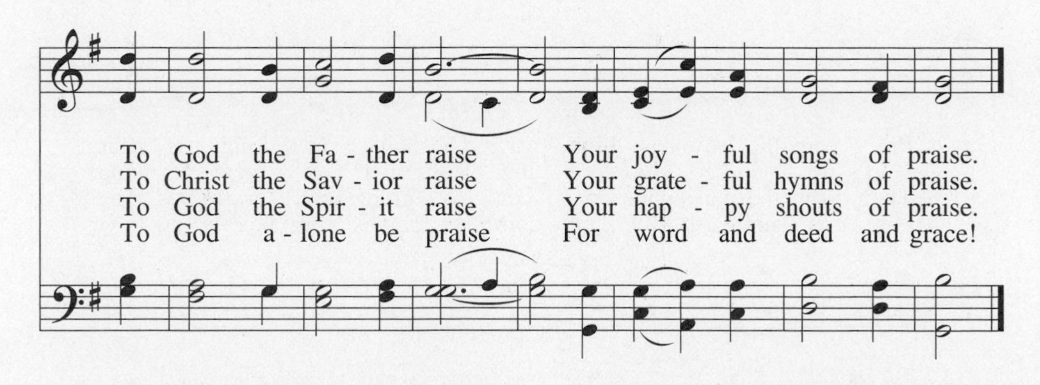
To God the Fa - ther raise Your joy - ful songs of praise.
To Christ the Sav - ior raise Your grate - ful hymns of praise.
To God the Spir - it raise Your hap - py shouts of praise.
To God a - lone be praise For word and deed and grace!

5 Redeemer, come and open wide
My heart to Thee; here, Lord, abide!
O enter with Thy grace divine;
Thy face of mercy on me shine.

Thy Holy Spirit guide us on
Until our glorious goal is won.
Eternal praise and fame
We offer to Thy name.

What Hope! An Eden Prophesied 342

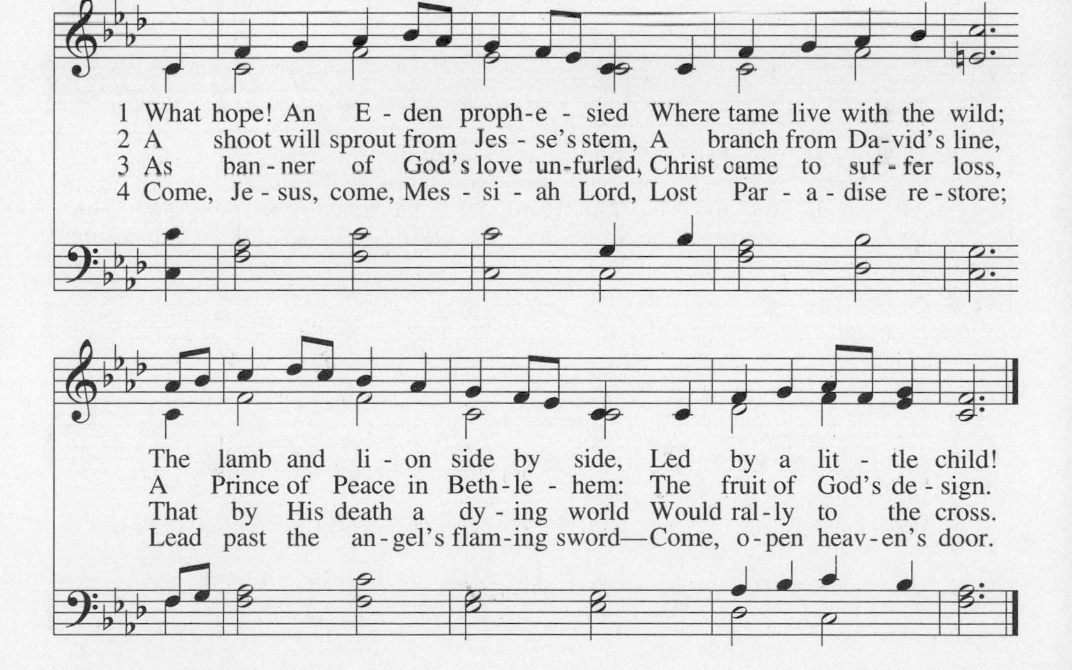
1 What hope! An E - den proph-e - sied Where tame live with the wild;
2 A shoot will sprout from Jes - se's stem, A branch from Da-vid's line,
3 As ban - ner of God's love un-furled, Christ came to suf - fer loss,
4 Come, Je - sus, come, Mes - si - ah Lord, Lost Par - a - dise re - store;
The lamb and li - on side by side, Led by a lit - tle child!
A Prince of Peace in Beth-le - hem: The fruit of God's de - sign.
That by His death a dy - ing world Would ral - ly to the cross.
Lead past the an - gel's flam-ing sword—Come, o - pen heav - en's door.

Text: Stephen P. Starke, b. 1955
Tune: *Repository of Sacred Music, Part Second*, Harrisburg, 1813, ed. John Wyeth;
setting: Kevin J. Hildebrand, b. 1973

CONSOLATION
C M

Is. 11:1, 6–10, 12–16

343 Prepare the Royal Highway

1 Pre - pare the roy - al high - way; The King of kings is near!
2 God's peo - ple, see Him com - ing: Your own e - ter - nal king!
3 Then fling the gates wide o - pen To greet your prom - ised king!
4 His is no earth - ly king - dom; It comes from heav'n a - bove.
Let ev - 'ry hill and val - ley A lev - el road ap - pear!
Palm branch - es strew be - fore Him! Spread gar - ments! Shout and sing!
Your king, yet ev - 'ry na - tion Its trib - ute too should bring.
His rule is peace and free - dom And jus - tice, truth, and love.
Then greet the King of Glo - ry Fore - told in sa - cred sto - ry:
God's prom - ise will not fail you! No more shall doubt as - sail you!
All lands, bow down be - fore Him! All na - tions, now a - dore Him!
So let your praise be sound - ing For kind - ness so a - bound - ing:
Refrain
Ho - san - na to the Lord, For He ful - fills God's Word!

Text: Frans Mikael Franzén, 1772–1847; tr. *Lutheran Book of Worship*, 1978, alt.
Tune: Swedish, 17th cent.; setting: Henry V. Gerike, b. 1948

BEREDEN VÄG FÖR HERRAN
76 76 77 and refrain

Is. 40:3–5; Matt. 21:1–11; Ps. 24:7–10; Is. 9:6–7

On Jordan's Bank the Baptist's Cry

1 On Jor - dan's bank the Bap - tist's cry An - nounc - es that the Lord is nigh; A - wake and hear - ken, for he brings Glad tid - ings of the King of kings!
2 Then cleansed be ev - 'ry life from sin; Make straight the way for God with - in, And let us all our hearts pre - pare For Christ to come and en - ter there.
3 We hail Thee as our Sav - ior, Lord, Our ref - uge and our great re - ward; With - out Thy grace we waste a - way Like flow'rs that with - er and de - cay.
4 Lay on the sick Thy heal - ing hand And make the fall - en strong to stand; Show us the glo - ry of Thy face Till beau - ty springs in ev - 'ry place.
△ 5 All praise, e - ter - nal Son, to Thee Whose ad - vent sets Thy peo - ple free, Whom with the Fa - ther we a - dore And Ho - ly Spir - it ev - er - more.

Text: Charles Coffin, 1676–1749; tr. composite
Tune: adapt. Michael Praetorius, 1571–1621; setting: George R. Woodward, 1848–1934

PUER NOBIS
L M

Matt. 3:1–6; Is. 40:3

345 Hark! A Thrilling Voice Is Sounding

1 Hark! A thrill - ing voice is sound - ing! "Christ is near," we hear it say. "Cast a - way the works of dark - ness, All you chil - dren of the day!"
2 Star - tled at the sol - emn warn - ing, Let the earth - bound soul a - rise; Christ, its sun, all sloth dis - pel - ling, Shines up - on the morn - ing skies.
3 See, the Lamb, so long ex - pect - ed, Comes with par - don down from heav'n. Let us haste, with tears of sor - row, One and all, to be for - giv'n;
4 So, when next He comes in glo - ry And the world is wrapped in fear, He will shield us with His mer - cy And with words of love draw near.
△ 5 Hon - or, glo - ry, might, do - min - ion To the Fa - ther and the Son With the ev - er - liv - ing Spir - it While e - ter - nal a - ges run!

The voice of John the Baptist proclaims that Christ's coming is near—news that thrills the longing hearts of all believers.

Text: Latin, c. 5th–10th cent.; tr. Edward Caswall, 1814–78, alt.
Music: William H. Monk, 1823–89

MERTON
87 87

Luke 1:76–79; Is. 60:1–3, 19–20; Eph. 5:8–14; Is. 25:7–9

When All the World Was Cursed 346

1 When all the world was cursed By Mo-ses' con-dem-na-tion,
2 Be-fore he yet was born, He leaped in joy-ful meet-ing,
3 Be-hold the Lamb of God That bears the world's trans-gres-sion,
4 O grant, dear Lord of love, That we re-ceive, re-joic-ing,
Saint John the Bap-tist came With words of con-so-la-tion.
Con-fess-ing Him as Lord Whose moth-er he was greet-ing.
Whose sac-ri-fice re-moves The dev-il's dread op-pres-sion.
The word pro-claimed by John, Our true re-pen-tance voic-ing,
With true fore-run-ner's zeal The great-er One he named,
By Jor-dan's roll-ing stream, A new E-li-jah bold,
Be-hold the Lamb of God, Who takes a-way our sin,
That glad-ly we may walk Up-on our Sav-ior's way
And Him, as yet un-known, As Sav-ior he pro-claimed.
He tes-ti-fied of Him Of whom the proph-ets told:
Who for our peace and joy Will full a-tone-ment win.
Un-til we live with Him In His e-ter-nal day.

Text: Johann Gottfried Olearius, 1635–1711; tr. Paul E. Kretzmann, 1883–1965, alt.
Tune: Ahasverus Fritsch, 1629–1701; setting: *Lutheran Service Book*, 2006

WAS FRAG ICH NACH DER WELT
67 67 66 66

John 1:6–9, 15–17, 23–31; Matt. 3:1–12; 11:9–14; Luke 1:41–44

347 Comfort, Comfort Ye My People

1 "Com - fort, com - fort ye My peo - ple, Speak ye peace," thus
2 Yea, her sins our God will par - don, Blot - ting out each
3 Hark, the her - ald's voice is cry - ing In the des - ert
4 Make ye straight what long was crook - ed; Make the rough - er
saith our God; "Com - fort those who sit in dark - ness, Mourn - ing
dark mis - deed; All that well de - served His an - ger He no
far and near, Call - ing sin - ners to re - pen - tance, Since the
plac - es plain. Let your hearts be true and hum - ble, As be -
'neath their sor - rows' load. Speak ye to Je - ru - sa - lem
more will see or heed. She hath suf - fered man - y a day,
King - dom now is here. O that warn - ing cry o - bey!
fits His ho - ly reign. For the glo - ry of the Lord
Of the peace that waits for them; Tell her that her
Now her griefs have passed a - way; God will change her
Now pre - pare for God a way; Let the val - leys
Now o'er earth is shed a - broad, And all flesh shall

Text: Johann Olearius, 1611–84; tr. Catherine Winkworth, 1827–78, alt.
Tune: *Trente quatre Pseaumes de David*, Geneva, 1551, ed. Louis Bourgeois; setting: *The Lutheran Hymnal*, 1941

FREU DICH SEHR
87 87 77 88

Is. 40:1–8

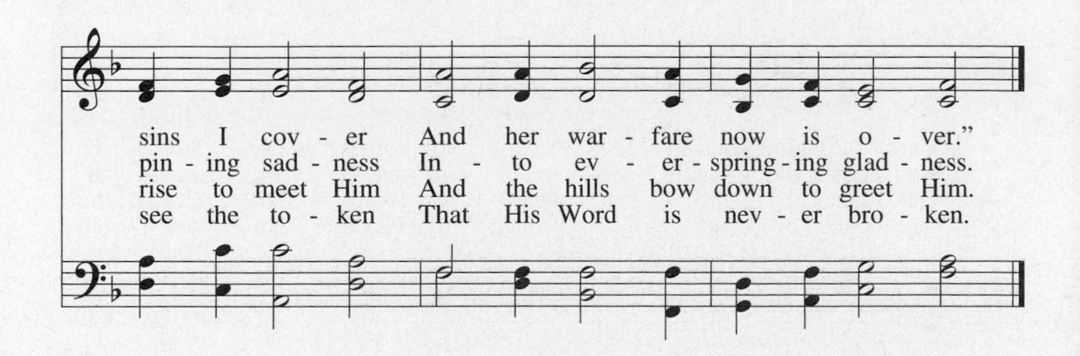
sins I cov - er And her war - fare now is o - ver."
pin - ing sad - ness In - to ev - er - spring - ing glad - ness.
rise to meet Him And the hills bow down to greet Him.
see the to - ken That His Word is nev - er bro - ken.

The King Shall Come When Morning Dawns

348

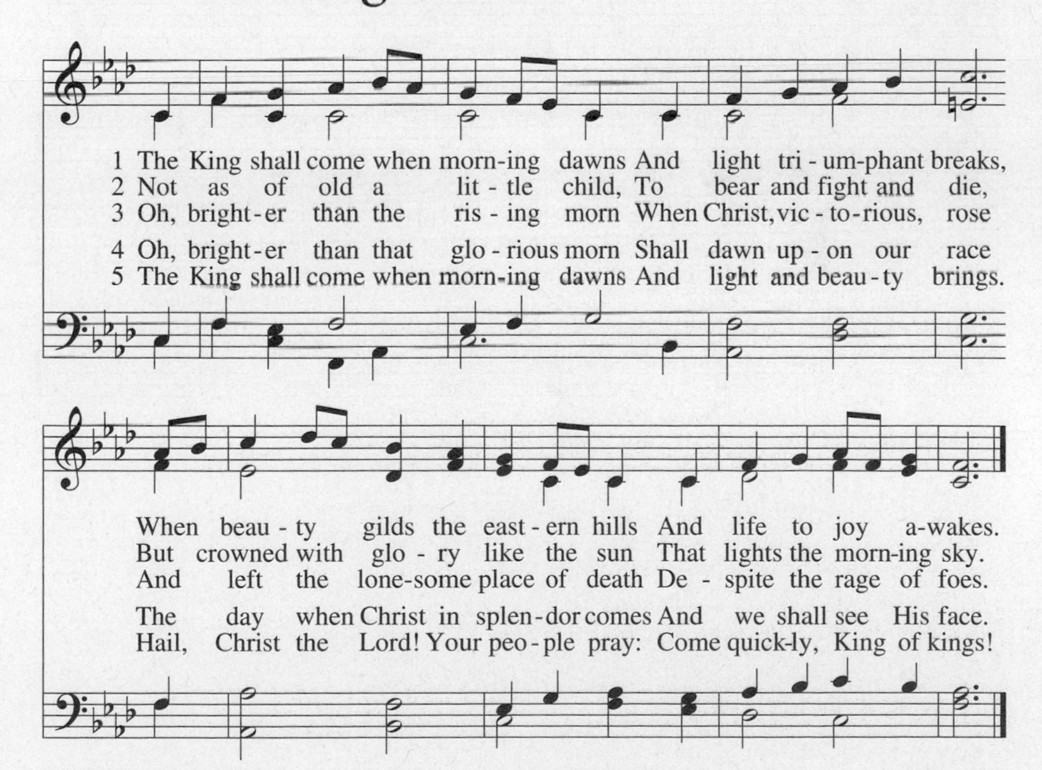
1 The King shall come when morn-ing dawns And light tri - um-phant breaks,
2 Not as of old a lit - tle child, To bear and fight and die,
3 Oh, bright-er than the ris - ing morn When Christ, vic - to-rious, rose
4 Oh, bright-er than that glo - rious morn Shall dawn up - on our race
5 The King shall come when morn-ing dawns And light and beau - ty brings.
When beau - ty gilds the east - ern hills And life to joy a-wakes.
But crowned with glo - ry like the sun That lights the morn-ing sky.
And left the lone-some place of death De - spite the rage of foes.
The day when Christ in splen-dor comes And we shall see His face.
Hail, Christ the Lord! Your peo - ple pray: Come quick-ly, King of kings!

Text: John Brownlie, 1859–1925, alt.
Tune: *Repository of Sacred Music, Part Second*, Harrisburg, 1813, ed. John Wyeth;
setting: Paul J. Grime, b. 1958

CONSOLATION
C M

Matt. 25:31; Rev. 22:20; Dan. 7:13–14

349 Hark the Glad Sound

1 Hark the glad sound! The Sav - ior comes, The Sav - ior prom - ised long; Let ev - 'ry heart pre - pare a throne And ev - 'ry voice a song.
2 He comes the pris - 'ners to re - lease, In Sa - tan's bond - age held. The gates of brass be - fore Him burst, The i - ron fet - ters yield.
3 He comes the bro - ken heart to bind, The bleed - ing soul to cure, And with the trea - sures of His grace To en - rich the hum - ble poor.
4 Our glad ho - san - nas, Prince of Peace, Thy wel - come shall pro - claim, And heav'n's e - ter - nal arch - es ring With Thy be - lov - ed name.

Text: Philip Doddridge, 1702–51
Tune: Thomas Haweis, 1734–1820; setting: *The Lutheran Hymnal*, 1941

CHESTERFIELD
C M

Luke 4:18–19; Is. 40:3; 61:1–2; Matt. 21:9

Come, Thou Precious Ransom, Come

1 Come, Thou pre - cious Ran - som, come, On - ly hope for
2 En - ter now my wait - ing heart, Glo - rious King and
3 My ho - san - nas and my palms Gra - cious - ly re -
4 Hail! Ho - san - na, Da - vid's Son! Je - sus, hear our
sin - ful mor - tals! Come, O Sav - ior of the world!
Lord most ho - ly. Dwell in me and ne'er de - part,
ceive, I pray Thee; Ev - er - more, as best I can,
sup - pli - ca - tion! Let Thy king - dom, scep - ter, crown,
O - pen are to Thee all por - tals. Come, Thy beau - ty
Though I am but poor and low - ly. Ah, what rich - es
Sav - ior, I will hom - age pay Thee, And in faith I
Bring us bless - ing and sal - va - tion, That for - ev - er
let us see; Anx - ious - ly we wait for Thee.
will be mine When Thou art my guest di - vine!
will em - brace, Lord, Thy mer - it through Thy grace.
we may sing: Hail! Ho - san - na to our King.

Text: Johann Gottfried Olearius, 1635–1711; tr. August Crull, 1845–1923, alt.
Tune: *Neu-verfertigtes Darmstädtisches Gesang-Buch*, Darmstadt, 1699;
setting: *The Lutheran Hymnal*, 1941

MEINEN JESUM LASS' ICH NICHT (DARMSTADT)
78 78 77

Matt. 20:28; 21:5; 1 Tim. 2:6; Ps. 49:7–8; Rev. 5:9

351 Creator of the Stars of Night

1 Cre - a - tor of the stars of night,
2 Thou, griev - ing that the an - cient curse
3 Thou cam'st the Bride - groom of the bride,
4 At whose dread name, ma - jes - tic now,
Thy peo - ple's ev - er - last - ing Light:
Should doom to death a u - ni - verse,
As drew the world to e - ven - tide,
All knees must bend, all hearts must bow;
O Christ, Re - deem - er, save us all
Hast found the heal - ing, full of grace,
The spot - less Vic - tim all di - vine
All things ce - les - tial Thee shall own,
And hear Thy ser - vants when they call.
To cure and save our ru - ined race.
Pro - ceed - ing from a vir - gin shrine.
And things ter - res - trial, Lord a - lone. A - men.

5 O Thou, whose coming is with dread
To judge the living and the dead,
Preserve us from the ancient foe
While still we dwell on earth below.

△ 6 To God the Father and the Son
And Holy Spirit, Three in One,
Praise, honor, might, and glory be
From age to age eternally.
Amen.

Setting available in hymn accompaniment edition.

Text: Latin, 5th–10th cent.; tr. John Mason Neale, 1818–66, alt.
Tune: Sarum plainsong, c. 9th cent., mode IV

CONDITOR ALME SIDERUM
L M

Col. 1:13–17; John 1:1–4, 14; Mal. 4:2; 1 Thess. 4:16–17

Let the Earth Now Praise the Lord 352

1 Let the earth now praise the Lord, Who has tru - ly
2 What the fa - thers most de - sired, What the proph - ets'
3 A - bram's prom - ised great re - ward, Zi - on's help - er,
4 As Your com - ing was in peace, Qui - et, full of
kept His word And at last to us did send
heart in - spired, What they longed for man - y a year,
Ja - cob's Lord— Him of two - fold race be - hold—
gen - tle - ness, Let the same mind dwell in me
Christ, the sin - ner's help and friend.
Stands ful - filled in glo - ry here.
Tru - ly came, as long fore - told.
Which is Yours e - ter - nal - ly.

5 Bruise for me the serpent's head
That, set free from doubt and dread,
I may cling to You in faith,
Safely kept through life and death.

6 Then when You will come again
As the glorious king to reign,
I with joy will see Your face,
Freely ransomed by Your grace.

Text: Heinrich Held, 1620–59; tr. Catherine Winkworth, 1827–78, alt.
Tune: *Geystliche gesangk Buchleyn*, Wittenberg, 1524, ed. Johann Walter;
setting: Seth Calvisius, 1556–1615

NUN KOMM, DER HEIDEN HEILAND
77 77

Acts 3:24–26; 13:32–33; Luke 24:27

353 Jesus Came, the Heavens Adoring

1 Je - sus came, the heav'ns a - dor - ing, Came with peace from realms on high; Je - sus came to win re - demp - tion, Low - ly came on earth to die; Al - le - lu - ia! Al - le - lu - ia! Came in deep hu - mil - i - ty.
2 Je - sus comes a - gain in mer - cy When our hearts are worn with care; Je - sus comes a - gain in an - swer To an ear - nest, heart - felt prayer; Al - le - lu - ia! Al - le - lu - ia! Comes to save us from de - spair.
3 Je - sus comes to hearts re - joic - ing, Bring - ing news of sins for - giv'n; Je - sus comes with words of glad - ness, Lead - ing souls re - deemed to heav'n. Al - le - lu - ia! Al - le - lu - ia! Hope to all the world is giv'n.
4 Je - sus comes in joy and sor - row, Shares a - like our hopes and fears; Je - sus comes, what - e'er be - falls us, Cheers our hearts and dries our tears; Al - le - lu - ia! Al - le - lu - ia! Com - forts us in fail - ing years.

Text: Godfrey Thring, 1823–1903, alt.
Tune: *Geistreiches Gesang-Buch*, Darmstadt, 1698; setting: *The Lutheran Hymnal,* 1941

SIEH, HIER BIN ICH
87 87 87

Zech. 9:9; Luke 2:14; John 14:18; Matt. 25:31–34

Arise, O Christian People 354

1 A - rise, O Chris - tian peo - ple! Pre - pare your - selves to - day; Pre - pare to greet the Sav - ior, Who takes your sins a - way. To us by grace a - lone The truth and light were giv - en; The prom - ised Lord from heav - en To all the world is shown.
2 Pre - pare the way be - fore Him; Pre - pare for Him the best. Cast out what would of - fend Him, This great, this heav'n - ly guest. Make straight, make plain the way: The low - ly val - leys rais - ing, The heights of pride a - bas - ing, His path all e - ven lay.
3 The hum - ble heart and low - ly God rais - es up on high; Be - neath His feet in ter - ror The haugh - ty soul shall lie. The heart sin - cere and right, That heeds God's in - vi - ta - tion And makes true prep - a - ra - tion— It is the Lord's de - light.
4 Pre - pare my heart, Lord Je - sus; Turn not from me a - side, And help me to re - ceive You This bless - ed Ad - vent - tide. From stall and man - ger low Come now to dwell wlth - in me; I'll sing Your prais - es glad - ly And forth Your glo - ry show.

Setting available in hymn accompaniment edition.

Text: Valentin Thilo, 1607–62; tr. Arthur T. Russell, 1806–74, alt.
Tune: *New Catechismus Gesangbüchlein*, Hamburg, 1598, alt.

AUS MEINES HERZENS GRUNDE
76 76 67 76

Luke 3:4–5; 1 Peter 5:5b–6; Ps. 51:10–12

355 O Savior, Rend the Heavens Wide

1 O Sav - ior, rend the heav - ens wide;
2 O Fa - ther, light from heav - en send;
3 O earth, in flow'r - ing bud be seen;
4 O Fount of hope, how long, how long?
5 O Morn - ing Star, O ra - diant Sun,
Come down, come down with might - y stride;
As morn - ing dew, O Son, de - scend.
Clothe hill and dale in garb of green.
When will You come with com - fort strong?
When will our hearts be - hold Your dawn?
Un - lock the gates, the doors break down;
Drop down, you clouds, the life of spring:
Bring forth, O earth, a blos - som rare,
O come, O come, Your throne fore - go;
O Sun, a - rise; with - out Your light
Un - bar the way to heav - en's crown.
To Ja - cob's line rain down the King.
Our Sav - ior, sprung from mead - ow fair.
Con - sole us in our vale of woe.
We grope in gloom and dark of night.

6 Sin's dreadful doom upon us lies;
Grim death looms fierce before our eyes.
O come, lead us with mighty hand
From exile to our promised land.

7 There shall we all our praises bring
And sing to You, our Savior King;
There shall we laud You and adore
Forever and forevermore.

Hymn accompaniment: 586

Text: Friedrich von Spee, 1591–1635; tr. Martin L. Seltz, 1909–67, alt.
Tune: *Rheinfelssisch Deutsches Catholisches Gesangbuch*, Augsburg, 1666

O HEILAND, REISS DIE HIMMEL AUF
L M

Is. 64:1; 45:8; 40:1–2; Luke 1:76–79

The Angel Gabriel from Heaven Came

1 The angel Gabriel from heaven came,
2 "For know a blessed mother thou shalt be,
3 Then gentle Mary meekly bowed her head;
4 Of her, Emmanuel, the Christ, was born
With wings as drifted snow, with eyes as flame:
All generations laud and honor thee;
"To me be as it pleaseth God," she said.
In Bethlehem all on a Christmas morn,
"All hail to thee, O lowly maiden Mary,
Thy son shall be Emmanuel, by seers foretold,
"My soul shall laud and magnify God's holy name."
And Christian folk throughout the world will ever say:
Most highly favored lady."
Most highly favored lady."
Most highly favored lady,
"Most highly favored lady."
Gloria!

Mary was uniquely favored among women—chosen by God to give birth to His Son! She responded with firm faith in God's word of promise carried to her by the angel Gabriel.

Text: Basque, c. 18th cent.; para. Sabine Baring-Gould, 1834–1924
Tune: Basque, c. 18th cent.; setting: C. Edgar Pettman, 1865–1943

GABRIEL'S MESSAGE
10 10 11 7 3

Luke 1:26–38; Is. 7:14

357 O Come, O Come, Emmanuel

1 O come, O come, Em - man - u - el, And ran - som cap - tive
2 O come, Thou Wis - dom from on high, Who or - d'rest all things
3 O come, O come, Thou Lord of might, Who to Thy tribes on
4 O come, Thou Branch of Jes - se's tree, Free them from Sa - tan's
5 O come, Thou Key of Da - vid, come, And o - pen wide our
Is - ra - el, That mourns in lone - ly ex - ile here
might - i - ly; To us the path of knowl - edge show,
Si - nai's height In an - cient times didst give the Law
tyr - an - ny That trust Thy might - y pow'r to save,
heav'n - ly home; Make safe the way that leads on high,
Refrain
Un - til the Son of God ap - pear.
And teach us in her ways to go.
In cloud and maj - es - ty and awe. Re - joice! Re - joice!
And give them vic - t'ry o'er the grave.
And close the path to mis - er - y.
Em - man - u - el Shall come to thee, O Is - ra - el!

This hymn is based on seven ancient antiphons (see facing page) that were used at Vespers during the last seven days of Advent.

Text: Latin, c. 12th cent.; *Psalteriolum Cantionum Catholicarum*, Köln, 1710; tr. John Mason Neale, 1818–66, alt.
Tune: French, 15th cent.; setting: C. Winfred Douglas, 1867–1944

VENI EMMANUEL
L M and refrain

Is. 7:10–14; Is. 11:1–5, 10–11; Matt. 1:23

6 O come, Thou Dayspring from on high,
And cheer us by Thy drawing nigh;
Disperse the gloomy clouds of night,
And death's dark shadows put to flight.
Refrain

7 O come, Desire of nations, bind
In one the hearts of all mankind;
Bid Thou our sad divisions cease,
And be Thyself our King of Peace.
Refrain

The Great "O" Antiphons

December 17
O Wisdom, proceeding from the mouth of the Most High, pervading and permeating all creation, mightily ordering | all things:*
Come and teach us the way of | prudence.

December 18
O Adonai and ruler of the house of Israel, who appeared to Moses in the burning bush and gave him the Law on | Sinai:*
Come with an outstretched arm and re- | deem us.

December 19
O Root of Jesse, standing as an ensign before the peoples, before whom all kings are mute, to whom the nations will do | homage:*
Come quickly to de- | liver us.

December 20
O Key of David and scepter of the house of Israel, You open and no one can close, You close and no one can | open:*
Come and rescue the prisoners who are in darkness and the shad- | ow of death.

December 21
O Dayspring, splendor of light ever- | lasting:*
Come and enlighten those who sit in darkness and in the shad- | ow of death.

December 22
O King of the nations, the ruler they long for, the cornerstone uniting all | people:*
Come and save us all, whom You formed | out of clay.

December 23
O Emmanuel, our king and our Lord, the anointed for the nations and their | Savior:*
Come and save us, O | Lord our God.

358

From Heaven Above to Earth I Come

1 "From heav'n a - bove to earth I come To bear good
2 "To you this night is born a child Of Mar - y,
3 "This is the Christ, our God Most High, Who hears your
4 "He will on you the gifts be - stow Pre - pared by
5 "These are the signs that you shall mark: The swad - dling
news to ev - 'ry home; Glad tid - ings of great
cho - sen vir - gin mild; This lit - tle child of
sad and bit - ter cry; He will Him - self your
God for all be - low, That in His king - dom,
clothes and man - ger dark. There you will find the
joy I bring, Where - of I now will say and sing:
low - ly birth Shall be the joy of all the earth.
Sav - ior be From all your sins to set you free.
bright and fair, You may with us His glo - ry share.
in - fant laid By whom the heav'ns and earth were made."

6 How glad we'll be to find it so!
Then with the shepherds let us go
To see what God for us has done
In sending us His own dear Son.

7 Come here, my friends, lift up your eyes,
And see what in the manger lies.
Who is this child, so young and fair?
It is the Christ Child lying there.

The first five stanzas declare the joyful words of the angel proclaiming the wondrous news of Jesus' birth.
The remaining stanzas declare the response of the shepherds and the meaning of the Savior's birth for all the world.

Text: Martin Luther, 1483–1546; tr. Catherine Winkworth, 1827–78, alt.
Tune: *Geistliche lieder*, Leipzig, 1539, ed. Valten Schumann; setting: *The Lutheran Hymnal*, 1941

VOM HIMMEL HOCH
L M

Luke 2:10–20

8 Welcome to earth, O noble Guest,
Through whom the sinful world is blest!
You came to share my misery
That You might share Your joy with me.

9 Ah, Lord, though You created all,
How weak You are, so poor and small,
That You should choose to lay Your head
Where lowly cattle lately fed!

10 Were earth a thousand times as fair
And set with gold and jewels rare,
It would be far too poor and small
A cradle for the Lord of all.

11 Instead of soft and silken stuff
You have but hay and straw so rough
On which as King, so rich and great,
To be enthroned in royal state.

12 And so it pleases You to see
This simple truth revealed to me:
That worldly honor, wealth, and might
Are weak and worthless in Your sight.

13 Ah, dearest Jesus, holy Child,
Prepare a bed, soft, undefiled,
A quiet chamber set apart
For You to dwell within my heart.

14 My heart for very joy must leap;
My lips no more can silence keep.
I, too, must sing with joyful tongue
That sweetest ancient cradlesong:

15 Glory to God in highest heav'n,
Who unto us His Son has giv'n!
While angels sing with pious mirth
A glad new year to all the earth.

359 Lo, How a Rose E'er Blooming

1 Lo, how a rose e'er bloom - ing From ten - der stem hath
2 I - sa - iah 'twas fore - told it, The rose I have in
3 This flow'r, whose fra - grance ten - der With sweet-ness fills the
4 O Sav - ior, child of Mar - y, Who felt our hu - man

sprung! Of Jes - se's lin - eage com - ing As proph-ets long have
mind; With Mar - y we be - hold it, The vir - gin moth - er
air, Dis - pels with glo - rious splen - dor The dark-ness ev - 'ry -
woe; O Sav - ior, King of glo - ry, Who dost our weak - ness

sung, It came, a flow - 'ret bright, A - mid the
kind. To show God's love a - right, She bore to
where. True man, yet ver - y God, From sin and
know: Bring us at length we pray To the bright

cold of win - ter, When half - spent was the night.
us a Sav - ior, When half - spent was the night.
death He saves us And light - ens ev - 'ry load.
courts of heav - en, And to the end - less day.

Text: German, 16th cent., sts. 1–2, 4; Friedrich L. C. Layriz, 1808–59, st. 3;
tr. Theodore Baker, 1851–1934, sts. 1–2, alt.; tr. Harriet R. K. Spaeth, 1845–1925, st. 3;
tr. John C. Mattes, 1876–1948, st. 4
Tune: *Alte Catholische Geistliche Kirchengeseng*, Köln, 1599; setting: Michael Praetorius, 1571–1621

ES IST EIN ROS (Rhythmic)
76 76 6 76

Is. 11:1–2; Matt. 1:20–21; Heb. 2:14–15; Luke 2:1–18

All My Heart Again Rejoices 360

1 All my heart a - gain re - joic - es As I hear Far and near
2 Hear! The Con - quer - or has spo - ken: "Now the foe, Sin and woe,
3 Should we fear our God's dis - plea - sure, Who, to save, Free - ly gave
4 See the Lamb, our sin once tak - ing To the cross, Suf - f'ring loss,
Sweet-est an - gel voic - es. "Christ is born!" their choirs are sing - ing
Death and hell are bro - ken!" God is man, man to de - liv - er,
His most pre-cious trea - sure? To re - deem us He has giv - en
Full a - tone-ment mak - ing. For our life His own He ten - ders,
Till the air Ev - 'ry-where Now with joy is ring - ing.
And the Son Now is one With our blood for - ev - er.
His own Son From the throne Of His might in heav - en.
And His grace All our race Fit for glo - ry ren - ders.

5 Softly from His lowly manger
Jesus calls
One and all,
"You are safe from danger.
Children, from the sins that grieve you
You are freed;
All you need
I will surely give you."

6 Come, then, banish all your sadness!
One and all,
Great and small,
Come with songs of gladness.
We shall live with Him forever
There on high
In that joy
Which will vanish never.

Text: Paul Gerhardt, 1607–76, abr., adapt.; tr. Catherine Winkworth, 1827–78, alt.
Tune: Johann Crüger, 1598–1662; setting: *Lutheran Book of Worship*, 1978

FRÖHLICH SOLL MEIN HERZE SPRINGEN
8 33 6 D

Luke 2:8–14; Rom. 8:31–34; 1 Peter 3:18–19; Eph. 1:3–14

361 O Little Town of Bethlehem

1 O lit - tle town of Beth - le - hem, How still we see thee lie!
2 For Christ is born of Mar - y, And, gath - ered all a - bove
3 How si - lent - ly, how si - lent - ly The won - drous gift is giv'n!
4 O ho - ly Child of Beth - le - hem, De - scend to us, we pray;
A - bove thy deep and dream-less sleep The si - lent stars go by;
While mor-tals sleep, the an - gels keep Their watch of won-d'ring love.
So God im - parts to hu - man hearts The bless - ings of His heav'n.
Cast out our sin, and en - ter in, Be born in us to - day.
Yet in thy dark streets shin - eth The ev - er - last - ing light.
O morn-ing stars, to - geth - er Pro - claim the ho - ly birth,
No ear may hear His com - ing; But in this world of sin,
We hear the Christ - mas an - gels The great glad tid - ings tell;
The hopes and fears of all the years Are met in thee to - night.
And prais - es sing to God the king And peace to all the earth!
Where meek souls will re - ceive Him, still The dear Christ en - ters in.
O come to us, a - bide with us, Our Lord Im - man - u - el!

Alternate tune: FOREST GREEN (362)

Text: Phillips Brooks, 1835–93
Tune: Lewis H. Redner, 1831–1908; setting: *Service Book and Hymnal*, 1958, alt.

ST. LOUIS
86 86 76 86

Luke 2:1–15; Luke 1:68–75; Eph. 3:16–19; Micah 5:2

O Sing of Christ

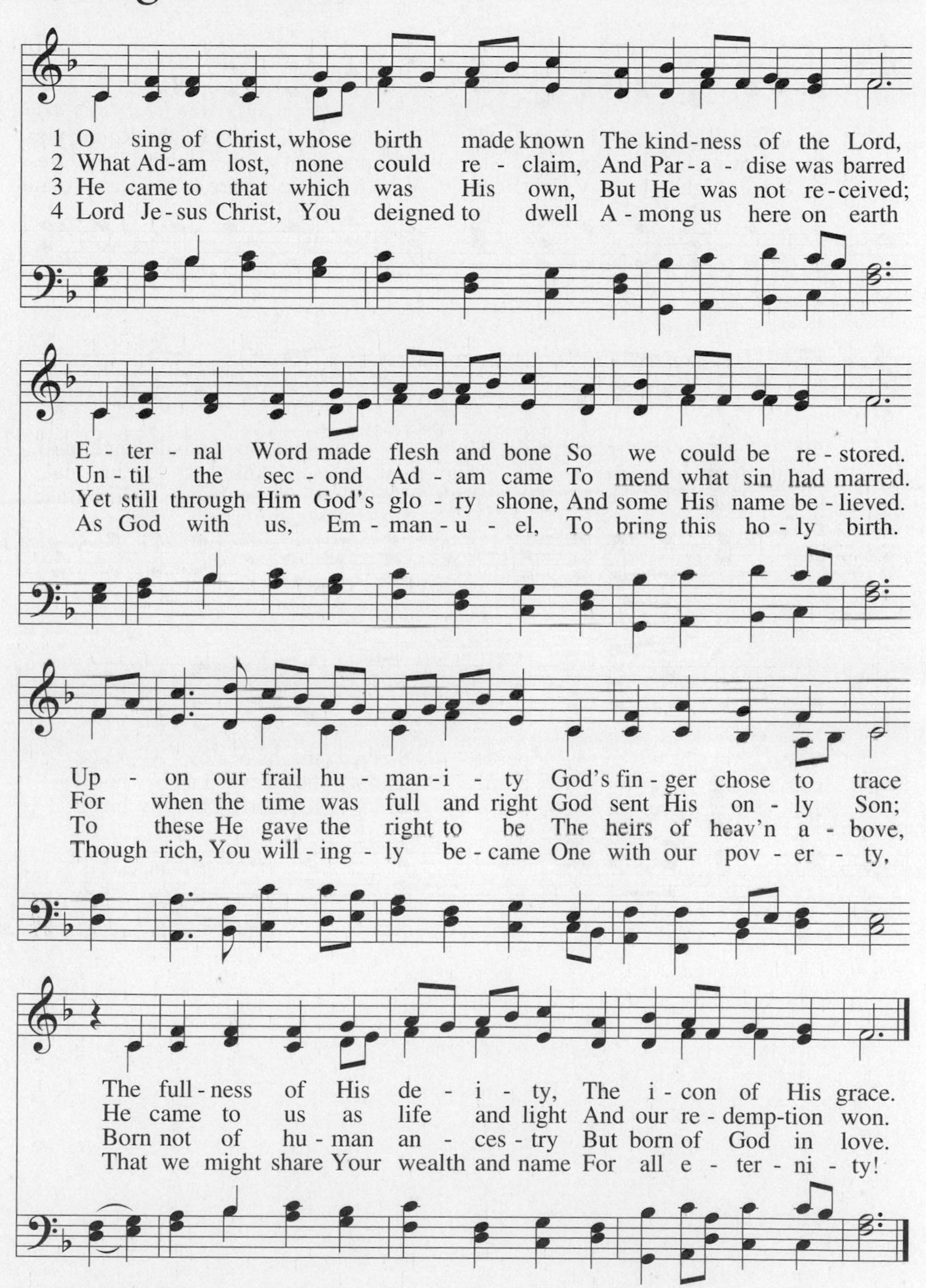
1 O sing of Christ, whose birth made known The kind-ness of the Lord,
2 What Ad-am lost, none could re - claim, And Par-a - dise was barred
3 He came to that which was His own, But He was not re-ceived;
4 Lord Je-sus Christ, You deigned to dwell A - mong us here on earth
E - ter - nal Word made flesh and bone So we could be re - stored.
Un - til the sec - ond Ad - am came To mend what sin had marred.
Yet still through Him God's glo - ry shone, And some His name be - lieved.
As God with us, Em - man - u - el, To bring this ho - ly birth.
Up - on our frail hu - man - i - ty God's fin - ger chose to trace
For when the time was full and right God sent His on - ly Son;
To these He gave the right to be The heirs of heav'n a - bove,
Though rich, You will - ing - ly be - came One with our pov - er - ty,
The full-ness of His de - i - ty, The i - con of His grace.
He came to us as life and light And our re - demp-tion won.
Born not of hu - man an - ces - try But born of God in love.
That we might share Your wealth and name For all e - ter - ni - ty!

Text: Stephen P. Starke, b. 1955
Tune: English; adapt. Ralph Vaughan Williams, 1872–1958;
setting: Ralph Vaughan Williams, 1872–1958, alt.

FOREST GREEN
C M D

John 1:1, 4, 10–14; Col. 1:15–20

363 Silent Night, Holy Night

1 Si - lent night, ho - ly night! All is calm, all is bright Round yon
2 Si - lent night, ho - ly night! Shep-herds quake at the sight; Glo - ries
3 Si - lent night, ho - ly night! Son of God, love's pure light Ra - diant
vir - gin moth-er and child. Ho - ly In-fant, so ten-der and mild,
stream from heav-en a - far, Heav'n-ly hosts sing, Al - le - lu - ia!
beams from Thy ho-ly face With the dawn of re-deem - ing grace,
Sleep in heav-en-ly peace, Sleep in heav - en - ly peace.
Christ, the Sav - ior, is born! Christ, the Sav - ior, is born!
Je - sus, Lord, at Thy birth, Je - sus, Lord, at Thy birth.

Text: Franz Joseph Mohr, 1792–1848; tr. John F. Young, 1820–85;
Spanish tr. Federico Fliedner, 1845–1901
Tune: Franz Xaver Gruber, 1787–1863; setting: Traditional

STILLE NACHT
66 88 66

Luke 2:7–16; Col. 1:13

1 *Stille Nacht, heilige Nacht!*
Alles schläft, einsam wacht
Nur das traute, hochheilige Paar.
Holder Knabe im lockigen Haar,
Schlaf in himmlischer Ruh,
Schlaf in himmlischer Ruh.

2 *Stille Nacht, heilige Nacht!*
Hirten erst kundgemacht,
Durch der Engel Halleluja
Tönt es laut von fern und nah:
Christ, der Retter, ist da,
Christ, der Retter, ist da!

3 *Stille Nacht, heilige Nacht!*
Gottes Sohn, o wie lacht
Lieb aus deinem göttlichen Mund,
Da uns schlägt die rettende Stund,
Christ, in deiner Geburt,
Christ, in deiner Geburt.

1 *¡Noche de paz, noche de amor!*
Todo duerme en derredor.
Entre los astros que esparcen su luz,
bella anunciando al niñito Jesús
brilla la estrella de paz,
brilla la estrella de paz.

2 *¡Noche de paz, noche de amor!*
Oye humilde el fiel pastor
coros celestes que anuncian salud,
gracias y glorias en gran plenitud,
por nuestro buen Redentor,
por nuestro buen Redentor.

3 *¡Noche de paz, noche de amor!*
Ved qué bello resplandor
luce en el rostro del niño Jesús
en el pesebre, del mundo la luz,
astro de eterno fulgor,
astro de eterno fulgor.

Note: The text below, known to some in The Lutheran Church—Missouri Synod, is an alternate wording of stanza 1.

Stille Nacht, heilige Nacht!
Alles schläft, einsam wacht
Nur das heilige Elternpaar,
Das im Stalle zu Bethlehem war,
Bei dem himmlischen Kind,
Bei dem himmlischen Kind.

364 Away in a Manger

1 A - way in a man - ger, no crib for a bed,
2 The cat - tle are low - ing, the ba - by a - wakes,
3 Be near me, Lord Je - sus; I ask Thee to stay
The lit - tle Lord Je - sus laid down His sweet head.
But lit - tle Lord Je - sus, no cry - ing He makes.
Close by me for - ev - er and love me, I pray.
The stars in the sky looked down where He lay,
I love Thee, Lord Je - sus! Look down from the sky,
Bless all the dear chil - dren in Thy ten - der care,
The lit - tle Lord Je - sus a - sleep on the hay.
And stay by my cra - dle till morn - ing is nigh.
And take us to heav - en to live with Thee there.

Text: *Little Children's Book*, Philadelphia, 1885, sts. 1–2; *Vineyard Songs*, Louisville, 1892, st. 3, alt.
Tune: James R. Murray, 1841–1905; setting: Joseph Herl, b. 1959

AWAY IN A MANGER
11 11 11 11

Luke 2:7; Mark 10:14–16; Matt. 1:23; 28:20

Away in a Manger

1 A - way in a man - ger, no crib for a bed,
2 The cat - tle are low - ing, the ba - by a - wakes,
3 Be near me, Lord Je - sus; I ask Thee to stay
The lit - tle Lord Je - sus laid down His sweet head.
But lit - tle Lord Je - sus, no cry - ing He makes.
Close by me for - ev - er and love me, I pray.
The stars in the bright sky looked down where He lay,
I love Thee, Lord Je - sus! Look down from the sky,
Bless all the dear chil - dren in Thy ten - der care,
The lit - tle Lord Je - sus a - sleep on the hay.
And stay by my cra - dle till morn - ing is nigh.
And take us to heav - en to live with Thee there.

Text: *Little Children's Book*, Philadelphia, 1885, sts. 1–2; *Vineyard Songs*, Louisville, 1892, st. 3, alt.
Tune: William J. Kirkpatrick, 1838–1921; setting: James E. Engel, 1925–89, alt.

CRADLE SONG
11 11 11 11

Luke 2:7; Mark 10:14–16; Matt. 1:23; 28:20

366 It Came upon the Midnight Clear

1 It came up-on the mid-night clear, That glo-rious song of old,
2 Still through the clo-ven skies they come With peace-ful wings un-furled,
3 All you, be-neath your heav-y load, By care and guilt bent low,
4 For lo, the days have come to pass By proph-ets seen of old,

From an-gels bend-ing near the earth To touch their harps of gold:
And still their heav'n-ly mu-sic floats O'er all the wea-ry world.
Who toil a-long a drea-ry way With pain-ful steps and slow:
When down in-to the cir-cling years Came Christ as was fore-told.

"Peace on the earth, good-will to all, From heav'n's all-gra-cious king."
A-bove its sad and low-ly plains They bend on hov-'ring wing,
Look up, for gold-en is the hour, Come swift-ly on the wing,
His word of peace shall to the earth God's an-cient prom-ise bring,

The world in sol-emn still-ness lay To hear the an-gels sing.
And ev-er o'er its ba-bel sounds The bless-ed an-gels sing.
The Prince was born to bring you peace; Of Him the an-gels sing.
And all who take this gift will hear The song the an-gels sing.

Text: Edmund H. Sears, 1810–76, alt.
Music: Richard S. Willis, 1819–1900

CAROL
C M D

Luke 2:13–14; Is. 9:4–5; Gen. 11:9

Angels from the Realms of Glory 367

1 An - gels from the realms of glo - ry, Wing your flight o'er all the earth; Ye who sang cre - a - tion's sto - ry, Now pro - claim Mes - si - ah's birth.
2 Shep - herds in the field a - bid - ing, Watch - ing o'er your flocks by night, God with us is now re - sid - ing, Yon - der shines the In - fant Light.
3 Sa - ges, leave your con - tem - pla - tions, Bright - er vi - sions beam a - far; Seek the great De - sire of na - tions, Ye have seen His na - tal star.
4 Saints be - fore the al - tar bend - ing, Watch - ing long in hope and fear, Sud - den - ly the Lord, de - scend - ing, In His tem - ple shall ap - pear.
△ 5 All cre - a - tion, join in prais - ing God the Fa - ther, Spir - it, Son, Ev - er - more your voic - es rais - ing To the e - ter - nal Three in One.
Refrain
Come and wor - ship, come and wor - ship; Wor - ship Christ, the new - born King.

Text: James Montgomery, 1771–1854, sts. 1–4, alt.; *Salisbury Hymn Book*, Salisbury, 1857, st. 5, alt.
Tune: Henry T. Smart, 1813–79; setting: *The Lutheran Hymnal*, 1941

REGENT SQUARE
87 87 87

Luke 2:8–17; John 1:4–5, 9, 14; Luke 2:25–38; Matt. 2:1–11

368 Angels We Have Heard on High

1 An - gels we have heard on high, Sweet - ly sing - ing o'er the plains,
2 Shep - herds, why this ju - bi - lee? Why your joy - ous strains pro - long?
3 Come to Beth - le - hem and see Him whose birth the an - gels sing;

And the moun - tains in re - ply, Ech - o - ing their joy - ous strains.
What the glad - some tid - ings be Which in - spire your heav'n - ly song?
Come, a - dore on bend - ed knee Christ the Lord, the new - born King.

Refrain

Glo - - - - ri - a in ex - cel - sis De - o. Glo - - -

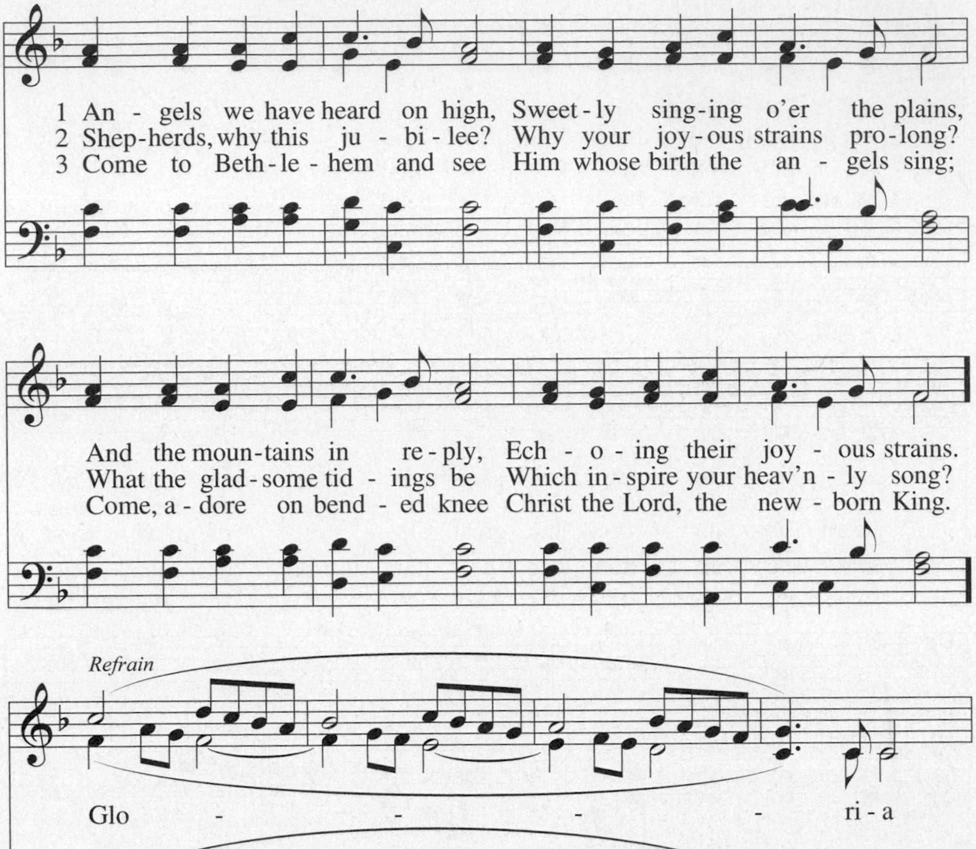

"Gloria in excelsis Deo" is Latin for "Glory to God in the highest" (Luke 2:14).

Text: French; tr. *The Crown of Jesus, Part 2*, London, 1862, alt.
Tune: French; setting: Edward S. Barnes, 1887–1958

GLORIA
77 77 and refrain

Luke 2:7–20

- - ri - a in ex - cel - sis De - o.

Where Shepherds Lately Knelt 369

1 Where shep-herds late - ly knelt and kept the an - gel's word,
2 In that un - like - ly place I find Him as they said:
3 How should I not have known I - sa - iah would be there,
4 Can I, will I for - get how Love was born, and burned
I come in half - be - lief, a pil - grim strange - ly stirred;
Sweet new-born babe, how frail! And in a man - ger bed:
His proph - e - cies ful - filled? With pound - ing heart I stare:
Its way in - to my heart— un - asked, un - forced, un - earned,
But there is room and wel - come there for me,
A still, small voice to cry one day for me,
A child, a son, the Prince of Peace for me,
To die, to live, and not a - lone for me,
But there is room and wel - come there for me.
A still, small voice to cry one day for me.
A child, a son, the Prince of Peace for me.
To die, to live, and not a - lone for me?

Setting available in hymn accompaniment edition.

Text: Jaroslav J. Vajda, 1919–2008
Tune: Carl F. Schalk, b. 1929

MANGER SONG
12 12 10 10

Luke 2:1–16; Is. 9:1–7

370 What Child Is This

1 What child is this, who, laid to rest, On Mar - y's lap is
2 Why lies He in such mean es - tate Where ox and ass are
3 So bring Him in - cense, gold, and myrrh; Come, peas - ant, king, to
sleep - ing? Whom an - gels greet with an - thems sweet While
feed - ing? Good Chris - tian, fear; for sin - ners here The
own Him. The King of kings sal - va - tion brings; Let
shep - herds watch are keep - ing? This, this is
si - lent Word is plead - ing. Nails, spear shall
lov - ing hearts en - throne Him. Raise, raise the
Christ the king, Whom shep - herds guard and an - gels sing;
pierce Him through, The cross be borne for me, for you;
song on high, The vir - gin sings her lul - la - by;

Text: William C. Dix, 1837–98
Tune: English, 16th cent.; setting: John Stainer, 1840–1901, alt.

GREENSLEEVES
87 87 68 67

Luke 2:1–20; Matt. 2:1–11; Phil. 2:5–8; Is. 53:3–6

Haste, haste to bring Him laud, The babe, the son of Mar-y!
Hail, hail the Word made flesh, The babe, the son of Mar-y!
Joy, joy, for Christ is born, The babe, the son of Mar-y!

Let Our Gladness Banish Sadness 371

1 Let our glad-ness Ban-ish sad-ness All through-out cre-a-tion!
2 Whom the sa-ges And the a-ges Ea-ger-ly a-wait-ed,
3 Child ap-peal-ing, Light re-veal-ing, Je-sus Christ, our plea-sure;
God, whose fa-vor Sent our Sav-ior, Praise with ad-o-ra-tion!
An-gels proud-ly Her-ald loud-ly In their songs e-lat-ed.
God, yet ver-y Son of Mar-y, Heav-en's gift and trea-sure.
He is born in a stall, Now He lies, in-fant small,
Let us, too, in these days, Thank-ful hearts glad-ly raise;
Might-y king, gen-tle friend, As our Lord to us bend,
In a man-ger, Heav'n-ly strang-er, Lord of all,
To the ten-der In-fant ren-der All our praise,
With Your bless-ing Us ca-ress-ing, Now de-scend,
In a man-ger, Heav'n-ly strang-er, Lord of all.
To the ten-der In-fant ren-der All our praise.
With Your bless-ing Us ca-ress-ing, Now de-scend.

Setting available in hymn accompaniment edition.

Text: Juraj Tranovský, 1591–1637; tr. Jaroslav J. Vajda, 1919–2008, alt.
Tune: Bohemian, 12th cent.

ČAS RADOSTI
86 86 66 11 11

Luke 2:1–16; John 1:1–4, 14; Gal. 4:4; Matt. 2:1–7

372 O Jesus Christ, Thy Manger Is

1 O Je - sus Christ, Thy man - ger is My
2 He whom the sea And wind o - bey Doth
3 Thy light and grace Our guilt ef - face, Thy
4 Thou Chris - tian heart, Who - e'er thou art, Be
par - a - dise at which my soul re - clin - eth.
come to serve the sin - ner in great meek - ness.
heav'n - ly rich - es all our loss re - triev - ing.
of good cheer and let no sor - row move thee!
For there, O Lord, Doth lie the Word Made
Thou, God's own Son, With us art one, Dost
Im - man - u - el, Thy birth doth quell The
For God's own Child, In mer - cy mild, Joins
flesh for us; here - in Thy grace forth shin - eth.
join us and our chil - dren in our weak - ness.
pow'r of hell and Sa - tan's bold de - ceiv - ing.
thee to Him; how great - ly God must love thee!

5 Remember thou
What glory now
The Lord prepared thee for all earthly sadness.
The angel host
Can never boast
Of greater glory, greater bliss or gladness.

6 The world may hold
Her wealth and gold;
But thou, my heart, keep Christ as thy true treasure.
To Him hold fast
Until at last
A crown be thine and honor in full measure.

Setting available in hymn accompaniment edition.

Text: Paul Gerhardt, 1607–76; tr. *The Lutheran Hymnal*, 1941
Tune: Kenneth T. Kosche, b. 1947

IN PARADISUM
4 4 11 D

Luke 2:4–16; John 1:14; Matt. 20:28; John 17:23

See amid the Winter's Snow 373

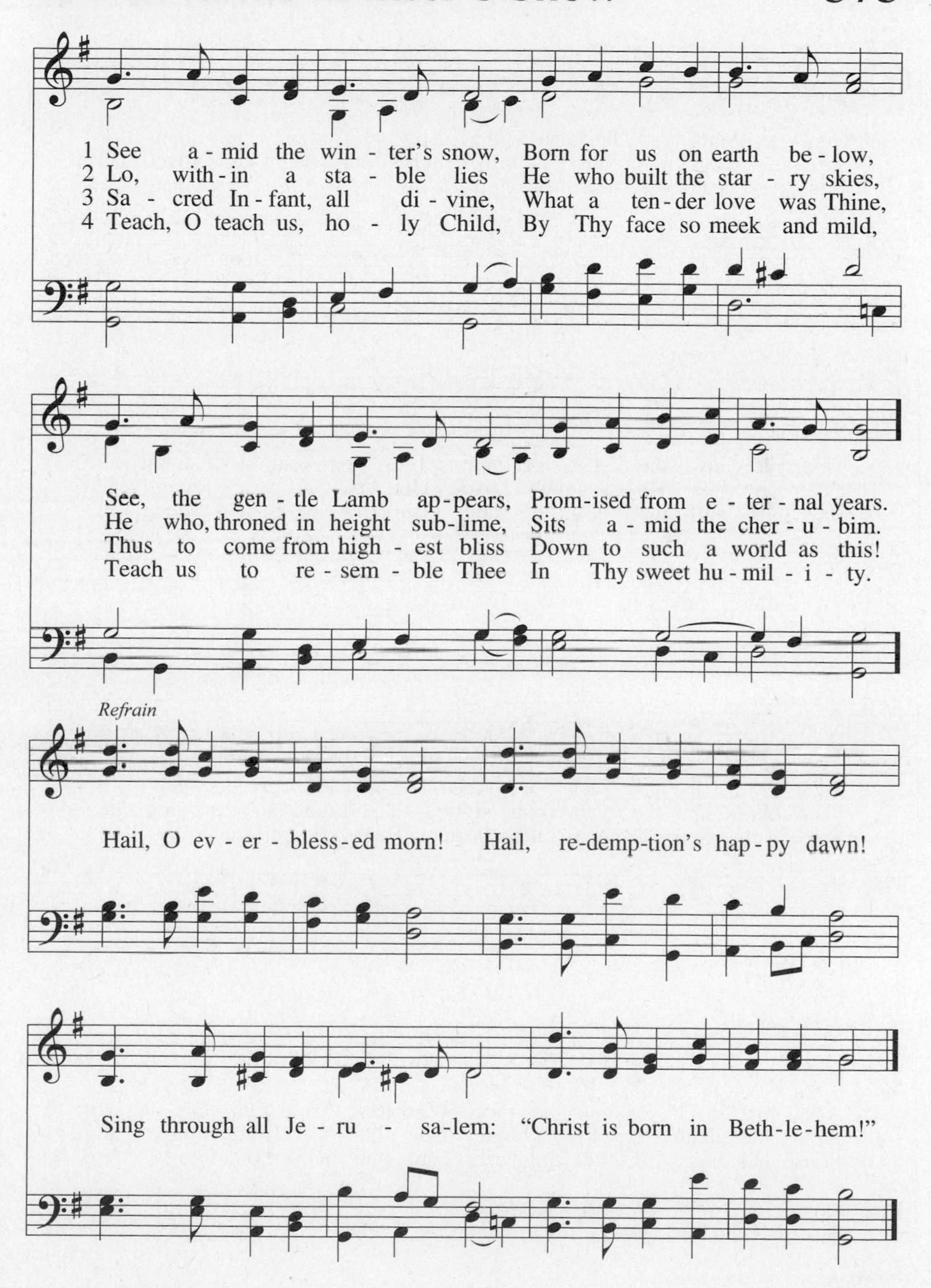

1 See a - mid the win - ter's snow, Born for us on earth be - low,
2 Lo, with - in a sta - ble lies He who built the star - ry skies,
3 Sa - cred In - fant, all di - vine, What a ten - der love was Thine,
4 Teach, O teach us, ho - ly Child, By Thy face so meek and mild,
See, the gen - tle Lamb ap - pears, Prom - ised from e - ter - nal years.
He who, throned in height sub - lime, Sits a - mid the cher - u - bim.
Thus to come from high - est bliss Down to such a world as this!
Teach us to re - sem - ble Thee In Thy sweet hu - mil - i - ty.
Refrain
Hail, O ev - er - bless - ed morn! Hail, re - demp - tion's hap - py dawn!
Sing through all Je - ru - sa - lem: "Christ is born in Beth - le - hem!"

Text: Edward Caswall, 1814–78, alt.
Music: John Goss, 1800–80

HUMILITY
77 77 and refrain

Luke 2:1–20; John 1:29; Phil. 2:3–8

374 Gentle Mary Laid Her Child

1 Gen - tle Mar - y laid her child Low - ly in a man - ger;
2 An - gels sang a - bout His birth, Wise Men sought and found Him;
3 Gen - tle Mar - y laid her child Low - ly in a man - ger;
There He lay, the Un - de-filed, To the world a strang - er.
Heav - en's star shone bright - ly forth Glo - ry all a - round Him.
He is still the Un - de - filed But no more a strang - er.
Such a babe in such a place, Can He be the Sav - ior?
Shep - herds saw the won - drous sight, Heard the an - gels sing - ing;
Son of God of hum - ble birth, Beau - ti - ful the sto - ry;
Ask the saved of all the race Who have found His fa - vor.
All the plains were lit that night, All the hills were ring - ing.
Praise His name in all the earth; Hail the King of glo - ry!

Text: Joseph Simpson Cook, 1859–1933
Tune: *Piae Cantiones Ecclesiasticae*, Griefswald, 1582; setting: *Common Praise* (Canada), 1998

TEMPUS ADEST FLORIDUM
76 76 D

Luke 2:1–20; Phil. 2:5–11; 1 John 3:5

Come, Your Hearts and Voices Raising

1 Come, your hearts and voic - es rais - ing, Christ the Lord with glad - ness prais - ing; Loud - ly sing His love a - maz - ing, Wor - thy folk of Chris - ten - dom.
2 Christ, from heav'n to us de - scend - ing And in love our race be - friend - ing; In our need His help ex - tend - ing, Saved us from the wi - ly foe.
3 Ja - cob's star in all its splen - dor Beams with com - fort sweet and ten - der, Forc - ing Sa - tan to sur - ren - der, Break - ing all the pow'rs of hell.
4 From the bond - age that op - pressed us, From sin's fet - ters that pos - sessed us, From the grief that sore dis - tressed us, We, the cap - tives, now are free.

5 Oh, the joy beyond expressing
When by faith we grasp this blessing,
And to You we come confessing
That Your love has set us free.

6 Gracious Child, we pray, O hear us,
From Your lowly manger cheer us,
Gently lead us and be near us
Till we join Your choir above.

Text: Paul Gerhardt, 1607–76; tr. *The Lutheran Hymnal*, 1941, alt.
Tune: German, 14th cent.; setting: *The Lutheran Hymnal*, 1941

QUEM PASTORES
88 87

Luke 1:68–71; Is. 61:1; Ps. 107:10–22

376 Once in Royal David's City

1 Once in roy - al Da - vid's cit - y Stood a
2 He came down to earth from heav - en, Who is
3 For He is our child - hood's pat - tern, Day by
4 And our eyes at last shall see Him, Through His
low - ly cat - tle shed, Where a moth - er laid her
God and Lord of all, And His shel - ter was a
day like us He grew; He was lit - tle, weak, and
own re - deem - ing love; For that child so dear and
ba - by In a man - ger for His bed: Mar - y
sta - ble, And His cra - dle was a stall; With the
help - less, Tears and smiles like us He knew; And He
gen - tle Is our Lord in heav'n a - bove; And He
was that moth - er mild, Je - sus Christ her lit - tle child.
poor and mean and low - ly Lived on earth our Sav - ior ho - ly.
feels for all our sad - ness, And He shares in all our glad - ness.
leads His chil - dren on To the place where He is gone.

Text: Cecil F. Alexander, 1818–95, alt.
Tune: Henry J. Gauntlett, 1805–76; setting: Arthur H. Mann, 1850–1929

IRBY
87 87 77

Luke 2:4–7; Heb. 4:14–16; Job 19:25–27; Rev. 7:9–12

5 Not in that poor, lowly stable
With the oxen standing by
Shall we see Him, but in heaven,
Set at God's right hand on high.
Then like stars His children, crowned,
All in white, His praise will sound!

On Christmas Night All Christians Sing 377

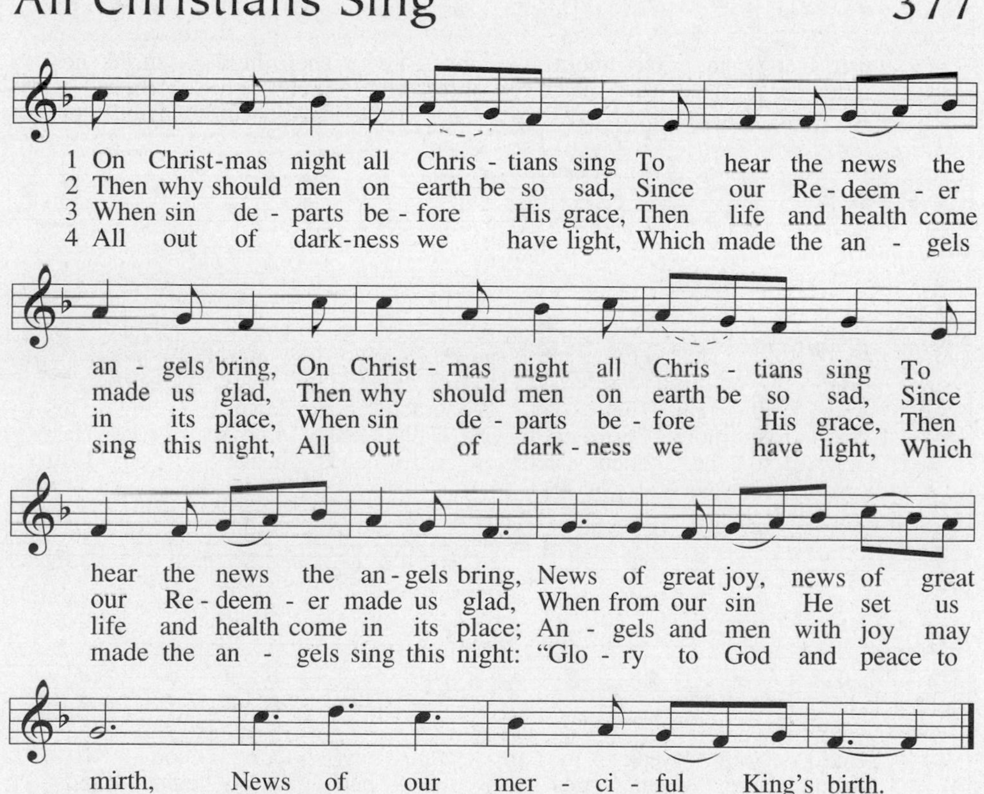
1 On Christ-mas night all Chris - tians sing To hear the news the an - gels bring, On Christ - mas night all Chris - tians sing To hear the news the an-gels bring, News of great joy, news of great mirth, News of our mer - ci - ful King's birth.
2 Then why should men on earth be so sad, Since our Re-deem - er made us glad, Then why should men on earth be so sad, Since our Re-deem - er made us glad, When from our sin He set us free, All for to gain our lib - er - ty?
3 When sin de - parts be - fore His grace, Then life and health come in its place, When sin de - parts be - fore His grace, Then life and health come in its place; An - gels and men with joy may sing, All for to see the new - born King.
4 All out of dark-ness we have light, Which made the an - gels sing this night, All out of dark - ness we have light, Which made the an - gels sing this night: "Glo - ry to God and peace to men Now and for - ev - er - more. A - men."

Setting available in hymn accompaniment edition.

Text: English
Tune: English

SUSSEX CAROL
L M

Luke 2:10–14, 20

378 Break Forth, O Beauteous Heavenly Light

1 Break forth, O beau - teous heav'n - ly light, And
2 O dear - est Child, whom I a - dore, Whose
3 All bless - ing, thanks, and praise to Thee, Lord
ush - er in the morn - ing. Ye shep - herds, shrink not
grace sur - pass - es mea - sure, My Broth - er, whom I
Je - sus Christ, be giv - en: Thou hast my Broth - er
with af - fright, The day of grace is dawn - ing. This
cher - ish more Than earth with all its trea - sure: Haste
deigned to be, Thou Lord of earth and heav - en. Help
Child, though weak in in - fan - cy, Our con - fi -
from Thy man - ger to de - part, O come and
me through - out this day of grace To praise Thy

Text: Johann Rist, 1607–67; tr. *Lutheran Hymnal* (Australia), 1973
Tune: Johann Schop, c. 1590–1667; setting: Johann Sebastian Bach, 1685–1750

ERMUNTRE DICH
87 87 88 77

Is. 9:2–7; 1 Tim. 2:5; John 1:1–5, 14; Eph. 2:14

dence and joy shall be, The pow'r of Sa - tan
dwell with - in my heart; With joy will I re -
love and seek Thy face; And when I stand be -
break - ing, Our peace with God now mak - ing.
ceive Thee, A cra - dle there will give Thee.
fore Thee For - ev - er to a - dore Thee.

O God, You make this most holy night to shine with the brightness of the true Light. Grant that as we have known the mysteries of that Light on earth we may also come to the fullness of His joys in heaven; through the same Jesus Christ, Your Son, our Lord, who lives and reigns with You and the Holy Spirit, one God, now and forever.

Collect for Christmas Midnight

---

379 O Come, All Ye Faithful

1 O come, all ye faith - ful, Joy - ful and tri - um - phant! O
2 High - est, most ho - ly, Light of Light e - ter - nal,
3 Sing, choirs of an - gels, Sing in ex - ul - ta - tion,
4 Yea, Lord, we greet Thee, Born this hap - py morn - ing;
come ye, O come ye to Beth - le - hem;
Born of a vir - gin, a mor - tal He comes;
Sing, all ye cit - i - zens of heav - en a - bove!
Je - sus, to Thee be glo - ry giv'n!
Come and be - hold Him Born the king of an - gels:
Son of the Fa - ther Now in flesh ap - pear - ing!
Glo - ry to God In the high - est:
Word of the Fa - ther Now in flesh ap - pear - ing!
Refrain
O come, let us a - dore Him, O come, let us a - dore Him,

Text: John F. Wade, c. 1711–86; tr. Frederick Oakeley, 1802–80, alt.;
Spanish tr. Juan Bautista Cabrera, 1837–1916
Tune: John F. Wade, c. 1711–86; setting: *The Hymnal* 1940

ADESTE FIDELES
Irregular meter

Luke 2:15

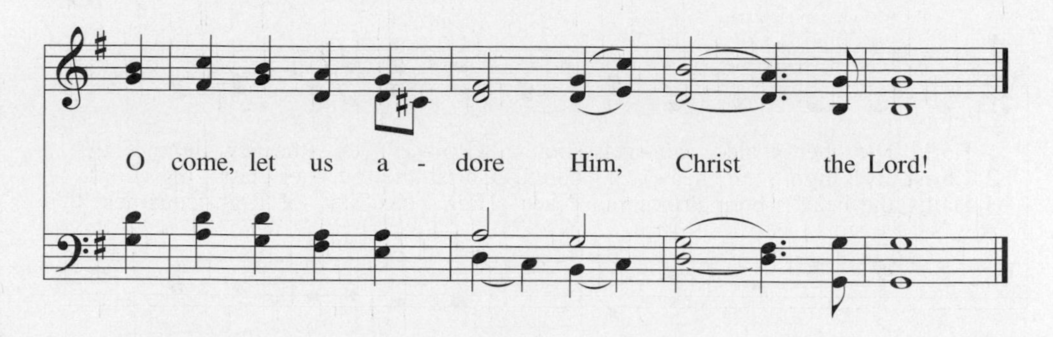
O come, let us a - dore Him, Christ the Lord!

1 *Venid, fieles todos, a Belén vayamos*
de gozo triunfantes henchidos de amor,
y al rey de los cielos humildes veremos:

Estribillo
Venid, adoremos, venid, adoremos,
venid, adoremos a Cristo el Señor.

2 *En pobre pesebre yace él reclinado,*
al hombre ofreciendo eternal salvación,
el santo Mesías, el Verbo humanado:
Estribillo

3 *Cantad jubilosas, celestes criaturas:*
resuenen los cielos con vuestra canción,
¡Al Dios bondadoso gloria en las alturas!
Estribillo

4 *Jesús, celebramos tu bendito nombre*
con himnos solemnes de grato loor;
por siglos eternos adórete el hombre:
Estribillo

380 Hark! The Herald Angels Sing

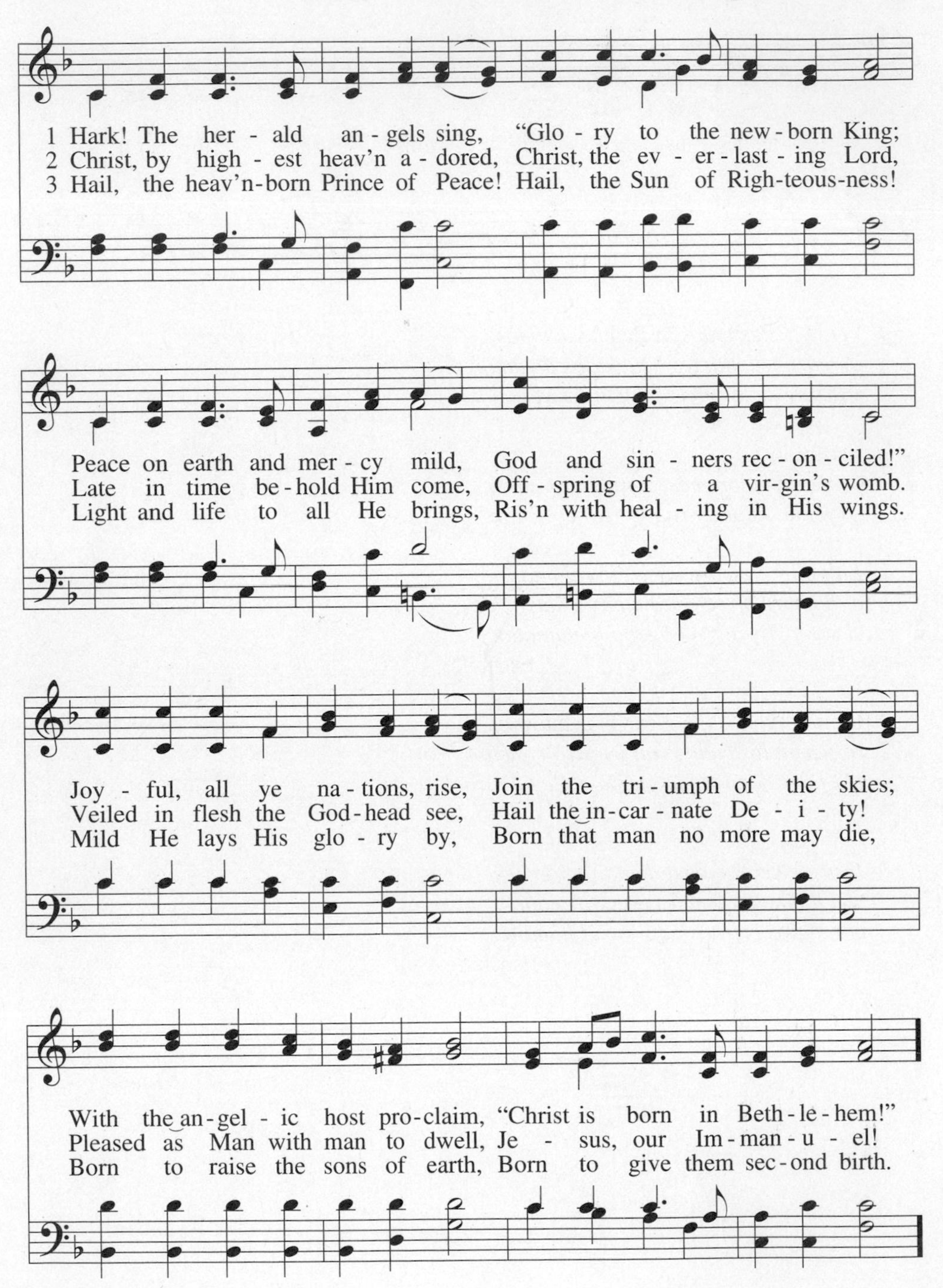
1 Hark! The her - ald an - gels sing, "Glo - ry to the new - born King;
2 Christ, by high - est heav'n a - dored, Christ, the ev - er - last - ing Lord,
3 Hail, the heav'n-born Prince of Peace! Hail, the Sun of Righ-teous-ness!
Peace on earth and mer - cy mild, God and sin - ners rec - on - ciled!"
Late in time be - hold Him come, Off - spring of a vir-gin's womb.
Light and life to all He brings, Ris'n with heal - ing in His wings.
Joy - ful, all ye na - tions, rise, Join the tri - umph of the skies;
Veiled in flesh the God - head see, Hail the in - car - nate De - i - ty!
Mild He lays His glo - ry by, Born that man no more may die,
With the an - gel - ic host pro - claim, "Christ is born in Beth - le - hem!"
Pleased as Man with man to dwell, Je - sus, our Im - man - u - el!
Born to raise the sons of earth, Born to give them sec - ond birth.

Text: Charles Wesley, 1707–88, alt.
Tune: Felix Mendelssohn, 1809–47; setting: William H. Cummings, 1831–1915

MENDELSSOHN
77 77 D and refrain

Luke 2:13–14; Rom. 5:10–11; John 1:1, 14; 11:26

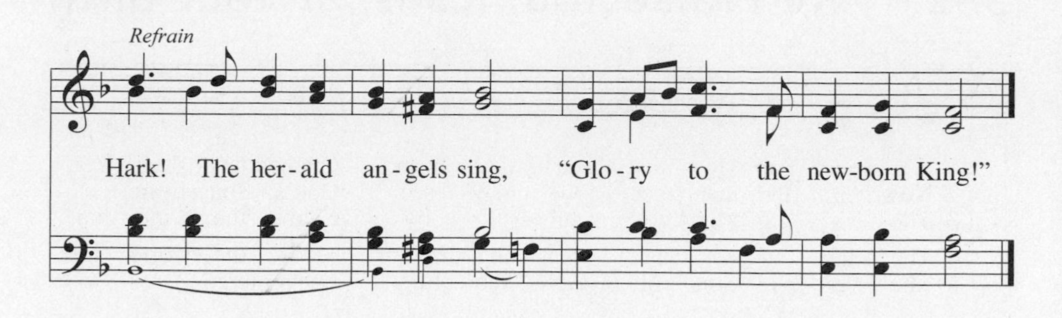
Refrain
Hark! The her-ald an-gels sing, "Glo-ry to the new-born King!"

Let Our Gladness Have No End 381

1 Let our glad-ness have no end, al-le-lu-ia! For to earth did Christ de-scend, al-le-lu-ia!
2 Proph-e-sied in days of old, al-le-lu-ia! God has sent Him as fore-told, al-le-lu-ia!
3 See, the love-liest bloom-ing rose, al-le-lu-ia! From the branch of Jes-se grows, al-le-lu-ia!
4 In-to flesh is made the Word, al-le-lu-ia! He, our ref-uge and our Lord, al-le-lu-ia!
Refrain
On this day God gave us Christ, His Son, to save us; Christ, His Son, to save us.

Text: Bohemian, 15th cent.; tr. unknown, sts. 1, 3–4, alt.; tr. Vincent Pisek, 1859–1930, st. 2
Tune: Bohemian, 15th cent.; setting: Richard W. Hillert, 1923–2010

NARODIL SE KRISTUS PÁN
74 74 and refrain

Rom. 5:11; 8:32–33; John 1:14; Gen. 3:15

382 We Praise You, Jesus, at Your Birth

1 We praise You, Je - sus, at Your birth; Clothed in flesh You came to earth. The vir - gin bears a sin - less boy And all the an - gels sing for joy. Al - le - lu - ia!
2 Now in the man - ger we may see God's Son from e - ter - ni - ty, The gift from God's e - ter - nal throne Here clothed in our poor flesh and bone. Al - le - lu - ia!
3 The vir - gin Mar - y's lul - la - by Calms the in - fant Lord Most High. Up - on her lap con - tent is He Who keeps the earth and sky and sea. Al - le - lu - ia!
4 The Light E - ter - nal, break - ing through, Made the world to gleam a - new; His beams have pierced the core of night, He makes us chil - dren of the light. Al - le - lu - ia!
5 The ver - y Son of God sub - lime En - tered in - to earth - ly time To lead us from this world of cares To heav - en's courts as bless - ed heirs. Al - le - lu - ia!

6 In poverty He came to earth
Showing mercy by His birth;
He makes us rich in heav'nly ways
As we, like angels, sing His praise.
Alleluia!

7 All this for us our God has done
Granting love through His own Son.
Therefore, all Christendom, rejoice
And sing His praise with endless voice.
Alleluia!

Text: German, c. 1380, st. 1; Martin Luther, 1483–1546, sts. 2–7; tr. Gregory J. Wismar, b. 1946, sts. 1, 6; tr. F. Samuel Janzow, 1913–2001, sts. 2, 4; tr. *Lutheran Service Book*, 2006, sts. 3, 5, 7
Tune: *Eyn Enchiridion oder Handbüchlein*, Erfurt, 1524; setting: Jan O. Bender, 1909–94

GELOBET SEIST DU
87 88 4

Luke 2:7–14; 1 Tim. 3:16; 1 John 1:1–3

A Great and Mighty Wonder 383

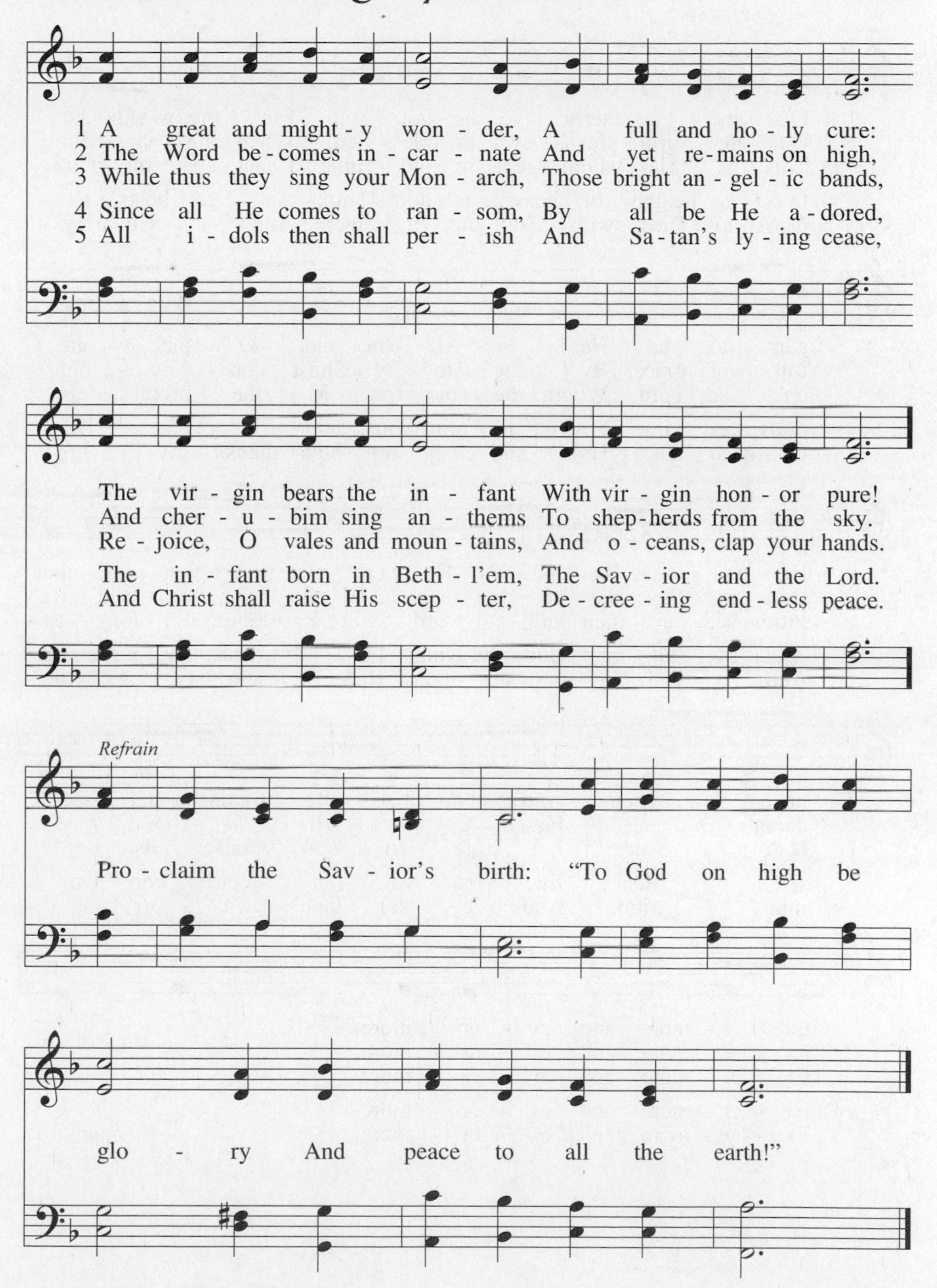
1 A great and might - y won - der, A full and ho - ly cure:
2 The Word be - comes in - car - nate And yet re - mains on high,
3 While thus they sing your Mon - arch, Those bright an - gel - ic bands,
4 Since all He comes to ran - som, By all be He a - dored,
5 All i - dols then shall per - ish And Sa - tan's ly - ing cease,
The vir - gin bears the in - fant With vir - gin hon - or pure!
And cher - u - bim sing an - thems To shep - herds from the sky.
Re - joice, O vales and moun - tains, And o - ceans, clap your hands.
The in - fant born in Beth - l'em, The Sav - ior and the Lord.
And Christ shall raise His scep - ter, De - cree - ing end - less peace.
Refrain
Pro - claim the Sav - ior's birth: "To God on high be
glo - ry And peace to all the earth!"

Text: Germanus, c. 634–c. 734; tr. John Mason Neale, 1818–66, alt.
Tune: *Alte Catholische Geistliche Kirchengeseng*, Köln, 1599;
setting: *The Lutheran Hymnal*, 1941

ES IST EIN ROS (Isorhythmic)
76 76 6 76

John 1:14; Luke 2:1–20; 1 Tim. 2:5–6; Heb. 2:14–15

384 Of the Father's Love Begotten

1 Of the Fa - ther's love be - got - ten Ere the worlds be -
2 Oh, that birth for - ev - er bless - ed, When the vir - gin,
3 This is He whom seers in old time Chant - ed of with
4 O ye heights of heav'n, a - dore Him; An - gel hosts, His
△ 5 Christ, to Thee, with God the Fa - ther, And, O Ho - ly
gan to be, He is Al - pha and O - me - ga,
full of grace, By the Ho - ly Ghost con - ceiv - ing,
one ac - cord, Whom the voic - es of the proph - ets
prais - es sing. Pow'rs, do - min - ions, bow be - fore Him
Ghost, to Thee Hymn and chant and high thanks - giv - ing
He the source, the end - ing He, Of the things that are, that
Bore the Sav - ior of our race, And the babe, the world's Re -
Prom - ised in their faith - ful word. Now He shines, the long - ex -
And ex - tol our God and King. Let no tongue on earth be
And un - end - ing prais - es be, Hon - or, glo - ry, and do -
have been, And that fu - ture years shall see
deem - er, First re - vealed His sa - cred face
pect - ed; Let cre - a - tion praise its Lord
si - lent, Ev - 'ry voice in con - cert ring
min - ion, And e - ter - nal vic - to - ry
Ev - er - more and ev - er - more.
Ev - er - more and ev - er - more.
Ev - er - more and ev - er - more.
Ev - er - more and ev - er - more.
Ev - er - more and ev - er - more. A - men.

Setting available in hymn accompaniment edition.

Text: Aurelius Prudentius Clemens, 348–c. 413; tr. John Mason Neale, 1818–66, sts. 1–4, alt.;
tr. Henry W. Baker, 1821–77, st. 5
Tune: Plainsong, 13th cent., mode V

DIVINUM MYSTERIUM
87 87 877

1 Tim. 3:16; Rev. 1:8; John 1:1; Phil. 2:11

From East to West

385

1 From east to west, from shore to shore Let ev - 'ry
2 Be - hold, the world's cre - a - tor wears The form and
3 For this how won - drous - ly He wrought! A maid - en,
4 And while the an - gels in the sky Sang praise a -
△ 5 All glo - ry for this bless - ed morn To God the
heart a - wake and sing The ho - ly child whom
fash - ion of a slave; Our ver - y flesh our
in her low - ly place, Be - came, in ways be -
bove the si - lent field, To shep - herds poor the
Fa - ther ev - er be; All praise to You, O
Mar - y bore, The Christ, the ev - er - last - ing king.
mak - er shares, His fall - en crea - tures all to save.
yond all thought, The cho - sen ves - sel of His grace.
Lord Most High, The one great Shep - herd, was re - vealed.
Vir - gin - born, And Ho - ly Ghost e - ter - nal - ly.

Text: Coelius Sedulius, 5th cent.; tr. John Ellerton, 1826–93, alt.
Tune: *Geistliche lieder*, Leipzig, 1539, ed. Valten Schumann;
setting: *The Lutheran Hymnal*, 1941

VOM HIMMEL HOCH
L M

Luke 1:26–31; 2:7–11; Ps. 95:1–6; Phil. 2:5–7

386 Now Sing We, Now Rejoice

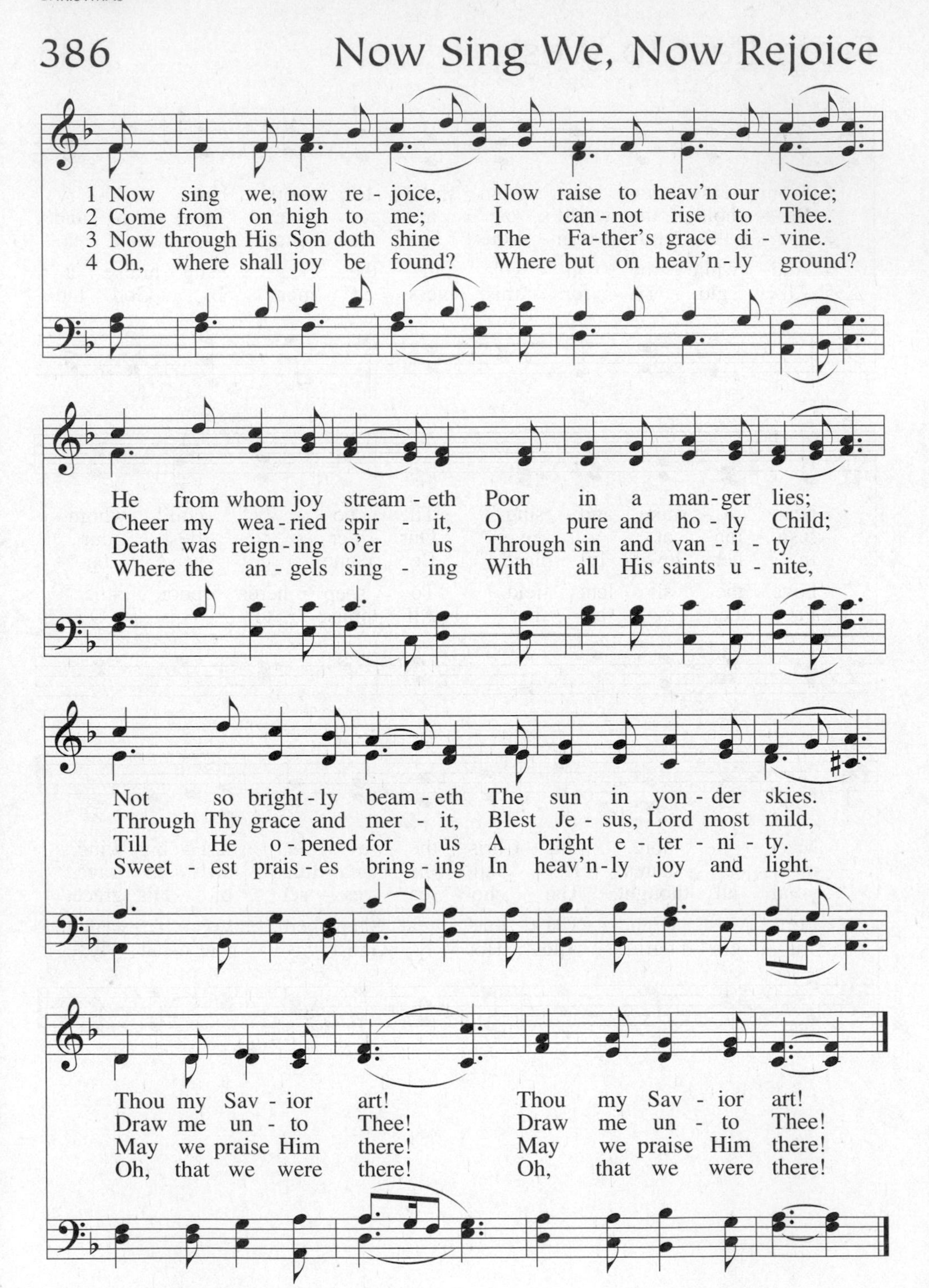
1 Now sing we, now re - joice, Now raise to heav'n our voice;
2 Come from on high to me; I can - not rise to Thee.
3 Now through His Son doth shine The Fa - ther's grace di - vine.
4 Oh, where shall joy be found? Where but on heav'n - ly ground?
He from whom joy stream - eth Poor in a man - ger lies;
Cheer my wea - ried spir - it, O pure and ho - ly Child;
Death was reign - ing o'er us Through sin and van - i - ty
Where the an - gels sing - ing With all His saints u - nite,
Not so bright - ly beam - eth The sun in yon - der skies.
Through Thy grace and mer - it, Blest Je - sus, Lord most mild,
Till He o - pened for us A bright e - ter - ni - ty.
Sweet - est prais - es bring - ing In heav'n - ly joy and light.
Thou my Sav - ior art! Thou my Sav - ior art!
Draw me un - to Thee! Draw me un - to Thee!
May we praise Him there! May we praise Him there!
Oh, that we were there! Oh, that we were there!

Text: Latin and German, 14th cent.; tr. Arthur T. Russell, 1806–74, alt.
Tune: German, 14th cent.; setting: Richard W. Hillert, 1923–2010, alt.

IN DULCI JUBILO
66 66 66 55

Luke 2:1–14; John 12:32; 1 Peter 1:8–9; Rev. 21:3–4

Joy to the World 387

1 Joy to the world, the Lord is come! Let earth re - ceive her King; Let ev - 'ry heart pre - pare Him room And heav'n and na - ture sing, And heav'n and na - ture sing, And heav'n, and heav'n and na - ture sing.
2 Joy to the earth, the Sav - ior reigns! Let men their songs em - ploy, While fields and floods, rocks, hills, and plains Re - peat the sound - ing joy, Re - peat the sound - ing joy, Re - peat, re - peat the sound - ing joy.
3 No more let sins and sor - rows grow Nor thorns in - fest the ground; He comes to make His bless - ings flow Far as the curse is found, Far as the curse is found, Far as, far as the curse is found.
4 He rules the world with truth and grace And makes the na - tions prove The glo - ries of His righ - teous - ness And won - ders of His love, And won - ders of His love, And won - ders, won - ders of His love.

Text: Isaac Watts, 1674–1748
Tune: George Frideric Handel, 1685–1759, adapt.; setting: Lowell Mason, 1792–1872

ANTIOCH
C M and refrain

Psalm 98; Rom. 5:16–19; Rev. 22:1–5

388 Go Tell It on the Mountain

Refrain

Go tell it on the moun - tain, O-ver the hills and ev - 'ry-where;

Go tell it on the moun - tain That Je-sus Christ is born!

1 While shep-herds kept their watch-ing O'er si - lent flocks by night,
2 The shep-herds feared and trem-bled When lo, a - bove the earth
3 Down in a lone - ly man - ger The hum-ble Christ was born;

Be - hold, through-out the heav-ens There shone a ho - ly light.
Rang out the an-gel cho-rus That hailed our Sav - ior's birth.
And God sent us sal - va - tion That bless - ed Christ-mas morn.

Refrain

Text: African American spiritual, refrain; John W. Work II, 1873–1925, stanzas, alt.
Tune: African American spiritual; setting: Hugh Porter, 1897–1960

GO TELL IT
78 76 76 76

Luke 2:7–20; Is. 40:9–11

Let All Together Praise Our God 389

1 Let all to - geth - er praise our God Be - fore His
2 He leaves His heav'n - ly Fa - ther's throne, Is born an
3 With - in an earth - born form He hides His all - cre -
4 He un - der - takes a great ex - change, Puts on our
5 He is a ser - vant, I a lord: How great a
glo - rious throne; To - day He o - pens heav'n a - gain To
in - fant small, And in a man - ger, poor and lone, Lies
at - ing light; To serve us all He hum - bly cloaks The
hu - man frame, And in re - turn gives us His realm, His
mys - ter - y! How strong the ten - der Christ Child's love! No
give us His own Son, To give us His own Son.
in a hum - ble stall, Lies in a hum - ble stall.
splen - dor of His might, The splen - dor of His might.
glo - ry, and His name, His glo - ry, and His name.
tru - er friend than He, No tru - er friend than He.

6 He is the key and He the door
To blessèd paradise;
The angel bars the way no more.
To God our praises rise,
To God our praises rise.

△ 7 Your grace in lowliness revealed,
Lord Jesus, we adore
And praise to God the Father yield
And Spirit evermore;
We praise You evermore.

Text: Nicolaus Herman, c. 1480–1561; tr. F. Samuel Janzow, 1913–2001, sts. 1, 3–7;
tr. August Crull, 1845–1923, st. 2, alt.
Tune: Nicolaus Herman, c. 1480–1561; setting: *The Lutheran Hymnal*, 1941

LOBT GOTT, IHR CHRISTEN
86 866

Luke 2:1–20; 2 Cor. 8:9; John 1:1–5, 10–14; Phil. 2:5–7

390 Let Us All with Gladsome Voice

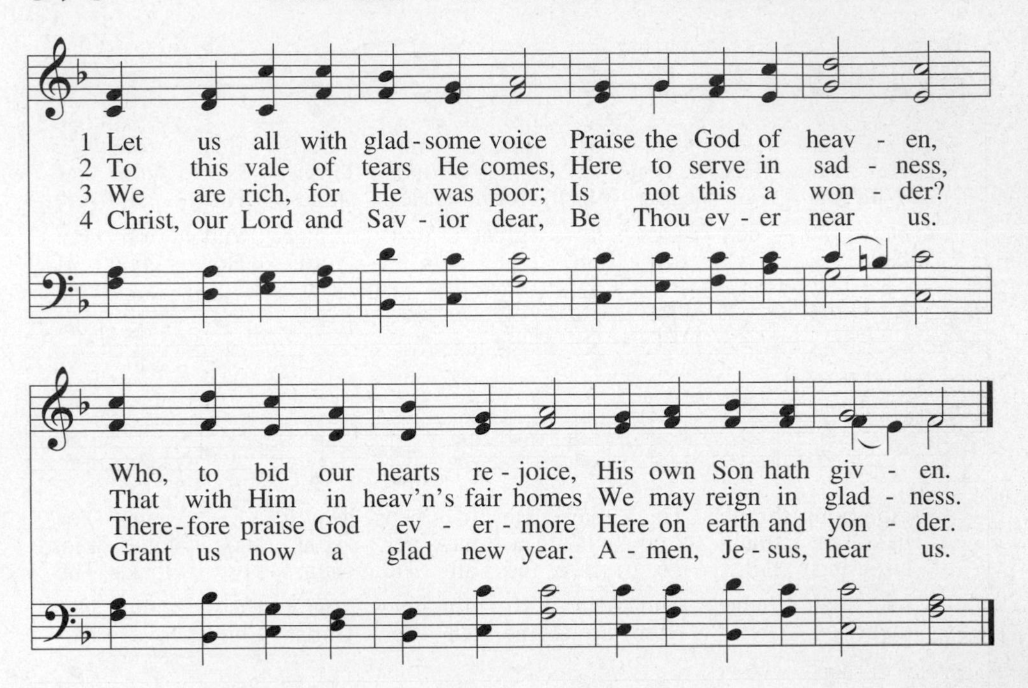
1 Let us all with glad-some voice Praise the God of heav - en,
2 To this vale of tears He comes, Here to serve in sad - ness,
3 We are rich, for He was poor; Is not this a won - der?
4 Christ, our Lord and Sav - ior dear, Be Thou ev - er near us.
Who, to bid our hearts re - joice, His own Son hath giv - en.
That with Him in heav'n's fair homes We may reign in glad - ness.
There-fore praise God ev - er - more Here on earth and yon - der.
Grant us now a glad new year. A - men, Je - sus, hear us.

Text: German, 17th cent.; tr. Catherine Winkworth, 1827–78, alt.
Tune: *Ander Theil Des Dreszdenischen GesangBuchs*, Dresden, 1632; setting: *The Lutheran Hymnal*, 1941

LASST UNS ALLE
76 76 (Trochaic)

Gal. 4:4–7; 1 Peter 1:8; Ps. 118:15; Rom. 5:10–12

391 Rejoice, Rejoice This Happy Morn

Rejoice, rejoice this happy morn,
A Savior unto us is born,
The Christ, the Lord of glory!
His lowly birth in Bethlehem
The angels from on high proclaim
And sing redemption's story!
My soul, extol
God's great favor;
Bless Him ever
For salvation;
Give Him praise and adoration!

Hymn accompaniment: 395

Text: Birgitte Katerine Boye, 1742–1824; tr. Carl Döving, 1867–1937

WIE SCHÖN LEUCHTET
887 887 4444 8

Luke 2:10–14, 20; Luke 1:46–47

God Loves Me Dearly 392

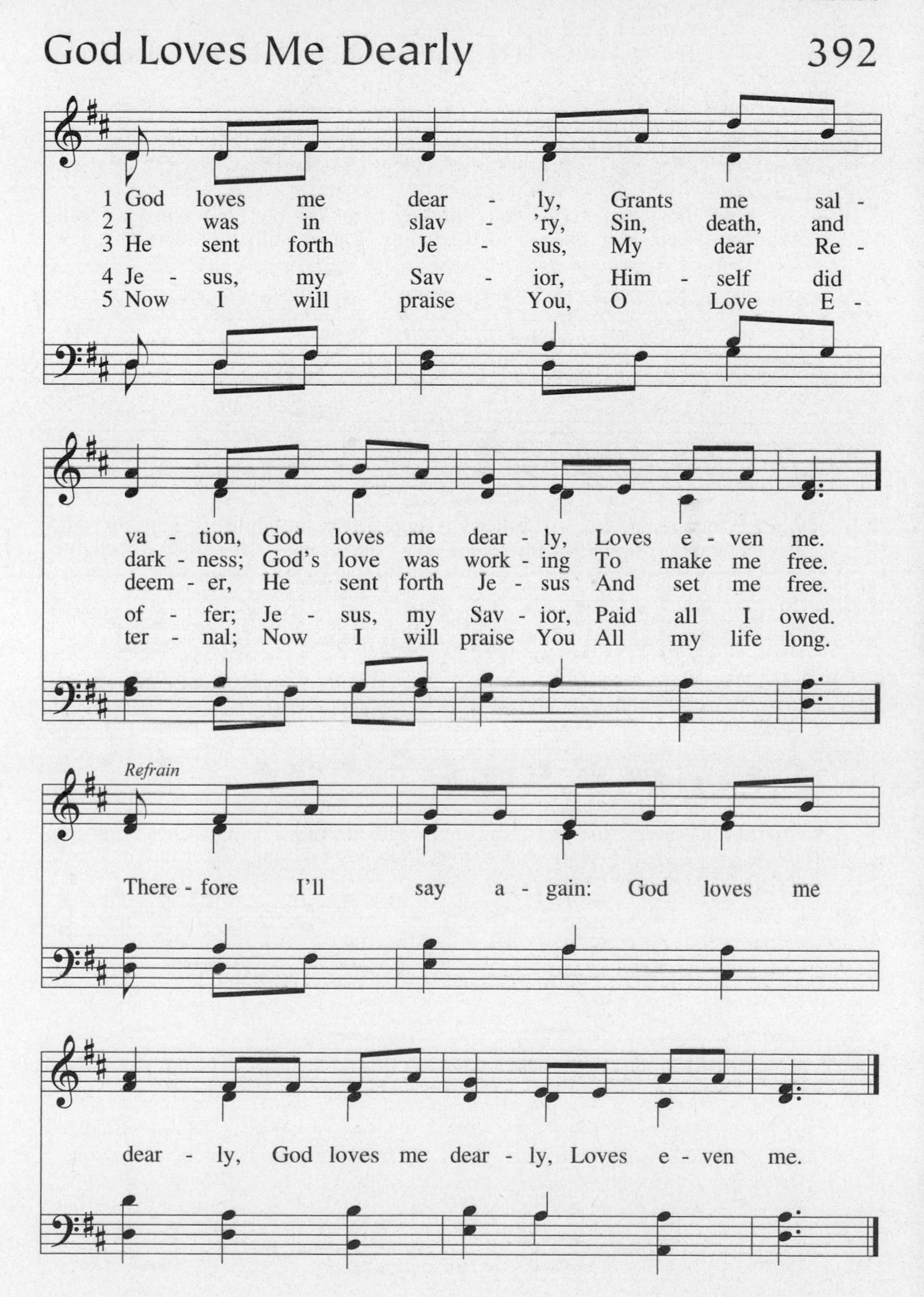
1 God loves me dear - ly, Grants me sal -
2 I was in slav - 'ry, Sin, death, and
3 He sent forth Je - sus, My dear Re -
4 Je - sus, my Sav - ior, Him - self did
5 Now I will praise You, O Love E -
va - tion, God loves me dear - ly, Loves e - ven me.
dark - ness; God's love was work - ing To make me free.
deem - er, He sent forth Je - sus And set me free.
of - fer; Je - sus, my Sav - ior, Paid all I owed.
ter - nal; Now I will praise You All my life long.
Refrain
There - fore I'll say a - gain: God loves me
dear - ly, God loves me dear - ly, Loves e - ven me.

Text: August Rische, 1819–1906; tr. composite
Tune: German; setting: *All God's People Sing!*, 1992

GOTT IST DIE LIEBE
55 54 and refrain

1 John 4:9–10; John 3:16; Rom. 5:8; Eph. 2:4–5

393 Infant Holy, Infant Lowly

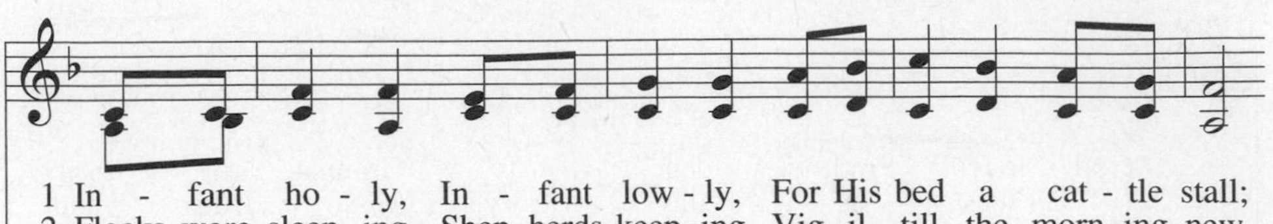

1 In - fant ho - ly, In - fant low - ly, For His bed a cat - tle stall;
2 Flocks were sleep - ing, Shep - herds keep - ing Vig - il till the morn - ing new

Ox - en low - ing, Lit - tle know - ing Christ the child is Lord of all.
Saw the glo - ry, Heard the sto - ry, Tid - ings of a Gos - pel true.

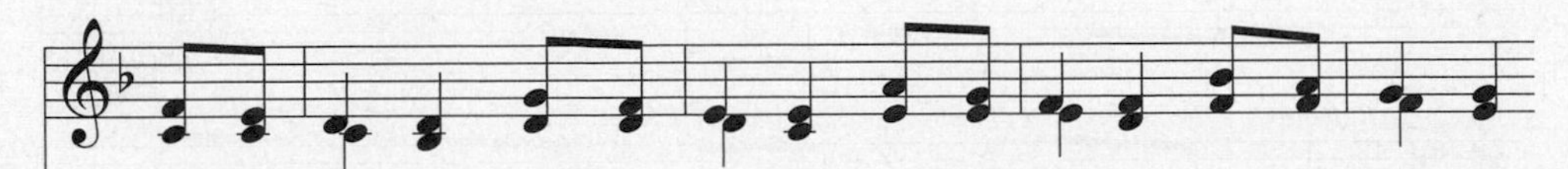

Swift - ly wing - ing, An - gels sing - ing, Bells are ring - ing, Tid - ings bring - ing:
Thus re - joic - ing, Free from sor - row, Prais - es voic - ing, Greet the mor - row:

Christ the child is Lord of all! Christ the child is Lord of all!
Christ the child was born for you! Christ the child was born for you!

Text: Polish; tr. Edith M. G. Reed, 1885–1933, alt.
Tune: Polish; setting: Joseph Herl, b. 1959

W ŻŁOBIE LEŻY
447 447 4444 77

Luke 2:1–20

Songs of Thankfulness and Praise 394

1 Songs of thank - ful - ness and praise, Je - sus, Lord, to Thee we raise,
2 Man - i - fest at Jor - dan's stream, Proph - et, Priest, and King su - preme;
3 Man - i - fest in mak - ing whole Pal - sied limbs and faint - ing soul;
4 Sun and moon shall dark - ened be, Stars shall fall, the heav'ns shall flee;
5 Grant us grace to see Thee, Lord, Pres - ent in Thy ho - ly Word—
Man - i - fest - ed by the star To the sa - ges from a - far,
And at Ca - na wed - ding guest In Thy God - head man - i - fest;
Man - i - fest in val - iant fight, Quell - ing all the dev - il's might;
Christ will then like light - ning shine, All will see His glo - rious sign;
Grace to im - i - tate Thee now And be pure, as pure art Thou;
Branch of roy - al Da - vid's stem In Thy birth at Beth - le - hem:
Man - i - fest in pow'r di - vine, Chang - ing wa - ter in - to wine;
Man - i - fest in gra - cious will, Ev - er bring - ing good from ill;
All will then the trum - pet hear, All will see the Judge ap - pear;
That we might be - come like Thee At Thy great e - piph - a - ny
An - thems be to Thee ad - dressed, God in man made man - i - fest.
An - thems be to Thee ad - dressed, God in man made man - i - fest.
An - thems be to Thee ad - dressed, God in man made man - i - fest.
Thou by all wilt be con - fessed, God in man made man - i - fest.
And may praise Thee, ev - er blest, God in man made man - i - fest.

Text: Christopher Wordsworth, 1807–85, alt.
Tune: George J. Elvey, 1816–93; setting: *The Lutheran Hymnal*, 1941

ST. GEORGE'S, WINDSOR
77 77 D

Is. 61:1–3; 1 Peter 1:20; Matt. 11:4–5; Rev. 19:1–16

395 O Morning Star, How Fair and Bright

1 O Morn-ing Star, how fair and bright! You shine with God's
2 Come, heav'n-ly Bride-groom, Light di - vine, And deep with - in
3 Lord, when You look on us in love, At once there falls
4 Al - might - y Fa - ther, in Your Son You loved us when
own truth and light, A - glow with grace and mer - cy!
our hearts now shine; There light a flame un - dy - ing!
from God a - bove A ray of pur - est plea - sure.
not yet be - gun Was this old earth's foun - da - tion!
Of Ja - cob's race, King Da - vid's son, Our Lord and mas -
In Your one bod - y let us be As liv - ing branch -
Your Word and Spir - it, flesh and blood Re - fresh our souls
Your Son has ran - somed us in love To live in Him
ter, You have won Our hearts to serve You on - ly!
es of a tree, Your life our lives sup - ply - ing.
with heav'n-ly food. You are our dear - est trea - sure!
here and a - bove: This is Your great sal - va - tion.

Text: Philipp Nicolai, 1556–1608; tr. *Lutheran Book of Worship*, 1978, alt.
Tune: Philipp Nicolai, 1556–1608; setting: *Choralbuch zum Evangelischen Kirchengesangbuch*, Berlin, 1955

WIE SCHÖN LEUCHTET
887 887 4444 8

Rev. 22:16; Luke 1:68–79; Eph. 1:3–7; Ps. 33:1–5

Low - ly, ho - ly! Great and glo-rious, All vic - to-rious,
Now, though dai - ly Earth's deep sad-ness May per-plex us
Let Your mer - cy Warm and cheer us! O draw near us!
Al - le - lu - ia! Christ the liv-ing, To us giv-ing
Rich in bless-ing! Rule and might o'er all pos-sess - ing!
And dis-tress us, Yet with heav'n-ly joy You bless us.
For You teach us God's own love through You has reached us.
Life for - ev - er, Keeps us Yours and fails us nev - er!

5 O let the harps break forth in sound!
Our joy be all with music crowned,
Our voices gladly blending!
For Christ goes with us all the way—
Today, tomorrow, ev'ry day!
His love is never ending!
Sing out! Ring out!
Jubilation!
Exultation!
Tell the story!
Great is He, the King of Glory!

6 What joy to know, when life is past,
The Lord we love is first and last,
The end and the beginning!
He will one day, oh, glorious grace,
Transport us to that happy place
Beyond all tears and sinning!
Amen! Amen!
Come, Lord Jesus!
Crown of gladness!
We are yearning
For the day of Your returning!

396 Arise and Shine in Splendor

1 A - rise and shine in splen - dor; Let night to day sur - ren - der. Your light is draw - ing near. A - bove, the day is beam - ing, In match - less beau - ty gleam - ing; The glo - ry of the Lord is here.
2 See earth in dark - ness ly - ing, The hea - then na - tions dy - ing In hope - less gloom and night. To you the Lord of heav - en— Your life, your hope— has giv - en Great glo - ry, hon - or, and de - light.
3 The world's re - mot - est rac - es, Up - on whose wea - ry fac - es The sun looks from the sky, Shall run with zeal un - tir - ing, With joy Your light de - sir - ing That breaks up - on them from on high.
4 Lift up your eyes in won - der— See, na - tions gath - er yon - der From sin to be set free. The world has heard Your sto - ry; Her sons come to Your glo - ry; Her daugh - ters haste Your light to see.

Text: Martin Opitz, 1597–1639; tr. Gerhard Gieschen, 1899–1987, alt.
Music: Heinrich Isaac, c. 1450–1517

O WELT, ICH MUSS DICH LASSEN
776 778

Is. 60:1–6; Col. 1:13; Is. 9:2; Acts 26:17–18

5 Your heart will leap for gladness
When from the realms of sadness
They come from near and far.
Your eyes will wake from slumber
As people without number
Rejoice to see the Morning Star.

As with Gladness Men of Old 397

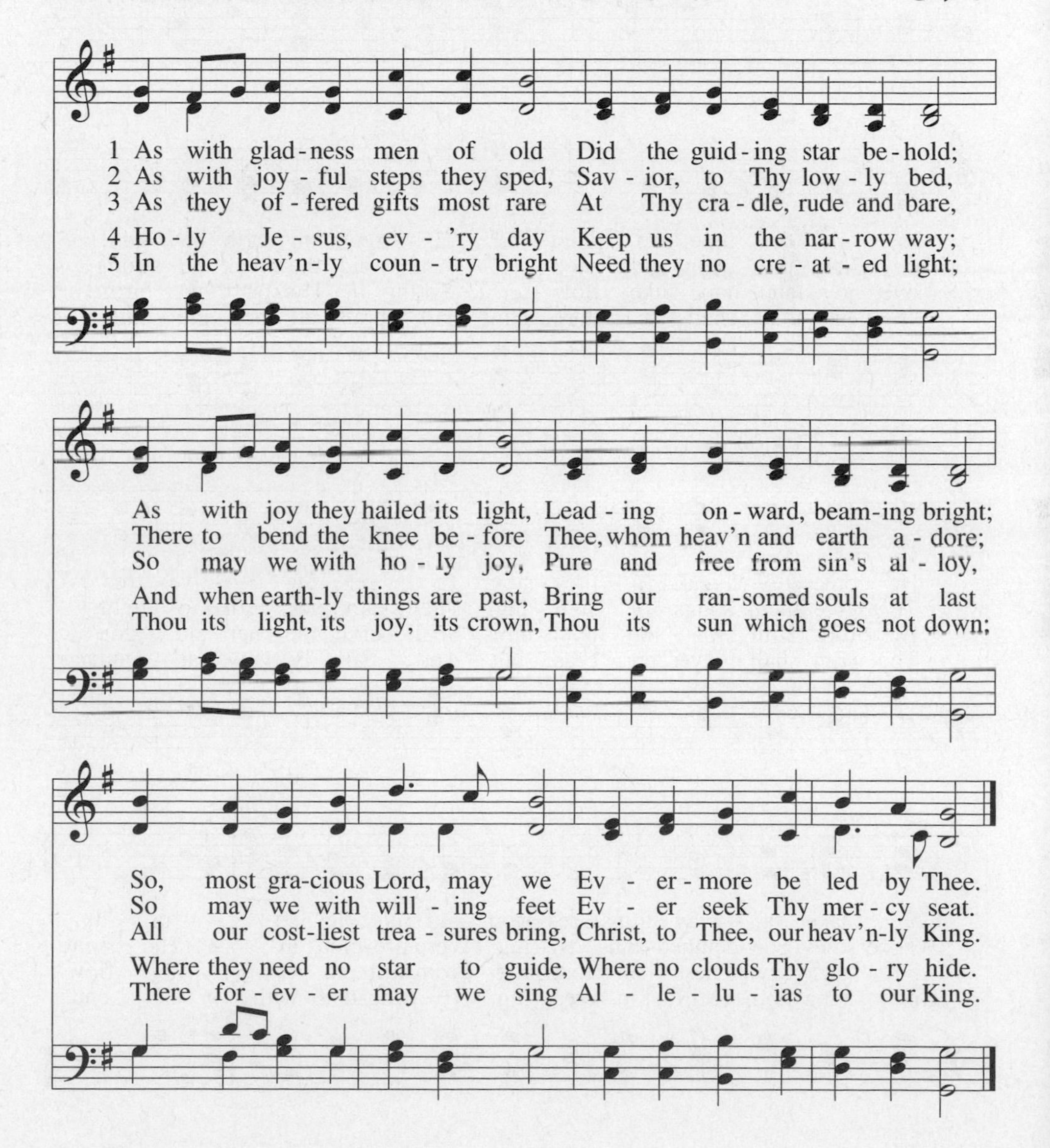
1 As with glad-ness men of old Did the guid-ing star be-hold;
2 As with joy-ful steps they sped, Sav-ior, to Thy low-ly bed,
3 As they of-fered gifts most rare At Thy cra-dle, rude and bare,
4 Ho-ly Je-sus, ev-'ry day Keep us in the nar-row way;
5 In the heav'n-ly coun-try bright Need they no cre-at-ed light;
As with joy they hailed its light, Lead-ing on-ward, beam-ing bright;
There to bend the knee be-fore Thee, whom heav'n and earth a-dore;
So may we with ho-ly joy, Pure and free from sin's al-loy,
And when earth-ly things are past, Bring our ran-somed souls at last
Thou its light, its joy, its crown, Thou its sun which goes not down;
So, most gra-cious Lord, may we Ev-er-more be led by Thee.
So may we with will-ing feet Ev-er seek Thy mer-cy seat.
All our cost-liest trea-sures bring, Christ, to Thee, our heav'n-ly King.
Where they need no star to guide, Where no clouds Thy glo-ry hide.
There for-ev-er may we sing Al-le-lu-ias to our King.

Text: William C. Dix, 1837–98, alt.
Tune: Conrad Kocher, 1786–1872; setting: *Service Book and Hymnal*, 1958

DIX
77 77 77

Matt. 2:1–11; Is. 60:19; Rev. 21:23

398 Hail to the Lord's Anointed

1 Hail to the Lord's a - noint - ed, Great Da - vid's great - er Son!
2 He comes with res - cue speed - y To those who suf - fer wrong,
3 He shall come down like show - ers Up - on the fruit - ful earth;
4 Kings shall fall down be - fore Him And gold and in - cense bring;
Hail, in the time ap - point - ed, His reign on earth be - gun!
To help the poor and need - y And bid the weak be strong;
Love, joy, and hope, like flow - ers, Spring in His path to birth.
All na - tions shall a - dore Him, His praise all peo - ple sing.
He comes to break op - pres - sion, To set the cap - tive free,
To give them songs for sigh - ing, Their dark - ness turn to light,
Be - fore Him on the moun - tains Shall peace, the her - ald, go;
To Him shall prayer un - ceas - ing And dai - ly vows as - cend;
To take a - way trans - gres - sion And rule in eq - ui - ty.
Whose souls, con - demned and dy - ing, Were pre - cious in His sight.
And righ - teous - ness in foun - tains From hill to val - ley flow.
His king - dom still in - creas - ing, A king - dom with - out end.

Text: James Montgomery, 1771–1854, alt.
Tune: Leonhart Schröter, c. 1532–c. 1601; setting: *The Lutheran Hymnal*, 1941

FREUT EUCH, IHR LIEBEN
76 76 D

Ps. 72:1–17; 2 Sam. 7:12; Acts 10:38; Psalm 2

5 O'er ev'ry foe victorious,
He on His throne shall rest,
From age to age more glorious,
All blessing and all-blest.

The tide of time shall never
His covenant remove;
His name shall stand forever—
That name to us is Love.

The Star Proclaims the King Is Here 399

1 The star pro - claims the King is here; But, Her - od, why this sense - less fear? For He who of - fers heav'n - ly birth Seeks not the king - doms of this earth.
2 The east - ern sa - ges saw from far And fol - lowed on His guid - ing star; And, led by light, to light they trod And by their gifts con - fessed their God.
3 With - in the Jor - dan's sa - cred flood The heav'n - ly Lamb in meek - ness stood That He, of whom no sin was known, Might cleanse His peo - ple from their own.
4 And oh, what mir - a - cle di - vine, When wa - ter red - dened in - to wine! He spoke the word, and forth it flowed In streams that na - ture ne'er be - stowed.
△ 5 For this Thy glad e - piph - a - ny All glo - ry, Je - sus, be to Thee, Whom with the Fa - ther we a- dore, And Ho - ly Spir - it ev - er - more.

Text: Coelius Sedulius, 5th cent.; tr. John Mason Neale, 1818–66, alt.
Tune: *Geistliche Lieder auffs new gebessert*, Wittenberg, 1535, ed. Joseph Klug; setting: *The Lutheran Hymnal*, 1941

WO GOTT ZUM HAUS
L M

Matt. 2:1–12; Eph. 1:9; John 18:36–37; John 1:29

Brightest and Best of the Stars of the Morning

1 Bright - est and best of the stars of the morn - ing,
2 Cold on His cra - dle the dew - drops are shin - ing;
3 Shall we not yield Him, in cost - ly de - vo - tion,
4 Vain - ly we of - fer each am - ple ob - la - tion,
Dawn on our dark - ness and lend us thine aid;
Low lies His head with the beasts of the stall;
Fra - grance of E - dom and of - f'rings di - vine,
Vain - ly with gifts would His fa - vor se - cure.
Star of the East, the ho - ri - zon a - dorn - ing,
An - gels a - dore Him in slum - ber re - clin - ing,
Gems of the moun - tain and pearls of the o - cean,
Rich - er by far is the heart's ad - o - ra - tion;
Guide where our in - fant Re - deem - er is laid.
Mak - er and Mon - arch and Sav - ior of all.
Myrrh from the for - est and gold from the mine?
Dear - er to God are the prayers of the poor.

Text: Reginald Heber, 1783–1826, alt.
Tune: James P. Harding, 1850–1911, adapt.; setting: *Service Book and Hymnal*, 1958

MORNING STAR
11 10 11 10

Matt. 2:1–11; Ps. 51:17

5 Brightest and best of the stars of the morning,
Dawn on our darkness and lend us thine aid;
Star of the East, the horizon adorning,
Guide where our infant Redeemer is laid.

From God the Father, Virgin-Born 401

1 From God the Fa - ther, vir - gin - born To us the
2 Be - gin - ning from His home on high, In hu - man
3 Glide on, O glo - rious Sun, and bring The gift of
4 A - bide with us, O Lord, we pray; The gloom of
on - ly Son came down; By death the font to con - se -
flesh He came to die; Cre - a - tion by His death re -
heal - ing on Your wing; To ev - 'ry dull and cloud - ed
dark - ness chase a - way; Your work of heal - ing, Lord, be -
crate, The faith - ful to re - gen - er - ate.
stored, And shed new joys of life a - broad.
sense The clear - ness of Your light dis - pense.
gin, And take a - way the stain of sin.

5 Lord, once You came to earth's domain
And, we believe, shall come again;
Be with us on the battlefield,
From ev'ry harm Your people shield.

△ 6 To You, O Lord, all glory be
For this Your blest epiphany;
To God, whom all His hosts adore,
And Holy Spirit evermore.

Text: Latin, c. 5th–10th cent.; tr. John Mason Neale, 1818–66, alt.
Tune: *Antiphoner*, Grenoble, 1753; setting: Janet Muth, b. 1962

DEUS TUORUM MILITUM
L M

John 1:14; Phil. 2:6–8; Luke 4:18; Acts 26:17–18

402 The Only Son from Heaven

1 The only Son from heaven, Foretold by ancient seers,
2 O time of God appointed, O bright and holy morn!
3 O Lord, our hearts awaken To know and love You more,
△ 4 O Father, here before You With God the Holy Ghost
By God the Father given, In human form appears.
He comes, the king anointed, The Christ, the virgin-born,
In faith to stand unshaken, In spirit to adore,
And Jesus, we adore You, O pride of angel host:
No sphere His light confining, No star so brightly
Grim death to vanquish for us, To open heav'n be-
That we, through this world moving, Each glimpse of heaven
Before You mortals lowly Cry, "Holy, holy,
shining As He, our Morning Star.
fore us And bring us life again.
proving, May reap its fullness there.
holy, O blessed Trinity!"

Text: Elisabeth Cruciger, c. 1500–35, sts. 1–3; *Lutheran Book of Worship*, 1978, st. 4; tr. Arthur T. Russell, 1806–74, sts. 1–3, alt.
Tune: *Eyn Enchiridion oder Handbüchlein*, Erfurt, 1524; setting: Joseph Herl, b. 1959

HERR CHRIST, DER EINIG GOTTS SOHN
76 76 776

Gal. 4:4–5; 2 Tim. 1:10; 1 John 4:9; Luke 1:30–35

O Savior of Our Fallen Race 403

1 O Sav - ior of our fall - en race, O Bright - ness
2 O Je - sus, ver - y Light of Light, Our con - stant
3 Re - mem - ber, Lord of life and grace, How once, to
4 To - day, as year by year its light Bathes all the
5 For from the Fa - ther's throne You came, His ban - ished
of the Fa - ther's face, O Son who shared
star in sin's deep night: Now hear the prayers
save our fall - en race, You put our hu -
world in ra - diance bright, One pre - cious truth
chil - dren to re - claim; And earth and sea
the Fa - ther's might Be - fore the world knew
Your peo - ple pray Through - out the world this
man ves - ture on And came to us as
out - shines the sun: Sal - va - tion comes from
and sky re - vere The love of Him who
day or night,
ho - ly day.
Mar - y's son. Al - le - lu - ia!
You a - lone.
sent You here.

6 And we are jubilant today,
For You have washed our guilt away.
O hear the glad new song we sing
On this, the birthday of our King!
Alleluia!

△ 7 O Christ, Redeemer virgin-born,
Let songs of praise Your name adorn,
Whom with the Father we adore
And Holy Spirit evermore.
Alleluia!

Hymn accompaniment: 874

Text: Latin, c. 5th–10th cent.; tr. Gilbert E. Doan, b. 1930
Tune: Stephen R. Johnson, b. 1966

PUTNAM
L M and alleluia

John 1:1–5, 14; 2 Cor. 4:6; John 14:6

404 Jesus, Once with Sinners Numbered

1 Je - sus, once with sin - ners num - bered, Had no blem - ish
2 John con - fessed Him as the Sav - ior— "Look, the sin - less
3 This the bap - tism that our Sav - ior Great - ly longed to
4 Je - sus, once with sin - ners num - bered, Full o - be - dience
of His own; In the wa - ters of the Jor - dan
Lamb of God!" Yet he dared not loose the san - dals
un - der - go; This the crim - son cleans - ing need - ed
was Your path; You, by death, have con - se - crat - ed
His true worth and work were shown: Heav - en o - pened
Of the One God's love had shod. Oh, how fair the
So the world God's love might know; This the mis - sion
Wa - ter in this sav - ing bath: Dy - ing to the
and the Spir - it There de - scend - ed like a
feet of Je - sus, Bring - ing news of peace to
of Mes - si - ah As He stepped from Jor - dan's
sin of Ad - am, Ris - ing to a life of
dove, As the Fa - ther's voice re - sound - ed,
us, Christ, the her - ald of sal - va - tion,
stream, He, the cho - sen and a - noint - ed
grace; We are count - ed with the righ - teous,
"Hear My Son, the One I love."
Preach - ing mer - cy from the cross:
Son of God, sent to re - deem.
O - ver us the cross You trace.

Setting available in hymn accompaniment edition.

Text: Stephen P. Starke, b. 1955
Tune: William B. Roberts, b. 1947

MISSISSIPPI
87 87 D

Is. 53:12; Matt. 3:13–17; John 1:29, 36; Gal. 4:4–5

To Jordan's River Came Our Lord 405

1 To Jor - dan's riv - er came our Lord, The Christ, whom
2 The Sav - ior came to be bap - tized— The Son of
3 As Je - sus in the Jor - dan stood And John bap -
4 Then from God's throne with thun - d'rous sound Came God's own
heav'n - ly hosts a - dored, The God from God, the
God in flesh dis - guised— To stand be - neath the
tized the Lamb of God, The Ho - ly Spir - it,
voice with words pro - found: "This is My Son," was
Light from Light, The Lord of glo - ry, pow'r, and might.
Fa - ther's will And all His righ - teous - ness ful - fill.
heav'n - ly dove, De - scend - ed on Him from a - bove.
His de - cree, "The one I love, who pleas - es Me."

5 The Father's word, the Spirit's flight
Anointed Christ in glorious sight
As God's own choice, from Adam's fall
To save the world and free us all.

6 Now rise, faint hearts, be resolute;
This man is Christ, our substitute!
He was baptized in Jordan's stream,
Proclaimed Redeemer, Lord supreme.

Text: James P. Tiefel, b. 1949, alt.
Tune: *Musicalisch Hand-Buch der Geistlichen Melodien*, Hamburg, 1690, alt.;
setting: William H. Monk, 1823–89, alt.

WINCHESTER NEW
L M

Matt. 3:13–17; Heb. 2:17; Luke 4:18; 2 Cor. 5:21

406 To Jordan Came the Christ, Our Lord

1 To Jor - dan came the Christ, our Lord, To do His
2 O hear and mark the mes - sage well, For God Him -
3 These truths on Jor - dan's banks were shown By might - y
4 There stood the Son of God in love, His grace to
Fa - ther's plea - sure; Bap - tized by John, the Fa - ther's Word
self has spo - ken. Let faith, not doubt, a - mong us dwell
word and won - der. The Fa - ther's voice from heav'n came down,
us ex - tend - ing; The Ho - ly Spir - it like a dove
Was giv - en us to trea - sure. This heav'n - ly wash - ing
And so re - ceive this to - ken. Our Lord here with His
Which we do well to pon - der: "This man is My be -
Up - on the scene de - scend - ing; The tri - une God as -
now shall be A cleans - ing from trans - gres - sion
Word en - dows Pure wa - ter, free - ly flow - ing.
lov - ed Son, In whom My heart has plea - sure.
sur - ing us, With prom - is - es com - pel - ling,
And by His blood and ag - o - ny Re - lease from death's
God's Ho - ly Spir - it here a - vows Our kin - ship while
Him you must hear, and Him a - lone, And trust in full -
That in our Bap - tism He will thus A - mong us find
op - pres - sion. A new life now a - waits us.
be - stow - ing The Bap - tism of His bless - ing.
est mea - sure The word that He has spo - ken."
a dwell - ing To com - fort and sus - tain us.

In his catechism hymn on Baptism, Luther uses the biblical narrative concerning Christ's Baptism to teach the meaning of Baptism for our lives. Setting available in hymn accompaniment edition.

Text: Martin Luther, 1483–1546; tr. Elizabeth Quitmeyer, 1911–88, alt.
Tune: *Geystliche gesangk Buchleyn*, Wittenberg, 1524, ed. Johann Walter

CHRIST, UNSER HERR
87 87 87 87 7

Luke 3:21–22; Acts 2:38; Gal. 3:26–27; Matt. 28:19–20

5 To His disciples spoke the Lord,
"Go out to ev'ry nation,
And bring to them the living Word
And this My invitation:
Let ev'ryone abandon sin
And come in true contrition
To be baptized and thereby win
Full pardon and remission
And heav'nly bliss inherit."

6 But woe to those who cast aside
This grace so freely given;
They shall in sin and shame abide
And to despair be driven.
For born in sin, their works must fail,
Their striving saves them never;
Their pious acts do not avail,
And they are lost forever,
Eternal death their portion.

7 All that the mortal eye beholds
Is water as we pour it.
Before the eye of faith unfolds
The pow'r of Jesus' merit.
For here it sees the crimson flood
To all our ills bring healing;
The wonders of His precious blood
The love of God revealing,
Assuring His own pardon.

Go therefore and make disciples of all nations, baptizing them in the name of the Father and of the Son and of the Holy Spirit, teaching them to observe all that I have commanded you. Matthew 28:19–20a

---

407 To Jordan Came the Christ, Our Lord

1 To Jor - dan came the Christ, our Lord, To do His Fa-ther's
2 O hear and mark the mes - sage well, For God Him-self has
3 These truths on Jor - dan's banks were shown By might - y word and
4 There stood the Son of God in love, His grace to us ex -
plea - sure; Bap - tized by John, the Fa - ther's Word
spo - ken. Let faith, not doubt, a - mong us dwell
won - der. The Fa - ther's voice from heav'n came down,
tend - ing; The Ho - ly Spir - it like a dove
Was giv - en us to trea - sure. This heav'n - ly wash - ing
And so re - ceive this to - ken. Our Lord here with His
Which we do well to pon - der: "This man is My be -
Up - on the scene de - scend - ing; The tri - une God as -
now shall be A cleans - ing from trans - gres - sion
Word en - dows Pure wa - ter, free - ly flow - ing.
lov - ed Son, In whom My heart has plea - sure.
sur - ing us, With prom - is - es com - pel - ling,
And by His blood and ag - o - ny Re - lease from death's op -
God's Ho - ly Spir - it here a - vows Our kin - ship while be -
Him you must hear, and Him a - lone, And trust in full - est
That in our Bap - tism He will thus A - mong us find a
pres - sion. A new life now a - waits us.
stow - ing The Bap - tism of His bless - ing.
mea - sure The word that He has spo - ken."
dwell - ing To com - fort and sus - tain us.

In his catechism hymn on Baptism, Luther uses the biblical narrative concerning Christ's Baptism to teach the meaning of Baptism for our lives. Setting available in hymn accompaniment edition.

Text: Martin Luther, 1483–1546; tr. Elizabeth Quitmeyer, 1911–88, alt.
Tune: David Lee, b. 1956

ELVET BANKS
87 87 87 87 7

Luke 3:21–22; Acts 2:38; Gal. 3:26–27; Matt. 28:19–20

5 To His disciples spoke the Lord,
"Go out to ev'ry nation,
And bring to them the living Word
And this My invitation:
Let ev'ryone abandon sin
And come in true contrition
To be baptized and thereby win
Full pardon and remission
And heav'nly bliss inherit."

6 But woe to those who cast aside
This grace so freely given;
They shall in sin and shame abide
And to despair be driven.
For born in sin, their works must fail,
Their striving saves them never;
Their pious acts do not avail,
And they are lost forever,
Eternal death their portion.

7 All that the mortal eye beholds
Is water as we pour it.
Before the eye of faith unfolds
The pow'r of Jesus' merit.
For here it sees the crimson flood
To all our ills bring healing;
The wonders of His precious blood
The love of God revealing,
Assuring His own pardon.

Come, Join in Cana's Feast 408

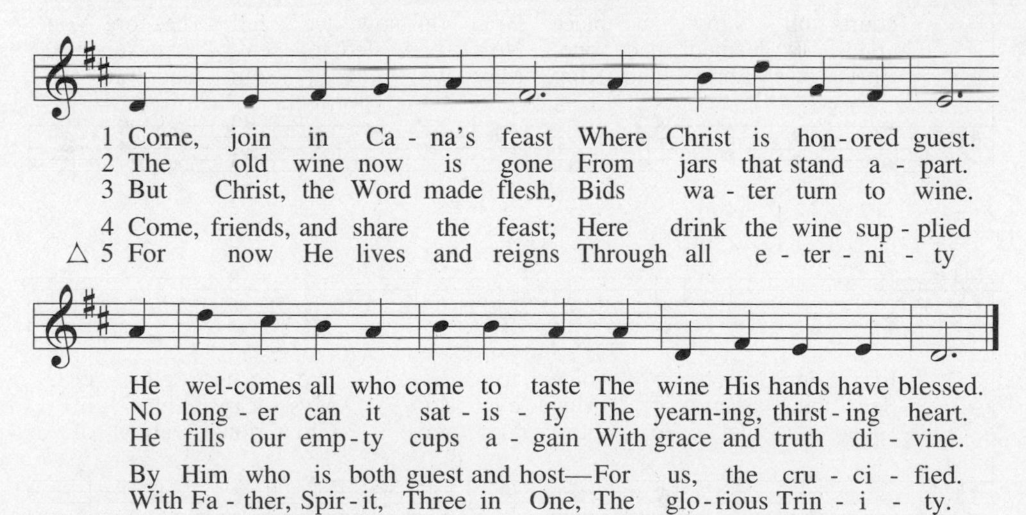
1 Come, join in Ca - na's feast Where Christ is hon-ored guest.
2 The old wine now is gone From jars that stand a - part.
3 But Christ, the Word made flesh, Bids wa - ter turn to wine.
4 Come, friends, and share the feast; Here drink the wine sup - plied
△ 5 For now He lives and reigns Through all e - ter - ni - ty
He wel-comes all who come to taste The wine His hands have blessed.
No long - er can it sat - is - fy The yearn-ing, thirst - ing heart.
He fills our emp - ty cups a - gain With grace and truth di - vine.
By Him who is both guest and host—For us, the cru - ci - fied.
With Fa - ther, Spir - it, Three in One, The glo - rious Trin - i - ty.

Hymn accompaniment: 410

Text: Herman G. Stuempfle, Jr., 1923–2007
Tune: Johann Balthasar König, 1691–1758; adapt. William H. Havergal, 1793–1870

FRANCONIA
S M

John 2:1–11; Rev. 19:7–9; 1 Cor. 11:23–26

409 Hail, O Source of Every Blessing

1 Hail, O Source of ev - 'ry bless - ing, Fa - ther of our
2 Once far off but now in - vit - ed, We ap - proach Your
3 Hail, O all - in - vit - ing Sav - ior! Gen - tiles now their
hu - man race! Gen - tiles now, Your grace pos - sess - ing, In Your
sa - cred throne, In Your cov - e - nant u - nit - ed, Rec - on -
of - f'rings bring, In Your tem - ples seek Your fa - vor, Je - sus
courts ob - tain a place. Grate - ful now, we fall be - fore You,
ciled, re - deemed, made one. Now re - vealed to east - ern sa - ges,
Christ, our Lord and King. May we, bod - y, soul, and spir - it,
In Your Church re - joice to live, See Your glo - ry
See the Star of Mer - cy shine, Mys - t'ry hid in
Live de - vot - ed to Your praise, Glo - rious realms of

Text: Basil Woodd, 1760–1831, alt.
Tune: *Geist-reiches Gesang-Buch*, Halle, 1704, ed. Johann A. Freylinghausen;
setting: *The Lutheran Hymnal*, 1941

O DURCHBRECHER
87 87 D

Is. 60:3–6; Rev. 21:22–27; Matt. 2:11

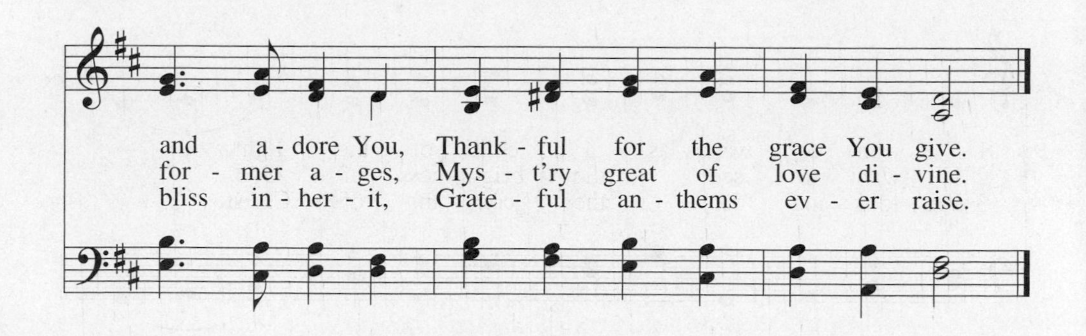
and a - dore You, Thank - ful for the grace You give.
for - mer a - ges, Mys - t'ry great of love di - vine.
bliss in - her - it, Grate - ful an - thems ev - er raise.

Within the Father's House 410

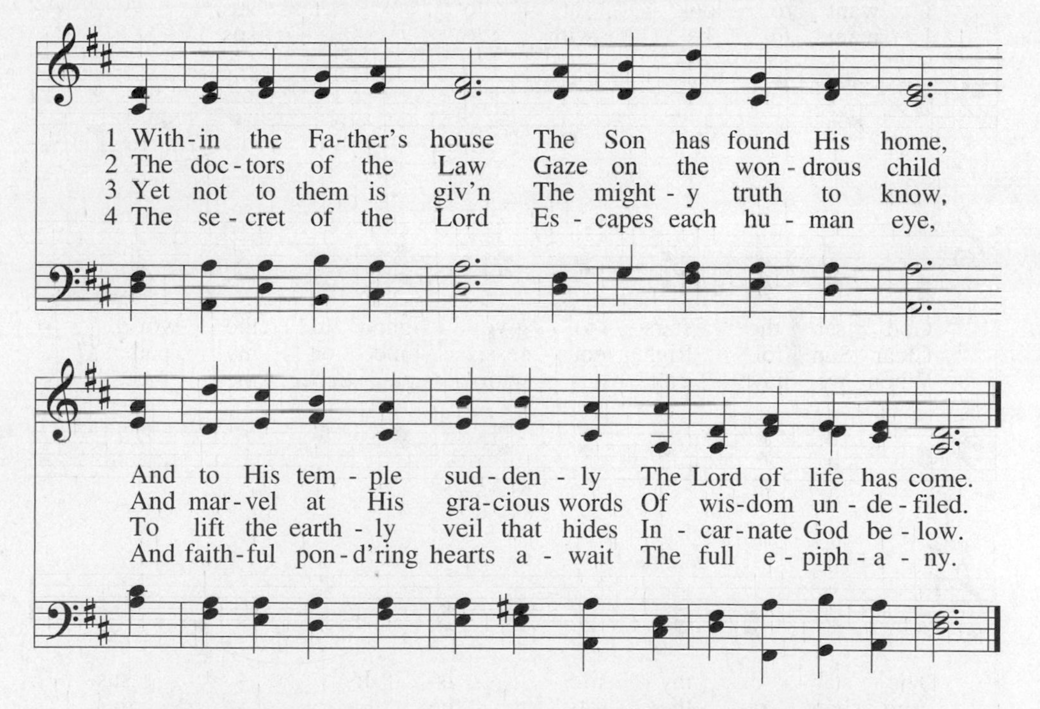
1 With-in the Fa-ther's house The Son has found His home,
2 The doc-tors of the Law Gaze on the won-drous child
3 Yet not to them is giv'n The might - y truth to know,
4 The se-cret of the Lord Es - capes each hu - man eye,
And to His tem - ple sud - den - ly The Lord of life has come.
And mar-vel at His gra-cious words Of wis-dom un - de - filed.
To lift the earth - ly veil that hides In - car-nate God be - low.
And faith-ful pon-d'ring hearts a - wait The full e - piph - a - ny.

5 Lord, visit Thou our souls
And teach us by Thy grace
Each dim revealing of Thyself
With loving awe to trace

△ 6 Till we behold Thy face
And know as we are known
Thee, Father, Son, and Holy Ghost,
Coequal Three in One.

Text: James R. Woodford, 1820–85, alt.
Tune: Johann Balthasar König, 1691–1758; adapt. William H. Havergal, 1793–1870; setting: *The Lutheran Hymnal*, 1941

FRANCONIA
S M

Luke 2:41–52; 1 Tim. 3:16; 1 Cor. 2:7–10; Eph. 1:9

411 I Want to Walk as a Child of the Light

1 I want to walk as a child of the light.
2 I want to see the bright-ness of God.
3 I'm look - ing for the com - ing of Christ.
I want to fol - low Je - sus.
I want to look at Je - sus.
I want to be with Je - sus.
God set the stars to give light to the world.
Clear Sun of Righ - teous - ness, shine on my path,
When we have run with pa - tience the race,
The star of my life is Je - sus.
And show me the way to the Fa - ther.
We shall know the joy of Je - sus.

Text: Kathleen Thomerson, b. 1934
Music: Kathleen Thomerson, b. 1934

HOUSTON
10 7 10 8 and refrain

2 Cor. 4:4–6; Heb. 12:1–2; 1 John 1:5; Rev. 21:23

Refrain
In Him there is no dark - ness at all.
The night and the day are both a - like.
The Lamb is the light of the cit - y of God.
Shine in my heart, Lord Je - sus.

412 The People That in Darkness Sat

1 The peo - ple that in dark - ness sat A glo - rious
2 To hail Thee, Sun of Righ - teous - ness, The gath - 'ring
3 To us a Child of hope is born, To us a
4 His name shall be the Prince of Peace, The Ev - er -
light have seen; The light has shined on them who long In
na - tions come; They joy as when the reap - ers bear Their
Son is giv'n, And on His shoul - der ev - er rests All
last - ing Lord, The Won - der - ful, the Coun - sel - or, The
shades of death have been, In shades of death have been.
har - vest trea - sures home, Their har - vest trea - sures home.
pow'r in earth and heav'n, All pow'r in earth and heav'n.
God by all a - dored, The God by all a - dored.

5 His righteous government and pow'r
Shall over all extend;
On judgment and on justice based,
His reign shall have no end,
His reign shall have no end.

△ 6 Lord Jesus, reign in us, we pray,
And make us Thine alone,
Who with the Father ever art
And Holy Spirit, one,
And Holy Spirit, one.

Text: John Morison, 1749–98, alt.
Tune: Nicolaus Herman, c. 1480–1561; setting: *The Lutheran Hymnal*, 1941

LOBT GOTT, IHR CHRISTEN
86 866

Is. 9:2, 6–7; Matt. 4:16

O Wondrous Type! O Vision Fair 413

1 O won - drous type! O vi - sion fair
2 With Mo - ses and E - li - jah nigh
3 With shin - ing face and bright ar - ray
4 And faith - ful hearts are raised on high
△ 5 O Fa - ther, with the e - ter - nal Son
Of glo - ry that the Church may share,
The in - car - nate Lord holds con - verse high;
Christ deigns to man - i - fest to - day
By this great vi - sion's mys - ter - y,
And Ho - ly Spir - it ev - er one,
Which Christ up - on the moun - tain shows,
And from the cloud the Ho - ly One
What glo - ry shall be theirs a - bove
For which in joy - ful strains we raise
We pray Thee, bring us by Thy grace
Where bright - er than the sun He glows!
Bears rec - ord to the on - ly Son.
Who joy in God with per - fect love.
The voice of prayer, the hymn of praise.
To see Thy glo - ry face to face.

Setting available in hymn accompaniment edition.

Text: *Sarum Breviary*, Salisbury, 1495; tr. John Mason Neale, 1818–66, alt.
Tune: English, 15th cent.

DEO GRACIAS
L M

Luke 9:28–36; John 1:14; 17:24

414 'Tis Good, Lord, to Be Here

1 'Tis good, Lord, to be here! Thy glory fills the night; Thy face and garments, like the sun, Shine with unborrowed light.
2 'Tis good, Lord, to be here, Thy beauty to behold Where Moses and Elijah stand, Thy messengers of old.
3 Fulfiller of the past And hope of things to be, We hail Thy body glorified And our redemption see.
4 Before we taste of death, We see Thy kingdom come; We long to hold the vision bright And make this hill our home.
5 'Tis good, Lord, to be here! Yet we may not remain; But since Thou bidst us leave the mount, Come with us to the plain.

Text: Joseph A. Robinson, 1858–1933, alt.
Tune: Johann Sebastian Bach, 1685–1750, adapt.; setting: *The Lutheran Hymnal*, 1941

POTSDAM
S M

Luke 9:28–36; Matt. 1:22–23; Ps. 130:7; Rev. 7:13–14

Jesus on the Mountain Peak 415

1 Je - sus on the moun - tain peak Stands a - lone in glo - ry blaz - ing; Let us, if we dare to speak, Join the saints and an - gels prais - ing.
2 Trem - bling at His feet we saw Mo - ses and E - li - jah speak - ing. All the proph - ets and the law Shout through them their joy - ful greet - ing:
3 Swift the cloud of glo - ry came: God pro - claim - ing in its thun - der Je - sus as the Son by name! Na - tions, cry a - loud in won - der,
4 This is God's be - lov - ed Son! Law and proph - ets sing be - fore Him, First and Last and on - ly One. All cre - a - tion shall a - dore Him!
Al - le - lu - ia!

Text: Brian Wren, b. 1936
Music: Theodore A. Beck, 1929–2003, alt.

SEWARD
78 78 4

2 Peter 1:16–19

416 Swiftly Pass the Clouds of Glory

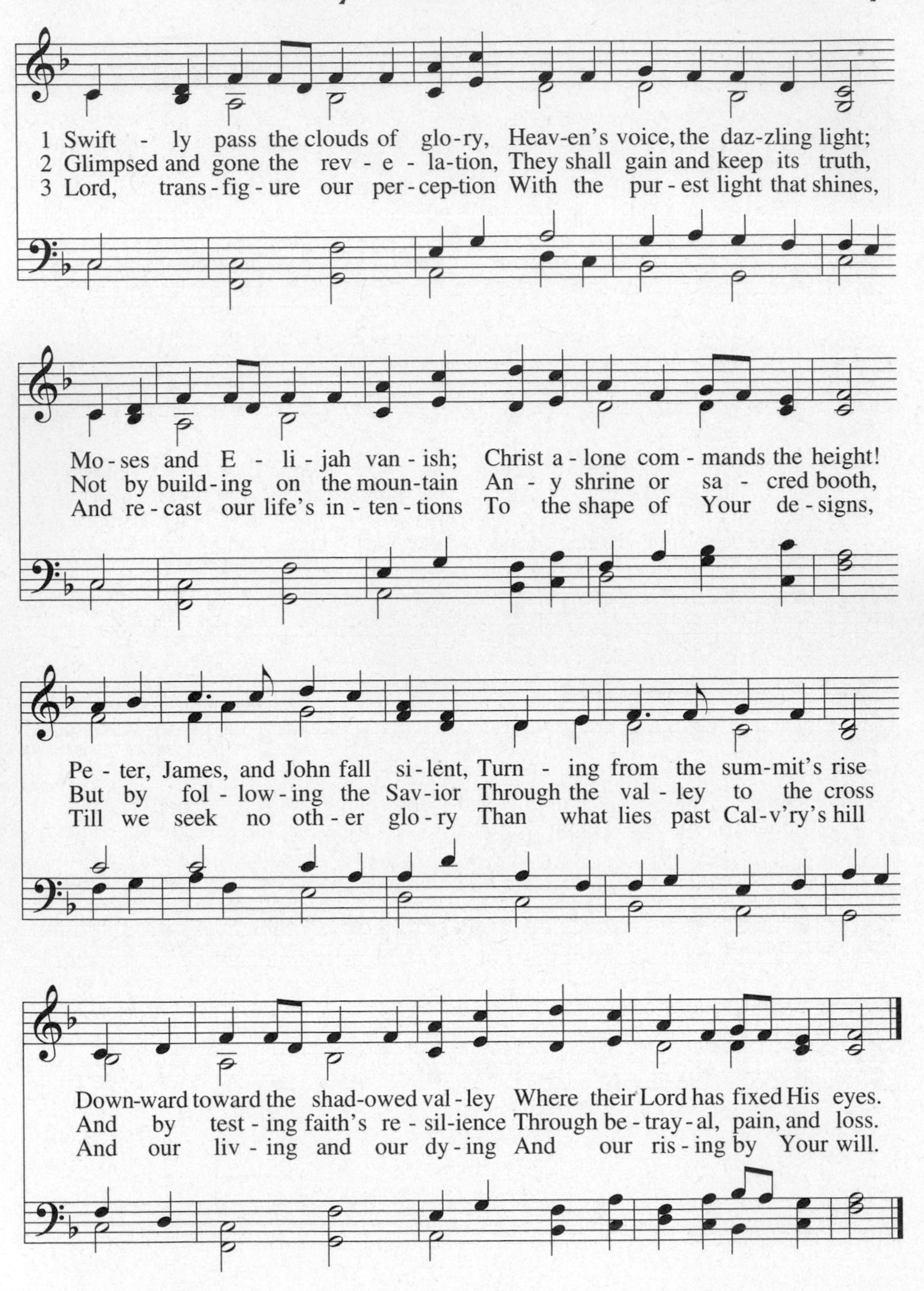
1 Swift - ly pass the clouds of glo-ry, Heav-en's voice, the daz-zling light;
2 Glimpsed and gone the rev - e - la-tion, They shall gain and keep its truth,
3 Lord, trans - fig - ure our per - cep-tion With the pur - est light that shines,
Mo - ses and E - li - jah van - ish; Christ a - lone com - mands the height!
Not by build - ing on the moun-tain An - y shrine or sa - cred booth,
And re - cast our life's in - ten - tions To the shape of Your de - signs,
Pe - ter, James, and John fall si - lent, Turn - ing from the sum-mit's rise
But by fol - low - ing the Sav - ior Through the val - ley to the cross
Till we seek no oth - er glo - ry Than what lies past Cal - v'ry's hill
Down-ward toward the shad-owed val - ley Where their Lord has fixed His eyes.
And by test - ing faith's re - sil-ience Through be - tray - al, pain, and loss.
And our liv - ing and our dy - ing And our ris - ing by Your will.

Text: Thomas H. Troeger, b. 1945
Music: Amanda Husberg, b. 1940

LOVE'S LIGHT
87 87 D

Matt. 17:2–9; 2 Peter 1:16

Alleluia, Song of Gladness 417

1 Al - le - lu - ia, song of glad - ness, Voice of joy that can - not die;
Al - le - lu - ia is the an - them Ev - er raised by choirs on high;
In the house of God a - bid - ing Thus they sing e - ter - nal - ly.
2 Al - le - lu - ia, thou re - sound - est, True Je - ru - sa - lem and free;
Al - le - lu - ia, joy - ful moth - er, All thy chil - dren sing with thee,
But by Bab - y - lon's sad wa - ters Mourn - ing ex - iles now are we.
3 Al - le - lu - ia can - not al - ways Be our song while here be - low;
Al - le - lu - ia, our trans - gres - sions Make us for a while for - go;
For the sol - emn time is com - ing When our tears for sin must flow.
4 There - fore in our hymns we pray Thee, Grant us, bless - ed Trin - i - ty,
At the last to keep Thine Eas - ter With Thy faith - ful saints on high;
There to Thee for - ev - er sing - ing Al - le - lu - ia joy - ful - ly.

We are mourning exiles who long to be in the heavenly Jerusalem, here referred to as "joyful mother." During Lent, the Church refrains from songs of "alleluia."

Text: Latin, c. 11th cent.; tr. John Mason Neale, 1818–66, alt.
Music: John Goss, 1800–80

LAUDA ANIMA
87 87 87

Ps. 137:1–6; Rev. 19:1–8

418 O Lord, throughout These Forty Days

1 O Lord, through - out these for - ty days You prayed and kept the fast; In - spire re - pen - tance for our sin, And free us from our past.
2 You strove with Sa - tan, and You won; Your faith - ful - ness en - dured; Lend us Your nerve, Your skill and trust In God's e - ter - nal Word.
3 Though parched and hun - gry, yet You prayed And fixed Your mind a - bove; So teach us to de - ny our - selves, Since we have known God's love.
4 Be with us through this sea - son, Lord, And all our earth - ly days, That when the fi - nal Eas - ter dawns, We join in heav - en's praise.

Text: based on Claudia F. Hernaman, 1838–98; para. Gilbert E. Doan, b. 1930
Tune: *The Psalmes of David in Prose and Meeter*, Edinburgh, 1635; setting: *The English Hymnal*, 1906

CAITHNESS
C M

Luke 4:1–13; Lev. 9:23

Savior, When in Dust to Thee 419

1 Sav - ior, when in dust to Thee Low we bow the a -
2 By Thy help - less in - fant years, By Thy life of
3 By Thine hour of dire de - spair, By Thine ag - o -
4 By Thy deep ex - pir - ing groan, By the sad se -
dor - ing knee; When, re - pen - tant, to the skies
want and tears, By Thy days of deep dis - tress
ny of prayer, By the cross, the nail, the thorn,
pul - chral stone, By the vault whose dark a - bode
Scarce we lift our weep - ing eyes; O, by all Thy
In the sav - age wil - der - ness, By the dread, mys -
Pierc - ing spear, and tor - turing scorn, By the gloom that
Held in vain the ris - ing God, O, from earth to
pains and woe Suf - fered once for us be - low, Bend - ing
te - rious hour Of the in - sult - ing tempt - er's pow'r, Turn, O
veiled the skies O'er the dread - ful sac - ri - fice, Lis - ten
heav'n re - stored, Might - y, re - as - cend - ed Lord, Bend - ing
from Thy throne on high, Hear our pen - i - ten - tial cry!
turn a fa - v'ring eye; Hear our pen - i - ten - tial cry!
to our hum - ble sigh; Hear our pen - i - ten - tial cry!
from Thy throne on high, Hear our pen - i - ten - tial cry!

Setting available in hymn accompaniment edition.

Text: Robert Grant, 1779–1838, alt.
Tune: Joseph Parry, 1841–1903

ABERYSTWYTH
77 77 D

Ezek. 18:30–32; Luke 18:13; Ps. 86:3; Job 42:6

420 Christ, the Life of All the Living

1 Christ, the life of all the liv - ing,
Christ, the death of death, our foe,
Who, Thy - self for me once giv - ing
To the dark - est depths of woe:
Through Thy suf - f'rings, death, and mer - it
I e - ter - nal life in - her - it.

2 Thou, ah! Thou, hast tak - en on Thee
Bonds and stripes, a cru - el rod;
Pain and scorn were heaped up - on Thee,
O Thou sin - less Son of God!
Thus didst Thou my soul de - liv - er
From the bonds of sin for - ev - er.

3 Thou hast borne the smit - ing on - ly
That my wounds might all be whole;
Thou hast suf - fered, sad and lone - ly,
Rest to give my wea - ry soul;
Yea, the curse of God en - dur - ing,
Bless - ing un - to me se - cur - ing.

4 Heart - less scof - fers did sur - round Thee,
Treat - ing Thee with shame - ful scorn
And with pierc - ing thorns they crowned Thee.
All dis - grace Thou, Lord, hast borne,
That as Thine Thou might - est own me
And with heav'n - ly glo - ry crown me.

Text: Ernst Christoph Homburg, 1605–81; tr. Catherine Winkworth, 1827–78, sts. 1–2, 5, 7, alt.; tr. *Evangelical Lutheran Hymn-Book*, St. Louis, 1912, sts. 3–4, 6
Tune: *Das grosse Cantional*, Darmstadt, 1687; setting: *The Lutheran Hymnal*, 1941

JESU, MEINES LEBENS LEBEN
87 87 88 77

Matt. 27:33–46; 1 Cor. 15:57; Is. 53:5; 1 Peter 2:24

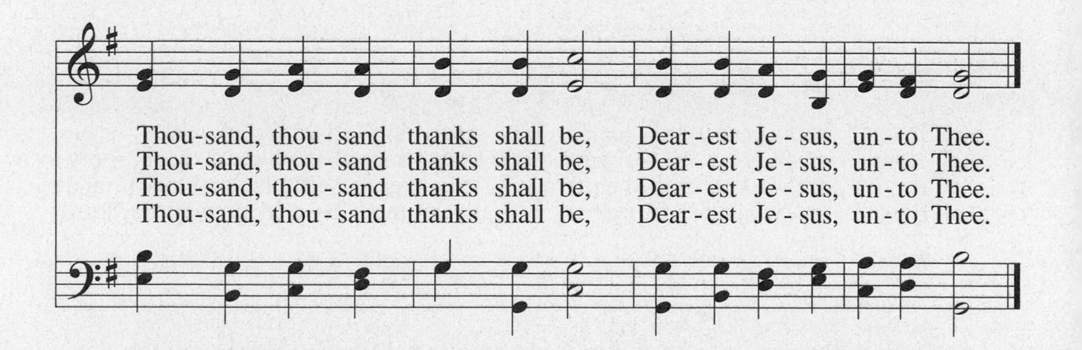
Thou-sand, thou - sand thanks shall be, Dear - est Je - sus, un - to Thee.
Thou-sand, thou - sand thanks shall be, Dear - est Je - sus, un - to Thee.
Thou-sand, thou - sand thanks shall be, Dear - est Je - sus, un - to Thee.
Thou-sand, thou - sand thanks shall be, Dear - est Je - sus, un - to Thee.

5 Thou hast suffered men to bruise Thee,
That from pain I might be free;
Falsely did Thy foes accuse Thee:
Thence I gain security;
Comfortless Thy soul did languish
Me to comfort in my anguish.
Thousand, thousand thanks shall be,
Dearest Jesus, unto Thee.

6 Thou hast suffered great affliction
And hast borne it patiently,
Even death by crucifixion,
Fully to atone for me;
Thou didst choose to be tormented
That my doom should be prevented.
Thousand, thousand thanks shall be,
Dearest Jesus, unto Thee.

7 Then, for all that wrought my pardon,
For Thy sorrows deep and sore,
For Thine anguish in the Garden,
I will thank Thee evermore,
Thank Thee for Thy groaning, sighing,
For Thy bleeding and Thy dying,
For that last triumphant cry,
And shall praise Thee, Lord, on high.

421 Jesus, Grant That Balm and Healing

1 Je - sus, grant that balm and heal - ing In Your ho - ly
2 Should some lust or sharp temp - ta - tion Fas - ci - nate my
3 If the world my heart en - tic - es With the broad and
4 Ev - 'ry wound that pains or grieves me By Your wounds, Lord,
wounds I find, Ev - 'ry hour that I am feel - ing Pains of
sin - ful mind, Draw me to Your cross and pas - sion, And new
eas - y road, With se - duc - tive, sin - ful vi - ces, Let me
is made whole; When I'm faint, Your cross re - vives me, Grant - ing
bod - y and of mind. Should some e - vil thought with - in
cour - age I shall find. Or should Sa - tan press me hard,
weigh the aw - ful load You were will - ing to en - dure.
new life to my soul. Yes, Your com - fort ren - ders sweet
Tempt my treach - 'rous heart to sin, Show the per - il, and from
Let me then be on my guard, Say - ing, "Christ for me was
Help me flee all thoughts im - pure And to mas - ter each temp -
Ev - 'ry bit - ter cup I meet; For Your all - a - ton - ing

Text: Johann Heermann, 1585–1647; tr. composite, alt.
Tune: Johann Balthasar König, 1691–1758; setting: *The Lutheran Hymnal*, 1941

DER AM KREUZ
87 87 77 88

Is. 53:4–5; 1 Peter 2:24; 1 Cor. 10:13; 2 Cor. 1:3–7

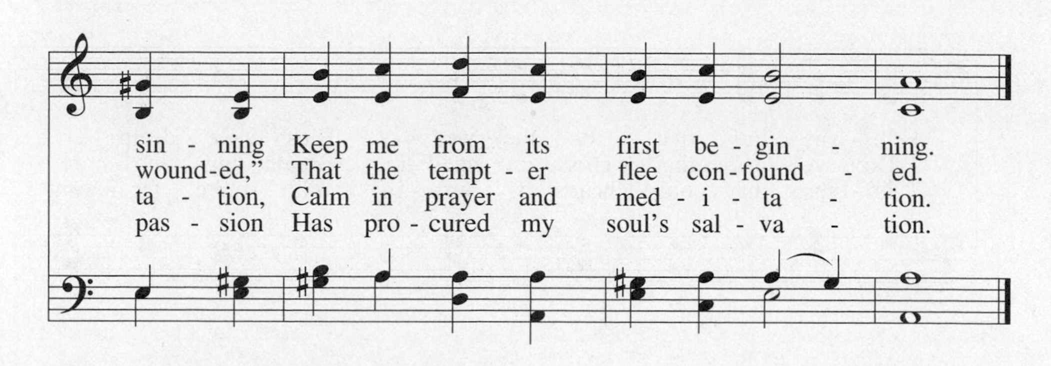
sin - ning Keep me from its first be - gin - ning.
wound-ed," That the tempt - er flee con-found - ed.
ta - tion, Calm in prayer and med - i - ta - tion.
pas - sion Has pro - cured my soul's sal - va - tion.

5 O my God, my rock and tower,
Grant that in Your death I trust,
Knowing death has lost its power
Since You crushed it in the dust.
Savior, let Your agony
Ever help and comfort me;
When I die be my protection,
Light and life and resurrection.

On My Heart Imprint Your Image 422

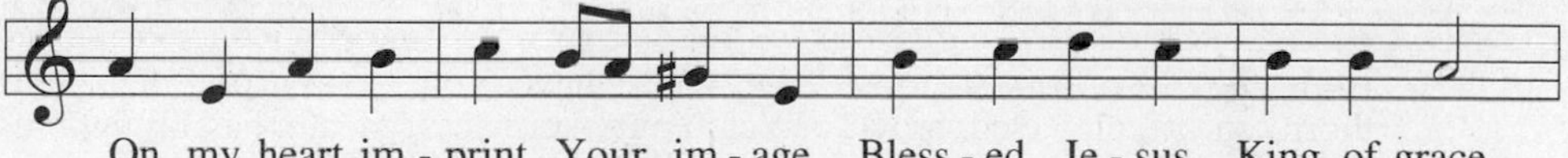
On my heart im - print Your im - age, Bless - ed Je - sus, King of grace,

That life's rich-es, cares, and plea-sures Nev - er may Your work e-rase;

Let the clear in - scrip-tion be: Je - sus, cru - ci - fied for me,

Is my life, my hope's foun - da - tion, And my glo - ry and sal - va - tion!

Hymn accompaniment: 421

Text: Thomas Hansen Kingo, 1634–1703; tr. Peer O. Strömme, 1856–1921, alt.
Tune: Johann Balthasar König, 1691–1758

DER AM KREUZ
87 87 77 88

Rom. 8:29; 2 Peter 1:4; Eph. 4:24; 2 Cor. 3:18

423 Jesus, Refuge of the Weary

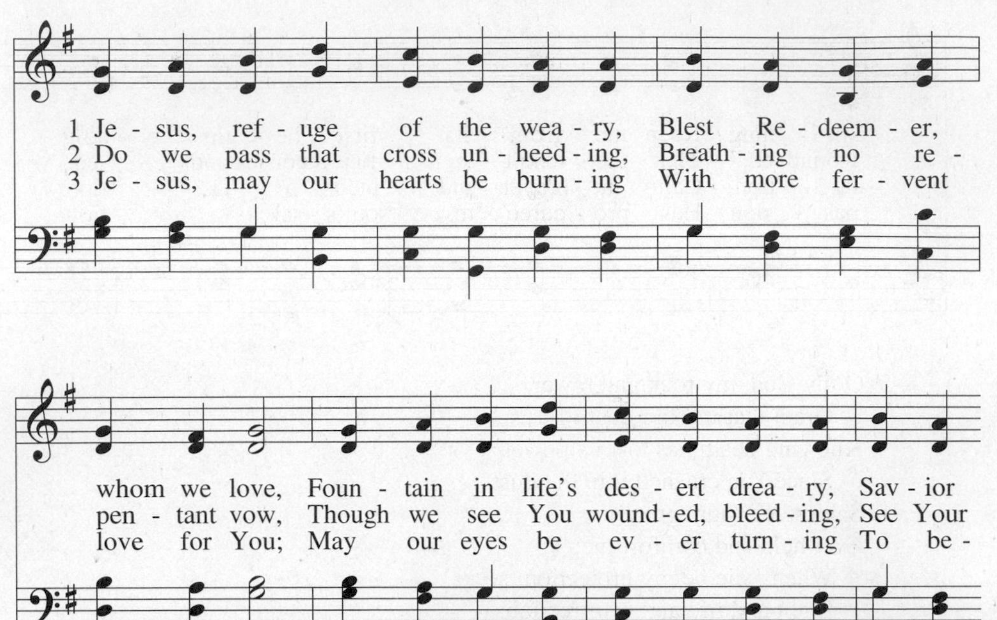
1 Je - sus, ref - uge of the wea - ry, Blest Re - deem - er,
2 Do we pass that cross un - heed - ing, Breath - ing no re -
3 Je - sus, may our hearts be burn - ing With more fer - vent
whom we love, Foun - tain in life's des - ert drea - ry, Sav - ior
pen - tant vow, Though we see You wound - ed, bleed - ing, See Your
love for You; May our eyes be ev - er turn - ing To be -

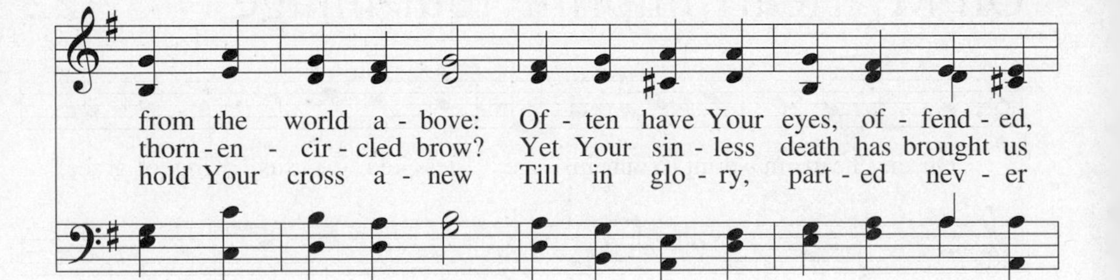
from the world a - bove: Of - ten have Your eyes, of - fend - ed,
thorn - en - cir - cled brow? Yet Your sin - less death has brought us
hold Your cross a - new Till in glo - ry, part - ed nev - er

Gazed up - on the sin - ner's fall; Yet up - on the
Life e - ter - nal, peace, and rest; On - ly what Your
From the bless - ed Sav - ior's side, Grav - en in our

Text: Girolamo Savonarola, 1452–98; tr. Jane F. Wilde, 1826–96, alt.
Tune: *Erbaulicher Musicalischer Christen-Schatz*, Basel, 1745; setting: *The Lutheran Hymnal*, 1941

O DU LIEBE MEINER LIEBE
87 87 D

Mark 15:29–30; Is. 53:4–5, 11

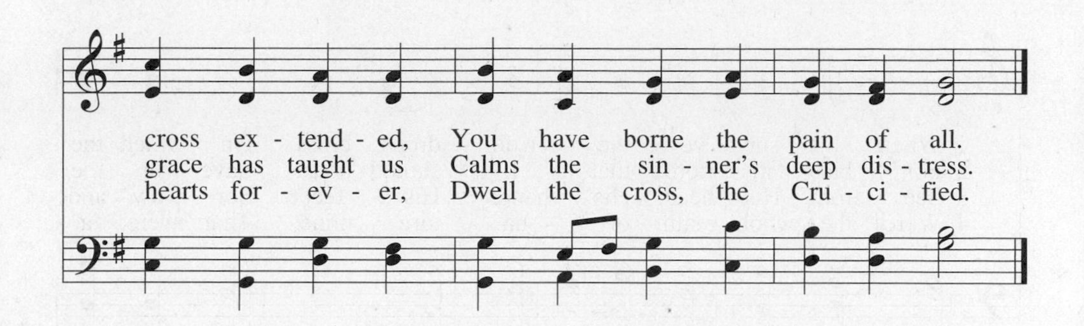
cross ex - tend - ed, You have borne the pain of all.
grace has taught us Calms the sin - ner's deep dis - tress.
hearts for - ev - er, Dwell the cross, the Cru - ci - fied.

O Christ, You Walked the Road 424

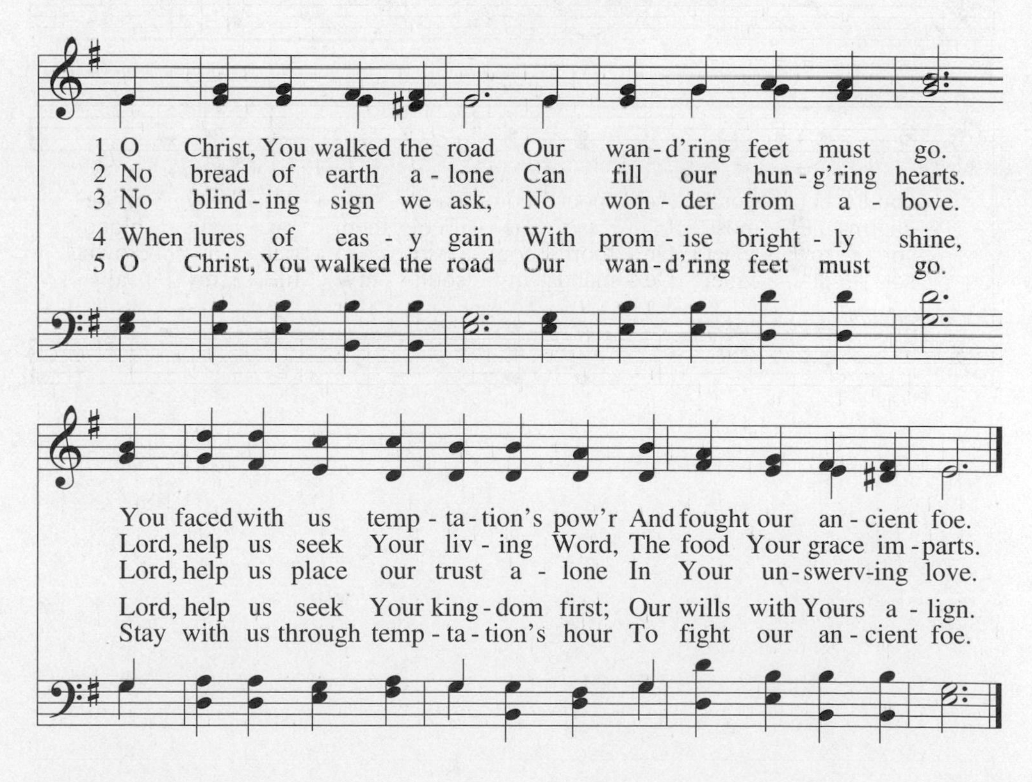
1 O Christ, You walked the road Our wan - d'ring feet must go.
2 No bread of earth a - lone Can fill our hun - g'ring hearts.
3 No blind - ing sign we ask, No won - der from a - bove.
4 When lures of eas - y gain With prom - ise bright - ly shine,
5 O Christ, You walked the road Our wan - d'ring feet must go.
You faced with us temp - ta - tion's pow'r And fought our an - cient foe.
Lord, help us seek Your liv - ing Word, The food Your grace im - parts.
Lord, help us place our trust a - lone In Your un - swerv - ing love.
Lord, help us seek Your king - dom first; Our wills with Yours a - lign.
Stay with us through temp - ta - tion's hour To fight our an - cient foe.

Text: Herman G. Stuempfle, Jr., 1923–2007
Tune: William Daman, c. 1540–91; setting: *New English Hymnal*, 1986

SOUTHWELL
S M

Matt. 4:1–11; Heb. 2:18; 4:15

425 When I Survey the Wondrous Cross

1 When I sur - vey the won - drous cross On which the
2 For - bid it, Lord, that I should boast Save in the
3 See, from His head, His hands, His feet Sor - row and
4 Were the whole realm of na - ture mine, That were a
Prince of Glo - ry died, My rich - est gain I
death of Christ, my God; All the vain things that
love flow min - gled down! Did e'er such love and
trib - ute far too small; Love so a - maz - ing,
count but loss And pour con - tempt on all my pride.
charm me most, I sac - ri - fice them to His blood.
sor - row meet Or thorns com - pose so rich a crown?
so di - vine, De - mands my soul, my life, my all!

Text: Isaac Watts, 1674–1748
Music: Lowell Mason, 1792–1872

HAMBURG
L M

Gal. 6:14; Phil. 3:8

When I Survey the Wondrous Cross 426

1 When I survey the wondrous cross On which the Prince of Glory died,
My richest gain I count but loss And pour contempt on all my pride.
2 Forbid it, Lord, that I should boast Save in the death of Christ, my God;
All the vain things that charm me most, I sacrifice them to His blood.
3 See, from His head, His hands, His feet Sorrow and love flow mingled down!
Did e'er such love and sorrow meet Or thorns compose so rich a crown?
4 Were the whole realm of nature mine, That were a tribute far too small;
Love so amazing, so divine, Demands my soul, my life, my all!

Text: Isaac Watts, 1674–1748
Tune: *Second Supplement to Psalmody in Miniature*, London, 1778; adapt. Edward Miller, 1731–1807;
setting: *The Worshipbook: Services and Hymns*, 1972

ROCKINGHAM OLD
L M

Gal. 6:14; Phil. 3:8

427 In the Cross of Christ I Glory

1 In the cross of Christ I glo - ry, Tow'r - ing o'er the wrecks of time. All the light of sa - cred sto - ry Gath - ers round its head sub - lime.
2 When the woes of life o'er - take me, Hopes de - ceive, and fears an - noy, Nev - er shall the cross for - sake me; Lo, it glows with peace and joy.
3 When the sun of bliss is beam - ing Light and love up - on my way, From the cross the ra - diance stream - ing Adds more lus - ter to the day.
4 Bane and bless - ing, pain and plea - sure By the cross are sanc - ti - fied; Peace is there that knows no mea - sure, Joys that through all time a - bide.

Text: John Bowring, 1792–1872
Tune: Ithamar Conkey, 1815–67; setting: *Service Book and Hymnal*, 1958, alt.

RATHBUN
87 87

Gal. 2:20; 6:14

Cross of Jesus, Cross of Sorrow

1 Cross of Je - sus, cross of sor - row,
2 Here the King of all the a - ges,
3 O mys - te - rious con - de - scend - ing!
4 Cross of Je - sus, cross of sor - row,
Where the blood of Christ was shed,
Throned in light ere worlds could be,
O a - ban - don - ment sub - lime!
Where the blood of Christ was shed,
Per - fect man on thee did suf - fer,
Robed in mor - tal flesh is dy - ing,
Ver - y God Him - self is bear - ing
Per - fect man on thee did suf - fer,
Per - fect God on thee has bled!
Cru - ci - fied by sin for me.
All the suf - fer - ings of time!
Per - fect God on thee has bled!

Text: William J. Sparrow Simpson, 1860–1952
Music: John Stainer, 1840–1901

CROSS OF JESUS
87 87

John 19:17–30; Col. 1:19–20; Phil. 2:5–11; Is. 53:10–11

429 We Sing the Praise of Him Who Died

1 We sing the praise of Him who died, Of Him who died up - on the cross. The sin - ner's hope let all de - ride; For this we count the world but loss.
2 In - scribed up - on the cross we see In shin - ing let - ters, "God is love." He bears our sins up - on the tree; He brings us mer - cy from a - bove.
3 The cross! It takes our guilt a - way; It holds the faint - ing spir - it up; It cheers with hope the gloom - y day And sweet - ens ev - 'ry bit - ter cup.
4 It makes the cow - ard spir - it brave And nerves the fee - ble arm for fight; It takes the ter - ror from the grave And gilds the bed of death with light;

5 The balm of life, the cure of woe,
The measure and the pledge of love,
The sinner's refuge here below,
The angels' theme in heav'n above.

6 To Christ, who won for sinners grace
By bitter grief and anguish sore,
Be praise from all the ransomed race
Forever and forevermore.

Text: Thomas Kelly, 1769–1855, sts. 1–5; *Hymns Ancient and Modern*, 1861, st. 6
Tune: attr. Daniel Read, 1757–1836; setting: *Lutheran Book of Worship*, 1978

WINDHAM
L M

Gal. 6:14; 1 John 4:8–10; Phil. 3:8; Rev. 5:12

My Song Is Love Unknown 430

1 My song is love un - known, My Sav - ior's love to me, Love to the love - less shown That they might love - ly be. Oh, who am I That for my sake My Lord should take Frail flesh and die?
2 He came from His blest throne Sal - va - tion to be - stow; But men made strange, and none The longed - for Christ would know. But, oh, my friend, My friend in - deed, Who at my need His life did spend!
3 Some - times they strew His way And His sweet prais - es sing; Re - sound - ing all the day Ho - san - nas to their King. Then "Cru - ci - fy!" Is all their breath, And for His death They thirst and cry.
4 Why, what hath my Lord done? What makes this rage and spite? He made the lame to run, He gave the blind their sight. Sweet in - ju - ries! Yet they at these Them - selves dis - please And 'gainst Him rise.
5 They rise and needs will have My dear Lord made a - way; A mur - der - er they save, The Prince of Life they slay. Yet cheer - ful He To suf - f'ring goes That He His foes From thence might free.

6 In life no house, no home
My Lord on earth might have;
In death no friendly tomb
But what a stranger gave.
What may I say?
Heav'n was His home
But mine the tomb
Wherein He lay.

7 Here might I stay and sing,
No story so divine!
Never was love, dear King,
Never was grief like Thine.
This is my friend,
In whose sweet praise
I all my days
Could gladly spend!

Setting available in hymn accompaniment edition.

Text: Samuel Crossman, c. 1624–83
Tune: John N. Ireland, 1879–1962

LOVE UNKNOWN
66 66 4444

Is. 52:13—53:3; Rom. 5:6, 10; Phil. 2:5–11; Acts 3:13–15

431 Not All the Blood of Beasts

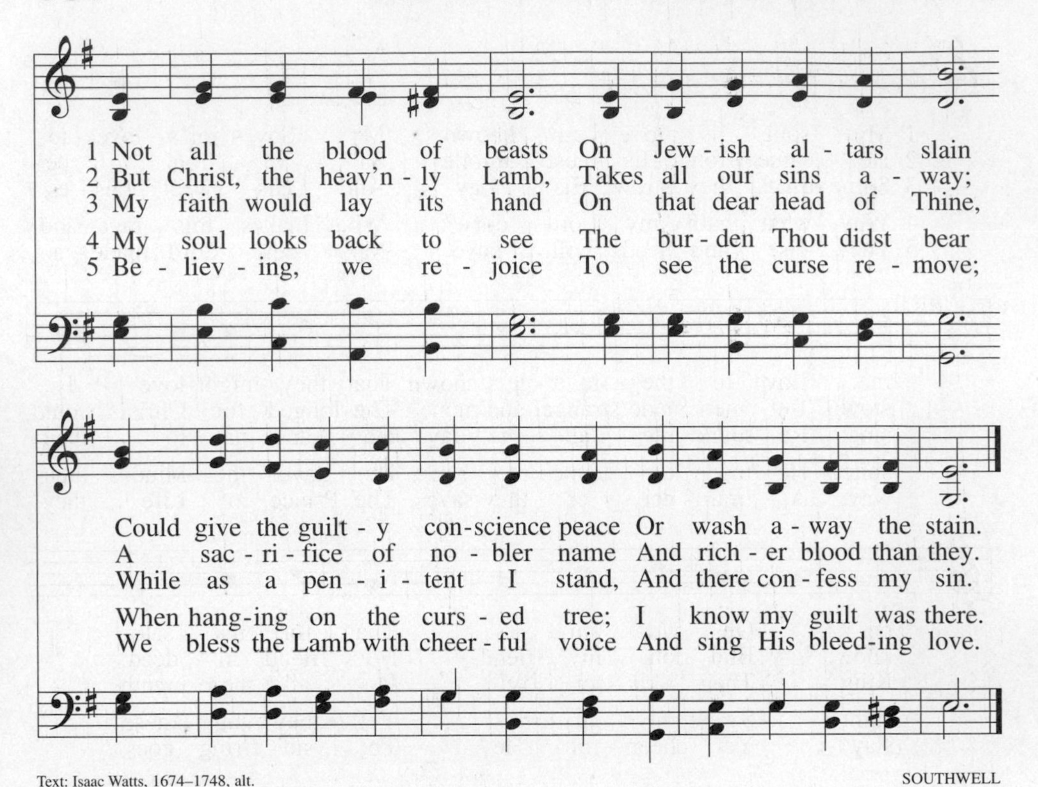
1 Not all the blood of beasts On Jew - ish al - tars slain
2 But Christ, the heav'n - ly Lamb, Takes all our sins a - way;
3 My faith would lay its hand On that dear head of Thine,
4 My soul looks back to see The bur - den Thou didst bear
5 Be - liev - ing, we re - joice To see the curse re - move;
Could give the guilt - y con-science peace Or wash a - way the stain.
A sac - ri - fice of no - bler name And rich - er blood than they.
While as a pen - i - tent I stand, And there con - fess my sin.
When hang-ing on the curs - ed tree; I know my guilt was there.
We bless the Lamb with cheer - ful voice And sing His bleed-ing love.

Text: Isaac Watts, 1674–1748, alt.
Tune: William Daman, c. 1540–91; setting: *The Lutheran Hymnal*, 1941

SOUTHWELL
S M

Heb. 10:1–4, 11; Heb. 9:12–14; Gal. 3:13; Rev. 5:6–14

432 In Silent Pain the Eternal Son

1 In si - lent pain the e - ter - nal Son Hangs der - e - lict and still;
2 He died that we might die to sin And live for righ-teous-ness;
3 For strife He came to bring a sword, The truth to end all lies;

In dark-ened day His work is done, Ful - filled, His Fa - ther's will.
The earth is stained to make us clean And bring us in - to peace.
To rule in us, our pa - tient Lord, Un - til all e - vil dies:

Our Lord tenderly reaches out to all the world with nail-scarred hands, inviting us to see in His eyes God's love from all eternity. Setting available in hymn accompaniment edition.

Text: Christopher M. Idle, b. 1938
Tune: John L. Bell, b. 1949

REALITY
86 86 88 86

Matt. 10:34–39; 27:45–54; 1 Peter 2:24

Up - lift - ed for the world to see He hangs in strang-est vic - to - ry,
For peace He came and met its cost; He gave Him - self to save the lost;
For in His hand He holds the stars, His voice shall speak to end our wars,

For in His bod - y on the tree He car - ries all our ill.
He loved us to the ut - ter - most And paid for our re - lease.
And those who love Him see His scars And look in - to His eyes.

Glory Be to Jesus 433

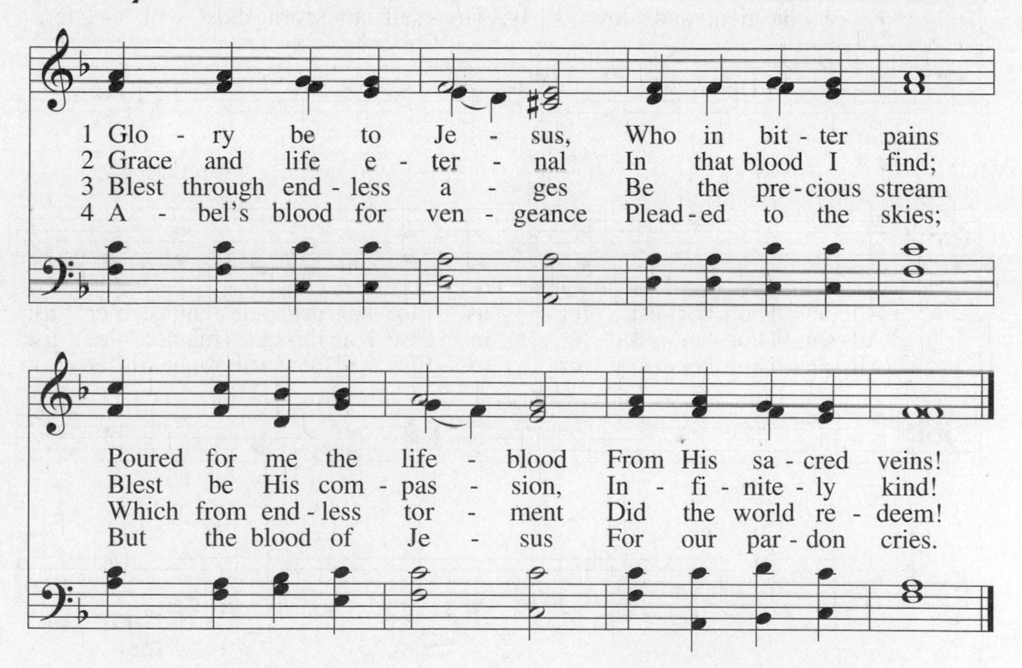
1 Glo - ry be to Je - sus, Who in bit - ter pains
2 Grace and life e - ter - nal In that blood I find;
3 Blest through end - less a - ges Be the pre - cious stream
4 A - bel's blood for ven - geance Plead - ed to the skies;
Poured for me the life - blood From His sa - cred veins!
Blest be His com - pas - sion, In - fi - nite - ly kind!
Which from end - less tor - ment Did the world re - deem!
But the blood of Je - sus For our par - don cries.

5 Oft as earth exulting
Wafts its praise on high,
Angel hosts rejoicing
Make their glad reply.

6 Lift we, then, our voices,
Swell the mighty flood;
Louder still and louder
Praise the precious blood!

Text: Italian, c. 18th cent.; tr. Edward Caswall, 1814–78, alt.
Tune: Friedrich Filitz, 1804–76; setting: *The Lutheran Hymnal*, 1941

WEM IN LEIDENSTAGEN
65 65

1 Peter 1:18–19; Eph. 1:6–8; Rev. 7:9–14

434 Lamb of God, Pure and Holy

1 Lamb of God, pure and ho - ly, Who on the cross didst suf - fer,
2 Lamb of God, pure and ho - ly, Who on the cross didst suf - fer,
3 Lamb of God, pure and ho - ly, Who on the cross didst suf - fer,
Ev - er pa - tient and low - ly, Thy - self to scorn didst of - fer.
Ev - er pa - tient and low - ly, Thy - self to scorn didst of - fer.
Ev - er pa - tient and low - ly, Thy - self to scorn didst of - fer.
All sins Thou bor - est for us, Else had de - spair reigned o'er us:
All sins Thou bor - est for us, Else had de - spair reigned o'er us:
All sins Thou bor - est for us, Else had de - spair reigned o'er us:
Have mer - cy on us, O Je - sus! O Je - sus!
Have mer - cy on us, O Je - sus! O Je - sus!
Thy peace be with us, O Je - sus! O Je - sus!

Text: Nicolaus Decius, c. 1485–after 1546; tr. *The Lutheran Hymnal*, 1941
Tune: Nicolaus Decius, c. 1485–after 1546; setting: *Lutheran Service Book*, 2006

O LAMM GOTTES, UNSCHULDIG
77 77 77 5 33

John 1:29, 35–36; Is. 53:6–7; 1 Peter 1:18–19; John 14:27

Come to Calvary's Holy Mountain 435

1 Come to Cal - v'ry's ho - ly moun - tain, Sin - ners, ru - ined by the fall; Here a pure and heal - ing foun - tain Flows for you, for me, for all, In a full, per - pet - ual tide, O - pened when our Sav - ior died.
2 Come in pov - er - ty and mean - ness, Come de - filed, with - out, with - in; From in - fec - tion and un - clean - ness, From the lep - ro - sy of sin, Wash your robes and make them white; Ye shall walk with God in light.
3 Come in sor - row and con - tri - tion, Wound - ed, im - po - tent, and blind; Here the guilt - y, free re - mis - sion, Here the trou - bled, peace may find. Health this foun - tain will re - store; They that drink shall thirst no more.
4 They that drink shall live for - ev - er; 'Tis a soul - re - new - ing flood. God is faith - ful; God will nev - er Break His cov - e - nant of blood, Signed when our Re - deem - er died, Sealed when He was glo - ri - fied.

Text: James Montgomery, 1771–1854, alt.
Tune: Ludvig M. Lindeman, 1812–87; setting: *Lutheran Book of Worship*, 1978

NAAR MIT ÖIE
87 87 77

Zech. 13:1; Heb. 9:14; Matt. 27:33–35; Is. 25:6–8

436 Go to Dark Gethsemane

1 Go to dark Geth - sem - a - ne, All who feel the
2 Fol - low to the judg - ment hall, View the Lord of
3 Cal - v'ry's mourn - ful moun - tain climb; There, a - dor - ing
4 Ear - ly has - ten to the tomb Where they laid His
tempt - er's pow'r; Your Re - deem - er's con - flict see,
life ar - raigned; Oh, the worm - wood and the gall!
at His feet, Mark that mir - a - cle of time,
breath - less clay; All is sol - i - tude and gloom.
Watch with Him one bit - ter hour; Turn not from His
Oh, the pangs His soul sus - tained! Shun not suf - f'ring,
God's own sac - ri - fice com - plete. "It is fin - ished!"
Who has tak - en Him a - way? Christ is ris'n! He
griefs a - way; Learn from Je - sus Christ to pray.
shame, or loss; Learn from Him to bear the cross.
hear Him cry; Learn from Je - sus Christ to die.
meets our eyes. Sav - ior, teach us so to rise.

Text: James Montgomery, 1771–1854
Tune: Richard Redhead, 1820–1901; setting: *The Lutheran Hymnal*, 1941

GETHSEMANE
77 77 77

Mark 14:32–38; 15:1–20; Luke 23:33–46; Matt. 27:33–50; John 20:1–18

Alas! And Did My Savior Bleed 437

1 A - las! And did my Sav - ior bleed, And did my sov - 'reign die? Would He de - vote that sa - cred head For such a worm as I?
2 Was it for crimes that I had done He groaned up - on the tree? A - maz - ing pit - y, grace un - known, And love be - yond de - gree!
3 Well might the sun in dark - ness hide And shut his glo - ries in When God, the might - y mak - er, died For His own crea - tures' sin.
4 Thus might I hide my blush - ing face While His dear cross ap - pears, Dis - solve my heart in thank - ful - ness, And melt mine eyes to tears.
5 But drops of grief can ne'er re - pay The debt of love I owe; Here, Lord, I give my - self a - way: 'Tis all that I can do.

Text: Isaac Watts, 1674–1748, alt.
Tune: Hugh Wilson, 1764–1824; setting: *The Lutheran Hymnal*, 1941

MARTYRDOM
C M

Matt. 27:45–50; Rom. 5:6–12; 12:1; 1 Peter 2:24

438 A Lamb Goes Uncomplaining Forth

1 A Lamb goes un - com - plain - ing forth, The
2 This Lamb is Christ, the soul's great friend, The
3 "Yes, Fa - ther, yes, most will - ing - ly I'll
4 Lord, when Your glo - ry I shall see And
guilt of sin - ners bear - ing And, lad - en with the
Lamb of God, our Sav - ior, Whom God the Fa - ther
bear what You com - mand Me. My will con - forms to
taste Your king - dom's plea - sure, Your blood my roy - al
sins of earth, None else the bur - den shar - ing; Goes
chose to send To gain for us His fa - vor. "Go
Your de - cree, I'll do what You have asked Me." O
robe shall be, My joy be - yond all mea - sure! When
pa - tient on, grows weak and faint, To slaugh - ter led with -
forth, My Son," the Fa - ther said, "And free My chil - dren
won - drous Love, what have You done! The Fa - ther of - fers
I ap - pear be - fore Your throne, Your righ - teous - ness shall

Text: Paul Gerhardt, 1607–76; tr. *The Lutheran Hymnal*, 1941, alt.
Tune: Wolfgang Dachstein, c. 1487–1553; setting: *Lutheran Service Book*, 2006

AN WASSERFLÜSSEN BABYLON
87 87 887 887

Is. 53:1–12; Ex. 12:5; John 1:29

out com-plaint, That spot-less life to of - fer, He bears the
from their dread Of guilt and con-dem-na - tion. The wrath and
up His Son, De - sir-ing our sal-va - tion. O Love, how
be my crown; With these I need not hide me. And there, in
stripes, the wounds, the lies, The mock-er - y, and
stripes are hard to bear, But by Your pas - sion
strong You are to save! You lay the One in -
gar - ments rich - ly wrought, As Your own bride shall
yet re - plies, "All this I glad - ly suf - fer."
they will share The fruit of Your sal - va - tion."
to the grave Who built the earth's foun - da - tion.
we be brought To stand in joy be - side You.

439 O Dearest Jesus, What Law Hast Thou Broken

1 O dear - est Je - sus, what law hast Thou bro - ken
2 They crown Thy head with thorns, they smite, they scourge Thee;
3 Whence come these sor - rows, whence this mor - tal an - guish?
4 What pun - ish - ment so strange is suf - fered yon - der!
5 The sin - less Son of God must die in sad - ness;
That such sharp sen - tence should on Thee be spo - ken?
With cru - el mock - ings to the cross they urge Thee;
It is my sins for which Thou, Lord, must lan - guish;
The Shep - herd dies for sheep that loved to wan - der;
The sin - ful child of man may live in glad - ness;
Of what great crime hast Thou to make con - fes - sion, What dark trans - gres - sion?
They give Thee gall to drink, they still de - cry Thee; They cru - ci - fy Thee.
Yea, all the wrath, the woe, Thou dost in - her - it, This I do mer - it.
The Mas - ter pays the debt His ser - vants owe Him, Who would not know Him.
Man for - feit - ed his life and is ac - quit - ted; God is com - mit - ted.

Text: Johann Heermann, 1585–1647; tr. Catherine Winkworth, 1827–78, alt.
Tune: Johann Crüger, 1598–1662; setting: *The Lutheran Hymnal*, 1941

HERZLIEBSTER JESU
11 11 11 5

Luke 23:20–24; Is. 53:4–6; John 10:11, 14–15; Rom. 12:1

6 There was no spot in me by sin untainted;
Sick with sin's poison, all my heart had fainted;
My heavy guilt to hell had well-nigh brought me,
Such woe it wrought me.

7 O wondrous love, whose depth no heart hath sounded,
That brought Thee here, by foes and thieves surrounded!
All worldly pleasures, heedless, I was trying
While Thou wert dying.

8 O mighty King, no time can dim Thy glory!
How shall I spread abroad Thy wondrous story?
How shall I find some worthy gifts to proffer?
What dare I offer?

9 For vainly doth our human wisdom ponder—
Thy woes, Thy mercy, still transcend our wonder.
Oh, how should I do aught that could delight Thee!
Can I requite Thee?

10 Yet unrequited, Lord, I would not leave Thee;
I will renounce whate'er doth vex or grieve Thee
And quench with thoughts of Thee and prayers most lowly
All fires unholy.

11 But since my strength will nevermore suffice me
To crucify desires that still entice me,
To all good deeds O let Thy Spirit win me
And reign within me!

12 I'll think upon Thy mercy without ceasing,
That earth's vain joys to me no more be pleasing;
To do Thy will shall be my sole endeavor
Henceforth forever.

13 Whate'er of earthly good this life may grant me,
I'll risk for Thee; no shame, no cross, shall daunt me.
I shall not fear what foes can do to harm me
Nor death alarm me.

14 But worthless is my sacrifice, I own it;
Yet, Lord, for love's sake Thou wilt not disown it;
Thou wilt accept my gift in Thy great meekness
Nor shame my weakness.

15 And when, dear Lord, before Thy throne in heaven
To me the crown of joy at last is given,
Where sweetest hymns Thy saints forever raise Thee,
I, too, shall praise Thee.

440 Jesus, I Will Ponder Now

1 Je - sus, I will pon - der now On Your ho - ly pas - sion;
2 Make me see Your great dis - tress, An - guish, and af - flic - tion,
3 Yet, O Lord, not thus a - lone Make me see Your pas - sion,
4 Grant that I Your pas - sion view With re - pen - tant griev - ing.
With Your Spir - it me en - dow For such med - i - ta - tion.
Bonds and stripes and wretch - ed - ness And Your cru - ci - fix - ion;
But its cause to me make known And its ter - mi - na - tion.
Let me not bring shame to You By un - ho - ly liv - ing.
Grant that I in love and faith May the im - age cher - ish
Make me see how scourge and rod, Spear and nails did wound You,
Ah! I al - so and my sin Wrought Your deep af - flic - tion;
How could I re - fuse to shun Ev - 'ry sin - ful plea - sure
Of Your suf - f'ring, pain, and death That I may not per - ish.
How for them You died, O God, Who with thorns had crowned You.
This in - deed the cause has been Of Your cru - ci - fix - ion.
Since for me God's on - ly Son Suf - fered with - out mea - sure?

Text: Sigismund von Birken, 1626–81; tr. August Crull, 1845–1923, alt.
Tune: Melchior Vulpius, c. 1570–1615; setting: *Lutheran Book of Worship*, 1978

JESU KREUZ, LEIDEN UND PEIN
76 76 D

Is. 53:3–6; John 3:16; Rom. 12:1–2; 1 John 4:19

5 If my sins give me alarm
And my conscience grieve me,
Let Your cross my fear disarm;
Peace of conscience give me.
Help me see forgiveness won
By Your holy passion.
If for me He slays His Son,
God must have compassion!

6 Graciously my faith renew;
Help me bear my crosses,
Learning humbleness from You,
Peace mid pain and losses.
May I give You love for love!
Hear me, O my Savior,
That I may in heav'n above
Sing Your praise forever.

Ride On, Ride On in Majesty 441

1 Ride on, ride on in maj - es - ty! Hark! All the tribes ho - san - na cry. O Sav - ior meek, pur - sue Thy road, With palms and scat - tered gar - ments strowed.
2 Ride on, ride on in maj - es - ty! In low - ly pomp ride on to die. O Christ, Thy tri - umphs now be - gin O'er cap - tive death and con - quered sin.
3 Ride on, ride on in maj - es - ty! The an - gel ar - mies of the sky Look down with sad and won - d'ring eyes To see the ap - proach - ing sac - ri - fice.
4 Ride on, ride on in maj - es - ty! Thy last and fierc - est strife is nigh. The Fa - ther on His sap - phire throne A - waits His own a - noint - ed Son.
5 Ride on, ride on in maj - es - ty! In low - ly pomp ride on to die. Bow Thy meek head to mor - tal pain, Then take, O God, Thy pow'r and reign.

Text: Henry H. Milman, 1791–1868, alt.
Tune: *Musicalisch Hand-Buch der Geistlichen Melodien*, Hamburg, 1690, alt.;
setting: William H. Monk, 1823–89, alt.

WINCHESTER NEW
L M

John 12:12–16; Ps. 118:25–26; Zech. 9:9

442 All Glory, Laud, and Honor

Refrain

All glo - ry, laud, and hon - or To You, Re-deem-er, King,
To whom the lips of chil - dren Made sweet ho - san - nas ring.

1 You are the King of Is - rael And Da - vid's roy - al Son,
2 The com-pa - ny of an - gels Is prais - ing You on high,
3 The mul - ti - tude of pil - grims With palms be - fore You went;
4 To You be - fore Your pas - sion They sang their hymns of praise;
5 As You re-ceived their prais - es, Ac - cept the prayers we bring,

Now in the Lord's name com - ing, Our King and Bless - ed One.
And we with all cre - a - tion In cho - rus make re - ply.
Our praise and prayer and an - thems Be - fore You we pre - sent.
To You, now high ex - alt - ed, Our mel - o - dy we raise.
O Source of ev - 'ry bless - ing, Our good and gra - cious King.

Refrain

Text: Theodulf of Orléans, c. 762–821; tr. John Mason Neale, 1818–66, alt.
Tune: Melchior Teschner, 1584–1635, alt.; setting: *Lutheran Book of Worship: Select Hymns*, 1985

VALET WILL ICH DIR GEBEN
76 76 D

John 12:12–15; Ps. 118:26; Ps. 24:7–9

Hosanna, Loud Hosanna

443

1 Ho - san - na, loud ho - san - na, The lit - tle chil - dren sang;
2 From Ol - i - vet they fol - lowed Mid an ex - ul - tant crowd,
3 "Ho - san - na in the high - est!" That an - cient song we sing;
Through pil - lared court and tem - ple The love - ly an - them rang.
The vic - tor palm branch wav - ing And chant-ing clear and loud.
For Christ is our Re - deem - er, The Lord of heav'n our King.
To Je - sus, who had blessed them, Close fold - ed to His breast,
The Lord of earth and heav - en Rode on in low - ly state
Oh, may we ev - er praise Him With heart and life and voice
The chil - dren sang their prais - es, The sim-plest and the best.
Nor scorned that lit - tle chil - dren Should on His bid - ding wait.
And in His bliss - ful pres - ence E - ter - nal - ly re - joice!

"Hosanna" is a Hebrew word of praise meaning "save us now."

Text: Jeannette Threlfall, 1821–80, alt.
Tune: *Gesangbuch der Herzogl. Hofkapelle*, Württemberg, 1784; setting: *The Lutheran Hymnal*, 1941

ELLACOMBE
76 76 D

Matt. 21:15; Mark 11:1–11; Ps. 118:25–26

444 No Tramp of Soldiers' Marching Feet

1 No tramp of sol - diers' march - ing feet
2 And yet He comes. The chil - dren cheer;
3 What fad - ing flow'rs His road a - dorn;
4 Now He who bore for mor - tals' sake
With ban - ners and with drums,
With palms His path is strown.
The palms, how soon laid down!
The cross and all its pains
No sound of mu - sic's
With ev - 'ry step the
No bloom or leaf but
And chose a ser - vant's
mar - tial beat: "The King of glo - ry comes!"
cross draws near: The King of glo - ry's throne.
on - ly thorn The King of glo - ry's crown.
form to take, The King of glo - ry reigns.
To greet what pomp of king - ly pride
A - stride a colt He pass - es by
The sol - diers mock, the rab - ble cries,
Ho - san - na to the Sav - ior's name

Text: Timothy Dudley-Smith, b. 1926
Music: English; adapt. and harm. Ralph Vaughan Williams, 1872–1958, alt.

KINGSFOLD
C M D

Luke 19:36–40; John 19:14–19; Phil. 2:5–8; Rev. 19:11–16

No bells in tri-umph ring, No cit - y gates swing
As loud ho - san-nas ring, Or else the ver - y
The streets with tu-mult ring, As Pi - late to the
Till heav - en's raf - ters ring, And all the ran - somed
o - pen wide: "Be - hold, be - hold your King!"
stones would cry "Be - hold, be - hold your King!"
mob re - plies, "Be - hold, be - hold your King!"
host pro - claim "Be - hold, be - hold your King!"

Almighty and everlasting God, You sent Your Son, our Savior Jesus Christ, to take upon Himself our flesh and to suffer death upon the cross. Mercifully grant that we may follow the example of His great humility and patience and be made partakers of His resurrection; through the same Jesus Christ, our Lord, who lives and reigns with You and the Holy Spirit, one God, now and forever.

Collect for the Sunday of the Passion

---

445 When You Woke That Thursday Morning

1 When You woke that Thurs - day morn - ing, Sav - ior, teach - er, faith-ful friend, Thoughts of self and safe - ty scorn - ing, Know - ing how the day would end; Lamb of God, fore - told for a - ges, Now at last the hour had come When but One could pay sin's
2 Nev - er so a - lone and lone - ly, Long - ing with tor - ment-ed heart To be with Your dear ones on - ly For a qui - et hour a - part: Sin - less Lamb and fall - en crea - ture, One last pas - chal meal to eat, One last les - son as their
3 What was there that You could give them That would nev - er be out - spent, What great gift that would out - live them, What last will and tes - ta - ment? "Show Me and the world you love Me, Know Me as the Lamb of God: Do this in re - mem - brance
4 One in faith, in love u - nit - ed, All one bod - y, You the head, When we meet, by You in - vit - ed, You are with us, as You said. One with You and one an - oth - er In a u - ni - ty sub - lime, See in us Your sis - ter,
5 One day all the Church will cap - ture That bright vi - sion glo - ri - ous, And Your saints will know the rap - ture That Your heart de - sired for us, When the longed - for peace and u - nion Of the Great - est and the least Meet in joy - ous, blest com -

Setting available in hymn accompaniment edition.

Text: Jaroslav J. Vajda, 1919–2008
Tune: Marty Haugen, b. 1950

JOYOUS LIGHT
87 87 D

John 1:29, 36; 13:1–9

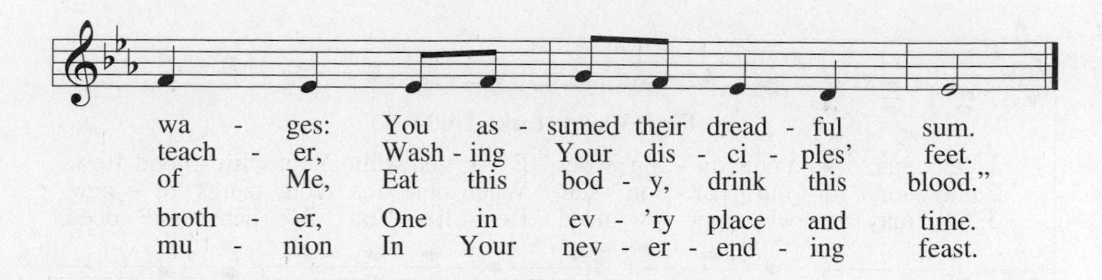
wa - ges: You as - sumed their dread - ful sum.
teach - er, Wash - ing Your dis - ci - ples' feet.
of Me, Eat this bod - y, drink this blood."
broth - er, One in ev - 'ry place and time.
mu - nion In Your nev - er - end - ing feast.

Jesus, Greatest at the Table 446

1 Je - sus, great - est at the ta - ble, The al - might - y Son of Man, Laid a - side His out - er cloth - ing, Poured some wa - ter in a pan; As the Twelve lay, hushed in si - lence, He the ser - vant's task be - gan.
2 Mar - vel how their Lord and teach - er Gent - ly taught them not to vie As He hum - bly knelt be - fore them, Dust - y feet to wash and dry, By His ten - der touch ex - press - ing True com - pas - sion from on high.
3 Je - sus took the role of ser - vant When up - on that grue - some span, For all hu - man sin He suf - fered As a vile and loath - some man; On the cross poured out like wa - ter To ful - fill the Fa - ther's plan.
4 Can we fath - om such deep mer - cy? Do we see what God has done? Who can grasp this great re - ver - sal: Love that gives His on - ly Son? Christ, the sin - less for the sin - ners, For the man - y dies the One.
5 Je - sus gave to His dis - ci - ples A com - mand - ment that was new: "Show My love to one an - oth - er, Do as I have done for you; All the world will know you love Me As you love each oth - er too."

Hymn accompaniment: 511

Text: Stephen P. Starke, b. 1955
Tune: David McCarthy, b. 1931

NEW MALDEN
87 87 87

John 13:1–17; Phil. 2:5–8; 2 Cor. 8:9; 1 John 4:9–11

447 Jesus, in Your Dying Woes

First Word: Luke 23:34
1 Je - sus, in Your dy - ing woes, E - ven while Your life-blood flows,
2 Sav - ior, for our par - don sue When our sins Your pangs re - new,
3 Oh, may we, who mer - cy need, Be like You in heart and deed,
Crav - ing par - don for Your foes:
For we know not what we do: Hear us, ho - ly Je - sus.
When with wrong our spir - its bleed:

Second Word: Luke 23:43

4 Jesus, pitying the sighs
Of the thief, who near You dies,
Promising him paradise:
Hear us, holy Jesus.

5 May we in our guilt and shame
Still Your love and mercy claim,
Calling humbly on Your name:
Hear us, holy Jesus.

6 May our hearts to You incline
And their thoughts Your cross entwine.
Cheer our souls with hope divine:
Hear us, holy Jesus.

Third Word: John 19:26–27

7 Jesus, loving to the end
Her whose heart Your sorrows rend,
And Your dearest human friend:
Hear us, holy Jesus.

8 May we in Your sorrows share,
For Your sake all peril dare,
And enjoy Your tender care:
Hear us, holy Jesus.

9 May we all Your loved ones be,
All one holy family,
Loving, since Your love we see:
Hear us, holy Jesus.

This hymn for Good Friday is based on the seven last words of Christ spoken from the cross.

Text: Thomas B. Pollock, 1836–96, alt.
Music: Bernhard Schumacher, 1886–1978

SEPTEM VERBA
777 6

Fourth Word: Matthew 27:46; Mark 15:34

10 Jesus, whelmed in fears unknown,
With our evil left alone,
While no light from heav'n is shown:
Hear us, holy Jesus.

11 When we seem in vain to pray
And our hope seems far away,
In the darkness be our stay:
Hear us, holy Jesus.

12 Though no Father seem to hear,
Though no light our spirits cheer,
May we know that God is near:
Hear us, holy Jesus.

Fifth Word: John 19:28

13 Jesus, in Your thirst and pain,
While Your wounds Your lifeblood drain,
Thirsting more our love to gain:
Hear us, holy Jesus.

14 Thirst for us in mercy still;
All Your holy work fulfill;
Satisfy Your loving will:
Hear us, holy Jesus.

15 May we thirst Your love to know.
Lead us in our sin and woe
Where the healing waters flow:
Hear us, holy Jesus.

Sixth Word: John 19:30

16 Jesus, all our ransom paid,
All Your Father's will obeyed;
By Your suff'rings perfect made:
Hear us, holy Jesus.

17 Save us in our soul's distress;
Be our help to cheer and bless
While we grow in holiness:
Hear us, holy Jesus.

18 Brighten all our heav'nward way
With an ever holier ray
Till we pass to perfect day:
Hear us, holy Jesus.

Seventh Word: Luke 23:46

19 Jesus, all Your labor vast,
All Your woe and conflict past,
Yielding up Your soul at last:
Hear us, holy Jesus.

20 When the death shades round us low'r,
Guard us from the tempter's pow'r,
Keep us in that trial hour:
Hear us, holy Jesus.

21 May Your life and death supply
Grace to live and grace to die,
Grace to reach the home on high:
Hear us, holy Jesus.

448 O Darkest Woe

1 O dark - est woe! Ye tears, forth flow! Has
2 O sor - row dread! Our God is dead, Up-
3 O child of woe: Who struck the blow That
4 Thy Bride - groom dead! God's Lamb has bled Up-
5 Such in - no - cence! His coun - te - nance A
earth so sad a won - der? God the Fa - ther's
on the cross ex - tend - ed. There His love en-
killed our gra - cious Mas - ter? "It was I," thy
on thy sin for - ev - er, Pour - ing out His
fount of faith un - dy - ing! Worlds on worlds canon - ly Son Now is bur - ied yon - der.
liv - ened us As His life was end - ed.
con - science cries, "I have wrought dis - as - ter!"
sin - less self In this vast en - deav - or.
not con - tain Grief at Him here ly - ing.

6 O Virgin's Son,
What Thou hast won
Is far beyond all telling:
How our God, detested, died,
Hell and devil felling.

7 O Jesus Christ,
Who sacrificed
Thy life for lifeless mortals:
Be my life in death and bring
Me to heaven's portals!

Text: Friedrich von Spee, 1591–1635, st. 1; Johann Rist, 1607–67, sts. 2–7;
tr. Catherine Winkworth, 1827–78, st. 1, alt.; tr. Joseph Herl, b. 1959, sts. 2–7
Tune: *Himmlische Harmony*, Mainz, 1628; setting: Joseph Herl, b. 1959

O TRAURIGKEIT
44 776

Matt. 27:57–60; 1 John 4:9–10; 1 Peter 1:18–19; Eph. 2:4–6

O Sacred Head, Now Wounded 449

1 O sa - cred Head, now wound - ed, With grief and shame weighed down,
2 What Thou, my Lord, hast suf - fered Was all for sin - ners' gain;
3 What lan-guage shall I bor - row To thank Thee, dear - est Friend,
4 Be Thou my con - so - la - tion, My shield, when I must die;
Now scorn-ful-ly sur - round - ed With thorns, Thine on - ly crown.
Mine, mine was the trans - gres - sion, But Thine the dead - ly pain.
For this Thy dy - ing sor - row, Thy pit - y with - out end?
Re - mind me of Thy pas - sion When my last hour draws nigh.
O sa - cred Head, what glo - ry, What bliss, till now was Thine!
Lo, here I fall, my Sav - ior! 'Tis I de - serve Thy place;
O make me Thine for - ev - er! And should I faint - ing be,
Mine eyes shall then be - hold Thee, Up - on Thy cross shall dwell,
Yet, though de - spised and gor - y, I joy to call Thee mine.
Look on me with Thy fa - vor, And grant to me Thy grace.
Lord, let me nev - er, nev - er, Out - live my love for Thee.
My heart by faith en - fold Thee. Who di - eth thus dies well.

Text: attr. Bernard of Clairvaux, 1091–1153; German version, Paul Gerhardt, 1607–76; tr. *The Lutheran Hymnal*, 1941, alt.
Tune: Hans Leo Hassler, 1564–1612; setting: Johann Sebastian Bach, 1685–1750

HERZLICH TUT MICH VERLANGEN (Isorhythmic)
76 76 D

Ps. 22:6–8; Is. 53:4–5; John 10:14–15, 27–28; Heb. 12:2

450 O Sacred Head, Now Wounded

1 O sa - cred Head, now wound - ed, With grief and shame weighed down,
2 How pale Thou art with an - guish, With sore a - buse and scorn!
3 What Thou, my Lord, hast suf - fered Was all for sin - ners' gain;
4 My Shep-herd, now re - ceive me; My Guard-ian, own me Thine.
Now scorn - ful - ly sur-round - ed With thorns, Thine on - ly crown.
How doth Thy face now lan - guish That once was bright as morn!
Mine, mine was the trans-gres - sion, But Thine the dead - ly pain.
Great bless - ings Thou didst give me, O Source of gifts di - vine.
O sa - cred Head, what glo - ry, What bliss, till now was Thine!
Grim death, with cru - el rig - or, Hath robbed Thee of Thy life;
Lo, here I fall, my Sav - ior! 'Tis I de - serve Thy place;
Thy lips have of - ten fed me With words of truth and love;
Yet, though de-spised and gor - y, I joy to call Thee mine.
Thus Thou hast lost Thy vig - or, Thy strength, in this sad strife.
Look on me with Thy fa - vor, And grant to me Thy grace.
Thy Spir - it oft hath led me To heav'n - ly joys a - bove.

Text: attr. Bernard of Clairvaux, 1091–1153; German version,
Paul Gerhardt, 1607–76; tr. *The Lutheran Hymnal*, 1941, alt.
Tune: Hans Leo Hassler, 1564–1612; setting: *The Lutheran Hymnal*, 1941

HERZLICH TUT MICH VERLANGEN (Rhythmic)
76 76 D

Ps. 22:6–8; Is. 53:4–5; John 10:14–15, 27–28; Heb. 12:2

5 What language shall I borrow
To thank Thee, dearest Friend,
For this Thy dying sorrow,
Thy pity without end?
O make me Thine forever!
And should I fainting be,
Lord, let me never, never,
Outlive my love for Thee.

6 My Savior, be Thou near me
When death is at my door;
Then let Thy presence cheer me,
Forsake me nevermore!
When soul and body languish,
O leave me not alone,
But take away mine anguish
By virtue of Thine own!

7 Be Thou my consolation,
My shield, when I must die;
Remind me of Thy passion
When my last hour draws nigh.
Mine eyes shall then behold Thee,
Upon Thy cross shall dwell,
My heart by faith enfold Thee.
Who dieth thus dies well.

He was wounded for our transgressions; He was crushed for our iniquities; upon Him was the chastisement that brought us peace, and with His stripes we are healed.

Isaiah 53:5

---

451 Stricken, Smitten, and Afflicted

1 Strick-en, smit-ten, and af - flict - ed, See Him dy - ing on the tree! 'Tis the Christ, by man re - ject - ed; Yes, my soul, 'tis He, 'tis He! 'Tis the long - ex - pect - ed Proph - et, Da - vid's Son, yet Da-vid's Lord; Proofs I
2 Tell me, ye who hear Him groan - ing, Was there ev - er grief like His? Friends through fear His cause dis - own - ing, Foes in - sult - ing His dis - tress; Man - y hands were raised to wound Him, None would in - ter - vene to save; But the
3 Ye who think of sin but light - ly Nor sup - pose the e - vil great Here may view its na - ture right - ly, Here its guilt may es - ti - mate. Mark the sac - ri - fice ap - point - ed, See who bears the aw - ful load; 'Tis the
4 Here we have a firm foun - da - tion, Here the ref - uge of the lost: Christ, the Rock of our sal - va - tion, Is the name of which we boast; Lamb of God, for sin - ners wound - ed, Sac - ri - fice to can - cel guilt! None shall

Text: Thomas Kelly, 1769–1855, alt.
Tune: *Geistliche Volkslieder*, Paderborn, 1850; setting: Paul G. Bunjes, 1914–98, alt.

O MEIN JESU, ICH MUSS STERBEN
87 87 D

Is. 53:3–6; Acts 4:11–12; Rom. 4:25

O Perfect Life of Love 452

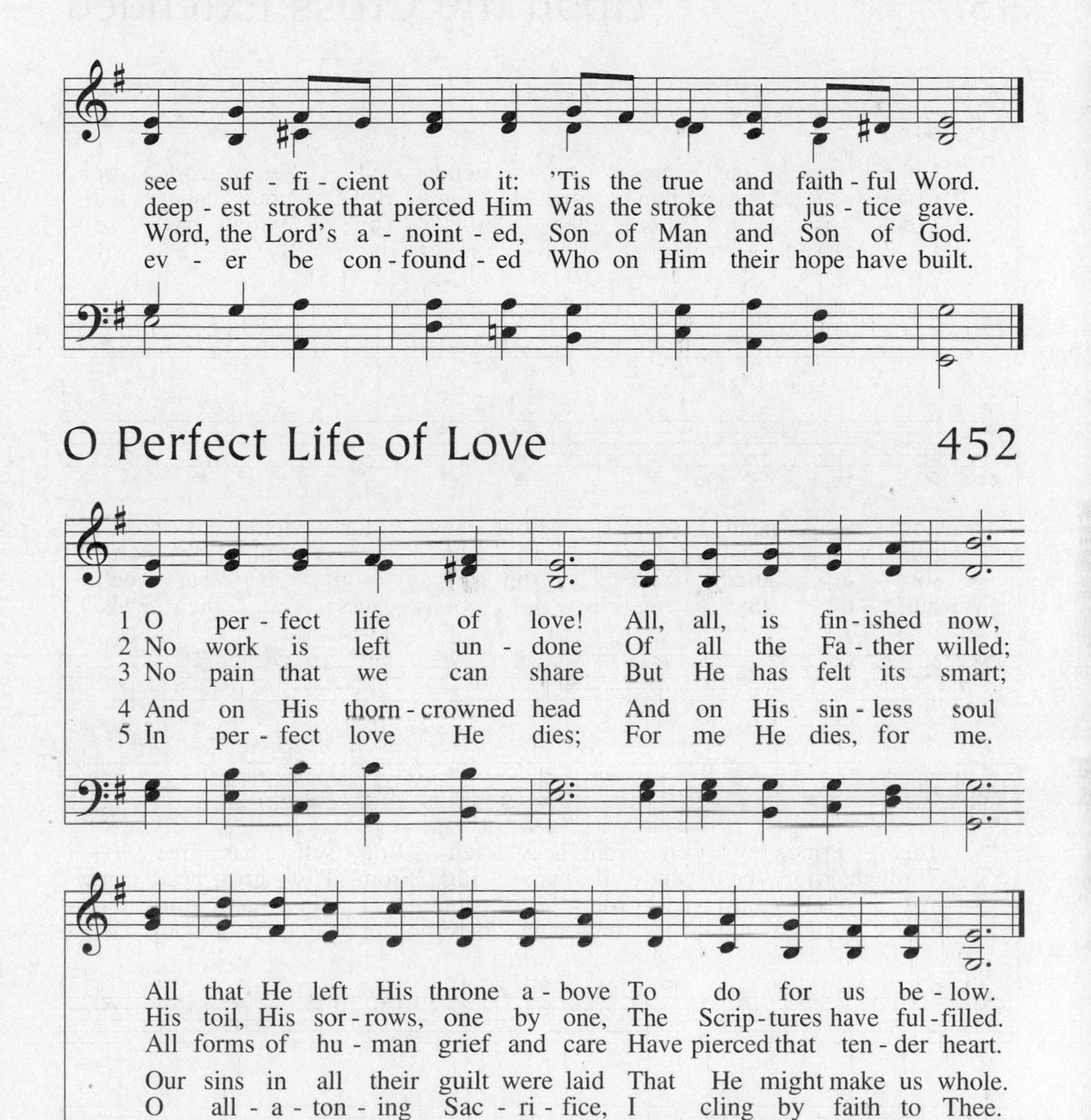
see suf - fi - cient of it: 'Tis the true and faith - ful Word.
deep - est stroke that pierced Him Was the stroke that jus - tice gave.
Word, the Lord's a - noint - ed, Son of Man and Son of God.
ev - er be con - found - ed Who on Him their hope have built.
1 O per - fect life of love! All, all, is fin - ished now,
2 No work is left un - done Of all the Fa - ther willed;
3 No pain that we can share But He has felt its smart;
4 And on His thorn - crowned head And on His sin - less soul
5 In per - fect love He dies; For me He dies, for me.
All that He left His throne a - bove To do for us be - low.
His toil, His sor - rows, one by one, The Scrip - tures have ful - filled.
All forms of hu - man grief and care Have pierced that ten - der heart.
Our sins in all their guilt were laid That He might make us whole.
O all - a - ton - ing Sac - ri - fice, I cling by faith to Thee.

6 In ev'ry time of need,
Before the judgment throne,
Thy work, O Lamb of God, I'll plead,
Thy merits, not mine own.

7 Yet work, O Lord, in me
As Thou for me hast wrought;
And let my love the answer be
To grace Thy love has brought.

Text: Henry W. Baker, 1821–77, alt.
Tune: William Daman, c. 1540–91; setting: *The Lutheran Hymnal*, 1941

SOUTHWELL
S M

John 19:30; Is. 53:3–12; Psalm 22; Luke 18:31–33

453 Upon the Cross Extended

1 Up - on the cross ex - tend - ed See, world, your Lord sus - pend - ed. Your Sav - ior yields His breath. The Prince of Life from heav - en Him - self has free - ly giv - en To shame and blows and bit - ter death.
2 Come, see these things and pon - der, Your soul will fill with won - der As blood streams from each pore. Through grief be - yond all know - ing From His great heart came flow - ing Sighs well - ing from its deep - est core.
3 Who is it, Lord, that bruised You? Who has so sore a - bused You And caused You all Your woe? We all must make con - fes - sion Of sin and dire trans - gres - sion While You no ways of e - vil know.
4 I caused Your grief and sigh - ing By e - vils mul - ti - ply - ing As count - less as the sands. I caused the woes un - num - bered With which Your soul is cum - bered, Your sor - rows raised by wick - ed hands.

Text: Paul Gerhardt, 1607–76; tr. John Kelly, 1833–90, alt.
Tune: Heinrich Isaac, c. 1450–1517; setting: *The Lutheran Hymnal*, 1941

O WELT, ICH MUSS DICH LASSEN
776 778

Isaiah 53; Heb. 9:28; 1 Peter 2:21–25

5 Your soul in griefs unbounded,
Your head with thorns surrounded,
You died to ransom me.
The cross for me enduring,
The crown for me securing,
You healed my wounds and set me free.

6 Your cords of love, my Savior,
Bind me to You forever,
I am no longer mine.
To You I gladly tender
All that my life can render
And all I have to You resign.

7 Your cross I place before me;
Its saving pow'r restore me,
Sustain me in the test.
It will, when life is ending,
Be guiding and attending
My way to Your eternal rest.

Almighty God, graciously behold this Your family for whom our Lord Jesus Christ was willing to be betrayed and delivered into the hands of sinful men to suffer death upon the cross; through the same Jesus Christ, Your Son, our Lord, who lives and reigns with You and the Holy Spirit, one God, now and forever. Collect for Good Friday

---

454 Sing, My Tongue, the Glorious Battle

1 Sing, my tongue, the glo - rious bat - tle; Sing the end - ing
2 Tell how, when at length the full - ness Of the ap-point - ed
3 Thus, with thir - ty years ac - com-plished, He went forth from
4 Faith - ful cross, true sign of tri - umph, Be for all the
△ 5 Un - to God be praise and glo - ry; To the Fa - ther
of the fray. Now a - bove the cross, the tro - phy,
time was come, He, the Word, was born of wom - an,
Naz - a - reth, Des - tined, ded - i - cat - ed, will - ing,
no - blest tree; None in fo - liage, none in blos - som,
and the Son, To the e - ter - nal Spir - it hon - or
Sound the loud tri - um - phant lay; Tell how Christ, the
Left for us His Fa - ther's home, Blazed the path of
Did His work, and met His death; Like a lamb He
None in fruit thine e - qual be; Sym - bol of the
Now and ev - er - more be done; Praise and glo - ry
world's re - deem - er, As a vic - tim won the day.
true o - be - dience, Shone as light a - midst the gloom.
hum - bly yield - ed On the cross His dy - ing breath.
world's re - demp - tion, For the weight that hung on thee!
in the high - est While the time - less a - ges run.

Hymn accompaniment: 521

Text: Venantius Honorius Fortunatus, c. 530–609; tr. John Mason Neale, 1818–66, alt.
Tune: Carl F. Schalk, b. 1929

FORTUNATUS NEW
87 87 87

Ps. 98:1–2; Is. 52:9–10; Gal. 4:4; John 19:30

The Royal Banners Forward Go 455

1 The roy - al ban - ners for - ward go;
2 Where deep for us the spear was dyed,
3 Ful - filled is all that Da - vid told
4 On whose hard arms, so wide - ly flung,
The cross shows forth re - demp - tion's flow, Where He, by
Life's tor - rent rush - ing from His side, To wash us
In sure pro - phet - ic song of old, That God the
The weight of this world's ran - som hung, The price of
whom our flesh was made, Our ran - som
in the pre - cious flood Where flowed the
na - tions' king should be And reign in
hu - man - kind to pay And spoil the
in His flesh has paid:
wa - ter and the blood.
tri - umph from the tree,
spoil - er of his prey. A - men.

5 O tree of beauty, tree most fair,
Ordained those holy limbs to bear:
Gone is thy shame, each crimsoned bough
Proclaims the King of Glory now.

△ 6 To Thee, eternal Three in One,
Let homage meet by all be done;
As by the cross Thou dost restore,
So guide and keep us evermore.
Amen.

Setting available in hymn accompaniment edition.

Text: Venantius Honorius Fortunatus, c. 530–609; tr. John Mason Neale, 1818–66, sts. 1–4, alt.; tr. *The Hymnal 1982*, sts. 5–6
Tune: Paul D. Weber, b. 1949

VEXILLA REGIS NOVA
L M

Is. 11:10, 12; 1 Peter 2:24; Matt. 20:28

456 Were You There

1 Were you there when they cru - ci - fied my Lord? Were you
2 Were you there when they nailed Him to the tree? Were you
3 Were you there when they laid Him in the tomb? Were you
4 Were you there when God raised Him from the tomb? Were you
there when they cru - ci - fied my Lord? Oh . . .
there when they nailed Him to the tree? Oh . . .
there when they laid Him in the tomb? Oh . . .
there when God raised Him from the tomb? Oh . . .
Some - times it caus - es me to trem-ble, trem-ble, trem-ble.
Some - times it caus - es me to trem-ble, trem-ble, trem-ble.
Some - times it caus - es me to trem-ble, trem-ble, trem-ble.
Some - times it caus - es me to trem-ble, trem-ble, trem-ble.
Were you there when they cru - ci - fied my Lord?
Were you there when they nailed Him to the tree?
Were you there when they laid Him in the tomb?
Were you there when God raised Him from the tomb?

Text: African American spiritual, 19th cent., alt.
Tune: African American spiritual, 19th cent., alt.; setting: C. Winfred Douglas, 1867–1944

WERE YOU THERE
10 10 14 10

Matt. 28:6; Luke 22:33, 53; Rom. 6:3–4

Jesus Christ Is Risen Today 457

1 Je - sus Christ is ris'n to - day,
2 Hymns of praise then let us sing,
3 But the pains which He en - dured,
△ 4 Sing we to our God a - bove,
Al - le - lu - ia!
Our tri - um - phant ho - ly day,
Un - to Christ, our heav'n - ly king,
Our sal - va - tion have pro - cured;
Praise e - ter - nal as His love;
Al - le - lu - ia!
Who did once up - on the cross,
Who en - dured the cross and grave,
Now a - bove the sky He's king,
Praise Him, all ye heav'n - ly host,
Al - le - lu - ia!
Suf - fer to re - deem our loss.
Sin - ners to re - deem and save.
Where the an - gels ev - er sing.
Fa - ther, Son, and Ho - ly Ghost.
Al - le - lu - ia!

Text: Latin, 14th cent., sts. 1–3; Charles Wesley, 1707–88, st. 4; tr. *Lyra Davidica*, London, 1708, sts. 1–3, alt.
Tune: *Lyra Davidica*, London, 1708; setting: *The Lutheran Hymnal*, 1941

EASTER HYMN
77 77 and alleluias

Luke 24:6–7; 1 Cor. 15:20; Rev. 1:18; Psalm 98

458 Christ Jesus Lay in Death's Strong Bands

1 Christ Je - sus lay in death's strong bands For our of - fens - es giv - en; But now at God's right hand He stands And brings us life from heav - en. There - fore let us joy - ful be And sing to God right thank - ful - ly
2 No son of man could con - quer death, Such ru - in sin had wrought us. No in - no - cence was found on earth, And there - fore death had brought us In - to bond - age from of old And ev - er grew more strong and bold
3 Christ Je - sus, God's own Son, came down, His peo - ple to de - liv - er; De - stroy - ing sin, He took the crown From death's pale brow for - ev - er: Stripped of pow'r, no more it reigns; An emp - ty form a - lone re - mains;
4 It was a strange and dread - ful strife When life and death con - tend - ed; The vic - to - ry re - mained with life, The reign of death was end - ed. Ho - ly Scrip - ture plain - ly saith That death is swal - lowed up by death,

Text: Martin Luther, 1483–1546; tr. Richard Massie, 1800–87, alt.
Tune: *Geystliche gesangk Buchleyn*, Wittenberg, 1524, ed. Johann Walter;
setting: *Lutheran Book of Worship*, 1978

CHRIST LAG IN TODESBANDEN
87 87 78 74

Acts 2:24; 1 Cor. 15:54–57; 1 Cor. 5:7b; 2 Tim. 1:10

Loud songs of al - le - lu - ia! Al - le - lu - ia!
And held us as its cap - tive. Al - le - lu - ia!
Its sting is lost for - ev - er. Al - le - lu - ia!
Its sting is lost for - ev - er. Al - le - lu - ia!

5 Here our true Paschal Lamb we see,
Whom God so freely gave us;
He died on the accursèd tree—
So strong His love—to save us.
See, His blood now marks our door;
Faith points to it; death passes o'er,
And Satan cannot harm us.
Alleluia!

6 So let us keep the festival
To which the Lord invites us;
Christ is Himself the joy of all,
The sun that warms and lights us.
Now His grace to us imparts
Eternal sunshine to our hearts;
The night of sin is ended.
Alleluia!

7 Then let us feast this Easter Day
On Christ, the bread of heaven;
The Word of grace has purged away
The old and evil leaven.
Christ alone our souls will feed;
He is our meat and drink indeed;
Faith lives upon no other!
Alleluia!

459 Christ Is Arisen

1 Christ is a - ris - en From the grave's dark pris - on.
So let our joy rise full and free; Christ our com-fort true will be.
Al - le-lu - ia! 2 Were Christ not a - ris - en,
Then death were still our pris - on. Now, with Him to life re-stored,
We praise the Fa-ther of our Lord. Al - le-lu - ia!
3 Al - le - lu - ia, al - le - lu - ia,
al - le - lu - ia! Now let our joy rise full and free;
Christ our com - fort true will be. Al - le-lu - ia!

Setting available in hymn accompaniment edition.

Text: German, 12th–15th cent.; tr. Martin L. Seltz, 1909–67, alt.
Tune: Latin, c. 1100; *Geistliche Lieder auffs new gebessert*, Wittenberg, 1533, ed. Joseph Klug

CHRIST IST ERSTANDEN
Peculiar meter

1 Cor. 15:17–20; Is. 26:19

Christians, to the Paschal Victim 460

Victimae Paschali

Christians, to the Paschal Victim
Offer your thankful praises!
The Lamb the sheep has ransomed:
Christ, who only is sinless,
Reconciling sinners to the Father.
Death and life have contended
In that combat stupendous:
The Prince of life, who died,
Reigns immortal.

(459, Stanza 1)

"Speak, Mary, declaring
What you saw when wayfaring."
"The tomb of Christ, who is living,
The glory of Jesus' resurrection;
Bright angels attesting,
The shroud and napkin resting.
My Lord, my hope, is arisen;
To Galilee He goes before you."

(459, Stanza 2)

Christ indeed from death is risen,
Our new life obtaining.
Have mercy, victor King, ever reigning!
Amen. Alleluia.

(459, Stanza 3)

Each stanza of the hymn "Christ Is Arisen" (459) may be sung following the corresponding section of the Victimae Paschali. *Music available in hymn accompaniment edition.*

Text: attr. Wipo of Burgundy, d. c. 1050; tr. *The English Hymnal*, 1906, alt.

VICTIMAE PASCHALI
Peculiar meter

1 Cor. 15:17–20; Mark 16:1–8

461 I Know That My Redeemer Lives

1 I know that my Re - deem - er lives; What com-fort this sweet sen - tence gives! He lives, He lives, who once was dead; He lives, my ev - er - liv - ing head.
2 He lives tri - um - phant from the grave; He lives e - ter - nal - ly to save; He lives all - glo - rious in the sky; He lives ex - alt - ed there on high.
3 He lives to bless me with His love; He lives to plead for me a - bove; He lives my hun - gry soul to feed; He lives to help in time of need.
4 He lives to grant me rich sup - ply; He lives to guide me with His eye; He lives to com - fort me when faint; He lives to hear my soul's com - plaint.

5 He lives to silence all my fears;
He lives to wipe away my tears;
He lives to calm my troubled heart;
He lives all blessings to impart.

6 He lives, my kind, wise, heav'nly friend;
He lives and loves me to the end;
He lives, and while He lives, I'll sing;
He lives, my Prophet, Priest, and King.

7 He lives and grants me daily breath;
He lives, and I shall conquer death;
He lives my mansion to prepare;
He lives to bring me safely there.

8 He lives, all glory to His name!
He lives, my Jesus, still the same;
Oh, the sweet joy this sentence gives:
I know that my Redeemer lives!

Text: Samuel Medley, 1738–99, abr.
Tune: attr. John C. Hatton, d. 1793; setting: *The Lutheran Hymnal*, 1941

DUKE STREET
L M

Job 19:25–27; Col. 1:18; Heb. 7:25; John 14:2–3

All the Earth with Joy Is Sounding 462

1 All the earth with joy is sound - ing: Christ has ris - en
2 Christ, the dev - il's might un - wind - ing, Leaves be-hind His
3 Je - sus, au - thor of sal - va - tion, Shared in our hu -
4 Praise the Lord, His reign com-menc - es, Reign of life and
from the dead! He, the great - er Jo - nah, bound-ing
bor - rowed tomb. Strong - er He, the strong man bind - ing,
man - i - ty; Crowned with ra - diant ex - al - ta - tion,
lib - er - ty— Pas - chal Lamb, for our of - fens - es,
From the grave, His three - day bed, Wins the prize:
Takes, dis - arms his house of doom; In the rout
Now He shares His vic - to - ry! From His face
Slain and raised to set us free! Ev - er - more
Death's de - mise— Songs of tri - umph fill the skies.
Cast - ing out Pow'rs of dark - ness, sin, and doubt.
Shines the grace Meant for all our fall - en race.
Bow be - fore Christ, the Lord of Life a - dore!

Jesus gave the people of His day "the sign of Jonah," pointing them to the day when He would rise from the grave. By His death and resurrection, Christ has indeed plundered the devil's house and won the victory.

Text: Stephen P. Starke, b. 1955
Music: Herbert Howells, 1892–1983

MICHAEL
87 87 33 7

Matt. 12:39–41; Mark 3:27; Heb. 2:7–15; 12:2

463 Christ the Lord Is Risen Today; Alleluia

1 Christ the Lord is ris'n to - day;
2 For the sheep the Lamb has bled,
3 Hail, the vic - tim un - de - filed,
4 Chris - tians, on this ho - ly day,
Al - le - lu - ia!
Chris - tians, has - ten on your way;
Sin - less in the sin - ner's stead.
God and sin - ners rec - on - ciled,
All your grate - ful hom - age pay;
Al - le - lu - ia!
Of - fer praise with love re - plete,
Christ the Lord is ris'n on high;
When con - tend - ing death and life,
Christ the Lord is ris'n on high;
Al - le - lu - ia!
At the pas - chal vic - tim's feet.
Now He lives, no more to die.
Met in strange and awe - some strife.
Now He lives, no more to die.
Al - le - lu - ia!

Text: attr. Wipo of Burgundy, d. c. 1050; tr. Jane E. Leeson, 1809–81, alt.
Tune: Robert Williams, c. 1781–1821; setting: John Roberts, 1822–77

LLANFAIR
77 77 and alleluias

Matt. 28:5–7; 1 Cor. 5:7–8; John 1:29; Rom. 6:9

The Strife Is O'er, the Battle Done 464

Refrain
Al - le - lu - ia, al - le - lu - ia, al - le - lu - ia!
1 The strife is o'er, the bat - tle done;
2 The pow'rs of death have done their worst,
3 The three sad days have quick - ly sped,
4 He broke the age - bound chains of hell;
5 Lord, by the stripes which wound - ed Thee,
Now is the vic - tor's tri - umph won;
But Christ their le - gions hath dis - persed.
He ris - es glo - rious from the dead.
The bars from heav'n's high por - tals fell.
From death's dread sting Thy ser - vants free
The Refrain is repeated after st. 5.
Now be the song of praise be - gun. Al - le - lu - ia!
Let shouts of ho - ly joy out - burst. Al - le - lu - ia!
All glo - ry to our ris - en Head! Al - le - lu - ia!
Let hymns of praise His tri - umph tell. Al - le - lu - ia!
That we may live and sing to Thee. Al - le - lu - ia!

The Refrain is sung once at the beginning of the hymn and a second time at the conclusion of the hymn.

Text: *Symphonia Sirenum Selectarum*, Köln, 1695; tr. Francis Pott, 1832–1909, alt.
Tune: Giovanni P. da Palestrina, c. 1525–94, adapt.; setting: *Hymns Ancient and Modern*, 1861

VICTORY
888 and alleluias

1 Cor. 15:55–57; 2 Tim. 1:10; Eph. 2:1, 4–6; Is. 53:5

465 Now All the Vault of Heaven Resounds

1 Now all the vault of heav'n re - sounds In praise of love that still a - bounds: "Christ has tri - umphed! He is liv - ing!" Sing, choirs of an - gels, loud and clear! Re - peat their song of glo - ry
2 E - ter - nal is the gift He brings, There - fore our heart with rap - ture sings: "Christ has tri - umphed! He is liv - ing!" Now still He comes to give us life And by His pres - ence stills all
3 O fill us, Lord, with daunt - less love; Set heart and will on things a - bove That we con - quer through Your tri - umph; Grant grace suf - fi - cient for life's day That by our lives we tru - ly
△ 4 A - dor - ing prais - es now we bring And with the heav'n - ly bless - ed sing: "Christ has tri - umphed! Al - le - lu - ia!" Be to the Fa - ther and our Lord, To Spir - it blest, most ho - ly

Text: Paul Z. Strodach, 1876–1947, alt.
Tune: *Geistliche Kirchengesäng*, Köln, 1623; setting: Ralph Vaughan Williams, 1872–1958

LASST UNS ERFREUEN
888 888 and alleluias

Rev. 5:13; 7:11–12; Rom. 8:11; Col. 3:1–12; 1 Cor. 15:57

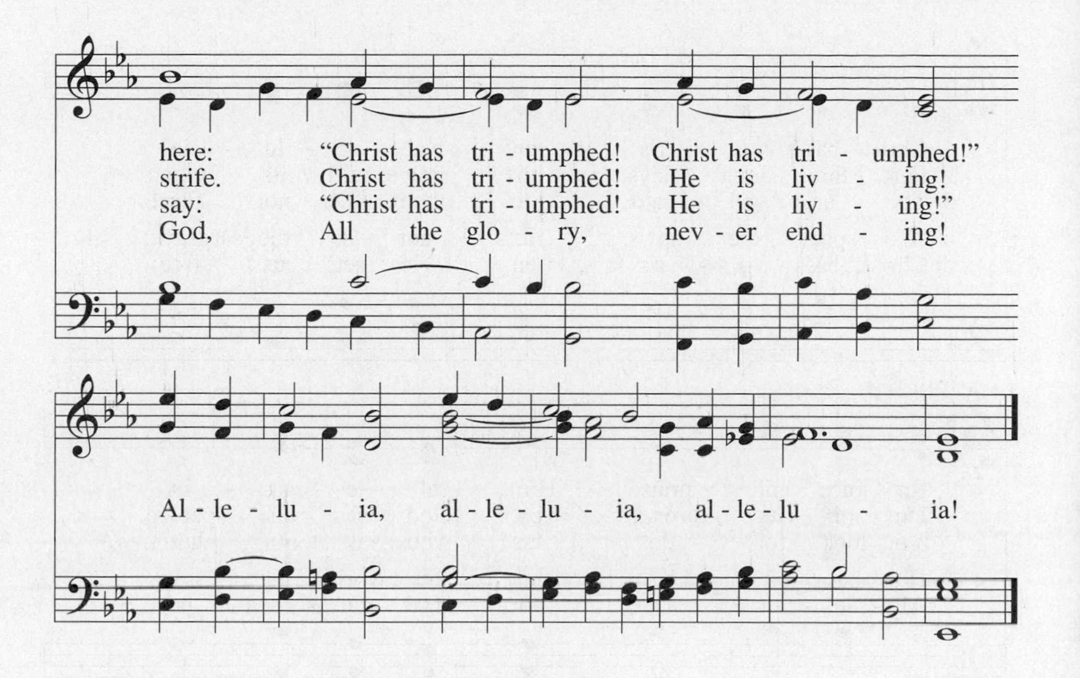
here: "Christ has tri - umphed! Christ has tri - umphed!"
strife. Christ has tri - umphed! He is liv - ing!
say: "Christ has tri - umphed! He is liv - ing!"
God, All the glo - ry, nev - er end - ing!
Al - le - lu - ia, al - le - lu - ia, al - le - lu - ia!

Almighty God, through Your only-begotten Son, Jesus Christ, You overcame death and opened to us the gate of everlasting life. We humbly pray that we may live before You in righteousness and purity forever; through the same Jesus Christ, our Lord, who lives and reigns with You and the Holy Spirit, one God, now and forever.

Collect for Easter Sunrise

466 Christ Has Arisen, Alleluia

1 Christ has a - ris - en, al - le - lu - ia.
2 For three long days the grave did its worst
3 The an - gel said to them, "Do not fear!
4 "Go spread the news: He's not in the grave;
5 Christ has a - ris - en; He sets us free;
Re - joice and praise Him, al - le - lu - ia.
Un - til its strength by God was dis - persed.
You look for Je - sus who is not here.
He has a - ris - en this world to save.
Al - le - lu - ia, to Him prais - es be.
For our Re - deem - er burst from the tomb,
He who gives life did death un - der - go;
See for your - selves the tomb is all bare;
Je - sus' re - deem - ing la - bors are done;
Je - sus is liv - ing! Let us all sing;
E - ven from death, dis - pel - ling its gloom.
And in its con - quest His might did show.
On - ly the grave cloths are ly - ing there."
E - ven the bat - tle with sin is won."
He reigns tri - um - phant, heav - en - ly King.

Text: Bernard Kyamanywa, b. 1938; tr. Howard S. Olson, 1922–2010
Music: Tanzanian

MFURAHINI HALELUYA
99 99 and refrain

Matt. 28:5–7; 1 Cor. 15:55–57

Refrain
Let us sing praise to Him with end - less joy;
Death's fear - ful sting He has come to de - stroy.
Our sin for - giv - ing, al - le - lu - ia!
Je - sus is liv - ing, al - le - lu - ia!

467 Awake, My Heart, with Gladness

1 A - wake, my heart, with glad - ness, See what to - day is done;
2 The foe in tri - umph shout - ed When Christ lay in the tomb;
3 This is a sight that glad - dens—What peace it doth im - part!
4 Now hell, its prince, the dev - il, Of all their pow'r are shorn;
Now, af - ter gloom and sad - ness, Comes forth the glo - rious sun.
But lo, he now is rout - ed, His boast is turned to gloom.
Now noth - ing ev - er sad - dens The joy with - in my heart.
Now I am safe from e - vil, And sin I laugh to scorn.
My Sav - ior there was laid Where our bed must be made
For Christ a - gain is free; In glo - rious vic - to - ry
No gloom shall ev - er shake, No foe shall ev - er take
Grim death with all its might Can - not my soul af - fright;
When to the realms of light Our spir - it wings its flight.
He who is strong to save Has tri - umphed o'er the grave.
The hope which God's own Son In love for me has won.
It is a pow'r - less form, How - e'er it rave and storm.

Text: Paul Gerhardt, 1607–76; tr. John Kelly, 1833–90, alt.
Tune: Johann Crüger, 1598–1662; setting: *Lutheran Service Book*, 2006

AUF, AUF, MEIN HERZ
76 76 66 66

Col. 2:15; Rom. 8:35–39; Gen. 3:15; Rom. 6:4

5 The world against me rages,
Its fury I disdain;
Though bitter war it wages,
Its work is all in vain.
My heart from care is free,
No trouble troubles me.
Misfortune now is play,
And night is bright as day.

6 Now I will cling forever
To Christ, my Savior true;
My Lord will leave me never,
Whate'er He passes through.
He rends death's iron chain;
He breaks through sin and pain;
He shatters hell's grim thrall;
I follow Him through all.

7 He brings me to the portal
That leads to bliss untold,
Whereon this rhyme immortal
Is found in script of gold:
"Who there My cross has shared
Finds here a crown prepared;
Who there with Me has died
Shall here be glorified."

468

I Am Content! My Jesus Ever Lives

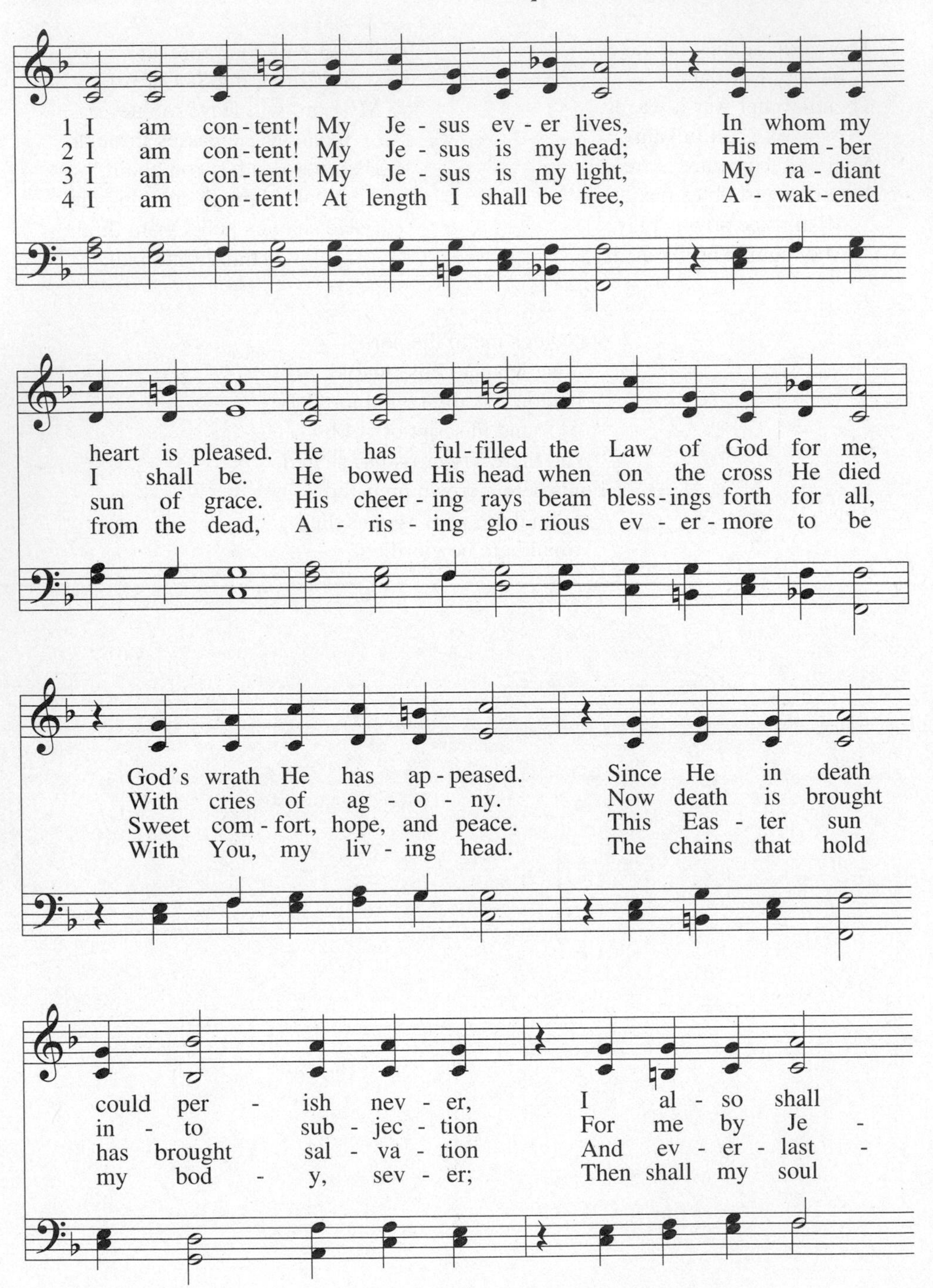
1 I am con-tent! My Je - sus ev - er lives, In whom my
2 I am con-tent! My Je - sus is my head; His mem - ber
3 I am con-tent! My Je - sus is my light, My ra - diant
4 I am con-tent! At length I shall be free, A - wak-ened
heart is pleased. He has ful-filled the Law of God for me,
I shall be. He bowed His head when on the cross He died
sun of grace. His cheer - ing rays beam bless-ings forth for all,
from the dead, A - ris - ing glo - rious ev - er - more to be
God's wrath He has ap - peased. Since He in death
With cries of ag - o - ny. Now death is brought
Sweet com - fort, hope, and peace. This Eas - ter sun
With You, my liv - ing head. The chains that hold
could per - ish nev - er, I al - so shall
in - to sub - jec - tion For me by Je -
has brought sal - va - tion And ev - er - last -
my bod - y, sev - er; Then shall my soul

Text: attr. Johann Joachim Möller, 1660–1733; tr. August Crull, 1845–1923, alt.
Tune: Johann Rudolph Ahle, 1625–73; setting: *The Lutheran Hymnal*, 1941

ES IST GENUG
10 6 10 6 99 44

John 11:25–26; Rom. 6:4–11; 8:1–4; 1 Cor. 15:55–57

not die for - ev - er. I am con - tent! I am con - tent!
sus' res - ur - rec - tion. I am con - tent! I am con - tent!
ing ex - ul - ta - tion. I am con - tent! I am con - tent!
re - joice for - ev - er. I am con - tent! I am con - tent!

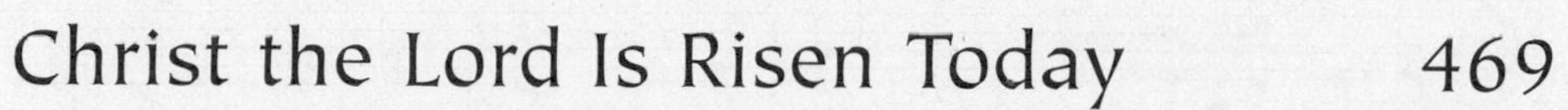

Christ the Lord Is Risen Today 469

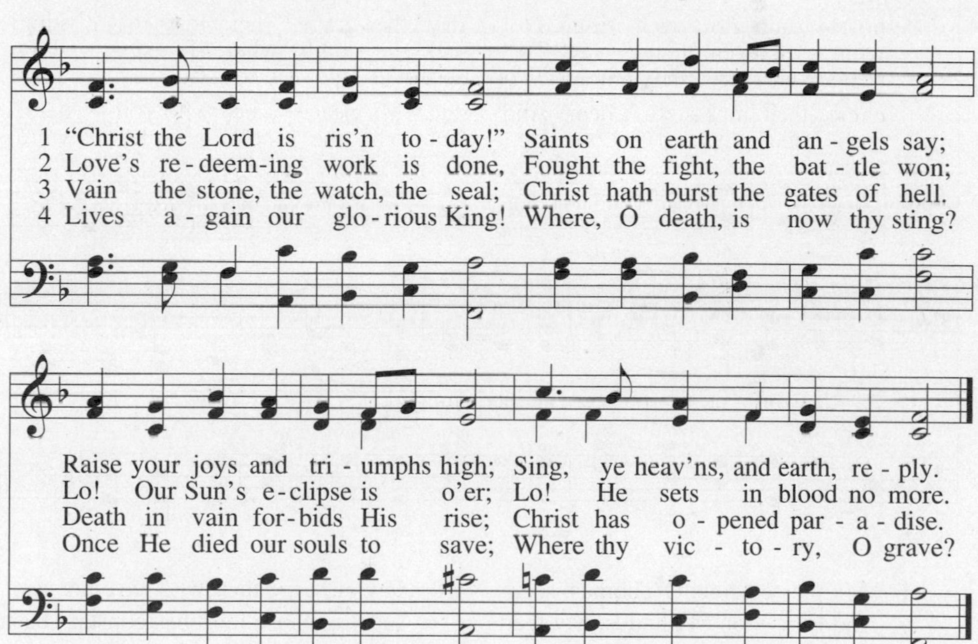
1 "Christ the Lord is ris'n to - day!" Saints on earth and an - gels say;
2 Love's re - deem - ing work is done, Fought the fight, the bat - tle won;
3 Vain the stone, the watch, the seal; Christ hath burst the gates of hell.
4 Lives a - gain our glo - rious King! Where, O death, is now thy sting?
Raise your joys and tri - umphs high; Sing, ye heav'ns, and earth, re - ply.
Lo! Our Sun's e - clipse is o'er; Lo! He sets in blood no more.
Death in vain for - bids His rise; Christ has o - pened par - a - dise.
Once He died our souls to save; Where thy vic - to - ry, O grave?

5 Soar we now where Christ has led;
Foll'wing our exalted Head.
Made like Him, like Him we rise;
Ours the cross, the grave, the skies.

6 Hail the Lord of earth and heav'n!
Praise to Thee by both be giv'n!
Thee we greet triumphant now:
Hail, the resurrection, Thou!

Text: Charles Wesley, 1707–88, alt.
Tune: French, 13th cent.; setting: *The Lutheran Hymnal*, 1941

ORIENTIS PARTIBUS
77 77

Luke 24:4–7; 1 Cor. 15:55–57; 1 Peter 1:18–21; Rev. 5:9–13

470 O Sons and Daughters of the King

1 O sons and daugh - ters of the King, Whom heav'n - ly
2 That Eas - ter morn, at break of day, The faith - ful
3 An an - gel clad in white they see, Who sits and
4 That night the a - pos - tles met in fear; A - mong them
5 When Thom - as first the tid - ings heard That they had
hosts in glo - ry sing, To - day the grave has lost its sting!
wom - en went their way To seek the tomb where Je - sus lay.
speaks un - to the three, "Your Lord will go to Gal - i - lee."
came their mas - ter dear And said, "My peace be with you here."
seen the ris - en Lord, He doubt-ed the dis - ci - ples' word.
Al - le - lu - ia, al - le - lu - ia, al - le - lu - ia!

6 "My piercèd side, O Thomas, see,
And look upon My hands, My feet;
Not faithless but believing be."
Alleluia, alleluia, alleluia!

7 No longer Thomas then denied;
He saw the feet, the hands, the side;
"You are my Lord and God!" he cried.
Alleluia, alleluia, alleluia!

8 How blest are they who have not seen
And yet whose faith has constant been,
For they eternal life shall win.
Alleluia, alleluia, alleluia!

9 On this most holy day of days
Be laud and jubilee and praise:
To God your hearts and voices raise.
Alleluia, alleluia, alleluia!

Text: attr. Jean Tisserand, d. 1494; tr. John Mason Neale, 1818–66, alt.
Tune: Melchior Vulpius, c. 1570–1615; setting: *The Lutheran Hymnal*, 1941

GELOBT SEI GOTT
888 and alleluias

Mark 16:5–7; John 20:24–29

O Sons and Daughters of the King 471

Refrain
Al - le - lu - ia, al - le - lu - ia, al - le-lu - ia!

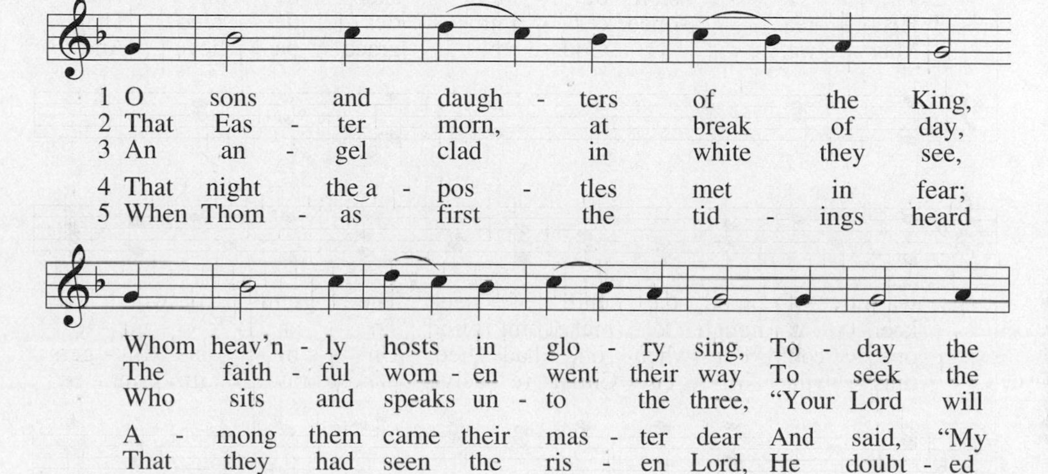
1 O sons and daugh - ters of the King,
2 That Eas - ter morn, at break of day,
3 An an - gel clad in white they see,
4 That night the a - pos - tles met in fear;
5 When Thom - as first the tid - ings heard
Whom heav'n - ly hosts in glo - ry sing, To - day the
The faith - ful wom - en went their way To seek the
Who sits and speaks un - to the three, "Your Lord will
A - mong them came their mas - ter dear And said, "My
That they had seen the ris - en Lord, He doubt - ed

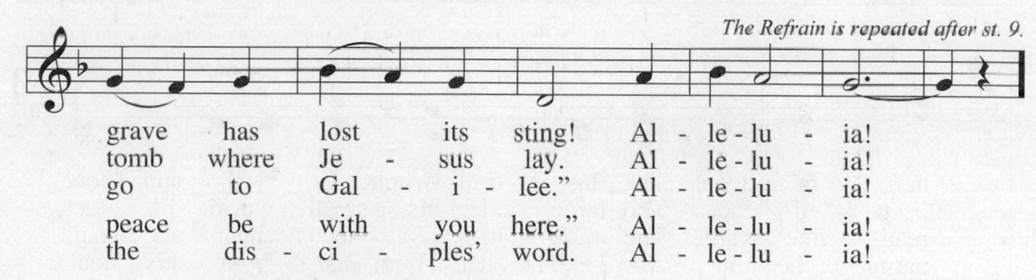
The Refrain is repeated after st. 9.
grave has lost its sting! Al - le - lu - ia!
tomb where Je - sus lay. Al - le - lu - ia!
go to Gal - i - lee." Al - le - lu - ia!
peace be with you here." Al - le - lu - ia!
the dis - ci - ples' word. Al - le - lu - ia!

6 "My piercèd side, O Thomas, see,
And look upon My hands, My feet;
Not faithless but believing be."
Alleluia!

7 No longer Thomas then denied;
He saw the feet, the hands, the side;
"You are my Lord and God!" he cried.
Alleluia!

8 How blest are they who have not seen
And yet whose faith has constant been,
For they eternal life shall win.
Alleluia!

9 On this most holy day of days
Be laud and jubilee and praise:
To God your hearts and voices raise.
Alleluia! *Refrain*

The Refrain is sung once at the beginning of the hymn and a second time at the conclusion of the hymn.
Setting available in hymn accompaniment edition.

Text: attr. Jean Tisserand, d. 1494; tr. John Mason Neale, 1818–66, alt.
Tune: French, 15th cent.

O FILII ET FILIAE
888 and alleluias

Mark 16:5–7; John 20:24–29

472 These Things Did Thomas Count as Real

1 These things did Thom - as count as real: The
2 The vi - sion of his skep - tic mind Was
3 His rea - soned cer - tain - ties de - nied That
4 May we, O God, by grace be - lieve And
warmth of blood, the chill of steel, The grain of wood, the
keen e - nough to make him blind To an - y un - ex -
one could live when one had died, Un - til his fin - gers
thus the ris - en Christ re - ceive, Whose raw im - print - ed
heft of stone, The last frail twitch of flesh and bone.
pect - ed act Too large for his small world of fact.
read like braille The mark - ings of the spear and nail.
palms reached out And beck - oned Thom - as from his doubt.

Text: Thomas H. Troeger, b. 1945
Music: Stephen R. Johnson, b. 1966

REALITER
L M

John 20:19–31

Our Paschal Lamb, That Sets Us Free

1 Our Pas - chal Lamb, that sets us free, Is sac - ri - ficed. O keep The feast of free - dom gal - lant - ly; Let al - le - lu - ias leap:
2 Let all our lives now cel - e - brate The feast; let mal - ice die. Let love grow strong a - new, and great, Let truth stamp out the lie.
3 Let all our deeds, u - nan - i - mous, Con - fess Him as our Lord Who by the Spir - it lives in us, The Fa - ther's liv - ing Word.
Refrain
Al - le - lu - ia! Al - le - lu - ia! Al - le - lu - ia! A - gain Sing al - le - lu - ia, cry a - loud: Al - le - lu - ia! A - men!

Text: Martin H. Franzmann, 1907–76
Music: Walter L. Pelz, b. 1926

REGION THREE
C M and refrain

1 Cor. 5:7–8; Eph. 5:2; Rom. 12:1–2

474 Alleluia! Jesus Is Risen

1 Al - le - lu - ia! Je - sus is ris - en! Trum - pets re - sound-ing in glo - ri - ous light! Splen-dor, the Lamb, Heav - en for - ev - er! Oh, what a mir - a - cle God has in sight!
2 Walk-ing the way, Christ in the cen - ter Tell - ing the sto - ry to o - pen our eyes; Break-ing our bread, Giv - ing us glo - ry: Je - sus our bless - ing, our con - stant sur - prise.
3 Je - sus the vine, We are the branch - es; Life in the Spir - it the fruit of the tree; Heav - en to earth, Christ to the peo - ple, Gift of the fu - ture now flow - ing to me.
4 Weep-ing, be gone; Sor - row, be si - lent: Death put a - sun - der, and Eas - ter is bright. Cher - u - bim sing: "O grave, be o - pen!" Clothe us in won - der, a - dorn us in light.
5 Cit - y of God, Eas - ter for - ev - er, Gold - en Je - ru - sa-lem, Je - sus the Lamb, Riv - er of life, Saints and arch- an - gels, Sing with cre - a - tion to God the I AM!
Refrain
Je - sus is ris - en and we shall a - rise:

Text: Herbert F. Brokering, 1926–2009
Tune: David N. Johnson, 1922–87; setting: Henry V. Gerike, b. 1948

EARTH AND ALL STARS
4 5 10 4 5 10 and refrain

Matt. 28:5–7; 1 Thess. 4:16–18; Rev. 5:6–14; John 15:1–8

Give God the glo - ry! Al - le - lu - ia!

Good Christian Friends, Rejoice and Sing 475

1 Good Chris - tian friends, re - joice and sing! Now is the tri - umph
2 The Lord of life is ris'n this day; Bring flow'rs of song to
3 Praise we in songs of vic - to - ry That love, that life which
4 Your name we bless, O ris - en Lord, And sing to - day with
of our King! To all the world glad news we bring:
strew His way; Let all the world re - joice and say:
can - not die, And sing with hearts up - lift - ed high:
one ac - cord The life laid down, the life re - stored:
Al - le - lu - ia, al - le - lu - ia, al - le - lu - ia!

Text: Cyril A. Alington, 1872–1955, alt.
Tune: Melchior Vulpius, c. 1570–1615; setting: *The Lutheran Hymnal*, 1941

GELOBT SEI GOTT
888 and alleluias

Ps. 118:24; Matt. 28:8; Is. 25:7–9; Rom. 6:9

476 Who Are You Who Walk in Sorrow

1 Who are you who walk in sor - row Down Em - ma - us'
2 Who is this who joins our jour - ney, Walk - ing with us
3 Who are You? Our hearts are o - pened In the break - ing
bar - ren road, Hearts dis - traught and hope de - feat - ed,
stride by stride? Un - known Strang - er, can You fath - om
of the bread— Christ the vic - tim, now the vic - tor
Bent be - neath grief's crush - ing load? Name - less mourn - ers,
Depths of grief for one who died? Then the won - der!
Liv - ing, ris - en from the dead! Great com - pan - ion
we will join you, We who al - so mourn our dead;
When we told You How our dreams to dust have turned,
on our jour - ney, Still sur - prise us with Your grace!
We have stood by graves un - yield - ing,
Then You o - pened wide the Scrip - tures
Make each day a new Em - ma - us;
Eat - en death's bare, bit - ter bread.
Till our hearts with - in us burned.
On our hearts Your im - age trace!

4 Who are we who travel with You
On our way through life to death?
Women, men, the young, the aging,
Wakened by the Spirit's breath!
At the font You claim and name us,
Born of water and the Word;
At the table still You feed us,
Host us as our risen Lord!

5 "Alleluia! Alleluia!"
Is the Easter hymn we sing!
Take our life, our joy, our worship
As the gift of love we bring.
You have formed us all one people
Called from ev'ry land and race.
Make the Church Your servant body,
Sent to share Your healing grace!

Setting available in hymn accompaniment edition.

Text: Herman G. Stuempfle, Jr., 1923–2007
Tune: *Southern Harmony*, New Haven, 1835

JEFFERSON
87 87 D

Luke 24:13–35

Alleluia, Alleluia! Hearts to Heaven 477

1 Al - le - lu - ia, al - le - lu - ia! Hearts to heav'n and voic - es raise:
2 Al - le - lu - ia, Christ is ris - en! Death at last has met de - feat:
△ 3 Al - le - lu - ia, al - le - lu - ia! Glo - ry be to God on high:
Sing to God a hymn of glad-ness, Sing to God a hymn of praise;
See the an-cient pow'rs of e - vil In con - fu - sion and re - treat;
Al - le - lu - ia to the Sav - ior Who has gained the vic - to - ry;
He who on the cross a vic - tim For the world's sal - va - tion bled—
Once He died, and once was bur - ied: Now He lives for - ev - er - more,
Al - le - lu - ia to the Spir - it, Fount of love and sanc - ti - ty!
Je - sus Christ, the King of Glo - ry, Now is ris - en from the dead.
Je - sus Christ, the world's Re - deem - er, Whom we wor - ship and a - dore.
Al - le - lu - ia, al - le - lu - ia To the tri - une Maj - es - ty!

Text: Christopher Wordsworth, 1807–85, sts. 1, 3; rev. Jubilate Hymns Ltd., st. 2
Music: Ludwig van Beethoven, 1770–1827; adapt. Edward Hodges, 1796–1867

HYMN TO JOY
87 87 D

1 Cor. 15:54b–57; Is. 25:7–9; Rev. 21:4; 2 Tim. 1:10

478 The Day of Resurrection

1 The day of res - ur - rec - tion! Earth, tell it out a - broad,
2 Let hearts be purged of e - vil That we may see a - right
3 Now let the heav'ns be joy - ful, Let earth its song be - gin,
△ 4 All praise to God the Fa - ther, All praise to God the Son,
The pass - o - ver of glad - ness, The pass - o - ver of God.
The Lord in rays e - ter - nal Of res - ur - rec - tion light
Let all the world keep tri - umph And all that is there - in.
All praise to God the Spir - it, E - ter - nal Three in One!
From death to life e - ter - nal, From sin's do - min - ion free,
And, lis - t'ning to His ac - cents, May hear, so calm and plain,
Let all things, seen and un - seen, Their notes of glad - ness blend;
Let all the ran - somed num - ber Fall down be - fore the throne
Our Christ has brought us o - ver With hymns of vic - to - ry.
His own "All hail!" and, hear - ing, May raise the vic - tor strain.
For Christ the Lord has ris - en, Our joy that has no end!
And hon - or, pow'r, and glo - ry As - cribe to God a - lone!

Text: John of Damascus, c. 696–c. 754; tr. John Mason Neale, 1818–66, alt.
Tune: Henry T. Smart, 1813–79; setting: *The Lutheran Hymnal*, 1941

LANCASHIRE
76 76 D

Ex. 12:22, 26–27; Ps. 105:43; 1 Cor. 5:7–8; Rev. 7:9–12

Christ Is Risen, Christ Is Living 479

1 Christ is ris - en, Christ is liv - ing, Dry your tears, be un - a - fraid!
2 If the Lord had nev - er ris - en, We'd have noth - ing to be - lieve.

1 ¡Cris - to vi - ve, fue - ra‿el llan - to, los la - men - tos y‿el pe - sar!
2 Que si Cris - to no vi - vie - ra va - na fue - ra nues - tra fe;

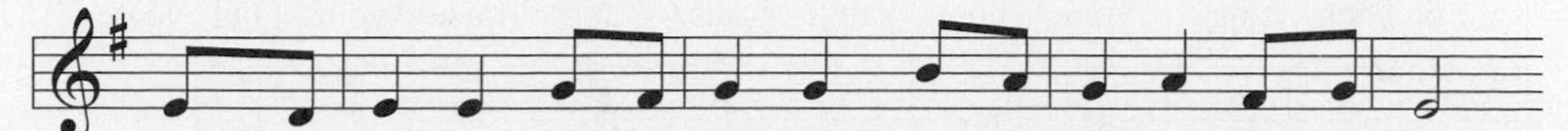

Death and dark - ness could not hold Him, Nor the tomb in which He lay.
But His prom - ise can be trust - ed: "You will live, be - cause I live."

Ni la muer - te ni‿el se - pul - cro lo‿han po - di - do su - je - tar.
mas se cum - ple su pro - me - sa: "Por - que vi - vo, vi - vi - réis."

Do not look a - mong the dead for One who lives for - ev - er - more;
As we share the death of Ad - am, So in Christ we live a - gain;

No bus - quéis en - tre los muer - tos al que siem - pre‿ha de vi - vir,
Si‿en A - dán en - tró la muer - te, por Je - sús la vi - da‿en - tró;

Tell the world that Christ is ris - en, Make it known He goes be - fore.
Death has lost its sting and ter - ror, Christ the Lord has come to reign.

¡Cris - to vi - ve! Es - tas nue - vas por do - quier de - jad o - ír.
no te - máis, el triun - fo‿es vues - tro: ¡El Se - ñor re - su - ci - tó!

3 Death has lost its old dominion,
Let the world rejoice and shout!
Christ, the firstborn of the living,
Gives us life and leads us out.
Let us thank our God, who causes
Hope to spring up from the ground;
Christ is risen, Christ is giving
Life eternal, life profound.

3 Si es verdad que de la muerte
el pecado es aguijón,
no temáis pues Jesucristo
nos da vida y salvación.
Gracias demos al Dios Padre
que nos da seguridad,
que quien cree en Jesucristo
vive por la eternidad.

Setting available in hymn accompaniment edition.

Text: Nicholas Martinez, 1917–72; tr. Fred Kaan, 1929–2009
Tune: Pablo D. Sosa, b. 1933

CENTRAL
87 87 D

1 Cor. 15:12–23, 55–57; John 14:19; Rom. 6:3–5

480 He's Risen, He's Risen

1 He's ris - en, He's ris - en, Christ Je - sus, the Lord;
2 The foe was tri - um - phant when on Cal - va - ry
3 But short was their tri - umph; the Sav - ior a - rose,
4 O, where is your sting, death? We fear you no more;
△ 5 Then sing your ho - san - nas and raise your glad voice;
He o - pened death's pris - on, the in - car - nate, true Word.
The Lord of cre - a - tion was nailed to the tree.
And death, hell, and Sa - tan He van - quished, His foes.
Christ rose, and now o - pen is fair E - den's door.
Pro - claim the blest tid - ings that all may re - joice.
Break forth, hosts of heav - en, in ju - bi - lant song
In Sa - tan's do - main did the hosts shout and jeer,
The con - quer - ing Lord lifts His ban - ner on high;
For all our trans - gres - sions His blood does a - tone;
Laud, hon - or, and praise to the Lamb that was slain:
And earth, sea, and moun - tain their prais - es pro - long.
For Je - sus was slain, whom the e - vil ones fear.
He lives, yes, He lives, and will nev - er - more die.
Re - deemed and for - giv - en, we now are His own.
With Fa - ther and Spir - it He ev - er shall reign.

Text: C. F. W. Walther, 1811–87, abr.; tr. Anna M. Meyer, 1867–1941, alt.
Tune: C. F. W. Walther, 1811–87; setting: *The Lutheran Hymnal*, 1941

WALTHER
11 11 11 11

1 Cor. 15:54–57; Rom. 5:9–11; Rev. 5:12–13

Scatter the Darkness, Break the Gloom

1 Scat - ter the dark - ness, break the gloom; Sun, re - veal an
2 Bear - ing the stan - dard from on high As the Lamb of
3 Ban - ners of tri - umph, be un - furled! Trum - pets, sound through-
emp - ty tomb Shin - ing with joy for all our sor - rows,
God to die; He who for us, so cruel - ly treat - ed,
out the world! Cry - ing and sighs, give way to sing - ing:
Hope and peace for all to - mor - rows, Life un - e-
Lives a - gain— our foes de - feat - ed! Where is your
Life from death, our Lord is bring - ing! Let there be-
clipsed by doubt and dread: Christ has ris - en from the dead!
sting, O death and grave? Christ has shown His strength to save!
gin the ju - bi - lee— Christ has gained the vic - to - ry!

Text: Stephen P. Starke, b. 1955
Tune: French; setting: Barry Rose, b. 1934, alt.

BESANÇON
8 7 9 8 8 7

Matt. 28:5–6; 1 Cor. 15:3–8, 20, 54–57

482 This Joyful Eastertide

1 This joy - ful Eas - ter - tide A - way with sin and sor - - - row! My love, the Cru - ci - fied, Has sprung to life this mor - - - row:
2 Death's flood has lost its chill Since Je - sus crossed the riv - - - er; Lov - er of souls, from ill My pass - ing soul de - liv - - - er:
3 My flesh in hope shall rest And for a sea - son slum - - - ber Till trump from east to west Shall wake the dead in num - - - ber:
Refrain
Had Christ, who once was slain, Not burst His three-day pris - on,

Text: George R. Woodward, 1848–1934
Tune: *Davids Psalmen*, Amsterdam, 1684; setting: Dale Grotenhuis, 1931–2012, alt.

VRUECHTEN
67 67 and refrain

1 Cor. 15:17–20, 51–52; Rev. 14:13

Our faith had been in vain: But now has Christ a - ris - en, a -
ris - en, a - ris - en; But now has Christ a - ris - en!

If Christ has not been raised, then our preaching is in vain and your faith is in vain. But in fact Christ has been raised from the dead, the firstfruits of those who have fallen asleep. 1 Corinthians 15:14, 20

---

483 With High Delight Let Us Unite

1 With high de-light Let us u-nite In songs of great jubilation. Ye pure in heart, All bear your part, Sing Jesus Christ, our salvation. To set us free Forever, He Is ris'n and sends To all earth's
2 True God, He first From death has burst Forth into life, all subduing. His enemy Doth vanquished lie; His death has been death's undoing. "And yours shall be Like victory O'er death and grave," Saith He, who
3 Let praises ring; Give thanks, and bring To Christ our Lord adoration. His honor speed By word and deed To ev'ry land, ev'ry nation. So shall His love Give us above, From misery And death set

Text: Georg Vetter, 1536–99; tr. Martin H. Franzmann, 1907–76
Tune: *Cinquante Pseaumes*, Geneva, 1543; setting: *Lutheran Book of Worship: Select Hymns*, 1985

MIT FREUDEN ZART
448 448 44 44 8

Is. 52:9–10; 1 Cor. 15:20–23; Mark 16:15

ends Good news to save ev - 'ry na - tion.
gave His life for us, life re - new - ing.
free, All joy and full con - so - la - tion.

Make Songs of Joy 484

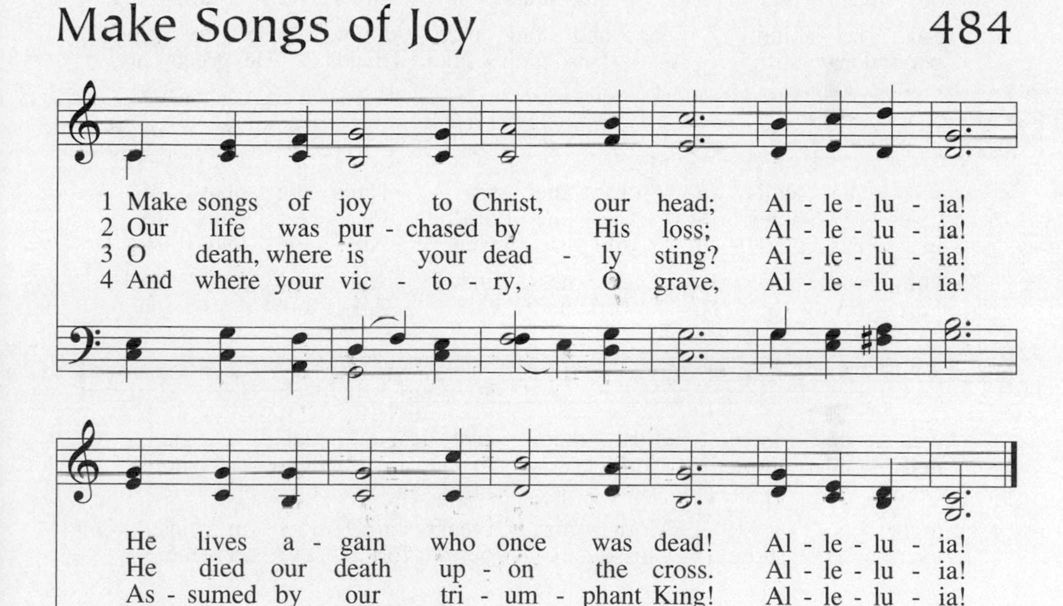
1 Make songs of joy to Christ, our head; Al - le - lu - ia!
2 Our life was pur - chased by His loss; Al - le - lu - ia!
3 O death, where is your dead - ly sting? Al - le - lu - ia!
4 And where your vic - to - ry, O grave, Al - le - lu - ia!
He lives a - gain who once was dead! Al - le - lu - ia!
He died our death up - on the cross. Al - le - lu - ia!
As - sumed by our tri - um - phant King! Al - le - lu - ia!
When one like Christ has come to save? Al - le - lu - ia!

5 Behold, the tyrants, one and all,
Alleluia!
Before our mighty Savior fall!
Alleluia!

△ 6 For this be praised the Son who rose,
Alleluia!
The Father, and the Holy Ghost!
Alleluia!

Text: Juraj Tranovský, 1591–1637; tr. Jaroslav J. Vajda, 1919–2008
Music: *Velká Partitúra*, 1936, ed. Juraj Chorvát

ZPIVEJMEŽ VŠICKNI VESELE
84 84

1 Cor. 15:55–57; Is. 53:4–5

485 Long before the World Is Waking

1 Long be - fore the world is wak - ing, Morn - ing mist on
2 So they cast, and all their heav - ing Can - not haul their
3 Char - coal em - bers bright - ly burn - ing, Bread and fish up -
4 Christ is ris - en! Grief and sigh - ing, Sins and sor - rows,
5 Morn - ing breaks, and Je - sus meets us, Feeds and com - forts,
Gal - i - lee, From the shore, as dawn is break - ing,
catch a - board; John in won - der turns, per - ceiv - ing,
on them laid: Je - sus stands at day's re - turn - ing
fall be - hind; Fear and fail - ure, doubt, de - ny - ing,
par - dons still; As His faith - ful friends He greets us,
Je - sus calls a - cross the sea; Hails the boat of
Cries a - loud, "It is the Lord!" Pe - ter waits for
In His ris - en life ar - rayed; As of old His
Full and free for - give - ness find. All the soul's dark
Part - ners of His work and will. All our days, on
wea - ry men, Bids them cast their net a - gain.
noth - ing more, Plung - es in to swim a - shore.
friends to greet, "Here is break - fast; come and eat."
night is past, Morn - ing breaks in joy at last.
ev - 'ry shore, Christ is ours for - ev - er - more!

Hymn accompaniment: 529

Text: Timothy Dudley-Smith, b. 1926
Tune: *Geistreiches Gesang-Buch*, Darmstadt, 1698

ALL SAINTS
87 87 77

John 21:1–17

If Christ Had Not Been Raised from Death

1 If Christ had not been raised from death Our faith would be in vain,
2 If Christ still lay with - in the tomb Then death would be the end,
3 If Christ had not been tru - ly raised His Church would live a lie;
Our preach - ing but a waste of breath, Our sin and guilt re - main.
And we should face our fi - nal doom With nei - ther guide nor friend.
His name should nev - er-more be praised, His words de - serve to die.
But now the Lord is ris'n in - deed; He rules in earth and heav'n:
But now the Sav - ior is raised up, So when a Chris-tian dies
But now our great Re - deem - er lives; Through Him we are re - stored;
His Gos - pel meets a world of need— In Christ we are for - giv'n.
We mourn, yet look to God in hope— In Christ the saints a - rise!
His Word en-dures, His Church re - vives In Christ, our ris - en Lord.

Text: Christopher M. Idle, b. 1938
Music: Phillip Magness, b. 1963

UNION CITY
C M D

1 Cor. 15:12–26; Job 19:25

487 Come, You Faithful, Raise the Strain

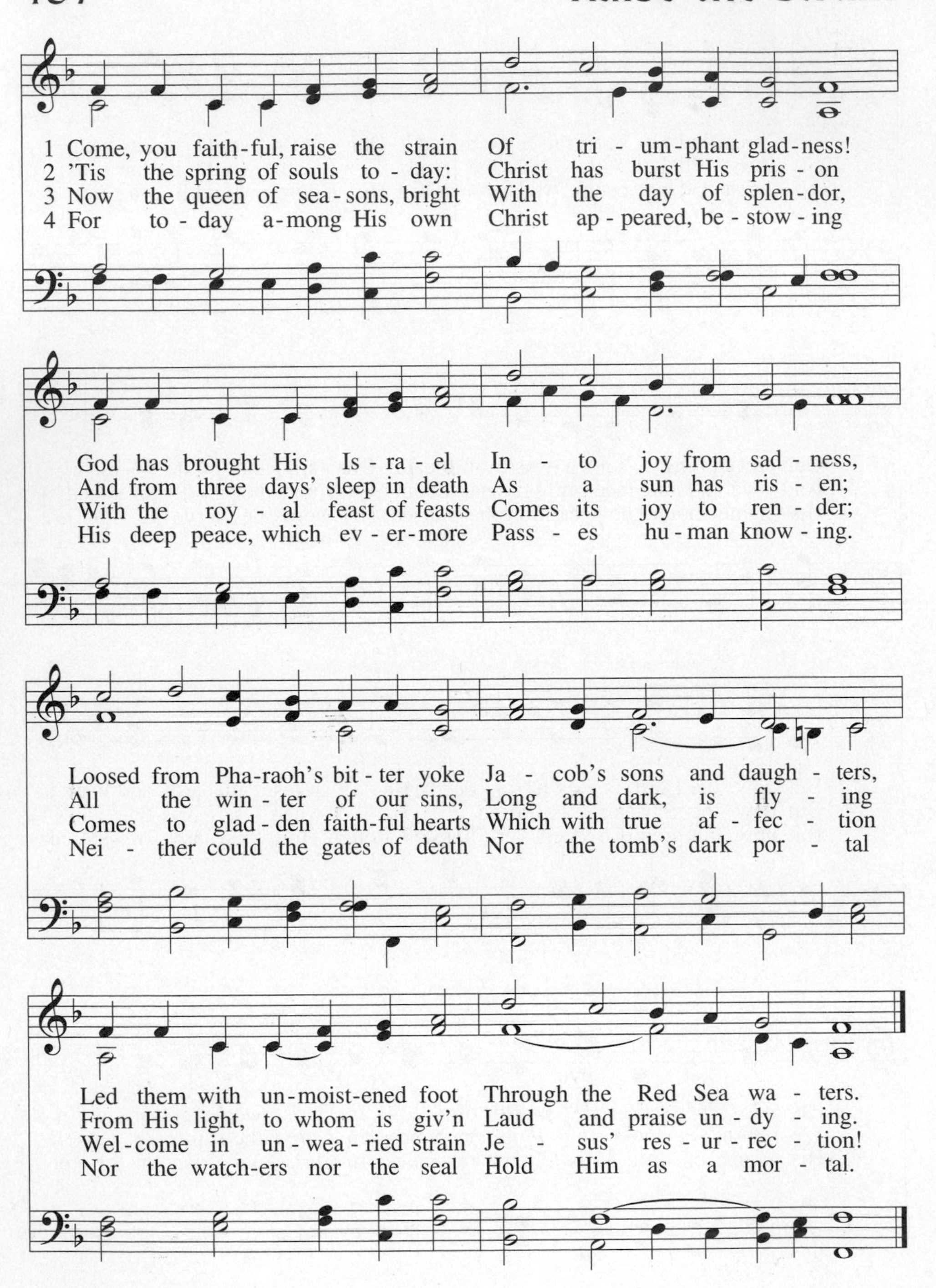
1 Come, you faith-ful, raise the strain Of tri - um-phant glad-ness!
2 'Tis the spring of souls to - day: Christ has burst His pris - on
3 Now the queen of sea - sons, bright With the day of splen - dor,
4 For to - day a - mong His own Christ ap - peared, be - stow - ing
God has brought His Is - ra - el In - to joy from sad - ness,
And from three days' sleep in death As a sun has ris - en;
With the roy - al feast of feasts Comes its joy to ren - der;
His deep peace, which ev - er - more Pass - es hu - man know - ing.
Loosed from Pha-raoh's bit - ter yoke Ja - cob's sons and daugh - ters,
All the win - ter of our sins, Long and dark, is fly - ing
Comes to glad - den faith-ful hearts Which with true af - fec - tion
Nei - ther could the gates of death Nor the tomb's dark por - tal
Led them with un-moist-ened foot Through the Red Sea wa - ters.
From His light, to whom is giv'n Laud and praise un - dy - ing.
Wel - come in un - wea - ried strain Je - sus' res - ur - rec - tion!
Nor the watch-ers nor the seal Hold Him as a mor - tal.

Text: John of Damascus, c. 696–c. 754; tr. John Mason Neale, 1818–66, alt.
Tune: Johann Horn, c. 1490–1547; setting: Theodore A. Beck, 1929–2003

GAUDEAMUS PARITER
76 76 D

Ex. 15:1–21; John 20:19–21; Rom. 6:9–11

5 Alleluia! Now we cry
To our King immortal,
Who, triumphant, burst the bars
Of the tomb's dark portal.
Come, you faithful, raise the strain
Of triumphant gladness!
God has brought His Israel
Into joy from sadness!

He Is Arisen! Glorious Word 488

He is a - ris - en! Glo - rious Word! Now rec - on - ciled
is God, my Lord; The gates of heav'n are o - pen.
My Je - sus did tri - um - phant die, And Sa - tan's ar -
rows bro - ken lie, De - stroyed hell's fierc - est weap - on.
O hear what cheer! Christ vic - to - rious, Ris - ing glo - rious,
Life is giv - ing. He was dead but now is liv - ing!

Hymn accompaniment: 395

Text: Birgitte Katerine Boye, 1742–1824; tr. George A. T. Rygh, 1860–1942, alt.
Tune: Philipp Nicolai, 1556–1608

WIE SCHÖN LEUCHTET
887 887 4444 8

1 Cor. 15:3–8, 12–23

489 Hail Thee, Festival Day

Refrain
All
Easter Hail thee, fes - ti - val day! Blest day to be hal - lowed for - ev - er;
Ascension Hail thee, fes - ti - val day! Blest day to be hal - lowed for - ev - er;
Pentecost Hail thee, fes - ti - val day! Blest day to be hal - lowed for - ev - er;
1st time only
Day when our Lord was raised, Break - ing the king - dom of death. death.
Day when our ris - en Lord Rose in the heav - ens to reign. reign.
Day when the Ho - ly Ghost Shone in the world with His grace. grace.
All
Easter 1 All the fair beau - ty of earth From the death of the win - ter a - ris - ing! Ev - 'ry good gift of the year Now with its mas - ter re - turns:
Ascension 1 He who was nailed to the cross Is rul - er and Lord of all peo - ple. All things cre - at - ed on earth Sing to the glo - ry of God:
Pentecost 1 Bright and in like - ness of fire, On those who a - wait His ap - pear - ing, He whom the Lord had fore - told Sud - den - ly, swift - ly de - scends:
3 God the Al - might - y, the Lord, The rul - er of earth and the heav - ens, Guard us from harm with - out; Cleanse us from e - vil with - in:
5 Spir - it of life and of pow'r, Now flow in us, fount of our be - ing, Light that en - light - ens us all, Life that in all may a - bide:
To next page

The Refrain is sung twice at the beginning of the hymn and then once after each stanza.
Setting available in hymn accompaniment edition.

Text: Venantius Honorius Fortunatus, c. 530–609; tr. *Lutheran Book of Worship*, 1978, sts. 1, 2-E, 2-A, 3–6, refrains, alt.; tr. *The English Hymnal*, 1906, st. 2-P, alt.
Tune: Ralph Vaughan Williams, 1872–1958

SALVE FESTA DIES
Irregular meter

Ps. 118:13–24; Eph. 1:19b–23; Rom. 6:4; Acts 2:1–4

Refrain
All
Easter Hail thee, fes - ti - val day! Blest day to be hal - lowed for - ev - er;
Ascension Hail thee, fes - ti - val day! Blest day to be hal - lowed for - ev - er;
Pentecost Hail thee, fes - ti - val day! Blest day to be hal - lowed for - ev - er;
Day when our Lord was raised, Break - ing the king - dom of death.
Day when our ris - en Lord Rose in the heav - ens to reign.
Day when the Ho - ly Ghost Shone in the world with His grace.
Choir
3
Easter 2 Rise from the grave now, O Lord, The au - thor of life and cre - a - tion. Tread - ing the path - way of death, New life You give to us all:
Ascension 2 Dai - ly the love - li - ness grows, A - dorned with the glo - ry of blos - som; Heav - en her gate - way un - bars, Fling - ing her in - crease of light:
Pentecost 2 Hark! For in myr - i - ad tongues Christ's own, His cho - sen a - pos - tles, Preached to the ends of the earth Christ and His won - der - ful works:
4 Je - sus, the health of the world, Cre - a - tor of all and re - deem - er, Son of the Fa - ther su - preme, On - ly - be - got - ten of God:
6 Praise to the giv - er of good! O Lov - er and Au - thor of con - cord, Pour out Your balm on our days; Or - der our ways in Your peace:
To previous page

490 Jesus Lives! The Victory's Won

1 Je - sus lives! The vic - t'ry's won! Death no long - er can ap -
2 Je - sus lives! To Him the throne High a - bove all things is
3 Je - sus lives! For me He died, Hence will I, to Je - sus
4 Je - sus lives! I know full well Noth - ing me from Him shall

pall me; Je - sus lives! Death's reign is done!
giv - en. I shall go where He is gone,
liv - ing, Pure in heart and act a - bide,
sev - er. Nei - ther death nor pow'rs of hell

From the grave will Christ re - call me. Bright - er
Live and reign with Him in heav - en. God is
Praise to Him and glo - ry giv - ing. All I
Part me now from Christ for - ev - er. God will

scenes will then com - mence; This shall be my con - fi - dence.
faith - ful; doubt-ings, hence! This shall be my con - fi - dence.
need God will dis - pense; This shall be my con - fi - dence.
be my sure de - fense; This shall be my con - fi - dence.

Text: Christian Fürchtegott Gellert, 1715–69; tr. Frances E. Cox, 1812–97, alt.
Tune: Johann Crüger, 1598–1662; setting: *The Lutheran Hymnal*, 1941

JESUS, MEINE ZUVERSICHT
78 78 77

Rom. 8:11, 35–39; 2 Cor. 5:15; Phil. 1:20–21

5 Jesus lives! And now is death
    But the gate of life immortal;
This shall calm my trembling breath
    When I pass its gloomy portal.
Faith shall cry, as fails each sense:
Jesus is my confidence!

O God, for our redemption You gave Your only-begotten Son to the death of the cross and by His glorious resurrection delivered us from the power of the enemy. Grant that all our sin may be drowned through daily repentance and that day by day we may arise to live before You in righteousness and purity forever; through Jesus Christ, our Lord, who lives and reigns with You and the Holy Spirit, one God, now and forever.

Collect for the Resurrection of Our Lord

---

491 Up through Endless Ranks of Angels

1 Up through end - less ranks of an - gels, Cries of tri - umph
2 Death - de - stroy - ing, life - re - stor - ing, Prov - en e - qual
3 To our lives of wan - ton wan - d'ring Send Your Spir - it,
△ 4 Al - le - lu - ia, al - le - lu - ia! Oh, to breathe the
in His ears, To His heav'n - ly throne as - cend - ing,
to our need, Now for us be - fore the Fa - ther
prom - ised guide; Through our lives of fear and fail - ure
Spir - it's grace! Al - le - lu - ia, al - le - lu - ia!
Hav - ing van - quished all their fears, Christ looks down up -
As our broth - er in - ter - cede; Flesh that for our
With Your pow'r and love a - bide; Wel - come us, as
Oh, to see the Fa - ther's face! Al - le - lu - ia,
on His faith - ful, Leav - ing them in hap - py tears.
world was wound - ed, Liv - ing, for the wound - ed plead!
You were wel - comed, To an end - less Eas - ter - tide.
al - le - lu - ia! Oh, to feel the Son's em - brace!

Text: Jaroslav J. Vajda, 1919–2008
Music: Henry V. Gerike, b. 1948

ASCENDED TRIUMPH
87 87 87

Mark 16:19; 1 John 2:1–2; John 14:16–18

On Christ's Ascension I Now Build 492

1 On Christ's as - cen - sion I now build The hope of my as - cen - sion; This hope a - lone has al - ways stilled All doubt and ap - pre - hen - sion; For where the Head is, there as well I know His mem - bers are to dwell When Christ will come and call them.
2 Since Christ re - turned to claim His throne, Great gifts for me ob - tain - ing, My heart will rest in Him a - lone, No oth - er rest re - main - ing; For where my trea - sure went be - fore, There all my thoughts will ev - er soar To still their deep - est yearn - ing.
3 O grant, dear Lord, this grace to me, Re - call - ing Your as - cen - sion, That I may serve You faith - ful - ly In thanks for my re - demp - tion; And then, when all my days will cease, Let me de - part in joy and peace In an - swer to my plead - ing.

Text: Josua Wegelin, 1604–40; tr. William M. Czamanske, 1873–1964, alt.
Tune: *Etlich Cristlich lider*, Wittenberg, 1524; setting: Paul G. Bunjes, 1914–98

NUN FREUT EUCH
87 87 887

John 14:3; Col. 3:1–4

493 A Hymn of Glory Let Us Sing

1 A hymn of glo - ry let us sing! New hymns through - out the world shall ring:
2 The ho - ly ap - os - tol - ic band Up - on the Mount of Ol - ives stand.
3 To them the shin - ing an - gels cry, "Why stand and gaze up - on the sky?"
4 "You see Him now, as - cend - ing high Up to the por - tals of the sky."
Al - le - lu - ia, al - le - lu - ia!
Christ, by a road be - fore un - trod,
And with His faith - ful fol - l'wers see
"This is the Sav - ior," thus they say;
"Here - af - ter Je - sus you shall see
As - cends un - to the throne of
Their Lord as - cend in maj - es -
"This is His glo - rious tri - umph
Re - turn - ing in great maj - es -

Text: Bede, 673–735; tr. *Lutheran Book of Worship*, 1978, alt.
Tune: *Geistliche Kirchengesäng*, Köln, 1623; setting: Ralph Vaughan Williams, 1872–1958

LASST UNS ERFREUEN
888 888 and alleluias

Acts 1:9–11; Col. 3:1–4; Ps. 47:5–9; Rev. 5:13

God.
ty.
day!"
ty."
Al - le - lu - ia, al - le - lu - ia! Al - le -
lu - ia, al - le - lu - ia, al - le - lu - ia!

5 Be now our joy on earth, O Lord,
And be our future great reward.
Alleluia, alleluia!
Then, throned with You forever, we
Shall praise Your name eternally.
Alleluia, alleluia!
Alleluia, alleluia, alleluia!

△ 6 O risen Christ, ascended Lord,
All praise to You let earth accord:
Alleluia, alleluia!
You are, while endless ages run,
With Father and with Spirit one.
Alleluia, alleluia!
Alleluia, alleluia, alleluia!

494 See, the Lord Ascends in Triumph

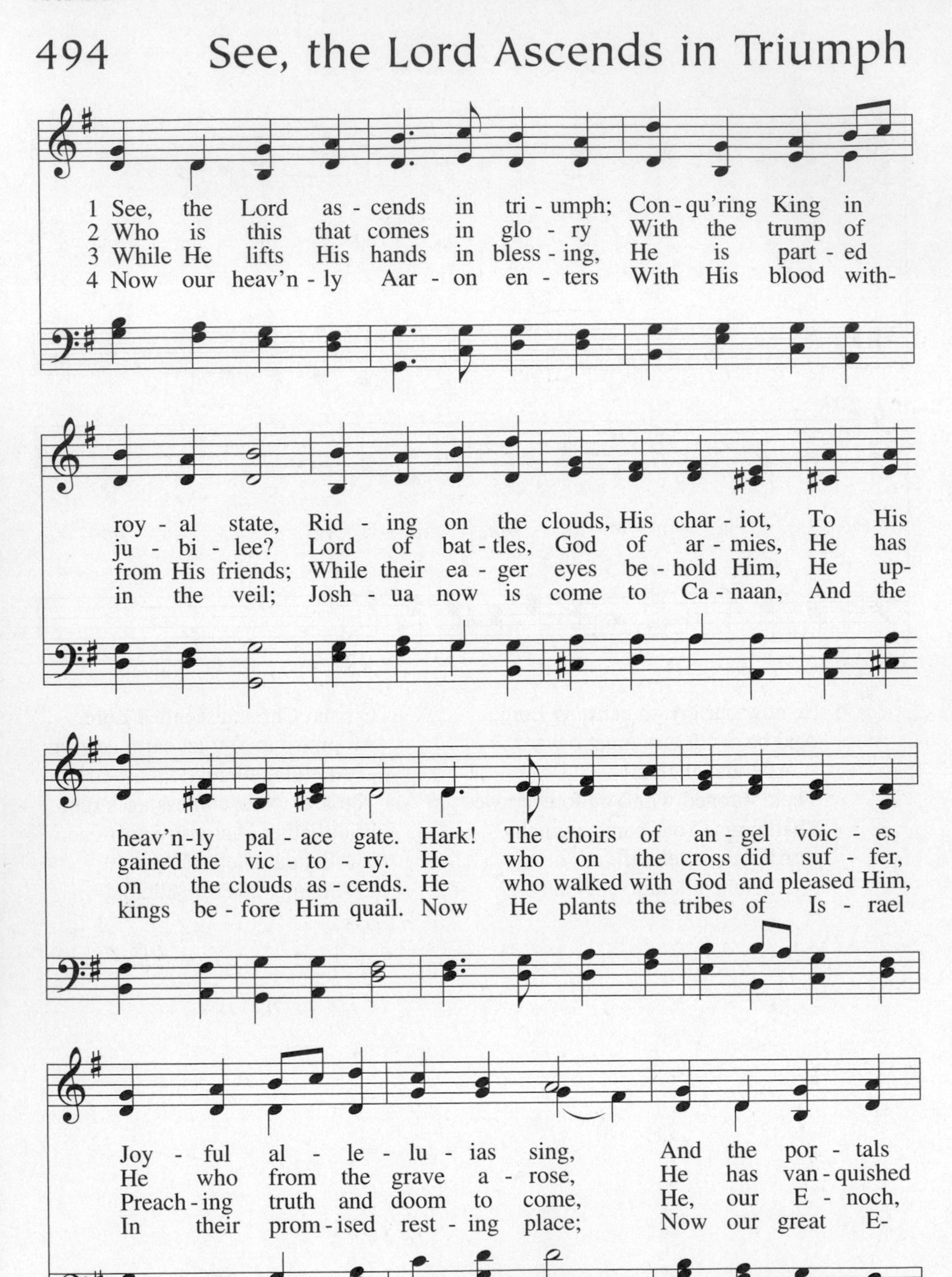
1 See, the Lord ascends in triumph; Con-qu'ring King in royal state, Riding on the clouds, His chariot, To His heav'nly palace gate. Hark! The choirs of angel voices Joyful alleluias sing, And the portals
2 Who is this that comes in glory With the trump of jubilee? Lord of battles, God of armies, He has gained the victory. He who on the cross did suffer, He who from the grave arose, He has vanquished
3 While He lifts His hands in blessing, He is parted from His friends; While their eager eyes behold Him, He upon the clouds ascends. He who walked with God and pleased Him, Preaching truth and doom to come, He, our Enoch,
4 Now our heav'nly Aaron enters With His blood within the veil; Joshua now is come to Canaan, And the kings before Him quail. Now He plants the tribes of Israel In their promised resting place; Now our great E-

The Old Testament saints—Enoch, Aaron, Joshua, and Elijah—all find their perfect fulfillment in Jesus Christ, who is indeed the greater Prophet, Priest, and ascended King of kings.

Text: Christopher Wordsworth, 1807–85, abr., alt.
Tune: Henry T. Smart, 1813–79; setting: Henry V. Gerike, b. 1948

REX GLORIAE
87 87 D

Mark 16:19; Col. 3:1–4; Ps. 110:1; Rev. 6:11–13

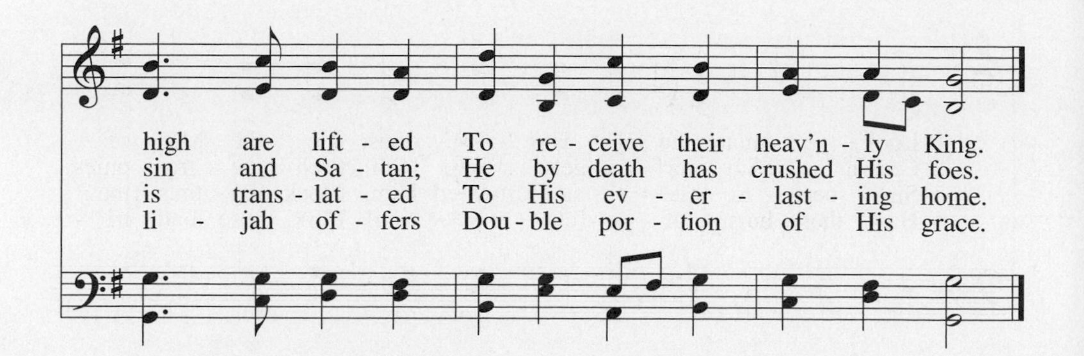
high are lift - ed To re - ceive their heav'n - ly King.
sin and Sa - tan; He by death has crushed His foes.
is trans - lat - ed To His ev - er - last - ing home.
li - jah of - fers Dou - ble por - tion of His grace.

5 He has raised our human nature
On the clouds to God's right hand;
There we sit in heav'nly places,
There with Him in glory stand.
Jesus reigns, adored by angels;
Man with God is on the throne.
By our mighty Lord's ascension
We by faith behold our own.

If then you have been raised with Christ, seek the things that are above, where Christ is, seated at the right hand of God. Set your minds on things that are above, not on things that are on earth. For you have died, and your life is hidden with Christ in God. When Christ who is your life appears, then you also will appear with Him in glory.

Colossians 3:1–4

495

Look, Ye Saints, the Sight Is Glorious

1 Look, ye saints, the sight is glo - rious; See the Man of
2 Crown the Sav - ior! An - gels, crown Him! Rich the tro - phies
3 Sin - ners in de - ri - sion crowned Him, Mock - ing thus the
4 Hark, those bursts of ac - cla - ma - tion! Hark, those loud tri -
Sor - rows now! From the fight re - turned vic - to - rious,
Je - sus brings; On the seat of pow'r en - throne Him
Sav - ior's claim; Saints and an - gels crowd a - round Him,
um - phant chords! Je - sus takes the high - est sta - tion;
Ev - 'ry knee to Him shall bow.
While the vault of heav - en rings.
Own His ti - tle, praise His name.
Oh, what joy the sight af - fords!
Crown Him! Crown Him!
Crown Him! Crown Him! Crown Him! Crown Him!
Crowns be - come the
Crown the Sav - ior
Spread a - broad the
King of kings and

Christ has ascended to the right hand of the Father. With eyes of faith, we now see Jesus—who suffered death for us all—crowned with glory and honor (Heb. 2:9).

Text: Thomas Kelly, 1769–1855
Tune: William Owen, 1813–93; setting: Joseph Herl, b. 1959

BRYN CALFARIA
87 87 444 77

Phil. 2:9–11; Rev. 7:9–14; Dan. 7:14; Acts 2:31–36

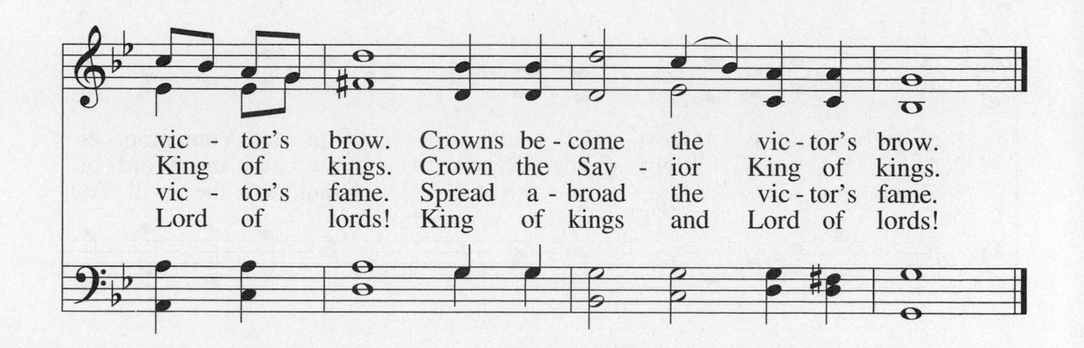
vic - tor's brow. Crowns be - come the vic - tor's brow.
King of kings. Crown the Sav - ior King of kings.
vic - tor's fame. Spread a - broad the vic - tor's fame.
Lord of lords! King of kings and Lord of lords!

Holy Spirit, Light Divine 496

1 Ho - ly Spir - it, light di - vine, Shine up - on this heart of mine;
2 Let me see my Sav - ior's face, Let me all His beau - ties trace;
3 Ho - ly Spir - it, pow'r di - vine, Cleanse this guilt - y heart of mine;
4 Ho - ly Spir - it, joy di - vine, Cheer this sad-dened heart of mine;
5 Ho - ly Spir - it, all di - vine, Dwell with - in this heart of mine;
Chase the shades of night a - way, Turn the dark - ness in - to day.
Show those glo - rious truths to me Which are on - ly known to Thee.
In Thy mer - cy pit - y me, From sin's bond - age set me free.
Yield a sa - cred, set - tled peace, Let it grow and still in - crease.
Cast down ev - 'ry i - dol throne, Reign su - preme, and reign a - lone.

Text: Andrew Reed, 1787–1862, alt.
Tune: Orlando Gibbons, 1583–1625; setting: based on Orlando Gibbons, 1583–1625

SONG 13
77 77

John 16:13; 1 Thess. 5:23; 1 Cor. 6:19; 2 Tim. 1:7

497 Come, Holy Ghost, God and Lord

1 Come, Ho - ly Ghost, God and Lord, With all Your grac - es
2 Come, ho - ly Light, guide di - vine, Now cause the Word of
3 Come, ho - ly Fire, com - fort true, Grant us the will Your
now out - poured On each be - liev - er's mind and heart;
life to shine. Teach us to know our God a - right
work to do And in Your ser - vice to a - bide;
Your fer - vent love to them im - part. Lord, by the
And call Him Fa - ther with de - light. From ev - 'ry
Let tri - als turn us not a - side. Lord, by Your
bright - ness of Your light In ho - ly faith Your Church u - nite;
er - ror keep us free; Let none but Christ our mas - ter be
pow'r pre - pare each heart, And to our weak - ness strength im - part

Text: German, 15th cent., st. 1; Martin Luther, 1483–1546, sts. 2–3;
tr. *The Lutheran Hymnal*, 1941, alt.
Tune: *Eyn Enchiridion oder Handbüchlein*, Erfurt, 1524; setting: *Lutheran Service Book*, 2006

KOMM, HEILIGER GEIST, HERRE GOTT
78 88 88 8 10 8

Luke 11:13; 1 Cor. 12:13; John 16:13–14; 2 Tim. 1:14

From ev - 'ry land and ev - 'ry tongue This to Your
That we in liv - ing faith a - bide, In Him, our
That brave - ly here we may con - tend, Through life and
praise, O Lord, our God, be sung:
Lord, with all our might con - fide. Al - le - lu - ia, al - le - lu - ia!
death to You, our Lord, as - cend.

Almighty and ever-living God, You fulfilled Your promise by sending the gift of the Holy Spirit to unite disciples of all nations in the cross and resurrection of Your Son, Jesus Christ. By the preaching of the Gospel spread this gift to the ends of the earth; through the same Jesus Christ, our Lord, who lives and reigns with You and the Holy Spirit, one God, now and forever.

Collect for Pentecost Eve

498 Come, Holy Ghost, Creator Blest

1 Come, Ho - ly Ghost, Cre - a - tor blest, And make
2 To You, the Coun - sel - or, we cry, To You,
3 In You, with grac - es sev - en - fold, We God's
4 Your light to ev - 'ry thought im - part, And shed
5 Drive far a - way our wi - ly foe, And Your
our hearts Your place of rest; Come with Your grace and
the gift of God Most High; The fount of life, the
al - might - y hand be - hold While You with tongues of
Your love in ev - 'ry heart; The weak - ness of our
a - bid - ing peace be - stow; With You as our pro -
heav'n-ly aid, And fill the hearts which You have made.
fire of love, The soul's a - noint - ing from a - bove.
fire pro - claim To all the world His ho - ly name.
mor - tal state With death - less might in - vig - or - ate.
tect - ing guide, No e - vil can with us a - bide.

6 Teach us to know the Father, Son,
And You, from both, as Three in One
That we Your name may ever bless
And in our lives the truth confess.

△ 7 Praise we the Father and the Son
And Holy Spirit, with them One,
And may the Son on us bestow
The gifts that from the Spirit flow!

This hymn may be sung in alternation with the version found on the facing page.

Text: attr. Rabanus Maurus, 776–856; tr. Edward Caswall, 1814–78, alt.
Tune: *Geistliche Lieder auffs new gebessert*, Wittenberg, 1533, ed. Joseph Klug; setting: *The Lutheran Hymnal*, 1941

KOMM, GOTT SCHÖPFER
L M

John 14:16, 26; Rom. 8:5–11; Titus 3:5–7; 1 Cor. 2:10–16

Come, Holy Ghost, Creator Blest 499

1 Come, Ho - ly Ghost, Cre - a - tor blest, And make our hearts Your place of rest; Come with Your grace and heav'n - ly aid, And fill the hearts which You have made.
2 To You, the Coun - sel - or, we cry, To You, the gift of God Most High; The fount of life, the fire of love, The soul's a - noint - ing from a - bove.
3 In You, with grac - es sev - en - fold, We God's al - might - y hand be - hold While You with tongues of fire pro - claim To all the world His ho - ly name.
4 Your light to ev - 'ry thought im - part, And shed Your love in ev - 'ry heart; The weak - ness of our mor - tal state With death - less might in - vig - or - ate.
5 Drive far a - way our wi - ly foe, And Your a - bid - ing peace be - stow; With You as our pro - tect - ing guide, No e - vil can with us a - bide. A - men.

6 Teach us to know the Father, Son,
And You, from both, as Three in One
That we Your name may ever bless
And in our lives the truth confess.

△ 7 Praise we the Father and the Son
And Holy Spirit, with them One,
And may the Son on us bestow
The gifts that from the Spirit flow!
Amen.

This hymn may be sung in alternation with the version found on the facing page.
Setting available in hymn accompaniment edition.

Text: attr. Rabanus Maurus, 776–856; tr. Edward Caswall, 1814–78, alt.
Tune: Sarum plainsong, c. 9th cent., mode VIII

VENI CREATOR SPIRITUS
L M

John 14:16, 26; Rom. 8:5–11; Titus 3:5–7; 1 Cor. 2:10–16

500 Creator Spirit, by Whose Aid

1 Cre - a - tor Spir - it, by whose aid The world's foun - da - tions
2 O Source of un - cre - at - ed light, The bear - er of God's
3 Giv - er of grace, de - scend from high; Your sev'n - fold gifts to
△ 4 Im - mor - tal hon - or, end - less fame At - tend the al - might - y

first were laid, Come, vis - it ev - 'ry hum - ble mind; Come,
gra - cious might, Thrice - ho - ly fount, thrice - ho - ly fire, Our
us sup - ply; Help us e - ter - nal truths re - ceive And
Fa - ther's name; The Sav - ior - Son be glo - ri - fied, Who

pour Your joys on hu - man - kind; From sin and sor - row
hearts with heav'n - ly love in - spire; Your sa - cred, heal - ing
prac - tice all that we be - lieve; Give us Your - self that
for all hu - man - kind has died; To You, O Par - a -

set us free; May we Your liv - ing tem - ples be.
mes - sage bring To sanc - ti - fy us as we sing.
we may see The glo - ry of the Trin - i - ty.
clete, we raise Un - end - ing songs of thanks and praise.

"Paraclete," another name for the Holy Spirit, comes from the Greek, meaning "comforter" or "counselor."

Text: attr. Rabanus Maurus, 776–856; tr. John Dryden, 1631–1700, alt.
Tune: *Gesangbuch . . . Psalmen, Geistliche Lieder*, Strassburg, 1541, alt.; setting: *The Lutheran Hymnal*, 1941

ALL EHR UND LOB
88 88 88

Rom. 8:9; 1 Cor. 3:16; John 16:13; Gen. 1:2

Come Down, O Love Divine 501

1 Come down, O Love di - vine; Seek Thou this soul of mine,
2 O let it free - ly burn, Till world - ly pas - sions turn
3 Let ho - ly char - i - ty Mine out - ward ves - ture be
4 And so the yearn - ing strong, With which the soul will long,
And vis - it it with Thine own ar - dor glow - ing;
To dust and ash - es in its heat con - sum - ing;
And low - li - ness be - come mine in - ner cloth - ing—
Shall far out - pass the pow'r of hu - man tell - ing;
O Com - fort - er, draw near; With - in my heart ap - pear,
And let Thy glo - rious light Shine ev - er on my sight,
True low - li - ness of heart, Which takes the hum - bler part,
No soul can guess His grace Till it be - come the place
And kin - dle it, Thy ho - ly flame be - stow - ing.
And clothe me round, the while my path il - lum - ing.
And o'er its own short - com - ings weeps with loath - ing.
Where - in the Ho - ly Spir - it makes His dwell - ing.

Text: Bianco da Siena, c. 1350–1434; tr. Richard F. Littledale, 1833–90
Music: Ralph Vaughan Williams, 1872–1958

DOWN AMPNEY
66 11 66 11

Rom. 5:5; Ezek. 36:26–28; John 14:16, 26; Rom. 15:13

502 Holy Spirit, the Dove Sent from Heaven

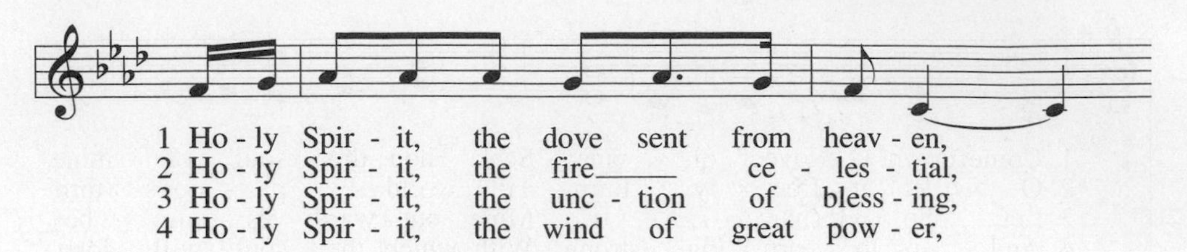
1 Ho - ly Spir - it, the dove sent from heav - en,
2 Ho - ly Spir - it, the fire ce - les - tial,
3 Ho - ly Spir - it, the unc - tion of bless - ing,
4 Ho - ly Spir - it, the wind of great pow - er,

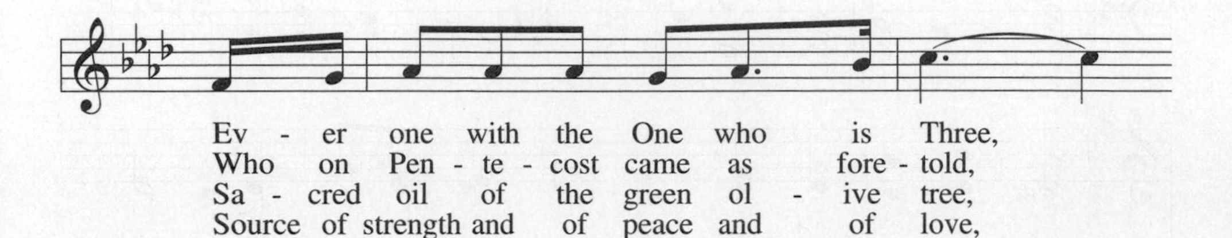
Ev - er one with the One who is Three,
Who on Pen - te - cost came as fore - told,
Sa - cred oil of the green ol - ive tree,
Source of strength and of peace and of love,

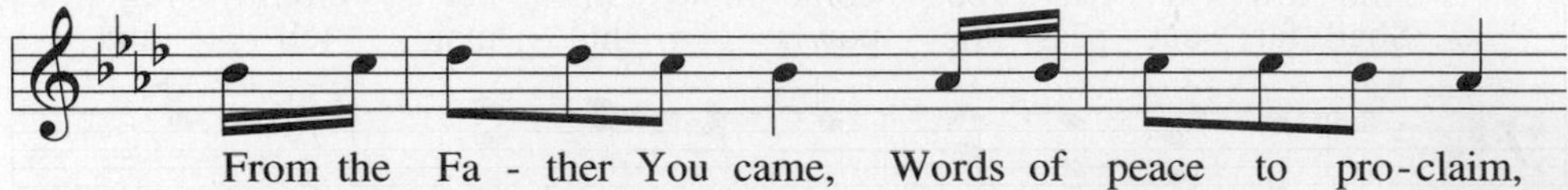

From the Fa - ther You came, Words of peace to pro-claim,
To de-scend from on high And the Church oc - cu - py
Giv - ing heat, giv - ing light, As the tent lamps ig - nite
Tru - est Com - fort - er, plead, As You bring all our need

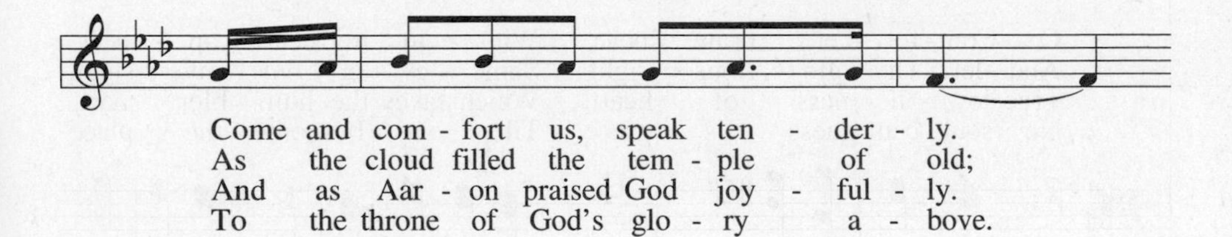
Come and com - fort us, speak ten - der - ly.
As the cloud filled the tem - ple of old;
And as Aar - on praised God joy - ful - ly.
To the throne of God's glo - ry a - bove.

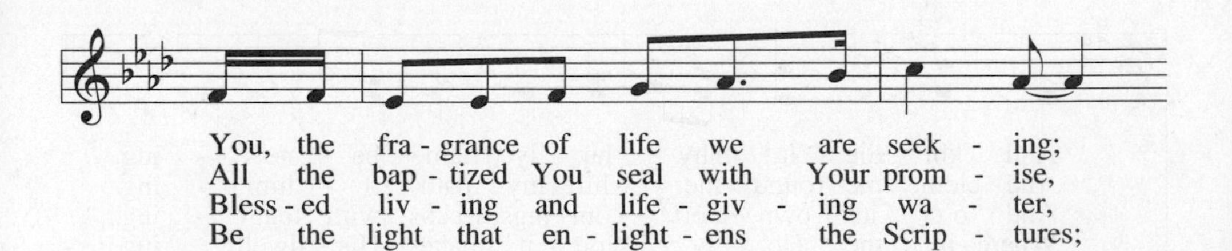
You, the fra - grance of life we are seek - ing;
All the bap - tized You seal with Your prom - ise,
Bless - ed liv - ing and life - giv - ing wa - ter,
Be the light that en - light - ens the Scrip - tures;

"Chrism" refers to the anointing of the baptized with oil to symbolize the Holy Spirit, whose powerful presence in Holy Baptism unites us to Christ's saving work.
Setting available in hymn accompaniment edition.

Text: Philip W. Blycker, b. 1939; tr. Stephen P. Starke, b. 1955
Tune: Philip W. Blycker, b. 1939

SANTO ESPÍRITU
10 9 6 6 9 D

Matt. 3:16–17; 2 Cor. 1:21–22; Titus 3:5–7; Rom. 8:26–27

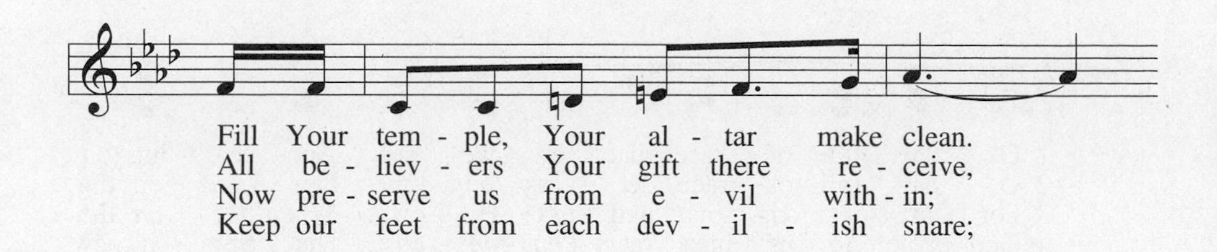
Fill Your tem - ple, Your al - tar make clean.
All be - liev - ers Your gift there re - ceive,
Now pre - serve us from e - vil with - in;
Keep our feet from each dev - il - ish snare;

Joy - ous shel - ter of love, Gra - cious friend from a - bove,
So that all the e - lect— All in Christ— may ex - pect
For in Je - sus, God's Son, All be - liev - ers are one
On - ly You can make whole All that trou - bles our soul;

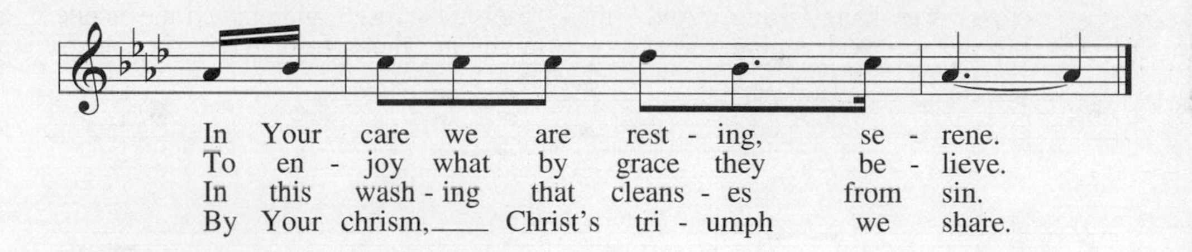
In Your care we are rest - ing, se - rene.
To en - joy what by grace they be - lieve.
In this wash - ing that cleans - es from sin.
By Your chrism,___ Christ's tri - umph we share.

1 *Santo Espíritu, excelsa paloma inmutable ser del Trino Dios;*
mensajero de paz que procedes del Padre hoy consuélanos con suave voz.
Tu vivífico aroma anhelamos; con él llena tu templo, tu altar;
que la sombra feliz de tus alas de gracia nos cobije, oh amigo sin par.

2 *Santo Espíritu, fuego celeste, que en el día de Pentecostés,*
cual la nube de gloria bajaste a la iglesia como al templo de Sión otra vez.
Para el nuevo cristiano eres sello, cada uno recibe tu don.
Todo hijo de Dios elegido es y goza ya las arras de tu salvación.

3 *Santo Espíritu, aceite bendito, fiel producto del verde olivar,*
luminaria y calor en la tienda sagrada donde Aarón se acercaba adorar.
Agua viva y regeneradora, santifícanos contra el mal;
somos uno en Jesús los creyentes del mundo por tu santo lavar bautismal.

4 *Santo Espíritu, viento potente, fuente y fuerza de paz y de amor;*
paracleto veraz que ante el trono del justo nuestra causa abogáis con ardor.
Sé la luz que ilumine la Biblia, nuestros pies dirige al caminar.
Hoy rendimos a ti nuestras almas ansiosas; sólo ungidos podremos triunfar.

503 O Day Full of Grace

1 O day full of grace that now we see Ap - pear - ing on
2 O day full of grace, O bless - ed time, Our Lord on the
3 For Christ bore our sins, and not His own, When He on the
4 God came to us then at Pen - te - cost, His Spir - it new
earth's ho - ri - zon, Bring light from our God that we may be
earth ar - riv - ing; Then came to the world that light sub - lime,
cross was hang - ing; And then He a - rose and moved the stone
life re - veal - ing, That we might no more from Him be lost,
Re - plete in His joy this sea - son. God, shine for us
Great joy for us all re - triev - ing; For Je - sus all
That we, un - to Him be - long - ing, Might join with an -
All dark - ness for us dis - pel - ling. His flame will the
now in this dark place; Your name on our hearts em - bla - zon.
mor - tals did em - brace, All dark - ness and shame re - mov - ing.
gel - ic hosts to raise Our voic - es in end - less sing - ing.
mark of sin ef - face And bring to us all His heal - ing.

Text: Scandinavian, c. 1450; tr. Gerald Thorson, 1921–2001
Tune: Christoph E. F. Weyse, 1774–1842; setting: *Lutheran Book of Worship*, 1978

DEN SIGNEDE DAG
98 98 98

Acts 2:1–4; 2 Cor. 1:21–22; 4:6; Col. 1:13–14

5 When we on that final journey go
That Christ is for us preparing,
We'll gather in song, our hearts aglow,
All joy of the heavens sharing,
And walk in the light of God's own place,
With angels His name adoring.

HOLY TRINITY

Father Most Holy 504

1 Fa - ther most ho - ly, mer - ci - ful, and ten - der; Je - sus, our
2 Trin - i - ty bless - ed, u - ni - ty un - shak - en, Good-ness un -
3 Mak - er of all things, all Thy crea-tures praise Thee; All for Thy
△ 4 Lord God Al - might - y, un - to Thee be glo - ry, One in three
Sav - ior, with the Fa - ther reign - ing; Spir - it of com - fort,
bound - ed, ver - y God of heav - en, Light of the an - gels,
wor - ship were and are cre - at - ed; Now, as we al - so
per - sons, o - ver all ex - alt - ed! Glo - ry we of - fer,
ad - vo - cate, de - fend - er, Light nev - er wan - ing;
joy of those for - sak - en, Hope of all liv - ing,
wor - ship Thee de - vout - ly, Hear Thou our voic - es.
praise Thee and a - dore Thee, Now and for - ev - er.

Text: Latin, c. 10th cent.; tr. Percy Dearmer, 1867–1936, alt.
Tune: *Antiphoner*, Paris, 1681; setting: Joseph Herl, b. 1959

CHRISTE SANCTORUM
11 11 11 5

Is. 6:2–3; 2 Cor. 13:14; Ps. 145:10, 21; Ps. 86:12

505 Triune God, Be Thou Our Stay

1 Tri - une God, be Thou our stay;
1 God the Fa - ther, be our stay;
2 Je - sus Christ, be Thou our stay;
3 Ho - ly Spir - it, be our stay;
O let us per - ish nev - er!

Cleanse us from our sins, we pray, And grant us life for - ev - er.

Keep us from the e - vil one; Up - hold our faith most ho - ly,

And let us trust Thee sole - ly With hum - ble hearts and low - ly.

Let us put God's ar - mor on, With all true Chris - tians run - ning

Our heav'n - ly race and shun - ning The dev - il's wiles and cun - ning.

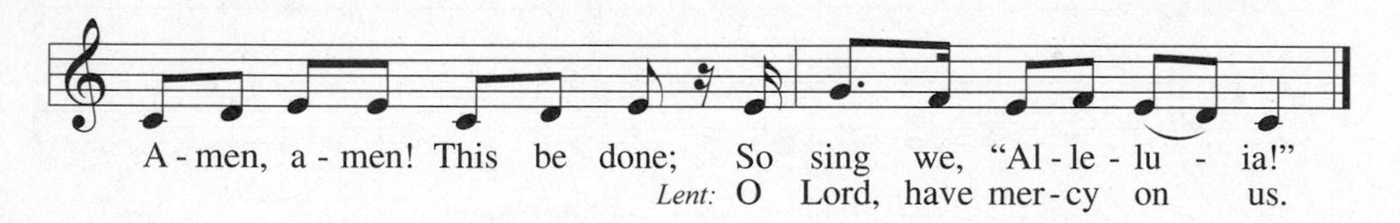

A - men, a - men! This be done; So sing we, "Al - le - lu - ia!"
Lent: O Lord, have mer - cy on us.

This hymn may be sung once, using the words "Triune God . . . ," or it may be sung three times, using the words in italic type. Setting available in hymn accompaniment edition.

Text: Martin Luther, 1483–1546, based on 15th-cent. German litany; tr. Richard Massie, 1800–87, alt.
Tune: *Geystliche gesangk Buchleyn*, Wittenberg, 1524, ed. Johann Walter

GOTT DER VATER, WOHN UNS BEI
77 77 77 7 D

Ps. 31:1–3; Eph. 6:10–17; Ps. 55:22; Is. 46:4

Glory Be to God the Father 506

1 Glo - ry be to God the Fa - ther, Glo - ry be to
2 Glo - ry be to Him who loved us, Washed us from each
3 Glo - ry to the King of an - gels, Glo - ry to the
4 Glo - ry, bless - ing, praise e - ter - nal! Thus the choir of

God the Son, Glo - ry be to God the Spir - it:
spot and stain; Glo - ry be to Him who bought us,
Church's King, Glo - ry to the King of na - tions;
an - gels sings; Hon - or, rich - es, pow'r, do - min - ion!

Great Je - ho - vah, Three in One! Glo - ry,
Made us kings with Him to reign! Glo - ry,
Heav'n and earth, your prais - es bring! Glo - ry,
Thus its praise cre - a - tion brings. Glo - ry,

glo - ry While e - ter - nal a - ges run!
glo - ry To the Lamb that once was slain!
glo - ry To the King of glo - ry sing!
glo - ry, Glo - ry to the King of kings!

Text: Horatius Bonar, 1808–89
Tune: Walter G. Whinfield, 1865–1919; setting: *The Lutheran Hymnal*, 1941

WORCESTER
87 87 47

Rev. 15:3–4; Rev. 7:9–14; Jude 25

507 Holy, Holy, Holy

1 Ho - ly, ho - ly, ho - ly! Lord God Al - might - y!
2 Ho - ly, ho - ly, ho - ly! All the saints a - dore Thee,
3 Ho - ly, ho - ly, ho - ly! Though the dark - ness hide Thee,
4 Ho - ly, ho - ly, ho - ly! Lord God Al - might - y!
Ear - ly in the morn - ing our song shall rise to Thee;
Cast - ing down their gold - en crowns a - round the glass - y sea;
Though the eye of sin - ful man Thy glo - ry may not see,
All Thy works shall praise Thy name in earth and sky and sea.
Ho - ly, ho - ly, ho - ly, mer - ci - ful and might - y!
Cher - u - bim and ser - a - phim fall - ing down be - fore Thee,
On - ly Thou art ho - ly; there is none be - side Thee,
Ho - ly, ho - ly, ho - ly, mer - ci - ful and might - y!
God in three per - sons, bless - ed Trin - i - ty!
Which wert and art and ev - er - more shalt be.
Per - fect in pow'r, in love, and pu - ri - ty.
God in three per - sons, bless - ed Trin - i - ty!

Text: Reginald Heber, 1783–1826; Spanish tr. Juan Bautista Cabrera, 1837–1916
Tune: John B. Dykes, 1823–76; setting: *The Worshipbook: Services and Hymns*, 1972

NICAEA
11 12 12 10

Is. 6:2–3; Rev. 4:2–11; Ex. 15:11; Rev. 7:9–12

1 *¡Santo! ¡Santo! ¡Santo! Señor omnipotente,*
siempre el labio mío loores te dará;
¡Santo! ¡Santo! ¡Santo! Te adoro reverente,
Dios en tres personas, bendita Trinidad.

2 *¡Santo! ¡Santo! ¡Santo! En numeroso coro*
santos escogidos te adoran con fervor,
de alegría llenos, y sus coronas de oro
rinden ante el trono glorioso del Señor.

3 *¡Santo! ¡Santo! ¡Santo! Por más que estés velado*
e imposible sea tu gloria contemplar,
santo tú eres sólo, y nada hay a tu lado
en poder perfecto, pureza y caridad.

4 *¡Santo! ¡Santo! ¡Santo! La gloria de tu nombre*
vemos en tus obras, en cielo, tierra y mar.
¡Santo! ¡Santo! ¡Santo! Te adorará todo hombre,
Dios en tres personas, bendita Trinidad.

508 The Day Is Surely Drawing Near

1 The day is sure - ly draw - ing near When Je - sus, God's a - noint - ed,
2 The fi - nal trum - pet then shall sound And all the earth be shak - en,
3 The books are o - pened then to all, A rec - ord tru - ly tell - ing
4 Then woe to those who scorned the Lord And sought but car - nal plea - sures,
In all His pow - er shall ap - pear As judge whom God ap -
And all who rest be - neath the ground Shall from their sleep a -
What each has done, both great and small, When he on earth was
Who here de - spised His pre - cious Word And loved their earth - ly
point - ed. Then fright shall ban - ish i - dle mirth, And flames on
wak - en. But all who live will in that hour, By God's al -
dwell - ing, And ev - 'ry heart be clear - ly seen, And all be
trea - sures! With shame and trem - bling they will stand And at the
flames shall rav - age earth As Scrip - ture long has warned us.
might - y, bound - less pow'r, Be changed at His com - mand - ing.
known as they have been In thoughts and words and ac - tions.
judg - e's stern com - mand To Sa - tan be de - liv - ered.

Text: Bartholomäus Ringwaldt, 1532–99; tr. Philip A. Peter, 1832–1919, alt.
Tune: *Geistliche Lieder auffs new gebessert*, Wittenberg, 1535, ed. Joseph Klug;
setting: *The Lutheran Hymnal*, 1941

ES IST GEWISSLICH
87 87 887

Luke 21:25–36; Matt. 25:31–46; 1 Thess. 4:13–18; 1 Cor. 15:51–57

5 My Savior paid the debt I owe
And for my sin was smitten;
Within the Book of Life I know
My name has now been written.
I will not doubt, for I am free,
And Satan cannot threaten me;
There is no condemnation!

6 May Christ our intercessor be
And through His blood and merit
Read from His book that we are free
With all who life inherit.
Then we shall see Him face to face,
With all His saints in that blest place
Which He has purchased for us.

7 O Jesus Christ, do not delay,
But hasten our salvation;
We often tremble on our way
In fear and tribulation.
O hear and grant our fervent plea:
Come, mighty judge, and set us free
From death and ev'ry evil.

Lord Jesus Christ, so govern our hearts and minds by Your Holy Spirit that, ever mindful of Your glorious return, we may persevere in both faith and holiness of living; for You live and reign with the Father and the Holy Spirit, one God, now and forever.

Collect for the Last Sunday of the Church Year, Series B

---

509 Christ Is Surely Coming

1 Christ is sure - ly com - ing Bring - ing His re - ward,
2 See the ho - ly cit - y! There they en - ter in,
3 Grace be with God's peo - ple! Praise His ho - ly name!
Al - pha and O - me - ga, First and Last and Lord:
All by Christ made ho - ly, Washed from ev - 'ry sin:
Fa - ther, Son, and Spir - it, Ev - er-more the same;
Root and Stem of Da - vid, Bril - liant Morn - ing Star;
Thirst - y ones, de - sir - ing All He loves to give,
Hear the cer - tain prom - ise From the e - ter - nal home:
Meet your Judge and Sav - ior, Na - tions near and far!
Come for liv - ing wa - ter, Free - ly drink, and live!
"Sure - ly I come quick - ly! Come, Lord Je - sus, come!"

Text: Christopher M. Idle, b. 1938
Music: Ralph Vaughan Williams, 1872–1958

KING'S WESTON
65 65 D

Rev. 3:11; 22:7, 12, 20; 2 Cor. 5:10; Eph. 5:25–27

A Multitude Comes from the East and the West

1 A mul - ti - tude comes from the east and the west
2 O God, let us hear when our Shep - herd shall call
3 All tri - als shall be like a dream that is past,
4 The heav - ens shall ring with an an - them more grand
To sit at the feast of sal - va - tion
In ac - cents per - sua - sive and ten - der,
For - got - ten all trou - ble and mourn - ing.
Than ev - er on earth was re - cord - ed.
With A - bra - ham, I - saac, and Ja - cob, the blest,
That while there is time we make haste, one and all,
All ques - tions and doubts have been an - swered at last,
The blest of the Lord shall re - ceive at His hand
O - bey - ing the Lord's in - vi - ta - tion.
And find Him, our might - y de - fend - er.
When ris - es the light of that morn - ing.
The crown to the vic - tors a - ward - ed.
Have mer - cy up - on us, O Je - sus!

Setting available in hymn accompaniment edition.

Text: Magnus Brostrup Landstad, 1802–80; tr. Peer O. Strömme, 1856–1921, adapt.
Tune: Swedish, 1694

DER MANGE SKAL KOMME
11 9 11 9 9

Matt. 8:11–12; Ps. 107:2–9; Rev. 7:9–17; Rev. 2:10

511 Herald, Sound the Note of Judgment

1 Her - ald, sound the note of judg - ment, Warn - ing us of right and wrong, Turn - ing us from sin and sad - ness Till once more we sing the song.
2 Her - ald, sound the note of glad - ness; Tell the news that Christ is here; Make a path - way through the des - ert For the one who brings God near.
3 Her - ald, sound the note of par - don— Those re - pent - ing are for - giv'n; God re - ceives His way - ward chil - dren, And to them new life is giv'n.
4 Her - ald, sound the note of tri - umph; Christ has come to share our life, Bring - ing God's own love and pow - er, Grant - ing vic - t'ry in our strife.
Refrain
Sound the trum-pet! Tell the mes-sage: Christ, the Sav-ior king, is come!

Text: Moir A. J. Waters, 1906–80
Music: David McCarthy, b. 1931

NEW MALDEN
87 87 87

Matt. 3:1–12; Luke 2:8–14; John 1:29–34

At the Name of Jesus 512

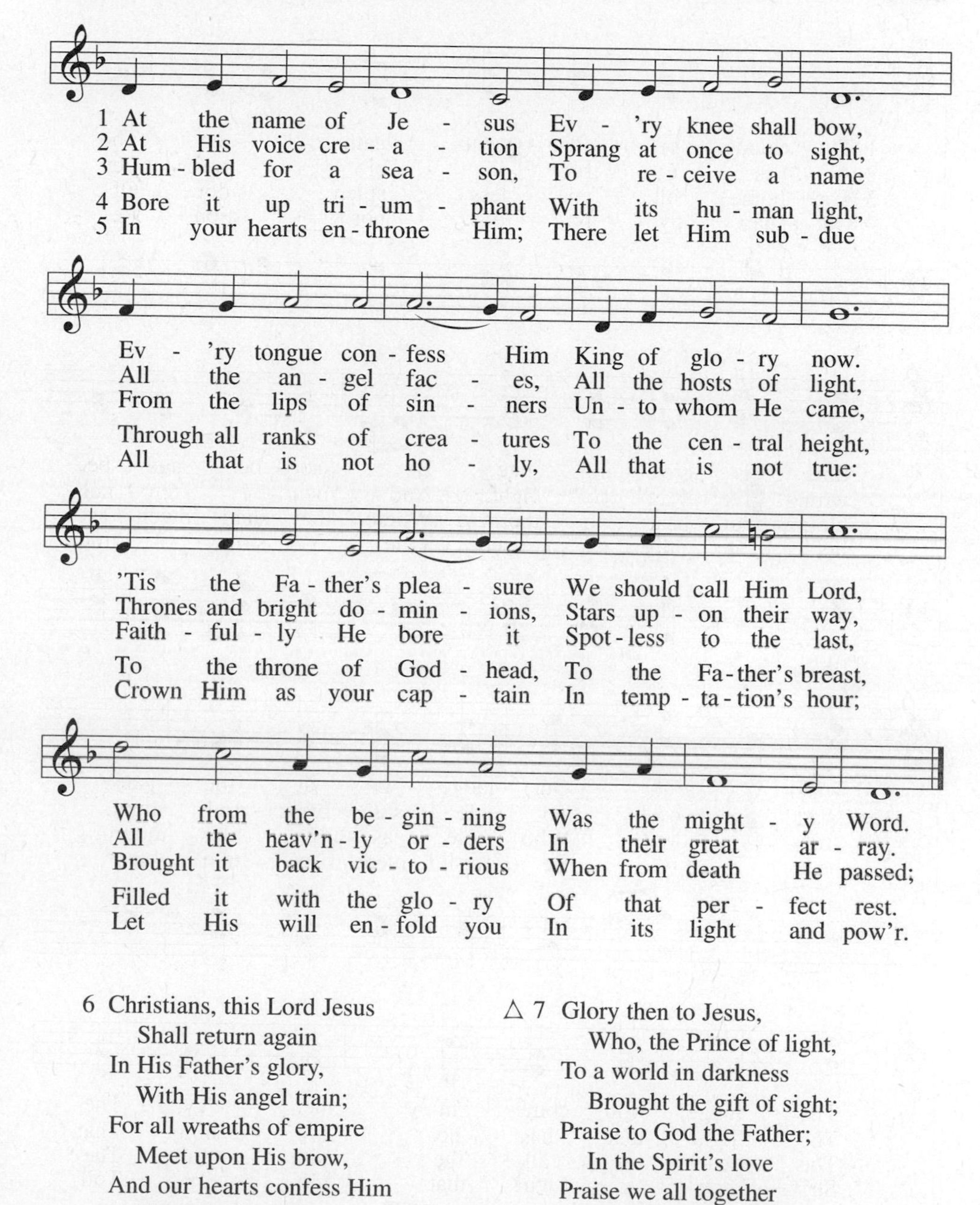
1 At the name of Je - sus Ev - 'ry knee shall bow,
2 At His voice cre - a - tion Sprang at once to sight,
3 Hum - bled for a sea - son, To re - ceive a name
4 Bore it up tri - um - phant With its hu - man light,
5 In your hearts en - throne Him; There let Him sub - due
Ev - 'ry tongue con - fess Him King of glo - ry now.
All the an - gel fac - es, All the hosts of light,
From the lips of sin - ners Un - to whom He came,
Through all ranks of crea - tures To the cen - tral height,
All that is not ho - ly, All that is not true:
'Tis the Fa - ther's plea - sure We should call Him Lord,
Thrones and bright do - min - ions, Stars up - on their way,
Faith - ful - ly He bore it Spot - less to the last,
To the throne of God - head, To the Fa - ther's breast,
Crown Him as your cap - tain In temp - ta - tion's hour;
Who from the be - gin - ning Was the might - y Word.
All the heav'n - ly or - ders In their great ar - ray.
Brought it back vic - to - rious When from death He passed;
Filled it with the glo - ry Of that per - fect rest.
Let His will en - fold you In its light and pow'r.

6 Christians, this Lord Jesus
  Shall return again
In His Father's glory,
  With His angel train;
For all wreaths of empire
  Meet upon His brow,
And our hearts confess Him
  King of glory now.

△ 7 Glory then to Jesus,
  Who, the Prince of light,
To a world in darkness
  Brought the gift of sight;
Praise to God the Father;
  In the Spirit's love
Praise we all together
  Him who reigns above.

Hymn accompaniment: 509

Text: Caroline M. Noel, 1817–77, alt.
Tune: Ralph Vaughan Williams, 1872–1958

KING'S WESTON
65 65 D

Phil. 2:5–11; Luke 1:31; John 1:1–4; Acts 1:10–11

513 The Clouds of Judgment Gather

1 The clouds of judg - ment gath - er, The
2 A - rise, O true dis - ci - ples; Let
3 The home of fade - less splen - dor, Of
4 Oh, hap - py, ho - ly por - tion, Re -
time is grow - ing late; Be so - ber and be
wrong give way to right, And pen - i - ten - tial
blooms that bear no thorn, Where they shall dwell as
lief for all dis - tressed, True vi - sion of true
watch - ful, Our judge is at the gate:
shad - ow To Je - sus' bless - ed light:
chil - dren Who here as ex - iles mourn;
beau - ty, Re - fresh - ment for the blest!
The judge who comes in mer - cy, The
The light that has no eve - ning, That
The peace of all the faith - ful, The
Strive now to win that glo - ry, Toil

Text: Bernard of Cluny, 12th cent.; tr. *Lutheran Book of Worship*, 1978
Tune: Welsh; setting: Ralph Vaughan Williams, 1872–1958

LLANGLOFFAN
76 76 D

1 Peter 1:3–9; Luke 21:36; John 12:46; Rev. 7:13–17

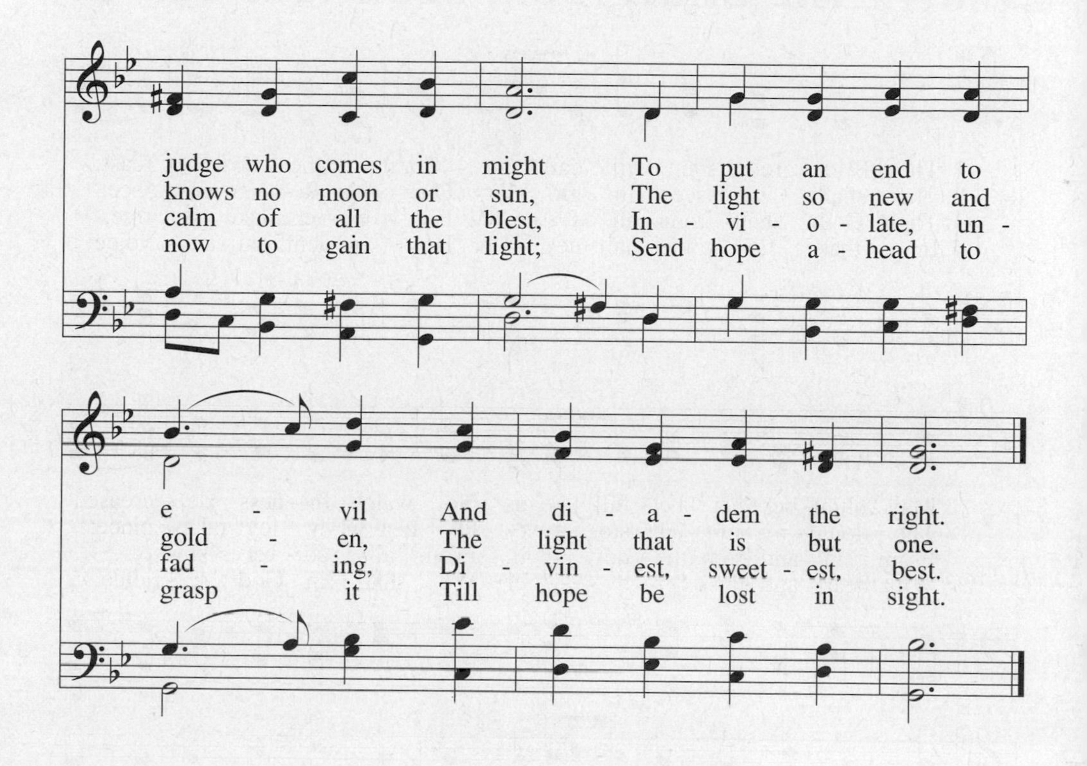
judge who comes in might To put an end to
knows no moon or sun, The light so new and
calm of all the blest, In - vi - o - late, un -
now to gain that light; Send hope a - head to
e - vil And di - a - dem the right.
gold - en, The light that is but one.
fad - ing, Di - vin - est, sweet - est, best.
grasp it Till hope be lost in sight.

Now to Him who is able to keep you from stumbling and to present you blameless before the presence of His glory with great joy, to the only God, our Savior, through Jesus Christ our Lord, be glory, majesty, dominion, and authority, before all time and now and forever. Amen.

Jude 24–25

---

514 The Bridegroom Soon Will Call Us

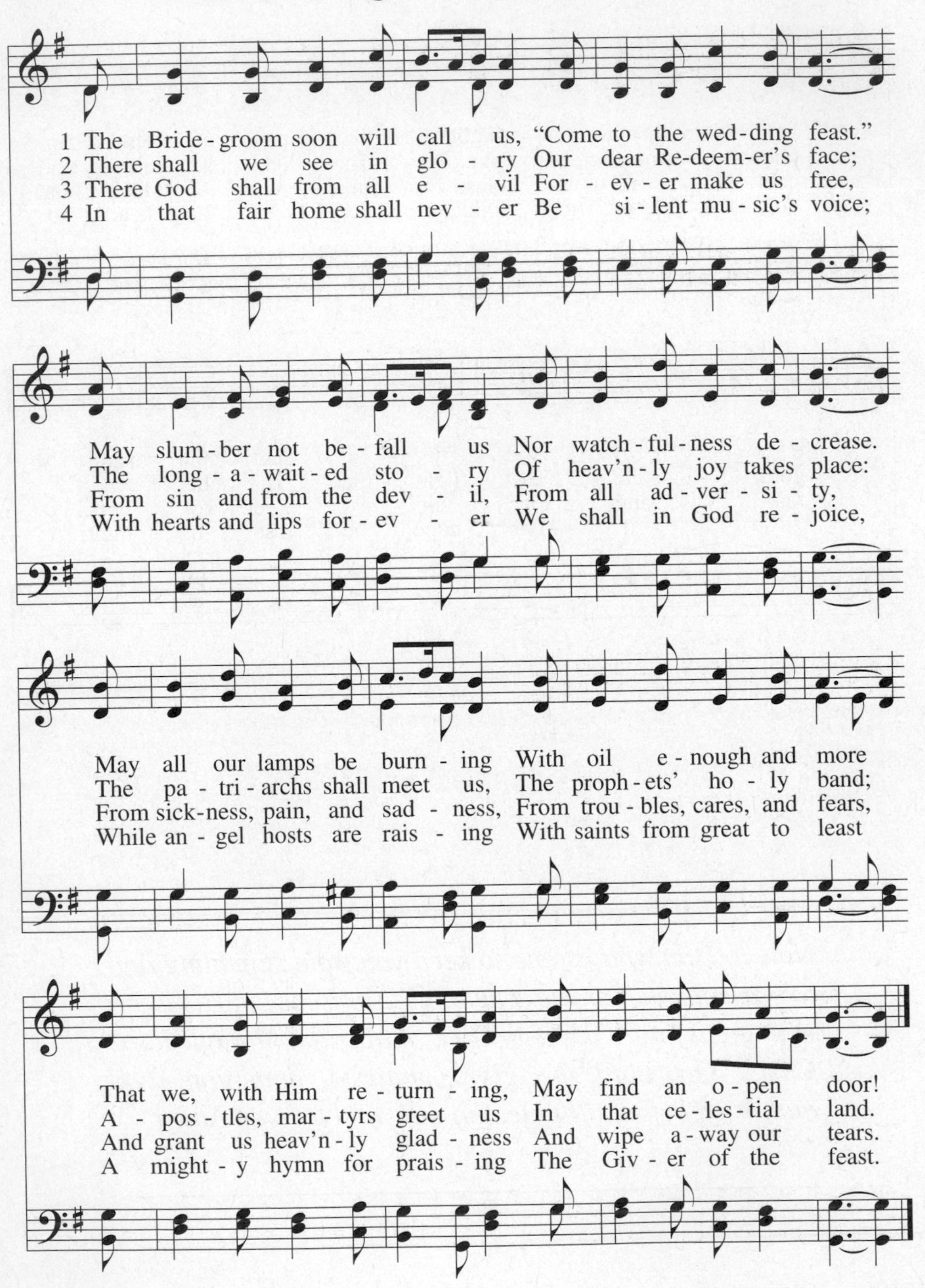
1 The Bride-groom soon will call us, "Come to the wed-ding feast."
May slum-ber not be-fall us Nor watch-ful-ness de-crease.
May all our lamps be burn-ing With oil e-nough and more
That we, with Him re-turn-ing, May find an o-pen door!
2 There shall we see in glo-ry Our dear Re-deem-er's face;
The long-a-wait-ed sto-ry Of heav'n-ly joy takes place:
The pa-tri-archs shall meet us, The proph-ets' ho-ly band;
A-pos-tles, mar-tyrs greet us In that ce-les-tial land.
3 There God shall from all e-vil For-ev-er make us free,
From sin and from the dev-il, From all ad-ver-si-ty,
From sick-ness, pain, and sad-ness, From trou-bles, cares, and fears,
And grant us heav'n-ly glad-ness And wipe a-way our tears.
4 In that fair home shall nev-er Be si-lent mu-sic's voice;
With hearts and lips for-ev-er We shall in God re-joice,
While an-gel hosts are rais-ing With saints from great to least
A might-y hymn for prais-ing The Giv-er of the feast.

Text: Johann Walter, 1496–1570; tr. F. Samuel Janzow, 1913–2001, st. 1; tr. Matthias Loy, 1828–1915, sts. 2–4, alt.
Tune: *Musae Sioniae,* vol. 7, Wolfenbüttel, 1609, ed. Michael Praetorius; setting: Joseph Herl, b. 1959

ACH GOTT VOM HIMMELREICHE
76 76 D

Matt. 25:1–13; Rev. 19:6–9; Rev. 7:9–17

Rejoice, Rejoice, Believers

1 Re - joice, re - joice, be - liev - ers, And let your lights ap - pear;
2 The watch - ers on the moun - tain Pro - claim the Bride - groom near;
3 The saints, who here in pa - tience Their cross and suf - f'rings bore,
4 Our hope and ex - pec - ta - tion, O Je - sus, now ap - pear;
The eve - ning is ad - vanc - ing, And dark - er night is near.
Go forth as He ap - proach - es With al - le - lu - ias clear.
Shall live and reign for - ev - er When sor - row is no more.
A - rise, O Sun so longed for, O'er this be - night - ed sphere.
The Bride - groom is a - ris - ing And soon is draw - ing nigh.
The mar - riage feast is wait - ing; The gates wide o - pen stand.
A - round the throne of glo - ry The Lamb they shall be - hold;
With hearts and hands up - lift - ed, We plead, O Lord, to see
Up, pray and watch and wres - tle; At mid - night comes the cry.
A - rise, O heirs of glo - ry; The Bride - groom is at hand.
In tri - umph cast be - fore Him Their di - a - dems of gold.
The day of earth's re - demp - tion That sets Your peo - ple free!

Text: Laurentius Laurenti, 1660–1722; tr. Sarah B. Findlater, 1823–1907, alt.
Tune: Swedish; setting: Henry V. Gerike, b. 1948

HAF TRONES LAMPA FÄRDIG
76 76 D

Matt. 25:1–6; Rev. 5:11–14; Mal. 4:2; Matt. 13:35–37

516 Wake, Awake, for Night Is Flying

1 "Wake, a - wake, for night is fly - ing," The watch - men on the
2 Zi - on hears the watch - men sing - ing, And all her heart with
3 Now let all the heav'ns a - dore Thee, Let saints and an - gels
heights are cry - ing; "A - wake, Je - ru - sa - lem, a - rise!"
joy is spring - ing; She wakes, she ris - es from her gloom.
sing be - fore Thee With harp and cym - bals' clear - est tone.
Mid - night hears the wel - come voic - es And at the thrill - ing
For her Lord comes down all - glo - rious, The strong in grace, in
Of one pearl each shin - ing por - tal, Where, join - ing with the
cry re - joic - es: "Oh, where are ye, ye vir - gins wise?
truth vic - to - rious; Her star is ris'n, her light is come.
choir im - mor - tal, We gath - er round Thy ra - diant throne.

Text: Philipp Nicolai, 1556–1608; tr. Catherine Winkworth, 1827–78, alt.
Tune: Philipp Nicolai, 1556–1608; setting: *Württembergisches Neues Choralbuch*, 1956

WACHET AUF
898 D 664 448

Matt. 25:1–13; Is. 62:5–12; Rev. 19:6–9; Rev. 7:9–17

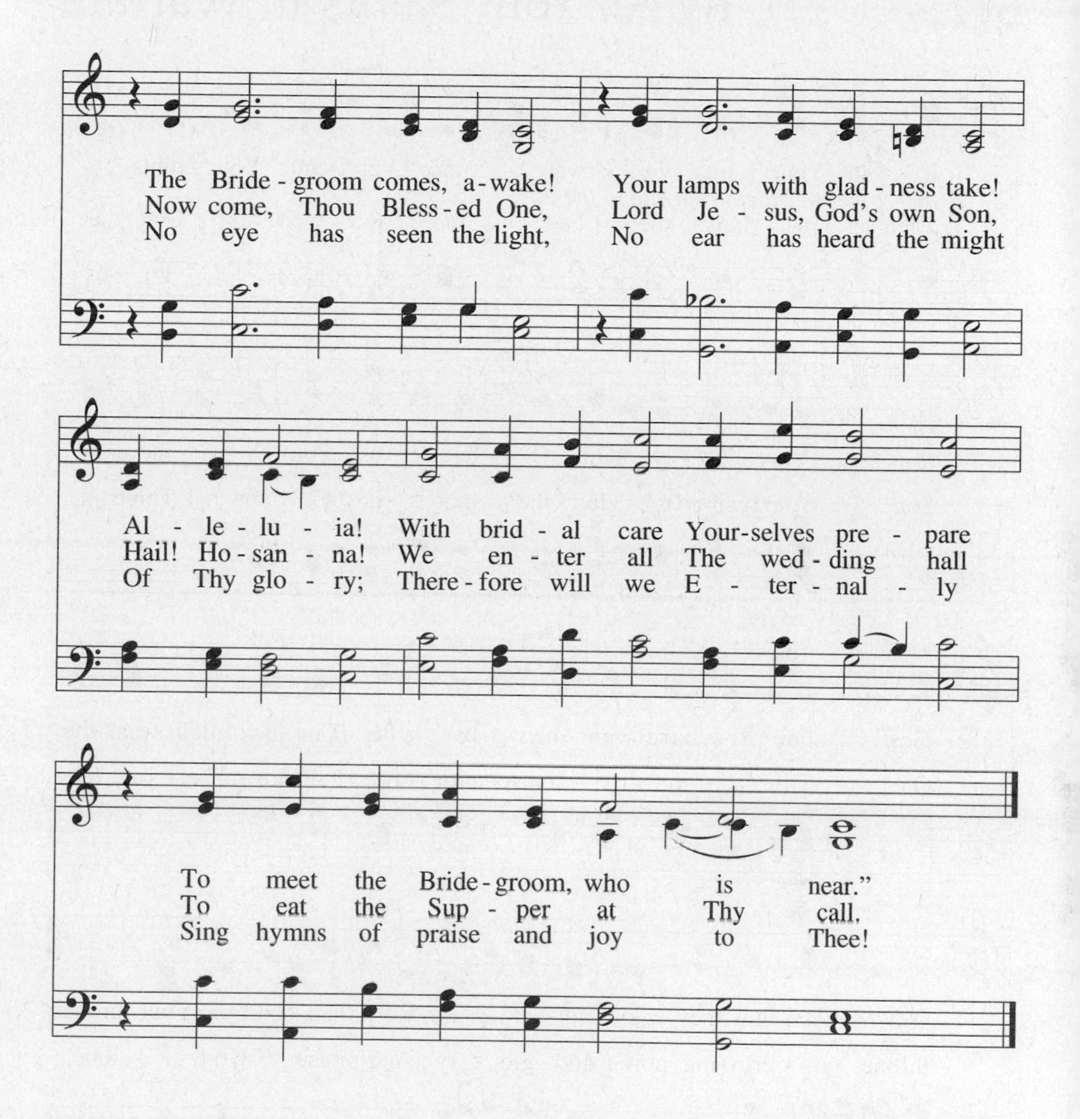
The Bride - groom comes, a - wake! Your lamps with glad - ness take!
Now come, Thou Bless - ed One, Lord Je - sus, God's own Son,
No eye has seen the light, No ear has heard the might
Al - le - lu - ia! With brid - al care Your-selves pre - pare
Hail! Ho - san - na! We en - ter all The wed - ding hall
Of Thy glo - ry; There - fore will we E - ter - nal - ly
To meet the Bride - groom, who is near."
To eat the Sup - per at Thy call.
Sing hymns of praise and joy to Thee!

517 By All Your Saints in Warfare

1 By all Your saints in war - fare, For all Your saints at rest, Your ho - ly name, O Je - sus, For - ev - er - more be blest! For You have won the bat - tle That they might wear the crown; And now they shine in glo - ry Re - flect - ed from Your throne.
2 Insert the stanza appropriate to the day.
△ 3 Then let us praise the Fa - ther And wor - ship God the Son And sing to God the Spir - it, E - ter - nal Three in One, Till all the ran - somed num - ber Fall down be - fore the throne, As - crib - ing pow'r and glo - ry And praise to God a - lone.

Saints and Martyrs (general)

4 Apostles, prophets, martyrs,
And all the noble throng
Who wear the spotless raiment
And raise the ceaseless song—
For these, passed on before us,
We offer praises due
And, walking in their footsteps,
Would live our lives for You.

Text: Horatio Bolton Nelson, 1823–1913, sts. 1–10, 12–13, 15–23, 25–26, 28, alt.;
Harlyn J. Kuschel, b. 1945, st. 11; Gregory J. Wismar, b. 1946, sts. 14, 24, 27
Tune: English; coll. and arr. Ralph Vaughan Williams, 1872–1958; setting: Paul G. Bunjes, 1914–98

KING'S LYNN
76 76 D

Heb. 13:7; 2 Tim. 4:8; Rev. 4:8–11; 7:9–17

St. Andrew, Apostle

5 All praise, O Lord, for Andrew,
The first to welcome You,
Whose witness to his brother
Named You Messiah true.
May we, with hearts kept open
To You throughout the year,
Confess to friend and neighbor
Your advent ever near.

St. Thomas, Apostle

6 All praise, O Lord, for Thomas,
Whose short-lived doubtings prove
Your perfect twofold nature,
The fullness of Your love.
To all who live with questions
A steadfast faith afford;
And grant us grace to know You,
True man, yet God and Lord.

St. Stephen, Martyr

7 Praise for the first of martyrs
Who saw You ready stand
To help in time of torment,
To plead at God's right hand.
Like You, our suff'ring Savior,
His enemies he blessed,
With "Lord, receive my spirit,"
His faith, by death, confessed.

St. John, Apostle and Evangelist

8 For Your belov'd disciple
Exiled to Patmos' shore,
And for his faithful record,
We praise You evermore.
Praise for the mystic vision
Through him to us revealed;
May we, in patience waiting,
With Your elect be sealed.

Holy Innocents, Martyrs

9 All praise for infant martyrs,
Whom Your mysterious love
Called early from their warfare
To share Your home above.
O Rachel, cease your weeping;
They rest from earthly cares!
Lord, grant us crowns as brilliant
And faith as sure as theirs.

The Confession of St. Peter

10 Praise for Your great apostle
So eager and so bold,
Thrice falling, yet repentant,
Thrice charged to feed Your fold.
Lord, make Your pastors faithful
To guard Your flock from harm,
And hold them when they waver
With Your almighty arm.

St. Timothy and St. Titus

11 All praise for faithful pastors,
Who preached and taught Your Word;
For Timothy and Titus,
True servants of their Lord.
Lord, help Your pastors nourish
The souls within their care,
So that Your Church may flourish
And all Your blessings share.

The Conversion of St. Paul

12 Praise for the light from heaven
And for the voice of awe;
Praise for the glorious vision
The persecutor saw.
O Lord, for Paul's conversion,
We bless Your name today;
Come shine within our darkness,
And guide us on our way.

St. Matthias, Apostle

13 For one in place of Judas,
Th'apostles sought God's choice;
The lot fell to Matthias
For whom we now rejoice.
May we like true apostles
Your holy Church defend,
And not betray our calling
But serve You to the end.

St. Joseph, Guardian of Jesus

14 We sing our thanks for Joseph,
The guardian of our Lord,
Who faithfully taught Jesus
Through craft and deed and word.
Grant wisdom, Lord, and patience
To parents ev'rywhere
Who guide and teach the children
Entrusted to their care.

518 By All Your Saints in Warfare

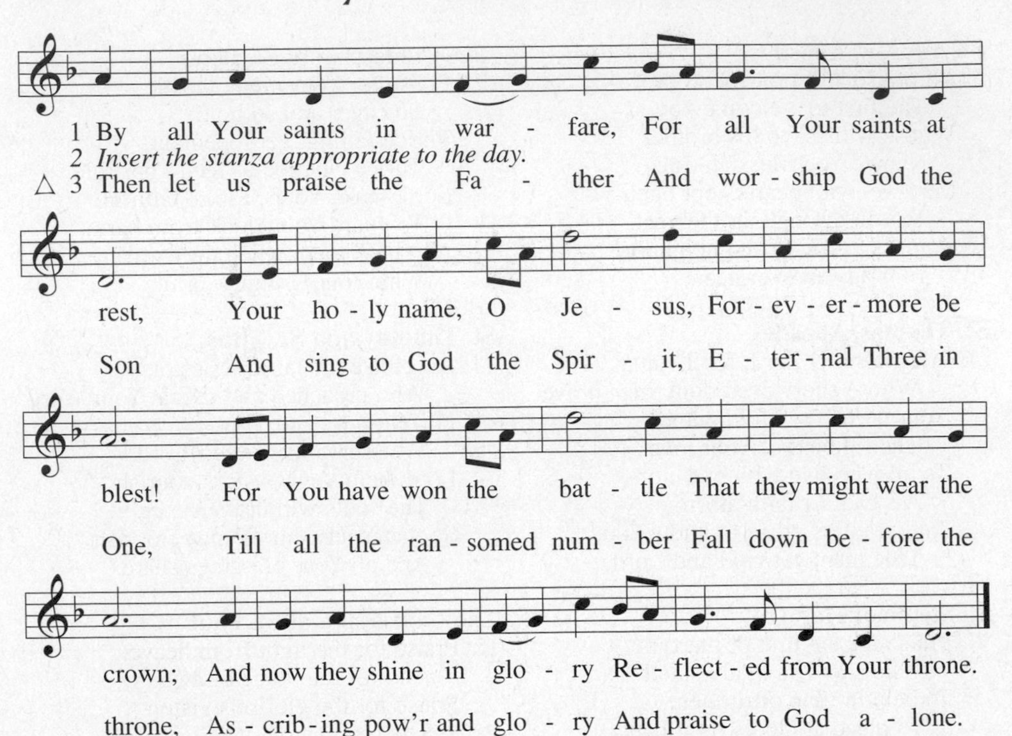
1 By all Your saints in war - fare, For all Your saints at rest, Your ho - ly name, O Je - sus, For - ev - er - more be blest! For You have won the bat - tle That they might wear the crown; And now they shine in glo - ry Re - flect - ed from Your throne.
2 Insert the stanza appropriate to the day.
△ 3 Then let us praise the Fa - ther And wor - ship God the Son And sing to God the Spir - it, E - ter - nal Three in One, Till all the ran - somed num - ber Fall down be - fore the throne, As - crib - ing pow'r and glo - ry And praise to God a - lone.

St. Mark, Evangelist

15 For Mark, O Lord, we praise You,
The weak by grace made strong,
Whose labors and whose Gospel
Enrich our triumph song.
May we, in all our weakness,
Reflect Your servant life
And follow in Your footsteps,
Enduring cross and strife.

St. Philip and St. James, Apostles

16 We praise You, Lord, for Philip,
Blest guide to Greek and Jew,
And for young James the faithful,
Who heard and followed You.
O grant us grace to know You,
The way, the truth, the life,
To wrestle with temptation,
To triumph in the strife.

St. Barnabas, Apostle

17 For Barnabas we praise You,
Who kept Your law of love
And, leaving earthly treasures,
Sought riches from above.
O Christ, our Lord and Savior,
Let gifts of grace descend,
That Your true consolation
May through the world extend.

The Nativity of St. John the Baptist

18 We praise You for the Baptist,
Forerunner of the Word,
Our true Elijah, making
A highway for the Lord.
The last and greatest prophet,
He saw the dawning ray
Of light that grows in splendor
Until the perfect day.

Hymn accompaniment: 517

Text: Horatio Bolton Nelson, 1823–1913, sts. 1–10, 12–13, 15–23, 25–26, 28, alt.;
Harlyn J. Kuschel, b. 1945, st. 11; Gregory J. Wismar, b. 1946, sts. 14, 24, 27
Tune: English; coll. and arr. Ralph Vaughan Williams, 1872–1958

KING'S LYNN
76 76 D

Heb. 13:7; 2 Tim. 4:8; Rev. 4:8–11; 7:9–17

St. Peter and St. Paul, Apostles

19 We praise You for Saint Peter;
We praise You for Saint Paul;
They taught both Jew and Gentile
That Christ is all in all.
To cross and sword they yielded
And saw Your kingdom come;
O God, these two apostles
Reached life through martyrdom.

St. Mary Magdalene

20 All praise for Mary Magdalene,
Whose wholeness was restored
By You, her faithful master,
Her Savior and her Lord.
On Easter morning early
A word from You sufficed;
For she was first to see You,
Her Lord, the risen Christ.

St. James the Elder, Apostle

21 O Lord, for James we praise You,
Who fell to Herod's sword;
He drank the cup of suff'ring
And thus fulfilled Your word.
Lord, curb our vain impatience
For glory and for fame,
Equip us for such suff'rings
As glorify Your name.

St. Mary, Mother of Our Lord

22 We sing with joy of Mary,
Whose heart with awe was stirred
When, youthful and astonished,
She heard the angel's word.
Yet she her voice upraises
To magnify God's name,
As once for our salvation
Your mother she became.

St. Bartholomew, Apostle

23 All praise for him whose candor
Through all his doubt You saw
When Philip at the fig tree
Disclosed You in the law.
Discern, beneath our surface,
O Lord, what we can be,
That by Your truth made guileless,
Your glory we may see.

The Martyrdom of St. John the Baptist

24 Our thanks for John the Baptist
Who, till his dying day,
Made straight paths for the Savior
And heralded His way!
In witnessing to Jesus
Through times of threat or shame
May we with faith and courage
The Lamb of God proclaim.

St. Matthew, Apostle and Evangelist

25 Praise, Lord, for him whose Gospel
Your human life declared,
Who, worldly gain forsaking,
Your path of suff'ring shared.
From all unrighteous mammon,
O raise our eyes anew
That we in our vocation
May rise and follow You.

St. Luke, Evangelist

26 For that belov'd physician
All praise, whose Gospel shows
The Healer of the nations,
The one who shares our woes.
Your wine and oil, O Savior,
Upon our spirits pour,
And with true balm of Gilead
Anoint us evermore.

St. James of Jerusalem

27 We sing of James, Christ's brother,
Who at Jerusalem
Told how God loved the Gentiles
And, in Christ, welcomed them.
Rejoicing in salvation
May we too, by God's grace,
Extend Christ's invitation
To all the human race.

St. Simon and St. Jude, Apostles

28 Praise, Lord, for Your apostles,
Saint Simon and Saint Jude.
One love, one hope impelled them
To tread the way, renewed.
May we with zeal as earnest
The faith of Christ maintain,
Be bound in love together,
And life eternal gain.

519 In His Temple Now Behold Him

1 In His tem - ple now be - hold Him, See the long - ex -
2 In the arms of her who bore Him, Vir - gin pure, be -
3 Je - sus, by Your pre - sen - ta - tion, When they blessed You,

pect - ed Lord; An - cient proph - ets had fore - told Him,
hold Him lie While His a - ged saints a - dore Him
weak and poor, Make us see Your great sal - va - tion,

God has now ful - filled His word. Now to praise Him,
Ere in per - fect faith they die. Al - le - lu - ia,
Seal us with Your prom - ise sure; And pre - sent us

His re - deem - ed Shall break forth with one ac - cord.
al - le - lu - ia! Lo, the in - car - nate God Most High!
in Your glo - ry To Your Fa - ther, cleansed and pure.

The Purification of Mary and the Presentation of Our Lord

Text: Henry J. Pye, c. 1825–1903, alt.
Music: Henry Purcell, 1659–95, adapt.

WESTMINSTER ABBEY
87 87 87

Luke 2:22–38

Stars of the Morning, So Gloriously Bright

1 Stars of the morn - ing, so glo - rious - ly bright,
2 These are Your min - is - ters, these are Your own,
3 Then, when the earth was first poised in mid - space,
4 Still let them aid us and still let them fight,
An - gels in heav - en, re - splen - dent in light,
Lord God of Sab - a - oth, near - est Your throne;
Then, when the plan - ets first sped on their race,
Lord of an - gel - ic hosts, bat - tling for right,
These, where no dark - ness the glo - ry can dim,
These are Your mes - sen - gers, these whom You send,
Then, when were end - ed the six days' em - ploy,
Till, where their an - thems they cease - less - ly pour,
Praise the Thrice Ho - ly One, serv - ing but Him.
Help - ing Your help - less ones, Help - er and Friend.
Then all the sons of God shout - ed for joy.
We with the an - gels may bow and a - dore.

St. Michael and All Angels

Text: Joseph the Hymnographer, c. 810–86; tr. John Mason Neale, 1818–66, alt.
Tune: *Antiphoner*, Paris, 1681; setting: John B. Dykes, 1823–76, alt.

O QUANTA QUALIA
10 10 10 10

Ps. 103:20–21; Heb. 1:14; Job 38:4–7; Rev. 5:13

521 Christ, the Lord of Hosts, Unshaken

1 Christ, the Lord of hosts, un - shak - en By the dev - il's
2 Mi - chael fought the heav'n - ly bat - tle, God - ly an - gels
3 Long on earth the bat - tle ra - ges, Since the ser - pent's
4 Je - sus came, this word ful - fill - ing, Tram - pled Sa - tan,
seeth - ing rage, Thwarts the plan of Sa - tan's min - ions;
by his side; Warred a - gainst the an - cient ser - pent,
first de - ceit; Twist - ed God's com - mand to Ad - am,
death de - fied; Bore the brunt of our temp - ta - tion,
Wins the strife from age to age; Con - quers sin and
Foiled the beast, so full of pride, Cast him earth - bound
Made for - bid - den fruit look sweet. Then the curse of
On the wretch - ed tree He died. Yet to life was
death for - ev - er; Slams them in their steel - y cage.
with his an - gels; Now he prowls, un - sat - is - fied.
God was spo - ken: "You'll lie crushed be - neath His feet!"
raised vic - to - rious; By His life our life sup - plied.

St. Michael and All Angels
Alternate tune: SIEH, HIER BIN ICH (353)

Text: Peter M. Prange, b. 1972
Music: Carl F. Schalk, b. 1929

FORTUNATUS NEW
87 87 87

Rev. 12:7–12; John 12:31–32; 1 Peter 5:8–9; 1 Cor. 15:54–57

5 Swift as lightning falls the tyrant
From his heav'nly perch on high,
As the word of Jesus' vict'ry
Floods the earth and fills the sky.
Wounded by a wound eternal
Now his judgment has drawn nigh!

6 Jesus, send Your angel legions
When the foe would us enslave.
Hold us fast when sin assaults us;
Come, then, Lord, Your people save.
Overthrow at last the dragon;
Send him to his fiery grave.

Lord God, to Thee We Give All Praise 522

1 Lord God, to Thee we give all praise, With grate - ful hearts our voic - es raise, That an - gel hosts Thou didst cre - ate A - round Thy glo - rious throne to wait.
2 They shine with light and heav'n - ly grace And con - stant - ly be - hold Thy face; They heed Thy voice, they know it well, In god - ly wis - dom they ex - cel.
3 They nev - er rest nor sleep as we; Their whole de - light is but to be With Thee, Lord Je - sus, and to keep Thy lit - tle flock, Thy lambs and sheep.
4 The an - cient drag - on is their foe; His en - vy and his wrath they know. It al - ways is his aim and pride Thy Chris - tian peo - ple to di - vide.

5 As he of old deceived the world
And into sin and death has hurled,
So now he subtly lies in wait
To undermine both Church and state.

6 A roaring lion, round he goes,
No halt nor rest he ever knows;
He seeks the Christians to devour
And slay them by his dreadful pow'r.

7 But watchful is the angel band
That follows Christ on ev'ry hand
To guard His people where they go
And break the counsel of the foe.

8 For this, now and in days to be,
Our praise shall rise, O Lord, to Thee,
Whom all the angel hosts adore
With grateful songs forevermore.

St. Michael and All Angels. Hymn accompaniment: 655

Text: Philipp Melanchthon, 1497–1560; German version, Paul Eber, 1511–69; tr. Emanuel Cronenwett, 1841–1931, alt.
Tune: *Geistliche Lieder auffs new gebessert*, Wittenberg, 1543, ed. Joseph Klug

ERHALT UNS, HERR
L M

Matt. 18:10; Heb. 1:14; Ps. 34:7; Rev. 7:9–17

523 O Word of God Incarnate

1 O Word of God in - car-nate, O Wis - dom from on high,
2 The Church from You, dear Mas-ter, Re-ceived the gift di - vine;
3 O make Your Church, dear Sav - ior, A lamp of bur-nished gold
O Truth un - changed, un - chang - ing, O Light of our dark sky:
And still that light is lift - ed O'er all the earth to shine.
To bear be - fore the na - tions Your true light as of old!
We praise You for the ra - diance That from the hal-lowed page,
It is the chart and com - pass That, all life's voy - age through,
O teach Your wan-d'ring pil - grims By this their path to trace
A lan - tern to our foot - steps, Shines on from age to age.
Mid mists and rocks and quick-sands Still guides, O Christ, to You.
Till, clouds and dark - ness end - ed, They see You face to face!

Text: William W. How, 1823–97, alt.
Tune: *Neu-vermehrtes . . . Gesangbuch*, 3rd ed., Meiningen, 1693;
setting: Felix Mendelssohn, 1809–47

MUNICH
76 76 D

John 1:14; 2 Sam. 22:29–33; Ps. 119:105; Rev. 1:20

How Sweet the Name of Jesus Sounds

REDEEMER

524

1 How sweet the name of Je - sus sounds In
2 It makes the wound - ed spir - it whole And
3 Dear name! The rock on which I build, My
4 O Je - sus, shep - herd, guard - ian, friend, My
a be - liev - er's ear! It soothes our sor - rows,
calms the heart's un - rest; 'Tis man - na to the
shield and hid - ing place; My nev - er - fail - ing
Proph - et, Priest, and King, My Lord, my life, my
heals our wounds, And drives a - way our fear.
hun - gry soul And to the wea - ry, rest.
trea - sury filled With bound - less stores of grace.
way, my end, Ac - cept the praise I bring.

5 How weak the effort of my heart,
How cold my warmest thought!
But when I see Thee as Thou art,
I'll praise Thee as I ought.

6 Till then I would Thy love proclaim
With ev'ry fleeting breath;
And may the music of Thy name
Refresh my soul in death!

Text: John Newton, 1725–1807, alt.
Tune: Alexander R. Reinagle, 1799–1877; setting: *Hymns Ancient and Modern*, 1861

ST. PETER
C M

Song 1:3; Acts 4:12; John 14:13; Acts 2:21

525 Crown Him with Many Crowns

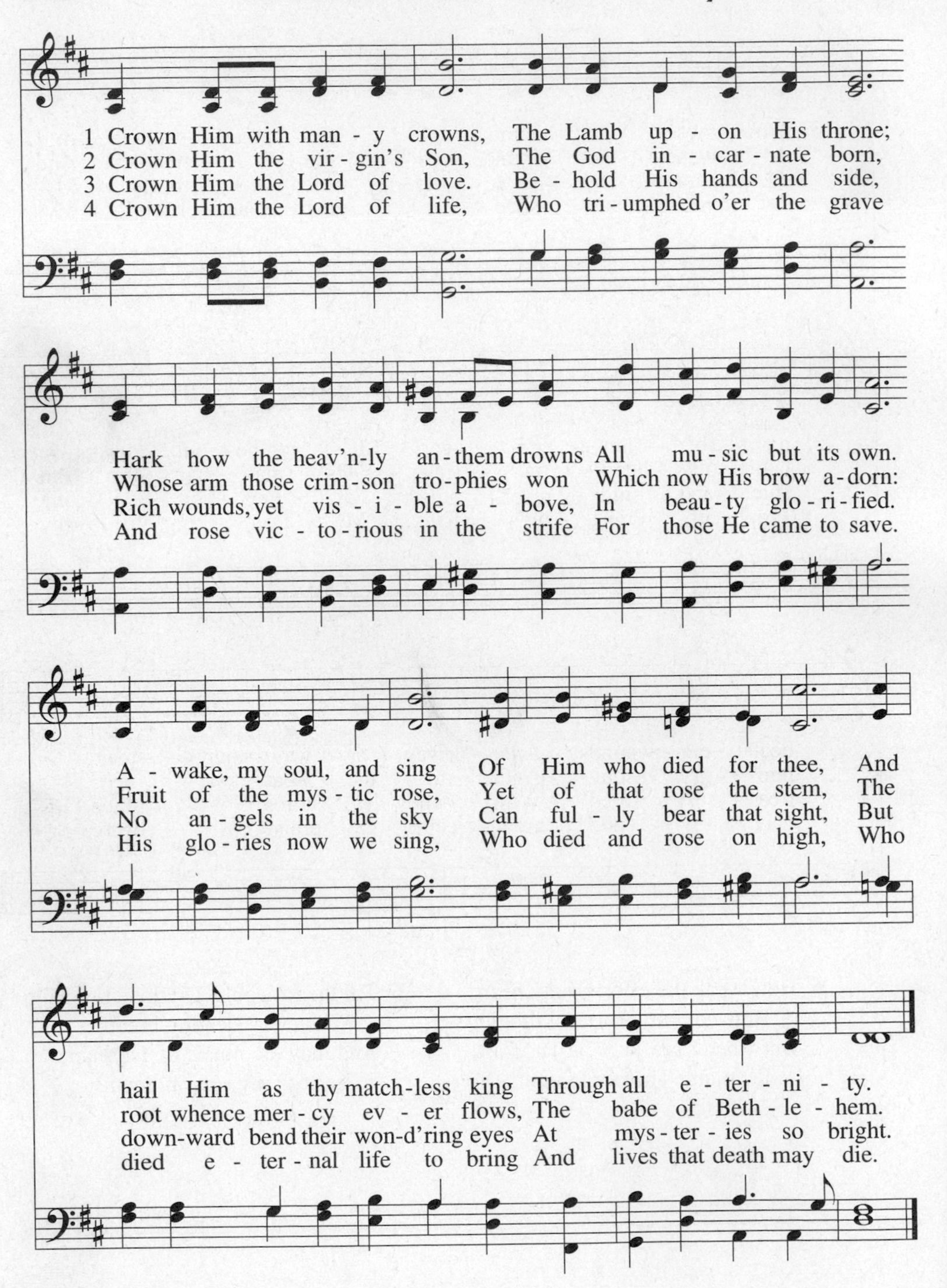
1 Crown Him with man - y crowns, The Lamb up - on His throne;
2 Crown Him the vir - gin's Son, The God in - car - nate born,
3 Crown Him the Lord of love. Be - hold His hands and side,
4 Crown Him the Lord of life, Who tri - umphed o'er the grave
Hark how the heav'n-ly an - them drowns All mu - sic but its own.
Whose arm those crim - son tro - phies won Which now His brow a - dorn:
Rich wounds, yet vis - i - ble a - bove, In beau - ty glo - ri - fied.
And rose vic - to - rious in the strife For those He came to save.
A - wake, my soul, and sing Of Him who died for thee, And
Fruit of the mys - tic rose, Yet of that rose the stem, The
No an - gels in the sky Can ful - ly bear that sight, But
His glo - ries now we sing, Who died and rose on high, Who
hail Him as thy match - less king Through all e - ter - ni - ty.
root whence mer - cy ev - er flows, The babe of Beth - le - hem.
down-ward bend their won - d'ring eyes At mys - ter - ies so bright.
died e - ter - nal life to bring And lives that death may die.

Text: Matthew Bridges, 1800–94, sts. 1–3, 5, alt.; Godfrey Thring, 1823–1903, st. 4
Tune: George J. Elvey, 1816–93; setting: *Service Book and Hymnal*, 1958

DIADEMATA
S M D

Rev. 19:12, 16; Heb. 2:9; Rev. 5:11–14; Phil. 2:9–11

5 Crown Him the Lord of heav'n,
  Enthroned in worlds above,
Crown Him the king to whom is giv'n
  The wondrous name of Love.
Crown Him with many crowns
  As thrones before Him fall;
Crown Him, ye kings, with many crowns,
  For He is king of all.

You Are the Way; through You Alone 526

1 You are the way; through You a - lone Can
2 You are the truth; Your Word a - lone True
3 You are the life; the emp - ty tomb Pro -
4 You are the way, the truth, the life; Grant
we the Fa - ther find; In You, O Christ, has
wis - dom can im - part; You on - ly can in -
claims Your con - qu'ring arm, And those who put their
us that way to know, That truth to keep, that
God re - vealed His heart and will and mind.
form the mind And pu - ri - fy the heart.
trust in You Not death nor hell shall harm.
life to win Whose joys e - ter - nal flow.

Text: George W. Doane, 1799–1859, alt.
Tune: *The CL Psalmes of David*, Edinburgh, 1615; setting: *The Lutheran Hymnal*, 1941

DUNDEE
C M

John 14:6; 1 Tim. 2:5; Acts 4:12

527 O Savior, Precious Savior

1 O Sav - ior, pre - cious Sav - ior, Whom yet un - seen we love;
2 O bring - er of sal - va - tion, Who won - drous - ly hast wrought
3 In Thee all full - ness dwell - eth, All grace and pow'r di - vine;
4 O grant the con - sum - ma - tion Of this our song a - bove
O name of might and fa - vor, All oth - er names a - bove,
Thy - self the rev - e - la - tion Of love be - yond our thought,
The glo - ry that ex - cel - leth, O Son of God, is Thine.
In end - less ad - o - ra - tion And ev - er - last - ing love;
We wor - ship Thee, we bless Thee, To Thee, O Christ, we sing;
We wor - ship Thee, we bless Thee, To Thee, O Christ, we sing;
We wor - ship Thee, we bless Thee, To Thee, O Christ, we sing;
Then shall we praise and bless Thee Where per - fect prais - es ring,
We praise Thee and con - fess Thee, Our ho - ly Lord and King.
We praise Thee and con - fess Thee, Our gra - cious Lord and King.
We praise Thee and con - fess Thee, Our glo - rious Lord and King.
And ev - er - more con - fess Thee, Our Sav - ior and our King!

Text: Frances R. Havergal, 1836–79
Music: Arthur H. Mann, 1850–1929

ANGEL'S STORY
76 76 D

1 Peter 1:8–9; Phil. 2:9; Col. 1:19; Rev. 7:9–14

Oh, for a Thousand Tongues to Sing

REDEEMER

1 Oh, for a thou - sand tongues to sing My
2 My gra - cious Mas - ter and my God, As -
3 Je - sus! The name that charms our fears, That
4 He breaks the pow'r of can - celed sin; He
5 Look un - to Him, ye na - tions; own Your
great Re - deem - er's praise, The glo - ries of my
sist me to pro - claim, To spread through all the
bids our sor - rows cease; 'Tis mu - sic in the
sets the pris - 'ner free. His blood can make the
God, ye fall - en race. Look and be saved through
God and King, The tri - umphs of His grace!
earth a - broad, The hon - ors of Thy name.
sin - ner's ears, 'Tis life and health and peace.
foul - est clean; His blood a - vails for me.
faith a - lone, Be jus - ti - fied by grace.

6 See all your sins on Jesus laid;
The Lamb of God was slain.
His soul was once an off'ring made
For ev'ry soul of man.

7 To God all glory, praise, and love
Be now and ever giv'n
By saints below and saints above,
The Church in earth and heav'n.

Text: Charles Wesley, 1707–88, alt.
Tune: Carl G. Gläser, 1784–1829; setting: Lowell Mason, 1792–1872

AZMON
C M

Ps. 96:1–3; 1 Peter 1:18–19; Rev. 5:11–13; Eph. 2:8–9

529 Since Our Great High Priest, Christ Jesus

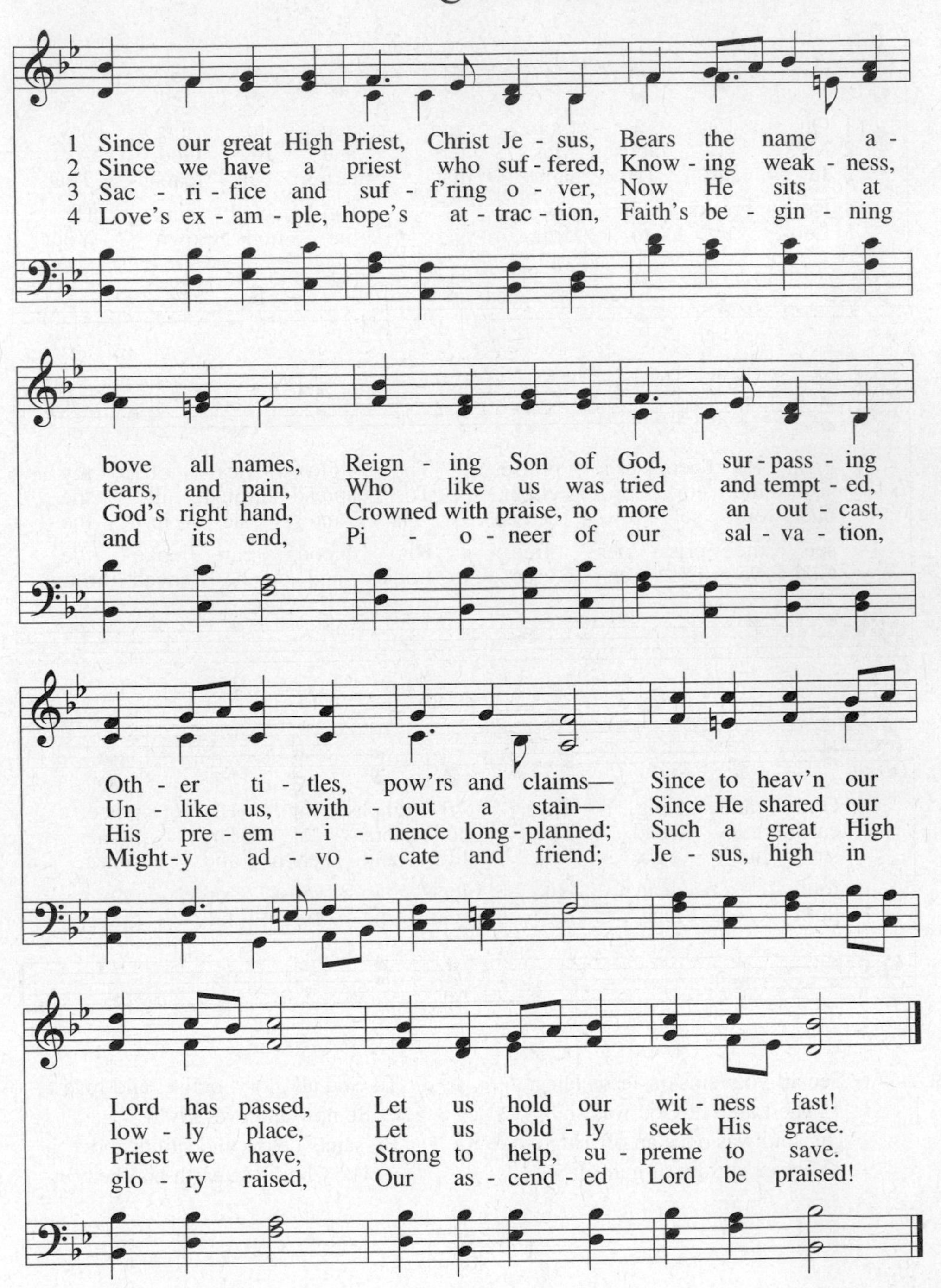
1 Since our great High Priest, Christ Je - sus, Bears the name a -
2 Since we have a priest who suf - fered, Know - ing weak - ness,
3 Sac - ri - fice and suf - f'ring o - ver, Now He sits at
4 Love's ex - am - ple, hope's at - trac - tion, Faith's be - gin - ning
bove all names, Reign - ing Son of God, sur - pass - ing
tears, and pain, Who like us was tried and tempt - ed,
God's right hand, Crowned with praise, no more an out - cast,
and its end, Pi - o - neer of our sal - va - tion,
Oth - er ti - tles, pow'rs and claims— Since to heav'n our
Un - like us, with - out a stain— Since He shared our
His pre - em - i - nence long - planned; Such a great High
Might - y ad - vo - cate and friend; Je - sus, high in
Lord has passed, Let us hold our wit - ness fast!
low - ly place, Let us bold - ly seek His grace.
Priest we have, Strong to help, su - preme to save.
glo - ry raised, Our as - cend - ed Lord be praised!

Text: Christopher M. Idle, b. 1938
Tune: *Geistreiches Gesang-Buch*, Darmstadt, 1698; setting: William H. Monk, 1823–89, alt.

ALL SAINTS
87 87 77

Heb. 1:3; 4:14; 9:24

No Temple Now, No Gift of Price 530

1 No temple now, no gift of price,
No priestly round of sacrifice,
Retain their ancient pow'rs.
As shadows fade before the sun
The day of sacrifice is done,
The day of grace is ours.

2 The dying Lord our ransom paid,
One final full self-offering made,
Complete in ev'ry part.
His finished sacrifice for sins
The covenant of grace begins,
The law within the heart.

3 In faith and confidence draw near,
Within the holiest appear,
With all who praise and pray;
Who share one family, one feast,
One great imperishable Priest,
One new and living way.

4 For Christ is ours! With purpose true
The pilgrim path of faith pursue,
The road that Jesus trod;
Until by His prevailing grace
We stand at last before His face,
Our Savior and our God.

Alternate tune: MERIBAH (698)

Text: Timothy Dudley-Smith, b. 1926
Music: Joseph Herl, b. 1959

KIRKWOOD
886 886

Heb. 9:11–28; 10:10–22; Jer. 31:31–34

531 Hail, Thou Once Despised Jesus

1 Hail, Thou once de - spis - ed Je - sus! Hail, Thou Gal - i - le - an King! Thou didst suf - fer to re - lease us; Thou didst free sal - va - tion bring. Hail, Thou u - ni - ver - sal Sav - ior, Bear - er of our sin and shame! By Thy mer - it
2 Pas - chal Lamb, by God ap - point - ed, All our sins on Thee were laid; By al - might - y love a - noint - ed, Thou hast full a - tone - ment made. All Thy peo - ple are for - giv - en Through the vir - tue of Thy blood; O - pened is the
3 Je - sus, hail! En - throned in glo - ry, There for - ev - er to a - bide; All the heav'n - ly hosts a - dore Thee, Seat - ed at Thy Fa - ther's side. There for sin - ners Thou art plead - ing; There Thou dost our place pre - pare, Ev - er for us
4 Wor - ship, hon - or, pow'r, and bless - ing Thou art wor - thy to re - ceive; High - est prais - es, with - out ceas - ing, Right it is for us to give. Help, ye bright an - gel - ic spir - its, All your no - blest an - thems raise; Help to sing our

Text: *Hymns Addressed to the Holy, Holy, Holy, Triune God*, London, 1757, sts. 1, 3a, 4a, alt.; *A Collection of Psalms and Hymns*, London, 1760, sts. 2, 3b, 4b, alt.
Tune: *Geist-reiches Gesang-Buch*, Halle, 1704, ed. Johann A. Freylinghausen; setting: *The Lutheran Hymnal*, 1941

O DURCHBRECHER
87 87 D

Isaiah 53; 1 Peter 1:18–20; Eph. 2:13–18; Rev. 5:9–14

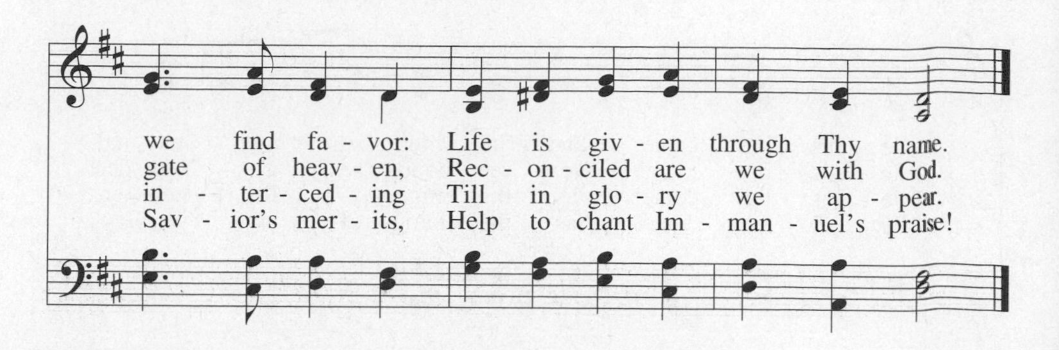
we find fa - vor: Life is giv - en through Thy name.
gate of heav - en, Rec - on - ciled are we with God.
in - ter - ced - ing Till in glo - ry we ap - pear.
Sav - ior's mer - its, Help to chant Im - man - uel's praise!

The Head That Once Was Crowned with Thorns 532

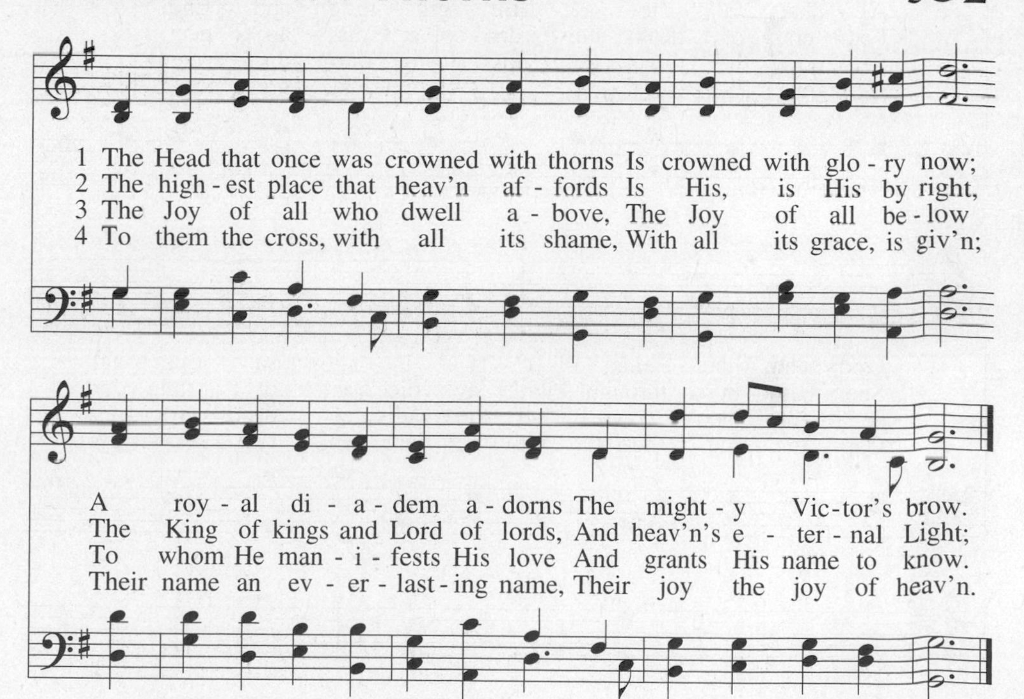
1 The Head that once was crowned with thorns Is crowned with glo - ry now;
2 The high - est place that heav'n af - fords Is His, is His by right,
3 The Joy of all who dwell a - bove, The Joy of all be - low
4 To them the cross, with all its shame, With all its grace, is giv'n;
A roy - al di - a - dem a - dorns The might - y Vic - tor's brow.
The King of kings and Lord of lords, And heav'n's e - ter - nal Light;
To whom He man - i - fests His love And grants His name to know.
Their name an ev - er - last - ing name, Their joy the joy of heav'n.

5 They suffer with their Lord below,
They reign with Him above,
Their profit and their joy to know
The myst'ry of His love.

6 The cross He bore is life and health,
Though shame and death to Him:
His people's hope, His people's wealth,
Their everlasting theme.

Text: Thomas Kelly, 1769–1855
Tune: Jeremiah Clarke, c. 1674–1707; setting: *The Lutheran Hymnal*, 1941

ST. MAGNUS
C M

Heb. 2:10; 1 Peter 4:16; Phil. 2:9–11; 3:10–11

REDEEMER

533 Jesus Has Come and Brings Pleasure

1 Je - sus has come and brings plea - sure e - ter - nal,
2 Je - sus has come! Now see bonds rent a - sun - der!
3 Je - sus has come as the might - y Re - deem - er.
4 Je - sus has come as the King of all glo - ry!
Al - pha, O - me - ga, Be - gin - ning and End;
Fet - ters of death now dis - solve, dis - ap - pear.
See now the threat - en - ing strong one dis - armed!
Heav - en and earth, O de - clare His great pow'r,
God - head, hu - man - i - ty, u - nion su - per - nal,
See Him burst through with a voice as of thun - der!
Je - sus breaks down all the walls of death's for - tress,
Cap - tur - ing hearts with the heav - en - ly sto - ry;
O great Re - deem - er, You come as our friend!
He sets us free from our guilt and our fear,
Brings forth the pris - 'ners tri - um - phant, un - harmed.
Wel - come Him now in this fast - fleet - ing hour!

Text: Johann Ludwig Conrad Allendorf, 1693–1773;
tr. Oliver C. Rupprecht, 1903–2000, alt.
Tune: Cöthen, c. 1733; setting: Paul G. Bunjes, 1914–98, alt.

JESUS IST KOMMEN, GRUND EWIGER FREUDE
11 10 11 10 11 11

Luke 1:68–79; 1 John 1:1–2; Isaiah 12

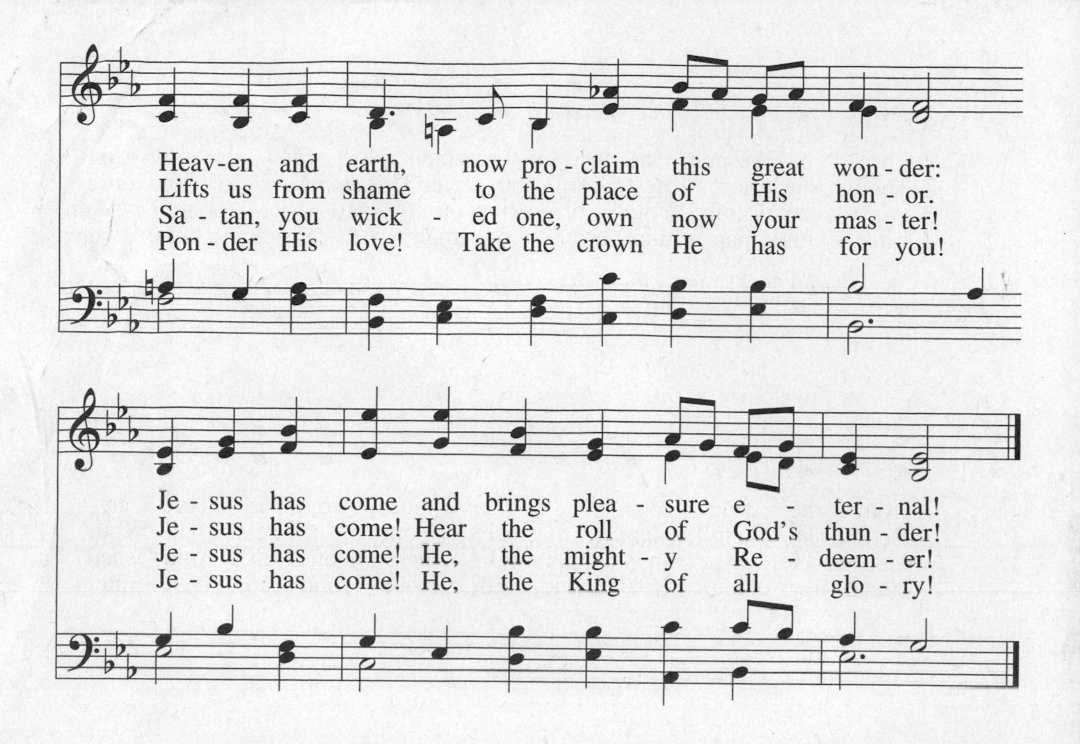
Heav-en and earth, now pro-claim this great won-der:
Lifts us from shame to the place of His hon-or.
Sa-tan, you wick-ed one, own now your mas-ter!
Pon-der His love! Take the crown He has for you!
Je-sus has come and brings plea-sure e-ter-nal!
Je-sus has come! Hear the roll of God's thun-der!
Je-sus has come! He, the might-y Re-deem-er!
Je-sus has come! He, the King of all glo-ry!

Almighty God, You exalted Your Son to the place of all honor and authority. Enlighten our minds by Your Holy Spirit that, confessing Jesus as Lord, we may be led into all truth; through the same Jesus Christ, our Lord, who lives and reigns with You and the Holy Spirit, one God, now and forever.

Collect for Proper 21, Series A

---

534 Lord, Enthroned in Heavenly Splendor

1 Lord, en-throned in heav'n - ly splen - dor, First - be - got - ten
2 Though the low - liest form now veil You As of old in
3 Pas - chal Lamb, Your of - f'ring, fin - ished Once for all when
4 Life - im - part - ing heav'n - ly man - na, Strick-en rock with
from the dead, You a - lone, our strong de - fend - er,
Beth - le - hem, Here as there Your an - gels hail You,
You were slain, In its full - ness un - di - min-ished
stream-ing side, Heav'n and earth with loud ho - san - na
Lift - ing up Your peo-ple's head.
Branch and flow'r of Jes - se's stem.
Shall for - ev - er - more re - main,
Wor - ship You, the Lamb who died,
Al - le - lu - ia,
al - le - lu - ia, al - le - lu - ia!
Je - sus, true and
We in wor - ship
Cleans - ing souls from
Ris'n, as - cend - ed,

Text: George H. Bourne, 1840–1925, alt.
Tune: William Owen, 1813–93; setting: Joseph Herl, b. 1959

BRYN CALFARIA
87 87 444 77

Rev. 1:5–6; 5:11–14; 7:9–17; 1 Cor. 5:7b

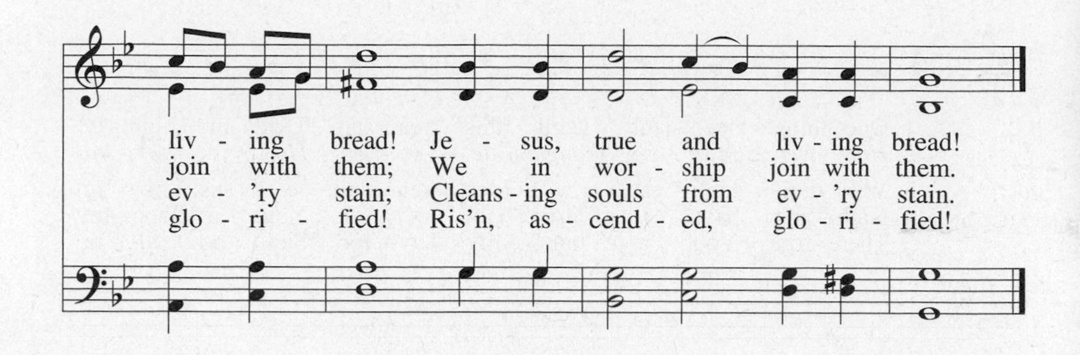
liv - ing bread! Je - sus, true and liv - ing bread!
join with them; We in wor - ship join with them.
ev - 'ry stain; Cleans - ing souls from ev - 'ry stain.
glo - ri - fied! Ris'n, as - cend - ed, glo - ri - fied!

How Wide the Love of Christ 535

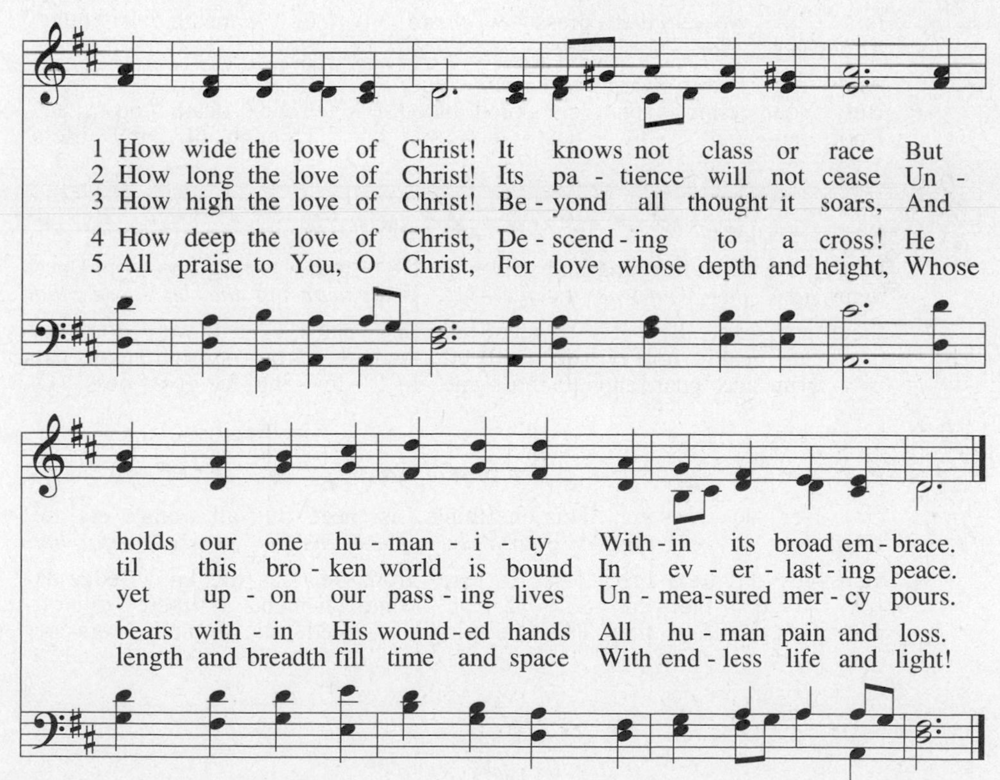
1 How wide the love of Christ! It knows not class or race But
2 How long the love of Christ! Its pa - tience will not cease Un -
3 How high the love of Christ! Be - yond all thought it soars, And
4 How deep the love of Christ, De - scend - ing to a cross! He
5 All praise to You, O Christ, For love whose depth and height, Whose
holds our one hu - man - i - ty With - in its broad em - brace.
til this bro - ken world is bound In ev - er - last - ing peace.
yet up - on our pass - ing lives Un - mea - sured mer - cy pours.
bears with - in His wound - ed hands All hu - man pain and loss.
length and breadth fill time and space With end - less life and light!

Text: Herman G. Stuempfle, Jr., 1923–2007
Tune: Johann M. Spiess, 1715–72; setting: *The Lutheran Hymnal*, 1941

SWABIA
S M

Eph. 3:17b–18

536 One Thing's Needful

1 One thing's need - ful; Lord, this trea - sure Teach me high - ly
2 How were Mar - y's thoughts de - vot - ed Her e - ter - nal
3 Wis - dom's high - est, no - blest trea - sure, Je - sus, is re -
4 Noth - ing have I, Christ, to of - fer, You a - lone, my
5 There - fore You a - lone, my Sav - ior, Shall be all in
to re - gard. All else, though it first give plea - sure,
joy to find As in - tent each word she not - ed,
vealed in You. Let me find in You my plea - sure,
high - est good. Noth - ing have I, Lord, to prof - fer
all to me; Search my heart and my be - hav - ior,
Is a yoke that press - es hard! Be - neath it the
At her Sav - ior's feet re - clined! How kin - dled her
And my way - ward will sub - due, Hu - mil - i - ty
But Your crim - son - col - ored blood. Your death on the
Root out all hy - poc - ri - sy. Through all my life's
heart is still fret - ting and striv - ing, No true, last - ing hap - pi - ness
heart, how de - vout was its feel - ing, While hear - ing the les - sons that
there and sim - plic - i - ty reign - ing, In paths of true wis - dom my
cross has death whol - ly de - feat - ed And there - by my righ - teous - ness
pil - grim - age, guard and up - hold me, In lov - ing for - give - ness, O
ev - er de - riv - ing. This one thing is need - ful; all oth - ers are
Christ was re - veal - ing! All earth - ly con - cerns she for - got for her
steps ev - er train - ing. If I learn from Je - sus this knowl - edge di -
ful - ly com - plet - ed; Sal - va - tion's white rai - ments I there did ob -
Je - sus, en - fold me. This one thing is need - ful; all oth - ers are

Stanza 2 may be reserved for occasions when Luke 10:38–42 is read.
Setting available in hymn accompaniment edition.

Text: Johann Heinrich Schröder, 1667–99; tr. Frances E. Cox, 1812–97, alt.
Tune: Adam Krieger, 1634–66

EINS IST NOT
87 87 12 12 11 11

Luke 10:42; Phil. 3:7–8; Heb. 9:14; John 13:15–17

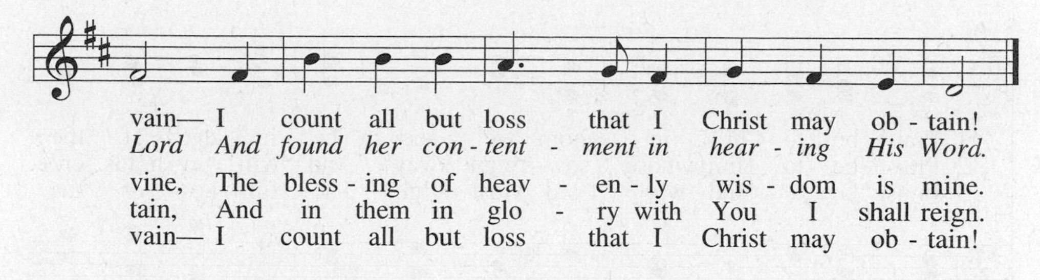
vain— I count all but loss that I Christ may ob - tain!
Lord And found her con - tent - ment in hear - ing His Word.
vine, The bless - ing of heav - en - ly wis - dom is mine.
tain, And in them in glo - ry with You I shall reign.
vain— I count all but loss that I Christ may ob - tain!

Beautiful Savior

537

1 Beau - ti - ful Sav - ior, King of cre - a - tion, Son of
2 Fair are the mead - ows, Fair are the wood - lands, Robed in
3 Fair is the sun - shine, Fair is the moon - light, Bright the
4 Beau - ti - ful Sav - ior, Lord of the na - tions, Son of
God and Son of Man! Tru - ly I'd love Thee, Tru - ly I'd
flow'rs of bloom - ing spring; Je - sus is fair - er, Je - sus is
spar - kling stars on high; Je - sus shines bright - er, Je - sus shines
God and Son of Man! Glo - ry and hon - or, Praise, ad - o -
serve Thee, Light of my soul, my joy, my crown.
pur - er, He makes our sor - r'wing spir - it sing.
pur - er Than all the an - gels in the sky.
ra - tion Now and for - ev - er - more be Thine!

Text: *Münsterisch Gesangbuch*, Münster, 1677; tr. Joseph A. Seiss, 1823–1904
Tune: Silesian, 19th cent.; setting: *Service Book and Hymnal*, 1958

SCHÖNSTER HERR JESU
557 558

Heb. 1:1–13; John 1:1–4, 14; Luke 1:30–33; John 12:46

538 Praise Be to Christ

1 Praise be to Christ in whom we see The im - age of the
2 Praise be to Him whose sov - 'reign sway And will up - holds cre -
3 Praise be to Him who, Lord Most High, The full - ness of the
Fa - ther shown, The first-born Son re - vealed and known, The truth and
a - tion's plan; Who is, be - fore all worlds be - gan And when our
God - head shares; And yet our hu - man na - ture bears, Who came as
grace of de - i - ty; Through whom cre - a - tion came to birth,
world has passed a - way: Lord of the Church, its life and head,
man to bleed and die. And from His cross there flows our peace
Whose fin - gers set the stars in place, The un - seen pow'rs, and
Re - demp - tion's price and source and theme, A - live, the first - born
Who chose for us the path He trod, That so might sins and

Text: Timothy Dudley-Smith, b. 1926
Tune: *Johann Störls . . . Schlag- Gesang- Und Noten-Buch*, Stuttgart, 1744;
setting: *The Lutheran Hymnal*, 1941

O GROSSER GOTT
L M D

Col. 1:15–20

this small earth, The fur - thest bounds of time and space.
from the dead, To reign as all - in - all su - preme.
sor - rows cease And all be rec - on - ciled to God.

Christ Is the World's Redeemer 539

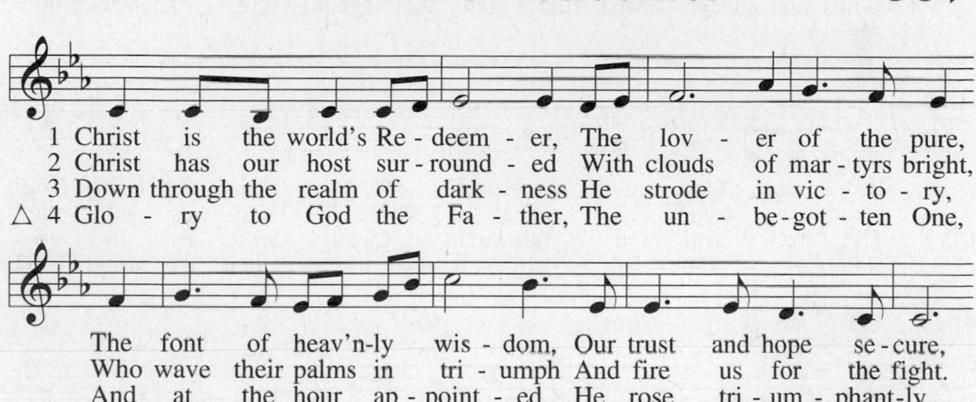
1 Christ is the world's Re - deem - er, The lov - er of the pure,
2 Christ has our host sur - round - ed With clouds of mar - tyrs bright,
3 Down through the realm of dark - ness He strode in vic - to - ry,
△ 4 Glo - ry to God the Fa - ther, The un - be - got - ten One,
The font of heav'n-ly wis - dom, Our trust and hope se - cure,
Who wave their palms in tri - umph And fire us for the fight.
And at the hour ap - point - ed He rose tri - um - phant-ly.
All hon - or be to Je - sus, His sole - be - got - ten Son,

The ar - mor of His sol - diers, The Lord of earth and sky,
Then Christ the cross as - cend - ed To save a world un - done
And now, to heav'n as - cend - ed, He sits up - on the throne
And to the Ho - ly Spir - it— The per - fect Trin - i - ty.

Our health while we are liv - ing, Our life when we shall die.
And, suf - f'ring for the sin - ful, Our full re - demp - tion won.
Whence He had ne'er de - part - ed, His Fa - ther's and His own.
Let all the worlds give an - swer: A - men! So let it be.

Setting available in hymn accompaniment edition.

Text: attr. Columba, 521–97; tr. Duncan MacGregor, 1854–1923, alt.
Tune: Irish

MOVILLE
76 76 D

Acts 2:21–36; Phil. 2:5–11; Heb. 12:2; Rev. 7:9–17

540 Christ, the Word of God Incarnate

1 Christ, the Word of God in - car - nate, Lord and Son of
2 Christ, the liv - ing bread from heav - en, Food for bod - y,
3 Christ, the shoot that springs tri - um - phant From the stump of
4 Christ, our good and faith - ful shep - herd, Watch - ing all Your

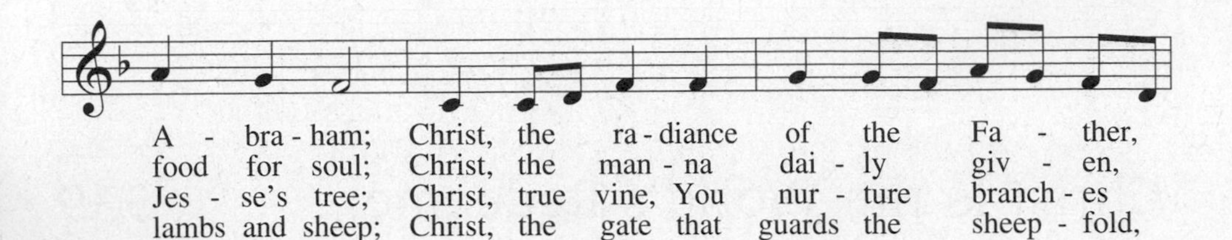

A - bra - ham; Christ, the ra - diance of the Fa - ther,
food for soul; Christ, the man - na dai - ly giv - en,
Jes - se's tree; Christ, true vine, You nur - ture branch - es
lambs and sheep; Christ, the gate that guards the sheep - fold,

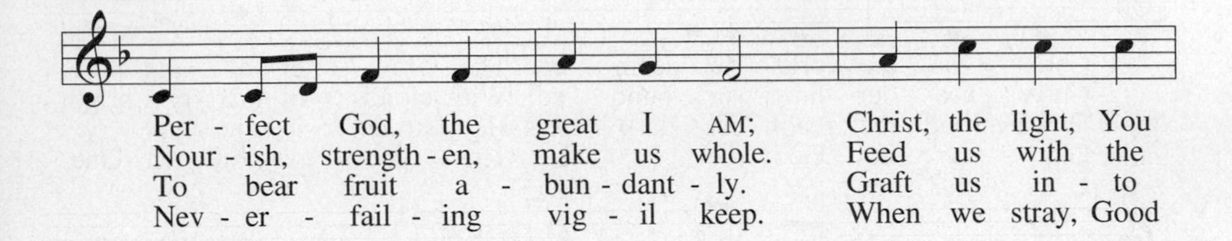

Per - fect God, the great I AM; Christ, the light, You
Nour - ish, strength - en, make us whole. Feed us with the
To bear fruit a - bun - dant - ly. Graft us in - to
Nev - er - fail - ing vig - il keep. When we stray, Good

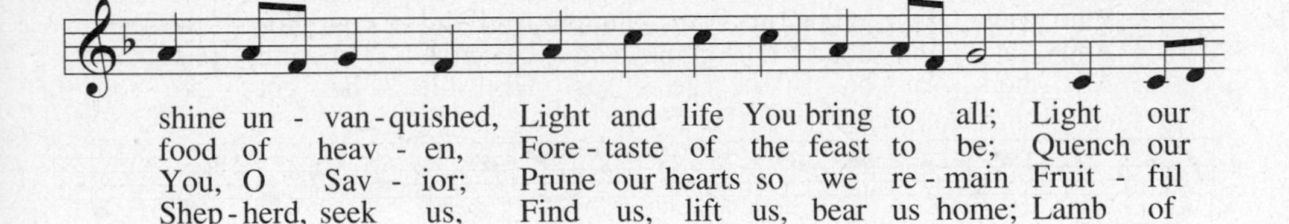

shine un - van - quished, Light and life You bring to all; Light our
food of heav - en, Fore - taste of the feast to be; Quench our
You, O Sav - ior; Prune our hearts so we re - main Fruit - ful
Shep - herd, seek us, Find us, lift us, bear us home; Lamb of

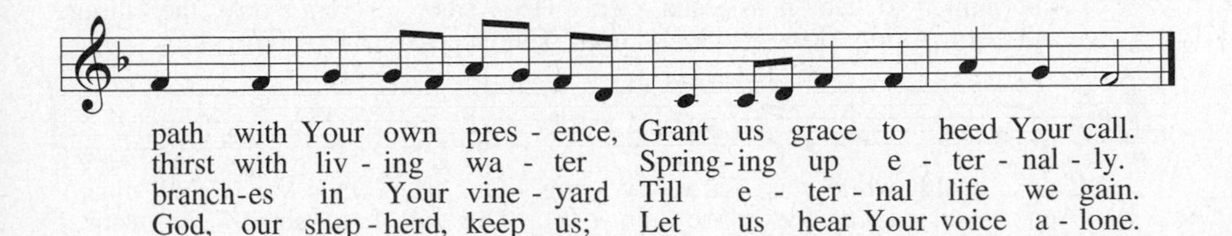

path with Your own pres - ence, Grant us grace to heed Your call.
thirst with liv - ing wa - ter Spring - ing up e - ter - nal - ly.
branch - es in Your vine - yard Till e - ter - nal life we gain.
God, our shep - herd, keep us; Let us hear Your voice a - lone.

Hymn accompaniment: 584, 782

Text: Steven P. Mueller, b. 1964
Tune: *Columbian Harmony*, Cincinnati, 1825

HOLY MANNA
87 87 D

John 1:1–14; 6:30–40, 48–58; 10:7–16, 27–28; 15:1–8

5 Christ, the way that leads unfailing
To the Father's home on high,
Christ, the truth that frees the captive,
Christ, the life that cannot die.
Mediator to the Father,
Sacrifice and great High Priest:
Lead us to Your heav'nly mansions,
There to share Your wedding feast.

△ 6 Christ, the Alpha and Omega,
Christ, the firstborn from the dead,
Christ, the life and resurrection,
Christ, the Church's glorious head:
Praise and thanks and adoration
And unending worship be
To the Father and the Spirit
And to You eternally.

"Away from Us!" the Demon Cried 541

1 "A - way from us!" the de - mon cried
2 But Je - sus spoke with God's own pow'r;
3 O ris - en Christ, God's liv - ing Word,
4 Drive out the doubt that crip - ples faith;
5 Then help us, Lord, to greet each day
When Christ, the Lord, drew near. "Our dark, dis - or - dered
"Come forth!" was His com - mand; For e - vil can - not
To us, we pray, draw near. Come, speak the truth that
Ex - pel our pride and greed That we, from pow'rs that
With hearts and wills made new And, when You call us
world is lost When You, the Light, ap - pear!"
bear the Light Nor sin the Truth with - stand.
cleans - es sin With love that con - quers fear.
threat - en us, May, by Your grace, be freed.
forth to serve, To rise and fol - low You.

Hymn accompaniment: 653
Alternate tune: CONSOLATION (348)

Text: Herman G. Stuempfle, Jr., 1923–2007
Tune: African American spiritual; adapt. Harry T. Burleigh, 1866–1949

MCKEE
C M

Mark 1:23–26; John 3:19–21; Eph. 5:8–14; Heb. 9:14

542 When I Behold Jesus Christ

1 When I be - hold Je - sus Christ, True God who died for me,
2 For me You gave all Your love, For me You suf-fered pain;
3 You had no sin, ho - ly Lord, But You were tor-tured, tried;
4 What love is this? Great - er love No one has ev - er known.

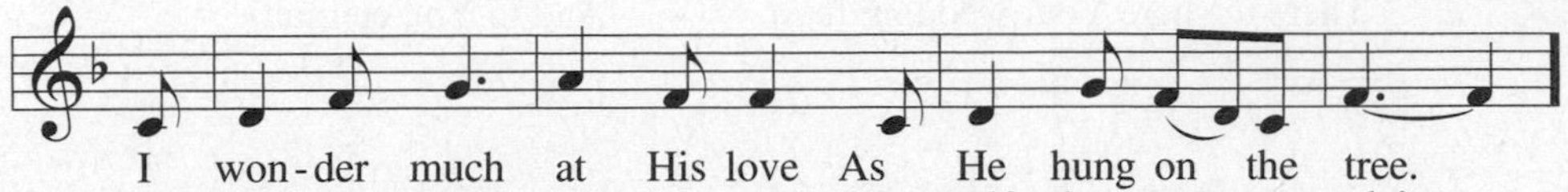

I won - der much at His love As He hung on the tree.
I find no words, noth - ing can Your self - less - ness ex - plain.
On Gol - go - tha there for all My sins You bled and died.
My life with God— this I owe To You, and You a - lone.

Refrain

What kind of love is this? What kind of love is this?

You showed Your love, Je - sus, there To me on Cal - va - ry.

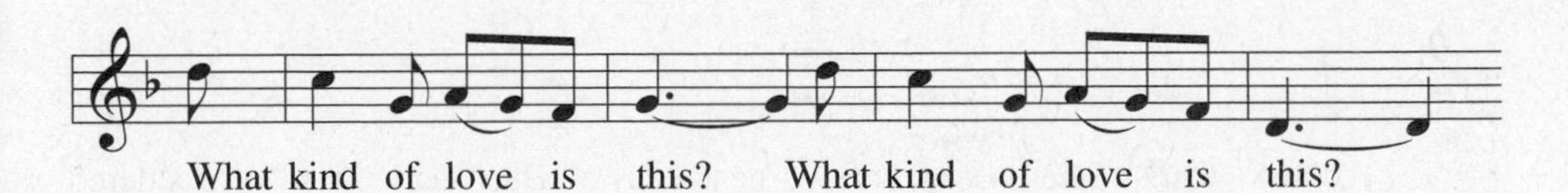

What kind of love is this? What kind of love is this?

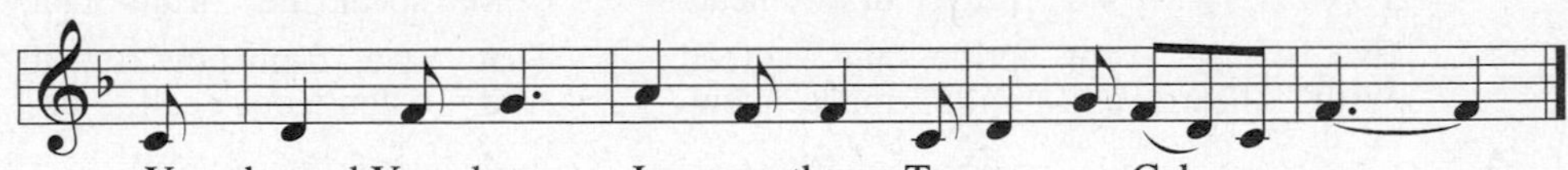

You showed Your love, Je - sus, there To me on Cal - va - ry.

Setting available in hymn accompaniment edition.

Text: Almaz Belhu, sts. 1–3; tr. Hartmut Schoenherr, with Jim and Aurelia Keefer, sts. 1–3;
Joseph Herl, b. 1959, st. 4
Tune: Almaz Belhu

MIN AYNET FIQIR NEW
76 76 and refrain

Rom. 5:8; 1 John 4:9–10; John 15:13

What Wondrous Love Is This

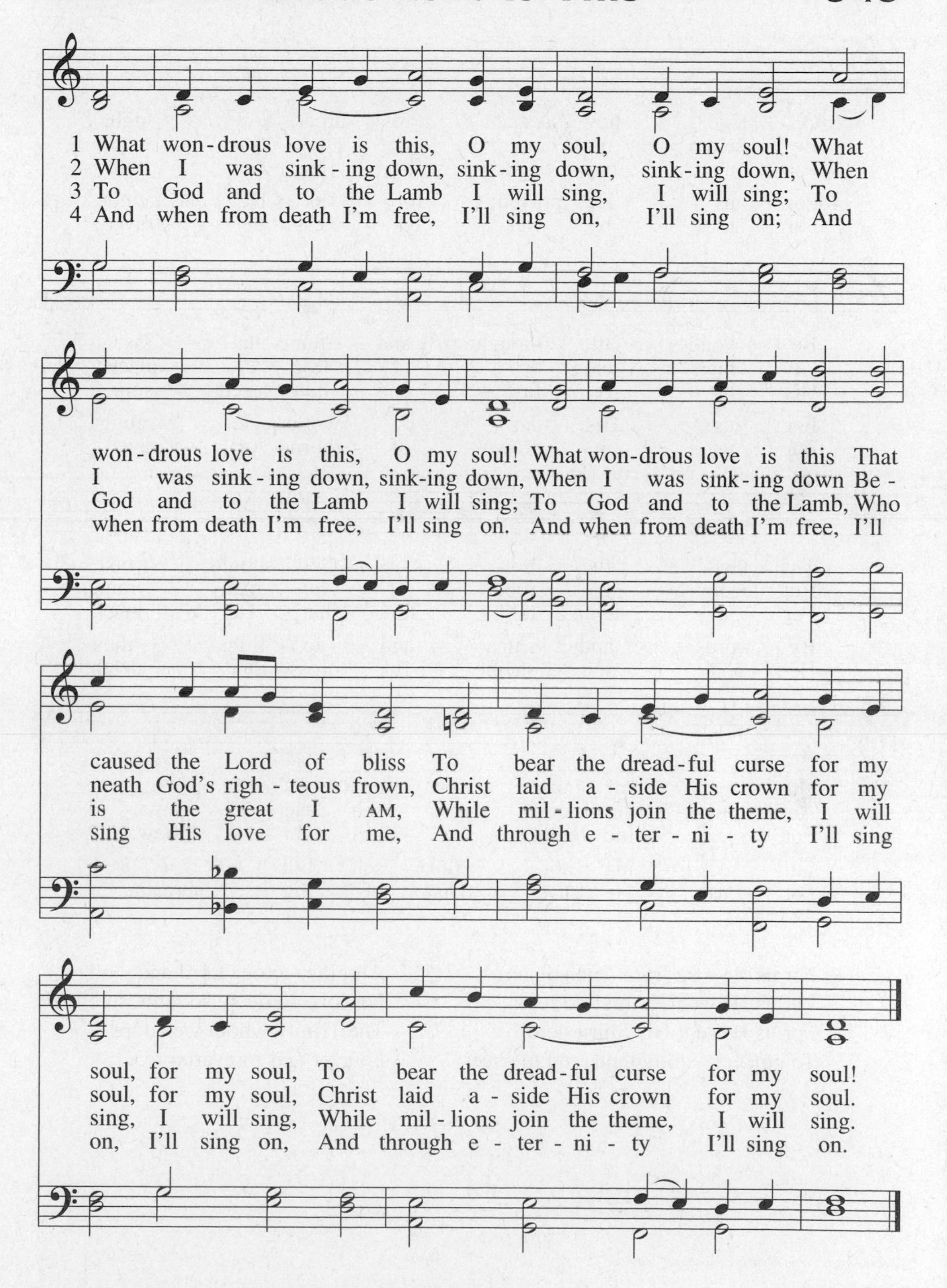
1 What won-drous love is this, O my soul, O my soul! What won-drous love is this, O my soul! What won-drous love is this That caused the Lord of bliss To bear the dread-ful curse for my soul, for my soul, To bear the dread-ful curse for my soul!
2 When I was sink-ing down, sink-ing down, sink-ing down, When I was sink-ing down, sink-ing down, When I was sink-ing down Be-neath God's righ-teous frown, Christ laid a-side His crown for my soul, for my soul, Christ laid a-side His crown for my soul.
3 To God and to the Lamb I will sing, I will sing; To God and to the Lamb I will sing; To God and to the Lamb, Who is the great I AM, While mil-lions join the theme, I will sing, I will sing, While mil-lions join the theme, I will sing.
4 And when from death I'm free, I'll sing on, I'll sing on; And when from death I'm free, I'll sing on. And when from death I'm free, I'll sing His love for me, And through e-ter-ni-ty I'll sing on, I'll sing on, And through e-ter-ni-ty I'll sing on.

Text: *A General Selection of . . . Hymns and Spiritual Songs*, Lynchburg, 1811, alt.
Tune: *Southern Harmony*, New Haven, 1835; setting: Donald A. Busarow, 1934–2011

WONDROUS LOVE
12 9 66 12 9

1 John 4:7–10; Rev. 5:6–13; John 8:58

544 O Love, How Deep

1 O love, how deep, how broad, how high,
2 He sent no an - gel to our race,
3 For us bap - tized, for us He bore
4 For us He prayed; for us He taught;
5 For us by wick - ed - ness be - trayed,
Be - yond all thought and fan - ta - sy,
Of high - er or of low - er place,
His ho - ly fast and hun - gered sore;
For us His dai - ly works He wrought,
For us, in crown of thorns ar - rayed,
That God, the Son of God, should take
But wore the robe of hu - man frame,
For us temp - ta - tion sharp He knew;
By words and signs and ac - tions thus
He bore the shame - ful cross and death;
Our mor - tal form for mor - tals' sake!
And to this world Him - self He came.
For us the tempt - er o - ver - threw.
Still seek - ing not Him - self but us.
For us He gave His dy - ing breath.

6 For us He rose from death again;
For us He went on high to reign;
For us He sent His Spirit here
To guide, to strengthen, and to cheer.

△ 7 All glory to our Lord and God
For love so deep, so high, so broad;
The Trinity whom we adore
Forever and forevermore.

Setting available in hymn accompaniment edition.

Text: attr. Thomas à Kempis, 1380–1471; tr. Benjamin Webb, 1819–85, alt.
Tune: English, 15th cent.

DEO GRACIAS
L M

Eph. 3:17b–21; Phil. 2:6–9; Heb. 2:9–10, 14–18; John 1:14

Word of God, Come Down on Earth

REDEEMER

545

1 Word of God, come down on earth, Liv - ing rain from
2 Word e - ter - nal, throned on high, Word that brought to
3 Word that caused blind eyes to see, Speak and heal our
4 Word that speaks God's ten - der love, One with God be -
heav'n de - scend - ing; Touch our hearts and bring to birth
life cre - a - tion, Word that came from heav'n to die,
mor - tal blind - ness; Deaf we are: our heal - er be;
yond all tell - ing, Word that sends us from a - bove,
Faith and hope and love un - end - ing. Word al - might - y,
Cru - ci - fied for our sal - va - tion, Sav - ing Word, the
Loose our tongues to tell Your kind - ness. Be our Word in
God the Spir - it, with us dwell - ing, Word of truth, to
we re - vere You; Word made flesh, we long to hear You.
world re - stor - ing, Speak to us, Your love out - pour - ing.
pit - y spo - ken, Heal the world, by sin now bro - ken.
all truth lead us; Word of life, with one bread feed us.

Text: James Quinn, 1919–2010
Tune: Johann Rudolph Ahle, 1625–73, alt.; setting: *The Lutheran Hymnal*, 1941

LIEBSTER JESU, WIR SIND HIER
78 78 88

John 1:1–3, 10, 14

546 O Jesus So Sweet, O Jesus So Mild

1 O Je - sus so sweet, O Je - sus so mild! For sin - ners You be - came a child. You came from heav - en down to earth In hu - man flesh through hu - man birth. O Je - sus so sweet, O Je - sus so mild!
2 O Je - sus so sweet, O Je - sus so mild! With God we now are rec - on - ciled. You have for all the ran - som paid, Your Fa - ther's righ - teous an - ger stayed. O Je - sus so sweet, O Je - sus so mild!
3 O Je - sus so sweet, O Je - sus so mild! Joy fills the world which sin de - filed. What - e'er we have be - longs to You; O keep us faith - ful, strong, and true. O Je - sus so sweet, O Je - sus so mild!

Text: Valentin Thilo, 1607–62, abr.; tr. Geoffrey W. Daisley, 1877–1939, st. 1, alt.; tr. Frieda Pietsch, 1904–82, sts. 2–3, alt.
Tune: *Geistliche Kirchengesäng*, Köln, 1623; setting: Johann Sebastian Bach, 1685–1750

O JESULEIN SÜSS
10 8 88 10

Gal. 4:4–5; Rom. 5:8–11

The Lamb

1 The Lamb, the Lamb, O Fa - ther, where's the sac - ri - fice?
2 The Lamb, the Lamb, One per - fect fi - nal of - fer - ing.
3 The Lamb, the Lamb, As way - ward sheep their shep - herd kill
4 He sighs, He dies, He takes my sin and wretch - ed - ness.
5 He rose, He rose, My heart with thanks now o - ver - flows.
Faith sees, be - lieves God will pro - vide the Lamb of price!
The Lamb, the Lamb, Let earth join heav'n His praise to sing.
So still, His will On our be - half the Law to fill.
He lives, for - gives, He gives me His own righ - teous - ness.
His song pro - long Till ev - 'ry heart to Him be - long.
Refrain
Wor - thy is the Lamb whose death makes me His
own! The Lamb is reign - ing on His throne!

Text: Gerald P. Coleman, b. 1953
Music: Gerald P. Coleman, b. 1953

WINTER
48 48 and refrain

Rev. 5:12–13; Gen. 22:7–8; 1 Peter 2:24–25

548 Thanks to Thee, O Christ, Victorious

1 Thanks to Thee, O Christ, vic - to - rious! Thanks to Thee, O
2 Thou hast died for my trans - gres - sion, All my sins on
3 For the joy Thine ad - vent gave me, For Thy ho - ly,
Lord of Life! Death hath now no pow - er o'er us,
Thee were laid; Thou hast won for me sal - va - tion,
pre - cious Word; For Thy Bap - tism, which doth save me,
Thou hast con-quered in the strife. Thanks be - cause Thou didst a -
On the cross my debt was paid. From the grave I shall a -
For Thy blest Com - mu - nion board; For Thy death, the bit - ter
rise And hast o - pened par - a - dise! None can ful - ly
rise And shall meet Thee in the skies. Death it - self is
scorn, For Thy res - ur - rec - tion morn, Lord, I thank Thee
sing the glo - ry Of the res - ur - rec - tion sto - ry.
tran - si - to - ry; I shall lift my head in glo - ry.
and ex - tol Thee, And in heav'n I shall be - hold Thee.

Hymn accompaniment: 589

Text: Thomas Hansen Kingo, 1634–1703; tr. George A. T. Rygh, 1860–1942
Tune: Johann Schop, c. 1590–1667

WERDE MUNTER
87 87 77 88

1 Cor. 15:51–57; Is. 53:4–6, 8, 11–12; 1 Thess. 4:16–17; 2 Cor. 9:15

All Hail the Power of Jesus' Name 549

1 All hail the pow'r of Je - sus' name! Let an - gels pros-trate fall;
2 Crown Him, ye mar - tyrs of our God, Who from His al - tar call;
3 Ye seed of Is - rael's cho - sen race, Ye ran - somed from the fall,
4 Hail Him, ye heirs of Da - vid's line, Whom Da - vid Lord did call,
5 Sin - ners, whose love can ne'er for - get The worm-wood and the gall,
Bring forth the roy - al di - a - dem And crown Him Lord of all.
Ex - tol the stem of Jes - se's rod And crown Him Lord of all.
Hail Him who saves you by His grace And crown Him Lord of all.
The God in - car - nate, man di - vine, And crown Him Lord of all.
Go, spread your tro - phies at His feet And crown Him Lord of all.
Bring forth the roy - al di - a - dem And crown Him Lord of all.
Ex - tol the stem of Jes - se's rod And crown Him Lord of all.
Hail Him who saves you by His grace And crown Him Lord of all.
The God in - car - nate, man di - vine, And crown Him Lord of all.
Go, spread your tro - phies at His feet And crown Him Lord of all.

6 Let ev'ry kindred, ev'ry tribe,
On this terrestrial ball
To Him all majesty ascribe
And crown Him Lord of all.
To Him all majesty ascribe
And crown Him Lord of all.

7 Oh, that with yonder sacred throng
We at His feet may fall!
We'll join the everlasting song
And crown Him Lord of all.
We'll join the everlasting song
And crown Him Lord of all.

Text: Edward Perronet, 1726–92, sts. 1–5, alt.; *A Selection of Hymns*, London, 1787, sts. 6–7, alt.
Tune: Oliver Holden, 1765–1844; setting: *Service Book and Hymnal*, 1958

CORONATION
86 86 86

Rev. 5:9–14; Heb. 2:9; Phil. 2:9–10; Rev. 19:16

550 Lamb of God

1 Your on - ly Son, no sin to hide, But You have sent Him from Your side To walk up - on this guilt - y sod, And to be - come the Lamb of God.
2 Your Gift of love they cru - ci - fied, They laughed and scorned Him as He died: The hum - ble King they named a fraud, And sac - ri - ficed the Lamb of God.
3 I was so lost, I should have died, But You have brought me to Your side To be led by Your staff and rod, And to be called a lamb of God.
Refrain
O Lamb of God, sweet Lamb of God, I love the ho - ly Lamb of God! O wash me in His pre - cious blood, My Je - sus Christ, the Lamb of God.

Setting available in hymn accompaniment edition.

Text: Twila Paris, b. 1958
Tune: Twila Paris, b. 1958

LAMB OF GOD
L M and refrain

John 1:29; Rev. 7:14

When to Our World the Savior Came

REDEEMER

551

1 When to our world the Sav - ior came The sick and
2 That good phy - si - cian! Night and day The peo - ple
3 His prais - es then were heard and sung By o - pened
4 Of long a - go: yet liv - ing still, Who died for
5 His sov - 'reign pur - pose still re - mains Who rose in
help - less heard His name, And in their weak - ness
thronged a - bout His way; And won - der ran from
ears and loos - ened tongue, While light - ened eyes could
us on Cal - v'ry's hill; Who tri - umphed o - ver
pow'r, and lives and reigns; Till ev - 'ry tongue con -
longed to see The heal - ing Christ of Gal - i - lee.
soul to soul, "The touch of Christ has made us whole!"
see and know The heal - ing Christ of long a - go.
cross and grave, His heal - ing hands stretched forth to save.
fess His praise, The heal - ing Christ of all our days.

Text: Timothy Dudley-Smith, b. 1926
Music: Robert Schumann, 1810–56

CANONBURY
L M

Acts 10:38; John 9:1–41

552 O Christ, Who Shared Our Mortal Life

1 O Christ, who shared our mor-tal life And end-ed death's long reign,
2–3 Insert appropriate stanzas.
4 Death's pow-er holds us still in thrall And bears us toward the tomb.
Who healed the sick and raised the dead And bore our grief and pain:
Death's dark-'ning cloud hangs like a pall That threat-ens earth with doom.
We know our years on earth are few, That death is al-ways near.
But You have bro-ken death's em-brace And torn a-way its sting.
Come now to us, O Lord of Life; Bring hope that con-quers fear!
Re-store to life our mor-tal race! Raise us, O Ris-en King!

Alternate tune: KINGSFOLD (444)

Text: Herman G. Stuempfle, Jr., 1923–2007, alt.
Music: Kevin J. Hildebrand, b. 1973

LORD OF LIFE
C M D

Raising of Jairus' Daughter (Matt. 9:18–19, 23–26 or Mark 5:21–43)

5 A ruler proud but bent by grief
Knelt down before Your feet:
"My precious daughter's gripped by death!
Come now and death defeat!"
A multitude had gathered round
To hear the truth You taught,
But, leaving them, You turned to help
A father sore distraught.

6 You pressed through crowds to reach the child
Whose limbs with death grew cold.
"She is not dead; she only sleeps!"
The weeping folk You told.
And then You took her hand and called,
"My child, I bid you rise!"
She rose! And all stood round You, Lord,
With awed and wond'ring eyes!

Raising of the Widow's Son (Luke 7:11–17)

7 The ranks of death with trophy grim
Through ancient streets once trod
And suddenly confronted You,
The mighty Son of God.
A widow's tears evoked Your Word;
You stopped the bearers' tread.
"Weep not!" in pity then You spoke
To her whose son was dead.

8 The ranks of death, the Lord of Life
Stood face to face that hour;
And You took up the age-old strife
With words of awesome pow'r.
"Young man, arise!" You ordered loud,
And death defeated lay.
The widow's son cast off his shroud
And strode from death away.

Raising of Lazarus (John 11:1–45)

9 Two weeping sisters, worn by grief
And mired in depths of gloom,
Stood watching where their brother lay
Within a rock-sealed tomb.
When, Lord, You met them as they mourned,
You wept compassion's tear.
But Martha, sore with sorrow, said,
"He'd lived had You been here!"

10 "I am the Lord of life and death!"
You answered Martha's cry,
"And all who hear and trust My Word
Shall live, although they die!"
You walked the path to Laz'rus' tomb,
You called him forth by name,
And living, loving once again,
From death to life he came!

553 O Christ, Our Hope, Our Hearts' Desire

1 O Christ, our hope, our hearts' de - sire, Cre - a - tion's might - y Lord, Re - deem - er of the fall - en world, By ho - ly love out - poured:
2 How vast Your mer - cy to ac - cept The bur - den of our sin And bow Your head in cru - el death To make us clean with - in.
3 But now the bonds of death are burst, The ran - som has been paid; You now as - cend the Fa - ther's throne In robes of light ar - rayed.
4 O let Your might - y love pre - vail To purge us of our pride That we may stand be - fore Your throne By mer - cy pu - ri - fied.

5 Christ Jesus, be our present joy,
Our future great reward;
Our only glory, may it be
To glory in the Lord!

△ 6 All praise to You, ascended Lord;
All glory ever be
To Father, Son, and Holy Ghost
Through all eternity!

Text: Latin, c. 5th–10th cent.; tr. John Chandler, 1806–76, adapt.
Tune: *Harmonischer Lieder-Schatz*, Frankfurt, 1738; setting: *The Lutheran Hymnal*, 1941

ICH SINGE DIR
C M

Col. 1:5, 20, 23, 27; Heb. 1:2; 1 Peter 2:24

O Jesus, King Most Wonderful 554

1 O Je - sus, King most won - der - ful!
2 When once You vis - it dark - ened hearts,
3 O Je - sus, light of all be - low,
4 May ev - 'ry heart con - fess Your name,
5 Oh, may our tongues for - ev - er bless,
O Con - quer - or re - nowned! O Source of peace in -
Then truth be - gins to shine, Then earth - ly van - i -
The fount of life and fire, Sur - pass - ing all the
For - ev - er You a - dore, And, seek - ing You, it -
May we love You a - lone And ev - er in our
ef - fa - ble, In whom all joys are found:
ty de - parts, Then kin - dles love di - vine.
joys we know, All that we can de - sire:
self in - flame To seek You more and more!
lives ex - press The im - age of Your own!

Text: attr. Bernard of Clairvaux, 1091–1153; tr. Edward Caswall, 1814–78, alt.
Music: John B. Dykes, 1823–76

ST. AGNES
C M

Luke 19:38; Phil. 2:10–11; Ps. 22:28; 45:1–3; 146:10; 1 Peter 2:7

555 Salvation unto Us Has Come

1 Sal - va - tion un - to us has come By God's free grace and fa - vor;
2 What God did in His Law de - mand And none to Him could ren - der
3 It was a false, mis - lead - ing dream That God His Law had giv - en
4 From sin our flesh could not ab - stain, Sin held its sway un - ceas - ing;
Good works can - not a - vert our doom, They help and save us nev - er.
Caused wrath and woe on ev - 'ry hand For man, the vile of - fend - er.
That sin - ners could them - selves re - deem And by their works gain heav - en.
The task was use - less and in vain, Our guilt was e'er in - creas - ing.
Faith looks to Je - sus Christ a - lone, Who did for all the
Our flesh has not those pure de - sires The spir - it of the
The Law is but a mir - ror bright To bring the in - bred
None can re - move sin's poi - soned dart Or pu - ri - fy our
world a - tone; He is our one Re - deem - er.
Law re - quires, And lost is our con - di - tion.
sin to light That lurks with - in our na - ture.
guile - ful heart— So deep is our cor - rup - tion.

Text: Paul Speratus, 1484–1551; tr. *The Lutheran Hymnal*, 1941, alt.
Tune: *Etlich Cristlich lider*, Wittenberg, 1524; setting: *The Lutheran Hymnal*, 1941

ES IST DAS HEIL
87 87 887

Rom. 3:10–31; 5:1–11; Gal. 3:1–25; Eph. 2:1–10

5 Yet as the Law must be fulfilled
Or we must die despairing,
Christ came and has God's anger stilled,
Our human nature sharing.
He has for us the Law obeyed
And thus the Father's vengeance stayed
Which over us impended.

6 Since Christ has full atonement made
And brought to us salvation,
Each Christian therefore may be glad
And build on this foundation.
Your grace alone, dear Lord, I plead,
Your death is now my life indeed,
For You have paid my ransom.

7 Let me not doubt, but truly see
Your Word cannot be broken;
Your call rings out, "Come unto Me!"
No falsehood have You spoken.
Baptized into Your precious name,
My faith cannot be put to shame,
And I shall never perish.

8 The Law reveals the guilt of sin
And makes us conscience-stricken;
But then the Gospel enters in
The sinful soul to quicken.
Come to the cross, trust Christ, and live;
The Law no peace can ever give,
No comfort and no blessing.

9 Faith clings to Jesus' cross alone
And rests in Him unceasing;
And by its fruits true faith is known,
With love and hope increasing.
For faith alone can justify;
Works serve our neighbor and supply
The proof that faith is living.

△ 10 All blessing, honor, thanks, and praise
To Father, Son, and Spirit,
The God who saved us by His grace;
All glory to His merit.
O triune God in heav'n above,
You have revealed Your saving love;
Your blessèd name we hallow.

For by grace you have been saved through faith. And this is not your own doing; it is the gift of God, not a result of works, so that no one may boast. Ephesians 2:8–9

---

556 Dear Christians, One and All, Rejoice

1 Dear Chris-tians, one and all, re-joice, With ex-ul-ta-tion spring-ing, And with u-nit-ed heart and voice And ho-ly rap-ture sing-ing, Pro-claim the won-ders God has done, How His right arm the vic-t'ry won. What price our ran-som cost Him!
2 Fast bound in Sa-tan's chains I lay; Death brood-ed dark-ly o'er me. Sin was my tor-ment night and day; In sin my moth-er bore me. But dai-ly deep-er still I fell; My life be-came a liv-ing hell, So firm-ly sin pos-sessed me.
3 My own good works all came to naught, No grace or mer-it gain-ing; Free will a-gainst God's judg-ment fought, Dead to all good re-main-ing. My fears in-creased till sheer de-spair Left on-ly death to be my share; The pangs of hell I suf-fered.
4 But God had seen my wretch-ed state Be-fore the world's foun-da-tion, And mind-ful of His mer-cies great, He planned for my sal-va-tion. He turned to me a fa-ther's heart; He did not choose the eas-y part But gave His dear-est trea-sure.

Text: Martin Luther, 1483–1546; tr. Richard Massie, 1800–87, alt.
Tune: *Etlich Cristlich lider*, Wittenberg, 1524; setting: *The Lutheran Hymnal*, 1941

NUN FREUT EUCH
87 87 887

Ps. 98:1–3; 2 Tim. 1:9–10; Gal. 4:4–5; Rom. 3:28

5 God said to His belovèd Son:
"It's time to have compassion.
Then go, bright jewel of My crown,
And bring to all salvation.
From sin and sorrow set them free;
Slay bitter death for them that they
May live with You forever."

6 The Son obeyed His Father's will,
Was born of virgin mother;
And God's good pleasure to fulfill,
He came to be my brother.
His royal pow'r disguised He bore;
A servant's form, like mine, He wore
To lead the devil captive.

7 To me He said: "Stay close to Me,
I am your rock and castle.
Your ransom I Myself will be;
For you I strive and wrestle.
For I am yours, and you are Mine,
And where I am you may remain;
The foe shall not divide us.

8 "Though he will shed My precious blood,
Me of My life bereaving,
All this I suffer for your good;
Be steadfast and believing.
Life will from death the vict'ry win;
My innocence shall bear your sin,
And you are blest forever.

9 "Now to My Father I depart,
From earth to heav'n ascending,
And, heavn'ly wisdom to impart,
The Holy Spirit sending;
In trouble He will comfort you
And teach you always to be true
And into truth shall guide you.

10 "What I on earth have done and taught
Guide all your life and teaching;
So shall the kingdom's work be wrought
And honored in your preaching.
But watch lest foes with base alloy
The heav'nly treasure should destroy;
This final word I leave you."

Since we have been justified by faith, we have peace with God through our Lord Jesus Christ. Through Him we have also obtained access by faith into this grace in which we stand, and we rejoice in hope of the glory of God.

Romans 5:1–2

---

557 Seek Where You May to Find a Way

1 Seek where you may To find a way That leads to your sal - va - tion. My heart is stilled, On Christ I build, He is the one foun - da - tion. His Word is sure, His works en - dure; He o - ver - throws All e - vil foes; Through Him I more than con - quer.
2 Seek whom you may To be your stay, None can re - deem his broth - er. All help - ers failed; This man pre - vailed, The God - man and none oth - er, Our Ser - vant-King Of whom we sing. We're jus - ti - fied Be - cause He died, The guilt - y be - ing guilt - less.
3 Seek Him a - lone Who did a - tone, Who did your souls de - liv - er. O seek Him first, All you who thirst For grace that fails you nev - er. In ev - 'ry need Seek Him in - deed; To ev - 'ry heart He will im - part His bless - ings with - out mea - sure.
4 My heart's de - light, My crown most bright, O Christ, my joy for - ev - er. Not wealth nor pride Nor for - tune's tide Our bonds of love shall sev - er. You are my Lord; Your pre - cious Word Shall guide my way And help me stay For - ev - er in Your pres - ence.

Setting available in hymn accompaniment edition.

Text: Georg Weissel, 1590–1635; tr. Arthur P. Voss, 1899–1955, alt.
Tune: Johann Stobäus, 1580–1646

SUCH, WER DA WILL
447 447 44447

John 6:68–69; Acts 4:12

Not unto Us

558

1 Not un - to us, not un - to us be glo - ry,
2 A - maz - ing grace— that chose us ere the worlds were
3 O faith - ful love— that shep - herd - ed through faith - less
4 Not un - to us but to Your name be glo - ry,
Lord; Not un - to us but to Your name be praise;
made; A - maz - ing grace— that sent Your Son to save;
years; For - giv - ing love— that led us to Your truth;
Lord, For grace so rich, so wide, so high, so free.
Not un - to us but to Your name all hon - or be
A - maz - ing grace— that robed us in Your righ - teous-
Un - yield - ing love— that would not let us turn from
A - bide with us till trav - 'ling days are o - ver and
giv'n For match - less mer - cy, for - give - ness, and grace.
ness And taught our lips to sing glo - ry and praise.
You But sent us forth to speak par - don and peace.
done, And pil - grim feet lead us home, Lord, to You.

Text: Kurt J. Eggert, 1923–93
Music: Kurt J. Eggert, 1923–93

NOT UNTO US
12 10 13 10

Ps. 115:1; Eph. 3:21; Phil. 3:8–9; Heb. 11:13–16

559 Oh, How Great Is Your Compassion

1 Oh, how great is Your com - pas - sion, Faith - ful Fa - ther, God of grace, That with all our fall - en race In our depth of deg - ra - da - tion You had mer - cy so that we Might be saved e - ter - nal - ly!
2 Your great love for this has striv - en That we may, from sin made free, Live with You e - ter - nal - ly. Your dear Son Him - self has giv - en And ex - tends His gra - cious call, To His sup - per leads us all.
3 Firm - ly to our soul's sal - va - tion Wit - ness - es Your Spir - it, Lord, In Your Sac - ra - ments and Word. There He sends true con - so - la - tion, Giv - ing us the gift of faith That we fear not hell nor death.
4 Lord, Your mer - cy will not leave me; Ev - er will Your truth a - bide. Then in You I will con - fide. Since Your Word can - not de - ceive me, My sal - va - tion is to me Safe and sure e - ter - nal - ly.

Text: Johann Olearius, 1611–84; tr. August Crull, 1845–1923, alt.
Tune: *Schäffer-Belustigung . . . Hirthen-Lieder*, Altdorf, 1653; setting: *The Lutheran Hymnal*, 1941

ACH, WAS SOLL ICH SÜNDER MACHEN
877 877

Titus 3:4–7; Eph. 2:4–9; 1 Peter 1:3–5; 2 Cor. 9:15

5 I will praise Your great compassion,
Faithful Father, God of grace,
That with all our fallen race
In our depth of degradation
You had mercy so that we
Might be saved eternally.

Drawn to the Cross, Which Thou Hast Blessed 560

1 Drawn to the cross, which Thou hast blessed With heal - ing gifts for souls dis - tressed, To find in Thee my life, my rest, Christ cru - ci - fied, I come.
2 Thou know - est all my griefs and fears, Thy grace a - bused, my mis - spent years; Yet now to Thee with con - trite tears, Christ cru - ci - fied, I come.
3 Wash me and take a - way each stain; Let noth - ing of my sin re - main. For cleans - ing, though it be through pain, Christ cru - ci - fied, I come.
4 And then for work to do for Thee, Which shall so sweet a ser - vice be That an - gels well might en - vy me, Christ cru - ci - fied, I come.

Text: Genevieve M. Irons, 1855–1928
Music: Joseph Barnby, 1838–96

DUNSTAN
888 6

John 12:32; Ps. 51:2, 17; Gal. 6:10

561 The Tree of Life

1 The tree of life with ev - 'ry good In E - den's
2 The still - ness of that sa - cred grove Was bro - ken,
3 What mer - cy God showed to our race, A plan of
4 Now from that tree of Je - sus' shame Flows life e -
ho - ly or - chard stood, And of its fruit so pure and
as the ser - pent strove With tempt - ing voice Eve to be -
res - cue by His grace: In send - ing One from wom - an's
ter - nal in His name; For all who trust and will be -
sweet God let the man and wom - an eat. Yet in this
guile And Ad - am too by sin de - file. O day of
seed, The One to fill our great - est need— For on a
lieve, Sal - va - tion's liv - ing fruit re - ceive. And of this
gar - den al - so grew An - oth - er tree, of which they
sad - ness when the breath Of fear and dark - ness, doubt and
tree up - lift - ed high His on - ly Son for sin would
fruit so pure and sweet The Lord in - vites the world to

Text: Stephen P. Starke, b. 1955
Tune: Bruce W. Becker, b. 1952; setting: Henry V. Gerike, b. 1948

TREE OF LIFE
88 88 88 88

Gen. 3:1–15; 1 Peter 2:24; Rev. 22:1–3; 1 Cor. 15:21–22

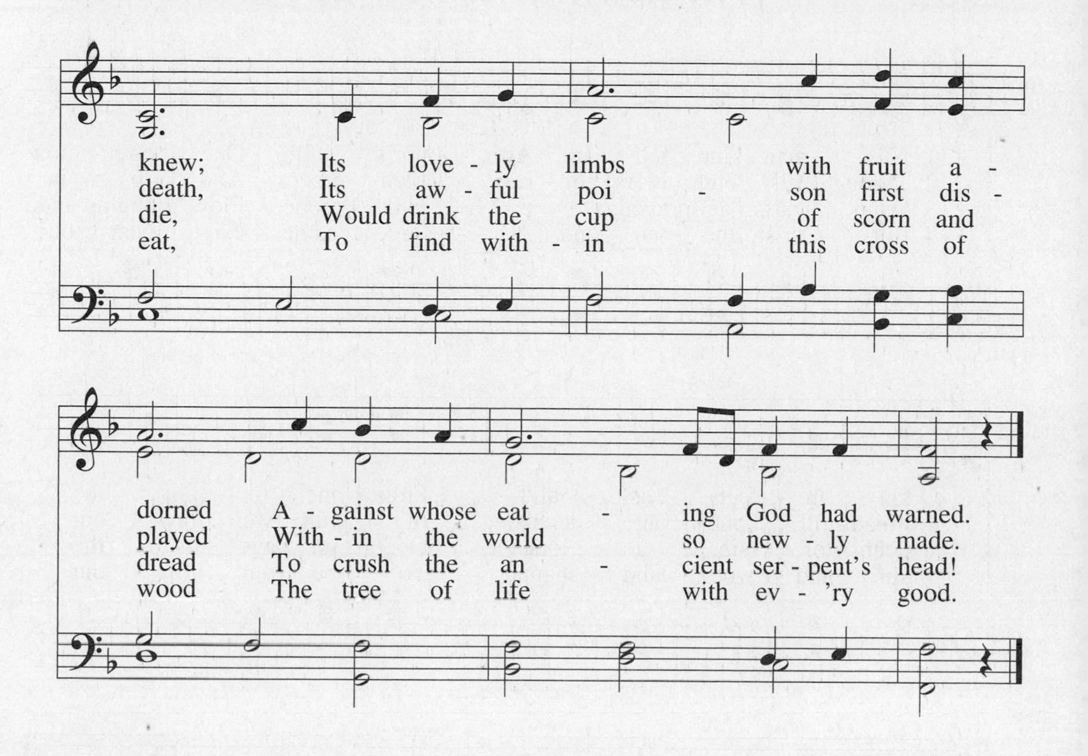
knew; Its love - ly limbs with fruit a -
death, Its aw - ful poi - son first dis -
die, Would drink the cup of scorn and
eat, To find with - in this cross of
dorned A - gainst whose eat - ing God had warned.
played With - in the world so new - ly made.
dread To crush the an - cient ser - pent's head!
wood The tree of life with ev - 'ry good.

Then the angel showed me the river of the water of life, bright as crystal, flowing from the throne of God and of the Lamb through the middle of the street of the city; also, on either side of the river, the tree of life with its twelve kinds of fruit, yielding its fruit each month. The leaves of the tree were for the healing of the nations.

Revelation 22:1–2

562 All Mankind Fell in Adam's Fall

1 All man - kind fell in Ad - am's fall; One com - mon sin in - fects us all. From one to all the curse de - scends, And o - ver all God's wrath im - pends.
2 Through all our pow'rs cor - rup - tion creeps And us in dread - ful bond - age keeps; In guilt we draw our in - fant breath And reap its fruits of woe and death.
3 From hearts de - praved, to e - vil prone, Flow thoughts and deeds of sin a - lone; God's im - age lost, the dark - ened soul Seeks not nor finds its heav'n - ly goal.
4 But Christ, the sec - ond Ad - am, came To bear our sin and woe and shame, To be our life, our light, our way, Our on - ly hope, our on - ly stay.

5 As by one man all mankind fell
And, born in sin, was doomed to hell,
So by one Man, who took our place,
We all were justified by grace.

6 We thank You, Christ; new life is ours,
New light, new hope, new strength, new pow'rs.
This grace our ev'ry way attend
Until we reach our journey's end.

Text: Lazarus Spengler, 1479–1534; tr. Matthias Loy, 1828–1915, alt.
Tune: Louis Bourgeois, c. 1510–61; setting: *The Lutheran Hymnal*, 1941

WENN WIR IN HÖCHSTEN NÖTEN SEIN
L M

Rom. 5:12–21; 1 Cor. 15:21–22, 45; Rom. 3:12; Gen. 3:1–19

Jesus, Thy Blood and Righteousness

1 Je - sus, Thy blood and righ - teous - ness My beau - ty are, my glo - rious dress; Midst flam - ing worlds, in these ar - rayed, With joy shall I lift up my head.
2 Bold shall I stand in that great day, Cleansed and re - deemed, no debt to pay; Ful - ly ab - solved through these I am From sin and fear, from guilt and shame.
3 Lord, I be - lieve Thy pre - cious blood, Which at the mer - cy seat of God Pleads for the cap - tives' lib - er - ty, Was al - so shed in love for me.
4 Lord, I be - lieve, were sin - ners more Than sands up - on the o - cean shore, Thou hast for all a ran - som paid, For all a full a - tone - ment made.

5 When from the dust of death I rise
To claim my mansion in the skies,
This then shall be my only plea:
Jesus hath lived and died for me.

6 Jesus, be endless praise to Thee,
Whose boundless mercy hath for me,
For me, and all Thy hands have made,
An everlasting ransom paid.

Text: Nicolaus Ludwig von Zinzendorf, 1700–60; tr. John B. Wesley, 1703–91, alt.
Tune: George J. Elvey, 1816–93; setting: *The Lutheran Hymnal*, 1941

ST. CRISPIN
L M

Is. 61:10; Heb. 12:24; 1 John 1:7; Rev. 7:9–14

564 Christ Sits at God's Right Hand

1 Christ sits at God's right hand, His sav - ing work com - plete,
2 Christ was that priest God swore, U - nique - ly First and Last,
3 Christ's al - tar was the tree, Where on the world's be - half
4 What cost - ly sac - ri - fice To cov - er hu - man sin!
To reign till ev - 'ry foe will lie Be - neath His feet—
Who would in righ - teous - ness and love Be un - sur - passed:
He shed a blood, un - like the blood Of goat or calf,
Who but Christ Je - sus had the right To en - ter in?
All that the Fa - ther planned, The Son sought to ful - fill,
"A priest for - ev - er - more," An oath God would not break,
To seal God's guar - an - tee Of grace that can - not fail;
His blood, that sprin - kled price, So we might be as - sured
When first He said, "Lord, here am I To do Your will."
"A priest with - in the or - der of Mel - chiz - e - dek."
With blood He en - tered for our good Be - hind the veil.
That our in - her - i - tance in light Has been se - cured.

Text: Stephen P. Starke, b. 1955
Tune: Hebrew; setting: *Hymns Ancient and Modern*, 1875

YIGDAL
6684 D

Heb. 7:15–28; 9:11–15; 10:19–23; Heb. 4:14–16

5 Then let us now draw near,
Washed in that precious flood
And enter the Most Holy Place
By Jesus' blood.
From hearts that are sincere,
Let tongues our hope profess,
And trust anew God's faithful grace
That we confess.

△ 6 All praise to Christ we bring,
Our Lord who intercedes,
Our great High Priest enthroned above
Who knows our needs;
And to the Father sing
Our songs of thankful praise,
Who with the Spirit reigns in love
For endless days.

Thy Works, Not Mine, O Christ 565

1 Thy works, not mine, O Christ, Speak glad - ness to this heart;
2 Thy wounds, not mine, O Christ, Can heal my bruis - ed soul;
3 Thy cross, not mine, O Christ, Has borne the crush - ing load
4 Thy death, not mine, O Christ, Has paid the ran - som due;
5 Thy righ - teous - ness, O Christ, A - lone can cov - er me;
They tell me all is done, They bid my fear de - part.
Thy stripes, not mine, con - tain The balm that makes me whole.
Of sins that none could bear But the in - car - nate God.
Ten thou - sand deaths like mine Would have been all too few.
No righ - teous - ness a - vails Save that which is of Thee.
Refrain
To whom save Thee, Who canst a - lone For sin a - tone, Lord, shall I flee?

Alternate tune: DARWALL'S 148TH (912)

Text: Horatius Bonar, 1808–89, alt.
Tune: *The Parish Choir*, London, 1850; setting: *The Lutheran Hymnal*, 1941

ST. JOHN
66 66 88

Titus 3:3–7; John 14:6; Phil. 3:7–9; Acts 4:12

566 By Grace I'm Saved

1 By grace I'm saved, grace free and bound-less; My soul, be-lieve and doubt it not. Why stag-ger at this word of prom-ise? Has Scrip-ture ev-er false-hood taught? No! Then this word must true re-main: By grace you too will life ob-tain.
2 By grace! None dare lay claim to mer-it; Our works and con-duct have no worth. God in His love sent our Re-deem-er, Christ Je-sus, to this sin-ful earth; His death did for our sins a-tone, And we are saved by grace a-lone.
3 By grace God's Son, our on-ly Sav-ior, Came down to earth to bear our sin. Was it be-cause of your own mer-it That Je-sus died your soul to win? No, it was grace, and grace a-lone, That brought Him from His heav'n-ly throne.
4 By grace! This ground of faith is cer-tain; As long as God is true, it stands. What saints have penned by in-spi-ra-tion, What in His Word our God com-mands, Our faith in what our God has done De-pends on grace— grace through His Son.

Text: Christian Ludwig Scheidt, 1709–61; tr. *The Lutheran Hymnal*, 1941, alt.
Tune: Cornelius Heinrich Dretzel, 1697–1775; setting: *The Lutheran Hymnal*, 1941

O DASS ICH TAUSEND ZUNGEN HÄTTE (DRETZEL)
98 98 88

Eph. 2:4–9; Titus 3:4–7; Is. 64:6; Rom. 3:23–24

5 By grace to timid hearts that tremble,
In tribulation's furnace tried,
By grace, in spite of fear and trouble,
The Father's heart is open wide.
Where could I help and strength secure
If grace were not my anchor sure?

6 By grace! On this I'll rest when dying;
In Jesus' promise I rejoice;
For though I know my heart's condition,
I also know my Savior's voice.
My heart is glad, all grief has flown
Since I am saved by grace alone.

Not What These Hands Have Done 567

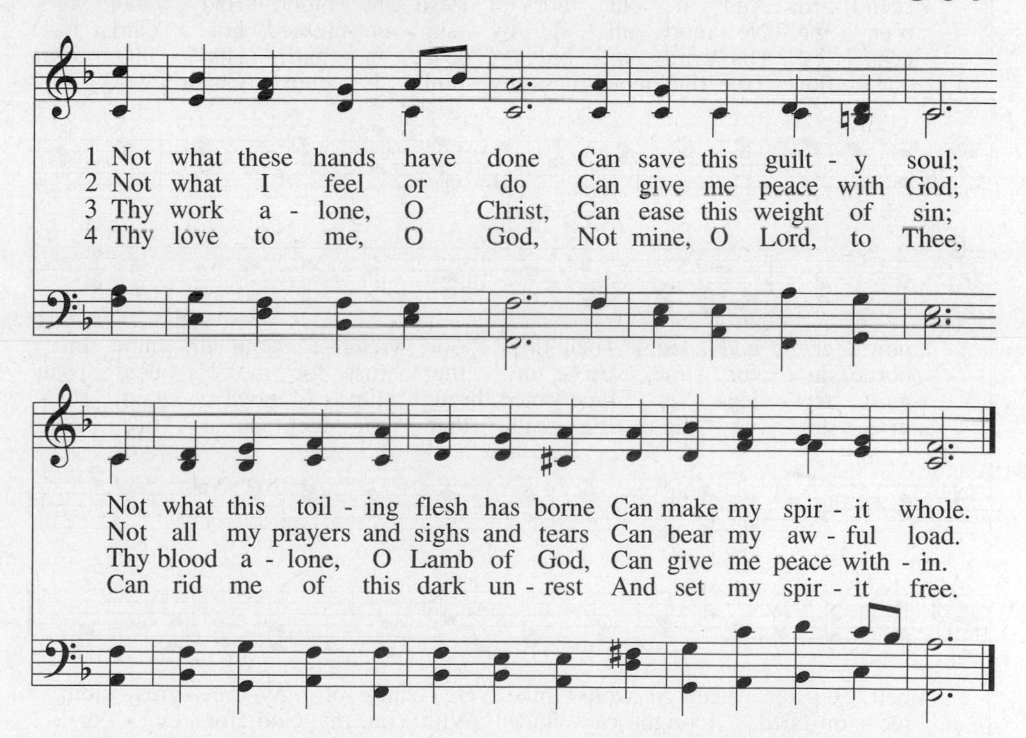
1 Not what these hands have done Can save this guilt - y soul;
2 Not what I feel or do Can give me peace with God;
3 Thy work a - lone, O Christ, Can ease this weight of sin;
4 Thy love to me, O God, Not mine, O Lord, to Thee,
Not what this toil - ing flesh has borne Can make my spir - it whole.
Not all my prayers and sighs and tears Can bear my aw - ful load.
Thy blood a - lone, O Lamb of God, Can give me peace with - in.
Can rid me of this dark un - rest And set my spir - it free.

5 Thy grace alone, O God,
To me can pardon speak;
Thy pow'r alone, O Son of God,
Can this sore bondage break.

6 I bless the Christ of God,
I rest on love divine,
And with unfalt'ring lip and heart
I call this Savior mine.

Text: Horatius Bonar, 1808–89
Tune: William H. Monk, 1823–89; setting: *The Lutheran Hymnal*, 1941

ENERGY
S M

Eph. 2:8–9; Rom. 3:28; 4:5

568 If Your Beloved Son, O God

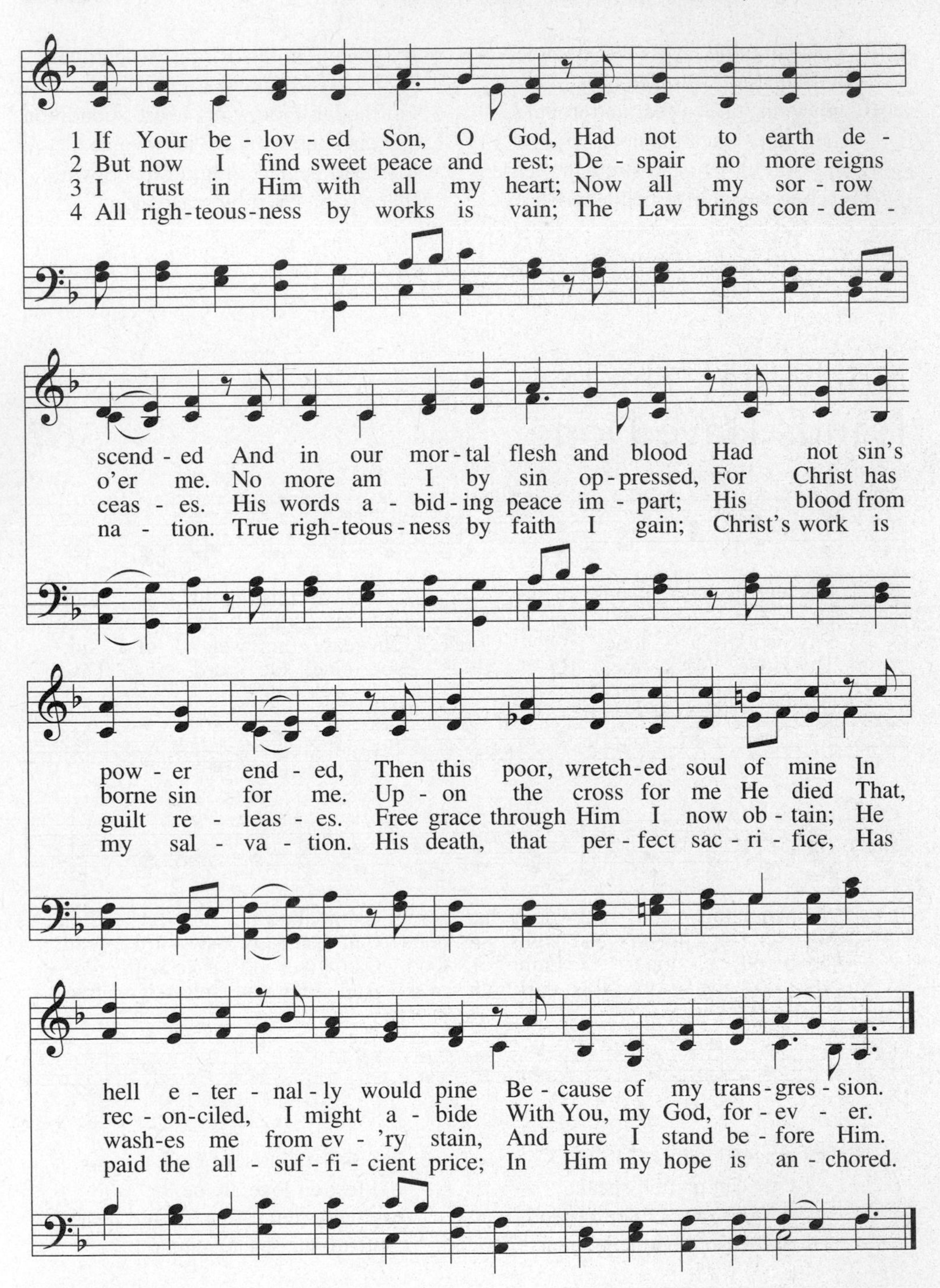
1 If Your be - lov - ed Son, O God, Had not to earth de - scend - ed And in our mor - tal flesh and blood Had not sin's pow - er end - ed, Then this poor, wretch - ed soul of mine In hell e - ter - nal - ly would pine Be - cause of my trans - gres - sion.
2 But now I find sweet peace and rest; De - spair no more reigns o'er me. No more am I by sin op - pressed, For Christ has borne sin for me. Up - on the cross for me He died That, rec - on - ciled, I might a - bide With You, my God, for - ev - er.
3 I trust in Him with all my heart; Now all my sor - row ceas - es. His words a - bid - ing peace im - part; His blood from guilt re - leas - es. Free grace through Him I now ob - tain; He wash - es me from ev - 'ry stain, And pure I stand be - fore Him.
4 All righ - teous - ness by works is vain; The Law brings con - dem - na - tion. True righ - teous - ness by faith I gain; Christ's work is my sal - va - tion. His death, that per - fect sac - ri - fice, Has paid the all - suf - fi - cient price; In Him my hope is an - chored.

Text: Johann Heermann, 1585–1647, sts. 1–4; *Neu-vermehrtes . . . Gesangbuch*, Braunschweig, 1661, st. 5; tr. *The Lutheran Hymnal*, 1941, alt.
Tune: *Etlich Cristlich lider*, Wittenberg, 1524; setting: Paul G. Bunjes, 1914–98, alt.

NUN FREUT EUCH
87 87 887

Gal. 2:16; Eph. 2:4–5, 8–9; Col. 1:21–22

△ 5 My guilt, O Father, You have laid
On Christ, Your Son, my Savior.
Lord Jesus, You my debt have paid
And gained for me God's favor.
O Holy Spirit, Fount of grace,
The good in me to You I trace;
In faith and hope preserve me.

In Adam We Have All Been One 569

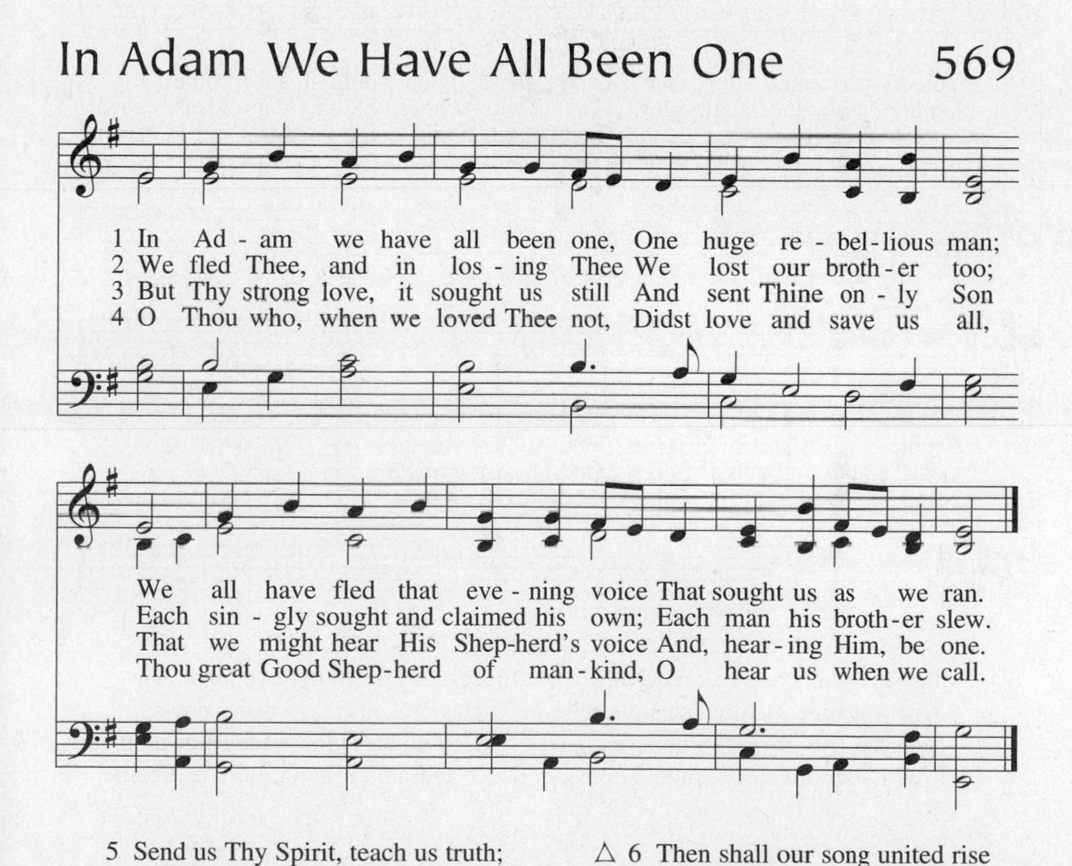
1 In Ad - am we have all been one, One huge re - bel-lious man;
2 We fled Thee, and in los - ing Thee We lost our broth - er too;
3 But Thy strong love, it sought us still And sent Thine on - ly Son
4 O Thou who, when we loved Thee not, Didst love and save us all,
We all have fled that eve - ning voice That sought us as we ran.
Each sin - gly sought and claimed his own; Each man his broth - er slew.
That we might hear His Shep-herd's voice And, hear - ing Him, be one.
Thou great Good Shep-herd of man - kind, O hear us when we call.

5 Send us Thy Spirit, teach us truth;
Thou Son, O set us free
From fancied wisdom, self-sought ways,
To make us one in Thee.

△ 6 Then shall our song united rise
To Thine eternal throne,
Where with the Father evermore
And Spirit Thou art one.

Text: Martin H. Franzmann, 1907–76
Tune: *Southern Harmony*, New Haven, 1835; setting: Leland B. Sateren, 1913–2007

THE SAINTS' DELIGHT
C M

Rom. 5:14, 17–19; John 10:14–16; John 8:31–32, 36; Gen. 3:1–13

570 Just as I Am, without One Plea

1 Just as I am, with - out one plea But that Thy
2 Just as I am and wait - ing not To rid my
3 Just as I am, though tossed a - bout With man - y a
4 Just as I am, poor, wretch - ed, blind; Sight, rich - es,
blood was shed for me And that Thou bidd'st me come to
soul of one dark blot, To Thee, whose blood can cleanse each
con - flict, man - y a doubt, Fight - ings and fears with - in, with -
heal - ing of the mind, Yea, all I need, in Thee to
Thee, O Lamb of God, I come, I come.
spot, O Lamb of God, I come, I come.
out, O Lamb of God, I come, I come.
find, O Lamb of God, I come, I come.

5 Just as I am, Thou wilt receive,
Wilt welcome, pardon, cleanse, relieve;
Because Thy promise I believe,
O Lamb of God, I come, I come.

6 Just as I am; Thy love unknown
Has broken ev'ry barrier down;
Now to be Thine, yea, Thine alone,
O Lamb of God, I come, I come.

Text: Charlotte Elliott, 1789–1871
Tune: William B. Bradbury, 1816–68; setting: George J. Elvey, 1816–93

WOODWORTH
L M

John 1:29; 6:37; Rev. 3:17

God Loved the World So That He Gave

1 God loved the world so that He gave His only Son the lost to save, That all who would in Him believe Should everlasting life receive.
2 Christ Jesus is the ground of faith, Who was made flesh and suffered death; All then who trust in Him alone Are built on this chief cornerstone.
3 God would not have the sinner die; His Son with saving grace is nigh; His Spirit in the Word declares How we in Christ are heaven's heirs.
4 Be of good cheer, for God's own Son Forgives all sins which you have done; And, justified by Jesus' blood, Your Baptism grants the highest good.

5 If you are sick, if death is near,
This truth your troubled heart can cheer:
Christ Jesus saves your soul from death;
That is the firmest ground of faith.

△ 6 Glory to God the Father, Son,
And Holy Spirit, Three in One!
To You, O blessèd Trinity,
Be praise now and eternally!

Text: *Heiliges Lippen- und Hertzens-Opffer*, Stettin, c. 1778; tr. August Crull, 1845–1923, alt.
Tune: George J. Elvey, 1816–93; setting: *The Lutheran Hymnal*, 1941

ST. CRISPIN
L M

John 3:16; Titus 3:4–7; 2 Tim. 1:9; Matt. 9:2

572 In the Shattered Bliss of Eden

1 In the shat - tered bliss of E - den Dawned the
2 Days and months and years un - fold - ing Clear - ly
3 What these sac - ri - fic - es prom - ised From a
4 Lamb of God, once slain for sin - ners, Host, who
day of sac - ri - fice, As our pri - mal par - ents
showed what sin had wrought: Fall - en Ad - am's chil - dren
God who sought to bless, Came at last— a sec - ond
spreads this meal di - vine, Here You pledge our sins are
shud - dered— Sin had caused this dread - ful price!
learn - ing Les - sons fall - en par - ents taught.
Ad - am— Priest and King of Righ - teous - ness:
cov - ered, Pledge re - ceived in bread and wine:
Faith em - barked with this dis - cern - ment: On - ly
All these sac - ri - fi - cial of - f'rings Crest - ed
Son of God, in - car - nate Sav - ior, Son of
"Take and eat; this is My bod - y, Giv - en

Alternate tune: O DURCHBRECHER (531)

Text: Stephen P. Starke, b. 1955
Music: C. Hubert H. Parry, 1848–1918

RUSTINGTON
87 87 D

Gen. 3:1–24; Lev. 16:6–19; Rom. 5:15–19; Rev. 7:9–17

God can cov - er sin, As He took their leaf - y
as a crim - son flood: Pa - tri - archs and priests a -
Man, both Christ and Lord, Who in na - ked shame would
on the cross for you. Take and drink; this cup of
gar - ments And He clothed their shame with skin.
ton - ing For their sins with cleans - ing blood.
of - fer On the cross His blood out - poured.
bless - ing Is My blood poured out for you."

5 Taste and see the bliss of heaven
  Known by saints around the throne,
Where the Lamb, in closest union,
  Lives to love and feed His own.
From His riven side forever
  Flows the purest stream of love,
Love that robes us with the raiment
  Worn by all who feast above.

6 Gone the bliss of Eden's garden,
  Gone the age of sacrifice;
Ours the time of grace and favor,
  Ours the call to paradise!
Ever, Lord, impress upon us:
  Only You can cover sin—
Take our worthless, self-made garments;
  Clothe our shame and cleanse within.

573 Lord, 'Tis Not That I Did Choose Thee

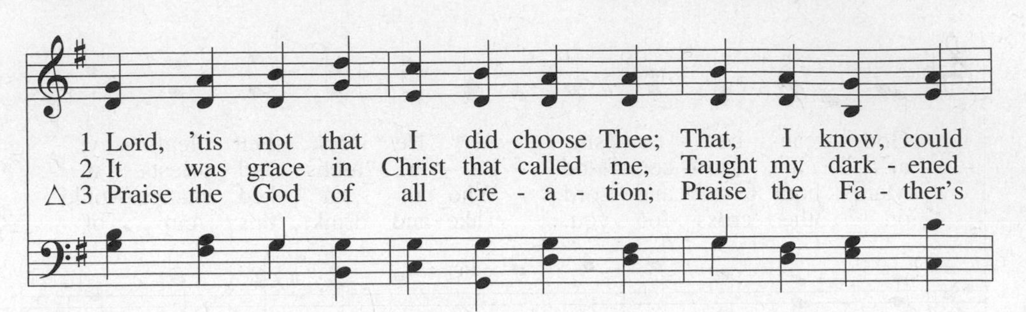
1 Lord, 'tis not that I did choose Thee; That, I know, could
2 It was grace in Christ that called me, Taught my dark - ened
△ 3 Praise the God of all cre - a - tion; Praise the Fa - ther's

nev - er be; For this heart would still re - fuse Thee Had Thy
heart and mind; Else the world had yet en-thralled me, To Thy
bound-less love. Praise the Lamb, our ex - pi - a - tion, Priest and

grace not cho - sen me. Thou hast from the sin that stained me
heav'n-ly glo - ries blind. Now I wor - ship none a - bove Thee;
King en - throned a - bove. Praise the Spir - it of sal - va - tion,

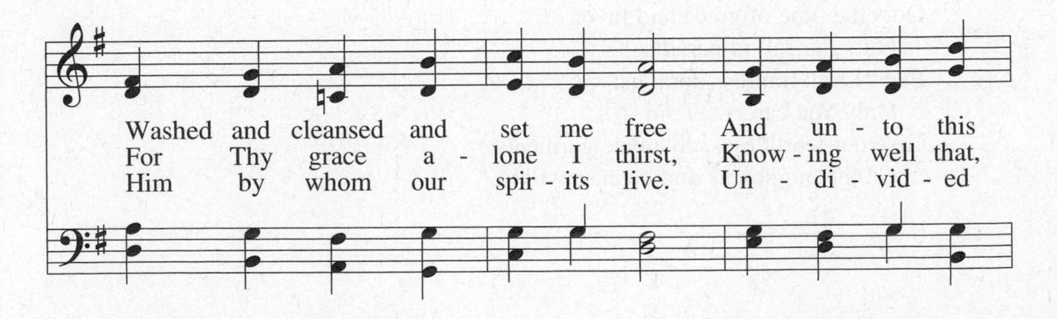
Washed and cleansed and set me free And un - to this
For Thy grace a - lone I thirst, Know - ing well that,
Him by whom our spir - its live. Un - di - vid - ed

Text: Josiah Conder, 1789–1855, alt.
Tune: *Erbaulicher Musicalischer Christen-Schatz*, Basel, 1745;
setting: *The Lutheran Hymnal*, 1941

O DU LIEBE MEINER LIEBE
87 87 D

John 15:16; Eph. 2:8–9; 1 Peter 2:9–10; 1 John 4:10, 19

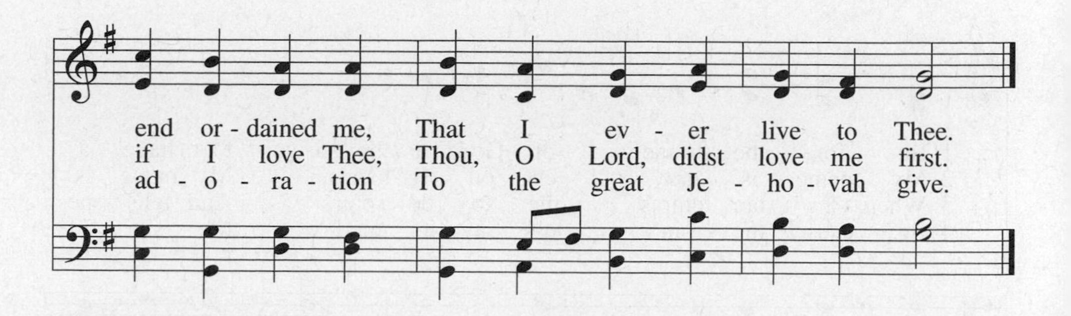
end or - dained me, That I ev - er live to Thee.
if I love Thee, Thou, O Lord, didst love me first.
ad - o - ra - tion To the great Je - ho - vah give.

Almighty and most merciful God, You sent Your Son, Jesus Christ, to seek and to save the lost. Graciously open our ears and our hearts to hear His call and to follow Him by faith that we may feast with Him forever in His kingdom; through the same Jesus Christ, our Lord, who lives and reigns with You and the Holy Spirit, one God, now and forever. Collect for Proper 5, Series A

574 Before the Throne of God Above

1 Be - fore the throne of God a - bove I have a strong, a per - fect plea: A great High Priest, whose name is Love, Who ev - er lives and pleads for me.
2 My name is grav - en on His hands, My name is writ - ten on His heart; I know that while in heav'n He stands No tongue can bid me thence de - part.
3 When Sa - tan tempts me to de - spair, And tells me of the guilt with - in, Up - ward I look, and see Him there Who made an end of all my sin.
4 Be - cause the sin - less Sav - ior died, My sin - ful soul is count - ed free; For God, the just, is sat - is - fied To look on Him and par - don me.

5 Behold Him there! The risen Lamb!
My perfect, spotless righteousness,
The great unchangeable I AM,
The King of glory and of grace!

6 At one with Him, I cannot die,
My soul is purchased by His blood;
My life is hid with Christ on high,
With Christ, my Savior and my God.

Text: Charitie L. de Chenez, 1841–1923
Music: Vernon Griffiths, 1894–1985

DUNEDIN
L M

Heb. 4:14—5:10; 7:24—8:2; 1 Peter 1:18–19; Rev. 7:9–14

My Hope Is Built on Nothing Less 575

1 My hope is built on noth - ing less Than Je - sus' blood and righ - teous - ness; No mer - it of my own I claim But whol - ly lean on Je - sus' name.
2 When dark - ness veils His love - ly face, I rest on His un - chang - ing grace; In ev - 'ry high and storm - y gale My an - chor holds with - in the veil.
3 His oath, His cov - e - nant and blood Sup - port me in the rag - ing flood; When ev - 'ry earth - ly prop gives way, He then is all my hope and stay.
4 When He shall come with trum - pet sound, Oh, may I then in Him be found, Clothed in His righ - teous - ness a - lone, Re - deemed to stand be - fore His throne!
Refrain
On Christ, the sol - id rock, I stand; All oth - er ground is sink - ing sand.

Our hope is secure because we are anchored to Christ. As our great High Priest and through His own body, He has opened a new and living way so that all believers may now approach God without fear (Heb. 10:20). Alternate tune: MELITA (717)

Text: Edward Mote, 1797–1874, alt.
Music: John Stainer, 1840–1901

MAGDALEN
L M and refrain

Acts 4:11–12; Matt. 16:18; Matt. 7:24; 16:24

576 My Hope Is Built on Nothing Less

1 My hope is built on noth - ing less Than
2 When dark - ness veils His love - ly face, I
3 His oath, His cov - e - nant and blood Sup -
4 When He shall come with trum - pet sound, Oh,
Je - sus' blood and righ - teous - ness; No mer - it of my
rest on His un - chang - ing grace; In ev - 'ry high and
port me in the rag - ing flood; When ev - 'ry earth - ly
may I then in Him be found, Clothed in His righ - teous -
own I claim But whol - ly lean on Je - sus' name.
storm - y gale My an - chor holds with - in the veil.
prop gives way, He then is all my hope and stay.
ness a - lone, Re - deemed to stand be - fore His throne!
Refrain
On Christ, the sol - id rock, I stand; All oth - er ground is

Our hope is secure because we are anchored to Christ. As our great High Priest and through His own body, He has opened a new and living way so that all believers may now approach God without fear (Heb. 10:20). Alternate tune: MELITA (717)

Text: Edward Mote, 1797–1874, alt.
Music: William B. Bradbury, 1816–68

THE SOLID ROCK
L M and refrain

Acts 4:11–12; Matt. 16:18; Matt. 7:24; 16:24

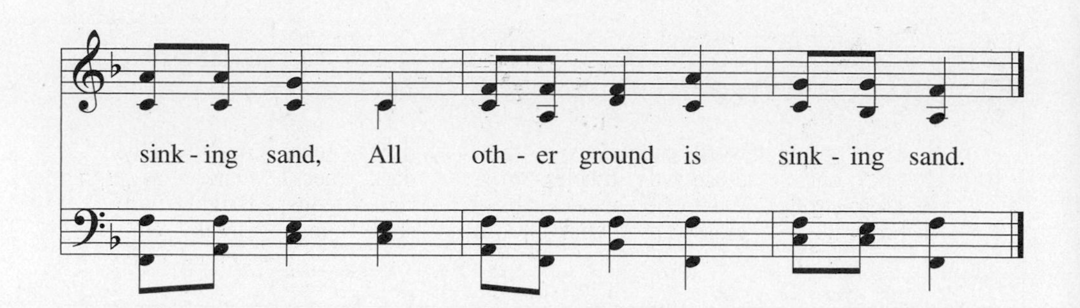
sink - ing sand, All oth - er ground is sink - ing sand.

Almighty God, Your Word Is Cast 577

1 Al - might - y God, Your Word is cast Like seed in - to the ground; Now let the dew of heav'n de - scend And righ - teous fruits a - bound.
2 Let not the sly sa - tan - ic foe This ho - ly seed re - move, But give it root in ev - 'ry heart To bring forth fruits of love.
3 Let not the world's de - ceit - ful cares The ris - ing plant de - stroy, But let it yield a hun - dred - fold The fruits of peace and joy.
4 So when the pre - cious seed is sown, Life - giv - ing grace be - stow That all whose souls the truth re - ceive Its sav - ing pow'r may know.

Text: John Cawood, 1775–1852, alt.
Tune: *The Whole Booke of Psalmes*, London, 1562; setting: Richard Redhead, 1820–1901

ST. FLAVIAN
C M

Matt. 13:3–9, 18–24; Mark 4:3–9, 13–20; Rom. 1:16

578 Thy Strong Word

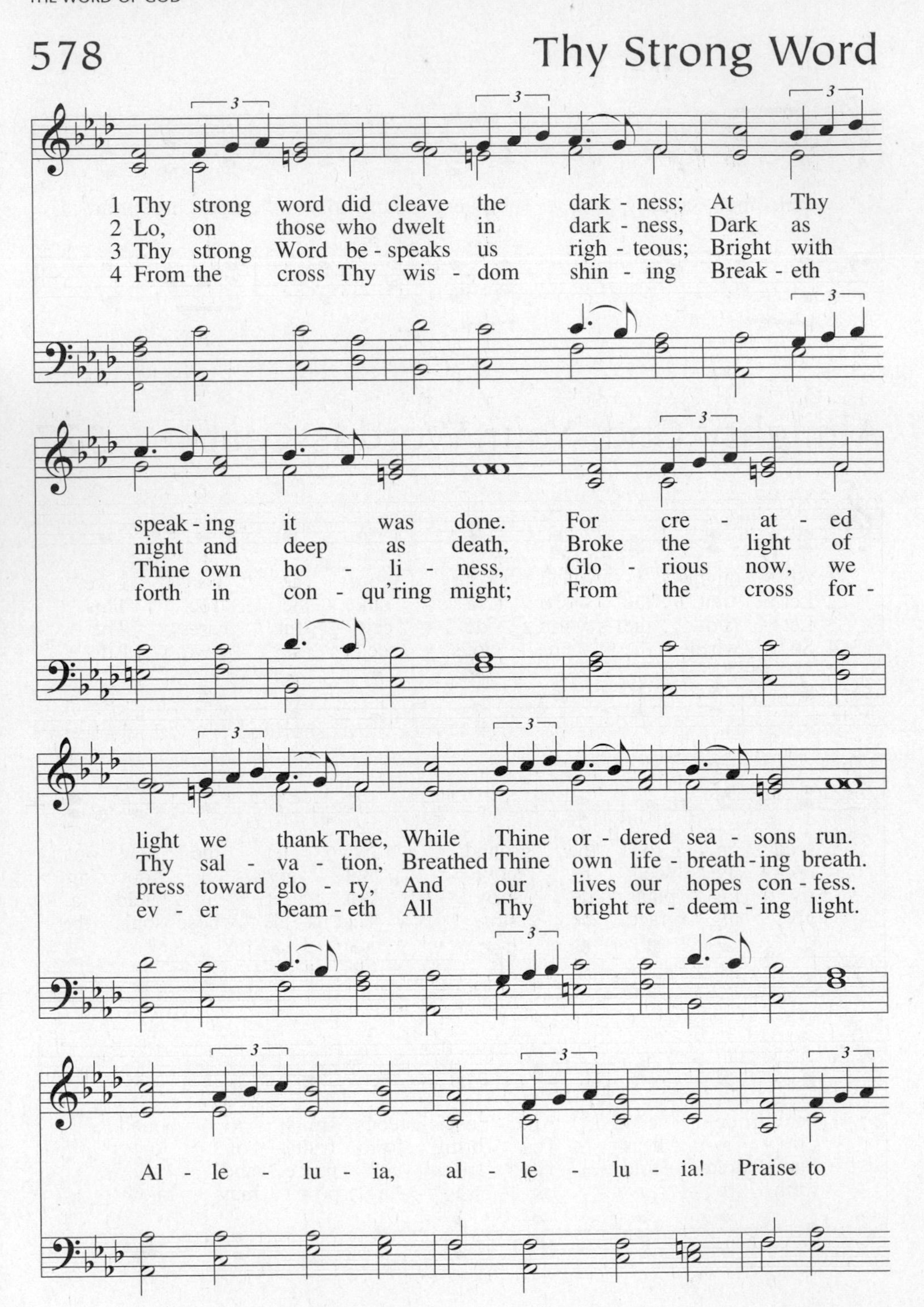
1 Thy strong word did cleave the dark - ness; At Thy speak - ing it was done. For cre - at - ed light we thank Thee, While Thine or - dered sea - sons run.
2 Lo, on those who dwelt in dark - ness, Dark as night and deep as death, Broke the light of Thy sal - va - tion, Breathed Thine own life - breath - ing breath.
3 Thy strong Word be - speaks us righ - teous; Bright with Thine own ho - li - ness, Glo - rious now, we press toward glo - ry, And our lives our hopes con - fess.
4 From the cross Thy wis - dom shin - ing Break - eth forth in con - qu'ring might; From the cross for - ev - er beam - eth All Thy bright re - deem - ing light.
Al - le - lu - ia, al - le - lu - ia! Praise to

Text: Martin H. Franzmann, 1907–76
Tune: Thomas J. Williams, 1869–1944; setting: Richard W. Hillert, 1923–2010, alt.

EBENEZER
87 87 D

Gen. 1:3; John 1:1–14; 2 Cor. 4:6; 1 Peter 2:9

Thee who light dost send! Al - le - lu - ia,
al - le - lu - ia! Al - le - lu - ia with - out end!

5 Give us lips to sing Thy glory,
Tongues Thy mercy to proclaim,
Throats that shout the hope that fills us,
Mouths to speak Thy holy name.
Alleluia, alleluia!
May the light which Thou dost send
Fill our songs with alleluias,
Alleluias without end!

△ 6 God the Father, light-creator,
To Thee laud and honor be.
To Thee, Light of Light begotten,
Praise be sung eternally.
Holy Spirit, light-revealer,
Glory, glory be to Thee.
Mortals, angels, now and ever
Praise the holy Trinity!

579 The Law of God Is Good and Wise

1 The Law of God is good and wise And sets His will be - fore our eyes, Shows us the way of righ - teous - ness, And dooms to death when we trans - gress.
2 Its light of ho - li - ness im - parts The knowl - edge of our sin - ful hearts That we may see our lost es - tate And turn from sin be - fore too late.
3 To those who help in Christ have found And would in works of love a - bound It shows what deeds are His de - light And should be done as good and right.
4 But those who scorn - ful - ly dis - dain God's Law shall then in sin re - main; Its ter - ror in their ear re - sounds And keeps their wick - ed - ness in bounds.

5 The Law is good; but since the fall
Its holiness condemns us all;
It dooms us for our sin to die
And has no pow'r to justify.

6 To Jesus we for refuge flee,
Who from the curse has set us free,
And humbly worship at His throne,
Saved by His grace through faith alone.

Text: Matthias Loy, 1828–1915, alt.
Tune: *Geistliche Lieder auffs new gebessert*, Wittenberg, 1543, ed. Joseph Klug;
setting: *Württembergisches Neues Choralbuch*, 1956

ERHALT UNS, HERR
L M

Ps. 19:7–8; Gal. 3:10–11; Gal. 2:15–16; Rom. 5:6–11

The Gospel Shows the Father's Grace

580

1 The Gos - pel shows the Fa - ther's grace, Who sent His
2 It sets the Lamb be - fore our eyes, Who made the a -
3 It brings the Sav - ior's righ - teous - ness To robe our
4 It is the pow'r of God to save From sin and
Son to save our race, Pro - claims how Je - sus
ton - ing sac - ri - fice, And calls the souls with
souls in roy - al dress; From all our guilt it
Sa - tan and the grave; It works the faith which
lived and died That we might thus be jus - ti - fied.
guilt op - pressed To come and find e - ter - nal rest.
brings re - lease And gives the trou - bled con - science peace.
firm - ly clings To all the trea - sures which it brings.

5 It bears to all the tidings glad
And bids their hearts no more be sad;
The weary, burdened souls it cheers
And banishes their guilty fears.

6 May we in faith its message learn
Nor thanklessly its blessings spurn;
May we in faith its truth confess
And praise the Lord, our righteousness.

Text: Matthias Loy, 1828–1915, alt.
Tune: *Cantionale Germanicum*, Gochsheim, 1628;
setting: *Württembergisches Neues Choralbuch*, 1956

HERR JESU CHRIST, DICH ZU UNS WEND
L M

Rom. 1:16–17; John 3:16; 1 John 4:9–10; Heb. 9:28

581 These Are the Holy Ten Commands

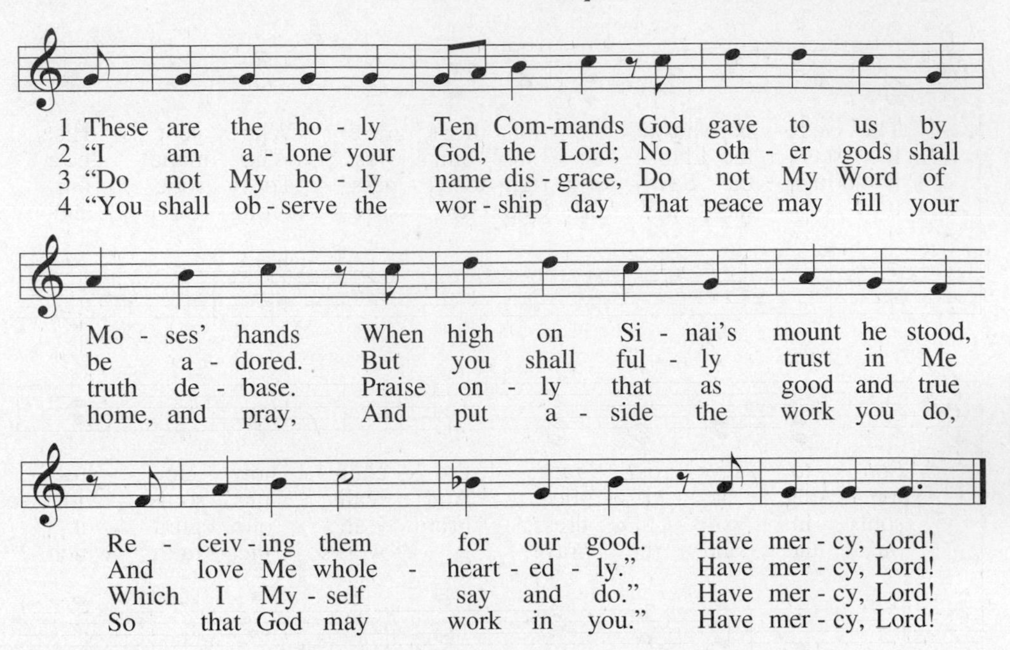
1 These are the ho - ly Ten Com-mands God gave to us by Mo - ses' hands When high on Si - nai's mount he stood, Re - ceiv - ing them for our good. Have mer - cy, Lord!
2 "I am a - lone your God, the Lord; No oth - er gods shall be a - dored. But you shall ful - ly trust in Me And love Me whole - heart - ed - ly." Have mer - cy, Lord!
3 "Do not My ho - ly name dis - grace, Do not My Word of truth de - base. Praise on - ly that as good and true Which I My - self say and do." Have mer - cy, Lord!
4 "You shall ob - serve the wor - ship day That peace may fill your home, and pray, And put a - side the work you do, So that God may work in you." Have mer - cy, Lord!

5 "You are to honor and obey
Your father, mother, ev'ry day,
Serve them each way that comes to hand;
You'll then live long in the land."
Have mercy, Lord!

6 "You shall not murder, hurt, nor hate;
Your anger dare not dominate.
Be kind and patient; help, defend,
And treat your foe as your friend."
Have mercy, Lord!

7 "Be faithful to your
marriage vow;
No lust or impure thoughts allow.
Keep all your conduct free from sin
By self-controlled discipline."
Have mercy, Lord!

8 "You shall not steal or take away
What others worked for night and day,
But open wide a gen'rous hand
And help the poor in the land."
Have mercy, Lord!

9 "Bear no false witness nor defame
Your neighbor nor destroy his name,
But view him in the kindest way;
Speak truth in all that you say."
Have mercy, Lord!

10 "You shall not crave your
neighbor's house
Nor covet money, goods, or spouse.
Pray God He would your neighbor bless
As you yourself wish success."
Have mercy, Lord!

A catechism hymn of Martin Luther.
Setting available in hymn accompaniment edition.

Text: Martin Luther, 1483–1546; tr. Joseph Herl, b. 1959, st. 1; tr. Michael A. Penikis, b. 1964, st. 2; tr. F. Samuel Janzow, 1913–2001, sts. 3–5, 7, 11, alt.; tr. *Christian Worship*, 1993, sts. 6, 8–10, 12, alt.
Tune: German, 13th cent.

IN GOTTES NAMEN FAHREN WIR
88 87 4

Ex. 20:1–17; Lev. 19:2; James 2:10; Rom. 3:21–24, 28

11 You have this Law to see therein
That you have not been free from sin
But also that you clearly see
How pure toward God life should be.
Have mercy, Lord!

12 Our works cannot salvation gain;
They merit only endless pain.
Forgive us, Lord! To Christ we flee,
Who pleads for us endlessly.
Have mercy, Lord!

God's Word Is Our Great Heritage 582

God's Word is our great her - i - tage And shall be ours for -
ev - er; To spread its light from age to age Shall be our
chief en - deav - or. Through life it guides our way, In death it
is our stay. Lord, grant, while worlds en - dure, We keep its
teach - ings pure Through - out all gen - er - a - tions.

Hymn accompaniment: 647
Alternate tune: EIN FESTE BURG (Isorhythmic) (657)

Text: Nikolai Fredrik Severin Grundtvig, 1783–1872; tr. Ole G. Belsheim, 1861–1925, alt.
Tune: Friedrich O. Reuter, 1863–1924

REUTER
87 87 65 66 7

Ps. 119:105, 111; John 14:23; Luke 11:28

583 God Has Spoken by His Prophets

1 God has spo - ken by His proph - ets, Spo - ken His un - chang - ing Word;
2 God has spo - ken by Christ Je - sus, Christ, the ev - er - last - ing Son,
3 God is speak-ing by His Spir - it, Speak-ing to our hearts a - gain,
Each from age to age pro-claim-ing God, the one, the righ-teous Lord.
Bright-ness of the Fa-ther's glo - ry, With the Fa - ther ev - er one;
In the age-less Word de - clar - ing His own mes-sage, now as then.
In the world's de - spair and tur - moil, One firm an - chor holds us fast:
Spo - ken by the Word In - car - nate, God of God, be - fore time was;
Through the rise and fall of na - tions One sure faith yet stand-ing fast;
God is king, His throne e - ter - nal; God the first, and God the last.
Light of Light, to earth de - scend - ing, He re - veals our God to us.
God a - bides, His Word un - chang - ing; God the first, and God the last.

Text: George W. Briggs, 1875–1959, alt.
Tune: Henry T. Smart, 1813–79; setting: Henry V. Gerike, b. 1948

REX GLORIAE
87 87 D

Heb. 1:1–3; John 1:1–14; 12:44–46, 49–50; 1 Cor. 2:12–13

Faith and Truth and Life Bestowing 584

1 Faith and truth and life be - stow - ing, O - pen now the Scrip - tures, Lord, Seed to life e - ter - nal sow - ing, Scat - tered on the wind a - broad. Let not hearts, Your Word re - ceiv - ing, Like a bar - ren field be found, Choked with thorns and un - be - liev - ing, Shal - low earth or ston - y ground.
2 May the Spir - it's pow'r un - ceas - ing Bring to life the hid - den grain, Dai - ly in our hearts in - creas - ing, Bear - ing fruit that shall re - main. So in Scrip - ture, song, and sto - ry, Sav - ior, may Your voice be heard. Till our eyes be - hold Your glo - ry Give us ears to hear Your Word.

Text: Timothy Dudley-Smith, b. 1926
Tune: *Columbian Harmony*, Cincinnati, 1825; setting: Margaret W. Mealy, b. 1922

HOLY MANNA
87 87 D

Matt. 13:3–23; Col. 1:3–6; 2 Cor. 9:10; Luke 4:16–22

585 Lord Jesus Christ, with Us Abide

1 Lord Je - sus Christ, with us a - bide, For round us falls the e - ven - tide. O let Your Word, that sav - ing light, Shine forth un - dimmed in - to the night.
2 In these last days of great dis - tress Grant us, dear Lord, true stead - fast - ness That we keep pure till life is spent Your ho - ly Word and Sac - ra - ment.
3 To hope grown dim, to hearts turned cold Speak tongues of fire and make us bold To shine Your Word of sav - ing grace In - to each dark and love - less place.
4 May glo - rious truths that we have heard, The bright sword of Your might - y Word, Spurn Sa - tan that Your Church be strong, Bold, u - ni - fied in act and song.

5 Restrain, O Lord, the human pride
That seeks to thrust Your truth aside
Or with some man-made thoughts or things
Would dim the words Your Spirit sings.

6 Stay with us, Lord, and keep us true;
Preserve our faith our whole life through—
Your Word alone our heart's defense,
The Church's glorious confidence.

Text: Philipp Melanchthon, 1497–1560, st. 1; German version, *Geistliche Psalmen*, Nuremberg, 1611, st. 1; Nicolaus Selnecker, 1532–92, sts. 2–6; tr. F. Samuel Janzow, 1913–2001, alt.
Tune: *Geistliche Lieder D. Martini Lutheri*, Leipzig, 1589; setting: *The Lutheran Hymnal*, 1941

ACH BLEIB BEI UNS
L M

Luke 24:29; John 8:31–32; Col. 2:8; 1 John 2:28

Preach You the Word 586

1 Preach you the Word and plant it home To men who like or like it not, The Word that shall en - dure and stand When flow'rs and men shall be for - got.
2 We know how hard, O Lord, the task Your ser - vant bade us un - der - take: To preach Your Word and nev - er ask What pride - ful prof - it it may make.
3 The sow - er sows; his reck - less love Scat - ters a - broad the good - ly seed, In - tent a - lone that all may have The whole - some loaves that all men need.
4 Though some be snatched and some be scorched And some be choked and mat - ted flat, The sow - er sows; his heart cries out, "Oh, what of that, and what of that?"

5 Of all his scattered plenteousness
One-fourth waves ripe on hill and flat,
And bears a harvest hundredfold:
"Ah, what of that, Lord, what of that!"

6 Preach you the Word and plant it home
And never faint; the Harvest Lord
Who gave the sower seed to sow
Will watch and tend His planted Word.

Alternate tune: WAREHAM (866)

Text: Martin H. Franzmann, 1907–76, alt.
Tune: *Rheinfelssisch Deutsches Catholisches Gesangbuch*, Augsburg, 1666; setting: Paul G. Bunjes, 1914–98, alt.

O HEILAND, REISS DIE HIMMEL AUF
L M

Luke 8:4–15; 1 Peter 1:24–25; 1 Tim. 4:15–16; 2 Tim. 2:3, 10

587 I Know My Faith Is Founded

1 I know my faith is found - ed On Je - sus Christ, my
2 In - crease my faith, dear Sav - ior, For Sa - tan seeks by
3 In faith, Lord, let me serve You; Though per - se - cu - tion,
God and Lord; And this my faith con - fess - ing, Un -
night and day To rob me of this trea - sure And
grief, and pain Should seek to o - ver - whelm me, Let
moved I stand on His sure Word. Our rea - son can - not
take my hope of bliss a - way. But, Lord, with You be -
me a stead - fast trust re - tain; And then at my de -
fath - om The truth of God pro - found; Who trusts in hu - man
side me, I shall be un - dis - mayed; And led by Your good
par - ture, Lord, take me home to You, Your rich - es to in -
wis - dom Re - lies on shift - ing ground. God's Word is
Spir - it, I shall be un - a - fraid. A - bide with
her - it As all You said holds true. In life and
all - suf - fi - cient, It makes di - vine - ly sure; And
me, O Sav - ior, A firm - er faith be - stow; Then
death, Lord, keep me Un - til Your heav'n I gain, Where
trust - ing in its wis - dom, My faith shall rest se - cure.
I shall bid de - fi - ance To ev - 'ry e - vil foe.
I by Your great mer - cy The end of faith at - tain.

Hymn accompaniment: 820

Text: Erdmann Neumeister, 1671–1756; tr. *The Lutheran Hymnal*, 1941, alt.
Tune: *Concentus novi*, Augsburg, 1540

NUN LOB, MEIN SEEL
78 78 76 76 76 76

2 Tim. 1:12; John 17:8; Luke 17:5; 1 Peter 1:3–9

Jesus Loves Me

1 Je - sus loves me! This I know, For the Bi - ble tells me so.
2 Je - sus loves me! He who died Heav-en's gates to o - pen wide.
Lit - tle ones to Him be-long; They are weak, but He is strong.
He has washed a - way my sin, Lets His lit - tle child come in.
Refrain
Yes, Je - sus loves me! Yes, Je - sus loves me!
Yes, Je - sus loves me! The Bi - ble tells me so.

1 *Cristo me ama, bien lo sé;*
su Palabra me hace ver
que los niños son de aquel
quien es nuestro amigo fiel.

2 *Cristo me ama, me salvó,*
en la cruz por mí murió;
mi pecado perdonó;
vida eterna me donó.

Estribillo *Sí, Cristo me ama; sí, Cristo me ama;*
sí, Cristo me ama; la Biblia dice así.

Text: Anna B. Warner, 1820–1915, alt.; Spanish tr. unknown
Music: William B. Bradbury, 1816–68

JESUS LOVES ME
77 77 and refrain

Matt. 19:14; Titus 3:4–7; John 15:9; Eph. 3:17b–19

589 Speak, O Lord, Your Servant Listens

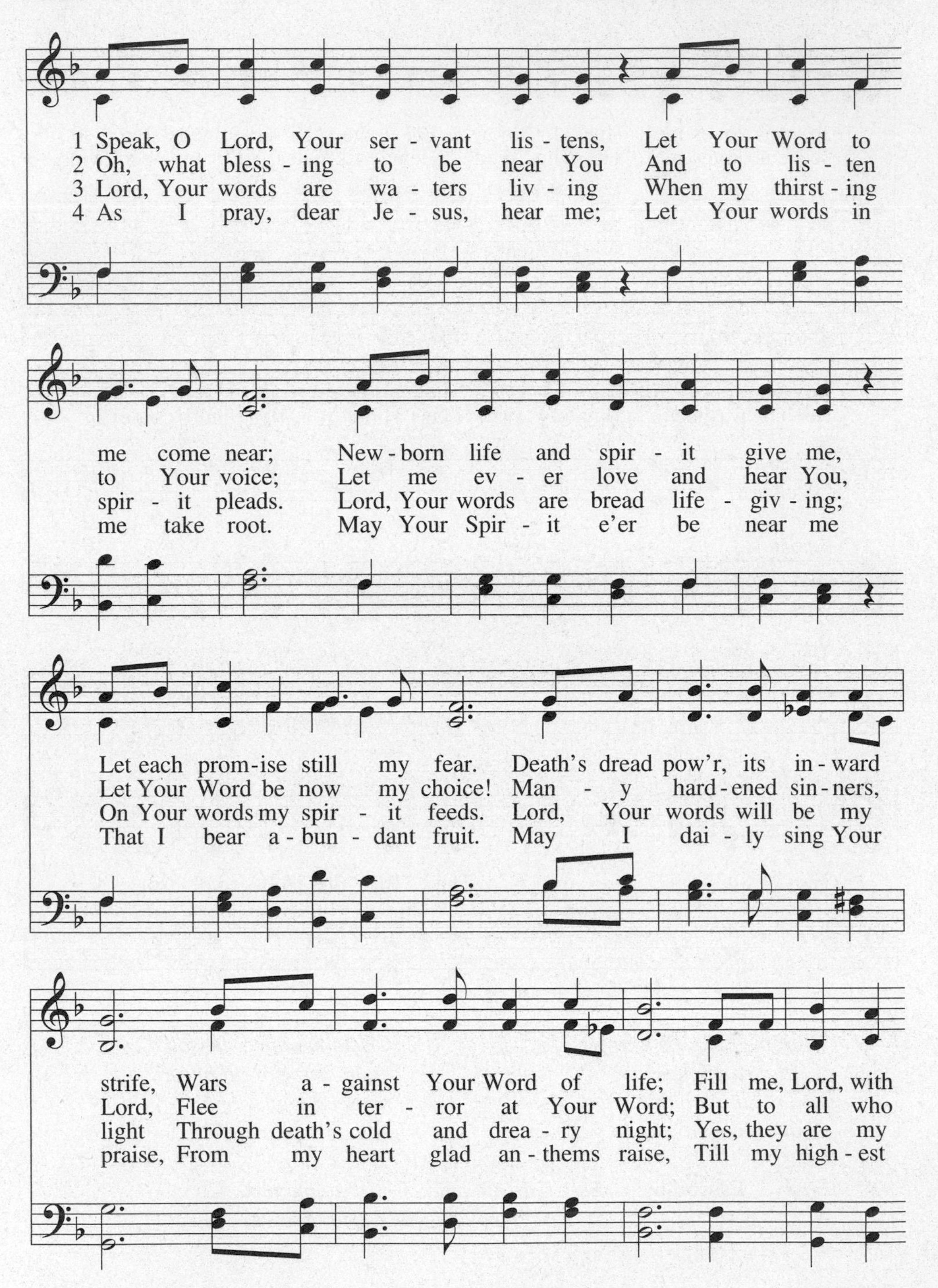
1 Speak, O Lord, Your servant listens, Let Your Word to me come near; New-born life and spirit give me, Let each promise still my fear. Death's dread pow'r, its inward strife, Wars against Your Word of life; Fill me, Lord, with
2 Oh, what blessing to be near You And to listen to Your voice; Let me ever love and hear You, Let Your Word be now my choice! Many hardened sinners, Lord, Flee in terror at Your Word; But to all who
3 Lord, Your words are waters living When my thirsting spirit pleads. Lord, Your words are bread life-giving; On Your words my spirit feeds. Lord, Your words will be my light Through death's cold and dreary night; Yes, they are my
4 As I pray, dear Jesus, hear me; Let Your words in me take root. May Your Spirit e'er be near me That I bear abundant fruit. May I daily sing Your praise, From my heart glad anthems raise, Till my highest

Text: Anna Sophia von Hessen-Darmstadt, 1638–83; tr. George A. T. Rygh, 1860–1942, sts. 1–3, alt.; tr. *Christian Worship,* 1993, st. 4
Tune: Johann Schop, c. 1590–1667; setting: Henry V. Gerike, b. 1948

WERDE MUNTER
87 87 77 88

1 Sam. 3:10; 1 Peter 1:23–25; John 6:63; 15:7–8

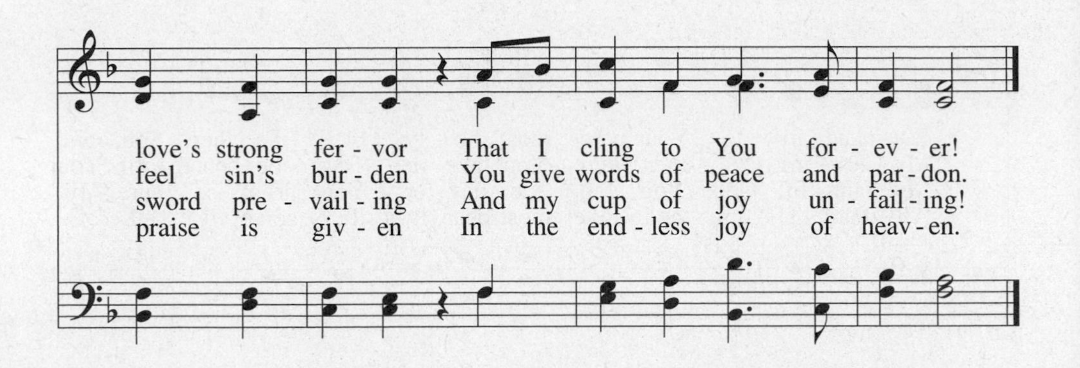
love's strong fer - vor That I cling to You for - ev - er!
feel sin's bur - den You give words of peace and par - don.
sword pre - vail - ing And my cup of joy un - fail - ing!
praise is giv - en In the end - less joy of heav - en.

Blessed Lord, since You have caused all Holy Scriptures to be written for our learning, grant that we may so hear them, read, mark, learn, and inwardly digest them that we may embrace and ever hold fast the blessed hope of everlasting life; through Jesus Christ, Your Son, our Lord, who lives and reigns with You and the Holy Spirit, one God, now and forever.

Collect for Proper 10, Series A

590 Baptized into Your Name Most Holy

1 Bap-tized in - to Your name most ho - ly, O Fa - ther, Son, and Ho - ly Ghost, I claim a place, though weak and low - ly, A - mong Your saints, Your cho - sen host. Bur - ied with Christ and dead to sin, Your Spir - it now shall live with - in.
2 My lov - ing Fa - ther, here You take me To be hence-forth Your child and heir. My faith - ful Sav - ior, here You make me The fruit of all Your sor - rows share. O Ho - ly Spir - it, com - fort me When threat-'ning clouds a - round I see.
3 My faith - ful God, You fail me nev - er; Your prom - ise sure - ly will en - dure. O cast me not a - way for - ev - er If words and deeds be - come im - pure. Have mer - cy when I come de - filed; For - give, lift up, re - store Your child.
4 All that I am and love most dear - ly— Re - ceive it all, O Lord, from me. Let me con - fess my faith sin - cere - ly; Help me Your faith - ful child to be! Let noth - ing that I am or own Serve an - y will but Yours a - lone.

Text: Johann Jacob Rambach, 1693–1735, abr.; tr. Catherine Winkworth, 1827–78, alt.
Tune: Cornelius Heinrich Dretzel, 1697–1775; setting: *The Lutheran Hymnal*, 1941

O DASS ICH TAUSEND ZUNGEN HÄTTE (DRETZEL)
98 98 88

Matt. 28:19; Rom. 6:2–4, 11; Gal. 3:26–27; Ps. 51:10–12

This Is the Spirit's Entry Now 591

1 This is the Spir - it's en - try now: The wa - ter and the Word, The cross of Je - sus on your brow, The seal both felt and heard.
2 This mir - a - cle of life re - born Comes from the Lord of breath; The per - fect Man from life was torn; Our life comes through Christ's death.
3 Let wa - ter be the sa - cred sign That we must die each day To rise a - gain by His de - sign As fol - l'wers of His way.
4 Re - new - ing Spir - it, hear our praise For Your bap - tis - mal pow'r That wash - es us through all our days; Lord, cleanse a - gain this hour.

Text: Thomas E. Herbranson, 1933–2009
Music: Roy Hopp, b. 1951

DAMASCUS ROAD
C M

Eph. 5:25b–27; Rom. 6:3–9

592 Dearest Jesus, We Are Here

1 Dear - est Je - sus, we are here, Glad - ly Your com-
2 Your com - mand is clear and plain, And we would o -
3 There - fore we have come to You, In our arms this
4 Gra - cious Head, Your mem - ber own; Shep - herd, take Your
mand o - bey - ing; With this child we now draw near
bey it du - ly: "You must all be born a - gain,
in - fant bear - ing. Tru - ly here Your grace we view;
lamb and feed it; Prince of Peace, make here Your throne;
In re - sponse to Your own say - ing That to You it
Heart and life re - new - ing tru - ly, Born of wa - ter
May this child, Your mer - cy shar - ing, In Your arms be
Way of Life, to heav - en lead it; Pre - cious Vine, let
shall be giv - en As a child and heir of heav - en.
and the Spir - it, And My king - dom thus in - her - it."
shield - ed ev - er, Yours on earth and Yours for - ev - er.
noth - ing sev - er From Your side this branch for - ev - er.

Text: Benjamin Schmolck, 1672–1737; tr. Catherine Winkworth, 1827–78, alt.
Tune: Johann Rudolph Ahle, 1625–73, alt.; setting: Paul G. Bunjes, 1914–98, alt.

LIEBSTER JESU, WIR SIND HIER
78 78 88

Mark 10:13–16; John 3:3–6

5 Now into Your heart we pour
Prayers that from our hearts proceeded.
Our petitions heav'nward soar;
May our hearts' desires be heeded!
Write the name we now have given;
Write it in the book of heaven!

See This Wonder in the Making 593

1 See this won - der in the mak - ing: God Him -
2 Mir - a - cle each time it hap - pens As the
3 Far more ten - der than a moth - er, Far more
4 Here we bring a child of na - ture; Home we

self this child is tak - ing As a lamb safe in His
door to heav - en o - pens And the Fa - ther beams, "Be -
car - ing than a fa - ther, God, in - to Your arms we
take a new - born crea - ture, Now God's pre - cious son or

keep - ing, His to be, a - wake or sleep - ing.
lov - ed, Heir of gifts a king would cov - et!"
place *him/her/them*, With Your love and peace em - brace *him/her/them*.
daugh - ter, Born a - gain by Word and wa - ter.

Text: Jaroslav J. Vajda, 1919–2008
Music: *Lofsånger och andeliga wisor*, Sweden, 1873

TRYGGARE KAN INGEN VARA
88 88 (Trochaic)

Matt. 3:16–17; Titus 3:3–7; Eph. 5:25b–26; Mark 10:16

594 God's Own Child, I Gladly Say It

1 God's own child, I glad - ly say it: I am bap-tized
2 Sin, dis - turb my soul no long - er: I am bap-tized
3 Sa - tan, hear this proc - la - ma - tion: I am bap-tized
4 Death, you can - not end my glad-ness: I am bap-tized
5 There is noth - ing worth com-par - ing To this life-long
in - to Christ! He, be - cause I could not pay it,
in - to Christ! I have com - fort e - ven strong-er:
in - to Christ! Drop your ug - ly ac - cu - sa - tion,
in - to Christ! When I die, I leave all sad - ness
com - fort sure! O - pen - eyed my grave is star - ing:
Gave my full re - demp - tion price. Do I need earth's
Je - sus' cleans-ing sac - ri - fice. Should a guilt - y
I am not so soon en - ticed. Now that to the
To in - her - it par - a - dise! Though I lie in
E - ven there I'll sleep se - cure. Though my flesh a -
trea - sures man - y? I have one worth
con - science seize me Since my Bap - tism
font I've trav - eled, All your might has
dust and ash - es Faith's as - sur - ance
waits its rais - ing, Still my soul con -
more than an - y That brought me sal -
did re - lease me In a dear for -
come un - rav - eled, And, a - gainst your
bright - ly flash - es: Bap - tism has the
tin - ues prais - ing: I am bap - tized

Setting available in hymn accompaniment edition.

Text: Erdmann Neumeister, 1671–1756; tr. Robert E. Voelker, b. 1957
Tune: Johann Caspar Bachofen, 1695–1755, alt.

BACHOFEN
87 87 88 77

Rom. 6:1–10; 1 Peter 3:18–22; Titus 3:4–7

va - tion free Last - ing to e - ter - ni - ty!
giv - ing flood, Sprin - kling me with Je - sus' blood?
tyr - an - ny, God, my Lord, u - nites with me!
strength di - vine To make life im - mor - tal mine.
in - to Christ; I'm a child of par - a - dise!

O Blessed Spring 595

1 O bless-ed spring, where Word and sign Em - brace us
2 Through sum-mer heat of youth-ful years, Un - cer - tain
3 When au-tumn cools and youth is cold, When limbs their
4 As win - ter comes, as win - ters must, We breathe our
5 Christ, ho - ly Vine, Christ, liv - ing Tree, Be praised for
in - to Christ the Vine: Here Christ en - joins each one to
faith, re - bel - lious tears, Sus - tained by Christ's in - fus - ing
heav - y har - vest hold, Then through us, warm, the Christ will
last, re - turn to dust; Still held in Christ, our souls take
this blest mys - ter - y: That Word and wa - ter thus re -
be A branch of this life - giv - ing Tree.
rain, The boughs will shout for joy a - gain.
move With gifts of beau - ty, wis - dom, love.
wing And trust the prom - ise of the spring.
vive And join us to Your Tree of Life.

Setting available in hymn accompaniment edition.

Text: Susan Palo Cherwien, b. 1953
Tune: English

O WALY WALY
L M

John 15:1–5; Gen. 2:9; Rev. 22:14

596 All Christians Who Have Been Baptized

1 All Chris-tians who have been bap-tized, Who know the God of
2 You were be-fore your day of birth, In-deed, from your con-
3 But all of that was washed a-way— Im-mersed and drowned for-
4 In Bap-tism we now put on Christ— Our shame is ful-ly
heav-en, And in whose dai-ly life is prized The name of
cep-tion, Con-demned and lost with all the earth, None good, with-
ev-er. The wa-ter of your Bap-tism day Re-stored a-
cov-ered With all that He once sac-ri-ficed And free-ly
Christ once giv-en: Con-sid-er now what God has done, The
out ex-cep-tion. For like your par-ents' flesh and blood, Turned
gain what-ev-er Old Ad-am and his sin de-stroyed And
for us suf-fered. For here the flood of His own blood Now
gifts He gives to ev-'ry-one Bap-tized in-to Christ Je-sus!
in-ward from the high-est good, You con-stant-ly de-nied Him.
all our sin-ful selves em-ployed Ac-cord-ing to our na-ture.
makes us ho-ly, right, and good Be-fore our heav'n-ly Fa-ther.

Text: Paul Gerhardt, 1607–76; tr. Jon D. Vieker, b. 1961
Tune: *Etlich Cristlich lider*, Wittenberg, 1524; setting: *The Lutheran Hymnal*, 1941

NUN FREUT EUCH
87 87 887

Rom. 6:1–10; Eph. 5:25b–26; Ezek. 36:25–27; Gal. 3:26–27

5 O Christian, firmly hold this gift
And give God thanks forever!
It gives the power to uplift
In all that you endeavor.
When nothing else revives your soul,
Your Baptism stands and makes you whole
And then in death completes you.

6 So use it well! You are made new—
In Christ a new creation!
As faithful Christians, live and do
Within your own vocation,
Until that day when you possess
His glorious robe of righteousness
Bestowed on you forever!

Water, Blood, and Spirit Crying 597

1 Water, blood, and Spirit crying, By their witness testifying To the One whose death-defying Life has come, with life for all.
2 In a wat'ry grave are buried All our sins that Jesus carried; Christ, the Ark of Life, has ferried Us across death's raging flood.
3 Dark the way, yet Christ precedes us, Past the scowl of death He leads us; Spreads a table where He feeds us With His body and His blood.
4 Though around us death is seething, God, His two-edged sword unsheathing, By His Spirit life is breathing Through the living, active Word.
5 Spirit, water, blood entreating, Working faith and its completing In the One whose death-defeating Life has come, with life for all.

Text: Stephen P. Starke, b. 1955
Music: Jeffrey N. Blersch, b. 1967

FILTER
88 87

1 John 5:5–8; John 10:10

598 Once in the Blest Baptismal Waters

1 Once in the blest bap - tis - mal wa - ters I put on Christ and made Him mine; Now num - bered with God's sons and daugh - ters, I share His peace and love di - vine.
2 His bod - y and His blood I've tak - en In His blest Sup - per, feast di - vine; Now I shall nev - er be for - sak - en, For I am His, and He is mine.
3 And thus I live in God con - tent - ed And die with - out a thought of fear; My soul has to God's plans con - sent - ed, For through His Son my faith is clear.
Refrain
O God, for Je - sus' sake I pray Your peace may bless my dy - ing day.

Alternate tune: O DASS ICH TAUSEND ZUNGEN HÄTTE (DRETZEL) (566)

Text: Emilie Juliane von Schwarzburg-Rudolstadt, 1637–1706; tr. *The Lutheran Hymnal*, 1941, abr., alt.
Tune: Christian Möck, 1737–1818; setting: *The Lutheran Hymnal*, 1941

WER WEISS, WIE NAHE
98 98 88

Gal. 3:26–27; Rom. 6:3; Luke 2:29–32

O Gracious Lord, with Love Draw Near

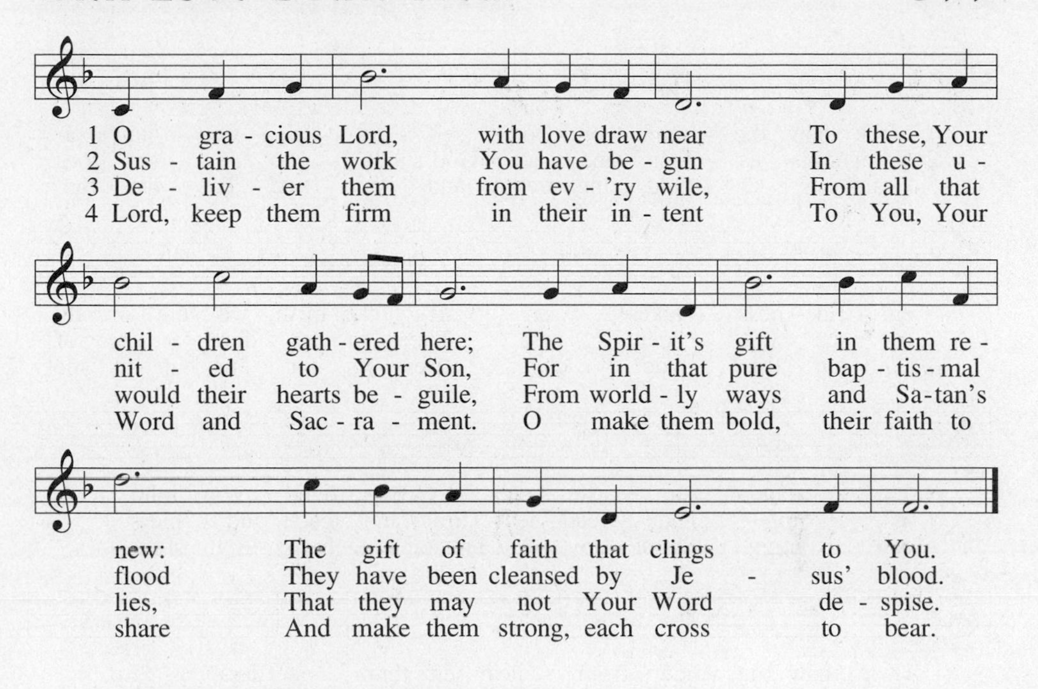
1 O gracious Lord, with love draw near To these, Your children gathered here; The Spirit's gift in them renew: The gift of faith that clings to You.
2 Sustain the work You have begun In these united to Your Son, For in that pure baptismal flood They have been cleansed by Jesus' blood.
3 Deliver them from ev'ry wile, From all that would their hearts beguile, From worldly ways and Satan's lies, That they may not Your Word despise.
4 Lord, keep them firm in their intent To You, Your Word and Sacrament. O make them bold, their faith to share And make them strong, each cross to bear.

5 O Father, grant that by Your grace
They may Your will each day embrace;
With fruits of faith their lives now bless,
Till they at death Your name confess.

6 Then robed in white before Your throne,
Your holy saints, by You foreknown—
Predestined, called, and justified,
Shall, crowned in light, be glorified.

Hymn accompaniment: 574

Text: Stephen P. Starke, b. 1955
Tune: Vernon Griffiths, 1894–1985

DUNEDIN
L M

Matt. 28:19; Mark 16:16; Titus 3:5–8; Rom. 6:4

600 Mark How the Lamb of God's Self-Offering

1 Mark how the Lamb of God's self - of - f'ring Our hu - man
2 From this as - sur - ance of God's fa - vor Je - sus goes
3 Grant us, O God, the strength and cour - age To live the
sin - ful - ness takes on In the birth - wa - ters of the
to the wil - der - ness, There to en - dure a time of
faith our lips de - clare; Bless us in our bap - tis - mal
Jor - dan As Je - sus is bap - tized by John.
test - ing That read - ied Him to teach and bless.
call - ing; Christ's roy - al priest - hood help us share.
Hear how the voice from heav - en thun - ders, "Lo,
So we, by wa - ter and the Spir - it Bap -
Turn us from ev - 'ry false al - le - giance, That
this is My be - lov - ed Son." See how in dove - like
tized in - to Christ's min - is - try, Are of - ten led to
we may trust in Christ a - lone: Raise up in us a
form the Spir - it De - scends on God's A - noint - ed One.
paths of ser - vice Through maz - es of ad - ver - si - ty.
cho - sen peo - ple Trans - formed by love to be Your own.

Hymn accompaniment: 792

Text: Carl P. Daw, Jr., b. 1944
Tune: attr. Louis Bourgeois, c. 1510–61

RENDEZ À DIEU
98 98 D

Matt. 3:13–16; 1 Peter 2:9

All Who Believe and Are Baptized

601

1 All who be - lieve and are bap-tized Shall see the Lord's sal - va - tion;
2 With one ac - cord, O God, we pray: Grant us Your Ho - ly Spir - it.
Bap-tized in - to the death of Christ, They are a new cre - a - tion.
Help us in our in - fir - mi - ty Through Je - sus' blood and mer - it.
Through Christ's re - demp-tion they shall stand A - mong the glo-rious,
Grant us to grow in grace each day That by this sac - ra -
heav'n - ly band Of ev - 'ry tribe and na - tion.
ment we may E - ter - nal life in - her - it.

Text: Thomas Hansen Kingo, 1634–1703; tr. George A. T. Rygh, 1860–1942, alt.
Tune: *Etlich Cristlich lider*, Wittenberg, 1524; setting: *The Lutheran Hymnal*, 1941

ES IST DAS HEIL
87 87 887

Mark 16:16; Col. 2:12–13; Acts 2:38; Rev. 7:13–15

602 The Gifts Christ Freely Gives

1 The gifts Christ free - ly gives He gives to you and me
2 The gifts flow from the font Where He calls us His own;
3 The gifts of grace and peace From ab - so - lu - tion flow;
4 The gifts are there each day The ho - ly Word is read;
To be His Church, His bride, His cho - sen, saved and free!
New life He gives that makes Us His and His a - lone.
The pas - tor's words are Christ's For us to trust and know.
God's chil - dren lis - ten, hear, Re - ceive, and they are fed.
Saints blest with these rich gifts Are chil - dren who pro - claim
Here He for - gives our sins With wa - ter and His Word;
For - give - ness that we need Is grant - ed to us there;
Christ fills them with Him - self, Blest words that give them life,
That they were won by Christ And cling to His strong name.
The tri - une God Him - self Gives pow'r to call Him Lord.
The Lord of mer - cy sends Us forth in His blest care.
Re - stor - ing and re - fresh - ing Them for this world's strife.

Text: Richard C. Resch, b. 1947
Music: Charles J. Dale, 1842–1912, alt.

DENBY
66 66 D

Eph. 1:3–7; 1 John 5:6–8

5 The gifts are in the feast,
Gifts far more than we see;
Beneath the bread and wine
Is food from Calvary.
The body and the blood
Remove our ev'ry sin;
We leave His presence in
His peace, renewed again.

6 All glory to the One
Who lavishes such love;
The triune God in love
Assures our life above.
His means of grace for us
Are gifts He loves to give;
All thanks and praise for His
Great love by which we live!

We Know That Christ Is Raised 603

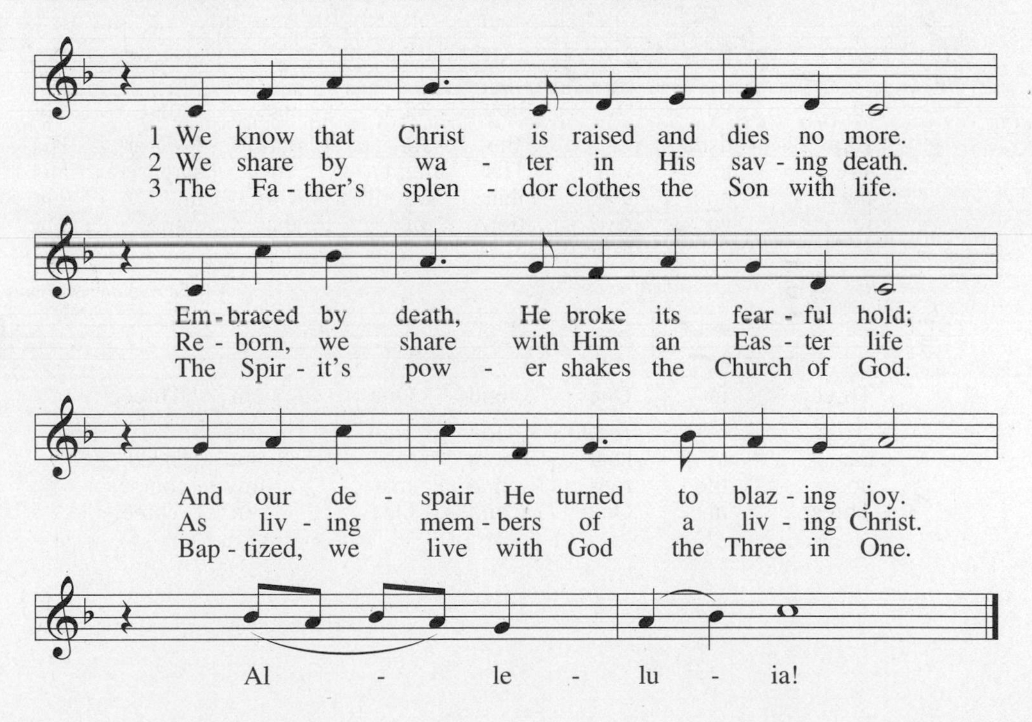
1 We know that Christ is raised and dies no more.
2 We share by wa - ter in His sav - ing death.
3 The Fa - ther's splen - dor clothes the Son with life.
Em - braced by death, He broke its fear - ful hold;
Re - born, we share with Him an Eas - ter life
The Spir - it's pow - er shakes the Church of God.
And our de - spair He turned to blaz - ing joy.
As liv - ing mem - bers of a liv - ing Christ.
Bap - tized, we live with God the Three in One.
Al - le - lu - ia!

Hymn accompaniment: 815

Text: John B. Geyer, b. 1932, alt.
Tune: Charles V. Stanford, 1852–1924

ENGELBERG
10 10 10 4

Rom. 6:3–11; John 3:1–6; Rom. 8:11

604 I Bind unto Myself Today

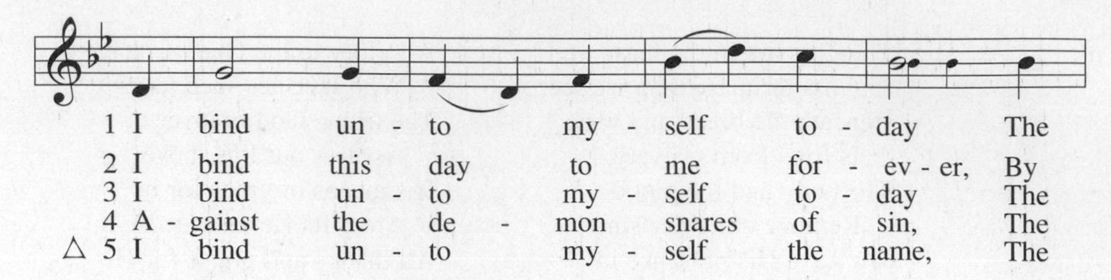
1 I bind un - to my - self to - day The
2 I bind this day to me for - ev - er, By
3 I bind un - to my - self to - day The
4 A - gainst the de - mon snares of sin, The
△ 5 I bind un - to my - self the name, The

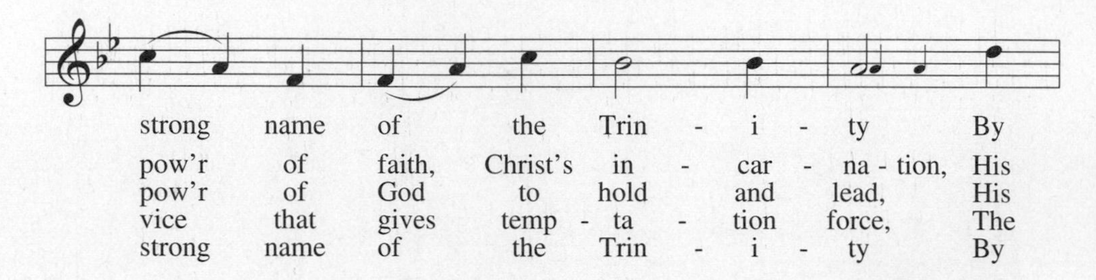
strong name of the Trin - i - ty By
pow'r of faith, Christ's in - car - na - tion, His
pow'r of God to hold and lead, His
vice that gives temp - ta - tion force, The
strong name of the Trin - i - ty By

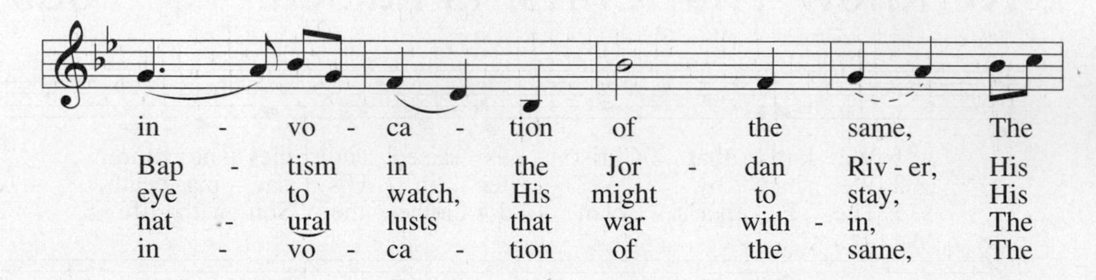
in - vo - ca - tion of the same, The
Bap - tism in the Jor - dan Riv - er, His
eye to watch, His might to stay, His
nat - ural lusts that war with - in, The
in - vo - ca - tion of the same, The

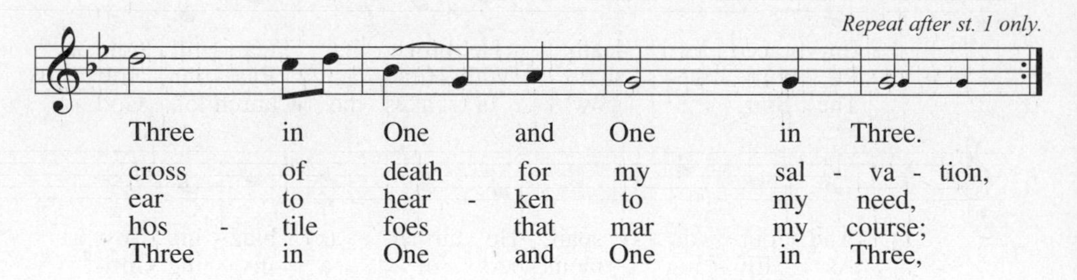
Repeat after st. 1 only.
Three in One and One in Three.
cross of death for my sal - va - tion,
ear to hear - ken to my need,
hos - tile foes that mar my course;
Three in One and One in Three,

Note that stanza 1 concludes at the end of the first page, at which point the singer returns to the beginning to sing stanza 2.
Setting available in hymn accompaniment edition.

Text: attr. Patrick, c. 372–466; tr. Cecil F. Alexander, 1818–95
Tune: Irish

ST. PATRICK'S BREASTPLATE
Irregular meter

1 Peter 1:1–9; Matt. 28:19; Rom. 6:4; John 6:39

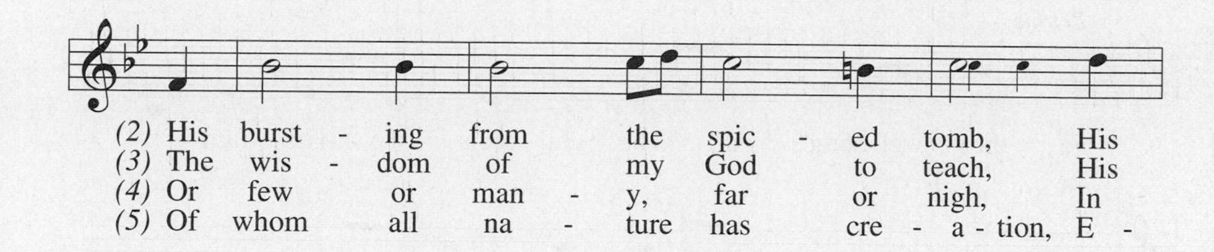
(2) His burst - ing from the spic - ed tomb, His
(3) The wis - dom of my God to teach, His
(4) Or few or man - y, far or nigh, In
(5) Of whom all na - ture has cre - a - tion, E -

rid - ing up the heav'n - ly way, His
hand to guide, His shield to ward, The
ev - 'ry place and in all hours, A -
ter - nal Fa - ther, Spir - it, Word. Praise

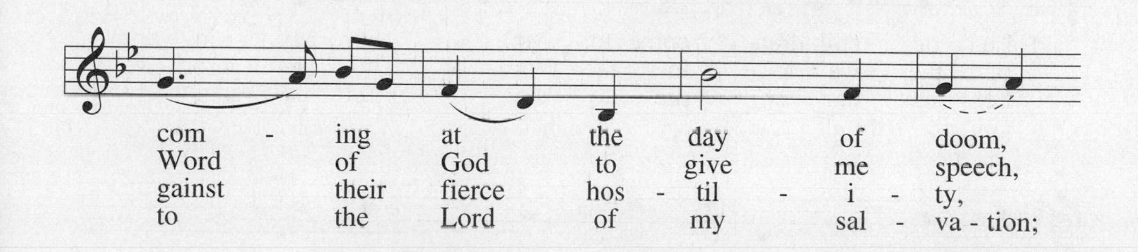
com - ing at the day of doom,
Word of God to give me speech,
gainst their fierce hos - til - i - ty,
to the Lord of my sal - va - tion;

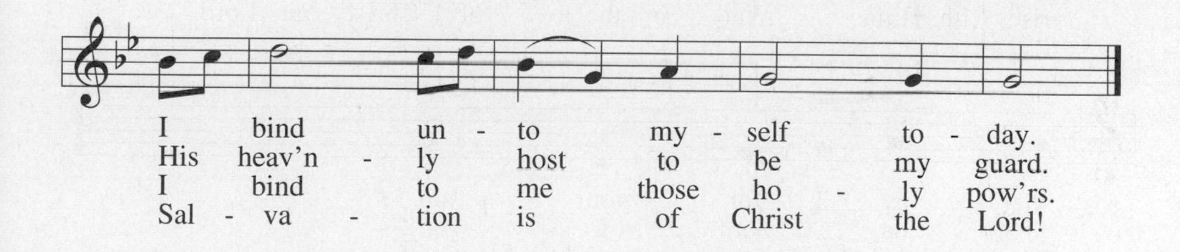
I bind un - to my - self to - day.
His heav'n - ly host to be my guard.
I bind to me those ho - ly pow'rs.
Sal - va - tion is of Christ the Lord!

605 Father Welcomes

Refrain
Fa - ther wel-comes all His chil-dren To His fam - 'ly
through His Son. Fa - ther giv - ing His sal - va - tion,
Life for - ev - er has been won.
1 Lit - tle chil-dren, come to Me, For My king-dom
2 In the wa - ter, in the Word, In His prom-ise,
3 Let us dai - ly die to sin; Let us dai - ly
is of these. Life and___ love I have to give,
be as - sured: Those who are bap - tized and be - lieve
rise with Him, Walk in the love of Christ our Lord,
Mer - cy___ for your sin.
Shall be___ born a - gain.
Live in the peace of God.
Refrain

Setting available in hymn accompaniment edition.

Text: Robin Mann, b. 1949
Tune: Robin Mann, b. 1949

FATHER WELCOMES
Irregular meter

Gal. 3:26–27; Rom. 6:1–7; Mark 16:16; John 3:3–6

I Lay My Sins on Jesus 606

1 I lay my sins on Je - sus, The spot - less Lamb of God;
2 I lay my wants on Je - sus; All full - ness dwells in Him;
3 I rest my soul on Je - sus, This wea - ry soul of mine;
He bears them all and frees us From the ac - curs - ed load.
He heals all my dis - eas - es; My soul He does re - deem.
His right hand me em - brac - es; I on His breast re - cline.
I bring my guilt to Je - sus To wash my crim - son stains
I lay my griefs on Je - sus, My bur - dens and my cares;
I love the name of Je - sus, Im - man - uel, Christ, the Lord;
Clean in His blood most pre - cious Till not a spot re - mains.
He from them all re - leas - es; He all my sor - rows shares.
Like fra - grance on the breez - es His name a - broad is poured.

Text: Horatius Bonar, 1808–89
Tune: *Neu-vermehrtes . . . Gesangbuch*, 3rd ed., Meiningen, 1693; setting: Felix Mendelssohn, 1809–47

MUNICH
76 76 D

1 John 1:7; Matt. 11:29; Eph. 1:7; Col. 1:14

607 From Depths of Woe I Cry to Thee

1 From depths of woe I cry to Thee, In trial and
2 Thy love and grace a - lone a - vail To blot out
3 There - fore my hope is in the Lord And not in
4 And though it tar - ry through the night And till the
5 Though great our sins, yet great - er still Is God's a -
trib - u - la - tion; Bend down Thy gra - cious
my trans - gres - sion; The best and ho - liest
mine own mer - it; It rests up - on His
morn - ing wak - en, My heart shall nev - er
bun - dant fa - vor; His hand of mer - cy
ear to me, Lord, hear my sup - pli - ca - tion.
deeds must fail To break sin's dread op - pres - sion.
faith - ful Word To them of con - trite spir - it
doubt His might Nor count it - self for - sak - en.
nev - er will A - ban - don us, nor wa - ver.
If Thou re - mem - b'rest ev - 'ry sin, Who then could heav - en
Be - fore Thee none can boast - ing stand, But all must fear Thy
That He is mer - ci - ful and just; This is my com - fort
O Is - rael, trust in God your Lord. Born of the Spir - it
Our shep - herd good and true is He, Who will at last His
ev - er win Or stand be - fore Thy pres - ence?
strict de - mand And live a - lone by mer - cy.
and my trust. His help I wait with pa - tience.
and the Word, Now wait for His ap - pear - ing.
Is - rael free From all their sin and sor - row.

Setting available in hymn accompaniment edition.

Text: Martin Luther, 1483–1546; tr. Catherine Winkworth, 1827–78, alt.
Tune: Martin Luther, 1483–1546, alt.

AUS TIEFER NOT
87 87 887

Psalm 130; Eph. 2:8–9; Rom. 5:20–21; 1 Tim. 1:14

Lord, to You I Make Confession 608

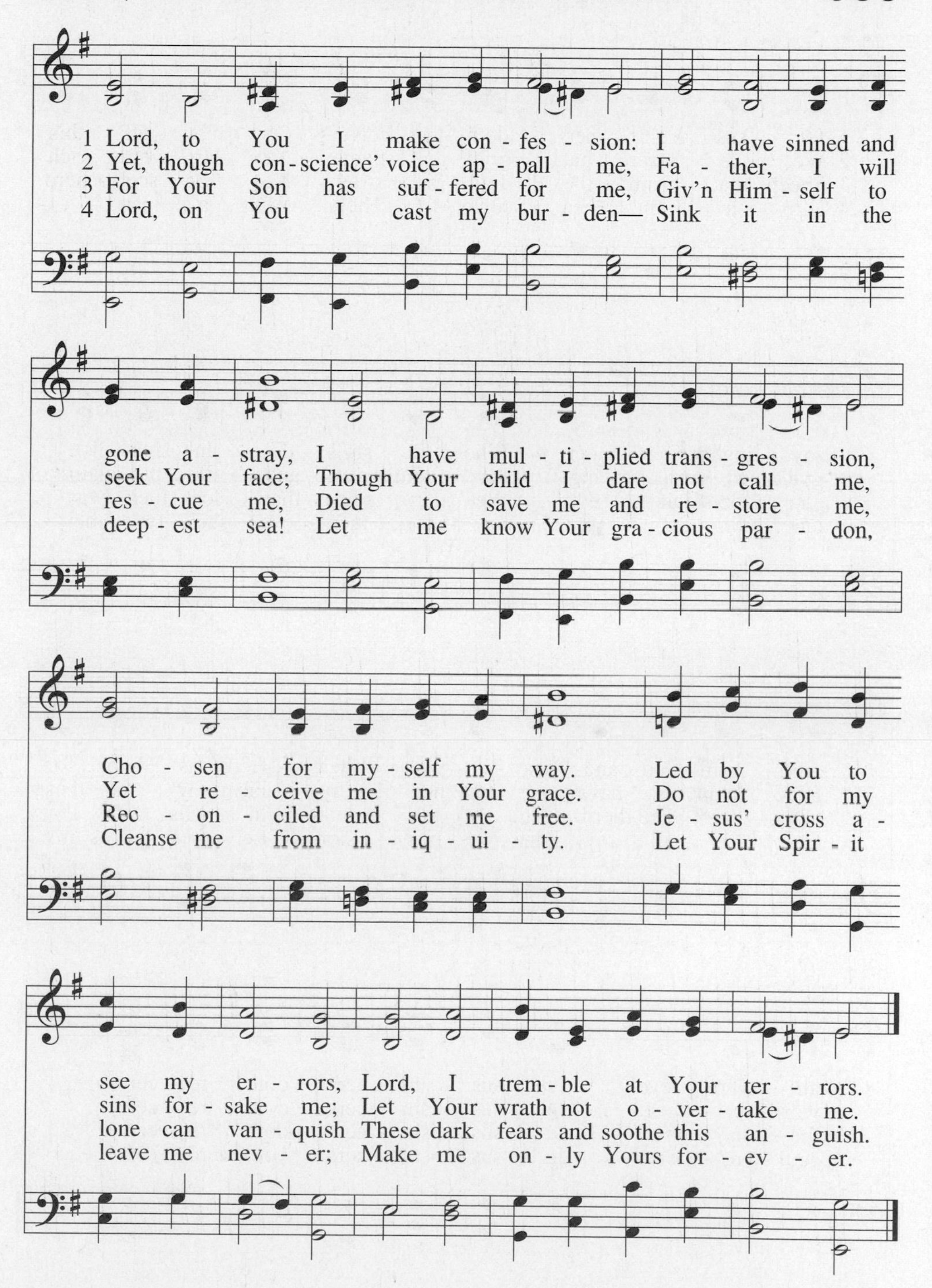
1 Lord, to You I make con - fes - sion: I have sinned and
2 Yet, though con - science' voice ap - pall me, Fa - ther, I will
3 For Your Son has suf - fered for me, Giv'n Him - self to
4 Lord, on You I cast my bur - den— Sink it in the
gone a - stray, I have mul - ti - plied trans - gres - sion,
seek Your face; Though Your child I dare not call me,
res - cue me, Died to save me and re - store me,
deep - est sea! Let me know Your gra - cious par - don,
Cho - sen for my - self my way. Led by You to
Yet re - ceive me in Your grace. Do not for my
Rec - on - ciled and set me free. Je - sus' cross a -
Cleanse me from in - iq - ui - ty. Let Your Spir - it
see my er - rors, Lord, I trem - ble at Your ter - rors.
sins for - sake me; Let Your wrath not o - ver - take me.
lone can van - quish These dark fears and soothe this an - guish.
leave me nev - er; Make me on - ly Yours for - ev - er.

Text: Johann Franck, 1618–77; tr. Catherine Winkworth, 1827–78, alt.
Tune: Johann Crüger, 1598–1662; setting: *The Lutheran Hymnal*, 1941

HERR, ICH HABE MISSGEHANDELT
87 87 88

Ps. 51:3–11, 17; 2 Cor. 5:18–20; Is. 59:12; Ps. 32:5

609 Jesus Sinners Doth Receive

1 Je - sus sin - ners doth re - ceive; Oh, may all this
2 We de - serve but grief and shame, Yet His words, rich
3 Sheep that from the fold did stray No true shep - herd
4 I, a sin - ner, come to Thee With a pen - i -
say - ing pon - der Who in sin's de - lu - sions live
grace re - veal - ing, Par - don, peace, and life pro - claim;
e'er for - sak - eth; Wea - ry souls that lost their way
tent con - fes - sion. Sav - ior, mer - cy show to me;
And from God and heav - en wan - der! Here is hope for
Here our ills have per - fect heal - ing. Firm - ly in these
Christ, the Shep - herd, gent - ly tak - eth In His arms that
Grant for all my sins re - mis - sion. Let these words my
all who grieve: Je - sus sin - ners doth re - ceive.
words be - lieve: Je - sus sin - ners doth re - ceive.
they may live: Je - sus sin - ners doth re - ceive.
soul re - lieve: Je - sus sin - ners doth re - ceive.

Text: Erdmann Neumeister, 1671–1756; tr. *The Lutheran Hymnal*, 1941, alt.
Tune: *Neu-verfertigtes Darmstädtisches Gesang-Buch*, Darmstadt, 1699; setting: *The Lutheran Hymnal*, 1941

MEINEN JESUM LASS' ICH NICHT (DARMSTADT)
78 78 77

Luke 15:2–4; Luke 5:31–32; Matt. 9:12–13; 1 Tim. 1:15–16; 1 Peter 1:18–19

5 Oh, how blest it is to know:
Were as scarlet my transgression,
It shall be as white as snow
By Thy blood and bitter passion;
For these words I now believe:
Jesus sinners doth receive.

6 Now my conscience is at peace;
From the Law I stand acquitted.
Christ hath purchased my release
And my ev'ry sin remitted.
Naught remains my soul to grieve:
Jesus sinners doth receive.

7 Jesus sinners doth receive;
Also I have been forgiven;
And when I this earth must leave,
I shall find an open heaven.
Dying, still to Him I cleave:
Jesus sinners doth receive.

Lord Jesus, Think on Me 610

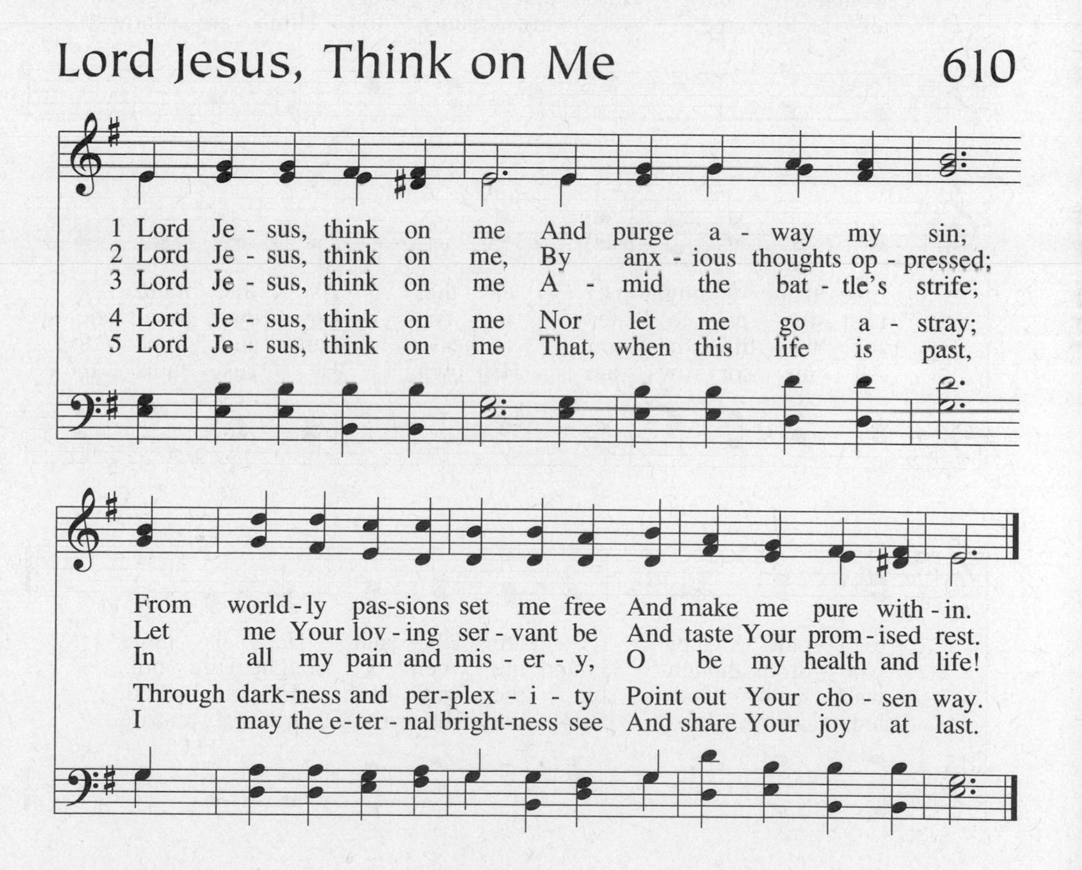
1 Lord Je - sus, think on me And purge a - way my sin;
2 Lord Je - sus, think on me, By anx - ious thoughts op - pressed;
3 Lord Je - sus, think on me A - mid the bat - tle's strife;
4 Lord Je - sus, think on me Nor let me go a - stray;
5 Lord Je - sus, think on me That, when this life is past,
From world - ly pas-sions set me free And make me pure with - in.
Let me Your lov - ing ser - vant be And taste Your prom - ised rest.
In all my pain and mis - er - y, O be my health and life!
Through dark-ness and per-plex - i - ty Point out Your cho - sen way.
I may the e - ter - nal bright-ness see And share Your joy at last.

Text: Synesius of Cyrene, c. 365–c. 414; tr. Allen W. Chatfield, 1808–96, alt.
Tune: William Daman, c. 1540–91; setting: *New English Hymnal*, 1986

SOUTHWELL
S M

Ps. 51:6–12; Heb. 4:15–16; Ps. 119:133; Luke 23:42–43

611 Chief of Sinners Though I Be

1 Chief of sin - ners though I be, Je - sus shed His blood for me, Died that I might live on high, Lives that I might nev - er die. As the branch is to the vine, I am His, and He is mine.
2 Oh, the height of Je - sus' love, High - er than the heav'ns a - bove, Deep - er than the depths of sea, Last - ing as e - ter - ni - ty! Love that found me— won - drous thought! Found me when I sought Him not.
3 On - ly Je - sus can im - part Balm to heal the wound - ed heart, Peace that flows from sin for - giv'n, Joy that lifts the soul to heav'n, Faith and hope to walk with God In the way that E - noch trod.
4 Chief of sin - ners though I be, Christ is all in all to me; All my wants to Him are known, All my sor - rows are His own. He sus - tains the hid - den life Safe with Him from earth - ly strife.

Text: William McComb, 1793–1873, alt.
Tune: Richard Redhead, 1820–1901; setting: *The Lutheran Hymnal*, 1941

GETHSEMANE
77 77 77

1 Tim. 1:15; Rom. 5:8–11; 1 John 4:10; Heb. 4:15–16

5 O my Savior, help afford
By Your Spirit and Your Word!
When my wayward heart would stray,
Keep me in the narrow way;
Grace in time of need supply
While I live and when I die.

As Rebels, Lord, Who Foolishly Have Wandered 612

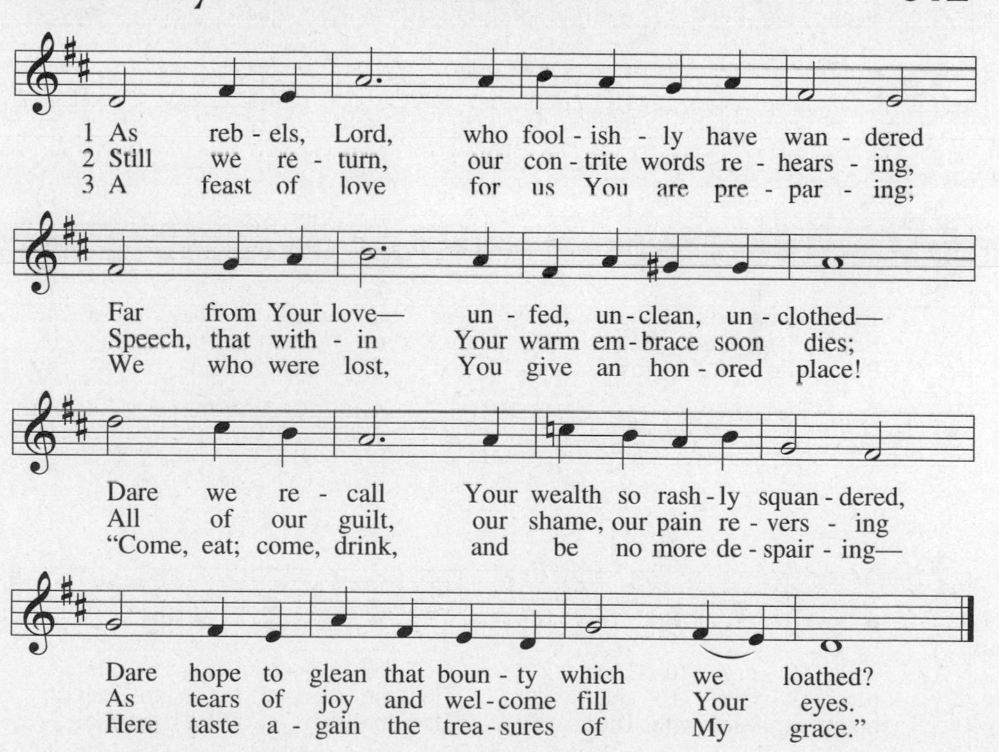
1 As reb - els, Lord, who fool - ish - ly have wan - dered
2 Still we re - turn, our con - trite words re - hears - ing,
3 A feast of love for us You are pre - par - ing;
Far from Your love— un - fed, un - clean, un - clothed—
Speech, that with - in Your warm em - brace soon dies;
We who were lost, You give an hon - ored place!
Dare we re - call Your wealth so rash - ly squan - dered,
All of our guilt, our shame, our pain re - vers - ing
"Come, eat; come, drink, and be no more de - spair - ing—
Dare hope to glean that boun - ty which we loathed?
As tears of joy and wel - come fill Your eyes.
Here taste a - gain the trea - sures of My grace."

Setting available in hymn accompaniment edition. Alternate tune: EIRENE (690)

Text: Stephen P. Starke, b. 1955
Tune: Jeffrey N. Blersch, b. 1967

WELCOME
11 10 11 10

Luke 15:11–24; Matt. 26:26–29

613 To Thee, Omniscient Lord of All

1 To Thee, om - ni - scient Lord of all, In grief and shame I hum - bly call; I see my sins a - gainst Thee, Lord, The sins of thought and deed and word. They press me sore; I cry to Thee: O God, be mer - ci - ful to me!
2 O Lord, my God, to Thee I pray: O cast me not in wrath a - way! Let Thy good Spir - it ne'er de - part, But let Him draw to Thee my heart That tru - ly pen - i - tent I be: O God, be mer - ci - ful to me!
3 O Je - sus, let Thy pre - cious blood Be to my soul a cleans - ing flood. Turn not, O Lord, Thy guest a - way, But grant that jus - ti - fied I may Go to my house at peace with Thee: O God, be mer - ci - ful to me!

Text: Magnus Brostrup Landstad, 1802–80; tr. Carl Döving, 1867–1937, alt.
Tune: attr. Martin Luther, 1483–1546; setting: *The Lutheran Hymnal*, 1941

VATER UNSER
88 88 88

Ps. 51:1–11; Ezra 9:15; Heb. 9:14; Luke 18:13

"As Surely as I Live," God Said 614

1 "As sure - ly as I live," God said, "I would not see the sin - ner dead. I want him turned from er - ror's ways, Re - pen - tant, liv - ing end - less days."
2 And so our Lord gave this com - mand: "Go forth and preach in ev - 'ry land; Be - stow on all My par - d'ning grace Who will re - pent and mend their ways.
3 "All those whose sins you thus re - mit I tru - ly par - don and ac - quit, And those whose sins you will re - tain Con - demned and guilt - y shall re - main.
4 "What you will bind, that bound shall be; What you will loose, that shall be free; To My dear Church the keys are giv'n To o - pen, close the gates of heav'n."

5 The words which absolution give
Are His who died that we might live;
The minister whom Christ has sent
Is but His humble instrument.

6 When ministers lay on their hands,
Absolved by Christ the sinner stands;
He who by grace the Word believes
The purchase of His blood receives.

7 All praise to You, O Christ, shall be
For absolution full and free,
In which You show Your richest grace;
From false indulgence guard our race.

△ 8 Praise God the Father and the Son
And Holy Spirit, Three in One,
As was, is now, and so shall be
World without end, eternally!

Alternate tune: ERHALT UNS, HERR (655)

Text: Nicolaus Herman, c. 1480–1561; tr. Matthias Loy, 1828–1915, alt.
Tune: Jeremiah Clarke, c. 1674–1707; setting: *The Lutheran Hymnal*, 1941

ST. LUKE
L M

Ezek. 33:11; John 20:21–23; Matt. 16:19; Rom. 3:23–24

615 When in the Hour of Deepest Need

1 When in the hour of deep - est need We know not where to look for aid; When days and nights of anx - ious thought No help or coun - sel yet have brought,
2 Then is our com - fort this a - lone That we may meet be - fore Your throne; To You, O faith - ful God, we cry For res - cue in our mis - er - y.
3 For You have prom - ised, Lord, to heed Your chil - dren's cries in time of need Through Him whose name a - lone is great, Our Sav - ior and our ad - vo - cate.
4 And so we come, O God, to - day And all our woes be - fore You lay; For sore - ly tried, cast down, we stand, Per - plexed by fears on ev - 'ry hand.

5 O from our sins, Lord, turn Your face;
Absolve us through Your boundless grace.
Be with us in our anguish still;
Free us at last from ev'ry ill.

6 So we with all our hearts each day
To You our glad thanksgiving pay,
Then walk obedient to Your Word,
And now and ever praise You, Lord.

Text: Paul Eber, 1511–69; tr. Catherine Winkworth, 1827–78, alt.
Tune: Louis Bourgeois, c. 1510–61; setting: *The Lutheran Hymnal*, 1941

WENN WIR IN HÖCHSTEN NÖTEN SEIN
L M

Ps. 102:1–2; Ps. 25:15–22; Rom. 9:17–19; Micah 7:7

Baptismal Waters Cover Me

1 Bap - tis - mal wa - ters cov - er me As I ap -
2 I look to Christ up - on the tree, His bod - y
3 Lord, may Your wound - ed hand im - part Your heal - ing
4 From Your own mouth comes forth a word; Your shep - herd
5 Bap - tis - mal wa - ters cov - er me; Christ's wound - ed
proach on bend - ed knee; My Fa - ther's mer - cy
bro - ken there for me; I lay be - fore Him
to my bro - ken heart; Your love a - lone can
speaks, but You are heard; Through him Your hand now
hand has set me free. Held in my Fa - ther's
here I plead, For griev - ous sins of thought and deed.
all my sin, My dark - est se - crets from with - in.
form in me A heart that serves You joy - ful - ly.
stretch - es out, For - giv - ing sin, de - stroy - ing doubt.
strong em - brace, With joy I praise Him for His grace.

Text: Kurt E. Reinhardt, b. 1969
Tune: *Sammlung alter und neuer . . . Melodien*, 1742; setting: *Lutheran Service Book*, 2006

GOTTLOB, ES GEHT NUNMEHR ZU ENDE
L M

Heb. 10:19–23; Ps. 51:1–2; Heb. 4:16; 1 John 1:9

617 O Lord, We Praise Thee

1 O Lord, we praise Thee, bless Thee, and a - dore Thee,
2 Thy ho - ly bod - y in - to death was giv - en,
3 May God be - stow on us His grace and fa - vor
In thanks - giv - ing bow be - fore Thee. Thou with Thy
Life to win for us in heav - en. No great - er
That we fol - low Christ our Sav - ior And live to -
bod - y and Thy blood didst nour - ish Our weak souls that
love than this to Thee could bind us; May this feast there -
geth - er here in love and u - nion Nor de - spise this
they may flour - ish: O Lord, have mer - cy!
of re - mind us! O Lord, have mer - cy!
blest Com - mu - nion! O Lord, have mer - cy!

Text: German, 14th cent., st. 1; Martin Luther, 1483–1546, sts. 2–3;
tr. *The Lutheran Hymnal*, 1941, alt.
Tune: *Geystliche gesangk Buchleyn*, Wittenberg, 1524, ed. Johann Walter;
setting: *The Lutheran Hymnal*, 1941

GOTT SEI GELOBET UND GEBENEDEIET
Peculiar meter

1 Cor. 11:23–26; Matt. 26:26–28; 1 Peter 2:24

May Thy bod - y, Lord, born of Mar - y, That our
Lord, Thy kind - ness did so con - strain Thee That Thy
Let not Thy good Spir - it for - sake us; Grant that
sins and sor - rows did car - ry, And Thy blood for us plead
blood should bless and sus - tain me. All our debt Thou hast paid;
heav'n - ly - mind - ed He make us; Give Thy Church, Lord, to see
In all tri - al, fear, and need: O Lord, have mer - cy!
Peace with God once more is made: O Lord, have mer - cy!
Days of peace and u - ni - ty: O Lord, have mer - cy!

618 I Come, O Savior, to Thy Table

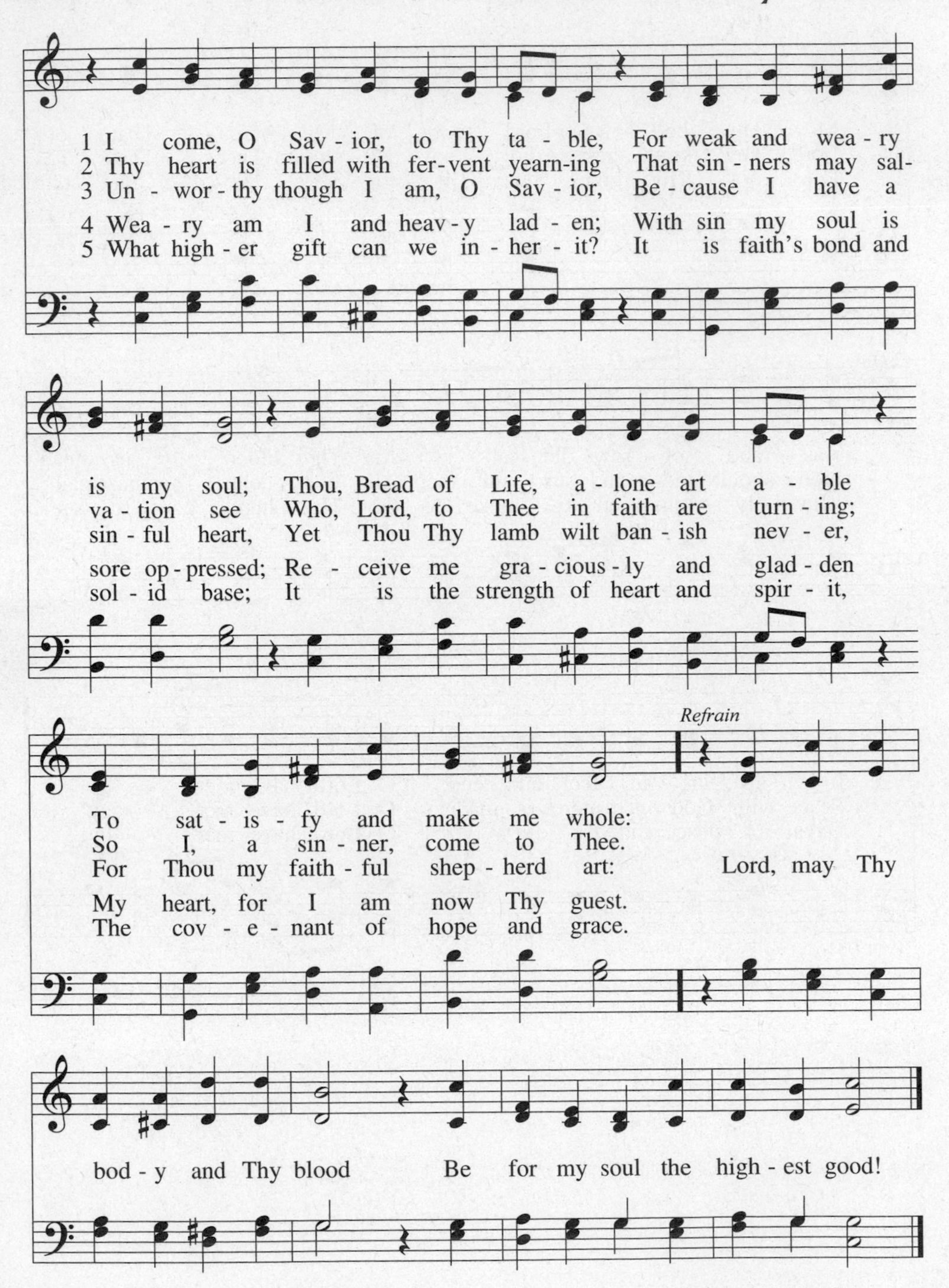
1 I come, O Sav - ior, to Thy ta - ble, For weak and wea - ry
2 Thy heart is filled with fer - vent yearn - ing That sin - ners may sal-
3 Un - wor - thy though I am, O Sav - ior, Be - cause I have a
4 Wea - ry am I and heav - y lad - en; With sin my soul is
5 What high - er gift can we in - her - it? It is faith's bond and
is my soul; Thou, Bread of Life, a - lone art a - ble
va - tion see Who, Lord, to Thee in faith are turn - ing;
sin - ful heart, Yet Thou Thy lamb wilt ban - ish nev - er,
sore op - pressed; Re - ceive me gra - cious - ly and glad - den
sol - id base; It is the strength of heart and spir - it,
To sat - is - fy and make me whole:
So I, a sin - ner, come to Thee.
For Thou my faith - ful shep - herd art:
My heart, for I am now Thy guest.
The cov - e - nant of hope and grace.
Refrain
Lord, may Thy
bod - y and Thy blood Be for my soul the high - est good!

Text: Friedrich Christian Heyder, 1677–1754; tr. *The Lutheran Hymnal*, 1941, abr.
Tune: *Emskirchner Choral-Buch*, Leipzig, 1756;
setting: *The Lutheran Hymnal*, 1941

ICH STERBE TÄGLICH
98 98 and refrain

1 Cor. 11:23–29; Luke 22:17–20; Mark 14:22–25; Matt. 26:26–28; Psalm 130

Thy Body, Given for Me, O Savior 619

1 Thy bod - y, giv'n for me, O Sav - ior, Thy blood which Thou for
2 With Thee, Lord, I am now u - nit - ed; I live in Thee and
3 Who can con-demn me now? For sure - ly The Lord is nigh, who
4 Though death may threat-en with dis - as - ter, It can - not rob me
5 My heart has now be-come Thy dwell-ing, O bless - ed, ho - ly

me didst shed, These are my life and strength for - ev - er,
Thou in me. No sor - row fills my soul, de - light - ed
jus - ti - fies. No hell I fear, and thus se - cure - ly
of my cheer; For He who is of death the mas - ter
Trin - i - ty. With an - gels I, Thy prais - es tell - ing,

By them my hun - gry soul is fed.
It finds its on - ly joy in Thee.
With Je - sus I to heav - en rise.
With aid and com - fort e'er is near.
Shall live in joy e - ter - nal - ly.

Refrain

Lord, may Thy bod - y and Thy blood Be for my soul the high - est good!

Text: Friedrich Christian Heyder, 1677–1754; tr. *The Lutheran Hymnal,* 1941, abr.
Tune: *Emskirchner Choral-Buch*, Leipzig, 1756;
setting: *The Lutheran Hymnal*, 1941

ICH STERBE TÄGLICH
98 98 and refrain

1 Cor. 11:23–29; Luke 22:17–20; Rom. 8:33–39

620 Jesus Comes Today with Healing

1 Je - sus comes to - day with heal - ing, Knock - ing at my
2 Christ Him - self, the priest pre - sid - ing, Yet in bread and
3 Un - der bread and wine, though low - ly, I re - ceive the
4 God de - scends with heav'n - ly pow - er, Gives Him - self to

door, ap - peal - ing, Of - f'ring par - don, grace, and peace.
wine a - bid - ing In this ho - ly sac - ra - ment,
Sav - ior ho - ly, Blood and bod - y, giv'n for me,
me this hour In this or - di - nar - y sign.

He Him - self makes prep - a - ra - tion, And I hear His
Gives the bread of life, once bro - ken, And the cup, the
Ver - y Lamb of God from heav - en, Who to bit - ter
On my tongue His pledge re - ceiv - ing, I ac - cept His

in - vi - ta - tion: "Come and taste the bless - ed feast."
pre - cious to - ken Of His sa - cred cov - e - nant.
death was giv - en, Hung up - on the curs - ed tree.
grace, be - liev - ing That I taste His love di - vine.

Text: Heinrich Puchta, 1808–58; tr. David W. Rogner, b. 1960
Tune: Johann Löhner, 1645–1705; adapt. Johann Balthasar König, 1691–1758;
setting: *The Lutheran Hymnal*, 1941

ALLES IST AN GOTTES SEGEN
887 887

Matt. 26:26–29; Heb. 7:23–27; 1 Peter 1:18–19; Rev. 7:13–17

5 Let me praise God's boundless favor,
Whose own feast of love I savor,
Bidden by His gracious call.
Wedding garments He provides me,
With a robe of white He hides me,
Fits me for the royal hall.

6 Now have I found consolation,
Comfort in my tribulation,
Balm to heal the troubled soul.
God, my shield from ev'ry terror,
Cleanses me from sin and error,
Makes my wounded spirit whole.

Let All Mortal Flesh Keep Silence 621

1 Let all mor - tal flesh keep si - lence And with fear and
2 King of kings yet born of Mar - y, As of old on
3 Rank on rank the host of heav - en Spreads its van - guard
4 At His feet the six - winged ser - aph, Cher - u - bim with
trem - bling stand; Pon - der noth - ing earth - ly - mind - ed,
earth He stood, Lord of lords in hu - man ves - ture,
on the way As the Light of Light, de - scend - ing
sleep - less eye, Veil their fac - es to the pres - ence
For with bless - ing in His hand Christ our God to earth de -
In the bod - y and the blood, He will give to all the
From the realms of end - less day, Comes the pow'rs of hell to
As with cease - less voice they cry: "Al - le - lu - ia, al - le -
scend - ing Comes our hom - age to de - mand.
faith - ful His own self for heav'n - ly food.
van - quish As the dark - ness clears a - way.
lu - ia! Al - le - lu - ia, Lord Most High!"

Setting available in hymn accompaniment edition.

Text: Liturgy of St. James, 5th cent.; tr. Gerard Moultrie, 1829–85, alt.
Tune: French, 17th cent.

PICARDY
87 87 87

Acts 1:10–11; 1 Thess. 4:16–17; 1 Cor. 11:23–26; Luke 2:8–15

622 Lord Jesus Christ, You Have Prepared

1 Lord Je - sus Christ, You have pre - pared This feast for our sal - va - tion; It is Your bod - y and Your blood, And at Your in - vi - ta - tion
2 Al - though You did to heav'n as - cend, Where an - gel hosts are dwell - ing, And in Your pres - ence they be - hold Your glo - ry, all ex - cel - ling,
3 Yet, Sav - ior, You are not con - fined To an - y hab - i - ta - tion; But You are pres - ent e - ven now Here with Your con - gre - ga - tion.
4 We eat this bread and drink this cup, Your pre - cious Word be - liev - ing That Your true bod - y and Your blood Our lips are here re - ceiv - ing.
As wea - ry souls, with sin op - pressed, We come to
And though Your peo - ple shall not see Your glo - ry
Firm as a rock this truth shall stand, Un - moved by
This Word re - mains for - ev - er true, All things are

Text: Samuel Kinner, 1603–68; tr. Emanuel Cronenwett, 1841–1931, alt.
Tune: Peter Sohren, c. 1630–92, alt.; setting: *The Lutheran Hymnal*, 1941

DU LEBENSBROT, HERR JESU CHRIST
87 87 887

1 Cor. 11:23–28; 1 Cor. 10:16; Matt. 11:28–29

You for need - ed rest, For com - fort, and for par - don.
and Your maj - es - ty Till dawns the judg - ment morn - ing,
an - y dar - ing hand Or sub - tle craft and cun - ning.
pos - si - ble with You, For You are Lord Al - might - y.

5 Though reason cannot understand,
Yet faith this truth embraces:
Your body, Lord, is even now
At once in many places.
I leave to You how this can be;
Your Word alone suffices me;
I trust its truth unfailing.

6 Lord, I believe what You have said;
Help me when doubts assail me.
Remember that I am but dust,
And let my faith not fail me.
Your supper in this vale of tears
Refreshes me and stills my fears
And is my priceless treasure.

7 Grant that we worthily receive
Your supper, Lord, our Savior,
And, truly grieving for our sins,
May prove by our behavior
That we are thankful for Your grace
And day by day may run our race,
In holiness increasing.

8 For Your consoling supper, Lord,
Be praised throughout all ages!
Preserve it, for in ev'ry place
The world against it rages.
Grant that this sacrament may be
A blessèd comfort unto me
When living and when dying.

623 Lord Jesus Christ, We Humbly Pray

1 Lord Je - sus Christ, we hum - bly pray That we may
2 Give us, who share this won-drous food, Your bod - y
3 By faith Your Word has made us bold To seize the
4 One bread, one cup, one bod - y, we, Re - joic - ing
5 Lord Je - sus Christ, we hum - bly pray: O keep us
feast on You to - day; Be - neath these forms of
bro - ken and Your blood, The grate - ful peace of
gift of love re - told; All that You are we
in our u - ni - ty, Pro - claim Your love un -
stead - fast till that day When each will be Your
bread and wine En - rich us with Your grace di - vine.
sins for - giv'n, The cer - tain joys of heirs of heav'n.
here re - ceive, And all we are to You we give.
til You come To bring Your scat - tered loved ones home.
wel - comed guest In heav - en's high and ho - ly feast.

Text: Henry E. Jacobs, 1844–1932, alt.
Tune: *Cantionale Germanicum,* Gochsheim, 1628; setting: *Service Book and Hymnal*, 1958

HERR JESU CHRIST, DICH ZU UNS WEND
L M

1 Cor. 10:16–17; 11:23–26; Rom. 5:1–2; Rev. 2:10b

The Infant Priest Was Holy Born

624

1 The in - fant Priest was ho - ly born For us un -
2 This great High Priest in hu - man flesh Was i - con
3 The ho - ly Lamb un - daunt - ed came To God's own
4 But death would not the vic - tor be Of Him who
5 The veil is torn, our Priest we see, As at the
ho - ly and for - lorn; From flesh - ly tem - ple
of God's righ - teous - ness. His hal - lowed touch brought
al - tar lit with flame; While weep - ing an - gels
hung up - on the tree. He leads us to the
rail on bend - ed knee Our hun - gry mouths from
forth came He, A - noint - ed from e - ter - ni - ty.
sanc - ti - ty; His hand re - moved im - pu - ri - ty.
hid their eyes, This Priest be - came a sac - ri - fice.
Ho - ly Place With - in the veil, be - fore God's face.
Him re - ceive The bread of im - mor - tal - i - ty.

6 The body of God's Lamb we eat,
A priestly food and priestly meat;
On sin-parched lips the chalice pours
His quenching blood
that life restores.

7 With cherubim and seraphim
Our voices join the endless hymn,
And "Holy, holy, holy" sing
To Christ, God's Lamb,
our Priest and King.

Text: Chad L. Bird, b. 1970
Tune: *Second Supplement to Psalmody in Miniature*, London, 1778; adapt. Edward Miller, 1731–1807;
setting: *The Worshipbook: Services and Hymns*, 1972

ROCKINGHAM OLD
L M

Heb. 9:11–28; John 1:29; 6:51–58

625 Lord Jesus Christ, Life-Giving Bread

1 Lord Je - sus Christ, life - giv - ing bread, May I in grace
2 To pas - tures green, Lord, safe - ly guide, To rest - ful wa -
3 O bread of heav'n, my soul's de - light, For full and free
4 I do not mer - it fa - vor, Lord, My weight of sin
pos - sess You. Let me with ho - ly food be fed,
ters lead me; Your ta - ble well for me pro - vide,
re - mis - sion I come with prayer be - fore Your sight
would break me; In all my guilt - y heart's dis - cord,
In hun - ger I ad - dress You. Pre - pare me well
Your wound - ed hand now feed me. Though wea - ry, sin -
In sor - row and con - tri - tion. Your righ - teous - ness,
O Lord, do not for - sake me. In my dis - tress
for You, O Lord, And, hum - bly by my prayer im - plored,
ful, sick, and weak, Ref - uge in You a - lone I seek,
Lord, cov - er me That I re - ceive You wor - thi - ly,
this com - forts me That You re - ceive me gra - cious - ly,

Text: Johann Rist, 1607–67; tr. Arthur T. Russell, 1806–74, alt.
Tune: *Theütsch kirchen ampt*, Strassburg, 1525; setting: *The Lutheran Hymnal*, 1941

HERR, WIE DU WILLST
87 87 887

John 6:33–35, 48–51; 1 Tim. 1:15–16; 1 Cor. 11:23–26; Psalm 23

Give me Your grace and mer - cy.
To share Your cup of heal - ing.
As - sured of Your full par - don.
O Christ, my Lord of mer - cy!

Come, Let Us Eat 626

Leader
1 Come, let us eat, for now the feast is spread,
2 Come, let us drink, for now the wine is poured,
3 In His pres - ence now we meet and rest,
4 Rise, then, to spread a - broad God's might - y Word,
All
Come, let us eat, for now the feast is spread.
Come, let us drink, for now the wine is poured.
In His pres - ence now we meet and rest.
Rise, then, to spread a - broad God's might - y Word.
Leader
Our Lord's bod - y let us take to - geth - er,
Je - sus' blood poured let us drink to - geth - er,
In the pres - ence of our Lord we gath - er,
Je - sus ris - en will bring in the King - dom,
All
Our Lord's bod - y let us take to - geth - er.
Je - sus' blood poured let us drink to - geth - er.
In the pres - ence of our Lord we gath - er.
Je - sus ris - en will bring in the King - dom.

Setting available in hymn accompaniment edition.

Text: Billema Kwillia, b. 1925, sts. 1–3; Gilbert E. Doan, b. 1930, st. 4, alt.;
tr. Margaret D. Miller, b. 1927, sts. 1–3, alt.
Tune: Billema Kwillia, b. 1925

A VA DE
10 10 10 10

Matt. 26:26–29; Matt. 18:20; Is. 52:7; 1 Cor. 15:20–26

627 Jesus Christ, Our Blessed Savior

1 Je - sus Christ, our bless - ed Sav - ior, Turned a - way God's
2 As His pledge of love un - dy - ing, He, this pre - cious
3 Je - sus here Him - self is shar - ing; Heed then how you
4 Praise the Fa - ther, who from heav - en To His own this
wrath for - ev - er; By His bit - ter grief and woe
food sup - ply - ing, Gives His bod - y with the bread,
are pre - par - ing, For if you do not be - lieve,
food has giv - en, Who, to mend what we have done,
He saved us from the e - vil foe.
And with the wine the blood He shed.
His judg - ment then you shall re - ceive.
Gave in - to death His on - ly Son.

5 Firmly hold with faith unshaken
That this food is to be taken
By the sick who are distressed,
By hearts that long for peace and rest.

6 Agony and bitter labor
Were the cost of God's high favor;
Do not come if you suppose
You need not Him who died and rose.

7 Christ says: "Come, all you that labor,
And receive My grace and favor:
Those who feel no pain or ill
Need no physician's help or skill.

8 "For what purpose was My dying
If not for your justifying?
And what use this precious food
If you yourself were pure and good?"

Text: John Hus, c. 1369–1415; German version, Martin Luther, 1483–1546;
tr. *The Lutheran Hymnal*, 1941, sts. 1–2, 4–5, 7, 9, alt.; tr. *Lutheran Service Book*, 2006, sts. 3, 8;
tr. F. Samuel Janzow, 1913–2001, sts. 6, 10, alt.
Tune: *Geistliche Lieder auffs new gebessert*, Wittenberg, 1533, ed. Joseph Klug, alt.;
setting: *The Lutheran Hymnal*, 1941

JESUS CHRISTUS, UNSER HEILAND
88 78

Rom. 5:9–10; 1 Cor. 11:23–29; John 6:50–57; 1 John 1:9

9 If your heart this truth professes
And your mouth your sin confesses,
You will be your Savior's guest,
Be at His banquet truly blest.

10 Let this food your faith so nourish
That its fruit of love may flourish
And your neighbor learn from you
How much God's wondrous love can do.

Your Table I Approach 628

1 Your ta - ble I ap - proach; Dear Sav - ior, hear my prayer.
2 Lord, I con - fess my sins And mourn their wretch - ed bands;
3 Your bod - y and Your blood, Once slain and shed for me,
4 Search not how this takes place, This won - drous mys - ter - y;
Let not an un - re - pen - tant heart Prove hurt - ful to me there.
A con - trite heart is sure to find For - give - ness at Your hands.
Are tak - en at Your ta - ble, Lord, In blest re - al - i - ty.
God can ac - com - plish vast - ly more Than what we think could be.

5 O grant, most blessèd Lord,
That earth and hell combined
May not about this sacrament
Raise doubt within my mind.

6 Oh, may I never fail
To thank You day and night
For Your true body and true blood,
O God, my peace and light.

Text: Gerhard Wolter Molanus, 1633–1722; tr. Matthias Loy, 1828–1915, alt.
Tune: *Trente quatre Pseaumes de David*, Geneva, 1551, ed. Louis Bourgeois; setting: *The Lutheran Hymnal*, 1941

ST. MICHAEL
S M

1 Cor. 11:23–29; Luke 5:31–32; Mark 2:17; 1 Cor. 10:16; Rom. 11:33–36

629 What Is This Bread

1 What is this bread? Christ's bod - y
2 What is this wine? The blood of
3 So who am I, That I should
4 Yet is God here? Oh, yes! By
5 Is this for me? I am for -
ris - en from the dead: This bread we break,
Je - sus shed for mine; The cup of grace
live and He should die Un - der the rod?
Word and prom - ise clear, In mouth and soul
giv - en and set free! I do be - lieve
This life we take, Was crushed to pay for our re -
Brings His em - brace Of life and love un - til I
My God, my God, Why have You not for - sak - en
He makes us whole— Christ, tru - ly pres - ent in this
That I re - ceive His ver - y bod - y and His
lease. O taste and see— the Lord is peace.
sing! O taste and see— the Lord is King.
me? O taste and see— the Lord is free.
meal. O taste and see— the Lord is real.
blood. O taste and see— the Lord is good.

Setting available in hymn accompaniment edition.

Text: Frederic W. Baue, b. 1946
Tune: Jean Neuhauser Baue, b. 1951

PREPARATION
48 44 88

1 Cor. 11:23–29; Ps. 34:8; 1 Peter 2:2–3

Now, My Tongue, the Mystery Telling

630

1 Now, my tongue, the mys - t'ry tell - ing Of the glo - rious
2 Giv'n for us, and con - de - scend - ing To be born for
3 That last night at sup - per ly - ing Mid the Twelve, His
4 Word made flesh, the bread He tak - eth, By His word His
△ 5 Glo - ry let us give and bless - ing To the Fa - ther
bod - y sing, And the blood, all price ex - cel - ling,
us be - low, He with us in con - verse blend - ing
cho - sen band, Je - sus, with the Law com - ply - ing,
flesh to be; Wine His sa - cred blood He mak - eth,
and the Son, Hon - or, thanks, and praise ad - dress - ing,
Which the Gen - tiles' Lord and King, Once on earth a -
Dwelt, the seed of truth to sow, Till He closed with
Keeps the feast its rites de - mand; Then, more pre - cious
Though the sens - es fail to see; Faith a - lone the
While e - ter - nal a - ges run; Ev - er too His
mong us dwell - ing, Shed for this world's ran - som - ing.
won - drous end - ing His most pa - tient life of woe.
food sup - ply - ing, Gives Him - self with His own hand.
true heart wak - eth To be - hold the mys - ter - y.
love con - fess - ing Who from both with both is One.

Hymn accompaniment: 847

Text: Thomas Aquinas, c. 1225–74; tr. *The Hymnal 1940*
Tune: *Chants ordinaires de l'Office Divin*, Paris, 1881

GRAFTON
87 87 87

1 Cor. 11:23–26; Matt. 26:26–28; John 1:1–3, 14

631 Here, O My Lord, I See Thee Face to Face

1 Here, O my Lord, I see Thee face to face;
2 Here would I feed up - on the bread of God,
3 This is the hour of ban - quet and of song;
4 I have no help but Thine; nor do I need
Here would I touch and han - dle things un - seen;
Here drink with Thee the roy - al wine of heav'n;
This is the heav'n - ly ta - ble spread for me;
An - oth - er arm but Thine to lean up - on.
Here grasp with firm - er hand the e - ter - nal grace,
Here would I lay a - side each earth - ly load,
Here let me feast and, feast - ing, still pro - long
It is e - nough, my Lord, e - nough in - deed;
And all my wea - ri - ness up - on Thee lean.
Here taste a - fresh the calm of sin for - giv'n.
The brief bright hour of fel - low - ship with Thee.
My strength is in Thy might, Thy might a - lone.

Text: Horatius Bonar, 1808–89, alt.
Tune: Henry Lawes, 1595–1662; setting: Carl F. Schalk, b. 1929

FARLEY CASTLE
10 10 10 10

John 6:35, 51, 58; 1 Cor. 11:23–26; 1 John 1:7; Rev. 19:7–9

5 Mine is the sin, but Thine the righteousness;
Mine is the guilt, but Thine the cleansing blood;
Here is my robe, my refuge, and my peace:
Thy blood, Thy righteousness, O Lord my God.

6 Too soon we rise; the vessels disappear;
The feast, though not the love, is past and gone;
The bread and wine remove, but Thou art here;
Nearer than ever; still my shield and sun.

7 Feast after feast thus comes and passes by,
Yet, passing, points to that glad feast above,
Giving sweet foretaste of the festal joy,
The Lamb's great marriage feast of bliss and love.

O Jesus, Blessed Lord, to Thee 632

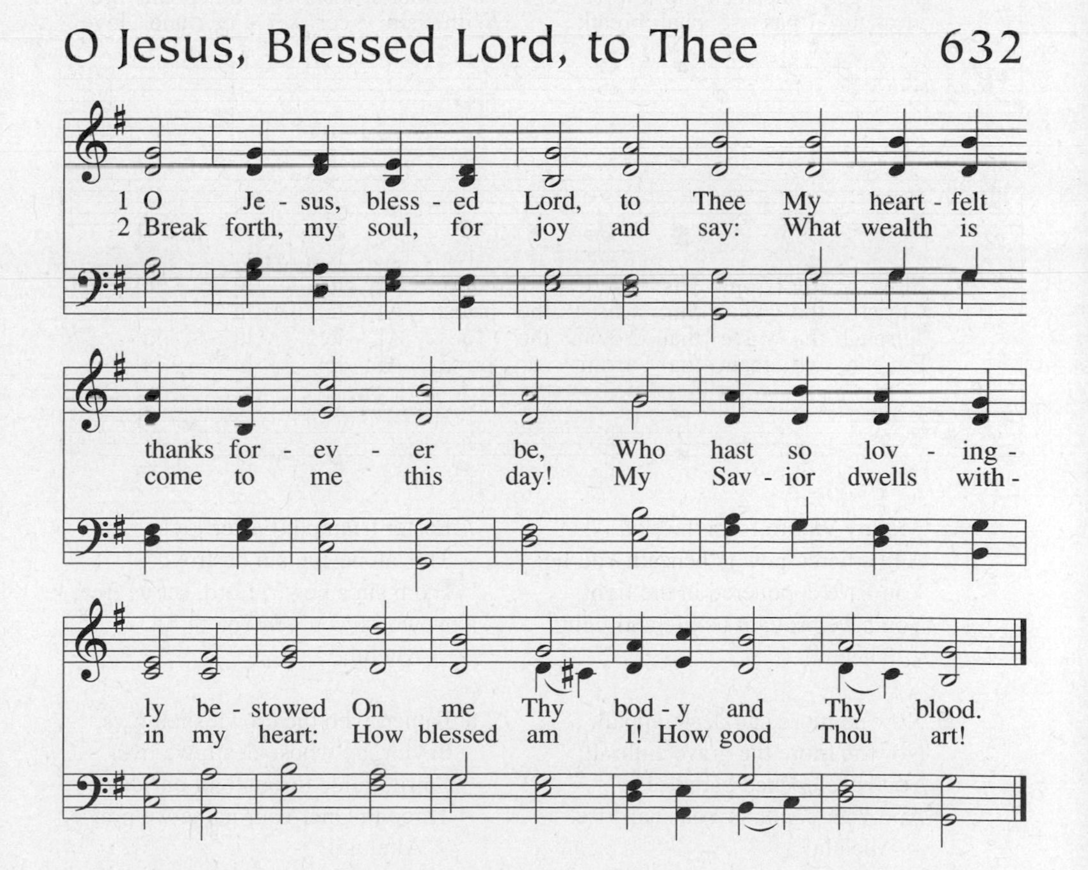
1 O Je - sus, bless - ed Lord, to Thee My heart - felt
2 Break forth, my soul, for joy and say: What wealth is
thanks for - ev - er be, Who hast so lov - ing -
come to me this day! My Sav - ior dwells with -
ly be - stowed On me Thy bod - y and Thy blood.
in my heart: How blessed am I! How good Thou art!

Text: Thomas Hansen Kingo, 1634–1703; tr. Arthur J. Mason, 1851–1928
Tune: *Trente quatre Pseaumes de David*, Geneva, 1551, ed. Louis Bourgeois; setting: *Common Praise*, 2000

OLD HUNDREDTH
L M

2 Cor. 9:15; 1 Cor. 11:23–26; 2 Cor. 8:9; 1 John 4:13

633 At the Lamb's High Feast We Sing

1 At the Lamb's high feast we sing Praise to our vic - to - rious King, Who has washed us in the tide Flow - ing from His pierc - ed side. Al - le - lu - ia!
2 Praise we Him, whose love di - vine Gives His sa - cred blood for wine, Gives His bod - y for the feast— Christ the vic - tim, Christ the priest. Al - le - lu - ia!
3 Where the pas - chal blood is poured, Death's dread an - gel sheathes the sword; Is - rael's hosts tri - um-phant go Through the wave that drowns the foe. Al - le - lu - ia!
4 Praise we Christ, whose blood was shed, Pas - chal vic - tim, pas - chal bread; With sin - cer - i - ty and love Eat we man - na from a - bove. Al - le - lu - ia!

5 Mighty Victim from the sky,
Hell's fierce pow'rs beneath You lie;
You have conquered in the fight,
You have brought us life and light.
Alleluia!

6 Now no more can death appall,
Now no more the grave enthrall;
You have opened paradise,
And Your saints in You shall rise.
Alleluia!

7 Easter triumph, Easter joy!
This alone can sin destroy;
From sin's pow'r, Lord, set us free,
Newborn souls in You to be.
Alleluia!

△ 8 Father, who the crown shall give,
Savior, by whose death we live,
Spirit, guide through all our days:
Three in One, Your name we praise.
Alleluia!

Text: Latin, c. 5th–10th cent.; tr. Robert Campbell, 1814–68, alt.
Tune: *Kirchengeseng*, Ivancice, 1566; setting: Jan O. Bender, 1909–94

SONNE DER GERECHTIGKEIT
77 77 4

Ex. 12:22; Matt. 26:26–28; John 6:32–35; 1 Cor. 15:54–57

The Death of Jesus Christ, Our Lord 634

1 The death of Je - sus Christ, our Lord, We cel - e - brate with one ac - cord; It is our com - fort in dis - tress, Our heart's sweet joy and hap - pi - ness.
2 He blot - ted out with His own blood The judg - ment that a - gainst us stood; For us He full a - tone - ment made, And all our debt He ful - ly paid.
3 That this for - ev - er true shall be He gives a sol - emn guar - an - tee: In this His ho - ly Sup - per here We taste His love so sweet, so near.
4 His Word pro - claims and we be - lieve That in this Sup - per we re - ceive His ver - y bod - y, as He said, His ver - y blood for sin - ners shed.

5 We dare not ask how this can be,
But simply hold the mystery
And trust this word where life begins:
"Given and shed for all your sins."

6 They who this word do not believe
This food unworthily receive,
Salvation here will never find—
May we this warning keep in mind!

7 But blest is each believing guest
Who in these promises finds rest;
For Jesus shall in love remain
With all who here His grace obtain.

8 Help us sincerely to believe
That we may worthily receive
Your Supper and in You find rest.
Amen! They who believe are blest.

Text: Haquin Spegel, 1645–1714, sts. 1–4, 6–8; composite, st. 5;
tr. Olof Olsson, 1841–1900, sts. 1–4, 6–8, alt.
Tune: *Sammlung alter und neuer . . . Melodien*, 1742; setting: *Lutheran Service Book*, 2006

GOTTLOB, ES GEHT NUNMEHR ZU ENDE
L M

Matt. 26:26–29; 1 Cor. 11:27–29; 1 Cor. 10:16; 1 Peter 1:18–19

635 O Gracious Lord, I Firmly Am Believing

1 O gra - cious Lord, I firm - ly am be - liev - ing
2 Lord, I have sinned, a thou - sand times of - fend - ing;
3 You see my sin yet seat me at Your ta - ble;
4 O Lamb of God, my faith - ful, lov - ing Sav - ior,
5 Heav - en - ly Bread, my life and ben - e - dic - tion,
Your bound - less love will bless each faith - ful soul,
My thank - less thoughts and words and deeds e - rase,
Lord, as a guest, I sure - ly am the least:
You I em - brace in faith and ho - ly love;
This cup You give can take a - way each ill.
As from this al - tar we are here re - ceiv - ing
To me Your hand of mer - cy now ex - tend - ing,
Un - clean, un - fit, of wor - thy deeds un - a - ble—
Grant me the strength to show by my be - hav - ior
Come and re - lieve my soul from all af - flic - tion;
Your bod - y and Your blood to make us whole,
O God, my Sav - ior, I im - plore Your grace,
My heart pre - pare for this most ho - ly feast,
A life now hid - den in Your reign a - bove,
Calm ev - 'ry sigh un - til my heart is still,
Your bod - y and Your blood to make us whole.
O God, my Sav - ior, I im - plore Your grace.
My heart pre - pare for this most ho - ly feast.
A life now hid - den in Your reign a - bove.
Calm ev - 'ry sigh un - til my heart is still.

Setting available in hymn accompaniment edition.

Text: Spanish or Latin American, 20th cent.; tr. Stephen P. Starke, b. 1955
Tune: H. León

OH BUEN JESÚS
11 10 11 10 10

Matt. 22:1–14; Rev. 19:9, 17

1 *¡Oh buen Jesús!, yo creo firmemente*
que por mi bien estás en el altar;
que das tu cuerpo y sangre juntamente
al alma fiel con infinito amor,
al alma fiel con infinito amor.

2 *Señor pequé: mil veces te he ofendido,*
ingrato fui, confieso mi maldad,
contrito ya, misericordia pido;
eres mi Dios, imploro tu piedad,
eres mi Dios, imploro tu piedad.

3 *Indigno soy de ser tu convidado;*
de recibir la Santa Comunión;
Jesús que ves mi nada y mi pecado,
prepara tú mi pobre corazón,
prepara tú mi pobre corazón.

4 *Señor Jesús, cordero fiel y amante*
mi corazón te abraza en santo ardor;
si te olvidé, hoy juro que constante
he de vivir tan sólo de tu amor,
he de vivir tan sólo de tu amor.

5 *Celeste pan, que das salud y vida,*
cáliz que quitas toda mi maldad,
ven a aliviar esta alma que afligida
por ti suspira: calma mi ansiedad,
por ti suspira: calma mi ansiedad.

636 Soul, Adorn Yourself with Gladness

1 Soul, a - dorn your - self with glad - ness, Leave the
2 Has - ten as a bride to meet Him, And with
3 He who craves a pre - cious trea - sure Nei - ther
4 Now in faith I hum - bly pon - der O - ver
gloom-y haunts of sad - ness, Come in - to the day-light's
lov - ing rev - 'rence greet Him. For with words of life im -
cost nor pain will mea - sure; But the price - less gifts of
this sur - pass - ing won - der That the bread of life is
splen - dor, There with joy your prais - es ren - der.
mor - tal He is knock - ing at your por - tal.
heav - en God to us has free - ly giv - en.
bound - less Though the souls it feeds are count - less:
Bless the One whose grace un - bound - ed This a - maz - ing
O - pen wide the gates be - fore Him, Say - ing, as you
Though the wealth of earth were prof - fered, None could buy the
With the choic - est wine of heav - en Christ's own blood to

Text: Johann Franck, 1618–77; tr. *Lutheran Book of Worship*, 1978, sts. 1, 4–5;
tr. Catherine Winkworth, 1827–78, sts. 2–3, 6–8, alt.
Tune: Johann Crüger, 1598–1662; setting: *The Lutheran Hymnal*, 1941

SCHMÜCKE DICH
88 88 D (Trochaic)

Is. 61:10; Rev. 19:7–8; 1 Cor. 11:23–26; John 6:35, 48–51, 57–58

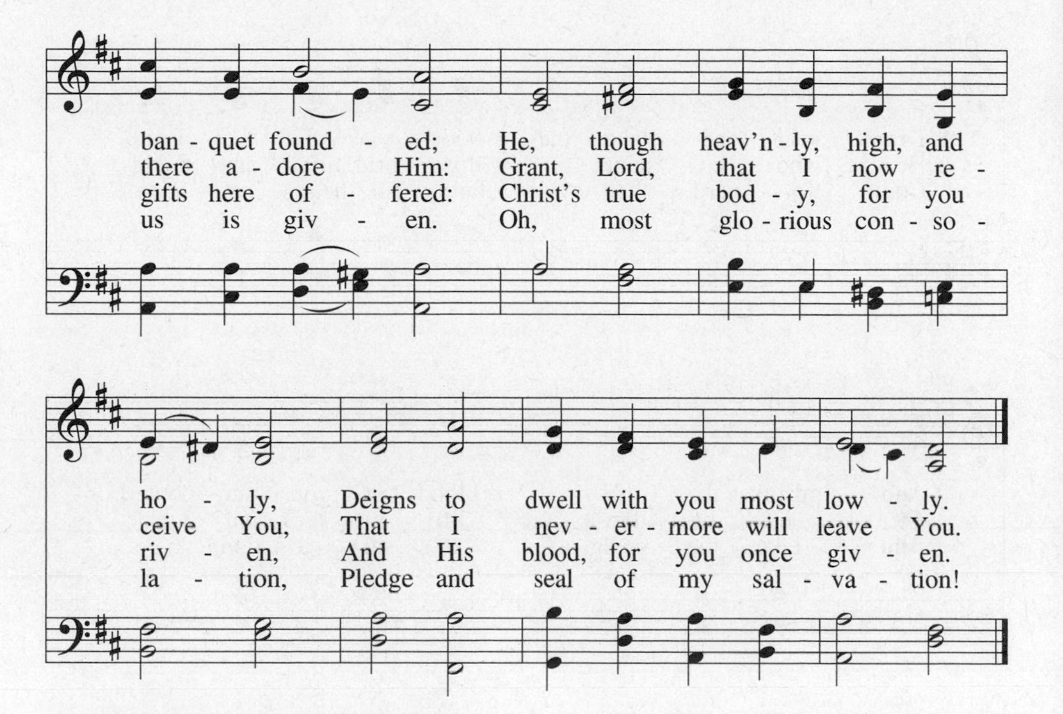
ban - quet found - ed; He, though heav'n - ly, high, and
there a - dore Him: Grant, Lord, that I now re -
gifts here of - fered: Christ's true bod - y, for you
us is giv - en. Oh, most glo - rious con - so -
ho - ly, Deigns to dwell with you most low - ly.
ceive You, That I nev - er - more will leave You.
riv - en, And His blood, for you once giv - en.
la - tion, Pledge and seal of my sal - va - tion!

5 Jesus, source of lasting pleasure,
Truest friend, and dearest treasure,
Peace beyond all understanding,
Joy into all life expanding:
Humbly now, I bow before You;
Love incarnate, I adore You;
Worthily let me receive You
And, so favored, never leave You.

6 Jesus, sun of life, my splendor,
Jesus, friend of friends, most tender,
Jesus, joy of my desiring,
Fount of life, my soul inspiring:
At Your feet I cry, my maker,
Let me be a fit partaker
Of this blessèd food from heaven,
For our good, Your glory, given.

7 Lord, by love and mercy driven,
You once left Your throne in heaven
On the cross for me to languish
And to die in bitter anguish,
To forego all joy and gladness
And to shed Your blood in sadness.
By this blood redeemed and living,
Lord, I praise You with thanksgiving.

8 Jesus, bread of life, I pray You,
Let me gladly here obey You.
By Your love I am invited,
Be Your love with love requited;
By this Supper let me measure,
Lord, how vast and deep love's treasure.
Through the gift of grace You give me
As Your guest in heav'n receive me.

637 Draw Near and Take the Body of the Lord

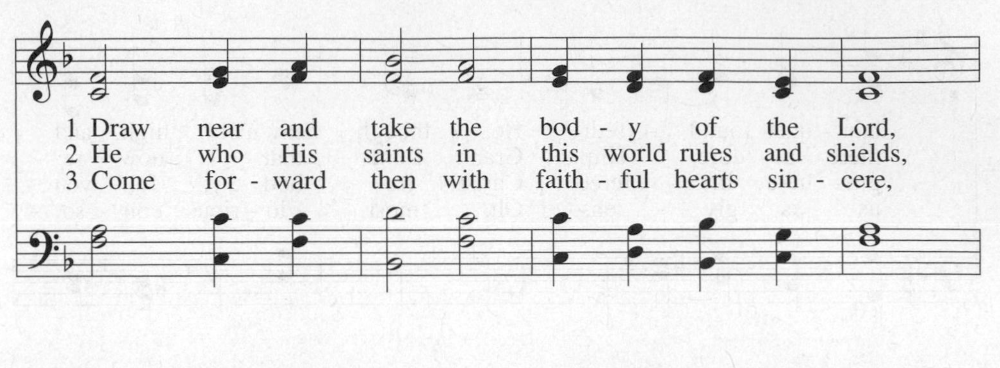
1 Draw near and take the bod - y of the Lord,
2 He who His saints in this world rules and shields,
3 Come for - ward then with faith - ful hearts sin - cere,

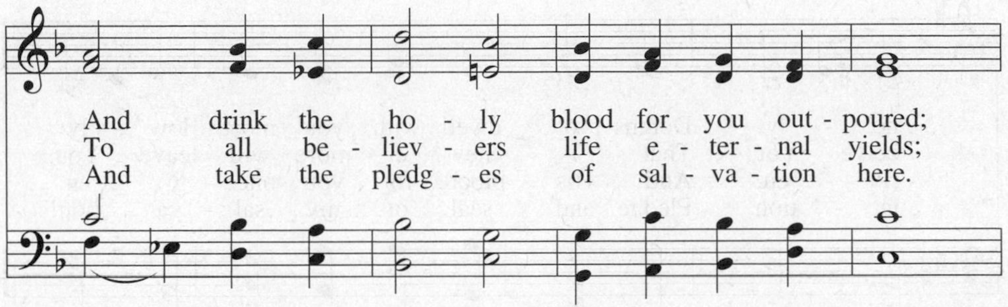
And drink the ho - ly blood for you out - poured;
To all be - liev - ers life e - ter - nal yields;
And take the pledg - es of sal - va - tion here.

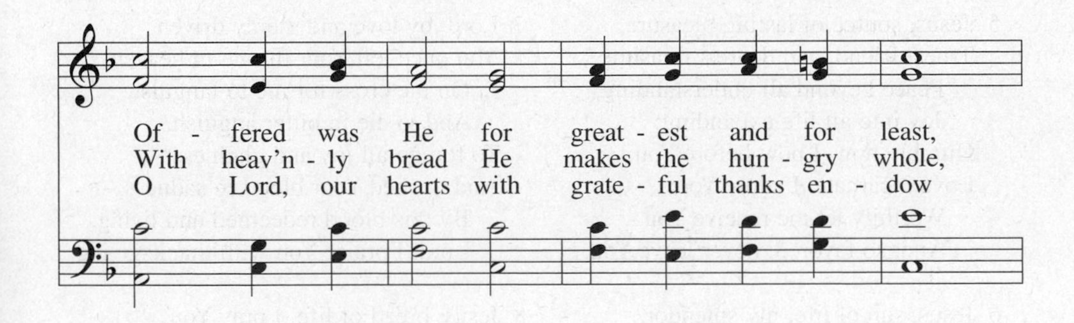
Of - fered was He for great - est and for least,
With heav'n - ly bread He makes the hun - gry whole,
O Lord, our hearts with grate - ful thanks en - dow

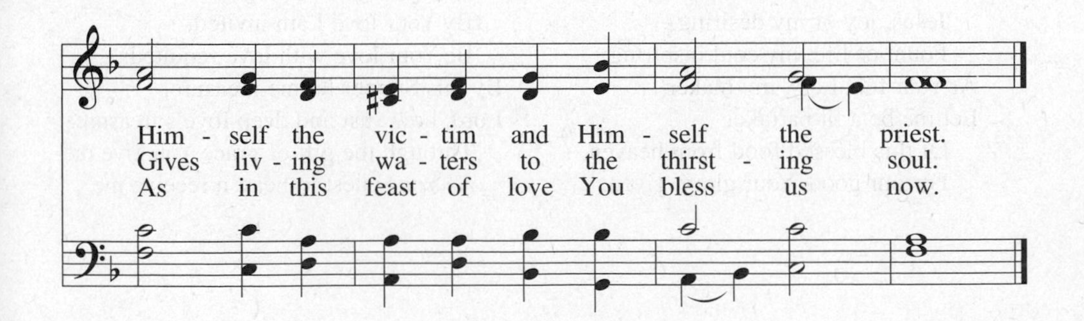
Him - self the vic - tim and Him - self the priest.
Gives liv - ing wa - ters to the thirst - ing soul.
As in this feast of love You bless us now.

Text: Latin, 7th cent.; tr. John Mason Neale, 1818–66, alt.
Tune: *Trente quatre Pseaumes de David*, Geneva, 1551, ed. Louis Bourgeois; setting: *The Lutheran Hymnal*, 1941

OLD 124TH, abbr.
10 10 10 10

1 Cor. 11:23–26; Ps. 34:8; 1 Cor. 10:16

Eat This Bread 638

Refrain
Eat this bread, drink this cup, Come to Him and nev - er be hun - gry.
Eat this bread, drink this cup, Trust in Him and you will not thirst.
Cantor or Choir
Refrain
1 This is His bod - y giv - en for you; this is His blood that was shed for you.
2 As of-ten as you eat this bread and drink this cup, you show His death un-til He comes a-gain.
3 Eat His flesh and drink His blood, and Christ will raise you up on the Last Day.
4 An - y - one who eats this bread will live for - ev - er.
5 If we be-lieve and eat this bread, we will have e - ter - nal life.
*

*Choose either part

Setting available in hymn accompaniment edition.

Text: Robert J. Batastini, b. 1942, and Taizé Community, Refrain and sts. 3–5; Stephen P. Starke, b. 1955, sts. 1–2
Music: Jacques Berthier, 1923–94

EAT THIS BREAD
Irregular meter

John 6:35; 1 Cor. 11:23–26; John 6:48–58

639 Wide Open Stand the Gates

1 Wide o - pen stand the gates a - dorned with pearl, While
2 He speaks the Word the bread and wine to bless: "This
3 The cher - u - bim, their fac - es veiled from light, While
round God's gold - en throne The choirs of saints in
is My flesh and blood!" He bids us eat and
saints in won - der kneel, Sing praise to Him whose
end - less cir - cles curl, And joy - ous praise the Son!
drink with thank - ful - ness This gift of ho - ly food.
face with glo - ry bright No earth - ly masks con - ceal.
They watch Him now de - scend - ing To vis - it wait-ing earth.
All hu - man thought must fal - ter— Our God stoops low to heal,
This sac - ra - ment God gives us Binds us in u - ni - ty,
The Lord of Life un - end - ing Brings dy - ing hope new birth!
Now pres - ent on the al - tar, For us both host and meal!
Joins earth with heav'n be - yond us, Time with e - ter - ni - ty!

Hymn accompaniment: 674

Text: J. K. Wilhelm Loehe, 1808–72; tr. Herman G. Stuempfle, Jr., 1923–2007
Tune: *Christlich Neu-vermehrt . . . Gesangbuch*, Erfurt, 1663

JERUSALEM, DU HOCHGEBAUTE STADT
10 6 10 6 76 76

Revelation 5; Is. 6:1–3; Rev. 21:12, 21, 25

Thee We Adore, O Hidden Savior 640

1 Thee we a - dore, O hid - den Sav - ior, Thee,
2 In this me - mo - rial of Thy death, O Lord,
3 Thou, like the pel - i - can to feed her brood,
4 Foun - tain of good - ness, Je - sus, Lord and God:
5 O Christ, whom now be - neath a veil we see,
Who in Thy Sac - ra - ment art pleased to be;
Thou dost Thy bod - y and Thy blood af - ford:
Didst pierce Thy - self to give us liv - ing food;
Cleanse us, un - clean, with Thy most cleans - ing blood;
May what we thirst for soon our por - tion be:
Both flesh and spir - it in Thy pres - ence fail,
Oh, may our souls for - ev - er feed on Thee,
Thy blood, O Lord, one drop has pow'r to win
In - crease our faith and love, that we may know
To gaze on Thee un - veiled and see Thy face,
Yet here Thy pres - ence we de - vout - ly hail.
And Thou, O Christ, for - ev - er pre - cious be.
For - give - ness for our world and all its sin.
The hope and peace which from Thy pres - ence flow.
The vi - sion of Thy glo - ry, and Thy grace. A - men.

Setting available in hymn accompaniment edition.

Text: Thomas Aquinas, c. 1225–74; tr. James R. Woodford, 1820–85, sts. 1, 2b, 4–5, alt.; Stephen P. Starke, b. 1955, sts. 2a, 3
Tune: *Processionale*, Paris, 1697, mode V

ADORO TE DEVOTE
10 10 10 10

Matt. 26:26–28; 1 John 1:7; John 10:17–18; 1 Cor. 13:12

641 You Satisfy the Hungry Heart

Refrain
You sat-is-fy the hun-gry heart With gift of fin-est wheat.

Come give to us, O sav-ing Lord, The bread of life to eat.

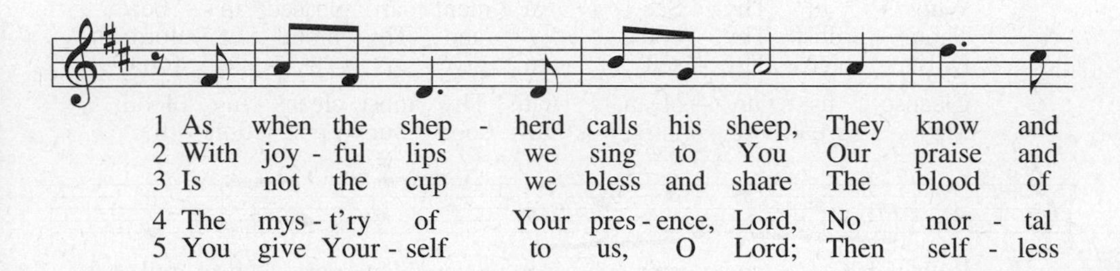
1 As when the shep - herd calls his sheep, They know and
2 With joy - ful lips we sing to You Our praise and
3 Is not the cup we bless and share The blood of
4 The mys - t'ry of Your pres - ence, Lord, No mor - tal
5 You give Your - self to us, O Lord; Then self - less

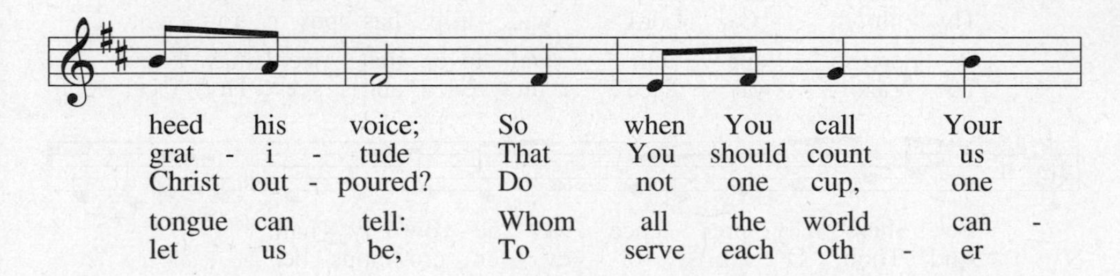
heed his voice; So when You call Your
grat - i - tude That You should count us
Christ out - poured? Do not one cup, one
tongue can tell: Whom all the world can -
let us be, To serve each oth - er

Refrain
fam - 'ly, Lord, We fol - low and re - joice.
wor - thy, Lord, To share this heav'n - ly food.
loaf, de - clare Our one - ness in the Lord?
not con - tain Comes in our hearts to dwell.
in Your name In truth and char - i - ty.

Setting available in hymn accompaniment edition.

Text: Omer E. Westendorf, 1916–97
Tune: Robert E. Kreutz, 1922–96

BICENTENNIAL
C M and refrain

Ps. 81:16; 1 Cor. 10:16–17; John 10:2–4; 1 John 4:7–21

O Living Bread from Heaven 642

1 O liv - ing Bread from heav - en, How well You
2 My Lord, You here have led me To this most
3 You gave me all I want - ed; This food can
4 Lord, grant me then, thus strength - ened With heav'n - ly
feed Your guest! The gifts that You have giv - en
ho - ly place And with Your - self have fed me
death de - stroy. And You have free - ly grant - ed
food, while here My course on earth is length - ened,
Have filled my heart with rest. Oh, won - drous food of
The trea - sures of Your grace; For You have free - ly
The cup of end - less joy. My Lord, I do not
To serve with ho - ly fear. And when You call my
bless - ing, Oh, cup that heals our woes! My heart, this
giv - en What earth could nev - er buy, The bread of
mer - it The fa - vor You have shown, And all my
spir - it To leave this world be - low, I en - ter,
gift pos - sess - ing, With prais - es o - ver - flows.
life from heav - en, That now I shall not die.
soul and spir - it Bow down be - fore Your throne.
through Your mer - it, Where joys un - min - gled flow.

Hymn accompaniment: 514

Text: Johann Rist, 1607–67; tr. Catherine Winkworth, 1827–78, alt.
Tune: *Musae Sioniae*, vol. 7, Wolfenbüttel, 1609, ed. Michael Praetorius

ACH GOTT VOM HIMMELREICHE
76 76 D

1 Cor. 11:23–26; John 6:35, 48–58; 1 Peter 1:18–19

643 Sent Forth by God's Blessing

1 Sent forth by God's bless-ing, Our true faith con-fess-ing,
2 With praise and thanks-giv-ing To God ev-er-liv-ing,
The peo-ple of God from His dwell-ing take leave.
The tasks of our ev-'ry-day life we will face.
The Sup-per is end-ed. O now be ex-tend-ed
Our faith ev-er shar-ing, In love ev-er car-ing,
The fruits of this ser-vice in all who be-lieve.
Em-brac-ing His chil-dren of each tribe and race.

Text: Omer E. Westendorf, 1916–97, alt.
Tune: Welsh; setting: Leland B. Sateren, 1913–2007

THE ASH GROVE
6 6 11 6 6 11 D

Luke 8:39; Col. 3:17; Num. 6:26; 1 Cor. 10:16

The seed of His teach-ing, Re-cep-tive souls reach-ing,
With Your feast You feed us, With Your light now lead us;
Shall blos-som in ac-tion for God and for all.
U-nite us as one in this life that we share.
His grace did in-vite us, His love shall u-nite us
Then may all the liv-ing With praise and thanks-giv-ing
To work for God's king-dom and an-swer His call.
Give hon-or to Christ and His name that we bear.

644 The Church's One Foundation

1 The Church's one foun - da - tion Is Je - sus Christ, her Lord;
2 E - lect from ev - 'ry na - tion, Yet one o'er all the earth;
3 Though with a scorn - ful won - der The world sees her op - pressed,
4 Through toil and trib - u - la - tion And tu - mult of her war
She is His new cre - a - tion By wa - ter and the Word.
Her char - ter of sal - va - tion: One Lord, one faith, one birth.
By schisms rent a - sun - der, By her - e - sies dis - tressed,
She waits the con - sum - ma - tion Of peace for - ev - er - more
From heav'n He came and sought her To be His ho - ly bride;
One ho - ly name she bless - es, Par - takes one ho - ly food,
Yet saints their watch are keep - ing; Their cry goes up, "How long?"
Till with the vi - sion glo - rious Her long - ing eyes are blest,
With His own blood He bought her, And for her life He died.
And to one hope she press - es With ev - 'ry grace en - dued.
And soon the night of weep - ing Shall be the morn of song.
And the great Church vic - to - rious Shall be the Church at rest.

Text: Samuel J. Stone, 1839–1900, alt.; Spanish tr. Lefferd M. A. Haughwout, 1873–1952
Music: Samuel S. Wesley, 1810–76

AURELIA
76 76 D

Eph. 2:20; 4:4–6; 1 Cor. 10:16–17; Rev. 7:14b–17

5 Yet she on earth has union
With God, the Three in One,
And mystic sweet communion
With those whose rest is won.
O blessèd heav'nly chorus!
Lord, save us by Your grace
That we, like saints before us,
May see You face to face.

---

1 Un solo fundamento y sólo un fundador
la santa iglesia tiene en Cristo, su Señor,
haciéndola su esposa, del cielo descendió,
y por su propia sangre su libertad compró.

2 Aunque es de muchas razas, disfruta de unidad:
solo una fe confiesa en santa caridad;
es uno su bautismo, un pan de santidad;
por gracia siempre espera una felicidad.

3 El mundo la contempla pasmado y con desdén:
de cismas desgarrada, de error y por vaivén.
Mas santos de vigilia no cesan en su orar,
y pronto por la noche oirán gozo y cantar.

4 Cercada de tumultos, de guerra y confusión,
la paz eterna espera, serena en su visión;
al fin, ya victoriosa, la iglesia terrenal
recibe por su premio descanso celestial.

5 Mas ella aquí disfruta celeste comunión
con Dios y con los santos en paz y perfección.
Jesús, cabeza nuestra, concédenos lugar
con los que habitan siempre en tu celeste hogar.

645 Built on the Rock

1 Built on the Rock the Church shall stand E - ven when
2 Sure - ly in tem - ples made with hands God, the Most
3 We are God's house of liv - ing stones, Built for His
4 Here stands the font be - fore our eyes, Tell - ing how
stee - ples are fall - ing. Crum - bled have spires in
High, is not dwell - ing; High a - bove earth His
own hab - i - ta - tion. He through bap - tis - mal
God has re - ceived us. The al - tar re - calls Christ's
ev - 'ry land; Bells still are chim - ing and call -
tem - ple stands, All earth - ly tem - ples ex - cel -
grace us owns Heirs of His won - drous sal - va -
sac - ri - fice And what His Sup - per here gives
ing, Call - ing the young and old to rest,
ling. Yet He who dwells in heav'n a - bove
tion. Were we but two His name to tell,
us. Here sound the Scrip - tures that pro - claim

Text: Nikolai Fredrik Severin Grundtvig, 1783–1872, abr.; tr. Carl Döving, 1867–1937, alt.
Tune: Ludvig M. Lindeman, 1812–87; setting: *The Lutheran Hymnal*, 1941

KIRKEN DEN ER ET GAMMELT HUS
88 88 88 8

Matt. 16:13–18; Eph. 2:19–22; 1 Cor. 3:11–16; Acts 17:24

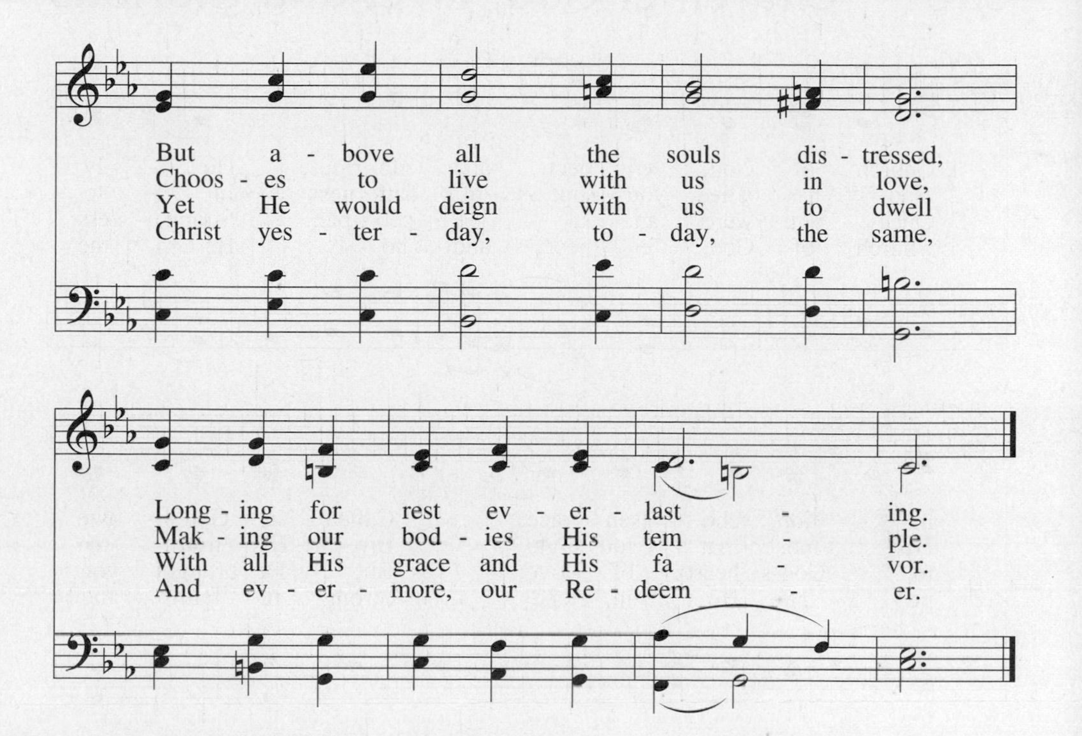
But a - bove all the souls dis - tressed,
Choos - es to live with us in love,
Yet He would deign with us to dwell
Christ yes - ter - day, to - day, the same,
Long - ing for rest ev - er - last - ing.
Mak - ing our bod - ies His tem - ple.
With all His grace and His fa - vor.
And ev - er - more, our Re - deem - er.

5 Grant, then, O God, Your will be done,
That, when the church bells are ringing,
Many in saving faith may come
Where Christ His message is bringing:
"I know My own; My own know Me.
You, not the world, My face shall see.
My peace I leave with you. Amen."

646 Church of God, Elect and Glorious

1 Church of God, e - lect and glo - rious, Ho - ly
2 God has called you out of dark - ness In - to
3 Once you were an al - ien peo - ple, Strang - ers
4 Church of God, e - lect and ho - ly, Be the
na - tion, cho - sen race; Called as God's own
His most mar - v'lous light; Brought His truth to
to God's heart of love; But He brought you
peo - ple He in - tends; Strong in faith and
spe - cial peo - ple, Roy - al priests and heirs of
life with - in you, Turned your blind - ness in - to
home in mer - cy, Cit - i - zens of heav'n a -
swift to an - swer Each com - mand your Mas - ter
grace: Know the pur - pose of your call - ing,
sight. Let your light so shine a - round you
bove. Let His love flow out to oth - ers,
sends: Roy - al priests, ful - fill your call - ing

Text: James Edward Seddon, 1915–83
Music: Cyril V. Taylor, 1907–92

ABBOT'S LEIGH
87 87 D

1 Peter 2:9–10; Eph. 2:19–22; 5:8–10; Rev. 5:9–10

Show to all His might - y deeds; Tell of love that
That God's name is glo - ri - fied And all find fresh
Let them feel a Fa - ther's care; That they too may
Through your sac - ri - fice and prayer; Give your lives in
knows no lim - its, Grace that meets all hu - man needs.
hope and pur - pose In Christ Je - sus cru - ci - fied.
know His wel - come And His count - less bless - ings share.
joy - ful ser - vice— Sing His praise, His love de - clare.

Almighty God, You have built Your Church on the foundation of the apostles and prophets with Christ Jesus Himself as the cornerstone. Continue to send Your messengers to preserve Your people in true peace that, by the preaching of Your Word, Your Church may be kept free from all harm and danger; through Jesus Christ, Your Son, our Lord, who lives and reigns with You and the Holy Spirit, one God, now and forever.

Collect for Proper 9, Series C

647 Lord Jesus Christ, the Church's Head

1 Lord Je - sus Christ, the Church's head, You are her one foun - da - tion; In You she trusts, be - fore You bows, And waits for Your sal - va - tion. Built on this rock se - cure, Your Church shall en - dure Though all the world de -
2 O Lord, let this Your lit - tle flock, Your name a - lone con - fess - ing, Con - tin - ue in Your lov - ing care, True u - ni - ty pos - sess - ing. Your sac - ra - ments, O Lord, And Your sav - ing Word To us, Lord, pure re -
3 Help us to serve You ev - er - more With hearts both pure and low - ly; And may Your Word, that light di - vine, Shine on in splen - dor ho - ly That we re - pen - tance show, In faith ev - er grow; The pow'r of sin de -
4 And for Your Gos - pel let us dare To sac - ri - fice all trea - sure; Teach us to bear Your bless - ed cross, To find in You all plea - sure. O grant us stead - fast - ness In joy and dis - tress, Lest we, Lord, You for -

Text: Johann Mentzer, 1658–1734; tr. William J. Schaefer, 1891–1976, alt.
Tune: Friedrich O. Reuter, 1863–1924; setting: *The Lutheran Hymnal*, 1941

REUTER
87 87 65 66 7

Eph. 2:19–21; Matt. 16:16–18; Eph. 4:3–6, 15–16

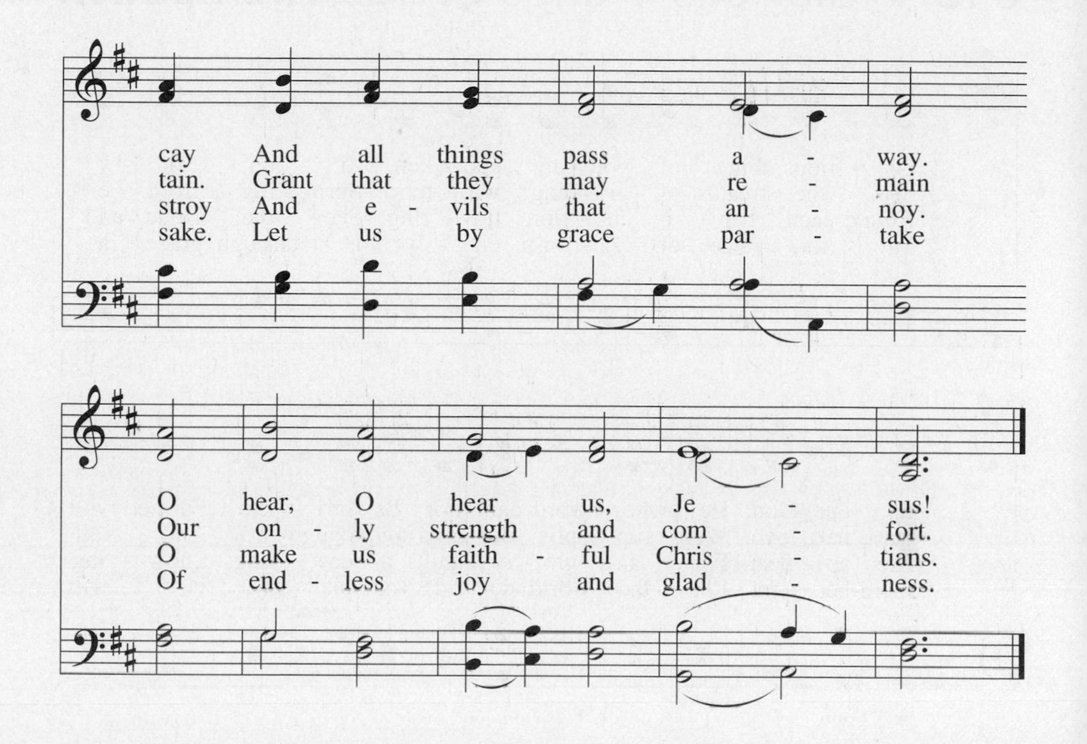
cay And all things pass a - way.
tain. Grant that they may re - main
stroy And e - vils that an - noy.
sake. Let us by grace par - take
O hear, O hear us, Je - sus!
Our on - ly strength and com - fort.
O make us faith - ful Chris - tians.
Of end - less joy and glad - ness.

You are no longer strangers and aliens, but you are fellow citizens with the saints and members of the household of God, built on the foundation of the apostles and prophets, Christ Jesus Himself being the cornerstone.

Ephesians 2:19–20

---

648 Glorious Things of You Are Spoken

1 Glo - rious things of you are spo - ken, Zi - on, cit - y
2 See, the streams of liv - ing wa - ters, Spring - ing from e -
3 Round each hab - i - ta - tion hov - 'ring, See the cloud and
4 Sav - ior, since of Zi - on's cit - y I through grace a
of our God; He whose word can - not be bro - ken Formed you
ter - nal love, Well sup - ply your sons and daugh - ters And all
fire ap - pear For a glo - ry and a cov - 'ring, Show - ing
mem-ber am, Let the world de - ride or pit - y, I will
for His own a - bode. On the Rock of A - ges found-ed,
fear of want re - move. Who can faint while such a riv - er
that the Lord is near. Thus de - riv - ing from their ban - ner
glo - ry in Your name. Fad - ing are the world's vain plea-sures,
What can shake your sure re - pose? With sal - va - tion's
Ev - er will their thirst as - suage? Grace, which like the
Light by night and shade by day, Safe they feed up -
All their boast - ed pomp and show; Sol - id joys and

Alternate tune: ABBOT'S LEIGH (646)

Text: John Newton, 1725–1807, alt.
Tune: Franz Joseph Haydn, 1732–1809; setting: *The Hymnal 1982*, alt.

AUSTRIA
87 87 D

Ps. 87; 48:1–14; 132:13–18; Is. 33:20–21; Ex. 13:21–22

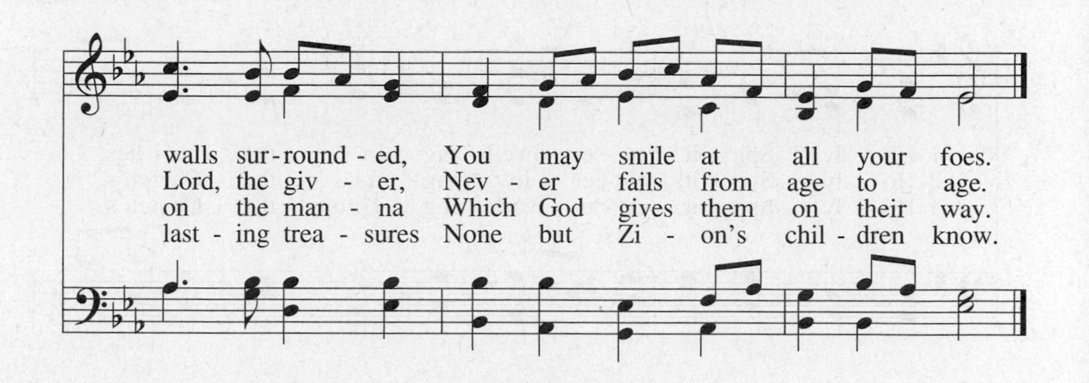
walls sur-round - ed, You may smile at all your foes.
Lord, the giv - er, Nev - er fails from age to age.
on the man - na Which God gives them on their way.
last - ing trea - sures None but Zi - on's chil - dren know.

Blest Be the Tie That Binds 649

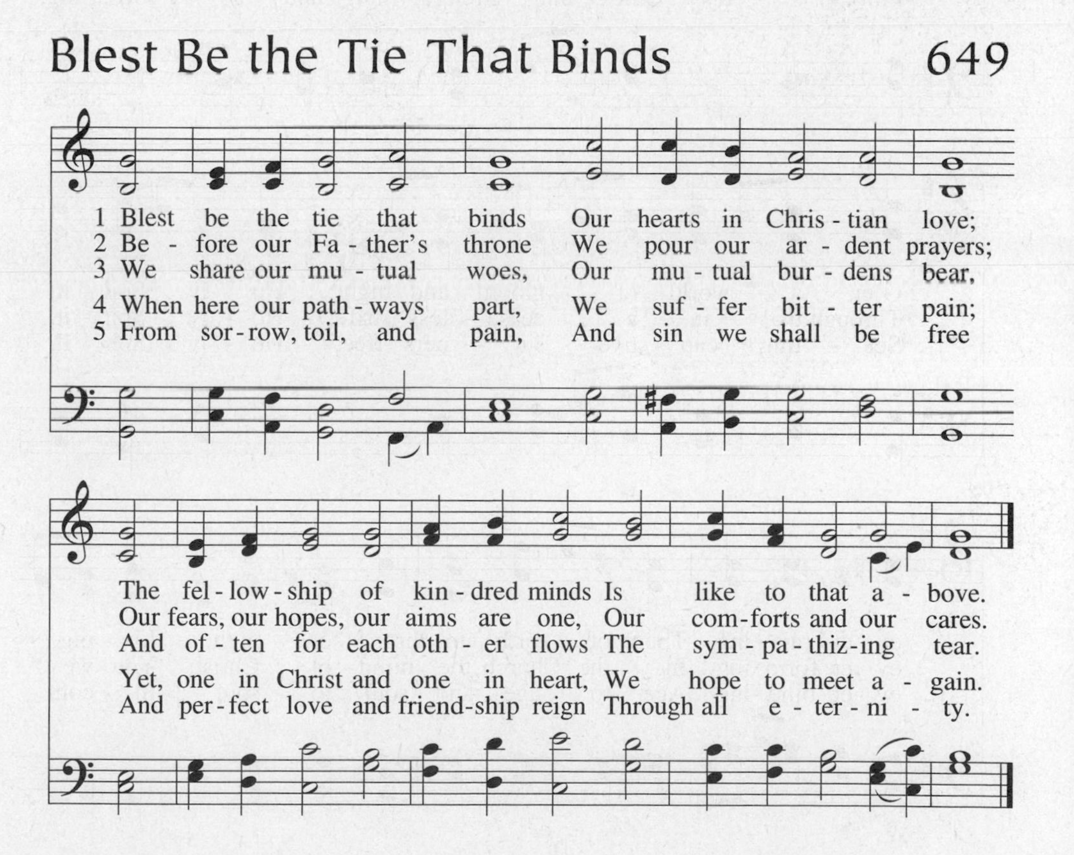
1 Blest be the tie that binds Our hearts in Chris - tian love;
2 Be - fore our Fa - ther's throne We pour our ar - dent prayers;
3 We share our mu - tual woes, Our mu - tual bur - dens bear,
4 When here our path - ways part, We suf - fer bit - ter pain;
5 From sor - row, toil, and pain, And sin we shall be free
The fel - low - ship of kin - dred minds Is like to that a - bove.
Our fears, our hopes, our aims are one, Our com - forts and our cares.
And of - ten for each oth - er flows The sym - pa - thiz - ing tear.
Yet, one in Christ and one in heart, We hope to meet a - gain.
And per - fect love and friend - ship reign Through all e - ter - ni - ty.

Text: John Fawcett, 1740–1817, alt.
Music: Lowell Mason, 1792–1872, alt.

BOYLSTON
S M

Eph. 4:3–6; Rom. 12:4–5; John 17:11, 20–23; Psalm 133

650 Holy Spirit, Ever Dwelling

1 Ho - ly Spir - it, ev - er dwell - ing In the ho - liest realms of light; Ho - ly Spir - it, ev - er brood - ing O'er a world of gloom and night; Ho - ly Spir - it, ev - er rais - ing Those of earth to thrones on high; Liv - ing,
2 Ho - ly Spir - it, ev - er liv - ing As the Church's ver - y life; Ho - ly Spir - it, ev - er striv - ing Through us in a cease - less strife; Ho - ly Spir - it, ev - er form - ing In the Church the mind of Christ: You we
3 Ho - ly Spir - it, ev - er work - ing Through the Church's min - is - try; Quick - 'ning, strength - 'ning, and ab - solv - ing, Set - ting cap - tive sin - ners free; Ho - ly Spir - it, ev - er bind - ing Age to age and soul to soul In com -

Text: Timothy Rees, 1874–1939, alt.
Tune: *Oude en Nieuwe Hollantse . . . Contradanseu*, Amsterdam, c. 1710;
setting: Henry V. Gerike, b. 1948

IN BABILONE
87 87 D

Gen. 1:1–2; 1 Cor. 12:12–14; Eph. 3:7–9

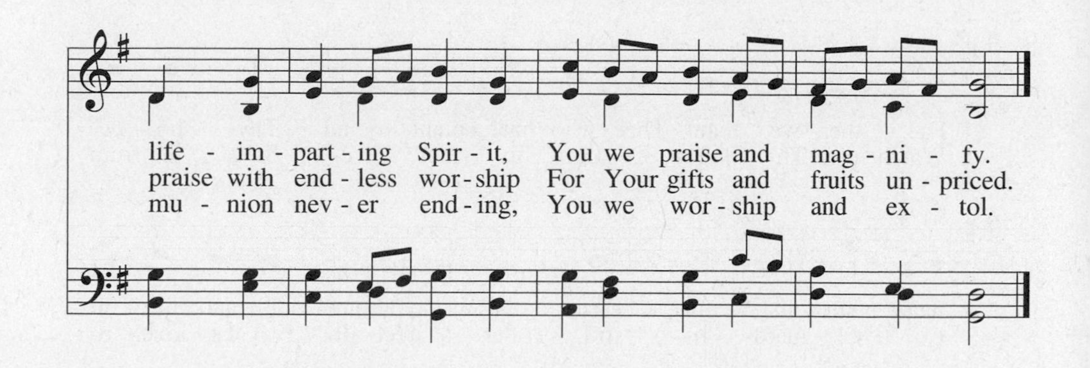
life - im - part - ing Spir - it, You we praise and mag - ni - fy.
praise with end - less wor - ship For Your gifts and fruits un - priced.
mu - nion nev - er end - ing, You we wor - ship and ex - tol.

I Love Your Kingdom, Lord 651

1 I love Your king - dom, Lord, The place of Your a - bode,
2 Be - yond my high - est joy I prize its heav'n - ly ways,
3 I love Your Church, O God, Your saints in ev - 'ry land,
4 For them my tears shall fall; For them my prayers as - cend;
5 Sure as Your truth shall last, To Zi - on shall be giv'n
The Church our blest Re - deem - er saved With His own pre - cious blood.
Its sweet com - mu - nion, sol - emn vows, Its hymns of love and praise.
Dear as the ap - ple of Your eye And grav - en on Your hand.
For them my cares and toils be giv'n Till toils and cares shall end.
The bright - est glo - ries earth can yield And bright - er bliss of heav'n.

Text: Timothy Dwight, 1752–1817, alt.
Tune: Aaron Williams, 1731–76; setting: *The Lutheran Hymnal*, 1941

ST. THOMAS
S M

Ps. 26:8; Col. 3:15–16; Eph. 6:18; Is. 30:19

652 Father, We Thank Thee

1 Fa - ther, we thank Thee who hast plant - ed Thy ho - ly
2 Watch o'er Thy Church, O Lord, in mer - cy, Save it from
name with - in our hearts. Knowl - edge and faith and life im -
e - vil, guard it still, Per - fect it in Thy love, u -
mor - tal Je - sus, Thy Son, to us im - parts.
nite it, Cleansed and con - formed un - to Thy will.
Thou, Lord, didst make all for Thy plea - sure, Didst
As grain, once scat - tered on the hill - sides, Was
give us food for all our days, Giv - ing in Christ the
in this bro - ken bread made one, So from all lands Thy
Bread e - ter - nal; Thine is the pow'r, be Thine the praise.
Church be gath - ered In - to Thy king - dom by Thy Son.

Hymn accompaniment: 792

Text: *Didache*, 2nd cent.; tr. F. Bland Tucker, 1895–1984
Tune: attr. Louis Bourgeois, c. 1510–61

RENDEZ À DIEU
98 98 D

John 6:22–58; 1 Cor. 10:16–17

In Christ There Is No East or West 653

1 In Christ there is no east or west,
2 With God there is no tribe or race;
3 So, broth - ers, sis - ters, praise His name
4 Join hands, dis - ci - ples of the faith,
5 In Christ now meet both east and west;
In Him no south or north, But one great fel - low -
In Him we all are one. He loves us as His
Who died to set us free From sin, di - vi - sion,
What - e'er your race may be; Who serves my Fa - ther
In Him meet south and north. All Chris - tian souls are
ship of love Through - out the whole wide earth.
chil - dren through Our faith in His dear Son.
hate, and shame, From spite and en - mi - ty!
as His child Is sure - ly kin to me.
one in Him Through - out the whole wide earth.

Text: John Oxenham, 1852–1941, sts. 1, 4–5, alt.; Mark A. Jeske, b. 1952, st. 2;
Michael A. Perry, 1942–96, st. 3
Music: African American spiritual; adapt. Harry T. Burleigh, 1866–1949

MCKEE
CM

Gal. 3:26–29; Col. 3:11–17; John 10:16; 17:11

654 Your Kingdom, O God, Is My Glorious Treasure

1 Your king - dom, O God, is my glo - ri - ous trea - sure,
2 Your king - dom, O God, is a - live with the pow - er
3 Your king - dom, O God, is a field for the grow - ing
My pearl of in - com - p'ra - ble worth.
Your Word and Your Spir - it be - stow.
Of seeds that Your mer - cy has sown;
Its val - ue ex - ceeds ev - 'ry stan - dard of mea - sure,
Like yeast, they af - fect the whole mea - sure of flour,
But still in our midst is the en - e - my sow - ing
Sur - pass - ing the wealth of the earth.
En - a - bling Your king - dom to grow.
The weeds that im - per - il Your own.
Lord, give me Your grace and the pow'r of the Spir - it
Em - pow - er me, Lord, as I live Your com - mis - sion,
Sus - tain me, O Lord, till Your day of re - turn - ing
To val - ue this trea - sure a - right
Though hum - ble my ser - vice may be,
And har - vest me home - ward at last,
That, nev - er al - lured by the world, I in - her - it
And bring ev - 'ry plant - ing to per - fect fru - i - tion,
To shine in the home - land that qui - ets all yearn - ing,

Setting available in hymn accompaniment edition.

Text: David W. Rogner, b. 1960
Tune: Joseph Herl, b. 1959

GLORIOUS TREASURE
12 8 12 8 D

Matt. 13:24–33, 45

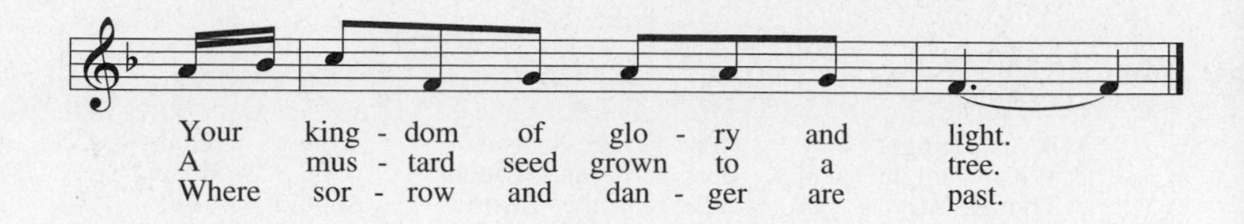
Your king - dom of glo - ry and light.
A mus - tard seed grown to a tree.
Where sor - row and dan - ger are past.

Lord, Keep Us Steadfast in Your Word

THE CHURCH MILITANT

655

1 Lord, keep us stead - fast in Your Word; Curb those who
2 Lord Je - sus Christ, Your pow'r make known, For You are
3 O Com - fort - er of price - less worth, Send peace and
by de - ceit or sword Would wrest the king - dom from Your
Lord of lords a - lone; De - fend Your ho - ly Church that
u - ni - ty on earth; Sup - port us in our fi - nal
Son And bring to naught all He has done.
we May sing Your praise e - ter - nal - ly.
strife And lead us out of death to life.

Text: Martin Luther, 1483–1546; tr. Catherine Winkworth, 1827–78, alt.
Tune: *Geistliche Lieder auffs new gebessert*, Wittenberg, 1543, ed. Joseph Klug; setting: Hans Leo Hassler, 1564–1612, alt.

ERHALT UNS, HERR
L M

Ps. 119:5–10; 2 John 9; John 8:31; Eph. 4:3–6

656 A Mighty Fortress Is Our God

1 A mighty - y for - tress is our God,
2 With might of ours can naught be done,
3 Though dev - ils all the world should fill,
4 The Word they still shall let re - main
A trust - y shield and weap - on;
Soon were our loss ef - fect - ed;
All ea - ger to de - vour us,
Nor an - y thanks have for it;
He helps us free from ev - 'ry need
But for us fights the val - iant One,
We trem - ble not, we fear no ill;
He's by our side up - on the plain
That hath us now o'er - tak - en.
Whom God Him - self e - lect - ed.
They shall not o - ver - pow'r us.
With His good gifts and Spir - it.

Text: Martin Luther, 1483–1546; tr. composite
Tune: Martin Luther, 1483–1546; setting: *The Lutheran Hymnal*, 1941

EIN FESTE BURG (Rhythmic)
87 87 55 56 7

Ps. 46:1, 7, 11; Rev. 19:11–16; Rom. 8:31–39; Eph. 6:10–17

The old e - vil foe Now means
Ask ye, Who is this? Je - sus
This world's prince may still Scowl fierce
And take they our life, Goods, fame,
dead - ly woe; Deep guile and great might
Christ it is, Of Sab - a - oth Lord,
as he will, He can harm us none.
child, and wife, Though these all be gone,
Are his dread arms in fight; On earth
And there's none oth - er God; He holds
He's judged; the deed is done; One lit -
Our vic - t'ry has been won; The King -
is not his e - qual.
the field for - ev - er.
tle word can fell him.
dom ours re - main - eth.

657 A Mighty Fortress Is Our God

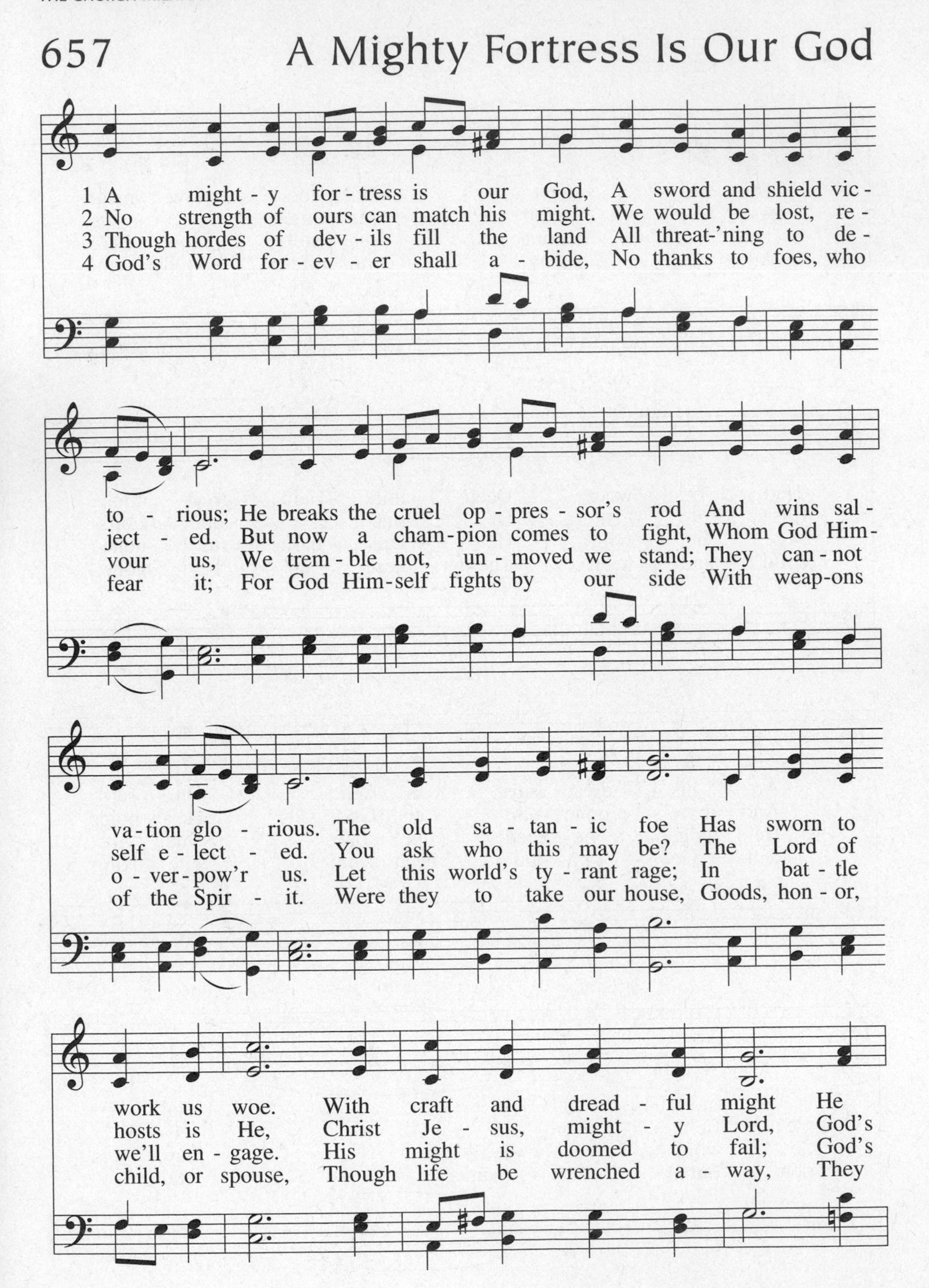
1 A mighty - y for - tress is our God, A sword and shield vic - to - rious; He breaks the cruel op - pres - sor's rod And wins sal - va - tion glo - rious. The old sa - tan - ic foe Has sworn to work us woe. With craft and dread - ful might He
2 No strength of ours can match his might. We would be lost, re - ject - ed. But now a cham - pion comes to fight, Whom God Him - self e - lect - ed. You ask who this may be? The Lord of hosts is He, Christ Je - sus, might - y Lord, God's
3 Though hordes of dev - ils fill the land All threat-'ning to de - vour us, We trem - ble not, un - moved we stand; They can - not o - ver - pow'r us. Let this world's ty - rant rage; In bat - tle we'll en - gage. His might is doomed to fail; God's
4 God's Word for - ev - er shall a - bide, No thanks to foes, who fear it; For God Him - self fights by our side With weap - ons of the Spir - it. Were they to take our house, Goods, hon - or, child, or spouse, Though life be wrenched a - way, They

Text: Martin Luther, 1483–1546; tr. *Lutheran Book of Worship*, 1978;
Spanish tr. Juan Bautista Cabrera, 1837–1916
Tune: Martin Luther, 1483–1546; setting: Johann Sebastian Bach, 1685–1750

EIN FESTE BURG (Isorhythmic)
87 87 66 66 7

Ps. 46:1, 7, 11; Rev. 19:11–16; Rom. 8:31–39; Eph. 6:10–17

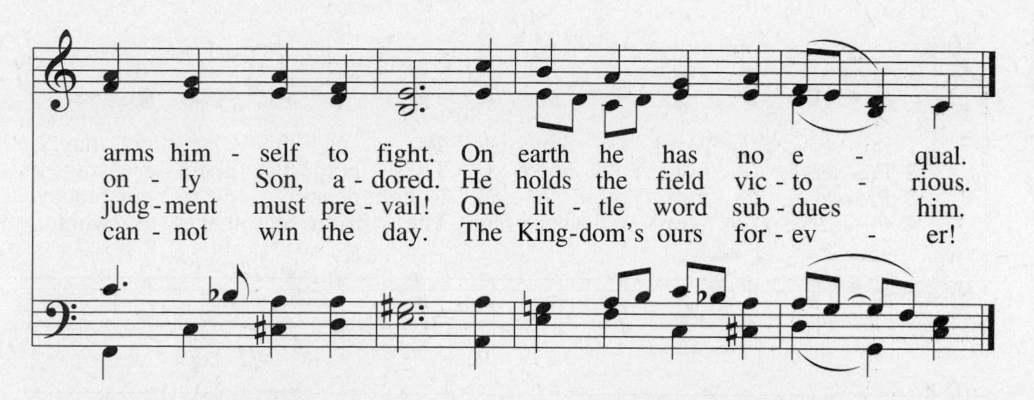
arms him - self to fight. On earth he has no e - qual.
on - ly Son, a - dored. He holds the field vic - to - rious.
judg - ment must pre - vail! One lit - tle word sub - dues him.
can - not win the day. The King - dom's ours for - ev - er!

1 *Castillo fuerte es nuestro Dios,*
defensa y buen escudo;
con su poder nos librará
en este trance agudo.
Con furia y con afán
acósanos Satán;
por armas deja ver
astucia y gran poder:
cual él no hay en la tierra.

2 *Nuestro valor es nada aquí,*
con él todo es perdido;
mas por nosotros pugnará
de Dios el escogido.
¿Sabéis quién es? Jesús,
el que venció en la cruz,
Señor de Sabaot,
y pues él sólo es Dios,
él triunfa en la batalla.

3 *Aun si están demonios mil*
prontos a devorarnos,
no temeremos, porque Dios
sabrá aún prosperarnos.
Que muestre su vigor
Satán, y su furor
dañarnos no podrá;
pues condenado es ya
por la Palabra santa.

4 *Sin destruirla dejarán,*
aún mal de su grado,
esta Palabra del Señor;
él lucha a nuestro lado.
Que lleven con furor
los bienes, vida, honor,
los hijos, la mujer . . .
todo ha de perecer:
de Dios el reino queda.

658 Preserve Your Word, O Savior

1 Pre-serve Your Word, O Sav-ior, To us this lat-ter day,
2 Pre-serve, O Lord, Your hon-or, The bold blas-phem-er smite;
3 Pre-serve, O Lord, Your Zi-on, Bought dear-ly with Your blood;
4 Pre-serve Your Word and preach-ing, The truth that makes us whole,
And let Your king-dom flour-ish; En-large Your Church, we pray.
Con-vince, con-vert, en-light-en The souls in er-ror's night.
Pro-tect what You have cho-sen A-gainst the hell-ish flood.
The mir-ror of Your glo-ry, The pow'r that saves the soul.
O keep our faith from fail-ing; Keep hope's bright star a-glow.
Re-veal Your will, dear Sav-ior, To all who dwell be-low,
Be al-ways our de-fend-er When dan-gers gath-er round;
Oh, may this liv-ing wa-ter, This dew of heav'n-ly grace,
Let noth-ing from truth turn us While liv-ing here be-low.
Great light of all the liv-ing, That all Your name may know.
When all the earth is crum-bling, Safe may Your Church be found.
Sus-tain us while here liv-ing Un-til we see Your face.

Text: Andreas Gryphius, 1616–64; tr. William J. Schaefer, 1891–1976, alt.
Tune: *Neu-vermehrtes . . . Gesangbuch*, 3rd ed., Meiningen, 1693; setting: Felix Mendelssohn, 1809–47

MUNICH
76 76 D

1 Peter 1:5–7; Jude 3, 17, 20–21

5 Preserve in wave and tempest
Your storm-tossed little flock;
Assailed by wind and weather,
May it endure each shock.
Stand at the helm, our pilot,
And set the course aright;
Then we will reach the harbor
In Your eternal light.

Lord of Our Life 659

1 Lord of our life and God of our sal - va - tion, Star of our night and hope of ev - 'ry na - tion: Hear and re - ceive Your Church's sup - pli - ca - tion, Lord God Al - might - y.
2 See round Your ark the hun - gry bil - lows curl - ing; See how Your foes their ban - ners are un - furl - ing And with great spite their fi - ery darts are hurl - ing, O Lord, pre - serve us.
3 Lord, be our light when world - ly dark - ness veils us; Lord, be our shield when earth - ly ar - mor fails us; And in the day when hell it - self as - sails us, Grant us Your peace, Lord:
4 Peace in our hearts, where sin - ful thoughts are rag - ing, Peace in Your Church, our trou - bled souls as - suag - ing, Peace when the world its end - less war is wag - ing, Peace in Your heav - en.

Text: Matthäus Apelles von Löwenstern, 1594–1648; tr. Philip Pusey, 1799–1855, alt.
Tune: *Antiphoner,* Poitiers, 1746; setting: *New English Hymnal,* 1986

ISTE CONFESSOR
11 11 11 5

Ps. 79:9; Rev. 12:10; Ps. 84:11; Matt. 16:18

660 Stand Up, Stand Up for Jesus

1 Stand up, stand up for Je - sus, Ye sol - diers of the cross.
2 Stand up, stand up for Je - sus; The trum - pet call o - bey;
3 Stand up, stand up for Je - sus; Stand in His strength a - lone.
4 Stand up, stand up for Je - sus; The strife will not be long;
Lift high His roy - al ban - ner; It must not suf - fer loss.
Stand forth in might - y con - flict In this His glo - rious day.
The arm of flesh will fail you, Ye dare not trust your own.
This day the din of bat - tle, The next the vic - tor's song.
From vic - t'ry un - to vic - t'ry His ar - my He shall lead
Let all His faith - ful serve Him A - gainst un - num - bered foes;
Put on the Gos - pel ar - mor; Each piece put on with prayer.
The sol - diers, o - ver - com - ing, Their crown of life shall see
Till ev - 'ry foe is van - quished, And Christ is Lord in - deed.
Let cour - age rise with dan - ger And strength to strength op - pose.
Where du - ty calls or dan - ger, Be nev - er want - ing there.
And with the King of Glo - ry Shall reign e - ter - nal - ly.

Text: George Duffield, Jr., 1818–88, alt.
Tune: George J. Webb, 1803–87; setting: *Service Book and Hymnal*, 1958

WEBB
76 76 D

Luke 9:23–26; 1 John 5:4–5; 1 Cor. 15:25, 55–57; Eph. 6:11–18

The Son of God Goes Forth to War 661

1 The Son of God goes forth to war A king - ly crown to gain.
2 The mar - tyr first, whose ea - gle eye Could pierce be - yond the grave,
3 A glo - rious band, the cho - sen few, On whom the Spir - it came,
4 A no - ble ar - my, men and boys, The ma - tron and the maid,
His blood - red ban - ner streams a - far; Who fol - lows in His train?
Who saw his mas - ter in the sky And called on Him to save.
Twelve val - iant saints—their hope they knew And mocked the cross and flame.
A - round the Sav - ior's throne re - joice, In robes of light ar - rayed.
Who best can drink His cup of woe, Tri - um - phant o - ver pain,
Like Him, with par - don on His tongue In midst of mor - tal pain,
They met the ty - rant's bran - dished steel, The li - on's gor - y mane;
They climbed the steep as - cent of heav'n Through per - il, toil, and pain.
Who pa - tient bears his cross be - low— He fol - lows in His train.
He prayed for those who did the wrong— Who fol - lows in his train?
They bowed their necks their death to feel— Who fol - lows in their train?
O God, to us may grace be giv'n To fol - low in their train!

Stanza 2 speaks of Stephen, the first Christian martyr.

Text: Reginald Heber, 1783–1826, alt.
Music: Henry S. Cutler, 1824–1902

ALL SAINTS NEW
C M D

Rev. 19:11–16; Luke 9:23–24; Acts 7:54–60; 1 Tim. 6:12

662 Onward, Christian Soldiers

1 On - ward, Chris - tian sol - diers, March - ing as to war,
2 Like a might - y ar - my Moves the Church of God;
3 Crowns and thrones may per - ish, King - doms rise and wane,
4 On - ward, then, ye faith - ful, Join our hap - py throng,
With the cross of Je - sus Go - ing on be - fore.
Broth - ers, we are tread - ing Where the saints have trod.
But the Church of Je - sus Con - stant will re - main.
Blend with ours your voic - es In the tri - umph song:
Christ, the roy - al mas - ter, Leads a - gainst the foe;
We are not di - vid - ed, All one bod - y we,
Gates of hell can nev - er 'Gainst that Church pre - vail;
Glo - ry, laud, and hon - or Un - to Christ, the king;
For - ward in - to bat - tle See His ban - ners go!
One in hope and doc - trine, One in char - i - ty.
We have Christ's own prom - ise, And that can - not fail.
This through count - less a - ges Men and an - gels sing.

Text: Sabine Baring-Gould, 1834–1924, alt.
Tune: Arthur S. Sullivan, 1842–1900; setting: *Service Book and Hymnal*, 1958

ST. GERTRUDE
65 65 65 D

Matt. 16:18; Ps. 145:13; Eph. 4:4–6; 6:10–18

Refrain
On-ward, Chris-tian sol - diers, March-ing as to war,
With the cross of Je - sus Go - ing on be - fore.

Be strong in the Lord and in the strength of His might. Put on the whole armor of God, that you may be able to stand against the schemes of the devil. Ephesians 6:10–11

663 Rise, My Soul, to Watch and Pray

1 Rise, my soul, to watch and pray; From your sleep a - wak - en! Be not by the e - vil day Un - a - wares o'er - tak - en; For the foe, Well we know, Is a har - vest reap - ing While the saints are sleep - ing.
2 Watch a - gainst the dev - il's snares Lest a - sleep he find you; For in - deed no pains he spares To de - ceive and blind you. Sa - tan's prey Oft are they Who se - cure are sleep - ing And no watch are keep - ing.
3 Watch! Let not the wick - ed world With its lies de - feat you Lest with bold de - cep - tions hurled It be - tray and cheat you. Watch and see Lest there be Faith - less friends to charm you, Who but seek to harm you.
4 Watch a - gainst your - self, my soul, Lest with grace you tri - fle; Let not self your thoughts con - trol Nor God's mer - cy sti - fle. Pride and sin Lurk with - in, All your hopes to shat - ter; Heed not when they flat - ter.

Text: Johann Burkhard Freystein, 1671–1718; tr. Catherine Winkworth, 1827–78, alt.
Tune: *Hundert . . . geistlicher Arien*, Dresden, 1694, alt.; setting: *Christian Worship*, 1993

STRAF MICH NICHT
76 76 33 66

Matt. 25:5, 13; 26:41; 1 Thess. 5:5–9; Rev. 16:15

5 But while watching, also pray
To the Lord unceasing.
God protects you day by day,
Strength and faith increasing,
So that still
Mind and will
Shall unite to serve Him
And forever love Him.

Fight the Good Fight 664

1 Fight the good fight with all your might; Christ is your strength, and Christ your right. Lay hold on life, and it shall be Your joy and crown e - ter - nal - ly.
2 Run the straight race through God's good grace; Lift up your eyes, and seek His face. Life with its way be - fore us lies; Christ is the path, and Christ the prize.
3 Cast care a - side, lean on your guide; His bound-less mer - cy will pro - vide. Trust, and en - dur - ing faith shall prove Christ is your life and Christ your love.
4 Faint not nor fear, His arms are near; He chang - es not who holds you dear; On - ly be - lieve, and you will see That Christ is all e - ter - nal - ly.

Text: John S. B. Monsell, 1811–75, alt.
Tune: *The Methodist Harmonist*, New York, 1821; setting: *The Lutheran Hymnal*, 1941

MENDON
L M

1 Tim. 6:12; 1 Cor. 9:24–27; 1 Peter 5:7; Ps. 55:22

665 Be Strong in the Lord

1 Be strong in the Lord In armor of light,
With helmet and sword, With shield for the fight;
On prayer be dependent, Be belted and shod,
In breastplate resplendent: The armor of God.
2 In integrity gird You round to impart
The truth of His Word As truth in your heart;
His righteousness wearing As breastplate of mail,
His victory sharing, Be strong to prevail.
3 With eagerness shod Stand firm in your place,
Or go forth for God With news of His grace;
No foe shall disarm you Nor force you to yield,
No arrow can harm you With faith as your shield.
4 Though Satan presume To test you and try,
In helmet and plume Your head shall be high;
Beset by temptation Be true to your Lord,
Your helmet salvation And Scripture your sword.

Alternate tune: HANOVER (804)

Text: Timothy Dudley-Smith, b. 1926
Music: C. Hubert H. Parry, 1848–1918

LAUDATE DOMINUM
55 55 65 65

Eph. 6:10–18; 1 Cor. 16:13; 1 Peter 5:8–10; 1 John 5:4–5

5 So wield well your blade,
Rejoice in its pow'rs,
Fight on undismayed
For Jesus is ours!
Then in Him victorious
Your armor lay down,
To praise, ever glorious,
His cross and His crown.

O Little Flock, Fear Not the Foe 666

1 O lit - tle flock, fear not the foe Who mad - ly
2 Be of good cheer; your cause be - longs To Him who
3 As true as God's own Word is true, Not earth nor
4 A - men, Lord Je - sus, grant our prayer; Great Cap - tain,
seeks your o - ver - throw; Dread not his rage and pow'r.
can a - venge your wrongs; Leave it to Him, our Lord.
hell's sa - tan - ic crew A - gainst us shall pre - vail.
now Thine arm make bare, Fight for us once a - gain!
And though your cour - age some-times faints, His seem - ing
Though hid - den yet from mor - tal eyes, His Gid - eon
Their might? A joke, a mere fa - cade! God is with
So shall Thy saints and mar - tyrs raise A might - y
tri - umph o'er God's saints Lasts but a lit - tle hour.
shall for you a - rise, Up - hold you and His Word.
us and we with God— Our vic - t'ry can - not fail.
cho - rus to Thy praise For - ev - er - more. A - men.

Setting available in hymn accompaniment edition.

Text: Jacob Fabricius, 1593–1654; tr. Catherine Winkworth, 1827–78, alt.
Tune: German, Nürnberg, 1534

KOMMT HER ZU MIR
886 886

Luke 12:32; 2 Tim. 4:18; Luke 18:7–8a; Rev. 7:9–17

667 Saints, See the Cloud of Witnesses

1 Saints, see the cloud of wit - ness - es sur - round us;
2 These saints of old re - ceived God's com - men - da - tion;
3 They call to us, "Your tim - id foot - steps length - en;
4 Come, let us fix our sight on Christ who suf - fered,
Their lives of faith en - cour - age and as - tound us.
They lived as pil - grim - heirs of His sal - va - tion.
Throw off sin's weight, your halt - ing weak - ness strength - en.
He faced the cross, His sin - less life He of - fered;
Hear how the Mas - ter praised their faith so
Through faith they con - quered flame and sword and
We kept the faith, we shed our blood, were
He scorned the shame, He died, our death en -
fer - vent: "Well done, My ser - vant!"
gal - lows, God's name to hal - low.
mar - tyred; Our lives we bar - tered."
dur - ing, Our hope se - cur - ing.

5 Lord, give us faith to walk where You are sending,
On paths unmarked, eyes blind as to their ending;
Not knowing where we go, but that You lead us—
With grace precede us.

6 You, Jesus, You alone deserve all glory!
Our lives unfold, embraced within Your story;
Past, present, future—You, the same forever—
You fail us never!

Hymn accompaniment: 825

Text: Stephen P. Starke, b. 1955
Tune: Dale Wood, 1934–2003

WOJTKIEWIECZ
11 11 11 5

Heb. 11:1—12:3; Matt. 25:21; Phil. 3:12–14

Rise! To Arms! With Prayer Employ You

1 Rise! To arms! With prayer em-ploy you, O Chris-tians, lest the
2 Cast a - far this world's vain plea - sure And bold - ly strive for
3 Wise - ly fight, for time is fleet - ing; The hours of grace are
foe de - stroy you; For Sa - tan has de - signed your fall.
heav'n-ly trea - sure. Be stead - fast in the Sav - ior's might.
fast re - treat - ing; Short, short is this our earth - ly way.
Wield God's Word, the weap - on glo - rious; A - gainst all foes be
Trust the Lord, who stands be - side you, For Je - sus from all
When the Lord the dead will wak - en And sin - ners all by
thus vic - to - rious, For God pro - tects you from them all.
harm will hide you. By faith you con - quer in the fight.
fear are shak - en, The saints with joy will greet that day.
Fear not the hordes of hell, Here is Em - man - u - el.
Take cour - age, wea - ry soul! Look for - ward to the goal!
Praise God, our tri - umph's sure. We need not long en - dure
Hail the Sav - ior! The strong foes yield To Christ, our shield,
Joy a - waits you. The race well run, Your long war won,
Scorn and tri - al. Our Sav - ior King His own will bring
And we, the vic - tors, hold the field.
Your crown shines splen - did as the sun.
To that great glo - ry which we sing.

Hymn accompaniment: 516

Text: Wilhelm Erasmus Arends, 1677–1721; tr. John M. Sloan, 1835–after 1890, alt.
Tune: Philipp Nicolai, 1556–1608

WACHET AUF
898 D 664 448

Eph. 6:10–18; Rom. 8:31–39; Phil. 1:27–28; 1 Cor. 9:24–25

669 Come, We That Love the Lord

1 Come, we that love the Lord, And let our joys be known; Join in a song with sweet accord, Join in a song with sweet accord And thus surround the throne, And thus surround the throne.
2 Let those refuse to sing Who never knew our God; But children of the heav'nly King, But children of the heav'nly King May speak their joys abroad, May speak their joys abroad.
3 The hill of Zion yields A thousand sacred sweets Before we reach the heav'nly fields, Before we reach the heav'nly fields, Or walk the golden streets, Or walk the golden streets.
4 Then let our songs abound, And ev'ry tear be dry; We're marching through Emmanuel's ground, We're marching through Emmanuel's ground To fairer worlds on high, To fairer worlds on high.

Text: Isaac Watts, 1674–1748, stanzas; Robert Lowry, 1826–99, refrain
Music: Robert Lowry, 1826–99

MARCHING TO ZION
S M and refrain

Is. 35:8–10; Ps. 48:2; Jer. 31:12; Ps. 149:2

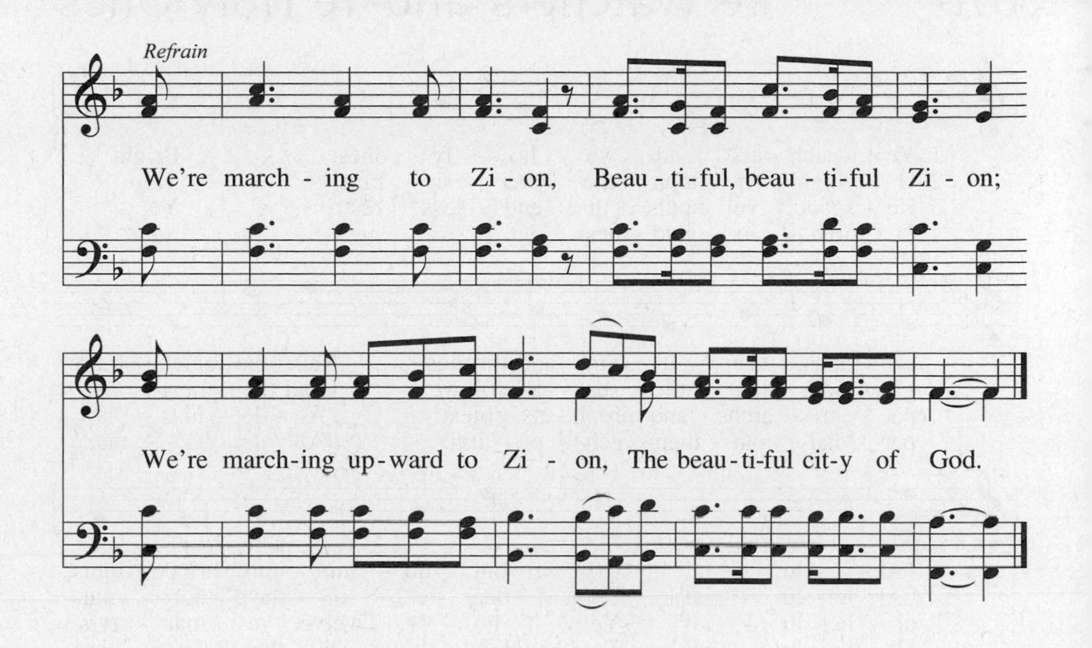
Refrain
We're march - ing to Zi - on, Beau - ti - ful, beau - ti - ful Zi - on;
We're march-ing up-ward to Zi - on, The beau-ti-ful cit-y of God.

Great is the Lord *and greatly to be praised*
in the city of our God!
His holy mountain, beautiful in elevation,
is the joy of all the earth,
Mount Zion, in the far north,
the city of the great King.

Psalm 48:1–2

670 Ye Watchers and Ye Holy Ones

1 Ye watch - ers and ye ho - ly ones, Bright
2 O high - er than the cher - u - bim, More
3 Re - spond, ye souls in end - less rest, Ye
△ 4 O friends, in glad - ness let us sing, Su -
ser - aphs, cher - u - bim, and thrones, Raise the glad strain:
glo - rious than the ser - a - phim, Lead their prais - es:
pa - tri - archs and proph - ets blest: "Al - le - lu - ia,
per - nal an - thems ech - o - ing: "Al - le - lu - ia,
"Al - le - lu - ia!" Cry out, do - min - ions, prince - doms,
"Al - le - lu - ia!" Thou bear - er of the e - ter - nal
al - le - lu - ia!" Ye ho - ly Twelve, ye mar - tyrs
al - le - lu - ia!" To God the Fa - ther, God the
pow'rs, Vir - tues, arch - an - gels, an - gels'
Word, Most gra - cious, mag - ni - fy the
strong, All saints tri - um - phant, raise the
Son, And God the Spir - it, Three in
choirs:
Lord:
song:
One:
"Al - le - lu - ia, al - le - lu - ia! Al - le -
lu - ia, al - le - lu - ia, al - le - lu - ia!"

Hymn accompaniment: 465

Text: J. Athelstan L. Riley, 1858–1945, alt.
Tune: *Geistliche Kirchengesäng*, Köln, 1623

LASST UNS ERFREUEN
888 888 and alleluias

Rev. 7:9–15; 14:1–3; Eph. 5:19; Luke 1:46–55

Sing with All the Saints in Glory 671

1 Sing with all the saints in glo - ry, Sing the res - ur - rec - tion song! Death and sor - row, earth's dark sto - ry, To the for - mer days be - long. All a - round the clouds are break - ing; Soon the storms of time shall cease; In God's like - ness we a - wak - en, Know - ing ev - er - last - ing peace.
2 Oh, what glo - ry, far ex - ceed - ing All that eye has yet per - ceived! Ho - liest hearts for a - ges plead - ing Nev - er that full joy con - ceived. God has prom - ised, Christ pre - pares it; There on high our wel - come waits. Ev - 'ry hum - ble spir - it shares it, Christ has passed the e - ter - nal gates.
3 Life e - ter - nal! Heav'n re - joic - es: Je - sus lives who once was dead. Shout with joy, O death - less voic - es! Child of God, lift up your head! Life e - ter - nal! Oh, what won - ders Crowd on faith; what joy un - known, When, a - mid earth's clos - ing thun - ders, Saints shall stand be - fore the throne!

Setting available in hymn accompaniment edition.

Text: William J. Irons, 1812–83, alt.
Tune: William B. Roberts, b. 1947

MISSISSIPPI
87 87 D

Rev. 7:9–17; 21:1–5; 1 Cor. 2:9; John 14:1–3

672 Jerusalem the Golden

1 Je - ru - sa - lem the gold - en, With milk and hon - ey blest—
2 With-in those walls of Zi - on Sounds forth the joy - ful song,
3 A - round the throne of Da - vid, The saints, from care re - leased,
△ 4 O sweet and bless - ed coun - try, The home of God's e - lect!
The prom - ise of sal - va - tion, The place of peace and rest—
As saints join with the an - gels And all the mar - tyr throng.
Raise loud their songs of tri - umph To cel - e - brate the feast.
O sweet and bless - ed coun - try That faith - ful hearts ex - pect!
We know not, oh, we know not What joys a - wait us there:
The Prince is ev - er with them; The day - light is se - rene;
They sing to Christ their lead - er, Who con - quered in the fight,
In mer - cy, Je - sus, bring us To that e - ter - nal rest
The ra - dian - cy of glo - ry, The bliss be - yond com - pare!
The cit - y of the bless - ed Shines bright with glo - rious sheen.
Who won for them for - ev - er Their gleam - ing robes of white.
With You and God the Fa - ther And Spir - it, ev - er blest.

Text: Bernard of Cluny, 12th cent.; tr. John Mason Neale, 1818–66, alt.
Tune: Alexander C. Ewing, 1830–95, alt.; setting: *Hymns Ancient and Modern*, 1861

EWING
76 76 D

Rev. 21:18–23; 2 Cor. 4:17–18; Rev. 7:9–17; Is. 60:19–20

Jerusalem, My Happy Home 673

1 Je - ru - sa - lem, my hap - py home,
2 O hap - py har - bor of the saints,
3 Thy gar - dens and thy gal - lant walks
4 There trees for - ev - er - more bear fruit
When shall I come to thee? When shall my sor - rows
O sweet and pleas - ant soil! In thee no sor - row
Con - tin - ual - ly are green; There grow such sweet and
And ev - er - more do spring; There ev - er - more the
have an end? Thy joys when shall I see?
may be found, No grief, no care, no toil.
pleas - ant flow'rs As no - where else are seen.
an - gels dwell And ev - er - more do sing.

5 Apostles, martyrs, prophets, there
Around my Savior stand;
And soon my friends in Christ below
Will join the glorious band.

6 O Christ, do Thou my soul prepare
For that bright home of love
That I may see Thee and adore
With all Thy saints above.

Text: F. B. P., 16th cent., alt.
Tune: American; setting: Charles H. Webb, b. 1933

LAND OF REST
C M

Text and tune: Public domain

Ps. 137:1–6; Heb. 12:22–24; Rev. 21:10–12; 22:1–2

674 Jerusalem, O City Fair and High

1 Je - ru - sa - lem, O cit - y fair and high, Your
2 O hap - py day, O yet far hap - pier hour, When
3 The pa - tri - archs' and proph - ets' no - ble train, With
4 Un - num - bered choirs be - fore the shin - ing throne Their

tow'rs I yearn to see; My long - ing heart to
will you come at last, When by my gra - cious
all Christ's fol - l'wers true, Who washed their robes and
joy - ful an - thems raise Till heav - en's arch - es

you would glad - ly fly, It will not stay with me.
Fa - ther's love and pow'r I see that por - tal vast?
cleansed sin's guilt - y stain, Sing prais - es ev - er new!
ech - o with the tone Of that great hymn of praise.

E - li - jah's char - iot take me A - bove the low - er skies, To
From heav - en's shin - ing re - gions To greet me glad - ly come Your
I see them shine for - ev - er, Re - splen-dent as the sun, In
And all its host re - joic - es, And all its bless - ed throng U -

Text: Johann Matthäus Meyfart, 1590–1642; tr. Catherine Winkworth, 1827–78, alt.
Tune: *Christlich Neu-vermehrt . . . Gesangbuch,* Erfurt, 1663;
setting: *The Lutheran Hymnal*, 1941

JERUSALEM, DU HOCHGEBAUTE STADT
10 6 10 6 76 76

Rev. 21:2–3; Rev. 7:9–12; Matt. 17:1–9

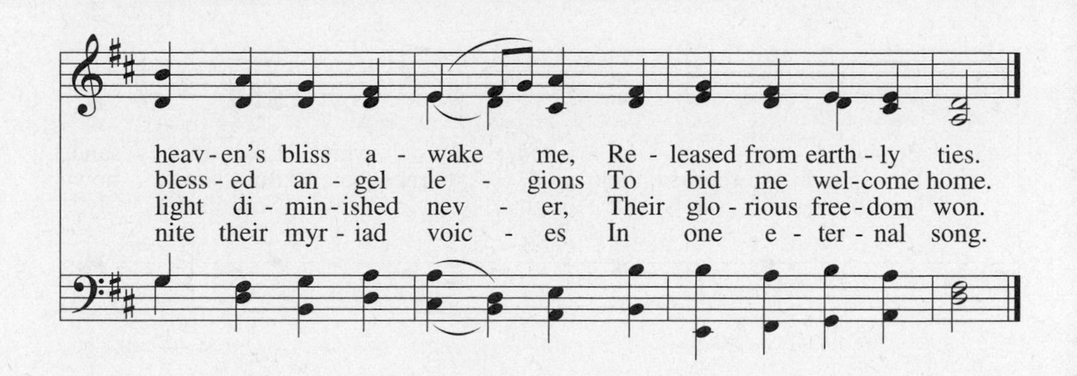
heav-en's bliss a - wake me, Re - leased from earth - ly ties.
bless - ed an - gel le - gions To bid me wel-come home.
light di - min - ished nev - er, Their glo - rious free - dom won.
nite their myr - iad voic - es In one e - ter - nal song.

Oh, What Their Joy 675

1 Oh, what their joy and their glo - ry must be,
2 In new Je - ru - sa - lem joy shall be found,
3 We, where no trou - ble dis - trac - tion can bring,
△ 4 Now let us wor - ship our Lord and our King,
Those end-less Sab - baths the bless - ed ones see!
Bless - ings of peace shall for - ev - er a - bound;
Safe - ly the an - thems of Zi - on shall sing;
Joy - ful - ly rais - ing our voic - es to sing:
Crowns for the val - iant, to wea - ry ones rest;
Wish and ful - fill - ment are not sev - ered there,
While for Your grace, Lord, their voic - es of praise
Praise to the Fa - ther, and praise to the Son,
God shall be all, and in all ev - er blest.
Nor the things prayed for come short of the prayer.
Your bless - ed peo - ple shall ev - er - more raise.
Praise to the Spir - it, to God, Three in One.

Hymn accompaniment: 520

Text: Peter Abelard, 1079–1142; tr. John Mason Neale, 1818–66, alt.
Tune: *Antiphoner*, Paris, 1681

O QUANTA QUALIA
10 10 10 10

Rev. 7:10–17; 21:2–7

676 Behold a Host, Arrayed in White

1 Be - hold a host, ar - rayed in white, Like thou - sand snow - clad moun - tains bright! With palms they stand; Who is this band Be - fore the throne of light? These are the saints of glo - rious fame, Who from the great af -
2 De - spised and scorned, they so - journed here; But now, how glo - rious they ap - pear! Those mar - tyrs stand, A priest - ly band, God's throne for - ev - er near. On earth they wept through bit - ter years; Now God has wiped a -
3 O bless - ed saints in bright ar - ray Now safe - ly home in end - less day, Ex - tol the Lord, Who with His Word Sus - tained you on the way. The steep and nar - row path you trod; You toiled and sowed the

Text: Hans Adolf Brorson, 1694–1764; tr. *The Lutheran Hymnal,* 1941, alt.
Tune: Norwegian, 17th cent.; setting: *The Lutheran Hymnal,* 1941

DEN STORE HVIDE FLOK
88446 88446 88446

Rev. 7:9–17; Heb. 9:14; 1 John 1:7; Rev. 6:11–13

flic - tion came And in the flood Of Je - sus' blood
way their tears, Trans - formed their strife To heav'n - ly life,
Word a - broad; Re - joice and bring Your fruits and sing
Are cleansed from guilt and shame. They now serve God both
And freed them from their fears. They now en - joy the
Be - fore the throne of God. The myr - iad an - gels
day and night; They sing their songs in end - less light. Their
Sab - bath rest, The heav'n - ly ban - quet of the blest; The
raise their song; O saints, sing with that hap - py throng! Lift
an - thems ring As they all sing With an - gels shin - ing bright.
Lamb, their Lord, At fes - tive board Him - self is host and guest.
up one voice; Let heav'n re - joice In our Re - deem - er's song!

677 For All the Saints

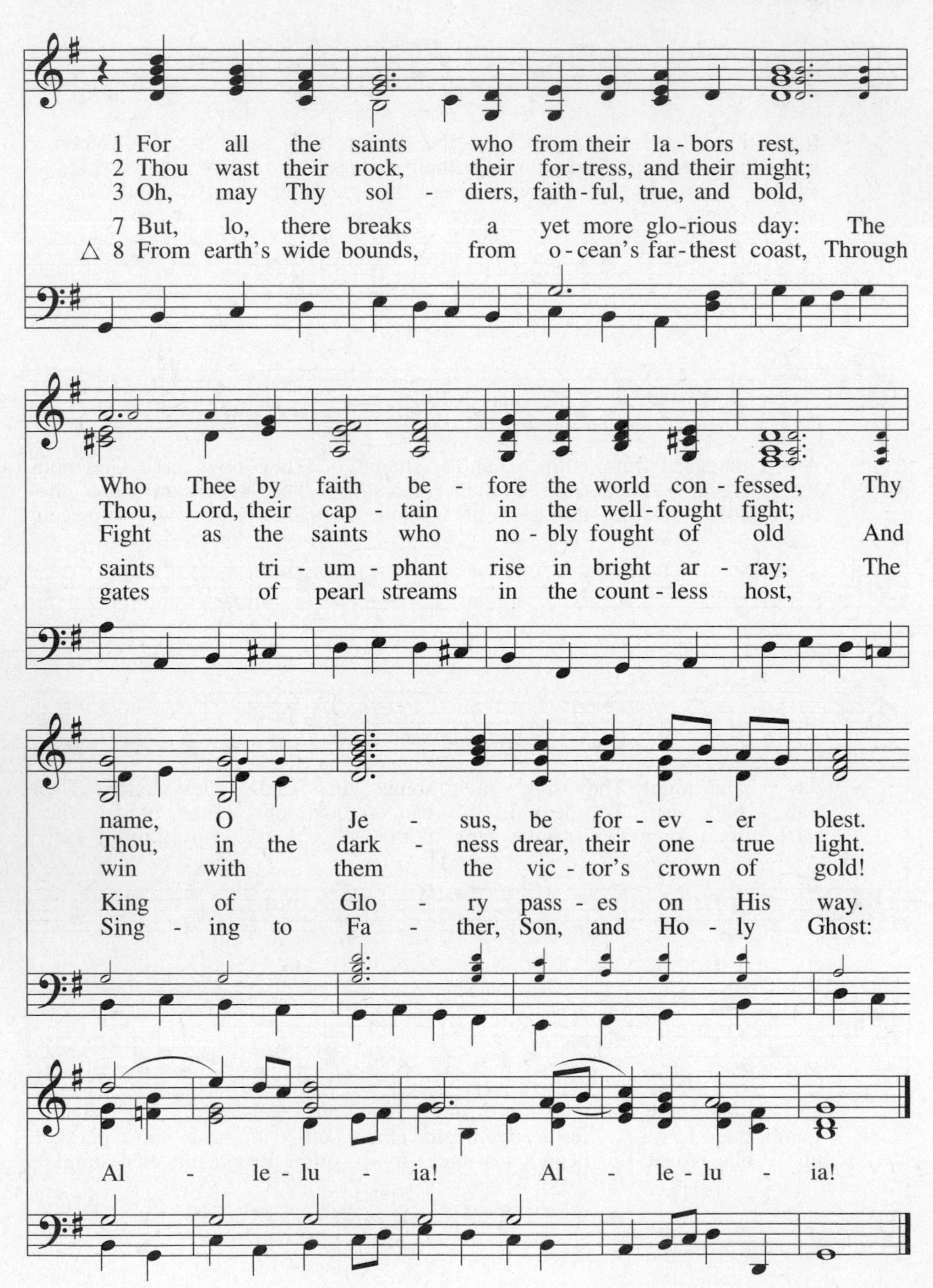
1 For all the saints who from their la - bors rest,
2 Thou wast their rock, their for - tress, and their might;
3 Oh, may Thy sol - diers, faith - ful, true, and bold,
7 But, lo, there breaks a yet more glo - rious day: The
△ 8 From earth's wide bounds, from o - cean's far - thest coast, Through
Who Thee by faith be - fore the world con - fessed, Thy
Thou, Lord, their cap - tain in the well - fought fight;
Fight as the saints who no - bly fought of old And
saints tri - um - phant rise in bright ar - ray; The
gates of pearl streams in the count - less host,
name, O Je - sus, be for - ev - er blest.
Thou, in the dark - ness drear, their one true light.
win with them the vic - tor's crown of gold!
King of Glo - ry pass - es on His way.
Sing - ing to Fa - ther, Son, and Ho - ly Ghost:
Al - le - lu - ia! Al - le - lu - ia!

Text: William W. How, 1823–97, alt.
Music: Ralph Vaughan Williams, 1872–1958

SINE NOMINE
10 10 10 and alleluias

Heb. 12:1–3; Rev. 2:10; 14:13; 17:14

4 Oh, blest com - mu - nion, fel - low - ship di - vine!
5 And when the fight is fierce, the war - fare long,
6 The gold - en eve - ning bright - ens in the west;
We fee - bly strug - gle, they in glo - ry shine; Yet
Steals on the ear the dis - tant tri - umph song, And
Soon, soon to faith - ful war - riors com - eth rest;
all are one in Thee, for all are Thine.
hearts are brave a - gain, and arms are strong.
Sweet is the calm of par - a - dise the blest.
Al - le - lu - ia! Al - le - lu - ia!

678 We Sing for All the Unsung Saints

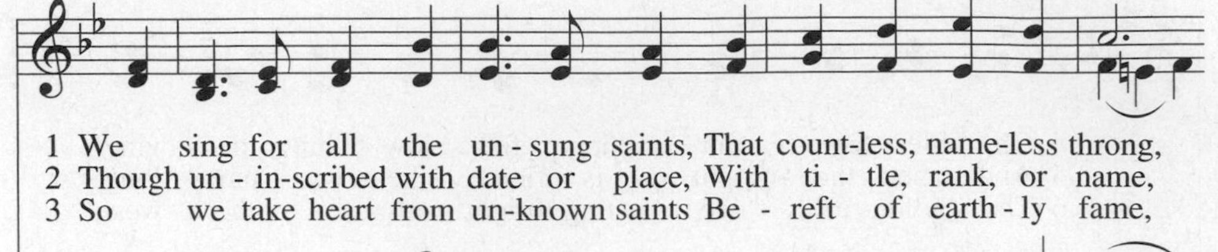

1 We sing for all the un - sung saints, That count-less, name-less throng,
2 Though un - in-scribed with date or place, With ti - tle, rank, or name,
3 So we take heart from un-known saints Be - reft of earth - ly fame,

Who kept the faith and passed it on With hope stead-fast and strong
As liv - ing stones their sto - ries join To form a hal-lowed frame
Those faith - ful ones who have re-ceived A more en - dur - ing name:

Through all the dai - ly griefs and joys No chron - i - cles re-cord,
A - round the mys-t'ry in their midst: The Lamb once sac - ri - ficed,
For they re-veal true bless - ing comes When we our pride ef-face

For - get - ful of their lack of fame, But mind - ful of their Lord.
The Love that wrest-ed life from death, The wound-ed, ris - en Christ.
And of - fer back our lives to be The ves - sels of God's grace.

Text: Carl P. Daw, Jr., b. 1944
Tune: Henry S. Cutler, 1824–1902; setting: *Service Book and Hymnal*, 1958

ALL SAINTS NEW
C M D

Hebrews 11; Rev. 7:9–10, 17

Oh, How Blest Are They 679

1 Oh, how blest are they whose toils are end - ed, Who through death have un - to God as - cend - ed! They have a - ris - en From the cares which keep us still in pris - on.
2 We are still as in a dun - geon liv - ing, Still op - pressed with sor - row and mis - giv - ing; Our un - der - tak - ings Are but toils and trou - bles and heart - break - ings.
3 They mean - while are in their cham - bers sleep - ing, Qui - et and set free from all their weep - ing; No cross or sad - ness There can hin - der their un - trou - bled glad - ness.
4 Christ has wiped a - way their tears for - ev - er; They have that for which we still en - deav - or. By them are chant - ed Songs that ne'er to mor - tal ears were grant - ed.
5 Come, O Christ, and loose the chains that bind us; Lead us forth and cast this world be - hind us. With You, the A - noint - ed, Finds the soul its joy and rest ap - point - ed.

Text: Simon Dach, 1605–59; tr. Henry W. Longfellow, 1807–92, alt.
Tune: *Johann Störls . . . Schlag- Gesang- Und Noten-Buch*, Stuttgart, 1744;
setting: *The Lutheran Hymnal*, 1941

O WIE SELIG
10 10 5 10

Rev. 14:13; Phil. 1:21; Rev. 21:4; 2 Cor. 4:16–17

680 Thine the Amen, Thine the Praise

1 Thine the a - men Thine the praise Al - le - lu - ias an - gels raise Thine the ev - er - last - ing head Thine the break - ing of the bread Thine the glo - ry Thine the
2 Thine the life e - ter - nal - ly Thine the prom - ise let there be Thine the vi - sion Thine the tree All the earth on bend - ed knee Gone the nail - ing gone the
3 Thine the tru - ly Thine the yes Thine the ta - ble we the guest Thine the mer - cy all from Thee Thine the glo - ry yet to be Then the ring - ing and the
4 Thine the king - dom Thine the prize Thine the won - der full sur - prise Thine the ban - quet then the praise Then the jus - tice of Thy ways Thine the glo - ry Thine the
5 Thine the glo - ry in the night No more dy - ing on - ly light Thine the riv - er Thine the tree Then the Lamb e - ter - nal - ly Then the ho - ly ho - ly

Text: Herbert F. Brokering, 1926–2009
Music: Carl F. Schalk, b. 1929

THINE
77 77 87 14

Matt. 26:26–29; Rev. 19:1–16; Rev. 7:9–14; Rev. 5:6–14

sto - ry Thine the har - vest then the cup Thine the
rail - ing Gone the plead - ing gone the cry Gone the
sing - ing Then the end of all the war Thine the
sto - ry Then the wel - come to the least Then the
ho - ly Cel - e - bra - tion ju - bi - lee Thine the
vine - yard then the cup is lift - ed
sigh - ing gone the dy - ing what was
liv - ing Thine the lov - ing ev - er -
won - der all in - creas - ing at Thy
splen - dor Thine the bright - ness on - ly
1–4
5
up lift - ed up. (2 Thine the)
loss lift - ed high. (3 Thine the)
more ev - er - more. (4 Thine the)
feast at Thy feast. (5 Thine the)
Thee on - ly Thee.

681 Send, O Lord, Your Holy Spirit

1 Send, O Lord, Your Ho - ly Spir - it On Your ser - vant
2 You, O Lord, Your - self have called him For Your pre - cious
3 Help, Lord Je - sus, help him nour - ish All our chil - dren
now, we pray; Let him prove a faith - ful shep - herd
lambs to care; But to pros - per in his call - ing,
with Your Word That in fer - vent love they serve You
That no lamb be led a - stray. Your pure teach - ing to pro -
He the Spir - it's gifts must share. Give him wis - dom from a -
Till in heav'n their song is heard. Bound - less bless - ings, Lord, be -
claim, To ex - tol Your ho - ly name, And to feed Your
bove, Fill his heart with ho - ly love; In his weak - ness,
stow On his faith - ful toil be - low Till by grace to
lambs, dear Sav - ior, Make his aim and sole en - deav - or.
Lord, be near him, In his prayers, Good Shep - herd, hear him.
him be giv - en His re - ward, the crown of heav - en.

Hymn accompaniment: 589

Text: *Lieder-Perlen*, St. Louis, 1905; tr. Frederick W. Herzberger, 1859–1930, alt.
Tune: Johann Schop, c. 1590–1667

WERDE MUNTER
87 87 77 88

John 20:21–23; 2 Tim. 1:13–14; 3:14–17; John 21:15–17

God of the Prophets, Bless the Prophets' Sons

1 God of the proph - ets, bless the proph - ets' sons;
2 A - noint them proph - ets, men who are in - tent
3 A - noint them priests, strong in - ter - ces - sors they,
4 A - noint them kings, yes, king - ly kings, O Lord.
5 Make them a - pos - tles, her - alds of Your cross;
E - li - jah's man - tle o'er E - li - sha cast.
To be Your wit - ness - es in word and deed,
For par - don and for love and hope and peace,
A - noint them with the Spir - it of Your Son.
Forth let them go to tell the world of grace.
Each age its sol - emn task may claim but once;
Their hearts a - flame, their lips made el - o - quent,
That, through their plead - ing, guilt - y sin - ners may
Theirs not a jew - eled crown, a blood - stained sword;
In - spired by You, may they count all but loss
Make each one no - bler, strong - er than the last.
Their eyes a - wake to ev - 'ry hu - man need.
Find Je - sus' mer - cy and from sin re - lease.
Theirs, by sweet love, for Christ a king - dom won.
And stand at last with joy be - fore Your face.

Text: Denis Wortman, 1835–1922, alt.
Tune: *Trente quatre Pseaumes de David*, Geneva, 1551, ed. Louis Bourgeois;
setting: *The Lutheran Hymnal,* 1941

OLD 124TH, abbr.
10 10 10 10

2 Kings 2:1–15; John 20:21–23; John 17:18; 1 Tim. 4:13–16

683 Jesus, Thy Boundless Love to Me

1 Je - sus, Thy bound-less love to me No thought can reach, no tongue de - clare; U - nite my thank - ful heart to Thee, And reign with-out a ri - val there! Thine whol - ly, Thine a - lone I am; Be Thou a - lone my con - stant flame.
2 O grant that noth - ing in my soul May dwell, but Thy pure love a - lone; Oh, may Thy love pos - sess me whole, My joy, my trea - sure, and my crown! All cold-ness from my heart re - move; My ev - 'ry act, word, thought be love.
3 This love un - wea - ried I pur - sue And daunt - less - ly to Thee as - pire. Oh, may Thy love my hope re - new, Burn in my soul like heav'n - ly fire! And day and night, be all my care To guard this sa - cred trea - sure there.
4 In suf - f'ring be Thy love my peace, In weak - ness be Thy love my pow'r; And when the storms of life shall cease, O Je - sus, in that fi - nal hour, Be Thou my rod and staff and guide, And draw me safe - ly to Thy side!

Text: Paul Gerhardt, 1607–76; tr. John B. Wesley, 1703–91, alt.
Music: Norman Cocker, 1889–1953

RYBURN
88 88 88

Eph. 3:16–21; Gal. 2:20; 1 John 3:24; John 15:9

Come unto Me, Ye Weary 684

1 "Come un - to Me, ye wea - ry, And I will give you rest."
2 "Come un - to Me, ye wan - d'rers, And I will give you light."
3 "Come un - to Me, ye faint - ing, And I will give you life."
4 "And who - so - ev - er com - eth, I will not cast him out."
O bless - ed voice of Je - sus, Which comes to hearts op - pressed!
O lov - ing voice of Je - sus, Which comes to cheer the night!
O cheer - ing voice of Je - sus, Which comes to aid our strife!
O pa - tient love of Je - sus, Which drives a - way our doubt,
It tells of ben - e - dic - tion, Of par - don, grace, and peace,
Our hearts were filled with sad - ness, And we had lost our way;
The foe is stern and ea - ger, The fight is fierce and long;
Which, though we be un - wor - thy Of love so great and free,
Of joy that hath no end - ing, Of love that can - not cease.
But Thou hast brought us glad - ness And songs at break of day.
But Thou hast made us might - y And strong - er than the strong.
In - vites us ver - y sin - ners To come, dear Lord, to Thee!

Text: William C. Dix, 1837–98, alt.
Tune: Friedrich K. Anthes, 1812–after 1857; setting: *The Lutheran Hymnal*, 1941

ANTHES
76 76 D

Matt. 11:28; John 6:37; Is. 60:20; Is. 40:31

685 Let Us Ever Walk with Jesus

1 Let us ev - er walk with Je - sus, Fol - low His ex -
2 Let us suf - fer here with Je - sus And with pa - tience
3 Let us glad - ly die with Je - sus. Since by death He
4 Let us al - so live with Je - sus. He has ris - en
am - ple pure, Through a world that would de - ceive us And to
bear our cross. Joy will fol - low all our sad - ness; Where He
con - quered death, He will free us from de - struc - tion, Give to
from the dead That to life we may a - wak - en. Je - sus,
sin our spir - its lure. On - ward in His foot - steps tread - ing,
is, there is no loss. Though to - day we sow no laugh - ter,
us im - mor - tal breath. Let us mor - ti - fy all pas - sion
You are now our head. We are Your own liv - ing mem - bers;
Pil - grims here, our home a - bove, Full of faith and
We shall reap ce - les - tial joy; All dis - com - forts
That would lead us in - to sin; And the grave that
Where You live, there we shall be In Your pres - ence

Text: Sigismund von Birken, 1626–81; tr. *Lutheran Book of Worship*, 1978, alt.
Tune: Georg G. Boltze, 18th cent.; setting: *The Lutheran Hymnal*, 1941

LASSET UNS MIT JESU ZIEHEN
87 87 877 877

Matt. 16:24; 1 Peter 4:12–13; Matt. 10:38–39; Rom. 6:2–5, 8

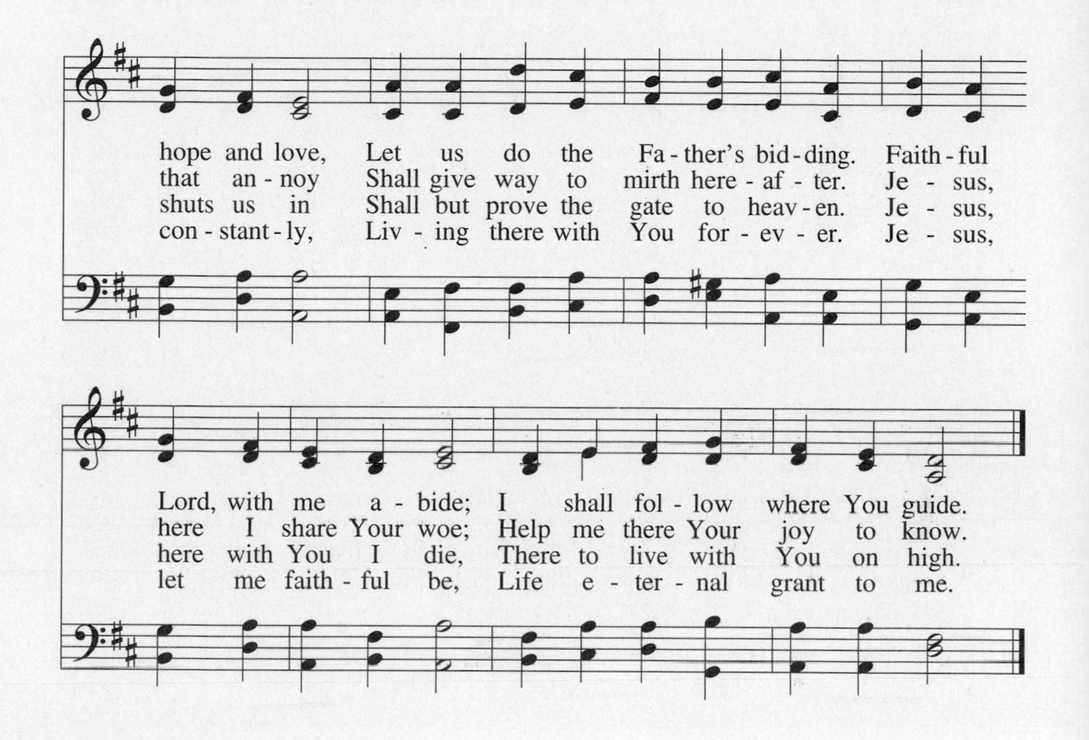
hope and love, Let us do the Fa - ther's bid - ding. Faith - ful
that an - noy Shall give way to mirth here - af - ter. Je - sus,
shuts us in Shall but prove the gate to heav - en. Je - sus,
con - stant - ly, Liv - ing there with You for - ev - er. Je - sus,
Lord, with me a - bide; I shall fol - low where You guide.
here I share Your woe; Help me there Your joy to know.
here with You I die, There to live with You on high.
let me faith - ful be, Life e - ter - nal grant to me.

Almighty God, Your Son willingly endured the agony and shame of the cross for our redemption. Grant us courage to take up our cross daily and follow Him wherever He leads; through the same Jesus Christ, our Lord, who lives and reigns with You and the Holy Spirit, one God, now and forever. Collect for Proper 17, Series A

---

686 Come, Thou Fount of Every Blessing

1 Come, Thou Fount of ev - 'ry bless - ing, Tune my heart to
2 Here I raise my Eb - en - e - zer, Hith - er by Thy
3 Oh, to grace how great a debt - or Dai - ly I'm con -
4 Oh, that day when freed from sin - ning, I shall see Thy
sing Thy grace; Streams of mer - cy, nev - er ceas - ing,
help I've come; And I hope, by Thy good plea - sure,
strained to be; Let that grace now like a fet - ter
love - ly face; Clothed then in the blood - washed lin - en,
Call for songs of loud - est praise. While the hope of end - less
Safe - ly to ar - rive at home. Je - sus sought me when a
Bind my wan-d'ring heart to Thee: Prone to wan - der, Lord, I
How I'll sing Thy won-drous grace! Come, my Lord, no long - er
glo - ry Fills my heart with joy and love, Teach me
strang - er, Wan - d'ring from the fold of God; He, to
feel it; Prone to leave the God I love. Here's my
tar - ry; Take my ran - som'd soul a - way; Send Thine

"Ebenezer" means "Thus far has the Lord helped us" and was the name given to the stone of remembrance that Samuel raised to God's glory (1 Sam. 7:12).

Text: Robert Robinson, 1735–90, alt.
Music: *Repository of Sacred Music, Part Second*, Harrisburg, 1813

NETTLETON
87 87 D

John 4:14; 1 Sam. 7:3–12; 1 Peter 1:18–19; Eph. 1:13–14

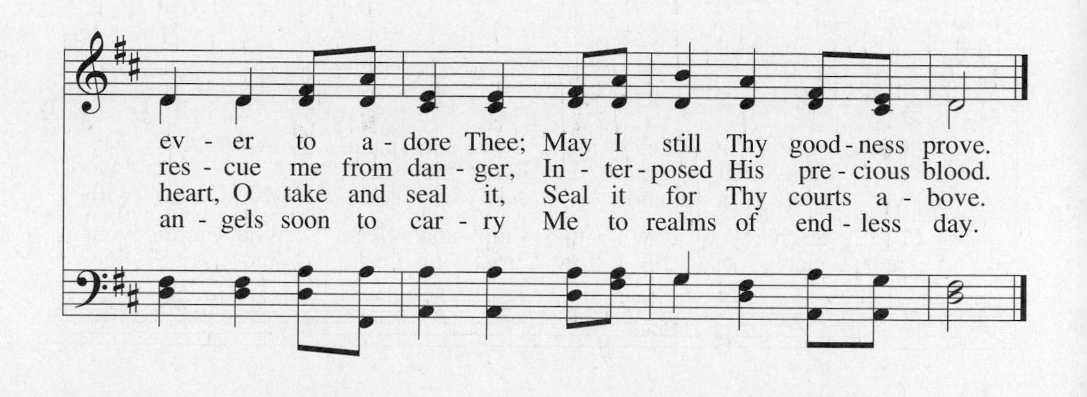
ev - er to a - dore Thee; May I still Thy good - ness prove.
res - cue me from dan - ger, In - ter - posed His pre - cious blood.
heart, O take and seal it, Seal it for Thy courts a - bove.
an - gels soon to car - ry Me to realms of end - less day.

Thine Forever, God of Love 687

1 Thine for - ev - er, God of love! Hear us from Thy throne a - bove;
2 Thine for - ev - er! Oh, how blest They who find in Thee their rest!
3 Thine for - ev - er, Lord of Life! Shield us through our earth - ly strife.
4 Thine for - ev - er! Shep - herd, keep These Thy frail and trem - bling sheep;
5 Thine for - ev - er! Thou our guide, All our wants by Thee sup - plied,
Thine for - ev - er may we be Here and in e - ter - ni - ty!
Sav - ior, guard - ian, heav'n - ly friend, O de - fend us to the end!
Thou, the life, the truth, the way, Guide us to the realms of day.
Safe a - lone be - neath Thy care, Let us all Thy good - ness share.
All our sins by Thee for - giv'n; Lead us, Lord, from earth to heav'n.

Text: Mary F. Maude, 1819–1913
Tune: Justin H. Knecht, 1752–1817; setting: *The Lutheran Hymnal*, 1941

VIENNA
77 77

Mal. 3:17; John 10:27–30; John 6:39

688 "Come, Follow Me," the Savior Spake

1 "Come, fol - low Me," the Sav - ior spake, "All in My way a - bid - ing; De - ny your - selves, the world for - sake, O - bey My call and guid - ing. O bear the cross, what - e'er be - tide, Take My ex - am - ple for your guide.
2 "I am the light, I light the way, A god - ly life dis - play - ing; I bid you walk as in the day; I keep your feet from stray - ing. I am the way, and well I show How you must so - journ here be - low.
3 "My heart a - bounds in low - li - ness, My soul with love is glow - ing; And gra - cious words My lips ex - press, With meek - ness o - ver - flow - ing. My heart, My mind, My strength, My all, To God I yield, on Him I call.
4 "I teach you how to shun and flee What harms your soul's sal - va - tion, Your heart from ev - 'ry guile to free, From sin and its temp - ta - tion. I am the ref - uge of the soul And lead you to your heav'n - ly goal."
5 Then let us fol - low Christ, our Lord, And take the cross ap - point - ed And, firm - ly cling - ing to His Word, In suf - f'ring be un - daunt - ed. For those who bear the bat - tle's strain The crown of heav'n - ly life ob - tain.

Text: Johann Scheffler, 1624–77, sts. 1–3, 5; *Geistliche Lieder und Lobgesänge*, 1695, st. 4; tr. Charles W. Schaeffer, 1813–96
Tune: Bartholomäus Gesius, c. 1555–1613, adapt.; setting: Johann Hermann Schein, 1586–1630

MACHS MIT MIR, GOTT
87 87 88

1 Peter 2:21–25; Matt. 16:24; John 8:12; Matt. 10:38–39

Let Me Be Thine Forever 689

1 Let me be Thine for - ev - er, My faith - ful God and Lord;
2 Lord Je - sus, my sal - va - tion, My light, my life di - vine,
3 And Thou, O Ho - ly Spir - it, My com - fort - er and guide,
Let me for-sake Thee nev - er Nor wan - der from Thy Word.
My on - ly con - so - la - tion, O make me whol - ly Thine!
Grant that in Je - sus' mer - it I al - ways may con - fide,
Lord, do not let me wa - ver, But give me stead - fast - ness,
For Thou hast dear - ly bought me With blood and bit - ter pain.
Him to the end con - fess - ing Whom I have known by faith.
And for such grace for - ev - er Thy ho - ly name I'll bless.
Let me, since Thou hast sought me, E - ter - nal life ob - tain.
Give me Thy con - stant bless - ing And grant a Chris - tian death.

Text: Nicolaus Selnecker, 1532–92, st. 1; *Gesang-Büchlein*, Rudolstadt, 1688, sts. 2–3;
tr. Matthias Loy, 1828–1915, alt.
Tune: *Musika Teutsch*, Nürnberg, 1532; setting: *The Lutheran Hymnal*, 1941

LOB GOTT GETROST MIT SINGEN
76 76 D

Ps. 119:10; Eph. 1:7; 2 Tim. 1:8–10; John 8:31

690 Hope of the World

1 Hope of the world, Thou Christ of great com - pas - sion;
2 Hope of the world, God's gift from high - est heav - en,
3 Hope of the world, a - foot on dust - y high - ways,
4 Hope of the world, who by Thy cross didst save us
Speak to our fear - ful hearts by con - flict rent.
Bring - ing to hun - gry souls the bread of life,
Show - ing to wan - d'ring souls the path of light,
From death and dark de - spair, from sin and guilt,
Save us, Thy peo - ple, from con - sum - ing pas - sion,
Still let Thy Spir - it un - to us be giv - en
Walk Thou be - side us lest the tempt - ing by - ways
We ren - der back the love Thy mer - cy gave us;
Who by our own false hopes and aims are spent.
To heal earth's wounds and end our bit - ter strife.
Lure us a - way from Thee to end - less night.
Take Thou our lives and use them as Thou wilt.

Text: Georgia Harkness, 1891–1974
Tune: Frances R. Havergal, 1836–79; setting: *The Lutheran Hymnal*, 1941

EIRENE
11 10 11 10

1 Tim. 1:1; Col. 2:13–15; Ps. 146:5–10; John 8:12

5 Hope of the world, O Christ, o'er death victorious,
Who by this sign didst conquer grief and pain,
We would be faithful to Thy Gospel glorious.
Thou art our Lord! Thou dost forever reign!

Fruitful Trees, the Spirit's Sowing 691

1 Fruit - ful trees, the Spir - it's sow-ing, May we rip - en and in - crease, Fruit to life e - ter - nal grow-ing, Rich in love and joy and peace.
2 Lad - en branch-es free - ly bear-ing Gifts the Giv - er loves to bless; Here is fruit that grows by shar - ing, Pa - tience, kind - ness, gen - tle - ness.
3 Root - ed deep in Christ our Mas-ter, Christ our pat - tern and our goal, Teach us, as the years fly fast - er, Good - ness, faith, and self - con - trol.
4 Fruit - ful trees, the Spir - it's tend-ing, May we grow till har - vests cease; Till we taste, in life un-end - ing, Heav - en's love and joy and peace.

Text: Timothy Dudley-Smith, b. 1926
Music: Ralph C. Schultz, b. 1932

DOROTHY
87 87

John 15:1–9; Gal. 5:22–23; Eph. 5:8–10; Luke 6:43–45

692 Praise to You and Adoration

1 Praise to You and ad - o - ra - tion, Bless - ed Je - sus,
2 Hold me ev - er in Your keep - ing; Com - fort me in
Son of God, Who, to serve Your own cre - a - tion, Came to
pain and strife. In my laugh - ter and my weep - ing Be with
share our flesh and blood. Guide me that I nev - er may
me through - out my life. Give me great - er love for You,
From Your fold or pas - tures stray, But with zeal and
And my faith and hope re - new In Your birth, Your
joy ex - ceed - ing Fol - low where Your steps are lead - ing.
life, and pas - sion, In Your death and res - ur - rec - tion.

Text: Thomas Hansen Kingo, 1634–1703; tr. Kristen Kvamme, 1866–1938, st. 1, alt.; tr. *Christian Worship,* 1993, st. 2
Tune: *Trente quatre Pseaumes de David*, Geneva, 1551, ed. Louis Bourgeois; setting: *The Lutheran Hymnal,* 1941

FREU DICH SEHR
87 87 77 88

2 Thess. 2:15–17; Matt. 20:26–28; John 10:27–28; 14:18

O Holy Spirit, Grant Us Grace 693

1 O Ho - ly Spir - it, grant us grace That we our Lord and Sav - ior
2 Help us that we Thy sav - ing Word In faith-ful hearts may trea - sure;
3 And when our earth - ly race is run, Death's bit - ter hour im - pend - ing,
In faith and fer - vent love em - brace And tru - ly serve Him ev - er.
Let e'er that Bread of Life af - ford New grace in rich - est mea - sure.
Then may Thy work in us be - gun Con - tin - ue till life's end - ing,
The hour of death can - not bring loss When we are shel - tered
O make us die to ev - 'ry sin, Each day cre - ate new
Un - til we glad - ly may com - mend Our souls in - to our
by the cross That can - celed our trans - gres - sions.
life with - in, That fruits of faith may flour - ish.
Sav - ior's hand, The crown of life ob - tain - ing.

Text: Bartholomäus Ringwaldt, 1532–99; tr. Oluf H. Smeby, 1851–1929, alt.
Tune: *Geistliche Lieder auffs new gebessert*, Wittenberg, 1535, ed. Joseph Klug;
setting: *The Lutheran Hymnal*, 1941

ES IST GEWISSLICH
87 87 887

Rom. 5:1–5; 1 Cor. 12:3; 1 Peter 2:21–25; 1 Cor. 9:24–25

Thee Will I Love, My Strength, My Tower

1 Thee will I love, my strength, my tow - er; Thee will I
2 Thee will I love, my life, my Sav - ior, Who art my
3 I thank Thee, Je - sus, Sun from heav - en, Whose ra - diance
4 O keep me watch - ful, then, and hum - ble; Per - mit me
love, my hope, my joy. Thee will I love with all my
best and tru - est friend. Thee will I love and praise for -
hath brought light to me; I thank Thee, who hast rich - ly
nev - er - more to stray. Up - hold me when my feet would
pow - er, With ar - dor time shall ne'er de - stroy. Thee will I
ev - er, For nev - er shall Thy kind - ness end. Thee will I
giv - en All that could make me glad and free; I thank Thee
stum - ble, And keep me on the nar - row way. Fill all my
love, O Light di - vine, So long as life is mine.
love with all my heart— Thou my Re - deem - er art!
that my soul is healed By what Thy lips re - vealed.
na - ture with Thy light, O Ra - diance strong and bright!

Text: Johann Scheffler, 1624–77; tr. Catherine Winkworth, 1827–78, alt.
Tune: *Harmonischer Lieder-Schatz*, Frankfurt, 1738; setting: *Christian Worship*, 1993

ICH WILL DICH LIEBEN
98 98 86

John 14:23; 1 John 4:19; John 8:12

5 Thee will I love, my crown of gladness;
Thee will I love, my God and Lord,
Amid the darkest depths of sadness,
And not for hope of high reward,
For Thine own sake, O Light divine,
So long as life is mine.

Not for Tongues of Heaven's Angels 695

1 Not for tongues of heav-en's an - gels, Not for wis - dom to dis - cern, Not for faith that mas-ters moun - tains, For this bet - ter gift we yearn:
2 Love is hum - ble, love is gen - tle, Love is ten - der, true, and kind; Love is gra - cious, ev - er pa - tient, Gen - er - ous of heart and mind:
3 Nev - er jeal - ous, nev - er self - ish, Love will not re - joice in wrong; Nev - er boast - ful nor re - sent - ful, Love be - lieves and suf - fers long:
4 In the day this world is fad - ing Faith and hope will play their part; But when Christ is seen in glo - ry Love shall reign in ev - 'ry heart:
May love be ours, O Lord.

Text: Timothy Dudley-Smith, b. 1926
Music: Peter W. Cutts, b. 1937

BRIDEGROOM
87 87 6

1 Corinthians 13

696 O God, My Faithful God

1 O God, my faith - ful God, True foun-tain ev - er flow - ing,
With - out whom noth - ing is, All per - fect gifts be - stow - ing:
Give me a health - y frame, And may I have with - in
A con - science free from blame, A soul un - stained by sin.

2 Grant me the strength to do With read - y heart and will - ing
What - ev - er You com - mand, My call - ing here ful - fill - ing;
That I do what I should While trust - ing You to bless
The out - come for my good, For You must give suc - cess.

3 Keep me from say - ing words That lat - er need re - call - ing;
Guard me lest i - dle speech May from my lips be fall - ing;
But when with - in my place I must and ought to speak,
Then to my words give grace Lest I of - fend the weak.

4 Lord, let me win my foes With kind - ly words and ac - tions,
And let me find good friends For coun - sel and cor - rec - tion.
Help me, as You have taught, To love both great and small
And by Your Spir - it's might To live in peace with all.

Text: Johann Heermann, 1585–1647; tr. Catherine Winkworth, 1827–78, alt.
Tune: *Neu-vermehrtes . . . Gesangbuch*, 3rd ed., Meiningen, 1693;
setting: *The Lutheran Hymnal*, 1941

O GOTT, DU FROMMER GOTT
67 67 66 66

1 John 5:14–15; James 1:5, 17; 1 Thess. 4:16–17

5 Let me depart this life
Confiding in my Savior;
By grace receive my soul
That it may live forever;
And let my body have
A quiet resting place
Within a Christian grave;
And let it sleep in peace.

6 And on that final day
When all the dead are waking,
Stretch out Your mighty hand,
My deathly slumber breaking.
Then let me hear Your voice,
Redeem this earthly frame,
And bid me to rejoice
With those who love Your name.

Awake, O Sleeper, Rise from Death 697

1 A - wake, O sleep - er, rise from death, And Christ shall give you light; So learn His love, its length and breadth, Its full - ness, depth, and height.
2 To us on earth He came to bring From sin and fear re - lease, To give the Spir - it's u - ni - ty, The ver - y bond of peace.
3 Then walk in love as Christ has loved, Who died that He might save; With kind and gen - tle hearts for - give As God in Christ for - gave.
4 For us Christ lived, for us He died, And con - quered in the strife; A - wake, a - rise, go forth in faith, And Christ shall give you life.

Text: F. Bland Tucker, 1895–1984
Tune: Carl G. Gläser, 1784–1829; setting: Lowell Mason, 1792–1872

AZMON
C M

Eph. 5:1–14; Eph. 3:16–19; 4:3–6

698 May We Thy Precepts, Lord, Fulfill

1 May we Thy pre - cepts, Lord, ful - fill And do on
2 So may we join Thy name to bless, Thy grace a -
3 Spir - it of life, of love and peace, U - nite our
earth our Fa - ther's will As an - gels do a - bove;
dore, Thy pow'r con - fess, From sin and strife to flee.
hearts, our joy in - crease, Thy gra - cious help sup - ply.
Still walk in Christ, the liv - ing way, With all Thy
One is our call - ing, one our name, The end of
To each of us the bless - ing give In Chris - tian
chil - dren and o - bey The law of Chris - tian love.
all our hopes the same, A crown of life with Thee.
fel - low - ship to live, In joy - ful hope to die.

Text: Edward Osler, 1798–1863, alt.
Music: Lowell Mason, 1792–1872

MERIBAH
886 886

Matt. 6:10; Ex. 20:3–17

I Heard the Voice of Jesus Say 699

1 I heard the voice of Je - sus say, "Come un - to Me and rest;
2 I heard the voice of Je - sus say, "Be - hold, I free - ly give
3 I heard the voice of Je - sus say, "I am this dark world's light.
Lay down, thou wea - ry one, lay down Thy head up - on My breast."
The liv - ing wa - ter; thirst - y one, Stoop down and drink and live."
Look un - to Me; thy morn shall rise And all thy day be bright."
I came to Je - sus as I was, So wea - ry, worn, and sad;
I came to Je - sus, and I drank Of that life - giv - ing stream;
I looked to Je - sus, and I found In Him my star, my sun;
I found in Him a rest - ing place, And He has made me glad.
My thirst was quenched, my soul re - vived, And now I live in Him.
And in that light of life I'll walk Till trav-'ling days are done.

Text: Horatius Bonar, 1808–89, alt.
Music: Amanda Husberg, b. 1940

SARAH-ELIZABETH
C M D

John 6:35; Matt. 11:28–29; John 7:37; 8:12

700 Love Divine, All Loves Excelling

1 Love divine, all loves excelling, Joy of heav'n, to earth come down! Fix in us Thy humble dwelling, All Thy faithful mercies crown. Jesus, Thou art all compassion, Pure, un-
2 Breathe, O breathe Thy loving Spirit Into ev'ry troubled breast; Let us all in Thee inherit; Let us find Thy promised rest. Take away the love of sinning; Alpha
3 Come, Almighty, to deliver; Let us all Thy life receive; Suddenly return, and never, Nevermore Thy temples leave. Thee we would be always blessing, Serve Thee
4 Finish then Thy new creation, Pure and spotless let us be; Let us see Thy great salvation Perfectly restored in Thee, Changed from glory into glory, Till in

Text: Charles Wesley, 1707–88
Tune: Rowland H. Prichard, 1811–87; setting: *Service Book and Hymnal*, 1958

HYFRYDOL
87 87 D

Ps. 85:7–8; 1 John 4:10; Rev. 7:9–17; 2 Cor. 5:17

bound - ed love Thou art; Vis - it us with
and O - me - ga be; End of faith, as
as Thy hosts a - bove, Pray and praise Thee
heav'n we take our place, Till we cast our
Thy sal - va - tion, En - ter ev - 'ry trem - bling heart.
its be - gin - ning, Set our hearts at lib - er - ty.
with - out ceas - ing, Glo - ry in Thy per - fect love.
crowns be - fore Thee, Lost in won - der, love, and praise!

In this the love of God was made manifest among us, that God sent His only Son into the world, so that we might live through Him. In this is love, not that we have loved God but that He loved us and sent His Son to be the propitiation for our sins. Beloved, if God so loved us, we also ought to love one another. 1 John 4:9–11

---

701 Draw Us to Thee

1 Draw us to Thee, For then shall we Walk in Thy steps for - ev - er And has - ten on Where Thou art gone To be with Thee, dear Sav - ior.
2 Draw us to Thee, Lord, lov - ing - ly; Let us de - part with glad - ness That we may be For - ev - er free From sor - row, grief, and sad - ness.
3 Draw us to Thee; O grant that we May walk the road to heav - en! Di - rect our way Lest we should stray And from Thy paths be driv - en.
4 Draw us to Thee That al - so we Thy heav'n - ly bliss in - her - it And ev - er dwell Where sin and hell No more can vex our spir - it.
5 Draw us to Thee Un - ceas - ing - ly, In - to Thy king - dom take us; Let us for - e'er Thy glo - ry share, Thy saints and joint heirs make us.

Text: Friedrich Funcke, 1642–99; tr. August Crull, 1845–1923, alt.
Tune: *As hymnodus sacer*, Leipzig, 1625; setting: *The Lutheran Hymnal*, 1941

ACH GOTT UND HERR
447 447

John 6:44–45; 1 Peter 2:21; Col. 1:12–14; Rom. 8:17

My Faith Looks Up to Thee 702

1 My faith looks up to Thee, Thou Lamb of Cal - va - ry,
2 May Thy rich grace im - part Strength to my faint - ing heart;
3 While life's dark maze I tread And griefs a - round me spread,
4 When ends life's tran - sient dream, When death's cold, sul - len stream
Sav - ior di - vine. Now hear me while I pray; Take all my
My zeal in - spire! As Thou hast died for me, Oh, may my
Be Thou my guide; Bid dark - ness turn to day, Wipe sor-row's
Shall o'er me roll, Blest Sav - ior, then, in love, Fear and dis -
guilt a - way; O let me from this day Be whol - ly Thine!
love to Thee Pure, warm, and change - less be, A liv - ing fire!
tears a - way, Nor let me ev - er stray From Thee a - side.
trust re-move; O bear me safe a - bove, A ran-somed soul!

Text: Ray Palmer, 1808–87
Music: Lowell Mason, 1792–1872

OLIVET
664 6664

John 1:29, 36; Heb. 12:2–3; Eph. 3:12; Rev. 2:10–11

703 How Can I Thank You, Lord

1 How can I thank You, Lord, For all Your lov - ing - kind - ness,
2 It is Your work a - lone That I am now con - vert - ed;
3 Lord, You have raised me up To joy and ex - ul - ta - tion
4 Grant that Your Spir - it's help To me be al - ways giv - en
That You have pa - tient - ly Borne with me in my blind - ness!
O'er Sa - tan's work in me You have Your pow'r as - sert - ed.
And clear - ly shown the way That leads me to sal - va - tion.
Lest I should fall a - gain And lose the way to heav - en.
When dead in man - y sins And tres - pass - es I lay,
Your mer - cy and Your grace That rise a - fresh each morn
My sins are washed a - way; For this I thank You, Lord.
Grant that He give me strength In my in - fir - mi - ty;
I kin - dled, ho - ly God, Your an - ger ev - 'ry day.
Have turned my ston - y heart In - to a heart new - born.
Now with my heart and soul All e - vil I ab - hor.
May He re - new my heart To serve You will - ing - ly.

Text: David Denicke, 1603–80; tr. August Crull, 1845–1923, alt.
Tune: *Neu-vermehrtes . . . Gesangbuch*, 3rd ed., Meiningen, 1693;
setting: *The Lutheran Hymnal*, 1941

O GOTT, DU FROMMER GOTT
67 67 66 66

Col. 1:12–14; Ps. 107:20–22; Eph. 2:8–10; Phil. 1:6

△ 5 O Father, God of love,
Now hear my supplication;
O Savior, Son of God,
Accept my adoration;
O Holy Spirit, be
My ever faithful guide
That I may serve You here
And there with You abide.

Renew Me, O Eternal Light 704

1 Re - new me, O e - ter - nal Light, And let my
2 Re - move the pow'r of sin from me And cleanse all
3 Cre - ate in me a new heart, Lord, That glad - ly
4 Grant that I on - ly You may love And seek those
heart and soul be bright, Il - lu - mined with the
my im - pu - ri - ty That I may have the
I o - bey Your Word. Let what You will be
things which are a - bove Till I be - hold You
light of grace That is - sues from Your ho - ly face.
strength and will Temp - ta - tions of the flesh to still.
my de - sire, And with new life my soul in - spire.
face to face, O Light e - ter - nal, through Your grace.

Text: Johann Friedrich Ruopp, 1672–1708; tr. August Crull, 1845–1923, alt.
Tune: *As hymnodus sacer*, Leipzig, 1625; setting: *The Lutheran Hymnal*, 1941

HERR JESU CHRIST, MEINS
L M

2 Cor. 3:18; Col. 3:1–10; Ps. 51:10–12

705 The Man Is Ever Blessed

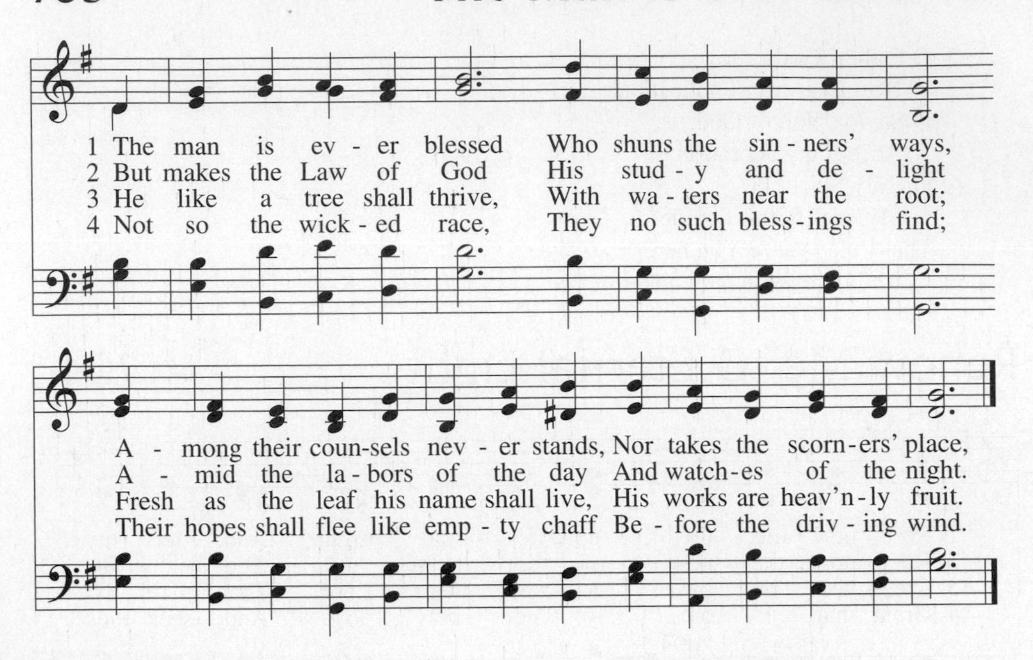
1 The man is ev - er blessed Who shuns the sin - ners' ways,
2 But makes the Law of God His stud - y and de - light
3 He like a tree shall thrive, With wa - ters near the root;
4 Not so the wick - ed race, They no such bless - ings find;
A - mong their coun - sels nev - er stands, Nor takes the scorn - ers' place,
A - mid the la - bors of the day And watch - es of the night.
Fresh as the leaf his name shall live, His works are heav'n - ly fruit.
Their hopes shall flee like emp - ty chaff Be - fore the driv - ing wind.

5 How will they bear to stand
Before the judgment seat
Where all the saints at
Christ's right hand
In full assembly meet?

6 He knows and He approves
The way the righteous go;
But sinners and their
works shall meet
A dreadful overthrow.

Text: Isaac Watts, 1674–1748, alt.
Tune: *Trente quatre Pseaumes de David*, Geneva, 1551, ed. Louis Bourgeois;
setting: *The Lutheran Hymnal*, 1941

ST. MICHAEL
S M

Ps. 1; 119:16, 35; Ps. 92:12–14; 145:20

706 Love in Christ Is Strong and Living

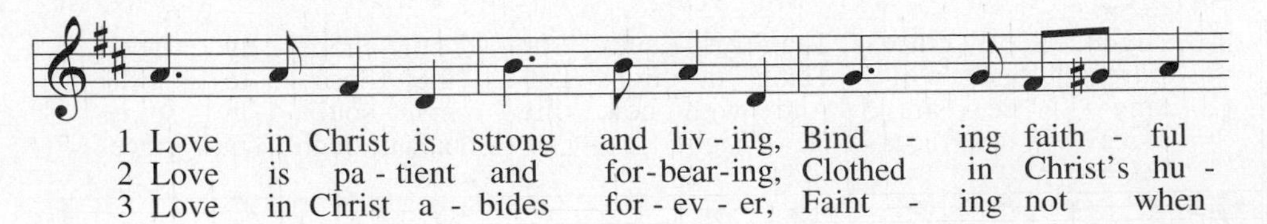
1 Love in Christ is strong and liv - ing, Bind - ing faith - ful
2 Love is pa - tient and for - bear - ing, Clothed in Christ's hu -
3 Love in Christ a - bides for - ev - er, Faint - ing not when

Hymn accompaniment: 691

Text: Dorothy R. Schultz, b. 1934
Tune: Ralph C. Schultz, b. 1932

DOROTHY
87 87

Col. 3:12–14; Eph. 5:2; 1 Corinthians 13; Eph. 4:2, 32

hearts in one; Love in Christ is true and giv - ing.
mil - i - ty, Gen - tle, self - less, kind, and car - ing,
ills at - tend; Love, for - giv - ing and for - giv - en,
May His will in us be done.
Reach - ing out in char - i - ty.
Shall en - dure un - til life's end.

Oh, That the Lord Would Guide My Ways 707

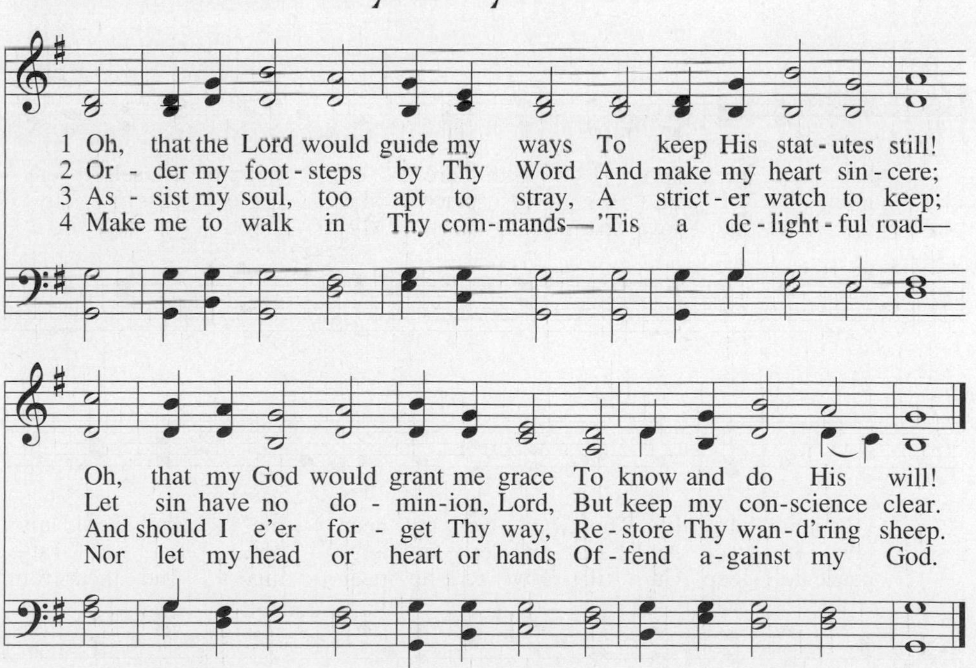
1 Oh, that the Lord would guide my ways To keep His stat - utes still!
2 Or - der my foot - steps by Thy Word And make my heart sin - cere;
3 As - sist my soul, too apt to stray, A strict - er watch to keep;
4 Make me to walk in Thy com - mands—'Tis a de - light - ful road—
Oh, that my God would grant me grace To know and do His will!
Let sin have no do - min - ion, Lord, But keep my con - science clear.
And should I e'er for - get Thy way, Re - store Thy wan - d'ring sheep.
Nor let my head or heart or hands Of - fend a - gainst my God.

Text: Isaac Watts, 1674–1748, alt.
Tune: William H. Havergal, 1793–1870; setting: *The Lutheran Hymnal*, 1941

EVAN
CM

Ps. 119:5, 33, 133, 176; Ezek. 34:11–12; Matt. 18:12–14

708 Lord, Thee I Love with All My Heart

1 Lord, Thee I love with all my heart; I pray Thee, ne'er from me de - part, With ten - der mer - cy cheer me. Earth has no plea - sure I would share. Yea, heav'n it - self were void and bare If Thou, Lord, wert not near me. And should my
2 Yea, Lord, 'twas Thy rich boun - ty gave My bod - y, soul, and all I have In this poor life of la - bor. Lord, grant that I in ev - 'ry place May glo - ri - fy Thy lav - ish grace And help and serve my neigh - bor. Let no false
3 Lord, let at last Thine an - gels come, To A - br'ham's bos - om bear me home, That I may die un - fear - ing; And in its nar - row cham - ber keep My bod - y safe in peace - ful sleep Un - til Thy re - ap - pear - ing. And then from

Text: Martin Schalling, 1532–1608; tr. Catherine Winkworth, 1827–78, alt.
Tune: *Zwey Bücher . . . Tabulatur*, Strassburg, 1577; setting: Friedrich Zipp, 1914–97

HERZLICH LIEB
887 887 88 88 88

1 John 4:19; 1 Peter 1:18–19; 4:11; 1 Thess. 4:14–17

heart for sor - row break, My trust in Thee can noth - ing shake.
doc - trine me be - guile; Let Sa - tan not my soul de - file.
death a - wak - en me, That these mine eyes with joy may see,
Thou art the por - tion I have sought; Thy pre - cious
Give strength and pa - tience un - to me To bear my
O Son of God, Thy glo - rious face, My Sav - ior
blood my soul has bought. Lord Je - sus Christ, my God and
cross and fol - low Thee. Lord Je - sus Christ, my God and
and my fount of grace. Lord Je - sus Christ, my prayer at -
Lord, my God and Lord, For - sake me not! I trust Thy Word.
Lord, my God and Lord, In death Thy com - fort still af - ford.
tend, my prayer at - tend, And I will praise Thee with - out end.

709 The King of Love My Shepherd Is

1 The King of love my shep - herd is, Whose good - ness
2 Where streams of liv - ing wa - ter flow, My ran - somed
3 Per - verse and fool - ish oft I strayed, But yet in
4 In death's dark vale I fear no ill With Thee, dear
fail - eth nev - er; I noth - ing lack if
soul He lead - eth And, where the ver - dant
love He sought me And on His shoul - der
Lord, be - side me, Thy rod and staff my
I am His And He is mine for - ev - er.
pas - tures grow, With food ce - les - tial feed - eth.
gent - ly laid And home re - joic - ing brought me.
com - fort still, Thy cross be - fore to guide me.

5 Thou spreadst a table in my sight;
Thine unction grace bestoweth;
And, oh, what transport of delight
From Thy pure chalice floweth!

6 And so through all the length of days
Thy goodness faileth never;
Good Shepherd, may I sing Thy praise
Within Thy house forever!

Text: Henry W. Baker, 1821–77
Tune: Irish, c. 18th cent.; setting: *Service Book and Hymnal*, 1958

ST. COLUMBA
87 87

Psalm 23; John 10:11; Luke 15:4–7; Rev. 7:17

The Lord's My Shepherd, I'll Not Want

1 The Lord's my shep - herd, I'll not want; He makes me down to lie In pas - tures green; He lead - eth me The qui - et wa - ters by.
2 My soul He doth re - store a - gain And me to walk doth make With - in the paths of righ - teous - ness, E'en for His own name's sake.
3 Yea, though I walk in death's dark vale, Yet will I fear no ill; For Thou art with me, and Thy rod And staff me com - fort still.
4 My ta - ble Thou hast fur - nish - ed In pres - ence of my foes; My head Thou dost with oil a - noint, And my cup o - ver - flows.
5 Good-ness and mer - cy all my life Shall sure - ly fol - low me; And in God's house for - ev - er - more My dwell - ing place shall be.

Text: *The Psalms of David in Meeter*, Edinburgh, 1650
Tune: William Gardiner, 1770–1853; setting: *The Lutheran Hymnal*, 1941

BELMONT
C M

Psalm 23; John 10:11; Rev. 7:17

711 Savior, like a Shepherd Lead Us

1 Sav - ior, like a shep - herd lead us; Much we
2 We are Yours; in love be - friend us, Be the
3 You have prom - ised to re - ceive us, Poor and
4 Ear - ly let us seek Your fa - vor, Ear - ly
need Your ten - der care. In Your pleas - ant pas - tures
guard - ian of our way; Keep Your flock, from sin de -
sin - ful though we be; You have mer - cy to re -
let us do Your will; Bless - ed Lord and on - ly
feed us, For our use Your fold pre - pare.
fend us, Seek us when we go a - stray.
lieve us, Grace to cleanse, and pow'r to free.
Sav - ior, With Your love our spir - its fill.
Bless - ed Je - sus, bless - ed Je - sus, You have
Bless - ed Je - sus, bless - ed Je - sus, Hear us
Bless - ed Je - sus, bless - ed Je - sus, Ear - ly
Bless - ed Je - sus, bless - ed Je - sus, You have

Text: *Hymns for the Young*, 4th ed., London, 1836, alt.
Music: William B. Bradbury, 1816–68

BRADBURY
87 87 87

Psalm 23; John 10:1–16; Eph. 2:4–5; Rom. 5:8

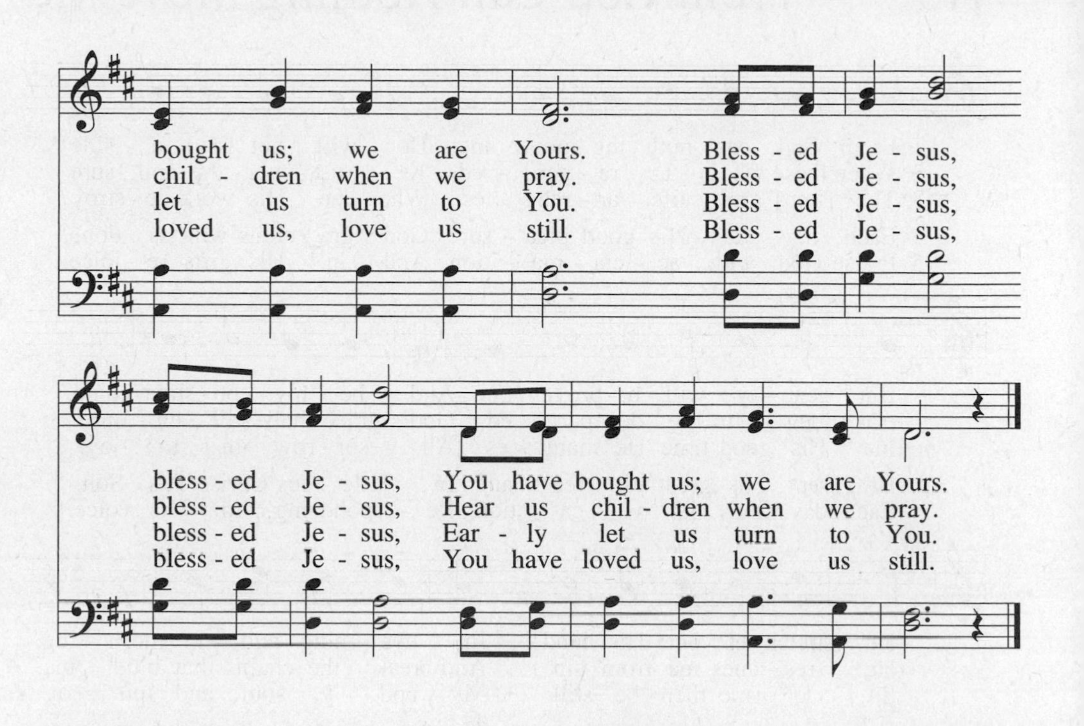

bought us; we are Yours. Bless - ed Je - sus,
chil - dren when we pray. Bless - ed Je - sus,
let us turn to You. Bless - ed Je - sus,
loved us, love us still. Bless - ed Je - sus,
bless - ed Je - sus, You have bought us; we are Yours.
bless - ed Je - sus, Hear us chil - dren when we pray.
bless - ed Je - sus, Ear - ly let us turn to You.
bless - ed Je - sus, You have loved us, love us still.

Seek Ye First 712

1 Seek ye first the king - dom of God, And His
2 Ask and it shall be giv - en un - to you, Seek and
3 Man does not live by bread a - lone, But by
righ - teous - ness. And all these things shall be
ye shall find, Knock and the door shall be
ev - 'ry word That pro - ceeds from the
add - ed un - to you! Al - le - lu, al - le - lu - ia!
o - pened un - to you, Al - le - lu, al - le - lu - ia!
mouth of the Lord, Al - le - lu, al - le - lu - ia!

Setting available in hymn accompaniment edition.

Text: Karen Lafferty, b. 1948
Tune: Karen Lafferty, b. 1948

SEEK YE FIRST
Irregular meter

Matt. 6:33; 7:7; Matt. 4:4

713 From God Can Nothing Move Me

1 From God can noth - ing move me; He will not step a - side
2 When those whom I re - gard - ed As trust - wor - thy and sure
3 The Lord my life ar - rang - es; Who can His work de - stroy?

4 Each day at His good plea - sure God's gra - cious will is done.
5 Praise God with ac - cla - ma - tion And in His gifts re - joice.

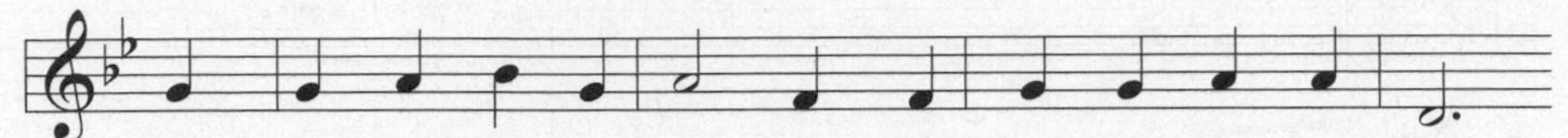

But gent - ly will re - prove me And be my con - stant guide.
Have long from me de - part - ed, God's grace shall still en - dure.
In His good time He chang - es All sor - row in - to joy.

He sent His great - est trea - sure In Je - sus Christ, His Son.
Each day finds its vo - ca - tion Re - spond - ing to His voice.

He stretch - es out His hand In eve - ning and in morn - ing,
He res - cues me from sin And breaks the chains that bind me.
So let me then be still: My bod - y, soul, and spir - it

He ev - 'ry gift im - parts. The bread of earth and heav - en
Soon years on earth are past; But time we spend ex - press - ing

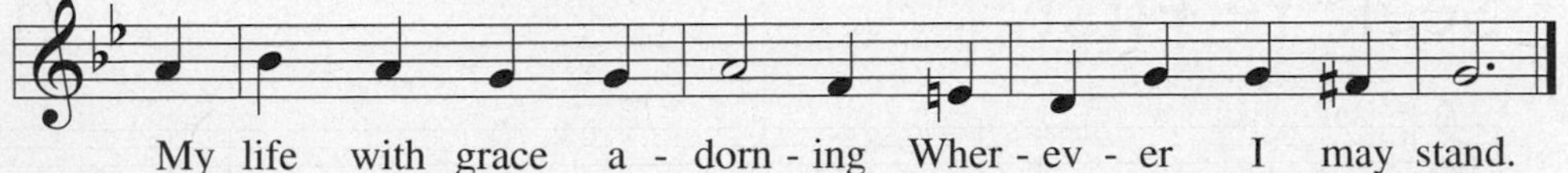

My life with grace a - dorn - ing Wher - ev - er I may stand.
I leave death's fear be - hind me; His peace I have with - in.
His ten - der care in - her - it Ac - cord - ing to His will.

Are by His kind - ness giv - en. Praise Him with thank - ful hearts!
The love of God brings bless - ing That will for - ev - er last!

6 Yet even though I suffer
The world's unpleasantness,
And though the days grow rougher
And bring me great distress,
That day of bliss divine,
Which knows no end or measure,
And Christ, who is my pleasure,
Forever shall be mine.

△ 7 For thus the Father willed it,
Who fashioned us from clay;
And His own Son fulfilled it
And brought eternal day.
The Spirit now has come,
To us true faith has given;
He leads us home to heaven.
O praise the Three in One!

Setting available in hymn accompaniment edition.

Text: Ludwig Helmbold, 1532–98; tr. Gerald Thorson, 1921–2001, sts. 1–2, 6, alt.; tr. *Lutheran Service Book*, 2006, st. 3; tr. Gregory J. Wismar, b. 1946, sts. 4–5; tr. Joseph Herl, b. 1959, st. 7
Tune: *Recueil de plusieurs chansons*, Lyons, 1557, alt.

VON GOTT WILL ICH NICHT LASSEN
76 76 67 76

Rom. 8:38–39; Joshua 24:16; Ps. 73:23

Who Trusts in God a Strong Abode 714

1 Who trusts in God A strong a - bode In heav'n and
2 Though Sa - tan's wrath Be - set our path And world - ly
3 In all the strife Of mor - tal life Our feet will
earth pos - sess - es; Who looks in
scorn as - sail us, While You are
stand se - cure - ly; Temp - ta - tion's
love To Christ a - bove, No fear that heart op -
near, We shall not fear; Your strength will nev - er
hour Will lose its pow'r, For You will guard us
press - es. In You a - lone, Dear Lord, we own Sweet
fail us. Your rod and staff Will keep us safe And
sure - ly. O God, re - new With heav'n - ly dew Our
hope and con - so - la - tion, Our shield from foes, Our balm for
guide our steps for - ev - er; Nor shades of death Nor hell be -
bod - y, soul, and spir - it Un - til we stand At Your right
woes, Our great and sure sal - va - tion.
neath Our lives from You will sev - er.
hand Through Je - sus' sav - ing mer - it.

Setting available in hymn accompaniment edition.

Text: Joachim Magdeburg, c. 1525–after 1587, st. 1; *Harmonia cantionum*, Leipzig, 1597, sts. 2–3; tr. Benjamin H. Kennedy, 1804–99, alt.
Tune: Claudin de Sermisy, c. 1490–1562

WAS MEIN GOTT WILL (Rhythmic)
87 87 D

Ps. 73:25–26; Heb. 12:2–3; Rom. 8:38–39; Titus 3:5–7

715 Jesus, Savior, Pilot Me

1 Je - sus, Sav - ior, pi - lot me O - ver life's tem - pes - tuous sea; Un - known waves be - fore me roll, Hid - ing rock and treach - 'rous shoal. Chart and com - pass come from Thee. Je - sus, Sav - ior, pi - lot me.
2 As a moth - er stills her child, Thou canst hush the o - cean wild; Bois - t'rous waves o - bey Thy will When Thou say'st to them, "Be still!" Won - drous Sov - 'reign of the sea, Je - sus, Sav - ior, pi - lot me.
3 When at last I near the shore And the fear - ful break - ers roar 'Twixt me and the peace - ful rest, Then, while lean - ing on Thy breast, May I hear Thee say to me, "Fear not, I will pi - lot thee."

Text: Edward Hopper, 1818–88
Music: John E. Gould, 1822–75

PILOT
77 77 77

Matt. 8:23–27

I Walk in Danger All the Way 716

1 I walk in dan - ger all the way. The thought shall nev - er
2 I pass through tri - als all the way, With sin and ills con -
3 And death pur - sues me all the way, No - where I rest se -
4 I walk with an - gels all the way, They shield me and be -
leave me That Sa - tan, who has marked his prey, Is plot - ting
tend - ing; In pa - tience I must bear each day The cross of
cure - ly; He comes by night, he comes by day, He takes his
friend me; All Sa - tan's pow'r is held at bay When heav'n - ly
to de - ceive me. This foe with hid - den snares
God's own send - ing. When in ad - ver - si - ty
prey most sure - ly. A fail - ing breath, and I
hosts at - tend me; They are my sure de - fense,
May seize me un - a - wares If I should fail to
I know not where to flee, When storms of woe my
In death's strong grasp may lie To face e - ter - ni -
All fear and sor - row, hence! Un - harmed by foes, do
watch and pray. I walk in dan - ger all the way.
soul dis - may, I pass through tri - als all the way.
ty to - day As death pur - sues me all the way.
what they may, I walk with an - gels all the way.

5 I walk with Jesus all the way,
His guidance never fails me;
Within His wounds I find a stay
When Satan's pow'r assails me;
And by His footsteps led,
My path I safely tread.
No evil leads my soul astray;
I walk with Jesus all the way.

6 My walk is heav'nward all the way;
Await, my soul, the morrow,
When God's good healing shall allay
All suff'ring, sin, and sorrow.
Then, worldly pomp, begone!
To heav'n I now press on.
For all the world I would not stay;
My walk is heav'nward all the way.

Setting available in hymn accompaniment edition.

Text: Hans Adolf Brorson, 1694–1764; tr. Ditlef G. Ristad, 1863–1938, alt.
Tune: *Geist-reiches Gesang-Buch*, 4th ed., Halle, 1708, ed. Johann A. Freylinghausen

DER LIEBEN SONNE LICHT UND PRACHT
87 87 66 88

1 Peter 5:8–9; John 10:4, 27–29; John 6:39; Is. 51:11

717 Eternal Father, Strong to Save

1 E - ter - nal Fa - ther, strong to save, Whose arm hath bound the rest - less wave, Who bidd'st the might - y o - cean deep Its own ap - point - ed lim - its keep: O hear us when we cry to Thee For those in per - il on the sea.
2 O Christ, the Lord of hill and plain, O'er which our traf - fic runs a - main By moun - tain pass or val - ley low; Wher - ev - er, Lord, Thy peo - ple go, Pro - tect them by Thy guard - ing hand From ev - 'ry per - il on the land.
3 O Spir - it, whom the Fa - ther sent To spread a - broad the fir - ma - ment; O Wind of heav - en, by Thy might Save all who dare the ea - gle's flight, And keep them by Thy watch - ful care From ev - 'ry per - il in the air.
4 O Trin - i - ty of love and pow'r, Our peo - ple shield in dan - ger's hour; From rock and tem - pest, fire and foe, Pro - tect them where - so - e'er they go; Thus ev - er - more shall rise to Thee Glad praise from air and land and sea.

This hymn is appropriate at times of travel.

Text: William Whiting, 1825–78, sts. 1, *2, *3, 4, alt.; Robert N. Spencer, 1877–1961, sts. 2–3, alt.
Music: John B. Dykes, 1823–76

MELITA
88 88 88

Gen. 1:1–10; Psalm 3; Matt. 8:23–27; 14:22–33

The following stanzas from the original Navy Hymn may be substituted:

*2 O Christ, whose voice the waters heard
And hushed their raging at Thy word,
Who walkedst on the foaming deep
And calm amid its rage didst sleep:
O hear us when we cry to Thee
For those in peril on the sea.

*3 Most Holy Spirit, who didst brood
Upon the chaos dark and rude,
And bid its angry tumult cease,
And give, for wild confusion, peace:
O hear us when we cry to Thee
For those in peril on the sea.

Jesus, Lead Thou On 718

1 Je - sus, lead Thou on Till our rest is won; And al-though the
2 If the way be drear, If the foe be near, Let not faith-less
3 When we seek re - lief From a long-felt grief, When temp - ta - tions
4 Je - sus, lead Thou on Till our rest is won. Heav'n-ly lead - er,
way be cheer - less, We will fol - low calm and fear - less.
fears o'er - take us; Let not faith and hope for - sake us;
come al - lur - ing, Make us pa - tient and en - dur - ing.
still di - rect us, Still sup - port, con - sole, pro - tect us,
Guide us by Thy hand To our fa - ther - land.
For through man - y a woe To our home we go.
Show us that bright shore Where we weep no more.
Till we safe - ly stand In our fa - ther - land.

Text: Nicolaus Ludwig von Zinzendorf, 1700–60; tr. Jane L. Borthwick, 1813–97, alt.
Tune: Adam Drese, 1620–1701; setting: Joseph Herl, b. 1959

SEELENBRÄUTIGAM
55 88 55

Luke 12:32; 1 Peter 2:20b–21; 1 Cor. 10:13; James 1:12

719 I Leave All Things to God's Direction

1 I leave all things to God's di - rec - tion; He loves me both in joy and woe. His will is good, sure His af - fec - tion; His ten - der love is true, I know. My for - tress and my rock is He: What pleas - es God, that pleas - es me.
2 God knows what must be done to save me; His love for me will nev - er cease. Up - on His hands He did en - grave me With pur - est gold of lov - ing grace. His will su - preme must ev - er be: What pleas - es God, that pleas - es me.
3 My God de - sires the soul's sal - va - tion; My soul He, too, de - sires to save. There - fore with Chris - tian res - ig - na - tion All earth - ly trou - bles I will brave. His will be done e - ter - nal - ly: What pleas - es God, that pleas - es me.
4 My God has all things in His keep - ing; He is the ev - er faith - ful friend. He gives me laugh - ter af - ter weep - ing, And all His ways in bless - ings end. His love en - dures e - ter - nal - ly: What pleas - es God, that pleas - es me.

Text: Salomo Franck, 1659–1725; tr. August Crull, 1845–1923, alt.
Tune: Georg Neumark, 1621–81; setting: *Service Book and Hymnal*, 1958

WER NUR DEN LIEBEN GOTT
98 98 88

Rom. 8:28; 2 Peter 3:9; Is. 38:17; Jer. 29:11

We Walk by Faith and Not by Sight 720

1 We walk by faith and not by sight, No gracious words we hear From Him who spoke as none e'er spoke, But we believe Him near.
2 We may not touch His hands and side, Nor follow where He trod; But in His promise we rejoice And cry "My Lord and God!"
3 Help then, O Lord, our unbelief; And may our faith abound To call on You when You are near And seek where You are found.
4 For You, O resurrected Lord, Are found in means divine: Beneath the water and the Word, Beneath the bread and wine.
5 Lord, when our life of faith is done, In realms of clearer light We may behold You as You are, With full and endless sight.

Text: Henry Alford, 1810–71, alt.
Tune: Marty Haugen, b. 1950; setting: Randall Sensmeier, b. 1948

SHANTI
C M

2 Cor. 5:7; Heb. 12:2; John 20:29

721 Lead Me, Guide Me

Refrain
Lead me, guide me, a - long the way;
For if You lead me, I can - not stray.
Lord, let me walk each day with Thee.
Lead me, O Lord, lead me.
1 I am weak and I need Thy strength and pow'r
2 Help me tread in the paths of righ - teous - ness,
3 I am lost if You take Your hand from me,
To help me o - ver my weak - est hour.
Be my aid when Sa - tan and sin op - press.
I am blind with - out Thy light to see.
Help me through the dark - ness Thy face to see.
I am put - ting all my trust in Thee.
Lord, al - ways let me Thy ser - vant be.
Refrain
Lead me, O Lord, lead me.

Setting available in hymn accompaniment edition.

Text: Doris M. Akers, 1922–95
Tune: Doris M. Akers, 1922–95

LEAD ME
Irregular meter

Ps. 5:8; 25:5

Lord, Take My Hand and Lead Me 722

1 Lord, take my hand and lead me Up - on life's way;
2 Lord, when the tem - pest ra - ges, I need not fear,
3 Lord, when the shad - ows length - en And night has come,
Di - rect, pro - tect, and feed me From day to day.
For You, the Rock of A - ges, Are al - ways near.
I know that You will strength - en My steps toward home.
With - out Your grace and fa - vor I go a - stray;
Close by Your side a - bid - ing, I fear no foe,
Then noth - ing can im - pede me, O bless - ed Friend;
So take my hand, O Sav - ior, And lead the way.
For when Your hand is guid - ing, In peace I go.
So take my hand and lead me Un - to the end.

Text: Julie von Hausmann, 1825–1901; tr. *Lutheran Book of Worship*, 1978, alt.
Tune: P. Friedrich Silcher, 1789–1860; setting: *Service Book and Hymnal*, 1958

SO NIMM DENN MEINE HÄNDE
74 74 D

John 10:27–28; Psalm 23; Ps. 5:8; 121:4–7

723 The Lord Is My Light

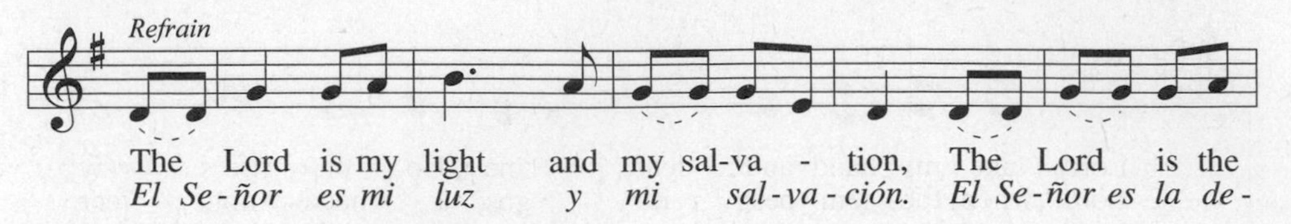
Refrain
The Lord is my light and my sal-va - tion, The Lord is the
El Se-ñor es mi luz y mi sal-va-ción. El Se-ñor es la de-

strong-hold of my life. Since the Lord is my life, my
fen - sa de mi vi - da. Si el Se - ñor es mi luz, ¿a

To Stanzas
strength, and my all, Whom then shall I fear?
quién te - me - ré? ¿Quién me ha - rá tem - blar?

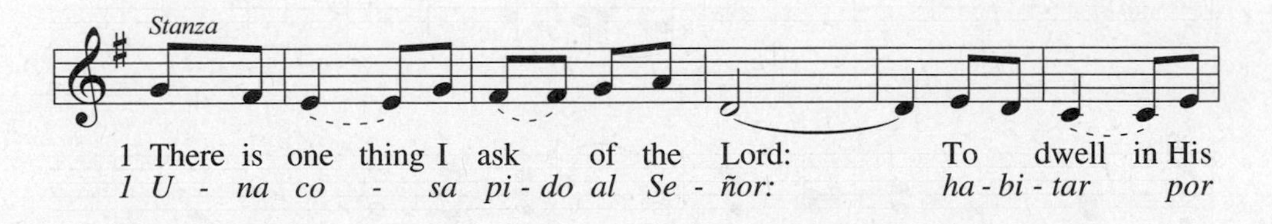
Stanza
1 There is one thing I ask of the Lord: To dwell in His
1 U - na co - sa pi - do al Se - ñor: ha - bi - tar por

house for - ev - er, To gaze on the beau-ty of the
siem - pre en su ca - sa, go - zar de la ter - nu - ra del Se -

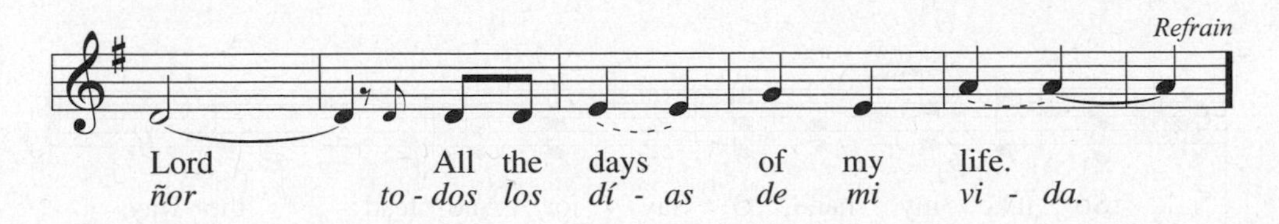
Refrain
Lord All the days of my life.
ñor to - dos los dí - as de mi vi - da.

Setting available in hymn accompaniment edition.

Text: Alberto Taulé, 1932–2007; tr. Lorraine Florindez, 1926–2011; tr. Jon D. Vieker, b. 1961
Tune: Alberto Taulé, 1932–2007

EL SEÑOR ES MI LUZ
Irregular meter

Psalm 27

Stanza
2 Do not hide Your face, O Lord; Ev-'ry day I will
2 No me es-con-das tu ros-tro, Se-ñor, bus-ca-ré to-do el
seek Your face. Though my fa-ther and moth-er may for-
dí-a tu ros-tro. Si mi pa-dre y mi ma-dre me a-ban-
Refrain
sake me, The Lord will re-ceive me.
do-nan, el Se-ñor me a-co-ge-rá.
Stanza
3 Teach me, Lord, and keep me on Your paths; Guide me, Lord, a-
3 Oh Se-ñor, en-sé-ña-me el ca-mi-no, guí-a-me por la
long a lev-el way. I will gaze on the good-ness of the
sen-da ver-da-de-ra. Go-za-ré de la di-cha del Se-
Refrain
Lord In the land of all the liv-ing.
ñor en la tie-rra de la vi-da.

724 If God Himself Be for Me

1 If God Him-self be for me, I may a host de-fy;
2 I build on this foun-da-tion, That Je-sus and His blood
3 Christ Je-sus is my splen-dor, My sun, my light, a-lone;
4 He can-celed my of-fens-es, De-liv-ered me from death;
5 For no one can con-demn me Or set my hope a-side;
6 Who clings with res-o-lu-tion To Him whom Sa-tan hates
For when I pray, be-fore me My foes, con-found-ed, fly.
A-lone are my sal-va-tion, My true, e-ter-nal good.
Were He not my de-fend-er Be-fore God's judg-ment throne,
He is the Lord who cleans-es My soul from sin through faith.
Now hell no more can claim me: Its fu-ry I de-ride.
Must look for per-se-cu-tion; For him the bur-den waits
If Christ, my head and mas-ter, Be-friend me from a-bove,
With-out Him all that pleas-es Is val-ue-less on earth;
I nev-er should find fa-vor And mer-cy in His sight,
In Him I can be cheer-ful, Cou-ra-geous on my way;
No sen-tence now re-proves me, No guilt de-stroys my peace;
Of mock-'ry, shame, and loss-es Heaped on his blame-less head;
What foe or what dis-as-ter Can drive me from His love?
The gifts I have from Je-sus A-lone have price-less worth.
But be de-stroyed for-ev-er As dark-ness by the light.
In Him I am not fear-ful Of God's great Judg-ment Day.
For Christ, my Sav-ior, loves me And shields me with His grace.
A thou-sand plagues and cross-es Will be his dai-ly bread.

7 From me this is not hidden,
Yet I am not afraid;
I leave my cares, as bidden,
To whom my vows were paid.
Though life from me be taken
And ev'rything I own,
I trust in You unshaken
And cleave to You alone.

8 No danger, thirst, or hunger,
No pain or poverty,
No earthly tyrant's anger
Shall ever vanquish me.
Though earth should break asunder,
My fortress You shall be;
No fire or sword or thunder
Shall sever You from me.

Setting available in hymn accompaniment edition.

Text: Paul Gerhardt, 1607–76; tr. *Evangelical Lutheran Hymn-Book*, Pittsburgh, 1907, sts. 1, 3–5, 10, alt.; tr. Richard Massie, 1800–87, sts. 2, 6–9, alt.
Tune: *Vierundzwanzig geistliche Lieder*, Augsburg, 1609

IST GOTT FÜR MICH
76 76 D

Rom. 8:31–39; Is. 50:7–9; Ps. 118:6; 1 Peter 1:3–9

9 No angel and no gladness,
No throne, no pomp, no show,
No love, no hate, no sadness,
No pain, no depth of woe,
No scheming, no contrivance,
No subtle thing or great
Shall draw me from Your guidance
Nor from You separate.

10 My heart with joy is springing;
I am no longer sad.
My soul is filled with singing;
Your sunshine makes me glad.
The sun that cheers my spirit
Is Jesus Christ, my King;
The heav'n I shall inherit
Makes me rejoice and sing.

Children of the Heavenly Father 725

1 Chil - dren of the heav'n - ly Fa - ther Safe - ly
2 God His own doth tend and nour - ish; In His
3 Nei - ther life nor death shall ev - er From the
4 Though He giv - eth or He tak - eth, God His

in His bos - om gath - er; Nest - ling bird nor star in
ho - ly courts they flour - ish. From all e - vil things He
Lord His chil - dren sev - er; Un - to them His grace He
chil - dren ne'er for - sak - eth; His the lov - ing pur - pose

heav - en Such a ref - uge e'er was giv - en.
spares them; In His might - y arms He bears them.
show - eth, And their sor - rows all He know - eth.
sole - ly To pre - serve them pure and ho - ly.

Text: Carolina Sandell Berg, 1832–1903; tr. Ernst W. Olson, 1870–1958
Music: *Lofsånger och andeliga wisor*, Sweden, 1873

TRYGGARE KAN INGEN VARA
88 88 (Trochaic)

Rom. 8:14–17, 35–39; Matt. 6:26–27; Eph. 5:25–27

726 Evening and Morning

1 Eve-ning and morn-ing, Sun-set and dawn-ing, Wealth, peace, and glad-ness, Com-fort in sad-ness: These are Thy works; all the glo-ry be Thine! Times with-out num-ber, A-wake or in slum-ber, Thine eye ob-serves us, From dan-ger pre-serves us, Caus-ing Thy mer-cy up-on us to shine.
2 Fa-ther, O hear me, Par-don and spare me; Calm all my ter-rors, Blot out my er-rors That by Thine eyes they may no more be scanned. Or-der my go-ings, Di-rect all my do-ings; As it may please Thee, Re-tain or re-lease me; All I com-mit to Thy fa-ther-ly hand.
3 Ills that still grieve me Soon are to leave me; Though bil-lows tow-er, And winds gain pow-er, Af-ter the storm the fair sun shows its face. Joys e'er in-creas-ing And peace nev-er ceas-ing: These shall I trea-sure And share in full mea-sure When in His man-sions God grants me a place.
4 To God in heav-en All praise be giv-en! Come, let us of-fer And glad-ly prof-fer To the Cre-a-tor the gifts He doth prize. He well re-ceiv-eth A heart that be-liev-eth; Hymns that a-dore Him Are pre-cious be-fore Him And to His throne like sweet in-cense a-rise.

Setting available in hymn accompaniment edition.

Text: Paul Gerhardt, 1607–76; tr. Richard Massie, 1800–87, sts. 1–2, alt.;
tr. Hermann H. M. Brueckner, 1866–1942, sts. 3–4, alt.
Tune: Johann G. Ebeling, 1637–76

DIE GÜLDNE SONNE
55 55 10 56 56 10

Psalm 145; Psalm 33; Ps. 40:5; 1 Peter 5:7

On Eagles' Wings 727

1 You who dwell in the shel - ter of the Lord, Who a -
2 snare of the fowl - er will nev - er cap - ture you, And
3 You need not fear the ter - ror of the night, Nor the
4 For to His an - gels He's giv - en a com - mand To
bide in His shad - ow for life,
fam - ine will bring you no fear;
ar - row that flies by day; Though
guard you in all of your ways; Up -
Say to the Lord: "My ref - uge, My
Un - der His wings your ref - uge, His
thou - sands fall a - bout you,
on their hands they will bear you up, Lest you
rock in whom I trust!"
faith - ful - ness your shield.
Near you it shall not come.
dash your foot a - gainst a stone.
Refrain
And He will raise you up on ea - gles' wings,
Bear you on the breath of dawn, Make you to shine like the
sun, And hold you in the palm of His hand. 2 The

Setting available in hymn accompaniment edition.

Text: Michael Joncas, b. 1951
Tune: Michael Joncas, b. 1951

ON EAGLES' WINGS
Irregular meter

Ps. 91:1–12; 103:5; Is. 40:31; Ex. 19:4

728 How Firm a Foundation

1 How firm a foun - da - tion, O saints of the Lord,
2 "Fear not! I am with you, O be not dis - mayed,
3 "The soul that on Je - sus has leaned for re - pose
4 "When through fi - ery tri - als your path - way will lie,
Is laid for your faith in His ex - cel - lent Word!
For I am your God and will still give you aid;
I will not, I will not, de - sert to his foes;
My grace, all - suf - fi - cient, will be your sup - ply.
What more can He say than to you He has said
I'll strength - en you, help you, and cause you to stand,
That soul, though all hell should en - deav - or to shake,
The flames will not hurt you; I on - ly de - sign
Who un - to the Sav - ior for ref - uge have fled?
Up - held by My righ - teous, om - nip - o - tent hand.
I'll nev - er, no nev - er, no nev - er, for - sake!
Your dross to con - sume and your gold to re - fine.

Text: *A Selection of Hymns*, London, 1787, alt.
Tune: *Genuine Church Music*, Winchester, 1832; setting: Joseph Herl, b. 1959

FOUNDATION
11 11 11 11

Is. 28:16; 41:10; 43:1–7; 2 Cor. 12:9

5 "Throughout all their lifetime My people will prove
My sov'reign, eternal, unchangeable love;
And then, when gray hairs will their temples adorn,
Like lambs they will still in My bosom be borne."

I Am Trusting Thee, Lord Jesus 729

1 I am trust-ing Thee, Lord Je - sus, Trust-ing on - ly Thee;
2 I am trust-ing Thee for par - don; At Thy feet I bow,
3 I am trust-ing Thee for cleans-ing In the crim-son flood;
4 I am trust-ing Thee to guide me; Thou a - lone shalt lead,
Trust-ing Thee for full sal - va - tion, Great and free.
For Thy grace and ten - der mer - cy Trust - ing now.
Trust-ing Thee to make me ho - ly By Thy blood.
Ev - 'ry day and hour sup - ply - ing All my need.

5 I am trusting Thee for power;
Thine can never fail.
Words which Thou Thyself shalt give me
Must prevail.

6 I am trusting Thee, Lord Jesus;
Never let me fall.
I am trusting Thee forever
And for all.

Text: Frances R. Havergal, 1836–79
Tune: Henry W. Baker, 1821–77; setting: *The Lutheran Hymnal*, 1941

STEPHANOS
85 83

Is. 12:2; Matt. 28:18–20; Is. 26:3

730 What Is the World to Me

1 What is the world to me With all its vaunt - ed plea - sure
2 The world seeks to be praised And hon - ored by the might - y
3 The world seeks af - ter wealth And all that mam - mon of - fers
4 What is the world to me! My Je - sus is my trea - sure,
When You, and You a - lone, Lord Je - sus, are my trea - sure!
Yet nev - er once re - flects That they are frail and flight - y.
Yet nev - er is con - tent Though gold should fill its cof - fers.
My life, my health, my wealth, My friend, my love, my plea - sure,
You on - ly, dear - est Lord, My soul's de - light shall be;
But what I tru - ly prize A - bove all things is He,
I have a high - er good, Con - tent with it I'll be:
My joy, my crown, my all, My bliss e - ter - nal - ly.
You are my peace, my rest. What is the world to me!
My Je - sus, He a - lone. What is the world to me!
My Je - sus is my wealth. What is the world to me!
Once more, then, I de - clare: What is the world to me!

Text: Georg Michael Pfefferkorn, 1645–1732; tr. August Crull, 1845–1923, alt.
Tune: Ahasverus Fritsch, 1629–1701; setting: *Lutheran Service Book*, 2006

WAS FRAG ICH NACH DER WELT
67 67 66 66

1 John 2:15–17; Phil. 3:7–9; Ps. 73:25; Rom. 12:2

O God, Forsake Me Not 731

1 O God, for-sake me not! Your gra-cious pres-ence lend me;
2 O God, for-sake me not! Take not Your Spir - it from me;
3 O God, for-sake me not! Lord, hear my sup-pli - ca - tion!
4 O God, for-sake me not! Lord, I am Yours for - ev - er.
Lord, lead Your help-less child; Your Ho-ly Spir-it send me
Do not per-mit the might Of sin to o-ver-come me.
In ev-'ry e-vil hour Help me re-sist temp-ta - tion;
O keep me strong in faith That I may leave You nev - er.
That I my course may run. O be my light, my lot,
In-crease my fee-ble faith, Which You a-lone have wrought.
And when the prince of hell My con-science seeks to blot,
Grant me a bless-ed end When my good fight is fought;
My staff, my rock, my shield— O God, for-sake me not!
O be my strength and pow'r— O God, for-sake me not!
Be then not far from me— O God, for-sake me not!
Help me in life and death— O God, for-sake me not!

Text: Salomo Franck, 1659–1725; tr. August Crull, 1845–1923, alt.
Tune: *Neu-vermehrtes . . . Gesangbuch*, 3rd ed., Meiningen, 1693;
setting: *The Lutheran Hymnal*, 1941

O GOTT, DU FROMMER GOTT
67 67 66 66

Ps. 38:21–22; Ps. 22:11, 19; Psalm 71; Ps. 27:9

732 All Depends on Our Possessing

1 All de - pends on our pos - sess - ing God's a - bun - dant
2 He who to this day has fed me And to man - y
3 Man - y spend their lives in fret - ting O - ver tri - fles
4 When with sor - row I am strick - en, Hope a - new my
grace and bless - ing, Though all earth - ly wealth de - part.
joys has led me Is and ev - er shall be mine.
and in get - ting Things that have no sol - id ground.
heart will quick - en; All my long - ing shall be stilled.
They who trust with faith un - shak - en By their God are
He who ev - er gent - ly schools me, He who dai - ly
I shall strive to win a trea - sure That will bring me
To His lov - ing - kind - ness ten - der Soul and bod - y
not for - sak - en And will keep a daunt - less heart.
guides and rules me Will re - main my help di - vine.
last - ing plea - sure And that now is sel - dom found.
I sur - ren - der, For on God a - lone I build.

Text: *Andächtige Haus-Kirche*, Nürnberg, 1676; tr. Catherine Winkworth, 1827–78, alt.
Tune: Johann Löhner, 1645–1705; adapt. Johann Balthasar König, 1691–1758;
setting: *The Lutheran Hymnal*, 1941

ALLES IST AN GOTTES SEGEN
887 887

Matt. 6:19–34; Col. 3:1–4; Rom. 8:31–32, 38–39; Ps. 143:8

5 Well He knows what best to grant me;
All the longing hopes that haunt me,
Joy and sorrow, have their day.
I shall doubt His wisdom never;
As God wills, so be it ever;
I commit to Him my way.

6 If my days on earth He lengthen,
God my weary soul will strengthen;
All my trust in Him I place.
Earthly wealth is not abiding,
Like a stream away is gliding;
Safe I anchor in His grace.

O God, Our Help in Ages Past 733

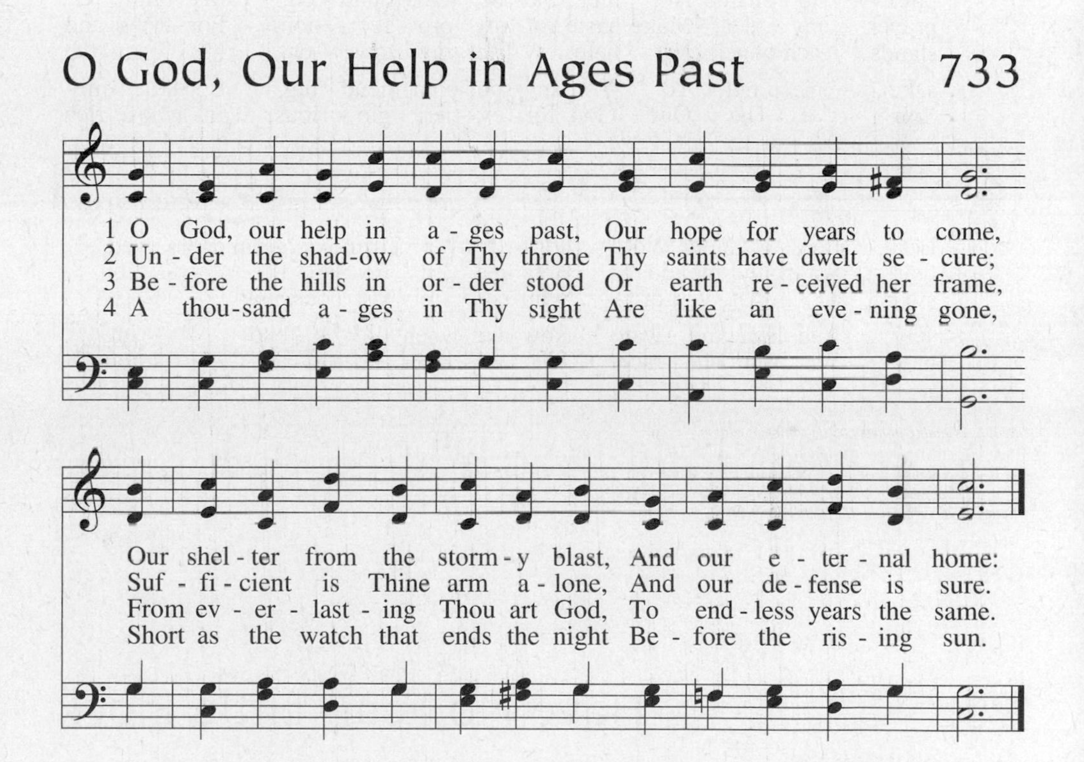

1 O God, our help in a - ges past, Our hope for years to come,
2 Un - der the shad-ow of Thy throne Thy saints have dwelt se - cure;
3 Be - fore the hills in or - der stood Or earth re - ceived her frame,
4 A thou-sand a - ges in Thy sight Are like an eve - ning gone,
Our shel - ter from the storm - y blast, And our e - ter - nal home:
Suf - fi - cient is Thine arm a - lone, And our de - fense is sure.
From ev - er - last - ing Thou art God, To end - less years the same.
Short as the watch that ends the night Be - fore the ris - ing sun.

5 Time, like an ever-rolling stream,
Soon bears us all away;
We fly forgotten as a dream
Dies at the op'ning day.

6 O God, our help in ages past,
Our hope for years to come,
Be Thou our guard while troubles last
And our eternal home!

An eight-stanza version of this hymn may be found in Lutheran Service Builder.

Text: Isaac Watts, 1674–1748, alt.
Tune: William Croft, 1678–1727; setting: *The Lutheran Hymnal*, 1941

ST. ANNE
C M

Psalm 90; 2 Cor. 4:16–18; Rom. 8:18; Ps. 46:1–3

734 I Trust, O Lord, Your Holy Name

1 I trust, O Lord, Your ho - ly name; O let me not be
2 Bow down Your gra - cious ear to me And hear my cry, my
3 You are my strength, my shield, my rock, My for - tress that with -
4 With You, O Lord, I cast my lot; O faith - ful God, for -
△ 5 All hon - or, praise, and maj - es - ty To Fa - ther, Son, and
put to shame Nor let me be con - found - ed. My faith, O
prayer, my plea; Make haste for my pro - tec - tion, For woes and
stands each shock, My help, my life, my tow - er, My bat - tle
sake me not, To You my soul com - mend - ing. Lord, be my
Spir - it be, Our God for - ev - er glo - rious, In whose rich
Lord, Be in Your Word For - ev - er firm - ly ground - ed.
fear Sur - round me here. Help me in my af - flic - tion.
sword, Al - might - y Lord— Who can re - sist Your pow - er?
stay, And lead the way Now and when life is end - ing.
grace We run our race Till we de - part vic - to - rious.

Setting available in hymn accompaniment edition.

Text: Adam Reusner, 1496–c. 1575; tr. Catherine Winkworth, 1827–78, sts. 1–4, alt.;
tr. *Evangelical Lutheran Hymn-Book*, Pittsburgh, 1907, st. 5, alt.
Tune: *Davids Himlische Harpffen*, Nürnberg, 1581

IN DICH HAB ICH GEHOFFET
887 447

Ps. 31:1–5; 40:4; 64:10

735 Have No Fear, Little Flock

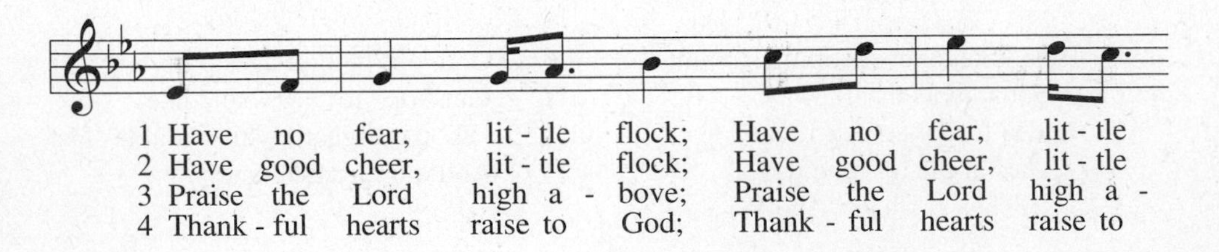
1 Have no fear, lit - tle flock; Have no fear, lit - tle
2 Have good cheer, lit - tle flock; Have good cheer, lit - tle
3 Praise the Lord high a - bove; Praise the Lord high a -
4 Thank - ful hearts raise to God; Thank - ful hearts raise to

Setting available in hymn accompaniment edition.

Text: Heinz Werner Zimmermann, b. 1930, st. 1; Marjorie A. Jillson, 1931–2010, sts. 2–4
Tune: Heinz Werner Zimmermann, b. 1930

LITTLE FLOCK
66 76 6

Luke 12:32; Matt. 25:34; Ps. 103:3–5; Matt. 28:20b

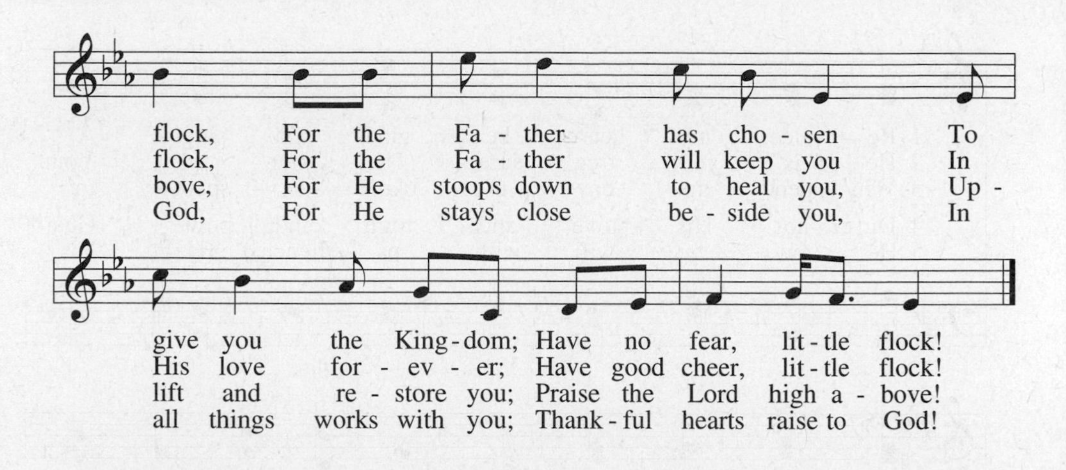
flock, For the Fa - ther has cho - sen To
flock, For the Fa - ther will keep you In
bove, For He stoops down to heal you, Up -
God, For He stays close be - side you, In
give you the King - dom; Have no fear, lit - tle flock!
His love for - ev - er; Have good cheer, lit - tle flock!
lift and re - store you; Praise the Lord high a - bove!
all things works with you; Thank - ful hearts raise to God!

Consider How the Birds Above 736

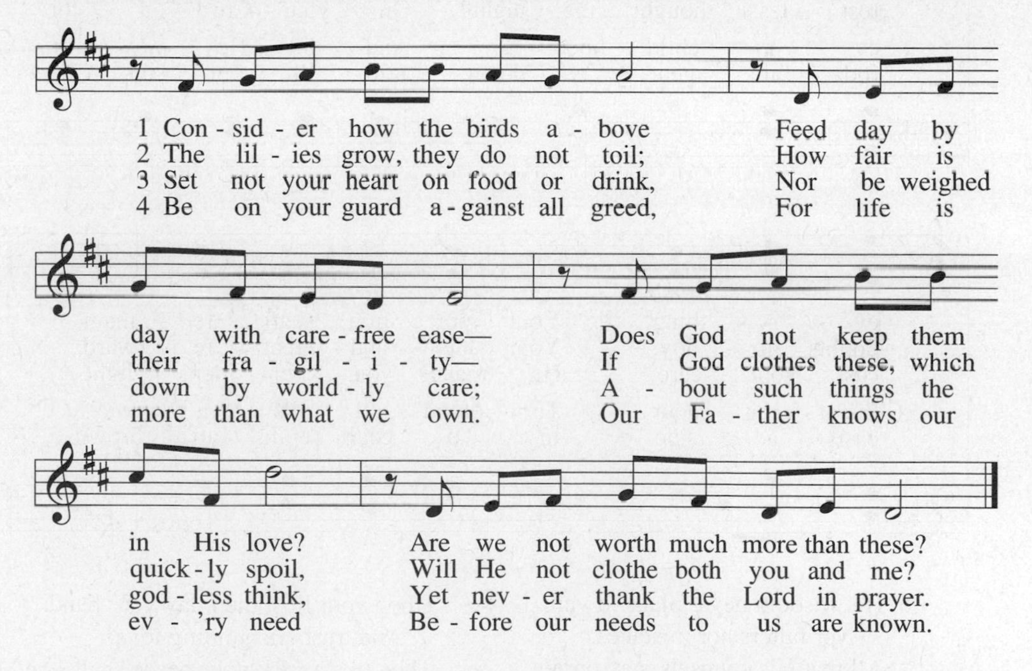
1 Con - sid - er how the birds a - bove Feed day by
2 The lil - ies grow, they do not toil; How fair is
3 Set not your heart on food or drink, Nor be weighed
4 Be on your guard a - gainst all greed, For life is
day with care - free ease— Does God not keep them
their fra - gil - i - ty— If God clothes these, which
down by world - ly care; A - bout such things the
more than what we own. Our Fa - ther knows our
in His love? Are we not worth much more than these?
quick - ly spoil, Will He not clothe both you and me?
god - less think, Yet nev - er thank the Lord in prayer.
ev - 'ry need Be - fore our needs to us are known.

5 Be not afraid to suffer loss
Of all the things for which you pray,
For He who faced for you the cross
Will give you strength to live each day.

6 Seek first God's reign, His boundless grace,
His holy name in all you do:
Christ first and last in ev'ry place;
All else will then be given you.

Setting available in hymn accompaniment edition.
Alternate tune: O JESU CHRISTE, WAHRES LICHT (839)

Text: Stephen P. Starke, b. 1955
Tune: Daniel Zager, b. 1951

NORTHCROFT
L M

Matt. 6:25–34; 10:29–31; 1 Tim. 6:8–10; 2 Cor. 12:7–10

737

Rejoice, My Heart, Be Glad and Sing

1 Re - joice, my heart, be glad and sing, A
2 He is your trea - sure, He your joy, Your
3 Why spend the day in blank de - spair, In
4 Did not His love and truth and pow'r Guard
5 He on - ly will with pa - tience chide, His
cheer - ful trust main - tain; For God, the source of
life and light and Lord, Your coun - sel - or when
rest - less thought the night? On your Cre - a - tor
ev - 'ry child - hood day? And did He not in
rod falls gent - ly down; And all your sins He
ev - 'ry - thing, Your por - tion shall re - main.
doubts an - noy, Your shield and great re - ward.
cast your care; He makes your bur - dens light.
threat - 'ning hour Turn dread - ed ills a - way?
casts a - side In o - cean depths to drown.

6 His wisdom never plans in vain
Nor falters nor mistakes.
All that His counsels may ordain
A blessèd ending makes.

7 Upon your lips, then, lay your hand,
And trust His guiding love;
Then like a rock your peace shall stand
Here and in heav'n above.

Text: Paul Gerhardt, 1607–76; tr. John Kelly, 1833–90, alt.
Tune: *Harmonischer Lieder-Schatz*, Frankfurt, 1738; setting: *The Lutheran Hymnal*, 1941

ICH SINGE DIR
C M

Ps. 28:7; Ps. 27:1–6; Micah 7:18–19; Ps. 73:25–26

Lord of All Hopefulness

1 Lord of all hope - ful - ness, Lord of all joy,
2 Lord of all ea - ger - ness, Lord of all faith,
3 Lord of all kind - li - ness, Lord of all grace,
4 Lord of all gen - tle - ness, Lord of all calm,
Whose trust, ev - er child - like, no cares could de - stroy:
Whose strong hands were skilled at the plane and the lathe:
Your hands swift to wel - come, Your arms to em - brace:
Whose voice is con - tent - ment, whose pres - ence is balm:
Be there at our wak - ing, and give us, we pray,
Be there at our la - bors, and give us, we pray,
Be there at our hom - ing, and give us, we pray,
Be there at our sleep - ing, and give us, we pray,
Your bliss in our hearts, Lord, at the break of the day.
Your strength in our hearts, Lord, at the noon of the day.
Your love in our hearts, Lord, at the eve of the day.
Your peace in our hearts, Lord, at the end of the day.

Text: Jan Struther, 1901–53
Tune: Irish; setting: Carlton R. Young, b. 1926

SLANE
Irregular meter

Ps. 55:16–17

739 Precious Lord, Take My Hand

1 Pre - cious Lord, take my hand, Lead me on, let me stand;
2 When my way grows drear, Pre - cious Lord, lin - ger near,
3 When the dark - ness ap - pears And the night draws near
I am tired, I am weak, I am worn.
When my life is al - most gone,
And the day is al - most gone,
Through the storm, through the night, Lead me on to the light.
Hear my cry, hear my call; Hold my hand lest I fall.
At the riv - er I stand; Guide my feet, hold my hand,
Take my hand, pre - cious Lord; lead me home.
Take my hand, pre - cious Lord; lead me home.
Take my hand, pre - cious Lord; lead me home.

Text: Thomas A. Dorsey, 1899–1993
Music: Thomas A. Dorsey, 1899–1993

PRECIOUS LORD
6 6 9 D

Is. 42:6; John 10:1–3, 27–28; Ps. 121:8

I Am Jesus' Little Lamb 740

1 I am Je - sus' lit - tle lamb, Ev - er glad at
2 Day by day, at home, a - way, Je - sus is my
3 Who so hap - py as I am, E - ven now the
heart I am; For my Shep - herd gent - ly guides me,
staff and stay. When I hun - ger, Je - sus feeds me,
Shep - herd's lamb? And when my short life is end - ed,
Knows my need and well pro - vides me, Loves me ev - 'ry
In - to pleas - ant pas - tures leads me; When I thirst, He
By His an - gel host at - tend - ed, He shall fold me
day the same, E - ven calls me by my name.
bids me go Where the qui - et wa - ters flow.
to His breast, There with - in His arms to rest.

Text: Henrietta L. von Hayn, 1724–82; tr. *The Lutheran Hymnal*, 1941
Tune: *Choral-Buch . . . Brüder-Gemeinen,* Leipzig, 1784; setting: Ewald Weiss, 1906–98

WEIL ICH JESU SCHÄFLEIN BIN
778 877

Psalm 23; Is. 40:11; 49:10; John 21:15

741 Jesus Christ, My Sure Defense

1 Je - sus Christ, my sure de - fense And my Sav - ior, now is
2 Je - sus, my Re - deem - er, lives; Like - wise I to life shall
3 No, too close - ly I am bound By my hope to Christ for -
4 I am flesh and must re - turn To the dust, whence I am

liv - ing! Know - ing this, my con - fi - dence
wak - en. He will bring me where He is;
ev - er; Faith's strong hand the Rock has found,
tak - en; But by faith I now dis - cern

Rests up - on the hope here giv - en, Though the
Shall my cour - age then be shak - en? Shall I
Grasped it, and will leave it nev - er; E - ven
That from death I shall a - wak - en With my

night of death be fraught Still with man - y an anx - ious thought.
fear, or could the Head Rise and leave His mem - bers dead?
death now can - not part From its Lord the trust - ing heart.
Sav - ior to a - bide In His glo - ry, at His side.

Text: Otto von Schwerin, 1616–79; tr. Catherine Winkworth, 1827–78, alt.
Tune: Johann Crüger, 1598–1662; setting: *The Lutheran Hymnal,* 1941

JESUS, MEINE ZUVERSICHT
78 78 77

1 Cor. 15:34–58; 1 Peter 1:3–5; 1 Cor. 15:20–23; Job 19:25–27

5 Glorified, I shall anew
With this flesh then be enshrouded;
In this body I shall view
God, my Lord, with eyes unclouded;
In this flesh I then shall see
Jesus Christ eternally.

6 Then take comfort and rejoice,
For His members Christ will cherish.
Fear not, they will hear His voice;
Dying, they will never perish;
For the very grave is stirred
When the trumpet's blast is heard.

7 Laugh to scorn the gloomy grave
And at death no longer tremble;
He, the Lord, who came to save
Will at last His own assemble.
They will go their Lord to meet,
Treading death beneath their feet.

8 O, then, draw away your hearts
From all pleasures base and hollow;
Strive to share what He imparts
While you here His footsteps follow.
As you now still wait to rise,
Fix your hearts beyond the skies!

For Me to Live Is Jesus 742

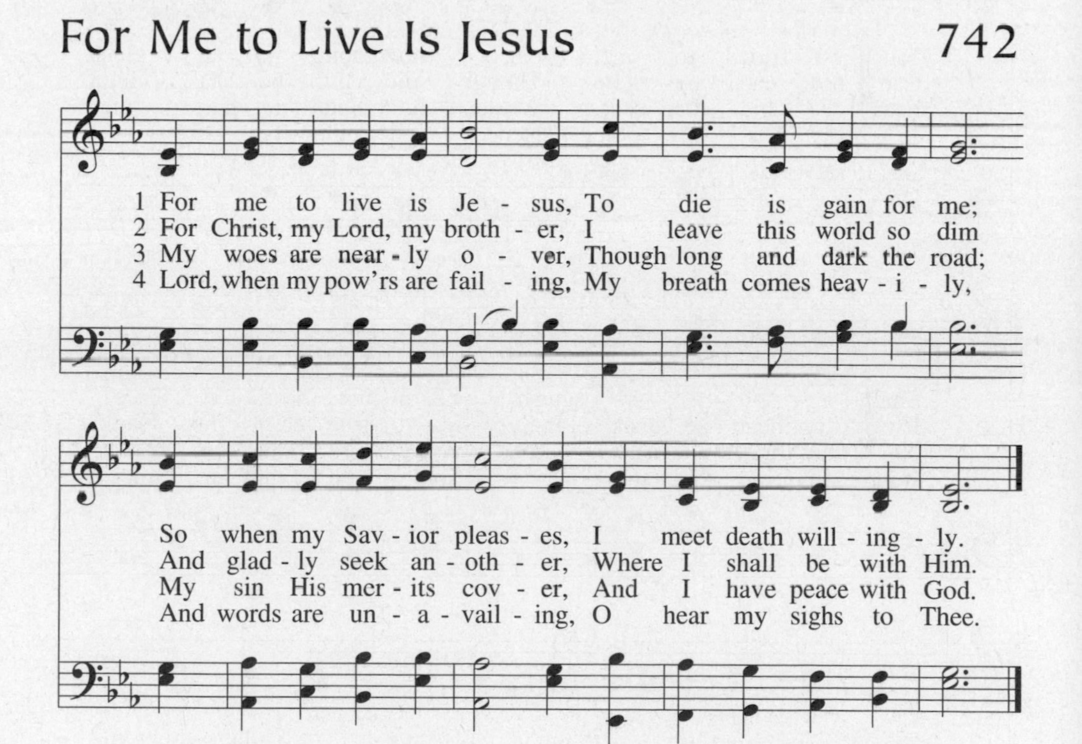

1 For me to live is Je - sus, To die is gain for me;
2 For Christ, my Lord, my broth - er, I leave this world so dim
3 My woes are near - ly o - ver, Though long and dark the road;
4 Lord, when my pow'rs are fail - ing, My breath comes heav - i - ly,
So when my Sav - ior pleas - es, I meet death will - ing - ly.
And glad - ly seek an - oth - er, Where I shall be with Him.
My sin His mer - its cov - er, And I have peace with God.
And words are un - a - vail - ing, O hear my sighs to Thee.

5 In my last hour, O grant me
A slumber soft and still,
No doubts to vex or haunt me,
Safe anchored in Thy will;

6 And so to Thee still cleaving
When death shall come to me,
I fall asleep believing
And wake in heav'n with Thee!

Text: *Ein schön geistlich Gesangbuch*, Jena, 1609; tr. Catherine Winkworth, 1827–78, alt.
Tune: Melchior Vulpius, c. 1570–1615; setting: *The Lutheran Hymnal*, 1941

CHRISTUS, DER IST MEIN LEBEN
76 76

Phil. 1:20–23; 2 Cor. 5:2, 8

743 Jesus, Priceless Treasure

1 Je - sus, price-less trea - sure, Fount of pur-est plea - sure,
2 In Thine arms I rest me; Foes who would mo-lest me
3 Sa - tan, I de - fy thee; Death, I now de - cry thee;
4 Hence, all earth-ly trea - sure! Je - sus is my plea - sure,
Tru - est friend to me, Ah, how long in an - guish
Can - not reach me here. Though the earth be shak - ing,
Fear, I bid thee cease. World, thou shalt not harm me
Je - sus is my choice. Hence, all emp - ty glo - ry!
Shall my spir - it lan - guish, Yearn - ing, Lord, for Thee?
Ev - 'ry heart be quak - ing, Je - sus calms my fear.
Nor thy threats a - larm me While I sing of peace.
Naught to me thy sto - ry Told with tempt - ing voice.
Thou art mine, O Lamb di - vine! I will suf - fer
Light - nings flash And thun - ders crash; Yet, though sin and
God's great pow'r Guards ev - 'ry hour; Earth and all its
Pain or loss, Or shame or cross, Shall not from my

Text: Johann Franck, 1618–77; tr. Catherine Winkworth, 1827–78, alt.
Tune: Johann Crüger, 1598–1662; setting: *Lutheran Book of Worship*, 1978

JESU, MEINE FREUDE
665 665 786

1 Peter 1:18–19; 1 Peter 1:6–9; Rom. 8:38–39; John 6:68–69

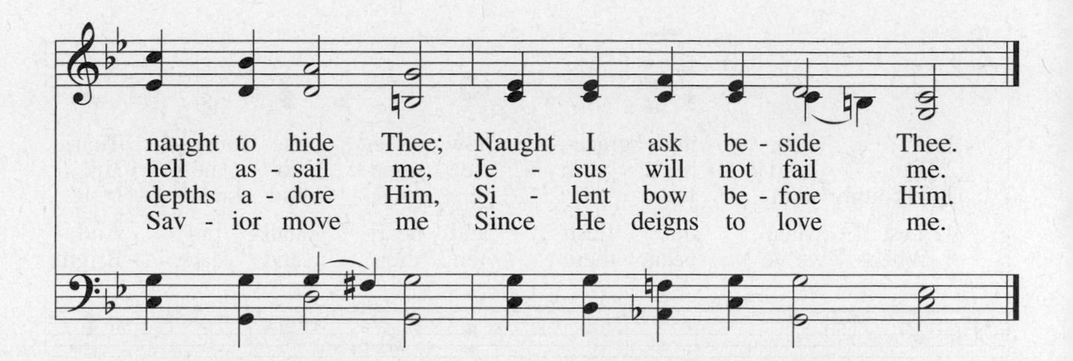
naught to hide Thee; Naught I ask be - side Thee.
hell as - sail me, Je - sus will not fail me.
depths a - dore Him, Si - lent bow be - fore Him.
Sav - ior move me Since He deigns to love me.

5 Evil world, I leave thee;
Thou canst not deceive me,
Thine appeal is vain.
Sin that once did blind me,
Get thee far behind me,
Come not forth again.
Past thy hour,
O pride and pow'r;
Sinful life, thy bonds I sever,
Leave thee now forever.

6 Hence, all fear and sadness!
For the Lord of gladness,
Jesus, enters in.
Those who love the Father,
Though the storms may gather,
Still have peace within.
Yea, whate'er
I here must bear,
Thou art still my purest pleasure,
Jesus, priceless treasure!

Lord Jesus Christ, our support and defense in every need, continue to preserve Your Church in safety, govern her by Your goodness, and bless her with Your peace; for You live and reign with the Father and the Holy Spirit, one God, now and forever. *Collect for Proper 19, Series B*

---

744 Amazing Grace

1 A - maz - ing grace— how sweet the sound— That
2 The Lord has prom - ised good to me, His
3 Through man - y dan - gers, toils, and snares I
4 Yes, when this flesh and heart shall fail And
5 When we've been there ten thou - sand years, Bright
saved a wretch like me! I once was lost but
Word my hope se - cures; He will my shield and
have al - read - y come; His grace has brought me
mor - tal life shall cease, A - maz - ing grace shall
shin - ing as the sun, We've no less days to
now am found, Was blind but now I see!
por - tion be As long as life en - dures.
safe thus far, His grace will lead me home.
then pre - vail In heav - en's joy and peace.
sing God's praise Than when we'd first be - gun.

1 Sublime gracia del Señor,
que a un pecador salvó;
perdido andaba, él me halló,
su luz me rescató.

2 Su gracia me enseñó a vencer,
mis dudas disipó.
¡Qué gozo siento en mi ser!
Mi vida él cambió.

Text: John Newton, 1725–1807, sts. 1–4, alt.; *A Collection of Sacred Ballads*, Richmond, 1790, st. 5;
Spanish tr. *¡Cantad al Señor!*, 1991
Tune: *Columbian Harmony*, Cincinnati, 1829; setting: Joseph Herl, b. 1959

NEW BRITAIN
C M

Eph. 2:1, 4–9; John 1:14, 16–17; Heb. 4:16; Rom. 3:22b–24

3 *Peligros, lucha y aflicción,*
los he tenido aquí;
su gracia siempre me libró,
consuelo recibí.

4 *Y cuando en Sión por siglos mil*
brillando esté cual sol,
yo cantaré por siempre allí
a Cristo el Salvador.

In God, My Faithful God 745

1 In God, my faith-ful God, I trust when dark my road;
2 My sins fill me with care, Yet I will not de-spair.
3 If death my por-tion be, It brings great gain to me;
4 O Je-sus Christ, my Lord, So meek in deed and word,
5 "So be it," then, I say With all my heart each day.
Great woes may o-ver-take me, Yet He will not for-sake me.
I build on Christ, who loves me; From this rock noth-ing moves me.
It speeds my life's en-deav-or To live with Christ for-ev-er.
You suf-fered death to save us Be-cause Your love would have us
Dear Lord, we all a-dore You, We sing for joy be-fore You.
My trou-bles He can al-ter; His hand lets noth-ing fal-ter.
To Him I will sur-ren-der, To Him, my soul's de-fend-er.
He gives me joy in sor-row, Come death now or to-mor-row.
Be heirs of heav'n-ly glad-ness When ends this life of sad-ness.
Guide us while here we wan-der Un-til we praise You yon-der.

Text: *Veer schöne nye Geistlike Leder*, Lübeck, before 1603; tr. Catherine Winkworth, 1827–78, alt.
Tune: *Kurtzweilige teutsche Lieder*, Nürnberg, 1576, alt.; setting: *The Lutheran Hymnal*, 1941

AUF MEINEN LIEBEN GOTT
66 77 77

Psalm 25; Phil. 1:21; 2 Thess. 3:3; Titus 3:4–7

746 Through Jesus' Blood and Merit

1 Through Je - sus' blood and mer - it I am at peace with God.
2 There's noth - ing that can sev - er From this great love of God;
3 For nei - ther life's temp - ta - tion Nor death's most try - ing hour
4 Nor an - y crea - ture ev - er Shall from the love of God
What, then, can daunt my spir - it, How - ev - er dark my road?
No want, no pain what - ev - er, No fam - ine, per - il, flood.
Nor an - gels of high sta - tion Nor an - y oth - er pow'r
This ran - somed sin - ner sev - er; For in my Sav - ior's blood
My cour - age shall not fail me, For God is on my side;
Though thou - sand foes sur - round me, For slaugh - ter mark His sheep,
Nor things that now are pres - ent Nor things that are to come
This love has its foun - da - tion; God hears my faith - ful prayer
Though hell it - self as - sail me, Its rage I may de - ride.
They nev - er shall con - found me, The vic - t'ry I shall reap.
Nor height, how - ev - er pleas - ant, Nor dark - est depths of gloom
And long be - fore cre - a - tion Named me His child and heir.

Text: Simon Dach, 1605–59; tr. *The Lutheran Hymnal*, 1941, alt.
Tune: *Musika Teutsch*, Nürnberg, 1532; setting: *The Lutheran Hymnal*, 1941

LOB GOTT GETROST MIT SINGEN
76 76 D

Rom. 8:35–39; Eph. 1:4–6

No Saint on Earth Lives Life to Self Alone

1 No saint on earth lives life to self a - lone Or dies a - lone, for we with Christ are one. So if we live, for Christ a - lone we live, And if we die, to Christ our dy - ing give. In liv - ing and in dy - ing this con - fess: We are the Lord's, safe in God's faith - ful - ness.
2 For to this end our Lord by death was slain, That to new life He might a - rise a - gain. Through sor - row on to tri - umph Christ has led, And reigns o'er all: the liv - ing and the dead. In liv - ing and in dy - ing, Him we bless; We are the Lord's, safe in God's faith - ful - ness.

Text: Norman J. Kansfield, b. 1940
Tune: Orlando Gibbons, 1583–1625; setting: Ralph Vaughan Williams, 1872–1958

SONG 1
10 10 10 10 10 10

Rom. 14:7–9; Rom. 8:38–39; Rom. 6:5–11

748 I'm But a Stranger Here

1 I'm but a strang - er here, Heav'n is my home;
2 What though the tem - pest rage, Heav'n is my home;
3 There - fore I mur - mur not, Heav'n is my home;
Earth is a des - ert drear, Heav'n is my home.
Short is my pil - grim - age, Heav'n is my home;
What - e'er my earth - ly lot, Heav'n is my home;
Dan - ger and sor - row stand Round me on ev - 'ry hand;
And time's wild win - try blast Soon shall be o - ver - past;
And I shall sure - ly stand There at my Lord's right hand;
Heav'n is my fa - ther - land, Heav'n is my home.
I shall reach home at last, Heav'n is my home.
Heav'n is my fa - ther - land, Heav'n is my home.

Text: Thomas R. Taylor, 1807–35
Tune: Arthur S. Sullivan, 1842–1900; setting: *The Lutheran Hymnal*, 1941

HEAVEN IS MY HOME
64 64 6664

Heb. 11:13–16; Phil. 3:20; Eph. 2:19; Heb. 4:9

There Is a Balm in Gilead

749

Refrain
There is a balm in Gil-e-ad To make the wound-ed whole;
There is a balm in Gil-e-ad To heal the sin-sick soul.
1 Some-times I feel dis-cour-aged And think my work's in vain,
2 If you can-not preach like Pe-ter, If you can-not pray like Paul,
3 Don't ev-er feel dis-cour-aged, For Je-sus is your friend;
But then the Ho-ly Spir-it Re-vives my soul a-gain.
You can tell the love of Je-sus And say He died for all.
And if you lack for knowl-edge, He'll ne'er re-fuse to lend.
Refrain

Text: African American spiritual
Music: African American spiritual

BALM IN GILEAD
Irregular meter

Jer. 8:18—9:2

750 If Thou But Trust in God to Guide Thee

1 If thou but trust in God to guide thee And hope in Him through all thy ways, He'll give thee strength, what-e'er be-tide thee, And bear thee through the e-vil days. Who trusts in God's un-chang-ing love Builds on the rock that naught can move.
2 What can these anx-ious cares a-vail thee, These nev-er-ceas-ing moans and sighs? What can it help if thou be-wail thee O'er each dark mo-ment as it flies? Our cross and tri-als do but press The heav-ier for our bit-ter-ness.
3 Be pa-tient and a-wait His lei-sure In cheer-ful hope, with heart con-tent To take what-e'er thy Fa-ther's plea-sure And His dis-cern-ing love hath sent, Nor doubt our in-most wants are known To Him who chose us for His own.
4 God knows full well when times of glad-ness Shall be the need-ful thing for thee. When He has tried thy soul with sad-ness And from all guile has found thee free, He comes to thee all un-a-ware And makes thee own His lov-ing care.

Text: Georg Neumark, 1621–81; tr. Catherine Winkworth, 1827–78, alt.
Tune: Georg Neumark, 1621–81; setting: *Service Book and Hymnal*, 1958

WER NUR DEN LIEBEN GOTT
98 98 88

Ps. 55:22; Prov. 3:5–6; Is. 41:10; Matt. 9:22

5 Nor think amid the fiery trial
That God hath cast thee off unheard,
That he whose hopes meet no denial
Must surely be of God preferred.
Time passes and much change doth bring
And sets a bound to ev'rything.

6 All are alike before the Highest;
'Tis easy for our God, we know,
To raise thee up, though low thou liest,
To make the rich man poor and low.
True wonders still by Him are wrought
Who setteth up and brings to naught.

7 Sing, pray, and keep His ways unswerving,
Perform thy duties faithfully,
And trust His Word; though undeserving,
Thou yet shalt find it true for thee.
God never yet forsook in need
The soul that trusted Him indeed.

O God of Love, O King of Peace 751

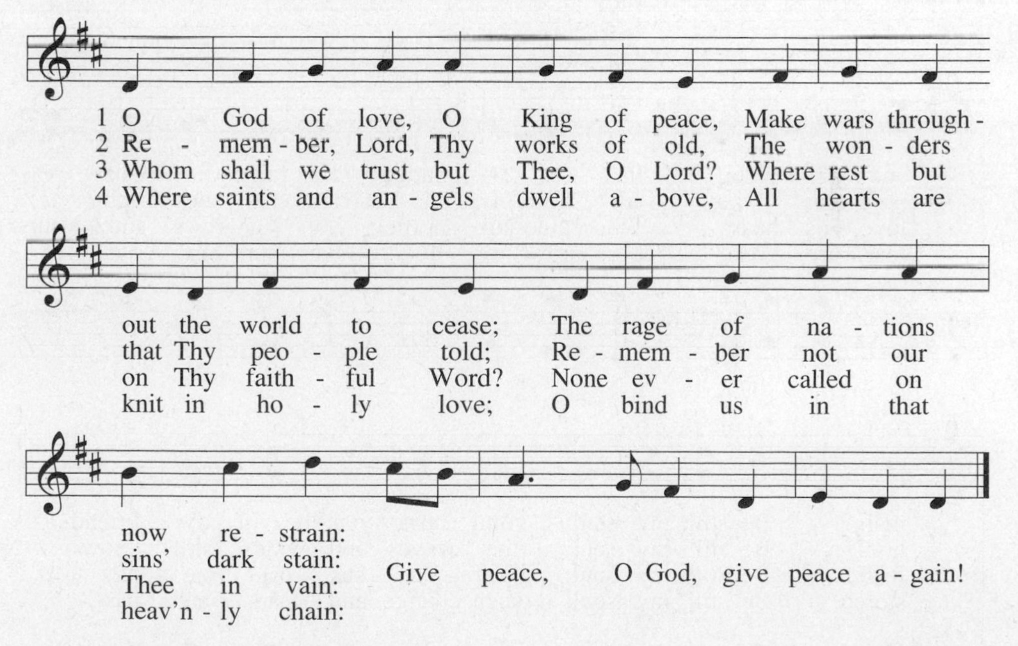
1 O God of love, O King of peace, Make wars through - out the world to cease; The rage of na - tions now re - strain: Give peace, O God, give peace a - gain!
2 Re - mem - ber, Lord, Thy works of old, The won - ders that Thy peo - ple told; Re - mem - ber not our sins' dark stain:
3 Whom shall we trust but Thee, O Lord? Where rest but on Thy faith - ful Word? None ev - er called on Thee in vain:
4 Where saints and an - gels dwell a - bove, All hearts are knit in ho - ly love; O bind us in that heav'n - ly chain:

Setting available in hymn accompaniment edition.

Text: Henry W. Baker, 1821–77, alt.
Tune: Sandra J. Voelker, b. 1952

NYLUNDA
L M

Ps. 46:9; 2 Thess. 3:16; Is. 43:25; 1 Thess. 5:23–24

752 Be Still, My Soul

1 Be still, my soul; the Lord is on your side; Bear pa - tient - ly the cross of grief or pain; Leave to your God to or - der and pro - vide; In ev - 'ry change He faith - ful will re - main. Be still, my soul; your best, your heav'n - ly Friend
2 Be still, my soul; your God will un - der - take To guide the fu - ture as He has the past. Your hope, your con - fi - dence let noth - ing shake; All now mys - te - rious shall be bright at last. Be still, my soul; the waves and winds still know
3 Be still, my soul; though dear - est friends de - part And all is dark - ened in this vale of tears; Then you will bet - ter know His love, His heart, Who comes to soothe your sor - rows and your fears. Be still, my soul; your Je - sus can re - pay
4 Be still, my soul; the hour is has - t'ning on When we shall be for - ev - er with the Lord, When dis - ap - point - ment, grief, and fear are gone, Sor - row for - got, love's pur - est joys re - stored. Be still, my soul; when change and tears are past,

Text: Catharina Amalia Dorothea von Schlegel, 1697–1752; tr. Jane L. Borthwick, 1813–97, alt.
Tune: Jean Sibelius, 1865–1957, adapt.; setting: *The Hymnbook*, 1955

FINLANDIA
10 10 10 10 10 10

Ps. 42:4–11; 46:10; John 11:1–44; Rev. 7:13–17

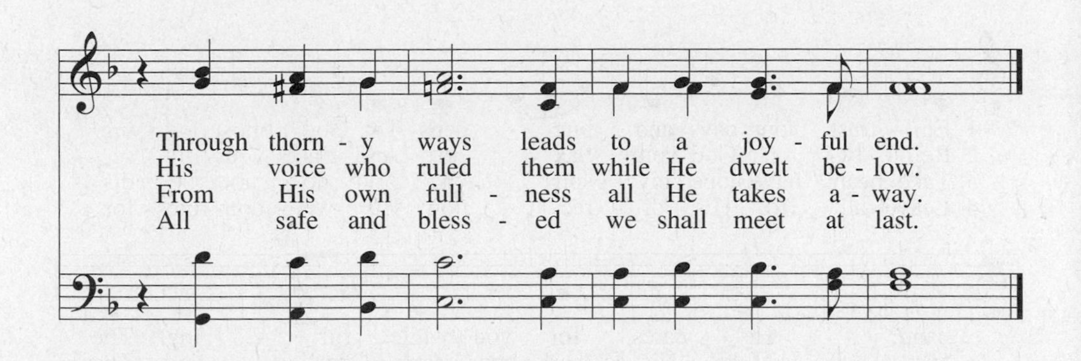
Through thorn - y ways leads to a joy - ful end.
His voice who ruled them while He dwelt be - low.
From His own full - ness all He takes a - way.
All safe and bless - ed we shall meet at last.

All for Christ I Have Forsaken 753

1 All for Christ I have for - sak - en And have
2 Who is sweet - er than Christ Je - sus? No good
3 Gone the past, un - known the fu - ture— Grace sup -
4 When God takes me home to heav - en, Should this
5 Though the road a - head be thorn - y, Though dark
tak - en up my cross; World - ly joy, its
thing in Him I lack! Hand to plow, at
plies my dai - ly breath; Strong in Christ through
be the day I die, God will keep my
clouds all light ob - scure, Though my cross - shaped
fame and for - tune, Now I count as worth-less dross.
peace I fol - low Where He leads me . . . why look back?
death's dark val - ley, Firm and faith - ful un - to death.
spouse and chil - dren As the ap - ple of His eye.
path grows steep - er, With the Lord, I am se - cure.

Setting available in hymn accompaniment edition.

Text: Calvin Chao, 1906–96; tr. Stephen P. Starke, b. 1955
Tune: *Southern Harmony*, New Haven, 1835

RESTORATION
87 87

Phil. 3:7–14; Matt. 10:38–39; Luke 9:62; Rev. 2:10

754 Entrust Your Days and Burdens

1 En - trust your days and bur - dens To God's most lov - ing
2 Re - ly on God your Sav - ior And find your life se -
3 Take heart, have hope, my spir - it, And do not be dis -
4 Leave all to His di - rec - tion; His wis - dom rules for
hand; He cares for you while rul - ing The
cure. Make His work your foun - da - tion That
mayed; God helps in ev - 'ry tri - al And
you In ways to rouse your won - der At
sky, the sea, the land. For He who guides the
your work may en - dure. No anx - ious thought, no
makes you un - a - fraid. A - wait His time with
all His love can do. Soon He, His prom - ise
tem - pests A - long their thun - d'rous ways Will
wor - ry, No self - tor - ment - ing care Can
pa - tience Through dark - est hours of night Un -
keep - ing, With won - der - work - ing pow'rs Will
find for you a path - way And guide you all your days.
win your Fa - ther's fa - vor; His heart is moved by prayer.
til the sun you hoped for De - lights your ea - ger sight.
ban - ish from your spir - it What gave you trou - bled hours.

5 O blessèd heir of heaven,
You'll hear the song resound
Of endless jubilation
When you with life are crowned.
In your right hand your maker
Will place the victor's palm,
And you will thank Him gladly
With heaven's joyful psalm.

6 Our hands and feet, Lord, strengthen;
With joy our spirits bless
Until we see the ending
Of all our life's distress.
And so throughout our lifetime
Keep us within Your care
And at our end then bring us
To heav'n to praise You there.

Setting available in hymn accompaniment edition.

Text: Paul Gerhardt, 1607–76; tr. F. Samuel Janzow, 1913–2001, sts. 1–5, alt.;
tr. *Lutheran Service Book*, 2006, st. 6
Tune: Stephen R. Johnson, b. 1966

SUFFICIENTIA
76 76 D

Ps. 37:5; 125:1; Phil. 4:6–7; 1 Peter 5:6–7

In the Very Midst of Life 755

1 In the ver - y midst of life Snares of death sur - round us;
2 In the midst of death's dark vale Pow'rs of hell o'er - take us.
3 In the midst of ut - ter woe When our sins op - press us,
Who shall help us in the strife Lest the foe con - found us?
Who will help when they as - sail, Who se - cure will make us?
Where shall we for ref - uge go, Where for grace to bless us?
Thou on - ly, Lord, Thou on - ly! We mourn that we have great - ly
Thou on - ly, Lord, Thou on - ly! Thy heart is moved with ten - der-
To Thee, Lord Je - sus, on - ly! Thy pre - cious blood was shed to
erred, That our sins Thy wrath have stirred. Ho - ly and righ - teous God!
ness, Pit - ies us in our dis - tress. Ho - ly and righ - teous God!
win Full a - tone - ment for our sin. Ho - ly and righ - teous God!
Ho - ly and might - y God! Ho - ly and all - mer - ci - ful
Ho - ly and might - y God! Ho - ly and all - mer - ci - ful
Ho - ly and might - y God! Ho - ly and all - mer - ci - ful
Sav - ior! E - ter - nal Lord God! Save us lest we per - ish
Sav - ior! E - ter - nal Lord God! Save us from the ter - ror
Sav - ior! E - ter - nal Lord God! Lord, pre - serve and keep us
In the bit - ter pangs of death. Have mer - cy, O Lord!
Of the fi - ery pit of hell. Have mer - cy, O Lord!
In the peace that faith can give. Have mer - cy, O Lord!

Setting available in hymn accompaniment edition.

Text: Martin Luther, 1483–1546; tr. *The Lutheran Hymnal*, 1941, alt.
Tune: Latin, 13th cent.; adapt. *Geystliche gesangk Buchleyn*, Wittenberg, 1524, ed. Johann Walter

MITTEN WIR IM LEBEN SIND
Peculiar meter

Rom. 14:7–8; 2 Cor. 1:9–10; 1 Cor. 15:53–54

756 Why Should Cross and Trial Grieve Me

1 Why should cross and tri - al grieve me? Christ is near With His cheer; Nev - er will He leave me. Who can rob me of the heav - en That God's Son For me won When His life was giv - en?
2 When life's trou - bles rise to meet me, Though their weight May be great, They will not de - feat me. God, my lov - ing Sav - ior, sends them; He who knows All my woes Knows how best to end them.
3 God gives me my days of glad - ness, And I will Trust Him still When He sends me sad - ness. God is good; His love at - tends me Day by day, Come what may, Guides me and de - fends me.
4 From God's joy can noth - ing sev - er, For I am His dear lamb, He, my Shep - herd ev - er. I am His be - cause He gave me His own blood For my good, By His death to save me.

Text: Paul Gerhardt, 1607–76; tr. *Christian Worship*, 1993, sts. 1–3; tr. Stephen P. Starke, b. 1955, sts. 4–5
Tune: Johann G. Ebeling, 1637–76; setting: *The Lutheran Hymnal*, 1941

WARUM SOLLT ICH MICH DENN GRÄMEN
8 33 6 D

1 Peter 1:6–9; James 1:2–4; 1 Peter 4:12; Matt. 11:29–30

5 Now in Christ, death cannot slay me,
Though it might,
Day and night,
Trouble and dismay me.
Christ has made my death a portal
From the strife
Of this life
To His joy immortal!

Lord, It Belongs Not to My Care 757

1 Lord, it be - longs not to my care Wheth - er I die or live; To love and serve Thee is my share, And this Thy grace must give.
2 If life be long, I will be glad That I may long o - bey; If short, yet why should I be sad To soar to end - less day?
3 Christ leads me through no dark - er rooms Than He went through be - fore; He that un - to God's king - dom comes Must en - ter by this door.
4 Come, Lord, when grace has made me meet Thy bless - ed face to see; For if Thy work on earth be sweet, What will Thy glo - ry be!

5 Then shall I end my sad complaints
And weary, sinful days
And join with the triumphant saints
Who sing my Savior's praise.

6 My knowledge of that life is small,
The eye of faith is dim;
But 'tis enough that Christ knows all,
And I shall be with Him.

Text: Richard Baxter, 1615–91, alt.
Music: Henry J. Gauntlett, 1805–76

ST. FULBERT
C M

Phil. 1:21–26; Luke 23:43

758 The Will of God Is Always Best

1 The will of God is al - ways best And shall be done for -
2 God is my com - fort and my trust, My hope and life a -
3 Lord, this I ask, O hear my plea, De - ny me not this
4 When life's brief course on earth is run And I this world am

ev - er; And they who trust in Him are blest;
bid - ing; And to His coun - sel, wise and just,
fa - vor: When Sa - tan sore - ly trou - bles me,
leav - ing, Grant me to say, "Your will be done,"

He will for - sake them nev - er. He helps in - deed In
I yield, in Him con - fid - ing. The ver - y hairs, His
Then do not let me wa - ver. O guard me well, My
Your faith - ful Word be - liev - ing. My dear - est Friend, I

time of need; He chas - tens with for - bear - ing. They who de -
Word de - clares, Up - on my head He num - bers. By night and
fear dis - pel, Ful - fill Your faith - ful say - ing: All who be -
now com - mend My soul in - to Your keep - ing; From sin and

Text: Albrecht von Preussen, 1490–1568; tr. *The Lutheran Hymnal*, 1941, alt.
Tune: Claudin de Sermisy, c. 1490–1562; setting: *The Lutheran Hymnal*, 1941

WAS MEIN GOTT WILL (Isorhythmic)
87 87 D

Matt. 6:10; 26:39, 42; 1 Cor. 10:13; Ps. 84:12

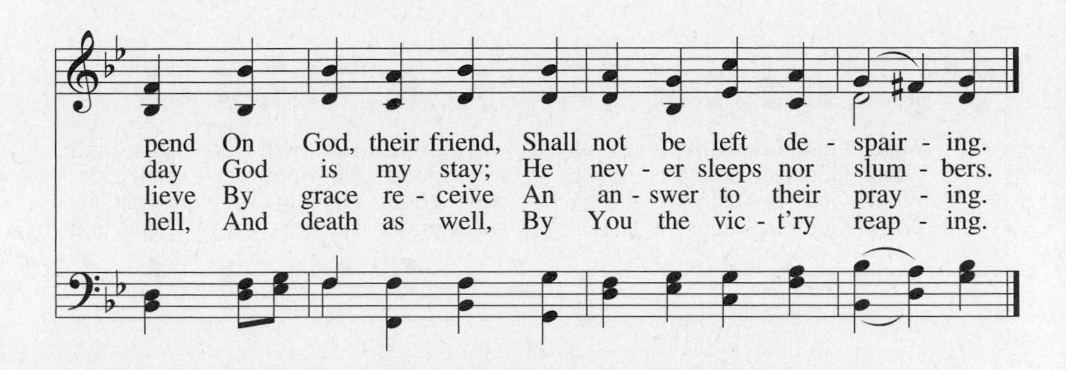
pend On God, their friend, Shall not be left de - spair - ing.
day God is my stay; He nev - er sleeps nor slum - bers.
lieve By grace re - ceive An an - swer to their pray - ing.
hell, And death as well, By You the vic - t'ry reap - ing.

This Body in the Grave We Lay 759

1 This bod - y in the grave we lay There to a - wait that sol - emn day When God Him - self shall bid it rise To mount tri - um - phant to the skies.
2 And so to earth we now en - trust What came from dust and turns to dust And from the dust shall rise that day In glo - rious tri - umph o'er de - cay.
3 The soul for - ev - er lives with God, Who free - ly hath His grace be - stowed And through His Son re - deemed it here From ev - 'ry sin, from ev - 'ry fear.
4 All tri - als and all griefs are past, A bless - ed end has come at last. Christ's yoke was borne with read - y will; Who di - eth thus is liv - ing still.
5 We have no cause to mourn or weep; Se - cure - ly shall this bod - y sleep Till Christ Him - self shall death de - stroy And raise the bless - ed dead to joy.

6 Then let us leave this place of rest
And homeward turn, for they are blest
Who heed God's warning and prepare
Lest death should find them unaware.

7 So help us, Jesus, ground of faith;
Thou hast redeemed us by Thy death
From endless death and set us free.
We laud and praise and worship Thee.

Setting available in hymn accompaniment edition.

Text: Michael Weisse, c. 1480–1534, sts. 1–6; *Gesangbuch*, Magdeburg, 1540, st. 7;
tr. William M. Czamanske, 1873–1964
Tune: *Newe deudsche geistliche Gesenge*, Wittenberg, 1544

NUN LASST UNS DEN LEIB
L M

John 5:24; 1 Cor. 15:51–57; 2 Cor. 5:4; 1 Thess. 4:13–14

760 What God Ordains Is Always Good

1 What God or - dains is al - ways good: His will is just and ho - ly. As He di - rects my life for me, I fol - low meek and low - ly. My God in - deed In ev - 'ry need Knows well how He will shield me; To Him, then, I will yield me.
2 What God or - dains is al - ways good: He nev - er will de - ceive me; He leads me in His righ - teous way, And nev - er will He leave me. I take con - tent What He has sent; His hand that sends me sad - ness Will turn my tears to glad - ness.
3 What God or - dains is al - ways good: His lov - ing thought at - tends me; No poi - son can be in the cup That my phy - si - cian sends me. My God is true; Each morn - ing new I trust His grace un - end - ing, My life to Him com - mend - ing.
4 What God or - dains is al - ways good: He is my friend and Fa - ther; He suf - fers naught to do me harm Though man - y storms may gath - er. Now I may know Both joy and woe; Some - day I shall see clear - ly That He has loved me dear - ly.

Text: Samuel Rodigast, 1649–1708; tr. *The Lutheran Hymnal*, 1941, alt.
Tune: Severus Gastorius, 1646–82; setting: *The Lutheran Hymnal*, 1941

WAS GOTT TUT
87 87 44 77

Rom. 8:28; Ps. 92:15; Deut. 32:4; Lam. 3:19–26

5 What God ordains is always good:
Though I the cup am drinking
Which savors now of bitterness,
I take it without shrinking.
For after grief
God gives relief,
My heart with comfort filling
And all my sorrow stilling.

6 What God ordains is always good:
This truth remains unshaken.
Though sorrow, need, or death be mine,
I shall not be forsaken.
I fear no harm,
For with His arm
He shall embrace and shield me;
So to my God I yield me.

Rock of Ages, Cleft for Me 761

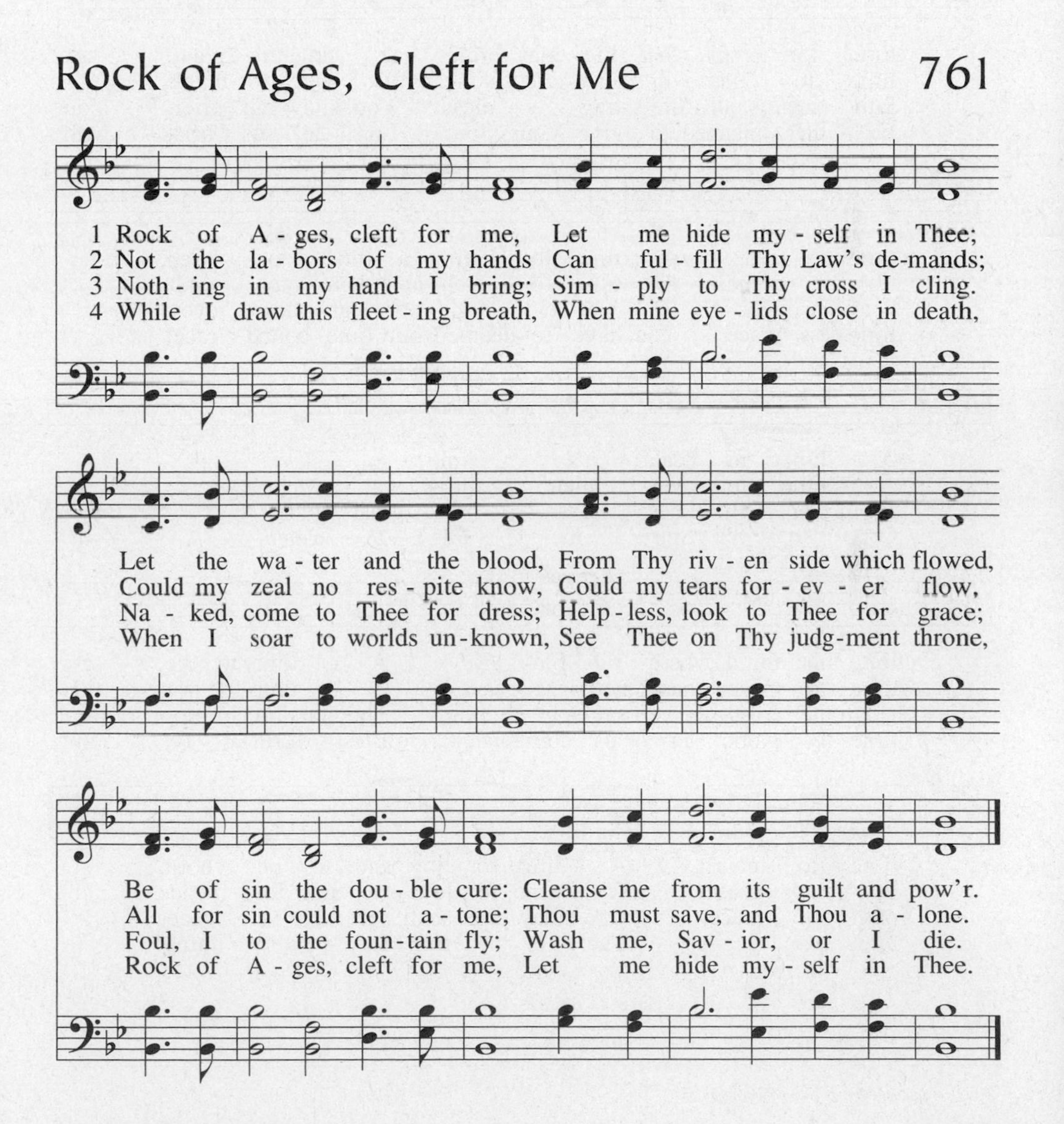
1 Rock of A - ges, cleft for me, Let me hide my - self in Thee;
2 Not the la - bors of my hands Can ful - fill Thy Law's de-mands;
3 Noth - ing in my hand I bring; Sim - ply to Thy cross I cling.
4 While I draw this fleet - ing breath, When mine eye - lids close in death,
Let the wa - ter and the blood, From Thy riv - en side which flowed,
Could my zeal no res - pite know, Could my tears for - ev - er flow,
Na - ked, come to Thee for dress; Help - less, look to Thee for grace;
When I soar to worlds un - known, See Thee on Thy judg - ment throne,
Be of sin the dou - ble cure: Cleanse me from its guilt and pow'r.
All for sin could not a - tone; Thou must save, and Thou a - lone.
Foul, I to the foun - tain fly; Wash me, Sav - ior, or I die.
Rock of A - ges, cleft for me, Let me hide my - self in Thee.

Text: Augustus M. Toplady, 1740–78
Tune: Thomas Hastings, 1784–1872; setting: *Lutheran Worship*, 1982

TOPLADY
77 77 77

1 Cor. 10:4; John 19:34; Heb. 9:14; Ezek. 36:25

762 There Is a Time for Everything

1 There is a time for ev - 'ry - thing, A
2 A time to hold, then be a - lone, A
3 E - ter - nal Lord, Your wis - dom sees And
△ 4 Be - fore all time had yet be - gun, You,
time for all that life may bring: A time to plant, a
time to gath - er scat - tered stone, A time to break, a
fath - oms all life's trag - e - dies; You know our grief, You
Fa - ther, planned to give Your Son; Lord Je - sus Christ, with
time to reap, A time to laugh, a time to weep,
time to mend, A time to search and then to end,
hear our sighs— In mer - cy, dry our tear - stained eyes.
time - less grace, You have re - deemed our time - bound race;
A time to heal, a time to slay, A
A time to keep, then throw a - way, A
From e - vil times, You bring great good; Be -
O Ho - ly Spir - it, Par - a - clete, Your
time to build where rub - ble lay, A time to die, a
time to speak, then noth - ing say, A time for war till
neath the cross, we've safe - ly stood. Though dim - ly now life's
time - ly work in us com - plete; Blest Trin - i - ty, Your
time to mourn, A time for joy and to be born,
ha - treds cease, A time for love, a time for peace.
path we trace, One day we shall see face to face.
praise we sing— There is a time for ev - 'ry - thing!

Setting available in hymn accompaniment edition.

Text: Stephen P. Starke, b. 1955
Tune: Stephen R. Johnson, b. 1966

ST. PETER'S NORWALK
L M D

Eccl. 3:1–8; Ps. 33:13–15; Gal. 4:4–5

When Peace, like a River

763

1 When peace, like a river, attendeth my way; When sorrows, like sea billows, roll; Whatever my lot, Thou hast taught me to say, It is well, it is well with my soul.
2 Though Satan should buffet, though trials should come, Let this blest assurance control, That Christ hath regarded my helpless estate And hath shed His own blood for my soul.
3 He lives— oh, the bliss of this glorious thought; My sin, not in part, but the whole, Is nailed to His cross, and I bear it no more. Praise the Lord, praise the Lord, O my soul!
4 And, Lord, haste the day when our faith shall be sight, The clouds be rolled back as a scroll, The trumpet shall sound and the Lord shall descend; Even so it is well with my soul.
Refrain
It is well with my soul, It is well, it is well with my soul.
It is well with my soul,

Text: Horatio G. Spafford, 1828–88, alt.
Music: Philip P. Bliss, 1838–76

IT IS WELL
11 8 11 9 and refrain

Is. 26:3; Luke 2:29; Rom. 5:1; Col. 3:15

764 When Aimless Violence Takes Those We Love

1 When aim - less vi - o - lence takes those we love,
2 When pass - ing years rob sight and strength and mind
3 Our faith may flick - er low, and hope grow dim,
4 Be - cause Your Son knew ag - o - ny and loss,
When ran - dom death strikes child - hood's prom - ise down,
Yet fail to still a strong - ly beat - ing heart,
Yet You, O God, are with us in our pain;
Felt des - o - la - tion, grief and scorn and shame,
When wrench - ing loss be - comes our dai - ly bread,
And grief be - comes the fab - ric of our days,
You grieve with us and for us day by day,
We know You will be with us, come what may,
We know, O God, You leave us not a - lone.
Dear Lord, You do not stand from us a - part.
And with us, shar - ing sor - row, will re - main.
Your lov - ing pres - ence near, al - ways the same.

Text: Joy F. Patterson, b. 1931
Tune: Alfred M. Smith, 1879–1971; setting: Richard W. Hillert, 1923–2010

SURSUM CORDA
10 10 10 10

2 Cor. 1:3–5; 1 Peter 2:21–24; 4:12–14, 19; Ps. 9:9–10

5 Through long grief-darkened days help us, dear Lord,
To trust Your grace for courage to endure,
To rest our souls in Your supporting love,
And find our hope within Your mercy sure.

God Moves in a Mysterious Way 765

1 God moves in a mys - te - rious way His won - ders to per - form; He plants His foot - steps in the sea And rides up - on the storm.

2 Judge not the Lord by fee - ble sense, But trust Him for His grace; Be - hind a frown - ing prov - i - dence Faith sees a smil - ing face.

3 His pur - pos - es will rip - en fast, Un - fold - ing ev - 'ry hour; The bud may have a bit - ter taste, But sweet will be the flow'r.

4 Blind un - be - lief is sure to err And scan His work in vain; God is His own in - ter - pret - er, And He will make it plain.

5 You fear - ful saints, fresh cour - age take; The clouds you so much dread Are big with mer - cy and will break In bless - ings on your head.

Text: William Cowper, 1731–1800, alt.
Tune: *The CL Psalmes of David*, Edinburgh, 1615; setting: *The Lutheran Hymnal*, 1941

DUNDEE
C M

Rom. 11:33; Is. 38:17; Rom. 8:28; Jer. 29:11

766 Our Father, Who from Heaven Above

1 Our Fa - ther, who from heav'n a - bove Bids all of us to live in love As mem - bers of one fam - i - ly And pray to You in u - ni - ty, Teach us no thought - less words to say But from our in - most hearts to pray.
2 Your name be hal - lowed. Help us, Lord, In pu - ri - ty to keep Your Word, That to the glo - ry of Your name We walk be - fore You free from blame. Let no false teach - ing us per - vert; All poor de - lud - ed souls con - vert.
3 Your king - dom come. Guard Your do - main And Your e - ter - nal righ - teous reign. The Ho - ly Ghost en - rich our day With gifts at - ten - dant on our way. Break Sa - tan's pow'r, de - feat his rage; Pre - serve Your Church from age to age.
4 Your gra - cious will on earth be done As it is done be - fore Your throne, That pa - tient - ly we may o - bey Through - out our lives all that You say. Curb flesh and blood and ev - 'ry ill That sets it - self a - gainst Your will.

This is a catechism hymn of Martin Luther.

Text: Martin Luther, 1483–1546; tr. *The Lutheran Hymnal*, 1941, sts. 1, 6, 8–9, alt.; tr. F. Samuel Janzow, 1913–2001, sts. 2–5, 7, alt.
Tune: attr. Martin Luther, 1483–1546; setting: *The Lutheran Hymnal*, 1941

VATER UNSER
88 88 88

Matt. 6:9–13

5 Give us this day our daily bread,
And let us all be clothed and fed.
Save us from hardship, war, and strife;
In plague and famine, spare our life,
That we in honest peace may live,
To care and greed no entrance give.

6 Forgive our sins, Lord, we implore,
That they may trouble us no more;
We, too, will gladly those forgive
Who hurt us by the way they live.
Help us in our community
To serve each other willingly.

7 Lead not into temptation, Lord,
Where our grim foe and all his horde
Would vex our souls on ev'ry hand.
Help us resist, help us to stand
Firm in the faith, a mighty host,
Through comfort of the Holy Ghost.

8 From evil, Lord, deliver us;
The times and days are perilous.
Redeem us from eternal death,
And, when we yield our dying breath,
Console us, grant us calm release,
And take our souls to You in peace.

9 Amen, that is, so shall it be.
Make strong our faith in You, that we
May doubt not but with trust believe
That what we ask we shall receive.
Thus in Your name and at Your Word
We say, "Amen, O hear us, Lord!"

Jesus, Remember Me 767

Je - sus, re-mem-ber me when You come in - to Your king-dom.
Je - sus, re-mem-ber me when You come in - to Your king-dom.

Text: Luke 23:42
Music: Jacques Berthier, 1923–94

REMEMBER ME
68 68

768 To God the Holy Spirit Let Us Pray

1 To God the Ho - ly Spir - it let us pray
2 O sweet - est Love, Your grace on us be - stow;
3 Tran - scen - dent Com - fort in our ev - 'ry need,
4 Shine in our hearts, O Spir - it, pre - cious light;
For the true faith need - ed on our way
Set our hearts with sa - cred fire a - glow
Help us nei - ther scorn nor death to heed
Teach us Je - sus Christ to know a - right
That He may de - fend us when life is end - ing And from
That with hearts u - nit - ed we love each oth - er, Ev - 'ry
That we may not fal - ter nor cour - age fail us When the
That we may a - bide in the Lord who bought us, Till to
ex - ile home we are wend - ing. Lord, have mer - cy!
strang - er, sis - ter, and broth - er. Lord, have mer - cy!
foe shall taunt and as - sail us. Lord, have mer - cy!
our true home He has brought us. Lord, have mer - cy!

Text: German, c. 13th cent., st. 1; Martin Luther, 1483–1546, sts. 2–4; tr. *Worship Supplement*, 1969, alt.
Tune: *Geystliche gesangk Buchleyn*, Wittenberg, 1524, ed. Johann Walter;
setting: *Lutheran Service Book*, 2006

NUN BITTEN WIR
10 9 11 9 4

John 16:13; Eph. 4:3–6; Rom. 8:26; 1 Cor. 12:3

Eternal Spirit of the Living Christ 769

1 E - ter - nal Spir - it of the liv - ing Christ,
2 Come, pray in me the prayer I need this day;
3 Come with the strength I lack, bring vi - sion clear

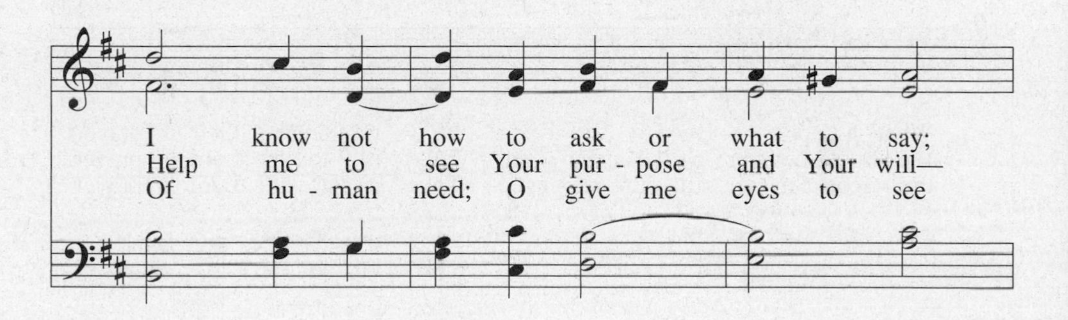
I know not how to ask or what to say;
Help me to see Your pur - pose and Your will—
Of hu - man need; O give me eyes to see

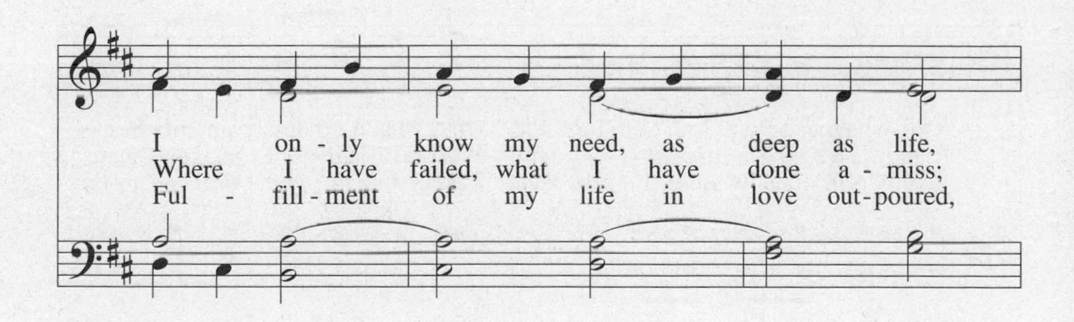
I on - ly know my need, as deep as life,
Where I have failed, what I have done a - miss;
Ful - fill - ment of my life in love out - poured,

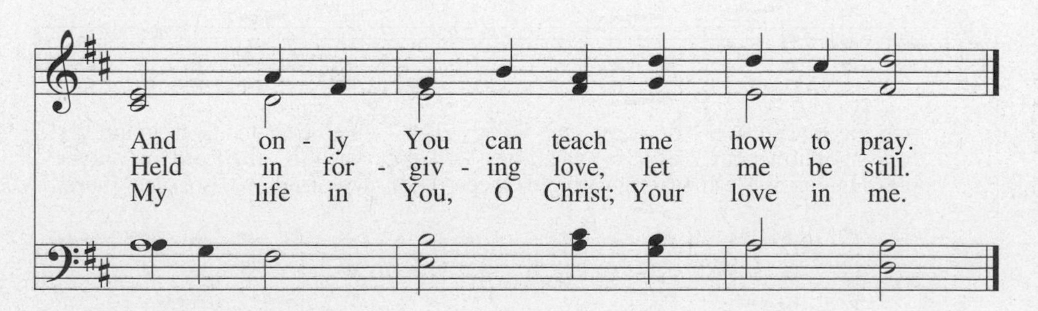
And on - ly You can teach me how to pray.
Held in for - giv - ing love, let me be still.
My life in You, O Christ; Your love in me.

Alternate tune: SURSUM CORDA (788)

Text: Frank von Christierson, 1900–96, alt.
Tune: Henry Lawes, 1595–1662; setting: Carl F. Schalk, b. 1929

FARLEY CASTLE
10 10 10 10

Rom. 8:26–27; Eph. 6:18; Luke 11:1–4; 22:42

770 What a Friend We Have in Jesus

1 What a friend we have in Je - sus, All our sins and griefs to bear!
2 Have we tri - als and temp-ta - tions? Is there trou-ble an - y-where?
3 Are we weak and heav - y lad - en, Cum - bered with a load of care?
What a priv - i - lege to car - ry Ev - 'ry-thing to God in prayer!
We should nev - er be dis-cour-aged— Take it to the Lord in prayer.
Pre - cious Sav-ior, still our ref - uge— Take it to the Lord in prayer.
Oh, what peace we of - ten for - feit; Oh, what need-less pain we bear—
Can we find a friend so faith - ful Who will all our sor-rows share?
Do thy friends de-spise, for-sake thee? Take it to the Lord in prayer.
All be - cause we do not car - ry Ev - 'ry-thing to God in prayer!
Je - sus knows our ev - 'ry weak-ness— Take it to the Lord in prayer.
In His arms He'll take and shield thee; Thou wilt find a sol-ace there.

Text: Joseph M. Scriven, 1819–86
Tune: Charles C. Converse, 1832–1918; setting: *The Hymn Book*, 1971

CONVERSE
87 87 D

Matt. 7:7–8; Heb. 4:15; John 15:14–16; 1 Peter 2:24

Be Still, My Soul, before the Lord 771

1 Be still, my soul, be - fore the Lord, For
2 You need not mul - ti - ply your words Nor
3 Wait, then, in qui - et con - fi - dence, Your
4 Be still, my soul, be - fore the Lord; On
God is al - ways near. Be - fore your mind is
pray with prac - ticed art. Be - yond all speech, God
anx - ious thoughts at rest. God knows your needs be -
God in pa - tience wait. God's love, un - seen, sur -
moved to pray, God lis - tens and will hear.
un - der - stands The hun - ger of your heart.
fore you ask And works for what is best.
rounds your life; God's help will not be late.

Text: Herman G. Stuempfle, Jr., 1923–2007
Music: Marty Haugen, b. 1950

SHANTI
C M

Matt. 7:7–8; Is. 65:24; 1 John 5:14; Ps. 27:13–14

772 In Holy Conversation

1 In ho-ly con-ver-sa-tion We speak to God in prayer,
2 These ho-ly con-ver-sa-tions Be-gin in child-like ways;
3 As ho-ly con-ver-sa-tion, In si-lence or by word,
And at His in-vi-ta-tion Our deep-est thoughts we share.
We bring our sup-pli-ca-tions And words of thanks and praise.
In ev-'ry sit-u-a-tion Through Je-sus, we are heard.
We come, His will o-bey-ing, As chil-dren bring-ing needs;
With care our Fa-ther lis-tens To ev-'ry thought ex-pressed,
So let us pray se-cure-ly, Ex-press-ing hopes and fears
And to sup-port our pray-ing, His Spir-it in-ter-cedes.
Then an-swers our pe-ti-tions In ways He knows are best.
With con-fi-dence that sure-ly Our Fa-ther ev-er hears.

Text: Gregory J. Wismar, b. 1946
Tune: Swedish; setting: *With One Voice*, 1995

BRED DINA VIDA VINGAR
76 76 D

Ps. 50:15; Phil. 4:6; Is. 65:24; 1 John 5:14

Hear Us, Father, When We Pray 773

1 Hear us, Father, when we pray,
Through Your Son and in Your Spirit.
By Your Spirit's Word convey
All that we through Christ inherit,
That as baptized heirs we may
Truly pray.

2 When we know not what to say
And our wounded souls are pleading,
May Your Spirit, night and day,
Groan within us interceding;
By His sighs, too deep for words,
We are heard.

3 Jesus, advocate on high,
Sacrificed on Calv'ry's altar,
Through Your priestly blood we cry:
Hear our prayers, though they may falter;
Place them on Your Father's throne
As Your own.

4 By Your Spirit now attend
To our prayers and supplications,
As like incense they ascend
To Your heav'nly habitations.
May their fragrance waft above,
God of love.

Text: Chad L. Bird, b. 1970
Tune: *Geist-reiches Gesang-Buch*, Halle, 1704, ed. Johann A. Freylinghausen;
setting: *The Lutheran Hymnal*, 1941

MORGENGLANZ DER EWIGKEIT
78 78 73

Matt. 6:9–13; Rom. 8:26–27; Heb. 4:14–16; Ps. 141:1–2

774 Feed Thy Children, God Most Holy

Feed Thy chil - dren, God most ho - ly; Com - fort sin - ners
poor and low - ly. O Thou Bread of Life from heav-en, Bless the
food Thou here hast giv - en! As these gifts the bod - y nour - ish,
May our souls in grac - es flour - ish Till with saints in
heav'n - ly splen - dor At Thy feast due thanks we ren - der.

Text: Johann Heermann, 1585–1647; tr. *The Lutheran Hymnal*, 1941
Tune: Johann Crüger, 1598–1662; setting: *The Lutheran Hymnal*, 1941

SCHMÜCKE DICH
88 88 D (Trochaic)

Ps. 145:15–17; John 6:35–38; Rev. 19:7–9

Be Present at Our Table, Lord 775

Be pres - ent at our ta - ble, Lord; Be here and
ev - 'ry - where a - dored; Thy crea - tures bless, and
grant that we May feast in par - a - dise with Thee.

Text: John Cennick, 1718–55
Tune: *Trente quatre Pseaumes de David*, Geneva, 1551, ed. Louis Bourgeois;
setting: *The Lutheran Hymnal*, 1941

OLD HUNDREDTH
L M

Ps. 145:15–16; Rev. 19:9; Is. 25:6

Come, Lord Jesus, Be Our Guest 776

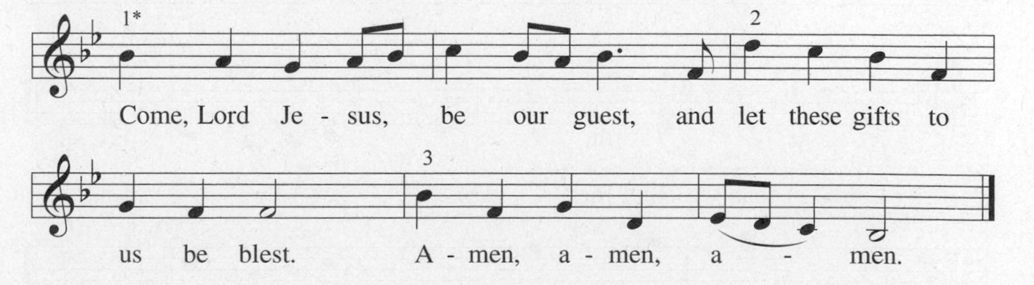
1*
2
Come, Lord Je - sus, be our guest, and let these gifts to
3
us be blest. A - men, a - men, a - men.

May be sung as a two- or three-part canon.

Text: German
Tune: German

KOMM, HERR JESU
Peculiar meter

Ps. 145:15–16; Luke 24:29–30; James 1:17a

777 Grant Peace, We Pray, in Mercy, Lord

Grant peace, we pray, in mer - cy, Lord; Peace
in our time, O send us! For there is
none on earth but You, None oth - er
to de - fend us. You on - ly,
Lord, can fight for us. A - men.

Text: Latin, c. 6th cent.; adapt. Martin Luther, 1483–1546; tr. *Laudamus*, Hannover, 1952
Music: Felix Mendelssohn, 1809–47

MENDELSSOHN DA PACEM
87 87 8

2 Thess. 3:16; Ps. 62:2, 6; Is. 31:5

Grant Peace, We Pray, in Mercy, Lord

Grant peace, we pray, in mer-cy, Lord; Peace in our time, O send us!
For there is none on earth but You, None oth-er to de-fend us.
You on - ly, Lord, can fight for us. A - men.

Text: Latin, c. 6th cent.; adapt. Martin Luther, 1483–1546; tr. *Laudamus*, Hannover, 1952
Tune: *Kirchen gesenge*, Nürnberg, 1531; setting: Carl F. Schalk, b. 1929

VERLEIH UNS FRIEDEN
87 87 8

2 Thess. 3:16; Ps. 62:2, 6; Is. 31:5

779 Come, My Soul, with Every Care

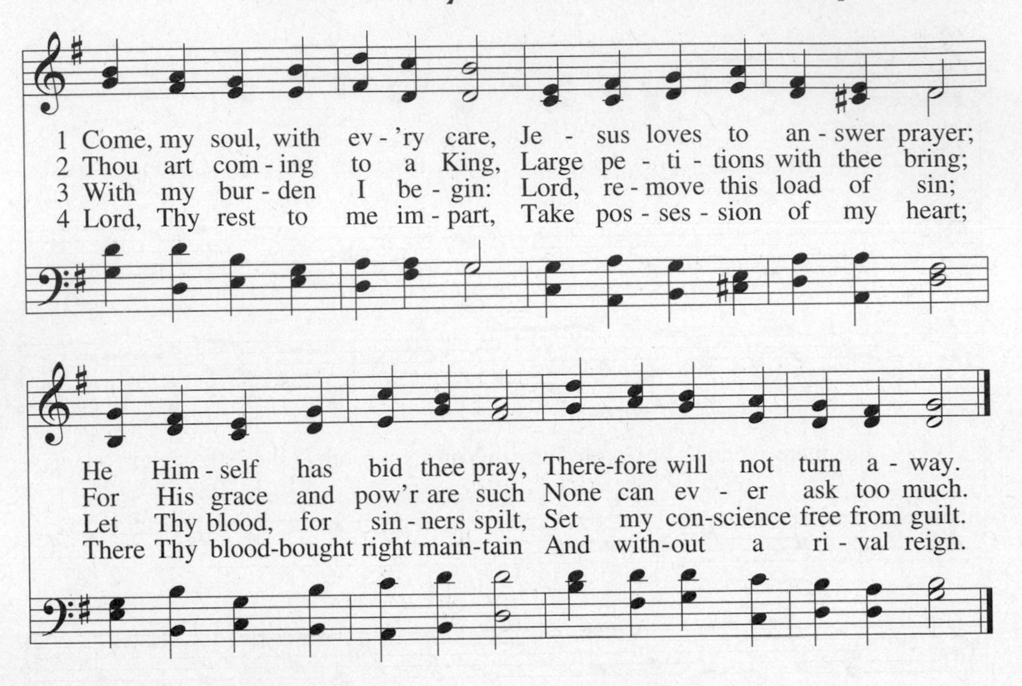
1 Come, my soul, with ev - 'ry care, Je - sus loves to an - swer prayer;
2 Thou art com - ing to a King, Large pe - ti - tions with thee bring;
3 With my bur - den I be - gin: Lord, re - move this load of sin;
4 Lord, Thy rest to me im - part, Take pos - ses - sion of my heart;
He Him - self has bid thee pray, There-fore will not turn a - way.
For His grace and pow'r are such None can ev - er ask too much.
Let Thy blood, for sin - ners spilt, Set my con-science free from guilt.
There Thy blood-bought right main-tain And with-out a ri - val reign.

5 While I am a pilgrim here,
Let Thy love my spirit cheer;
As my guide, my guard, my friend,
Lead me to my journey's end.

6 Show me what is mine to do;
Ev'ry hour my strength renew.
Let me live a life of faith;
Let me die Thy people's death.

Text: John Newton, 1725–1807, alt.
Tune: Justin H. Knecht, 1752–1817; setting: *The Lutheran Hymnal*, 1941

VIENNA
77 77

Matt. 6:5–13; 7:7–11; Luke 11:5–13; Heb. 4:16

780 O Lord, Hear My Prayer

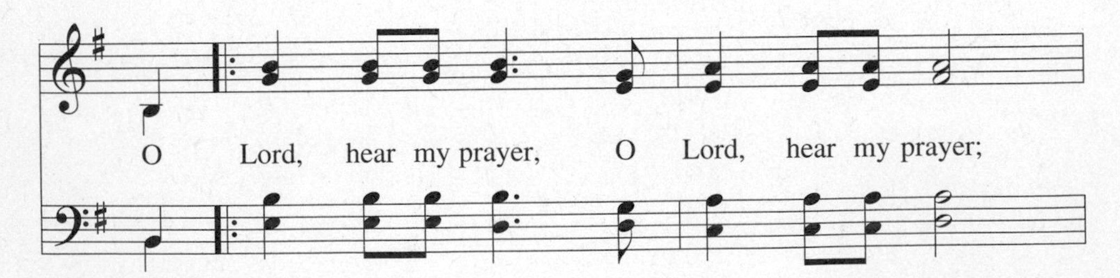
O Lord, hear my prayer, O Lord, hear my prayer;

Text: Taizé Community
Music: Jacques Berthier, 1923–94

HEAR MY PRAYER
55 6 D

Ps. 31:12; 102:1–2

When I call an - swer me. O Lord, hear my prayer, O
Lord, hear my prayer; Come and lis-ten to me. O me.
1
2

We Give Thee But Thine Own 781

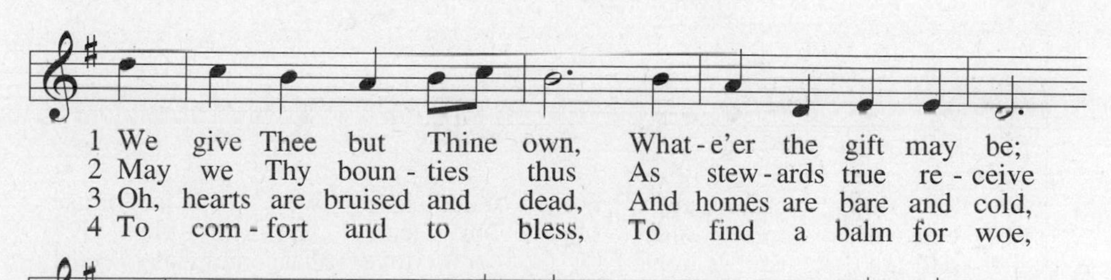
1 We give Thee but Thine own, What-e'er the gift may be;
2 May we Thy boun-ties thus As stew-ards true re-ceive
3 Oh, hearts are bruised and dead, And homes are bare and cold,
4 To com-fort and to bless, To find a balm for woe,
All that we have is Thine a-lone, A trust, O Lord, from Thee.
And glad-ly, as Thou bless-est us, To Thee our first-fruits give!
And lambs for whom the Shep-herd bled Are stray-ing from the fold.
To tend the lone and fa-ther-less Is an-gels' work be-low.

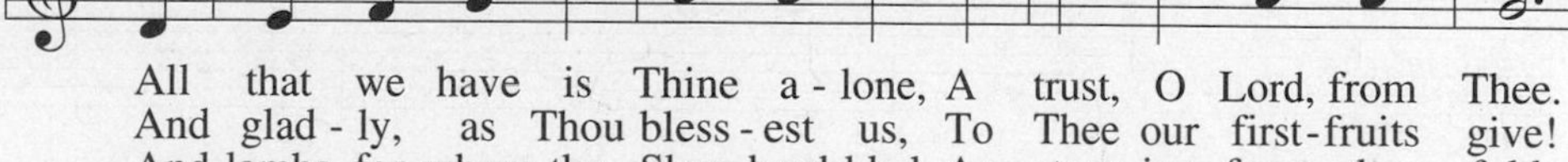

5 The captive to release,
To God the lost to bring,
To teach the way of life and peace,
It is a Christ-like thing.

6 And we believe Thy Word,
Though dim our faith may be:
Whate'er for Thine we do, O Lord,
We do it unto Thee.

Hymn accompaniment: 567

Text: William W. How, 1823–97
Tune: William H. Monk, 1823–89

ENERGY
S M

1 John 3:16–18; Matt. 25:40; Ex. 23:19a; James 1:27

782 Gracious God, You Send Great Blessings

1 Gra - cious God, You send great bless - ings
2 By Your Word You formed cre - a - tion
3 In His earth - ly life, our Sav - ior
△ 4 Heav'n - ly Fa - ther, may our car - ing
New each morn - ing all our days. For Your mer - cies
Filled with crea - tures large and small; As we tend that
Knew the care of faith - ful friends; May our deeds of
Bear the im - print of Your grace; With the Son and
nev - er end - ing, For Your love we of - fer praise.
end - less trea - sure May our care en - cir - cle all.
ded - i - ca - tion Of - fer love that nev - er ends.
Ho - ly Spir - it, Praise be Yours in ev - 'ry place!
Refrain
Lord, we pray that we, Your peo - ple Who Your gifts un - num - bered claim,

Text: Gregory J. Wismar, b. 1946
Tune: *Columbian Harmony*, Cincinnati, 1825; setting: Norman E. Johnson, 1928–83, alt.

HOLY MANNA
87 87 D

Lam. 3:22–23; 1 Peter 4:10–11; 1 John 3:16–18; Matt. 5:16

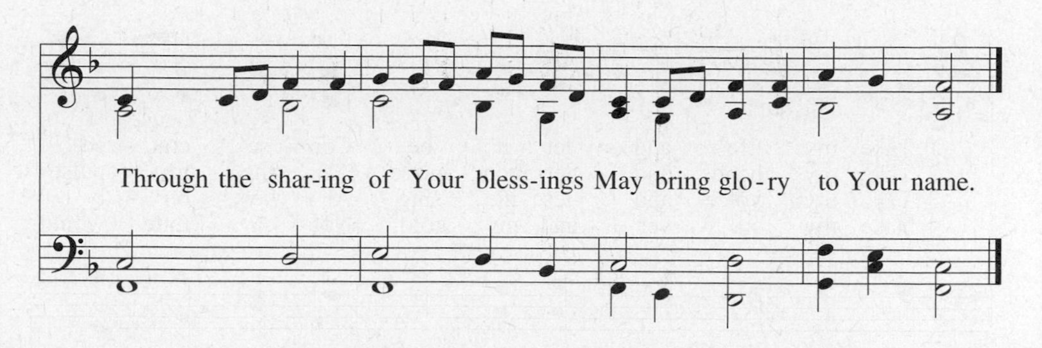
Through the shar-ing of Your bless-ings May bring glo-ry to Your name.

Take My Life and Let It Be 783

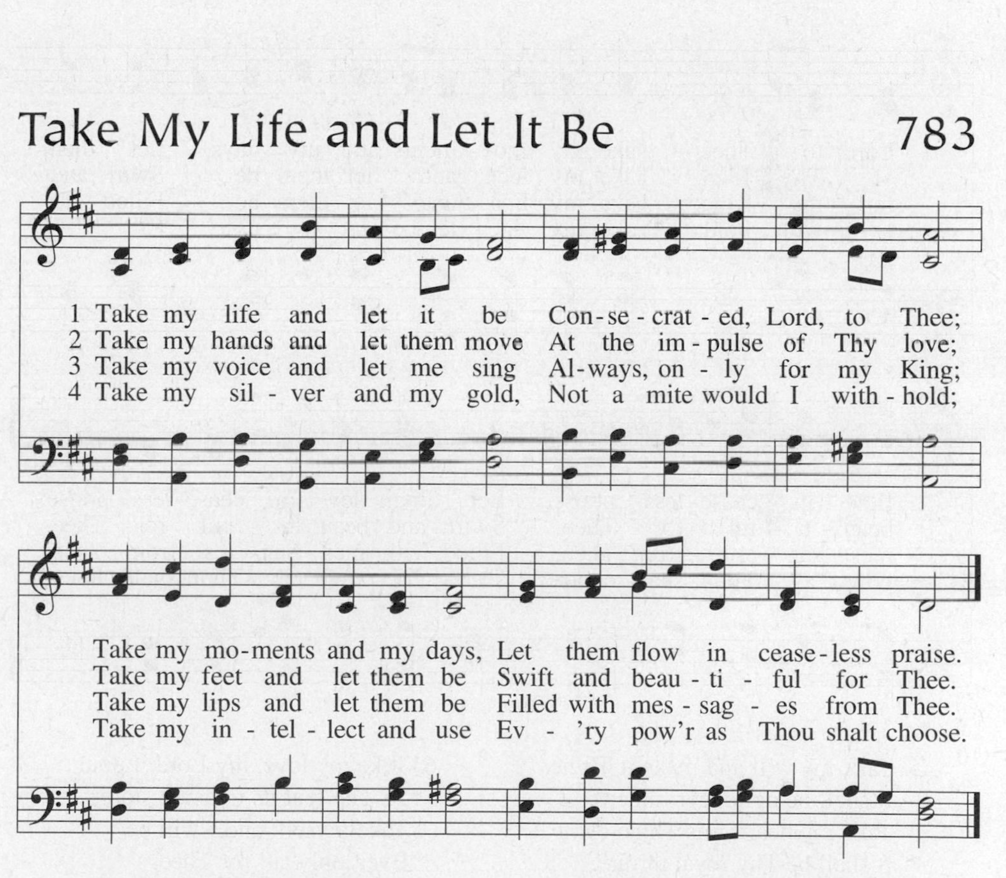
1 Take my life and let it be Con-se-crat-ed, Lord, to Thee;
2 Take my hands and let them move At the im-pulse of Thy love;
3 Take my voice and let me sing Al-ways, on-ly for my King;
4 Take my sil-ver and my gold, Not a mite would I with-hold;
Take my mo-ments and my days, Let them flow in cease-less praise.
Take my feet and let them be Swift and beau-ti-ful for Thee.
Take my lips and let them be Filled with mes-sag-es from Thee.
Take my in-tel-lect and use Ev-'ry pow'r as Thou shalt choose.

5 Take my will and make it Thine,
It shall be no longer mine;
Take my heart, it is Thine own,
It shall be Thy royal throne.

6 Take my love, my Lord, I pour
At Thy feet its treasure store;
Take myself, and I will be
Ever, only, all for Thee.

Text: Frances R. Havergal, 1836–79
Music: William H. Havergal, 1793–1870

PATMOS
77 77

Rom. 12:1–2; Rom. 6:13; 1 Cor. 6:20; 2 Cor. 5:15

784 Take My Life and Let It Be

1 Take my life and let it be Con - se - crat - ed,
2 Take my hands and let them move At the im - pulse
3 Take my voice and let me sing Al - ways, on - ly
4 Take my sil - ver and my gold, Not a mite would
Lord, to Thee; Take my mo - ments and my days, Let them
of Thy love; Take my feet and let them be Swift and
for my King; Take my lips and let them be Filled with
I with - hold; Take my in - tel - lect and use Ev - 'ry
flow in cease - less praise, Let them flow in cease - less praise.
beau - ti - ful for Thee, Swift and beau - ti - ful for Thee.
mes - sag - es from Thee, Filled with mes - sag - es from Thee.
pow'r as Thou shalt choose, Ev - 'ry pow'r as Thou shalt choose.

5 Take my will and make it Thine,
It shall be no longer mine;
Take my heart, it is Thine own,
It shall be Thy royal throne,
It shall be Thy royal throne.

6 Take my love, my Lord, I pour
At Thy feet its treasure store;
Take myself, and I will be
Ever, only, all for Thee,
Ever, only, all for Thee.

Text: Frances R. Havergal, 1836–79
Music: Henri A. C. Malan, 1787–1864

HENDON
77 77

Rom. 12:1–2; Rom. 6:13; 1 Cor. 6:20; 2 Cor. 5:15

We Praise You, O God

1 We praise You, O God, our Re - deem - er, Cre - a - tor;
2 We wor - ship You, God of our fa - thers, we bless You;
3 With voic - es u - nit - ed our prais - es we of - fer
In grate - ful de - vo - tion our trib - ute we bring.
Through tri - al and tem - pest our guide You have been.
And glad - ly our songs of thanks - giv - ing we raise.
We lay it be - fore You, we kneel and a - dore You;
When per - ils o'er - take us, You will not for - sake us,
With You, Lord, be - side us, Your strong arm will guide us.
We bless Your ho - ly name, glad prais - es we sing.
And with Your help, O Lord, our strug - gles we win.
To You, our great Re - deem - er, for - ev - er be praise!

Text: Julia B. Cory, 1882–1963, alt.
Tune: *Nederlandtsch Gedenckclanck*, Haarlem, 1626; setting: *Service Book and Hymnal*, 1958

KREMSER
12 11 12 11

Ps. 107:31–32; Ps. 44:1–8; 95:1–7

786 Lord of All Good

1 Lord of all - good, our gifts we bring You now;
2 We give our minds to un - der - stand Your ways;
△ 3 Fa - ther, whose boun - ty all cre - a - tion shows;
Use them Your ho - ly pur - pose to ful - fill.
Hands, eyes, and voice to serve Your great de - sign;
Christ, by whose will - ing sac - ri - fice we live;
To - kens of love and pledg - es they shall be
Hearts with the flame of Your own love a - blaze—
Spir - it, from whom all life in full - ness flows:
That our whole life is of - fered to Your will.
Thus for Your glo - ry all our pow'rs com - bine.
To You with grate - ful hearts our - selves we give.

Text: Albert F. Bayly, 1901–84, alt.
Tune: Henry Lawes, 1595–1662; setting: *New English Hymnal*, 1986

FARLEY CASTLE
10 10 10 10

Rom. 12:1; 1 Peter 4:10–11

The Temple Rang with Golden Coins

1 The tem - ple rang with gold - en coins The rich in bright ar - ray Con - trib - ut - ed from gleam - ing hoards Their scales could scarce - ly weigh.
2 A wid - ow came with cop - per coins And of - fered them in praise. They were the last she had to give Or save for dark - er days.
3 When Je - sus saw her cost - ly gift And knew she had no more, He praised a love that spared not self And called her rich, though poor.
4 At last He brought His of - fer - ing And laid it on a tree; There gave Him - self, His life, His love For all hu - man - i - ty.
5 Lord, help us all, with You, to yield What - ev - er love de - mands And free - ly give, as You have giv'n, With o - pen hearts and hands.

Text: Herman G. Stuempfle, Jr., 1923–2007
Tune: *The Whole Booke of Psalmes*, London, 1562; setting: Kermit G. Moldenhauer, b. 1949

ST. FLAVIAN
CM

Mark 12:41–44; Heb. 10:4–12

Forgive Us, Lord, for Shallow Thankfulness

1 For - give us, Lord, for shal - low thank - ful - ness,
2 Teach us to thank You, Lord, for love and grace,
3 For - give us, Lord, for self - ish thanks and praise,
4 Teach us, O Lord, true thank - ful - ness di - vine,
For dull con - tent with warmth and shel - tered care,
For life and vi - sion, for a pur - pose clear,
For words that speak at var - i - ance with deeds;
That gives as Christ gave, nev - er count - ing cost,
For songs of praise for food and har - vest press,
For Christ Your Son, and for each hu - man face
For - give our thanks for walk - ing pleas - ant ways
That knows no bar - ri - er of "yours" and "mine,"
While of Your rich - er gifts we're un - a - ware:
That shows Your mes - sage ev - er new and near.
Un - mind - ful of a bro - ken broth - er's needs:
As - sured that on - ly what's with - held is lost.

Text: William Watkins Reid, Sr., 1890–1983, alt.
Tune: Alfred M. Smith, 1879–1971; setting: Richard W. Hillert, 1923–2010

SURSUM CORDA
10 10 10 10

Phil. 1:9–11; Eph. 4:32—5:2; Rom. 2:4; Gal. 6:9–10

5 Forgive us, Lord, for feast that knows not fast,
For joy in things that meanwhile starve the soul,
For walls and wars that hide Your mercies vast
And blur our vision of the Kingdom goal:

6 Open our eyes to see Your love's intent,
To know with minds and hearts its depth and height;
May thankfulness be days in service spent,
Reflection of Christ's life and love and light.

Praise and Thanksgiving 789

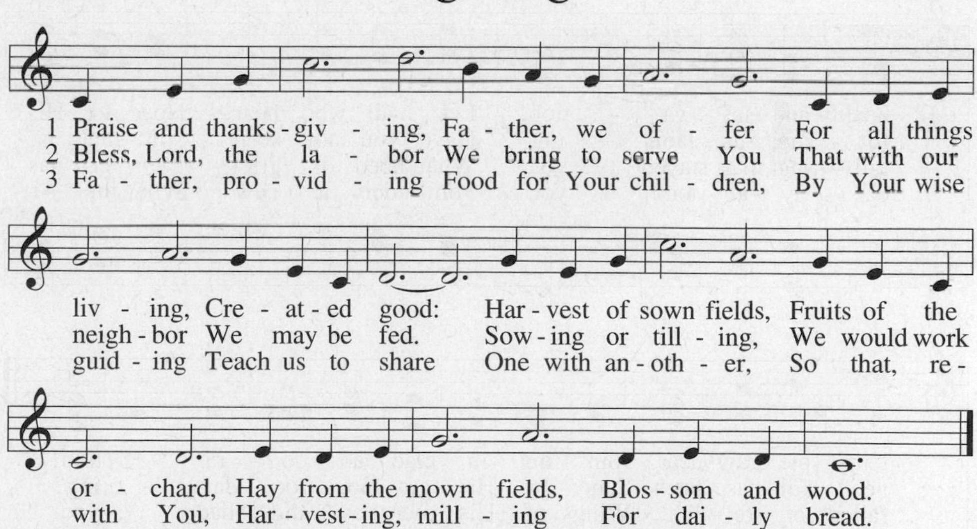
1 Praise and thanks - giv - ing, Fa - ther, we of - fer For all things
2 Bless, Lord, the la - bor We bring to serve You That with our
3 Fa - ther, pro - vid - ing Food for Your chil - dren, By Your wise
liv - ing, Cre - at - ed good: Har - vest of sown fields, Fruits of the
neigh - bor We may be fed. Sow - ing or till - ing, We would work
guid - ing Teach us to share One with an - oth - er, So that, re -
or - chard, Hay from the mown fields, Blos - som and wood.
with You, Har - vest - ing, mill - ing For dai - ly bread.
joic - ing With us, all oth - ers May know Your care.

Setting available in hymn accompaniment edition.

Text: Albert F. Bayly, 1901–84
Tune: Gaelic, 19th cent.

BUNESSAN
55 54 D

Eph. 5:19–20; Ps. 105:1–2; 107:31–38

790 Praise to the Lord, the Almighty

1 Praise to the Lord, the Al - might - y, the King of cre - a - tion! O my soul, praise Him, for He is your health and sal - va - tion! Let all who hear Now to His tem - ple draw near, Join - ing in glad ad - o - ra - tion!
2 Praise to the Lord, who o'er all things is won - drous - ly reign - ing And, as on wings of an ea - gle, up - lift - ing, sus - tain - ing. Have you not seen All that is need - ful has been Sent by His gra - cious or - dain - ing?
3 Praise to the Lord, who has fear - ful - ly, won - drous - ly, made you, Health has be - stowed and, when heed - less - ly fall - ing, has stayed you. What need or grief Ev - er has failed of re - lief? Wings of His mer - cy did shade you.
4 Praise to the Lord, who will pros - per your work and de - fend you; Sure - ly His good - ness and mer - cy shall dai - ly at - tend you. Pon - der a - new What the Al - might - y can do As with His love He be - friends you.

Text: Joachim Neander, 1650–80; tr. Catherine Winkworth, 1827–78, alt.
Tune: *Ander Theil Des Erneuerten Gesang-Buchs*, Stralsund, 1665;
setting: *The Chorale Book of England*, 1863, alt.

LOBE DEN HERREN
14 14 4 78

1 Chron. 16:23–26; Ps. 103:1–11; 106:48

5 Praise to the Lord! O let all that is in me adore Him!
All that has life and breath, come now with praises before Him!
  Let the Amen
  Sound from His people again;
Gladly forever adore Him!

All People That on Earth Do Dwell 791

1 All peo - ple that on earth do dwell, Sing to the
2 Know that the Lord is God in - deed; With - out our
3 O en - ter then His gates with praise; Ap - proach with
4 For why? The Lord our God is good: His mer - cy
△ 5 To Fa - ther, Son, and Ho - ly Ghost, The God whom
Lord with cheer - ful voice. Him serve with mirth, His
aid He did us make. We are His folk, He
joy His courts un - to. Praise, laud, and bless His
is for - ev - er sure. His truth at all times
heav'n and earth a - dore, From us and from the
praise forth - tell; Come ye be - fore Him and re - joice.
doth us feed, And for His sheep He doth us take.
name al - ways, For it is seem - ly so to do.
firm - ly stood And shall from age to age en - dure.
an - gel host Be praise and glo - ry ev - er - more.

Text: William Kethe, d. c. 1593, alt.
Tune: *Trente quatre Pseaumes de David*, Geneva, 1551, ed. Louis Bourgeois; setting: *Common Praise*, 2000

OLD HUNDREDTH
L M

Psalm 100

792 New Songs of Celebration Render

1 New songs of cel - e - bra - tion ren - der To Him who
2 Joy - ful - ly, heart - i - ly re - sound - ing, Let ev - 'ry
3 Riv - ers and seas and tor - rents roar - ing, Hon - or the
has great won - ders done; Love sits en - throned in age - less
in - stru - ment and voice Peal out the praise of grace a -
Lord with wild ac - claim; Moun - tains and stones, look up a -
splen - dor; Come and a - dore the might - y One.
bound - ing, Call - ing the whole world to re - joice.
dor - ing, And find a voice to praise His name.
He has made known His great sal - va - tion Which
Trum - pets and or - gans, set in mo - tion Such
Righ - teous, com - mand - ing, ev - er glo - rious, Prais -

Text: Erik Routley, 1917–82
Tune: attr. Louis Bourgeois, c. 1510–61; setting: *Hymnal Supplement 1998*

RENDEZ À DIEU
98 98 D

Psalm 98

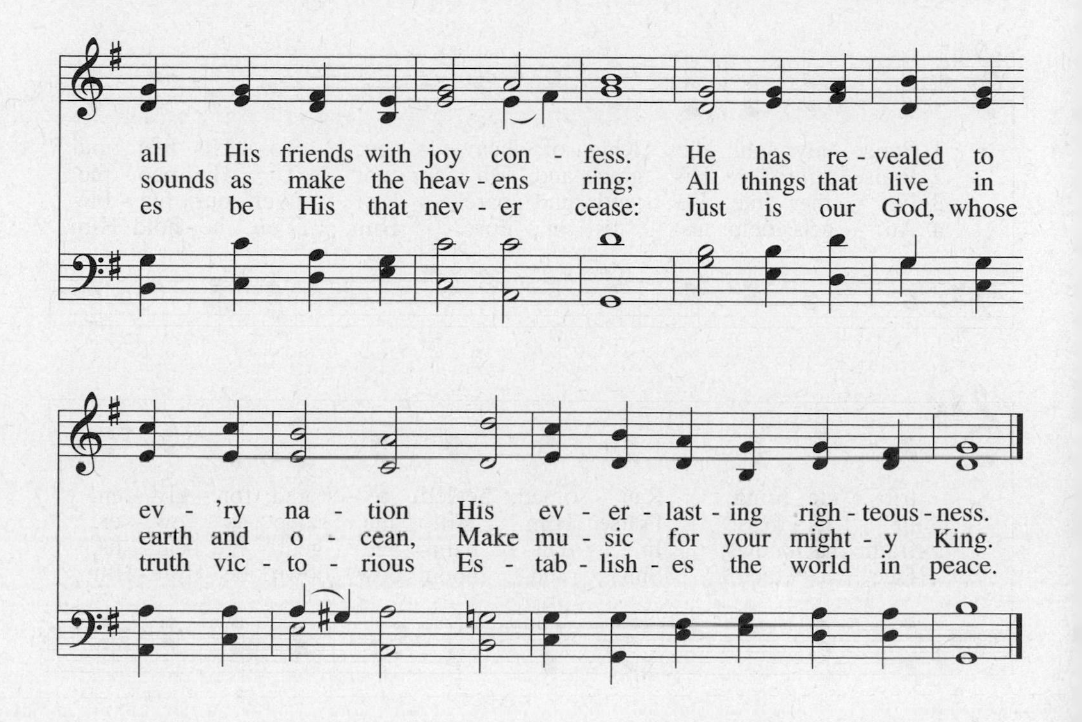
all His friends with joy con - fess. He has re - vealed to
sounds as make the heav - ens ring; All things that live in
es be His that nev - er cease: Just is our God, whose
ev - 'ry na - tion His ev - er - last - ing righ - teous - ness.
earth and o - cean, Make mu - sic for your might - y King.
truth vic - to - rious Es - tab - lish - es the world in peace.

Let the word of Christ dwell in you richly, teaching and admonishing one another in all wisdom, singing psalms and hymns and spiritual songs, with thankfulness in your hearts to God.

Colossians 3:16

793 Praise, My Soul, the King of Heaven

1 Praise, my soul, the King of heav - en; To His feet your trib - ute bring; Ran - somed, healed, re - stored, for - giv - en, Ev - er - more His prais - es sing: Al - le - lu - ia, al - le - lu - ia! Praise the ev - er - last - ing King.
2 Praise Him for His grace and fa - vor To His peo - ple in dis - tress; Praise Him still the same as ev - er, Slow to chide and swift to bless: Al - le - lu - ia, al - le - lu - ia! Glo - rious in His faith - ful - ness.
3 Fa - ther - like He tends and spares us; Well our fee - ble frame He knows; In His hand He gent - ly bears us, Res - cues us from all our foes. Al - le - lu - ia, al - le - lu - ia! Wide - ly yet His mer - cy flows.
4 An - gels, help us to a - dore Him; You be - hold Him face to face; Sun and moon, bow down be - fore Him, All who dwell in time and space. Al - le - lu - ia, al - le - lu - ia! Praise with us the God of grace.

Text: Henry F. Lyte, 1793–1847
Music: John Goss, 1800–80

LAUDA ANIMA
87 87 87

Psalm 103

The Lord, My God, Be Praised 794

1 The Lord, my God, be praised, My light, my life from heav - en;
2 The Lord, my God, be praised, My trust, my life from heav - en,
3 The Lord, my God, be praised, My hope, my life from heav - en,
△ 4 The Lord, my God, be praised, My God, the ev - er - liv - ing,
My mak - er, who to me Has soul and bod - y giv - en;
The Fa - ther's own dear Son, Whose life for me was giv - en,
The Spir - it, whom the Son In love to me has giv - en.
To whom the heav'n - ly host Their laud and praise are giv - ing.
My Fa - ther, who will shield And keep me day by day
Who for my sin a - toned With His most pre - cious blood
His grace re - vives my heart And gives my spir - it pow'r,
The Lord, my God, be praised, In whose great name I boast,
And make each mo - ment yield New bless - ings on my way.
And gives to me by faith The high - est heav'n - ly good.
Help, com - fort, and sup - port In sor - row's gloom - y hour.
God Fa - ther, God the Son, And God the Ho - ly Ghost.

Text: Johann Olearius, 1611–84; tr. August Crull, 1845–1923, alt.
Tune: Johann Crüger, 1598–1662; setting: *The Lutheran Hymnal*, 1941

NUN DANKET ALLE GOTT
67 67 66 66

Deut. 32:3; Ps. 5:11–12; Rom. 3:24–25a; 8:26–27

795 Voices Raised to You We Offer

1 Voic - es raised to You we of - fer; Tune them, God, for
2 All cre - a - tion joins to praise You; Earth and sky Your
3 Christ, the song of Love in - car - nate, Touch - ing earth with
4 Spir - it, flam - ing through cre - a - tion, Kin - dle faith with -
songs of praise. Hearts and hands we bring in trib - ute
works dis - play. Art and mu - sic, gifts You lend us,
heav - en's grace, For Your liv - ing, suf - f'ring, dy - ing,
in each heart. Lift our voic - es high in cho - rus;
For Your gifts through all our days. Al - le - lu - ia!
We re - turn to You to - day. Al - le - lu - ia!
For Your ris - ing, hear our praise! Al - le - lu - ia!
Through our hands Your love im - part. Al - le - lu - ia!
Al - le - lu - ia! Tri - une God, to You we sing!
Al - le - lu - ia! God, Cre - a - tor, source of life!
Al - le - lu - ia! Christ, Re - deem - er, Lord of life!
Al - le - lu - ia! Spir - it, Help - er, breath of life!

Text: Herman G. Stuempfle, Jr., 1923–2007
Music: Carolyn Jennings, b. 1936

SONG OF PRAISE
87 87 87

Col. 3:16; Is. 12:2; 2 Cor. 4:13; Ps. 147:1

5 How can any praise we offer
Measure all the thanks we owe?
Take our hearts and hands and voices—
Gifts of love we can bestow.
Alleluia! Alleluia!
Triune God, to You we sing!

When in Our Music God Is Glorified

796

1 When in our mu - sic God is glo - ri - fied
2 How of - ten, mak - ing mu - sic, we have found
3 So has the Church, in lit - ur - gy and song,
4 And did not Je - sus sing a psalm that night
5 Let ev - 'ry in - stru - ment be tuned for praise!
And ad - o - ra - tion leaves no room for pride,
A new di - men - sion in the world of sound
In faith and love, through cen - tu - ries of wrong,
When ut - most e - vil strove a - gainst the light?
Let all re - joice who have a voice to raise!
It is as though the whole cre - a - tion cried:
As wor - ship moved us to a more pro - found
Borne wit - ness to the truth in ev - 'ry tongue:
Then let us sing, for whom He won the fight:
And may God give us faith to sing al - ways:
Al - le - lu - ia!

Hymn accompaniment: 815

Text: Fred Pratt Green, 1903–2000
Tune: Charles V. Stanford, 1852–1924

ENGELBERG
10 10 10 4

1 Chron. 16:4–36; 2 Chron. 5:13–14; Col. 3:16–17; Mark 14:26

797 Praise the Almighty

1 Praise the Al - might - y, my soul, a - dore Him!
2 Trust not in rul - ers; they are but mor - tal;
3 Bless - ed, oh, bless - ed are they for - ev - er
4 Pen - i - tent sin - ners, for mer - cy cry - ing,
Yes, I will laud Him un - til death; With songs and
Earth - born they are and soon de - cay. Vain are their
Whose help is from the Lord Most High, Whom from sal -
Par - don and peace from Him ob - tain; Ev - er the
an - thems I come be - fore Him As long as
coun - sels at life's last por - tal, When the dark
va - tion can noth - ing sev - er, And who in
wants of the poor sup - ply - ing, Their faith - ful
He al - lows me breath. From Him my life and
grave en - gulfs its prey. Since mor - tals can no
hope to Christ draw nigh. To all who trust in
God He will re - main. He helps His chil - dren

Text: Johann Daniel Herrnschmidt, 1675–1723; tr. Alfred E. R. Brauer, 1866–1949, alt.
Tune: *New-vermehrte Christliche Seelenharpf*, Ansbach, 1665; setting: *Christian Worship*, 1993

LOBE DEN HERREN, O MEINE SEELE
10 8 10 8 88 8

Psalm 146

all things came; Bless, O my soul, His ho - ly name.
help af - ford, Place all your trust in Christ, our Lord.
Him, our Lord Will aid and coun - sel now af - ford.
in dis - tress, The wid - ows and the fa - ther - less.
Al - le - lu - ia, al - le - lu - ia!

△ 5 Praise, all you people, the name so holy
Of Him who does such wondrous things!
All that has being, to praise Him solely,
With happy heart its amen sings.
Children of God, with angel host
Praise Father, Son, and Holy Ghost!
Alleluia, alleluia!

798 The God of Abraham Praise

1 The God of A - br'ham praise, Who reigns en - throned a - bove;
2 The God of A - br'ham praise, At whose su - preme com - mand
3 The God of A - br'ham praise, Whose all - suf - fi - cient grace
4 He by Him - self has sworn; I on His oath de - pend.
An - cient of ev - er - last - ing days And God of love.
From earth I rise and seek the joys At His right hand.
Shall guide me all my pil - grim days In all my ways.
I shall, on ea - gle wings up - borne, To heav'n as - cend.
Je - ho - vah, great I AM! By earth and heav'n con - fessed;
I all on earth for - sake, Its wis - dom, fame, and pow'r,
He deigns to call me friend; He calls Him - self my God.
I shall be - hold His face; I shall His pow'r a - dore
I bow and bless the sa - cred name For - ev - er blest.
And Him my on - ly por - tion make, My shield and tow'r.
And He shall save me to the end Through Je - sus' blood.
And sing the won - ders of His grace For - ev - er - more.

Text: Thomas Olivers, 1725–99, alt.
Tune: Hebrew; setting: *Hymns Ancient and Modern*, 1875

YIGDAL
6684 D

Ex. 3:6, 14; Ps. 142:5–6; Ps. 9:7–11; Rev. 4:8

5 Though nature's strength decay,
And earth and hell withstand,
To Canaan's bounds I urge my way
At His command.
The wat'ry deep I pass,
With Jesus in my view,
And through the howling wilderness
My way pursue.

6 The goodly land I see,
With peace and plenty blest:
A land of sacred liberty
And endless rest.
There milk and honey flow,
And oil and wine abound,
And trees of life forever grow
With mercy crowned.

7 There dwells the Lord our king,
The Lord our righteousness,
Triumphant o'er the world and sin,
The Prince of Peace.
On Zion's sacred height
His kingdom He maintains
And glorious with His saints in light
Forever reigns.

8 The God who reigns on high
The great archangels sing,
And "Holy, holy, holy!" cry,
"Almighty King!
Who was and is the same
And evermore shall be:
Jehovah, Father, great I AM!
We worship Thee!"

△ 9 The whole triumphant host
Give thanks to God on high.
"Hail, Father, Son, and Holy Ghost!"
They ever cry.
Hail, Abr'ham's God and mine!
I join the heav'nly lays:
All might and majesty are Thine
And endless praise!

799 Alabaré — I

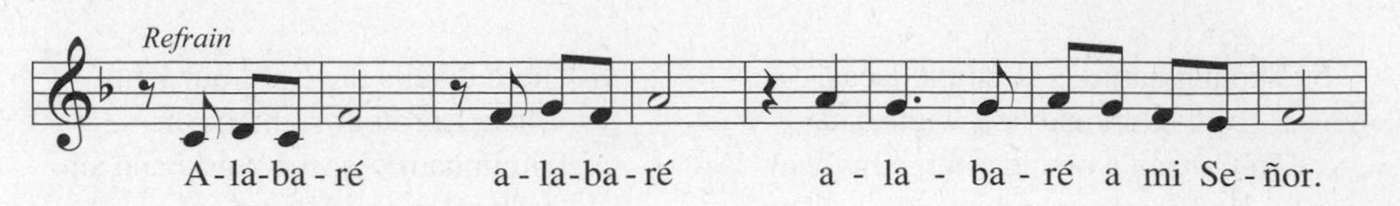
Refrain
A-la-ba-ré a-la-ba-ré a - la - ba-ré a mi Se-ñor.

A-la-ba-ré a-la-ba-ré a - la - ba-ré a mi Se - ñor.

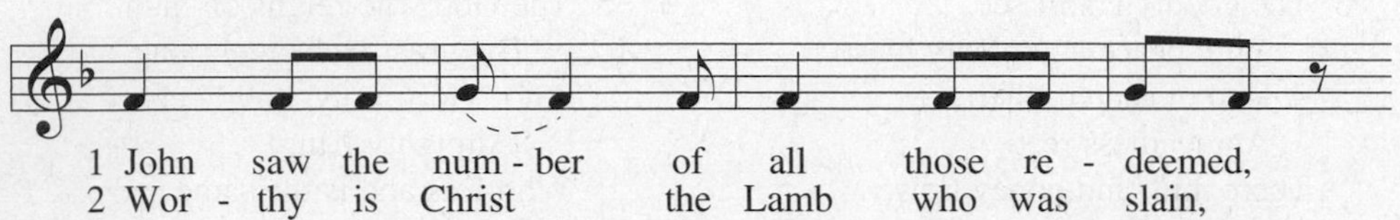
1 John saw the num-ber of all those re - deemed,
2 Wor - thy is Christ the Lamb who was slain,
3 Sing with the peo-ple, the peo - ple of God,

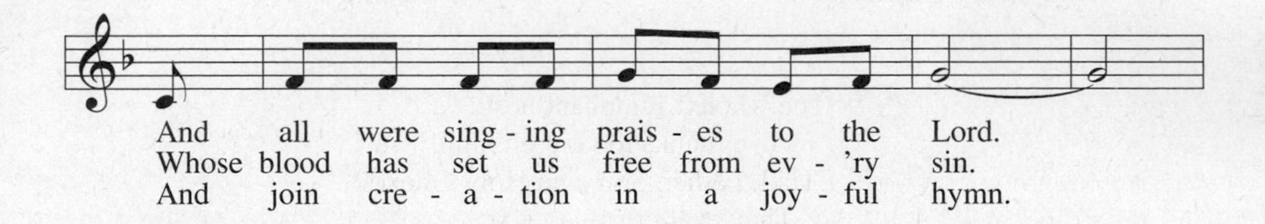
And all were sing-ing prais-es to the Lord.
Whose blood has set us free from ev - 'ry sin.
And join cre - a - tion in a joy - ful hymn.

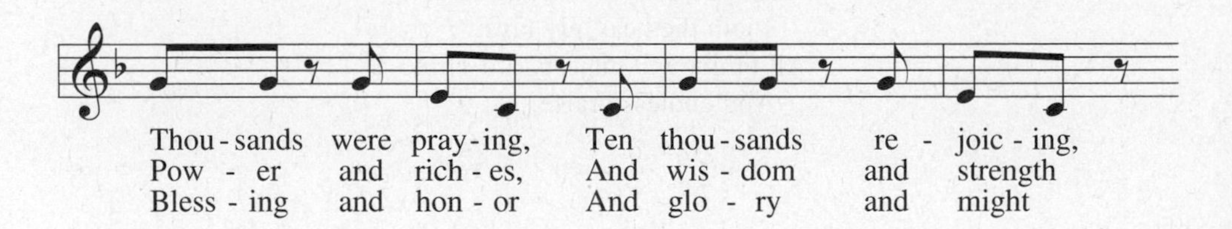
Thou-sands were pray-ing, Ten thou-sands re - joic-ing,
Pow - er and rich-es, And wis-dom and strength
Bless-ing and hon-or And glo - ry and might

Refrain
And all were sing-ing prais-es to the Lord.
And hon - or and all bless-ing shall be His.
To God and to the Lamb be with - out end.

Alabaré a mi Señor (Ah-lah-bah-RAY ah mee sen-YOR): I will praise my Lord.
Setting available in hymn accompaniment edition.

Text: Manuel José Alonso, refrain; José Pagán, 1916–2009, refrain; tr. *Libro de Liturgia y Cántico*, 1998, st. 1; John Ylvisaker, b. 1937, sts. 2–3
Tune: Manuel José Alonso; José Pagán, 1916–2009

ALABARÉ
Irregular meter

Rev. 5:8–13; 7:9–15

Alabaré — II

800

Refrain/Estribillo

Alabaré alabaré alabaré a mi Señor.
Alabaré alabaré alabaré a mi Señor.

1 John saw the number of all those redeemed,
And all were singing praises to the Lord.
Thousands were praying,
Ten thousands rejoicing,
And all were singing praises to the Lord.
Refrain

1 Juan vio el número de los redimidos,
y todos alababan al Señor:
unos oraban,
otros cantaban,
mas todos alababan al Señor.
Estribillo

2 Voices united in joy and in singing,
We offer praise and glory to our God:
To God the Father,
To Christ the Savior,
And to the Holy Spirit, Three in One.
Refrain

2 Todos unidos, alegres cantemos
gloria y alabanzas al Señor:
gloria al Padre,
gloria al Hijo,
y gloria al Espíritu de amor.
Estribillo

3 We are Your people, O God everlasting,
The people You created out of love.
Mercy and justice,
Power and wisdom:
We bless You, we adore You without end.
Refrain

3 Somos tu pueblo, Dios Padre eterno;
tú nos has creado por amor.
Te adoramos,
te bendecimos,
y todos cantamos en tu honor.
Estribillo

Alabaré a mi Señor (Ah-lah-bah-RAY ah mee sen-YOR): I will praise my Lord.
This text is sung to the same melody as on the facing page.

Text: Manuel José Alonso, Spanish; José Pagán, 1916–2009, Spanish;
English tr. *Libro de Liturgia y Cántico*, 1998

ALABARÉ
Irregular meter

Rev. 5:8–13; 7:9–15

801 How Great Thou Art

1 O Lord my God, when I in awe-some won - der Con - sid - er
2 When through the woods and for - est glades I wan - der, I hear the
3 But when I think that God, His Son not spar - ing, Sent Him to
4 When Christ shall come with shout of ac - cla - ma - tion And take me
all the works Thy hand hath made, I see the stars, I hear the might - y
birds sing sweet - ly in the trees; When I look down from loft - y moun - tain
die, I scarce can take it in— That on the cross my bur - den glad - ly
home, what joy shall fill my heart! Then I shall bow in hum - ble ad - o-
thun - der, Thy pow'r through - out the u - ni - verse dis - played;
gran - deur And hear the brook and feel the gen - tle breeze;
bear - ing He bled and died to take a - way my sin;
ra - tion And there pro - claim: "My God, how great Thou art!"
Refrain
Then sings my soul, my Sav - ior God, to Thee, How great Thou

Text: Carl Gustaf Boberg, 1859–1940; tr. Stuart W. K. Hine, 1899–1989
Tune: Swedish; arr. and harm. Stuart W. K. Hine, 1899–1989

O STORE GUD
11 10 11 10 and refrain

Rev. 15:3b–4; Gen. 1:1–25; Is. 53:3–12; 1 Thess. 4:16–17

art! How great Thou art! Then sings my soul, my Sav - ior God, to
Thee, How great Thou art! How great Thou art!

Living God, Your almighty power is made known chiefly in showing mercy and pity. Grant us the fullness of Your grace to lay hold of Your promises and live forever in Your presence; through Jesus Christ, Your Son, our Lord, who lives and reigns with You and the Holy Spirit, one God, now and forever. Collect for Proper 27, Series C

802 Immortal, Invisible, God Only Wise

1 Im - mor - tal, in - vis - i - ble, God on - ly wise,
2 Un - rest - ing, un - hast - ing, and si - lent as light,
3 To all life Thou giv - est— to both great and small—
4 Great Fa - ther of glo - ry, pure Fa - ther of light,
In light in - ac - ces - si - ble hid from our eyes,
Nor want - ing, nor wast - ing, Thou rul - est in might;
In all life Thou liv - est, the true Life of all;
Thine an - gels a - dore Thee, all veil - ing their sight;
Most bless - ed, most glo - rious, the An - cient of Days,
Thy jus - tice like moun - tains high soar - ing a - bove
We blos - som and flour - ish as leaves on the tree
All laud we would ren - der: O help us to see
Al - might - y, vic - to - rious, Thy great name we praise.
Thy clouds which are foun - tains of good - ness and love.
And with - er and per - ish— but naught chang - es Thee.
'Tis on - ly the splen - dor of light that hides Thee.

Text: W. Chalmers Smith, 1824–1908, alt.
Tune: Welsh; setting: Richard W. Hillert, 1923–2010

ST. DENIO
11 11 11 11

Ps. 104:1–5, 31–35; Dan. 7:13; 1 Tim. 1:17; 6:15–16

Joyful, Joyful We Adore Thee 803

1 Joy - ful, joy - ful we a - dore Thee, God of glo - ry, Lord of love!
2 All Thy works with joy sur-round Thee, Earth and heav'n re - flect Thy rays,
△ 3 Thou art giv - ing and for - giv - ing, Ev - er bless-ing, ev - er blest,

Hearts un - fold like flow'rs be - fore Thee, Prais-ing Thee, their sun a - bove.
Stars and an-gels sing a-round Thee, Cen - ter of un - bro-ken praise.
Well-spring of the joy of liv - ing, O - cean-depth of hap - py rest!

Melt the clouds of sin and sad - ness, Drive the gloom of doubt a - way.
Field and for - est, vale and moun-tain, Flow - 'ry mead-ow, flash-ing sea,
Fa - ther, Son, and Ho - ly Spir - it, Foun - tain - head of love di - vine:

Giv - er of im - mor - tal glad-ness, Fill us with the light of day.
Chant-ing bird, and flow - ing foun-tain Call us to re - joice in Thee.
Joy - ful, we Thy heav'n in - her - it! Joy - ful, we by grace are Thine!

Text: Henry Van Dyke, 1852–1933, alt.
Music: Ludwig van Beethoven, 1770–1827; adapt. Edward Hodges, 1796–1867

HYMN TO JOY
87 87 D

Ps. 5:11; Phil. 4:4; Ps. 8:3

804 O Worship the King

1 O wor - ship the King, all - glo - rious a - bove.
2 O tell of His might, O sing of His grace,
3 This earth, with its store of won - ders un - told,
4 Thy boun - ti - ful care what tongue can re - cite?
O grate - ful - ly sing His pow'r and His love;
Whose robe is the light, whose can - o - py space;
Al - might - y, Thy pow'r hath found - ed of old,
It breathes in the air, it shines in the light,
Our shield and de - fend - er, the An - cient of Days,
His char - iots of wrath the deep thun - der - clouds form,
Es - tab - lished it fast by a change - less de - cree,
It streams from the hills, it de - scends to the plain,
Pa - vil - ioned in splen - dor and gird - ed with praise.
And dark is His path on the wings of the storm.
And round it hath cast, like a man - tle, the sea.
And sweet - ly dis - tills in the dew and the rain.

Text: Robert Grant, 1779–1838, alt.
Tune: William Croft, 1678–1727; setting: *The Lutheran Hymnal*, 1941

HANOVER
10 10 11 11

Psalm 104; Ps. 103:20–22; Is. 66:15; Luke 1:78

5 Frail children of dust
and feeble as frail,
In Thee do we trust,
nor find Thee to fail.
Thy mercies, how tender,
how firm to the end,
Our maker, defender,
redeemer, and friend!

6 O measureless Might,
ineffable Love,
While angels delight
to hymn Thee above,
Thy humbler creation,
though feeble their lays,
With true adoration
shall sing to Thy praise.

Praise God, from Whom All Blessings Flow 805

△ Praise God, from whom all bless - ings flow; Praise Him, all
crea - tures here be - low; Praise Him a - bove, ye heav'n - ly
host: Praise Fa - ther, Son, and Ho - ly Ghost. A - men.

Text: Thomas Ken, 1637–1711
Tune: *Trente quatre Pseaumes de David,* Geneva, 1551, ed. Louis Bourgeois;
setting: *The Lutheran Hymnal*, 1941

OLD HUNDREDTH
L M

Psalm 150; Is. 6:1–4; Rev. 4:8

806 Give Thanks with a Grateful Heart

Give thanks with a grate - ful heart, Give thanks to the
Ho - ly One, Give thanks be - cause He's giv - en Je - sus
Christ His Son. Give thanks with a grate - ful heart, Give
thanks to the Ho - ly One, Give thanks be-cause He's giv-en
Je - sus Christ His Son. And now let the weak say "I am
strong," Let the poor say "I am rich," Be-cause of
what the Lord has done for us. And now let the
weak say "I am strong," Let the poor say "I am
rich," Be - cause of what the Lord has done for us.
Give thanks, give thanks.

Setting available in hymn accompaniment edition.

Text: Henry Smith, b. 1952
Tune: Henry Smith, b. 1952

GIVE THANKS
Peculiar meter

2 Cor. 9:15; 12:9–10; 2 Cor. 8:9

When Morning Gilds the Skies 807

1 When morn-ing gilds the skies, My heart, a - wak - ing, cries,
2 When mirth for mu - sic longs, This is my song of songs:
3 No love-lier an - ti - phon In all high heav'n is known
4 Ye na - tions of man - kind, In this your con - cord find:
5 Sing, suns and stars of space, Sing, ye that see His face,

"May Je - sus Christ be praised!" When eve - ning shad-ows fall,
"May Je - sus Christ be praised!" God's ho - ly house of prayer
Than "Je - sus Christ be praised!" There to the e - ter - nal Word
"May Je - sus Christ be praised!" Let all the earth a - round
Sing, "Je - sus Christ be praised!" God's whole cre - a - tion o'er,

This rings my cur - few call: "May Je - sus Christ be praised!"
Hath none that can com - pare With "Je - sus Christ be praised!"
The e - ter - nal psalm is heard: "May Je - sus Christ be praised!"
Ring joy - ous with the sound: "May Je - sus Christ be praised!"
Both now and ev - er - more Shall Je - sus Christ be praised!

Text: *Katholisches Gesangbuch*, Würzburg, 1828; tr. Robert S. Bridges, 1844–1930, alt.
Tune: Joseph Barnby, 1838–96; setting: *Service Book and Hymnal*, 1958

LAUDES DOMINI
666 666

Luke 19:37–38; Phil. 2:9–11; John 1:1–4, 14; Rev. 6:11–14

808 O Sing to the Lord

1 O sing to the Lord, O sing God a new song. O sing to the Lord, O sing God a new song. O sing to the Lord, O sing God a new song. O sing to our God, O sing to our God.

2 For God is the Lord! And God has done wonders. For God is the Lord! And God has done wonders. For God is the Lord! And God has done wonders. O sing to our God, O sing to our God.

1 Cantad al Señor un cántico nuevo, cantad al Señor un cántico nuevo, cantad al Señor un cántico nuevo. ¡Cantad al Señor, cantad al Señor!

2 Pues nuestro Señor ha hecho prodigios, pues nuestro Señor ha hecho prodigios, nuestro Señor ha hecho prodigios. ¡Cantad al Señor, cantad al Señor!

Text: Brazilian; Spanish and English tr. Gerhard Cartford, b. 1923
Tune: Brazilian; setting: Jack Schrader, b. 1942

CANTAD AL SEÑOR
56 56 56 55

Psalm 98; Psalm 150; 1 Cor. 12:3

3 So dance for our God
And blow all the trumpets.
So dance for our God
And blow all the trumpets.
So dance for our God
And blow all the trumpets.
And sing to our God,
And sing to our God.

4 O shout to our God,
Who gave us the Spirit.
O shout to our God,
Who gave us the Spirit.
O shout to our God,
Who gave us the Spirit.
O sing to our God,
O sing to our God.

5 For Jesus is Lord!
Amen! Alleluia!
For Jesus is Lord!
Amen! Alleluia!
For Jesus is Lord!
Amen! Alleluia!
O sing to our God,
O sing to our God.

3 Cantad al Señor,
alabadle con arpa,
cantad al Señor,
alabadle con arpa,
cantad al Señor,
alabadle con arpa.
¡Cantad al Señor,
cantad al Señor!

4 Es él que nos da
el Espíritu Santo,
es él que nos da
el Espíritu Santo,
es él que nos da
el Espíritu Santo.
¡Cantad al Señor,
cantad al Señor!

5 ¡Jesús es Señor!
¡Amén, aleluya!
¡Jesús es Señor!
¡Amén, aleluya!
¡Jesús es Señor!
¡Amén, aleluya!
¡Cantad al Señor,
cantad al Señor!

809 Great Is Thy Faithfulness

1 Great is Thy faith - ful - ness, O God my Fa - ther;
2 Sum - mer and win - ter and spring - time and har - vest,
3 Par - don for sin and a peace that en - dur - eth,
There is no shad - ow of turn - ing with Thee.
Sun, moon, and stars in their cours - es a - bove
Thine own dear pres - ence to cheer and to guide;
Thou chang - est not: Thy com - pas - sions, they fail not;
Join with all na - ture in man - i - fold wit - ness
Strength for to - day and bright hope for to - mor - row,
As Thou hast been, Thou for - ev - er wilt be.
To Thy great faith - ful - ness, mer - cy, and love.
Bless - ings all mine, with ten thou - sand be - side!

Text: Thomas O. Chisholm, 1866–1960
Music: William M. Runyan, 1870–1957

FAITHFULNESS
11 10 11 10 and refrain

Lam. 3:22–24; James 1:17; Gen. 8:20–22; Ps. 89:1–2

Refrain
Great is Thy faith-ful-ness! Great is Thy faith-ful-ness!
Morn-ing by morn-ing new mer-cies I see;
All I have need - ed Thy hand hath pro - vid - ed;
Great is Thy faith - ful-ness, Lord, un - to me!

810 O God of God, O Light of Light

1 O God of God, O Light of Light, O Prince of Peace and King of kings: To You in heav-en's glo - ry bright The song of praise for - ev - er rings. To Him who sits up - on the throne, The Lamb once slain but raised a - gain, Be all the glo - ry
2 For deep in proph - ets' sa - cred page, And grand in po - ets' wing-ed word, Slow - ly in type, from age to age The na - tions saw their com - ing Lord; Till through the deep Ju - de - an night Rang out the song, "Good - will to men!" Sung once by first - born
3 That life of truth, those deeds of love, That death so steeped in hate and scorn— These all are past, and now a - bove He reigns, our King once crowned with thorn. Lift up your heads, O might - y gates! So sang that host be - yond our ken. Lift up your heads, your
4 Then raise to Christ a might - y song, And shout His name, His mer-cies tell! Sing, heav'n-ly host, your praise pro - long, And all on earth, your an - them swell! All hail, O Lamb for sin - ners slain! For - ev - er let the song as - cend! Wor - thy the Lamb, en -

The Old Testament contains many "types"—people, like Moses, or things, like the temple—that pointed people forward in some way to the coming Christ. The hosts of heaven and their angelic song are beyond our "ken" (stanza 3), that is, beyond our knowledge and realm of experience in this life.

Text: John Julian, 1839–1913, alt.
Tune: *Johann Störls . . . Schlag- Gesang- Und Noten-Buch*, Stuttgart, 1744;
setting: *The Lutheran Hymnal*, 1941

O GROSSER GOTT
L M D

Rev. 5:12–13; Acts 2:22–24, 36; Rev. 19:4–6

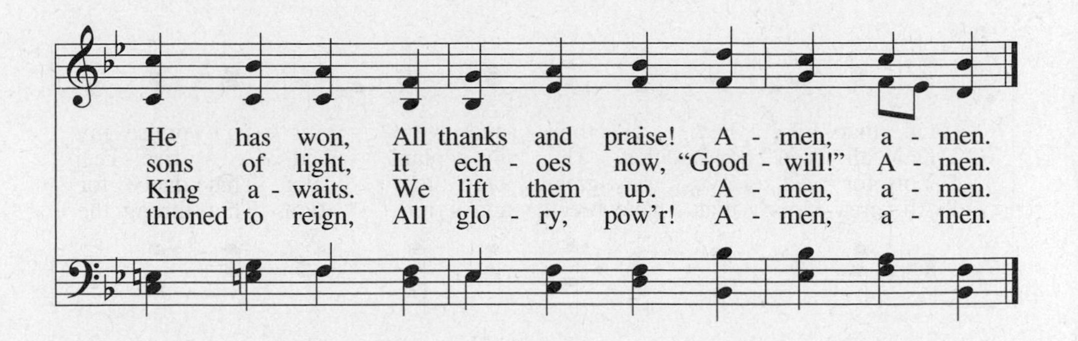
He has won, All thanks and praise! A - men, a - men.
sons of light, It ech - oes now, "Good - will!" A - men.
King a - waits. We lift them up. A - men, a - men.
throned to reign, All glo - ry, pow'r! A - men, a - men.

Then I looked, and I heard around the throne and the living creatures and the elders the voice of many angels, numbering myriads of myriads and thousands of thousands, saying with a loud voice, "Worthy is the Lamb who was slain, to receive power and wealth and wisdom and might and honor and glory and blessing!"

Revelation 5:11–12

811 Oh, That I Had a Thousand Voices

1 Oh, that I had a thou - sand voic - es To praise my
2 O all you pow'rs that He im - plant - ed, A - rise, keep
3 You for - est leaves so green and ten - der That dance for
4 All crea - tures that have breath and mo - tion, That throng the
God with thou - sand tongues! My heart, which in the Lord re -
si - lence now no more; Put forth the strength that God has
joy in sum - mer air, You mead - ow grass - es, bright and
earth, the sea, the sky, Come, share with me my heart's de -
joic - es, Would then pro - claim in grate - ful songs To all, wher-
grant - ed! Your no - blest work is to a - dore. O soul and
slen - der, You flow'rs so fra - grant and so fair, You live to
vo - tion, Help me to sing God's prais - es high. My ut - most
ev - er I might be, What great things God has done for me.
bod - y, join to raise With heart - felt joy our Mak - er's praise.
show God's praise a - lone. Join me to make His glo - ry known.
pow'rs can nev - er quite De - clare the won - ders of His might.

Text: Johann Mentzer, 1658–1734; tr. *The Lutheran Hymnal*, 1941, alt.
Tune: Johann Balthasar König, 1691–1758; setting: *The Lutheran Hymnal*, 1941

O DASS ICH TAUSEND ZUNGEN HÄTTE (KÖNIG)
98 98 88

1 Chron. 16:31–36; Ps. 126:3; Joel 2:26; Ps. 95:6

5 Creator, humbly I implore You
To listen to my earthly song
Until that day when I adore You,
Together with the angel throng
And learn with choirs of heav'n to sing
Eternal anthems to my King.

Come, Let Us Join Our Cheerful Songs

812

1 Come, let us join our cheer - ful songs With an - gels round the throne; Ten thou - sand thou - sand are their tongues, But all their joys are one.
2 "Wor - thy the Lamb that died," they cry, "To be ex - alt - ed thus!" "Wor - thy the Lamb," our lips re - ply, "For He was slain for us!"
3 Je - sus is wor - thy to re - ceive Hon - or and pow'r di - vine; And bless - ings more than we can give Be, Lord, for - ev - er Thine.
4 Let all cre - a - tion join in one To bless the sa - cred name Of Him who sits up - on the throne And to a - dore the Lamb.

Text: Isaac Watts, 1674–1748
Tune: Johann Crüger, 1598–1662; setting: *The Lutheran Hymnal*, 1941

NUN DANKET ALL
C M

Rev. 5:6–14; Ps. 95:1–2

813 Rejoice, O Pilgrim Throng

1 Re - joice, O pil - grim throng! Re - joice, give thanks, and sing; Your fes - tal ban - ner wave on high, The cross of Christ your king.
2 With voice as full and strong As o - cean's surg - ing praise, Send forth the stur - dy hymns of old, The psalms of an - cient days.
3 With all the an - gel choirs, With all the saints on earth Pour out the strains of joy and bliss, True rap - ture, no - blest mirth.
4 Yet on and on - ward still, With hymn and chant and song, Through gate and porch and col - umned aisle The hal - lowed path - ways throng.
5 Still lift your stan - dard high, Still march in firm ar - ray, As pil - grims through the dark - ness wend Till dawns the gold - en day.
Refrain
Re - joice! Re - joice! Re - joice, give thanks, and sing!

Text: Edward H. Plumptre, 1821–91, alt.
Tune: Arthur H. Messiter, 1834–1916; setting: *Service Book and Hymnal*, 1958

MARION
S M and refrain

Ps. 20:5; 118:15–26; Col. 3:16; Heb. 13:14

6 At last the march shall end;
The wearied ones shall rest;
The pilgrims find their home at last,
Jerusalem the blest.
Refrain

△ 7 Praise Him who reigns on high,
The Lord whom we adore:
The Father, Son, and Holy Ghost,
One God forevermore.
Refrain

O Bless the Lord, My Soul 814

1 O bless the Lord, my soul! Let all with - in me join
2 O bless the Lord, my soul, Nor let His mer - cies lie
3 'Tis He for - gives thy sins; 'Tis He re - lieves thy pain;
4 He crowns thy life with love When ran - somed from the grave;
And aid my tongue to bless His name Whose fa - vors are di - vine.
For - got - ten in un - thank - ful - ness And with - out prais - es die!
'Tis He that heals thy sick - ness - es And makes thee young a - gain.
He that re - deemed my soul from hell Hath sov - 'reign pow'r to save.

5 He fills the poor with good;
He gives the suff'rers rest.
The Lord hath judgments for the proud
And justice for th'oppressed.

6 His wondrous works and ways
He made by Moses known,
But sent the world His truth and grace
By His belovèd Son.

Text: Isaac Watts, 1674–1748
Tune: Aaron Williams, 1731–76; setting: *The Lutheran Hymnal*, 1941

ST. THOMAS
S M

Psalm 103; John 1:1–4, 14

815 All Praise to Thee, for Thou, O King Divine

1 All praise to Thee, for Thou, O King di - vine,
2 Thou cam'st to us in low - li - ness of thought;
3 Let this mind be in us which was in Thee,
4 Where - fore, by God's e - ter - nal pur - pose, Thou
5 Let ev - 'ry tongue con - fess with one ac - cord,
Didst yield the glo - ry that of right was Thine,
By Thee the out - cast and the poor were sought;
Who wast a ser - vant that we might be free,
Art high ex - alt - ed o'er all crea - tures now,
In heav'n and earth, that Je - sus Christ is Lord,
That in our dark - ened hearts Thy grace might shine.
And by Thy death was God's sal - va - tion wrought.
Hum - bling Thy - self to death on Cal - va - ry.
And giv'n the name to which all knees shall bow.
And God the Fa - ther be by all a - dored.
1–4
Al - le - lu - ia!
5
Al - le - lu - ia!

Text: F. Bland Tucker, 1895–1984
Tune: Charles V. Stanford, 1852–1924; setting: Ralph C. Schultz, b. 1932

ENGELBERG
10 10 10 4

Phil. 2:5–11; Mark 10:45; Is. 55:10–11

From All That Dwell Below the Skies

816

1 From all that dwell be - low the skies Let the Cre - a - tor's praise a - rise;
2 E - ter - nal are Thy mer - cies, Lord; E - ter - nal truth at - tends Thy Word.
△ 3 All praise to God the Fa - ther be, All praise, e - ter - nal Son, to Thee.
Al - le - lu - ia, al - le - lu - ia!
Let the Re - deem - er's name be sung Through ev - 'ry land by ev - 'ry tongue.
Thy praise shall sound from shore to shore Till suns shall rise and set no more.
Whom with the Spir - it we a - dore For - ev - er and for - ev - er - more:
Al - le - lu - ia, al - le - lu - ia!
Al - le - lu - ia, al - le - lu - ia, al - le - lu - ia!

Hymn accompaniment: 493

Text: Isaac Watts, 1674–1748, sts. 1–2; William W. How, 1823–97, st. 3
Tune: *Geistliche Kirchengesäng*, Köln, 1623

LASST UNS ERFREUEN
888 888 and alleluias

Psalm 117; Is. 45:22–23; Phil. 2:5–11

817 Earth and All Stars

1 Earth and all stars! Loud rush-ing plan - ets! Sing to the Lord a new song! Oh, vic - to - ry! Loud shout-ing ar - my! Sing to the Lord a new song!
2 Hail, wind, and rain! Loud blow-ing snow - storm! Sing to the Lord a new song! Flow - ers and trees! Loud rus - tling dry leaves! Sing to the Lord a new song!
3 Trum - pet and pipes! Loud clash-ing cym - bals! Sing to the Lord a new song! Harp, lute, and lyre! Loud hum-ming cel - los! Sing to the Lord a new song!
4 En - gines and steel! Loud pound-ing ham - mers! Sing to the Lord a new song! Lime-stone and beams! Loud build-ing work - ers! Sing to the Lord a new song!

Refrain

He has done mar - vel - ous things.

Text: Herbert F. Brokering, 1926–2009
Tune: David N. Johnson, 1922–87; setting: Henry V. Gerike, b. 1948

EARTH AND ALL STARS
457 457 and refrain

Ps. 96:1; 149:1–3; Is. 42:10–12; Ex. 15:1–2

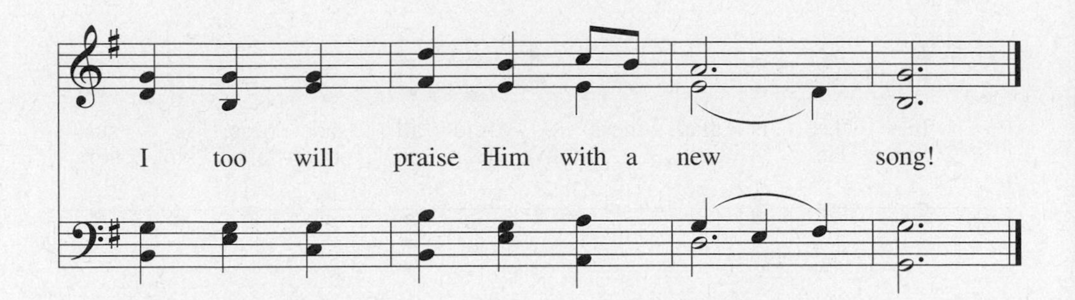
I too will praise Him with a new song!

5 Classroom and labs!
Loud boiling test tubes!
Sing to the Lord a new song!
Athlete and band!
Loud cheering people!
Sing to the Lord a new song!
Refrain

6 Knowledge and truth!
Loud sounding wisdom!
Sing to the Lord a new song!
Daughter and son!
Loud praying members!
Sing to the Lord a new song!
Refrain

7 Children of God,
Dying and rising,
Sing to the Lord a new song!
Heaven and earth,
Hosts everlasting,
Sing to the Lord a new song!
Refrain

818 In Thee Is Gladness

1 In Thee is glad - ness A - mid all sad - ness, Je - sus,
2 Since He is ours, We fear no pow - ers, Not of
sun - shine of my heart. By Thee are giv - en The gifts of
earth nor sin nor death. He sees and bless - es In worst dis -
heav - en, Thou the true Re - deem - er art. Our souls Thou
tress - es; He can change them with a breath. Where - fore the
wak - est, Our bonds Thou break - est; Who trusts Thee sure - ly Has built se -
sto - ry Tell of His glo - ry With hearts and voic - es; All heav'n re -
cure - ly; He stands for - ev - er: Al - le - lu - ia! Our hearts are
joic - es In Him for - ev - er: Al - le - lu - ia! We shout for

Text: Johann Lindemann, 1549–1631; tr. Catherine Winkworth, 1827–78, alt.
Tune: Giovanni Giacomo Gastoldi, c. 1556–c. 1622;
setting: *Württembergisches Neues Choralbuch*, 1956

IN DIR IST FREUDE
557 D 55554 D

John 16:20–22; 1 Peter 1:6–9; Ps. 30:11–12; Rom. 8:38–39

pin - ing To see Thy shin - ing, Dy - ing or liv - ing
glad - ness, Tri - umph o'er sad - ness, Love Him and praise Him
To Thee are cleav - ing; Naught can us sev - er: Al - le - lu - ia!
And still shall raise Him Glad hymns for - ev - er: Al - le - lu - ia!

You have turned for me my mourning into dancing;
You have loosed my sackcloth and clothed me with gladness,
that my glory may sing Your praise and not be silent.
O LORD my God, I will give thanks to You forever!

Psalm 30:11–12

---

819 Sing Praise to God, the Highest Good

1 Sing praise to God, the high - est good, The au - thor of cre -
2 What God's al - might - y pow'r has made, In mer - cy He is
3 We sought the Lord in our dis - tress; O God, in mer - cy
4 He nev - er shall for - sake His flock, His cho - sen gen - er -
a - tion, The God of love who un - der - stood
keep - ing. By morn - ing glow or eve - ning shade
hear us. Our Sav - ior saw our help - less - ness
a - tion; He is their ref - uge and their rock,
Our need for His sal - va - tion. With heal - ing balm our
His eye is nev - er sleep - ing. With - in the king - dom
And came with peace to cheer us. For this we thank and
Their peace and their sal - va - tion. As with a moth - er's
souls He fills And ev - 'ry faith - less mur - mur stills:
of His might All things are just and good and right:
praise the Lord, Who is by one and all a - dored:
ten - der hand, He leads His own, His cho - sen band:

Text: Johann Jacob Schütz, 1640–90; tr. Frances E. Cox, 1812–97, adapt., sts. 1–3, 5;
tr. Catherine Winkworth, 1827–78, adapt., st. 4
Tune: Melchior Vulpius, c. 1570–1615; setting: *The Lutheran Hymnal*, 1941

LOBT GOTT DEN HERREN, IHR
87 87 887

Deut. 32:3; Ps. 96:1–8; Eph. 1:3–8; John 11:27–28

To God all praise and glo - ry!

5 All who confess Christ's holy name,
  Give God the praise and glory.
Let all who know His pow'r proclaim
  Aloud the wondrous story.
Cast ev'ry idol from its throne,
For God is God, and He alone:
  To God all praise and glory!

Sing to the L*ORD a new song;*
  sing to the L*ORD, all the earth!*
Sing to the L*ORD, bless His name;*
  tell of His salvation from day to day. *Psalm 96:1–2*

---

820 My Soul, Now Praise Your Maker

1 My soul, now praise your Mak - er! Let all with - in me
2 He of - fers all His trea - sure Of jus - tice, truth, and
3 For as a ten - der fa - ther Has pit - y on His
4 His grace re - mains for - ev - er, And chil - dren's chil - dren
bless His name Who makes you full par - tak - er Of
righ - teous - ness, His love be - yond all mea - sure, His
chil - dren here, God in His arms will gath - er All
yet shall prove That God for - sakes them nev - er Who
mer - cies more than you dare claim. For - get Him not whose
yearn - ing pit - y o'er dis - tress; Nor treats us as we
who are His in child - like fear. He knows how frail our
in true fear shall seek His love. In heav'n is fixed His
meek - ness Still bears with all your sin, Who heals your ev - 'ry
mer - it But sets His an - ger by. The poor and con - trite
pow - ers, Who but from dust are made. We flour - ish like the
dwell - ing, His rule is o - ver all; O hosts with might ex -

Text: Johann Gramann, 1487–1541; tr. Catherine Winkworth, 1827–78, alt.
Tune: *Concentus novi*, Augsburg, 1540; setting: *Lutheran Service Book*, 2006

NUN LOB, MEIN SEEL
78 78 76 76 76 76

Psalm 103; Is. 40:6–8; 57:15–16; Ps. 119:89–90

weak - ness, Re - news your life with - in; Whose grace and
spir - it Finds His com - pas - sion nigh; And high as
flow - ers, And e - ven so we fade; The wind but
cel - ling, With praise be - fore Him fall. Praise Him for -
care are end - less And saved you through the past; Who
heav'n a - bove us, As dawn from close of day, So
through them pass - es, And all their bloom is o'er. We
ev - er reign - ing, All you who hear His Word— Our
leaves no suf - f'rer friend - less But rights the wronged at last.
far, since He has loved us, He puts our sins a - way.
with - er like the grass - es; Our place knows us no more.
life and all sus - tain - ing. My soul, O praise the Lord!

821 Alleluia! Sing to Jesus

1 Al - le - lu - ia! Sing to Je - sus; His the scep - ter, His the throne; Al - le - lu - ia! His the tri - umph, His the vic - to - ry a - lone.
2 Al - le - lu - ia! Not as or - phans Are we left in sor - row now; Al - le - lu - ia! He is near us; Faith be - lieves, nor ques - tions how.
3 Al - le - lu - ia! Bread of heav - en, Here on earth our food, our stay; Al - le - lu - ia! Here the sin - ful Flee to You from day to day.
4 Al - le - lu - ia! King e - ter - nal, Lord om - nip - o - tent we own; Al - le - lu - ia! Born of Mar - y, Earth Your foot - stool, heav'n Your throne.
Hark! The songs of peace - ful Zi - on Thun - der
Though the cloud from sight re - ceived Him When the
In - ter - ces - sor, Friend of sin - ners, Earth's Re -
As with - in the veil You en - tered, Robed in

Text: William C. Dix, 1837–98, alt.
Music: Rowland H. Prichard, 1811–87

HYFRYDOL
87 87 D

Rev. 7:9–14; Heb. 9:11–28; John 6:31–35, 48–51; 14:18–19

like a might - y flood: "Je - sus out of
for - ty days were o'er, Shall our hearts for -
deem - er, hear our plea Where the songs of
flesh, our great High Priest, Here on earth both
ev - 'ry na - tion Has re - deemed us by His blood."
get His prom - ise: "I am with you ev - er - more"?
all the sin - less Sweep a - cross the crys - tal sea.
priest and vic - tim In the eu - cha - ris - tic feast.

5 Alleluia! Sing to Jesus;
His the scepter, His the throne;
Alleluia! His the triumph,
His the victory alone.
Hark! The songs of peaceful Zion
Thunder like a mighty flood:
"Jesus out of ev'ry nation
Has redeemed us by His blood."

822 Alleluia! Let Praises Ring

1 Al - le - lu - ia! Let prais - es ring! To God the Fa - ther let us bring Our songs of ad - o - ra - tion.
2 Al - le - lu - ia! Let prais - es ring! Un - to the Lamb of God we sing, In whom we are e - lect - ed.
3 Al - le - lu - ia! Let prais - es ring! Un - to the Ho - ly Ghost we sing For our re - gen - er - a - tion.
4 Al - le - lu - ia! Let prais - es ring! Un - to our tri - une God we sing; Blest be His name for - ev - er!
To Him through ev - er - last - ing days Be wor - ship, hon - or, pow'r, and praise, Whose hand sus - tains cre - a - tion.
He bought His Church with His own blood, He cleansed her in that bless - ed flood, And as His bride se - lect - ed.
The sav - ing faith in us He wrought And us un - to the Bride - groom brought, Made us His cho - sen na - tion.
With an - gel hosts let us a - dore And sing His prais - es ev - er - more For all His grace and fa - vor!

Text: *Geistreiches Gesang-Buch*, Darmstadt, 1698; tr. *The Lutheran Hymnal*, 1941, alt.
Tune: Philipp Nicolai, 1556–1608; setting: *Choralbuch zum Evangelischen Kirchengesangbuch*, Berlin, 1955

WIE SCHÖN LEUCHTET
887 887 4444 8

Rev. 19:1; Ps. 145:15–16; Rev. 7:9–17; Titus 3:4–7

Sing - ing, ring - ing: Ho - ly, ho - ly, God is ho - ly;
Ho - ly, ho - ly Is our u - nion And com - mu - nion.
Glo - ry! Glo - ry! Joy e - ter - nal, Bliss su - per - nal;
Sing - ing, ring - ing: Ho - ly, ho - ly, God is ho - ly;
Spread the sto - ry Of our God, the Lord of glo - ry.
His be - friend - ing Gives us joy and peace un - end - ing.
There is man - na And an end - less, glad ho - san - na.
Spread the sto - ry Of our God, the Lord of glo - ry!

All the angels were standing around the throne and around the elders and the four living creatures, and they fell on their faces before the throne and worshiped God, saying, "Amen! Blessing and glory and wisdom and thanksgiving and honor and power and might be to our God forever and ever! Amen." Revelation 7:11–12

823 May God Bestow on Us His Grace

1 May God be-stow on us His grace, With bless-ings rich pro-
2 Thine o - ver all shall be the praise And thanks of ev - 'ry
△ 3 O let the peo-ple praise Thy worth, In all good works in-
vide us; And may the bright-ness of His face
na - tion; And all the world with joy shall raise
creas - ing; The land shall plen-teous fruit bring forth,
To life e - ter - nal guide us, That we His
The voice of ex - ul - ta - tion. For Thou shalt
Thy Word is rich in bless - ing. May God the
sav - ing health may know, His gra-cious will and plea - sure,
judge the earth, O Lord, Nor suf - fer sin to flour - ish;
Fa - ther, God the Son, And God the Spir - it bless us!
And al - so to the na-tions show Christ's rich - es with-out
Thy peo-ple's pas - ture is Thy Word Their souls to feed and
Let all the world praise Him a - lone, Let sol-emn awe pos-
mea - sure And un - to God con - vert them.
nour - ish, In righ - teous paths to keep them.
sess us. Now let our hearts say, "A - men!"

Setting available in hymn accompaniment edition.

Text: Martin Luther, 1483–1546; tr. Richard Massie, 1800–87, alt.
Tune: *Der Lxvj. Deus Misereatur*, Magdeburg, 1524

ES WOLLE GOTT UNS GNÄDIG SEIN
87 87 87 87 7

Ps. 67:1–2; 96:10–13; Is. 55:10–11; 62:1–2

May God Bestow on Us His Grace 824

1 May God be - stow on us His grace, With bless - ings rich pro -
2 Thine o - ver all shall be the praise And thanks of ev - 'ry
△ 3 O let the peo - ple praise Thy worth, In all good works in -
vide us; And may the bright - ness of His face
na - tion; And all the world with joy shall raise
creas - ing; The land shall plen - teous fruit bring forth,
To life e - ter - nal guide us, That we His sav - ing
The voice of ex - ul - ta - tion. For Thou shalt judge the
Thy Word is rich in bless - ing. May God the Fa - ther,
health may know, His gra - cious will and plea - sure,
earth, O Lord, Nor suf - fer sin to flour - ish;
God the Son, And God the Spir - it bless us!
And al - so to the na - tions show Christ's rich - es with - out
Thy peo - ple's pas - ture is Thy Word Their souls to feed and
Let all the world praise Him a - lone, Let sol - emn awe pos -
mea - sure And un - to God con - vert them.
nour - ish, In righ - teous paths to keep them.
sess us. Now let our hearts say, "A - men!"

Setting available in hymn accompaniment edition.

Text: Martin Luther, 1483–1546; tr. Richard Massie, 1800–87, alt.
Tune: David Lee, b. 1956

ELVET BANKS
87 87 87 87 7

Ps. 67:1–2; 96:10–13; Is. 55:10–11; 62:1–2

825 Rise, Shine, You People

1 Rise, shine, you peo - ple! Christ the Lord has en - tered
2 See how He sends the pow'rs of e - vil reel - ing;
3 Come, cel - e - brate, your ban - ners high un - furl - ing,
4 Tell how the Fa - ther sent His Son to save us.

Our hu - man sto - ry; God in Him is cen - tered.
He brings us free - dom, light and life and heal - ing.
Your songs and prayers a - gainst the dark - ness hurl - ing.
Tell of the Son, who life and free - dom gave us.

He comes to us, by death and sin sur -
All men and wom - en, who by guilt are
To all the world go out and tell the
Tell how the Spir - it calls from ev - 'ry

round - ed, With grace un - bound - ed.
driv - en, Now are for - giv - en.
sto - ry Of Je - sus' glo - ry.
na - tion His new cre - a - tion.

Text: Ronald A. Klug, b. 1939, alt.
Music: Dale Wood, 1934–2003

WOJTKIEWIECZ
11 11 11 5

Eph. 5:14; Col. 2:13–15; Is. 60:1; Matt. 28:18–20

Hark, the Voice of Jesus Crying 826

1 Hark, the voice of Je - sus cry - ing, "Who will go and work to - day?
2 If you can - not speak like an - gels, If you can - not preach like Paul,
3 If you can - not be a watch - man, Stand - ing high on Zi - on's wall,
4 Let none hear you i - dly say - ing, "There is noth - ing I can do,"
Fields are white and har - vests wait - ing— Who will bear the sheaves a - way?"
You can tell the love of Je - sus, You can say He died for all.
Point - ing out the path to heav - en, Of - f'ring life and peace to all,
While the mul - ti - tudes are dy - ing And the Mas - ter calls for you.
Loud and long the Mas - ter call - eth; Rich re - ward He of - fers thee.
If you can - not rouse the wick - ed With the judg - ment's dread a - larms,
With your prayers and with your boun - ties You can do what God com - mands;
Take the task He gives you glad - ly, Let His work your plea - sure be;

Who will an - swer, glad - ly say - ing, "Here am I, send me, send me"?
You can lead the lit - tle chil - dren To the Sav - ior's wait - ing arms.
You can be like faith - ful Aar - on, Hold - ing up the proph - et's hands.
An - swer quick - ly when He call - eth, "Here am I, send me, send me!"

Text: Daniel March, 1816–1909, sts. 1–2, 4, alt.; unknown, st. 3, alt.
Tune: Joseph Barnby, 1838–96; setting: *The Lutheran Hymnal*, 1941

GALILEAN
87 87 D

Is. 6:8; Luke 10:2; Matt. 9:37–38; Col. 4:3–4

827 Hark, the Voice of Jesus Calling

1 Hark, the voice of Je - sus call - ing, "Who will go and work to - day?
2 Some take up His task in morn - ing, To their Lord re - spond - ing soon;
3 For as rain and snow from heav - en Wa - ter seeds in dust - y soil,
4 Hear - ken to the Lord whose com - ing Marks the time when grace shall end,

Fields are white and har - vests wait - ing— Who will bear the sheaves a - way?"
Some are called in heat of mid - day, Oth - ers late in af - ter - noon;
Caus - ing them to bud and flow - er, Giv - ing bread to those who toil;
When with His an - gel - ic reap - ers He in glo - ry shall de - scend.

Loud and long the Mas - ter call - eth; Rich re - ward He of - fers thee.
E - ven as the sun is set - ting, Some are sent in - to the fields,
So the Lord sends forth His prom - ise, Words of life and joy and peace—
Soon the night, the fi - nal har - vest; Soon the time for work shall cease.

Who will an - swer, glad - ly say - ing, "Here am I, send me, send me"?
There to gath - er in the boun - ty That God's Word so rich - ly yields.
Nev - er void to Him re - turn - ing, Bear - ing fruit with great in - crease.
Then the souls His grace has gar - nered Shall en - joy His Sab - bath peace.

Text: Daniel March, 1816–1909, st. 1, alt.; Stephen P. Starke, b. 1955, sts. 2–4
Tune: Joseph Barnby, 1838–96; setting: *The Lutheran Hymnal*, 1941

GALILEAN
87 87 D

Is. 6:8; 55:10–11; Luke 10:2

We Are Called to Stand Together 828

1 We are called to stand to - geth - er With the saints of
2 Those whom Je - sus called a - pos - tles Jour - neyed with Him
3 Through the in - ter - ven - ing a - ges Round the world the
4 Now in man - y tongues and cul - tures Songs of cel - e -
5 To each com - ing gen - er - a - tion Tell the truth, per -
a - ges past, With the pa - tri - archs and proph - ets
side by side, Heard His teach - ing, felt His pow - er,
Gos - pel spread: Faith - ful her - alds took the mes - sage,
bra - tion ring; Mil - lions who con - fess our Sav - ior
suade, ex - plain, Till the time when time is end - ed,
In the faith they once held fast; Prom - is - es and
Saw the way He lived and died; Then the news of
Guid - ed where the Spir - it led; So the bod - y
Hon - or Him as Lord and King And, for cour - age,
Till the Sav - ior comes a - gain— Till the saints are
hopes they trea - sured Now we find ful - filled at last!
res - ur - rec - tion They de - liv - ered far and wide.
grew in stat - ure, Serv - ing Christ, the liv - ing head.
grace and guid - ance Ev - 'ry day their prayers they bring.
all u - nit - ed Un - der Christ's e - ter - nal reign!

Hymn accompaniment: 491

Text: Martin E. Leckebusch, b. 1962
Tune: Henry V. Gerike, b. 1948

ASCENDED TRIUMPH
87 87 87

Hebrews 11; Luke 24:48; Matt. 28:19–20; 2 Tim. 4:1–5

829 Christ the Eternal Lord

1 Christ the e - ter - nal Lord, Whose prom - ise here we claim,
2 Christ the un - chang - ing Word To ev - 'ry pass - ing age,
3 Christ the re - deem - ing Son, Who shares our hu - man birth,
4 Christ the un - fad - ing Light Of ev - er - last - ing day,
Whose gifts of grace are free - ly poured On all who name Your name;
Whose time - less teach - ings still are heard Set forth on Scrip - ture's page;
And by His death sal - va - tion won For ev - 'ry child of earth;
Our Morn - ing Star in splen - dor bright, The Life, the Truth, the Way;
With thank - ful - ness and praise We stand be - fore Your throne,
Trans - form our thought and mind, En - light - en all who read,
In - spire our hearts, we pray, To tell Your love a - broad,
That light of truth You give To ser - vants as to friends,
In - tent to serve You all our days And make Your glo - ry known.
With - in Your Word by faith to find The bread of life in - deed.
That all may hon - or Christ to - day And fol - low Him as Lord.
Your way to walk, Your life to live, Till earth's brief jour - ney ends.

Text: Timothy Dudley-Smith, b. 1926
Tune: George J. Elvey, 1816–93; setting: *Service Book and Hymnal*, 1958

DIADEMATA
S M D

Matt. 28:18–20; John 1:1–18; 14:6; 1 Peter 1:8–9

5 Christ the ascended King
Exalted high above,
Whose praise unending ages sing,
Whom yet unseen we love;
When mortal life is past
Your voice from heaven's throne
Shall call Your children home at last
To know as we are known.

Spread the Reign of God the Lord 830

1 Spread the reign of God the Lord, Spo - ken, writ - ten, might-y Word;
2 Tell how God the Fa - ther's will Made the world, up - holds it still,
3 Tell of our Re-deem - er's grace, Who, to save our hu - man race
4 Tell of God the Spir - it giv'n Now to guide us on to heav'n,
Ev - 'ry - where His crea-tures call To His heav'n - ly ban-quet hall.
How His own dear Son He gave Us from sin and death to save.
And to pay re - bel-lion's price, Gave Him - self as sac - ri - fice.
Strong and ho - ly, just and true, Work - ing both to will and do.

5 Enter, mighty Word, the field;
Ripe the promise of its yield.
But the reapers, oh, how few
For the work there is to do!

6 Lord of harvest, great and kind,
Rouse to action heart and mind;
Let the gath'ring nations all
See Your light and heed Your call.

Text: Jonathan Friedrich Bahnmaier, 1774–1841; tr. composite
Tune: *Geist-reiches Gesang-Buch*, Halle, 1704, ed. Johann A. Freylinghausen, alt.;
setting: *The Lutheran Hymnal*, 1941

GOTT SEI DANK
77 77

Ps. 96:1–5; Matt. 22:9–10; Luke 10:2; 24:47–48; Rom. 8:32; 10:15

831 "How Shall They Hear," Who Have Not Heard

1 "How shall they hear," who have not heard
2 "To all the world," to ev - 'ry place,
3 "Whom shall I send?" Who hears the call,
4 "Lord, here am I:" Your fire im - part
News of a Lord who loved and came;
Neigh - bors and friends and far - off lands,
Con - stant in prayer, through toil and pain,
To this poor cold self - cen - tered soul;
Nor known His rec - on - cil - ing word,
Preach the good news of sav - ing grace;
Tell - ing of One who died for all,
Touch but my lips, my hands, my heart,
Nor learned to trust a Sav - ior's name?
Go while the great com - mis - sion stands.
To bring a lost world home a - gain?
And make a world for Christ my goal.

Text: Timothy Dudley-Smith, b. 1926
Tune: Georg Joseph, 17th cent., adapt.; setting: *Cantica Spiritualia*, 1847

ANGELUS
L M

Rom. 10:14–15; Matt. 28:18–20; Is. 6:5–8; Acts 4:29–31

5 Spirit of love, within us move:
Spirit of truth, in pow'r come down!
So shall they hear and find and prove
Christ is their life, their joy, their crown.

Jesus Shall Reign 832

1 Je - sus shall reign wher - e'er the sun Does its suc - ces - sive jour - neys run; His king - dom stretch from shore to shore Till moons shall wax and wane no more.
2 To Him shall end - less prayer be made, And end - less prais - es crown His head; His name like sweet per - fume shall rise With ev - 'ry morn - ing sac - ri - fice.
3 Peo - ple and realms of ev - 'ry tongue Dwell on His love with sweet - est song; And in - fant voic - es shall pro - claim Their ear - ly bless - ings on His name.
4 Bless - ings a - bound wher - e'er He reigns: The pris - 'ners leap, un - loose their chains, The wea - ry find e - ter - nal rest, And all who suf - fer want are blest.
5 Let ev - 'ry crea - ture rise and bring Hon - ors pe - cu - liar to our King; An - gels de - scend with songs a - gain, And earth re - peat the loud a - men.

Text: Isaac Watts, 1674–1748, alt.
Tune: attr. John C. Hatton, d. 1793; setting: *The Lutheran Hymnal*, 1941

DUKE STREET
L M

Ps. 72:5–11, 17; Rev. 11:15; Ps. 8:2; Matt. 21:15–16; Matt. 11:28

833 Listen, God Is Calling

Refrain
Leader
All
Lis - ten, lis-ten, God is call-ing Through the Word in - vit-ing,
Of - fer - ing for - give-ness, Com - fort, and joy. joy.
1
2
Leader
All
1 Je - sus gave His man-date: Share the good news
2 Let none be for - got - ten Through - out the world.
3 Help us to be faith - ful, Stand - ing stead - fast,
Leader
All
Refrain
That He came to save us And set us free.
In the tri - une name of God Go and bap - tize.
Walk-ing in Your pre - cepts, Led by Your Word.

Text: Kenyan; tr. Howard S. Olson, 1922–2010
Tune: Kenyan; setting: Austin C. Lovelace, 1919–2010

NENO LAKE MUNGU
64 64 and refrain

2 Thess. 2:14; Matt. 28:18–20; Mark 16:15–16; 1 Cor. 15:58

O God, O Lord of Heaven and Earth

1 O God, O Lord of heav'n and earth, Thy liv - ing
2 Our fa - tal will to e - qual Thee, Our reb - el
3 Thou cam - est to our hall of death, O Christ, to
△ 4 O Spir - it, who didst once re - store Thy Church that
fin - ger nev - er wrote That life should be an aim -
will wrought death and night. We seized and used in pride -
breathe our poi - soned air, To drink for us the dark
it might be a - gain The bring - er of good news
less mote, A death - ward drift from fu - tile birth.
ful spite Thy won - drous gift of lib - er - ty.
de - spair That stran - gled our re - luc - tant breath.
to men, Breathe on Thy clo - ven Church once more,
Thy Word meant life tri - um - phant hurled In splen - dor through
We housed us in this house of doom, Where death had roy -
How beau - ti - ful the feet that trod The road that leads
That in these gray and lat - ter days There may be those
Thy bro - ken world. Since light a - woke and life be - gan,
al scope and room, Un - til Thy ser - vant, Prince of Peace,
us back to God! How beau - ti - ful the feet that ran
whose life is praise, Each life a high dox - ol - o - gy
Thou hast de - sired Thy life for man.
Breached all its walls for our re - lease.
To bring the great good news to man!
To Fa - ther, Son, and un - to Thee.

Setting available in hymn accompaniment edition.

Text: Martin H. Franzmann, 1907–76, alt.
Tune: Jan O. Bender, 1909–94

WITTENBERG NEW
L M D

John 1:1–7; Heb. 2:14–15; Rom. 5:17; 15:5–6

835 On Galilee's High Mountain

1 On Gal - i - lee's high moun - tain Christ gave the great com - mand
2 The Lord who, born of Mar - y, Came down as man and died,
3 His strength with - in my weak - ness Will make me bold to say
4 And not a - lone to na - tions In far - a - way re - treats,
In words of strength and prom - ise Which all can un - der - stand:
Who preached to all who lis - tened, For us was cru - ci - fied—
How His re - deem - ing pow - er Trans - forms my stub - born clay;
But ev - 'ry - where I broad - cast His love through crowd - ed streets:
"All pow'r to Me is giv - en To do what I shall choose;
This Lord, our liv - ing broth - er, In pow'r at God's right hand,
His touch of fire ig - nites me, With cour - age I am sent,
The lives that my life touch - es, How - ev - er great or small—
There - fore I send My chil - dren, Their wit - ness I will use."
Has cho - sen us to car - ry His truth to ev - 'ry land.
My tongue - tied si - lence bro - ken, With grace made el - o - quent.
Let them through me see Je - sus, Who served and saved us all.

Text: Henry L. Lettermann, 1932–96
Music: Lowell Mason, 1792–1872

MISSIONARY HYMN
76 76 D

Matt. 28:16–20; Is. 49:6; 2 Cor. 12:9–10; 2 Cor. 4:10–11

5 That ev'ryone He chooses,
For reasons of His own,
Will find in Christ his calling
To live His love alone.
His presence always leads us
Till time no more shall be;
Christ's strength, His love, His comfort
Give us His victory.

△ 6 Lord, gather all Your children,
Wherever they may be,
And lead them on to heaven
To live eternally
With You, our loving Father,
And Christ, our brother dear,
Whose Spirit guards and gives us
The joy to persevere.

O God of Light 836

1 O God of light, Your Word, a lamp un - fail - ing,
2 From days of old, through blind and will - ful a - ges,
3 Un - dimmed by time, those words are still re - veal - ing
4 To all the world Your sum - mons You are send - ing,
Shall pierce the dark - ness of our earth - bound way
Though we re - belled, You gent - ly sought a - gain
To sin - ful hearts Your jus - tice and Your grace;
Through all the earth, to ev - 'ry land and race,
And show Your grace, Your plan for us un - veil - ing,
And spoke through saints, a - pos - tles, proph - ets, sa - ges,
And quest - ing spir - its, long - ing for Your heal - ing,
That myr - iad tongues, in one great an - them blend - ing,
And guide our foot - steps to the per - fect day.
Who wrote with ea - ger or re - luc - tant pen.
See Your com - pas - sion in the Sav - ior's face.
May praise and cel - e - brate Your gift of grace.

Setting available in hymn accompaniment edition. Alternate tune: EIRENE (690)

Text: Sarah E. Taylor, 1883–1954, alt.
Tune: H. Barrie Cabena, b. 1933

ATKINSON
11 10 11 10

Ps. 119:105; 1 Peter 1:10–12; Is. 51:4

837 Lift High the Cross

Refrain
Unison
Lift high the cross, the love of Christ pro-claim Till
all the world a-dore His sa-cred name.
Harmony
1 Come, Chris-tians, fol-low where our Cap-tain trod,
2 Led on their way by this tri-um-phant sign,
3 All new-born sol-diers of the Cru-ci-fied
4 O Lord, once lift-ed on the glo-rious tree,
Our king vic-to-rious, Christ, the Son of God.
The hosts of God in con-qu'ring ranks com-bine.
Bear on their brows the seal of Him who died.
As Thou hast prom-ised, draw us all to Thee.
Refrain

Text: George W. Kitchin, 1827–1912; rev. Michael R. Newbolt, 1874–1956, alt.;
Spanish tr. Leopoldo Gros, b. 1925
Music: Sydney H. Nicholson, 1875–1947

CRUCIFER
10 10 10 10

John 12:32; Heb. 13:12–15; Is. 11:10, 12; Matt. 16:24

5 Let ev'ry race and ev'ry language tell
Of Him who saves our lives from death and hell.
Refrain

6 So shall our song of triumph ever be:
Praise to the Crucified for victory!
Refrain

Estribillo
¡Alzad la cruz! ¡A Cristo pregonad!
¡Del buen Jesús el nombre proclamad!

1 Venid, creyentes, a Jesús seguid,
al rey de reyes vuestro amor rendid.
Estribillo

2 La senda sigue del triunfal Señor,
cristiana hueste, con total valor.
Estribillo

3 Soldados fieles del Señor Jesús,
alzad valientes la triunfante cruz.
Estribillo

4 Jesús clavado en la enhiesta cruz,
¡Por ti salvados, llénanos de luz!
Estribillo

5 Himnos de gloria sin cesar alzad,
¡La gran victoria de Jesús cantad!
Estribillo

838 The Saints in Christ Are One in Every Place

1 The saints in Christ are one in ev - 'ry place
2 In chains for Christ! His pris'n-ers love to sing,
3 To live is Christ, for us, to die is gain;
4 Lord Je - sus Christ! Heav'n's praise let earth re - peat;
To serve the Gos - pel of His cost - ly grace;
For slaves and free re - joice to praise our King;
Where then shall be our hun - ger, dan - ger, pain?
The work that You be - gan, You will com - plete.
From those first days to this, our hope the same:
What though the Church on earth still suf - fers wrong?
Our joy to preach good news to rich and poor,
By grace let ev - 'ry foe be - come Your friend;
The love of Christ, one Lord, one sav - ing name.
The cross of Christ re - mains our pil - grim song.
Then be with Christ, to live for - ev - er - more.
Your day, O Christ, shall dawn and nev - er end.

Text: Christopher M. Idle, b. 1938, alt.
Tune: Walter Greatorex, 1877–1949; setting: Janette Cooper, b. 1937

WOODLANDS
10 10 10 10

Phil. 1:1–21

O Christ, Our True and Only Light 839

1 O Christ, our true and on - ly light, En - light - en
2 Fill with the ra - diance of Your grace The souls now
3 O gent - ly call those gone a - stray That they may
4 Shine on the dark - ened and the cold; Re - call the
5 That they with us may ev - er - more Such grace with
those who sit in night; Let those a - far now
lost in er - ror's maze; En - light - en those whose
find the sav - ing way! Let ev - 'ry con - science
wan - d'rers to Your fold. U - nite all those who
won - d'ring thanks a - dore And end - less praise to
hear Your voice And in Your fold with us re - joice.
in - most minds Some dark de - lu - sion haunts and blinds.
sore op - pressed In You find peace and heav'n - ly rest.
walk a - part; Con - firm the weak and doubt - ing heart,
You be giv'n By all Your Church in earth and heav'n.

Text: Johann Heermann, 1585–1647; tr. Catherine Winkworth, 1827–78, alt.
Tune: *Andächtige Haus-Kirche*, Nürnberg, 1676; setting: Johannes C. A. Zahn, 1817–95

O JESU CHRISTE, WAHRES LICHT
L M

Is. 60:1–3; Luke 1:78–79; John 8:12; Eph. 5:8–14

840 Christ High-Ascended, Now in Glory Seated

1 Christ high-as-cend-ed, now in glo-ry seat-ed, Throned and ex-alt-ed, vic-to-ry com-plet-ed, Death's dread do-min-ion fi-nal-ly de-feat-ed, We are His wit-ness-es.
2 Christ from the Fa-ther ev-'ry pow'r pos-sess-ing, Who on His cho-sen lift-ed hands in bless-ing, Sends forth His ser-vants, still in faith con-fess-ing, We are His wit-ness-es.
3 Christ, who in dy-ing won for us sal-va-tion, Lives now the first-born of the new cre-a-tion; To win dis-ci-ples out of ev-'ry na-tion, We are His wit-ness-es.
4 Christ in His splen-dor, all do-min-ion gain-ing, Christ with His peo-ple ev-er-more re-main-ing, Christ to all a-ges glo-ri-ous-ly reign-ing, We are His wit-ness-es.
5 As at His part-ing, joy shall ban-ish griev-ing, Faith in His pres-ence strength-en our be-liev-ing; Filled with His Spir-it, love and pow'r re-ceiv-ing, We are His wit-ness-es.

Text: Timothy Dudley-Smith, b. 1926
Tune: *Antiphoner*, Poitiers, 1746; setting: Joseph Herl, b. 1959

ISTE CONFESSOR
11 11 11 6

Matt. 28:18–20; Acts 1:8; Phil. 2:9–11; John 16:19–24

O Son of God, in Galilee 841

1 O Son of God, in Gal - i - lee You
2 O lis - ten to the si - lent prayer Of
3 The speech - less tongue, the life - less ear You
4 Mean - while to them the lis - t'ning ear Of
5 Then in Your prom - ised hap - py land Each
made the deaf to hear, The mute to speak, the
Your af - flict - ed ones. O bid them cast on
can re - store, O Lord; Your "Eph - pha - tha," O
stead - fast faith im - part, And let Your Word bring
loss will prove a gain; All mys - t'ries we shall
blind to see; O bless - ed Lord, be near.
You their care; Your grace to them make known.
Sav - ior dear, Can in - stant help af - ford.
light and cheer To ev - 'ry trou - bled heart.
un - der - stand, For You will make them plain.

Text: Anna B. D. Hoppe, 1889–1941, alt.
Music: Lucius Chapin, 1760–1842

TWENTY-FOURTH
C M

Mark 7:32–37

842 Son of God, Eternal Savior

1 Son of God, e - ter - nal Sav - ior, Source of life and truth and grace, Word made flesh, whose birth a - mong us Hal - lows all our hu - man race, You our Head, who, throned in glo - ry, For Your own will ev - er plead: Fill us with Your
2 As You, Lord, have lived for oth - ers, So may we for oth - ers live. Free - ly have Your gifts been grant - ed; Free-ly may Your ser - vants give. Yours the gold and Yours the sil - ver, Yours the wealth of land and sea; We but stew-ards
3 Come, O Christ, and reign a - mong us, King of love and Prince of Peace; Hush the storm of strife and pas - sion, Bid its cru - el dis - cords cease. By Your pa - tient years of toil - ing, By Your si - lent hours of pain, Quench our fe - vered
4 Son of God, e - ter - nal Sav - ior, Source of life and truth and grace, Word made flesh, whose birth a - mong us Hal - lows all our hu - man race: By Your pray - ing, by Your will - ing That Your peo - ple should be one, Grant, O grant our

Text: Somerset T. C. Lowry, 1855–1932, alt.
Tune: *Oude en Nieuwe Hollantse . . . Contradanseu*, Amsterdam, c. 1710;
setting: Henry V. Gerike, b. 1948

IN BABILONE
87 87 D

1 Peter 1:20–23; Heb. 7:25; John 13:34–35; 17:20–21

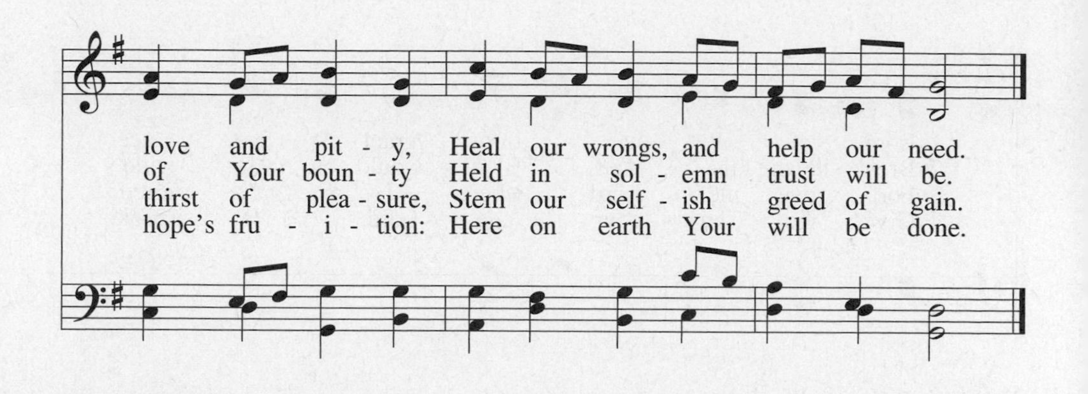
love and pit - y, Heal our wrongs, and help our need.
of Your boun - ty Held in sol - emn trust will be.
thirst of plea - sure, Stem our self - ish greed of gain.
hope's fru - i - tion: Here on earth Your will be done.

"Forgive Our Sins as We Forgive" 843

1 "For - give our sins as we for - give,"
2 How can Your par - don reach and bless
3 In blaz - ing light Your cross re - veals
4 Lord, cleanse the depths with - in our souls
You taught us, Lord, to pray; But You a - lone can
The un - for - giv - ing heart That broods on wrongs and
The truth we dim - ly knew: What triv - ial debts are
And bid re - sent - ment cease; Then, bound to all in
grant us grace To live the words we say.
will not let Old bit - ter - ness de - part?
owed to us, How great our debt to You!
bonds of love, Our lives will spread Your peace.

Setting available in hymn accompaniment edition.

Text: Rosamond E. Herklots, 1905–87, alt.
Tune: *A Supplement to the Kentucky Harmony*, Harrisonburg, 1820

DETROIT
C M

Luke 11:4; Matt. 18:21–35; Eph. 4:31–32; Matt. 5:23–24

844 Lord of All Nations, Grant Me Grace

1 Lord of all na - tions, grant me grace
2 Break down the wall that would di - vide
3 For - give me, Lord, where I have erred
4 Give me Thy cour - age, Lord, to speak
To love all peo - ple, ev - 'ry race;
Thy chil - dren, Lord, on ev - 'ry side.
By love - less act and thought - less word.
When - ev - er strong op - press the weak.
And in each per - son may I see
My neigh - bor's good let me pur - sue;
Make me to see the wrong I do
Should I my - self the vic - tim be,
My kin - dred, loved, re - deemed by Thee.
Let Chris - tian love bind warm and true.
Will grieve my wound - ed Lord a - new.
Help me for - give, re - mem - b'ring Thee.

Text: Olive Wise Spannaus, b. 1916, alt.
Tune: Georg Joseph, 17th cent., adapt.; setting: *Cantica Spiritualia*, 1847

ANGELUS
L M

Phil. 1:9; Lev. 19:34; 1 John 4:12

5 With Thine own love may I be filled
And by Thy Holy Spirit willed,
That all I touch, where'er I be,
May be divinely touched by Thee.

Where Charity and Love Prevail 845

1 Where char - i - ty and love pre - vail There God is ev - er found; Brought here to - geth - er by Christ's love By love are we thus bound.
2 With grate - ful joy and ho - ly fear His char - i - ty we learn; Let us with heart and mind and soul Now love Him in re - turn.
3 For - give we now each oth - er's faults As we our faults con - fess, And let us love each oth - er well In Chris - tian ho - li - ness.
4 Let strife a - mong us be un - known; Let all con - ten - tion cease; Be God's the glo - ry that we seek; Be ours His ho - ly peace.

5 Let us recall that in our midst
Dwells Christ, His only Son;
As members of His body joined
We are in Him made one.

6 For love excludes no race or clan
That names the Savior's name;
His family embraces all
Whose Father is the same.

Text: Latin, c. 9th cent.; tr. Omer E. Westendorf, 1916–97, alt.
Music: Lucius Chapin, 1760–1842

TWENTY-FOURTH
C M

John 13:1–17; 1 John 4:7–21; Eph. 4:29–32

846 Your Hand, O Lord, in Days of Old

1 Your hand, O Lord, in days of old
2 Your touch then, Lord, brought life and health,
3 O be our great de - liv - 'rer still,
Was strong to heal and save; It tri - umphed o - ver
Gave speech and strength and sight; And youth re - newed and
The Lord of life and death; Re - store and quick - en,
ills and death, O'er dark - ness and the grave.
fren - zy calmed Re - vealed You, Lord of light.
soothe and bless, With Your life - giv - ing breath.
To You they came, the blind, the mute,
And now, O Lord, be near to bless,
To hands that work and eyes that see
The pal - sied and the lame, The lep - ers in their
Al - might - y as be - fore, In crowd - ed street, by
Give wis - dom's heal - ing pow'r That whole and sick and
mis - er - y, The sick with fe - vered frame.
beds of pain, As by Gen - nes - 'ret's shore.
weak and strong May praise You ev - er - more.

Hymn accompaniment: 444

Text: Edward H. Plumptre, 1821–91, alt.
Tune: English; adapt. Ralph Vaughan Williams, 1872–1958

KINGSFOLD
C M D

Luke 19:10; Matt. 9:35; John 10:10; 1 Peter 2:9

Christ, Our Human Likeness Sharing

1 Christ, our hu - man like - ness shar - ing, Heav - en's love on earth por - trayed; Christ the Shep - herd, tend - ing, car - ing, In His death our ran - som paid: Christ the Sav - ior, Christ the Ser - vant, Be Your life in us dis - played.
2 Hear the word that Christ has spo - ken, Help the weak, the hun - gry feed; See the pow'rs of dark - ness bro - ken, Sin - ners par - doned, cap - tives freed: Christ the Sav - ior, Christ the Ser - vant, Help us meet our neigh - bor's need.
3 Christ, in ev - 'ry con - gre - ga - tion Build Your tem - ple, stone by stone, With Your word as firm foun - da - tion For a faith ma - tured and grown: Christ the Sav - ior, Christ the Ser - vant, Make in us Your Gos - pel known.
4 Come, O liv - ing Christ, re - new us, As of old in wind and flame; With the Spir - it's pow'r en - due us, Ser - vants of Your sav - ing name: Christ the Sav - ior, Christ the Ser - vant, Christ whose king - dom we pro - claim.

Text: Timothy Dudley-Smith, b. 1926
Tune: *Chants ordinaires de l'Office Divin*, Paris, 1881; setting: *Songs of Praise*, 1925, alt.

GRAFTON
87 87 87

Titus 3:4–8; Eph. 2:10; Titus 2:11–14; Rom. 12:1–2

848 Lord, Whose Love through Humble Service

1 Lord, whose love through hum - ble ser - vice Bore the weight of
2 Still Your chil - dren wan - der home - less; Still the hun - gry
3 As we wor - ship, grant us vi - sion, Till Your love's re -
4 Called by wor - ship to Your ser - vice, Forth in Your dear
hu - man need, Who up - on the cross, for - sak - en,
cry for bread; Still the cap - tives long for free - dom;
veal - ing light In its height and depth and great - ness,
name we go, To the child, the youth, the a - ged,
Of - fered mer - cy's per - fect deed, We, Your ser - vants, bring the
Still in grief we mourn our dead. As, O Lord, Your deep com-
Dawns up - on our quick - ened sight, Mak - ing known the needs and
Love in liv - ing deeds to show; Hope and health, good - will and
wor - ship Not of voice a - lone, but heart, Con - se -
pas - sion Healed the sick and freed the soul, Use the
bur - dens Your com - pas - sion bids us bear, Stir - ring
com - fort, Coun - sel, aid, and peace we give, That Your

Text: Albert F. Bayly, 1901–84, alt.
Tune: *The Sacred Harp,* Philadelphia, 1844; setting: Ronald A. Nelson, b. 1927

BEACH SPRING
87 87 D

Matt. 25:34–40; Gal. 6:10; Rom. 12:1

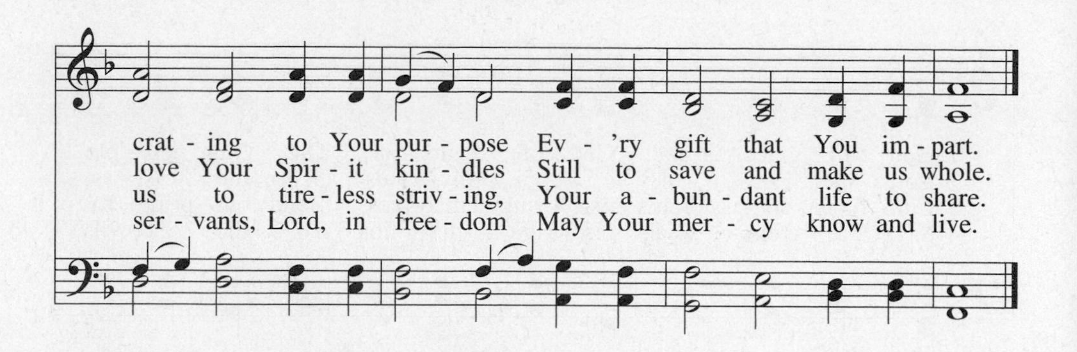
crat - ing to Your pur - pose Ev - 'ry gift that You im - part.
love Your Spir - it kin - dles Still to save and make us whole.
us to tire - less striv - ing, Your a - bun - dant life to share.
ser - vants, Lord, in free - dom May Your mer - cy know and live.

Praise the One Who Breaks the Darkness 849

1 Praise the One who breaks the dark - ness With a lib - er - at - ing light; Praise the One who frees the pris - 'ners, Turn - ing blind - ness in - to sight. Praise the One who preached the Gos - pel, Heal - ing ev - 'ry dread dis - ease, Calm - ing storms, and feed - ing thou - sands With the ver - y Bread of peace.
2 Praise the One who blessed the chil - dren With a strong, yet gen - tle, word; Praise the One who drove out de - mons With the pierc - ing, two - edged sword. Praise the One who brings cool wa - ter To the des - ert's burn - ing sand; From this Well comes liv - ing wa - ter, Quench - ing thirst in ev - 'ry land.
3 Let us praise the Word In - car - nate, Christ, who suf - fered in our place. Je - sus died and rose vic - to - rious That we may know God by grace. Let us sing for joy and glad - ness, See - ing what our God has done; Let us praise the true Re - deem - er, Praise the One who makes us one.

Hymn accompaniment: 848

Text: Rusty Edwards, b. 1955
Tune: *The Sacred Harp,* Philadelphia, 1844

BEACH SPRING
87 87 D

Luke 4:16–21; Mark 10:13–16; John 1:1, 14, 29; 4:5–14

850 God of Grace and God of Glory

1 God of grace and God of glo - ry, On Your peo - ple
2 Lo, the hosts of e - vil round us Scorn the Christ, as -
3 Cure Your chil - dren's war - ring mad - ness; Bend our pride to
4 Save us from weak res - ig - na - tion To the e - vils
pour Your pow'r; Crown Your an - cient Church's sto - ry;
sail His ways! From the fears that long have bound us
Your con - trol; Shame our wan - ton, self - ish glad - ness,
we de - plore; Let the gift of Your sal - va - tion
Bring its bud to glo - rious flow'r. Grant us wis - dom,
Free our hearts to faith and praise. Grant us wis - dom,
Rich in things and poor in soul. Grant us wis - dom,
Be our glo - ry ev - er - more. Grant us wis - dom,
grant us cour - age For the fac - ing of this
grant us cour - age For the liv - ing of these
grant us cour - age Lest we miss Your king - dom's
grant us cour - age, Serv - ing You whom we a -

Text: Harry Emerson Fosdick, 1878–1969
Tune: John Hughes, 1873–1932; setting: Henry V. Gerike, b. 1948

CWM RHONDDA
87 87 877

Ps. 80:14–19; 2 Tim. 1:7; Rom. 15:13; Luke 12:32

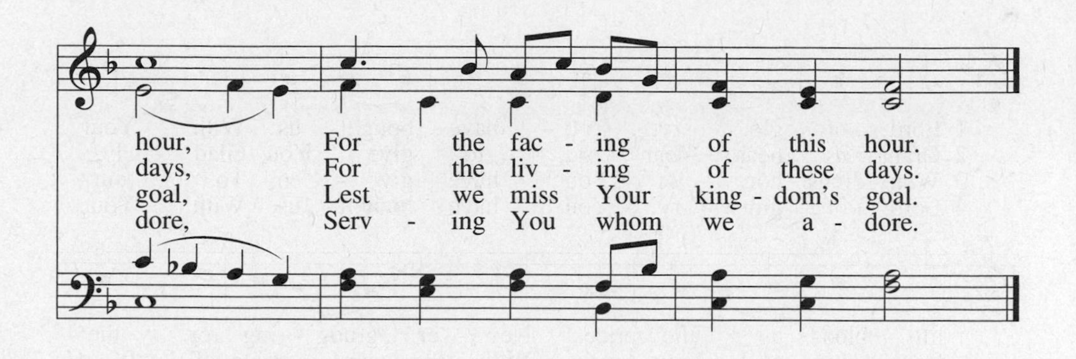
hour, For the fac - ing of this hour.
days, For the liv - ing of these days.
goal, Lest we miss Your king - dom's goal.
dore, Serv - ing You whom we a - dore.

Lord of all power and might, author and giver of all good things, instill in our hearts the love of Your name, impress on our minds the teachings of Your Word, and increase in our lives all that is holy and just; through Jesus Christ, Your Son, our Lord, who lives and reigns with You and the Holy Spirit, one God, now and forever.

Collect for Proper 4, Series A

851 Lord of Glory, You Have Bought Us

1 Lord of glo - ry, You have bought us With Your
2 Grant us hearts, dear Lord, to give You Glad - ly,
3 Won - drous hon - or You have giv - en To our
4 Lord of glo - ry, You have bought us With Your
life - blood as the price, Nev - er grudg - ing for the
free - ly of Your own. With the sun - shine of Your
hum - blest char - i - ty In Your own mys - te - rious
life - blood as the price, Nev - er grudg - ing for the
lost ones That tre - men - dous sac - ri - fice;
good - ness Melt our thank - less hearts of stone
sen - tence, "You have done it all to Me."
lost ones That tre - men - dous sac - ri - fice.
And with that have free - ly giv - en Bless - ings
Till our cold and self - ish na - tures, Warmed by
Can it be, O gra - cious Mas - ter, That You
Give us faith to trust You bold - ly, Hope, to
count - less as the sand To the un - thank - ful
You, at length be - lieve That more hap - py
deign for alms to sue, Say - ing by Your
stay our souls on You; But, oh, best of
and the e - vil With Your own un - spar - ing hand.
and more bless - ed 'Tis to give than to re - ceive.
poor and need - y, "Give as I have giv'n to you"?
all Your grac - es, With Your love our love re - new.

Hymn accompaniment: 821

Text: Eliza S. Alderson, 1818–89, alt.
Tune: Rowland H. Prichard, 1811–87

HYFRYDOL
87 87 D

1 John 3:16–19; Heb. 13:16; Matt. 25:40; Rom. 8:32

O God of Mercy, God of Might 852

1 O God of mer - cy, God of might, In love and pit - y in - fi - nite, Teach us, as ev - er in Thy sight, To live our lives in Thee.
2 And Thou, who cam'st on earth to die That our lost world might live there - by, O hear us; for to Thee we cry, In hope, O Lord, to Thee.
3 Teach us the les - son Thou hast taught: To feel for those Thy blood hath bought, That ev - 'ry word and deed and thought May work a work for Thee.
4 All are re - deemed, both far and wide, Since Thou, O Lord, for all hast died. Grant us the will and grace pro - vide To love them all in Thee!

5 In sickness, sorrow, want, or care,
May we each other's burdens share;
May we, where help is needed, there
Give help as unto Thee!

6 And may Thy Holy Spirit move
All those who live to live in love
Till Thou shalt greet in heav'n above
All those who live in Thee.

Text: Godfrey Thring, 1823–1903, alt.
Tune: Samuel Howard, 1710–82; setting: *The Lutheran Hymnal*, 1941

ISLEWORTH
888 6

Deut. 10:12; Gal. 5:22–26; Matt. 25:40; Luke 10:36–37

853 How Clear Is Our Vocation, Lord

1 How clear is our vo - ca - tion, Lord,
2 But if, for - get - ful, we should find
3 We mar - vel how Your saints be - come
4 In what You give us, Lord, to do,
When once we heed Your call: To live ac - cord - ing
Your yoke is hard to bear; If world - ly pres - sures
In hin - dranc - es more sure; Whose joy - ful vir - tues
To - geth - er or a - lone, In old rou - tines or
to Your Word And dai - ly learn, re - freshed, re - stored,
fray the mind, And love it - self can - not un - wind
put to shame The cas - ual way we wear Your name
ven - tures new, May we not cease to look to You,
That You are Lord of all And will not let us fall.
Its tan - gled skein of care: Our in - ward life re - pair.
And by our faults ob - scure Your pow'r to cleanse and cure.
The cross You hung up - on— All You en - deav - ored done.

With a variety of images, the hymn writer reminds Christians of their calling in life as it is lived under the cross. The word "skein" (pronounced SKANE) in stanza 2 reminds us that we depend on God to untangle our sin-filled lives.

Text: Fred Pratt Green, 1903–2000
Music: C. Hubert H. Parry, 1848–1918, alt.

REPTON
86 88 66

Luke 5:1–11; Matt. 11:28–30; Heb. 12:1–4

Forth in Thy Name, O Lord, I Go 854

1 Forth in Thy name, O Lord, I go, My dai - ly
2 The task Thy wis - dom has as - signed, O let me
3 Thee may I set at my right hand, Whose eyes my
4 Give me to bear Thine eas - y yoke, And ev - 'ry
5 For Thee de - light - ful - ly em - ploy What - e'er Thy
la - bor to pur - sue, Thee, on - ly Thee, re -
cheer - ful - ly ful - fill; In all my works Thy
in - most sub - stance see, And la - bor on at
mo - ment watch and pray, And still to things e -
boun - teous grace has giv'n, And run my course with
solved to know In all I think or speak or do.
pres - ence find, And prove Thy good and per - fect will.
Thy com - mand, And of - fer all my works to Thee.
ter - nal look, And has - ten to Thy glo - rious day.
e - ven joy, And close - ly walk with Thee to heav'n.

Alternate tune: WINCHESTER NEW (405)

Text: Charles Wesley, 1707–88, alt.
Music: Barry L. Bobb, b. 1951

LAKEWOOD
L M

1 Cor. 15:58; Col. 3:17; John 6:27; Matt. 11:29–30

855 For All the Faithful Women

1 For all the faith - ful wom - en Who served in days of old,
To You shall thanks be giv - en; To all, their sto - ry told.
They served with strength and glad - ness In tasks Your wis - dom gave.
To You their lives bore wit - ness, Pro - claimed Your pow'r to save.
2 Insert appropriate stanza(s).
3 O God, for saints and ser - vants, Those named and those un - known
In whom through all the a - ges Your light of glo - ry shone,
We of - fer glad thanks - giv - ing And fer - vent prayer we raise
That, faith - ful in Your ser - vice, Our lives may sing Your praise.
△ 4 All praise to God the Fa - ther! All praise to Christ the Son!
All praise the Ho - ly Spir - it, Who binds the Church in one!
With saints who went be - fore us, With saints who wit - ness still,
We sing glad Al - le - lu - ias And strive to do Your will.

Text: Herman G. Stuempfle, Jr., 1923–2007, alt.
Tune: Finnish, 19th cent.; setting: Joseph Herl, b. 1959

KUORTANE
76 76 D

Heb. 12:1; Rev. 7:9–17

Miriam

5 We praise Your name for Miriam
Who sang triumphantly
While Pharaoh's vaunted army
Lay drowned beneath the sea.
As Israel marched to freedom,
Her chains of bondage gone,
So may we reach the kingdom
Your mighty arm has won.
Exodus 15:19–21

Hannah

6 To Hannah, praying childless
Before Your throne of grace,
You gave a son and called him
To serve before Your face.
Grant us her perseverance;
Lord, teach us how to pray
And trust in Your deliv'rance
When darkness hides our way.
1 Samuel 1:1—2:10

Ruth

7 For Ruth, who left her homeland
And ventured forth in faith,
Who pledged to serve and worship
Naomi's God till death,
We praise You, God of Israel,
And pray for hearts set free
To bind ourselves to others
In love and loyalty.
Ruth 1:8–18

Mary, Mother of Our Lord

8 We sing of Mary, mother,
Fair maiden, full of grace.
She bore the Christ, our brother,
Who came to save our race.
May we, with her, surrender
Ourselves to Your command
And lay upon Your altar
Our gifts of heart and hand.
Luke 1:26–38

Martha and Mary

9 We sing of busy Martha,
Who toiled with pot and pan
While Mary sat in silence
To hear the Word again.
Christ, keep our hearts attentive
To truth that You declare,
And strengthen us for service
When work becomes our prayer.
Luke 10:38–42

The Woman at the Well

10 Recall the outcast woman
With whom the Lord conversed;
Christ gave her living water
To quench her deepest thirst.
Like hers, our hearts are yearning;
Christ offers us His Word.
Then may our lips be burning
To witness to our Lord.
John 4:1–42

Mary Magdalene

11 We sing Your praise for Mary,
Who came at Easter dawn
To look for Jesus' body
And found her Lord was gone.
But, as with joy she saw Him
In resurrection light,
May we by faith behold Him,
The Day who ends our night!
John 20:1–18

Dorcas

12 Lord, hear our thanks for Dorcas,
Who served the sick and poor.
Her hands were cups of kindness,
Her heart an open door.
Send us, O Christ, Your Body,
Where people cry in pain,
And touch them with compassion
To make them whole again.
Acts 9:36

Eunice and Lois

13 For Eunice and for Lois
We sing our thanks and praise.
Young Timothy they nurtured
And led him in Your ways.
Raise up in ev'ry household
True teachers of Your Word
Whose lives will bear clear witness
To Christ, our risen Lord.
2 Timothy 1:5

856 O Christ, Who Called the Twelve

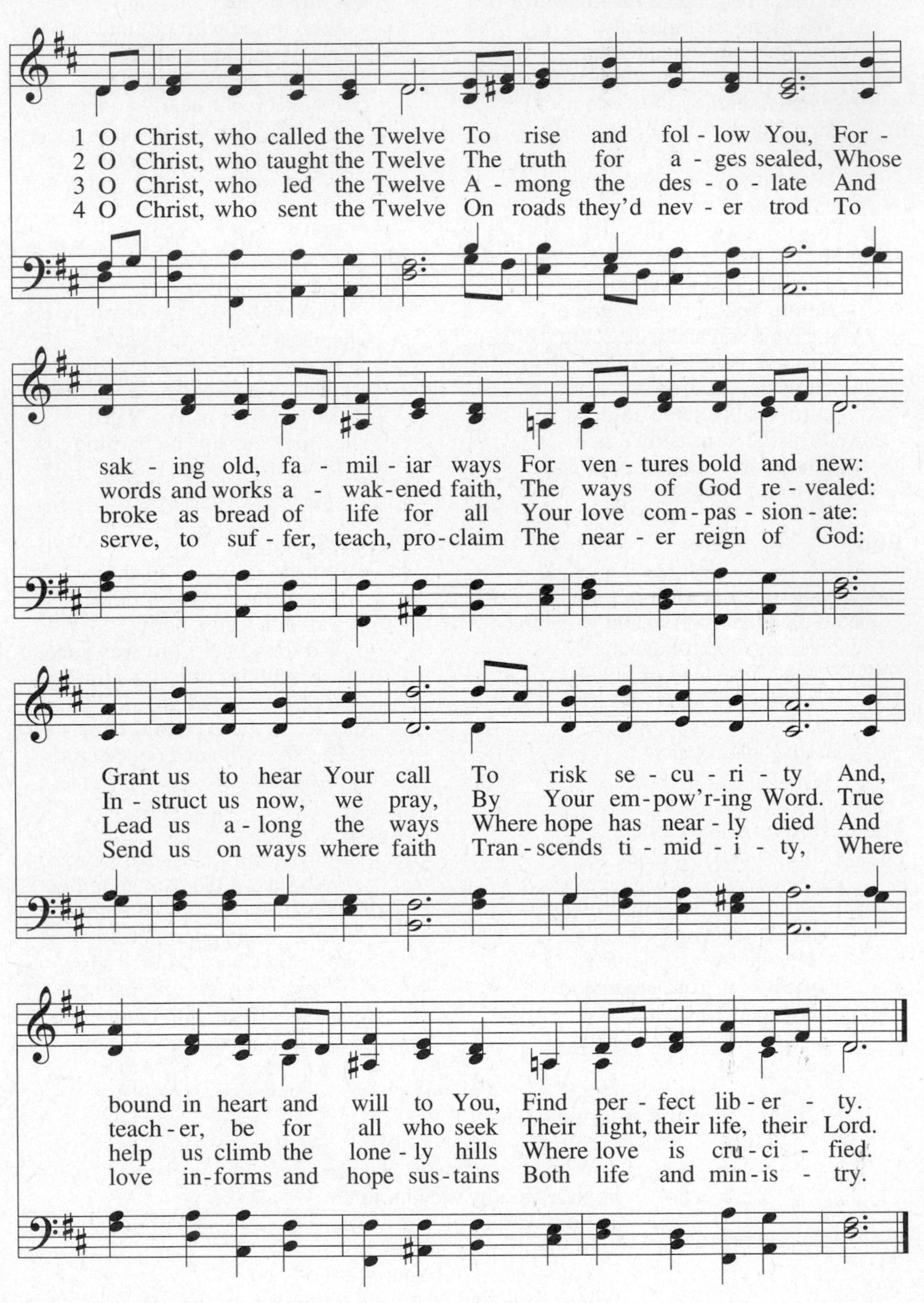
1 O Christ, who called the Twelve To rise and fol - low You, For - sak - ing old, fa - mil - iar ways For ven - tures bold and new: Grant us to hear Your call To risk se - cu - ri - ty And, bound in heart and will to You, Find per - fect lib - er - ty.
2 O Christ, who taught the Twelve The truth for a - ges sealed, Whose words and works a - wak - ened faith, The ways of God re - vealed: In - struct us now, we pray, By Your em - pow'r - ing Word. True teach - er, be for all who seek Their light, their life, their Lord.
3 O Christ, who led the Twelve A - mong the des - o - late And broke as bread of life for all Your love com - pas - sion - ate: Lead us a - long the ways Where hope has near - ly died And help us climb the lone - ly hills Where love is cru - ci - fied.
4 O Christ, who sent the Twelve On roads they'd nev - er trod To serve, to suf - fer, teach, pro - claim The near - er reign of God: Send us on ways where faith Tran - scends ti - mid - i - ty, Where love in - forms and hope sus - tains Both life and min - is - try.

Text: Herman G. Stuempfle, Jr., 1923–2007
Tune: English; adapt. Franklin L. Sheppard, 1852–1930; setting: Stanley Oliver, 1892–1964

TERRA BEATA
S M D

Matt. 10:1–42; Matt. 4:18–22

5 O Christ, th'apostles' Lord,
The martyrs' strength and song,
The crucified and risen King
To whom the saints belong:
Though generations pass,
Our tribute still we bring,
Our hymns a sacrifice of praise,
Our lives an offering.

Lord, Help Us Walk Your Servant Way 857

1 Lord, help us walk Your ser - vant way Wher - ev - er love may lead And, bend - ing low, for - get - ting self, Each serve the oth - er's need.
2 You came to earth, O Christ, as Lord, But pow'r You laid a - side. You lived Your years in ser - vant - hood; In low - li - ness You died.
3 No gold - en scep - ter but a towel You place with - in the hands Of those who seek to fol - low You And live by Your com - mands.
4 You bid us bend our hu - man pride Nor count our - selves a - bove The low - est place, the mean - est task That waits the gift of love.
5 Lord, help us walk Your ser - vant way Wher - ev - er love may lead And, bend - ing low, for - get - ting self, Each serve the oth - er's need.

Text: Herman G. Stuempfle, Jr., 1923–2007
Tune: *The Whole Booke of Psalmes*, London, 1562; setting: Richard Redhead, 1820–1901

ST. FLAVIAN
C M

Mark 10:35–45

858 O Father, All Creating

1 O Fa - ther, all cre - at - ing, Whose wis - dom, love, and pow'r
2 With good wine, Lord, at Ca - na The wed - ding feast You blessed.
3 O Spir - it of the Fa - ther, Breathe on them from a - bove,
4 Un - less You build it, Fa - ther, The house is built in vain;
First bound two lives to - geth - er In E - den's pri - mal hour,
Grant al - so these Your pres - ence, And be their dear - est guest.
So search - ing in Your pure - ness, So ten - der in Your love
Un - less You, Sav - ior, bless it, The joy will turn to pain.
To - day to these Your chil - dren Your ear - liest gifts re - new:
Their store of earth - ly glad - ness Trans - form to heav'n - ly wine,
That, guard - ed by Your pres - ence And kept from strife and sin,
But noth - ing breaks the u - nion Of hearts in You made one;
A home by You made hap - py, A love by You kept true.
And teach them, in the test - ing, To know the gift di - vine.
Their hearts may heed Your guid - ance And know You dwell with - in.
The love Your Spir - it hal - lows Is end - less love be - gun.

Text: John Ellerton, 1826–93, alt.
Music: Samuel S. Wesley, 1810–76

AURELIA
76 76 D

Matt. 19:4–6; Gen. 2:18, 21–24; John 2:1–11; Ps. 127:1

Lord, When You Came as Welcome Guest

1 Lord, when You came as wel - come guest
2 Now give Your pres - ence from a - bove
3 Pre - serve the vow these two shall make,
4 Your dai - ly mer - cies let them share,
To Ca - na's wed - ding feast, The brid - al pair, di-
That these, by vow - ing true, May show their pledge is
This cir - cle round their life, This gold - en ring that
All threats of harm de - stroy; By this their vow divine - ly blest, Found all their joy in - creased.
like the love Be - tween the Church and You.
none may break Which makes them hus - band, wife.
vide their care And dou - ble all their joy.

5 On all who thus before You kneel
Your joyous Spirit pour
That each may wake the other's zeal
To love You more and more.

6 O grant them here in peace to live,
In purity and love,
And after this life to receive
The crown of life above.

Text: F. Samuel Janzow, 1913–2001
Tune: American; setting: Charles H. Webb, b. 1933

LAND OF REST
C M

John 2:1–11

860 Gracious Savior, Grant Your Blessing

1 Gra - cious Sav - ior, grant Your bless - ing To this
2 Lord, if You are not the build - er, Then the
3 Ca - na's guest, this u - nion hal - low; Ten - der -
4 Make their love a liv - ing pic - ture Show - ing
△ 5 Fa - ther, You cre - at - ed Ad - am, Craft - ed
hus - band and this wife, That in peace they
house is built in vain, For a home with -
ly em - brace this pair. Clothe this cou - ple
how You loved Your bride: When You gave Your -
Eve, and made them one; Je - sus, from their
live to - geth - er In Your love through - out their life.
out Your pres - ence Shall with - out true love re - main.
with the gar - ments They will dai - ly need to wear:
self to cleanse her, When for her You bled and died.
sin You saved us, As God's true in - car - nate Son;
Christ, de - fend them from the tempt - er And from
Yet when You with - in a mar - riage Come and
Pa - tience, kind - ness, and com - pas - sion, Gen - tle -
Je - sus, You have made her ho - ly, Pure and
Ho - ly Spir - it, You for - give us; From our
all that would de - stroy Love's foun - da - tion
dwell with grace di - vine, There You fill the
ness, hu - mil - i - ty; Robe them, Lord, with
fair her ra - diant train; To Your - self, Your
sins we are re - leased. Bring us, Lord, at

Hymn accompaniment: 821

Text: Stephen P. Starke, b. 1955
Tune: Rowland H. Prichard, 1811–87

HYFRYDOL
87 87 D

Eph. 5:22–33; Matt. 19:4–6; John 2:1–11; Rev. 19:6–9

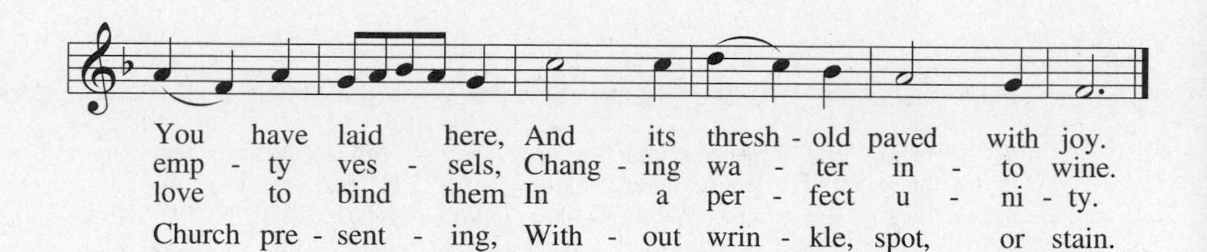
You have laid here, And its thresh - old paved with joy.
emp - ty ves - sels, Chang - ing wa - ter in - to wine.
love to bind them In a per - fect u - ni - ty.
Church pre - sent - ing, With - out wrin - kle, spot, or stain.
last to heav - en, To the end - less wed - ding feast.

Christ Be My Leader 861

1 Christ be my Lead - er by night as by day; Safe through the dark - ness, for He is the way. Glad - ly I fol - low, my fu - ture His care, Dark - ness is day - light when Je - sus is there.
2 Christ be my Teach - er in age as in youth, Drift - ing or doubt - ing, for He is the truth. Grant me to trust Him; though shift - ing as sand, Doubt can - not daunt me; in Je - sus I stand.
3 Christ be my Sav - ior in calm as in strife; Death can - not hold me, for He is the life. Nor dark - ness nor doubt - ing nor sin and its stain Can touch my sal - va - tion: with Je - sus I reign.

Text: Timothy Dudley-Smith, b. 1926
Tune: Irish; setting: *Lutheran Service Book*, 2006

SLANE
Irregular meter

John 8:12; John 1:4, 14, 17; 14:6

862 Oh, Blest the House

1 Oh, blest the house, what - e'er be - fall, Where Je - sus Christ is all in all! A home that is not whol - ly His— How sad and poor and dark it is!
2 Oh, blest that house where faith is found And all in hope and love a - bound; They trust their God and serve Him still And do in all His ho - ly will!
3 Oh, blest the par - ents who give heed Un - to their chil - dren's fore - most need And wea - ry not of care or cost. May none to them and heav'n be lost!
4 Oh, blest that house; it pros - pers well. In peace and joy the par - ents dwell, And in their chil - dren's lives is shown How rich - ly God can bless His own.
5 Then here will I and mine to - day A sol - emn prom - ise make and say: Though all the world for - sake His Word, I and my house will serve the Lord!

Text: Christoph Carl Ludwig von Pfeil, 1712–84; tr. Catherine Winkworth, 1827–78, sts. 1–2, 4–5, alt.; tr. *Evangelical Lutheran Hymnal,* Columbus, 1880, st. 3
Tune: *Geistliche Lieder auffs new gebessert,* Wittenberg, 1535, ed. Joseph Klug; setting: *The Lutheran Hymnal,* 1941

WO GOTT ZUM HAUS
L M

Joshua 24:15b; Eph. 6:4; Luke 2:41–52; 10:38–42

Our Father, by Whose Name 863

1 Our Fa - ther, by whose name All fa - ther-hood is known,
2 O Christ, Thy - self a child With - in an earth - ly home,
3 O Spir - it, who dost bind Our hearts in u - ni - ty,
Who dost in love pro - claim Each fam - i - ly Thine own,
With heart still un - de - filed, Thou didst to man-hood come;
Who teach - est us to find The love from self set free,
Bless Thou all par - ents, guard - ing well, With con - stant love as
Our chil - dren bless in ev - 'ry place That they may all be-
In all our hearts such love in - crease That ev - 'ry home by
sen - ti - nel, The homes in which Thy peo - ple dwell.
hold Thy face, And know - ing Thee may grow in grace.
this re - lease May be the dwell - ing place of peace.

Text: F. Bland Tucker, 1895–1984
Tune: John D. Edwards, 1805–85; setting: *The Hymnal 1940*

RHOSYMEDRE
66 66 888

Joshua 24:15; Is. 63:16; Luke 18:15–17; Eph. 4:3

864 Shepherd of Tender Youth

1 Shep - herd of ten - der youth, Guid - ing in love and truth Through de - vious ways; Christ, our tri - um - phant king, We come Your name to sing And here our chil - dren bring To join Your praise.
2 You are the ho - ly Lord, O all - sub - du - ing Word, Heal - er of strife. Your - self You did a - base That from sin's deep dis - grace You so might save our race And give us life.
3 You are the great High Priest; You have pre - pared the feast Of ho - ly love; And in our mor - tal pain None calls on You in vain; Our plea do not dis - dain; Help from a - bove.
4 O ev - er be our guide, Our shep - herd, and our pride, Our staff and song. Je - sus, O Christ of God, By Your en - dur - ing Word Lead us where You have trod; Make our faith strong.

Text: attr. Clement of Alexandria, c. 170–c. 220; tr. Henry M. Dexter, 1821–90, alt.
Tune: Felice de Giardini, 1716–96; setting: *Lutheran Book of Worship: Select Hymns*, 1985

ITALIAN HYMN
664 66 64

Is. 40:11; John 10:11

5 So now, and till we die,
Sound we Your praises high
And joyful sing:
Infants and all the throng,
Who to the Church belong,
Unite to swell the song
To Christ, our king!

Lord, Help Us Ever to Retain 865

1 Lord, help us ev - er to re - tain The Cat - e - chism's doc-trine plain As Lu - ther taught the Word of truth In sim - ple style to ten - der youth.
2 Help us Your ho - ly Law to learn, To mourn our sin and from it turn In faith to You and to Your Son And Ho - ly Spir - it, Three in One.
3 Hear us, dear Fa - ther, when we pray For need - ed help from day to day That as Your chil - dren we may live, Whom You bap - tized and so re - ceived.
4 Lord, when we fall or go a - stray, Ab - solve and lift us up, we pray; And through the Sac - ra - ment in - crease Our faith till we de - part in peace.

Text: Ludwig Helmbold, 1532–98; tr. Matthias Loy, 1828–1915, alt.
Tune: *As hymnodus sacer*, Leipzig, 1625; setting: *The Lutheran Hymnal*, 1941

HERR JESU CHRIST, MEINS
L M

Ps. 119:9–12; Ex. 20:1–17; Deut. 6:4–9

866 Lord Jesus Christ, the Children's Friend

1 Lord Je - sus Christ, the chil - dren's friend, To each of
2 In Chris - tian homes, Lord, let them be Your bless - ing
3 That car - ing par - ents, gra - cious Lord, And faith - ful
4 For by Your Word we clear - ly see That we have
them Your pres - ence send; Call them by name and
to their fam - i - ly; Let Chris - tian schools Your
teach - ers find re - ward In lead - ing these, to
sinned con - tin - ual - ly; But show us too, for -
keep them true In lov - ing faith, dear Lord, to You.
work ex - tend In liv - ing truth as You in - tend.
whom You call, To find in Christ their all in all.
giv - ing Lord, Your sav - ing Gos - pel's great re - ward.

5 That all of us, Your children dear,
By Christ redeemed, may Christ revere;
Lead us in joy that all we do
Will witness to our love for You.

6 Then guard and keep us to the end,
Secure in You, our gracious friend,
That in Your heav'nly family
We sing Your praise eternally.

Text: Henry L. Lettermann, 1932–96
Tune: William Knapp, 1698–1768; setting: based on James Turle, 1802–82

WAREHAM
L M

Ps. 78:1–8; 128:3–6; Ps. 34:11

Let Children Hear the Mighty Deeds

1 Let chil - dren hear the might - y deeds Which God per - formed of old, Which in our youn - ger days we saw, And which our par - ents told.
2 So make to them His glo - ries known, His works of pow'r and grace; And we'll con - vey His won - ders down Through ev - 'ry ris - ing race.
3 Our sons and daugh - ters we shall tell And they a - gain to theirs That gen - er - a - tions yet un - born May teach them to their heirs.
4 O teach them with all dil - i - gence The truths of God's own Word, To place in Him their con - fi - dence, To fear and trust their Lord,
5 To learn that in our God a - lone Their hope se - cure - ly stands, That they may nev - er doubt His love But walk in His com - mands.

Text: Isaac Watts, 1674–1748, sts. 1–3, 5, alt.; Bernhard Schumacher, 1886–1978, st. 4
Tune: Johann Crüger, 1598–1662; setting: *Lutheran Service Book*, 2006

NUN DANKET ALL
C M

Ps. 78:5–8; Deut. 4:9–10; 6:7; 11:19–20

868 Awake, My Soul, and with the Sun

1 A - wake, my soul, and with the sun Thy dai - ly
2 In con - ver - sa - tion be sin - cere, Thy con - science
3 All praise to Thee, who safe hast kept And hast re -
4 Lord, I my vows to Thee re - new; Dis - perse my
stage of du - ty run; Shake off dull sloth and
as the noon - day clear; Think how the all - see - ing
freshed me while I slept; Grant, Lord, when I from
sins as morn - ing dew; Guard my first springs of
joy - ful rise To pay thy morn - ing sac - ri - fice.
God thy ways And all thy se - cret thoughts sur - veys.
death shall wake, I may of end - less light par - take.
thought and will And with Thy - self my spir - it fill.

5 Direct, control, suggest this day
All I design or do or say
That all my pow'rs with all their might
In Thy sole glory may unite.

△ 6 Praise God, from whom all blessings flow;
Praise Him, all creatures here below;
Praise Him above, ye heav'nly host:
Praise Father, Son, and Holy Ghost.

Text: Thomas Ken, 1637–1711, alt.
Tune: François H. Barthélémon, 1741–1808; setting: *Lutheran Worship*, 1982

MORNING HYMN
L M

Ps. 59:16–17; 92:1–4; 108:1–2; 1 Cor. 10:31

With the Lord Begin Your Task 869

1 With the Lord be - gin your task; Je - sus will di - rect it.
2 Let each day be - gin with prayer, Praise, and ad - o - ra - tion.
3 With your Sav - ior at your side, Foes need not a - larm you;
4 If your task be thus be - gun With the Sav - ior's bless - ing,
5 Thus, Lord Je - sus, ev - 'ry task Be to You com - mend - ed;
For His aid and coun - sel ask; Je - sus will per - fect it.
On the Lord cast ev - 'ry care; He is your sal - va - tion.
In His prom - is - es con - fide, And no ill can harm you.
Safe - ly then your course will run, Toward the prom - ise press - ing.
May Your will be done, I ask, Un - til life is end - ed.
Ev - 'ry morn with Je - sus rise, And when day is end - ed,
Morn - ing, eve - ning, and at night Je - sus will be near you,
All your trust and hope re - pose In the might - y Mas - ter,
Good will fol - low ev - 'ry - where While you here must wan - der;
Je - sus, in Your name be - gun Be the day's en - deav - or;
In His name then close your eyes; Be to Him com - mend - ed.
Save you from the tempt - er's might, With His pres - ence cheer you.
Who in wis - dom tru - ly knows How to stem dis - as - ter.
You at last the joy will share In the man - sions yon - der.
Grant that it may well be done To Your praise for - ev - er.

Text: *Morgen- und Abend-segen*, Waldenburg, 1734; tr. W. Gustave Polack, 1890–1950, alt.
Tune: Peter Frank, 1616–75; setting: *The Lutheran Hymnal*, 1941

FANG DEIN WERK
76 76 D

Col. 3:17; Ps. 5:3, 11–12; 55:22

870 Now That the Daylight Fills the Sky

1 Now that the day - light fills the sky,
2 Would guard our hearts and tongues from strife;
3 So we, when this new day is gone
△ 4 "All praise to You, cre - a - tor Lord!
We lift our hearts to God on high,
From an - ger's din would shield our life;
And night in turn is draw - ing on,
All praise to You, e - ter - nal Word!
That He, in all we do or say,
From e - vil sights would turn our eyes,
With con - science by the world un - stained
All praise to You, O Spir - it wise!"
Would keep us free from harm to - day;
And close our ears to van - i - ties.
Shall praise His name for vic - t'ry gained.
We sing as day - light fills the skies.

Text: Latin, c. 5th–6th cent.; tr. John Mason Neale, 1818–66, alt.
Music: Dale Wood, 1934–2003

LAUREL
L M

Ps. 143:8–12; Phil. 4:5–8; Ps. 59:16–17; Ps. 4:1–3

Greet the Rising Sun

1 Greet the ris - ing sun, Shin - ing with bright force,
2 Fa - ther, hear my prayer, Keep me safe to - day;
3 Lord, I will to - day On Your love re - ly;
Like an ath - lete strong, Set to run the course;
Sanc - ti - fy my thoughts, All I do and say:
Let no e - vil thought Cloud the clear blue sky.
Birds soar high a - bove, Wild-flow'rs bloom be - low;
As I teach the young And es - teem the old,
Joy - ful and con - tent With life's sim - pler things,
With the day's new light, Glad to work I go.
May Your boun - teous grace By my life be told.
Know-ing all I need From Your kind - ness springs.

Text: Zhao Zichen, 1888–1979; tr. Stephen P. Starke, b. 1955
Tune: Chinese; setting: John R. Eggert, b. 1946

LE P'ING
55 55 55 55

Ps. 4:1–3; 143:8–10; Phil. 4:7

872 Come, Thou Bright and Morning Star

1 Come, Thou bright and Morn - ing Star, Light of Light with -
2 Let Thy grace, like morn - ing dew Fall - ing soft on
3 May Thy fer - vent love de - stroy Our cold works, in
4 Ah! Thou Day - spring from on high, Grant that at Thy
out be - gin - ning; Shine up - on us from a - far
bar - ren plac - es, Com - fort, quick - en, and re - new
us a - wak - ing Ar - dent zeal and ho - ly joy
next ap - pear - ing We who in the graves do lie
That we may be kept from sin - ning.
Our dry souls and dy - ing grac - es;
At the pur - ple morn's first break - ing.
May a - rise, Thy sum - mons hear - ing,
Drive a - way by Thy clear light Our dark night.
Bless Thy flock from Thy rich store Ev - er - more.
Let us tru - ly rise ere yet Life has set.
And re - joice in our new life, Far from strife.

Text: Christian Knorr von Rosenroth, 1636–89; tr. Richard Massie, 1800–87
Tune: *Geist-reiches Gesang-Buch*, Halle, 1704, ed. Johann A. Freylinghausen;
setting: *The Lutheran Hymnal*, 1941

MORGENGLANZ DER EWIGKEIT
78 78 73

Ps. 5:3; John 12:46; Is. 45:8; Rom. 12:11

5 Light us to those heav'nly spheres,
Sun of grace, in glory shrouded;
Lead us through this vale of tears
To the land where days unclouded,
Purest joy, and perfect peace
Never cease.

Christ, Whose Glory Fills the Skies 873

1 Christ, whose glo - ry fills the skies, Christ, the true and on - ly light,
2 Dark and cheer - less is the morn Un - ac - com - pa - nied by Thee;
3 Vis - it then this soul of mine, Pierce the gloom of sin and grief;
Sun of righ - teous - ness, a - rise; Tri - umph o'er the shades of night.
Joy - less is the day's re - turn Till Thy mer - cy's beams I see,
Fill me, ra - dian - cy di - vine, Scat - ter all my un - be - lief;
Day - spring from on high, be near; Day - star, in my heart ap - pear.
Till they in - ward light im - part, Glad my eyes, and warm my heart.
More and more Thy - self dis - play, Shin - ing to the per - fect day.

Text: Charles Wesley, 1707–88
Tune: attr. Johann G. Werner, 1777–1822; setting: *The Lutheran Hymnal*, 1941

RATISBON
77 77 77

John 8:12; Mal. 4:2; 2 Peter 1:19; Luke 1:78–79

874 O Splendor of God's Glory Bright

1 O Splen - dor of God's glo - ry bright, O Thou that
2 Come, ver - y Sun of truth and love; Pour down Thy
3 With prayer the Fa - ther we im - plore: O Fa - ther,
4 To guide what - e'er we no - bly do, With love all
bring - est light from light, O Light of Light, light's
ra - diance from a - bove And shed the Ho - ly
glo - rious ev - er - more, We plead with Thee for
en - vy to sub - due, To give us grace our
liv - ing spring, O Day, all days il - lu - min - ing:
Spir - it's ray On all we think or do or say.
grace and pow'r To con - quer in temp - ta - tion's hour,
wrongs to bear, To make ill for - tune turn to fair.
1–5
6
Al - le - lu - ia!
ia!

Text: Ambrose of Milan, 340–397; tr. Robert S. Bridges, 1844–1930, sts. 1, 3–4, 6, alt.;
tr. *Hymns Ancient and Modern*, 1904, sts. 2, 5, alt.
Music: Stephen R. Johnson, b. 1966

PUTNAM
L M and alleluia

2 Cor. 4:6; John 1:14; 1 Cor. 10:13; John 6:35, 41, 48, 51

5 On Christ, the true bread, let us feed;
Let Him to us be drink indeed;
And let us taste with joyfulness
The Holy Spirit's plenteousness.
Alleluia!

△ 6 All laud to God the Father be;
All praise, eternal Son, to Thee;
All glory to the Spirit raise
In equal and unending praise.
Alleluia!

Father, We Praise Thee 875

1 Fa - ther, we praise Thee, now the night is o - ver, Ac - tive and watch - ful, stand we all be - fore Thee; Sing - ing, we of - fer prayer and med - i - ta - tion: Thus we a - dore Thee.

2 Mon - arch of all things, fit us for Thy man - sions; Ban - ish our weak - ness, health and whole - ness send - ing; Bring us to heav - en, where Thy saints u - nit - ed Joy with - out end - ing.

△ 3 All - ho - ly Fa - ther, Son, and e - qual Spir - it, Trin - i - ty bless - ed, send us Thy sal - va - tion; Thine is the glo - ry, gleam - ing and re - sound - ing Through all cre - a - tion.

Text: attr. Gregory I, c. 540–604; tr. Percy Dearmer, 1867–1936
Tune: *Antiphoner*, Paris, 1681; setting: Joseph Herl, b. 1959

CHRISTE SANCTORUM
11 11 11 5

Ps. 5:3; 92:1–2; Rev. 7:9–17

876 O Blessed, Holy Trinity

1 O bless - ed, ho - ly Trin - i - ty, Di - vine, e - ter - nal U - ni - ty, O Fa - ther, Son, and Ho - ly Ghost, This day Your name be up - per - most.
2 My soul and bod - y keep from harm, And o - ver all ex - tend Your arm; Let Sa - tan cause me no dis - tress Nor bring me shame and wretch - ed - ness.
3 The Fa - ther's love shield me this day; The Son's pure wis - dom cheer my way; The Ho - ly Spir - it's joy and light Drive from my heart the shades of night.
4 My Mak - er, hold me in Your hand; O Christ, for - giv - en let me stand; Blest Com - fort - er, do not de - part; With faith and love en - rich my heart.
5 Lord, bless and keep me as Your own; Lord, look in kind - ness from Your throne; Lord, shine un - fail - ing peace on me By grace sur - round - ed; set me free.

Text: Martin Behm, 1557–1622; tr. Conrad H. L. Schuette, 1843–1926, alt.
Tune: Nicolaus Herman, c. 1480–1561; setting: *The Lutheran Hymnal*, 1941

O HEILIGE DREIFALTIGKEIT
L M

Ps. 59:16–17; Num. 6:24–26; 2 Cor. 13:14

God, Who Made the Earth and Heaven

877

1 God, who made the earth and heav-en, Dark-ness and light:
2 And when morn a-gain shall call us To run life's way,
3 Guard us wak-ing, guard us sleep-ing, And when we die,
△ 4 Ho-ly Fa-ther, throned in heav-en, All-ho-ly Son,
You the day for work have giv-en, For rest the night. May Your
May we still, what-e'er be-fall us, Your will o-bey. From the
May we in Your might-y keep-ing All peace-ful lie. When the
Ho-ly Spir-it, free-ly giv-en, Blest Three in One: Grant us
an-gel guards de-fend us, Slum-ber sweet Your mer-cy send us,
pow'r of e-vil hide us, In the nar-row path-way guide us,
last dread call shall wake us, Then, O Lord, do not for-sake us,
grace, we now im-plore You, Till we lay our crowns be-fore You
Ho-ly dreams and hopes at-tend us All through the night.
Nev-er be Your smile de-nied us All through the day.
But to reign in glo-ry take us With You on high.
And in wor-thier strains a-dore You While a-ges run.

Text: Reginald Heber, 1783–1826, st. 1, alt.; William Mercer, 1811–73, sts. 2, 4, alt.; Richard Whately, 1787–1863, st. 3, alt.
Tune: Welsh, 18th cent.; setting: Ralph Vaughan Williams, 1872–1958

AR HYD Y NOS
84 84 88 84

Psalm 121; 2 Tim. 4:18; Ps. 91:9–12; Ps. 32:7

878 Abide with Me

1 A - bide with me, fast falls the e - ven - tide.
2 I need Thy pres - ence ev - 'ry pass - ing hour;
3 Come not in ter - rors, as the King of kings,
4 Swift to its close ebbs out life's lit - tle day;
The dark - ness deep - ens; Lord, with me a - bide.
What but Thy grace can foil the tempt - er's pow'r?
But kind and good, with heal - ing in Thy wings;
Earth's joys grow dim, its glo - ries pass a - way;
When oth - er help - ers fail and com - forts flee,
Who like Thy - self my guide and stay can be?
Tears for all woes, a heart for ev - 'ry plea.
Change and de - cay in all a - round I see;
Help of the help - less, O a - bide with me.
Through cloud and sun - shine, O a - bide with me.
Come, Friend of sin - ners, thus a - bide with me.
O Thou who chang - est not, a - bide with me.

Text: Henry F. Lyte, 1793–1847, alt.
Tune: William H. Monk, 1823–89; setting: *The Lutheran Hymnal*, 1941

EVENTIDE
10 10 10 10

Luke 24:29; Ps. 63:6–8; 73:23–26; 1 Cor. 10:13

5 I fear no foe with Thee at hand to bless;
Ills have no weight and tears no bitterness.
Where is death's sting? Where, grave, thy victory?
I triumph still if Thou abide with me!

6 Hold Thou Thy cross before my closing eyes;
Shine through the gloom, and point me to the skies.
Heav'n's morning breaks, and earth's vain shadows flee;
In life, in death, O Lord, abide with me.

Stay with Us 879

1 Stay with us, till night has come: Our praise to
2 Walk with us, our spir - its sigh: Hear when our
3 Walk with us, the road will bend: Make all our
4 Talk with us, till we be - hold A joy - ful
5 Stay with us, till day is done: No tears nor
You this day be sung. Bless our bread, O - pen our
wea - ry spir - its cry, Feel a - gain Our loss, our
weep-ing, wail - ing end. Wipe our tears, For - give our
life You will un - fold: Heal our eyes To see the
dark shall dim the sun. Cheer the heart, Your grace im-
eyes: Je - sus, be our great sur - prise.
pain: Je - sus, take us to Your side.
fears: Je - sus, lift the heav - y cross.
prize: Je - sus, take us to the light.
part: Je - sus, bring e - ter - nal life.

Setting available in hymn accompaniment edition.

Text: Herbert F. Brokering, 1926–2009
Tune: Walter L. Pelz, b. 1926

STAY WITH US
78 77

Luke 24:13–35

880 Now Rest beneath Night's Shadow

1 Now rest be - neath night's shad - ow The wood - land,
2 The ra - diant sun has van - ished, Its gold - en
3 Now all the heav'n - ly splen - dor Breaks forth in
4 Lord Je - sus, since You love me, Now spread Your
field, and mead - ow; The world in slum - ber lies.
rays are ban - ished From dark - 'ning skies of night;
star - light ten - der From myr - iad worlds un - known;
wings a - bove me And shield me from a - larm.
But you, my heart, a - wak - ing And prayer and mu - sic
But Christ, the Sun of glad - ness, Dis - pel - ling all our
And we, this mar - vel see - ing, For - get our self - ish
Though Sa - tan would de - vour me, Let an - gel guards sing
mak - ing, Let praise to your Cre - a - tor rise.
sad - ness, Shines down on us in warm - est light.
be - ing For joy of beau - ty not our own.
o'er me: This child of God shall meet no harm.

Text: Paul Gerhardt, 1607–76; tr. *The Lutheran Hymnal*, 1941, alt.
Tune: Heinrich Isaac, c. 1450–1517; setting: *The Lutheran Hymnal*, 1941

O WELT, ICH MUSS DICH LASSEN
776 778

Ps. 4:8; 91:4, 11–12; Luke 1:78–79; Ps. 139:11–14

5 My loved ones, rest securely,
For God this night will surely
From peril guard your heads.
Sweet slumbers may He send you
And bid His hosts attend you
And through the night watch o'er your beds.

Christ, Mighty Savior 881

1 Christ, might - y Sav - ior, Light of all cre - a - tion,
2 Now comes the day's end as the sun is set - ting,
3 There - fore we come now eve - ning rites to of - fer,
4 Give heed, we pray You, to our sup - pli - ca - tion,
5 Though bod - ies slum - ber, hearts shall keep their vig - il,
You make the day - time ra - diant with the sun - light
Mir - ror of day - break, pledge of res - ur - rec - tion;
Joy - ful - ly chant - ing ho - ly hymns to praise You,
That You may grant us par - don for of - fens - es,
For - ev - er rest - ing in the peace of Je - sus,
And to the night give glit - ter - ing a -
While in the heav - ens choirs of stars ap -
With all cre - a - tion join - ing hearts and
Strength for our weak hearts, rest for ach - ing
In light or dark - ness wor - ship - ing our
dorn - ment, Stars in the heav - ens.
pear - ing Hal - low the night - fall.
voic - es Sing - ing Your glo - ry.
bod - ies, Sooth - ing the wea - ry.
Sav - ior Now and for - ev - er.

Setting available in hymn accompaniment edition.

Text: Latin, c. 7th cent.; tr. Alan McDougall, 1895–1966; rev. Anne K. LeCroy, b. 1930
Tune: Richard W. Dirksen, 1921–2003

INNISFREE FARM
11 11 11 5

John 1:1–5; Psalm 4; Heb. 4:8–10; Psalm 134

882 O Christ, Who Art the Light and Day

1 O Christ, who art the light and day,
2 All - ho - ly Lord, in hum - ble prayer
3 Our sleep be pure from sin - ful stain;
4 A - sleep though wea - ried eyes may be,
Thou driv - est night and gloom a - way;
We ask to - night Thy watch - ful care.
Let not the tempt - er van - tage gain
Still keep the heart a - wake to Thee;
O Light of Light, whose Word doth show
O grant us calm re - pose in Thee,
Or our un - guard - ed flesh sur - prise
Let Thy right hand out - stretched a - bove
The light of heav'n to us be - low.
A qui - et night, from per - ils free.
And make us guilt - y in Thine eyes.
Guard those who serve the Lord they love. A - men.

5 Behold, O God, our shield, and quell
The crafts and subtleties of hell;
Direct Thy servants in all good,
Whom Thou hast purchased with Thy blood.

6 O Lord, remember us who bear
The burden of the flesh we wear;
Thou who dost e'er our souls defend,
Be with us even to the end.

△ 7 All praise to God the Father be,
All praise, eternal Son, to Thee,
Whom with the Spirit we adore
Forever and forevermore.
Amen.

Setting available in hymn accompaniment edition. Alternate tune: TALLIS' CANON (883)

Text: Latin, c. 6th cent.; tr. William J. Copeland, 1804–85
Tune: Sarum plainsong, c. 9th cent., mode IV

CONDITOR ALME SIDERUM
L M

John 8:12; 12:35–36; 1 Thess. 5:5

All Praise to Thee, My God, This Night

1 All praise to Thee, my God, this night For all the blessings of the light. Keep me, O keep me, King of kings, Beneath Thine own almighty wings.
2 Forgive me, Lord, for Thy dear Son, The ill that I this day have done, That with the world, myself, and Thee, I, ere I sleep, at peace may be.
3 Teach me to live that I may dread The grave as little as my bed. Teach me to die that so I may Rise glorious at the awe-full day.
4 Oh, may my soul in Thee repose, And may sweet sleep mine eyelids close, Sleep that shall me more vig'rous make To serve my God when I awake!

5 When in the night I sleepless lie,
My soul with heav'nly thoughts supply;
Let no ill dreams disturb my rest,
No pow'rs of darkness me molest.

△ 6 Praise God, from whom all blessings flow;
Praise Him, all creatures here below;
Praise Him above, ye heav'nly host:
Praise Father, Son, and Holy Ghost.

Text: Thomas Ken, 1637–1711, alt.
Tune: Thomas Tallis, c. 1505–85; setting: *The Lutheran Hymnal*, 1941

TALLIS' CANON
L M

Ps. 92:1–2; Ps. 4:8; Psalm 91

884 Lord, Support Us All Day Long

1 Lord, sup - port us all day long, Guide and strength - en.
2 Be our light in dark - ness, Lord, Our de - fend - er;
3 With Your pres - ence, Lord, draw near Those who la - bor
4 Gra - cious Lord, we give You thanks, Praise and bless You,
Eve - ning comes, the world is hushed, Shad - ows length - en,
In Your pres - ence per - ils all Must sur - ren - der.
Through the night - time on be - half Of their neigh - bor.
As the giv - er of all good We con - fess You.
Work is done, life's fe - vered pace Now has end - ed;
Drive all dark sa - tan - ic snares From each dwell - ing;
Grant them cour - age for each fear, Faith - ful car - ing:
This past day we now com - mit To Your keep - ing
Christ, to You, our fi - nal rest Is com - mend - ed.
Then, at peace, our hearts Your praise Will be tell - ing.
Your com - pas - sion and Your love Tru - ly shar - ing.
And en - trust to You the hours Of our sleep - ing.

Text: Stephen P. Starke, b. 1955
Music: Joseph D. Jones, 1827–70, alt.

GWALCHMAI
74 74 D

Ex. 13:21; Ps. 25:5; Ps. 4:8; 2 Sam. 22:29

I Lie, O Lord, within Your Care 885

1 I lie, O Lord, with - in Your care, A - wake or when I'm sleep - ing. Who - ev - er trusts in Your strong arms Is safe with - in Your keep - ing.
2 Lord, You a - lone keep con - stant watch; My rest - less heart You qui - et. When dark - ness fills the night with fear, I will by faith de - fy it.
3 When shad - ows fall, I will not dwell On trou - bles that dis - tress me, Nor let some pain - ful mem - o - ry Em - bit - ter and op - press me.
4 It is e - nough that You are near; I need not now dis - cov - er What hid - den plans You have for me, My fu - ture's path un - cov - er.

5 Tomorrow's road I cannot trace
Nor know what ills will meet me.
You only ask that I be still
And trust You there will greet me.

6 Each dawning day to which I wake
Will show Your hand still guiding
And ev'ry good my life requires
Your grace again providing.

7 Though troubles still may cloud the sky,
I'll see beyond them shining
A light to show some hidden way—
A way of Your designing.

8 Since You have gently touched my eyes,
I'll sleep through tears of sorrow.
Though long the night, my God, my friend,
Will be my guide tomorrow.

Text: Jochen Klepper, 1903–42; tr. Herman G. Stuempfle, Jr., 1923–2007
Music: Joseph Herl, b. 1959

ICH LIEGE, HERR, IN DEINER HUT
87 87

Psalm 121; Ps. 91:1–5; Ps. 17:15; 37:5–6

886 The Day Thou Gavest

1 The day Thou gav - est, Lord, is end - ed,
2 We thank Thee that Thy Church, un - sleep - ing
3 As o'er each con - ti - nent and is - land
4 The sun, that bids us rest, is wak - ing
The dark - ness falls at Thy be - hest;
While earth rolls on - ward in - to light,
The dawn leads on an - oth - er day,
Thy saints be - neath the west - ern skies,
To Thee our morn - ing hymns as - cend - ed,
Through all the world her watch is keep - ing,
The voice of prayer is nev - er si - lent,
And hour by hour, as day is break - ing,
Thy praise shall sanc - ti - fy our rest.
And nev - er rests by day or night.
Nor dies the strain of praise a - way.
Fresh hymns of thank - ful praise a - rise.

Text: John Ellerton, 1826–93, alt.
Music: Clement C. Scholefield, 1839–1904

ST. CLEMENT
98 98

Ps. 113:2–4; Rom. 13:11–12; 1 Thess. 5:5–10; Rev. 7:9–12

5 So be it, Lord! Thy throne shall never,
Like earth's proud empires, pass away;
Thy kingdom stands and grows forever,
Till all Thy creatures own Thy sway.

Now the Light Has Gone Away 887

1 Now the light has gone a - way; Fa - ther, lis - ten while I pray,
2 Je - sus, Sav - ior, wash a - way All that has been wrong to - day;
3 Let my near and dear ones be Al - ways near and dear to Thee;
4 Now my eve-ning praise I give; Thou didst die that I might live.
5 Thou, my best and kind - est Friend, Thou wilt love me to the end.

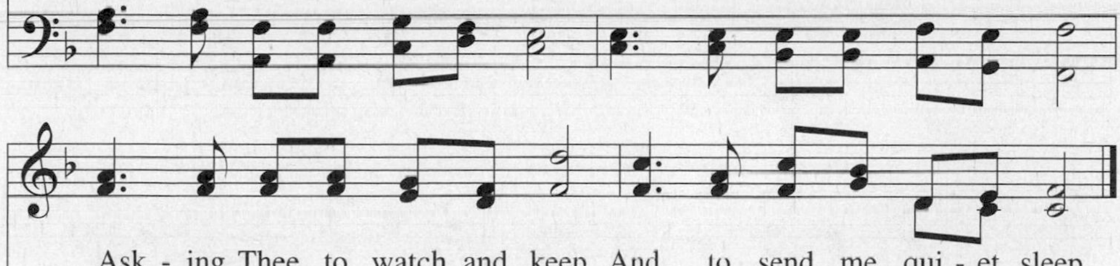

Ask - ing Thee to watch and keep And to send me qui - et sleep.
Help me ev - 'ry day to be Good and gen - tle, more like Thee.
O bring me and all I love To Thy hap - py home a - bove.
All my bless-ings come from Thee; Oh, how good Thou art to me!
Let me love Thee more and more, Al - ways bet - ter than be - fore.

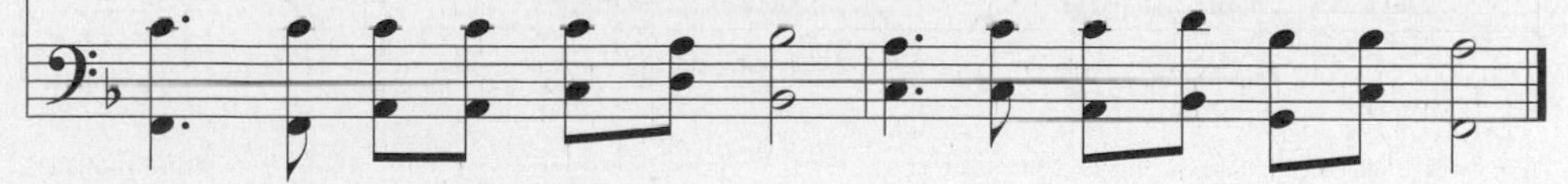

1 Müde bin ich, geh zur Ruh,
Schließe meine Äuglein zu:
Vater, laß die Augen dein
Über meinem Bette sein.

2 Hab ich Unrecht heut getan,
Sieh es, lieber Gott, nicht an.
Deine Gnad und Christi Blut
Macht ja allen Schaden gut.

3 Alle, die mir sind verwandt,
Gott, laß ruhn in deiner Hand;
Alle Menschen groß und klein
Sollen dir befohlen sein.

4 Kranken Herzen sende Ruh,
Nasse Augen schließe zu.
Laß den Mond am Himmel stehn
Und die stille Welt besehn.

The text of the German hymn "Müde bin ich, geh zur Ruh," also sung to this tune, is provided for those who remember it as their bedtime prayer during childhood.

Text: Frances R. Havergal, 1836–79, alt.; Luise Hensel, 1798–1876, German
Tune: *Liederbuch für Kleinkinder-Schulen*, Kaiserswerth, 1842; setting: *The Lutheran Hymnal*, 1941

MÜDE BIN ICH
77 77

Ps. 4:8; 1 John 1:7b, 9; 4:10, 19; John 14:1–3

888 O Gladsome Light, O Grace

1 O glad-some Light, O Grace Of God the Fa-ther's face,
2 As day-light turns to night, We see the fad-ing light,
3 To Thee of right be-longs All praise of ho-ly songs,
E-ter-nal splen-dor wear-ing: Ce-les-tial, ho-ly, blest,
Our eve-ning hymn out-pour-ing, Fa-ther of might un-known,
O Son of God, Life-giv-er; Thee, there-fore, O Most High,
Our Sav-ior Je-sus Christ, Joy-ful in Thine ap-pear-ing!
Thee, His in-car-nate Son, And Ho-ly Ghost a-dor-ing.
The world doth glo-ri-fy And shall ex-alt for-ev-er.

Text: Greek, c. 4th cent.; tr. Robert S. Bridges, 1844–1930, alt.
Tune: attr. Louis Bourgeois, c. 1510–61; setting: Claude Goudimel, 1514–72

NUNC DIMITTIS
667 667

John 1:9, 14; 2 Cor. 4:6; John 8:12; Col. 3:16

889 Before the Ending of the Day

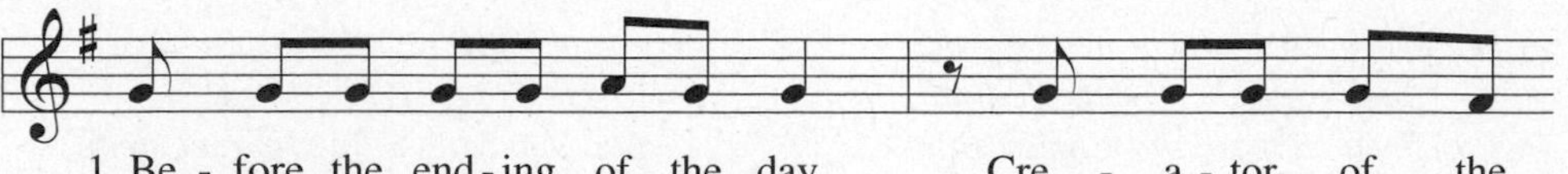
1 Be-fore the end-ing of the day, Cre-a-tor of the
2 From all the ter-rors of the night, From e-vil dreams de-
△ 3 O Fa-ther, this we ask be done Through Je-sus Christ, Thine

Setting available in hymn accompaniment edition.

Text: Latin, c. 5th–10th cent.; tr. John Mason Neale, 1818–66, alt.
Tune: Benedictine plainsong, mode VI

JAM LUCIS
L M

Psalm 121; Ps. 91:1–12; John 16:23

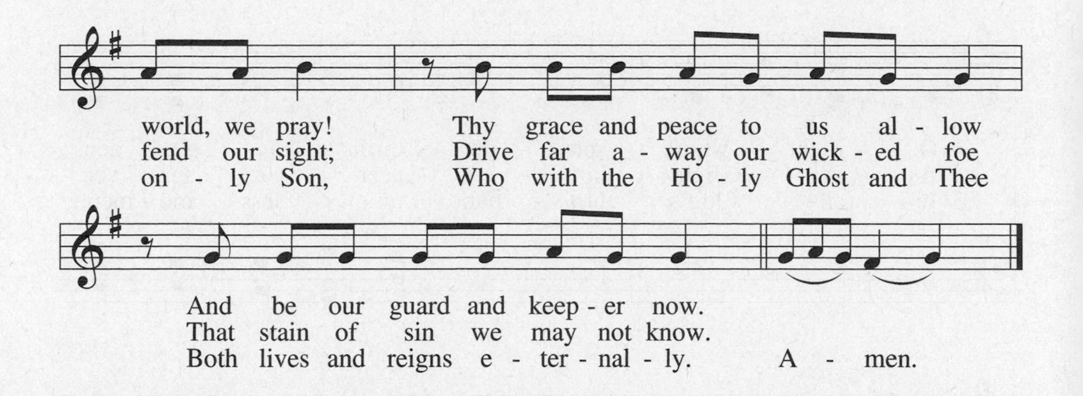
world, we pray! Thy grace and peace to us al - low
fend our sight; Drive far a - way our wick - ed foe
on - ly Son, Who with the Ho - ly Ghost and Thee
And be our guard and keep - er now.
That stain of sin we may not know.
Both lives and reigns e - ter - nal - ly. A - men.

O Blessed Light, O Trinity 890

1 O bless - ed Light, O Trin - i - ty, O ev - er -
2 To You our morn - ing song of praise, To You our
△ 3 All glo - ry be to God a - bove And to the
last - ing U - ni - ty: As now the fi - ery
eve - ning prayer we raise; We praise Your light in
Son, the Prince of love, And to the Spir - it,
sun de - parts, Send forth Your light in - to our hearts.
ev - 'ry age, The glo - ry of our pil - grim - age.
One in Three! We praise You, bless - ed Trin - i - ty.

Text: attr. Ambrose of Milan, 340–397; tr. *Lutheran Service Book*, 2006, st. 1;
tr. Gracia Grindal, b. 1943, sts. 2–3
Tune: Nicolaus Herman, c. 1480–1561; setting: *The Lutheran Hymnal*, 1941

O HEILIGE DREIFALTIGKEIT
L M

1 John 1:5–7; 2 Cor. 4:6; Eph. 5:8–14; Ps. 113:2–3

891 O Light Whose Splendor

1 O Light whose splen - dor thrills and glad - dens
2 As twi - light hov - ers near at sun - set,
3 In all life's bril - liant time - less mo - ments,
With ra - diance bright - er than the sun,
And lamps are lit, and chil - dren nod,
Let faith - ful voic - es sing Your praise,
Pure gleam of God's un - end - ing glo - ry,
In eve - ning hymns we lift our voic - es
O Son of God, our Life - be - stow - er,
O Je - sus, blest A - noint - ed One;
To Fa - ther, Spir - it, Son: one God.
Whose glo - ry light - ens end - less days.

Text: Carl P. Daw, Jr., b. 1944
Music: Clement C. Scholefield, 1839–1904

ST. CLEMENT
98 98

Rev. 21:22–27; Rev. 1:16b; John 8:12; Ps. 113:2–4

Come, Ye Thankful People, Come 892

1 Come, ye thank-ful peo - ple, come; Raise the song of har - vest home.
2 All the world is God's own field, Fruit un - to His praise to yield;
3 For the Lord, our God, shall come And shall take His har - vest home,
4 E - ven so, Lord, quick - ly come To Thy fi - nal har - vest home;
All be safe - ly gath - ered in Ere the win - ter storms be - gin;
Wheat and tares to - geth - er sown, Un - to joy or sor - row grown.
From His field shall in that day All of - fens - es purge a - way,
Gath - er Thou Thy peo - ple in, Free from sor - row, free from sin,
God, our mak - er, doth pro - vide For our wants to be sup-plied.
First the blade and then the ear, Then the full corn shall ap - pear.
Give His an - gels charge at last In the fire the tares to cast,
There, for - ev - er pu - ri - fied, In Thy gar - ner to a - bide:
Come to God's own tem - ple, come; Raise the song of har - vest home.
Lord of har - vest, grant that we Whole-some grain and pure may be.
But the fruit - ful ears to store In His gar - ner ev - er - more.
Come with all Thine an - gels, come, Raise the glo - rious har - vest home.

Text: Henry Alford, 1810–71, alt.
Tune: George J. Elvey, 1816–93; setting: *The Lutheran Hymnal*, 1941

ST. GEORGE'S, WINDSOR
77 77 D

Matt. 13:24–30, 37–43; Rev. 22:7, 12, 20; Is. 9:3

893 Sing to the Lord of Harvest

1 Sing to the Lord of har - vest, Sing songs of love and praise;
2 God makes the clouds rain good - ness, The des - erts bloom and spring,
3 Bring to this sa - cred al - tar The gifts His good - ness gave,

With joy - ful hearts and voic - es Your al - le - lu - ias raise.
The hills leap up in glad - ness, The val - leys laugh and sing.
The gold - en sheaves of har - vest, The souls Christ died to save.

By Him the roll - ing sea - sons In fruit - ful or - der move;
God fills them with His full - ness, All things with large in - crease;
Your hearts lay down be - fore Him When at His feet you fall,

Sing to the Lord of har - vest A joy - ous song of love.
He crowns the year with bless - ing, With plen - ty and with peace.
And with your lives a - dore Him Who gave His life for all.

Text: John S. B. Monsell, 1811–75, alt.
Tune: Johann Steurlein, 1546–1613; setting: Healey Willan, 1880–1968

WIE LIEBLICH IST DER MAIEN
76 76 D

Ps. 65:9–13; 1 Cor. 6:20

For the Fruits of His Creation 894

1 For the fruits of His cre - a - tion, Thanks be to God.
2 In the just re - ward of la - bor, God's will is done.
3 For the har-vests of the Spir - it, Thanks be to God.
For His gifts to ev - 'ry na - tion, Thanks be to God. For the
In the help we give our neigh-bor, God's will is done. In our
For the good we all in - her - it, Thanks be to God. For the
plow - ing, sow-ing, reap - ing, Si - lent growth while we are sleep-ing,
world-wide task of car - ing For the hun - gry and de - spair-ing,
won - ders that as - tound us, For the truths that still con-found us,
Fu - ture needs in earth's safe-keep - ing, Thanks be to God.
In the har-vests we are shar - ing, God's will is done.
Most of all, that love has found us, Thanks be to God.

Of all the gifts for which we are thankful to God, the greatest by far is that His love in Christ has found us.

Text: Fred Pratt Green, 1903–2000
Tune: Welsh, 18th cent.; setting: Ralph Vaughan Williams, 1872–1958

AR HYD Y NOS
84 84 88 84

Mark 4:26–27; 2 Cor. 9:6–12, 15

895 Now Thank We All Our God

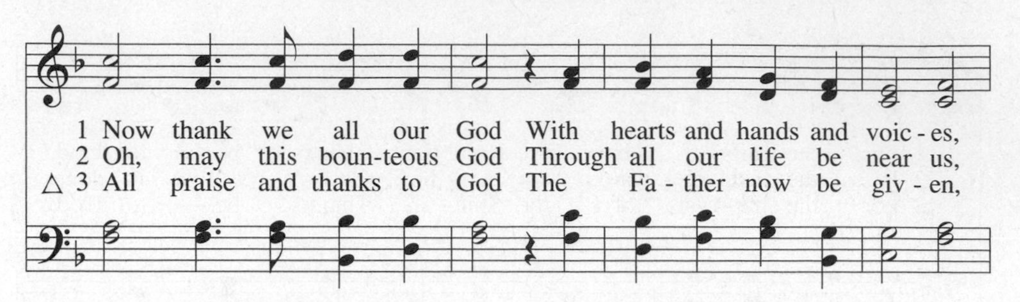
1 Now thank we all our God With hearts and hands and voic - es,
2 Oh, may this boun-teous God Through all our life be near us,
△ 3 All praise and thanks to God The Fa - ther now be giv - en,

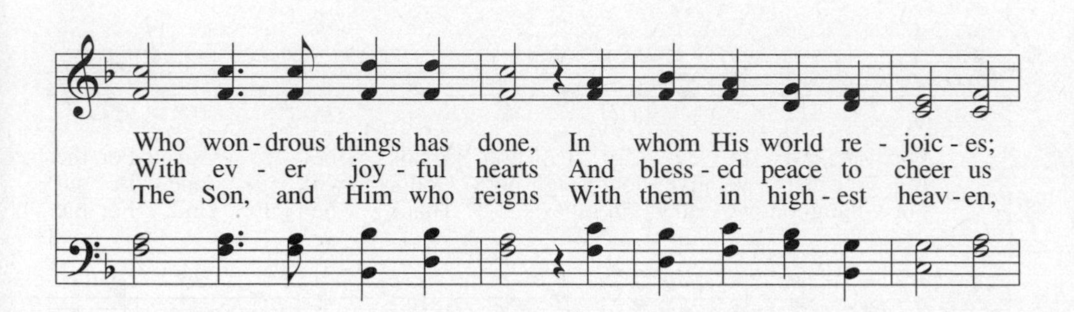
Who won - drous things has done, In whom His world re - joic - es;
With ev - er joy - ful hearts And bless - ed peace to cheer us
The Son, and Him who reigns With them in high - est heav - en,

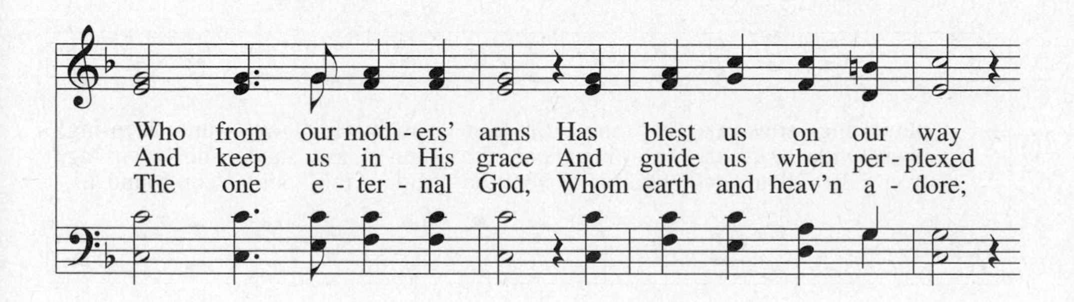
Who from our moth - ers' arms Has blest us on our way
And keep us in His grace And guide us when per - plexed
The one e - ter - nal God, Whom earth and heav'n a - dore;

With count - less gifts of love And still is ours to - day.
And free us from all ills In this world and the next!
For thus it was, is now, And shall be ev - er - more.

Text: Martin Rinckart, 1586–1649; tr. Catherine Winkworth, 1827–78, alt.
Tune: Johann Crüger, 1598–1662; setting: *The Lutheran Hymnal*, 1941

NUN DANKET ALLE GOTT
67 67 66 66

Ps. 107:21–22; Eph. 5:19; Ps. 105:1–2; Ps. 37:5–6, 39–40

Now Greet the Swiftly Changing Year

896

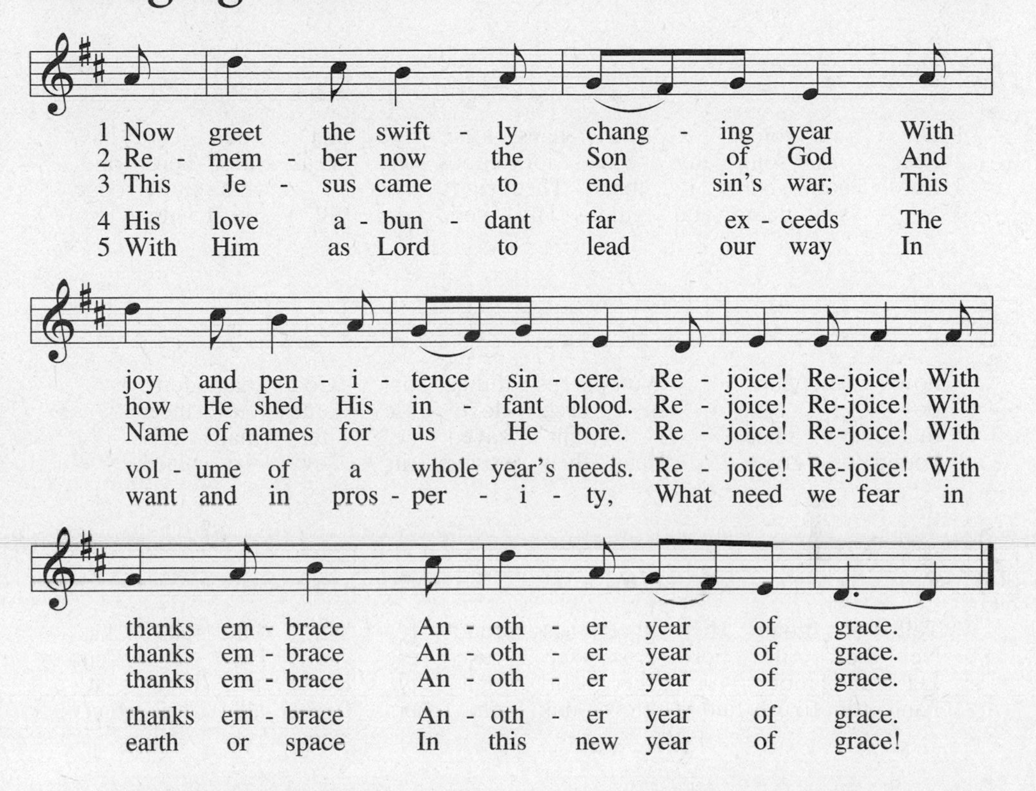
1 Now greet the swift - ly chang - ing year With joy and pen - i - tence sin - cere. Re - joice! Re-joice! With thanks em - brace An - oth - er year of grace.
2 Re - mem - ber now the Son of God And how He shed His in - fant blood. Re - joice! Re-joice! With thanks em - brace An - oth - er year of grace.
3 This Je - sus came to end sin's war; This Name of names for us He bore. Re - joice! Re-joice! With thanks em - brace An - oth - er year of grace.
4 His love a - bun - dant far ex - ceeds The vol - ume of a whole year's needs. Re - joice! Re-joice! With thanks em - brace An - oth - er year of grace.
5 With Him as Lord to lead our way In want and in pros - per - i - ty, What need we fear in earth or space In this new year of grace!

6 "All glory be to God on high,
And peace on earth!" the angels cry.
Rejoice! Rejoice! With thanks embrace
Another year of grace.

△ 7 God, Father, Son, and Spirit, hear!
To all our pleas incline Your ear;
Upon our lives rich blessing trace
In this new year of grace.

Setting available in hymn accompaniment edition.

Text: *Cithara Sanctorum*, Levoca, 1636; tr. Jaroslav J. Vajda, 1919–2008, alt.
Tune: Alfred V. Fedak, b. 1953

SIXTH NIGHT
88 86

Ps. 65:11; 107:8; Luke 2:21; Eph. 3:20–21

897 O Rejoice, Ye Christians, Loudly

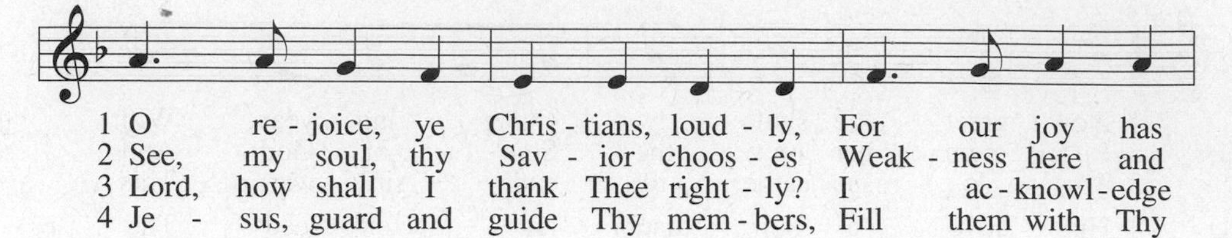
1 O re - joice, ye Chris - tians, loud - ly, For our joy has
2 See, my soul, thy Sav - ior choos - es Weak - ness here and
3 Lord, how shall I thank Thee right - ly? I ac - knowl - edge
4 Je - sus, guard and guide Thy mem - bers, Fill them with Thy

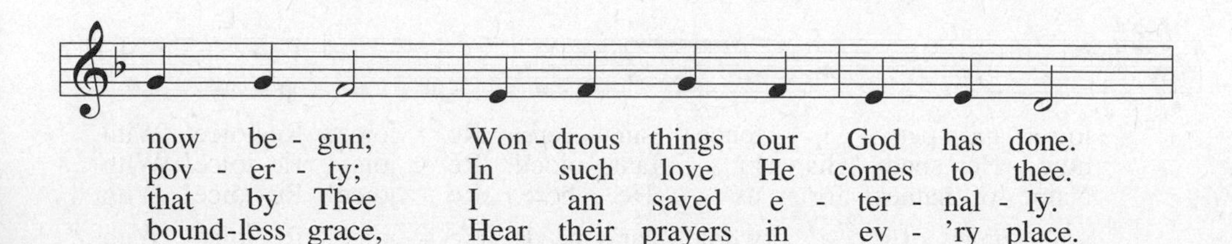
now be - gun; Won - drous things our God has done.
pov - er - ty; In such love He comes to thee.
that by Thee I am saved e - ter - nal - ly.
bound - less grace, Hear their prayers in ev - 'ry place.

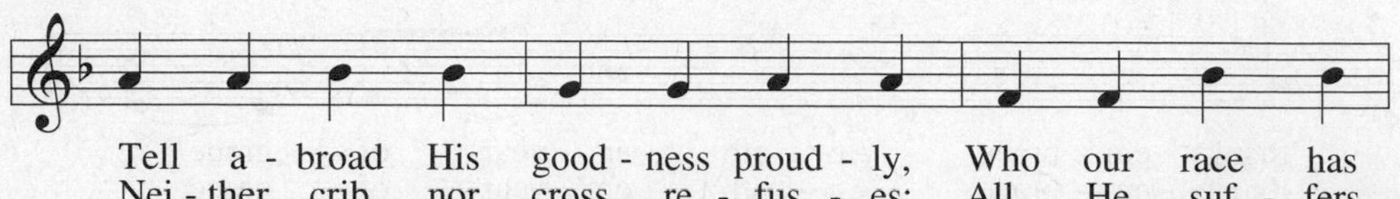
Tell a - broad His good - ness proud - ly, Who our race has
Nei - ther crib nor cross re - fus - es; All He suf - fers
Let me not for - get it light - ly, But to Thee at
Fan to flame faith's glow - ing em - bers; Grant all Chris - tians,

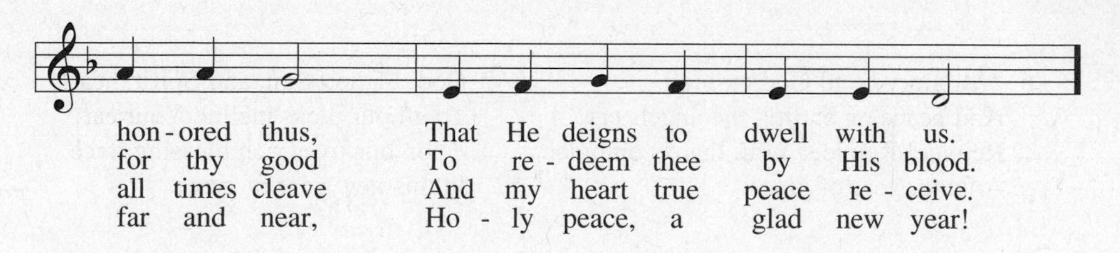
hon - ored thus, That He deigns to dwell with us.
for thy good To re - deem thee by His blood.
all times cleave And my heart true peace re - ceive.
far and near, Ho - ly peace, a glad new year!

Refrain
Joy, O joy, be - yond all glad - ness, Christ has done a -

Setting available in hymn accompaniment edition.

Text: Christian Keimann, 1607–62; tr. Catherine Winkworth, 1827–78, alt.
Tune: Andreas Hammerschmidt, c. 1611–75

FREUET EUCH, IHR CHRISTEN
877 877 and refrain

Luke 2:10–14; 2 Cor. 8:9; Phil. 2:5–8; John 14:27

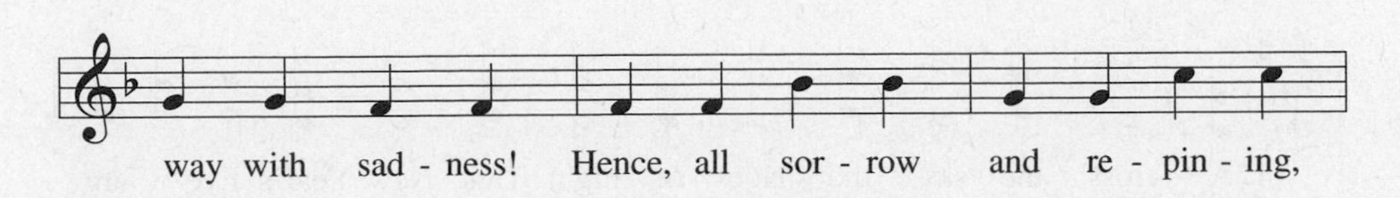
way with sad - ness! Hence, all sor - row and re - pin - ing,

For the Sun of Grace is shin - ing!

The Ancient Law Departs 898

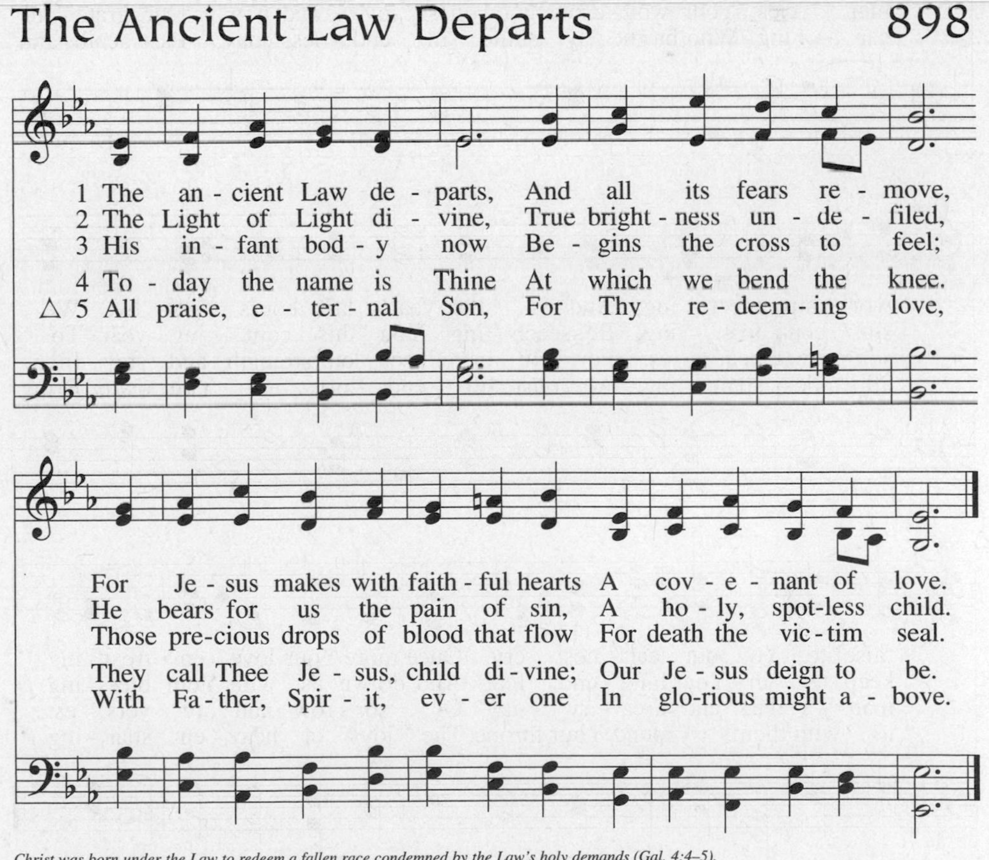
1 The an - cient Law de - parts, And all its fears re - move,
2 The Light of Light di - vine, True bright - ness un - de - filed,
3 His in - fant bod - y now Be - gins the cross to feel;
4 To - day the name is Thine At which we bend the knee.
△ 5 All praise, e - ter - nal Son, For Thy re - deem - ing love,
For Je - sus makes with faith - ful hearts A cov - e - nant of love.
He bears for us the pain of sin, A ho - ly, spot-less child.
Those pre-cious drops of blood that flow For death the vic - tim seal.
They call Thee Je - sus, child di - vine; Our Je - sus deign to be.
With Fa - ther, Spir - it, ev - er one In glo-rious might a - bove.

Christ was born under the Law to redeem a fallen race condemned by the Law's holy demands (Gal. 4:4–5). The circumcision of our Lord signified that His saving, substitutionary work on our behalf had begun.

Text: Sebastian Besnault, d. 1724; tr. *The Lutheran Hymnal*, 1941
Tune: Johann Sebastian Bach, 1685–1750, adapt.; setting: *The Lutheran Hymnal*, 1941

POTSDAM
S M

Luke 2:21; Matt. 1:21

899 Across the Sky the Shades of Night

1 A - cross the sky the shades of night This New Year's Eve are
2 Be - fore the cross sub - dued we bow, To You our prayer ad -
3 We gath - er up in this brief hour The mem - 'ry of Your
4 We now re - mem - ber, as we pray, Our dear ones in Your
fleet - ing. We deck Your al - tar, Lord, with light, In sol - emn
dress - ing, Re - count - ing all Your mer - cies now, And all our
mer - cies: Your won - drous good - ness, love, and pow'r Our grate - ful
car - ing Who bright - ly shine in end - less day, Past death and
wor - ship meet - ing; And as the year's last hours go by, We
sins con - fess - ing; Be - seech - ing You this com - ing year To
song re - hears - es; For You have been our strength and stay In
all de - spair - ing. At our life's end, Lord, as Your own, Bring
raise to You our ear - nest cry, Once more Your love en - treat - ing.
keep us in Your faith and fear And crown us with Your bless - ing.
man - y a dark and drea - ry day Of sor - row and re - vers - es.
us with them a - round Your throne, The joys of heav - en shar - ing.

Text: James Hamilton, 1819–96, sts. 1–3, 5, alt.; Gregory J. Wismar, b. 1946, st. 4
Tune: attr. Nicolaus Decius, c. 1485–after 1546; setting: Joseph Herl, b. 1959

ALLEIN GOTT IN DER HÖH
87 87 887

Ps. 121:1; 136:1; Ps. 100:5; Ps. 68:19

5 Then, gracious God, in years to come,
We pray Your hand may guide us,
And, onward through our journey home,
Your mercy walk beside us
Until at last our ransomed life
Is safe from peril, toil, and strife
When heav'n itself shall hide us.

Jesus! Name of Wondrous Love 900

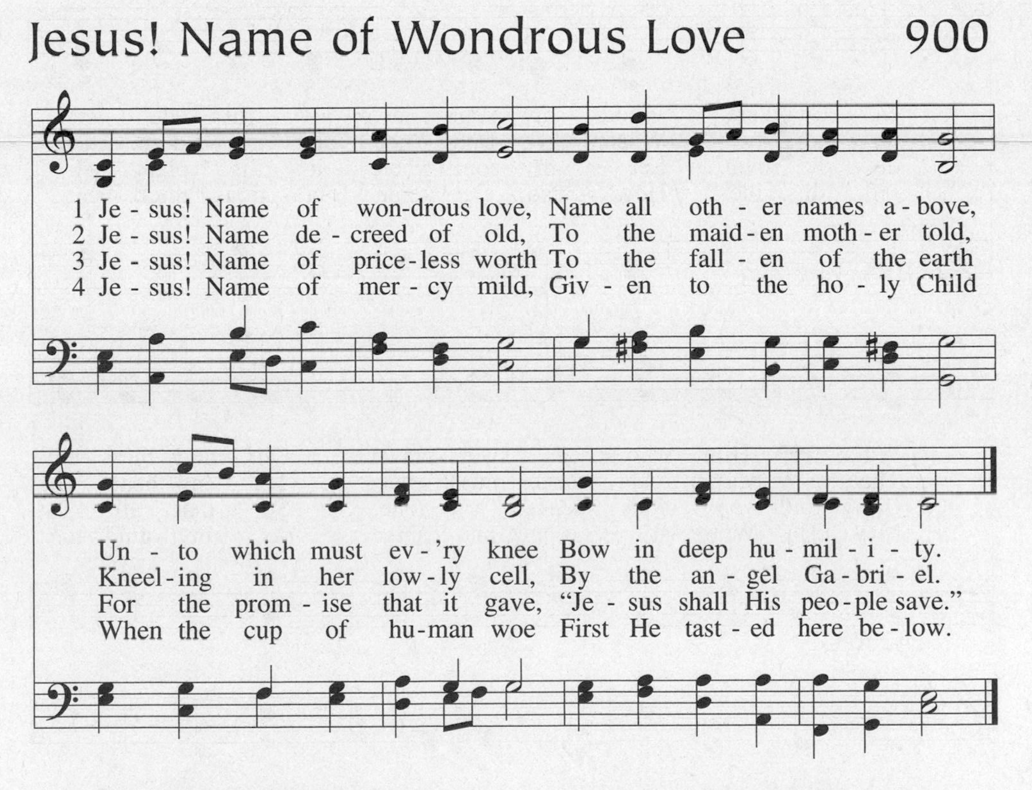
1 Je - sus! Name of won-drous love, Name all oth - er names a - bove,
2 Je - sus! Name de - creed of old, To the maid-en moth - er told,
3 Je - sus! Name of price-less worth To the fall - en of the earth
4 Je - sus! Name of mer - cy mild, Giv - en to the ho - ly Child
Un - to which must ev - 'ry knee Bow in deep hu - mil - i - ty.
Kneel-ing in her low - ly cell, By the an - gel Ga - bri - el.
For the prom - ise that it gave, "Je - sus shall His peo-ple save."
When the cup of hu-man woe First He tast - ed here be - low.

5 Jesus! Only name that's giv'n
Under all the mighty heav'n
Whereby those to sin enslaved
Burst their fetters and are saved.

6 Jesus! Name of wondrous love,
Human name of God above;
Pleading only this, we flee
Helpless, O our God, to Thee.

On the eighth day after His birth, Jesus was circumcised according to the Mosaic Law (Ex. 13:12–13) and was given the name "Jesus," which means "He saves."

Text: William W. How, 1823–97, alt.
Tune: *Geist-reiches Gesang-Buch*, Halle, 1704, ed. Johann A. Freylinghausen, alt.;
setting: *The Lutheran Hymnal*, 1941

GOTT SEI DANK
77 77

Acts 4:12; Matt. 1:21; Acts 10:43; Phil. 2:9–11

901 Open Now Thy Gates of Beauty

1 O - pen now thy gates of beau - ty; Zi - on, let me
2 Gra - cious God, I come be - fore Thee; Come Thou al - so
3 Here Thy praise is glad - ly chant - ed; Here Thy seed is
4 Thou my faith in - crease and quick - en; Let me keep Thy
en - ter there, Where my soul in joy - ful du - ty
un - to me. Where we find Thee and a - dore Thee,
du - ly sown. Let my soul, where it is plant - ed,
gift di - vine, How - so - e'er temp - ta - tions thick - en;
Waits for Him who an - swers prayer. Oh, how bless - ed
There a heav'n on earth must be. To my heart, O
Bring forth pre - cious sheaves a - lone, So that all I
May Thy Word still o'er me shine As my guid - ing
is this place, Filled with sol - ace, light, and grace!
en - ter Thou; Let it be Thy tem - ple now!
hear may be Fruit - ful un - to life in me.
star through life, As my com - fort in all strife.

Text: Benjamin Schmolck, 1672–1737; tr. Catherine Winkworth, 1827–78, alt.
Tune: Joachim Neander, 1650–80; setting: *The Lutheran Hymnal*, 1941

UNSER HERRSCHER
87 87 77

Ps. 100:4; 118:19–26; Is. 26:2–4; 2 Cor. 6:16

5 Speak, O God, and I will hear Thee;
Let Thy will be done indeed.
May I undisturbed draw near Thee
While Thou dost Thy people feed.
Here of life the fountain flows;
Here is balm for all our woes.

Lord Jesus Christ, Be Present Now 902

1 Lord Je - sus Christ, be pres - ent now; Our hearts in
2 Un - seal our lips to sing Your praise In end - less
3 Then shall we join the hosts that cry, "O ho - ly,
△ 4 All glo - ry to the Fa - ther, Son, And Ho - ly
true de - vo - tion bow. Your Spir - it send with
hymns through all our days. In - crease our faith and
ho - ly Lord Most High!" And in the light of
Spir - it, Three in One! To You, O bless - ed
light di - vine, And let Your truth with - in us shine.
light our minds; And set us free from doubt that blinds.
that blest place We then shall see You face to face.
Trin - i - ty, Be praise through-out e - ter - ni - ty!

Text: *Lutherisch Hand-Büchlein*, Altenburg, 1648; tr. Catherine Winkworth, 1827–78, alt.
Tune: *Cantionale Germanicum*, Gochsheim, 1628; setting: *Service Book and Hymnal*, 1958

HERR JESU CHRIST, DICH ZU UNS WEND
L M

Ps. 43:3–4; Heb. 13:15; Is. 6:3; Ps. 95:2

903 This Is the Day the Lord Has Made

1 This is the day the Lord has made; He calls the
2 To - day He rose and left the dead, And Sa - tan's
3 Ho - san - na to the a - noint - ed King, To Da - vid's
4 Bless - ed is He who comes to us With mes - sag -
5 Ho - san - na in the high - est strains The Church on
hours His own. Let heav'n re - joice, let
em - pire fell; To - day the saints His
ho - ly Son! Help us, O Lord; de -
es of grace; He, in the Lord's name,
earth can raise. The high - est heav'ns, in
earth be glad And praise sur - round the throne.
tri - umphs spread And all His won - ders tell.
scend and bring Sal - va - tion from Your throne.
comes to us To save our fall - en race.
which He reigns, Shall give Him no - bler praise.

Text: Isaac Watts, 1674–1748, alt.
Tune: Johann Crüger, 1598–1662; setting: *The Lutheran Hymnal*, 1941

NUN DANKET ALL
C M

Ps. 118:24–26; Matt. 21:9; Luke 1:68–75; Heb. 2:14–15

Blessed Jesus, at Your Word 904

1 Bless - ed Je - sus, at Your Word We are gath - ered
2 All our knowl - edge, sense, and sight Lie in deep - est
3 Gra - cious Sav - ior, good and kind, Light of Light, from
△ 4 Fa - ther, Son, and Spir - it, Lord, Praise to You and

all to hear You. Let our hearts and souls be stirred
dark - ness shroud - ed Till Your Spir - it breaks our night
God pro - ceed - ing, O - pen now our heart and mind;
ad - o - ra - tion! Grant that we may trust Your Word,

Now to seek and love and fear You, By Your teach-ings,
With the beams of truth un - cloud - ed. You a - lone to
Help us by Your Spir - it's plead - ing. Hear the cry Your
Con - fi - dent of our sal - va - tion, While we here be -

sweet and ho - ly, Drawn from earth to love You sole - ly.
God can win us; You must work all good with - in us.
Church now rais - es; Hear and bless our prayers and prais - es.
low must wan - der, Till we sing Your prais - es yon - der.

Text: Tobias Clausnitzer, 1619–84, sts. 1–3; *Geistreiches Gesang-Büchlein*, Berlin, 1707, st. 4;
tr. Catherine Winkworth, 1827–78, sts. 1–3, alt.; tr. unknown, st. 4, alt.
Tune: Johann Rudolph Ahle, 1625–73, alt.; setting: Paul G. Bunjes, 1914–98, alt.

LIEBSTER JESU, WIR SIND HIER
78 78 88

John 6:63–68; 8:31b–32; Heb. 4:12; 1 Cor. 2:14

905 Come, Thou Almighty King

1 Come, Thou al - might - y King, Help us Thy
2 Come, Thou in - car - nate Word, Gird on Thy
3 Come, ho - ly Com - fort - er, Thy sa - cred
△ 4 To Thee, great One in Three, E - ter - nal
name to sing; Help us to praise; Fa - ther all -
might - y sword; Our prayer at - tend. Come and Thy
wit - ness bear In this glad hour! Thou, who al -
prais - es be Hence ev - er - more! Thy sov-'reign
glo - ri - ous, O'er all vic - to - ri - ous,
peo - ple bless, And give Thy Word suc - cess,
might - y art, Now rule in ev - 'ry heart,
maj - es - ty May we in glo - ry see,
Come and reign o - ver us, An - cient of Days.
And let Thy righ - teous - ness On us de - scend.
And ne'er from us de - part, Spir - it of pow'r.
And to e - ter - ni - ty Love and a - dore.

Text: English, before 1760, alt.
Tune: Felice de Giardini, 1716–96; setting: *Lutheran Book of Worship: Select Hymns*, 1985

ITALIAN HYMN
664 66 64

1 Tim. 6:14–16; John 1:14; 14:25–26; Rev. 4:8

O Day of Rest and Gladness 906

1 O day of rest and glad - ness, O day of joy and light,
2 This day at earth's cre - a - tion The light first had its birth;
3 This day, God's peo - ple meet - ing, His Ho - ly Scrip - ture hear;
△ 4 That light our hope sus - tain - ing, We walk the pil - grim way,
O balm of care and sad - ness, Most beau - ti - ful, most bright;
This day for our sal - va - tion Christ rose from depths of earth;
His liv - ing pres - ence greet - ing, Through bread and wine made near.
At length our rest at - tain - ing, Our end - less Sab - bath day.
This day the high and low - ly, Through a - ges joined to bless,
This day our Lord vic - to - rious The Spir - it sent from heav'n,
We jour - ney on, be - liev - ing, Re - newed with heav'n - ly might,
We sing to Thee our prais - es, O Fa - ther, Spir - it, Son;
Sing, "Ho - ly, ho - ly, ho - ly," The tri - une God con - fess.
And thus this day most glo - rious A three - fold light was giv'n.
From grace more grace re - ceiv - ing, On this blest day of light.
The Church her voice up - rais - es To Thee, blest Three in One.

Text: Christopher Wordsworth, 1807–85, sts. 1–2, alt.; Charles P. Price, 1920–99, st. 3; *The Hymnal 1982*, st. 4
Tune: *Gesangbuch der Herzogl. Hofkapelle*, Württemberg, 1784; setting: *The Lutheran Hymnal*, 1941

ELLACOMBE
76 76 D

Heb. 4:1; Matt. 28:1; Ps. 118:24; Is. 6:3

907 God Himself Is Present

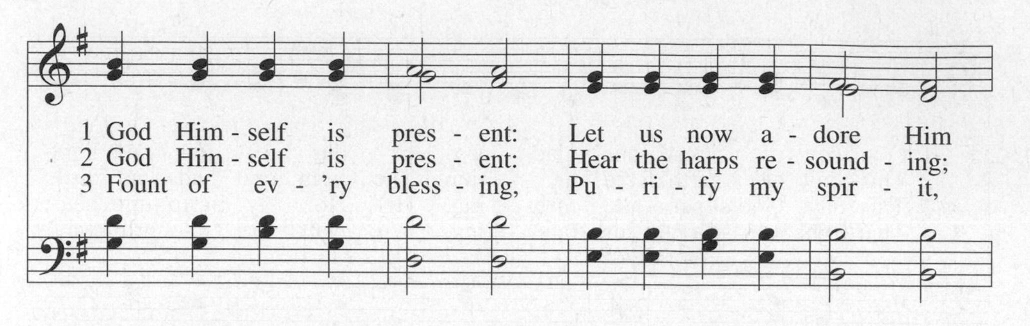
1 God Him - self is pres - ent: Let us now a - dore Him
2 God Him - self is pres - ent: Hear the harps re - sound - ing;
3 Fount of ev - 'ry bless - ing, Pu - ri - fy my spir - it,

And with awe ap - pear be - fore Him. God is in His
See the hosts the throne sur - round - ing. "Ho - ly, ho - ly,
Trust-ing on - ly in Your mer - it. Like the ho - ly

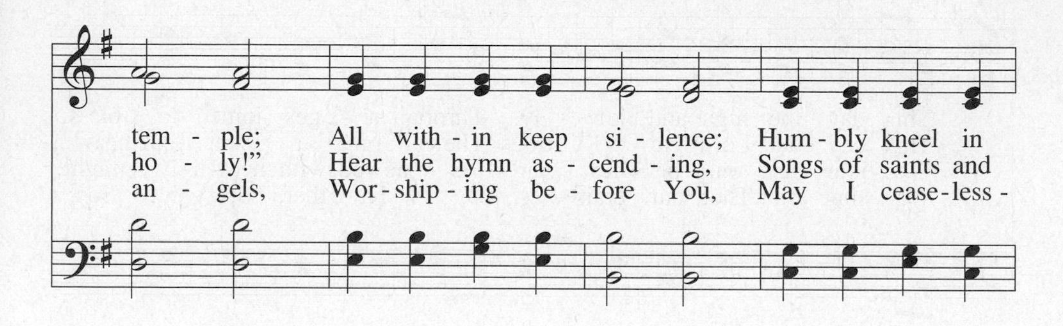
tem - ple; All with - in keep si - lence; Hum - bly kneel in
ho - ly!" Hear the hymn as - cend - ing, Songs of saints and
an - gels, Wor - ship - ing be - fore You, May I cease - less -

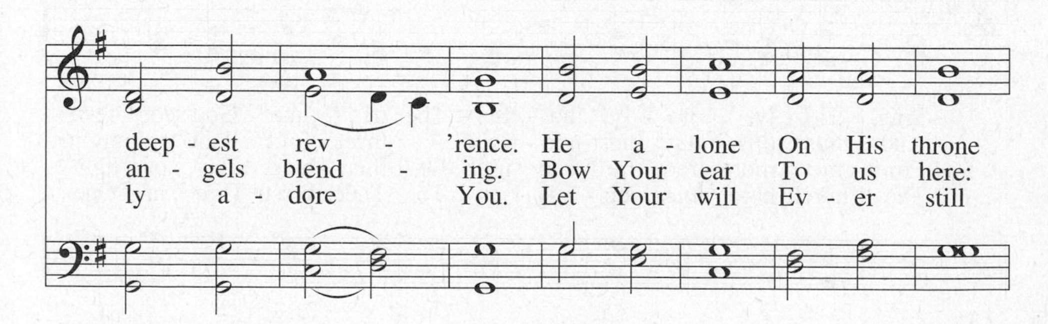
deep - est rev - 'rence. He a - lone On His throne
an - gels blend - ing. Bow Your ear To us here:
ly a - dore You. Let Your will Ev - er still

Text: Gerhard Tersteegen, 1697–1769, abr.; tr. Frederick W. Foster, 1760–1835, and John Miller, 1756–90, alt.
Tune: Joachim Neander, 1650–80, alt.; setting: *The Lutheran Hymnal,* 1941

WUNDERBARER KÖNIG
668 668 33 66

Ex. 15:11–13; Hab. 2:20; Rev. 7:9–12; Is. 6:2–3

Is our God and Sav - ior; Praise His name for - ev - er!
Hear, O Christ, the prais - es That Your Church now rais - es.
Rule Your Church ter - res - trial As the hosts ce - les - tial.

Lord, Open Now My Heart to Hear 908

1 Lord, o - pen now my heart to hear, And through Your
2 Your Word in - spires my heart with - in; Your Word grants
△ 3 To God the Fa - ther, God the Son, And God the
Word to me draw near; Let me Your Word e'er pure re -
heal - ing from my sin; Your Word has pow'r to guide and
Spir - it, Three in One, Shall glo - ry, praise, and hon - or
tain; Let me Your child and heir re - main.
bless; Your Word brings peace and hap - pi - ness.
be Now and through - out e - ter - ni - ty.

Text: Johann Olearius, 1611–84; tr. Matthias Loy, 1828–1915, sts. 1, 3, alt.; tr. Mark A. Jeske, b. 1952, st. 2
Tune: *Geistliche Lieder auffs new gebessert*, Wittenberg, 1543, ed. Joseph Klug; setting: *Württembergisches Neues Choralbuch*, 1956

ERHALT UNS, HERR
L M

Ps. 119:131–133, 140; 143:8

909 Christ Is Made the Sure Foundation

1 Christ is made the sure foun - da - tion, Christ, our head and
2 To this tem - ple, where we call You, Come, O Lord of
3 Grant, we pray, to all Your faith - ful All the gifts they
△ 4 Praise and hon - or to the Fa - ther, Praise and hon - or
cor - ner - stone, Cho - sen of the Lord and pre - cious,
hosts, and stay; Come with all Your lov - ing - kind - ness,
ask to gain; What they gain from You, for - ev - er
to the Son, Praise and hon - or to the Spir - it,
Bind - ing all the Church in one; Ho - ly Zi - on's
Hear Your peo - ple as they pray; And Your full - est
With the bless - ed to re - tain; And here - af - ter
Ev - er three and ev - er one: One in might and
help for - ev - er And our con - fi - dence a - lone.
ben - e - dic - tion Shed with - in these walls to - day.
in Your glo - ry Ev - er - more with You to reign.
one in glo - ry While un - end - ing a - ges run!

Text: Latin, c. 8th cent.; tr. John Mason Neale, 1818–66, alt.
Music: Henry Purcell, 1659–95, adapt.

WESTMINSTER ABBEY
87 87 87

Eph. 2:20–22; 4:15–16; 2 Chron. 6:18–21; Rev. 21:1–4

Now the Silence

910

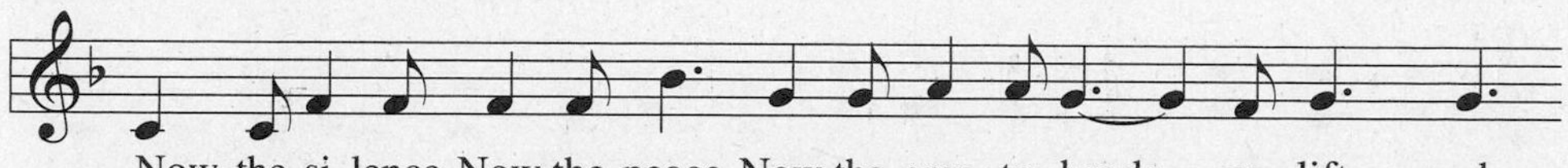
Now the si-lence Now the peace Now the emp-ty hands up-lift - ed

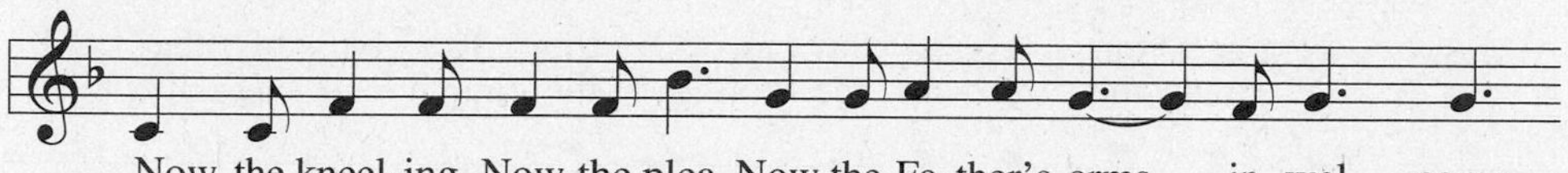
Now the kneel-ing Now the plea Now the Fa-ther's arms in wel - come

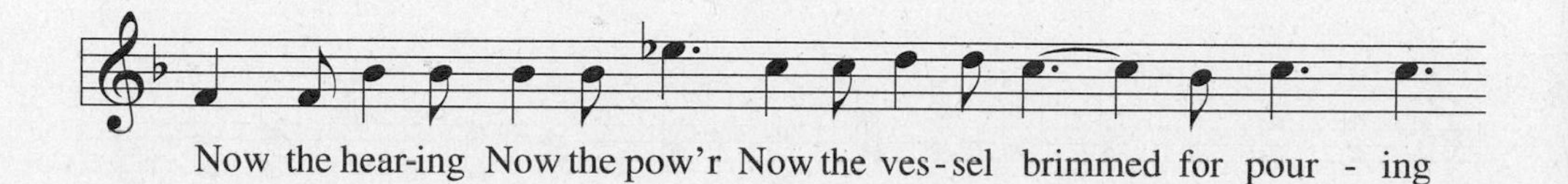
Now the hear-ing Now the pow'r Now the ves-sel brimmed for pour - ing

Now the bod - y Now the blood Now the joy-ful cel - e - bra - tion

Now the wed-ding Now the songs Now the heart for-giv - en leap - ing

Now the Spir - it's vis - i - ta - tion Now the Son's e-piph - a - ny

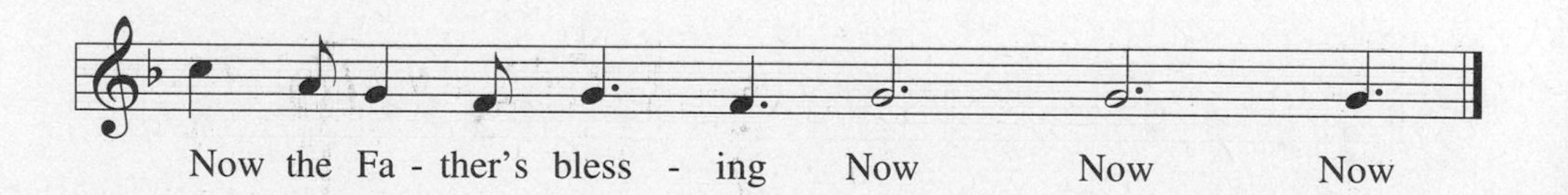
Now the Fa - ther's bless - ing Now Now Now

This text traces the path of the Divine Service: from confession and absolution through Word and Sacrament. Earthly worship, centered in these precious means of grace, is a joyful foretaste of the heavenly wedding banquet to come. Setting available in hymn accompaniment edition.

Text: Jaroslav J. Vajda, 1919–2008
Tune: Carl F. Schalk, b. 1929

NOW
Peculiar meter

Rev. 19:7–9; Matt. 26:26–29; Luke 15:20–24; Rev. 22:1–5

911 Lord, This Day We've Come to Worship

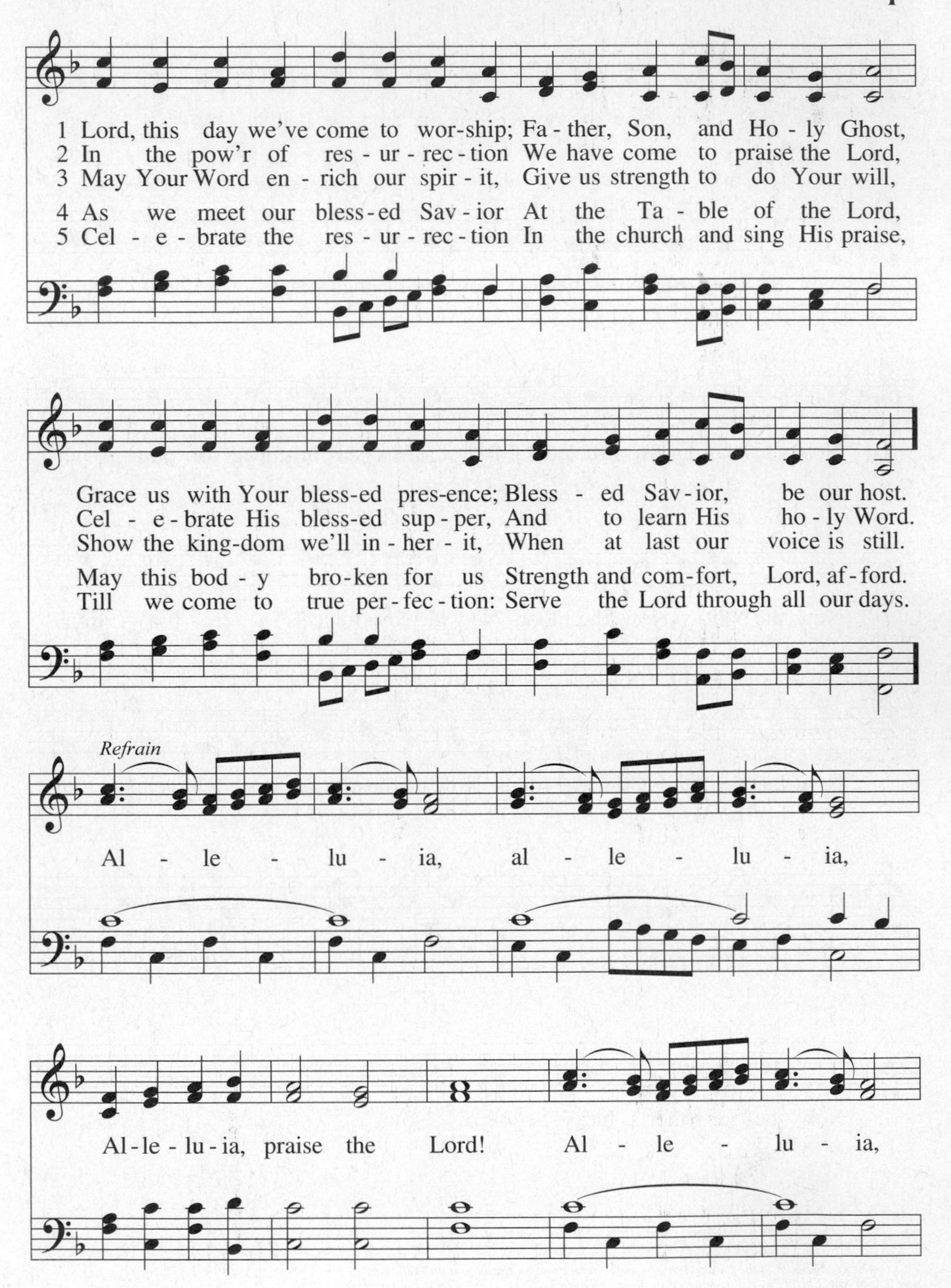
1 Lord, this day we've come to wor-ship; Fa - ther, Son, and Ho - ly Ghost,
2 In the pow'r of res - ur - rec - tion We have come to praise the Lord,
3 May Your Word en - rich our spir - it, Give us strength to do Your will,
4 As we meet our bless-ed Sav - ior At the Ta - ble of the Lord,
5 Cel - e - brate the res - ur - rec - tion In the church and sing His praise,
Grace us with Your bless-ed pres-ence; Bless - ed Sav - ior, be our host.
Cel - e - brate His bless-ed sup - per, And to learn His ho - ly Word.
Show the king-dom we'll in - her - it, When at last our voice is still.
May this bod - y bro-ken for us Strength and com-fort, Lord, af - ford.
Till we come to true per - fec - tion: Serve the Lord through all our days.
Refrain
Al - le - lu - ia, al - le - lu - ia,
Al - le - lu - ia, praise the Lord! Al - le - lu - ia,

Text: Richard C. Dickinson, 1925–2010
Music: B. B. McKinney, 1886–1952, alt.

GLORIOUS NAME
87 87 and refrain

Ps. 86:12; Acts 2:42; Deut. 31:11–13; Luke 24:13–35

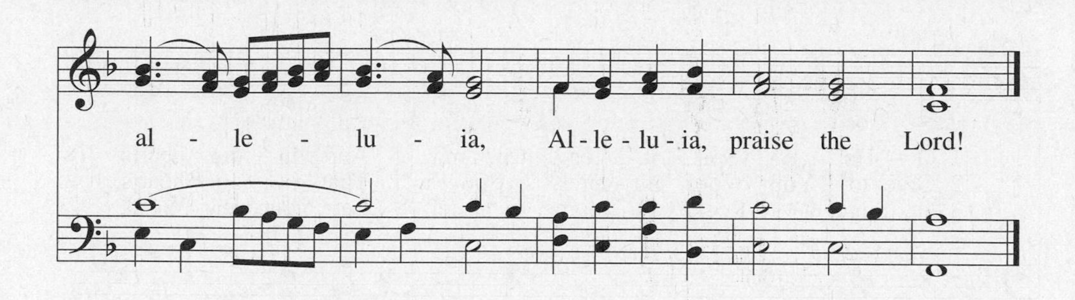
al - le - lu - ia, Al - le - lu - ia, praise the Lord!

Christ Is Our Cornerstone 912

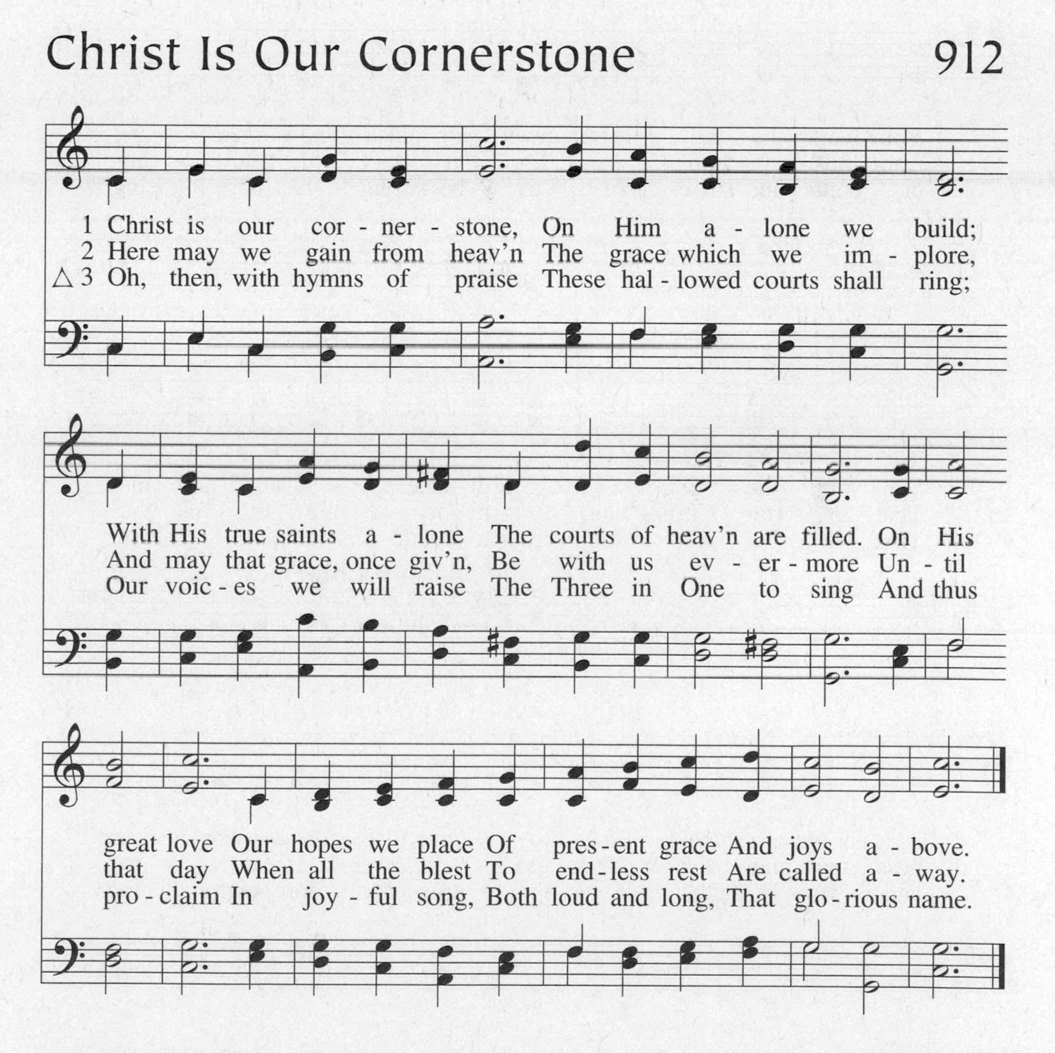
1 Christ is our cor - ner - stone, On Him a - lone we build;
2 Here may we gain from heav'n The grace which we im - plore,
△ 3 Oh, then, with hymns of praise These hal - lowed courts shall ring;
With His true saints a - lone The courts of heav'n are filled. On His
And may that grace, once giv'n, Be with us ev - er - more Un - til
Our voic - es we will raise The Three in One to sing And thus
great love Our hopes we place Of pres - ent grace And joys a - bove.
that day When all the blest To end - less rest Are called a - way.
pro - claim In joy - ful song, Both loud and long, That glo - rious name.

Text: Latin, c. 8th cent.; tr. John Chandler, 1806–76, alt.
Tune: John Darwall, 1731–89; setting: *Lutheran Book of Worship*, 1978

DARWALL'S 148TH
66 66 88

Eph. 2:19–21; 1 Peter 2:4–9; Acts 4:10–12; Ps. 118:22

913 O Holy Spirit, Enter In

1 O Ho - ly Spir - it, en - ter in, And in our hearts
2 Give to Your Word im - pres - sive pow'r, That in our hearts
3 O might - y Rock, O Source of life, Let Your dear Word,
Your work be - gin, Your dwell - ing place now make us.
from this good hour As fire it may be glow - ing,
in doubt and strife, In us be strong - ly burn - ing
Sun of the soul, O Light di - vine, A - round and in
That in true Chris - tian u - ni - ty We faith - ful wit -
That we be faith - ful un - to death And live in love
us bright - ly shine, To joy and glad - ness wake us
ness - es may be, Your glo - ry ev - er show - ing.
and ho - ly faith, From You true wis - dom learn - ing.

Text: Michael Schirmer, 1606–73, adapt.; tr. Catherine Winkworth, 1827–78, sts. 1, 3, alt.; tr. *The Lutheran Hymnal*, 1941, st. 2, alt.
Tune: Philipp Nicolai, 1556–1608; setting: *Choralbuch zum Evangelischen Kirchengesangbuch*, Berlin, 1955

WIE SCHÖN LEUCHTET
887 887 4444 8

1 Cor. 3:16; Ezek. 36:27; 1 Cor. 2:13; Rev. 2:10

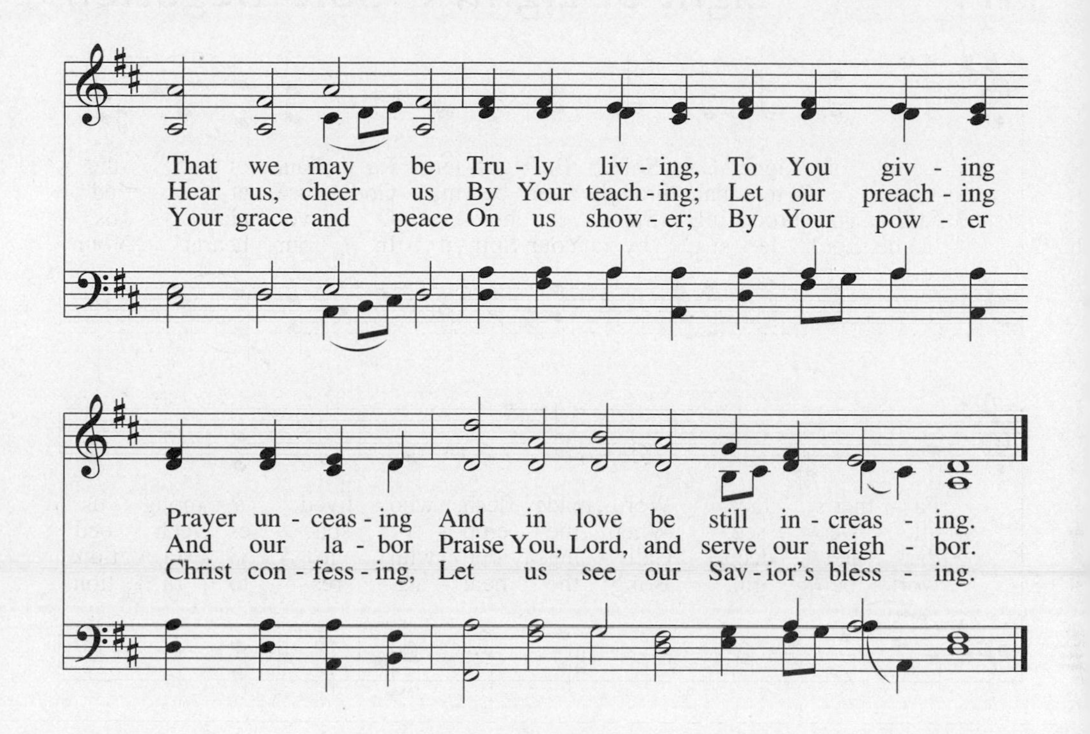
That we may be Tru - ly liv - ing, To You giv - ing
Hear us, cheer us By Your teach - ing; Let our preach - ing
Your grace and peace On us show - er; By Your pow - er
Prayer un - ceas - ing And in love be still in - creas - ing.
And our la - bor Praise You, Lord, and serve our neigh - bor.
Christ con - fess - ing, Let us see our Sav - ior's bless - ing.

Almighty God, by the working of Your Holy Spirit, grant that we may gladly hear Your Word proclaimed among us and follow its directing; through Jesus Christ, Your Son, our Lord, who lives and reigns with You and the Holy Spirit, one God, now and forever. Collect for Proper 8, Series A

914 Light of Light, O Sole-Begotten

1 Light of Light, O Sole - Be - got - ten Ra - diance of the
2 Word e - ter - nal, through Your be - ing God cre - at - ed
3 Still Your brood - ing Spir - it hov - ers O - ver cha - os,
4 Come, Lord Je - sus, by Your Spir - it In our hearts Your
Fa - ther's face, Word made flesh, who lived a - mong us
all we see, When the emp - ty spac - es ech - oed
dark and deep, Call - ing out with in - vi - ta - tion:
work be - gin, Bring the heal - ing res - to - ra - tion
Full of truth and full of grace, Shine up - on our
With the Fa - ther's "Let there be . . ." Light and life burst
"Rise, a - wak - en from your sleep; Christ the Lord will
Of Your im - age lost by sin; From Your full - ness
hu - man dark - ness; Pierce the night that shrouds our race.
from the glo - rious Pow - er of Your maj - es - ty!
shine up - on you And from death your soul shall keep."
all re - ceiv - ing Grace on grace, new life with - in!

Text: Stephen P. Starke, b. 1955
Music: Henry Purcell, 1659–95, adapt.

WESTMINSTER ABBEY
87 87 87

John 1:1–17; Col. 1:15–16

Today Your Mercy Calls Us 915

1 To - day Your mer - cy calls us To wash a - way our sin.
2 To - day Your gate is o - pen, And all who en - ter in
3 To - day our Fa - ther calls us; His Ho - ly Spir - it waits;
4 O all - em - brac - ing Mer - cy, O ev - er - o - pen Door,
How - ev - er great our tres - pass, What - ev - er we have been,
Shall find a Fa - ther's wel - come And par - don for their sin.
His bless - ed an - gels gath - er A - round the heav'n - ly gates.
What should we do with - out You When heart and eye run o'er?
How - ev - er long from mer - cy Our hearts have turned a - way,
The past shall be for - got - ten, A pres - ent joy be giv'n,
No ques - tion will be asked us How of - ten we have come;
When all things seem a - gainst us, To drive us to de - spair,
Your pre - cious blood can wash us And make us clean to - day.
A fu - ture grace be prom - ised, A glo - rious crown in heav'n.
Al - though we oft have wan - dered, It is our Fa - ther's home.
We know one gate is o - pen, One ear will hear our prayer.

Text: Oswald Allen, 1816–78, alt.
Tune: Friedrich K. Anthes, 1812–after 1857; setting: *The Lutheran Hymnal*, 1941

ANTHES
76 76 D

Is. 1:18; Luke 15:20–24; Heb. 9:14; John 10:9

916 Only-Begotten, Word of God Eternal

1 On - ly - be - got - ten, Word of God e - ter - nal, Lord of cre - a - tion, mer - ci - ful and might - y: Hear us, Your ser - vants, as our tune - ful voic - es Rise in Your pres - ence.
2 Ho - ly this tem - ple where our Lord is dwell - ing; This is none oth - er than the gate of heav - en. Ev - er Your chil - dren, year by year re - joic - ing, Chant in Your tem - ple.
3 Hear us, O Fa - ther, as we throng Your tem - ple. By Your past bless - ings, by Your pres - ent boun - ty, Smile on Your chil - dren, and in grace and mer - cy Hear our pe - ti - tion.
△ 4 God in three per - sons, Fa - ther ev - er - last - ing, Son co - e - ter - nal, ev - er bless - ed Spir - it: To You be prais - es, thanks, and ad - o - ra - tion, Glo - ry for - ev - er.

Text: Latin, c. 9th cent.; tr. Maxwell J. Blacker, 1822–88, alt.
Tune: *Antiphoner*, Poitiers, 1746; setting: *New English Hymnal*, 1986

ISTE CONFESSOR
11 11 11 5

1 Kings 8:27–30; Ps. 20:1–5

Savior, Again to Thy Dear Name We Raise

1 Sav - ior, a - gain to Thy dear name we raise
With one ac - cord our part - ing hymn of praise;
Once more we bless Thee ere our wor - ship cease,
Then, low - ly bend - ing, wait Thy word of peace.
2 Grant us Thy peace up - on our home - ward way;
With Thee be - gan, with Thee shall end, the day.
Guard Thou the lips from sin, the hearts from shame,
That in this house have called up - on Thy name.
3 Grant us Thy peace, Lord, through the com - ing night;
Turn Thou for us its dark - ness in - to light.
From harm and dan - ger keep Thy chil - dren free;
For dark and light are both a - like to Thee.
4 Grant us Thy peace through - out our earth - ly life,
Our balm in sor - row and our stay in strife;
Then, when Thy voice shall bid our con - flict cease,
Call us, O Lord, to Thine e - ter - nal peace.

Text: John Ellerton, 1826–93
Tune: Edward J. Hopkins, 1818–1901; setting: *The Lutheran Hymnal*, 1941

ELLERS
10 10 10 10

Num. 6:22–26; John 16:33; Ps. 85:8; 2 Cor. 4:6

918 Guide Me, O Thou Great Redeemer

1 Guide me, O Thou great Re - deem - er, Pil - grim through this
2 O - pen now the crys - tal foun - tain Whence the heal - ing
3 When I tread the verge of Jor - dan, Bid my anx - ious
bar - ren land. I am weak, but Thou art might - y;
stream doth flow; Let the fi - ery, cloud - y pil - lar
fears sub - side; Death of death and hell's de - struc - tion,
Hold me with Thy pow'r - ful hand. Bread of heav - en,
Lead me all my jour - ney through. Strong de - liv - 'rer,
Land me safe on Ca - naan's side. Songs of prais - es,
bread of heav - en, Feed me till I want no
strong de - liv - 'rer, Be Thou still my strength and
songs of prais - es I will ev - er give to

Text: William Williams, 1717–91, abr.; tr. Peter Williams, 1722–96, st. 1, alt.;
tr. William Williams, 1717–91, sts. 2–3
Music: John Hughes, 1873–1932

CWM RHONDDA
87 87 877

Ex. 15:13; Ex. 13:21–22; John 6:32–35; John 4:14

more; Feed me till I want no more.
shield; Be Thou still my strength and shield.
Thee; I will ev - er give to Thee.

Abide, O Dearest Jesus

919

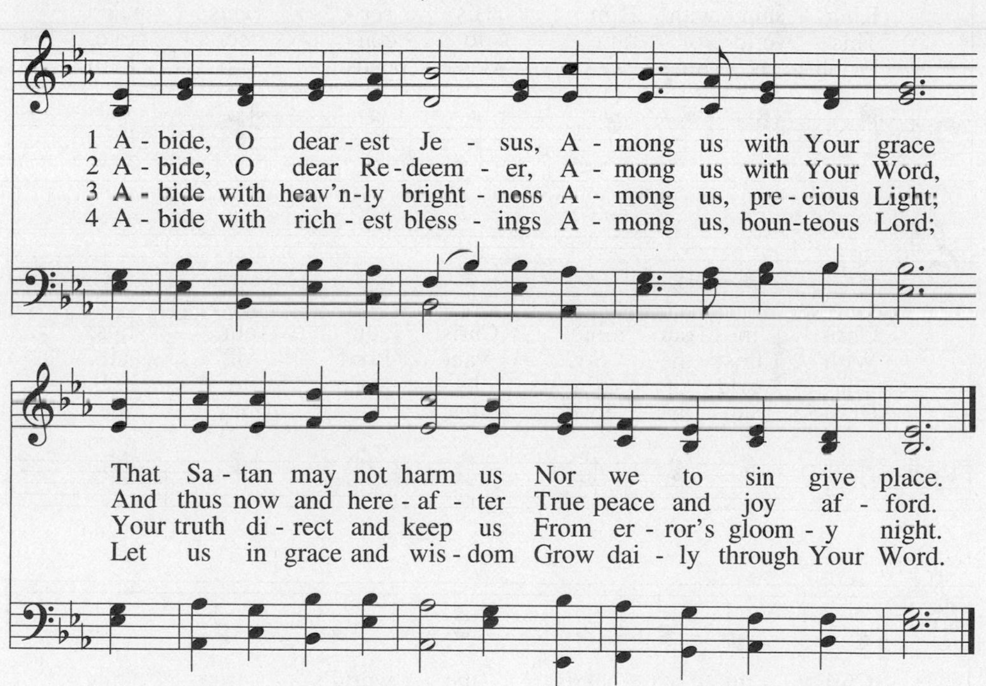
1 A - bide, O dear - est Je - sus, A - mong us with Your grace
2 A - bide, O dear Re - deem - er, A - mong us with Your Word,
3 A - bide with heav'n-ly bright - ness A - mong us, pre - cious Light;
4 A - bide with rich - est bless - ings A - mong us, boun-teous Lord;
That Sa - tan may not harm us Nor we to sin give place.
And thus now and here - af - ter True peace and joy af - ford.
Your truth di - rect and keep us From er - ror's gloom - y night.
Let us in grace and wis - dom Grow dai - ly through Your Word.

5 Abide with Your protection
Among us, Lord, our strength,
Lest world and Satan fell us
And overcome at length.

6 Abide, O faithful Savior,
Among us with Your love;
Grant steadfastness and help us
To reach our home above.

Text: Josua Stegmann, 1588–1632; tr. August Crull, 1845–1923, alt.
Tune: Melchior Vulpius, c. 1570–1615; setting: *The Lutheran Hymnal*, 1941

CHRISTUS, DER IST MEIN LEBEN
76 76

Luke 24:29; John 1:4–5, 14, 17; 12:46; 2 Thess. 3:3

920 Forth in the Peace of Christ We Go

1 Forth in the peace of Christ we go;
2 King of our hearts, Christ makes us kings;
3 Priests of the world, Christ sends us forth
4 Christ's are our lips, His Word we speak;
Christ to the world with joy we bring;
King - ship with Him His ser - vants gain;
This world of time to con - se - crate,
Proph - ets are we whose deeds pro - claim
Christ in our minds, Christ on our lips,
With Christ the Ser - vant - Lord of all,
This world of sin by grace to heal,
Christ's truth in love that we may be
Christ in our hearts, the world's true king.
Christ's world we serve to share Christ's reign.
Christ's world in Christ to re - cre - ate.
Christ in the world, to spread Christ's name.

Text: James Quinn, 1919–2010
Tune: Georg Joseph, 17th cent., adapt.; setting: *Cantica Spiritualia*, 1847

ANGELUS
L M

1 Peter 2:9; Col. 3:16–17; Rev. 5:10; 20:6

5 We are the Church; Christ bids us show
That in His Church all nations find
Their hearth and home where Christ restores
True peace, true love to all mankind.

On What Has Now Been Sown 921

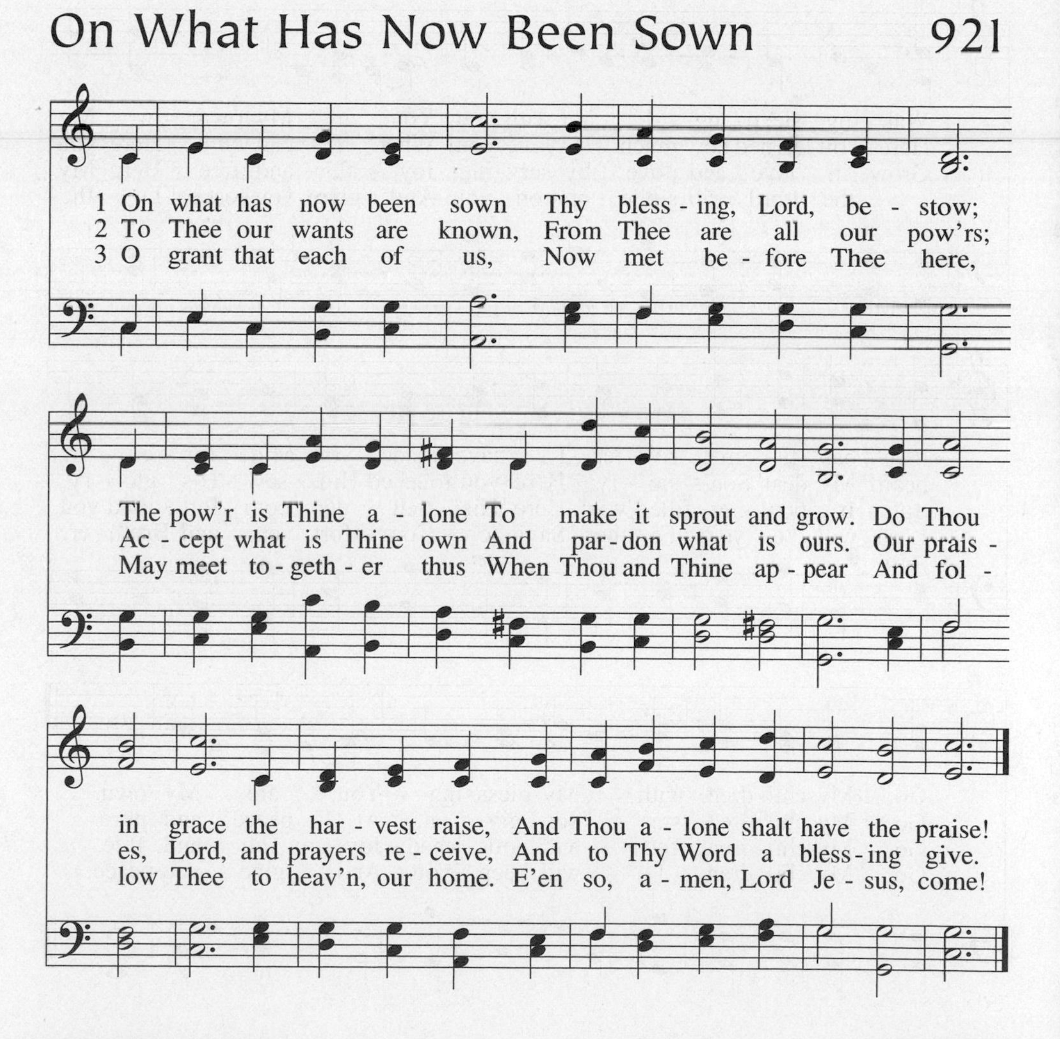
1 On what has now been sown Thy bless - ing, Lord, be - stow;
2 To Thee our wants are known, From Thee are all our pow'rs;
3 O grant that each of us, Now met be - fore Thee here,
The pow'r is Thine a - lone To make it sprout and grow. Do Thou
Ac - cept what is Thine own And par - don what is ours. Our prais -
May meet to - geth - er thus When Thou and Thine ap - pear And fol -
in grace the har - vest raise, And Thou a - lone shalt have the praise!
es, Lord, and prayers re - ceive, And to Thy Word a bless - ing give.
low Thee to heav'n, our home. E'en so, a - men, Lord Je - sus, come!

Text: John Newton, 1725–1807, alt.
Tune: John Darwall, 1731–89; setting: *Lutheran Book of Worship*, 1978

DARWALL'S 148TH
66 66 88

Mark 4:26–29; 1 Cor. 3:6–7; Phil. 1:6; 1 Thess. 5:23–24

922 Go, My Children, with My Blessing

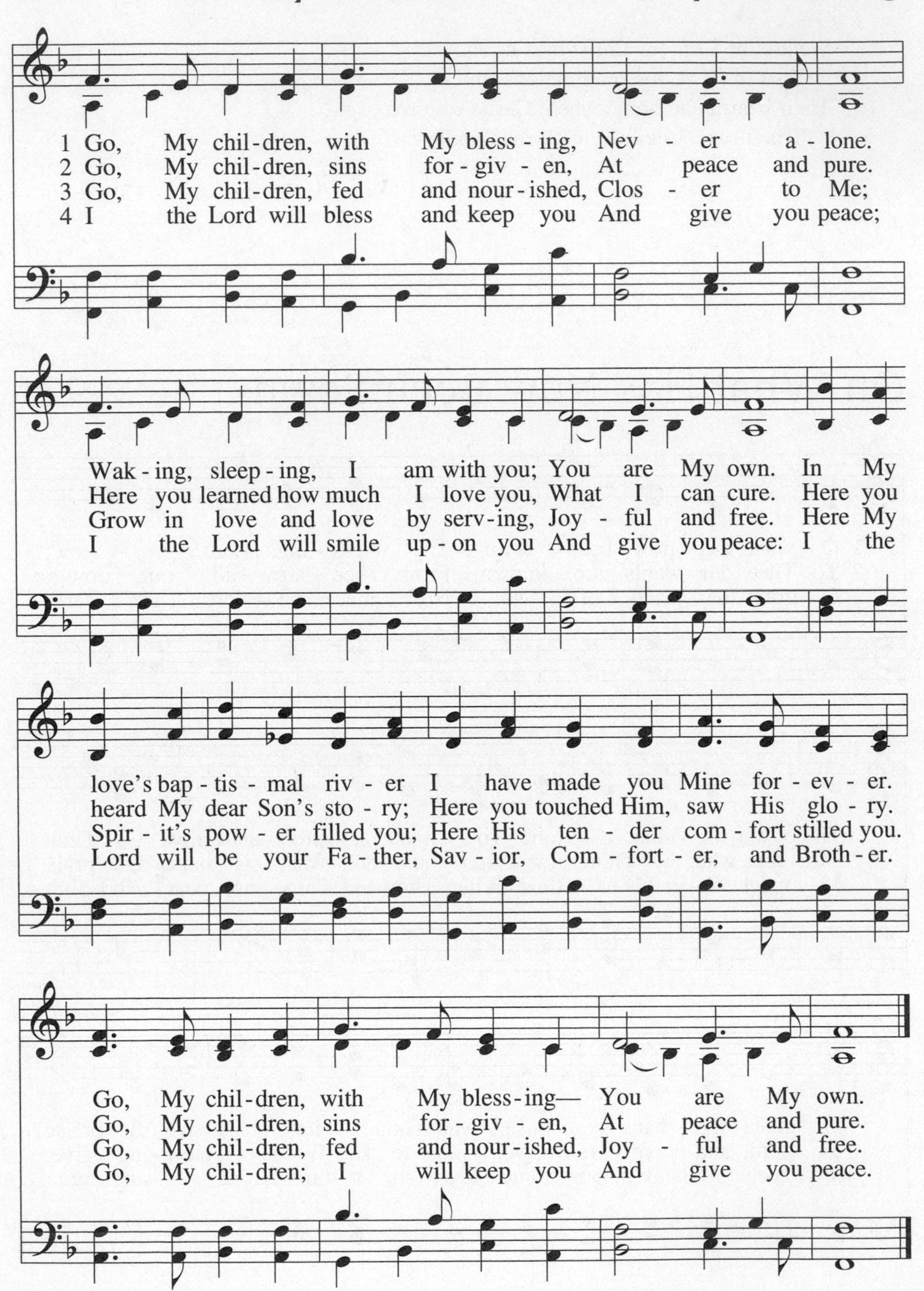
1 Go, My chil-dren, with My bless-ing, Nev-er a-lone.
2 Go, My chil-dren, sins for-giv-en, At peace and pure.
3 Go, My chil-dren, fed and nour-ished, Clos-er to Me;
4 I the Lord will bless and keep you And give you peace;
Wak-ing, sleep-ing, I am with you; You are My own. In My
Here you learned how much I love you, What I can cure. Here you
Grow in love and love by serv-ing, Joy-ful and free. Here My
I the Lord will smile up-on you And give you peace: I the
love's bap-tis-mal riv-er I have made you Mine for-ev-er.
heard My dear Son's sto-ry; Here you touched Him, saw His glo-ry.
Spir-it's pow-er filled you; Here His ten-der com-fort stilled you.
Lord will be your Fa-ther, Sav-ior, Com-fort-er, and Broth-er.
Go, My chil-dren, with My bless-ing— You are My own.
Go, My chil-dren, sins for-giv-en, At peace and pure.
Go, My chil-dren, fed and nour-ished, Joy-ful and free.
Go, My chil-dren; I will keep you And give you peace.

Text: Jaroslav J. Vajda, 1919–2008
Tune: Welsh, 18th cent.; setting: Ralph Vaughan Williams, 1872–1958

AR HYD Y NOS
84 84 88 84

Titus 3:4–7; John 20:19–29; John 14:26–27; Num. 6:22–27

For use at weddings, the following stanza may be sung in place of stanzas 2 and 3:

In this union I have joined you
  Husband and wife,
Now, My children, live together
  As heirs of life:
 Each the other's gladness sharing,
 Each the other's burdens bearing,
Now, My children, live together
  As heirs of life.

Almighty Father, Bless the Word 923

1 Al - might - y Fa - ther, bless the Word Which through Your
2 We praise You for the means of grace As home - ward
△ 3 Praise God, from whom all bless - ings flow; Praise Him, all

grace we now have heard. Oh, may the pre - cious
now our steps we trace. Grant, Lord, that we who
crea - tures here be - low; Praise Him a - bove, ye

seed take root, Spring up, and bear a - bun - dant fruit!
wor - shiped here May all at last in heav'n ap - pear.
heav'n - ly host: Praise Fa - ther, Son, and Ho - ly Ghost.

Text: *Church Poetry*, Philadelphia, 1823, sts. 1–2, alt.; Thomas Ken, 1637–1711, st. 3
Tune: *Trente quatre Pseaumes de David*, Geneva, 1551, ed. Louis Bourgeois;
  setting: *The Lutheran Hymnal*, 1941

OLD HUNDREDTH
L M

Mark 4:26–29; Matt. 13:8–9

924 Lord, Dismiss Us with Your Blessing

1 Lord, dis - miss us with Your bless - ing, Fill our hearts with joy and peace; Let us each, Your love pos - sess - ing, Tri - umph in re - deem - ing grace. O re - fresh us; O re - fresh us, Trav - 'ling through this wil - der - ness.
2 Thanks we give and ad - o - ra - tion For Your Gos - pel's joy - ful sound. May the fruits of Your sal - va - tion In our hearts and lives a - bound. Ev - er faith - ful, ev - er faith - ful To Your truth may we be found.
3 Sav - ior, when Your love shall call us From our strug - gling pil - grim way, Let not fear of death ap - pall us, Glad Your sum - mons to o - bey. May we ev - er, may we ev - er Reign with You in end - less day.

Text: attr. John Fawcett, 1740–1817, sts. 1–2, alt.; Godfrey Thring, 1823–1903, st. 3, alt.
Tune: Henry T. Smart, 1813–79; setting: *The Lutheran Hymnal*, 1941

REGENT SQUARE
87 87 87

Num. 6:24–26; John 8:31; Phil. 1:21

Song of Moses and Israel

925

Cantemus Domino

Refrain
I will sing to the LORD, for He has tri-umphed glo-rious-
ly; the horse and his rid-er He has thrown in - to the sea.

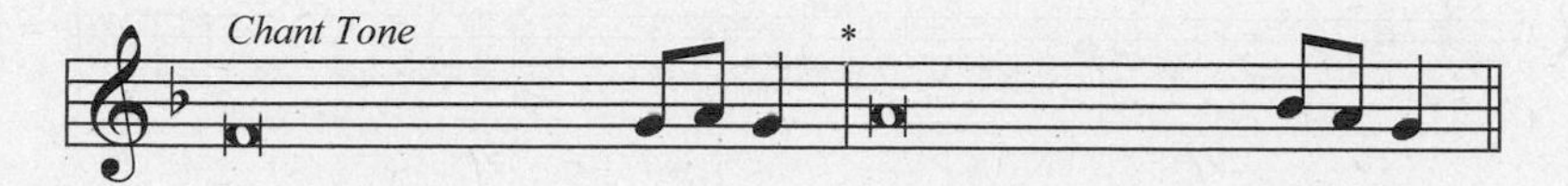
Chant Tone
*

[1] The LORD is my strength | and my song,*
and He has become my sal- | vation;

[2] this is my God, and I will | praise Him,*
my father's God, and I will ex- | alt Him.

Refrain

[3] The LORD is a | man of war;*
the LORD | is His name.

[4] Pharaoh's chariots and his host He cast in- | to the sea,*
and his chosen officers were sunk in the | Red Sea.

[5] The floods | covered them;*
they went down into the depths | like a stone.

[6] Your right hand, O LORD, glorious | in power,*
Your right hand, O LORD, shatters the | enemy.

Refrain

[7] Who is like You, O LORD, a- | mong the gods?*
Who is like You, majestic in holiness, awesome in glorious deeds, doing | wonders?

[8] You stretched out Your | right hand;*
the earth | swallowed them.

[9] You have led in Your steadfast love the people whom You | have redeemed;*
You have guided them by Your strength to Your ho- | ly abode.

[10] You will bring them in and plant them on Your own | mountain,*
the place, O Lord, which You have made for | Your abode,

[11] the sanctuary, O LORD, which Your hands have es- | tablished.*
The LORD will reign forever and | ever.

Glory be to the Father and | to the Son*
and to the Holy | Spirit;
as it was in the be- | ginning,*
is now, and will be forever. | Amen.

Refrain

Setting available in hymn accompaniment edition.

Text: Exodus 15:1–6, 11–13, 17–18 ESV
Tune: Jeffrey N. Blersch, b. 1967

926 Song from Deuteronomy

Audite, coeli

Refrain
The LORD will vin - di - cate His peo - ple and
have com - pas - sion on His ser - vants.
Chant Tone

[1] Give ear, O heavens, and | I will speak,*
and let the earth hear the words | of my mouth.

[2] May my teaching drop as the rain, my speech distill | as the dew,*
like gentle rain upon the tender grass, and like showers up- | on the herb.

[3] For I will proclaim the name | of the LORD;*
ascribe greatness | to our God!

[4] The Rock, His work is perfect, for all His ways are | justice.*
A God of faithfulness and without iniquity, just and up- | right is He.

Refrain

[5] When the Most High gave to the nations their inheritance, when He divided | mankind,*
He fixed the borders of the peoples according to the number of the | sons of God.

[6] But the LORD's portion is His | people,*
Jacob His allotted | heritage.

[7] He found him in a | desert land,*
and in the howling waste of the | wilderness;

[8] He encircled him, He | cared for him,*
He kept him as the apple | of His eye.

[9] Like an eagle that stirs up its nest, that flutters over | its young,*
spreading out its wings, catching them, bearing them on its | pinions,

[10] the LORD alone | guided him,*
no foreign god was | with him.

Refrain

[11] "See now that I, even I, am He, and there is no god be- | side Me;*
I kill and I make alive; I wound and I heal; and there is none that can deliver out of | My hand."

[12] Rejoice with Him, O | heavens;*
bow down to | Him, all gods,

[13] for He avenges the blood of His | children*
and takes vengeance on His adver- | saries.

Setting available in hymn accompaniment edition.

Text: Deuteronomy 32:1–4, 8–12, 36a, 39, 43 ESV
Tune: Jonathan R. Mueller, b. 1964

[14] He repays those who | hate Him*
and cleanses His | people's land.

Glory be to the Father and | to the Son*
and to the Holy | Spirit;
as it was in the be- | ginning,*
is now, and will be forever. | Amen.

Refrain

First Song of Isaiah 927

Confitebor tibi, Domine

Refrain
The LORD GOD is my strength and my song, and
He has be-come my sal - va - tion.
Chant Tone
*

[1] I will give thanks to You, | O LORD,*
for though You were angry | with me,

[2] Your anger | turned away,*
that You might | comfort me.

[3] Behold, God is my sal- | vation;*
I will trust, and will not | be afraid;

[4] for the LORD GOD is my strength | and my song,*
and He has become my sal- | vation.

Refrain

[5] With joy you will draw | water*
from the wells of sal- | vation.

[6] Give thanks | to the LORD,*
call up- | on His name,

[7] make known His deeds among the | peoples,*
proclaim that His name is ex- | alted.

Refrain

[8] Sing praises to the LORD, for He has done | gloriously;*
let this be made known in | all the earth.

[9] Shout, and sing for joy, O inhabitant of | Zion,*
for great in your midst is the Holy One of | Israel.

Glory be to the Father and | to the Son*
and to the Holy | Spirit;
as it was in the be- | ginning,*
is now, and will be forever. | Amen.

Refrain

Setting available in hymn accompaniment edition.

Text: Isaiah 12:1–6 ESV
Tune: Henry V. Gerike, b. 1948

928 Song of Hannah

Exultavit cor meum

Refrain
My heart ex-ults in the LORD; I re-joice in Your sal - va - tion.

Chant Tone
*
*

[1] My heart exults in the LORD; my strength is exalted | in the LORD.*
My mouth derides my enemies, because I rejoice in Your sal- | vation.

[2] There is none holy like the LORD; there is none be- | sides You;*
there is no rock | like our God.

[3] Talk no more so very | proudly,*
let not arrogance come | from your mouth;

[4] for the LORD is a God of | knowledge,*
and by Him actions | are weighed.

Refrain

[5] The bows of the mighty are | broken,*
but the feeble | bind on strength.

[6] Those who were full have hired themselves | out for bread,*
but those who were hungry have ceased to | hunger.

[7] The barren has borne | seven,*
but she who has many children | is forlorn.

[8] The LORD kills and | brings to life;*
He brings down to Sheol and | raises up.

[9] The LORD makes poor and | makes rich;*
He brings low and | He exalts.

[10] He raises up the poor | from the dust;*
He lifts the needy from the ash heap to make them sit with princes and inherit a seat of | honor.

Refrain

[11] For the pillars of the earth | are the LORD'S,*
and on them He has | set the world.

[12] He will guard the feet of His faithful ones, but the wicked shall be cut off in | darkness,*
for not by might shall a | man prevail.

[13] The adversaries of the LORD shall be broken to | pieces;*
against them He will thunder in | heaven.

[14] The LORD will judge the ends | of the earth;*
He will give strength to His king and exalt the power of His a- | nointed.

Glory be to the Father and | to the Son*
and to the Holy | Spirit;
as it was in the be- | ginning,*
is now, and will be forever. | Amen.

Refrain

Setting available in hymn accompaniment edition.

Text: 1 Samuel 2:1–10 ESV
Tune: Kurt E. von Kampen, b. 1960, Refrain; Paul J. Grime, b. 1958, Chant Tone

I Will Greatly Rejoice in the Lord 929

Gaudens gaudebo

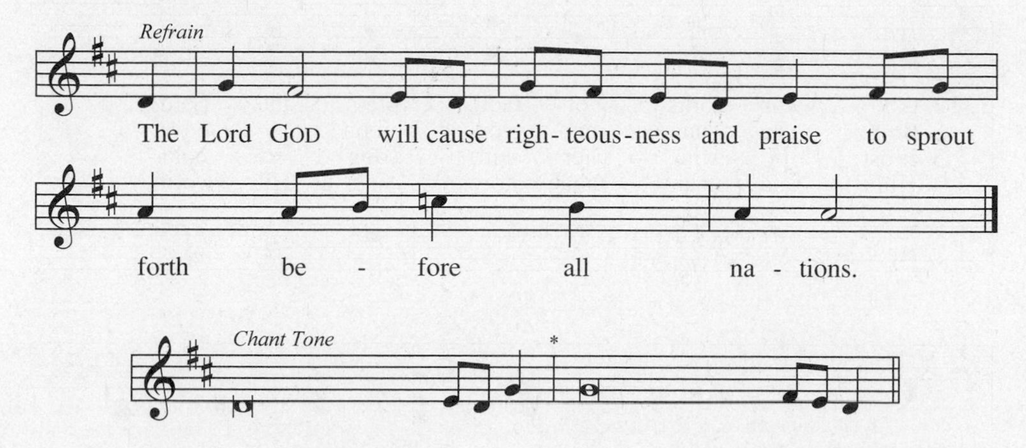

Refrain
The Lord GOD will cause righ-teous-ness and praise to sprout
forth be - fore all na - tions.
Chant Tone
*

[1] I will greatly rejoice | in the LORD;*
my soul shall exult | in my God,

[2] for He has clothed me with the garments of sal- | vation;*
He has covered me with the robe of | righteousness,

[3] as a bridegroom decks himself like a priest with a beautiful | headdress,*
and as a bride adorns herself with her | jewels.

Refrain

[4] For as the earth brings | forth its sprouts,*
and as a garden causes what is sown in it to | sprout up,

[5] so the Lord GOD will cause righteous- | ness and praise*
to sprout up before all the | nations.

Glory be to the Father and | to the Son*
and to the Holy | Spirit;
as it was in the be- | ginning,*
is now, and will be forever. | Amen.

Refrain

Setting available in hymn accompaniment edition.

Text: Isaiah 61:10–11 ESV
Tune: Phillip Magness, b. 1963

All You Works of God, Bless the Lord

1 All you works of God, bless the Lord!
2 Sing, you sun and you moon a - bove,
3 Frost of win - ter with song so cold,
4 Hills and moun - tains, now sing His worth,
All you an - gels, now bless the Lord;
Stars of heav - en, now sing His love;
Dews of sum - mer, your song un - fold;
All you green things that grow on earth;
Come, you heav - ens and pow'rs that be,
Dew and show - ers, you winds that blow,
Light and dark - ness, you day and night,
Seas and riv - ers, you springs and wells,
Praise the Lord and His maj - es - ty:
Heat and fire, ___ you ice and snow:
Clouds of thun - der, you light - nings bright:
Beasts and cat - tle, you birds and whales:

This hymn is a paraphrase of the "Song of the Three Young Men."

Text: Stephen P. Starke, b. 1955
Music: Jamaican; adapt. Doreen Potter, 1925–80

LINSTEAD
88 88 and refrain

Song of the Three Young Men; Ps. 103:20–22

Refrain
Raise your voic - es high, praise and mag - ni - fy,
All you works of God, bless the Lord!
Raise your voic - es high, praise and mag - ni - fy,
All you works of God, bless the Lord!

5 Come, humanity, sing along,
Sing, you people of God, a song;
Priests and servants, your Lord now bless,
Join, you spirits and souls at rest:
Refrain

△ 6 Bless the Lord, all you pure of heart;
All you humble, His praise impart;
God the Father and Son adore,
Bless the Spirit forevermore!
Refrain

931 All You Works of the Lord

Benedicite, omnia opera

Chant Tone
*
*
Refrain
Praise Him and mag-ni-fy Him for-ev-er.

[1] All you works of the Lord, | bless the Lord—*
praise Him and magnify Him for- | ever.*
You angels of the Lord, | bless the Lord: ***Refrain***

[2] You heavens, | bless the Lord;*
all you waters above the heavens, | bless the Lord;*
all you powers of the Lord, | bless the Lord: ***Refrain***

[3] You sun and moon, | bless the Lord;*
you stars of heaven, | bless the Lord;*
all you showers and dew, | bless the Lord: ***Refrain***

[4] All you winds of God, | bless the Lord;*
you fire and heat, | bless the Lord;*
you winter and summer, | bless the Lord: ***Refrain***

[5] You dews and frost, | bless the Lord;*
you frost and cold, | bless the Lord;*
you ice and snow, | bless the Lord: ***Refrain***

[6] You nights and days, | bless the Lord;*
you light and darkness, | bless the Lord;*
you lightnings and clouds, | bless the Lord: ***Refrain***

[7] Let the earth | bless the Lord;*
you mountains and hills, | bless the Lord;*
all you green things that grow on the earth, | bless the Lord: ***Refrain***

[8] You wells and springs, | bless the Lord;*
you rivers and seas, | bless the Lord;*
you whales and all who move in the waters, | bless the Lord: ***Refrain***

[9] All you birds of the air, | bless the Lord;*
all you beasts and cattle, | bless the Lord;*
all you children of men, | bless the Lord: ***Refrain***

[10] O Israel, | bless the Lord;*
you priests of the Lord, | bless the Lord;*
you servants of the Lord, | bless the Lord: ***Refrain***

[11] You spirits and souls of the righteous, | bless the Lord;*
you pure and humble of heart, | bless the Lord;*
let us bless the Father and the Son and the Holy | Spirit: ***Refrain***

Setting available in hymn accompaniment edition.

Text: Song of the Three Young Men
Tune: Paul J. Grime, b. 1958

Jesus Sat with His Disciples 932

1 Je - sus sat with His dis - ci - ples On a moun - tain - side one day; As the crowds of peo-ple gath - ered, He be - gan to teach and say: "Bless-ed are the poor in spir - it, Heav - en's king - dom they will share. Bless-ed are the sad and mourn - ing, Joy and com - fort will be theirs.
2 "Bless-ed are the meek and hum - ble, All the earth to them is willed. Those who hun - ger to be ho - ly, They are bless'd and will be filled. Yes, the mer - ci - ful are bless - ed, Mer - cy will to them be shown. And the pure in heart are bless - ed, They have eyes for God a - lone.
3 "Bless-ed are God's sons and daugh - ters, Mak - ing peace where there is strife. Bless - ed are the per - se - cut - ed, Who for righ - teous - ness lose life; Their re - ward is great in heav - en, In the king - dom up a - bove— So be glad to share My suf - f'ring And re - joice to know My love."

This hymn is a versification of the "Beatitudes," the opening verses of Jesus' Sermon on the Mount. "Beatitude" is from the Latin word for "blessed." Setting available in hymn accompaniment edition.

Text: Stephen P. Starke, b. 1955
Tune: Marty Haugen, b. 1950

JOYOUS LIGHT
87 87 D

Matt. 5:1–12; Luke 6:20–23

933 My Soul Rejoices

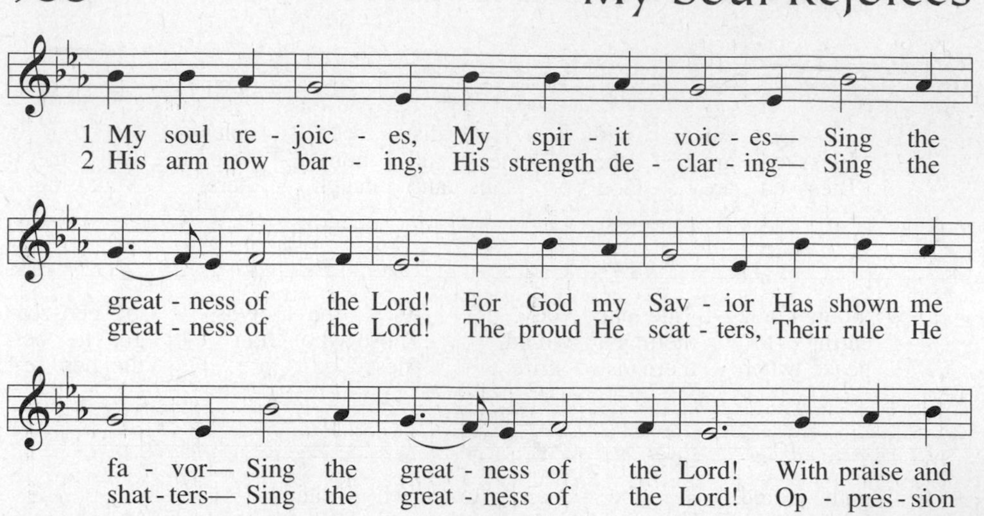
1 My soul re - joic - es, My spir - it voic - es— Sing the
2 His arm now bar - ing, His strength de - clar - ing— Sing the
great - ness of the Lord! For God my Sav - ior Has shown me
great - ness of the Lord! The proud He scat - ters, Their rule He
fa - vor— Sing the great - ness of the Lord! With praise and
shat - ters— Sing the great - ness of the Lord! Op - pres - sion

bless-ing, Join in con - fess - ing God, who is sole - ly Might-y and
halt - ed; The meek ex - alt - ed. Full are the hun - gry; Emp - ty, the

ho - ly— O sing the great - ness of God the Lord! His mer - cy
wealth - y— O sing the great - ness of God the Lord! Here is the

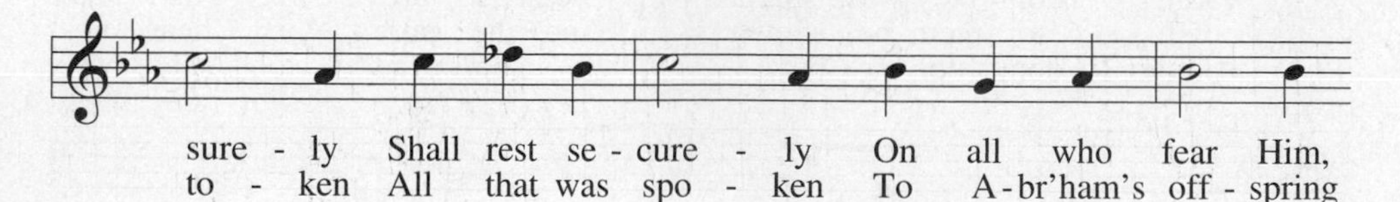
sure - ly Shall rest se - cure - ly On all who fear Him,
to - ken All that was spo - ken To A - br'ham's off - spring

Love and re - vere Him— O sing the great - ness of God the Lord!
God is ful - fill - ing— O sing the great - ness of God the Lord!

This hymn is based on the Magnificat. *Hymn accompaniment: 818*

Text: Stephen P. Starke, b. 1955
Tune: Giovanni Giacomo Gastoldi, c. 1556–c. 1622

IN DIR IST FREUDE
557 D 55554 D

Luke 1:46–55

My Soul Now Magnifies the Lord 934

1 My soul now mag - ni - fies the Lord; My spir - it
2 For He a - lone who shows such might Has done a -
3 His arm is strong; His strength is great. He scat - ters
4 He feeds the hun - gry as His own; The wealth - y
leaps for joy in Him. He keeps me in His kind re -
maz - ing things to me. His mer - cy flows; His name like
those of proud in - tent And casts them down from high es -
leave with emp - ty hands. He gives His help to Is - ra -
gard, And I am blest for time to come.
light Re - mains in time per - pet - ual - ly.
tate, Then gives the low His nour - ish - ment.
el; His gra - cious prom - ise al - ways stands.

This hymn is a versification of the Magnificat.

Text: Luke 1:46–55; adapt. Stephanie K. Frey, b. 1952
Tune: *Geistliche Lieder auffs new gebessert*, Wittenberg, 1535, ed. Joseph Klug;
setting: *The Lutheran Hymnal*, 1941

WO GOTT ZUM HAUS
L M

935 Tell Out, My Soul, the Greatness of the Lord

1 Tell out, my soul, the great - ness of the Lord!
2 Tell out, my soul, the great - ness of His name!
3 Tell out, my soul, the great - ness of His might!
4 Tell out, my soul, the glo - ries of His Word!
Un - num - bered bless - ings, give my spir - it voice;
Make known His might, the deeds His arm has done;
Pow'rs and do - min - ions lay their glo - ry by.
Firm is His prom - ise, and His mer - cy sure.
Ten - der to me the prom - ise of His Word;
His mer - cy sure, from age to age the same;
Proud hearts and stub - born wills are put to flight,
Tell out, my soul, the great - ness of the Lord
In God my Sav - ior shall my heart re - joice.
His ho - ly name, the Lord, the Might - y One.
The hun - gry fed, the hum - ble lift - ed high.
To chil - dren's chil - dren and for - ev - er - more!

This hymn is based on the Magnificat.

Text: Timothy Dudley-Smith, b. 1926
Music: Walter Greatorex, 1877–1949

WOODLANDS
10 10 10 10

Luke 1:46–55

Sing Praise to the God of Israel 936

1 Sing praise to the God of Is - ra - el! Sing praise for His
2 God spoke by the proph - ets long a - go, His prom - ise on
3 You, child, will go on be - fore the Lord As proph - et, His
4 O bright, ris - ing Sun, now shine on us In need of il -

vis - i - ta - tion! Re - deem - ing His peo - ple from their sin,
oath re - call - ing— To A - bra - ham made in for - mer years:
way pre - par - ing; To speak on be - half of God Most High,
lu - mi - na - tion; Come scat - ter the shades of sin and death

Ac - com - plish - ing their sal - va - tion, Up - rais - ing a
Of van - quish - ing foes ap - pall - ing, That those He de -
His coun - sel of truth de - clar - ing: Rich mer - cy and
And shat - ter their dom - i - na - tion. Be guid - ing our

might - y horn with - in The house of His ser - vant Da - vid!
liv - ered from their fears Might glad - ly and tru - ly serve Him.
grace for all where - by In - iq - ui - ty is for - giv - en.
foot - steps on the path Of peace, in Your pres - ence dawn - ing!

This hymn is a versification of the Benedictus.

Text: Stephen P. Starke, b. 1955
Tune: Christoph E. F. Weyse, 1774–1842; setting: *Lutheran Book of Worship*, 1978

DEN SIGNEDE DAG
98 98 98

Luke 1:68–79; Jer. 33:15–16; Gen. 22:16–18; Is. 9:2

937 Lord, Bid Your Servant Go in Peace

1 Lord, bid Your ser - vant go in peace,
2 This is the Sav - ior of the world,
△ 3 With saints of old, with saints to come,
Your word is now ful - filled. These eyes have seen sal -
The Gen - tiles' prom - ised light, God's glo - ry dwell - ing
To You we lift our voice; To Fa - ther, Son, and
va - tion's dawn, This child so long fore - told.
in our midst, The joy of Is - ra - el.
Spir - it blest Be hon - or, love, and praise.

This hymn is a versification of the Nunc Dimittis.

Text: James Quinn, 1919–2010
Tune: American; setting: Henry V. Gerike, b. 1948

LAND OF REST
C M

Luke 2:29–32

938 In Peace and Joy I Now Depart

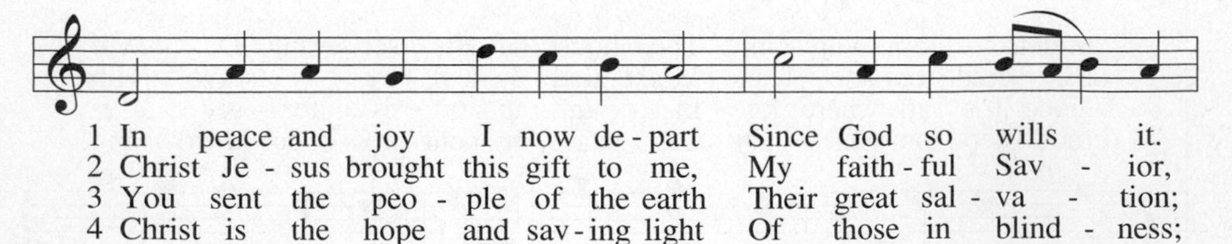
1 In peace and joy I now de - part Since God so wills it.
2 Christ Je - sus brought this gift to me, My faith - ful Sav - ior,
3 You sent the peo - ple of the earth Their great sal - va - tion;
4 Christ is the hope and sav - ing light Of those in blind - ness;

This hymn is based on the Nunc Dimittis. *Setting available in hymn accompaniment edition.*

Text: Martin Luther, 1483–1546; tr. F. Samuel Janzow, 1913–2001, st. 1, alt.; tr. *Christian Worship*, 1993, sts. 2–4, alt.
Tune: *Geystliche gesangk Buchleyn*, Wittenberg, 1524, ed. Johann Walter

MIT FRIED UND FREUD
85 84 77

Luke 2:29–32; Is. 42:6–7; 52:10; Is. 49:6

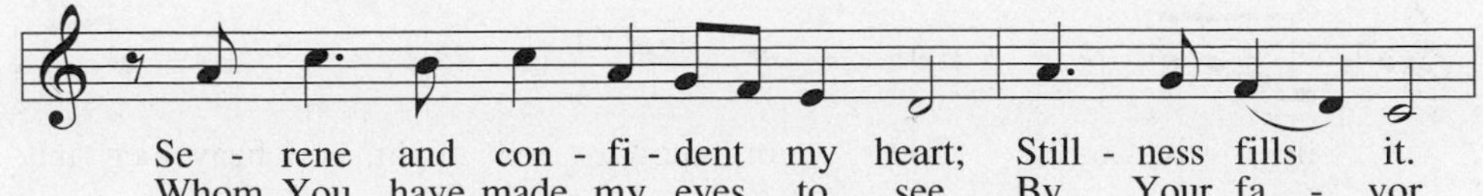

Se - rene and con - fi - dent my heart; Still - ness fills it.
Whom You have made my eyes to see By Your fa - vor.
Your in - vi - ta - tion sum - mons forth Ev - 'ry na - tion
He guides and com - forts those in night By His kind - ness.

For the Lord has prom - ised me That death is but a slum - ber.
Now I know He is my life, My friend when I am dy - ing.
By Your ho - ly, pre - cious Word, In ev - 'ry place re - sound - ing.
For Your peo - ple Is - ra - el In Him find joy and glo - ry.

You Are God; We Praise You 939

When this setting of the Te Deum *is sung with the Paschal Blessing, it is preceded by the words ". . . The Son of Man must be delivered into the hands of sinful men, be crucified, and on the third day be raised again."*

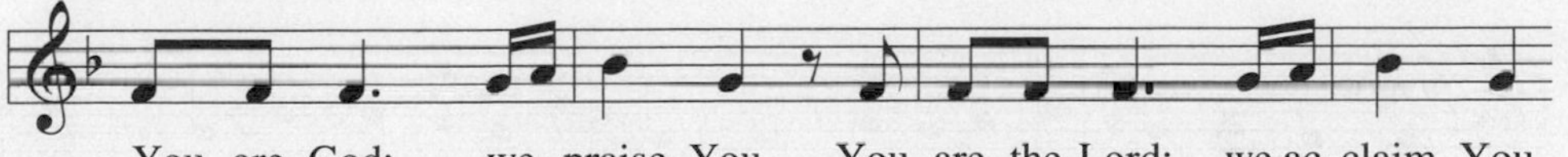

You are God; we praise You. You are the Lord; we ac - claim You.

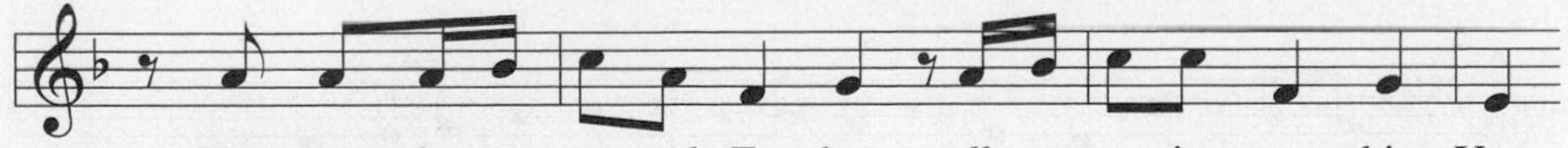

You are the e - ter - nal Fa - ther; all cre - a - tion wor - ships You.

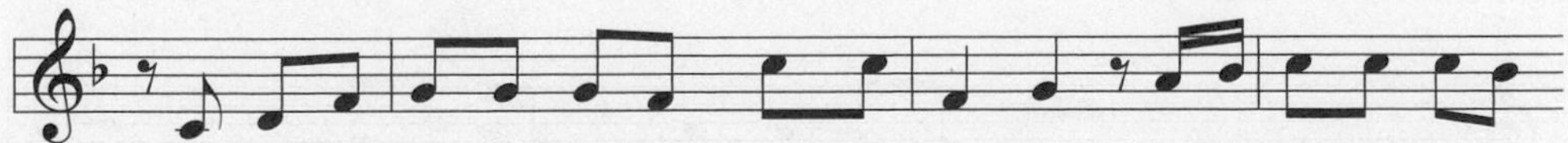

To You all an - gels, all the pow'rs of heav - en, cher - u - bim and ser - a -

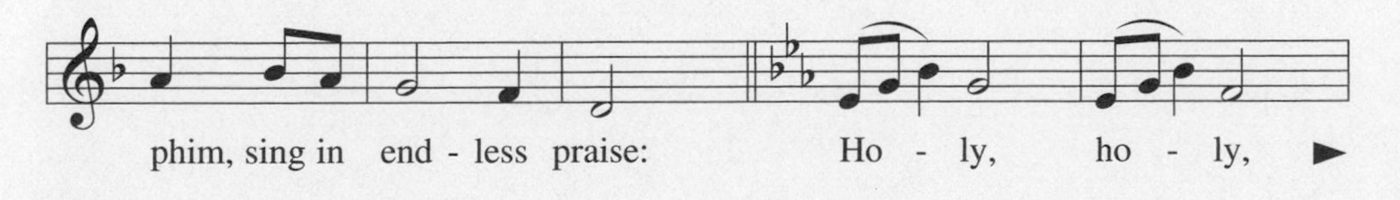

phim, sing in end - less praise: Ho - ly, ho - ly, ►

This canticle is a setting of the Te Deum laudamus. *Setting available in hymn accompaniment edition.*

Text: Latin, c. 4th cent.; tr. International Consultation on English Texts
Tune: Richard W. Hillert, 1923–2010

Is. 6:1–3; Rev. 6:9; 7:9–12; Phil. 2:6–11; Dan. 7:13–14; Heb. 1:3

ho - ly Lord, God of pow'r and might, heav - en and
earth are full of Your glo - ry. The glo-rious com-pa-ny
of a-pos-tles praise You. The no-ble fel-low-ship of proph-ets
praise You. The white-robed ar-my of mar-tyrs praise You.
Through-out the world the ho-ly Church ac-claims You:
Fa-ther, of maj-es-ty un-bound-ed; Your true and on-ly Son,
wor-thy of all wor-ship; and the Ho-ly Spir-it, ad-vo-cate and guide.
You, Christ, are the king of glo-ry, the e-ter-nal Son of the

Fa - ther. When You be - came man to set us
free, You did not spurn the vir - gin's womb.
You o - ver - came the sting of death and o - pened the
king - dom of heav - en to all be - liev - ers. You are seat - ed at
God's right hand in glo - ry. We be - lieve that You will
come and be our judge. Come, then, Lord, and
help Your peo - ple, bought with the price of Your own blood, and
bring us with Your saints to glo - ry ev - er - last - ing.

When this setting of the Te Deum *is sung with the Paschal Blessing, the service concludes with a collect and Benediction.*

940 Holy God, We Praise Thy Name

1 Ho - ly God, we praise Thy name; Lord of all, we
2 Hark! The glad ce - les - tial hymn An - gel choirs a -
3 Lo, the a - pos - tles' ho - ly train Join Thy sa - cred
4 Thou art King of Glo - ry, Christ; Son of God, yet
△ 5 Ho - ly Fa - ther, ho - ly Son, Ho - ly Spir - it,
bow be - fore Thee. All on earth Thy scep - ter claim,
bove are rais - ing; Cher - u - bim and ser - a - phim,
name to hal - low; Proph - ets swell the glad re - frain,
born of Mar - y. For us sin - ners sac - ri - ficed,
three we name Thee; Though in es - sence on - ly one,
All in heav'n a - bove a - dore Thee. In - fi - nite Thy
In un - ceas - ing cho - rus prais - ing, Fill the heav'ns with
And the white - robed mar - tyrs fol - low, And from morn to
As to death a Trib - u - tar - y, First to break the
Un - di - vid - ed God we claim Thee And, a - dor - ing,
vast do - main, Ev - er - last - ing is Thy reign.
sweet ac - cord: Ho - ly, ho - ly, ho - ly Lord!
set of sun Through the Church the song goes on.
bars of death, Thou hast o - pened heav'n to faith.
bend the knee While we own the mys - ter - y.

A "tributary" is one who pays a tribute that is owed. From the cross, Christ paid the penalty of death on our behalf.
The complete, seven-stanza version of this versification of the Te Deum laudamus *may be found in* Lutheran Service Builder.

Text: Latin, c. 4th cent.; German version, *Katholisches Gesangbuch*, Vienna, 1774;
tr. Clarence A. Walworth, 1820–1900, alt.
Tune: *Katholisches Gesangbuch*, Vienna, 1774; setting: *The Worshipbook: Services and Hymns*, 1972

GROSSER GOTT
78 78 77

Rev. 7:9–14; 1 Peter 1:18–19; 1 Cor. 15:20–23; Ps. 31:1–4

We Praise You and Acknowledge You, O God

941

1 We praise You and ac - knowl-edge You, O God, to be the Lord,
2 The band of the a - pos - tles in glo - ry sing Your praise;
3 You, Christ, are King of glo - ry, the ev - er - last - ing Son,
4 You sit in splen - did glo - ry, en-throned at God's right hand,
The Fa - ther ev - er - last - ing, by all the earth a - dored.
The fel - low - ship of proph - ets their death-less voic - es raise.
Yet You, with bound-less love, sought to res - cue ev - 'ry - one:
Up - hold - ing earth and heav - en by forc - es You com - mand.
To You all an - gel pow - ers cry a - loud, the heav - ens sing,
The mar - tyrs of Your king - dom, a great and no - ble throng,
You laid a - side Your glo - ry, were born of vir - gin's womb,
We know that You will come as our Judge that fi - nal day,
The cher - u - bim and ser - a - phim their prais - es to You bring:
Sing with the ho - ly Church through-out all the world this song:
Were cru - ci - fied for us and were placed in - to a tomb;
So help Your ser - vants You have re - deemed by blood, we pray;
"O ho - ly, ho - ly, ho - ly Lord God of Sab - a - oth;
"O all - ma - jes - tic Fa - ther, Your true and on - ly Son,
Then by Your res - ur - rec - tion You won for us re - prieve—
May we with saints be num - bered where prais - es nev - er end,
Your maj - es - ty and glo - ry fill the heav - ens and the earth!"
And Ho - ly Spir - it, Com-fort-er— for - ev - er Three in One!"
You o - pened heav - en's king - dom to all who would be - lieve.
In glo - ry ev - er - last - ing. A - men, O Lord, a - men!

This hymn is a versification of the Te Deum laudamus. *Setting available in hymn accompaniment edition.*

Text: Stephen P. Starke, b. 1955
Tune: Gustav Holst, 1874–1934, alt.

THAXTED
13 13 13 13 13 13

Rev. 7:9–17; Phil. 2:5–11; Ps. 89:26

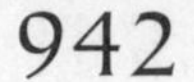

942 Kyrie! God, Father

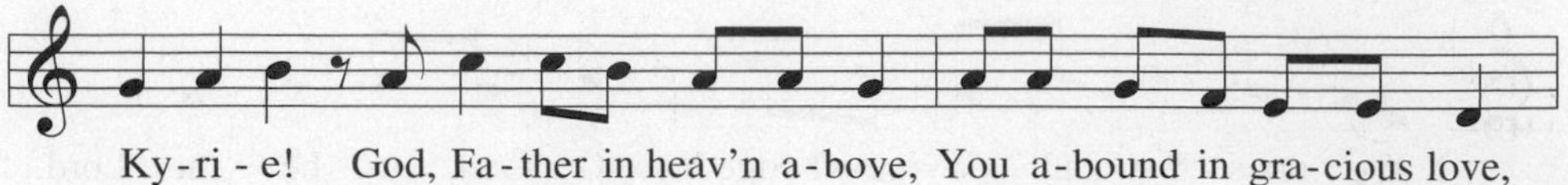

Ky-ri - e! God, Fa - ther in heav'n a - bove, You a - bound in gra - cious love,

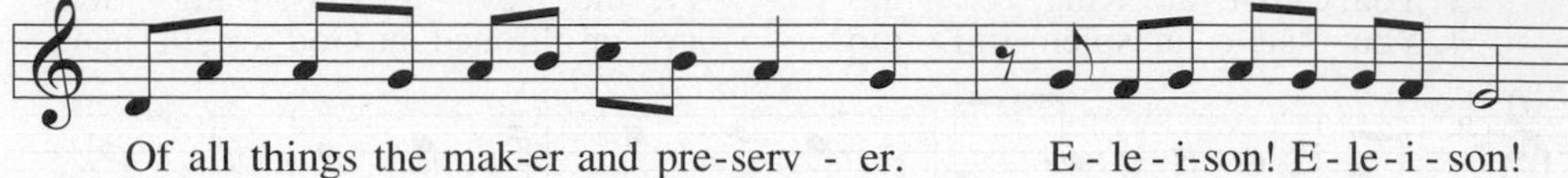

Of all things the mak-er and pre-serv - er. E - le - i-son! E - le - i - son!

Ky-ri - e! O Christ, our king, Sal - va - tion for all You came to bring.

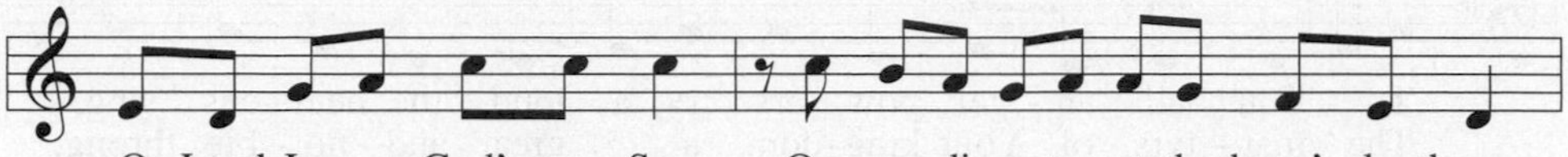

O Lord Je - sus, God's own Son, Our me - di - a - tor at the heav'n-ly throne:

Hear our cry and grant our sup-pli - ca - tion. E - le - i-son! E - le - i - son!

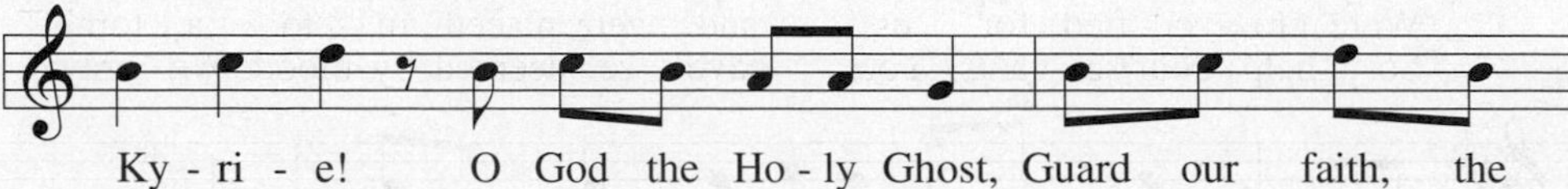

Ky - ri - e! O God the Ho - ly Ghost, Guard our faith, the

gift we need the most, And bless our life's last hour, That we leave this

sin - ful world with glad - ness. E - le - i-son! E - le - i - son!

Kyrie eleison (KIH-ree-ay eh-LAY-ee-sohn): Lord, have mercy.
This setting of the Kyrie *follows the ancient practice of expanding a liturgical text.*
Here the stanzas express a trinitarian interpretation of the threefold Kyrie.
Setting available in hymn accompaniment edition.

Text: Latin, 9th cent.; German version, *Ordenung der ceremonien*, Naumburg, 1537/38;
tr. W. Gustave Polack, 1890–1950, alt.
Tune: Latin, 9th cent.; adapt. *Kirchen ampt Deutsch*, Erfurt, 1525

KYRIE, GOTT VATER
Peculiar meter

Ps. 28:2; 103:13; Heb. 4:15–16; Phil. 1:6

Kyrie — I 943

Lord, Have Mercy

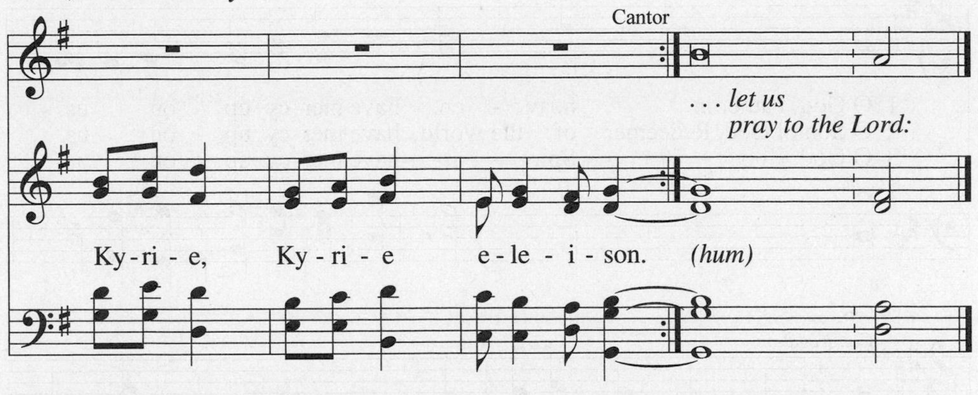
Cantor
. . . let us
pray to the Lord:
Ky-ri-e, Ky-ri-e e-le-i-son. (hum)

Kyrie eleison (KIH-ree-ay eh-LAY-ee-sohn): Lord, have mercy.

Text: Traditional
Music: Jacques Berthier, 1923–94

Mark 10:47

Kyrie — II 944

Lord, Have Mercy

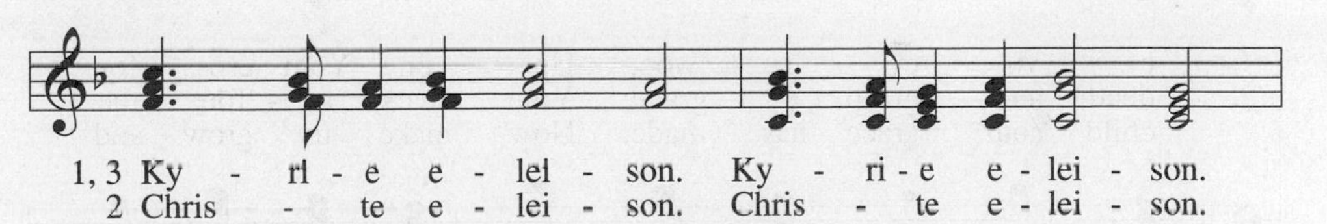
1, 3 Ky - ri - e e - lei - son. Ky - ri - e e - lei - son.
2 Chris - te e - lei - son. Chris - te e - lei - son.
1, 3 Lord, have mer - cy. Lord, have mer - cy.
2 Christ, have mer - cy. Christ, have mer - cy.

Ky - ri - e e - le - i - son.
Chris - te e - le - i - son.
Lord, have mer - - - cy.
Christ, have mer - - - cy.

Kyrie eleison (KIH-ree-ay eh-LAY-ee-sohn); Christe (KRIS-tay)

Text: Traditional
Music: Russian Orthodox

Ps. 51:1; Luke 17:13; Matt. 20:30

945 Your Heart, O God, Is Grieved

Cantor
1 O God, Father in heav - en, have mer-cy up - on us.
2 O Son of God, Redeemer of the world, have mer-cy up - on us.
3 O God, Holy Spir - it, have mer-cy up - on us.
Congregation
Your heart, O God, is grieved, we know, By ev - 'ry
Your arms ex - tend, O Christ, to save From sting of
O lav - ish Giv - er, come to aid The fee - ble
e - vil, ev - 'ry woe; Up - on Your cross - for -
death and grasp of grave; Your scars be - fore the
child Your grace has made. Now make us grow and
sak - en Son Our death is laid, and peace is won.
Fa - ther move His heart to mer - cy at such love.
help us pray; Bring joy and com - fort; come to stay.

This setting of the Kyrie *follows the ancient practice of expanding a liturgical text. Here the stanzas express a trinitarian interpretation of the threefold* Kyrie.

Text: Juraj Tranovský, 1591–1637; tr. Jaroslav J. Vajda, 1919–2008
Tune: *Cithara Sanctorum*, Levoca, 1636; setting: Michael Kútsky, 1828–99

ZNÁME TO, PANE BOŽE NÁŠ
Irregular meter

Heb. 4:16; Is. 53:3–6; 1 Cor. 15:55–58; Rom. 8:26

Glory to God, We Give You Thanks and Praise

1 Glo - ry to God, we give You thanks and praise;
2 Lord Je - sus Christ, the Fa - ther's on - ly Son,
△ 3 A - lone, O Christ, You on - ly are the Lord,
Of heav'n - ly joy and earth - ly peace we sing.
You bore for us the load of this world's sin.
At God's right hand in maj - es - ty most high:
We wor - ship You, to You our hearts we raise,
O Lamb of God, Your glo - rious vic - t'ry won,
Who with the Spir - it wor - shiped and a - dored,
Lord God, al - might - y Fa - ther, heav'n - ly King.
Re - ceive our prayer, grant us Your peace with - in.
With all the heav'n - ly host we glo - ri - fy.

This hymn is a versification of the Gloria in Excelsis.

Text: Edwin Le Grice, 1911–92
Music: Walter Greatorex, 1877–1949

WOODLANDS
10 10 10 10

Luke 2:14; John 1:29, 36; Rev. 5:9–14; Eph. 1:20–21

947 All Glory Be to God on High

1 All glo - ry be to God on high And thanks for all His
2 We praise and laud and wor - ship You; We give You thanks for -
3 O Je - sus Christ, the on - ly Son Be - got - ten of the
4 O Ho - ly Spir - it, our de - light And source of con - so -

fa - vor; No harm can touch or ter - ri - fy A child of
ev - er, O Fa - ther, for Your rule is true And just and
Fa - ther, Your sav - ing death has made us one With God and
la - tion, Pro - tect us from the dev - il's might Through Je - sus,

God for - ev - er. God shows His good and gra - cious will And
chang - es nev - er. With bound - less pow'r, Your might - y reign Ful -
with each oth - er. O Lamb of God, to You on high In
our sal - va - tion, Who by His death up - on a tree Has

grants His peace, the world to fill— All strife at last has end - ed.
fills what - ev - er You or - dain. Lord, grant us ev - 'ry bless - ing!
our dis - tress we sin - ners cry, Have mer - cy on us, a - men!
res - cued us from mis - er - y: To this we hold for - ev - er.

This hymn is a versification of the Gloria in Excelsis.

Text: Nicolaus Decius, c. 1485–after 1546; tr. *Lutheran Service Book*, 2006
Tune: attr. Nicolaus Decius, c. 1485–after 1546; setting: Joseph Herl, b. 1959

ALLEIN GOTT IN DER HÖH
87 87 887

Luke 2:14; John 1:29, 36; Rev. 5:9–14; Eph. 1:20–21

All Glory Be to God Alone 948

1 All glo - ry be to God a - lone, For - ev - er - more the
2 We praise You, God; Your name we bless And wor - ship You in
3 Lord God, our King on heav - en's throne, Our Fa - ther, the Al-
4 You take the whole world's sin a - way; Have mer - cy on us,
5 You on - ly are the Ho - ly One And o - ver all are
high - est one, Who did our sin - ful race be - friend And
hum - ble - ness; From day to day we glo - ri - fy The
might - y One. O Lord, the sole - be - got - ten One, Lord
Lord, we pray. You take the whole world's sin a - way; O
Lord a - lone. O Je - sus Christ, we glo - ri - fy You
grace and peace to us ex - tend. A - mong us may His
ev - er - last - ing God on high. Of Your great glo - ry
Je - sus Christ, the Fa - ther's Son, True God from all e -
Lord, re - ceive our prayer this day. From God's right hand Your
and the Spir - it, Lord Most High; With Him You ev - er -
gra - cious will All hearts with deep thanks - giv - ing fill.
do we sing, And to Your throne our thanks we bring.
ter - ni - ty, O Lamb of God, to You we flee.
mer - cy send, To all the world Your grace ex - tend.
more shall be One in the Fa - ther's maj - es - ty.

This hymn is a versification of the Gloria in Excelsis.

Text: attr. Martin Luther, 1483–1546, abr.; tr. W. Gustave Polack, 1890–1950, alt.
Tune: *Gesangbuch . . . Psalmen, Geistliche Lieder*, Strassburg, 1541, alt.;
setting: *The Lutheran Hymnal*, 1941

ALL EHR UND LOB
88 88 88

Luke 2:10–14; John 1:29, 36; Rev. 5:9–14; 1 John 2:2

949 Heavenly Hosts in Ceaseless Worship

1 Heav'n-ly hosts in cease-less wor-ship "Ho-ly, ho-ly, ho-ly" cry;
2 All cre-a-tion, all re-demp-tion, Join to sing the Sav-ior's worth;
"He who is, who was and will be, God Al-might-y, Lord Most High."
Lamb of God, whose blood has bought us, Kings and priests, to reign on earth.
Praise and hon-or, pow'r and glo-ry, Be to Him who reigns a-lone!
Wealth and wis-dom, pow'r and glo-ry, Hon-or, might, do-min-ion, praise,
We, with all His hands have fash-ioned, Fall be-fore the Fa-ther's throne.
Now be His from all His crea-tures And to ev-er-last-ing days!

This versification of the Dignus es *is drawn from selected hymns of praise in the book of Revelation.*

Text: Timothy Dudley-Smith, b. 1926
Music: Amanda Husberg, b. 1940

LOVE'S LIGHT
87 87 D

Rev. 4:1–11; 5:1–14; Is. 6:1–4; Rev. 7:9–17

Splendor and Honor

950

1 Splen - dor and hon - or, maj - es - ty and pow - er
2 Praised be the true Lamb, slain for our re - demp - tion,
3 To the Al - might - y, throned in heav'n - ly splen - dor,
Are Yours, O Lord God, fount of ev - 'ry bless - ing,
By whose self - of - f'ring we are made God's peo - ple:
And to the Sav - ior, Christ our Lamb and Shep - herd,
For by Your bid - ding was the whole cre -
A priest - ly king - dom, from all tongues and
Be ad - o - ra - tion, praise, and glo - ry
a - tion Called in - to be - ing.
na - tions, Called to God's ser - vice.
giv - en, Now and for - ev - er.

This versification of the Dignus es *is drawn from selected hymns of praise in the book of Revelation.*

Text: Carl P. Daw, Jr., b. 1944
Music: K. Lee Scott, b. 1950

SHADES MOUNTAIN
11 11 11 5

Rev. 4:11; 5:9–10; 6:16; 7:9, 14, 17

951 Alleluia — I

Al - le - lu - ia, al - le - lu - ia, al - le - lu -
ia. Al - le - lu - ia, al - le - lu - ia, al - le - lu -
Cantor (Psalms)
Al - le - lu - ia.
ia. (hum)

The appointed Verse of the Day may be sung by a cantor.

Text: Traditional
Music: Jacques Berthier, 1923–94

952 Alleluia — II

Al - le - lu - ia, al - le - lu - ia!

Text: Traditional
Music: Fintan O'Carroll, d. 1977

Al - le - lu - ia, al - le - lu - ia!

We All Believe in One True God 953

1 We all be-lieve in one true God, Fa - ther, Son, and Ho - ly Ghost,
2 We all be-lieve in Je - sus Christ, Son of God and Mar - y's son,
3 We all con-fess the Ho - ly Ghost, Who from both in truth pro-ceeds,
Ev - er - pres - ent help in need, Praised by all the heav'n - ly host;
Who de - scend - ed from His throne And for us sal - va - tion won;
Who sus - tains and com - forts us In all tri - als, fears, and needs.
All He made His love en - folds, All cre - a - tion He up - holds.
By whose cross and death are we Res - cued from all mis - er - y.
Bless - ed, ho - ly Trin - i - ty, Praise for - ev - er be to Thee!

Text: Tobias Clausnitzer, 1619–84; tr. Catherine Winkworth, 1827–78, alt.
Tune: *Neu-vermehrtes . . . Gesangbuch*, 3rd ed., Meiningen, 1693;
setting: *The Lutheran Hymnal*, 1941

WIR GLAUBEN ALL (Metrical)
87 77 77

Heb. 1:1–8; Rom. 8:26–27; Ps. 145:15–16; John 11:25–27

954 We All Believe in One True God

1 We all be - lieve in one true God, Who cre - at - ed
2 We all be - lieve in Je - sus Christ, His own Son, our
3 We all con - fess the Ho - ly Ghost, Who, in high - est

earth and heav - en, The Fa - ther, who to us in love
Lord, pos - sess - ing An e - qual God - head, throne, and might,
heav - en dwell - ing With God the Fa - ther and the Son,

Has the right of chil - dren giv - en. He in soul and
Source of ev - 'ry grace and bless - ing; Born of Mar - y,
Com - forts us be - yond all tell - ing; Who the Church, His

bod - y feeds us; All we need His hand pro - vides us;
vir - gin moth - er, By the pow - er of the Spir - it,
own cre - a - tion, Keeps in u - ni - ty of spir - it.

Through all snares and per - ils leads us, Watch - ing that no
Word made flesh, our el - der broth - er; That the lost might
Here for - give - ness and sal - va - tion Dai - ly come through

harm be - tide us. He cares for us by
life in - her - it, Was cru - ci - fied for
Je - sus' mer - it. All flesh shall rise, and

day and night; All things are gov - erned by His might.
all our sin And raised by God to life a - gain.
we shall be In bliss with God e - ter - nal - ly.

This is a catechism hymn of Martin Luther. Setting available in hymn accompaniment edition.

Text: Martin Luther, 1483–1546; tr. *The Lutheran Hymnal*, 1941, alt.
Tune: Latin, 14th cent., adapt.

WIR GLAUBEN ALL (Chant)
8888 8888 88

Is. 43:1–7; Rom. 8:14–17; John 1:1–4, 14; 2 Cor. 4:13–14

OR
A - men, a - - men. A - men.

Let the Vineyards Be Fruitful 955

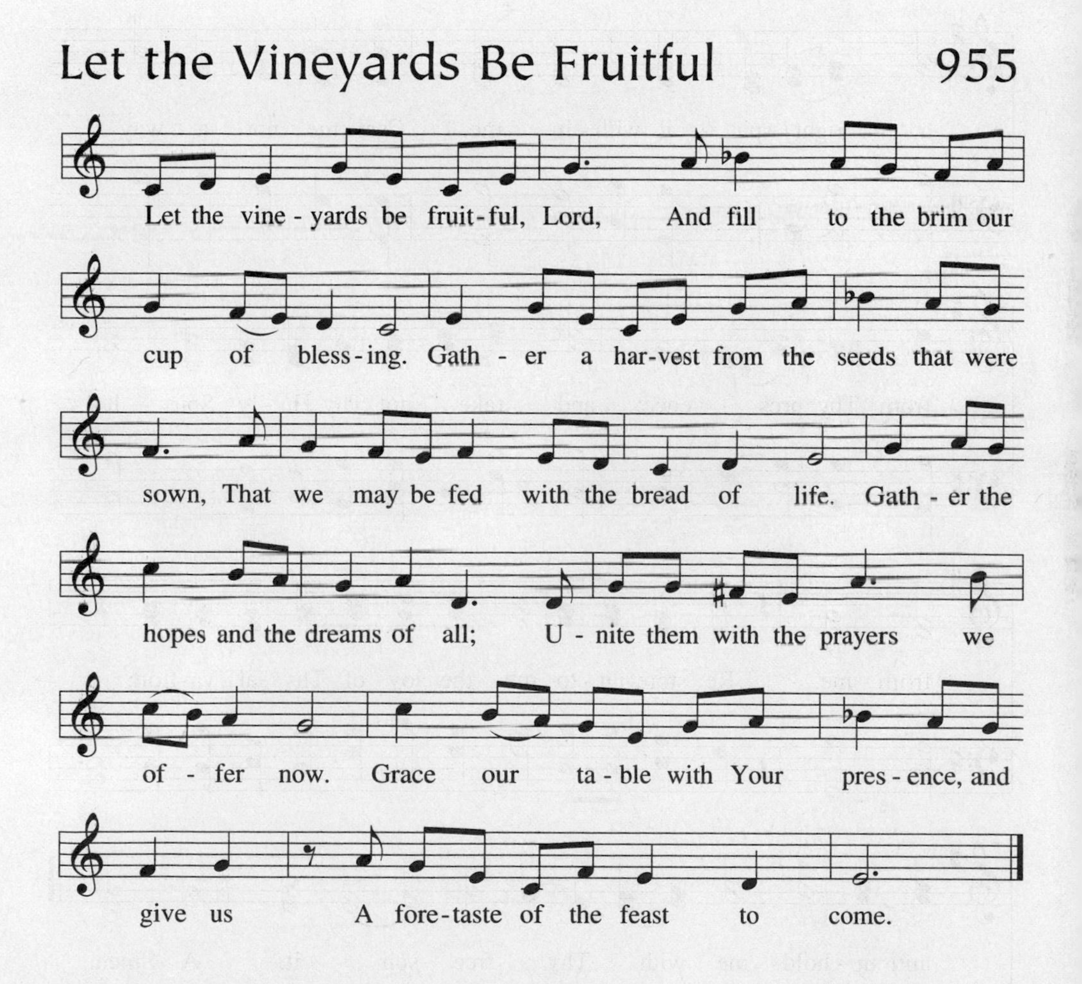
Let the vine - yards be fruit - ful, Lord, And fill to the brim our
cup of bless - ing. Gath - er a har - vest from the seeds that were
sown, That we may be fed with the bread of life. Gath - er the
hopes and the dreams of all; U - nite them with the prayers we
of - fer now. Grace our ta - ble with Your pres - ence, and
give us A fore - taste of the feast to come.

Setting available in hymn accompaniment edition.

Text: John W. Arthur, 1922–80
Tune: Richard W. Hillert, 1923–2010

Ps. 104:14–15; Is. 25:6; 1 Cor. 5:7

956 Create in Me

Cre-ate in me a clean heart, O God, and re-new
a right spir - it with-in me. Cast me not a-way
from Thy pres - ence; and take not Thy Ho-ly Spir - it
from me. Re-store un-to me the joy of Thy sal-va-tion;
and up-hold me with Thy free spir - it. A - men.

Text: Psalm 51:10–12
Tune: Johann Georg Winer, 1583–1651, adapt.; setting: *The Lutheran Hymnal*, 1941

SCHAFFE IN MIR, GOTT
Peculiar meter

Our Father Who Art in Heaven — I

Our Fa - ther who art in heav - en, hal-low - ed be Thy name,
Thy king - dom come, Thy will be done on earth as
it is in heav - en; give us this day our dai - ly
bread; and for - give us our tres - pass - es as we for - give
those who tres - pass a - gainst us; and lead us not in -
to temp - ta - tion, but de - liv - er us from e - vil.
For Thine is the king - dom and the pow'r and the glo -
ry for - ev - er and ev - er. A - men.

Text: Traditional
Tune: Plainsong, mode VII

Matt. 6:9–13; Rom. 8:15; Gal. 4:6

958 Our Father Who Art in Heaven — IIa

Refrain
Our Fa - ther who art in

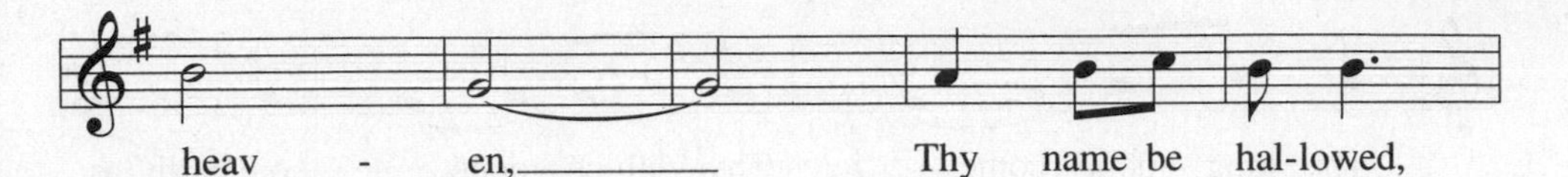
heav - en, Thy name be hal-lowed,

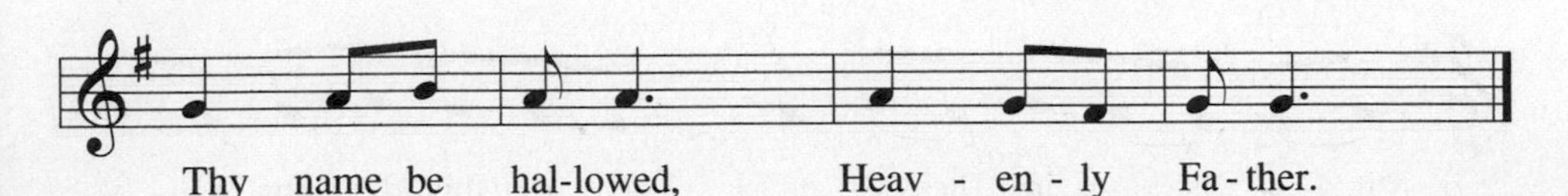
Thy name be hal-lowed, Heav - en - ly Fa - ther.

1 May Thy king - dom come to us, O
2 Give us this day, O Lord, our dai - ly
3 Lead us not in - to temp - ta - tion,

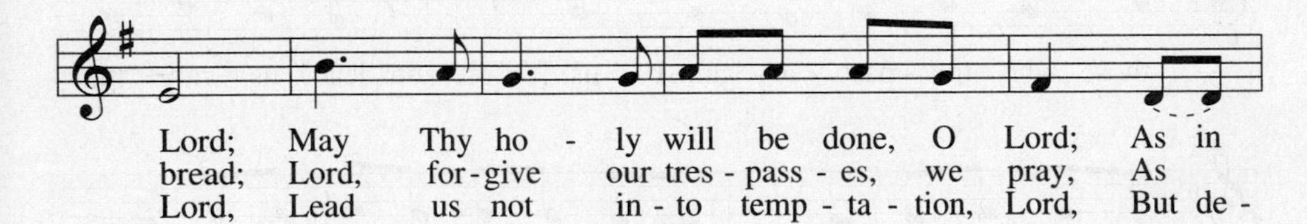
Lord; May Thy ho - ly will be done, O Lord; As in
bread; Lord, for - give our tres - pass - es, we pray, As
Lord, Lead us not in - to temp - ta - tion, Lord, But de -

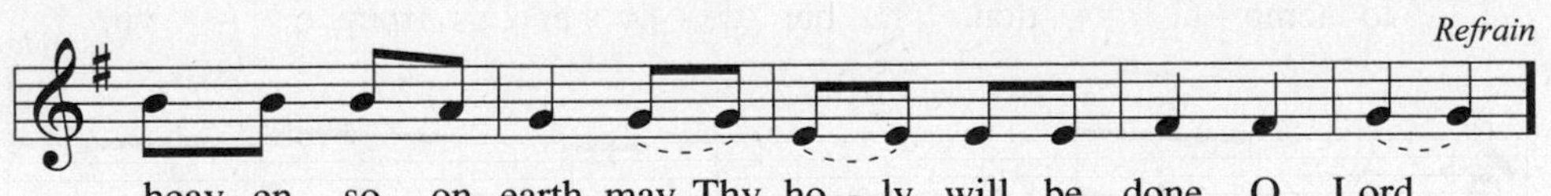
Refrain
heav - en so on earth may Thy ho - ly will be done, O Lord.
we for - give all those who tres - pass a - gainst us, Lord.
liv - er us from e - vil, Lord, de - liv - er us from e - vil.

Setting available in hymn accompaniment edition.

Text: Carlos Rosas, b. 1939; tr. Daniel Zager, b. 1951
Tune: Carlos Rosas, b. 1939

PADRE NUESTRO
Irregular meter

Matt. 6:9–13; Rom. 8:15; Gal. 4:6

Our Father Who Art in Heaven — IIb

Estribillo
Pa-dre nues - tro___ que es-tás en el
cie - lo,___ san - ti - fi - ca-do,
san - ti - fi - ca-do se - a tu nom-bre.
1 Vén - ga-nos tu rei-no, Se-ñor;
2 Da - nos hoy, dá-nos-lo Se-ñor:
3 No nos de-jes ca-er en ten-ta-ción;

há - ga-se tu san-ta vo-lun-tad en el cie-lo y en la
nues - tro pan, el pan de ca-da dí - a. Y per-do-na nues-tras
an - tes bien, lí-bra-nos del mal. No nos de-jes ca-

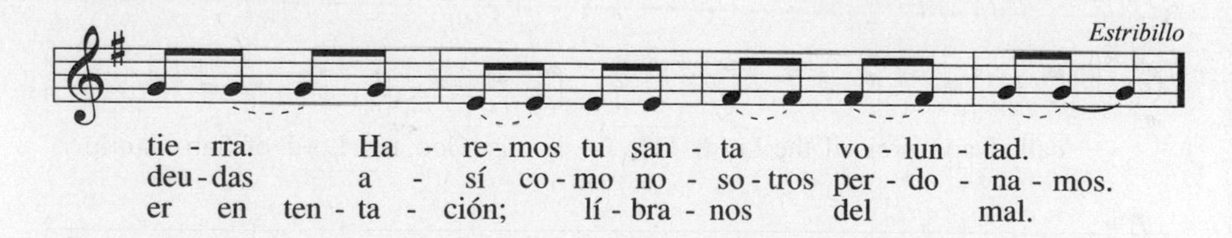
Estribillo
tie-rra. Ha - re-mos tu san - ta vo-lun - tad.
deu-das a - sí co-mo no - so-tros per - do - na - mos.
er en ten - ta - ción; lí - bra - nos del mal.

Setting available in hymn accompaniment edition.

Text: Carlos Rosas, b. 1939
Tune: Carlos Rosas, b. 1939

PADRE NUESTRO
Irregular meter

Matt. 6:9–13; Rom. 8:15; Gal. 4:6

960 Isaiah, Mighty Seer in Days of Old

I - sa - iah, might-y seer in days of old, The Lord of all in spir - it

did be-hold High on a loft - y throne, in splen-dor bright, With robes that

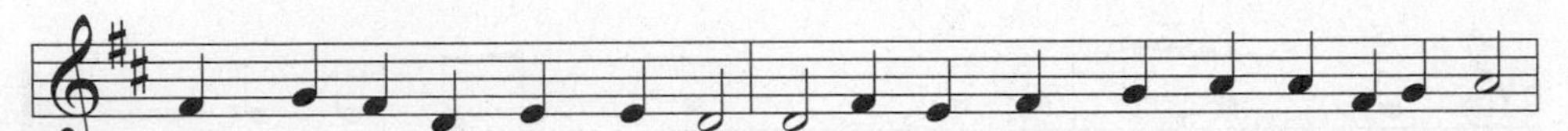

filled the tem-ple courts with light. A-bove the throne were flam-ing ser-a-phim;

Six wings had they, these mes-sen-gers of Him. With two they veiled their

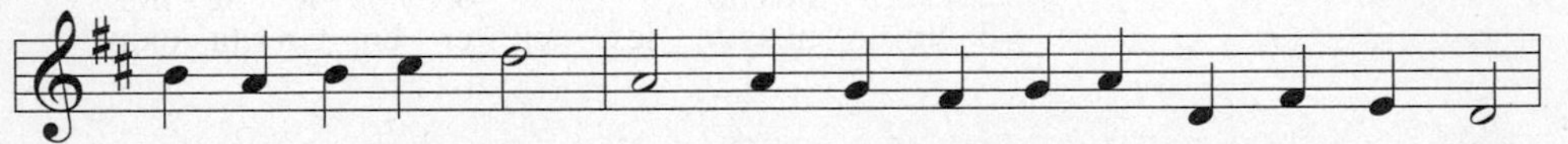

fac-es as was right, With two they hum-bly hid their feet from sight,

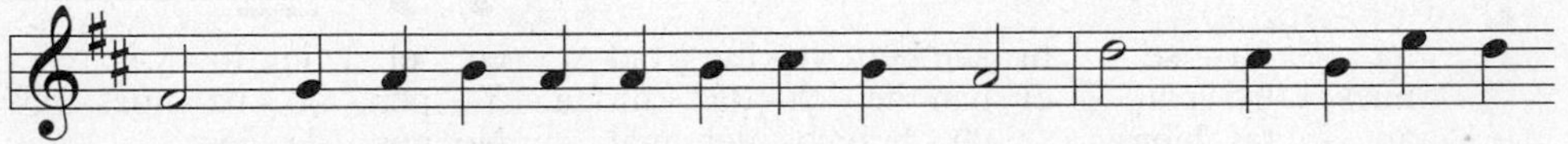

And with the oth - er two a - loft they soared; One to the oth - er

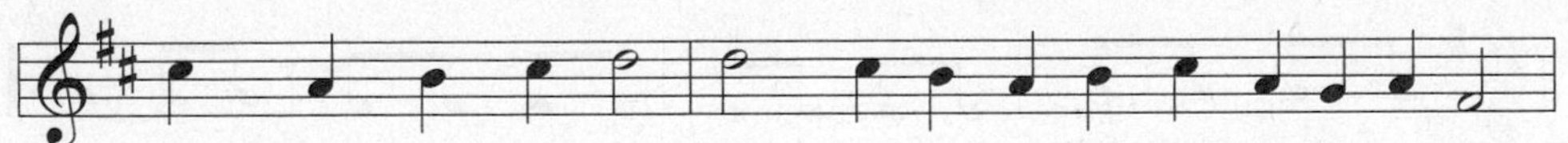

called and praised the Lord: "Ho - ly is God, the Lord of Sab - a - oth!

Ho - ly is God, the Lord of Sab - a - oth! Ho - ly is God, the Lord of

This hymn is a versification of Isaiah's vision of heaven (Is. 6:1–4). Sabaoth (SAH-bay-oath) is Hebrew for "heavenly hosts." Setting available in hymn accompaniment edition.

Text: Martin Luther, 1483–1546; tr. *The Lutheran Hymnal*, 1941, alt.
Tune: Martin Luther, 1483–1546

JESAIA, DEM PROPHETEN
Peculiar meter

Is. 6:1–4; Rev. 4:8

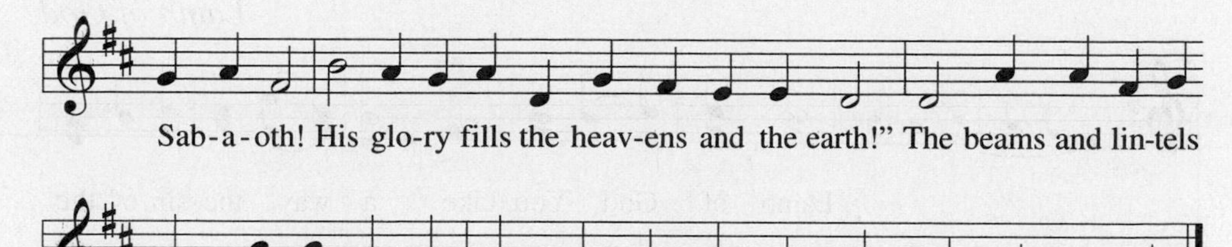
Sab-a-oth! His glo-ry fills the heav-ens and the earth!" The beams and lin-tels
trem-bled at the cry, And clouds of smoke en-wrapped the throne on high.

Sanctus

961

Holy, Holy, Holy

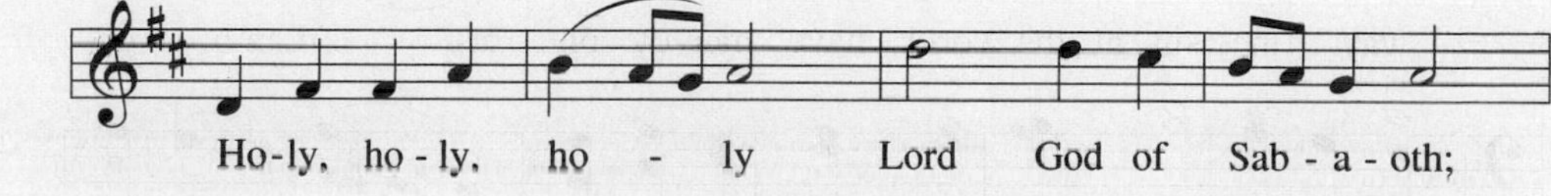
Ho-ly, ho-ly, ho - ly Lord God of Sab-a-oth;

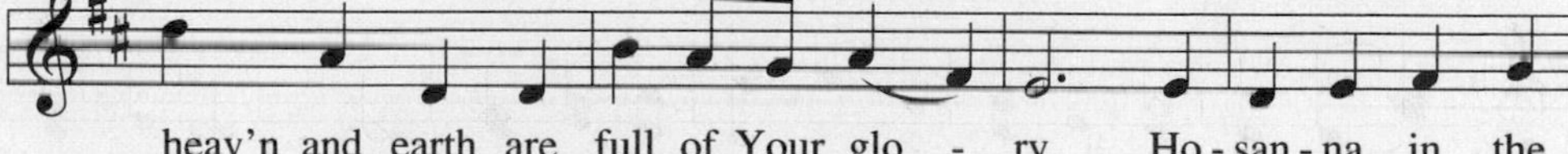
heav'n and earth are full of Your glo - ry. Ho-san-na in the

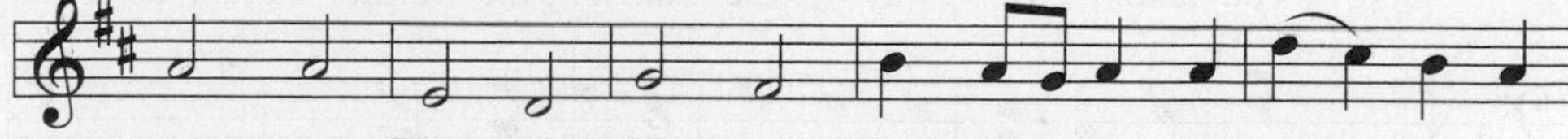
high-est. Bless-ed, bless-ed, bless-ed is He who comes in the

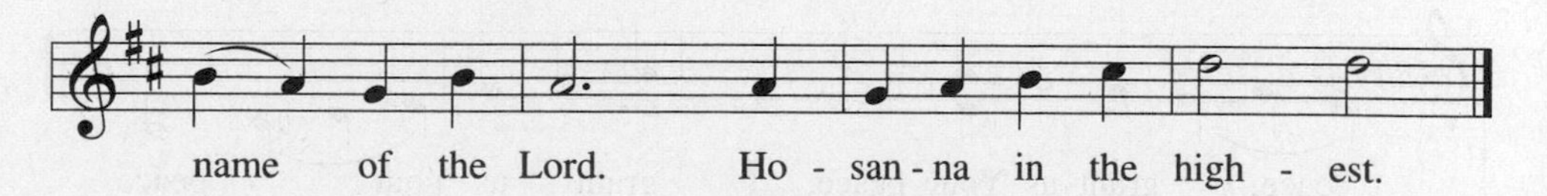
name of the Lord. Ho - san-na in the high - est.

Setting available in hymn accompaniment edition.

Text: Traditional; tr. International Consultation on English Texts, alt.
Tune: Mark L. Bender, b. 1951

Is. 6:3; Matt. 21:9

962 Agnus Dei — I

Lamb of God

Lamb of God, You take a - way the sin of the
world; have mer - cy on us. Lamb of God, You take a -
way the sin of the world; have mer - cy on us. Lamb of
God, You take a - way the sin of the world; grant us Your
peace, grant us Your peace, grant us Your peace.

Text: Traditional; tr. International Consultation on English Texts, alt.
Music: Paul D. Weber, b. 1949

John 1:29; 1 Cor. 5:7

Agnus Dei — II

Lamb of God

Lamb of God, You take a-way the sin of the
world; have mer - cy on us.
Lamb of God, You
take a-way the sin of the world;
have mer - cy on us.
Lamb of God, You take a-way the sin of the world;
grant us Your peace,
grant us Your peace.

Text: Traditional; tr. International Consultation on English Texts, alt.
Music: Jeffrey N. Blersch, b. 1967

John 1:29; 1 Cor. 5:7

964 Lift Every Voice and Sing

1 Lift ev - 'ry voice and sing Till earth and heav - en ring,
2 Ston - y the road we trod, Bit - ter the chas - t'ning rod
3 God of our wea - ry years, God of our si - lent tears,
Ring with the har - mo - nies of lib - er - ty.
Felt in the days when hope un - born had died;
Thou who hast brought us thus far on the way;
Let our re - joic - ing rise High as the lis - t'ning skies,
Yet with a stead - y beat, Have not our wea - ry feet
Thou who hast by Thy might Led us in - to the light,
Let it re - sound loud as the roll - ing sea.
Come to the place for which our par - ents sighed?
Keep us for - ev - er in the path, we pray.

Text: James Weldon Johnson, 1871–1938
Music: J. Rosamond Johnson, 1873–1954

LIFT EVERY VOICE
Peculiar meter

Ex. 15:1–21; Ps. 85:1–7

Sing a song full of the faith that the dark past has taught us;
We have come o - ver a way that with tears has been wa - tered;
Lest our feet stray from the plac - es, our God, where we met Thee;
Sing a song full of the hope that the pres - ent has brought us;
We have come, tread - ing our path through the blood of the slaugh - tered,
Lest, our hearts drunk with the wine of the world, we for - get Thee;
Fac - ing the ris - ing sun Of our new day be - gun,
Out from the gloom - y past, Till now we stand at last
Shad - owed be - neath Thy hand, May we for - ev - er stand,
Let us march on till vic - to - ry is won.
Where the white gleam of our bright star is cast.
True to our God, true to our na - tive land.

965 God Bless Our Native Land

1 God bless our na - tive land; Firm may she ev - er stand
2 So shall our prayers a - rise To God a - bove the skies;
Through storm and night. When the wild tem - pests rave, Rul - er of
On Him we wait. Thou who art ev - er nigh, Guard-ing with
wind and wave, Do Thou our coun - try save By Thy great might.
watch-ful eye, To Thee a - loud we cry: God save the state!

Text: Charles T. Brooks, 1813–83, st. 1, alt.; John S. Dwight, 1813–93, st. 2, alt.
Tune: *Thesaurus Musicus*, London, c. 1740; setting: *The Lutheran Hymnal*, 1941

NATIONAL ANTHEM
664 6664

Rom. 13:1–7

Before You, Lord, We Bow 966

1 Be - fore You, Lord, we bow, Our God who reigns a - bove And rules the world be - low, Bound - less in pow'r and love, Our thanks we bring In joy and praise, Our hearts we raise To You, our King!
2 The na - tion You have blest May well Your love de - clare, From foes and fears at rest, Pro - tect - ed by Your care. For this bright day, For this fair land— Gifts of Your hand— Our thanks we pay.
3 May ev - 'ry moun - tain height, Each vale and for - est green, Shine in Your Word's pure light, And its rich fruits be seen! May ev - 'ry tongue Be tuned to praise And join to raise A grate - ful song.
4 Earth, hear your Mak - er's voice; Your great Re - deem - er own; Be - lieve, o - bey, re - joice, And wor - ship Him a - lone. Cast down your pride, Your sin de - plore, And bow be - fore The Cru - ci - fied.
5 And when in pow'r He comes, Oh, may our na - tive land From all its rend - ing tombs Send forth a glo - rious band, A count - less throng, With joy to sing To heav'n's high King Sal - va - tion's song!

Text: Francis Scott Key, 1779–1843, alt.
Tune: John Darwall, 1731–89; setting: William H. Monk, 1823–89

DARWALL'S 148TH
66 66 88

Ps. 145:1; Ps. 29:11; 46:9; 72:3, 7

ACKNOWLEDGMENTS

The material on pages i–xxvi and 151–1024 is covered by the copyright of this book except where noted.

Prayers We Have in Common © 1970, 1971, 1975 International Consultation on English Texts (ICET).

Lutheran Book of Worship © 1978 Lutheran Church in America, The American Lutheran Church, The Evangelical Lutheran Church in Canada, and The Lutheran Church—Missouri Synod.

Lutheran Worship © 1982 Concordia Publishing House.

Small Catechism © 1986 Concordia Publishing House.

Scripture quotations marked "NIV" are taken from the HOLY BIBLE, NEW INTERNATIONAL VERSION®. Copyright © 1973, 1978, 1984 by International Bible Society. Used by permission of Zondervan Publishing House. All rights reserved.

Scripture quotations marked "NKJV" are taken from the New King James Version. Copyright © 1979, 1980, 1982 by Thomas Nelson, Inc. Used by permission. All rights reserved.

Divine Service—Settings One and Two

Text ("Glory to God," Preface, "Holy, holy, holy," "Lamb of God," and "Lord, now You let Your servant"): © ICET; liturgical texts ("Alleluia, Lord, to whom shall we go," "Return to the Lord, your God," "What shall I render," "Thank the Lord"): © 1978 *Lutheran Book of Worship*; "This is the feast": John W. Arthur (1922–80) © 1978 *Lutheran Book of Worship.*

Music (Setting One): Richard W. Hillert (1923–2010) © 1978 *Lutheran Book of Worship*, except "This is the feast": © 1975, 1988 Richard Hillert, admin. OCP Publications; (Setting Two): Ronald A. Nelson (b. 1927), alt. © 1978 *Lutheran Book of Worship*, except "Return to the Lord" and "Lord, now You let Your servant": Richard W. Hillert © 1978 *Lutheran Book of Worship.*

Divine Service—Setting Three

Text: Public domain; drawn from *The Lutheran Hymnal*, © 1941 Concordia Publishing House.

Music: © 2006 Concordia Publishing House; adapted from *The Lutheran Hymnal*, © 1941 Concordia Publishing House.

Divine Service—Setting Four

Kyrie—text: public domain. Music: Amanda Husberg (b. 1940) © 2006 Concordia Publishing House.

Gloria in Excelsis—text: Stephen P. Starke (b. 1955) © 2001 Stephen P. Starke, admin. Concordia Publishing House. Tune: ES FLOG EIN KLEINS WALDVÖGELEIN, German folksong; setting: Paul J. Grime (b. 1958) © 2006 Concordia Publishing House.

Alleluia—text: public domain. Music (refrain): Howard Hughes (b. 1930) © 1972, 1983 GIA Publications, Inc.; (verse): composite © 1998 Concordia Publishing House.

Sanctus—text: Stephen P. Starke © 1998 Concordia Publishing House. Music: THINE, Carl F. Schalk (b. 1929) © 1983 Augsburg Publishing House, admin. Augsburg Fortress.

Agnus Dei—text: Stephen P. Starke © 1998 Concordia Publishing House. Music: ANGELUS, Georg Joseph (17th cent.), public domain.

Nunc Dimittis—text (st. 1): Ernest Ryden (1886–1981) © Board of Publications, Lutheran Church in America, admin. Augsburg Fortress; (st. 2) Stephen P. Starke © 1998 Concordia Publishing House. Tune: KUORTANE, Finnish folksong (19th cent.), public domain; setting: Joseph Herl (b. 1959) © 1998 Concordia Publishing House.

Divine Service—Setting Five

Texts drawn from Martin Luther's *German Mass* (1526) and *The Lutheran Hymnal*, alt.

Matins and Vespers

Text: *The Lutheran Hymnal*, alt., © 1941 Concordia Publishing House.

Music (Venite, Te Deum, Benedictus, and liturgical responses): *The Lutheran Hymnal*, alt. © 1941 Concordia Publishing House; (Gloria Patri, Responsory, Magnificat): *Lutheran Worship*, alt. © 1982 Concordia Publishing House.

Morning Prayer

Text ("Blessed be the Lord"): © ICET; ("O come, let us sing" and liturgical texts, alt.): © 1978 *Lutheran Book of Worship.*

Music ("O come, let us sing"): Richard W. Hillert; ("Blessed be the Lord"): Dale Wood (1923–2003); liturgical responses © 1978 *Lutheran Book of Worship*.

Evening Prayer

Text ("Joyous light of glory"): tr. Roger T. Petrich (b. 1938) © 1978 *Lutheran Book of Worship*; ("Let my prayer rise before You"): *Book of Common Prayer*, The Episcopal Church 1979; liturgical texts, alt.: © 1978 *Lutheran Book of Worship*.

Music ("Joyous light of glory"): Roger T. Petrich; ("Let my prayer rise before You"): David Schack (b. 1947); (liturgical texts): © 1978 *Lutheran Book of Worship*; ("My soul magnifies the Lord") refrain: David Schack; verse: Paul J. Grime © 2006 Concordia Publishing House.

Compline

Text ("Lord, now You let Your servant"): © ICET; liturgical texts, alt.: © 1978 *Lutheran Book of Worship.*

Music: Carlos R. Messerli (b. 1927), alt. © 1978 *Lutheran Book of Worship.*

Service of Prayer and Preaching

Text: © 2001 Crossway Bibles

Music (Old Testament Canticle): Phillip Magness (b. 1963); (New Testament Canticle): Carl F. Schalk © 2006 Concordia Publishing House.

Psalm Tones

Tone D: Mark Bangert (b. 1938) and tone I: Richard W. Hillert © 1978 *Lutheran Book of Worship*.

Tones A, E, F, G, H: © 1982 Concordia Publishing House.

Tone B: Henry V. Gerike © 1998 Concordia Publishing House.

Tones C and K: Paul J. Grime and tone J: Phillip Magness © 2006 Concordia Publishing House

The Commission on Worship of The Lutheran Church—Missouri Synod serving 1998–2006

Members—Mark Bender (chairman, 2001–04), Barbara Bradfield, Stephen Everette, Ronald Feuerhahn, Daniel Q. Johnson, Reed Lessing, Allen Loesel, James Lowitzer, Mary Mountford, Janet Muth, William Otte, Roger Pittelko (chairman, 1992–98), Richard Resch (chairman, 1998–2001), Linda Stoterau, Kurt von Kampen, Elizabeth Werner, Gregory Wismar (chairman, 2004–10).

Staff—Rachel Asburry, Paul Grime (executive director and *LSB* project director), Lynda Lorenz, and Jon Vieker (assistant director).

Committees and Other Contributors

**Indicates committee chairman and member of hymnal steering committee.*

Liturgy—Mark Bender, Kent Burreson, William Cwirla, *Ronald Feuerhahn, Naomichi Masaki, Timothy Quill, Elizabeth Werner, Thomas Winger.

Hymnody—Stephen Everette, Lorraine Florindez, Henry Gerike, Joseph Herl, Janet Muth, Richard Resch, *Stephen Starke, Daniel Zager.

Lectionary—James Brauer, *Arthur Just, Daniel Reuning, Richard Stuckwisch, Gregory Wismar.

Translations—Erik Ankerberg, Frederic Baue, David Berger, James Lowitzer, Christopher Mitchell, *Gene Edward Veith, Kari Vo.

Agenda—Peter Bender, John Fenton, William Otte, Frank Pies, *Roger Pittelko, John Pless, David Saar.

Introductory—Jeffrey Blersch, William Heide, Sally Hiller, John Hooper, James Lowitzer, Phillip Magness, Mary Mountford, David Reed.

Others who served on the committees for varying lengths of time include Barry Bobb, Katharine Borst, Joel Brondos, Robert Clancy, Charles Evanson, John Nunes, Bruce Schuchard, Timothy Seals, Harold Senkbeil, John Stephenson, and Dien Taylor.

Additional assistants, consultants, and contributors—Christopher Ahlman, Randy Asburry, Chad Bird, Richard Bucher, Paul Cain, Albert Collver III, Joseph Das, J. Bart Day, Karen Eggemeyer, Karl Fabrizius, Charles Ferry, David Fleming, Daniel Gard, David Gottschalk, Brian Hamer, Kent Heimbigner, William Hoesman, Allen Hoger, Cindy Holden, James Kellerman, Gerald Kieschnick, Aaron Koch, Gerald Krispin, Brent Kuhlman, Peter Ledic, Dale Lewis, Reena Linke, Kevin Loughran, Lee Maxwell, John Nordling, Louis Nuechterlein, Dean Pittelko, Timothy Saleska, J. Richard Sawyer, David Scaer, Robert Schaibley, Carl Schalk, Scott Schilbe, Ruth Ann Stautzenberger, Karen Stevenson, William Thompson, Kent Tibben, Keith Vieregge, James Voelz, William Weedon, Kirby Wilbur, Adolph H. Wismar, Jr., Daniel Woodring.

In addition to those listed above, special thanks and acknowledgment are given to all other individuals, as well as congregations, who participated in the review and field testing of *Lutheran Service Book.*

Generous funding from The Marvin M. Schwan Charitable Foundation for the research and development of *Lutheran Service Book* is hereby acknowledged.

Concordia Publishing House

Editorial—Nancy Adams, David Johnson (director), Peter Reske (editor), Dawn Weinstock.

Leadership council—Bruce Kintz, Paul McCain, Jonathan Schultz.

Engraving—Gerald Near, Randy L. Scheffel.

Copyrights and permissions—Gloria Clark, Norma Muench.

Lutheran Service Builder—Robert Lail (developer), Ryan Markel.

Layout—Ruth Brown, Christopher Loemker.

Multiethnic consultants—Elissa Fowler, Héctor Hoppe.

Technology consultants—Kevin Applegate, Scott Busacker, Richard Futrell, Eric Glantz, Steve Harris, Brad Wheeling.

Art—Tim Agnew, Jackie Appelt, Chris Johnson, Ed Luhmann, Tom Openlander.

Production—Pam Burgdorf, Karen Capps, Robert Duggan, Anne Francisco, Connie Goodson, Marcia Passanise, Jim Stange.

Proofreading—Jeff Caithamer, Mary Carbello, Don Petering, Rachel Peters, Laine Rosin, Jim Wiemers.

Advisory staff—Peggy Anderson, James Bennett, Collin Bivens, Dana Neuhaus, Denise Walsh.

Communications—Susie Alles, Amy Brotcke, Don Brown, Pam Cunningham, Sharon Fagin, Laura Hawkins, Brenda Nelson, Gerry Puglisi, Phyllis Shremp, Kim Thiele.

Soli Deo Gloria

COPYRIGHT HOLDERS AND ADMINISTRATORS

Alfred Publishing Co., Inc.
PO Box 10003
Van Nuys, CA 91410-0003
818-891-5999
Fax: 818-891-4875

Archdiocese of Philadelphia
222 N. 17th St.
Philadelphia, PA 19103
215-587-3537

Augsburg Fortress
PO Box 1209
100 S. 5th St., Suite 700
Minneapolis, MN 55402
800-421-0239
Fax: 612-330-3252

Bärenreiter Music Corporation
224 King St.
Englewood, NJ 07631
201-569-2898
Fax: 201-569-7023

Bavarian Lutheran Church
(*See* Strube Verlag GmbH)

Church Publishing Incorporated
(Church Pension Fund)
Copyrights and Permissions
445 Fifth Avenue
New York, NY 10016
800-223-6602 x 360
Fax: 212-779-3392

Community of Celebration
PO Box 309
809 Franklin Avenue
Aliquippa, PA 15001
724-375-1510
Fax: 724-375-1138

The Copyright Company
1025 16th Avenue South, Suite 204
PO Box 128139
Nashville, TN 37212-8139
800-779-1177
Fax: 615-321-1099

EMI CMG Publishing
(*See* Music Services)

Ethiopian Evangelical Church Mekane Yesus
PO Box 2087
Addis Ababa
Ethiopia
Fax: 251-1-534148

Faber Music Limited
3 Queen Square
London WC1N 3AU
Tel: +44 (0)20 7833 7900
Fax: +44 (0)20 7833 7939

Faith Alive Christian Resources
2850 Kalamazoo Ave., SE
Grand Rapids, MI 49560
616-224-0785
Fax: 616-224-0834

For the most recent addresses of copyright holders, please see our Web site, www.cph.org, or call 800-325-0191.

Genevox
c/o Lifeway Worship Music Group
127 9th Ave. N.
Nashville, TN 37234
800-436-3869
Fax: 615-251-3810

GIA Publications
7404 S. Mason St.
Chicago, IL 60638
800-442-1358
Fax: 708-496-3828

Hal Leonard Corporation
PO Box 13819
7777 West Bluemound Rd.
Milwaukee, WI 53213
414-774-3630
Fax: 414-774-3259

Hope Publishing Co.
380 South Main Pl.
Carol Stream, IL 60188
800-323-1049
630-665-2552

Integrity Media, Inc.
1000 Cody Road
Mobile, AL 36695
251-776-5025
Fax: 251-776-5036

The John Ireland Charitable Trust
1st Floor, Lynton House
7–12 Tavistock Square
London WC1H 9LT
Great Britain

Kevin Mayhew Publishers
Buxhall
Stowmarket
Suffolk IP14 3BW
United Kingdom
011-44-449-73-7978
Fax: 011-44-449-73-7834

The Lutheran World Federation
150, route de Ferney
PO Box 2100
CH-1211 Geneva 2
Switzerland
011-41-22-791 61 11
Fax: 011-41-22-791 66 30

Makumira University College
(formerly Lutheran Theological College)
Makumira
PO Box 55
Usa River
Tanzania
255-27-255-3634

Manna Music, Inc.
PO Box 218
35255 Brooten Road
Pacific City, OR 97135
503-965-6112
Fax: 503-965-6880

MorningStar Music Publishers
1727 Larkin Williams Rd.
Fenton, MO 63026
800-647-2117
636-305-0121

Music Sales Corporation & G. Schirmer, Inc.
257 Park Avenue South, 20th Fl.
New York, NY 10010
212-254-2100
Fax: 212-254-2013

Music Services
1526 Otter Creek Road
Nashville, TN 37215
615-371-1320
Fax: 615-371-1351

National Association of Pastoral Musicians
962 Wayne Avenue, Suite 210
Silver Spring, MD 20910-4461
240-247-3000
Fax: 240-247-3001

Novello
(*See* Music Sales)

Openbook Publishers
205 Halifax
GPO Box 1368
Adelaide SA 5000
Australia
011-61-8-8124-0049
Fax: 011-61-8-8223-4552

Oregon Catholic Press (OCP)
5536 NE Hassalo
Portland, OR 97213
800-548-8749
Fax: 800-843-8181

Oxford University Press
198 Madison Avenue
New York, NY 10016
800-334-4249 x6048
212-726-6037
Fax: 212-726-6444

Presbyterian Board of Christian Education
Presbyterian Church (USA)
100 Witherspoon Street
Louisville, KY 40202-1396
800-523-1631
Fax: 502-569-5113

Selah Publishing Co., Inc.
4143 Brownsville Rd., Suite 2
Pittsburgh, PA 15227
412-886-1020
Fax: 412-886-1022

Strube Verlag GmbH
Pettenkoferstraße 24
80336 München
Germany
011-49-89-544-266-11
Fax: 011-49-89-544-266-30

World Library Publications
3708 River Rd. Suite 400
Franklin Park, IL 60131
800-566-6150
Fax: 888-957-3291

INDEXES

TOPICAL INDEX OF HYMNS AND SONGS

AUTHORS, TRANSLATORS, AND SOURCES OF HYMNS AND SONGS

Numbers in italics indicate translations.

COMPOSERS AND SOURCES OF HYMNS AND SONGS

Numbers in italics indicate settings. Hymn settings not included in this book are included in Lutheran Service Book: Accompaniment for the Hymns.

TUNES—METRICAL

TUNES—ALPHABETICAL

Indented lines indicate names by which some tunes in this book may also be known.

FIRST LINES OF HYMNS AND SONGS

Indented lines indicate first lines by which some hymns were known in earlier hymnals.

FOREIGN LANGUAGE HYMNS

HOLY BAPTISM

In Cases of Emergency

In urgent situations, in the absence of the pastor, any Christian may administer Holy Baptism.

If time permits, the following may precede the Baptism.

Jesus said, "Assuredly, I say to you, whoever does not receive the kingdom of God as a little child will by no means enter it." And He took them up in His arms, put His hands on them, and blessed them. *Mark 10:15–16 NKJV*

Eternal God, Father of our Lord Jesus Christ, give *name(s)* Your grace through rebirth by the Holy Spirit. Receive *him/her/them* according to Your promise: "Ask, and it will be given to you; seek, and you will find; knock, and it will be opened to you," that through this heavenly washing *he/she/they* may receive the gift of the Holy Spirit and the forgiveness of all *his/her/their* sins and come to the eternal kingdom which You have prepared for *him/her/them*; through Jesus Christ, our Lord. Amen. (508) *Matthew 7:7*

Lord's Prayer

Apostles' Creed

Take water, call the child or adult by name, and pour or sprinkle the water on the head of the candidate while saying:

Name, I baptize you in the name of the Father and of the Son and of the Holy Spirit. Amen.

Holy Baptism administered by a layperson shall immediately be reported to the pastor for its recognition by the congregation.

Library of Congress Cataloging-in-Publication Data

Lutheran Church—Missouri Synod.
Lutheran service book / prepared by the Commission on Worship of the Lutheran Church—Missouri Synod.
p. cm.
Includes index.
ISBN 0-7586-1217-6
ISBN 978-0-7586-1217-5
1. Hymns, English. 2. Lutheran Church—Hymns. 3. Lutheran Church—Liturgy—Texts. I. Lutheran Church—Missouri Synod. Commission on Worship. II. Title.
BX8067.L4L865 2006
264'.041322034—dc22 2006009041

ISBN 13: 978-0-7586-1217-5
ISBN 10: 0-7586-1217-6

9 780758 612175
Church & Ministry/Worship & Liturgy
03-1170

NICENE CREED

C **I believe in one God,**
the Father Almighty,
maker of heaven and earth
and of all things visible and invisible.

And in one Lord Jesus Christ,
the only-begotten Son of God,
begotten of His Father before all worlds,
God of God, Light of Light,
very God of very God,
begotten, not made,
being of one substance with the Father,
by whom all things were made;
who for us men and for our salvation came down from heaven
and was incarnate by the Holy Spirit of the virgin Mary
and was made man;
and was crucified also for us under Pontius Pilate.
He suffered and was buried.
And the third day He rose again according to the Scriptures
and ascended into heaven
and sits at the right hand of the Father.
And He will come again with glory to judge both the living and the dead,
whose kingdom will have no end.

And I believe in the Holy Spirit,
the Lord and giver of life,
who proceeds from the Father and the Son,
who with the Father and the Son together is worshiped and glorified,
who spoke by the prophets.
And I believe in one holy Christian and apostolic Church,
I acknowledge one Baptism for the remission of sins,
and I look for the resurrection of the dead
and the life ✠ of the world to come. Amen.

Us men means all people.
Christian: the ancient text reads "catholic," meaning the whole Church as it confesses the wholeness of Christian doctrine.